THE SHORTER DICTIONARY OF

ENGLISH FURNITURE

Painted serpentine Commode; ground ivory colour with a green diaper pattern and ovals filled with figure subjects after Angelica Kauffmann and Adam Buck; colonnettes and bandings gilt. c. 1795. Ht. 3ft., L. 4ft. 2in., Depth 1ft. 11in. (Arundel Castle, Sussex.)

THE SHORTER DICTIONARY OF

ENGLISH FURNITURE

From the Middle Ages to the Late Georgian period

BY

RALPH EDWARDS

C.B.E., F.S.A.

COUNTRY LIFE
LONDON · NEW YORK · SYDNEY · TORONTO

Published for Country Life Books by
THE HAMLYN PUBLISHING GROUP LIMITED
LONDON · NEW YORK · SYDNEY · TORONTO
Hamlyn House, Feltham, Middlesex, England

© Copyright 1964 Country Life Limited
Fourth impression 1972

ISBN 0 600 43082 0

Printed in England by
Chapel River Press, Andover

FOREWORD

The first edition of *The Dictionary of English Furniture* (published in 1924-25), in which I collaborated with the late Percy Macquoid (his *History* of the subject, a pioneer work, dates back to the beginning of the century), was followed by a revised edition in three folio volumes in 1954; a shorter version, in a single volume, will, it is hoped, bring this work within the reach of a wider public.

The omission of a few articles has been found necessary. Tapestry, Carpets and Hangings have been excluded, with some minor accessories, as not being furniture in the primary and commonly accepted sense of the term. On the other hand, because Needlework is inseparably connected with movables, particularly seat-furniture, an article on that subject has again been included. This abbreviated *Dictionary* is concerned only with domestic furniture, and therefore the evolutions of bookcases and desks from medieval, collegiate or ecclesiastical prototypes have been omitted.

In condensing the text I have sought to retain all important historical and literary references (even adding some which seemed of special interest), while confining descriptive detail mainly to the captions. Limitations of space have, however, imposed a reduction of acknowledgments of indebtedness for information to a minimum, and the abbreviations in the short sections have been enforced by the same consideration.

If the text has been condensed, it has also been revised, and a certain amount of information not in the larger edition has been incorporated. The initials of original contributors are appended to their articles and notes, except in cases where the changes made are so extensive that it has not seemed proper to credit them with responsibility. These contributors were:

Oliver Brackett	W. A. Propert
Francis W. Galpin	John C. Rogers
Ingleson C. Goodison	H. Clifford Smith
Margaret Jourdain	H. Avray Tipping
John Seymour Lindsay	W. G. Thompson

For convenience of reference, cabinet-makers, decorative artists and other craftsmen are grouped together at the end of the volume, instead of being dispersed as formerly throughout the text. To include all those, an enormous number, known to have been concerned in the production of furniture over a period of several centuries, clearly is impossible in a work of this kind, and the selection from among the minor makers and craftsmen must inevitably appear arbitrary.

The number of illustrations has been reduced by about one third, but even so there are upwards of 1,900 in this volume. Some examples have been substituted as being finer or more representative; or because the makers are known. To trace changes of ownership in the years that have elapsed since the previous edition has not been attempted; they have been noted only in comparatively few instances.

It would not have been possible within the scope of this volume to pass beyond the *terminus ad quem*, that is *circa* 1820, and include Victorian and later developments. Space has not sufficed for presenting the evidence on which conclusions are based, though in some instances it has led to a change of opinion; as on the question of Chippendale's responsibility for designs in *The Director*.

I am grateful to Mr Edward T. Joy for valuable help in the preparation of this shorter edition.

RALPH EDWARDS

INTRODUCTION

THIS work is intended to give an insight into the history of English domestic furniture and its place in the changing social habits of the people of this island. It shows a movement extending over six centuries from little to much, from simple to complex, from roughly wrought to skilfully constructed. The development begins with the carpenter; later the joiner takes over most of his functions and from the mid-17th century onwards is, in his turn, largely superseded by the cabinet-maker and upholsterer. Craftsmen, designers, materials, technical terms, processes and styles are discussed under their respective headings.

As, under all heads, survivals from medieval times and from the early Tudor age are exceedingly rare, in tracing the evolution of English furniture from its beginnings, it is necessary to rely largely on inventories and contemporary allusions for the material of the text, and on illuminated manuscripts for pictorial representation. The latter, though mainly of continental origin, afford a valuable record, because the household gear possessed by the medieval English peasantry was so rough as hardly to deserve the name of furniture, while the prosperous classes were almost as continental as English, and therefore had furniture that either came from Flanders and France or differed from it only in a minor degree.

An analysis of inventories strengthens the conclusion that we can get a general impression of what English 15th-century rooms were like from those depicted with such minute finish in manuscript books of the time, although wrought by foreigners. Fig. 2, taken from a historical work made in Flanders for Edward IV and dating from about 1475, shows Richard II feasting. He is under a canopy, but is not seated apart on a chair of state. He shares with others a settle which, although not against a wall, has a rectangular return, and belongs to the fixed category. Over the settle a cloth or 'banker' of rich material is thrown, but the bench along the third side of the table is bare of carpet or cushions. Against the back wall of the room is set a cupboard covered with a cloth and with a carved back. On it silver plate is displayed; the cloth hangs so near to the ground as to hide the trestles. There is no chair, but another Flemish illumination (Fig. 3) shows us a king sitting in one of X-shaped framework to which the material forming the seat and back is attached. This was a shape that represented the lighter type of the age and was of a kind much imported to or imitated in England.

An inventory taken of the contents of The Vyne in Hampshire after the death of William, Lord Sandys, in 1542 shows that in the whole of the 52 rooms enumerated there are only 19 chairs, and of them 7 are described as 'fflaunders chayers'. There were 3 in one parlour, a table with trestles and several forms

and stools, described as 'joyned'. Tables also were soon to be joyned. This was not so at The Vyne, for in the 'Great Dynyng Chamber', hung with 11 pieces of imagery 'with borders of Anticke and my lordes Armes', there was a trestle table 15 feet long, and—what was rather exceptional—with a top made of fir and not of oak. As no benches are mentioned they were probably fixed, and so went with the freehold, but cushions were plentiful, for 30 'cusshens' are entered as belonging to the room. There was one chair, reserved, no doubt, for his lordship's use, unless a greater man was present, as King Henry twice was. The 'Cuppord of boardes' covered with a Turkey carpet was evidently merely for the display of plate. But elsewhere in the house we find a piece described as a 'Cuppord with 11 Ambres', showing that some part of it was enclosed with doors.

1. *Church Doctor reading: Chapter House doorway, Rochester Cathedral, representing 14th-century chair and reading desk.*

2. *Richard II feasting:* Les Chroniques d'Angleterre, *Bruges, c. 1475, when English and Flemish furniture very similar* (*B.M. Royal* 14 *E IV, f.* 2656).

The most sumptuous of Lord Sandys's furniture (and this remains true in general for two centuries onwards) were some of the beds. Costly draperies, forming canopy and curtains, enclosed a frame on which was set ample bedding and rich coverlet. Green velvet and cloth of gold were among the materials, and these were enriched with fringes of gold and of silk, and with embroidery, floral and heraldic. As a rule no woodwork showed, but the carved oak or walnut bed of Elizabethan times is foreshadowed by '1 trussing bed of waynscot with iij pillars carved'. In such great houses as The Vyne joyned forms and stools were not the only evidence of the joiner's advent, for by this date panelled framing had been introduced from the Continent—an epoch-making revolution in construction (*see* Construction).

Passing on to pieces of Elizabeth's time we observe the considerable advance noted by that observant Berkshire parson, William Harrison, in his *Description of England* (1587). In his chapter on 'The Manner of Building and Furniture of our Houses,' he writes that:

The furniture of our houses also exceedeth, and is growne in manner even to passing delicacie: and herein I doo not speake of the nobilitie and gentrie onelie, but likewise of the lowest sort in most places of our south countrie, that haue anie thing at all to take to. Certes in noble mens houses it is not rare to see abundance of Arras, rich hangings of tapistrie, siluer vessels, and so much other plate, as may furnish sundrie cupboards, to the summe oftentimes of a thousand or two pounds at the least: whereby the value of this and the rest of their stuffe dooth grow to be almost inestimable. Likewise in the houses of knights, gentlemen, merchantmen, and some other wealthie citizens, it is not geson to behold generallie their great prouision of tapistrie, Turkie worke, pewter, brasse, fine linen, and thereto costlie cupboards of plate, worth five or six hundred or a thousand pounds, to be deemed by estimation. But as herein all these sortes doo far exceed their elders and predecessors, and in neatnesse and curiositie, the merchant all other; so in time past, the costlie furniture staied there, whereas now it is descended yet lower, euen vnto the inferiour artificers and manie farmers. . . .

Ingatestone Hall in Essex was built and furnished by Sir William Petre, a great acquirer of monastic lands, and Secretary

of State under Henry VIII. An inventory was taken in 1600, a quarter of a century after his death, and lists much furniture in the newest manner. But there remained pieces of older fashion and in the hall are listed:

A long thick elm planke for a Table lying upon iiij dormers.
A shorte thick oke planke for a Table lying upon ij dormers.

Even in the hall, however, there were innovations, such as an oak table on a joined frame and with the 'draw' system of sections to pull out at either end. Ingatestone was evidently an 'up-to-date' house, as to the disposition as well as the furnishing of the rooms. It had both a 'Dyning Chamber' and a dining parlour very fully equipped. In each were a 'longe Table of Walnuttree upon a frame with two leaves to drawe out' and a dozen 'highe joyned stoolls', the one set of oak and the other of walnut. The dining chamber also had an oak 'Groom Porter's' table 'for a carvinge bourde'. No chair is mentioned here, whereas the 'Dyninge Parler' had four of them, two high and two low. But the most elaborate example of a seat was that in the garden chamber described as 'a high chaire of Walnuttree with Armes' covered in crimson velvet with gold lace and crimson silk fringe.

Hardwick Hall in Derbyshire (finished in 1597) preserves the character of a great Elizabethan house in its decoration; and its amazing assemblage of tapestry and needlework, carpets, curtains and hangings can be estimated by the full inventory of its contents taken in 1601. Several pieces of furniture in the Presence Chamber (the High Great Chamber, Fig. 4) are identifiable in this list. It contained one 'long table of white wood', 'an inlayed table in the windowe', 'a cubberde guild and carved, with tills', 'a chare of needlework with golde and

3. *A King seated: from* La Bible Historiale, *Flemish, c.* 1470 (*B.M. Royal* 15 *D,* 111).

4. *Presence Chamber, Hardwick Hall, Derbys. Tudor and later furniture.*

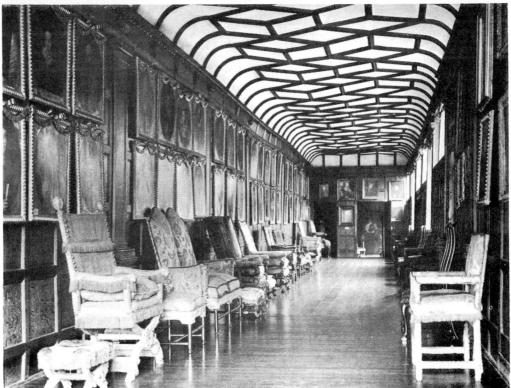

5. *Brown Gallery, Knole, Kent, c. 1605: chair and stool to left of same period, the other furniture late 17th and early 18th century.*

6. Hall at Kildwick: typical furniture of small Yorkshire manor house c. 1650.

silke fringe', a footstool, three forms 'covered with watchet satin embroidered with cloth of gold and needlework flowers', 14 stools with needlework seats and 2 'French Stools set with marble stones'. The large inlaid table which displays the Countess of Shrewsbury's arms in the centre may be 'the inlaid table in the window' listed in the inventory.

There still exists at Knole sumptuous upholstered furniture, although not of walnut, and dating a few years later. Such are the X-chair and stool seen on the left of the illustration of the Brown Gallery (Fig. 5). But perhaps the most wonderful collection of furniture in the possession of a subject, both as to quality and quantity, in Elizabethan England must have been that inventoried for Lord Lumley in 1590. He was son-in-law and co-heir to the last of the Fitzalan Earls of Arundel, who had travelled and collected in Italy, and had owned the Palace of Nonsuch which was inherited by Lumley, who also owned Lumley Castle and a great London house. Only an epitome of the inventories survives. From that we learn that Lumley possessed 17 chairs, 57 stools, 20 forms, 25 tables, 8 cupboards, and 23 beds, all described as 'of Walnuttree and Markatre', showing the extent to which walnut with inlay, both of English and continental origin, was used by the wealthy Elizabethans. Of oak there was about twice the amount as of walnut. A few

beds were gilt, while of upholstered chairs and stools, 119 of the former and 80 of the latter were covered in velvet, silk, or cloth of gold.

These Lumley and Ingatestone inventories, with specimens still surviving at Hardwick, show that before the close of the 16th century rich and cultivated men were supplementing oak with walnut furniture, often having geometric and other simple forms of inlay. But only a few great nobles like Lord Lumley and Robert Sydney, Earl of Leicester, possessed great quantities of walnut furniture. Examples of this period are rare, and the wood was not adopted in this country to the displacement of oak until after 1660 (*see* WALNUT).

As furniture was still scarce, and as rooms generally contained very few pieces, no feeling of overcrowding and over-decoration was produced by the very rich and elaborate wainscotings that were being introduced. The stone- or brick- or timber-framed halls of medieval interiors had been left bare, except where hidden by sets of tapestries, hung on tenter-hooks, and therefore easily movable. The fashion of framed wood linings came earlier in Flanders than in England. In 1516 Erasmus finds Bishop Fisher living at the Palace at Rochester in rooms where the walls of 'brick and mortar' exhale 'noxious vapours', and afterwards writes to suggest that a wainscoted

7. *Long Gallery, Ham House, Surrey: panelled* 1639, *furniture and picture frames of Charles II period.*

room would be much better. Such were not infrequent before Henry VIII died, and under Elizabeth, Harrison writes:

> The walls of our houses on the inner sides in like sort be either hanged with tapisterie arras work, or painted cloths, wherein either diurse histories, or hearbes, beasts, knots, and such like are stained, or else they are seeled with oke of our owne or wainescot brought hither out of the east countries whereby the rooms are not a little commended, made warme, and much more close than otherwise they would be.

This extract shows that the word 'wainscot' then referred to foreign as opposed to English oak, and that the process we term wainscoting was then known as 'ceiling' the walls of a room. It was soon brought to a pitch of great elaboration. The hall at Kildwick in Yorkshire (Fig. 6) may be taken as typical of Elizabethan times. Yet both structure and contents date from a good many years after the Queen's death; indeed, the settle to the right of the chimney has inscribed on it the initials 'I.A.A.' and the date 1691. Although these are subsequent additions, yet the conservatism of our provincial and hereditarily trained joiners make their production possible even so near the end of the century. The panelled walls, the beam and rafter ceiling, the massive stone fire arch and window mullions of the hall, combine to render it an excellent setting for the representative and regional examples of chairs and tables.

Although the south and east of England did not share the extreme conservatism of the west and north—which, with no more than slight variations of design and detail, carried the style of the beginning of the 17th century on to its end—yet, even in London, the reigns of the first two Stuarts did not witness any radical changes. There is merely some variation of form and ornament, some perceptible influence from the Continent and developments from native needs. Even these were checked by the political and social conditions that prevailed from 1640 to 1660. But with the return of Charles II and his court in the latter year came a revolution in social habits, and therefore of the disposition and furnishing of the rooms that society occupied. There was a strong tinge of the continental tastes which the Royalists had imbibed during the time of exile; an impulse towards portability attained by smaller designs carried out in a lighter wood, and marked multiplication of specialised types. There was also an advance in craftsmanship which continued until, within a few years, the English cabinet-maker could rival, where he did not excel, his continental brethren in the output of fine domestic furniture; although, in the palatial manner, the Paris *ébénistes* retained their pre-eminence.

11

8. *Venetian Ambassador's Room, Knole, Kent: gilt furniture hung and upholstered in cut Genoese velvet, 1685-8, armchairs and stools by Thomas Roberts.*

The revolution in the character of furniture that occurred under Charles II is well indicated by John Evelyn, who in 1690 contrasts the light tea-table that ladies of fashion were then obtaining for their dressing-rooms with conditions at his boyhood home, where 'the shovel board and other long tables both in hall and parlour were as fixed as the freehold'. These remained in many halls, and may, on occasions, have been used for meals. But the fashion was to dine in small parties at different tables, as Duke Cosmo II's secretary noted when the Duke was in England in 1669. These were probably of the gate-leg type and oval in form. Surviving examples are of oak or much more rarely walnut. That tables of other light woods were not uncommon is shown by the 1679 inventory of Ham House, which enumerates 8 cedarwood tables in the 'Great Eating Room'. In the gallery (Fig. 7) chairs and cabinets of the period are arranged down each side, and above them hang, on earlier wainscoting, the 'Two and Twenty Pictures with

Carv'd Guild Frames' mentioned in the inventory. Sets of portraits thus framed were one of the fashionable wall decorations of the day. They were essentially furniture.

Another form of wall covering was tapestry. In the lofty rooms that then began to prevail the tapestries were set above a dado, but when adapted to rooms that were structurally of earlier date and less elevation they descended to the skirting, as in the 'Venetian' Room at Knole (Fig. 8). It contains a splendid set of carved and gilt furniture which can be assigned to the craftsman Thomas Roberts. The set is hung and covered with Genoa velvet and probably dates from 1686-8. It was made for James II and on the bed the royal cypher and crown appear repeatedly in the carved decoration. After the Revolution of 1688 it was removed to Knole by the sixth Earl of Dorset, William III's Lord Chamberlain.

But if tapestry-hung rooms were frequent towards the end of the century, oak, cedar or chestnut wainscotings of large

12

9. *Great Chamber, Chatsworth, Derbys.: joinery by H. Lobb and R. Owen, carvings by J. Lobb, W. Davis and S. Watson, c. 1692; side tables c. 1730.*

bolection-moulded panels were still more usual, and they were often enriched with carvings by Grinling Gibbons and his school. Such can be seen in the 'Great Chamber' at Chatsworth (Fig. 9). The wainscoting, prepared in London by Henry Lobb and Robert Owen, joiners, was sent down in time for the carvers, Joel Lobb, William Davis and Samuel Watson, to enrich with their carvings in 1692. In the furnishing of this room the later development of side-tables will be observed. They occur in pairs on both the chimney and window sides of the room. Elaborately carved and gilt wooden frames support marble slabs. The Chatsworth 'Great Chamber' was used as a state dining-room, and it was the dining-room of the period that was most usually supplied with such side-tables. But they were also placed elsewhere, proportionate to the rooms they were for, and habitually placed between windows and in conjunction with mirrors. Quite modest in the ordinary country gentleman's home, both tables and mirrors assumed lordly

size and richness in the great Whig palaces of the 18th century.

Under the late Stuarts specialised forms of tables increased. This development is marked in those tables and cognate forms of furniture which, while primarily intended to write on, were also adapted to keep writing materials in. They were fitted with one or more drawers, and the development, the dominance almost, of the drawer is one of the most marked features of post-Restoration furniture. An impetus was given by the importation, beginning, indeed, in late Tudor and early Stuart days, of cabinets from Italy and Flanders which, whether they were open or closed with a hinged flap, equally served for nests of drawers. They continued to be imported under Charles II, and although many were then being made in England, the walnut and kingwood veneered writing cabinets on carved twisted-legged stands at Ham House—which were the 'scriptors' used by the Duke and Duchess of Lauderdale and

13

10. *From Hogarth's 'Marriage à la Mode', 1744 (Nat. Gallery): furniture earlier in style.*

were included in the 1679 inventory (*see* BUREAUX, Fig. 1)—are unusually fine examples of the native production. In this instance the 'German' or Dutch craftsmen employed by the Duke may, however, have been responsible.

The lacquered cabinets from China and Japan, and the screens which also came in large quantities gave rise to an active school of English japanners, who produced drawer-fitted furniture of various types. Thus the light oblong table with a single drawer was finished in japan as well as in plain or marquetried walnut. The use of such was not necessarily confined to writing or study, but specialised forms for such purposes soon developed. Desks on stands, scrutoires, writing bureaux and writing cabinets were evolved and multiplied, assuming varying forms and styles throughout the 18th century. We may add to the list of drawer-fitted furniture cabinets, commodes, chests of drawers and tallboys.

In days when social habits kept the centres of rooms clear of furniture for the assemblage of people, there would naturally arise a demand for light side-tables easily brought forward and replaced. If, when brought forward for occasional use, they could assume a larger surface than when stored against the wall, the advantage was obvious. Thus there are examples in oak,

and dating from the early 17th century, of small semi-circular tables with a flap to open and rest on a hinged leg. After the Restoration they are, like other furniture, often of walnut, while in Georgian times they were made at first of solid mahogany, and then of satinwood. Moreover, they became specialised, as for card playing, and for that purpose, by the time of Queen Anne, they present, when open, a surface of woven material, such as velvet or cloth. The round form then becomes largely superseded by one of rectangular shape with a curved outline, such as that represented in Hogarth's 'Marriage à la Mode' (Fig. 10).

Other forms of gaming tables also arose under Charles II, while the tea-tables were especially intended for the display of the Oriental porcelain that the East India Company was importing in considerable quantities before Charles II died. Thus in July, 1684, Abigail Harley writes from the country to her brother Robert (the future Prime Minister) in London, asking him to procure and send down 'some China pots and cups for tea'. Tea-tables were either cabriole-legged or supported on a tripod such as was then also used for fire-screens, lamp-stands and other purposes. It was usual for both these types to have a raised edge or gallery running round as a pro-

11. *Saloon, Houghton, Norfolk: decorations and furniture 1730-5, designed by W. Kent.*

12. *Drawing-Room, Syon House, Middx.: designed by R. Adam, c. 1765, carpet by Moore, dated 1769.*

13. *Eating Room, Osterley, Middx.: decorations, sideboard and pedestals by R. Adam, c. 1767.*

14. *End of Dining-Room (originally Library), Saltram, Devon: decoration by R. Adam, carpet (Moorfields or Axminster) design resembling that of ceiling; sideboard and pedestals designed by Adam, 1780.*

tection against the sweeping off of the fragile and expensive ware. The double purpose of display and use continued to the time of Chippendale, who in his *Director* (3rd ed., 1762) describes them as:

> Tables for holding each a Set of China, and may be used as Tea Tables.

Portability was likewise aimed at in chairs, which, after the Restoration, appear not merely as single specimens, but often in sets. The combination of walnut wood and caning made for lightness, not greatly affected by the height of the back and the considerable area of the carved crestings and front stretchers which were then fashionable. But comfort as well as mobility was sought, and several types of armed and upholstered chairs were introduced. Those with wings occasionally had ratchets to let down the back at any angle, as in the Duke and Duchess of Lauderdale's 'sleeping chayres' at Ham House (*see* CHAIRS, Fig. 44). There also, as seen in the illustration of the gallery (Fig. 7), other forms of upholstered armchairs of the period survive, still retaining their original upholstery of silks or velvet with gold or silk fringes. Such chairs also appear, beyond those of the James I period, in the Knole Brown Gallery (Fig. 5); while the very elaborately carved and gilt set also in that house has already been noticed. There the leg takes the form of a human figure, while a set at Ham has dolphins carved not only on the legs, but on the arms and stretchers (*see* CHAIRS, Fig. 50).

Such fanciful elaboration was rare, the result of continental influence when not the work of immigrant craftsmen. The more modest and usual English type began the reign of Charles II with straight legs, but ended it with a frequent use of the single or double scroll, the carved front stretcher and turned side ones being retained. Under William III this was in great measure superseded by the straight leg. It was baluster-shaped, sometimes turned, but often square or octagonal, starting from a cap and diminishing as it descended to meet stretchers inserted between the base of the leg and a bulbous foot, and formed of flat serpentines meeting centrally, where a turned or carved vase was often placed.

Stools had not yet lost their early importance as the usual seat for ordinary people, for on all occasions of ceremony only personages of importance occupied chairs. When Duke Cosmo of Tuscany dined at Wilton and at Althorp in 1669, for him only was a chair provided, the rest of the company being seated on stools. Even in 1736 Lord Hervey relates how Frederick, Prince of Wales, after his marriage wished his brothers and sisters, who were to dine with him, to sit on stools, while he and his bride had armchairs. At Hampton Court (when William III was furnishing it), with one chair of state and one footstool for its occupant, were provided at least half a dozen stools and 4 forms; stools and forms being of the same design as, and forming a set with, the chair, not only in its frame, but its upholstery. Like in character, only wider, and fitted with an adjustable end, was the day-bed, and gradually new kinds of settees and developments of the couch came into vogue. To the latter the word 'sofa', introduced by Eastern travellres, became attached, and appears in the Chatsworth furnishing accounts of 1702, which show that £7 were paid 'For 2 large Saffaws carved'. They did not, however, become numerous until curved forms had again become fashionable. The straight leg did not supplant, but for a while existed side by side with, the scroll. But under Queen Anne a new form arose that dominated English furniture design for nearly half a century (*see* CABRIOLE).

While the chair (or the settee, now often in the form of a double- or treble-backed chair) gave scope for the best expression of this style in the curves of the legs, seat-rail, back and cresting, it was present in every other variety of furniture. It was at its full during the earlier part of the reign of George II, but the style in vogue when Hogarth painted 'Marriage à la Mode' (Fig. 10) was very soon superseded by more exuberant forms. The rococo style was mixed with the 'Chinese' and 'Gothic' fancies of the cabinet-makers' books of designs, as seen in Chippendale's *Director* (1754). But over the mass of production English sobriety and reserve still reigned. Fine material and consummate workmanship, in conjunction with thoughtful and often masterly design, marked the output of our cabinet-makers during the 'cabriole period'.

With the accession of George III a reaction from rococo fantasy once more established the pre-eminence of the straight line. Under the heading ADAM, ROBERT, something is said as to the characteristics of his style and the influence of his furniture designs on Thomas Chippendale in his later years, and then on Hepplewhite and Sheraton. There was a change of material and treatment as well as of style. When, after the Restoration, walnut became the cabinet-maker's prevalent wood, it was largely employed in the solid by joiners. But for large and uncarved surfaces veneer became more and more fashionable, and with it marquetry, also of veneer thickness and not, like Elizabethan inlay, let into the solid. The walnut veneer enabled choice pieces of the wood, rich in figure and 'burr', to go a long way and to be used to give the greatest effect. It was therefore soon greatly in demand, so that, under Queen Anne, even chairs had quite as much veneered as solid surface. The large importation of mahogany towards the end of George I's reign checked to some extent the demand for veneer. The wood was much used in the solid. Other choice woods also came into vogue. Veneering in satinwood and other exotic woods with characteristic inlaid or painted decorations holds the field, with gilding, during the prevalence of the 'Adam' style—that is, until nearly the end of the century.

Despite the excellence of our designers and craftsmen, that period saw the continuance of the considerable importation of French furniture which had set in after the peace of Utrecht in 1713, and was but little interrupted by the Austrian Succession and Seven Years' wars. Commodes and suites of chairs and sofas arrived in numbers. Tapestries and carpets were also imported. The latter, indeed, were being made of excellent quality at Wilton and Axminster, Kidderminster and Moorfields, often from designs by Adam and other architects. But the output appears to have been limited, and the number of Aubusson carpets that came across the Channel—sometimes, as for Stowe, with the arms of the Englishman for whose new or altered house they were specially made—was certainly very large. Few tapestries were made in England in the earlier half of the 18th century and even fewer in the latter half, yet there was a considerable demand for them; and even in houses where decoration and furniture were in Robert Adam's charge, as at Osterley, there were one or more rooms hung with the products of the Gobelins looms. This form of wall decoration was also used at Moor Park, Newby, Croome Court and Nostell Priory.

15. *Room, Crawley House, Beds.: paper-hangings, furniture and carpet, all dating from* 1806.

But for much of the furniture at these and other houses Adam was responsible. Thus in the Osterley 'Eating Room' (Fig. 13) there is the characteristic side-table flanked by urns, and another example, specially designed for and fitted to the curved end of the room, occurs at Saltram (Fig. 14). The dining-tables are of the kind that extend by putting in one or more complete sections between the ends; the expanding table becoming general under George III. The chairs are of the round and fluted straight-legged type very usual about 1780. A desire to supplement, if not wholly to supersede, wainscot and woven fabrics by paper as a wall hanging arose soon after the advent of the Hanoverians, and English wallpaper makers developed their trade. The accounts of Thomas Chippendale show that he undertook general decoration, including paper hanging.

The practice of publishing trade-catalogues continued and increased in the last quarter of the 18th century. These illustrated pattern-books had a far-reaching influence on the character of English furniture in the final phase of the neo-classic style; for their purpose was not only 'to exhibit the present taste' but also to provide intending purchasers with a wide repertory of designs. At this period cabinet-making attained the zenith of technical accomplishment. Marquetry

remained fashionable, and a wide variety of exotic woods was employed, the broadly designed classical ornament favoured at the outset of the neo-classic revival being succeeded by motives which were often naturalistic and inlaid on a much reduced scale towards the century's close. There was also a large output of furniture in beech, birch and other soft woods, painted to accord with the delicately coloured walls and soft-toned hangings of contemporary rooms. Such 'japanned' and inlaid furniture formed an integral part of a carefully co-ordinated scheme; and some of the more important commodes and side-tables are painted, like the ceilings under which they stood, with figure subjects and mythological scenes after the designs of Angelica Kauffmann, Cipriani and other decorative artists.

The so-called Regency taste (*q.v.*) which became current in England at the turn of the century covered the whole range of decoration and furniture. The most gifted exponent of the early phase was Henry Holland, who may be held to have introduced the French version of classicism which captured the imagination of the Prince Regent and his circle. After Holland's death in 1806 a new and more intense study of classical precedents set in, and leading designers and decorators, inspired by the ideal set before them by Percier and Fontaine in their *Recueil de*

19

décorations intérieures, sought to achieve a synthesis of architecture, decoration and furniture. The style now acquired an archaeological bias and marked eclectic character, its elements being drawn from the remains of three civilisations— the Roman, Greek and Egyptian—though in later phases 'Grecian severity' became the rule. Mahogany was supplemented by rosewood in boudoirs and drawing-rooms, and metal inlays and appliqués were freely used.

In interior decoration an effect of dignified simplicity was sought. The use of traditional structural elements such as columns and entablatures was discouraged by Soane and other arbiters of contemporary taste; but the resulting severity was to some extent mitigated by wall-papers and elaborately festooned window draperies, often in primary colours and decorated with classical patterns to harmonise with the contents. The drawing-room at Crawley House gives an adequate impression of a style which its votaries held to be the final expression of enlightened taste. The 'handsome Grecian couches with squabbs' and the 'Japanned bugle-horn polescreens' were supplied by Collis, an upholsterer, in 1806. In the yellow and black carpet griffins figure among the motives of the design. The plain grey wall-paper is enriched with a border in which mummies and sphinxes are introduced, and the 'burnished gould frame' of the overmantel mirror has elongated terms ending in Egyptian female heads.

By far the larger number of the makers of English domestic furniture in the long evolution here briefly surveyed are unknown to us as individuals; though some particulars have been recorded of the guilds and fraternities to which they belonged (*see* CABINET-MAKERS, CARPENTERS, JOINERS). With few exceptions, they remain anonymous until towards the end of the Stuart period, but from that time onwards the obscurity hitherto enveloping them has been partly dispelled by recent research.

Chippendale's name no longer completely overshadows that of his contemporaries: he is now known to have had a formidable rival, perhaps a superior, in William Vile during the ascendancy of rococo taste. If Hepplewhite and Sheraton (*q.v.*) still retain their status as formative influences on late 18th-century design, their names should be used as generic terms to indicate phases of style. Of Georgian cabinet-makers whose names survive, the great majority are commemorated only by their trade cards and labels, which announce their places of business and the goods they supplied. But those of whom we possess fuller information will be found recorded: their number has increased considerably since the publication of earlier editions of this work.

THE SHORTER DICTIONARY
OF ENGLISH FURNITURE

ACACIA (*Robinia pseud-acacia*). Appears in 18th-century furniture, chiefly in country work, being employed for inlay and bandings. English acacia not the true genus, actually the locust wood of America; from whence originally brought. A dull yellow with brown veins and markings; for durability ranks next to oak. Evelyn (*Sylva*, 1664) refers to its use by inlayers when requiring a yellow wood. He writes that 'The French have lately brought in the Virginian Acacia'.

ACANTHUS. In architecture and decoration, a term applied to the conventional representation of *Acanthus spinosus*. Conventional acanthus foliage is employed on the capitals of the Corinthian and Composite order. First freely used during the Early Renaissance on furniture (in England generally in a rude form); widely exploited as a motif in the late Stuart period and again after introduction of mahogany until towards end of the 18th century.

ACROTER or **ACROTERIUM.** Pedestals for figures and other ornaments placed on apex and corners of pediments (*see* BUREAUX, Figs. 20 and 21). 1706, Philips: *Acroteres in Architecture, Pedestals upon the Corners and middle of a Pediment to support statues.*

ALDER (*Alnus*). Used in the 18th century for country-made furniture, tables, chairs, etc. After cutting fades to a flesh tint and so remains when dried. For furniture old trees were selected, which, being full of knots, polished with a fine figure like curled maple.

ALKANET. Several varieties of English plants are known by this name. *Alkanna tinctoria* mixed with linseed oil used in the 18th century to darken mahogany (*see* POLISHES).

ALLGOOD (the family of). Manufacturers of 'Pontypool' Japan. Thomas Allgood, of Northampton (d. c. 1710), settled in Pontypool, Monmouthshire, in 1660. He discovered a by-product of coal, which he applied as a varnish to local wares made of thin rolled iron plate, and appears to have founded the first Pontypool Japan factory, which was developed by his sons Edward (1681-1763) and John. The former is described on a mural tablet (now in the Caerleon Museum) as 'having first invented the art of tinning iron in England'. In 1761 three other members of the family set up a rival factory at Usk, but the business was still carried on at Pontypool. William Allgood, great-grandson of the founder, died about 1800 and after that date the manufacture steadily declined. Among the chief products were dressing-boxes, large urns for sideboards and lamps. (*See* JAPANNING AND LACQUER; also *Guide to the Collections of Pontypool and Usk Japan*, Nat. Museum of Wales, 1926.)

AMBOYNA (*Pterospermun indicum*). Imported from the West Indies in the 18th century, and employed in furniture in veneers both for whole surfaces and with other woods in inlay and bandings. Grain full of small knots and curls; polishes to a light warm brown tone. Often confused with Thuja wood; usually lighter in tone and richer in figure than the latter. (*See* BUREAUX, Fig. 45.)

ANDIRONS. *See* CHIMNEY FURNITURE.

ANTEFIX. An architectural term, in furniture applied to ornamental corners hipped above angles of cornices designed in classical style (*see* BEDS, Fig. 33).

APPLEWOOD (*Malus*). Employed for inlay, veneer and applied carving in 17th-century work, including cases of some long clocks, and for much country furniture in the following century. Little distinction between wood of wild and cultivated apple: both are hard, but the latter has a finer grain. The tone light and warm.

APPLIQUE (or **APPLIED WORK**). *See* NEEDLEWORK.

APRON PIECE. The ornamental shaped portion below the seat-rail of a chair, or underframing of tables and stands, etc. (*See* CHAIRS, Fig. 53, for inception of apron piece and Fig. 112 for a fine specimen of c. 1755.)

ARABESQUE. A term (meaning Arabian) used for a form of decorative design in which flowing lines are interlaced and generally disposed symmetrically, springing from a central core. Arabesques were used in inlay in light and dark woods during the late 16th and early 17th century, and again in the marquetry of the reigns of William III and Anne (*see* MARQUETRY). This form of decoration (known as the 'anticke' or grotesque) is described in Peacham's *Gentleman's Exercise* (1612), where he writes that it is 'a general and (as I may say) an unnaturall or disorderly composition for delight's sake, of men, beasts, birds, fishes, flowers, etc., without . . . Rime or Reason'. In furniture arabesques are used to some extent in the painted and inlaid furniture of George III's reign.

ARCHITRAVE. In classical architecture lowest division of the entablature, also mouldings around doors and windows;

1. *Ark, 16th century: oak with canted top, framework secured by wooden pegs. Ht. 3 ft. 7 in., L. 4 ft. 3 in., W. 2 ft. 5 in. (Aston Hall, Birmingham.)*

hence applied in same sense to furniture in which the motifs are borrowed direct from classical architecture.

ARK. A term applied in the North of England to a chest with a canted top. 1557 Lancs. Wills (857) 'II great Arkes standinge in the nurserie.' An example (Fig. 1) has a panelled front and wide stiles, the framework being secured by wedges and wooden pins.

ASH (*Fraxinus excelsior*). Much in demand for cheap country furniture, though examples rare before 1700. Used chiefly for chairs, for entire construction in early part of 18th century, and later for seats of many Windsor chairs; in chests of drawers sometimes used for drawer linings from second half of 17th century onwards. The wood tough and elastic, hard and heavy, but very subject to worm. White, veined in direction of its growth, with yellowish-brown streaks. The knots and bosses of trunk and branches when cut are highly marbled and veined, and were used for forms of veneer in late Georgian times. Evelyn (*Sylva*, 1664):

> Some ash is curioysly camleted and vein'd, I say, so differently from other timber, that our skilful cabinet-makers prize it equal with Ebony. . . .

ASTRAGAL. A small semi-circular moulding or bead in architecture, and in furniture a term often applied to glazing-bars of cabinets and bookcases

ATLAS. An Indian fabric with a cotton warp or back, and silk woof with a satin surface. Sometimes used for bed hangings in late 17th century. 'Rich Atlasses in imitation of those made in India' are advertised in the *London Gazette* (July 23, 27, 1702).

AUMBRY (AMBRY, ALMERY, ARMOIRE). The French term 'armoire' is translated in Cotgrave's *Dictionary* (1611) as 'an aumbrie, cupboard or little book-presse'. A term of wide application: in the Middle Ages a variety of receptacles were commonly so described, and until the 16th century the word 'cupboard' had not acquired its modern significance (*see* CUPBOARDS and WARDROBES). In the Privy Purse expenses of Elizabeth of York, queen of Henry VII, an entry occurs of a payment for making 'of almerys' in her council chamber 'for to put in the bokes', and they were used for this purpose from a very early date (*see* BOOKCASES). Passages in medieval documents prove that the term was applied impartially to receptacles contrived in the wall and to those of wainscot. The name seems to have been derived from the aumbry's original use as a receptacle for that portion of the provisions which, being left after the feast, was reserved for alms. In the Marshalsea, in 1483, there was 'a litell olde almery in the logge at the gate', no doubt for the deposit of gifts of food for the relief of prisoners. Distributions of this kind from the tables of princes and great nobles were often lavish; and in the Statutes of Eltham Henry VIII is found providing for the due observance of the ancient custom, commanding that:

> All the relics and fragments be gathered by the officers of the Almery, and to be given to the poore people at the utter gate by oversight of the almener.

The custom of dispensing hospitality to all comers declined rapidly after the Reformation.

By the 15th century the aumbry had also come to be regarded as an enclosed receptacle made for security. 'Ther averice', says Piers Plowman satirically, 'hath almeries and yren bounden cofres.' It was a safe, and in early glossaries is described as a 'gardiviance'. In 1440 Dean Lisieux of St Paul's caused the archives of the cathedral to be placed in coffers and pixes and then enclosed in aumbries. The cupboards of that time were still, in many instances, entirely open structures (*see* CUPBOARDS) constructed of shelves for the display of plate, but the

1. *Oak Aumbry, York Minster: battlemented cornice and 6 lockers: ironwork original. Late 15th century.*

2. *Oak Aumbry, fixture in vestry, St Mary's, Woodbridge, Suffolk: doors panelled with linen-fold, hinges original, top of cornice modern. c. 1525.*

more secure form was fitted with tills or enclosed divisions, and in inventories 'cubbordes with aumbreys' sometimes occur. In 1530, Henry VIII paid 43 shillings 'to a joyner for viii cupboards with aumbreys and some without'. In the inventory of a nunnery at Boston in 1534 'a playne arombry wᵗ ii litill chambers wʸᵗⁿ wᵗ too lockes' is recorded. By an aumbry is now understood 'a niche or cupboard by the side of an altar to contain the utensils belonging thereunto'; but in monastic establishments, the term originally had a far wider connotation. An account of St Cuthbert's Feritorye at Durham, written within a generation of the Dissolution, records that both on 'The North side and the South, there was almeryes of fine wenscote, beinge varnished and finelye painted and guilted finely over with little images, verye seemly and beautiful to behould, for the Reliques belonging to Saint Cuthbert to lye in'.

A medieval example at York (Fig. 1) has a battlemented cornice and is divided into six lockers and a single narrow receptacle, probably intended for processional crosses: the handles, hinges and lock-plates are all original and very representative of late 15th-century ironwork.

Aumbries continued to be used in churches for vestments and ornaments up to the Reformation. An example dating from about 1525 is divided into three cupboards, the panels being decorated with long linen-fold (Fig. 2). The term was still in use, as applied to a cupboard, under Elizabeth, and in 1570 Ralph Collingwood, of Titlington, County Durham, bequeathed to one of his daughters 'the best new almeri'.

AVENTURINE. A term applied to the minute clippings of gold wire sometimes sprinkled over the surface during japanning of furniture. Evelyn writes in *Sylva* (1664):

By Venturine is meant the most delicate and slender golden wyre such as Embroideres use, reduced to a kind of powder as small as you can clip it, this strew'd upon the first layer of pure Vernish, when dry, superinduce what colour you please; and this is prettily imitated in several lackes.

BABY-CAGES or **GOING-CARTS.** Pieces of nursery furniture constructed to teach children to walk; the top supports the child in an upright position, leaving its arms free, while wheels or castors permit of easy movement; the outward inclination of the legs making it difficult for the cage to be overturned. This device was known on the Continent in the Middle Ages. Among the German woodcuts of the early 15th century in the British Museum there is one representing a man bent double by age in a square going-cart supported by six legs. The design typifies second childhood.

By the 17th century going-carts had become familiar in the Low Countries and in England. An etching by Rembrandt shows a child in one being taught to walk by its mother or nurse, and a print in Francis Quarles's *Emblems* of 1635 represents the soul as a child in a square going-cart beckoned by an angel. In a portrait group of three children dated 1613, the circular top, covered with velvet and trimmed with fringe, rests upon turned supports. Fig. 1 shows another variety, dating from the end of the century and made of yew. The circle opens with a catch, and the castors and feet working in every direction permit the child far greater liberty of movement.

In the *Howard Household Books* there is an entry of a payment to one of the servants for two days' work when making a going-cart in 1620, and a passage in *The Lady's Delight* of 1715, a miscellany of information for mothers and housewives, emphasises the use of these devices. Going-carts remained in favour until late in the 18th century. In *Nollekins and His Times* (1828) J. T. Smith states that when he was a boy they were common in every toy shop in London, but in the greatest abundance in the far-famed turners' shops in Spinning-Wheel Alley, Moorfields. Mrs Papendeik records in her *Journal* (1784) that her baby ran about in one.

1. *Baby-cage of yew, turned uprights and stretchers: top opens and feet (with wooden castors) work in every direction. c. 1700. (Ockwells Manor, Berks.)*

1. *Backgammon Board, with parquetry of lignum vitae, etc.: on reverse of each leaf, initials below coronet. c. 1670. Ht. 1 ft. 8½ in., W. (closed) 1 ft. 5¾ in. (V. & A. Mus.)*

BACKGAMMON AND CHESS BOARDS. The favourite medieval games of chance, before the introduction of cards in the 15th century, were chess, dice and backgammon (then called 'tables'); in contemporary illuminations such games are shown being played on boards set on another piece of furniture (*see* SETTLES and TABLES). In the inventory of Bishop Thomas Britton of Exeter (d. 1307) *I Seaccarum cum familia*, or chess board with men, is entered. Boards for these purposes, sometimes of multiple form with folding leaves for various games, were used in the Tudor period. Henry VIII possessed costly 'bourdes' or 'pairs of tables', for the 'Pleasant and Wittie Plaie of the Cheastes', and the inventories of Katherine of Aragon mention several enriched specimens contained in cases. At Kenilworth Castle in 1588 there was a chess board of ebony elaborately decorated, which was probably of Dutch origin, in view of the Earl of Leicester's connections with the Netherlands. It is described in the inventory as 'A chess boarde of ebanie, with checkars of christall and other stones layed with silver, garnished with beares and ragged staves'. When the contents of Charles I's palaces were dispersed by order of the Council of State, there was at Somerset House 'a payre of playing Tables of Inlaid Wood garnished with silver gilt sett with stones and pearles, ye men of Wood part white part Silver gilt with a box and Suite of chessmen of silver'.

From the 17th century gaming boards made of inlaid oak and walnut survive. The most ornamental are for backgammon, or tric-trac, this game lending itself more readily to decorative treatment than chess, in which dark and light squares alternately monopolise the area for play. The example (Fig. 1) dates from about 1670, the inner surfaces being decorated with oyster-shell parquetry (*q.v.*) in lignum vitae. On the outside of each leaf within an oval is a monogram formed of the letters G.S.K.V. surmounted by a coronet. With the board are 32 original pieces of light and dark wood, each carved with a rosette. (*See* TABLES, CARD AND GAMING.)

BACK-STOOL. A chair without arms, a stool with a back. In the furniture 'in the Greate Gallerye' at Leicester House, The Strand, in 1588 were 'twoe backe stooles . . . covered wthe greene Velvett'. At Ham House in 1679 the Withdrawing Room contained a set of '6 armchairs and 6 back stools (*i.e.* single chairs) carved and gilt'. The term was still used in the middle of the 18th century. Ince and Mayhew in the *Universal System* (1759-63) illustrate 2 'back stool chairs', in type corresponding with other single chairs in the book.

BALL-AND-CLAW FOOT. Derived from the oriental design of a dragon's claw holding a ball or pearl, frequently found on early Chinese bronzes; introduced in English furniture early in the 18th century, succeeding the club-foot, which, however, continued to be employed. An eagle's claw was at times substituted; by 1760 this treatment had ceased to be fashionable (*see* CHAIRS, Fig. 62 and Fig. 78, for an eagle's claw).

BALL-FOOT. Spherical and mainly employed on the oak and walnut furniture of the 16th and 17th centuries (*see* BUREAUX, CABINETS, etc.).

BALUSTERS. A short pillar or column, spiral, vase-shaped, straight, tapered or in a variety of other forms; at first turned by hand, but from the 17th century onwards by foot lathe, and employed as supports in chairs, tables, stands, etc. Split-baluster ornament was applied to many varieties of furniture about the middle of the 17th century.

BAMBOO FURNITURE. The bamboo, a genus of giant grasses (*genus Bambusa*) having a light, jointed stem, was defined in Sheraton's *Cabinet Dictionary* (1803) as 'a kind of Indian reed, which in the East is used for chairs. They are in some degree imitated in England by turning beech in the same form, and making chairs of this fashion, painting them to match the colour of the reeds and cane.' Other colour schemes were also employed. Peter Nicholson states that 'bamboo is employed in chairs and tables' (*The Practical Cabinet-Maker and Upholsterer*, 1826). Bamboo furniture was considered appropriate for interiors in the Chinese taste. The vogue for bamboo furniture continued into Victorian times.

BANDING. A term employed for borders on furniture (*see* CHESTS OF DRAWERS, CONSTRUCTION, TABLES).

BANK. A term applied to a long seat in the Middle Ages; the *New English Dictionary* gives several forms of the word.

BANKER (BANCORS, BANQUER). A cushion or covering for a seat. All the above forms occur in the Account Rolls of the Priory of Finchale (Surtees). Under the date 1446 there is an entry 'Banqueres pro scabellis' (benches). There are many references in later Tudor wills and inventories.

BANTAM WORK. *See* JAPANNING AND LACQUER.

BARBERRY or **BERBERRY** (*Berberis vulgaris* of the order Berberidaceae). A shrub yielding a close-grained yellow wood from which a yellow dye is obtained; used in 17th-century inlay.

BARGELLO WORK. *See* NEEDLEWORK.

BAROMETER CASES AND FRAMES. The Barometer or Baroscope—terms used indiscriminately as early as the 17th century—is an instrument for indicating impending changes in the weather, the type employing a column of mercury for registering variations in atmospheric pressure (and known as the 'Quick-Silver Weather-Glass') superseding, before the end of the 17th century, the former primitive weather glasses. The Mercurial Barometer originated from the experiments of Torricelli, a disciple of Galileo, during investigations in connection with the force pump in 1643. In England, following the Restoration of 1660, this form of weather-glass engaged the attention of the newly-formed Royal Society. Robert Boyle first brought it into use, while Robert Hooke and Sir Samuel Morland identified themselves with its development; in addition to whom leading horologists and instrument makers, such as Henry Jones, Thomas Tompion, Daniel Quare, John Patrick and Charles Orme, gave the cases or frames beauty and elegance of form.

Early Baroscopes or Barometers took five principal forms:

1. The Balance, Statical or Steelyard Baroscope; 'fitter for the Closets and Speculations of Philosophers than to be introduced into common use,' and calling for no further mention here.

2. Cistern Barometers.

3. The Inclined, Diagonal, 'Sign-Post' or 'Yard-Arm' Barometer.

4. The Rectangular or Horizontal Barometer. Unlike the

3. *Diagonal Barometer, turned walnut case. Daniel Quare, London, c. 1695. (Hampton Court Palace.)*

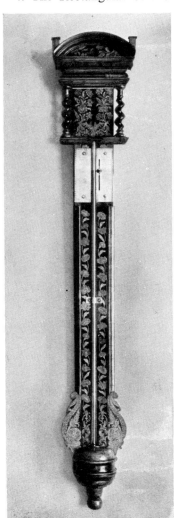 

4. *Diagonal Barometer and Thermometer, walnut mirror-frame. J. Patrick, London, c. 1715. (Mr A. Wade.)*

1. *Torricellian Barometer, oak frame veneered with walnut, decorated floral marquetry. J. Shaw, Holborn, c. 1695. (Mr F. Garrett.)* 2. *Torricellian Barometer, walnut frame with pedimented hood, flanked by twisted columns. Anon., c. 1700.*

Diagonal Barometer, which long survived, the rectangular type proved defective in practical application.

5. The Siphon Barometer.

First adapted as a wheel barometer by Dr Robert Hooke and illustrated and described in his *Micography* (1665), it was not generally adopted until the time of George III. A few exceptionally fine examples, however, were produced in the reign of William III (Figs. 5 and 6). *A Complete Discourse of . . . the Baroscope or Quick-Silver Weather Glass* (1688) by John Smith, Clockmaker, states that 'The Frame is Wood, of which any sort may serve, but for Ornament sake, the Choicest are generally made use of, such as Ebony, Walnut or Olive-Wood. The Shape or Figure is various according to the Fancies of Them that either make or use them.'

In 1695 Daniel Quare, the celebrated clock-maker, patented

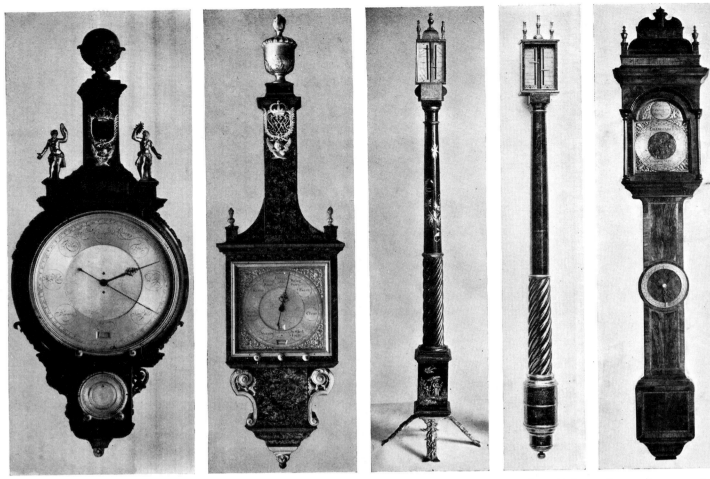

5. *Siphon Wheel Barometer, walnut case, mounted with ormolu, T. Tompion, c. 1695. (Buckingham Palace: By gracious permission of Her Majesty the Queen.)* 6. *Siphon Wheel Barometer, stained burr-maple case, walnut mouldings mounted with ormolu. Made for William III (royal cypher) by Thomas Tompion, c. 1695. (Hampton Court Palace.)* 7. *Portable, or Independent Barometer, case decorated black and gold japan. D. Quare, c. 1695. (P. Griffiths Coll.)* 8. *'Pillar' or 'Stick' Barometer, turned wood case decorated with reddish-brown and gold japan. Anon., c. 1705. (V. & A. Mus.)* 9. *Pendant Wheel Barometer, clock-like case of walnut. J. Hallifax, Barnsley, c. 1715. (P. Griffiths Coll.)*

his well-known 'Portable Weather Glass', a portable form of cistern barometer. Derham, in 1696, refers to some experiments and observations made at the Monument, on Fish Street Hill, with 'Two of Mr. Quare's best Portable Barometers,' and a number of these instruments—inscribed *Invented and Made by Danl Quare*—are in various public and private collections (Fig. 7). Certain of Quare's portable instruments, which are double-sided, are lettered in English on one face and in French on the other. In ancient barometers the grace and excellence of both lettering and numerals, framed within borders or scrolls and flourishes, contribute greatly to the decorative effect.

Probably the earliest mention of a barometer in England occurs in the inventory of the possessions of King Charles I, sold by order of Parliament, between 1648 and 1652. It includes 'A Barometer' valued at 10s. Possibly this refers to one of the primitive 'weather glasses' to which reference has already been made. A mercurial barometer was acquired for Lyme Hall, Cheshire, in 1675, the owner writing on May 8 of that year:

The Carrier will bring a long deale box with a bottle that hath

Quick-silver in itt. Prithee command there be great care of itt, that neither of them—the box or bottle—be stirred till I come home. 'Tis a device I had of Sir Jonas Moore to know the weather by.

Sir Jonas was the patron of Flamsteed, the first Astronomer-Royal, the foundation of the Royal Observatory at Greenwich dating from this very year.

Barometers with a siphon tube were also made in considerable numbers at the beginning of the 18th century. This type, not externally distinguishable from the pendant barometer with the straight or Torricellian tube, was often mounted in a walnut frame and provided with a turned wood cistern-cover.

Two types of cistern barometer, the Torricellian and the Diagonal, appear to have been popular during the first three-quarters of the 18th century, rare exceptions being indicated in the examples illustrated in Figs. 8 and 12. A remarkable wheel barometer, corresponding closely in design with contemporary clock-cases (Fig. 9) dates probably early in the 18th century and is finely executed in walnut.

Examples of barometer-frames, or cases decorated with japan, are generally in the form of the portable or 'stick' barometer in vogue about 1700. The specimen (Fig. 12) is interest-

10. *Diagonal Barometer and Thermometer, frame incorporating 'Perpetual Calendar of Time'. Watkins and Smith, London, c. 1755. (Science Mus., London.)*

11. *Diagonal Barometer, walnut frame, dated 1742. C. Orme, Ashby-de-la-Zouch.*

 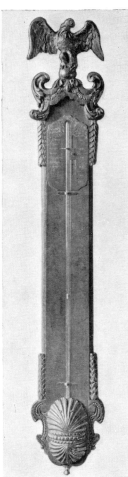  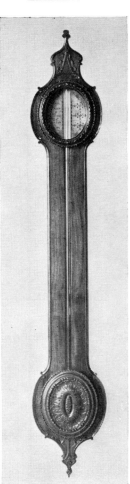 

12. *Siphon Barometer and Thermometer, frame decorated black and gold japan, dated 1719. I. Robelou, London. (Science Mus.)*
13. *Torricellian Barometer, carved walnut case, c. 1730. (Levens Hall, Westmorland.)* 14. *Torricellian Barometer and Thermometer, carved and painted rococo frame, 'sun-in-splendour' gilded. J. Ayscough, c. 1755. (V. & A. Mus.)* 15. *Torricellian Barometer, carved mahogany frame. Anon., c. 1760. (P. Griffiths Coll.)* 16. *Wheel Barometer, Thermometer, Hygrometer and Time-Piece, case inlaid mahogany. J. Somalvico, London, c. 1780. (M. L. Meyer Coll.)*

ing because of its uncommon form, and bears the name of the maker and date—'Isaac Robelou, Fecit, Lond. 1719.' The frame is charmingly decorated in gold upon black japan.

During the early and mid-Georgian periods, the instruments principally favoured were of the cistern type with either the straight or inclined tube. Diagonal barometers, mounted in large rectangular frames enclosing mirrors, were made at the beginning of the 18th century. One of John Patrick's barometers of this kind is illustrated in Fig. 4. This method of mounting the diagonal barometer was no doubt devised to overcome the objection to the 'Inconveniences . . . in the Shape', to which John Smith refers in his *Discourse* of 1688. Examples indicate that the type was still popular in the latter half of the 18th century. Between the years 1720 and 1740 a considerable number of diagonal barometers of the 'sign-post' or 'yard-arm' variety appear to have been constructed by the well-known maker Charles Orme of Ashby-de-la-Zouch (Fig. 11).

Another diagonal barometer is mounted in a large rectangular frame of mahogany (Fig. 10). It closely resembles the earlier instrument by Patrick (Fig. 4), but encloses a calendar entitled 'A Perpetual Regulation of Time', from which the days of the month, zodiacal signs, sun's right ascension, declination, and time of rising and setting, high-water at London Bridge, and phases of the moon can be ascertained.

The barometer case (Fig. 13) is a rare example, the scrolled cresting supporting an eagle recalling the decoration of contemporary mirror frames.

Towards the middle of the 18th century the decoration of barometer frames or cases shows the influence of the rococo style (Fig. 14). The barometer (Fig. 15) foreshadows the classical reaction and the motives popularised by Robert Adam—the carved elliptical patera, forming the cistern-cover, and the delicate enrichments framing the barometric scale.

The wheel principle of construction, although seldom made when first invented, was revived under George III. Known as the Wheel or Dial Barometer (Fig. 16), during the last quarter of the 18th century it was the most popular type for domestic purposes, the cases being usually made of finely figured mahogany or satinwood, inlaid with neo-classic motifs and containing—in addition to the silvered dial framed within a moulded ring or bezel of polished brass, filled with convex or flattened crown glass—a thermometer, hygrometer and spirit-level. Rosewood was occasionally used for the cases of late wheel barometers, cross-banded with contrasting woods, or inlaid with brass or mother-of-pearl. At this period many barometers appear to have been constructed by immigrant Italian chamber-masters and workmen domiciled in this country. After remarking upon the utility of the barometer, in the third edition of his Historical and Philosophical Account of that instrument, published in 1766, the Rev. Edward Saul adds in conclusion:

> And all such Persons as would be curious in them, and well assured of the Truth and Exactness of those Instruments, upon which they ground their Observations, must not grudge the Expense of purchasing them from the very best Hands. As for such Weather-Glasses, as have been lately hawked about the Country, by needy Foreigners, or pedling Philosophers; it may not be improper to caution my Readers, that they are, generally speaking very great cheats and Impositions upon those, who, for the Sake of the Meanness of the Price, are persuaded to buy them.

In the early decades of the 19th century the most popular forms were the 'wheel' type and the Common 'chamber' or Torricellian weather-glass, the case of the first generally incorporating a thermometer and hygrometer, while examples of the second are frequently found with narrow, upright, convex-fronted frames or cases of mahogany, the silvered register-plates being protected by 'bow glasses'.

BAROQUE. A French term originally employed as an adjective meaning whimsical, grotesque, irregularly shaped. As applied to the arts, it did not obtain any wide currency until towards the middle of the 19th century, when it was used in a derisive sense, *e.g.* in the *Architectural Dictionary* (1863): 'The word baroque involves the idea of anything unintentionally absurd.' Though its precise significance still remains debatable, in its modern connotation baroque implies composition in mass with a thorough exploitation of plastic values, a dynamic sense of movement, and a bold scenic use of light and shade; also a considerable element of grotesque. As a descriptive term baroque relates primarily to architecture and painting, but its use has been extended to the decorative arts. Late Stuart carving affords many examples. The second phase of the style is seen in the carved and gilt furniture designed by Kent and other architects for the great Palladian houses of the early 18th century, which is fully baroque in spirit and form. Baroque precedes the rococo style (*q.v.*) and passes into it by almost imperceptible stages.

BASES or **BASSES.** A term commonly used to describe the lower valances of a bed. Basses are frequently mentioned in connection with state beds in the accounts for the furnishing of the royal palaces from 1667 onwards. Chippendale refers to 'bases of stuff' in connection with bedposts.

BASKERVILLE, JOHN (1706-75). Famous typographer, also manufacturer of japanned wares. John Taylor began business as a japanner in Birmingham about 1736 and developed his manufacture. Baskerville, then a poor teacher of penmanship, studied Taylor's technical methods in order to produce 'goods painted and japanned as they had never been painted or japanned before'. His workshop was at 22 Moor Street, until 1749. He had obtained a patent in 1742 'for a new method of making and flat grinding thin metal plates'. These plates were to be japanned and varnished, and were to 'produce fine glowing mahogany colour, a black no way inferior to that of the most perfect Indian goods, or an imitation Tortoise-shell'. Among the uses to which these plates were to be applied were 'to Veneer the Frames of Paintings and Pictures of all sizes, Looking-Glass Frames, the Fronts of Cabinets, Buroes, Glass Frames, Chimney Pieces . . . and every other sort of Household Furniture'. Samuel Derrick, Master of the Ceremonies at Bath, after a visit to Birmingham, writes:

> This ingenious artist carries on a great trade in the Japan way, in which he showed me several useful articles. . . . One of his workmen has manifested fine talents for fruit painting in several pieces which he showed me.

Though the japanning business appears to have been carried on by Baskerville until towards the end of his career, its productions have not been identified, the bulk of Birmingham japan wares being of later date (*see* JAPANNING AND LACQUER and *John Baskerville*, Ralph Straus and R. K. Kent, 1907).

BASON STAND. So called in trade catalogues of the 18th century (*see* WASHING-STANDS).

BAS-RELIEF. Sculptured work the figures of which project less than half their true proportions from the surface on which they are carved; when the projection is equal to half the true proportions it is called *mezzo-relievo*, when more than half, *alto-relievo*.

BATTLEMENTED. Notched or indented, a form of cornice derived from medieval architecture (*see* AUMBRY, (Fig. 1).

BAUDEKIN. A very rich silk woven with gold (Du Cange). A rich cloth, now called brocade. Name is said to have been derived from Baldacus, Babylon, whence originally brought. First woven with a warp of gold thread, but name came to be applied to rich shot silks, and finally even to plain silk webs. Sometimes mentioned in connection with bed-hangings in the later Middle Ages, and probably introduced into England in the 13th century. 'Baldekyn of silke at xxxiiis iiiid. the pece' (Wardrobe Accounts of Edward VI).

BAYES, BAYS. A coarse woollen stuff having a long nap used chiefly for linings, coverings, curtains, etc., the manufacture being introduced into England in the 16th century by fugitives from France and the Netherlands. 1635 Camden's *Hist. Eliz.* i. 101: *These light stuffes which they call Bayes and Sayes* (*see* BEDS, descriptions of Cromwell's at Hampton Court Palace). Two shillings and sixpence a yard was the average cost of 'blewe and black bayse' (Howard Household Books), but in 1622 scarlet bays cost 6s. a yard.

BAYWOOD. A term formerly used to distinguish Honduras mahogany from the West Indian varieties (*see* MAHOGANY).

BEAD. A small half-round moulding of very frequent occurrence in 18th-century furniture: sometimes arranged in a sequence as 'beading.'

BEAD AND REEL. A variety of the bead moulding in which rounds and oblongs are combined. In the form of inlay

1. *Bed; tester suspended from ceiling, from Burgundian MS. c. 1480. (B.M. Harley MS. 4431.)*

2. *Oak Posts and linen-fold panels from head of bed: on right-hand post, eagle, symbol of St John. c. 1525. Ht. (posts) 4 ft. 1½ in., L. 4 ft. 2½ in. (V. & A. Mus.)*

also commonly used to decorate framework, and invariably found on 'Nonsuch Chests' (*see* CHESTS). In the mid-18th century adopted by cabinet-makers on a smaller scale.

BEDS. From the Middle Ages onwards great attention has been bestowed upon beds, householders spending more money on their construction and decoration than on any other type of furniture. Minute descriptions of them are found in early inventories. In wills dating from the 14th century to late Tudor times 'the best bed' often headed the list of legacies. In royal palaces an officer was placed in charge of them, and in the Privy Purse Expenses of Elizabeth of York, queen of Henry VII, there are frequent allusions to the 'grome of the beddes' and to sums paid to him for superintending the removal of this part of the Queen's furniture on her progress through the country.

Though Alexander Neckham (*De Naturis Rerum*) implies that a roof and hangings were introduced at the end of the 12th century, there were neither posts, cornices, nor high wooden backs to beds until the close of the Middle Ages. When nobles and princely testators bequeathed their beds, they thought primarily of the costly draperies. These were an integral part of the decoration of the room, and the apparel of the bed with 'all hallyngs belongyng to ye saide bed and chamber' is a frequent form in such bequests. In the medieval domestic economy rooms set apart for sleeping in were unknown. In Sir John Fastolphe's great house at Caister there were beds in almost every room. In 1492, a Canon of Wells had a bed in his parlour, and even in Elizabeth's reign the practice was still continued. The Great Chamber, which would contain the most splendid bed, was also the private dining-room of the lord and lady of the house. The herald who attended Princess Margaret, daughter of Henry VII, into Scotland to marry King James, relates that in the chamber at Holyrood where the banquet was served after the wedding 'ther was also a riche Bed of Astat'. Beds were commonly used as couches and seats in the

3. *Oak Bed, posts fluted and carved with cusps and diapers. Early 16th century. Ht. 5 ft. 10 in., L. 6 ft. 2 in., W. 5 ft. 4 in. (Saffron Walden Mus., Essex.)*

daytime, and the curtains, which, when drawn, completely surrounded the bedding, are generally shown looped up in the form of a bag (Fig. 1).

At the head of the bed was a 'celour' (*see* CELURE AND TESTER) of silk, damask or linen, while the tester was often embroidered with some heraldic or other device. Voluminous curtains to protect the sleeper from draughts completed the medieval state bed. The framework, of negligible value, is never separately mentioned in inventories.

From the 14th century onwards, hangings of the richest velvets, satins, silks, and even cloth of gold are described in inventories. Hunting and hawking were favourite subjects. To the Duke of Exeter, Henry V bequeathed a complete and costly 'bed of hawkying' with the figures worked in gold. Tapestry was also employed for the hangings, and was occasionally the product of English looms, 'beds of Norfolk' (*i.e.* Lynn or—Norwich) being mentioned in early inventories.

The curtains were often suspended by rings from the 'tester', and that they might be drawn backwards and forwards 'poles or beltis of Yren' were provided, or they were raised and lowered by cords. The draperies of a bed so suspended are implied by the bequest of John Baret, a wealthy citizen of Bury, to his niece in 1463 of 'my greene hangyyd bedde steyned (*i.e.* painted) with my armys that hanggeth in the chambyr over kitchene with the greene keveryng longgyng thereto'. The sides and ends of the oak-framed 'bedstock' (*q.v.*) were pierced and ropes drawn through them to support the mattress. Records of the time show that the bedding usually consisted of a straw or wool pallet, two feather-beds, sheets (sometimes of silk), blankets, another feather-bed, and over all an embroidered quilt, often trimmed with fur. In the medieval period people generally slept unclothed. Some cynical lines of the *Reliquiae Antiquae* inveigh against the pomp and vanity of dress in

women, who are told that, however gay may be their raiment during the day, they know well they must lie in bed as naked as they were born. On their periodical progresses from house to house, great magnates carried their valuable bedding, curtains and valances with them, leaving the common wood framings.

This type of bed was in use until the beginning of the 16th century. Within the next 50 years a new type was evolved, wood taking the place of fabric in the principal parts. At the four corners carved posts were now placed, while the head was filled with panelling. Later a tester was added, but the evidence afforded by the few surviving Tudor beds indicates that this member was not introduced until about the middle of the century.

'Stande Beddes', of a more stable structure, were known in the 15th century, some having a low panelled head. One in Dürer's well-known woodcut of the Death of the Virgin has a head of late Gothic panelling and a wooden tester hung from the ceiling in the ancient manner. The earliest recorded set of bedposts are four now supporting the West Gallery of St Mary's Church, Broughton, Cheshire. The heraldic escutcheons with which they are decorated suggest that the bed belonged to Henry VII, being made about the time of his marriage to Elizabeth of York.

In the Victoria and Albert Museum there is a collection of posts which are all of slender proportions, but show various types of ornament including profile heads. Four, diapered with late Gothic foliage, have bosses carved as split pomegranates and may be dated before Henry VIII's divorce from Katherine of Aragon in 1533, the split pomegranate being one of the badges of the Queen.

Fig. 2 shows a pair of about the same date, and in this case

4. *Oak Bed, octagonal post, carving early Renaissance style; panel of tester modern. Ht. 6 ft. 6 in., L. 7 ft. 1 in., W. 4 ft. 8 in. (V. & A. Mus.)*

they represent the head of a bed flanking linen-pattern panels of simple character; the posts are carved with vase shapes and foliage of Early Renaissance character. At each of the four corners once stood symbols of the Evangelists, though only the eagle of St John now remains. Beds of this date in which the framework has survived are very rare and the majority are freely restored. In Fig. 3, from the Saffron Walden Museum, the main interest is in the carved posts, those at the foot having deep flutes with Gothic cusps and Early Renaissance ornament above.

Inventories prove that in the opening years of the century the wainscot head was coming into general use. A 'sillour del waynscot' is included among the goods of Master Martin Colyns, Treasurer of York in 1508, and The Vyne Inventory of 1541 mentions 'i trussing bed of wynscot with iiii pillars carved'.

Probably in many of these early Tudor beds the suspended canopy with its valance and curtains had not yet given place to a panelled ceiling and a carved frieze, this view gaining support from the inventories and account books of the age. The 'well kerved bedsteade' of Henry Fitzroy, created Duke of Richmond in 1525, was adorned with a tester of cloth of gold, while a few years later the mistress of Grafton bought 'xii yards and a half of russet greye fustyon to lyne the tester' of her best bed-stead. At Mendham Hall, Suffolk, in 1548, the 'joyned' beds in the principal chambers had testers and celours of fabric, implying that only the frame and carved posts were of wood.

About in the middle of the century the posts at the head were discarded, the wainscot being sufficiently solid to carry that end of the tester. This departure is seen in the remarkable bedstead (Fig. 4) from Crackenthorpe Hall, near Appleby. It probably dates from about 1530, and the decoration is of transitional character—a mixture of Gothic and Renaissance detail. The

5. *Head (Celour) of Bed (Fig. 4): Gothic lettering on upper panels.*

6. *Oak Bed. Anne Hathaway's house, Shottery, Stratford-on Avon: original mattress. c. 1580*

panels of the celour are carved with doves and conventional flowers, while the upper row are inscribed in burnt Gothic lettering 'Drede God', 'Love God', 'Prayes God'. A crocketed cornice surmounts a carved frieze, but there is no indication that originally the bedstead possessed a wooden tester. The octagonal posts merge into square plinths and are intersected by shield-shaped bosses. The 'bedstock', which has the frame-work carved with leaf patterns and trails of foliage, stands clear of the end posts, but the length seems to have been reduced.

In the fully developed Elizabethan type a panelled tester was supported on posts of bulbous form which reach their maximum girth early in the 17th century, after which time they tend to diminish. Fig. 6 illustrates the more simple bedstead of the time. The proportions are falsified, for the posts have been cut down, while the tester has been raised by nearly a foot. The original height of an oak bedstead was seldom more than 7 feet 6 inches.

Early in Elizabeth's reign carved beds appear to have been confined to the wealthy, but within the next 25 years a higher standard of domestic comfort had brought them within the reach of the yeoman class. In a familiar passage William Harrison writes that in his time three things are 'marvellously altered', one of them being the great improvement in beds and bedding among countryfolk, who had hitherto been content to lie on a straw pallet with a sack of chaff for a pillow.

Tudor and Jacobean oak and walnut bedsteads were some-times varnished soon after they were made (*see* VARNISHES); while an entry in the Grafton Accounts early in Elizabeth's reign records that a workman was set to stain a bed of inferior wood to resemble walnut. In 1569 'a pentare of Worcester' was employed to paint 'my Mr's armes in coulours' on 'a walnot tree bed'.

Bed staves or wooden pegs were used to provide some lateral support for the mountainous pile of clothes within the 'bed-

stock'. The vertical holes in the sides of the bed in Fig. 6 and in many others were intended, no doubt, to contain these staves. The sides and ends of the 'bedstock' also continued to be pierced horizontally, and on the ropes as a foundation was laid a mattress of plaited rushes. In Warwickshire inventories of Shakespeare's time these 'mattes of flagges' are a common item. The mat still preserved on the bed in Fig. 6 is in excellent condition and may well be contemporary with the bed. That such mats were commonly used for this purpose is proved by the sepulchral monuments of the age. Carved in marble or alabaster they figure on many elaborate tombs; for example, in the Beauchamp Chapel at Warwick, Ambrose Dudley is lying on a mat of this kind.

The Hathaway example (Fig. 6) was probably the work of the local joiner, but the bed from Great Fulford (Fig. 7) is of higher quality. It is said to have belonged to the second Sir John Fulford, who owned the house from 1546 to 1580; and the ruff worn by the figures on the stiles, in the fashion of the last decade of his ownership, supports the tradition. The studied proportions and well-applied ornament are typical of the finer work of this period. The bulbous supports to the columns are admirably modelled, and the pedestals have gadrooned mouldings enclosing the upper section.

In most of these panelled backs the arches start from a ledge or shelf-rail on which rushlights were placed, and the marks of burning are often visible on specimens that have survived this dangerous practice. Below the shelf-rail the panels were generally left plain, as the bolsters and pillows would have covered any carving.

7. *Oak Bed, elaborately carved; posts of bulbous form. c. 1580. (Great Fulford. Devon.)*

8. *Great Bed of Ware; carved oak, inlay and painted decoration, c. 1595. Ht. 8 ft. 9 in., L. and W. 10 ft. 8 in. (V. & A. Mus.)*

The 'Great Bed of Ware' (Fig. 8) has long been celebrated on account of its gigantic proportions. In 1596, within a few years of its construction, it was mentioned in the *Poetical Itinerary* of Prince Ludwig of Anhalt-Köhten as among the memorable curiosities near London; while that its fame soon became proverbial is proved by the reference in *Twelfth Night* to a sheet 'big enough for the bed of Ware in England'. Possibly made for Sir Henry Fanshaw (b. 1569) of Ware Park, it was apparently already at The White Hart in 1612, and then at other inns in Ware, until its removal in 1869 to Rye House, Hoddesdon. It has been the subject of many jests and allusions by dramatists, poets, travellers and antiquarians. In the *History of Hertfordshire* (1700) Sir Henry Chauncey relates that on one occasion 'six citizens and their wives came from London' and slept in it.

Apart from its gigantic proportions, the bed is a fine example of the lavishly enriched Elizabethan type. The back is divided by terminal figures flanked by columns with composite capitals, two grotesque satyrs in profile flanking the outer stiles. Within round arches are panels of inlay in various coloured woods, representing the elevation of a Tudor house with swans on water in the foreground; this decoration, closely resembling perspective inlay in contemporary overmantels, being adapted from designs by J. V. de Vries (1527-1604), a Dutch commercial artist whose engravings circulated widely in England. The richly carved posts rest on arcaded canopies supported on pillars with square plinths below. The cappings have been mutilated to enable the bed to stand in a low room; while the original cornice has been replaced by a copy. The tester still retains traces of colour decoration, but many panel mouldings have been renewed.

A good specimen made of walnut in the more restrained architectural style is shown in Fig. 9. It was originally at

10. *Oak Bed, inlaid in box and holly, lower portion restored. c. 1590 (Astley Hall, Lancs.)*

9. *Walnut Bed, posts with Ionic capitals, frieze inlaid with a corbeau (crest of Corbets) and dated 1593. Ht. 7 ft. 4 in., L. 7 ft. 11 in., W. 5 ft. 8 in. (V. & A. Mus.)*

Astley Corbet, Shropshire, and bears the corbeau crest of the Corbets. The frieze is inlaid with the initials J.C. and the date 1593. The Red Book (1590) at Lumley Castle lists no fewer than 23 beds of 'Walnutree and Markatree'.

In a list of the contents of Kenilworth Castle made after the death of Robert, Earl of Leicester, in 1588, many 'beddestedes of walnuttree' are listed with hangings of satin, velvet, silk and 'clothe of gould tysshue'. One had 'five plumes of coloured feathers standing in cuppes knitt all over with goulde silver and crymson silke'—an early instance of a kind of ornament which became normal on the testers of state beds in the following century. Several field bedsteads were made 'toppe fashion', probably resembling in shape the 'waggon tilt' canopied bedsteads of medieval times. This variety, apparently designed for use in war, continued to be made for travelling and other pacific purposes until a much later date (*see* BEDS, FIELD).

The inlaid decoration of the back is a notable feature in Tudor beds. The bog oak, holly, box, poplar and sycamore, almost the only available inlays, did not permit of more than a restricted scale of chromatic effect. Inlay of exceptional excellence is found on all the flat surfaces of the Astley Hall example (Fig. 10). The bedstock, panelled ends and pedestals are much restored, but the corbelled-out cornice, the tester with its wealth of mouldings and inlay of floral sprigs and stars, the fanciful elaboration of the panels, delicate vine tendrils and faceted ornament of the posts all contribute to the magnificence of the effect. Queen Elizabeth had one of these marquetry beds at Whitehall, described by Paul Hentzner (1578) as 'ingeniously composed of woods of different colours'.

11. *Oak Bed, posts with bulbous supports richly carved, plinths and arcaded back inlaid. c. 1600. Ht. 7 ft. 2 in., L. 8 ft., W. 5 ft. 7 in. (Aston Hall, Birmingham.)*

12. *Oak Bed, carved and painted with coats of arms and floral sprays. c. 1610-15. Ht. 7 ft. 1¾ in., L. 7 ft. 4 in., W. 6 ft. 5¾ in. (V. & A. Mus.)*

In the Great Bed of Ware painting and inlay are combined in the decoration, and another remarkable specimen of this treatment is given in Fig. 12. The back is arcaded in the upper stage and has shell-headed niches below; while at the sides are pierced scrolls surmounted by obelisks. Various coats of arms blazoned in colours occupy the panels of the headboard and tester. The rest of the structure is lavishly painted with floral sprays, foliage and berried trees. The decoration is carried out on a dark background, while the plain portions are of light unvarnished oak. This is a rare survival from the painted furniture fashionable under Elizabeth and James I.

Among the contents of Northampton House, near Charing Cross, were several pieces of furniture painted in imitation of oriental lacquer; and thus long anticipating the general inception of the vogue. In the Bed Chamber was 'a Field bedstead of china worke black and silver branched with silver'. The Household Books of Lord Howard of Naworth record a payment in 1621 'To Mr. Hesketh for gilding a bedstead, drawing Mrs. Elizabeth and Marye's pictures'—a curious combination of functions. Though no gilded example survives, the Earl of Leicester's inventory and other Elizabethan and early Stuart domestic records suggest there was a fashion for such bedsteads in great houses. One at Windsor Castle, with '4 pillars and a headpiece of walnuttree gilt with ye furniture belonging' was sold for £40, then a very large sum, by order of the Council of State after Charles I's execution.

The display of heraldry, so common in that age, and denounced by Philip Stubbes in his *Anatomie of Abuses* (1583), is seen again in Fig. 13. On the centre of the headboard are the arms of James I with the initials J.R.; the shield to the left bearing the badge of Henry, Prince of Wales, and that to the right the arms of Frederick, Count Palatine. These shields date the bed within a year, as Frederick married Elizabeth, James's eldest daughter, in 1613; while Henry died in 1612, and Charles I was not created Prince of Wales until four years later. The posts are remarkable for the variety in the cup and cover enlargements, the lower portion being of columnar form.

Though in all the illustrated examples of Tudor beds the hangings are lacking, originally they were draped in a variety of materials such as velvets, silks, tapestry, embroidered linen, or even, in the most costly specimens, cloth of gold. Humbler people formed their hangings of fustian or 'steyned' cloth representing events in sacred history. In 1538 Alice Harvy, a widow of Bury, bequeathed to her son 'one seller steyned clothe wyth 5 Woundes (of Christ) and 3 curtyens thereunto steyned'. In Stuart times embroidered linen and crewel work were often employed. Lady Anne Drury of Hardwicke, Suffolk, bequeathed 'a cloth bed of my own working' in 1621.

It is often difficult to determine if the gorgeously upholstered beds described in 16th- and early 17th-century inventories were survivals from a past age or newly made. Some were certainly handed down through several generations. When Paul Hentzner visited Windsor Castle in 1578, he was shown a chamber containing the royal beds of Henry VII and his Queen and of Henry VIII and Anne Boleyn, each one 11 feet square and furnished with hangings of gold and silver; Queen Elizabeth's bed had crimson coverings of embroidery, and was not quite so long as the others. Beds with a light framework had never become really obsolete, and they continued to be made on medieval lines throughout the 16th century. In a list of the goods of Katherine of Aragon (1535) there are many descriptions of 'celours' and 'testours' of prodigal magnificence, but no mention of a wainscot bed.

Again, at Hampton Court Palace, Hentzner saw a bed, the tester of which was worked by Anne Boleyn and presented by her to Henry VIII. Even as late as 1620, for one 'waynscot' bedstead at Farringdon or Walton there were a dozen in which the tester and head are expressly stated to have been formed of material. The hangings and bedding for a bed of this kind were sent by one Symondes to Knole Park in July, 1642:

> Packed up in a fardel, viz. in ye black bed chamber . . . 5 curtains of crimson and white taffeta, the valance of it white satin embroidered with crimson and white silk, and a deep fringe suitable; . . . tester of white satin suitable to the valance.

This evidence shows the prevalence of two distinct types at the same period, one with a light framework and very elaborate hangings, the other the 'joined' bed in which carved woodwork constituted the main interest.

Only one elaborately draped bedstead dating before the Restoration is now known to be extant and is preserved at Knole (Fig. 14). Those at Hampton Court were sold with the bulk of Charles I's furniture, with the exception of a few retained by Cromwell. An inventory of goods at the latter's death in 1659 included:

> In the Rich Bedchamber a bedstead with a sackcloth bottom, the furniture of rich incarnadine velvett embroidered very rich with gold and silver conteyning, Three Courtines, Fower cantoines, deep Vallons and bases, Fower capps (*i.e.* cup-shaped finials) of the same velvett and imbroidered suitable for the same bed. The ceeler and head cloth . . . is of rich cloth of gold with inward vallons, cases for the posts and lynyngs of the curtains and cantoines all of the same.

The cantoins, or *cantonnières*, were narrow, shaped panels of the same material, which united the valances at the corners. When fine materials were employed, they were protected by extra coverings, and the incarnadine velvet bed had '3 large courtines of scarlet blazes being a case about the bed'. Beds hung with 'a liver collour serge' or with 'courtines of sad collour bazes' were clearly the outcome of Cromwell's sombre taste, while several are described as 'halfe headed bedsteads'—either with the tester extending only part of the length and not supported on posts at the foot, or with a low-panelled back without canopy or curtains. Such beds were in use in Elizabethan times, and in 1634 Lettice, Countess of Leicester, possessed one which the inventory states to have been already old.

Bed linen was familiar in the early Middle Ages, but detailed descriptions are not found until much later. The eight mattresses of Wolsey's bed were 'every of them stuffed with 13 pounds of carded wulle and covered with 12 elles of fyne hollande cloth'. His pillow-cases were of the same material, '2 of them seamed with black silk and fleur-de-lys of gold; and the other 2 with white silk and fleur-de-lys of red silk'. Leaves were also used for stuffing mattresses, and in *Sylva* (1664) Evelyn writes that 'the leaves of the beech being gathered about the fall, and somewhat before they are frostbitten' for this purpose. Fringes and valances are mentioned early in the 16th century, and bases, or lower valances, are described in Henry VIII's inventory (1547).

Although richly carved oak bedsteads continued to be used, for the type descended from the medieval draped bedstead, oak

13. *Oak Bed, carved with arms of James I, badge of Henry. Prince of Wales, and arms of Frederick V, Count Palatine of the Rhine. c. 1612-13. Ht. 7 ft. 8½ in., L. 7 ft. 7¼ in., W. 6 ft. 2 in. (Montacute, Som. National Trust.)*

14. *Bed; hangings and quilt red satin, appliqué pattern silver tissue. c. 1610-20. (Knole, Kent.)*

15. *State Bed, hung with cloth of gold, lined with coral taffeta.*
c. 1670-80. (Knole, Kent.)

also described by Fanny Burney, who adds 'but the third state-room (the King's Bedroom) was magnificence itself: it was fitted up for King William. The bed-curtains, tester, quilt, and valance were all of gold flowers, worked upon a silver ground: its value, even in those days, was £7,000.' Since her time tradition has associated James I with this magnificent bed (Fig. 15) instead of with the one in the 'Spangled Room' actually dating from his time. It represents the type which came into fashion after the Restoration, and is one of the most extravagant ever made in England. The curtains, valances, tester and bases are composed of cloth of gold lined with brilliant coral taffeta, now much faded, all closely embroidered in a floral design in gold, silver and coloured silks.

A bed of comparable magnificence was formerly at Glemham Hall, Suffolk, having been made about 1685 for the London house of Sir Dudley North and moved to Glemham after his death in 1691 (Fig. 16). The straight moulded cornice is covered with crimson velvet, lavishly trimmed with tawny and brown tasselled fringe; the ceiling of the tester, back and bedstead being of cream satin embroidered in a delicate floral pattern. The slender octagonal posts finish in removable bases, painted and carved with gilt cherubs. The illustration shows two of the remarkable armchairs from the set to match the bed. The set, and that in the Venetian Ambassador's Room at Knole, can be assigned to Thomas Roberts (q. v.).

Until well into the next century the four corners of the tester

16. *State Bed, crimson velvet hangings trimmed with tassel fringe; tester and back lined with embroidered silk. c. 1685. (Formerly at Glemham Hall, Suff.)*

was discarded for a beechwood frame, the testers, cornices and backs being covered with the same material as the curtains. The tall and slender posts were covered with taffeta, the valances were deep, the whole construction much higher, and the 'bedstok' was united to the posts. This type of bed, complete with hangings, was enormously costly, but most important houses had at least one, destined for state occasions and distinguished guests, and not for ordinary domestic purposes. Oak bedsteads now declined in quality, the posts becoming more simple and attenuated, until they degenerated into plain balusters.

At Knole Park there are several specimens of upholstered beds dating from about 1625 to late Stuart times. In her *Diary* for 1779 Fanny Burney records a visit to Knole and gives a description of three State-rooms. The first, she says, 'was fitted up by an "Earle of Dorsette" for the bedchamber of James I'. This may be identified with the 'Spangle Bedroom', and contains a bed (Fig. 14) of which the hangings and quilt are of the same material—red satin with an *appliqué* pattern of silver tissue—as that on a set of early Jacobean stools and the X-framed armchair with which it is contemporary; and therefore the only state bedstead of the type known to survive from that time. The cornice is straight and surmounts a frieze with an ogee moulding; the headboard has a lunette-shaped top.

The second, or Venetian Room, in which the bed bears the crowned cypher of James II (*see* INTRODUCTION, Fig. 8) is were generally surmounted by vase-shaped finials covered with the material of the valances and holding large bunches of ostrich plumes, a fashion dating back to c. 1560. In the Ingatestone inventory of 1600, 'fower guilt topps for the iiii corners of ye bed teaster' are mentioned, and among the items delivered by Symondes at Knole in 1624 were a large number of these 'cups' or finials. In the bills for furnishing the royal palaces under Charles II and William III, there are many entries for sums paid to Richard Chase and Robert Crofts, 'Feather Dressers', 'for scowering a set of Bedd Plumes for his mat^{ie}'. Similar ornaments were also fashionable in France at this time.

In the great houses of the 17th century a mourning bed was commonly provided. In 1624 a bedstead of black velvet with taffeta curtains is listed among the contents of the Black Chamber at Walton, and at Claydon, twenty years later, Sir Ralph Verney is continually lending his great 'blake bedde' when a death occurs in the family. Evelyn records (March 5, 1685) that 'there came over divers envoyes and greate persons to condole the death of the late king (Charles II) who were receiv'd by the Queen Dowager on a bed of mourning'. The bed and hangings of the lying-in chambers were likewise objects of special attention, for the birth of an heir was regarded as a very important event, and receptions and even card parties were held in the bedchamber.

After the Restoration the height of bedsteads gradually

18. *William III's Bed, Hampton Court Palace; crimson velvet trimmed silver galon: vase-shaped finials with ostrich plumes. c. 1690. Ht. 17 ft. (By gracious permission of Her Majesty the Queen.)*

increased, in some cases reaching the ceiling of the loftiest room. A carved wooden cornice was also introduced, covered with the same material as the valances and curtains. Catherine of Braganza's bed, which Evelyn saw in 1662 at Hampton Court Palace, was 'an embroidery of silver on crimson velvet and cost £8,000, being a present made by the States of Holland when his Majesty returned'. In the private dining-room at Hampton Court may be seen a bed (Fig. 18) hung with crimson velvet trimmed with silver galon and a deep fringe. The corners of the tester are surmounted by openwork vase-shaped finials holding ostrich plumes. The present height to the top of the plumes is 17 feet, but the cornice has been removed, which accounts for the vases appearing out of scale. The Palace accounts mention the purchase from Lord Jersey of a crimson velvet bed 'for his Mat^{ies} State bed-chamber at Hampton Court', which almost certainly refers to this example. Between 1699 and 1701 many items relate to repairs and alterations to 'his Mat^{ies} Crimson Velvett Bed'. There was an enormous disparity between the cost of the hangings and the frames of such beds. The first Duke of Devonshire, for example, paid Francis Lapierre £15 in 1697 for a large wainscot bedstead with carved ornament and £470 for the hangings.

Of beds based upon designs by Daniel Marot and other prominent French architects of the late 17th century only a few specimens survive, but the blue damask bed from Hampton

17. *State Bed, crimson velvet hangings and tasselled fringe: back decorated in oyster colour silk damask, cypher in openwork of 1st Earl of Melville. 1690. Ht. 15 ft. 2 in., L. 9 ft., W. 8 ft. (V. & A. Mus.)*

19. *State Bed, coved cornice surmounted by scrolled cresting; valances and head-board drapery festooned and heavily fringed. c. 1700. (Formerly at Hampton Court, Herefords.)*

20. *State Bed made for Queen Anne, hung with figured velvet on white satin ground; urn-shaped finials. 1714. (Hampton Court Palace. By gracious permission of Her Majesty the Queen.)*

Court, Leominster (Fig. 19), is typical. The coved cornice of the tester is surmounted by a cresting of fretted scrollwork. The headboard is formed of a cartouche with elaborate scrolling and drapery below. The ornament is carved wood with the material glued on. The pattern of the damask is identical with that of a canopy of state in the First Presence Chamber at Hampton Court Palace, for which a large quantity of this damask was supplied in crimson at 24s. per yard in 1700. Beds of this type were formerly at Combe Abbey and Stoke Edith. Marot is now known to have received large payments from William III for designs supplied to Hampton Court (*see* MAROT, DANIEL), and the resemblance of some of these state beds and his published designs suggest that he exercised considerable influence.

The bed from Melville House, Fife (Fig. 17), reminiscent of Marot's style, is probably the finest surviving specimen of the last decade of the century. It was made for George Melville, first Earl of Melville (created 1690), and bears his monogram C.M.G. on an escutcheon above the headboard with an earl's coronet on either side. The cornice, fancifully carved in open-work and decorated with six coronets, is covered with crimson velvet, the festooned and tasselled valances and curtains being of the same material. The interior is lined with figured oyster-coloured damask of Chinese origin, the tester and headboard

being outlined with silk braid trimmed with fringe. The original coverlet is decorated with Lord Melville's monogram in an escutcheon below a coronet within an elaborate scrollwork design. The *cantonnières* (*q.v.*) are projected on curved iron supports, an apparently unique arrangement.

Allusions to 'French beds' in the royal upholsterers' accounts indicate that, if not actually imported, their design was based on contemporary French models. Several leading contemporary craftsmen, like the upholsterer Francis Lapierre, had emigrated from France.

Though early in the 18th century some important state beds had the cornice formed of bold architectural mouldings which reflected this foreign influence, the ornate character of the hangings sometimes dictated a more austere design. In the Queen's Bedroom at Hampton Court is a state bed which has no elaborate carving or complex mouldings (Fig. 20). It is hung with a large-patterned velvet in claret, green and gold on a white satin ground. A straight, projecting cornice is covered with velvet pasted over the mouldings; the hangings are simply trimmed with narrow galon, for fringes and tassels were out of fashion in 1714, the date of the bed. A warrant signed by the Lord Chamberlain proves that it was originally made for Queen Anne's use at Windsor, whence it was later removed to Hampton Court.

21. *Half-tester or 'Angel' Bed, serpentine cornice and head surmounted by whorls. c. 1710. (Leeds Castle, Kent.)*

22. *State Bed made for George, Prince of Wales, 1715, hangings of rose damask; curtains missing. (Hampton Court Palace. By gracious permission of Her Majesty the Queen.)*

Furniture for Her Majesty at Windsor:

For the bedchamber a standing bed without bedding, a large arm chair and 8 square stools, all of Crimson gold and white figured velvet trimmed with a figured silk arras lace of the same colours, and false cases, and a case curtain to the bed of gold coloured silk; the curtains of the bed to be lined with white satin, likewise 3 pair of large window curtains.

sgd. Shrewsbury.

27th Day of July, 1714.

The bill for these splendid hangings was sent in by John Johnson and Company, Mercers, in May of that year. The 321 yards of velvet at 1s. 8d. a yard included the material for window curtains and the armchair. These hangings have been attributed to Spitalfields; they are not, like most costly velvets at that period, described as 'Genoa' in the accounts, while their pattern supports the inference that they are of native origin.

Another fine example is in the King's bedroom at Hampton Court (Fig. 22). The cornice is formed of bold architectural mouldings with projecting corbels supporting vase-shaped finials at the corners. The bed is hung throughout with a large-patterned rose damask silk, the deep valances projecting in scrolls at the lower corners to receive the *cantonnières*. The invoices show that this bed was made for George, Prince of Wales, in 1715. The structure in this instance is of oak, and the head bears the Prince of Wales's feathers. Fig. 23 illustrates a state bed made about 1710 for William Blathwayt, who held various important offices under William III and Anne. The cornice is very elaborately moulded and the back, composed of a headboard supporting 2 columns with foliated capitals, is highly characteristic of baroque design. The hangings are of red velvet with yellow *appliqué*, the curtains being panelled in olive green. The back panel matches the quilt, which is of cream satin embroidered in yellow and red with a pattern of scrolls.

At this date beds of the 'Angel' or half-tester type were occasionally made, which, save for the absence of posts at the foot, have nothing to differentiate them from the prevalent fashion (Fig. 21). In 1698 Celia Fiennes found two 'half bedsteads' in the Duke of Norfolk's bedchamber, one being of 'fine Indian quilting and embroidery of silk'.

The bed with embroidered satin hangings and gilded enrichments at Erthig, Denbighshire (though no longer in pristine state), is of this type (Fig. 24), and a letter from Simon Yorke, who married the heiress of Erthig, dated April 17, 1720, gives the upholsterer's name and shows that the carving and joinery were done elsewhere: 'I called on Mr. Hunt (*see* HUNT, PHILIP) to press his sending the Bed he is making on

23. *State Bed, hung with crimson velvet curtains panelled in olive green, valances decorated with yellow silk* appliqué; *head-board with fluted pilasters. c. 1710. Ht. 12 ft. 7 in., L. 7 ft. 3 in., W. 6 ft. 6 in. (Lady Lever Art Gall., Port Sunlight; formerly at Dyrham Park, Glos.)*

Monday next; his Wife told me that the Bed as to their worke hath been finished long since; but the gilding and Carving is not ready nor will be 'till towards the latter end of next week; she saith she is very desirous of having the Bed out of her hands, and for that purpose hath sent severall times to hasten them.' The hangings are all of white satin embroidered with silks in the Chinese manner, a style of decoration known as 'Indian needlework'. Brilliantly coloured peacocks are applied at the corners and centre of the tester, and within the elaborately scrolled headboards, bordered with gesso ornament. Below are two gilt eagles' heads vigorously carved in relief.

The plainer type of bed in more common use is well represented by the example (Fig. 27) at Hampton Court, supposed to have been used by George II, and dating from c. 1725. The large lozenge-shaped pattern of the damask in no way resembles the florid silk designs fashionable in the early years of the century. Hangings were now made of linen, chintz, China silk, or needlework, the curtains still shutting the sleeper in. Another fine example of 'Indian needlework' is in the 'Embroidered Bed-chamber' at Houghton (Fig. 25); Horace Walpole records in his *Aedes Walpolianae* that this bed was occupied by Francis, Duke of Lorraine, in 1731, during a visit to Sir Robert Walpole. The white background is quilted with leaf

pattern in white silk thread, the coloured design of flowers and birds being all in chain stitch. In the Green Velvet Bedchamber at Houghton there is a bed (Fig. 26) designed by William Kent (q. v.). The bill of 'Turner Hill, and Pitter in the Strand' for the hangings is dated 1732, and amounts to £1,219 3s. 11d.

The gold embroidery was worked, as the bill shows, on a vellum ground and the items enumerated—'rich gold bullion roses, flowers for the Tester Pedesta and Counterpain', etc.—can all be identified. The bed reaches within two feet of the ceiling of the 18-foot room, the back thus affording an ample field for a shell of gigantic proportions.

On mahogany bedsteads of the first half of the century a panelled back was reintroduced, cabriole legs with lion-paw feet, and posts with vase-shaped plinths replacing the silk-covered uprights. The delicate inlay in Fig. 28 contrasts with the decorative figure of the Cuban mahogany in the back and with the boldly carved ornament of frieze and cornice. The cornice and valance were still designed in relation to each other, the former under rococo influence being carved in a flamboyant style, and sometimes covered with velvet or silk, a process demanding great skill, as cornices became more and more elaborate (Fig. 30). In some cases the silk covering was abandoned, the mahogany woodwork being either left in the natural state or gilt. Few of such beds retain the original hangings of velvet, flowered brocade or embroidered linen.

Of a design for an immensely ponderous state bed with allegorical figures, military trophies and other fantastic devices,

24. *'Angel' Bed, hangings of embroidered satin, carved enrichments gilded. Philip Hunt, 1720. (Erthig Park, Denbighs.)*

25. *State Bed, hung with 'Indian needlework', Walpole arms on frieze escutcheons c. 1730. (Houghton Hall, Norf.)*

26. *State Bed, designed by W. Kent, hung with green velvet embroidered with gold. Bill dated 1732. Ht. 16 ft. (Houghton Hall, Norf.)*

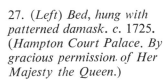

27. *(Left) Bed, hung with patterned damask. c. 1725. (Hampton Court Palace. By gracious permission of Her Majesty the Queen.)*

28. *(Right) Mahogany Bed, head-board inlaid, cornice carved with gadroons, lion-paw feet. c. 1740. (B. Coppinger Prichard Coll.)*

29. *Mahogany Bed, gadrooned cornice, cluster column posts; modern hangings. c. 1755. (Tabley, Cheshire.)*

30. *Mahogany Bed, the carved cornice covered with yellow velvet. c. 1755. (Corsham Court, Wilts.)*

Chippendale observes that 'There are found magnificence, proportion and harmony', but 'a workman of genius' is required to comprehend the design. Fashion demanded many varieties, including field beds and the type termed 'French'.

Japanned bedsteads were also in demand, and an example from Badminton (Fig. 31) was probably made by Chippendale for the fourth Duke of Beaufort. Japanned in scarlet, the original colour having been lately recovered from beneath a coating of black japan (the canopy retained its original black and gold decoration), it is in the Chinese style with a pagoda-shaped tester, and gilt dragons on scrolled finials ornament the corners. This form of tester hung with bells is illustrated in the *Director* (1754), cluster columns being sometimes favoured as an alternative for the posts. The original curtains were probably of painted Chinese silk.

Constant allusions in contemporary corresppndence to beds of red damask and moreen suggest that this was the favourite colour. In the *Guide* (1788) Hepplewhite writes that white dimity gives 'an effect of elegance and neatness truly agreeable'. In state rooms he recommends silk or satin, figured or plain, and velvet with a gold fringe; if these were of a dark pattern, a green silk lining 'may be used with good effect'. Valances on 'Elegant beds' should always be gathered full, and when so arranged are known as *petticoat valances*.

By 1775 the cornice had become simple in outline, straight or serpentine, often with vase finials at the four corners; the surface was now carved, carved and gilt, or painted in colours

on satinwood or mahogany. The cheaper examples, of beechwood, were painted throughout. With the introduction of the classical style the posts became simpler and curtains less voluminous and costly, but state beds retained the old extravagant fashion (as at Chatsworth, Blenheim and Osterley).

The fine bed in the Queen's Presence Chamber at Hampton Court (Fig. 33) was made for Queen Charlotte, wife of George III. A gilt cornice in the classical style rests upon carved gilt posts; the valances and curtains are of shot lilac silk embroidered with garlands of flowers, brilliant in colour and tasteful in design, the back and quilt being of cream satin with similar embroidery. *Cantonnières* are still retained at the corners of the valances to hold the small extra curtains that excluded any possible draught at the foot of the bed, those to correspond at the head being termed 'bonegraces'. All the Hampton Court beds possess their original thin feather mattresses, sometimes three or four in number, on which was placed the feather bed, with blankets, sheets and a counterpane. Pillows were small and resembled cushions, being often supported by wedge-shaped bolsters. In the *Guide* Hepplewhite commends a stuffed headboard above the pillows. Sheraton writes of French beds that 'square bolsters are now often introduced'. Embroidered linen is minutely described in the Walton inventory drawn up for Sir William Fairfax in 1642, and by the end of Charles II's reign cotton sheets were in regular use.

In its initial phase the classical style, though it began to

31. *Bed, japanned scarlet, canopy black and gold; original Curtains missing. c. 1755. Ht. 12 ft. 6 in., W. 7 ft. 11 in., L. 8ft. 6 in. (V. & A. Mus.)*

32. *Gilt Bed, posts and cornice simulating palm trees; original blue damask curtains. c. 1765. (Kedleston, Derbys.)*

33. *Gilt Bed made for Queen Charlotte; embroidered silk hangings, carved decoration in neo-classic style. c. 1775–8. (Hampton Court Palace. By gracious permission of Her Majesty the Queen.)*

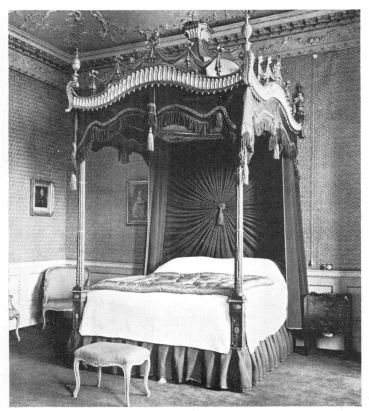

34. *Mahogany Bed, domed tester, cornice decorated in blue and gold, blue cloth hangings trimmed with gold braid, carved and gilt appliqué ornament on posts. c. 1780. (Formerly at Lulworth Castle, Dorset.)*

35. *State Bed, designed by R. Adam in 1776, satinwood inlaid, bases and capital of chased metal. (Osterley Park, Middx.)*

affect all furniture shortly after 1760, had little influence on the design of bedsteads. One of the most bizarre of 18th-century examples dates from about this time and is in the State bedroom at Kedleston (Fig. 32). A palm-tree appears from root to crown, the curving branches sweeping above and below the valances of the tester. The palm torchères (*see* STANDS, CANDLE) in this room, three large mirrors, and the gilt suite that accompanies these pieces are all treated with the palm motive, which is strongly reminiscent of some of Vardy's decoration at Spencer House, c. 1760.

For Osterley, Adam designed a State bed of satinwood inlaid with green laurel ornament and upholstered in green silks and velvets (Fig. 35), the drawing for which is in the Soane Museum (*see* ADAM, R., Fig. 4). Horace Walpole adversely criticised this bed in a letter (July 16, 1778) as being 'too like a modern head-dress', for round the outside of the dome are festoons of artificial flowers: 'What would Vitruvius think of a dome decorated by a milliner?'

Throughout the 18th century the cornices and valances of the window hangings were made to match those of the bed. Lady Elizabeth Smithson (later Duchess of Northumberland) writes to her mother in August, 1740: 'I must now speak of my bedchamber; my bed in cotton flowered with large natural flowers lined with grass green lutestring with fluted posts . . . the window curtains, chairs, arm-chair and *Peché Mortel* and the Hangings are all of the same.'

The type of bed in common use c. 1775-1800 is well represented in Hepplewhite's *Guide* (1788) and Sheraton's *Drawing*

Book (1791-4). The slender posts were fluted and carved with wheat ears or husks and the lunette-shaped frieze inlaid with shells and paterae, in coloured woods, or painted with ribbons and garlands of flowers, like those shown in Fig. 36. Sometimes a scalloped edging of wood heads the valances, which were formed of swags of silk or other material disposed, writes Sheraton, 'to hang easy'. Festoons of cords with large tassels were favourite decoration, while it was usual for the curtains to be drawn up by pulleys and tied to the posts. At the corners of the tester plumes or vase-shaped finials were often employed, as in earlier times (Fig. 37).

Beds of the early 19th century were designed in a version of the Empire style, ostensibly based on classical precedents, and resulting from 'the reciprocal exchanges of British and French taste'. Many varieties are shown in George Smith's *Designs for Household Furniture* (1808) and Ackermann's *Repository*. The turned posts, which had lost the former elegance, were of mahogany or rosewood enriched with 'Grecian ornaments' bronzed or gilt, while chased metal *appliqués* were also employed. The tester was often dome-shaped and the hangings were of silk or calico in primary colours, embroidered, or with borders of velvet, and liberally trimmed with lace or fringe (Fig. 38). 'Tasteful simplicity' was proclaimed as the ideal. An attempt was made to provide beds suited to the particular circumstances of the individual, and Smith shows one intended for a military officer ornamented with 'war trophies' and having a cornice formed of spears. Smith also produced a design for a very ambitious Gothic bed, but remarks that this style is 'applicable only in a real Gothic mansion'. Towards 1820 most elegantly furnished sleeping-rooms are stated to have been 'fitted up in the French style', an essential part of the scheme being a bed of couch form below a canopy attached to the wall, which supported the curtains. Many beds of this kind were imported, but the taste was short-lived, and the majority of English examples seem to have been destroyed or transformed into couches in Victorian times.

BEDS, ANGEL. Defined by Edward Phillips in *A New World of Words* (1706) as 'a sort of open bed without bed-posts', *i.e.* in which the tester, or canopy, usually extends over only part of the bedstock and is not supported on posts (*see* Fig. 21).

BEDS, DUCHESSE. The French equivalent of an Angel bed. Sheraton explains in the *Drawing Book* (1791-4) that what is 'sometimes named a duchesse amongst us is merely 2 barjier chairs (*see* BIRJAIR) fastened to a stool in the middle'. The French duchesse bed is 'more stately': it was fully draped.

BEDS, FIELD. Often referred to in medieval inventories, presumably for use in war and travelling; but not apparently intended for rough usage in second half of the 16th century, as the inventory of furniture belonging to Robert Dudley, Earl of Leicester at Kenilworth (1588) lists eight 'Fielde beddestedes' of walnut, several elaborately carved with rich woven and embroidered hangings. In the *Academie of Armory* (MS. dated 1649) Randle Holme writes: 'Beds made higher with an head, so that they may be set in a chamber corner, or under a cant roof are called field beds.' The term was still in use in the second half of the 18th century (*see* Ince and Mayhew's *Universal System*, 1759-63), though descriptions do not indicate any specialised character.

36. *Mahogany Bed; frieze decorated with rose trails centres in tablet above festooned valance of painted wood. c. 1790. (Chatsworth Derbys.)* 37. *Bed, carved mahogany posts, cornice painted with trophies and foliated scrolls. c. 1780. (Hedingham Castle, Essex.)*

38. *Bed, carved and gilt, the domed tester and posts surmounted by ostrich plumes; prepared for George IV when Prince of Wales. c. 1810. (Wimpole Hall, Cambs.)* 39. *Design for a Bed with dome-shaped canopy from George Smith's* Household Furniture, 1808.

BEDS, LIVERY. For servants' use, frequently referred to in 16th- and 17th-century inventories.

BEDS, MOURNING. *See* BEDS, p. 37.

BEDS, PRESS. Made to fit into a cupboard or wardrobe; referred to in Stuart inventories, and still made in the 18th century. Fully described by a foreign traveller visiting Oxford in 1710:

> It is a press into which a bed is shut, and which neither takes up space in a room nor is any inconvenience. The door forms a tester which, when it is let down, covers the whole front of the bed and shuts up so that one cannot see that a bed is concealed behind it. If one wants to set up the bed, the door is lifted and the poles placed under it; the bed itself is lowered outwards from its position inside the press, and, on account of this movement, is joined to it by two hinges which support the back portion, while the front is maintained exactly in line with it by means of two feet. These feet are hung on hinges underneath the bed, so that when it is closed up again, they lie flat . . . (*The Travels of Zacharias Von Uffenbach*; Blackwell, 1928.)

Horace Walpole writes (August 4, 1755) concerning the Duke of Newcastle's house at Chelsea: 'In one of the rooms is a bed for the duke, and a press-bed for his footman; for he never dares lie alone.' Hepplewhite in the *Guide* (1788) draws attention to a wardrobe which has 'all the appearance' of a press-bed and could be adapted by making the door 'to turn up all in one piece and form a tester'. At Harewood House, Yorkshire, there is a mahogany wardrobe of the late 18th century which formerly contained a bed.

BEDS, SPARVER and **TENT.** Apparently beds with a tent-shaped or 'waggon-tilt' canopy. The arms of the Upholsterers Company, granted 1447, bear tents or 'spervers' as a charge. In 'Lord Warwickes bed-chamber' at Leicester House in 1588 was 'an old sparver bedstead of walnuttree' with richly embroidered velvet hangings. Tent beds were still in use towards the end of the 18th century, and George III slept in one on a visit to Wilton in January, 1779. (*Letters and Diaries of Henry, 10th Earl of Pembroke*, 1939, p. 139.)

BEDS, TRUCKLE, TRUNDLE or **WHEILBED.** A low bed on wheels, in use from late Middle Ages until mid-Georgian period. The Statutes of Corpus Christi College, Oxford (late 15th century) provided that scholars of the college should sleep in truckle beds below the fellows. Listed in

1. *Oak Truckle Bed, the wheel feet are restorations. 17th century. L. 5 ft. 6 in. (National Mus. of Wales.)*

large numbers in Elizabethan and early Stuart inventories, and were sometimes provided with hangings, probably suspended on a light framework. Anthony Place of Dynsdall, County Durham, gent., in 1570 had in his Little Chamber a 'truckle bed and hangings'. Later the low price paid suggests that their use was confined to servants, the sums expended on 'trundle beds' in the Shuttleworth Accounts for first years of 17th century varying between 4s. 6d. and 6s. each. They continued to be occupied by servants in their masters' bedrooms until a desire for greater privacy put an end to the practice. Pepys records that his man, Will, slept in his chamber 'in a truckle bed' on the night of May 1, 1662.

BEDS, TRUSSING. A variety, frequently mentioned in medieval and Tudor inventories, made to pack up and often used for travel and military service. Nature of mechanism not known. When owner changed houses, such beds were packed into bags. The inventory of Katherine of Aragon mentions a trussing bedstead with '2 leather cases to trusse it'. John of Gaunt (died 1399) demises to his wife beds 'made for his body and called in England trussing beds'. Those owned by Wolsey were of elaborate character and solid construction, one having '4 posts partly gilte and paynted' and another being made of alabaster. Sir John Gage, of West Firle, Sussex, in 1556 had, among other equipment for campaigning, 'a trussing bedsted for the field'. They were still used by great persons in the 17th century.

BEDSTAFF. A staff or stick used in some way about a bed (N.E.D.). Apparently used in more than one sense. (1) Sticks or staves 'stuck anciently in the sides of the bedstead to hold the clothes from slipping on either side' (Johnson's *Dictionary*. 1755). (2) When a bed was fixed in a recess, a stick or staff was used to help in making it and sometimes called a bedstick— e.g. Baker Gessier's *Jewel of Health* (1596): 'sturring it well about with a short bedde staffe'. Aubrey, writing of William Oughtred in *Brief Lives*, relates that he 'studyed late at night; and in the top of his bedstaffe, he had his inke-horne fixit'.

BEDSTOCK. That part of a bed which supported the mattress and clothes. In Elizabethan beds the posts at the foot often stood clear of the bedstock (*see* BEDS).

BEECH (*Fagus sylvatica*). Constantly in demand for inexpensive furniture from the mid-17th century. So subject to worm that Evelyn writes in *Sylva* (1664): 'I wish the use of it were by a law prohibited all joyners, cabinetmakers, and such as furnish tables, chairs, bed-steads, cofers, etc. They have a way to black and polish it so as to render it like ebony, and with a mixture of soot and urine, imitate the wall-nut.' When stained, used for carved chairs of Restoration period, also for painted chairs of the late 18th century, and often employed for the seat-rails of 'stuffed over' mahogany chairs and couches. Also used for bedframes, presses, etc. A comparatively soft wood, colour varying from white to pale brown; when split transversely has satiny markings like silver grain of oak, but much smaller and less numerous.

BEER WAGON. *See* COASTERS.

BEERES, or **PILLOWBERES.** A word used for pillowcases in the Middle Ages: 'Pillowes of Fustyn, stufyd with Downe, every each with *Beeres* of Raines' (MS. Account of

1. *Bench, panelled back of linen-fold pattern. c. 1520. Ht. 3 ft. 8 in., L. 11 ft. 2 in. (V. & A. Mus.)*

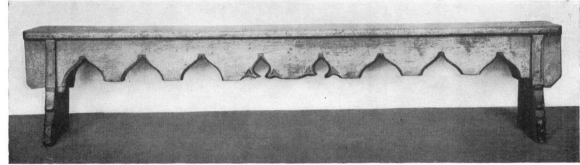

2. *Oak Bench of trestle form. c. 1400. Ht. 1 ft. 9 in., L. 7 ft. 11 in. (V. & A. Mus.)*

Christening of a Prince, etc., in Leland's *Collectanea*, c. 1552). Pillowberes figure under heading 'Diaper' in inventory of Robert Dudley, Earl of Leicester (1588).

BEETLE. *See* WOOD-WORM.

BENCHES AND FORMS. In the medieval hall, benches and settles were the ordinary seats. Two distinct varieties of bench were in use—the movable form and the bench structurally united to the wall. The bench or form (the terms are interchangeable) has remained essentially the same throughout its history, though shaped board supports developed into legs. Medieval tables were generally movable, being boards laid upon trestles and flanked by forms of the simplest type; but tables and forms were sometimes fixtures. In the inventories of the Essex monasteries (1536) (*see Essex Archaeological Society Transactions*, vol. ix), 'trestyll' forms constantly occur in halls and parlours. These were, no doubt, moved about at will, but in the halls of Henry VIII's palaces the forms were 'dormante', implying that they were stationary and of joined construction. The building contract for Hengrave (c. 1525) provides that the hall and parlours are to be 'benched about', while the Ingatestone inventory (1600) mentions a bench 'at the upp ende of the hall lyinge upon brackets'. These halls resembled those still in use at the Inns of Court and in the Colleges of Oxford and Cambridge, with tables extending from the 'screens' to the dais, and benches running around the walls against the panelling. An example in a private house is at Ockwells, Berkshire, where the medieval hall was 'benched

about' in the 17th century, and the seats, supported on turned legs, are backed against the wainscot and carried round the window recess.

In houses without wall panelling these forms were sometimes provided with a panelled back, when it needed only the addition of arms at either end for them to become settles (*q.v.*). A bench of this type, dating from early in the 16th century, was formerly at Orchard Farm, Monkleigh, Devon (Fig. 1). Although set against a side wall, it appears never to have had ends. Formed of wide linen-fold panels, framed in moulded stiles, it is surmounted by a moulding of interlaced leaves deeply undercut. The cresting, pierced and carved with dolphins, is in early Renaissance style. Part is missing: the finials, in the form of poppy-heads set on a square moulded base above each panel, are still of Gothic character. As such benches were part of the freehold, descending with it, they are omitted from inventories, where the 'bankers', or cloths that covered them, figure constantly.

Movable medieval forms are as scarce as Gothic chairs, but the fine example given in Fig. 2, of which the arcaded underframing has ogee-headed cusping, probably dates from about 1400, though the uprights closely resemble those of stools of much later date. Beyond the uprights the underframing is extended to the ends of the seat. This form was discovered in Barningham Hall, Norfolk, built by Sir William Paston under James I, and may well have figured among the household goods in an earlier home of the Pastons. It lacks the framing at the back, but is otherwise perfect, the wood being almost in the

3. *Oak Bench, shaped and pierced underframing, buttressed ends. c. 1550. (National Mus. of Wales.)*

4. *Oak 'joyned' Bench or Form, with stretchers, turned supports and decorated frieze. c. 1650. (Lawrence Cadbury Coll.)*

natural state. Another specimen, probably made c. 1550, has a deep shaped under-framing enclosed by a bar and buttressed ends (Fig. 3).

'Flanders Forms' were among the many articles imported into England from the Low Countries in the 15th century. The Prior's Chamber at Finchale contained such seats in 1411. Many, no doubt, were made in England by Flemish craftsmen settled in the eastern counties. By no means invariably of oak, sometimes the wood is stated to have been fir or ash. From the end of the 12th century benches were commonly placed at the foot of the bed, where they served for conversation, and are shown in illuminations throughout the Middle Ages.

Seats constructed in this 'fashion of a form' continued to be made throughout the 16th and 17th centuries, when they were generally supported by turned legs. In the 17th century large oak tables were often provided with a nest of stools, which were ranged along the stretchers when not in use, and consequently forms were seldom made. A rare specimen is shown in Fig. 4 which, with massive blocks forming the feet, and finely turned pillars, dates from about the middle of the century.

At this time a number of benches were made to accord with farthingale chairs (*see* CHAIRS) and other upholstered furniture of the period. They were often very long, the legs united by foot-rails which support several pairs of plainly turned pillars; this particular variety was copied from France, and few indubitably English examples exist. With the Restoration the bench became more ornamental, the design being merely an enlargement of contemporary walnut stools. Fig. 5 is a rare variety. The legs carved with masks end in volutes and are

united by scrolled stretchers set in pairs and enriched with cherubs' heads. These ornamental stretchers being confined to one side, it was obviously intended to stand against a wall; upholstered in old material, no doubt originally it was caned. Plain oak specimens were made throughout the 18th century, but in great houses benches were largely superseded by day-beds and settees. Though still used in galleries and halls, at this date they are scarcely distinguishable from long stools (*q.v.*).

BERGERE. *See* BIRJAIR.

BIBLE BOX. *See* BOXES.

BILLIARD TABLES. *See* TABLES, BILLIARD.

BIRCH (*Betula alba*). 'Of all others the worst of Timber'— Evelyn, *Sylva* (1664). In 18th century (possibly earlier) used in chair-making and for other furniture. Certain cuts strongly resembled satinwood, and used as substitute for it; after c. 1780, in solid and as veneer. English birch is white, shaded and tinged with red; North American variety (*Betula lenta*) seems to have been imported 1750-1800.

BIRD-CAGES. A number of references in late medieval literature prove that, towards the end of the Middle Ages in England, jays, magpies and other birds were kept in cages as pets. Chaucer in his *Squieres Tale* (1386) speaks of 'briddes . . . that men in cases fede'; Lydgate writes of a 'chorle' who was 'so gladde that his birdde hadde take' that in 'al haste he cast for to make within his house a pratie litelle cage, and with his songs to rejoice his corage'; while passages in Skelton and

5. *Walnut Bench or Long Stool. c. 1680. (Formerly at Layer Marney, Essex.)*

other early 16th-century poets suggest that this caging was common. A taste for exotic birds had always been widespread among the upper classes in France, and innumerable documents mention cages and their prices. Some were made of copper or brass wire, but in Charles V's inventory (1380) cages of gold are mentioned, garnished with precious stones. Many of these costly ornaments, however, were not for real birds, as it was then customary to hang an ornate cage in the chief apartment containing a stuffed bird.

One of the miniatures in a French late medieval manuscript shows a cage with a domed top of a more practical type. It hangs from the ceiling, being raised and lowered by a pulley, and a number of small birds are seen behind the bars (Fig. 1). The kitchen seems to be supplied from this source, for the cook is plucking a bird like those in the cage; while others are on the plate with which the master of the house is being served. When mentioned in English inventories, cages are

2. *Mahogany Bird-cage, wirework filling, turned baluster uprights, metal inlay. c. 1720-30. (Mr H. G. Fenwick.)*

1. *Miniature, from translation of* Valerius Maximus, *illuminated by François Foucquet c. 1475; cage containing small birds suspended from ceiling. (B.M. Harley MS., 4374.)*

the fingers of the sitter. Sir Thomas More was among the most enthusiastic English fanciers of that age, and Erasmus, in a letter (1519) describing More's Chelsea home, represents him as desiring 'most ardently' to buy any kind of exotic species.

Bird-cages were certainly freely used in Tudor England, and references abound in Shakespeare's plays. In woodcuts, such as those in Whitney's *Emblems* (1585), they are generally surprisingly modern in design. Contemporary English specimens are unknown, and it is probable that they were fashioned of perishable materials such as basket work. Webster refers to the custom of putting turfs into larks' cages in the *Duchess of Malfi* (1614): 'Did'st thou ever see a lark in a cage? Such is the soul in the body; this world is like her little turf of grass.'

A bird-cage which antedates the earliest surviving English example is sculptured on a monument (c. 1630, in St Andrew's Church, Norwich) to Sir John Suckling and his wife, parents

generally among the contents of the kitchen, there used for fattening capons and quails, and this practice continued until well into the 17th century.

But elaborate cages were also in use, either imported or made in England, from the late Middle Ages. In a beautiful little poem, Chaucer describes the misery of the captive bird who will pine for liberty 'although his cage of gold be never so gay'. Magpies in cages were favourite pets at this time. The burgess in the English version of the *Seven Sages* had a pie in his hall:

> That couthe tell tales alle
> Apertliche (openly) in French language
> And heng in a faire cage.

A love of birds for the sake of their bright plumage was fostered in the Renaissance by the rapidly-growing commerce with tropical and subtropical countries, and imported parrots were in great demand for their plumage and imitative powers. In early Renaissance pictures, goldfinches and other bright-plumaged birds are occasionally depicted in the hand of the Child Christ, while in portraits they are shown perched upon

3. *Mahogany Bird-cage, in form of house with dormer windows, gilded cones at corners of eaves. Late 18th century. (Edward Hudson Coll.)*

4. Bird-cage, gilded wires, base painted with floral swags and paterae. c. 1770. (Syon House, Middx.) 5. Sheffield-plated Bird-cage, headed by royal crown. c. 1790. (Edward Hudson Coll.) 6. Glass Bird-cage, base decorated with sprays of roses on white ground, surmounted by band of ormolu and spear-headed points of red and white glass. Early 19th century.

of the cavalier poet, and was apparently copied from a small wire cage with a wooden cross-piece and domed wire top. The door is open, the bird about to soar into the air (typical of the spirit escaping from the body) recalling Webster's simile.

It is not until the third quarter of the century that a variety of bird-cages are shown in the pictures of Vermeer, Jan Steen and other Dutch genre painters. They were also becoming common in England. The sad plight of a bird in confinement appealed to Cowley as strongly as to earlier poets. In his *Ode upon Liberty* he writes that no bird would exchange 'his native liberty'

> For a more plentiful and constant Food,
> Nor ever did Ambitious rage
> Make him into a painted cage,
> Or the false forest of a well-hung Room,
> For Honour and Preferment come.

Charles II kept a considerable collection of birds. The long avenue, familiar as Bird Cage Walk, is still reminiscent of the King's pastime of feeding his birds, but the cages, planned by the celebrated gardener Le Notre, were so large as more accurately to be classed as aviaries. Pepys notes in his diary (January 25, 1661) that two cages have just been delivered 'which I bought this evening for my canary birds'. These were sent to Pepys by Captain Rooth of the *Dartmouth*, no doubt brought back by him on one of his voyages. In 1675 Sir Robert Shirley paid £11 5s. 6d. for '4 Virginia nightingales and 4 canary birds and one red Linnicke, with seed and cages' (*Historical MS. Commission*).

In the 18th century English bird-cages became more abundant, but their pattern is again of Dutch inspiration. An inventory of the contents of Dyrham Park (1710) mentions three in the Great Hall, and another described as a 'large Bird Cage' in the Ante Hall. The balustered uprights and gilt metal inlay in Fig. 2 are of about this date. In most examples the glass for the seed has been renewed. In the mid-18th century

a number of mahogany cages were made, the more elaborate being designed as decorative objects rather than for actual use. They do not conform to any particular style, though some were architectural in character. The influence of late Georgian houses is apparent in Fig. 3; the knocker is missing, but to carry out the illusion of an inhabited dwelling, the number 37 is painted on the door. A gilded bird-cage in neo-classic style, and in harmony with the general decorative scheme, hangs from the centre of the dome in the round closet or boudoir opening out of the gallery at Syon House. The base is painted with garlands of flowers and a clock framed into the underside (Fig. 4). Cages for ordinary use were generally of mahogany inlaid with shells. Fig. 5 shows a Sheffield-plated cage, probably made for George III towards the end of the century, the pierced decoration of the tray and the cone that forms the pendant being in the style of contemporary silver plate. From this time onwards the modern shape was generally adopted, and with the disappearance of all traces of architectural design, it becomes difficult to assign an approximate date. In Fig. 6 the cutting of the finial recalls the fashion of late chandeliers.

BIRJAIR or **BURJAIR**, etc. The French term, Bergère, a winged armchair of a type introduced about 1725, anglicised by cabinet-makers and applied to couches by Ince and Mayhew (*Universal System*, 1759-63). An inventory taken at Bedford House (1771) mentions among the furniture in Her Grace's Bed Chamber 'a walnut-tree burgier in red Morocco leather'. A letter from Chippendale, Haig & Co. to Sir Edward Knatchbull of Mersham Hatch (May 7, 1773) states: 'Lady Knatchbull seem'd to want 4 larger chairs, what we call *Barjairs*. . . . We would rather recommend 2 large *Berjairs* as we think it would be of more propriety in one room.'

BLACK WORK (also Spanish Work). Black silk needlework on linen or holland cloth, probably introduced by Katherine

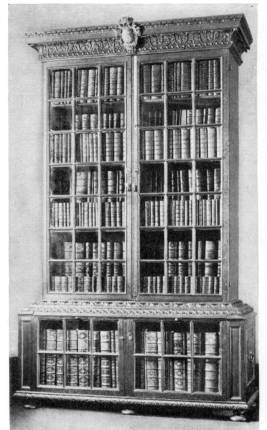

1. Oak Bookcase, one of twelve made for Samuel Pepys. c. 1666. (Pepys Library, Magdalene Coll., Cambridge.) 2. Oak Bookcase; arcaded lower portion supported on turned baluster stand. c. 1695. (West Farleigh Hall, Kent.) 3. Walnut Bookcase, lower portion fitted with oak drawers. c. 1710. Ht. 7 ft. 8 in., L. 4 ft., Depth 1 ft. 3 in. (Assheton Smith Coll.)

of Aragon. Of common occurrence in the Tudor period, dying out in early 17th century.

BLACKSTONE. 'A portable desk is called a blackstone'— from an advertisement inside a small writing cabinet or croft (*q.v.*) made by Seddon's c. 1790; presumably after Sir W. Blackstone, author of the *Commentaries*.

BLAZE. Term applied to chandeliers. The inventory of Cannons drawn up for the first Duke of Chandos (1725) records in 'The Salone' 'A Blaze with 3 branches crimson silk line and ballance weight' valued at £35. Several other 'blazes' occur in the inventory.

BLUE-JOHN. *See* DERBYSHIRE SPAR.

BOARD. Old name for table, perpetuated in Board of Directors, etc. Also used to denote any kind of wood cut into quarter, half, three-quarters, and inch thicknesses.

BOG OAK. *See* OAK.

BOLECTION. Moulding in projection above surface of framework enclosing a panel, having an outward roll and of ogee shape in section. In early 17th century run on the solid round small panels, but after the Restoration and in 18th century applied round panels of larger size.

BOMBE. French term for furniture with swelling outline towards the base.

BONEGRACES. French *Bonne graces,* narrow curtains fixed at junction of large ones on 17th- and 18th-century beds at the back to protect sleeper from draughts.

BOOKCASES. Domestic bookcases are not found before Charles II's reign. The early history of this type of furniture is as closely connected with the medieval fittings of collegiate libraries as with the aumbry, or wall cupboard, of private houses and monastic establishments, and such fittings cannot be classified as domestic furniture. Long after the invention of printing, books continued to be regarded as so great a luxury that in most households a chest, hutch, or shelf beneath a desk sufficed to contain them (*see* CHESTS and DESKS). But aumbries, or wall cupboards, were introduced to supplement chests as receptacles for books at a very early date. These cupboards were sometimes used for the permanent storage of books. At the end of the 12th century, Simon, Abbot of St Albans, had a large collection placed in a painted aumbry 'against the tomb of Roger the Hermit'.

Many of the most beautiful volumes transcribed and bound in the late Middle Ages are known to have been the property of laymen; and as they were exceedingly costly they can scarcely have been produced to be locked away in chests. An opportunity for displaying a few precious volumes was afforded by small hanging shelves, and in illuminations of domestic interiors they are often shown bracketed out and hung against the wall one above another (*see* SHELVES).

When permanent libraries were established at the Universities in the 14th century, the fittings were adapted from the desk of double lectern form, a composite piece of furniture used by medieval scholars and often represented by the illuminator with a shelf enclosed by doors in the lower portion (*see* DESKS).

The introduction of the stall system, the next step in the evolution, was apparently delayed until the Elizabethan period. The two halves of the sloping desk were at first divided by a wide shelf with one or more shelves fixed above it. Later the desk was entirely discarded and narrow presses were introduced.

Yet another system was introduced in the latest portion of the Bodleian Library, Oxford, built and fitted by Sir Thomas Bodley in 1610-12. The presses running out into the room were abandoned, and the shelves were carried up to so great a height that for convenience of access a light gallery was provided with seats for readers. In the great Palladian houses of the first half of the 18th century this wall system was frequently employed, and in the libraries of Holkham and Houghton shelves were designed as part of the architectural scheme.

It is said that in Elizabethan and early Jacobean days a room at the top of the house was often set apart as a library. Such rooms retaining their original fittings do not appear to have survived, but they probably resembled the Kederminster Library in Langley Parish Church, Bucks., dating from 1613. There the presses are contained in the deal wainscoting, their doors being elaborately painted to correspond with the panels. At Longleat, Wilts., there is a room at the top of the house fitted with shelves as a library for Bishop Ken by the first Viscount Weymouth, c. 1700.

4. *Bookcase, painted pine in style of W. Kent, gilt enrichments. c. 1730. Ht. 7 ft. 1½ in., W. 5 ft. 7 in., Depth 1 ft. 9 in. (V. & A. Mus.)*
5. *(Below) Mahogany Break-front Bookcase, doors carved with applied pendants of fruit and flowers. c. 1750. (C. D. Rotch Coll.)*
6. *(Right) Bookcase, one of pair, veneered with rosewood and inlaid with brass; dolphins at base and floral swags gilded. J. Channon, c. 1750. (Powderham Castle, Devon.)*

7. *Mahogany Bookcase; eagle heads with foliated terminations in pediment. c. 1740.* 8. *Mahogany Bookcase; ogee-headed panels on lower portion. c. 1745. Ht. 6 ft. 6 in., L. 5 ft. 3 in., Depth 1 ft. 3 in. (J. Thursby Pelham Coll.)*

9. *Mahogany Bookcase; panels carved with enriched oval foliage and floral pendants. c. 1750. (Coppinger Prichard Coll.)* 10. *Mahogany Bookcase, based on design (Pl. LXVII) in* Director *(1st ed., dated 1753). (Longford Castle, Wilts.)*

11. (*Left*) *Rosewood Bookcase parcel gilt; supplied by Chippendale to Earl of Dumfries in 1759.* (*Dumfries House, Ayrs.*)

12. (*Right*) *Mahogany Bookcase, based on Plate LXXIII in the* Director (*1st ed., dated* 1753). (*Hotspur Ltd.*)

The oak bookcases (Fig. 1), designed to contain the library of Samuel Pepys, are the earliest domestic examples to which a definite date can be assigned. Pepys held the first of several deliberations on this matter with 'Simpson the joiner' on July 23, 1666, when they were engaged 'with great pains contriving presses to put my books up in: they now growing numerous, and lying one upon another on my chairs'. A month later he has obtained them, for he spends the morning with Simpson in setting them up. By January, 1668, he appears to have added two more cases. There are twelve in the Bibliotheca Pepysiana at Magdalene, Cambridge. In the centre of each entablature is a scrolled escutcheon, the frieze being decorated with a pattern of scrolls and foliage above a ribbon moulding. The lower portion is also finely carved, and here the glazed panels slide up and down in grooves. The bookcases are of oak stained a reddish brown, and the thin glass of the period is framed in plain moulded bars. An example now in the Victoria and Albert Museum is one of a pair from Dyrham Park, Glos., which are probably by the same maker. Other bookcases of similar design are in existence.

Fig. 2, dating from c. 1695, is an interesting instance of the combination of desk and bookcase in a domestic specimen, ledges being provided on a sloping front to support volumes taken from the shelves. Below the flaps are a series of drawer fronts to give the appearance of drawers, the arcade beneath being supported on balusters united by shaped stretchers.

The bookcases of Queen Anne's reign are marked by extreme simplicity, depending for effect on excellence of proportion and the finely figured walnut with which the oak carcase is veneered (Fig. 3). The straight front is retained, the lower portion when open disclosing drawers, and the glazing bars are some-

times shaped in baluster form. In these examples architectural character is almost entirely absent, though a few years later it becomes prominent. Fig. 4 represents the type designed by Kent and his school, a broken pediment surmounting an arch, a corbelled out cornice and trusses heading pilasters faced with pendants being favourite motives. Batty Langley claims that bookcases are within the architect's province, though when a good design has been supplied to a client, he is too often influenced by cabinet-makers who complain that ' 'tis not possible to make cabinet-works look well that are proportioned by the Rules of Architecture'. In his *Treasury of Designs* (1740) Langley illustrates a number of bookcases 'true after any of the Five Orders', with glazed doors divided by plain bars into 6 panes, and pediments with urns at the corners. A bookcase reminiscent of these designs (Fig. 7) has in the pediment a plinth flanked by eagles' heads finishing in foliage. The frieze of the lower stage pulls out to form two slides, while the panel mouldings are delicately enriched with egg and dart. Fig. 5, of about a decade later, is of the type with a centre and two wings introduced about this time, and destined to enjoy long popularity. The framework is decorated with applied pendants of fruit and flowers, and the drawers in the centre section are edged with narrow cock-beading. In a few examples made c. 1750 architectural influence is still noticeable, though the decorative motives of the new rococo style are found in the carving.

A pair of bookcases at Powderham Castle (Fig. 6) by J. Channon (*q.v.*), an obscure maker, are remarkable and highly exceptional examples in the baroque style. When recently coats of dirt and varnish were removed, they were found to be veneered with carefully selected rosewood, not mahogany as formerly supposed. Corinthian columns, frieze

13. *Mahogany Bookcase; glazing in Gothic taste. c. 1760.*
L. 5 ft. 9 in. (Percival Griffiths Coll.)
14. *Mahogany bookcase, made for Queen Charlotte by Vile and*
Cobb in 1762. L. 8 ft. 7½ in., Ht. from base of columns to top of
pediment, 6 ft. 4 in. (Buckingham Palace. By gracious permission
of Her Majesty the Queen.)
15. *Mahogany break-front Bureau Bookcase; in centre com-*
partment frame and musical trophies carved with rococo
ornament. Attributed to Chippendale. c. 1760. (Wilton, Wilts.)

and door frames are inlaid with brass, while the carved
enrichments, which include pairs of dolphins, are gilded.

The splendid bookcase (Fig. 14), which formed the frontispiece to both of the larger editions of this work, embodies rococo
decoration and yet, in Langley's words, is 'proportioned by the
Rules of Architecture'. It was made for George III by the firm
of Vile and Cobb in 1762 at a cost of £107 14s. 0d. For the construction the finest Cuban mahogany is employed, and the
design shows a masterly adaptation of Palladian principles.
The elevation, classical in style, consists of a wide projecting
centre and two wings. The double broken pediment and the
cornice are richly carved, the frieze being decorated with C-
scrolls and acanthus sprays in high relief. This entablature is
supported on four columns with Corinthian capitals, while
over the glazed doors, originally divided into panes, hang
admirably carved floral swags. In the lower portion the panels
of the cupboard doors are decorated with pendants, wreaths
and borders of rococo scrollwork, the Garter Star forming the
centre ornament. Imposing in design and faultlessly executed,
this bookcase is the most remarkable example of its period, and
takes high rank among the masterpieces of English furniture.

16. *Mahogany Bookcase, scrolled pediment with pierced ornament. c. 1770. Ht. 9 ft. 5 in., W. 4 ft. 7 in., Depth 2 ft. ½ in. (Commonwealth Relations Office.)*

17. *Bookcases in Library of Brocket Hall, Herts., probably designed by James Paine, c. 1765.*

18. *Bookcase of deal, carved, painted white and parcel gilt, pilasters finish below frieze in consoles. c. 1765. (Castle Howard, Yorks.)*

It was given by George IV to Augusta, Duchess of Cambridge, and came into the possession of H.R.H. Victoria Mary, Princess of Wales, later Queen Mary, in 1904.

About 1750 bookcases were affected by new tendencies in design, the architectural character becoming less pronounced, and astragals in various patterns replacing solid glazing bars. Most large examples are 'break-fronted' or in three divisions: the pediment above the projecting centre is sometimes pierced and the wings enclosed by a fretwork gallery, while the framework is noticeably lighter. This treatment is found in the *Director*, which gives 14 designs for bookcases in the third edition (1762). Glazing bars are extremely elaborate, pilasters

and scrollwork being freely introduced. Bookcases of a more serviceable type are not lacking, and even of his most ornate examples Chippendale writes, 'the trusses, pilasters and drops of flowers are pretty ornaments . . . but all may be omitted if required'. Fig. 10 is based on one of the *Director* designs (1st ed., 1754); the wings are surmounted by arched cornices, their curves repeated in the acanthus foliage springing from small capitals on the central glazing bars.

The next example (Fig. 11) was supplied by Chippendale's firm to the Earl of Dumfries at Dumfries House, Ayrshire, in 1759, and is entered in the accounts as 'a rosewood bookcase with rich carved and gilt ornaments on the top and doors, and

19. *Mahogany Bookcase, designed by R. Adam for Sir Watkin Williams-Wynn. c. 1770. Ht. 11 ft., L. 12 ft., Depth 2 ft. (Formerly at 20 St James's Square.)* 20. *Mahogany break-front Bookcase in neo-classic style; centre portion pulls out as writing drawer. c. 1770. (F. Partridge and Sons.)*

a writing drawer in the underpart'. The slender glazing bars are carved and gilt, and the centre and wings surmounted by light carved scrollwork. Though the use of rosewood was exceptional at this date, it is mentioned as being used for two dressing tables in the *Director* (*see* TABLES, DRESSING, Fig. 11) and here the parquetry on the lower stage emphasises the rich colour of the material.

At Wilton a break-fronted bookcase (Fig. 15) can be assigned to Chippendale on stylistic grounds: the fact that in the *Director* he is stated to have supplied a couch (Plate XLVI) for the Earl of Pembroke's house in Whitehall and that payments to him are recorded in the Wilton accounts, afford strong corroborative evidence. This bookcase is perhaps the most original and remarkable example of Chippendale's case-furniture in the rococo style. On the upper stage the advanced centre has, instead of glazing bars, a carved frame headed by musical trophies applied to the glass, a treatment represented in several designs in the *Director*. The inlaid stars are another exceptional feature, while the urns with swags of drapery on the wings foreshadow the classical revival.

Gothic bookcases figure in all three editions of the *Director*, but probably few of these extravagant designs were executed without considerable modification. Horace Walpole in 1754 had bookcases designed in the Gothic taste with 'arches and pinnacles and pierced columns' to match the other furniture at Strawberry Hill. In Fig. 13 the Gothic motive is suggested in the arrangement of the glazing and the mouldings of the cornice; but the pierced cresting of acanthus scrolls is rococo in character. The carving throughout is remarkably delicate, and in the lower portion the centre compartment is of serpen-

tine form. The smaller examples are equally serviceable for books or china; such pieces exhibit great variety in the design of glazing bars. A number of composite specimens, impossible to classify, were made between 1750 and 1800.

From c. 1770 the classical revival began to affect bookcases, of which some were made from the designs of fashionable architects. The tendency was now towards simplicity and breadth of treatment, seen in entablatures, mouldings and astragals of almost Grecian severity, combined with restrained detail. A remarkable example of this neo-classical, architectural type was designed by Robert Adam for Sir Watkin Williams-Wynn's house in St James's Square (Fig. 19). The admirably distributed ornament is carved in mahogany almost the colour of bronze. In the furnishing of his libraries Adam supervised the most trivial details even to ink-stands, and his bookcases, many of which were intended to stand in a recess, are distinguished by perfection of line and reticence of ornament, according with the architectural treatment of the room. James Paine was probably responsible for the two examples in Fig. 17, in the library of Brocket Hall, built for Sir Matthew Lamb (d. 1768), from Paine's designs. They are in pinewood painted white, with gilt enrichments; the doors are filled with a small metal trellis-work with pleated purple silk suspended behind, the gilded astragals with scrolled terminations being particularly graceful. Fig. 18 from Castle Howard is a fine specimen of the large library bookcase in the classical taste; the alcove supporting the central compartment gives architectural character to the design. Fig. 20 shows classical motives applied to a mahogany bookcase, while in a large example (Fig. 21), veneered with curled mahogany, the front forms a

21. *Break-front Bookcase, veneered with curled mahogany. Ht. 9 ft. 2½ in., W. 12 ft. 5 in., Depth 2 ft. ½ in. (Dr A. Wollaston.)*

22. *Mahogany Bookcase fitted with apothecary's dispensary and pedestal writing table. c. 1780. (M. Harris & Sons.)*

double break, each wing being constructed in two sections. In the pediment's centre is a medallion by John Flaxman, from a series of Muses designed by him for Wedgwood in 1775-6. With its vase- and oval-shaped glazing bars and delicate enrichment this bookcase is a fine example of the architectural type. It was made for General West Hyde (1735-97) about 1775. Many of these large bookcases have a drawer fitted for writing.

The bookcases in Hepplewhite's *Guide* (1788) have straight moulded cornices, occasionally surmounted by urns or scroll-work. These 'library cases' are to be made of the finest mahogany, and the doors of waved or curled wood, sometimes banded and inlaid. Hepplewhite writes that 'the ornamental glazing bars are intended to be of metal . . . painted of a light colour, or gilt'. All the bookcases in the *Guide* have ring handles with circular back plates. Designs of similar character are illustrated by Shearer, while bureau-bookcases by Gillows of Lancaster in design and quality rival the work of the best London makers.

Fig. 22 shows a remarkable composite bookcase, the central recess being fitted with a pedestal library table which draws out beyond the cupboards on either side. The lowest shelf of the cupboard above is faced with a row of 'dummy' folio volumes, forming doors; while behind are small drawers and compartments containing glass bottles and an apothecary's weights and scales.

A miniature variety, made at this time for recesses or the space between windows in sitting-rooms, is described in Gillow's cost book in 1799 as a 'moving library'. Examples, generally between 3 and 4 feet high, have a brass or wooden

23. *Satinwood Bookcase, brass gallery and turned feet; type designed for space between windows. c. 1785. (Macquoid Coll.)*
24. *Mahogany Bookcase inlaid with satinwood and sycamore. c. 1790. 25. Mahogany glazed Bookcase, corresponding with design Pl. 39, Sheraton's* Drawing Book. *c. 1795.*

26. *Mahogany Bookcase with satinwood bandings; bears label of Morgan and Saunders. c. 1800. (Lord David Ogilvy.) 27. Mahogany Bookcase, painted lead astragals; brass handles attached to pierced paterae. c. 1795. (The late Mrs H. Cordes.)*

28. *Mahogany Bookcase designed by T. Hope, female masks of bronze. c. 1810. (Mr J. Brandreth.)* 29. *Mahogany Bookcase, domed centre and concave wings. c. 1800. (Mr J. B. Wheatley.)*

gallery and a series of fixed shelves with a drawer or cupboard. Fig. 23, of solid satinwood, illustrates this type, which occasionally had sides of lattice work.

Sheraton's bookcase designs are marked by increased height in the lower portion, a reduction of width, and a tendency to stilted proportions. To achieve elegance, makers relied chiefly on a light scrolled or lunette-shaped pediment, vase finials and delicate mouldings; these, with use of satinwood and other veneers, produced a lively and graceful appearance. Sheraton introduced several novelties in the design: for instance, he shows a large bookcase with 'elliptic breaks' in the wings. He paid special attention to astragals or glazing bars, producing a variety of graceful patterns, often of oval and vase forms. The earlier practice of filling the doors with brass trellis-work continued, various coloured silks forming an ornamental background to this 'wirework'; while in some examples wooden

30. *Bookcase, veneered with zebra wood, divided by reeded pilasters headed by brass lions' masks. c. 1810. Ht. 3 ft., L. 5 ft. 6½ in. (Brocklesby Park, Lincs.)* 31. *Mahogany revolving Bookcase; label of Mack Williams and Gibbon. c. 1800.*

astragals were replaced by painted lead (Fig. 27). The example shown in Fig. 25 corresponds with a design in Sheraton's *Drawing Book* (Appendix, Plate 39, 2nd and 3rd eds.). Above the pediment, carved with a draped urn, is a 'foliated' spray with branches extending to the finials. The graceful tracing of the glazing has squares in the centre intended for mirror plates or a painted panel 'which has a pretty effect'; while the borders are of deep-toned satinwood, slender pilasters with carved capitals and bases forming the outer stiles. The mechanism of the writing drawer is explained at length in Sheraton's notes. It is thrown out by a spring operated by touching the centre of the patera at each end of the drawer. Below are sliding trays or 'clothes press shelves'.

To appeal to the jaded public taste Sheraton towards the end of his career produced a variety of eccentric designs, notably 'The Sisters' Cylinder Bookcase', 'for the use of two ladies'; formerly at Arundel Castle there was a mahogany example closely corresponding with Sheraton's plate. Fig. 29 suggests the search for novelty characteristic of this phase, the concave wings being ill-adapted for books, while the finials headed by the Prince of Wales's feathers are fancifully elongated.

The archaeological revival, which so strongly affected furniture in the early 19th century, is particularly noticeable in the design of bookcases. As no true antique precedents could be found, classical detail was applied to cases of traditional form. A representative selection is given in George Smith's *Household Furniture* (1808). He writes of an example with metal terminals in the upper stage that it should be made of rosewood or satinwood with the figures of bronze, but 'if mahogany is preferred, the less contrast that is used the better'. The silk backing to a wire trellis remained in favour, 'for nothing can distress the eye more than the sight of a countless number of volumes occupying one entire space'. The Egyptian taste was considered specially appropriate for libraries, and a bookcase with stiles tapered towards the top to produce a pyramidal effect is designed to be carried round three sides of such a room. Mahogany is recommended with ornaments of inlaid ebony and 'figures in imitation of bronzed metal'.

Dwarf bookcases were favoured as being susceptible of classical treatment. They are shown in Smith's *Household Furniture* with pedestals at each end supporting busts, and enriched with laurel leaves and medallions. They were intended to be placed one at each end of a room or gallery, with a library table between them, to produce 'a grand pleasing efect', the 'lowness adopted in the present design' being intended 'to leave space on the walls for paintings'. Smith shows designs for 'Chinese, Egyptian and Gothic Bookcase Doors', recommending yellow or pink silk behind the glass. Thomas Hope's designs for this variety of furniture exhibit a more learned interpretation of the prevailing style. One of his bookcases, formerly at Deepdene (Fig. 28) is of mahogany with metal enrichments, the modelling of the terminal sphinxes being remarkably good.

Another favoured type midway between a low bookcase and a commode had shelves in the centre flanked by panels or doors, 'calculated to contain all the books that may be required in a sitting-room without reference to the library'. Gilt columns, terminals carved in the Egyptian style and applied metal ornaments are characteristic of this type. These were also supplemented by book stands in which circular shelves

1. *Oak Book Rest. c.* 1700. *Ht.* 1 *ft.* 8 *in., W.* 1 *ft.* 9 *in.* (*V. & A. Mus.*)

revolve round a central column. In a patent for this variety, taken out in 1808 by Benjamin Crosby, it is described as 'a machine or stand for books . . . which may be turned or moved at pleasure.' The difficulty of arranging books on a circular shelf was overcome by inserting wedge-shaped blocks at intervals.

In Fig. 31 the vertical divisions in each stage are fitted with a key, and open to allow brass rods protecting the books to be removed. On the central column is pasted a label inscribed 'Mack Williams and Gibbon Furniture Warehouse 39, Strafford Street. Upholders to the Rt. Honble and Honble His Majesty's Board of Works'.

BOOK RESTS. Intended to support manuscripts or folio volumes in 18th-century libraries. Portable, of light construction, with turned cross-bars pivoting in rectangular blocks of uprights; upper bar supported by strut adjustable by means of a ratchet. Early example in oak (Fig. 1) has carved scrolls and foliage on top and bottom rails. Most surviving rests are mahogany; rosewood used in early 19th century. Similar supports sometimes in bureau flaps or library tables.

BOOK SHELVES. *See* SHELVES.

BOOK STANDS. *See* BOOKCASES and DESKS.

BOSS. Projecting ornament used as stop or finishing to mouldings, to cover them where they intersect.

BOW FRONT. Convex curved front on 18th-century furniture, chiefly chests of drawers and commodes.

BOWL STAND. *See* WASHING-STANDS.

BOXES AND CASKETS. As a receptacle for precious possessions the box is coeval with the chest, and is distinguished from it generically, merely by difference in size. Of the enormous variety of boxes and caskets relatively few can be classed as furniture. For the most part boxes escape notice in early inventories, no doubt being held of too small account to de-

1. *Oak Box, front carved with profile heads in medallions and lion's mask; hinges and handles original, lock-plate later. c. 1545.* (*Ockwells Manor, Berks.*)

2. *Oak Box carved with foliated scrolls and lozenges. Late 16th century. Ht. 10 in., L. 1 ft. 2 in., Depth 1 ft. 4½ in.* (*H. Clifford Smith Coll.*)

serve mention; and if entered are seldom described, though an account of their contents is sometimes given. In the will of John of Gaunt 'a little box of Cypress wood' is the depository of rings, diamonds and rubies.

English medieval boxes in the category of furniture, unlike chests, have not survived. Some, fitted with padlocks, were used for the dispatch of confidential communications, one key

being kept by each correspondent. A box *pro pulvere* in the cellarium of Hugh Grantham of York in 1410 was probably used to contain the sand for drying ink. It is more difficult to account for the scarcity of allusions in 16th- and 17th-century inventories, which often list trifling articles in every room in the house. There are, however, some notable exceptions and in *The second parte of the inventorye of our late soverangne, Lord King Henry VIII* (1547) a remarkable variety of boxes are given. In the closet 'next the kynges privy chamber' were 'a boxe of leather full of painted antiques', a 'little boxe of leather for table men', one covered with velvet, 'wherein were pictures of needlework', and a wooden box 'with xii payers of hawkes belles smalle and greate, and a fawconer's glove'. One held slippers of velvet for women, while another was 'a boxe with burnynge perfumes in'. Several boxes are listed which contained dolls, probably used by Mary, Elizabeth and Edward VI as children. Katherine of Aragon also possessed a large collection, among them a 'blacke boxe of chestmen of ivorye, lacking the cheste boarde', probably of Spanish or Italian

3. *Casket, inlaid with bone and dark woods, dated 1570. Ht. 1 ft. 3½ in., L. 1 ft. 3½ in., Depth 10 in.* (*Melford Hall, Suffolk.*)

4. *Box of ash, inlaid with pearwood, holly and bog-oak: figures in late Elizabethan costume. c. 1600. Ht. 10 in., L. 2 ft. 6½ in., Depth 1 ft. 10 in.* (*V. & A. Mus.*)

5. *Oak Box, front and sides decorated with flutings. c. 1600. Ht. 10 in., L. 2 ft. 2 in., Depth 1 ft. 6½ in. (The late Mr O. Baker.)*

6. *Oak Box carved with scrolls painted red and blue. c. 1620. Ht. 8 in., L. 2 ft., Depth 1 ft. 2 in. (M. Buckmaster Coll.)*

7. *Oak Box, with mitred mouldings and split balusters. c. 1650. (F. Skull Coll.)*

origin and made of ebony. Paul Hentzner records that at Whitehall Queen Elizabeth kept her bracelets, etc., in a little chest or box ornamented all over with pearls.

More modest boxes were certainly much used in Elizabethan and Jacobean times for small articles of personal apparel, documents and private papers. In a rare black-letter quarto (1598) entitled *A Health to the Gentlemanly Profession of Servingmen*, we are told that when a lady rides abroad one of her serving men 'is to carrie her boxe with ruffles and other accessories'.

Surgical instruments cases were often covered with shagreen. In *The Merry Wives of Windsor* (1598) Doctor Caius calls for 'a box, a green-a box' from his closet. Between 1617 and 1621 the Steward of the Shuttleworths of Gawthorpe paid various small sums for boxes—for instance, 3s. for a handbox for the lawn or lace bands worn at the neck by men. There is also an entry 'for a little E.O. Boxe and sending yt downe xiid'. This was a small cylindrical box for a game of hazard, much in vogue at the time (*see* TABLES, CARD AND GAMING). The box-makers were already incorporated at this date, and are several times mentioned in 17th-century records of the Joiners' Company.

Boxes are found with a sloping lid, sometimes so carved as to preclude their use as a desk (*see* DESKS), while others are divided into compartments with a drawer in the lower portion. From the early Renaissance, a few boxes survive carved with profile heads in medallions. Fig. 1 is a specimen of c. 1545, for a frill at the neck—precursor of a ruff—is perceptible in the male and female costume.

In Fig. 2 the front is vigorously carved, the scrolls on either side terminating in broad leaves; the nicking of the framework is very characteristic of these Elizabethan specimens. An inlaid casket, of a form extremely rare at this time, is shown in Fig. 3, the decoration consisting of diamond-shaped ornaments enclosed within bandings in which bone is used with dark and light woods. The canted top is raised on a hinge and the lower part of the front slides to one side, revealing a set of little tills. Another inlaid specimen is seen in Fig. 4, the ornament being glued to the foundation and some portions further secured by pegs forming part of the pattern. The box is of ash, inlaid with figures in late Elizabethan costume, cocks and small birds, roundels and roses, the inlay being of pear-wood, holly and bog-oak; the lock-plate is a later addition. The interior is lined with hand-block-printed paper, decorated with a diaper pattern of Tudor roses, some sheets of Camden's

8. *Oak Box, decorated with chip carving, dated 1648. Ht. 12½ in., L. 1 ft. 8 in., Depth 1 ft. 2 in. (V. & A. Mus.)*

9. *Oak Box on stand, with arcaded front and incised decoration. c. 1670. Ht. 2 ft. 10 in., L. 2 ft., Depth 1 ft. 5 in. (Mr Ralph Edwards.)*

Remaines Concerning Britaine (1st ed., 1605) having been used. Fig. 5 depends on large and small flutings and a well-moulded base for effect; hinge and lock-plate being original. In Fig. 6 scrolls in juxtaposition fill front and sides, painted alternately in reds and blues, an instance of the taste for gaily coloured wood that persisted from medieval times well into the 17th century.

A number of boxes were covered with incised leather, a traditional treatment copied so closely from Spanish and Portuguese originals that it is difficult in some instances to determine their nationality. In Fig. 8 the date 1648 and initials E.W. are incised in a half-circle below the lid. The decorative areas are skilfully filled with elaborate interlaced bandings, the interspaces being carved with faceted ornament, the border and spandrels corresponding in treatment. This specimen has little in common with chest fronts or boxes of its

age, the decoration, though more refined, closely resembling the chip carving on 13th-century chests, and illustrating an interesting departure from contemporary taste. In Fig. 7 the decoration is confined to mitred mouldings and baluster ornament carved in the solid, with an incised chevron pattern on the frieze. Many of these boxes were made to contain Bibles, while others were intended for lace or the elaborate gloves of the period. An entry of 16d. 'for a box for my Lords bouks' occurs in the Howard Household Accounts for 1620.

A box on its original stand, c. 1670, is seen in Fig. 9; the front is arcaded on either side of the lock-plate, the remaining decoration being incised. Towards the end of the century glove and lace boxes were sometimes mounted on walnut stands with spiral or baluster-turned uprights united by shaped diagonal stretchers, but genuine examples of such stands are extremely rare owing to the fragility of the supports.

10. *Box, cut from the 'Boscobel Oak'; original silver mounts. c. 1670. Ht. 3 in., L. 11 in., Depth 9 in. (Percival Griffiths Coll.)*

11. *Stump-work Box, banded with tortoise-shell, interior fitted with tray above series of small drawers. c. 1665. (Mrs Gratrix.)*

12. *Walnut Box, decorated with marquetry of various woods and ivory. c. 1680. Ht. 6½ in., L. 1 ft. 8½ in., Depth 1 ft. 4½ in. (Mr Ralph Edwards.)*

13. *(Left) Casket, worked in flat stitch, interior fitted with drawers. c. 1640. (Percival Griffiths Coll.)*

14. *(Right) Casket, decorated with cut paper and floss silk; figures of Charles II and Catherine of Braganza on the doors; silver mounts. c. 1670. (Percival Griffiths Coll.)*

15. *Workbox*, decorated with designs in cut paper-work, painted and gilded; framed in ebonised mouldings, dated 1687. Ht. 5½ in., L. 1 ft. 6 in., Depth 1 ft. 2½ in. (*V. & A. Mus.*)

16. *Satinwood Box; front inlaid with seaweed in vase on green oval. c. 1755. Ht. 9½ in., L. 1 ft. 3 in., Depth 1 ft.*

17. *Mahogany Box, carved with rococo ornament, ormolu handle. c. 1755. Ht. 4¾ in., L. 1 ft. 1½ in., Depth 9 in. (H. Hirsch Coll.)*

18. *Japanned Workbox on stand, gilt and carved with rococo ornament. c. 1735. (Longford Castle, Wilts.)*

Fig. 10 is made from the Boscobel oak in which Charles II hid after the battle of Worcester. The silver mounts are engraved in the style of early Restoration plate, the shield with foliated borders bearing a representation of the tree, among the branches of which the king's head may be seen, together with an inscription in doggerel verse.

Under the Tudors and Stuarts, the giving of presents played an important part in diplomacy, and a number of highly ornamented boxes containing specie or jewels are said to have been presented by Charles II to foreign ambassadors. Walnut boxes of the reign are often decorated with marquetry (like the tables and chests of drawers on which they were placed). In an unusual example (Fig. 12) the top forms a continuous pattern pictorially composed. Birds and butterflies are introduced amid the flowers, and leaves of bone stained green are scattered freely in contrast with jessamine petals left unstained. A few years later the whole surface is covered with sprays of acanthus in marquetry of quieter tones, or with the arabesque variety in oval panels. Others were veneered with 'oyster-shell' walnut, the top being divided into panels by boxwood lines. In *Sylva* (1664) Evelyn writes that many boxes for writing were made of the lamina or scale of beechwood 'superinduc'd with thin leather or paper'.

The caskets and boxes set with needlework, so typical of the Stuart reigns, were used by ladies for many purposes; they contain bottles for perfume, and receptacles for ink and sand, wafers, combs, writing-paper, cosmetics, and needle cases, also a pin-cushion and looking-glass. The lower portion consists of a nest of small drawers, some placed at the back of others, and found by pulling out the partitions. The ring drawer is nearly always concealed in this way, but it is sometimes found in the top compartment, and the three jewel drawers are usually hidden behind a sliding partition in front, or in the sides under the upper compartments.

These specimens may be divided into four groups: (1) The double casket with domed top in which the lid carries a box with a well beneath. (2) The square casket, with a mirror in the lid, sometimes with a pin-pad on either side. (3) The square casket with tray and a deep compartment. (4) The plain shallow box for gloves, lace, etc. The various linings are coral red, pale blue, green and occasionally yellow. The top edges of the dividing partitions are bound with a mauve or white paper, impressed with a silver design or a fine silver braid. The back of the doors is often prettily decorated with braided patterns, and in some elaborate specimens a needlework picture is found. There is often realistic detail—leather for a horses' bridle, gold for sceptres and crowns, and seed pearls for head-dresses and necklaces, the faces being occasionally modelled in wood with silk glued over.

Fig. 13 is a casket worked in flat stitch in quiet shades of red, blue, yellow and brown, the silver tone of the ground predominating; the interior is fitted with tiny drawers lined and faced with coral silk. Fig. 11 was given to William Whitton, Ranger of Woodstock Park, by Charles II. It is of box-like form, but the interior is fitted with drawers and the front opens as doors. The decoration of figures, landscapes and architectural subjects is in very high relief in polychrome on a white satin ground. A mirror is framed under the lid. Another example (Fig. 14) is decorated with full-length figures of Charles II and Catherine of Braganza, butterflies, birds and

19. *Painted birchwood Box, cylindrical shape, lid decorated with coloured engraving of Tonbridge castle and bridge. c.* 1800. (*Miss H. E. Hewitt.*)

floral sprays in that peculiar work in which cut paper has floss silk spread over it, the whole being covered with mica as a preservative. This treatment is occasionally found combined with stump work. Other decorations were japan, shells and even rolled paper (*see* FILIGREE), a fanciful treatment popular with ladies until the end of the 18th century. In Fig. 15 rolled paper and shells are combined, the mouldings being of ebonised wood and the top and sides covered with yellow silk as a background. The top centre panel is filled with shells, while flanking it are the initials M.W. (Mary Wright) and the date 1687.

Throughout the 17th century candles were generally kept in the small till fitted inside chests, tallow being regarded as a preservative against moth; but both square and cylindrical candle boxes were also made in oak, silver, pewter and brass.

Boxes continued to be used for a variety of purposes in the 18th century. The Dyrham Inventory (1710) mentions one 'Peruke Box', and Gerreit Jensen made a 'box and stand for her Majesties service' at a cost of £1 5s. in 1713. Another to contain counters, given by the Duchess of Marlborough to Queen

20. *Box, veneered with thuya, banded with tulip and rosewood. c.* 1790. (*Mr A. Hewitt.*)

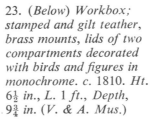

21. (*Left*) *Satinwood Box on stand, inlaid in neo-classic taste. c. 1780. (Pepys Cockerill Coll.)*

22. (*Right*) *Harewood octagonal Box on stand, decorated with coloured engravings. c. 1780. Ht. 2 ft. 4 in., W. 1 ft. 2½ in. (Leopold Hirsch Coll.)*

23. (*Below*) *Workbox; stamped and gilt teather, brass mounts, lids of two compartments decorated with birds and figures in monochrome. c. 1810. Ht. 6½ in., L. 1 ft., Depth, 9¾ in. (V. & A. Mus.)*

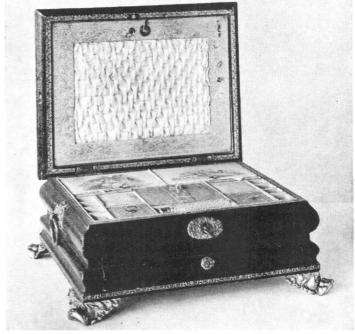

Anne, had the Royal Arms in ivory on the outside and on each of the four small boxes in the interior. In 1740 Benjamin Goodison received 7s. from the Countess of Cardigan for 'taking the brass work of a Japand Box and reparing the Box and brass work and new lackered Do'. The Countess also paid a guinea to Edward Griffiths for a 'neat wallnuttree box with a Drawer a Good Lock and a Neat Key'. At this time boxes were often decorated with japan. At Longford Castle, to which Goodison supplied some of the finest furniture for the first Lord Folkestone, there is a japanned casket of about this date mounted on a gilt stand, in the most florid rococo style (Fig. 18).

The royal accounts for this period afford almost as many instances of elaborate boxes as the Tudor inventories. John Bradburn, cabinet-maker to George III, charged £1 15s. 6d. 'ffor putting silver hinges to 2 Ivory Boxes in the Snuff Box way', for the Queen's House, St James's Park, in 1766. For Richmond Lodge in the same year he lined two ivory boxes with mahogany and fitted them with new trays. For the King's own use a few months later he made 'a neat mahogany Box with Compartments to hold a set of Chess-men', lining it with white satin and quilting the lid. Few elaborately carved mahogany boxes of the 18th century have survived, but in Fig. 17 is a fine specimen, the decoration carved in low relief on a matted ground consisting of sprays of husks and acanthus springing from shell centres.

As early as 1727 there was a large output of boxes and many other small articles at Tunbridge Wells, Kent, in the particular style of inlaid decoration known as 'Tunbridge Ware' (*q.v.*). A box (Fig. 19), veneered with polished birchwood, is from the adjacent town of Tonbridge, the lid being decorated with a coloured engraving of the Castle and Bridge, and the floral border skilfully painted in greens, reds and blues. A small

printed label inside states that it was made at '*Wise's Manufactory, Tonbridge*'. Fig. 16 is an unusually elaborate specimen decorated with marquetry. The top is veneered with figured satinwood, inlaid with an oval patera surrounded by husks of green stained wood. The sides are plain and the front has a vase on a green oval. Fig. 21 shows another fine satinwood box, mounted on its original stand and decorated with festoons of oak-leaves and acorns tied by ribbons; here there is a drawer in the lower portion. On the octagonal harewood box (Fig. 22) the coloured engravings of amatory subjects are in the manner of Bartolozzi, the angles being enriched with boxwood

1. *Wall-Bracket, carved and gilded soft wood. c. 1695. Ht. 1 ft. 4 in., W. 1 ft. 4 in. (V. & A. Mus.)* 2. *Wall-Bracket; carved soft wood. originally painted. c. 1740. (The late Mr F. C. Harper.)* 3. *Triple Console Bracket; carved, painted and partly gilded soft wood. c. 1735. (Rousham, Oxon.)*

and ebony; the interior lined with its original pink silk suggests that it was used as a workbox. An inlaid specimen (Fig. 20) c. 1790 is in a more sober style, but the thuya ground makes an effective contrast with bandings of tulip and rosewood.

Boxes of this kind rarely figure in trade catalogues of the time, though tea-caddies and knife-boxes decorated with marquetry are largely represented. Sheraton, however, in his *Drawing Book* (1791-4), gives a design for a lady's travelling-box 'with conveniences for writing, dressing and working'. It contains a writing drawer, a desk, dressing-glass, and another drawer for a kind of windlass or roller for 'fixing and winding up lace as it is worked'. The middle division is fitted with scissors, etc., while in the boxes on each side are powder, pomatum, scent bottles and rings.

From c. 1800 caskets and boxes covered with tooled leather and fitted for the toilet and needlework became popular. An example in green leather (Fig. 23) has brass mounts characteristic of this period, the lids of the two larger compartments being decorated with transfer prints. Boxes were not suitable subjects for the archaeological motives of the Regency period, but many workboxes and tea-caddies were elaborately decorated in a pseudo-Chinese style, the landscapes, figures, etc., being 'reserved' or stopped out against a brown or black background, and shaded with a pen by hand.

BOXWOOD (*Buxus sempervirens*). Hard, firm wood; light brown tone when polished, with silky lustre. Used extensivehy in 16th and 17th centuries for inlay and marquetry, and in latler 18th century as inlay and border lines. Figured wood from the roots used by cabinet-makers and inlayers (Evelyn in *Sylva*, 1664).

BRACKET CLOCKS. *See* CLOCK CASES.

BRACKETS. The bracket which falls within the category of furniture (as distinct from architecture and decorative woodwork) is rare before the end of the 17th century, and few, if any, surviving examples date before William and Mary's reign. Many detachable brackets of this era are probably of foreign origin, made by skilled Huguenot craftsmen in England, though commissioned here and used in English houses.

Daniel Marot, in one of his published designs, possibly for Queen Mary's private sitting-room at Hampton Court, shows a number of wall-brackets disposed throughout the apartment for the display of China and Delft ware, of which the Queen was an enthusiastic collector; and in a further series of plates he has designs for such brackets to a larger scale.

The contemporary passion for collecting china perhaps explains the vogue for brackets of various shapes and sizes, with the characteristic decorative motives of the period, such as the foliated female mask, male mask, and lambrequin (Fig. 1)—a tabbed, fringed and tasselled drapery—or so-called 'Indian' head.

French influence prevailed under William III, Anne and George I, lingering until the Palladian revival modified the design of the wall-bracket by the increasing use of sculpture as decoration and the adoption of a more massive and monumental scale in accessory objects. The bracket, now used to support marble and bronze busts and porphyry or alabaster vases, assumed matching proportions, a type much in favour being known as a console—scroll-shaped in profile, the curves terminating above and below in a volute and surmounted by a horizontal tablet. The Palladian mansions of Houghton, Ragley, Holkham and Rousham are equipped with sets of these large-scale brackets, or consoles, still bearing the 'bustos' or bronzes for which they were originally designed.

William Kent's name is associated with the design of many early Georgian brackets for busts, vases or candelabra, and examples in Figs. 2 and 3 are characteristic of the style of this versatile designer and of contemporary architects such as Campbell, Gibbs and Ripley.

From c. 1750 brackets were important articles of furniture as the pattern books of Chippendale, Ince and Mayhew, Lock, Johnson, and others attest. In this period the panelling of the interior was becoming less general and was being often replaced

4. Wall-Bracket, carved pinewood (gilding renewed); mask of Venus, one of pair based on design in Director *(3rd ed., Pl. CLXI). c. 1762. Ht. 2 ft. 2 in., W. 1 ft. 9 in. (V. & A. Mus.) 5. Eagle Bracket; carved and gilded limewood. c. 1745. (Mr Montague L. Meyer.) 6. Carved mahogany Bracket. c. 1750. (Sir Harry and Lady Hague Coll.)*

with silk damask or similar material or with hand-painted wallpaper. This involved a less formal disposition of pictures and other ornaments, among which the girandoles and brackets of painted or gilded wood, with a spirited blending of rococo and Chinese motives, were freely used to support lights and for the display of porcelain vases and figurines. Mahogany was only occasionally employed.

Chippendale's *Director* (1st ed., 1754) has a number of designs for 'Brackets for Bustoes', both symmetric and asymmetric, carved and pierced, and adorned with *Chinoiserie* motifs—rock-work, dripping water, stalactites, long-billed stork-like birds, pagoda tops, etc. For much of the second half of the 18th century fret-cut brackets (Fig. 8) were popular and, made with well-chosen mahogany, are stronger than their fragile appearance suggests. They were primarily intended to support bright-hued, true and soft-paste porcelain. More baroque in conception is the fine carved and gilt bracket for

a bust (Fig. 4), one of a pair, formerly at Langley Park, Norfolk, dating from c. 1760 and closely resembling a design in the *Director* (3rd ed., Plate CLXI). Wall-brackets were extensively used to support clocks and timepieces in the latter half of the 18th century (*see* CLOCK CASES).

After c. 1765 wall-brackets came under the influence of the classical revival. Among Adam's original drawings in the Soane Museum are several designs for these, notably an important 'Clock-Bracket for the King' (George III), and a clock-bracket for 20, Portman Square, designed for the Countess of Home in 1775. The six designs for brackets in Hepplewhite's *Guide*, and such an example as Fig. 9, show how even minor varieties of furniture were made to conform with the restrained simplicity of the final phase of the neo-classical style. Brackets carved with birds, chimeras or other ornament in the Egyptian style figure in Smith's *Household Furniture* (1808, Pl. 116), but surviving specimens are rare.

7. Wall-Bracket, carved and gilded in rococo style. c. 1755. (Blair Castle, Perths.) 8. Mahogany Wall-Bracket, carved with fretwork c. 1760. 9. Wall-Bracket, carved and painted soft wood. c. 1775. (Percival Griffiths Coll.)

BRANCH VENEER. Cut from smaller branches of a tree, used from c. 1650 onwards; generally from laburnum and kingwood (*see* CONSTRUCTION).

BRANCHES. Name often used for chandeliers in 17th and 18th centuries.

BRAND DOGS. *See* CHIMNEY FURNITURE, ANDIRONS.

BRASIER. A portable metal pan or hearth in which coke or charcoal was burnt. The brasier (brasero or brasera in the 17th century) is thus defined in the *Fops Dictionary* (1690): 'A large vessel or moving hearth of silver for coaks transportable into any room.' The portable hearths, termed 'court chimneys' in the list of Henry VIII's furniture in the Royal palaces, made 'grate wise' upon wheels, were brasiers, not grates standing in a fireplace. In the larger rooms, such as the Great Chamber and Long Gallery, brasiers supplemented the fire on the hearth, and several specimens, resembling the one in Fig. 1, are still preserved at Knole in the rooms in which they were used. When the fashion for silver furniture was at its height towards the end of Charles II's reign, brasiers were occasionally made of that metal. At Christ Church, Oxford, there is a charcoal brasier in the form of a copper bowl on an iron stand with scrolled supports probably c. 1750. M.J.

BRASS (INLAY OF). The Boulle technique of metal inlay was employed by Gerreit Jensen (*q.v.*) for some of the furniture supplied by him to William and Mary. It was also used in the 18th century by immigrant craftsmen, *e.g.* Peter Langlois and Abraham Roentgen (*q.v.*; also BUREAUX, Fig. 26). An inlay of brass lines or fret-cut ornament is often found on rosewood and mahogany furniture of the Regency period. Sheraton tried these new combinations. In his *Cabinet Dictionary* (1803) the old inlay of wood is passed over as a very 'expensive mode of decorating furniture used in the cabinet-making of twenty and thirty years back: the present mode of inlaying with brass is more durable, and looks well into the black woods of any kind'. (*See* BUHL.)

BRASS MOUNTS. *See* METAL MOUNTS.

BRATTISHING (Bratticing, etc.). Generally used to denote a carved cresting.

BRAZIL WOOD (*Caesalpinia brasilensis*). Originally known as an Oriental and East Indian tree; but allied species discovered in South America by Portuguese; similar species also in West Indies. Heavy, hard, red wood with strong markings resembling certain cuts of Cuban mahogany; beautiful rich colour when polished. Used by inlayer (Evelyn in *Sylva*, 1664), but seldom in 18th-century furniture.

BROADCLOTH. Fine, plain, woven, double-width cloth sometimes mentioned in inventories as bed-hangings. In the 'Dyninge Chamber' at Ingatestone, 1600, a 'long carpete (table-cloth) of *grene broad clothe*'.

BROCADE. Textile fabric woven with contrasting design, originally in gold or silver; later silk introduced as ground for ornaments of gold and silver thread. Frequently used for bed-hangings and chair upholstery in 17th and 18th centuries.

BROCATELLE (BROCATEL, BROCADEL). Diminutive of brocade, *i.e.* an imitation brocade with tissue, coarse silk or cotton; used for upholstery and hangings. Horace

1. *Brass Brasier, first half 18th century. Ht. 1 ft. 2½ in., L. 1 ft. 9 in., Depth 1 ft. 1½ in. (Knole Park, Kent.)*

1. *Buffet of carved pinewood. c. 1700. Ht. 9 ft. 9 in., L. 3 ft. 9 in., Depth 1 ft. 8 in. (V. & A. Mus.)*

Walpole writes of English brocatelles in 1760: 'of two colours they make them very well but they cannot arrive at three'.

BROCHED. Worked or embroidered with ornaments; '*som broched with golde*' (Wardrobe Accounts of Edward IV).

BROKEN FRONT. Applied to 18th-century bookcases, wardrobes, etc., in which front surfaces are on two or more planes divided by vertical breaks.

BROKEN PEDIMENT. *See* PEDIMENT.

BROOM, HEARTH. *See* CHIMNEY FURNITURE.

BUCKRAM. At first denoted thin fabric of cotton and linen, ranking with finest silks and used in early 14th century for hangings, covers, etc. Also applied, from early 15th century, to canvas stiffened with glue and paste. At Ingatestone, 1600, 'two old window curtaines—lyned with old blew buckeram'.

BUFFET (BEAUFETE, BUFFETTE, etc.). Until lately this French term has been applied to early varieties of the sideboard, but there is conclusive evidence that such sideboards were described as 'Court Cupboards' in Elizabethan and Jacobean times (see CUPBOARDS, COURT). In contemporary inventories the term is always employed as a compound, e.g. 'Buffet stool', i.e. padded (see STOOLS), or 'buffet cupboard', of which there were two described as 'courte' (short) in the 'Dyninge Parlor' at Ingatestone (1600). Though the exact meaning cannot be determined, there are occasional references to buffets in contemporary translations of accounts by foreigners of their travels in England, e.g. in Estienne Perlin's *Description d'Angleterre* (1588): 'The servants wait on their masters bare-headed, and leave their caps on the buffet.' At the banquet given by James I to the Constable of Castile at Whitehall in 1604 the Constable directed that a jewelled cup supplied by him should remain in the king's buffet.

In the 18th century an alcove in the panelling of a room with shelves in tiers for the display of china was described as a 'buffet'. A fine example of carved pinewood, c. 1700, is illustrated (p. 71). Sheraton in his *Cabinet Dictionary* (1803) applies the term to a piece of furniture with cupboard doors in the lower portion and tiers of shelves above.

BUFFET CHAIRS, FORMS AND STOOLS (buffed or stuffed). 1612, 'buffet cheyre' (Warrack, *Domestic Life in Scotland*, 1488-1688). 1703, Lady G. Baillie: 'For a big buffet eassi chair with cushon £18.' Ingatestone Inventory (1600): 'a little lowe buffet stoole' and 'a little buffet forme a yearde longe'.

BUHL. A popular term for a process of inlay derived from the name of the French artist and decorator, André Charles Boulle (1642-1732), who brought this art to perfection and had many imitators. Very thin layers of brass and tortoiseshell, glued together, were cut out with a fine saw in varied patterns, scrolls and arabesques being the favourite motives. This technique was practised in England by the royal cabinet-maker, Gerreit Jensen, at the end of the 17th century (see BRASS, INLAY OF, and JENSEN, G.), and by others, notably Peter Langlois (q.v.), in the mid-Georgian period. Much fine Boulle furniture found its way into English palaces and great houses from the time of the style's inception; but English imitations do not appear to have been made to any considerable extent until c. 1815, when a Buhl factory, owned by a Frenchman, Louis Gaigneur, was started at 10, Queen Street, Edgware Road. This establishment supplied the Prince Regent with a writing table inlaid with metal for £250. Another firm, Town and Emanuel, 103, New Bond Street, describe themselves on their trade label as 'Manufacturers of buhl, marqueterie, Resner, Furniture, etc. of the finest and most superb designs of the times of Louis XIVth'.

BUN FOOT. Flattened form of ball-foot introduced c. 1660 and largely used on oak and walnut furniture.

BUREAUX, BUREAU TABLES AND WRITING CABINETS (ESCRITOIRE, SCRIPTOR, SCRUTOIRE, SECRETAIRE, SECRETARY, etc.). The bureau, as distinguished from the desk and writing cabinet, is not found in England until after the end of Charles II's reign. The word has never been clearly defined, and to many of the examples illustrated the terms scrutoire, escritoire, scriptor or secretary would have been applied by their original owners. In his *Cabinet Dictionary* (1803) Sheraton states that in England the term has 'generally been applied to common desks with drawers under them, such as are made very frequently in country towns'; when a bookcase is added to the upper part 'they are called Bureau Bookcase'.

Throughout the 16th century a small desk with a sloping front met the wants of the ordinary householder, who wrote few letters and, like his ancestors, kept his papers in chests. Even in royal palaces pieces of furniture for writing were often extremely primitive under the Tudors. The earliest French and Italian examples in existence date from the beginning of the 16th century and are composed of a nest of drawers with inner compartments, enclosed by a flap which lets down as a writing board. These small portable escritoires appear to have been occasionally made in England, and the traditional form is preserved in two well-known writing cabinets at Ham House, entered as 'scriptors' in the 1679 inventory, one being veneered with walnut, the other with a parquetry of kingwood (described as 'Prince Wood' in the inventory). This cabinet (Fig. 1) is 'garnished with silver' and mounted on a 'frame' with turned baluster legs, having vase-shaped bases carved with foliage. The highly-figured veneer has bleached on the outside to a golden brown, while on the interior drawers it retains the original strong reddish tone.

Before the Restoration this type had already been superseded on the Continent by an entirely new form with a centre recessed to accommodate the writer's knees and small drawers on either side; a little later carried down to the ground, walnut being the wood commonly used for the veneer. Fig. 2 is an English example of this rare form. The top opens and a writing flap lets down, disclosing five small drawers. The tulip-shaped cappings of the legs and the bun feet are richly carved with acanthus, the flat surfaces including the stretchers being entirely covered with arabesque marquetry. In 1693 Gerreit Jensen (q.v.) charges for 'a large Bouro of fine markatrie with drawers to stand upon the topp carv'd and gilt pillars' supplied to the Crown—an early use of the term.

In Fig. 3 the evolution is carried a stage further, a desk with a falling front fitted with drawers and pigeon-holes taking the place of the writing flap. The baluster legs are of graceful profile, the centre legs swinging forward to support the front when the desk is open. The drawers are oak lined, the knobs of ivory, and the flap is inlaid with a delicate feather banding. In front of the centre drawer is a well to which access is gained by pushing back a slide, and within is a receptacle for coins and jewels. An example of this type decorated with finely cut arabesque marquetry is given in Fig. 4. In the Dyrham Park inventory (1710) 'Skrewtores' are listed in two of the living-rooms, being distinguished from the more abundant 'tables for writing'.

In the type popularly known as a 'knee-hole writing table', introduced early in the 18th century, the centre compartment is deeply recessed, most of such pieces being veneered with walnut cross-banded (see TABLES, LIBRARY, Fig. 8). In another variety the flap lets down and is supported on sliders fitted at the corners; the knee-hole is omitted, and the lower portion is composed of three long and two short drawers. In Fig. 6 the variety of woods is remarkable, the exterior being

1. *'Scriptor' veneered with parquetry of kingwood; turned and carved stand of same wood, silver mounts. c. 1675. Ht. 4 ft. 1 in., W. 2 ft. 5 in., Depth 1 ft. 3¼ in. (Ham House, Surrey.)*

2. *Walnut Bureau Table, decorated with arabesque marquetry; legs carved with acanthus, stretchers inlaid on upper surface; top opens and fitted with drawers, front lets down as writing flap. c. 1690. (H. C. Moffat Coll.)*

3. *Walnut Secretaire, on stand with turned baluster legs hinged in front to support flaps. c. 1700. (G. L. Riley Coll.)*

4. *Walnut Secretaire; decorated with arabesque marquetry in holly; on stand with turned taper legs. c. 1690. (Ramsden Coll.)*

5. *Walnut Bureau, inlaid with seaweed marquetry, drawers with feather bandings. c. 1700. (Col. N. R. Colville.)* 6. *Bureau, veneered with yew and walnut, interior with amboyna; ivory mounts. c. 1720. Ht. 3 ft. 5 in., L. 3 ft., Depth 1 ft. 11 in. (V. & A. Mus.)*

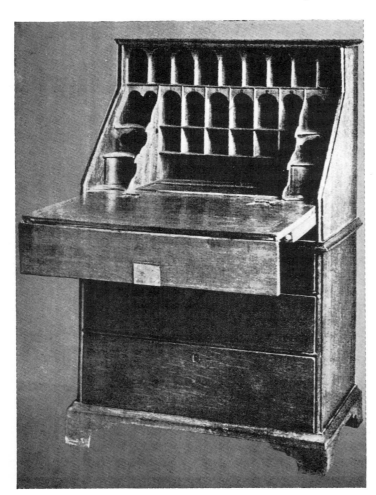

7. *Oak Bureau of country make, with pigeon-holes in three tiers; hinged portion of flap fits into compartment above desk when closed. First half of 18th century.*

veneered with yew and walnut on a ground of mahogany while amboyna is employed for the writing flap and the fittings of the desk. A few examples are decorated with seaweed marquetry, and in a fine bureau of this kind (Fig. 5) the narrow projecting desk is characteristic of the type and marks an early stage of the evolution. Fig. 7 shows an oak rustic specimen, the desk being surmounted by a narrow compartment into which a hinged portion of the flap fits when the bureau is closed.

In examples of the type forming a desk on stand dating from early in the 18th century the drawers below the writing flap were supported on cabriole legs, finishing in club feet, and carved on the knees with escalloped shells. A belated survival from the previous style is Fig. 8. The stand has tapered faceted legs, reminiscent of William III's reign, but an inscription on the flap records that the piece was made from a tree which fell in Stratton Park in the great storm of 1703. As several years would be required for the seasoning of the wood, the bureau probably dates from c. 1710.

In an admirably designed and carefully finished example (Fig. 9) the fittings of the desk are inlaid with a fine chequer pattern in sycamore; the concave shaping of the drawer beneath is a pleasing feature, and the interior, including the drawer linings, is of walnut instead of the more usual oak or deal. A small secretaire (Fig. 10) is veneered with laburnum and walnut to produce a symmetrical and highly decorative effect. The walnut stand has a fancifully shaped apron. In later examples of this small type the stands are sometimes decorated with lion masks and pendant acanthus finishing in paw feet, as in Fig. 11, which has an egg and dart moulding heading the lower drawer, while the apron also is finely carved. This bureau, which is veneered with burr walnut of golden hue, was originally surmounted by a dressing glass, a feature found intact on some specimens and indicating that they were for feminine use (Fig. 12). The pedestal knee-hole form continued to be

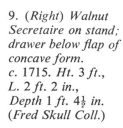

8. (*Left*) *Walnut Secretaire on stand; made from tree blown down in great gale of 1703. (Percival Griffiths Coll.)*

9. (*Right*) *Walnut Secretaire on stand; drawer below flap of concave form. c. 1715. Ht. 3 ft., L. 2 ft. 2 in., Depth 1 ft. 4½ in. (Fred Skull Coll.)*

made, but the sloping desk appears to have been discarded a few years later, the flat top being veneered in walnut and the table serving either as a desk or for the toilet. These bureaux were also made of oak and sometimes japanned.

Bureaux in two stages (called 'desks and bookcases' and other names in 18th-century trade catalogues) cannot be regarded as representing a further stage in the evolution, for they appeared shortly after the introduction of the sloping front; the advantages of an upper structure on the shelf at the top of the bureau being appreciated when the increased height of rooms led to a demand for tall pieces of furniture. These bureaux followed the fashion of contemporary cabinets and may be divided into two groups—those decorated with japan (*see* JAPANNING AND LACQUER) and those of walnut. Fig. 13 is a fine example in red japan with a double-hooded cornice surmounted by an elaborate cresting (of a type very rarely found on a bureau-bookcase), which is here silvered; a treatment repeated in the spandrels of the recess where there are finely carved cherubs' heads. The doors frame bevelled mirrors and the oak panels backing them are painted black, powdered with gold and ornamented with large groups of flowers delicately drawn, while the remainder of the cabinet is decor-

10. (*Left*) *Secretaire, veneered with figured laburnum on walnut stand. c. 1720. (The late Mrs William Mosenthal.)*

11. (*Right*) *Walnut Secretaire-Dressing Table on stand; legs carved with lion masks, front veneered with burr walnut, drawers lined with Virginia walnut. (Percival Griffiths Coll.)*

12. *Walnut Secretaire on stand, top surmounted by dressing glass with border of gilt gesso. c. 1715.* 13. *Red Japanned Bureau; doors with bevelled mirrors, cresting carved with foliated scrolls and silvered. c. 1690. (S. Greville Coll.)* 14. *Bureau-Cabinet, japanned in gold on olive-green ground, cresting carved and gilt. c. 1720. Ht. 6 ft. 2 in., L. 1 ft. 10 in., Depth 3 ft. (Mrs David Gubbay.)*

ated with smaller subjects in the Chinese taste, in gold and black on a red ground. The upper portion has drawers and open compartments for ledgers, the semi-circular sections of the hood being hinged at the bottom and supplied with keys. The drawers in the lower stage open by means of a key only. Fig. 17 is a fine bureau of rather later date, and here the red ground on the inside of the upper portion has retained its original clear and lustrous colour. The arrangement of the fittings closely corresponds with Fig. 13, but here the looking-glass panels are dipped at the corners.

Very few genuine bureau-cabinets in yellow or cream japan survive, though Stalker and Parker include yellow among their recommendations for the ground. The small bureau (Fig. 14) is japanned in a colour rarely found, the full olive-green of the ground being relieved by birds, flowers and figures in gold, and a carved and gilt cresting. The pigeon-holes and upper section are painted red in effective contrast with the olive-coloured japan, and the door is faced with a shaped mirror plate. Examples of this type constructed and decorated in the East were imported into England, the design conforming fairly closely to Western models.

The two-staged walnut bureaux contemporary with this japanned series were constructed on the same lines, with moulded panels in the upper doors, or Vauxhall mirrors bevelled and engraved in the finer specimens. The interior fittings show much ingenuity and regard for practical convenience, the central cupboard (as in japanned examples) being often flanked by columns or pilasters fixed to the front of narrow, vertical compartments. Sometimes the central compartment draws out disclosing secret receptacles, while drawers often had curved fronts, concave or convex. Like chairs, bureaux of this time often show obvious signs of Dutch influence. But the design of Fig. 19 is unmistakably English, a late Stuart crown being introduced in the inlaid spandrels of the central cupboard. The marquetry decoration is of fine quality. A scrolled, swan-necked pediment ends in gilt acanthus whorls and a foliated escutcheon, also gilt, bears a female bust. On removing one of the drawers the pilasters framing the upper cupboard pull out, and in the desk the centre compartment slides forward, disclosing a number of small drawers. The whole piece is veneered with finely figured burr walnut, and the drawers below the writing flap run in grooves; an arrangement rare at so late a date. The door lock is concealed in the plate of one of the side handles. The name 'Samuel Bennett' with 'London *fecit*' is inlaid at the base of the inner pilasters. This fine example is the work of an exceptionally gifted craftsman who alone among contemporary English workers in marquetry has handed down his name by inscriptions (*see* BENNETT,

15. (Left) Walnut Writing Cabinet; fall-down front, on chest of drawers, floral marquetry and acanthus foliage in various coloured woods. c. 1685. (Shawford House, Hants.)

16. (Right) Walnut Writing Cabinet; fall-down front, seaweed marquetry, light on dark ground. c. 1700. (Assheton-Smith Coll.)

17. (Left) Bureau in two stages, japanned in red, gold and silver. c. 1715. Ht. 7 ft. 6 in., L. 3 ft. 2 in. (Macquoid Coll.)

18. (Right) Bureau-Cabinet; burr elm inlaid with bandings of kingwood and pewter stringing. c. 1700. (M. Harris & Sons.)

19. (*Left*) *Bureau-Cabinet, veneered with burr walnut, inlaid with seaweed marquetry; scrolled pediment with gilt acanthus leaves and escutcheon; interior pilasters inlaid at bases 'Samuel Bennett London Fecit'. c. 1700. Ht. 8 ft. 9 in. (V. & A. Mus.)*

20. (*Right*) *Bureau in two stages veneered with burr walnut; cornice serpentined, interior fittings designed on curve; gilt figures on pediment. (Sir William Burrell Coll.)*

SAMUEL). Another bureau-cabinet by this maker was formerly in the Donaldson Collection.

Though domestic bureau-cabinets of this period tended to become standardised, there are some interesting exceptions. The makers of Fig. 18, G. Coxed and T. Woster (*q.v.*), are recorded by their trade label pasted in one of the drawers. This bureau is veneered with burr elm, and the firm's label has also been found on several other examples. A bureau-cabinet in the Victoria and Albert Museum is again exceptional, because the double-hooded cornice is crowned by a cresting silvered and carved with foliate scrolls like the contemporary japanned bureau (Fig. 13).

In a type of bureau, found in considerable numbers, the whole front of the upper portion lets down as a writing flap disclosing drawers and a cupboard, the pigeon-holes concealing secret drawers. This model was clearly derived from the writing cabinet enclosed by a flap of the previous century, then placed on a table or stand, but now on a chest of drawers. They were made in this form from c. 1675, embellished with floral inlay (Fig. 15), superseded by japanning or by seaweed marquetry, of which Fig. 16 is an exceptional specimen. So late as 1730, Bailey's *Dictionary* defines a scrutoire as 'a kind of long Cabinet, with a Door or Lid opening downwards for the conveniency of writing on'—a description relating to this type.

Of the more elaborate bureaux made in two stages, Fig. 20 is a fine example. The serpentine hooded cornice supports small plinths on which stand carved and gilt figures of baroque character. The interior fittings in both stages are of serpentine form, and the central cupboard is flanked by fluted pilasters with gilt capitals. In Fig. 21 the fittings are again arranged on

21. *Walnut Bureau Cabinet in three parts; bevelled plates on outer doors, central cupboard framed in glass pilasters. c. 1715. (Belton House, Lincs.)*

22. *Walnut Bureau-Cabinet, on claw-and-ball feet; carved enrichments of limewood gilt; rosewood pilasters framing bevelled mirror.* c. 1730. (*Percival Griffiths Coll.*)   23. *Walnut Tallboy-Bureau, inlaid with holly and ebony; badge of Prince of Wales and pediment mouldings, gilt. c.* 1730. (*Lady Bicester.*)   24. *Mahogany Bureau-Cabinet, broken pediment with deep embrasure supports, vase-shaped finials. c.* 1730. (*Arbury Manor, Warwicks.*)

the curve, and this example is of exceptional quality; at the corners of the pediment figures or finials are missing.

The combined tallboy and bureau was a piece primarily intended for use in a bedroom, one of the drawers pulling out to serve as a desk. The walnut tallboy-bureau (Fig. 23) was presumably made for Frederick, Prince of Wales, who arrived here from Hanover in 1728. It displays the Prince's badge within the open pediment, of which the mouldings, like the three feathers, are gilt. The handles also bear this badge on the back plate. The writing cabinet (Fig. 25) was given by George I to the British Ambassador at the Russian court. In the interior is a compartment with double doors decorated with engravings set off by painted floral borders and reflecting mirrors. The engravings represent George I and members of his family. Within the break of the pediment is a shield with a crown and the royal supporters. Fig. 22 concludes this series of walnut specimens, and here design and execution are alike remarkable, the narrow proportions and admirable carving producing an effect of remarkable elegance. The bureau is veneered throughout with burr walnut on a foundation of oak, the carved enrichments are of limewood gilt and the pilasters are of rosewood. In Fig. 24 dark Cuban mahogany takes the place of walnut, which had long remained the fashionable material. The mouldings, applied on the drawer fronts instead of on the carcase, indicate a date c. 1730.

25. *Walnut Writing Cabinet, decorated with engravings of George I and members of his family within painted floral borders. c.* 1725.

A number of fine mahogany specimens were produced at this date in which the influence of Palladian architecture is apparent. The central compartment is in projection, those at the sides forming wings, an arrangement found in contemporary china cabinets with which they closely correspond in design (*see* CABINETS, Fig. 23). Such pieces seem cumbrous out of their appropriate setting, but they were carefully planned to accord with the dignified simplicity and large scale of the mouldings in early Georgian rooms. A bureau in the style of William Kent is shown in Fig. 28, where originality of construction is combined with unusual elegance. The mahogany, now bleached to a light tone, is bordered with olive-wood intersected with spear-headed points of box, and all the enrichments are gilt. Pilasters, faced with pendants, are supported on consoles which open as secret drawers, eagle heads with acanthus sprays and oak leaves, heavily carved, being introduced on the front of the desk. The mouldings of the glazing and the raised mahogany drawer fronts in the lower portion are serpentined.

The writing cabinet (Fig. 26) departs very freely from the types in vogue c. 1750. It is of serpentine outline on the front and sides, setting the maker an exacting task in laying the figured veneers. Here the ornament is as original as the design, for the cupboard doors are inlaid in brass with arabesques, winged monsters, pendants of leaves and recumbent classical figures (Mars and Pomona?), the arabesque ornament of the spandrels being repeated on the drawers. The writing cabinet is enriched with ormolu mounts—chased or 'finely graved', like a 'Bookcase of the most curious workmanship and ornamented with brass' sold at Sir William Stanhope's house in Arlington Street in 1733. In these mounts rococo influence is distinctly perceptible. Below, the top drawer, enclosed by a writing

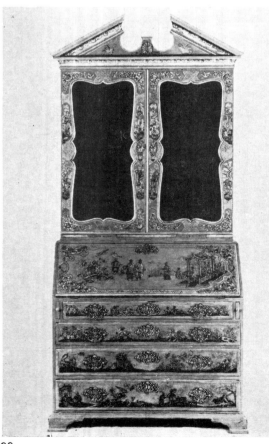

26. (*Above*) *Mahogany Writing Cabinet, inlaid with brass; chased ormolu mounts show rococo influence; top drawer in lower stage covered with a writing board.* c. 1750. Ht. 8 ft., L. 3 ft. 8 in., Depth 2 ft. 5 in. (*Major Arthur Bull.*)

27. (*Left*) *Cabinet Secretary, japanned in gold on scarlet ground; bears trade label of Giles Grendey.* c. 1745.

28. (*Right*) *Mahogany Bureau-Cabinet, bordered with olivewood and box; serpentine mouldings and enrichments gilt; top drawer fitted for writing.* c. 1735. (*Donaldson Coll.*)

29. *Mahogany Bureau-Cabinet; fretted cornice centring in swan-necked pediment; doors panelled in ogee mouldings, base gadrooned, and cabriole lion-paw feet. c. 1750. L. 3 ft. 6 in. (Percival Griffiths Coll.)* 30. *Mahogany Bureau-Bookcase; stiles decorated with floral pendants, desk front veneered with parquetry. c. 1745-50. (Formerly at Langley Park, Norf.)*

board, pulls out with the ormolu mounted corners. Another secretaire of very similar design is in existence, and in these two remarkable examples the finest figured mahogany is used and the craftsmanship is of the highest order. It is impossible to identify the maker, though the technique of metal inlay, introduced by Gerreit Jensen (*q.v.*), was practised by several immigrant craftsmen (*see* ROENTGEN, A., HINTS, F., and LANGLOIS, P.). A cabinet-secretary (Fig. 27) by Giles Grendey (*q.v.*) is a reminder that about the middle of the century japanning was still sometimes employed for the decoration.

A fine specimen, probably made about 1750, is shown in Fig. 29. The door panels are framed within serpentine mouldings in slight relief and the interior, fitted with pigeon-holes, drawers and compartments for ledgers, reproduces the arrangement of japanned examples of the previous century. The cornice is surmounted by a fretted gallery centring in a swan-necked pediment; the lower portion is plain, with original handles and lock plates, and the gadrooned base rests on lion-paw feet.

This group of mahogany bureaux, dating c. 1750, is the result of gradual evolution and marks no abrupt break with the past. But contemporary trade publications disclose new tendencies. Chippendale's *Director* (1754) shows a variety of bureaux in two stages—'Desks and Bookcases'—which range from traditional examples enriched with rococo detail (Fig. 57) to elaborate specimens in the Chinese taste. The upper portion in

each case is intended for glazing, tracery of fanciful character framing the glass. The division into a centre with recessed wings, seen in the bureau-bookcase (Fig. 30), distinguishes several of these designs. A Chinese example has a pagoda cresting hung with bells, while on rococo bureaux the pediments are curved or arched and enriched with carved scrollwork. Chippendale shows a new version of the 'Lady's Secretary' on cabriole legs, the glass in the upper part divided by a pilaster and the pediment crowned by a tall finial. Ince and Mayhew (*Universal System*, 1759-63) also devote attention to this type, illustrating a secretaire in the Gothic taste. Instead of a sloping desk, they provide a top drawer with the front letting down on a quadrant. Another example has open fret-work shelves above this writing drawer and a 'green silk curtain' to hang behind them is proposed. In 1773 Chippendale charges £26 for a 'Lady's Secretary' in the state bedchamber at Harewood House, 'Japann'd and part gilt, the front of the Secretary to rise with Ballance Weights'. Few of these japanned specimens now survive.

The remarkable bureau (Fig. 33), in the Royal Collection, was made for Queen Charlotte in 1761 by William Vile, the partner of John Cobb in St Martin's Lane (*see* VILE, W.). The admirable proportions show to perfection when the writing flap is lowered. The lines of the *bombé* base gradually merge into the vertical sides and are met by the curves of the recessed canopy supporting a royal crown of later date. The

31. *Mahogany Secretaire-Bookcase, attributed to William Vile; lower portion decorated with frets. c. 1760. (Longford Castle, Wilts.)*
32. *Bureau-Bookcase of carved mahogany; perhaps made for George, Prince of Wales (afterwards George III), by William Vile.*
c. 1755. 33. 'An exceedingly ffine mahogy. secretary'; upper portion enclosed with carved lattice work. Made by William Vile
in 1761. Ht. 7 ft., L. 3 ft. 1 in., Depth 1 ft. 6 in. (Buckingham Palace: By gracious permission of Her Majesty the Queen.)

34. *Mahogany Bureau-Cabinet in Chinese style; roof of pagoda form· centre drawer fitted as bureau. c. 1755. (Formerly at Holme Lacy, Hereford.)*

extremely delicate carving enhances brilliantly flashed mahogany veneer. The upper cupboards are filled with carved lattice-work in the Chinese taste and headed by a delicate classical cornice. The two top drawer fronts let down to form a writing flap, disclosing a series of small inner drawers faced with thuya wood. The scrolled base is consummately carved in the rococo style, the handles are fine specimens of metalwork, and this piece is certainly among the outstanding masterpieces of English craftsmanship. A bureau-bookcase, perhaps made for George III just before his accession, by Vile (Fig. 32), has the Prince of Wales's feathers in the embrasure of the pediment. Reeded columns with Corinthian capitals support the architrave, and colonettes flank the drawers in the lower portion. Another example from Longford Castle (Fig. 31) may also be assigned to Vile. The lower portion is decorated with applied frets in double X form, resembling a detail on the front and sides of a work-table made by Vile for Queen Charlotte in 1761.

The combined bureau and china-cabinet (Fig. 34) is an attractive specimen of the Chinese style. The centre compartment rises as a roof of pagoda form with fretwork in the cornice, the front and sides of the upper part being enclosed with lattice-work. The base is composed of side drawers and a central cupboard with a pull-out writing drawer above it; the doors of fine clouded mahogany are panelled with decorated serpentine mouldings, and the Chinese motive is repeated in

  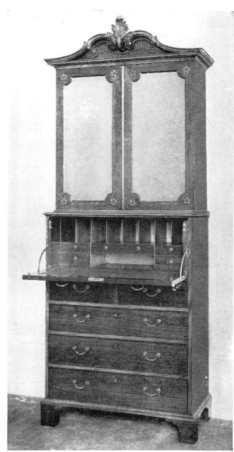

35. *Secretaire-Cabinet, carved mahogany; centre compartment of lattice-work superstructure, enclosed by doors. c. 1760*
36. *Mahogany Bureau-Cabinet with pierced pediment and brackets for china; top drawer lets down for writing. Ht. 6 ft., L. 2 ft 10 in., Depth 1 ft. 4 in. c. 1760. (Capel Cure Coll.)* 37. *Mahogany Bureau Bookcase; made in 1774 by John Bradburn for the Princess Royal. Ht. 7 ft. (Buckingham Palace: By gracious permission of Her Majesty the Queen.)*

the design of the feet. In Fig. 35 the fretwork is of unusual intricacy, the upper stage being divided into open shelves and a cupboard for china enclosed by open-work doors. The writing flap is in the form of two drawer-fronts, fitted with a keyhole and brass handles in the form of entwined serpents, while the straight legs are richly carved with pendants of fruit and leaves.

Fig. 36 is another of these combined pieces, the top drawer-front letting down to disclose the usual writing arrangements. Here the china-cabinet forming the upper portion is in English taste, but the interior is fitted with lattice-work brackets for Oriental vases, and the top drawer is surmounted by a wide pagoda moulding. A lattice-work superstructure for china was often added to small bureaux and secretaires designed for a bedroom. Of furniture made by Bradburn for the Crown, Fig. 37 shows one of three identified examples. In the secretary (Fig. 39) the lattice-work shows Gothic influence. This piece is designed on the lines of a Louis XV commode, and has ormolu acanthus mounts on the keel-shaped corners and feet. The superstructure of this type is described by Vile as 'a set of shelves at top, the sides and back all handsome cuttwork'.

Early in George III's reign classical detail in the style of Adam and other prominent architects was introduced in the decoration of bureaux. Satinwood and mahogany were used in contrasting veneers, inlaid and painted ornament replacing

38. *Mahogany Bureau, banded with applewood; writing drawer slides forward, and doors are reeded on outer surfaces. c. 1775.*

39. (Left) Secretaire; serpentine form, veneered with fiddle-back mahogany; lattice-work superstructure. c. 1770. (Mulliner Coll.)

40. (Right) Secretaire inlaid with various woods; recumbent figure of ivory on ebony ground. Attributed to T. Chippendale. c. 1770–5. (Harewood House, Yorks.)

41. (Left) Bureau-Cabinet, one of a pair; cupboards of superstructure painted with classical subjects after designs by Angelica Kauffmann; front falls down as writing desk, ormolu mouldings. c. 1790. (M. Harris & Sons.)

42. (Right) Bureau-Cabinet veneered with satinwood and mahogany; in centre of upper stage, figures in grisaille after Sir Joshua Reynolds. c. 1787. (Lady Lever Art Gallery, Port Sunlight.)

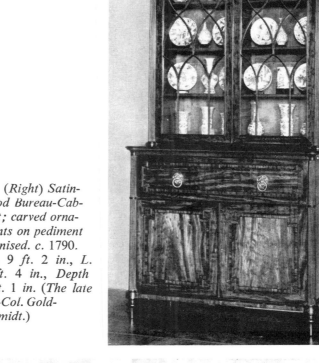

43. (*Left*) *Mahogany Bureau-Bookcase with satinwood inlay, bearing initials 'T. S.'. c. 1790. (James Ivory Coll.)*

44. (*Right*) *Satinwood Bureau-Cabinet; carved ornaments on pediment ebonised. c. 1790. Ht. 9 ft. 2 in., L. 4 ft. 4 in., Depth 2 ft. 1 in. (The late Lt.-Col. Goldschmidt.)*

45. *Secretaire on stand, veneered with amboyna; drawers lined with cedar. c. 1790. Ht. 4 ft. 2½ in., L. 1 ft. 8¾ in., Depth 1 ft. 5 in. (Mrs Ralph Edwards.)*

46. *Secretaire on stand, veneered with satinwood; 'cheveret' upper portion made to lift off; stamped 'Gillows, Lancaster'. c. 1795. (Mr Anthony Twiston-Davies.)*

47. *Bureau-Cabinet, veneered with harewood banded with rosewood; top drawer fitted as desk with cylindrical top. c. 1795. Ht. 5 ft. 6 in., L. 2 ft.*

48. (*Left*) *Satin-wood Bureau-Book-case with arcaded glazing; top drawer fitted for writing; fall-down front, bandings of mahogany. c. 1790.* (*Archdale Porter Coll.*)

49. (*Right*) *Secretaire veneered with satinwood and panels of sabicu wood; top drawer fitted for writing. c. 1790. Ht. 4 ft 5 in., L. 2 ft. 10 in., Depth 1 ft. 7 in.* (*Leopold Hirsch Coll.*)

carving. New designs supplemented the traditional types; but the upright secretary with a falling front and enclosed lower stage, so popular in France from the time of Louis XIV, was seldom produced, though affording an admirable field foɪ inlay. Fig. 40 shows a rare specimen from Harewood House, which though not in the accounts for furniture supplied by Chippendale and Haig from 1772 to 1775, can be attributed to the firm, while Adam was probably responsible for the design. Veneered with finely figured West Indian satinwood and decorated with marquetry in various woods, the central oval of the front is inlaid with a delicately drawn recumbent figure in ivory on an ebony ground.

In another rare type (Fig. 38) the desk slides forward and is enclosed by doors which, like the sides and drawer fronts, are of mahogany reeded to imitate 'tambour' construction. This treatment is also applied to the feet, veneered with applewood and inlaid. A shaped shield of the same wood backs the ornate side handles of gilt brass.

A combined cabinet and bureau (Fig. 41), one of a pair, again is remarkable for novelty of design. The top opens in

50. *Mahogany Bureau-Writing-Table of pedestal form; columns with leaved capitals at corners. c. 1800. Ht. 2 ft. 11 in., L. 5 ft. 1½ in., Depth 2 ft. 7½ in.*

51. Bureau-Cabinet of painted satinwood, surmounted by spindle gallery. c. 1795. (Frank Partridge & Sons). 52. Satinwood Secretaire stamped 'Gillows, Lancaster'. c. 1795. (The late Lt.-Col. Goldschmidt.) 53. Secretaire-Cabinet, mahogany, veneered with zebra-wood; Egyptian heads and ormolu feet on pilasters; water-colour drawings in upper stage signed 'J. Baynes, 1808'. Ht. 5 ft. 2½ in., W. 2 ft. 6¾ in. (V. & A. Mus.)

three cupboards; the doors, enamelled a rich cream, are painted in grisaille with medallions of classical subjects after Angelica Kauffmann. Below, the medallions, garlands and husks are on a black ground bordered in blue and framed in ormolu mouldings. The front pulls down as a writing desk, which has another coloured oval panel in the centre.

The bureaux in two stages designed c. 1775-1800 bear a strong generic resemblance to contemporary bookcases. The upper portion changes notably in design, the former scrolled pediment being replaced by a straight cornice carved with paterae or pointed dentils forming an arcade, sometimes with scrollwork above; or by a shallow pediment often of lunette shape. Instead of plain panels or bevelled mirrors, the doors were glazed with simple arcaded tracery or astragals in long sweeping lines. Vases and urns on the pediment, and tapered supports, or outward curving feet, completed the design in the neo-classic style. These changes are illustrated in Hepple-white's *Guide*. He distinguishes between a 'Desk and Bookcase' which has a sloping front, and a 'Secretary and Bookcase' which has the same general use but is not 'sloped in front', the top drawer letting down as a quadrant. The general proportions are: length, 3 feet 6 ins.; depth, 22 ins.; height of desk, 3 feet 2 ins.; total height about 6 feet; depth of bookcase about 12 ins.

In these lighter and simpler types the sense of elegance was enhanced by Sheraton in his *Drawing Book* (1791-4), where the plates of bureaux show great fertility of invention. The type with projecting centre and wings was revived, and Sheraton illustrates a 'Gentleman's Secretary' of this kind, which has a fitted writing drawer with a 'fall' front, and cupboards at the

sides with silk behind the glass, 'for a gentleman to write at, to keep his accounts and serve as a library'. One of these composite examples (Fig. 43) has the incised initials 'T.S.' and might plausibly be assigned to Sheraton, were there sufficient evidence that he ever had a workshop; it also recalls the designs of Thomas Shearer. In another 'Secretary-bookcase' (Fig. 44) the colonettes at the sides finishing in capitals recall Sheraton's designs; the carved eagle and vases on the pediment are ebonised to contrast with the golden tone of the mahogany. Sheraton recommends that some of the ornaments in his designs should be japanned. In his *Cabinet Dictionary* (1803) he notes that the type with drawers in the lower portion is 'nearly obsolete in London . . . among fashionable people'. He has 'endeavoured to retrieve their obscurity' by adding an open bookcase and modernising the lower part.

In Fig. 42 the pediment and spandrels over the wings are painted in the classical style, while the centre door is fitted with grisaille paintings after Sir Joshua Reynolds's designs for the west window of New College Chapel, Oxford, the three figures representing Temperance, Fortitude and Justice. The side doors are filled with rippled decoration in green and gold. This highly finished piece, which has a fitted writing drawer, was doubtless made c. 1787 when Thomas Jervis transferred Reynolds's designs to the chapel window. In a bureau-bookcase (Fig. 48) the top opens in arcaded doors with delicate glazing bars. The top drawer pulls out, the front letting down and disclosing fittings for writing. The doors are veneered with mottled satinwood in diamond shapes intersected by circles, with bandings and mouldings of mahogany. At this time the

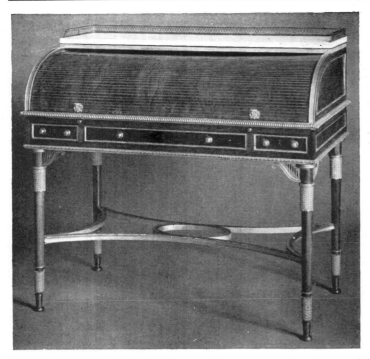

54. *Rosewood Secretaire; tambour front, brass gallery and ormolu mounts. c.* 1800. (*Southill, Beds.*)

intricate 'manufacturing part' with a diagram to explain how the cylinder rises to disclose the fittings of the interior. Fig. 47 shows a bureau-cabinet of about the date of the *Drawing Book* which is veneered with harewood banded with rosewood, the effect heightened by a little delicately painted ornament. When the desk is pulled out the cylinder front slides back; a single long drawer, fitted with trays for pens and silver-topped ink bottles, is concealed behind the main drawer front and pulls out on the right-hand side of the bureau.

Secretaires mounted on taper legs, with cupboards or shelves in the upper portion, were also made in large numbers at this time in response to the demand for lightness and elegance. Hepplewhite gives several designs with a tambour enclosing drawers and pigeon-holes, calling them 'Tambour Writing Tables'. Sheraton also illustrates this type (Fig. 60) for which the desk, fitted with various conveniences, was sometimes retained as an alternative to the tambour. Green silk flutings with swags of drapery behind the glass afford a decorative background, while the notes state that the square shape of the doors 'is much in the fashion now'. The ornament in the diamond centres is meant to be carved and gilt and laid on a silk ground, brass being proposed for the rim round the top. Such pieces combined elegance and utility; the desk had small receptacles for pens, sand, etc., while a cupboard below with a tambour shutter sometimes served as a knee-hole.

Fig. 45 is a lady's small secretaire depending for decorative effect on the figure of the amboyna veneer. The shaping of the sides of the superstructure recalls the small bookcases designed by Sheraton to be placed between windows (*see* BOOKCASES). Another specimen of this type, in satinwood, is stamped 'Gillows, Lancaster' (*q.v.*), and in both the 'cheveret' upper portion is made to lift off. Veneers of different woods were often combined by late 18th-century makers (Fig. 49). In Fig. 52

increased height of the upper stage is generally noticeable, but this piece is an exception.

Bureaux and secretaires with a 'roll-top' (tambour) or cylinder front do not appear in pattern books until towards the end of the 18th century. Sheraton writes that this 'style of furnishing is somewhat elegant, being made of satinwood, cross-banded and varnished'. A full description is given of the

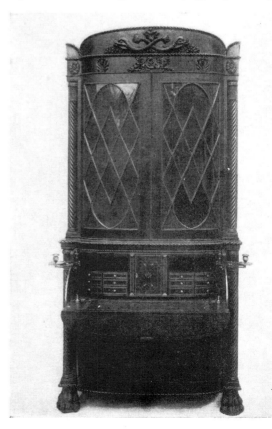

55. (*Left*) *Rosewood Secretaire, with two tiers of brass shelves; mounted with gilt brass; secretary drawer with fall front interior fitted for writing. John McLean, c.* 1810. *Ht.* 4 *ft.* 9¾ *in.,* *W.* 3 *ft.* ½ *in.* (*V. & A. Mus.*)

56. (*Right*) *Mahogany Bureau-Book-case; cornice carved with dolphins and classical motives; desk front lets down as double flap, interior inlaid with boxwood. c.* 1800. (*Lady Lever Art Gallery, Port Sunlight.*)

57. (*Left*) *Desk and Bookcase; Chippendale's* Director, 3rd ed., 1762, *Pl. CVIII.*

58. (*Right*) *Desk and Bookcase; Hepplewhite's* Guide, 1st ed., 1788, *Pl. 40.*

59. (*Left*) *Secretary and Bookcase; Sheraton's* Drawing Book (1791-4), *Pl.* 28

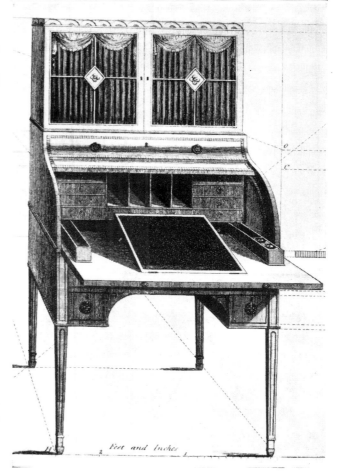

60. (*Right*) *A Cylinder Desk and Bookcase; Sheraton's* Drawing Book, *Pl.* 47.

again by Gillows, the deep secretaire drawer is panelled to represent two, satinwood being contrasted with flutings and borders of mahogany. In an ornamental 'lady's secretary' (Fig. 51) painting has supplanted inlay, and the designs on the cupboard doors already suggest Regency taste, the many-hued sprays and garlands of flowers lacking the delicate refinement of the Adam school. A few years later rosewood banded with satinwood was extensively used for small secretaires and bureaux. Fig. 50 dates from the end of the century, the secretaire portion being supported on two pedestals and the design corresponding with that of contemporary library tables (*q.v.*).

In the early 19th century rosewood was much used for bureaux, the ornament often being of bronzed metal or brass. In his *Household Furniture* (1808) George Smith made an attempt, with apparently little success, to popularise the upright secretaire with a falling front (cf. Fig. 40). One of his 'escritoires' is mounted on a stand with metal caryatides as supports, while another has drawers in the lower stage 'to contain coins and other articles'. Fantastic adaptations of the French Empire style are illustrated in Smith's book, Ackermann's *Repository* and other contemporary publications. Few of these extravagant designs seem to have been executed, most bureaux of this period being in pseudo-classic or Egyptian style and of clumsy proportions. A notable exception is the rosewood bureau with tambour front and ormolu mounts (Fig. 54) probably designed by Henry Holland. A secretaire-cabinet (Fig. 53) is veneered with zebra-wood and has Egyptian terminals at the corners. Behind the arched tracery of the glazing are mounted water-colour drawings, signed 'J. Baynes' and dated 1808, which formed part of the original decoration.

A rosewood secretary (Fig. 55) has the superstructure of shelves often found at this period, and bears the label of John McLean (*q.v.*) of Upper Marylebone Street. The mounts are of exceptional excellence for English ormolu, and other pieces authenticated by McLean's label show that this firm maintained a high standard. In Fig. 56 the cornice, carved with dolphins, is hipped acroter fashion at the corners, and a twisted cable is dominant throughout. The face of the piece is convex, the pattern of the glazing very original, and in the upper portion of the double flap a number of small drawers are ingeniously concealed.

BUREAU BOOKCASE. *See* BUREAUX.

BUREAU CABINET. *See* BUREAUX.

BURR WOOD. Malformations on the trunk of a tree. 'They may grow several feet across, their wood being very irregular and, owing to slow formation, very dense.' (*Woods*, G. S. Boulger.) Burrs from alder, elm, maple, oak, walnut and yew used for inlay and veneers from the 16th century.

BUSTIAN. Probably coarse kind of fustian (*q.v.*), twilled cotton cloth frequently used for bed-hangings in Middle Ages.

BUTTERFLY HINGE. *See* METAL MOUNTS.

BUTTRESS. Motive borrowed from Perpendicular architecture by cofferers to decorate chests (*see* CHESTS) where buttresses divided front into panels; carved out of solid in 14th century, later applied.

CABINETS. The earliest cabinets were generally employed for writing or the storage of papers and valuables; those of 16th-century date, fitted with drawers and a pull-down flap, are discussed under Bureaux, where they illustrate the evolutionary sequence, the examples in this section being either entirely open or enclosed by doors. In the possession of drawers both types represent a distinct innovation, and it is probable such cabinets originated in Italy. They made their appearance in France early in the 16th century, and by 1536, writes Havard, 'the cabinet had already received its letters of full naturalisation among us'. By c. 1560 it had become '*un petit meuble plus ou moins portatif, avec ou sans pied, posé parfois sur un buffet, une chaise, une table, mais toujours carré de forms et portant une infinité de menus tiroirs*'. Under the Valois kings the evolution was carried a stage further, and cabinets, generally of walnut, were designed in two stages on architectural lines. Early in Louis XIII's reign French courtiers possessed many cabinets enriched with bas-reliefs, mosaic, ivory or precious stones.

In England under Henry VIII the 'nest of drawers' was already known, and the King's cofferer had one committed to his care, covered with 'fustyan of Naples and being full of drawer boxes lyned with red and green sarcynet to put in stores of divers sorts'. King Henry also possessed others more elaborate and probably of larger size, for among the royal possessions 'remayning in sundrie of the King's Majesties Houses and Wardrobes' in the third year of Edward VI, 'three cabinetts set in the wall covered with crimson velvet and

1. *Cabinet painted gold and silver on black ground, mother-of-pearl inlay. Early 17th century. Ht. 2 ft., L. 1 ft. 7 in., Depth 11 in. (V. & A. Mus.)*

2. *Cedar Cabinet made for Archbishop Laud (while Bishop of London, 1628-33); door panels of architectural design, carved strapwork on pilasters; stand c. 1730. (Arbury Hall, Warwicks.)*

3. *Cabinet, one of a pair, veneered with lignum vitae and mounted with embossed silver; probably made by Dutch craftsmen in England. c. 1665. Ht. 6 ft. 3½ in., L. 4 ft. 11 in., Depth 1 ft. 7½ in. (Windsor Castle: By gracious permission of Her Majesty the Queen.)*

garnished with golde and silver' are mentioned in the 'secrete Juelhouse'. Twenty years later 'fustian of Naples' is mentioned again in an inventory taken at Kenilworth Castle, after the death of Robert Dudley, Earl of Leicester, a jewel cabinet 'with sundrie pieces, and partitions of redd leather gilte', being covered with that material and 'nailed all over with yello nails'; it was barred with iron and had four locks and keys. Among the Earl's splendid furniture was another 'cabinett of purple vellet, richelye embroidered withe gold and silver, with three braunches of flowers of golde and silke, and a case for the same'. Paul Hentzner noticed at Whitehall in 1578 'two little silver cabinets of exquisite work in which the Queen keeps her papers, and which she uses for writing boxes'.

A few surviving cabinets inlaid with delicate floral designs in rosewood, walnut and various stained woods are so Italian-ate in ornament and construction that, though some may be the work of foreigners domiciled in this country, they cannot be classified as English furniture.

The earliest native examples are of small size and intended to be mounted on a stand or on another low piece of furniture. The inner face of one of the doors in Fig. 1 bears the initials E.W., which also appear incised beneath a circular box in the Victoria and Albert Museum containing a set of roundels painted with figures wearing James I costume and inscribed with verses first published in 1608. The decoration consists of

gold and silver arabesques with flowers in vases on the larger doors and sides, the effect being heightened by mother-of-pearl inlay. The door in the interior bears a shield of arms charged with *three lozenges conjoined ermine*, an achievement borne by the families of Gifford, Devon, and Harrison, of Goudhurst, Kent. In the upper stage, of pedimental form, the doors enclose a case containing four drawers, which is fitted at the back with a looking-glass and has a floor covered with paper printed in a chequer pattern. This and another cabinet in the Museum with conventional floral ornament of a pseudo-Oriental character represent the earliest native type still surviving in England. The decoration of these cabinets, and that of a ballot box in the possession of the Sadlers Company, antedate by nearly half a century the fashion for japanned furniture in imitation of Oriental lacquer.

That cabinets were now becoming plentiful among the wealthy classes is suggested by contemporary inventories and accounts. A list of the goods and household stuff of the Earl of Northampton enumerates a number at Northampton House in 1614. In a bedchamber there were 'two Cabinettes whereof one is of ebony inlaied with white bone the other of crimson velvett laid with silver and gold lace'. Another in the With-drawing Chamber is described as 'a Danesque cabinett inlaid with coloured wood the fore front three stories of colombes', and an ebony cabinet inlaid with mother-of-pearl may also

4. *Walnut Cabinet, decorated in stumpwork with arms of Haynes of Fordington and portraits of Charles II and Catherine of Braganza; turned supports modern. c.* 1670. (*Stanford Mountain Coll.*)

have been of foreign origin, as at this period ebony was very fashionable on the Continent. The inventory mentions several decorated with needlework, one being richly 'embroidered in coulors'. The demand for ebony cabinets was, no doubt, stimulated by the visit of Prince Charles and Buckingham to Spain at the time of the negotiations for the Spanish marriage. The sum of £8 'paide for a Spanish Cabonett of Ebony' is included among Buckingham's expenses in Spain in a *Book of Accompt*. After Charles I's execution 'one large ebony cabinette with five silver images with silver supporters and studs' at Somerset House was sold for £30.

In Fig. 2 the architectural influence of Inigo Jones is apparent. The panels on the doors are supported by winged cherubim and surmounted by broken pediments, the pilasters being delicately carved with strapwork. The arms in the cartouches are those of Laud impaling London and London impaling Laud respectively, thus proving that the cabinet was made for the Archbishop during his five years' tenure of the See of London, to which he was translated in 1628. The front, opening as double doors, gives access to a series of small drawers.

Passages in contemporary memoirs suggest that small cabinets were frequently used to contain private papers, and the owner's supply of ready money when travelling. When Colonel Jeffries captured Cork for Cromwell, Lady Fanshawe writes that before making her escape she packed up her husband's cabinet 'with all his writings and near £1,000 in gold and silver'. They were still scarce at this date, and those in existence were generally imported like 'the Dutch Cabinett in my closett in which is the lands kipp inamiled upon gold' bequeathed by Sir Edmund Bacon to Lady Wootton in 1648. The rare allusions to them in correspondence of the period generally baffle conjecture as to their character. A letter from Lady

5. *Cabinet, decorated with floral marquetry on ebony panels, walnut 'oyster-pieces' and bandings of holly; turned supports of chestnut. c.* 1675. *Ht. 5 ft. 4 in., L. 3 ft. 6 in.* (*Assheton-Smith Coll.*)

6. *Walnut Cabinet, decorated with floral marquetry, ivory jessamine and green-stained leaves; drawers of central cupboard flanked by glass pilasters. c.* 1685. *Ht. 5 ft. 11½ in., L. 3 ft. 11¾ in., Depth 1 ft. 8½ in.* (*Francis Mallett Coll.*)

7. Cabinet, veneered with oyster-pieces and cross-cuttings of contrasted walnut; stand with turned uprights. c. 1685. (Donaldson Coll.)   8. Oak China Cabinet, veneered with walnut and yew; split baluster ornament on frieze and stand uprights of yew. c. 1685. Ht. 4 ft. 9½ in., L. 3 ft. 6 in., Depth 1 ft. 5 in. (J. Thursby Pelham Coll.)

Verney to Sir Ralph in this same year contains a reference to 'ye guilte cabbenett that was your mothers'—possibly of foreign origin, as the family obtained much furniture from abroad.

After the Restoration cabinets came into general use as decorative furniture. In design the new types betray strong foreign influence, and there is reason to suppose that some of the earliest specimens are the work of aliens resident in England. Besides cabinets veneered with figured walnut, many were decorated with floral marquetry or with parquetry of olivewood, lignum vitae, kingwood or laburnum. Needlework was also employed for the decoration, while the new process of japanning in imitation of Eastern lacquer was widely exploited. The first phase is represented by one of a celebrated pair of cabinets, now at Windsor Castle, which were made for Queen Henrietta Maria, probably as part of the furnishing of Somerset House, which she occupied after the Restoration (Fig. 3). They are veneered with parquetry of lignum vitae, and mounted with silver elaborately embossed. There is a key plate on each drawer, while the Queen's monogram appears on the central door and is repeated on the pendant below. The turned legs of the stand, also decorated with silver, are united by flat stretchers.

These remarkable cabinets must date between 1660 and 1669, the year of the Queen's death. She gave them to Henry Jermyn, Earl of St Albans, her Vice-Chamberlain, Secretary and reputed lover, who died in 1683 and bequeathed them to his nephew, Sir Thomas Jermyn of Rushbrook Hall, Bury St Edmunds, where they remained until presented to George V in 1910. In style and workmanship they display foreign characteristics; notably in the finely run panel mouldings of the central door. Doubtless, they are the work of accomplished immigrant craftsmen, like some of the furniture at Holyrood Palace and Ham House, which a correspondence between the Master Mason to the Crown in Scotland and the Duke of Lauderdale shows to have been produced by Dutch cabinet-makers later in the reign.

Fig. 4 is decorated with stumpwork (*see* NEEDLEWORK). The original owner's arms appear in the needlework between the top drawers, and the panels are in a remarkable state of preservation. The cornice, veneered with oyster-pieces of walnut, is fitted for jewels, and lined with its original pink silk. On the front the doors are inlaid with ebony and floral scrolls on sycamore ovals. The centre door opens to disclose a temple-like structure with mirrors and gilt columns concealing secret drawers, an arrangement derived from contemporary Flemish and Italian cabinets. The interesting needlework includes portraits of Charles II and Catherine of Braganza, Herod with Salome and the Baptist's head, and the finding of Moses.

In the majority of inlaid cabinets of this period there are certain distinctive features. Below the moulded cornices is a barrel frieze which pulls out as a drawer. A pair of doors enclose the interior in which a series of small drawers are arranged

9. *Walnut Cabinet decorated with marquetry of arabesques and birds; stand with scrolled legs; dated 1698. Ht. 5 ft. 2 in., L. 3 ft. 2 in., Depth 1 ft. 4 in. (Macquoid Coll.)*

10. *Walnut Cabinet inlaid with seaweed marquetry; legs of stand veneered on all four sides, feet carved with acanthus. c. 1695. (Chatsworth, Derbyshire.)*

symmetrically around a central cupboard. The top edge of the stand has a projecting convex moulding, while below the frame is fitted with one or more drawers and supported on a stand having turned legs united by flat, shaped stretchers.

In Fig. 5 the design on the doors corresponds with that found on tables of c. 1675, spandrelled panels of coloured flowers and ivory leaves stained green on an ebony ground surrounding an oval centre, the bandings and mouldings being of holly and bleached walnut. The original stands of such cabinets were generally of walnut and many have perished; but here the supports are of chestnut (*q.v.*), a heavy and more durable wood.

Fig. 6 shows a cabinet mounted on a chest of drawers. In the marquetry jessamine figures prominently; it is of ivory

11. *Cabinet, decorated with red and gold japanning; design of gilt pinewood cresting and stand shows strong French influence. c. 1695. (E. F. Wythes Coll.)*

(for the leaves stained green), and birds are introduced amid flowers in vases. In the centre of the interior is a temple-like structure, an architectural feature common in this type. The stiles in the lower portion conceal a series of small secret drawers fitted in the sides throughout their height.

This highly-coloured marquetry was supplemented by less ostentatious use of walnut veneer. In Fig. 7, a cabinet with parquetry decoration (*q.v.*), the effect is obtained by veneers of different cross-cuttings of walnut boughs placed in contrast.

At this time cabinets were also designed to contain Oriental porcelain and Delft ware, these being imported in considerable quantities. Such cabinets were made with doors glazed in half-round mouldings resembling those found on drawer fronts at the time, framings and sides being veneered with walnut cut on the straight or arranged in transverse sections. They had straight cornices and were supported on turned legs and stretchers, a later variety having drawers in the lower portion resting on bun feet. Fig. 8 is a specimen of the early type veneered with walnut and yew, and mounted on a stand with turned uprights, also of yew, a hard and close grained wood.

In Fig. 9 the inner surfaces of the doors are inlaid with macaws perched on cherry trees in rich red-browns and blacks on a ground of walnut, the design being repeated on the sides of the cabinet. The stand is formed of scrolled legs of plain walnut, a pattern first adopted c. 1680. This example supplies a link between the floral inlay of Charles II and the finer arabesque type of the succeeding period. Accounts of the tradesmen who furnished the royal palaces afford some interesting particulars of cabinets in the possession of Charles II and William III. Some were made of olivewood and 'Prinse's wood', while for *Ye Ladies of ye Sweete Coffers* Richard Pigge in September 1668 supplied at a cost of £25 'one large cabbinett covered with Turkey leather with the Drawers all lyned with Sarcenett and quilted with perfume with the lock handles and hing silvered'. Among those mentioned at Kensington Palace in a list drawn

12. *Walnut Cabinet on Chest of Drawers inlaid with seaweed marquetry. c. 1705. Ht. 5 ft. 8 in., L. 3 ft. 2 in. (Assheton-Smith Coll.)*

13. *Walnut Cabinet, doors decorated with arms of Bowes and Blakiston, endive, floral sprays and foliage tied with ribbons. c. 1691. Ht. 8 ft. 10 in., L. 4 ft., Depth 1 ft. 9½ in. (Formerly at Streatlam Castle, Durham.)*

up after Queen Mary's death in 1694 is 'a walnut tree cabbenett full of things locked up'.

In Fig. 10 the whole surface is closely inlaid with fine arabesque patterns in the final phase of this form of decoration, a style inspired by the workshops of Boulle, but with fine inlay of walnut or sycamore replacing metal and tortoiseshell. The legs are decorated on all four sides, the scrolled feet being carved with acanthus. In Fig. 12 the circular designs are filled with the same type of marquetry in sycamore, edged with a sand-burnt feather border, the ground being formed of oyster-pieces of walnut; and the stand is supported on short cabriole legs.

The imposing cabinet from Streatlam Castle, Durham (Fig. 13), reverts to floral inlay, though the delicacy and naturalistic grace of the ornament have nothing in common with the florid taste of Charles II's reign. The high pediment is framed in bolection mouldings and inlaid with a device of six arrows tied with ribbons which Sir William Bowes, who rebuilt Streatlam c. 1700, derived from the seal of his great-grandfather Knight,

95

14. *Walnut Cabinet, decorated with arabesque marquetry; supplied to Queen Mary by Gerreit Jensen,* 1693. (*Windsor Castle: By gracious permission of Her Majesty the Queen.*)   15. *Cabinet, japanned in high relief in reds and greens on black and gold ground; stand of carved and silvered pinewood. c.* 1678. *Ht.* 5 *ft.* 2¾ *in., L.* 4 *ft.* 6 *in., Depth* 2 *ft.* 2 *in.* (*V. & A. Mus.*)

16. *Cabinet, japanned in black and gold with figures, flowering tree and pagoda-roofed building; stand elaborately carved. c.* 1685. *Ht.* 5 *ft.* 5½ *in., L.* 3 *ft.* 6 *in.* (*The Vyne, Hants.*)

Marshal of Berwick under Queen Elizabeth. William Bowes married Elizabeth Blakiston, the heiress of Gibside on the Derwent, in 1691, and the doors are inlaid with, on the left, the Bowes, and on the right, the Blakiston arms, in a mantling of endive sprays and flowers, light on a darker ground, the surrounds and borders being formed of finely figured walnut. The drawers in the lower portion are decorated with a very unusual design of sprays of berries tied with ribbons. On the inner side the doors are inlaid with large eight-pointed stars in a darker walnut, also employed to form borders to the drawers, a remarkable decorative effect being obtained by the contrast that it affords to the figured veneer.

Another cabinet inlaid with similar motives is in the Victoria and Albert Museum. Both these fine cabinets came from the north of England. Design and decoration point to a common origin, and it is possible that they represent a now forgotten provincial workshop, an inference supported by the construction and marquetry cutting, which technically is not of high quality.

Cabinets with glazed doors and shelves in the interior were innovations at this time, and examples dating from the end of the century are rare. The cabinet in the Royal Collection (Fig. 14) is decorated with arabesque marquetry, and may be identified with the 'glass case of fine markatree upon a cabinett with doors' supplied to Queen Mary by Gerreit Jensen in 1693 for £30.

Evelyn records that Catherine of Braganza 'brought over with her from Portugal such Indian cabinets as had never before been seen here' (*Diary*, June 9, 1662), and many Chinese and Japanese lacquer cabinets were imported into England in Charles II's reign. Those illustrated are of native origin,

17. *Cabinet, japanned in black and gold with carved and gilt stand and cresting. c. 1690. Ht. 7 ft. 5¼ in., L. 3 ft. 5½ in., Depth 2 ft. ½ in. (V. & A. Mus.)* 18. *Lacquered Cabinet (Japanese), carved and gilt stand; attributed to Benjamin Goodison. c. 1730. (Windsor Castle: By gracious permission of Her Majesty the Queen.)* 19. *Cabinet, japanned in black and gold on Chest of Drawers, surmounted by double-hooded cornice; feet not original. c. 1710. Ht. 6 ft. 4 in., L. 3 ft. 5 in., Depth 1 ft. 9½ in. (Basil Oxenden Coll.)*

executed according to the precepts of Stalker and Parker or one of the later exponents of the art. (For the differences between Oriental lacquer and English japanning *see* JAPANNING.)

The experimental character of early attempts at imitation is shown in Fig. 15. The outside doors are decorated in high relief with water-birds and groups of figures beneath a tree in reds and greens on a black and gold ground; the drawers in the interior are japanned with a variety of smaller patterns in the same coarse but effective manner; on the inside of the doors are representations of a crane spiritedly drawn and a tree with buildings set in a peculiar tumulous landscape, this form of decoration being characteristic of early English japanning. The greens employed are of a viridian tone, never repeated on later examples. These cabinets were generally mounted on ornate stands of soft wood, gilt or silvered, the front legs, scrolled and often connected by a deep apron, being enriched with acanthus foliage, festoons of flowers, and amorini amid foliated scrolls. The stand of Fig. 15 is carved in the florid baroque manner of c. 1675, the coarse anatomy of the terminal figures being characteristic of contemporary English treatment.

Fig. 16, a cabinet decorated at about the date of Stalker and Parker's *Treatise* (1688), is noticeably more refined than the experiments of Charles II's reign. Although the decoration is bold and pictorial, it lacks the Oriental instinct for composition; while the background is not nearly so smooth and brilliant as in true Chinese lacquer. The stand represents the last phase of Charles II taste, when the scale of ornament

20. *Cabinet, japanned in silver on scarlet ground; legs of stand headed with scrolls, apron centres in female mask. c. 1725. (Formerly at Hornby Castle, Yorks.)*

and figure anatomy is becoming noticeably finer. Among colours recommended for the ground in the *Treatise* of 1688 tortoiseshell and red seem to have been used very sparingly, while on genuine examples chestnut, blue, olive or green are extremely rare. Fig. 11 is an example of the red. On the outer doors are sportsmen and dogs in pursuit of game; the sides are decorated with large single figures, the great cranes on the inner doors showing the same large scale of drawing. On the drawers in the interior are plants in full bloom, dragons, landscapes and figure subjects drawn with great delicacy and certainty of touch; the decoration of the whole is carried out in gold with slight relief, heightened in effect with black and brown. In the stand French inspiration is very apparent; the broken cresting is also of foreign character.

The interest of the carved and gilt woodwork predominates in a black and gold japanned cabinet (Fig. 17), where the cresting is complete and again shows French influence in the *lambrequin* ornament below the basket of flowers. The stand has a finely designed apron of foliage scrolls and tasselled drapery on the tapered supports, but the finials are missing from the scrolled cross stretchers. Few of these ornamental crestings survive as, carved in a soft wood, they were easily broken.

Cabinets decorated with cut lacquer are usually made up of imported panels, and though Stalker and Parker gave some directions for imitating 'Bantam Work', they state it to have been out of fashion by 1688. Imported specimens were sold at so-called Indian shops where Oriental china was also displayed, and large numbers are included in lists of imports from the Far East at the end of the century.

Fig. 19 shows a form of cabinet much in use at this time; the upper portion, surmounted by the bold-hooded cornice first adopted c. 1700, opens with two doors enclosing a series of small drawers, the lower stage being formed of a chest of drawers. The decoration in slight relief is probably the work of an amateur, the inferior quality of the japan supporting this inference. Small drop-handles have now given place to a ring-handle and plate, though the brass corners and hinges correspond with earlier specimens. Many cabinets at this period were decorated by amateurs (*see* JAPANNING AND LACQUER). Lockhart of Carnwath relates (*Papers*, Vol. I, p. 267) that in 1706 'one, Mrs. Dalrymple brought up from Scotland a very fine japanned cabinet, which, being her own work she presented to the queen; but it was more than six months before her Majesty could be mistress of fifty guineas which she designed to give in return for the compliment—that sum indeed being scarcely the value of it'.

In the fine cabinet (Fig. 20) the decoration is in silver; also the hinges, lock-plates and handle-rings. The colour of the ground is not of the crimson generally found on the inner surfaces of these cabinets when they have been unexposed to the light, but of the pale vermillion which Stalker and Parker mention as one of the three tints for red lacquer (*see* JAPANNING AND LACQUER). The design outside the doors represents the familiar pseudo-Chinese landscape in high relief, the inside being decorated with spiritedly drawn cocks and hens. When new, this silver and pale scarlet must have been far more attractive than the ordinary combination of red and gold; but in the course of time the silver has invariably tarnished. The stand of the same colour is original in design, the contrasting scrolls preluding the rococo.

Bouquets of flowers in vases of a type derived from Dutch

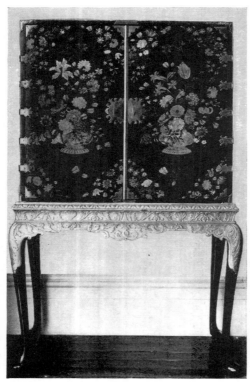

21. *Cabinet, japanned with bouquets of flowers in natural colours on black ground. c. 1730. Ht. of Cabinet 2 ft. 10½ in., L. 3 ft. 2 in., Ht. of stand, 2 ft. 8¼ in. (The late Lady Florence Pery.)*   22. *Walnut Cabinet on cabriole-leg stand; doors framed in fluted pilasters and inlaid with holly; interior drawers arranged on curve, pull-out writing slide. c. 1714. (Frank Green Coll.)*   23. *Cabinet of architectural design, japanned in black and gold; scroll-shaped brackets finely carved. c. 1740. (Milton, Northants.)*

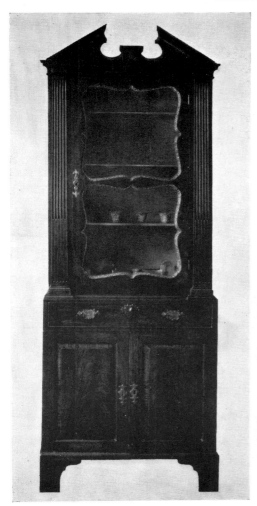

24. Mahogany China Cabinet; broken pediment supported on fluted pilasters, serpentine door mouldings gilt. c. 1720. 25. Cabinet and Stand in Chinese style; doors veneered on interior with rosewood, on exterior with amboyna wood; drawers with various coloured woods. Ht. 8 ft. 8½ in., L. 6 ft. 4 in., Depth 1 ft. 8 in. c. 1755. (Lady Lever Art Gallery, Port Sunlight.)

still-life painting are sometimes substituted for Oriental motives on later Stuart cabinets, a style of decoration also found on Georgian examples but with the flowers less formally composed and sometimes scattered over the surface of the doors (Fig. 21). In most of these later cabinets the character of the japanning is very degenerate. The strong demand for japanned cabinets in the first half of the century is suggested by the catalogue of Sir William Stanhope's furniture sold at his house in Albemarle Street in April, 1733. There were nine 'Japan' cabinets of various sizes, mostly on 'frames' or stands, the most notable being described as 'of the very rare brown Japan'. This shade is not specified among the considerable variety of colours given by Stalker and Parker, but may have corresponded to the 'chestnut colour' or to the 'Counterfeit Tortoiseshell' to which they allude.

China cabinets of the early 18th century with the upper stage glazed are severely simple in design, and so closely resemble contemporary bookcases that it is sometimes impossible to determine for which use they were intended. The variety with small drawers, so fashionable in the Stuart period, continued to be produced in walnut. The design in Fig. 22 is unusual, the cabinet being constructed in two stages with a deep moulded frieze and cornice. The doors are inlaid with fine lines of holly

and cross-banded in walnut; the interior is fitted with a series of drawers arranged on the curve above a writing slide and a single long drawer. The cabriole legs of the stand, scrolled and carved with shells, appear slight for the weight of the piece. In Fig. 24 the cornice is surmounted by a broken pediment with a deep embrasure supported on fluted columns, the door framings being of serpentine shape with the carved mouldings gilt; the cupboard doors are fielded and the figure of the Cuban mahogany is exceptionally good.

Cabinets designed under the influence of William Kent and other architects are again scarcely distinguishable from contemporary bookcases; there is the same broken pediment and pronounced architectural feeling, but the size of the doors and their obvious inconvenience as receptacles for books show in most cases that they were designed as china cabinets. Fig. 23 shows a japanned break-front specimen. The cornice is shouldered by scroll-shaped brackets which pull out forming secret drawers and terminate in eagles' heads holding pendants of oak-leaves. The face of these brackets is filled with a fine design of acanthus and husks; the central compartment is arched, and the mouldings are richly carved. In some examples of similar design rococo influence is already perceptible in the carved floral ornaments.

26. (*Left*) *Kingwood Cabinet made for Horace Walpole in 1743; enriched with ivory plaques and Walpole arms. Ht. 5 ft., L. 3 ft. 8½ in. (V. & A. Mus.)*

27. (*Right*) *Mahogany China Cabinet in Chinese style, surmounted by fretwork gallery; stand headed by pagoda moulding. c. 1760. Ht. 6 ft. 2½ in., L. 4 ft. 6 in., Depth 1 ft. 4 in. (Capel Cure Coll.)*

28. (*Left*) *Mahogany Hanging China Cabinet; fretwork doors and sides in Chinese style. c. 1755. Total Ht. 3 ft., L. 2 ft., Depth 7¾ in. (Percival Griffiths Coll.)*

29. (*Right*) *China Cabinet, japanned black and gold; lattice-work gallery of mahogany. c. 1760. (Assheton-Smith Coll.)*

30. (*Left*) Cabinet
japanned in black
and gold on carved
fretwork stand.
c. 1760. (*Formerly at
Trent Park, Herts.*)

31. (*Right*) Mahog-
any Hanging
Cabinet; pediment
carved with rosettes
and foliage. c. 1760.
Ht. 3 ft. 10 in.,
L. 2 ft. 4 in., Depth
1 ft. 8 in. (*Mr Ralph
Edwards.*)

Fig. 26 shows a kingwood and ivory hanging cabinet designed and made for Horace Walpole. In the pediment are the Walpole arms, supported by a cupid and lion with festoons of flowers, and surmounted by three ivory statuettes of Inigo Jones, Palladio and Duquesnoy (Fiammingo), the Flemish carver, these statuettes being by Verskovis. The doors are enriched with plaques, and ivory eagle-heads in the plinth support a festooned garland carved in mahogany. Walpole writes to Sir Horace Mann in July, 1743: 'I have a new cabinet for my enamels and miniatures just come home, which I am sure you would like; it is of rosewood, the doors inlaid with carvings in ivory.' The mistake concerning the veneer is curious. A very similar cabinet, also framing a set of ivory reliefs, but in this instance of rosewood, was formerly at The Hoo, near Welwyn, having been made for Walpole's friend, Thomas Brand. The maker of these two remarkable cabinets is unknown.

At this period the Early Georgian style as applied to cabinets became modified and in great measure transformed by new influences, rococo ornament derived from France being fused with Chinese and Gothic detail; while many cabinets in both design and decoration were in the Chinese style.

An important example with strong Chinese influence is given in Fig. 25. It is composed of a centre with two wings of serpentine shape, all the doors being veneered with sheets of fine amboyna wood, now toned to the colour of deep amber, and bordered with light rosewood inlaid with a fine chequer pattern of ebony and holly, the insides being veneered with plain panels of rosewood. A carved pagoda-shaped roof surmounts the centre compartment, bearing an escutcheon and two bracket candlesticks with ivory bells; a lattice-work gallery with small corner vases hung with ivory bells completes the structure of

32. *Queen Charlotte's Jewel Cabinet; mahogany framework veneered with padouk; tulipwood oval panels with centres of amboyna bordered and inlaid with ivory. Made by Vile and Cobb in 1761. (By gracious permission of Her Majesty the Queen.)*

33. (*Left*) *Mahogany Medal Cabinet, one of a pair; upper stage centres in Garter Star; probably part of 'grand medal case' altered by William Vile for George III in* 1761. (*From Stratfield Saye House, Berks.*)

34. (*Right*) *Mahogany Break-front Cabinet, finely carved in rococo taste. c.* 1755-60. *Attributed to William Vile. Ht. 7 ft. 1 in., L. 3 ft. 4 in., Depth 1 ft. 8 in. (Mrs Scudamore.)*

the wings. The stand is decorated with card-cut lattice-work and scrolled brackets. The interior contains nearly 100 drawers, each veneered with a different wood. Of a cabinet of the pagoda type in the *Director* (3rd ed. P1. CXLVII) Chippendale writes: 'This is not only the richest and most magnificent in the whole, but perhaps in all Europe. I had a particular pleasure in retouching and finishing this design, but should have much more in the execution of it, as I am confident I can make the work more beautiful and striking than the drawing.' He illustrates six of the glazed variety which he calls 'china cases' and his cabinets are mounted on stands with straight legs.

A cabinet (Fig. 27) is composed of a centre compartment and two wings surmounted by a fret-work gallery, the longitudinal glazing emphasising the Oriental character. The usual perforated brackets are here prolonged below the frieze of the stand, wh ch is headed by a wide pagoda moulding. Many of these cabiinets in the Chinese taste were japanned, and in their *Universal System* (1759-63) Ince and Mayhew describe a specimen as 'a china case for Japanning the inside all of looking-glass, in that manner it has been executed, and has a very elegant effect'. Fig. 29, decorated in black and gold, is surmounted by a Chinese railing, while a gilt fret on a black ground decorates the drawer fronts. In a small cabinet on a stand (Fig. 30) the woodwork affords the chief interest and in the ornament of the stand Chinese and Gothic motives are blended.

From Charles II's reign onwards imported panels of Eastern lacquer were often employed in the construction of cabinets and other varieties of furniture. In a fine hanging cabinet (Fig.

37) the back is faced with four Japanese panels in black and gold decorated with dragons, while the sides are also composed of Eastern lacquer. The design of the cabinet embodies the familiar Chinoiserie motive exploited by Chippendale and Ince and Mayhew, a degenerate imitation of a Persian pattern somewhat incongruously framing the gilt tracery.

Many small hanging cabinets to contain china were made enclosed by fretwork doors and sides, while others to contain jewels, medals or coins were among the specialised varieties made at this period; though as in some instances the purpose is conjectural they do not demand separate classification. When designed for medals or coins they are generally fitted with numerous shallow drawers or trays. The superlatively fine jewel cabinet (Fig. 32) was made at a cost of £138 10s. by Vile and Cobb (*q.v.*) to contain the diamonds, valued at £50,000, given by George III to Queen Charlotte and worn by her at their coronation in September, 1761. It is of mahogany richly carved in rococo taste, and veneered with various woods—padouk, amboyna, tulip, olive and rosewood—the doors being inlaid in ivory with a trophy and horned cornucopias, within a foliated cartouche. The top is also inlaid with engraved ivory on a panel of amboyna, and shows the arms of England impaling Mecklenburg. The interior is fitted with small drawers, and the cabriole legs finish in scroll feet. In Vile's bill this cabinet, a *tour-de-force* of design and craftsmanship, is described as:

a very handsome jewel cabinet of many different kinds of fine wood, on a mahogany frame, richly carved, the fronts, ends and top inlaid with ivory in compartments neatly engraved, the top to lift up and two doors, the drawers all lined with black velvet.

A pair of medal cabinets (Fig. 33) are probably the wings of 'his Majesty's grand medal case' which was altered for George III by William Vile in 1761. They are in three stages, all richly decorated. The uppermost is carved on the front with the Garter Star set within acanthus foliage. At the corners foliations spring from lion heads in full relief. In the middle stage Corinthian columns support a projecting section of the entablature. On the lowest stage the shaped panel mouldings, simplified to provide a foil to those above, are clasped at the corners by foliage, a motif employed by Vile and other contemporary makers. A charge for making the 'medal case' is not entered in the Royal Accounts.

In cabinets designed by Chippendale and his contemporaries in the Chinese taste, touches of rococo frequently occur. In the first edition of the *Director* (1754), cabinets in this style preponderate, and there is a similar emphasis upon it, with obvious plagiarism of Chippendale's ideas, in Ince and Mayhew's *Universal System* (1759-63); in both works Oriental motives imperfectly understood are grafted upon the prevalent European style to produce a highly distinctive creation. A

36. *Mahogany China Cabinet, made by firm of Ince and Mayhew. c. 1765. (Copenhagen Mus.)*

break-front example designed in the manner of contemporary bookcases (Fig. 34) shows with what skill this amalgamation was sometimes achieved. In the perforated galleries and the lower frieze surmounted by a pagoda moulding there is a hint of the Chinese, but all else is what Chippendale termed the 'best French manner'. This cabinet may be attributed to Vile, and the sculpturesque wreath of laurel and acanthus on the central door resembles those on the wings of the bookcase made by Vile for Queen Charlotte and now at Buckingham Palace (*see* BOOKCASES, Fig. 14). In Fig. 35 the cresting is of Chinese lattice-work, and in the lower stage the frieze and bracket feet correspond in treatment; but the door panels are carved with rococo foliage.

The cabinet shown in Fig. 36 is of exceptional interest, because affixed to it is the trade label of Ince and Mayhew (*q.v.*). The tracery bars are gracefully shaped, and carved with delicate scrolls; while the cupboard doors below are enriched in the same style. Mahogany hanging corner cabinets glazed for the display of china, surmounted by pediments and decorated with Gothic and rococo motives (Fig. 31), were also produced at this time, though apparently in smaller numbers than cupboards of similar form.

The new ideals of the classical style appreciably modified the design and decoration of cabinets from c. 1765. Cornices were sometimes surmounted by a scrolled and pierced pediment

35. *Mahogany China Cabinet, lattice-work pediment, lower frieze and feet in Chinese style. c. 1755. (Penshurst Place, Kent.)*

37. *Hanging Cabinet, decorated with black and gold japan. c. 1760. (Formerly at Raynham Hall, Norfolk.)*

38. *Hanging Cabinet; carved and gilt, roof of double pagoda form, with upper portion supported on columns. c. 1760.*

39. *Inlaid Satinwood Cabinet, with ormolu mounts and panels of Italian landscapes in marble mosaic. Design by Adam dated 1771. Formerly at Kimbolton, Hunts. (V. & A. Mus.)* 40. *Satinwood Cabinet; lattice-work pediment with mahogany urns, doors inlaid with architectural subjects in classical taste, interior with English castles and cathedrals. c. 1770. (Formerly at Combe Abbey, Warwicks.)*

41. *Mahogany Cabinet, one of pair, veneered with satinwood and inlaid with various exotic woods, mounts of chased ormolu. c. 1770. Attributed to T. Chippendale. (Viscountess Gage.)*

42. *Mahogany China Cabinet in neo-classic style; doors framed in fluted columns with gilt capitals and mouldings. c. 1770. (Balls Park, Herts.)*

with an urn in the centre and at the corners, while friezes were carved with delicate arabesques and anthemion ornament. The doors and cupboards of this new type were framed in tapered and fluted columns and pilasters (Fig. 42), curvilinear forms gracefully disposed being much employed for the glazing bars. Mahogany at first remained the ordinary material, but was soon supplemented by satinwood and a variety of exotic veneers, in which classical motives were inlaid with remarkable technical perfection. The mouldings were smaller than those of the preceding style, and in many instances, especially when Adam was responsible, the design and detail bore a definite relation to its architectural background. A pair of china cabinets formerly at Panshanger (Fig. 41) may confidently be attributed to Chippendale's firm, and are among the capital achievements of the neo-classic style. They are of mahogany veneered with East Indian satinwood and inlaid with various exotic woods, the detail of the ornament being delicately engraved. The mounts are of finely carved ormolu and correspond with those on pieces of inlaid furniture which Chippendale supplied to Harewood House.

Some cabinets on stands retain the pierced galleries of the rococo phase, but the new classical influence may be seen in the paterae enrichments on the pediments and doors and in the fluted taper legs. A mahogany example at Hitchin Priory, Herts., has curved cupboards fitted with shelves, and the canted door, inlaid in neo-classic taste, encloses a set of drawers labelled on engraved plates for bills, receipts and letters.

In June, 1767, Chippendale's firm supplied to Nostell Priory another cabinet made for a special purpose, which is described as having 'drawers and a medal case, with a glass door to ditto elegantly ornamented with carved work'. The example given in Fig. 44 also was probably made for coins and medals. The outer mahogany banding frames curved panels and on a field of pollarded veneers are placed cameo heads carved out of boxwood in high relief suspended by swags and ribbons. Lady Shelburne's *Diary* for 1768 records a visit to Ince and Mayhew's establishment to buy cabinets for Landsdowne House, which she was at that time furnishing under Adam's direction. She ordered 'two pretty glass cases for one of the rooms in my apartments, which though they are only deal, and

43. *Mahogany China Cabinet on stand, in 'Gothic' taste. c. 1760. Ht. 8 ft. 4 in., L. 4 ft., Depth 1 ft. 9½ in. (V. & A. Mus.)* 44. *Cabinet, veneered with figured mahogany; swags and cameo heads of boxwood. c. 1770. Ht. 4 ft. 6 in., L. 2 ft. 6 in., Depth 1 ft. 6 in. (Formerly at Streatlam Castle, Durham.)* 45. *Satinwood Cabinet; doors centring in mirrors, convex drawers inlaid with swags of laurel in harewood. c. 1775. Ht. 6 ft. 10 in., extreme L. 4 ft. (The Earl of Limerick.)*

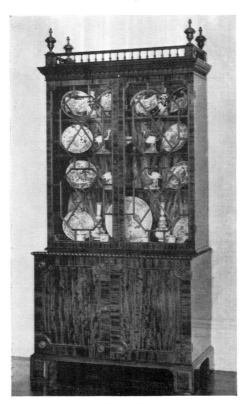
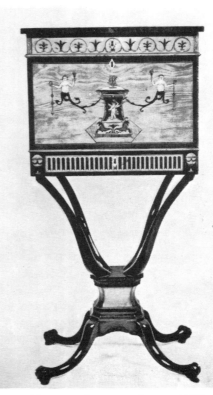

46. *Mahogany China Cabinet; spindle gallery with urns above cornice. c. 1785. (Bassett Down, Wilts.)* 47. *Cabinet on Stand, mahogany and satinwood; flap inlaid in neo-classic taste, drawers framed in ebony, top banded with kingwood. c. 1775. (Frank Partridge & Sons.)* 48. *Ebony Cabinet, with gilt enrichments in Gothic taste, designed by Edward Edwards, A.R.A., made for Horace Walpole in 1784 and decorated with drawings by Lady Diana Beauclerk. (Mr W. S. Lewis.)*

49. *Mahogany China Cabinet; cresting centres in Prince of Wales's feathers, satinwood finials headed by metal urns. c. 1790. Ht. 7 ft. 1 in., L. 2 ft. 1 in. (J. Thursby Pelham Coll.)* 50. *Satinwood Cabinet, banded with mahogany; central oval and side doors mounted with mirror panels, secretary drawer in lower stage. c. 1790. (Melbourne Art Gallery, Australia.)* 51. *Satinwood Cabinet; domed fluted top and painted decoration. c. 1795. (Irwin Untermyer Coll.)*

to be painted white, he charges £50 for'. When Adam dined at Landsdowne House in August of that year, 'I showed him', writes Lady Shelburne, 'my best Japan cabinet and asked him for a design for the frame of it.'

In the elaborate character of the ornament the Panshanger cabinet is highly exceptional, and marquetry decoration was generally confined to conventional decorative motives, swags, garlands and urns. Architectural effects were seldom attempted, though the Italians had long used this manner of decorating furniture. A cabinet on a stand (Fig. 39) which shows an English adaptation of this style was designed by Adam for the Duchess of Manchester. It is mounted in ormolu, the wooden surface being of satinwood inlaid in darker wood with foliated arabesques and other classical motives, and faced with land- and seascapes in coloured marbles (pietre dure) and the pilasters with strips of this material framed in brass. The drawing in the Soane Museum is dated June 1, 1771, and inscribed 'Design for a Cabinet for her Grace The Duchess of Manchester made to receive eleven pieces of scagliola Land-skips. The Parts Shaded Yellow Shew what may be gilt or done in Brass or Or Moulu. The Plain parts may be executed in woods of various kinds.' On the back of one of the panels is scratched the maker's name—'Baccio Cappelli Fecit Anno 1709 Fiorenza.' These attractive specimens of 18th-century marble inlay were no doubt bought in Florence, the centre of

production, and sent home as curiosities. The design in the museum, which shows the cabinet with an arcaded stand, and classical figures at the corners of the frieze, was apparently not acceptable without considerable modification, and Adam was misinformed as to the material of which the panels are composed. The cabinet is really a decorative frame for the pietre dure, since the interior is hollow and the panels only simulate drawers. A remarkable cabinet (Fig. 40) is also decorated in an Italianate style. In the centre is Salisbury Cathedral, while the other buildings are all named on ribbon labels inlaid on the top margins of the drawers.

Panels composed of Wedgwood's jasper ware are found introduced into cabinets at this time, their classical character harmonising admirably with the prevailing style.

A china cabinet in West Indian satinwood of beautiful golden tone (Fig. 45) is one of a pair originally designed for No. 5, Stratford Place. In the centre of the doors are convex mirrors set in bars of carved foliage; the lower portion, formed of a series of convex drawers, is decorated with swags of laurel. The refinement of the mouldings is characteristic of this style. The remarkable satinwood cabinet (Fig. 51), originally the property of Sir Richard Arkwright (1732-92), the inventor of the water frame, has a decorated domed top with three carved giltwood floral ornaments, and, on the bow-fronted upper portion, oval mahogany panels painted in the manner of

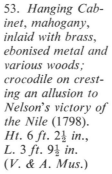

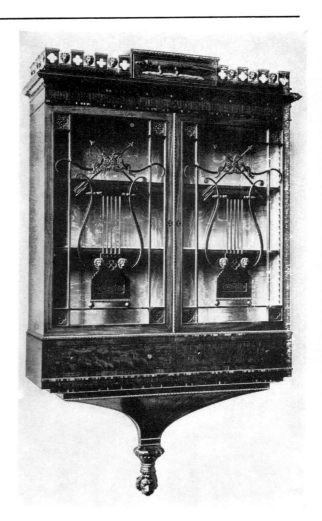

52. *China Cabinet, veneered with sabicu and East India satinwood; pediment frames a clock. c. 1795. (Assheton-Smith Coll.)*

53. *Hanging Cabinet, mahogany, inlaid with brass, ebonised metal and various woods; crocodile on cresting an allusion to Nelson's victory of the Nile (1798). Ht. 6 ft. 2½ in., L. 3 ft. 9½ in. (V. & A. Mus.)*

Angelica Kauffmann (*q.v.*) and surrounded by painted peacocks' feathers. The handles are of Sheffield plate.

The Gothic taste (*q.v.*) ran contemporaneously with the Chinese craze, being largely fostered by Horace Walpole and a small group of enthusiasts. Some china cabinets conform in design throughout to the 'true Gothic' without any admixture of rococo detail (Fig. 43). An example of the taste is given in Fig. 48, a belated specimen made for Walpole in 1784 to display a set of drawings by Lady Diana Beauclerk. The cabinet and stand of ebony with ormolu enrichments was designed by Edward Edwards, A.R.A.

One of the many small decorative cabinets produced at this period for boudoirs and drawing-rooms is illustrated in Fig. 47. The mahogany ground is veneered with satinwood enriched with various inlays. The front depicts a classical altar; on either side, as supporters, are nereids bearing torches. This front lets down disclosing drawers, and a centre recess opening in small partitions, which pulls out to reveal a further series of still smaller drawers all faced with satinwood framed in ebony. The top is decorated with a polygonal panel, inlaid in satinwood, representing Neptune and Venus. In colouring and treatment this panel rivals the work of the finest contemporary French *marqueteurs*.

The ordinary domestic cabinets of this period are scarcely distinguishable from bookcases in their structural lines and decoration; so close is the similarity that in Hepplewhite's *Guide* (1788) bookcases figure to the exclusion of cabinets, the cornices and astragals illustrated on a separate plate being considered appropriate to both varieties of furniture. Sheraton's designs mark the apotheosis of the cabinet as a decorative object for feminine use. He writes that 'the style of finishing them is elegant, being often richly japanned and veneered with the finest satinwood'; marquetry on a small scale in a large variety of woods was also freely employed.

Fig. 55 from the *Drawing Book* (1791-4) is to be of painted satinwood with drapery sewed to the silk in the arched door, which encloses sliding shelves for small books. A small china cabinet (Fig. 49) shows the more practical application of the style. The pediment, surrounded by satinwood finials headed by metal urns, centres in the Prince of Wales's feathers, the remainder of the piece being without ornament and depending on excellence of execution for effect. A cabinet made for Lady Hamilton c. 1790 and sent out to Sir William Hamilton at Naples is given in Fig. 50. The slender foliage scrolls of the pediment and the case finials are finely executed, four slender pilasters supporting the cornice. In the centre of the upper stage is an oval mirror panel, and the wings are also faced with looking-glass. Small cabinets, the doors painted with mythological subjects and mounted on stands, were produced at this time to accord with the decoration of walls and ceilings.

Fig. 52 represents neo-classic design before the Regency archaeological revival. The wings with the pediment framing a clock are curved and above the stiles are delicate mahogany

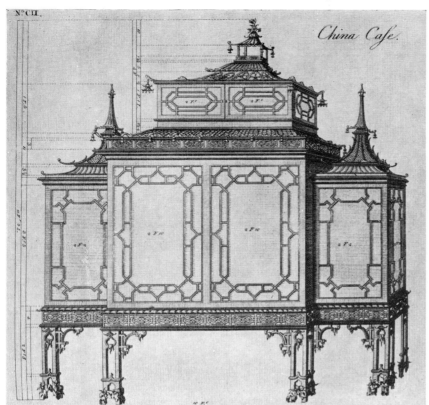

54. 'China Case'; Plate CII, Chippendale's Director, 1754.   55. Lady's Cabinet to be made of satinwood japanned; Sheraton's Drawing Book, 1st ed. (1791-4), Plate XLVIII.

urns. In the lower portion the upper drawer contains numerous small partitions and ivory fittings; the corners project in fluted colonnettes headed by leaf capitals, and a metal banding forms the cornice. Of the later archaeological phase the hanging cabinet (Fig. 53), one of a pair, is a fine example. On the central tablet of the cresting is a crocodile, a motif commemorative of Nelson's Victory of the Nile in 1798. A lyre with trophies is in the centre of each glazed door, and the applied mouldings are of brass, which about this time was coming into favour, the metal inlay and parts of the ornament being ebonised.

Because cabinets for the display of china were no doubt regarded as incongruous with the austerities of the Regency style in its more pedantic form, they do not figure among the designs of Thomas Hope and George Smith for household furniture. When made, they were designed and decorated on the lines of contemporary bookcases. A specimen by William Marsh (q.v.), probably from Henry Holland's design, shows the style in its early phase (Fig. 56). The Rev. Samuel Johnes, on a visit to Southill in 1800, writes that 'Marsh's cabinets are superb' when describing Mrs Whitbread's boudoir and dressing-room.

CABINETS, COIN; CORNER; JEWEL; MEDAL. See CABINETS, Figs. 33 and 44.

CABINET, DRESSING-TABLE. A table with 'every requisite for a lady to dress at' (see Sheraton's *Drawing Book* and TABLES, DRESSING).

56. *China Cabinet of rosewood; columns and applied ornaments of ormolu, by Marsh and Tatham. c. 1800. (Southill Park, Beds.)*

CABINET-MAKERS. Artificers who make furniture are still called 'cabinet-makers', although cabinets are only a minor part of their work. An early use of this term occurs in Adrian Bolte's petition (1660) for readmission to the office of cabinet-maker which he had held in Charles I's reign (*State Papers Domestic*, June, 1660). His name appears as Royal Cabinet-maker after the Restoration. Unlike carpenters, joiners and turners, cabinet-makers were not among the City Companies, nor were they organised in a separate guild.

The advance in skill of cabinet-makers, joiners and locksmiths at this period is noted by Evelyn: 'from very vulgar and pitiful artists', they had, he writes, 'come to produce works as curious for their fitting and admirable for their dexterity in contriving as any we meet with abroad' (*Account of Architects . . .* 1664). Pepys, visiting Mr Povy's house (March 15, 1667) found him 'at work with a cabinet-maker, of a new inlaid table'. Gerreit Jensen (*q.v.*), who supplied furniture to the Crown from Charles II's reign to the end of Queen Anne's, was a liveryman of the Joiners' Company, but was appointed cabinet-maker to the Crown, and is so described in the accounts for furnishing Kensington Palace. The Duke of Lauderdale when furnishing Ham House writes to Sir William Bruce (April 15, 1673) that he has engaged two joiners, 'Germans' who 'have made the double chassee (sash) windows' and are 'most excellent Workmen, both at that trade, and for making of cabinets'; these instances, among many, showing that there was no rigid differentiation at that period between the functions of the two crafts.

In the royal accounts from the late 17th century, the work of the cabinet-maker is distinguished to some extent from the joiner's, the former providing case furniture, tables and stands, and the latter seat furniture, stools and beds. But in some instances the same artificer was both cabinet-maker and joiner, and is thus described in trade-cards or advertisements.

In the mid-18th century, the large firms became complex organisations, combining the functions of cabinet-maker, chair-maker, joiner and upholsterer; and later some leading firms extended their scope to include the papering of rooms, gilding and other activities. About this time cabinet-makers and upholsterers founded a special Society to promote their interests by publishing trade catalogues. In 1760 the Society of Upholders and Cabinet-makers brought out *Household Furniture in Genteel Taste*, and continued to issue catalogues at intervals until well into the 19th century. About 100 cabinet-makers subscribed to the first edition of Chippendale's *Director* (1754), and nearly 650 from all parts of England to Sheraton's *Drawing Book* (1791-4). Though 'cabinet-maker' was generally adopted at this time by furniture-makers, there was a high degree of specialisation in large establishments.

In a *General Description of All Trades* (1747) cabinet-makers are described as prosperous—'many of their Shops are so richly set out they look more like Palaces, and their stocks are of exceeding great value.' Sheraton observes (*Cabinet Dictionary*, 1803) that the trade was considered 'one of the leading mechanical professions in every polite nation in Europe'.

CABLE MOULDING. Moulding cut in imitation of twisted rope, occasionally found on Gothic and early Renaissance furniture.

CABOCHON. Convex oval ornament, derived from the cutting of a precious stone, much used in 16th and 17th centuries, and revived in kidney shape on cabriole (*see* infra) knees of chairs and tables c. 1750 (*see* CHAIRS, Figs. 110 and 112).

CABRIOLE. French dancing term meaning bound or leap (apparently from Italian *capriola*, goat's leap), applied to a curved form of support adapted from quadruped's leg, and introduced in English furniture c. 1700. (For evolution, *see* CHAIRS and TABLES.) The seat-rail was at first united by cappings to the narrow cabriole legs (CHAIRS, Fig. 59), but soon after stretchers disappeared the knee became wider and stronger to compensate for their removal (CHAIRS, Fig. 62). The 'broken' cabriole leg was adapted in a few chairs (*e.g.* Fig. 64) and tables towards the end of Queen Anne's reign; another rare treatment can be seen in Fig. 67, where the legs are square-sided.

Early cabriole legs are plain or carved with honeysuckle or escallop shell on the knee (cf. CHAIRS, Fig. 62), which was occasionally divided by a channel, the lower part of the leg being intersected by a banding. This treatment was succeeded c. 1725 by acanthus decoration—lion, female and Indian masks (CHAIRS, Figs. 78, 85, 91), the feathering of the eagle or the hair of the lion being other variations of these motives (Figs. 88 and 90); and c. 1770 a taper leg or one of cylindrical shape, based on Louis XVI models, was introduced, but the cabriole was still employed for another decade or so on a few fashionable chairs and console tables. The word is also used to denote a kind of small armchair (Littré), and, by Hepplewhite, one with a stuffed back (*see* CHAIRS).

CADDY. *See* TEA-CADDIES.

CAFFOY. Fabric with a slight pile, imported in 18th century and also made in England—Beawes, *Lex Mercat* (1750), *Products of Abbeville as Plush, Caffoy*.

CALAMANDER WOOD (*Diospyros quaesita*). Employed to some extent in Regency furniture for veneer and bandings. From Ceylon; name derived from Singhalese *Kalu-mindrie* ('black flowering'), the wood being member of ebony family. Very hard fine grain of light brown colour, mottled and striped with black.

CALICO. General name for cotton cloth of all kinds imported from East, originally derived from Calicut, city on Malabar coast, in 16th-century chief port after Goa for Indian trade. Later, various cotton fabrics of European manufacture (sometimes also with linen warp) were thus designated. Heylin, *Cosmography*, iii (1682): 'A smock of Calicute a kind of linnen cloth here made, and from hence so called.' Chambers's *Cyclopaedia* (1753) states that 'Callicoes are of divers kinds, plain, printed, painted, stain'd, dyed, chints, muslins and the like'.

CAMLET, CHAMLET. Term of disputed etymology for a fine woollen material; early reference occurs in the wardrobe accounts of Edward IV (1480), where camlets of divers colours cost 30s. a piece. Much used for bed hangings down to mid-18th century. Camlet was imported in large quantities in early 17th century, but was also made in England, and Camden (*Britannia*, 1610) writes that the wealth of Coventry 'arose in the last age from its woollen and *camblet* manufacture'. It was often of mixed material, sometimes of wool, sometimes of silk, hair with wool or silk, etc.

CANDLE BOX. *See* BOXES.

CANDLESTAND. *See* STANDS, PEDESTAL and CANDLE.

CANDYLBEME. Form of chandelier (*q.v.*). In use during Middle Ages and down to Elizabethan times; made of cross-pieces of wood with candles affixed to arms.

CANING. Caning for seat furniture was introduced soon after the Restoration. The cane was obtained from a class of palms known as rattans, included under the genera *Calamus* and *Daemonorops*, and brought into England by East India Co. from Malay Peninsula.

An undated petition of the cane-chair makers states that caning came into use 'about the year 1664' and gave much satisfaction for its durability, lightness and cleanness. In 1689 a petition for the suppression of cane-chair making was forwarded by the Town of Bradford 'and the parts adjacent to the County of York'.

Early references in inventories are scarce, but there were footstools of 'Indian cane' with gilt frames in the Queen's Bedroom, and six armchairs with 'cane bottoms' in the Duke of Lauderdale's dressing room at Ham House (inventory, 1679). Caning was occasionally used for tables, and in a bill of Thomas Roberts (*q.v.*), 1691, there is an entry of 'a fine cane table, wrought handsome with a scrolled frame and scrolled pillars'; and at Ham House a carved stand (originally gilt) of about this date has a caned top. At first caning was large in the mesh, becoming finer towards the end of the 17th century.

After the introduction of vase and fiddle-shaped splats on chairs c. 1700, caning gradually became obsolete—'now almost out of use' (*London Tradesman*, 1747). In the mid-18th century, however, some chairs in the Chinese style had caned seats. Sheraton writes (*Cabinet Dictionary*, 1803) that caning 'about thirty years since was quite gone out of fashion.... But on the revival of japanning furniture it began to be brought gradually into use and to a state of improvement.'

CANOPY. Architectural term for ornamental projection; canopies frequently formed structural part of medieval aumbries, chairs, dressers, etc. Often also made of rich textile material, particularly when suspended above chairs of estate. Late 17th-century specimens survive—*e.g.* at Hampton Court.

CANTEEN. Small case divided into compartments for flasks or bottles. 1737, Ozell, *Rabelais*, II, 235: *The best Cantines are sold at Charing Cross.*

CANTERBURY. Sheraton (*Cabinet Dictionary*, 1803) writes that the term 'has of late years been applied to some pieces of cabinet work because, as the story goes, the bishop of that See first gave orders for these pieces. One piece is a small music stand.... The other piece ... is a supper tray, made to stand by a table at supper, with a circular end, and three partitions cross-wise, to hold knives, forks, and plates, at that end.' (*See* STANDS, MUSIC and PLATE.)

CANTONNIERES, CANTOINES, CANTONEERS. Narrow embroidered bands hung from pendants uniting the corners of the top valances outside the curtains at the foot of a bed (*see* BEDS).

CANTOON. Strong kind of fustian showing fine cording on one side and smooth bright surface on other. 1688, *London Gazette*, No. 2328/4: '*A Cantoon grey cloth Bed and Tester.*'

CAPITAL. Head of column or pilaster; capitals of each of the five classic orders being employed in furniture decoration, though generally somewhat freely adapted. Posts of Tudor beds occasionally headed by Ionic capitals (*see* BEDS, Fig. 9). Corinthian, Composite and Ionic varieties frequently used on furniture in first half of 18th century (*see* ORDERS).

CAQUETOIRE (CAQUETEURE, CAQUETEUSE). From *Caqueter*, to chatter. The French term for a light movable seat appears in Henri Estienne's *Apologie pour Herodote* (1556) in which he writes of women: 'It cannot be said that their mouths are frozen, at all events I will answer for it on behalf of the ladies of Paris, who could not refrain from calling their chairs *caquetoires*.' The term is employed in French inventories at the close of the 16th century and denotes a small, low chair. Also applied to form of armchair, derived from French models, with narrow back and outward-bowed arms (*see* CHAIRS, Fig. 7).

CARCASE. The main structure of a piece of furniture, the foundation on which veneers are applied (*see* CONSTRUCTION).

CARD-CUT. Applied to lattice ornaments carved in low relief.

CARD-TABLE. *See* TABLES, CARD.

CARLTON TABLE. *See* TABLES, LIBRARY and WRITING.

CARPENTERS. While medieval and Early Renaissance houses were largely timber-framed, carpenters were responsible for the construction and also for a very considerable proportion of the furnishing. The 'Boke' of the Ordinances of the Brotherhood of Carpenters carries back the history of the Guild to 1333, when it included both men and women and was chiefly religious and charitable in character. New Ordinances were issued in 1455; the Guild had changed 'from a Brotherhood of fellow-craftsmen to a fully organised "lesser Company" in almost complete control of an important handicraft'. The first charter was granted in 1477.

In 1632 the Committee of the Court of Aldermen, to end a dispute between the two Guilds, decided that joiners were entitled to the exclusive manufacture of most varieties of furniture 'made with mortesses and tennants, duftalled pynned or glued'. (For the list *see* JOINERS.) Continual disputes arose from the jealousy with which joiners and carpenters regarded attempted encroachments in their respective spheres. In 1672, the Company of Joiners and Ceilers petitioned the Lord Mayor and Aldermen to enforce the rules of 1632, persistently ignored by the carpenters, 'which if not speedily rectified the Joyners trade will be involved in the Carpenters and soe your petitioners inevitably ruined'. The carpenters replied that they originally dealt with every kind of woodwork, and that the joiners, carvers and sundry other companies 'were formerly but limbes, members and a part of the carpentry and Branches taken from them'. The joiners in particular were an offshoot penalised by their own action in Elizabeth's time, when they obtained the status of a separate company. They had 'made their eleccon to Joynery.... Yett by their Act the carpenters are not nor cannot be barred from their inherent right and privilege of using both occupations.'

No satisfactory solution was arrived at, but the Court of Aldermen decided their former order should remain a by-law between the two companies. Their jurisdiction was confined to London (that of the carpenters was extended to four miles around the capital by their Charter of 1640), and in the provinces one man would often practise both trades. Inventories prove that the estate carpenter was often responsible for Elizabethan oak and walnut furniture. (*See* Jupp, *An Historical Account of the Worshipful Company of Carpenters*, 1848, 2nd ed. 1887, and Bower Marsh, *Records of The Worshipful Carpenters' Company*, 1914.)

CARSEY. Woollen material used for bed hangings. 'Your Honour hath bought within 20 yeares . . . many *carsey* bedds' ('An Account of the Expenses of Robert Sidney, Earl of Leicester, by his Steward, c. 1600,' *Antiq. Repertory*).

CARTEL CLOCK. *See* CLOCK CASES.

CARTOUCHE. Term adopted from the French for tablet; sometimes purely ornamental, but more often with arms, initials, etc.; shape generally oval with edges curled or rolled over. In early 18th century carved and gilt cartouches sometimes set within embrasures in pediments.

CARVERS. Artisans who enrich a substance (*e.g.* stone, wood or ivory) by ornamenting it with cutting tools. The carver was in most cases distinct from the joiner, but some carvers were Freemen of the Joiners' Company; in 1707 Jonathan Maine, celebrated carver employed at St Paul's Cathedral Library, took up his livery (*Annals of the Joiners' Company*, H. L. Phillips, 1915). There is reason to suppose that in the 16th and 17th centuries in many instances the carver decorated the furniture which the chair-maker made. Mirrors, picture frames and some elaborate stands for cabinets were of course almost entirely his work. An answer of the cane-chair makers to a petition for their suppression by the makers of various textile materials (c. 1690) states that 'cane-chairs coming in time to be carved, many carvers took apprentices, and brought them up for carving of cane-chairs stools, couches and squobs only'.

By c. 1750 carving had become highly specialised, particularly for frames of tables and mirrors. The *London Tradesman* (1747) states there is 'a class of carvers who do nothing else but carve frames for looking glasses'. Two sorts of carving are described, in one of which the work was carried out entirely in wood, to be painted or gilded, and in the other 'the figures are just roughly cut out in the wood, the whole covered with two or three coats of whiting to the thickness of a quarter of an inch; when this is dry, the carver wets the whiting with a brush, then finishes the figures by making such flourishes in the whiting as is agreeable to his pattern'. This was carving carried out in the gesso preparation (*see* GESSO). It is also stated that cabinet-makers or upholders 'employ a species of carvers peculiar to themselves, who are employed in carving chairs, posts and testers of beds, or any other furniture whereon carving is used' (*ibid.*); and that owing to the vogue for carving, carvers were 'very much wanted and never out of business' (*The Parent's and Guardian's Directory*, J. Collyer, 1761).

During the neo-classic revival carving played a relatively minor part and was largely superseded by inlay and painted decoration. Sheraton (*Cabinet Dictionary*, 1803) recognises two distinct classes of carvers: (1) pier glasses and bed cornices, etc.; (2) for chairs, sofas, couches, etc.; and writes that in spite of this specialisation 'there are to be found persons, though rarely, of such universal genius in this ingenious art', that they are capable of combining all varieties of carving. But at this period the craft decayed rapidly, and in the early years of the 19th century there were only eleven master carvers in London and about 60 journeymen. In 1819 carving in wood had been 'long in the background as a branch of the Arts'. M. J. (*New Circle of the Mechanical Arts*). (*See* GRINLING GIBBONS, MATTHIAS LOCK, and THOMAS JOHNSON.)

CARYATIDES. Architectural term of Greek origin given to terminal figures of women; in furniture forming pilasters to backs of beds; used also for table legs, cabinet stands, etc. Similar male figures are called Atlantes.

CASE. Comprehensive term for receptacle; box or chest in oldest sense. In lists of contents of middle-class houses in 17th century case or casse often recorded in hall or kitchen (cf. *Beds. Hist. Records Soc.*, Vol. XX, 1938). Sometimes employed in second half of 18th century for large composite wardrobes. In Chippendale and Haig's accounts for the furnishing of David Garrick's house in the Adelphi in 1772 the following occurs: 'To a very large Inlaid case of Fustick (*q.v.*) and fine black Rosewood with Sundry other ornaments curiously inlaid with various fine woods . . . £65 10s.' (*See* BAROMETERS, CELLARETS, CLOCK CASES, KNIFE CASES, WINE CISTERNS.)

CASKET. Small box or chest for jewels, letters or other valuables, itself often of precious material and richly ornamented. 1467, *Eng. Gilds* (1870), p. 379: 'The same quayer to be put in a box called a casket.' Cotgrave: 'Boiste (or Boite): a box . . . little casket.' Cf. also Shakespeare, where many references occur—*e.g.* the caskets which Portia (*Merchant of Venice*, 1594) offers to her suitors (*see* BOXES AND CASKETS).

CASSOLETTE. *See* PERFUME BURNERS.

CASTORS. Small solid wheels attached to the lower extremities of a piece of furniture to enable it to move without lifting. They appear to have been introduced in England towards the end of the 17th century, though on the Continent they were in use at a much earlier date, a rude form of sunk wooden castor being clearly represented in Catena's picture of the Holy Family painted c. 1520. By 1690 the manufacture had become a distinct trade in England, for in that year the *London Gazette* Nos. 359/4 mentions Charles Mansell, 'a castor-maker'.

At first they were of hard wood rotating in wooden axles, which did not permit of lateral movement. This defect is remedied in an example dating from c. 1700 (BABY-CAGES, Fig. 1), where the axles are secured by pins which allow them to work in every direction. A boxwood ball running in a metal axle was the next improvement, and this form was soon superseded by a boxwood roller. About 1750 leather castors came into use on fashionable furniture, a number of leather discs being strung together on the axle and held in position by brass 'horns' attached to a flat metal plate. In the MS. account

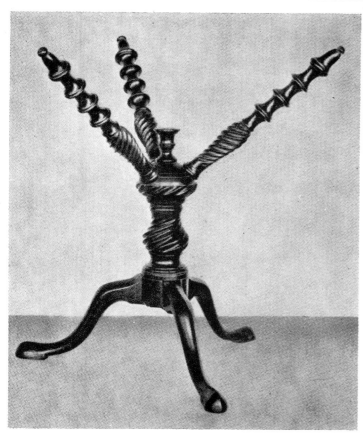

1. *Mahogany 'Cat', spiral turning and legs of cabriole form. Ht. 1 ft. 2 in., W. 12¾ in. (V. & A. Mus.)*

book of the fourth Earl and Countess of Cardigan for 1740 there is an entry of £3 3s. paid to Benjamin Goodison for fixing '18 setts' of castors at 3s. 6d. the set. Henry Williams (*q.v.*) about the same date charges for 'large brass socket castors with leather wheels' supplied to Kensington Palace.

By 1770 castors all of brass were available in three styles, each in 15 stock sizes. In his *Cabinet Dictionary* (1803) Sheraton distinguishes several varieties. He also enumerates five kinds of castors for bedposts. In tables of the Regency period, the socket often takes the form of a lion's paw-foot of brass or the surfaces are decorated with acanthus, honeysuckle or other designs, in relief, some of these paw castors containing several wheels. Many varieties are illustrated in pattern books of the period.

CAT. Tripod rest of metal or turned wood standing on tripod feet, used to support plates or dish to be kept warm in the fireplace. Whether the name derives from its fireside place, or from its way of falling on its feet either way up, is unknown. Such stands are found dating from the mid-18th century onwards, finer specimens being of mahogany with spiral turning and cabriole legs (Fig. 1). In 1798-9 two mahogany 'cats' were purchased by the Joiners' Company.

CAVETTO. Hollow moulding, quadrant of circle in profile; in furniture used chiefly as dominating member of cornices on cabinets, etc., veneered in walnut (*see* CONSTRUCTION).

CEDAR. *Juniperus virginiana*, North American cedar; *Cedrela odorata*, West Indian variety; similar trees also obtained from Honduras forests. Both varieties known as red cedar, and from c. mid-18th century used for drawer lining, wardrobe trays,

boxes and travelling chests. Evelyn (*Sylva*, 1664) advocates its shipment from the West Indies and that it should be used by 'our more wealthy citizens of London . . . at least for shelves, comptoires, chests, tables, wainscot, etc.' Cedar of Lebanon (*Cedrus Libani*), a very inferior variety, does not appear to have been used for furniture.

CELLARETS. Cases and receptacles to contain wine. As early as 1690 Gerreit Jensen (*q.v.*), the Royal cabinet-maker, charges for such a receptacle—'a cellar for six large bottles covered with seale skinne'; but the term cellaret does not seem to have come into general use until c. 1750.

Early Georgian sideboards were in the form of side tables without cupboards, and cellarets were placed under them. They had a lock, were lined with lead, with partitioning for bottles, and were provided with castors. The cellaret of octagon plan (Fig. 1), which has divisions for nine bottles and is one of the earliest known examples, has a base carved with foliage.

Robert Adam (*The Works in Architecture*) observes that Englishmen are 'accustomed by habit, or induced by the nature of our climate to indulge more largely in the enjoyment of the bottle' than the French; and this preoccupation with drinking accounts for the care bestowed on the design and finish of cellarets and other sideboard accessories.

When the fitted sideboard was introduced c. 1780, one of the drawers was generally fitted as a cellaret (*see* SIDEBOARDS); but such an arrangement afforded little space for wine or spirits and was often supplemented by a separate cellaret or *garde de vin*. Both terms are used in Hepplewhite's *Guide* (1788). He writes that they 'are generally made of mahogany hooped with brass lacquered; the inner part is divided with partitions, and lined with lead for bottles; they may be of any shape'. The two patterns illustrated are the plain oval and the circular tub.

Sheraton (*Cabinet Dictionary*, 1803) draws no distinction between cellarets and wine cisterns (*q.v.*), and writes that they 'are not strictly made to the dimensions of the bottles, but large enough to hold six light, or ten round wine bottles, and have an ornamental appearance'. In his *Encyclopaedia* (1803) he observes that they 'are not so generally used as they were, and amongst the higher classes are wholly laid aside', their place being taken by the sarcophagus form 'in the figure of ancient stone coffins'.

The word 'wine-keeper' (a translation of the French *garde-vin*) occurs in the sale catalogue of John Dryden, carver and

1. *Octagonal Mahogany Cellaret, base carved with foliage. c. 1740. Ht. 1 ft. 11 in., W. 1 ft. 11 in. (Percival Griffiths Coll.)*

2. Mahogany Cellaret of sarcophagus form, carved with husks and foliage and supported on cabriole legs. c. 1770. 3. Mahogany Cellaret on stand, corners of cellaret chamfered and fluted. c. 1770. Ht. 1 ft. 3 in. (Anthony White Coll.) 4. Mahogany Cellaret with chamfered, fluted corners; inlaid with tulipwood and decorated with satinwood paterae. c. 1785.

5. Mahogany Cellaret inlaid with ebony, gilt paw feet. Formerly in possession of Lord Nelson. c. 1800. (Nat. Maritime Mus., Greenwich.)

6. (Below) Mahogany Cellaret, reeded baluster supports; brass lion mask handles. c. 1820. (Mr W. Meyer.)

gilder, in 1807. At this period there was an increasing tendency towards specialisation, and Benjamin Banks (a cabinet-maker employed by John Cobb), who is described by J. T. Smith (*Nollekens and His Times*, 1828) as a 'cellaret-maker', affords an instance of this.

The example in Fig. 2 dates from the early years of the neo-classic revival. It is of sarcophagus form resting upon slender cabriole legs, the base of the cellaret being carved with upright leaves. Some pieces dating from the late 18th century are inlaid (Fig. 4).

Early in the 19th century cellarets came into more general use, and in some cases were of considerable size. Among the relics of Lord Nelson formerly at Trafalgar House is a circular cellaret which contains its contemporary cut glass decanters and glasses (Fig. 5).

Thomas Hope (*Household Furniture*, 1807) illustrates a cellaret decorated with 'amphorae and with figures allusive to the liquid element'. An example of Regency design with oval container is given in Fig. 6. In sideboards flanked by pedestals a cellaret drawer was provided in one of them, and in George Smith's *Household Furniture* (1808) such a pedestal is described as having 'a tray capable of holding six or eight bottles'. H.C.S. (*See also* WINE CISTERNS AND COOLERS.)

CELURE (CEELER, SELOUR) AND TESTER. The derivation of 'celure' is obscure. *Celatura* and *celatorium* occur in medieval Latin chiefly in the sense of 'canopy'. The term is constantly mentioned in connection with beds in medieval inventories and accounts, but what part of the hangings was intended is doubtful. The N.E.D. explains it as 'a canopy covering', but it was generally applied to the back above the pillows; which, until the introduction of wainscot beds in the 16th century, was of some kind of textile. Celour and Testour are very frequently mentioned together, the latter being 'a canopy over a bed supported on the posts of a bed-stead or suspended from the ceiling'. The terms were sometimes interchangeable, Palsgrave (1530) defining a tester for a bed as dossier, *i.e.* back. When mentioned alone *celure* was often applied to the canopy, but when the terms are used in conjunction the *tester* apparently always signified the canopy. Du Cange takes the various Latin forms all to imply 'the upper part, top, or upper covering of a bed'.

That tester was generally understood to imply a canopy by the middle of the 16th century is proved by Withal's *Dictionary* (1568 ed.), which renders *canopus* 'a teaster over the bedde', while Drayton writes of 'rich and sumptuous beds with tester-covering plumes' (*Polyolbion*, 1622, XXVI, 88).

CHAFING-DISH. Portable grate to hold burning charcoal or other fuel for heating food or anything placed upon it. References occur in the Middle Ages, and a testator bequeathes 'a chaffyn dish' in 1538.

CHAIRS. In the Middle Ages benches, settles, and forms were the ordinary seats in hall and chamber, and movable chairs were exceedingly scarce. The throne-like structures of fantastic shape in Saxon illuminations are always represented as the seats of persons of exalted rank, and probably bore little resemblance to actual objects. Throughout the Middle Ages the chair continued to be regarded as a symbol of authority, which none but the owner of the house or distinguished strangers might occupy. This rule was observed even in royal palaces. The herald who accompanied Princess Margaret, daughter of Henry VII, on her journey into Scotland to marry James IV (1503), relates that when the King came to supper at the Castle of Newboltell before the wedding he 'because the Stole of the Qwene was not for hyr Ease . . . gaffe hyr the said Chayre'.

The earliest surviving examples date from the 13th and 14th centuries and are of ecclesiastical origin; but at that period furniture of similar character was made for both religious and secular use. The well-known 'Prior's Chair' at Little Dunmow, Essex, shows the influence of early Pointed Architecture. Though mutilated, it retains enough of its original form to suggest that this characteristic medieval type was evolved from chests by the addition of a panelled back and sides. Seats of this kind were not confined to churches. In 1397 the Priory of Finchale had 'II Cathedrae,' or stalls, in the hall, doubtless for the use of the Prior and Sub-Prior.

The fine and important civic chair from St Mary's Guildhall, Coventry (Fig. 2), is all that remains of a triple seat, made for the Masters of the United Guild of St Mary, St John and St Catherine c. 1450. The outer side is carved with tracery; opposite, the lower portion is plain and there are mortises to join the centre portion of the seat, now missing. Late Gothic tracery decorates both surfaces of the back, and a richly carved vine trail forms the borders. The pinnacles are the Royal lions of England, and the Elephant and Castle, the Arms of Coventry.

Chairs resembling those shown in Fig. 1 were placed on the dais in feudal halls. They were often of great height, with crocketed and pinnacled canopies, cushions (*q.v.*) on the seat, and a 'dosser' (*q.v.*), or backing, of rich material. Such chairs sometimes accompanied the owner on his periodical progresses from house to house. The Ewelme Inventory (1466) of the Duke of Suffolk's possessions contains an entry for 'a chaire of tymbre of astate covered w^t blue cloth of gold and panells of copper', which has 'a case of lether thereto', into which it would be packed when taken to pieces.

For convenience of transport, however, other chairs were designed of more practical character and the second state chair of 'yren' listed in the same inventory was probably of the 'X'

1. *Two Chairs of Estate of form common to England and France; one canopy of wainscot, other of fabric. (From French MS.—Cotton MS. Augustus A.V. f. 103—B.M. c. 1470.)* 2. *Oak Chair, part of triple throne; finials carved as royal lions of England and arms of Coventry. c. 1450. Ht. 6 ft. 3 in., L. 3 ft. 9 in., Depth 1 ft. 11 in. (St Mary's Cathedral, Coventry.)*

3. Oak 'Joyned Chair', linen-fold panels and top panel carved with Renaissance ornament. Second quarter of 16th century. (V. & A. Mus.) 4. Oak 'Joyned Chair' carved with medallion heads and Renaissance ornament; sides of linen-fold. Second quarter of 16th century. (The late Sir Edward Barry.) 5. Oak Armchair (Caquetoire type), back carved with Renaissance ornament and female head within lozenge. c. 1535. (V. & A. Mus.)

pattern, a form which long remained in favour and resembled the modern camp stool in construction, being in some instances made to fold up. The chair of box-like form with panelled sides and back described as a 'close' or 'joyned cheyre', was introduced c. 1500. Figs. 3 and 4 are examples of this solid type, carved with linenfold and Italianate ornament of the early English Renaissance. It is to this type that Randle Holme's observations in *The Academy of Armory* may be taken to apply (MS. dated 1649), where he writes of 'the old way of making the chaire'. He states that 'some term it a settle chair, being so weighty that it cannot be moved from place to place but still abideth in its own station, having a kind of box or cubbert in the seate of it'.

In late medieval and early Tudor inventories references frequently occur to chairs of 'Flaunders Worke'. (In 1452 William Duffield of York had in a chamber one *Cathedrae operis Flandrensis* XX^d.) The character of these chairs cannot be determined from the descriptions. Another unidentified variety is stated to have been made *Ad Modum Anglicanum*; while chairs described as 'thrown' or 'turned' are often recorded. The original pattern with its triangular seat may perhaps have been introduced from Byzantium to Scandinavia, thence coming west with the Normans. Certainly, the type was made in England at a very early date and continued to be produced well into the Stuart period. In the Eadwine Psalter at Trinity College, Cambridge (c. 1150), faldstools and elbow chairs built up of knob-turning are clearly represented and, after the accession of James I, the Shuttleworths of Gawthorpe are found employing a dish-thrower to make them a chair of

this traditional pattern of which Fig. 9 is a very elaborate example. Similar chairs were also produced in Germany and Flanders. In a plainer variety the turned ornament was omitted from the back. There were two of this type in the 'Abbots Dyninge Chamber' at Tyltey in Essex, prior to the Dissolution in 1536.

It is to such chairs that Horace Walpole alludes in a letter to George Montague, written in August, 1761, when he recounts that one of his friends had 'picked up a whole cloisterful in Herefordshire. They were of wood, the Seats triangular, the backs loaded with turnery.' Joined wainscot chairs and those of the 'throwne' type are sometimes differentiated in inventories and wills of the 16th century. Thus John Hedge of Bury in 1504 bequeathed his son "II cheyres' in the hall of his house, 'on turnyd and the other close'.

In the long lists of Henry VIII's possessions drawn up in 1547 many magnificent chairs are described, which, if not actually of foreign origin, were derived from French and Italian prototypes, and mark the point of departure for the richly upholstered furniture of the succeeding age. Among the chairs enumerated at Hampton Court Palace are the following:

9 chaires of wood covered with cloth of gold Reized with crimson vellat fringed wythe Venice gold and crimson silke one of them being a Woman's chaire with H.A. carved on it. One chaire of wood covered with murrey vellat all over embraudered with Venice gold having the Kinges Armes crowned holden by his Majesties beastes wth back fringed with Venice gold and silke wth pommells of silver and gilt. One cheir of wood turned and painted walnut-tree colour and parcell guilte the seate and backe covered with blacke vellat embroidered with Venice gold and fringed with

6. *Oak Chair, originally covered in blue velvet garnished with gilt nails; capped with metal finials. c. 1550. (Winchester Cathedral.)*
7. *Oak Armchair (Caquetoire type). Back panel carved with flowers in vase flanked by lions; cresting centres in winged head. c. 1600.*
(Mr R. T. Gwynn.) 8. *Oak Armchair with folding frame-work, arches carved with guilloche pattern. c. 1600. (V. & A. Mus.)*

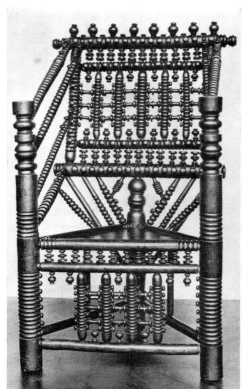

9. *'Turned Chair' of oak and ash, with triangular seat. Early 17th century. (V. & A. Mus.).* 10. *Oak Armchair, inlaid with various woods; cresting and brackets carved with foliage; legs and arm supports fluted. c. 1600. (V. & A. Mus.)* 11. *Oak Armchair, carved and inlaid with various woods; top rail carved with guilloche. c. 1600. (Sir William Burrell Coll.)*

yellowe and blake silke. One chair of walnuttree colour painted with a trayle of white parcell guilte with 2 toppes guilte. One chaire of yren covered all over with nedle worke all over wrought with silke and golde with the late Quene Annes Sipher—the posts and backe fringed with Venice gold with foure pomells of silver and gilte with the Kings and the said Quene Annes Armes in theym the seat covered with clothe of gold.

These painted or fabric-covered chairs were confined to the royal palaces and a few great houses, and no specimens corresponding to these descriptions survive.

Although chairs continued to be so scarce that at The Vyne (Hampshire) in 1541 the 52 rooms contained only 19, a number of lighter forms were now provided. The X-shape was again restored to favour, and many examples on Italian models were made in England. The woodwork of such chairs was completely covered with silk or velvet, the seat consisting of loose cushions resting on webbing ('girthweb') between the side rails of the frame. The more important of Henry VIII's richly embroidered chairs were doubtless of this kind; while they are found represented in portraits of the age, and a tradition that the chair in Fig. 6 was used by Mary Tudor at her marriage to Philip in July, 1554, gains support from the fact that when Antonio Mor painted the Queen he represented her as sitting on a similar chair. So late as 1807 (*Antiquarian Repertory*) it still retained a brass plate on one of the pommels embossed with the Sacred Monogram.

In Cardinal Wolsey's inventory a large number of chairs are noted covered with red, blue or black velvet, with fringes of gold or silk. That some were of English manufacture is shown by the entry '5 chairs with high backs new made and bought of Richard Gresham, embroidered with Cardinal hats and pome-

granates having gilt pomels.' In a list of Sir John Gage's goods at West Firle, Sussex, drawn up in 1556, there is some interesting information as to whence he obtained his furniture. A chair 'garnyshed with collored woode' was of 'Spanish making', while another of wainscot came from France; these being distinguished from 'wooden chaiers of the country makinge'—that is of native production.

At the end of Henry VIII's reign and early in that of Elizabeth a number of very elaborate and enormously costly 'X' chairs, and others with frames carved, painted, gilded and richly upholstered, were supplied to the Crown by the royal coffer-maker, William Greene (*q.v.*). The evidence suggests that fabric-covered chairs with web seats of the X-type were at this time generally supplied by coffer-makers.

By the mid-16th century the maker of 'joyned chairs' had evolved a much lighter seat. The chair (Fig. 5) is of the French type called *caquetoire* (*q.v.*) and was found about sixty years ago in Devon. The tall, slightly tapered back is boldly carved in the Renaissance manner, and centres in a female head set within a lozenge, the heraldic attribute of a woman. Walnut was generally employed for *caquetoire* chairs in France, and there are many examples in French collections, exhibiting a considerable variety of design. Here the blunt and summary carving, the ogee-shaped seat-rail and the plain rectangular framework (apparently without parallel in continental examples) point to the conclusion that the chair is of native origin and an early specimen of the type.

A number of such chairs were produced in England under Elizabeth and in the first quarter of the 17th century; though the descriptions of 'joyned chairs' in contemporary inventories

12. *Armchair, softwood carved, painted and parcel gilt; one of pair formerly at Holland House. Probably designed by Francis Cleyn. c. 1625. (Earl of Ilchester.)* 13. *Oak Armchair richly carved, in centre panel lions supporting pear tree. c. 1620. (Bodleian Library, Oxford.)* 14. *Oak Armchair, with reeded mouldings and uprights, top and seat rail carved. Initials and date 1625. (Lygon Arms, Broadway, Worcs.)*

15. *Oak Armchair elaborately carved, bases of arm supports bear initials E.P.; seat (restored) bears other initials and later date c. 1660. (V. & A. Mus.)* 16. *Oak Armchair, one of set made for a family, each bearing initials of owner; cresting carved with plumes. Lancashire type. c. 1660.* 17. *Oak Armchair, back carved in low relief commemorates marriage of Charles II and Catherine of Braganza in 1662. (The late Mr Francis Harper.)*

do not permit of their identification. A later specimen (Fig. 7) has the characteristic wedge-shaped seat and widely splayed arms, but the proportions of the back, surmounted by a cresting and carved in the style of c. 1600, conform to those of the familiar panel variety.

The close alliance of the French and Scottish Crowns at this period led to the adoption of the *caquetoire* form in Scotland. At Trinity Hall, Aberdeen, there is a remarkable series of such chairs belonging to the Deacons of the Incorporated Trades, one dated 1574, another 1627.

A distinctive type was introduced about the end of the 16th century (Fig. 8), closely resembling some earlier Italian models. The frame is formed of planks fastened together by wooden pins, the back has a pronounced rake, and the arms, hinged by a wooden bar passing through the front legs and sides of the seat, are shaped underneath and ramp upwards to support the elbows. The same motives appear always to have been introduced in the carving of the back on English specimens, the design taking the form of a conventional flower set within a lozenge and enclosed by a round-headed arch decorated with a guilloche pattern, having a half sunflower in the arc of the circle.

Although several varieties were in use in the second half of the century, chairs were still few even in large houses. At Hengrave in 1603, the Great Chamber contained 32 joined stools and only 4 chairs. On ceremonial occasions they retained their ancient significance. At court they were reserved exclusively for the Sovereign. When the Constable of Castile was entertained by James I at Whitehall in 1604, 'Their Majesties sat at the head of the table on chairs of brocade with cushions, and at the Queen's side sat the Constable, a little apart, on a tabouret (stool) of brocade with a high cushion of the same'; Prince Henry being provided with a similar seat.

Among English chairs of this period no counterpart to the example (Fig. 12) is known. It is one of a set formerly at Holland House. These chairs, painted stone colour and parcel gilt, with the backs formed as shells, are stated by Horace Walpole to be 'undoubtedly' from the designs of Francis Cleyn (*q.v.*) and 'evidences of his taste'.

Early panel-back chairs are of massive construction. As the evolution proceeds the turning of legs and arm supports becomes lighter; the arms develop a marked downward droop; the seat is narrower; while the back, often surmounted by a scrolled cresting, has brackets attached to the sides. An armchair in the Bodleian Library (Fig. 13) shows the picturesque richness of the earlier phase.

At this date inlay forms an important feature in the decoration of finer chairs, box, holly, pear, bog oak, and sycamore being the woods commonly employed. A design of conventional floral sprays, often springing from a vase and with small birds introduced, was the favourite decoration of the back panel (Figs. 10 and 11). In Fig. 11 the arms are inlaid on their upper surfaces.

In the provinces patterns continued to be reproduced long after they had become obsolete in fashionable furniture. The arms of a simple country chair (Fig. 14) preserve the earlier horizontal line, the turning is of Elizabethan character. Later in the century the decorative areas were covered with a profusion of carving, in which a medley of motives was rendered with a growing poverty of invention (Fig. 15).

Such chairs continued to be made in the country into mid-Georgian times; they are for the most part decadent in design

18. *Oak Armchair, shaped cresting and back panel carved with scrolls and conventional floral ornament. Lancashire type. c. 1660. (Chetham's Hospital, Manchester.)* 19. *Oak 'Derbyshire Chair' with arcaded back, split balusters on uprights; original dished seat replaced by cushion. c. 1650. (V. & A. Mus.)* 20. *Oak Chair elaborately turned, seat dished for cushion. c. 1660. (The late Mr C. H. F. Kindermann-Walker.)*

and mechanically ornamented. However, the armchair (Fig. 17) is apparently without parallel in the character of the ornament. The back uprights are carved with the Lion and Unicorn supporters of the royal arms, the panel bearing a representation in low relief of Charles II and Catherine of Braganza, while an angel hovers above the crown. This panel is probably based on a hitherto unidentified woodcut or engraving.

Fig. 16 is of Lancashire origin, made on the lines of contemporary walnut chairs. A solid panel is set high above the seat in place of caning, and the cresting, resembling the feather mantling found in Charles II silver, is boldly carved with plumes centring in a shell. This specimen is one of a set of five armchairs, each bearing the owner's initials. Save in a few areas, subsequent movements from the locality of production preclude the identification of regional types, but the richly carved example (Fig. 18) has again characteristics which it is possible to associate with Lancashire and West Yorkshire design.

About the time of the Restoration the panel-back was supplemented in Yorkshire and Derbyshire by a lighter type, in which the space between the uprights is filled with an arcade of turned balusters supported on a central rail and ornamented with knobbed finials (Fig. 19), while others have broad and flat rails, hooped and escalloped, with pendants attached (Fig. 21). A remarkable feature of these 'Derbyshire chairs' is the frequent introduction of a head with a pointed beard on the top rail, possibly commemorative of Charles I. In another variety (Fig. 20) the whole structure, with the exception of the points of junction, is formed of knob turning. The existence of chairs of very similar design in Portugal and Italy suggests that

imports from those countries may have been copied here; but possibly the inspiration was derived from the 'turned' or 'thrown' chairs of earlier days (cf. Fig. 9). They are occasionally found made in yew. The 'dishing' of the seats was intended for a cushion, and similar chairs were probably in Mary Verney's mind when she wrote to Lady Elmes in 1664: 'For a drawing room i should have 2 squobs (upholstered stools) and 6 turned woden chars.' Lady Elmes reported that 'tolerable chairs' would cost 7s. a piece and the squabs 10s.

Towards the end of Elizabeth's reign richly upholstered chairs were becoming plentiful in great establishments, rivalling continental standards of luxury. When an inventory was taken of the contents of Kenilworth Castle in 1583 it may be assumed that such chairs as the following were in rooms of state:

> A chaire of crimson velvett, the seate and back partlie embrothered with R.L. in clothe of golde, and the beare and ragged staffe in clothe of silver, garnished withe lace and fringe of golde, silver and crimson silk, the frame covered withe velvett bounde about the edges withe golde lace and studded withe gilt nailes.
>
> A chaire of Wallnutree, carved withe sinquefoile and the ragged staffe, covered with crimson velvett, the backe richelie embrothered withe sinquefoiles of silver with two beares and ragged staves standing on the toppe the seate all lozenged withe silver twist trymmed with fringe of crimson silke and silver, the backe of the chaire lyned withe crimson satten, and a case of buckram to the same.

The first was probably of X-form, the other being an elaborately carved chair with upholstery secured to the back and seat. The reference to 'the backe . . . lyned with crimson satten' in addition to the embroidery, indicates that the material was stretched between the uprights. The bears were the badge of the Earl of Leicester's family.

21. *Oak 'Derbyshire Chair', rails centre in head with pointed beard; arms, rare feature, coarsely scaled. c. 1660. (C. G. Stirling Coll.)*
22. *Upholstered Chair covered with appliqué of cloth of gold on red satin ground; shield-shaped escutcheon at intersection of legs has been reversed. c. 1610-20. (Knole Park, Kent.)* 23. *Walnut 'Farthingale Chair' covered in blue cloth embroidered in silks: front legs of columnar form. c. 1610. (V. & A. Mus.)*

Nearly all the chairs in the principal chambers at Hardwick Hall, Derbyshire, in 1600 were covered with fabrics of comparable splendour. The frame of one of these chairs was gilt. The back and seat were padded, and the covering finished off with a galon or fringe fastened to the frame by nails. The richly upholstered X-shaped type, supplied to the royal palaces under Elizabeth, continued to be made in the succeeding reign, but of the stately houses furnished by the great men of that age, none but Knole has retained any considerable number of examples, the perishable nature of the beechwood frames accounting for the almost total disappearance of such furniture. The X chair illustrated (Fig. 22) dates from early in James I's reign, the embroidered satin upholstery matching that of the contemporary bed (*see* BEDS, Fig. 14). There are four of these chairs at Knole of exactly the same size and with framework of very similar pattern. Though each is covered with a different material, all the covers are original. Every portion of these four chairs is upholstered, the backs being divided into two panels by a cut fringe, also used to trim the framework and fixed to it by gilt-headed nails. There is an X chair of rather smaller size, of which the framework is not covered with fabric, but painted vermilion with delicate geometric lines and floral sprigs in white.

Another armchair of this pattern, covered with faded crimson velvet, with tarnished gold fringe, once belonged to Archbishop Juxon, who attended Charles I on the scaffold. In the inventory of Charles's magnificent furniture, sold after his execution by the Council of State, a number of chairs of this type are described, among them one 'covered with murrey velvet all over embrawdered with venice gold', also with 'his

majisties beastes' and the Royal arms, the back being surmounted with two 'pomells' of 'silver and gilt'. In the portrait by Edward Bower of Charles I at his trial, the King is represented seated in an armchair resembling Juxon's, which is now in the Victoria and Albert Museum.

In square upholstered chairs of this period the woodwork was frequently covered with fabric to match the padded seats and backs. In design they closely resemble contemporary Flemish and Dutch examples and those represented in the engravings of domestic interiors by Abraham Bosse. Many were made without arms, a practice accounted for by the extravagant dimensions attained by the farthingale. These 'farthingale' chairs were not the first variety to be made in sets. In 1590, after the death of Robert, Earl of Leicester, the 'Dyninge Chamber' at Leicester House contained 'three suites of Chaires, all ymbrodered, with their stooles and long cushions'; while in the Ingatestone inventory of 1600 many chairs are listed without arms, covered with 'blew carsay (Kersey) suitable unto the bed', or with 'the same sutelike'; showing that towards the end of Elizabeth's reign if chairs were not actually made to match each other, they were at least upholstered *en suite*.

At the Victoria and Albert Museum are two 'farthingale chairs', still retaining their original upholstery. One (Fig. 23) is of walnut, the upholstery being finished with a narrow galon and fastened to the frame by brass-headed nails. The other chair (Fig. 24) is covered with Turkey work (*q.v.*). In Fig. 25, formerly at Boughton, Northants., the legs are also of columnar form, and the back, formed of faded velvet lined with leather, is raised high above the seat rail; while the arms,

24. (*Left*) *Oak 'Farthingale Chair' with chamfered legs and uprights; covered in 'Turkey work'. c. 1620. (V. & A. Mus.)*

25. (*Right*) *Armchair covered with velvet, originally red, faded to dull green; front legs and arm supports, walnut, back legs, beech; oak stretchers of later date. From Boughton House, Northants. c. 1630. (V. & A. Mus.)*

covered with this material on their upper surfaces, resemble those of oak panel-back chairs of c. 1625.

The chairs with knobbed legs and stretchers, in favour during the Protectorate, in design reflect the austerity of the times. Their seats and back panels are upholstered in leather, sometimes lightly tooled, and fastened to the frame by rows of brass-headed nails. This type continued to be made after the Restoration, and transitional examples (Fig. 28) have scrolled front stretchers, soon to become a stock ornament on walnut hairs. The leather coverings were sometimes painted and

embossed. Mr Butterfield, rector of Claydon, in 1658 writes to Sir Ralph Verney that he needs 'painted lether' to cover chairs and stools.

The use of walnut in conjunction with caning on seats and backs dates from after the Restoration, when Charles II and his courtiers introduced this new continental type (*see* CANING). In undecorated specimens, uprights and legs have a simple twist, and are connected on a plan that combines rigidity with economic use of material, the turned members being mortised and tenoned into rectangular sections. In

26. (*Left*) *Oak Armchair, with turned legs, uprights and front stretcher; re-upholstered in leather. c. 1650. (The late Mr A. de Navarro.)*

27. (*Right*) *Oak Chair, one of set of fifteen; frame decorated with knob turning. c. 1660-70. (Doddington Hall, Lincs.)*

28. *Oak Chair, upholstered in leather, front stretcher carved with scrolls; one of set of twenty-four. c. 1660. (Chetham's Hospital, Manchester.)*
29. *Oak Chair, legs and uprights of spiral turning. c. 1665. (Mr Ralph Edwards.)*
30. *Walnut Armchair, with cane back and seat; structure of spiral turning. c. 1665. (V. & A. Mus.)*

Fig. 30 the arms are flat and bowed, plain knob finials are now found for the first time, the oblong panel of the back, separated from the uprights, is on the same level as the arms; and in its lightness and mobility this chair marks a new departure. In some of these plain turned chairs the framework is incised with lozenge or lattice-work patterns, while the mesh of the caning is large. Descriptions in the Wardrobe accounts indicate that chairs 'turned all over' were supplied to the Crown from soon after the Restoration until c. 1675, when they were superseded by a more ornate variety.

Even after the Restoration the chair still retained its function as the seat of honour, and when a great personage was present he would occupy it, lesser folk sitting on stools. Even at Court, at a time when chairs were made in sets and produced in large numbers, on ceremonial occasions they continued to be regarded with a degree of reverence as serving to indicate differences in station. This traditional view of the dignity conferred by the possession of a chair is illustrated in a letter from Lord Conway to the Earl of Essex of 1673, in which he relates that when the King ordered one to be brought for the Duchess of Modena in the Queen's Presence Chamber, 'Ladyes to the number of 20 that were of the nobility ran out of the room, as thinking themselves of equall quality to the Duchess of Modena'. More than fifty years later a dispute of a similar character arose on the occasion of the marriage of Frederick, Prince of Wales (eldest son of George II). The English princesses refused to sit on stools while Frederick and his bride

31. *Walnut Armchair, elaborately carved; on cresting, arms of Earl of Pembroke. c. 1665. (Sir John Ramsden Coll.)*

32. (*Left*) *Armchair of carved beech; on cresting and stretcher cherubs supporting crown; in back, narrow cane panel framed in foliated scrollwork. Dated 1695. (Col. N. R. Colville.)*

33. (*Right*) *Walnut Armchair, carved, painted and gilt; on cresting Royal arms of Charles II. c. 1680. (Glasgow Art Gallery, Burrell Coll.)*

34. (*Left*) *Walnut Armchair, with thistle decoration, splat filled with three split balusters; woodwork painted. c. 1690. (Martin Buckmaster Coll.)*

35. (*Right*) *Walnut Armchair, high front stretcher carved with ribbon motive. c. 1690. (Donaldson Coll.)*

36. Walnut Chair, back carved with symmetrically arranged scrolls. c. 1690. (Formerly at Quenby Hall, Leics.) 37. Walnut Ladder-Back Chair, back composed of scrolls; caned seat of scrolled outline. c. 1690. (Layer Marney Towers, Essex.) 38. Walnut Armchair, surface painted to enhance figure of wood. c. 1690. (Col. N. R. Colville.)

occupied chairs at dinner, and remained in the ante-chamber until they carried their point.

In the ornate type of chair introduced into England about the middle of Charles II's reign, front stretcher, cresting, and back-panel frame are developed into decorative areas. The arms are of rounded section with a downward curve, while the mesh of the caning is considerably reduced. The ornament, in the more familiar form, consists of a crown supported by amorini, a motive adopted before the Restoration in decorative woodwork (cf. PICTURE FRAMES, Fig. 3), acanthus leaves and flat-petalled flowers.

This new type appears to have originated in Holland, from where the fashion spread to England. The turning affords the most reliable guide to nationality. The English spiral twist has a narrow rope with deep hollows, whereas in Dutch turning the rope is thick, the resulting twist being close and rapid. In 1683 Richard Price, a joiner who supplied furniture to the Crown, charges for 'an elbow chair with walnuttree turned of the Dutch turning'—a description which recognises the distinction, and suggests that this foreign variety of turning was deliberately imitated at this date by English makers. In continental chairs the stretcher between the back legs is often omitted; while with comparatively few exceptions examples with an oval panel in the back are of Dutch origin. The ornament of such imported chairs is generally more crisply cut, of thinner material and noticeably lighter in handling. But the

general form of these walnut cane-back chairs was widely spread in North-West Europe.

In English chairs of this period there is remarkable variety, the pattern being modified by successive phases of continental influence. Instead of straight turned legs, a scrolled form was often employed, the supports of the arms forming complementary curves. To such examples as Figs. 36 and 41 the description 'cutt with scrowles all over', which occurs in the Lord Chamberlain's accounts, obviously applies.

On fine Carolean chairs the carved ornament is bold and summary, suited to a soft material, but lacking sculpturesque quality and high finish. The most elaborate chairs are thoroughly baroque in character. Such specimens are given in Figs. 31 and 32, the forms, in both design and craftsmanship, being among the finest armchairs of the type. Another remarkable specimen of the baroque spirit is the armchair (Fig. 33), of walnut carved and painted with gilt enrichments on a gesso ground. On the cresting are the arms of Charles II and Catherine of Braganza. At the arm extremities are unicorns couchant on gilt eagles' heads, which point downwards towards supporting dragons bearing shields with, on the dexter, the arms of France, on the sinister the harp of Ireland. The legs are highly exceptional, being carved with baskets of flowers resting on couped lions' paws. This armchair was probably made for the king towards the end of his reign. An entry in the Lord Chamberlain's accounts of a sum paid to a cabinet-maker for

39. *Walnut Chair, with fluted uprights and baluster legs. c. 1695. (Donaldson Coll.)* 40. *Walnut Chair, caned panels divided by carved and perforated splat; gadrooned taper legs, scroll feet, serpentine stretchers. c. 1695.* 41. *Walnut Chair, carved with amorini and interlaced scrolls; front stretcher repeats motives of cresting. c. 1690.*

models of walnut chairs 'to show the King' is proof that Charles concerned himself with the furnishing of his palaces. From shortly after the Restoration the Wardrobe Accounts show that large numbers of caned chairs of 'walnuttree' were supplied for the royal apartments and for the lodgings of members of the Court.

Beech stained to resemble walnut was often employed for the sake of economy. A fine armchair in this material proves the persistence of the Charles II type into the last years of the century, when new fashions had been introduced (Fig. 32). The volutes of the S-shaped scrolls on the cresting are incised with the date 1695. The fashionable models were also rendered in oak by country craftsmen, whose individual fancies inspired attractive variations.

By the end of the century cane-backed chairs had become lighter in treatment. The uprights are now of baluster form and, instead of being tenoned in between, the cresting rests upon them. This member and the front stretcher are sometimes arched and ornamented with a boldly-conceived arrangement of scrolls. The front legs, which are either scrolled or of baluster form, are joined to the seat rail or base of the arm supports by a small turned knob, a sacrifice of sound principles of construction. The back increases in height, producing a sense of instability; while in some instances its entire area is occupied by canework, which becomes still finer in the last phase of this type. On many of these late Stuart chairs the arms turn out-

wards and terminate in volutes. A walnut chair, formerly at Hampton Court, Leominster, is a fine specimen of these developments (Fig. 38). Within the delicate pierced cresting are interlaced C's for Thomas Coningsby (1656-1729), created a baron in 1695. This chair is remarkable as affording an instance of graining, the walnut being mottled and streaked on a ground of light paint.

In some of these Late Stuart chairs the space between the uprights is filled with carved and pierced foliage and symmetrical scrollwork. The seats instead of being caned were upholstered. Fig. 41 shows a particularly graceful arrangement of scrolls with lively amorini introduced, and is notable for the delicacy of the execution. In Fig. 34 the thistle decoration suggests a Scottish origin, and the woodwork is varnished and painted throughout in a design of flowers and birds. In the royal accounts of Charles II's reign there are references to this rare form of decoration, Richard Price (*q.v.*) charging for a set of chairs 'of the China varnish', implying that they were japanned like other furniture of this time in Oriental taste. In the bills of Thomas Roberts (*q.v.*) under Charles II there are charges for chairs 'varnisht purple', and green was among the colours employed. Fig. 37 is an early specimen of the ladder-back type with horizontal slats and scrolls. On the cresting appears the crowned head of James II, while the bust on the front stretcher is, doubtless, intended to represent his Queen.

42. (Left) Walnut Chair, carved with scrolls and foliage; turned uprights with voluted capitals, tapered front legs, serpentine stretchers. c. 1695.

43. (Right) Arm-chair, beechwood painted black and parcel gilt. c. 1695. (Knole Park, Kent.)

44. (Left.) 'Sleep-ing Chayre', one of pair, covered in cherry-coloured brocade; woodwork gilt, back lets down by ratchets. c. 1675. (Ham House, Surrey.)

45. (Right) Winged Armchair, covered with velvet; front legs scrolled, stretcher carved with scrolls and foliage. c. 1680. (Boughton House, Northants.)

46. (*Left*) *Armchair, upholstered in Italian cut velvet; walnut woodwork painted black. c. 1685. (Formerly at Kimbolton, Hunts.)*

47. (*Right*) *Walnut Armchair, carved, gilded and covered in Italian cut velvet with original tasselled fringe; draped male figures form front legs. Attributed to Thomas Roberts. c. 1688. (Knole Park, Kent.)*

About 1690 vertical forms became fashionable for front legs. The cappings are often pear- or mushroom-shaped, carved with gadroons, and below is a turned section tapered to a rectangular block above an octagonal or spherical foot. Sometimes the leg is enriched with mouldings, with small sunk panels on the square sections. The stretchers on such chairs are not, as hitherto, attached midway to the front leg, but set back and tenoned into the side stretchers at a lower level (Fig. 39). The carved front rail was abandoned on certain models and replaced by flat, diagonal, moulded stretchers of serpentine form, with a turned finial at their junction. In Fig. 40 the front feet are scrolled (the so-called 'Braganza foot') and the pierced

48. *Walnut Armchair, scrolled arms and wings covered in blue and silver damask; turned walnut legs and stretchers. c. 1690. (Boughton House, Northants.)* 49. *Armchair, painted, gilt and carved; on stretcher recumbent angels trumpeting, original crimson velvet. c. 1685. (Right) Detail of the Armchair. (Formerly at Glemham Hall, Suffolk.)*

50. (*Left*) *Arm-chair; carved with dolphins, gilt and painted; one of set of six; original covering of embroidered silk. c. 1675. (Ham House, Surrey.)*

51. (*Right*) *Walnut Armchair, upholstered in crimson velvet with tasselled fringe; arms voluted and gadrooned cappings. c. 1690. (Boughton House, Northants.)*

apron is unusual. The carved splat framed in canework is a novel departure.

Some of these Late Stuart chairs were decorated to match other varieties of the japanned furniture for which at this period there was so great a demand. In the Blue Drawing Room at Ham House, Surrey, there are seven chairs of this kind, the survivors from separate, but almost identical, sets, and probably those described in the 1683 inventory as '12 back stooles with cane bottoms japanned'. The crestings bear the coronet and cipher of Elizabeth Dysart, Duchess of Lauderdale, thus suggesting the chairs were made for her just after the Duke's death (1682). Japanned in dark green with chinoiserie motives, the design represents a naïve attempt to reproduce an Oriental form. Obviously the makers of japanned chairs sought to produce decorative objects with little regard for utilitarian consideration or durability, and it is doubtless owing to their personal associations with Elizabeth Dysart that these chairs at Ham have been preserved by generations of her descendants. It seems unlikely that the craftsman who made chairs so original in conception was also responsible for the design; possibly in this and other instances drawings were provided to serve as a guide.

Some of the more elaborately carved chairs dating from William III's reign recall the designs of Daniel Marot (*see* MAROT, D.). Though pronouncedly foreign in character, many were doubtless made in England by immigrant craftsmen, and on this account have claims to be regarded as native productions (Fig. 42).

The evidence afforded by the royal tradesmen's accounts indicates that upholstered chairs with low backs, turned framework, and arms padded on their upper surfaces were the first variety of this type to become fashionable after the Restoration. This variety, which has become rare, is well represented in the remarkable aggregation of Carolean furniture at Knole. Large winged armchairs, padded and upholstered throughout, which are described as 'easie' chairs in contemporary inventories, were introduced about the middle of the reign. At Ham House and Knole there are examples of Charles II winged chairs with original velvet coverings. Fig. 44 shows one of a pair of winged armchairs described in the Ham inventory (1679) as 'two sleeping chayres carv'd and guilt frames covered with crimson and gould stuff with gould fringe. Cases of crimson sarsnet.' The central and side stretchers are formed of scrolls, that in the front being more elaborately carved; the feet terminate in seahorses supporting spirally twisted legs. Fig. 45 shows a chair of this type covered in the original velvet, the curved wings finishing in small elbow rests. The front legs and the stretcher carved with scrolls and acanthus are in the style of c. 1680. In the winged armchair (Fig. 52) the upholstery is again original. The sweep of the arms is particularly graceful, their lines being emphasised by the guilloched moulding that frames the back·

Towards the end of Charles II's reign much of the carved woodwork of chairs was gilt and painted, silk appliqués and gorgeous coloured Genoa velvet being employed in the upholstery. Fig. 49 is one of a set of six formerly at Glemham Hall, Suffolk, splendid examples which can be assigned to Thomas Roberts (*q.v.*). The original upholstery matches the hangings of Sir Dudley North's state bed (*see* BEDS, Fig. 16). The carving throughout is of exceptional excellence, the plain surfaces of the arms being decorated with delicate floral patterns in colour. The scrolled legs are formed as cherub terminals, and on the front stretchers the recumbent angels are sculpturesque and Italianate in treatment. At Burghley House there is a pair of armchairs identical in design and decoration. In a set at Ham House (Fig. 50) the arms finish in dolphins' heads, while legs and stretchers are carved with the interlaced bodies of the fish, gilding and colour being combined in the enrichment. This ornate set may be identified with '6 arm

52. *Armchair, one of pair, covered with rose damask and appliqué of velvet and coloured silks; gilding original. Probably by Thomas Roberts. c. 1690. (Penshurst Place, Kent.)*

53. *Walnut Armchair, original velvet upholstery, perforated mushroom-shaped cappings and arm-supports; one front leg original, others restored. c. 1690. (Formerly at Rushbrooke Hall, Suffolk.)*

54. *Gilt Chair, covered with Italian velvet; mushroom cappings to fluted baluster legs. c. 1690. (Formerly at Kimbolton, Hunts.*
55. *Walnut Armchair, covered with red velvet, decorated with applied panels of silver embroidery. c. 1700. Attributed to Thomas Roberts. (Hardwick Hall, Derbys.)* 56. *Walnut Armchair, scrolled legs and arm supports and flat shaped stretchers; covered with 'Turkey' work. c. 1690. (Hardwick Hall, Derbys.)*

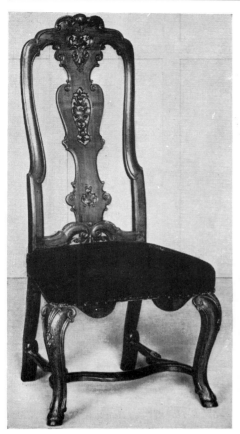

57. *Walnut Chair; 'shoe' connected with seat rail; cabriole legs and hoof-shaped feet. c. 1715. (Donaldson Coll.)* 58. *Chair of carved and gilt beech, one of pair; covered with original crimson velvet trimmed with fringe. c. 1695. (Col N. R. Colville)* 59. *Walnut Chair, one of set, splat carved and pierced; cabriole legs and scrolled feet. c. 1700. (Leopold Hirsch Coll.)*

60. *Walnut Chair, plain splat and turned stretchers; narrow cabriole legs end in club feet. c. 1710. (The late Mr H. Avray Tipping.)*
61. *Walnut Chair, enriched with marquetry; splat vase-shaped, turned uprights above sunk panels. c. 1710. (Donaldson Coll.)*
62. *Chair, veneered with burr walnut; cabriole legs, claw-and-ball feet; knees and seat-rail carved with shell. c. 1715. (Formerly at Hornby Castle, Yorks.)*

63. Walnut Chair, one of set; splat inlaid with design of arabesques and profile heads; curved central stretcher. c. 1710. (Mr Ralph Edwards.) 64. Walnut Chair, splat inlaid with arms of Skipwith impaling Dashwood; 'broken' cabriole legs hipped on seat-rail and inlaid. c. 1710. (Formerly at Honington Hall, Warwicks.) 65. Armchair, veneered with burr walnut; splat and uprights carved with paterae and acanthus. c. 1720. (Percival Griffiths Coll.)

chairs, 6 back stools carved and gilt, covered with rich brocade' which were in the Withdrawing Room when an inventory was taken in 1679.

In the chair (Fig. 46) the high back and the boldly designed open-work scrolls point to a date late in Charles II's reign. This example is upholstered with cut Genoa velvet of c. 1700. Fig. 47 shows one of an elaborate gilt suite in the Venetian Room at Knole. As the bed has the Royal arms and cipher of James II, it dates between 1685 and 1688. This set can also be assigned to Thomas Roberts, and closely resembles Fig. 49. The stretchers are almost identical, but here the front legs consist of draped male figures on scrolled acanthus feet.

In contrast to these highly ornate specimens is a walnut chair with scrolled legs and arm supports (Fig. 56), the flat looped stretchers resembling those of the gilt 'easy chair' (Fig. 52). The back and seat are covered with floral Turkey work (*q.v.*), this material being used early in the century on farthingale chairs (*see* Fig. 24).

A restored armchair (Fig. 53) shows a fanciful and highly effective treatment of the mushroom cappings to the legs. It is covered with original faded green velvet and festooned with a tasselled fringe. The velvet coverings are removable, the chair itself being covered in cream taffeta silk, a system reversing that of later times when furniture was upholstered in velvet or silk with loose covers generally of cheaper materials (*see* UPHOLSTERY). The legs and arm supports are carved into an open-work looped cup. A few stools and chairs of similar character are in existence, probably from the same unidentified hand. There are many entries in the royal tradesmen's accounts and the Treasury warrants at this period for the outer coverings which were provided to protect the costly upholstery of chairs. In Fig. 55 French influence is perceptible, notably in the back framed in enriched mouldings and the pierced cresting projecting in volutes, from which fall long pendants of husks. The sharply tapered arm supports are fluted and carved with a bold nulling while the original upholstery enhances the interest of this remarkable chair. It is probably the work of Thomas Roberts. This inference is supported by detailed descriptions of his work in the Lord Chamberlain's Accounts, among the items in 1697 being 'ffour large handsome chaires of state the back made spreading and the elboes to turne on the corner'. These accounts and other bills of the Late Stuart period afford some evidence of specialisation among makers of furniture. Chairs appear to have represented a considerable proportion of Roberts's total output, and early in George I's reign he is described as 'Chairmaker to His Majesty'.

In tall upholstered chairs without arms in the early years of William III the back is sometimes shaped at the top. The seats are supported at the front on fluted pillar legs with 'mushroom' cappings sometimes carved with gadroons. A pair of beech chairs (Fig. 58) have the ornate and picturesque character of gilt furniture made shortly before Anne's accession. They are covered with the original crimson velvet, the two rows of tufted fringe being secured by small buttons edged with silver wire. The treatment of the gesso recalls the 'cut-card' ornament of contemporary plate, while the rake of the back legs gives a pronounced sense of style.

66. Chair veneered with burr walnut, splat connected with uprights and carved with acanthus volutes; seat covered in needlework. c. 1720. (Percival Griffiths Coll.) 67. Walnut Chair, covered in original petit-point needlework; back scrolls over, stretchers united by turned baluster. c. 1710. (Canons Ashby, Northants.) 68. Walnut Armchair, covered with painted silk; turned and tapered front legs. c. 1720. (The late Sir George Leon, Bt.)

Soon after 1700 a new and distinctive type of walnut chair was introduced from Holland. They have curved uprights enclosing a wide shaped splat pierced and carved, and legs of cabriole form (*see* CABRIOLE) united by shaped stretchers. These legs are at first narrow at the knee and without the attached brackets which later become usual, while they end in scrolls or hoof-shaped feet. Some of the earliest specimens have ornate pierced carving, arched crestings, and recessed, scrolled front stretchers in the Marot style (cf. Figs. 42 and 59). In another variety a shoulder is formed on the uprights, which merge into the cresting and approximate a hoop shape. The splat is reduced in width, and in outline now suggests a vase, the base being for the first time connected with the seat framing. At the Rijksmuseum, Amsterdam, there are chairs closely resembling Fig. 57, while at Hampton Court Palace there is a set of six covered with needlework. This set is apparently indicated in a description of chairs supplied to the Palace by Thomas Roberts so late as 1717; they are stated to have 'India backs', presumably in reference to the pierced carving of the splats.

In Queen Anne's reign these new types became naturalised. The curved line dominates the design, while sound construction, elegance and utility are united in the best chairs. At first the uprights retain the vertical line and are of convex section, the seat rail is straight, and the narrow cabriole legs ending in club feet are united by plain turned stretchers (Fig. 60). Later the bowed shape of the uprights becomes more pronounced, the seat rail serpentine or convex, and the legs of greater width—changes accompanied by the abolition of

stretchers which were rendered superfluous (Fig. 62). Soon after 1710 the claw-and-ball, an Oriental motif of great antiquity, was adopted as a terminal for cabriole legs; though the club foot continued to be employed on many chairs throughout the first half of the 18th century. The splat follows the curve of the sitter's back rising from a moulded shoe-piece, and the normal vase or fiddle shapes are sometimes replaced by a more complex outline. The seats were either stuffed over or upholstered on a removable framework, needlework, tapestry or velvet being the usual coverings. Though it is possible to trace a broad structural evolution, a variety of types were in fashion simultaneously, while those discarded by the wealthy continued to be employed by people of smaller means. There were many variations inspired by the fancy of individual makers.

In the finest chairs of this period the splats, uprights and seat rail are veneered with figured burr walnut, while the carved ornament, consisting of shells and foliage, is sometimes applied, the junction between veneer and carving being rarely perceptible to the naked eye. A small group is enriched with marquetry, and a cartouche inlaid with the arms of the owner sometimes enlivened the splat. This treatment, together with the 'broken' cabriole leg, a variant of the ordinary form, is seen in Fig. 64. Some of these chairs were japanned, a form of decoration often mentioned in contemporary inventories and accounts. Thus, shortly before Anne's accession, Lord Ferrers's steward records the purchase of '8 very fine Japan chairs at 26s. each'. Green and gold appears to have been the favourite scheme of decoration, but other colours were also employed; a large set, exported by Giles Grendey to Spain and now in the

69. (*Left*) *Winged Armchair, upholstered in original crimson velvet trimmed with festooned and tasselled fringe; slender cabriole legs of walnut. c. 1710. (Col N. R. Colville.)*

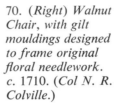

70. (*Right*) *Walnut Chair, with gilt mouldings designed to frame original floral needlework. c. 1710. (Col N. R. Colville.)*

Metropolitan Museum, New York, is japanned sealing-wax red with the detail in gold and silver. There was also a considerable importation from trading-stations in China of chairs made from European models and decorated with lacquer.

The highly enriched specimens of the curvilinear type probably were not made before 1720 and represent the initial phase of Georgian design. By that date the vase-shaped splat was sometimes ornamented with acanthus-carved volutes, elaborately shaped, and united to the uprights by short strappings (Fig. 66). The seats become wider, the rails being decorated with shells, or shaped in apron form with repetitive curves; while there is a noticeable increase in weight and solidity. In armchairs of the period, the arm supports no longer rise immediately above the front legs in the traditional manner, but are set back on the seat rail. The arms are bowed and 'dished' on their upper surfaces, scrolling over on the supports, or in still later specimens projecting beyond them and finishing in volutes or eagles' heads, introduced from France at this time. In Fig. 80 the arms and their supports are of original design with an incurving eagle's head at the junction.

Many upholstered chairs of Queen Anne's reign have tall backs shaped at the top, like their late seventeenth century predecessors. In the pattern of the legs they follow the veneered walnut chairs of this time. The finest specimens were covered with velvet, needlework, damask or tapestry. Less expensive materials were also used. At Dyrham Park in 1710, ten elbow chairs in the Gilt Leather Parlour were covered with 'Strip'd plush'; while in an ante-room another set had red serge upholstery with gold fringes. 'Russia', red Morocco and black leather were already in use, probably for sets made for dining-rooms, early in the century.

Fig. 70 was clearly designed to set off the embroidery. The framework is relieved by gilt mouldings, and cut back to take the broad scroll borders in blue and white, which enclose

bouquets of flowers. In Fig. 67 the flat side stretchers, united by a turned baluster, recall the style of c. 1690 and point to a country origin. An early specimen of a winged chair with cabriole legs (Fig. 69), one of a pair formerly at Hornby Castle, is covered in the original crimson velvet festooned with two rows of tasselled fringe, a style of upholstery now becoming obsolete. At this period, winged armchairs (commonly called 'easie chairs' in the royal accounts and other contemporary records) tend towards uniformity of design, the wings being prolonged in padded arm-rests with an outward scroll (Fig. 71).

A few years later the height of the back in upholstered chairs was considerably reduced, while the cabriole legs lost their attenuated appearance. There are, however, numerous exceptions, especially among provincial furniture, which often preserved traditional forms, and is, therefore, difficult to date with accuracy. Mahogany was first extensively employed for chairs c. 1725; before which time it was used very sparingly. As the fashionable material it gradually displaced walnut, though fine examples made of that wood are found dating from the mid-18th century. The earliest mahogany chairs include some interesting variations from the prevailing style. In Fig. 74 the shape of the back and seat is exceptional.

Many mahogany chairs of George I's reign are scarcely distinguishable in design from the 'Queen Anne' models, but in the new material, often used with remarkable prodigality, surfaces were not veneered. Though in much of the furniture made c. 1720-5 the tendency towards more elaborate ornament can be detected, in some examples the feeling for dignified simplicity recalls the outgoing style. This influence is noticeable in the walnut example, Fig. 72, in which the legs are of a rare form and finish in hoof feet, gilding being introduced on the edges and carving. In Fig. 77 the carving is far more elaborate: the heads are realistically modelled and the

71. (*Left*) *Winged Armchair, upholstered in needlework; back lets down on ratchet; cabriole walnut legs with shell ornament on knees. c. 1720. (Donaldson Coll.*)

72. (*Right*) *Walnut Chair with gilt enrichments; covered in green velvet. c. 1715. (Houghton Hall, Norfolk.*)

cabriole legs finish in scaled feet. French influence is strongly marked in Fig. 76. Here the walnut is overlaid with the gilt gesso decoration now becoming fashionable, while the richly carved legs rest on dolphin heads, an ornament revived about the mid-century. The central decoration of the seat-rail and 'hipping' of the shoulders are characteristic features in some fine upholstered chairs of this time. By a comparison of such details it is occasionally possible to recognise the work of an unknown craftsman.

There is abundant evidence that much of the furniture in fashionable houses at this period was made of walnut, despite the largely increased use of mahogany. When the contents of Sir

73. *Chair japanned green with gold and black detail; front legs of 'broken' cabriole form. c. 1715. (Erthig Park, Denbigh.).*
74. *Mahogany Chair, covered in needlework; top shaped, seat circular, and carved enrichments gilt. c. 1720. (Donaldson Coll.)*
75. *Chair, beechwood with gesso ornament; covered with Italian cut velvet. Made for Sir William Humphreys, Lord Mayor of London (1714-15). (V. & A. Mus.)*

76. Walnut gilt upholstered Armchair, scaled legs, finishing in dolphins' heads; upholstery modern. c. 1725. (Donaldson Coll.)

William Stanhope's house in Albemarle Street, St James's, were sold in 1733, the bedrooms contained a large number of luxuriously upholstered chairs, some of the sets having settees to match. In the 'Blue Mohair Bed Chamber' there were two settees and 'six walnut-tree chairs with blue mohair seats, and

an arm-chair ditto'; while the fashionable gesso decoration was represented in the principal drawing-room by a set of ten chairs 'the backs and seats covered with crimson velvet, the frames carv'd and gilt'.

A tendency towards specialisation may be observed in some of the chairs produced at this period. The 'writing chairs' shown in Figs. 81 and 99 represent distinct types produced early in the 18th century; though the purpose for which they were intended is not clearly established. The armchair which has three legs in front and one at the back is of remarkable quality and the figured veneers are of a beautiful golden tone.

Between 1720 and 1735 furniture decorated with the lion mask represented the latest development of fashionable design, and during these years the head, legs, and hair of the animal constituted the most important ornamental features on chairs and other furniture. The broad mask almost covers the shoulders, which finish off under the seat-rail in wide brackets, acanthus foliage travels down the leg, while the undersurface is realistically carved to represent the animal's hock with a feathering of hair. A set of single chairs from the Treasury (Fig. 82), covered in green morocco leather, shows the difficulty of dating such specimens on the evidence of style. They formed part of the original furnishings of the 'New Treasury Offices,' for which the bill was passed for payment in Dec., 1739 (Calendar of Treasury Books, Vol. IV, No. 206).

In a splendid armchair (Fig. 84), the colour of bronze, the arms finish in lion heads, the shaggy manes, carved with extraordinary realism, extending down the curved supports. Fig. 87 shows one of the chairs of apparently excessive width, made to accommodate the enormous hoop-skirts of this period, the rake of the arm supports also contributing to that purpose. A noticeable feature is the apron uniting the legs, which is finely carved with foliage on a trellised ground, a motive apparently favoured by Giles Grendey (*q.v.*),

77. (Left) Walnut Armchair, covered in velvet; arms terminate in eagles' heads, cabriole legs scaled. c. 1735. (V. & A. Mus.)

78. (Right) Mahogany Chair, one of set covered in petit-point needlework; cabriole legs finely carved with lions' masks; brackets below seat-rail. c. 1725-30. (Formerly at Copped Hall, Essex.)

79. (*Left*) *Walnut Chair, covered in needlework; seat-rail centres in shell, cabriole legs carved with honeysuckle. c. 1720. (Macquoid Coll.)*

80. (*Right*) *Arm-chair, veneered with figured walnut; scrolled arms finishing in eagles' heads on curved supports. c. 1720. (Sir John Ramsden Coll.)*

who was also probably responsible for the fine parcel-gilt mahogany arm-chair (Fig. 86) from Longford, part of a set obtained for that house by the first Lord Folkestone. This maker's label has been found attached to other chairs in a similar style, and in 1739 the Longford accounts record a payment of £68 to 'Greenday, chairmaker'. In this remarkable set the pierced guilloche moulding is *appliqué* over the green Italian velvet employed to cover the back and seat. On the rounded corners of the top rail, the acanthus foliage ends in recurving

eagles' heads carved with great virtuosity, while the lions' masks at the extremities of the padded arms are forcibly modelled. A female mask of the classical type is found in Fig. 85 in conjunction with lion-headed arms, the veil forming a pendant in place of the usual husks and acanthus. These lion-headed chairs were made both in walnut and mahogany.

An early example of a chair entirely decorated with gilt gesso (Fig. 75) was made for Sir William Humphreys, Lord Mayor of London, and can be dated 1717 when the arms, carved on

81. (*Left*) '*Writing Chair*', *veneered with burr walnut; arms end in eagles' heads with open beaks. c. 1720. (Col N. R. Colville.)*

82. (*Right*) *Mahogany Chair, one of set covered with green morocco leather; all four legs carved with lion masks. c. 1739. (Treasury, Whitehall.)*

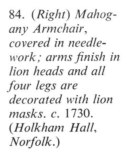

83. (*Left*) Mahogany Chair, spla' carved with acanthus volutes; wide cabriole legs decorated with lion masks; seat covered in needlework. c. 1730. (*Percival Griffiths Coll.*)

84. (*Right*) Mahogany Armchair, covered in needlework; arms finish in lion heads and all four legs are decorated with lion masks. c. 1730. (*Holkham Hall, Norfolk.*)

the cresting, were granted. In Fig. 88, a fine gilt armchair, an eagle motive is adopted throughout and, indeed, is as characteristic of the period as lion decoration. The arm headings are carved with great force, the massive supports being covered with the neck feathers of the bird; in the legs, also imitative of the eagle, the unfeathered portions are realistically modelled. Even in the needlework eagles' heads are introduced. In Fig. 90, a magnificent variant of the customary type, the conventional treatment of the lion-headed arms and fur-clad legs is particularly masterly.

Among the gilt chairs of this period, none are more distinctive than those designed by the fashionable architect William Kent. They are inspired by Venetian models in the florid baroque style, with which he had become familiar during his long stay in Italy from c. 1710 to 1719. But they are no mere transcripts, the originals being freely adapted to accord with the Palladian architectural setting for which Kent's chairs were destined. They are marked by peculiarities of proportion, and in the ornament motives drawn from a variety of sources are audaciously blended. A set of twelve armchairs (Fig. 89) in

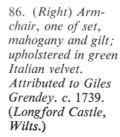

85. (*Left*) Mahogany Armchair, covered in needlework; arms terminating in lions' heads; cabriole legs carved on knees with female masks. c. 1730. (*The Duke of Buccleuch.*)

86. (*Right*) Armchair, one of set, mahogany and gilt; upholstered in green Italian velvet. Attributed to Giles Grendey. c. 1739. (*Longford Castle, Wilts.*)

87. *Mahogany Armchair, covered in needlework; carved with lion masks, paw feet and foliage on trellised ground Attributed to Giles Grendey. c. 1740. (Thursby Pelham Coll.)*

88. *Armchair, mahogany gilt; carved with eagle motif on leg and arms; eagles' heads introduced in pattern of original needlework. c. 1725. (Arundel Castle, Sussex.)*

89. *Mahogany Armchair, carved and gilt, one of set; covered in cut velvet, legs headed by female masks. c. 1730. (Houghton Hall, Norfolk.)*

90. *Mahogany Armchair, gilt and covered in original needlework; arms terminate in lions' heads; tufted legs realistically modelled. c. 1730. (Arundel Castle, Sussex.)*

91. *Mahogany Armchair, carved and gilt, covered in Italian cut velvet; 'broken' cabriole legs headed by Indian masks. c. 1730. (Houghton Hall, Norfolk.)*

92. *Mahogany Armchair, carved and gilt, covered in green velvet trimmed with silver galon; seat-rail centres in satyr mask. c. 1730. (Houghton Hall, Norfolk.)*

93. *Gilt Armchair of X form, arms lion-headed, cresting carved with acanthus; designed by William Kent. c. 1730. (Formerly at Devonshire House.)*

94. *Gilt Armchair, covered with Italian cut velvet, one of set made by James Miller in earlier style. c. 1760. (Holkham Hall, Norfolk.)*

95. (Left) Mahogany Chair, one of set; cabriole legs carved with shells. c. 1735. (Ammerdown House, Som.)

96. (Right) Chair, decorated with gilt gesso; front legs carved with lion masks; one of set. c. 1735. (Formerly at Stowe, Bucks.)

the Saloon at Houghton Hall, Norfolk, represent one of his most successful attempts to naturalise Italian principles of design. They are of mahogany, part gilt, covered with a Spitalfields velvet matching that on the walls. The back is low and surmounted by an elaborate cresting; while beneath the seat-rail the boldly carved scrolls centre in a double shell, one of Kent's favourite decorative motifs. Another fine set of twelve chairs, four with arms (Fig. 91), in the same house may also be assigned to him. The shape of the back and the broken

cabriole of the legs suggest 1715 rather than 1730 as the date, but Kent's taste was eclectic, and he frequently looked a little backward in borrowing his ideas. The baluster arms have scale decoration, and, in place of a female head, the legs shoulder in the mask of an Indian, the feathered head-dress being hipped above the seat-rail. In the winged armchair (Fig. 92) the undulating apron carved in low relief is decorated with acanthus scrolls and centres in a satyr's mask, the legs being lion-headed.

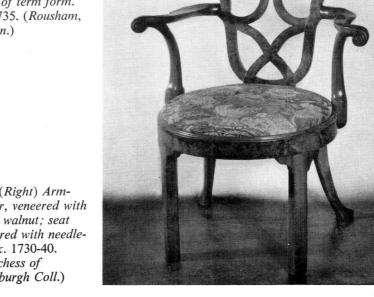

97. (Left) Mahogany Armchair, parcel gilt; seat-rail carved with wave pattern and legs of term form. c. 1735. (Rousham, Oxon.)

98. (Right) Armchair, veneered with burr walnut; seat covered with needlework. 1730-40. (Duchess of Roxburgh Coll.)

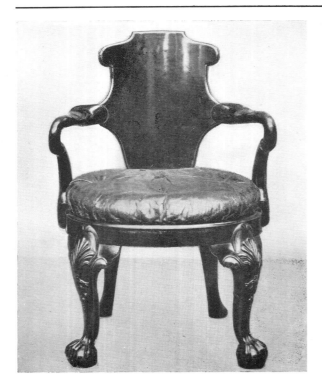

99. (*Left*) *Walnut 'Writing Chair' with concave solid back: legs covered with honeysuckle. c. 1720. (Boyton House, Wilts.)*

100. (*Right*) *Walnut 'Writing Chair', fluted uprights and strapwork splats; arms and cabriole legs eagle-headed. c. 1740. (Henry Hirsch Coll.)*

Fig. 93 shows one of a pair of gilt armchairs which were in the Saloon at Devonshire House before its demolition. The arms terminate in lions' heads, the cresting of the back being heavily scrolled acanthus. The lower portion represents a revival of the traditional X form which is also found in a few painted and mahogany chairs of this period (Fig. 101). In these examples Venetian influence is apparent; but the inspiration is imperfectly assimilated, and they afford some justification for Horace Walpole's stricture that the architect's hand was 'immeasurably ponderous'.

A fine set at Holkham (Fig. 94), probably designed by Kent, were carved by James Miller (*q.v.*) and covered with Genoa velvet supplied by the firm of Goodison (*q.v.*). Chairs enriched with gesso decoration, in which much of the more delicate ornament is carved in the preparation, are rare, and the specimen illustrated (Fig. 96) is one of a large set of seat furniture formerly at Stowe. Here the shells and strapwork in low relief on a pounced ground are in effective contrast to the bold lion masks and scroll foliage of the lower portion. The armchair (Fig. 97) has taper

101. (*Left*) *Mahogany Armchair, matching a settee; supports of X form. c. 1755. (Formerly at Langley Park, Norfolk.)*

102. (*Right*) *Mahogany Armchair, upholstered in Soho tapestry; early example of 'French' type. c. 1740. (Harewood House, Yorks.)*

103. (*Left*) *Mahogany Armchair; cabriole legs, united to seat-rail by brackets carved with acanthus, end in scrolled feet. c. 1740. (Chatsworth, Derbys.)*

104. (*Right*) *Mahogany Chair, with scrolled and pierced splat headed by shell motif; cabriole legs carved with foliage. c. 1740.*

legs, a rare form at this date, and is possibly by William Hallett (*q.v.*).

About 1745 the influence of the French *rocaille* style becomes increasingly apparent in the design of English chairs and led to the creation of a lighter and more fanciful fashion in which sinuous lines, subtle curves, and delicate carving in low relief usurped the place of baroque solidity. A noticeable change occurs in the treatment of the back. The solid splat is opened out into simple tracery, strapwork, or a symmetrical arrange-

ment of scrolls. The vase-like shape was still favoured, though sometimes the design occupies the whole area of the back (Fig. 107). In the majority of examples, the hoop shape was abandoned for the uprights and their lines became almost vertical, tapering with an outward curve to meet the top rail. Baroque ornament was gradually superseded by the naturalistic motives of the rococo style, never exploited in an extreme degree on chairs. Fig. 95 is an interesting example of the transitional phase and is notable for its fine proportions; the

105. *Mahogany Chair, with open-work vase-shaped splat; legs carved with cabochon ornament. c. 1750. (Penshurst Place, Kent.)*
106. *Mahogany 'Ribband-Back' Chair, one of set; scrolls and interlaced ribbons form splat. c. 1755. (Nostell Priory, Yorks.)*
107. *Walnut Chair, with gilt enrichments; open-work back in form of shell. c. 1750. (Stourhead, Wilts.)*

decoration of the cabriole legs is traditional, but the back is of the new rectangular form, with a pierced splat and a top rail finishing in bold volutes. One of a set of walnut armchairs (Fig. 98) has straight front legs in conjunction with a rounded seat. The back with its ingenious arrangement of interlaced curves is reminiscent of the earlier hoop shape; but this example probably dates from c. 1740.

An armchair (Fig. 101), one of a set matching a settee, shows a reversion to the X-shaped underframing introduced in the Middle Ages. In the walnut armchair (Fig. 109), ornate carving, which recalls the school of Kent, is combined with marked originality of design, notable peculiarities being the scaled fan-shaped cresting, the contrasted curves of the uprights, and the legs, which are hipped on the seat-rail and finish in claw-and-ball. At this stage in the evolution a chronological sequence again cannot be established exactly, the solidity of the baroque phase persisting in some models while the traditional structural forms are invaded by rococo detail. The idiosyncrasies of individual designers and makers must be taken into account in attempting to trace an evolution. The patterns, for instance, in Manwaring's *Chairmakers' Guide* (1766) suggest a predilection for massive forms and large-scale carving at a time when delicate ornament was in vogue and the framework of fashionable chairs had become noticeably lighter.

A walnut 'writing chair' (Fig. 100) conforms to a type made earlier in the century, but the pierced strap-work splats indicate a date c. 1740. The arms end in eagle-headed volutes, and the cabriole legs, of which eagle heads form the bracket, in claw-and-ball feet, the centre leg having ivory claws. This particular variety with three legs in front is not found described in bills and inventories, and there is no conclusive evidence that they were made specially for writing.

Before the publication of Chippendale's *Director* in 1754 chair-makers in England had been mainly dependent on their own ideas, carrying on business without the aid of engraved designs: Darly's *New Book of Chinese, Gothic and Modern Chairs* (1752), a mere pamphlet, is the only work of earlier date which aimed at providing assistance to the trade. The *Director* for the first time supplied a large variety of patterns which exercised a powerful influence on contemporary designs and aroused a spirit of emulation. In subsequent trade catalogues, such as Ince and Mayhew's *Universal System of Household Furniture* (1759-63) and the publications by the Society of Upholsterers and Cabinet-makers, chairs occupy a prominent place; while Manwaring's *Chairmakers' Guide* is an instance of the tendency towards specialisation.

Though some of the plates in the *Director* are free adaptations of contemporary French chairs, the divided aims of the period and its craving for novelty are expressed by excursions into the Chinese and Gothic styles; of which Darly's book may be taken to mark the inception. The former amounts to a distinct decorative convention, but Chippendale's interpretation of the 'Gothic taste' in chairs is limited to details of cusping and tracery. He aimed at presenting the latest fashion, and it is noticeable that the claw-and-ball foot, though used on many fine walnut and mahogany chairs of this time, is not represented in the *Director* save for one plate of 'hall chairs' in the third edition (1762). In its place Chippendale substituted a scrolled foot in conjunction with the cabriole leg, a motive borrowed

108. *Mahogany Chair; carved and parcel gilt, cabriole legs end in volutes. c. 1757. (Holkham Hall, Norfolk.)* 109. *Walnut Armchair, with gilt enrichments, scaled cresting, scrolled uprights; arm supports carved with foliage. c. 1750. (Kunstindustrimuseet, Oslo.)* 110. *Mahogany Armchair, cresting carved with crowned head of Neptune, legs with dolphins. c. 1755. (Trinity House. London.)*

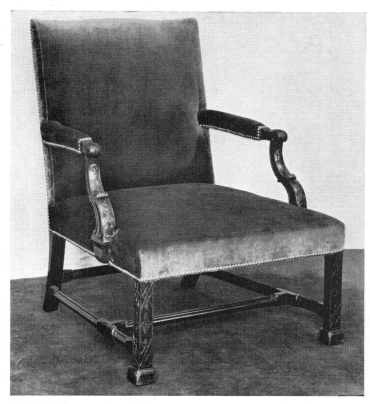

111. *Mahogany Armchair; arm supports carved with rococo ornament; fluted stretchers. Attributed to John Bradburn. c. 1760. (Mr. Ralph Edwards.)*

112. *Mahogany Armchair; in carving, dolphin motif combined with fine acanthus foliage and rococo ornament. c. 1755. (Lady Lever Art Gallery.)*

from French furniture. This new form of terminal was also adopted by Ince and Mayhew, a few years later, in their *Universal System*. For chairs in the Chinese and Gothic styles square straight legs with small block feet were favoured, while a tapered leg with a pierced and moulded foot was sometimes employed.

The progress towards lighter and more elegant design based on rhythmical structural lines is clearly seen in the upholstered chairs made between 1740 and 1765. An armchair of uncommon proportions (Fig. 102) has the high back and wide seat reminiscent of an earlier period. The padded arms are set well back on the seat-rail, doubtless to accommodate a lady's skirt, hoops having at this time attained their widest dimensions. In one of a set of 24 armchairs and 6 settees (Fig. 103) the width of the acanthus brackets and the short, bold cabriole indicate a date c. 1740. It is a late example of the baroque style. Though the chair has been recovered, the original system of upholstery has been preserved, the velvet being fastened to the frame by gilt-headed nails between bands of carved moulding. A pronounced change of style is seen in Fig. 135, where the legs and seat-rail are carved with rococo ornament. This example closely resembles Chippendale's designs for 'French' armchairs, and has the characteristic curved arms and scrolled feet. For the covering, tapestry or needlework is recommended in the *Director*, and here the embroidery is of remarkable quality. In the descriptive notes the measurements given for this kind of chair are '2 ft. 3 ins. in front; 1 ft. 11 ins. behind, and 1 ft. 10 ins. from front to back'.

After visiting Hardwick in 1757 Miss Caroline Girle (later

Mrs Lybbe Powys) writes 'if any one was to compare three or four hundred years hence a chair from the drawing-room of Queen Elizabeth's days and the light French ones of George II, it would never be possible to suppose them to belong to the same race of people, as the one is altogether gigantic, and the other quite liliputian'. By this date there was a pronounced reaction from the ponderous, monumental character of the upholstered chairs for drawing-rooms and saloons during the baroque phase. That lightness of effect was deliberately aimed at in the French type is indicated by Chippendale's observation that 'some of them are intended to be open below (*i.e.* the upholstered back raised on short supports above the seat), which makes them very light, without having a bad effect'. The armchair, Fig. 136, is taken with only trifling alterations from Plate XXII (right) in the third edition of the *Director* (1762), the skilfully contrasted scrolls enriched with rococo foliage representing a highly successful essay in curvilinear design. Fig. 137 represents one of a large set, also dating from c. 1765. The shape of this winged armchair is derived from the contemporary French *bergère*.

Although masks and animal terminals had been superseded, the dolphin, an early Georgian decorative motive, was revived on a few of the finest upholstered chairs in the rococo style. It figures in the *Director* and among the designs of Thomas Johnson (*q.v.*). In Fig. 112, one of a set, the light framework of the back and seat is designed to enclose needlework or tapestry. The legs and arms are dolphin-headed, the scaling on the latter merging into florid and delicate sprays of acanthus which centre on the seat-rail in cabochon ornament, a favourite rococo

113. (Left) Design for a Chair, from Chippendale's Director (1st ed., 1754), Plate XII.

114. (Right) Mahogany Armchair; splat corresponds with design in Chippendale's Director. c. 1755. (V. & A. Mus.)

detail. About this date straight legs came into use and stretchers were again reinstated on dining-room chairs after a lapse of about fifty years.

Mahogany and walnut chairs with carved backs at this period show an extraordinary variety of design, partly explained by the diffusion of engraved patterns over a wide area. About 1750 the splat, usually filled with symmetrical scroll-work, becomes noticeably more delicate, 'the effect of lightness being obtained largely by cutting back the return faces of each member so that they are narrower at the back'. In this process strength was rarely sacrificed to appearance. Fig. 105 shows an early example of a finely cut splat, retaining the traditional vase shape. The legs finish in flattened claw-and-ball feet, but they are carved on the knee with cabochon ornament surrounded by foliage. Here the seat-rail is square, but in Fig. 115 it is of apron form, merging into the legs with graceful curves. The delicate ornament is admirably distributed, and the proportions are remarkably fine. Such characteristics are confined to chairs by the fashionable metropolitan makers established in the neighbourhood of St Martin's Lane; while in those produced for the middle classes in the City and provinces the proportions are often clumsy and the detail is coarsely rendered, a profusion of decoration obscuring the structural lines.

Nostell Priory, Harewood and a few other houses contain chairs proved by invoices to have been made by Chippendale's firm. Some chairs of high quality, for which bills are lacking, correspond more or less closely with designs in the *Director*, thus affording evidence of its author's responsibility; though his designs were freely plagiarised and adapted by others. The splat of Fig. 114 has its counterpart on Plate XII of the first edition, and this chair is again remarkable for fine proportions and crisply cut carving. One of a set at Nostell Priory (Fig. 106) is an example of the 'ribband-back' chairs illustrated in the

Director. Here C-scrolls form the top rail and the framework of the splat, in which the arrangement of the ribbons is remarkably graceful. It may be noticed that the claw-and-ball (not shown in the *Director*) is retained. Chippendale observes that such chairs 'will have a fine effect' if covered in red morocco leather.

A chair (Fig. 119) closely resembles a design in the third edition of the *Director*, and is among the finest of Chippendale's designs in the full rococo style. The uprights merge with bold curves into the 'Cupid's bow' cresting, while Gothic motives are discernible in the tracery of the splat. The carving of the gracefully scrolled legs united by a shallow apron is of the highest quality. In Fig. 118 the fan-shaped filling of the back reverses the motives seen in Fig. 107. This armchair probably represents an eclectic design from hints afforded by the *Director*. A plate in that work dated 1753 shows similar tracery in the back, and the tapering fluted leg is illustrated by Chippendale. The design of the front legs in Fig. 120 may also be traced to the *Director* (3rd ed. Pl. XXV) where it is given as an alternative to 'Gothick Chairs'. The back is filled with palm foliage merging into scrolls to form the cresting.

Relatively few chairs of the mid-18th century can be traced to any pattern book, and the endless variations from the published designs are evidence of the makers' fertility of invention. Fig. 116 is reminiscent of *Director* types, the splat showing a characteristic rendering of Gothic cusping. In this restrained form it provides an attractive substitute for the pseudo-Oriental ornament so freely employed at this time; but by Horace Walpole, Bentley and other advocates of the style a far more thorough exploitation of Gothic detail was demanded (Fig. 125). For such chairs Walpole appears to have relied on the cabinet-maker William Hallet (*q.v.*), whose bill in 1755 includes an item of £30 for '8 black gothic chairs' supplied to Strawberry Hill. Fig. 121 suggests the style of Robert Man-

115. *Mahogany Chair, with carved uprights and pierced splat; legs and apron finely carved with acanthus. c. 1750. (Nostell Priory, Yorks.)* 116. *Mahogany Chair, with splat perforated in Gothic tracery; straight legs concave and filleted. c. 1755. (Macquoid Coll.)* 117. *Mahogany Chair, back of scrolled outline, motif repeated in design of front legs. c. 1760. (Leopold Hirsch Coll.)*

waring, whose trade catalogues afford many instances of this thick-set type. He was a designer of originality with an eccentric sense of line, of which this example is representative. Another unusual chair (Fig. 123), with rushes interlaced in the back, is also probably by Manwaring, or by a maker familiar with the *Chairmakers' Guide*; while Fig. 122 corresponds with

a design (Pl. IX) in Ince and Mayhew's *Universal System*, and is stamped 'I.M.' below the seat-rail, initials also found on a few other contemporary chairs.

The Chinese taste (*q.v.*) was more consistently exploited than the Gothic for chairs in the mid-18th century, and a great variety of designs in this style are given in the works of Darly,

118. (*Left*) Mahogany Armchair, back filled with fan-shaped design; arms and front taper legs fluted. c. 1760. (*Percival Griffiths Coll.*)

119. (*Right*) Mahogany Chair, with bow-shaped top rail; splat corresponds with design, Plate XIV, in Director (3rd ed.). c. 1762. (*Arundel Castle, Sussex.*)

120. *Mahogany Chair, pillar legs resemble those in designs for 'Gothic chairs' in* Director *(3rd ed.), Plate XXV. c. 1765. (Althorp. Northants.)* 121. *Mahogany Chair, back formed of interlaced loopings; rococo foliage. Style of Robert Manwaring. c. 1760-5. (V. & A. Mus.)* 122. *Mahogany Armchair; splat corresponds with a design in Ince and Mayhew's* Universal System, *1759-63, (Messrs. Hotspur Ltd.).*

Chippendale and Halfpenny. Sir William Chambers, in *Designs of Chinese Buildings* (1757), reproduced two drawings from chairs used in China, and noted that rosewood, ebony and bamboo were the chief woods employed in their manufacture. These authoritative patterns had little influence upon a convention already established, and the majority of chairs in the Anglo-Chinese style were made of mahogany. The backs were filled with lattice-work or 'Chinese railing', while the arms, which inclined outwards, were treated in the same manner. The legs were generally square in section, finishing in small blocks. They were solid, hollowed out with a turned shaft set in the angle, or built up in sections; in a few specimens they are rounded in imitation of bamboo (Fig. 131). In fine examples the top rail rises to a pagoda cresting, a motive also introduced in the ingeniously designed lattice-work of the back. A Chinese fret was the favourite enrichment for the uprights and legs, the latter being united to the seat-rail by pierced brackets. Chippendale considered such chairs suitable for a bedroom in the Chinese style, particularly if the room was hung with India paper. The pierced trellis-work in the back in Fig. 128 is echoed in the incised decoration within sunk panels on legs and uprights, while the blossoms carved on the top rail are an attractive variant of the favourite pagoda motif.

Sometimes these chairs were japanned black on the surface, the returns being painted in red or gold to enhance the pseudo-oriental appearance, while a few specimens are found with the bars and frame decorated with parquetry of dark and light woods (Fig. 133). In the *Director* Chippendale observes that they 'have commonly cane bottoms with loose cushions, but if required, they have stuffed seats and brass nails'; a printed or woven oriental silk representing flowers, small birds and

insects was also employed. Chinese and rococo ornament are often combined with charming effect, the oriental motives being usually confined to the legs and pierced stretchers (Fig. 130). The ladder back, of which an early example has been illustrated (Fig. 37), was again revived c. 1750, the model being produced in large numbers with trifling modifications, though it does not figure in pattern books of the time (Fig. 144).

In view of the many luxurious models available, notably those in the 'French taste', it is surprising to find Madame de Boçage writing in 1750 of contemporary London houses, 'there are scarcely any armchairs in their apartments they are satisfied with common ones'.

Early in George III's reign the neo-classical style began to affect the design and decoration of fashionable chairs. No trace of this new influence can be detected in the patterns illustrated in the third edition of the *Director* (1762), and the transformation proceeded slowly, classical motives in the decoration preceding structural change. A gilt armchair (Fig. 138) made from Adam's design for Sir Lawrence Dundas in 1764 is an interesting example of the transitional phase, retaining the curvilinear form of Chippendale's 'French' type in association with finely carved classic detail. After c. 1770, most of Adam's ceremonial chairs for drawing-rooms and saloons closely correspond with contemporary French models. They were made of beech or some other soft wood, with the framework painted in light colours or entirely gilt. The oval backs and the seats were padded and covered with damask or tapestry, such fabrics replacing the elaborate needlework of earlier times. The frames of these drawing-room chairs are moulded and the legs, turned and fluted, finish in small blocks or plinth-shaped feet.

123. *Walnut Chair, back carved with interlaced rushes and legs with diaper pattern. Style of Robert Manwaring. c. 1760. (Stephen Winkworth Coll.)* 124. *Armchair, of painted wood with back and legs formed of loopings; seat 'dished'. c. 1765. (Edward Hudson Coll.)* 125. *Armchair, in Gothic style, one of set; painted black and gold. c. 1765. (Hon. Sherman Stonor.)*

Curved supports spring from cappings at the corners of the seat to meet the bowed arms, which are padded on their upper surfaces. In some early specimens the arm supports are straight and, instead of finishing above the legs, they are tenoned into the side rails of the seat as in the rococo phase of design.

An armchair (Fig. 139), in the neo-classic style, shows a more original treatment. It has an arched top rail with small urn finials at the corners, the framework being delicately carved with foliate scrolls. The ordinary gilt drawing-room chairs of this period so closely resemble French models that it is often difficult to determine the nationality; but the scale of the carving is generally larger on the English examples.

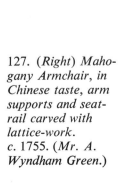

126. (*Left*) *Mahogany Armchair, legs finish in dolphin heads. c. 1755. (Leopold Hirsch Coll.)*

127. (*Right*) *Mahogany Armchair, in Chinese taste, arm supports and seat-rail carved with lattice-work. c. 1755. (Mr. A. Wyndham Green.)*

128. *Mahogany Chair, one of set; back filled with 'Chinese railing'. c. 1760. (The late Lt-Col. S. Goldschmidt.)* 129. *Mahogany Chair, filling of back connected to uprights by rosettes; seat-rail filled with pierced lattice-work. c. 1765. (Lulworth Castle, Dorset.)* 130. *Mahogany Chair, carved with foliated scrolls and lattice-work, one of set. c. 1755-60. (V. & A. Mus.)*

The concave oval back characteristic of this type is seen in the fine armchair from Osterley (Fig. 140), one of a set made from Adam's design, which has admirably modelled female sphinxes at the base of the back. The tub-shaped back of the contemporary French *bergère* was sometimes imitated, but few examples of this more luxurious type survive.

In their severe and graceful outline the mahogany chairs made under neo-classic influence afford a striking contrast to the extravagances of the rococo style. They are distinguished by a skilful use of contrasted curves, dignity of form and a sense of fitness in the choice of ornament. In early specimens the back is sometimes square with an open-work splat shaped to resemble a classical lyre (Fig. 147). This motif was employed by Adam and other designers, such as John Linnell, who

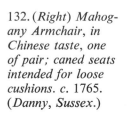

131. (*Left*) *Mahogany Armchair, in Chinese taste; back and arms filled with lattice-work, legs turned in imitation of bamboo. c. 1760. (Leopold Hirsch Coll.)*

132. (*Right*) *Mahogany Armchair, in Chinese taste, one of pair; caned seats intended for loose cushions. c. 1765. (Danny, Sussex.)*

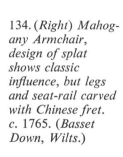

133. (*Left*) Armchair, beechwood veneered with parquetry of walnut and sycamore. c. 1760. (*V. & A. Mus.*)

134. (*Right*) Mahogany Armchair, design of splat shows classic influence, but legs and seat-rail carved with Chinese fret. c. 1765. (*Basset Down, Wilts.*)

worked under his influence. Horace Walpole, visiting Osterley in 1773, notes that 'the chairs are taken from antique lyres and make a charming harmony'. The shape of the lyre is ingeniously varied (Figs. 146 and 151), and the three sets in which it is introduced are masterpieces of craftsmanship and in a perfect state of preservation. Another armchair (Fig. 152) is from a set in a room at Osterley decorated and furnished in the Etruscan taste (*q.v.*).

As the style developed, oval, heart- and shield-shaped backs became fashionable, slender curved ribs, looped drapery or geometrical tracery occupying the main area. Cabriole legs are

replaced in most examples by those of turned or quadrilateral form, fluted and tapering to finish in small moulded feet. The arm supports, as in gilt upholstered chairs, were at first secured to the side rails of the seat; but later they spring from cappings on the front legs and sweep backwards with a sharp curve to meet the shaped arms. The decoration, rigorously subordinated to the interest of the design, consisted of orthodox classical detail; husks, honeysuckle, wheat ears, foliage and paterae, carved in low relief or inlaid, the framework being enriched with delicate mouldings or repeated ornament. Satinwood, though in general use as a veneer at this

135. (*Left*) Mahogany Armchair, of type termed 'French' in Director; covered with needlework, one of pair. c. 1760. (*Waldershare Park, Kent.*)

136. (*Right*) Mahogany 'French' Armchair, carved with rococo ornament; after design in Director (*3rd ed.*), Plate XXII. c. 1765. (*V. & A. Mus.*)

137. *Mahogany Armchair, part of set; carved enrichments gilt, design shows French influence. c. 1765. (Formerly at Hornby Castle, Yorks.)*

138. *Gilt Armchair, one of set; carved with sphinxes and shells. Designed by Robert Adam in 1764. (V. & A. Mus.)*

period, was employed very sparingly for the construction of chairs.

The design of an armchair (Fig. 154) suggests the hand of an architect with leanings to the 'Greek taste', which was in the ascendant in the later phase of the neo-classic revival. The shield-shaped back is filled with finely carved classical tripod and vase, and the finials at each corner take the form of small acroteria carved with anthemion. The top rail is mounted with a blue Wedgwood medallion.

Hepplewhite's *Guide* (1788) affords a representative selection of the types in vogue about the time of its publication. It was his aim 'to unite elegance with utility', and the designs show a skilful blending of fanciful ornament with the familiar classical motives. Though many strong and serviceable chairs were made for dining-rooms and ordinary domestic use (Fig. 145), taste was now inclining towards extreme lightness and feminine grace. The survival of so many fashionable models in a good state of preservation, despite their fragile appearance, must be attributed to the technical excellence of their construction and to a careful selection of woods.

Oval, heart- and shield-shapes are popularly associated with Hepplewhite's style, but chairs with rectilinear backs figure prominently among his designs; they are indeed eclectic rather than original, and in the first edition of the *Guide* cabriole legs of the attenuated form seen in Figs. 141, 150 are still retained for upholstered 'state chairs'. In the notes 'cabriole' does not refer to the shape of the legs, but describes chairs with 'stuffed' backs; and of these one in the newest fashion and with arms much higher than usual 'has been executed with good effect for the Prince of Wales'. Hepplewhite was possibly the

first maker to employ the familiar three feathers, popular at that time as the badge of the Prince's party, and a painted armchair (Fig. 166) closely corresponds with a design in the first edition of the *Guide*.

Hepplewhite draws attention to the scrolled 'French foot' as a desirable terminal, and also to the concave shaping of the back, 'the bars and frame sunk in a hollow, or rising in a round projection with a band or list on the inner and outer edges'. He gives the 'general dimensions' as, height 3 feet 1 inch, width 1 foot 8 inches, and depth 1 foot 5 inches, but explains they are liable to variations.

Though few contemporary chairs are obviously derived from Hepplewhite's designs, Fig. 153 shows another of these rare cases, the back, with trifling modifications, answering to a design on Plate IV of the first edition of the *Guide*. The slender tracery bars and scattered ornaments are highly characteristic. Among the patterns which are not illustrated in trade catalogues of the time, some are very representative of the style, while it still retained the dignity derived from its classical origin (*e.g.* Figs. 143, 148, 152). These chairs, reminiscent of Adam's designs, are distinguished by fine proportions and admirable craftsmanship. The original coverings are missing, Hepplewhite counselling the use of horsehair 'plain, striped, chequered etc., at pleasure', in place of needlework on chairs of this kind. That the *Guide* represented 'the prevailing mode' in chair design (as in other varieties of furniture) rather than any important innovation is shown by Figs. 158 and 159, the one inscribed below the seat-rail 'Samuel Fairhead, August 1783' (five years before the publication of the *Guide*), the other acquired between 1776 and 1781.

139. *Gilt Armchair, framework carved in neo-classic style. c. 1775. (Alnwick Castle, Northumberland.)*

140. *Armchair, carved and gilt, one of set; design by Robert Adam, dated 1777. (Osterley Park, Middx.)*

At this period there is endless variety in the treatment of the back; interlaced ovals and festoons of drapery forming the heart shape, and slender curved ribs swelling upwards with a slight entasis being among the more familiar treatments (Fig. 148). In the centre of the splat an elongated vase was often introduced, and oval paterae became an almost universal ornament. Wheat ears with rippled blades take the place of curved ribs in Fig. 149, while in a pair of armchairs (Fig. 157) the back is filled with radiating honeysuckle patterns.

In the preface to the *Guide* Hepplewhite observes that 'a new and very elegant fashion has arisen within these few years' of finishing chairs with painted or japanned decoration, 'which gives a rich and splendid appearance to the minute parts of the ornament which are generally thrown in by the painter'. Some early examples of this fashion were designed by Adam. The decoration usually consists of floral garlands, sprays, and medallions painted in natural colours or grisaille, while on less expensive chairs the framework is japanned black with gilt enrichments. The majority of these chairs were made of beech and, owing to the perishable nature of that wood and the delicacy of the ornament, they are seldom found in original condition. Fig. 166 shows a highly decorative example, part of a set including a settee, other chairs, stands and pole screens. Satinwood examples thus treated are comparatively rare, but Fig. 169 shows one from a set of 18 which are included in the bills of Seddon, Sons and Shackleton, for furniture supplied to Hauteville House, Guernsey, in 1790. They are described as 'neatly japanned, ornamented with roses on the back and peacock feather border', the cost being 79s. 6d. each.

Though winged armchairs dating from the second half of the

18th century are also rare, Hepplewhite provides a design for one, which he terms a 'Saddle Cheek or Easy Chair'. They should be covered with leather or horsehair, instead of the needlework of earlier times, 'or have a leather case to fit over the canvas stuffing, as is most usual and convenient'. In the example illustrated the legs are straight, but those of the arm-chair (Fig. 141) are of the slender cabriole form shown else-where in the *Guide*. It dates, however, from the earlier phase of the classical revival, and is of exceptional interest because when it was reupholstered the framework of the seat was found inscribed 'J. John Woodford, St Paul's Churchyard, London, April 17th, 1772'—doubtless the name of the chair-maker employed.

In gilt chairs of the ornate French type the splats are some-times found painted with figure subjects after designs by Angelica Kauffmann and other well-known decorative artists. Inexpensive painted chairs of this time were often based on the fashionable models. Hepplewhite singles out three of his 'banister-back' chairs as being particularly adapted to this treatment. He observes that it 'allows a framework less massy than is requisite for mahogany, and by assorting the prevailing colour to the furniture and light of the room, affords oppor-tunity by the variety of grounds which may be introduced to make the whole accord in harmony, with a pleasing and striking effect to the eye'. The notes state that such chairs should have linen or cotton cases over cushions to accord with the general hue. Caning had been reintroduced a few years earlier, and for chairs with caned bottoms, in mahogany or japanned, Hepplewhite recommends 'cushions of linen or leather'. Of another variety in which the top rail is formed of a

141. (*Left*) *Mahogany upholstered Armchair, made by John Woodford in 1772.*

142. (*Right*) *Mahogany Armchair, back carved with gadrooning, legs fluted and reeded, c. 1770.*

carved oblong panel or a painted medallion Hepplewhite writes that this 'more elegant kind' should have seats of red or blue morocco leather tied down with tassels of silk or thread.

The backs are square in this particular group, anticipating Sheraton, who adopted rectilinear forms in preference to the oval and heart shapes hitherto in vogue. Fertility of invention is strikingly displayed in his early designs for chairs, which are both practical and elegant. Horizontal lines are strongly emphasised, the arms are set high on the back uprights, and the supports are shaped as a concave curve, or form an extension of the turned and tapered front legs. Fig. 167 represents an accurate rendering of a design given on Plate 28 of Sheraton's *Drawing Book* (1791-4), and shows the sobriety and reticence of ornament which distinguishes so many of the carved mahogany chairs of this date. The splat is formed of a classical urn headed by ostrich plumes and flanked by fluted columns supporting an

143. *Mahogany Armchair, downward sweep of arms is unusual. c. 1780. (The Duke of Hamilton.)* 144. *Mahogany Chair, 'ladder' back; rails pierced and carved with foliage. c. 1775. (V. & A. Mus.)* 145. *Mahogany Chair, frame of back reeded and tripod splat headed by honeysuckle decoration. c. 1775.*

146. (*Left*) *Mahogany Armchair, lyre-shaped splat decorated with paterae and honeysuckle motives. Probably by John Linnell. c. 1775. (Osterley Park, Middx.)*

147. (*Right*) *Mahogany Armchair, strings of lyre splat and filling of arms, metal; covering original. c. 1775. (V. & A. Mus.)*

arch, the tapered legs being faced by pendants of husks. For the manufacture of such chairs Sheraton recommended the use of Spanish or Cuban mahogany of a clear straight grain 'which will rub bright, and keep cleaner than any Honduras wood'; yet it is explained that, if properly selected, the latter variety is permissible where lightness is desired. In Sheraton's designs for this type, sometimes made in satinwood, the top rail is often arched or ramped on each side of an oblong panel, while in the back curved bars form a splat of vase outline festooned with carved drapery. A favourite variation was a filling of latticework enclosed within bars raised above the seat (Fig. 176), a pattern which lent itself to a variety of treatment and continued to be produced in the early 19th century. The structural members are generally fluted and reeded; a narrow fillet often edges the top rail; the front legs are square sided and sharply tapered, or turned throughout their length.

148. *Mahogany Armchair, framework carved with guilloche moulding. c. 1780. (Copinger Prichard Coll.)* 149. *Mahogany Armchair, bars of back carved with wheat-ears, flowers and leaves. c. 1775. (Copinger Prichard Coll.)* 150. *Mahogany Armchair, back arcaded and carved with paterae, slender cabriole legs fluted. c. 1775. (V. & A. Mus.)*

151. (*Left*) *Arm-chair; frame veneered with rose-wood, inlaid decoration and lyre-shaped splat of satinwood. Probably by John Linnell. c. 1775. (Osterley Park, Middx.)*

152. (*Right*) *Arm-chair, of painted beechwood in Etruscan taste. Design by Robert Adam dated 1776. (Osterley Park, Middx.)*

In japanned chairs of this period the framework is decorated with delicate floral detail, while figure subjects, musical trophies or floral garlands are introduced on an entablature or an oval panel in the centre of the back, gilding being freely employed to enhance the effect. The wide demand for painted chairs receives full recognition in the *Drawing Book*. Some designs are specially indicated as 'suitable for japanning', or for finishing in white and gold; and to these are added a variety of 'new patterns of backs for painting'. The explanatory notes show that the most elaborate and fashionable models were intended for this treatment, and directions are given for 'retrenching' the designs so that they might be rendered in mahogany and made available for those to whom their excessively ornate character failed to appeal.

153. *Mahogany Chair, inlaid with boxwood paterae; splat closely resembles design in Hepplewhite's* Guide (*1st ed., Plate 4*). *c. 1788. (Fred Skull Coll.)* 154. *Armchair, one of set, mahogany decorated with paterae and foliage in holly-wood; top rail centres in Wedgwood plaque. c. 1780. (Brocklesby Park, Lincs.)* 155. *Mahogany Armchair, splat carved with drapery and ostrich feathers. c. 1780. (V. & A. Mus.)*

156. (*Left*) Mahogany Armchair, pierced splats centring in paterae, and top rail curved with wheat-ears. c. 1775. (*C. D. Rotch Coll.*)

157. (*Right*) Mahogany Armchair, one of pair; back filled with radiating design of honeysuckle; oval painted with Mitton arms. c. 1775. (*J. Thursby Pelham Coll.*)

Sheraton distinguishes between ordinary japanned chairs and the ceremonial type designed for drawing-rooms, of which the frames were usually finished in 'burnished gold' (Fig. 180). These had stuffed over round seats covered, like the backs, with printed silk, or with chintz 'which may now be had of various patterns on purpose for chair-seats, together with borders to suit them'. The effect of this style of upholstery is well suggested in a design (Fig. 172) from the *Drawing Book*,

where it is explained that 'the figures in the tablets above the front rails are on French printed silk or satin sewed on to the stuffing with borders round them. The seat and back of the same kind.'

In the last years of the 18th century the design of chairs was greatly influenced by the new and more intense archaeological revival introduced in emulation of the French *Directoire* style. At first the change was mainly confined to structural lines and

158. *Mahogany Chair. Inscribed Samuel Fairhead, August 1783. (V. & A. Mus.)* 159. *Mahogany Armchair, one of set, acquired 1776-81 by Jonathan Pytts of Kyre Park, Worcs. (V. & A. Mus.)* 160. *Mahogany Armchair, framework carved with beading and splats with paterae. c. 1780. (J. Thursby Pelham Coll.)*

161. (*Left*) *Armchair of beech, japanned black with gilt enrichments. c. 1780. (Edward Hudson Coll.)*

162. (*Right*) *Mahogany Armchair, circular back filled with radiating design of palm leaves and festoons of husks. c. 1785. (Sir Sydney Greville Coll.)*

minor detail, the results of the excavations at Pompeii and Herculaneum being closely studied in an endeavour to reproduce the forms of classical antiquity. With this end in view a pronounced scroll over was given to the back uprights, while the front legs were often shaped in bold concave or 'sabre' curves.

Thomas Hope, the chief exponent of this style in England, writes in 1807 that the French Revolution 'has restored the pure taste of the antique reproduction of ancient Greek forms

for chairs, etc.,' and recommends antique heads of helmeted warriors, winged figures emblematical of freedom, and lances surmounted by a Phrygian cap of Liberty as proper ornaments. Napoleon's campaign of 1797-8 had awakened an interest in Egyptian archaeology, and Hope experimented in adapting such ornament for the furniture of his own house. The armchair (Fig. 184) represents one of Hope's experiments in this manner, and with minor variations follows Plate 22 in his *Household Furniture* (1807). In George Smith's book, published

163. (*Left*) *Armchair, one of set painted in green, brown and yellow on ivory ground. c. 1785. (Southill, Beds.)*

164. (*Right*) *Gilt Armchair, with painted vase-shaped splat. c. 1785. Lady Lever Art (Gallery, Port Sunlight.)*

165. (*Left*) *Arm-chair, one of a set, painted and parcel gilt; oval in style of Angelica Kauffman. (Bolling Hall Mus., Bradford.)*

166. (*Right*) *Arm-chair of painted softwood, back closely resembles design (Plate 8) in Hepplewhite's Guide (1st ed.). c. 1788. (Formerly at Woodhall Park, Herts.)*

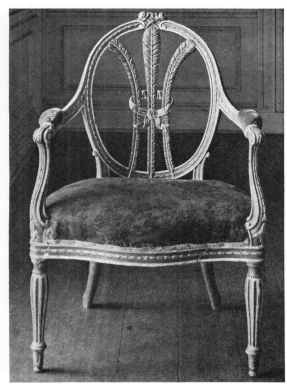

under the same title (1808), Egyptian motives, archaic lions, gryphons, sphinxes and owls are sedulously exploited, one of his most successful experiments in this manner being the arm-chair with lion terminals (Fig. 188). The plate is dated 1804. In addition to the Egyptian and Grecian styles, a debased form of Gothic is found represented in Smith's book, such chairs, with arcades of pointed arches in the back, finials and other tra-

vesties of medieval ornament, being made of 'brown oak varnished . . . of a close and tough grain greatly undercut', and covered with leather.

Smith's 'parlour chairs' have wide oblong panels with shaped ends forming the top rail, resting upon curved uprights with a sharp backward rake; the legs are of the 'sabre' shape so characteristic of the time, and carved, in some cases, as animal

167. *Mahogany Chair, design given in Sheraton's* Drawing Book, *Plate 28. c. 1795. (Fred Skull Coll.)* 168. *Armchair, carved and gilt; top rail painted in grisaille. c. 1790. (Brocklesby, Lincs.)* 169. *Armchair, of painted satinwood; one of set made by Seddon, Sons and Shackleton. 1790. (M. Harris and Sons.)*

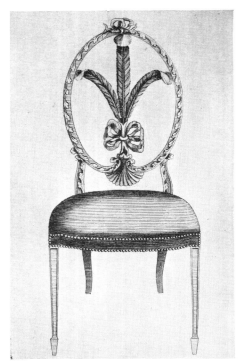 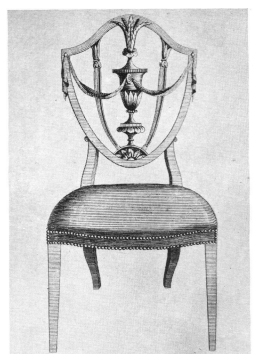 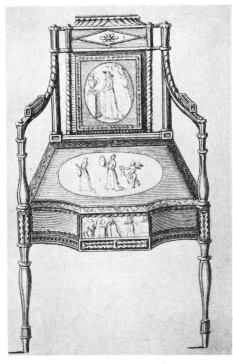

170. *Chair, Plate 8, Hepplewhite's* Guide (1788). 171. *Chair Plate 2, Hepplewhite's* Guide (1788). 172. *Drawing-room Chair, Plate 32, Sheraton's* Drawing Book (1791-4).

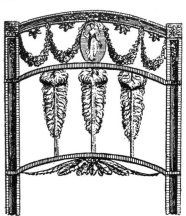

173. *Chair, Plate 12, Hepplewhite's* Guide (3rd ed., 1794).

174. *Mahogany Armchair, carved with husks, paterae and foliated ornament; uprights and front legs reeded. c. 1790. (V. & A. Mus.)* 175. *Mahogany upholstered Armchair, carved with paterae, foliage and fluting. c. 1790. (V. & A. Mus.)* 176. *Mahogany Armchair, veneered with satinwood; framework reeded. c. 1795. (Edward Hudson Coll.)*

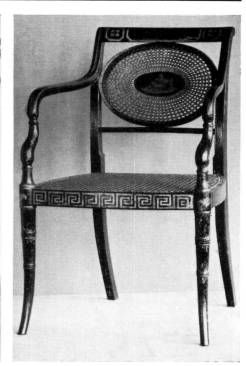

177. *Armchair, beechwood japanned and gilt. c. 1800. (V. & A. Mus.)* 178. *Chair, beechwood japanned, lattice-work splat supports an entablature. c. 1795. (Edward Hudson Coll.)* 179. *Armchair, beechwood japanned and gilt. c. 1800. (V. & A. Mus.)*

terminals. The notes explain that 'the frames of these chairs should be made of bright Spanish mahogany, the ornaments partly carved and partly inlaid with ebony; or the ornaments may be executed with good effect, of inlaid brass'. The seats were intended to be stuffed and covered in red morocco leather 'on the border of which may be printed a Grecian ornament in black'. In drawing-room chairs no attempt was made to preserve the austerity of classical exemplars, for this type 'admit of great elegance as well as variety, and are constructed of rich and costly materials in accordance with the room; the

180. *Drawing-room Chair, one of pair carved and gilt, panel painted by L. A. Delabrière. c. 1790. (Southill, Beds.)* 181. *Armchair, painted black and gilt; arm supports carved with busts in Egyptian style. c. 1805. (Brympton, Som.)* 182. *Mahogany Spoon-back Chair; ebonised inlay. c. 1800. (Caledon, County Tyrone.)*

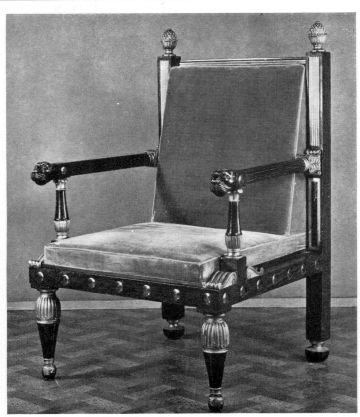

183. *Armchair, gilt, one of set; carved with 'Grecian' ornament. Probably made by Marsh and Tatham. c. 1805. (Southill, Beds.)*

184. *Armchair, grained in imitation of rosewood and parcel gilt. Based on Plate 22 of Thomas Hope's* Household Furniture *(1807). (V. & A. Mus.)*

185. *Mahogany Armchair, back filled with trellis-work. One of set supplied in 1809 by David Bruce. (Bank of England.)*

186. *Upholstered Armchair, gilt and carved with dolphins; one of a set probably by Marsh and Tatham. 1797-9. (Powderham Castle, Devon.)*

187. *Armchair, beechwood carved, japanned and gilded; arm supports formed as winged female terminals. c. 1810. (V. & A. Mus.)*

188. *Armchair, beechwood carved, painted and gilt in Egyptian style. (V. & A. Mus.)*

189. *Mahogany Armchair, in Gothic style. c. 1800. (Formerly at Eaton Hall, Cheshire).* 190. *Armchair of painted beech, with decoration in Pompeian style. c. 1805. (Edward Hudson Coll.)* 191. *Satinwood Armchair, inlaid with lines of ebony, made by Thomas Chippendale, junior, for Sir Richard Colt Hoare in 1802. (Stourhead, Wilts.)*

192. (*Left*) *Mahogany 'Hunting Chair'; made by Thomas Chippendale, junior, for Sir Richard Colt Hoare in 1816.* (*Stourhead, Wilts.*)

193. (*Right*) *Mahogany Writing Chair, scrolled arms supported on Egyptian heads, made by Thomas Chippendale, junior, for Sir Richard Colt Hoare in 1802.* (*Stourhead, Wilts.*)

frames of satinwood, burnished gold with parts of bronze, or otherwise highly enriched'. For the upholstery silks, painted satins, painted velvets, 'superfine cloth' or chintz were recommended.

Though many of these Regency drawing-room chairs were of an extremely grotesque character, a more rational style showing intelligent adaptation of contemporary French fashions is found in the examples made at this time for Southill, Beds., for which Marsh and Tatham (*q.v.*) seem to have supplied much of the furniture. The upholstered armchairs (Figs. 183, 186) are probably by these makers. In some of these chairs

of soft wood japanned and gilt symbolism was fully exploited. The dolphins of Fig. 186 represent the Courtenay crest.

At Stourhead, Wilts., there are a large number of chairs made by Thomas Chippendale, junior, for Sir Richard Colt Hoare, the celebrated antiquary, in the early years of the 19th century. Among those invoiced in the bills, which extend from 1795 to 1820, are Figs. 191-193 and 195, all being described in the bills. These serviceable and admirably executed specimens are typical of the 'ordinary chairs', in which Sir Walter Scott detected 'something of Grecian massiveness' and elegance, contrasting them in the *Quarterly Review* (1828) with the

194. (*Left*) *Mahogany upholstered Armchair, arm supports scrolled and carved with foliage. c. 1805.* (*Brocklesby Hall, Lincs.*)

195. (*Right*) *Mahogany Armchair, with gilt enrichments; made by Thomas Chippendale, junior, for Sir Richard Colt Hoare in 1812.* (*Stourhead, Wilts.*)

196. (*Left*) *Armchair, carved and gilt; legs formed in lion terminals. c. 1805. (Caledon, County Tyrone.)*

197. (*Right*) *Rosewood Armchair, ornament inlaid in brass. c. 1815. (Bank of England.)*

fashion twenty or thirty years earlier, when they were 'mounted on four tapering and tottering legs, resembling four tobacco pipes'.

After c. 1805 'Grecian symmetry' became the professed aim of fashionable designers, but it was found necessary to make large concessions to the public taste by way of excursions into other and more exciting styles. Sheraton in his later designs frequently introduced a medley of uncouth animal motives. In the *Cabinet Dictionary* (1803) he justifies this practice by Gallic precedent, remarking that he has been favoured with a view of some of the later specimens of French chairs in the antique taste in which 'various heads of animals' are introduced. In

this book and the *Encyclopaedia*, issued in parts 1804-7, many fantastic plates are given. A passage on the subject of drawing-room chairs suggests how jaded was Sheraton's invention. They should, he says, 'always be the produce of studied elegance, though it is extremely difficult to attain to anything really novel'. Extant specimens show to what lengths designers were prepared to go in an attempt to justify this mania for novelties. But the more eccentric aberrations were confined for the most part to drawing-rooms and 'rooms of state,' and throughout the period 1800-25 many unpretentious and serviceable chairs were made for general use in mahogany and rosewood, carved or inlaid with brass.

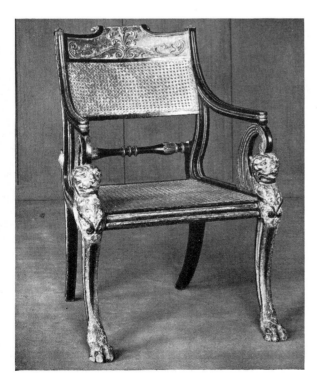

198. (*Left*) *Painted and Gilt Armchair, front legs formed as lion terminals. c. 1815. (The late Mr Goodhart-Rendel.)*

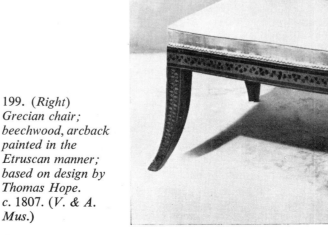

199. (*Right*) *Grecian chair; beechwood, arcback painted in the Etruscan manner; based on design by Thomas Hope. c. 1807. (V. & A. Mus.)*

200. *Armchair, carved and gilt, one of six made by Morel and Hughes in* 1812. (*Buckingham Palace. By gracious permission of Her Majesty the Queen.*)

CHAIRS, BARBERS' or SHAVING. Specialised varieties of chairs were made for barbers' use in the 18th century. Early Georgian chairs with triangular seats (*see* CHAIRS, Fig. 81) sometimes have an additional splat enclosed within turned uprights mounted on the top rail of the back, presumably for this purpose.

CHAIRS, BERGERE. See BIRJAIR.

CHAIRS, CABRIOLE. Cabriole chairs are defined in Hepplewhite's *Guide* (1788) as 'chairs with stuffed backs'. In the drawing-room of Dr Samuel Parr's rectory at Hatton, Warwickshire, 'was an old and costly cabriole chair covered with Gobelin tapestry', which was acquired by Parr in 1814.

CHAIRS, CAQUETOIRE. See CAQUETOIRE.

CHAIRS, CHILDREN'S. References occur in Tudor inventories to chairs made specially for children. Among the furniture of Robert Sidney, Earl of Leicester, in the Wardrobe at Leicester House in 1588 was 'a little chair for a childe, of carnation and greene clothe and tinsell', valued at 20s. The earliest extant examples date from the first half of the 17th century, and they continued to be made in two forms, one low on the ground so that a baby or small child might occupy the chair without risk of falling (Fig. 5); the other elevated on supports to permit attendance to the child without stooping.

Children's chairs of the Stuart period were of oak, and are miniature versions of the panel back. In Fig. 2 the legs and uprights are inclined at an angle, thus contributing to the stability of the structure. Here the back is surmounted by

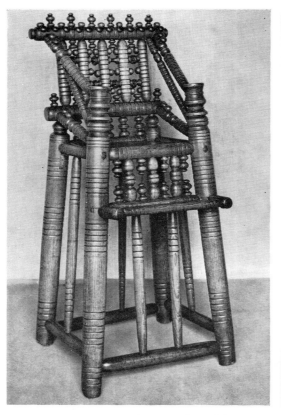

1. *Child's Chair of oak, turned or 'thrown'. Early 17th century. Ht. 3 ft. 6 in., W. 1 ft. 7 in. (Wolsey. Ltd.)* 2. *Oak Child's Chair, with knobbed legs and stretchers. c. 1660. Ht. 3 ft. 4½ in., W. 1 ft. 7½ in. (V. & A. Mus.)* 3. *Walnut Child's Chair, foot rest and bar to secure child missing; caning modern. c. 1675. (Clevedon Court, Som.)*

4. (Left) Child's Armchair, oak inlaid in holly and bog-wood; on back of top rail initials R.W. and date 1680. (V. & Mus.)

5. (Right) Child's Armchair, carved with initials E.C. and date 1724; Yorkshire. Ht. 2 ft. 5½ in., W. 1 ft. 5 in. (V. & A. Mus.)

turned finials, but the majority of oak children's chairs have, like Fig. 4, the cresting and brackets of their more massive contemporaries. This fine specimen is made in two stages, a wide platform being provided for the child's feet; it is dated 1680, the inlaid ornament being earlier in style.

The carved and caned walnut chairs introduced after the Restoration were also copied in miniature for children, but this variety, ill-adapted for hard wear, is seldom found in perfect condition. In Fig. 3 the upper section of the front supports is formed of knob-turning in order to take the foot rest. At Ham House in 1683 there were 'two chayres for children, the one black and the other japanned', the first probably being of stained beechwood. In the 18th century children's chairs continued to be based on fashionable models, and a few specimens in walnut and mahogany survive with the splats solid and vase-shaped or filled with tracery in the *Director* style.

6. *Mahogany Child's Chair, with looped splat and legs of double cabriole form united by turned stretchers. c. 1745. (Frank Partridge & Sons.)* 7. *Child's Armchair, mahogany with 'Gothic' splat; upholstered seat of later date. c. 1770. Ht. 2 ft. 1½ in., W. 1 ft. 6½ in. (V. & A. Mus.)* 8. *Child's Armchair, turned birchwood. c. 1800. Ht. 2 ft. 7½ in. (Mrs Alan Renwick.)*

CHAIRS, CONVERSATION. In the *Cabinet Dictionary* (1803) Sheraton writes 'the manner of conversing amongst some of the highest circles of company, on some occasions, is copied from the French, by lounging upon a chair. Hence we have the term conversation chair, which is peculiarly adapted for this kind of idle position.' He illustrates a design for one of these chairs which 'give scope for variety', and observes that 'they are made extraordinary long between back and front, for purpose of space for the fashionable posture'; and also are 'narrow in front and back, as an accommodation for this mode of conversing'.

CHAIRS, CURRICLE. A variety of upholstered chair with rounded or tub-shaped back in fashion at the beginning of the 19th century, and 'so-called', according to Sheraton's *Cabinet Dictionary* (1803), where two examples (Plate 6) are illustrated. Such chairs derive their name from 'a chaise on two wheels'.

CHAIRS, DRESSING. A variety presumably intended for use by ladies at their toilets in the 18th century. At Sir William Stanhope's house in Arlington Street in 1733 there were 'two fine dressing-chairs curiously wrought in Tent stitch'. Manwaring's *Chairmaker's Real Friend and Companion* (1765) shows four designs for 'Ladies Dressing Chairs' with upholstered backs and seats, which do not differ in type from his other drawing-room chairs; nor is there anything to indicate that the 'dressing chairs' in the Chinese style illustrated by Ince and Mayhew in the *Universal System* (1759-63) are a specialised variety.

CHAIRS, EASY. A padded chair 'adapted for ease or repose' or 'for sitting or half reclining in an easy posture'. A 'large easy elbow chair with cheekes down the sides' was supplied for Queen Mary's dressing room at Whitehall in 1692 (Lord Chamberlain's Accounts). Sometimes 'easy' (or great) chairs were made 'conformable' (*i.e.* to match a set of chairs), and when they are separately priced in accounts the disparity in their cost compared with other chairs is noticeable. An example is illustrated in Hepplewhite's *Guide* (1788), where it is described in the text as a 'saddle-cheek and easy chair'. An easy chair of tub shape is described in Sheraton's *Cabinet Dictionary* (1803) as 'stuffed all over and intended for sick persons'.

CHAIRS, ELBOW = ARMCHAIRS.

CHAIRS, EXERCISING. See CHAMBER HORSE.

CHAIRS, FARTHINGALE. A term applied to an upholstered chair of a type introduced under Elizabeth and made without arms; on the assumption that such chairs were designed to accommodate the farthingale, or verchingale, 'a petticoat borne out with graduated hoops' of Spanish origin. The term is without contemporary authority. (*See* CHAIRS, Figs. 23, 24 and p. 121.)

CHAIRS, FOLDING. References to such chairs, which were probably of X form with a collapsible frame, occur in 17th century inventories, *e.g.* at Somerset House in 1649 were 'six folding chaires of crimson vellvett trymmd with gold lace'.

CHAIRS, HALL. A special variety introduced early in the 18th century for halls and corridors, particularly those of great Palladian houses, in which furniture of a formal character was favoured. In a MS. book of accounts kept by the fourth Earl and Countess of Cardigan they are recorded to have paid £7 16s. for 'six mahogany hall chairs' in 1741. An example of

1. Mahogany Hall Chair, carved back headed with lion mask and drapery. Mid-18th century.   2. Hall Chair, carved with classical ornament; coronet and crest of first Earl Spencer painted. c. 1760. (Formerly at Spencer House.)   3. Hall Chair, of painted beechwood made by Chippendale for Nostell Priory in 1766.

about that date (Fig. 1) has the upper part of the back carved with a lion mask and drapery, while the straight legs are united by stretchers. In Chippendale's *Director* (3rd ed., 1762) six designs are given, and they are also recommended for summer houses. The notes state that 'they may be made of mahogany or any other wood, and painted, and have commonly wooden seats'. One of them is an armchair in the Gothic style, another has a circular panel to be painted with the owner's cipher and coronet above. The formal character of hall chairs and their solid backs rendered them highly suitable for classical treatment. An example at Nostell Priory (Fig. 3) was supplied by Chippendale's firm in 1766, while of about the same date is a set of 12 armchairs from Spencer House, with the crest and coronet of the first Earl Spencer painted in colours in the centre of the back. In Hepplewhite's *Guide* (1788) three hall chairs are illustrated, to be either carved or painted. The solid vase-shaped back of one is reproduced as a novelty which has been 'much approved'. Sheraton (*Cabinet Dictionary*, 1803) describes such chairs as 'for the use of servants or strangers waiting for business'. They are 'generally made all of mahogany with the crest of the family painted on the centre of the back'. The two examples illustrated have X-shaped underframing.

CHAIRS, HUNTING. Sheraton states (*Cabinet Dictionary*, 1803) that such chairs 'are stuffed all over except the legs, which are of mahogany'. He illustrates (Plate 8) a specimen with a frame which slides out in front, and supporting a cushion 'forms a temporary resting place for one that is fatigued, as hunters generally are'. In the bills of the younger Thomas Chippendale for furnishing Stourhead (1795-1820) the term is applied to armchairs in which the framework is filled with caning (*see* CHAIRS, Fig. 192).

1. *Mahogany Reading Chair, upholstered in leather, adjustable board and hinged trays below arms. c. 1720-25. (V. & A. Mus.)*

CHAIRS, LIBRARY AND READING. Early in the 18th century a specialised form of chair for use in libraries was introduced, padded and generally covered with leather. They were made in walnut and mahogany, other surviving examples closely resembling Fig. 1. It has an adjustable wooden rest for reading and writing, and below the arms are hinged trays with three circular wells, brass candle brackets (now missing)

2. *Walnut Reading Chair, scrolled uprights and vase-shaped splat; seat covered with leather. c. 1720. (Queen's College, Oxford.)*
3. *Mahogany Reading Chair, with extending foot-rest. c. 1820. (Stratfield Saye, Hants.)*

1. *Porter's Chair, covered with leather; cabriole legs of mahogany. c.* 1750. (*Blenheim Palace, Oxon.*)

folding underneath. Below the seat is a drawer and behind it a secret receptacle secured by a bolt.

A variant, of walnut and probably a few years earlier in date, with vase-shaped back and moulded top rail, is given in Fig. 2. Such chairs are erroneously associated with cock-fighting; but though perhaps used on occasion by the judge when a 'main' was fought, they were not designed for that purpose. Sheraton writes (*Cabinet Dictionary*, 1803), 'they are intended to make the exercise of reading easy, and for the convenience of taking down a note or quotation from any subject. The reader places himself with his back to the front of the chair and rests his arms on the top yoke.'

Walnut and mahogany armchairs with serpentine seat rails, three cabriole legs in front and one straight turned support behind are commonly called 'writing-chairs', but there is no evidence that they were intended for writing. They had wide vase-shaped splats within hooped uprights, or a top rail resting on three moulded supports, a pair of splats, solid or formed of pierced scrollwork, being enclosed between them. (*See* CHAIRS, Figs. 81 and 100.) A reading chair at Stratfield Saye, fitted with an adjustable swinging desk (Fig. 3), corresponds in form with a 'hunting chair' (*q.v.*) illustrated in Sheraton's *Cabinet Dictionary* (1803) and has a similar extending foot rest.

CHAIRS, MENDLESHAM. A distinct variety, which has affinities with the Windsor type, was made in Suffolk (the 'Mendlesham chair') by a wheelwright, Daniel Day of Mendlesham, in the early 19th century. The seat and legs are of Windsor type. The back has a straight top rail and the space between this and a cross rail is filled with turned balls. There is a narrow vertical splat, and the uprights and rails are sometimes inlaid with boxwood lines.

CHAIRS, PAGE AND PORTER. Used by menservants on duty as door openers, etc., in halls of town and country houses in the 18th century, and generally made with wings and arched top to exclude draughts, and upholstered in leather. An example at Blenheim Palace (Fig. 1) is of exceptional height and supported on cabriole legs carved with foliage. In another variety the lower portion is enclosed and the framework of the base supported on castors.

CHAIRS, SADDLE-CHEEK. *See* CHAIRS, EASY.

CHAIRS, WICKER. In the 16th and 17th centuries an inexpensive variety of chair made of twigs or osiers, probably by basket-makers, was in common use, but examples of that period have long since disappeared owing to the perishable nature of the material. In the will of Elizabeth Coddington of Ixworth, Suffolk, 'a wicker chaire' is mentioned in 1571, while the inventory of Thomas Beard of Sutton, Beds., in 1617 lists 'one wicker chair' in the hall, valued at 5s. Randle Holme (*Academy of Armory*, pub. 1681) wrote: 'There is another kind of these chaires called Twiggem chaires because they are made of Owsiers and Withen twigs; haveing round covers over the heads of them like a canapy. These are principally used by sick and infirm people, and such women as have bine lately brought to bed; from whence they are generally termed ... Child-bed chaires....' This description implies an armchair with wings and hood, and some examples of wicker enclosed chairs of this type, possibly dating from the 18th century, are extant.

CHAIRS, WINDSOR. An all-wooden seat in which the bow and spindles of the back and legs are dowelled into the seat and the stretchers into the legs. Lord Percival, writing in 1724 of his visit to the garden of Hall Barn, Bucks., observes that 'the narrow winding walks and paths cut in it are innumerable, and a woman in full health cannot walk them all, for which reason my wife was carry'd in a Windsor chair like those at Versailles, by which means she lost nothing worth seeing'. From sources such as trade cards and contemporary letters, it is clear that the Windsor served two main purposes, as an indoor seat in an inn or tavern, and as an outdoor seat in gardens, summerhouses and piazzas. Windsor chairs appear in a picture by Zoffany showing a Scotch landowner, William Ferguson, and his friends commemorating his succession to the estate of Raith in 1781. (*See* WINE CISTERNS, etc., Fig. 7.)

This type is made partly of beech, and its manufacture has centred for more than two centuries in the beechwoods of the Chilterns, Bucks., with High Wycombe as its focus. Daniel Defoe notices in 1725 the vast quantity of beech 'which grows in the woods of Buckinghamshire more plentifully than in any other part of England' (*Tour in Great Britain*,

1. (*Left*) *Elm Windsor Chair, crown on cresting, spiral-turned uprights in back. Legs much worn; one stretcher original. First half 18th century. (Fred Skull Coll.)*

2. (*Right*) *Windsor Chair, of yew with hooped back and cabriole legs. c. 1760. (Great Fosters, Surrey.)*

1725). The industry, however, was not of great importance before the 19th century. A chair factory was established at High Wycombe by Thomas Widgington *c.* 1810.

The seat, of saddle form, is nearly always of elm, and the bow of ash or yew, while leg spindles are normally of beech. When used as an outdoor seat, the chairs were painted as protection against wet weather. The most popular colour, green, would blend with the open-air background. Red and yellow Windsor chairs are also recorded.

The elasticity and durability of the type make it an ideal seat for tea-gardens, inns and taverns. In one variety fitted with two bracing spindles running from the crown of the hoop into the bob-tail at the back, the construction is an additional insurance against damage. The cheapness and lightness of the chair were further merits for the service of places of humble resort; but it was not confined to them, for in the library of the Duke of Chandos at Cannons in 1725 were 'seaven Japan'd Windsor chairs' and in 1729 Henry Williams (*q.v.*) supplied 3 mahogany Windsor chairs (2 'richly carved') to St James's Palace. In Sir William Stanhope's lavishly furnished house

3. (*Left*) *Windsor Chair, of yew and ash with elm seat. c. 1770. (V. & A. Mus.)*

4. (*Right*) *Windsor Chair, wood painted black. Formerly in possession of Oliver Goldsmith. c. 1750. (V. & A. Mus.)*

in Arlington Street in 1733 was 'a Windsor chair covered with quilted crimson damask'.

From about the middle of the century two main types were in general use—the comb-back with horizontal top rail curved at the ends and the hoop back, the filling consisting of a pierced, fret-cut splat flanked by turned spindles or of turned spindles only. A horizontal bar was bent to a semicircle to form the arms, which rest on supports with a backward rake; the front legs were sometimes of cabriole form in imitation of more costly furniture, and the stretcher uniting them was often curved (Fig. 2). From the existing examples of armchairs fitted with a lateral attachment for a book-rest or desk, it is evident that this type was in general use as a writing or reading chair.

Owing to its cheapness (Josiah Wedgwood writes to Bentley of some he had ordered about 5s. or 6s. each) the Windsor found its way into farmhouses and humble homes, and also into places where numbers of reasonably priced chairs were desired. Jackson (*Oxford Journal*, Nov. 29, 1766) records the introduction of Windsor chairs, 'so admirably calculated for ornament and repose', in the Bodleian library.

The aristocrat among Windsors is the Gothic variety, which dates from the revival of c. 1750. In such chairs the splats are opened out in cuspings and the back is sometimes shaped as a pointed arch. The legs are cabrioled, and the particular pattern seems to have been standardised, for many similar examples exist. Shop bills in the Banks Collection advertising 'all sorts of yew tree, Gothic and Windsor chairs' date from 1785 to 1788. Except for the Gothic influence there is little to mark fluctuations of taste. In late Georgian Windsors the splat is pierced with a wheel form or Prince of Wales's plume; and the wheel or star form has continued to the present day. M.J. (revised).

CHAIRS, WING. Easy chairs with cheeks or wings.

CHAIRS, YORKSHIRE AND DERBYSHIRE. Type of oak chair introduced c. 1650, particularly associated with Yorkshire and Derbyshire. The back filling takes the form of an arcade of turned balusters or broad rails, hooped and escalloped. (*See* CHAIRS, Figs. 19, 22 and p. 120.)

CHAIR-MAKERS. In the Middle Ages and far into the 17th century most domestic chairs were made by carpenters and joiners; the practice continued much later in country districts and has never been entirely discontinued. There is no reason to suppose that 'joyned chairs' which figure frequently in medieval and Tudor inventories were a monopoly of the joiners, for it was not until later that an attempt was made to draw a clear distinction between the two Guilds. Recent evidence shows that under Henry VIII and Elizabeth upholstered chairs with webbed seats of X-shape were supplied to the Crown by the royal coffer-makers (*see* GRENE FAMILY, and CHAIRS, Fig. 21), who also probably made those for palaces and great houses early in the next century.

In 1632 a committee of the Court of Aldermen, seeking to end a dispute between the Carpenters and Joiners assigned among other furniture 'All sorts of Chayres . . . which are made with mortesses or tennants' to the Joiners, though the Carpenters continued to ignore these provisions. In 1633 the Turners (*q.v.*), having complained that the Joiners 'assume unto themselves the art of turning', the Court ruled that 'whatsoever is done with the foot as have treddle or wheele for turning of any

wood . . . it properly belongs to the Turners'—a decision which would make the latter responsible for the turned members of chairs; and so, where turning largely predominated in the structure (*see* CHAIRS, Fig. 20), for the chair itself. The jurisdiction of the Guilds, however, was confined to the capital and the immediate neighbourhood, York, and two or three other cities.

References to individual 'chayre-makers' occur in James I's reign, but unlike the Carpenters, Joiners and Turners, the craft was not organised as a distinct guild. In 1699 cane-chair makers were enrolled in the Joiners' Company, and appealed to it for support against the basket-makers, who were apparently threatening to encroach on their business in the caning of chairs. At this period and into the second half of the 18th century, several leading providers of chairs to the Crown described themselves as 'joiners' and were members of that company.

The royal accounts of the Late Stuart period suggest that upholstered chairs with webbed seats were generally provided by upholsterers, but there is no indication that the roles of cabinet-maker, joiner or chair-maker were sharply differentiated. Thus, Thomas Roberts, 'joiner', supplied William III and Anne with screens and specialised in chairs and stools.

Though early in the 18th century 'chairmaker' occurs in advertisements, the same firm provides both seat furniture and cabinet goods. William Old and John Ody, for instance, c. 1720 advertise that they 'make and sell all sorts of cane and Dutch chairs, chair frames . . . and also all sorts . . . of the best . . . cabinet work.' A few years later Francis Croxford in the *Daily Post* is described as 'chair- and cabinet-maker eminent in his profession', his stock including, besides a large quantity of case furniture, 'about one hundred dozen of chaires of several sorts'. Giles Grendey, who was Master of the Joiners' Company in 1766, announces that he makes and sells 'all sorts of cabinet goods'—and chairs.

From the Restoration onwards there was a tendency towards specialisation, and the tradesmen who in the royal accounts describe themselves as cabinet-makers, joiners or upholders respectively may be assumed to have relied on employees trained in the craft for the chairs entered in their bills. But the making of cane chairs, produced in enormous quantities between 1675-1700, was apparently regarded as a special trade. When the demand declined, the makers turned their attention to other varieties, and in 1747 *The London Tradesman* observes that 'cane chair-makers not only make this sort (now almost out of use) but the better sort of leather bottomed and wooden chairs'. While in the fashionable firms of cabinet-makers and upholsterers (*e.g.* Chippendale's), chair-making was an important part of the business, according to *The Parents and Guardians Directory* (1761), tradesmen who had hitherto practised as chair-makers now greatly enlarged their activities. Formerly they are stated to have dealt in nothing but chairs, and to have been often employed by cabinet-makers, 'but now they keep large shops themselves and sell almost all kinds of household goods . . . as well as chairs of all sorts . . . '.

There is no evidence of a rigid subdivision of labour in cabinet-makers' shops of the early Georgian period. The side-tables and chairs designed *en suite* by architects for great Palladian houses were probably made by the same workmen, to be subsequently decorated by the same carver; but the making of seat furniture in general was recognised as a special branch of the industry. In Seddon's (*q.v.*) great manufactory in Aldersgate Street there was (c. 1785) a department devoted to 'chairs, sofas and stools'. 'Chair-making', writes Sheraton (*Cabinet Dictionary*, 1803), 'is a branch generally confined to itself; as those who professedly work at it seldom engage to make cabinet furniture. In the country manufactories it is otherwise, yet even these pay some regard to keeping their workmen constantly at the chair, or to cabinet work. The two branches seem evidently to require different talents in the workmen to become proficient. In the chair branch it requires a particular turn in the handling of shapes to make them agreeable and easy.' He adds that the difference is very remarkable in 'some chairs of precisely the same pattern, when executed by different chair-makers, arising chiefly in the want of taste concerning the beauty of an outline, of which we judge by the eye more than the rigid rules of geometry'—an interesting observation, since elegance of line is one of the chief characteristics of contemporary chairs. In the *Dictionary* Sheraton lists four 'japanned chair makers'. In the same year Joseph Farrington, R.A., records in his *Diary* 'that a Journeyman chairmaker can earn from 2 to 3 guineas a week. They work by *piecework*—and begin at 6 in the morning and sometimes till 9 at night.'

CHAIR-TABLES. A convertible form of furniture, in which the back of a chair swings over on a pivot to form a table, in use from late medieval times, and made in considerable numbers in the 17th century. An early example with buttressed sides of Gothic character is shown in Fig. 1.

1. *Oak Chair-Table, top with pierced and shaped underframing, revolves on movable pegs. c. 1500. Ht. 2 ft. 4½ in., W. 2 ft. 9 in. (The late Mr Fred Roe.)*

2. *Oak Chair-Table, showing top tilted up to form back of chair; elaborately carved and dated 1627. (Cotehele House, Cornwall.)*
3. *Oak Chair-Table, back carved with arch enclosing conventional floral ornament. c. 1650. (Nat. Mus. of Wales.)* 4. *Oak Chair-Table, carved with arms of Alexander Cockie and dated 1673. (Trinity Hall, Aberdeen.)*

The top (renewed) has a pierced and shaped underframing revolving on movable pegs. In 1558 Andrew Cranewise of Bury bequeathed to his son 'my round chaire table in the plour', the description referring to the shape of the top. The inventory of Gilling Castle, York, drawn up for Sir Thomas Fairfax in 1624 lists 'a chare uncovered with a falling back for a table'. An example from Cotehele, Cornwall, is dated 1627. A chair-table from the old Trades Hall, Aberdeen, elaborately carved, presented by Alexander Cockie in 1673, bears his arms (Fig. 4) and initials. The demand lasted into the 18th century, and Archbishop Sancroft, after his expulsion from Canterbury as a non-juror under William III, removed two chair-tables from the cathedral to Redenhall Church, Norfolk, where one still remains.

CHAISE LONGUE. French term for couch or day-bed with upholstered back. Sheraton (*Drawing Book*, 1791-4) illustrates one similar in form to the late 17th-century example at Hornby (*see* COUCHES and DAY-BEDS, Fig. 10) and he writes: 'These have their name from the French, which imports a long chair. Their use is to rest or loll upon after dinner.'

CHAMBER HORSE. Contrivance used for exercising in second half of the 18th century. The leather-covered seat had a concertina movement and was formed of boards supported on blocks, round which strong wire was twisted. The weight of

1. *Mahogany Chamber Horse, with removable back and standards; below foot-board, drawer supported on reeded legs. c. 1760. Ht. 4 ft. 8 in., W. 2 ft. 9¾ in. (V. & A. Mus.)*

the sitter compressed the air, thus securing an upward and downward movement.

These seats do not figure in early trade catalogues, but an example of c. 1760 is in Fig. 1. The back, filled with four interlaced slats, lifts off, and the standards, which facilitate exercising, are also removable: below the shaped footboard is a drawer. Sheraton (*Drawing Book*, 1791-4) gives detailed instructions for the manufacture of 'chamber horses', and writes 'the top board is stuffed with hair as a chair seat and the leather is fixed to each board with brass nails tacked all round'. An example illustrated by Sheraton is of stool form with arms to give a grip at each end.

CHAMBER ORGAN. Small form of organ used in private houses in 17th and 18th centuries (*see* MUSICAL INSTRUMENTS).

CHAMFER. Surface produced by bevelling off an angle; often found on Gothic woodwork, and sometimes on corners of walnut and mahogany tallboys and clothes presses in 18th century (*see* CHESTS OF DRAWERS: Figs. 23 and 31). Term 'canted' also applied to a chamfered corner.

CHANDELIERS. A variety of names have been used in successive periods to designate hanging lights—'branch', 'lustre', 'sconce', and 'hanging candlestick' being among those most widely employed between the 15th and the end of the 18th centuries. The name 'chandelier' is of considerable antiquity—it occurs in John of Trevisa's translation of Glanvil's *De Proprietatibus Rerum* (1398), where he writes that 'candels and other prickets be set on candelsticks and chandeliers'—and 'four chaundelers gilt, prykettes' are mentioned in the inventory drawn up for Henry Fitzroy, Duke of Richmond, in 1526—but it does not appear to have come into common use in England before Georgian times. In 1714 John Gumley (*q.v.*) advertises 'Glass Schandelieres' in the *London Gazette*. William Stukeley, the antiquary, in his *Paleographica Sacra* (1736), refers to 'branches or chandeliers, as we now modishly call them'. The name has gained wide currency since that period, and is here adopted for lights with branches suspended from a ceiling or roof.

Hanging lights were employed in churches and cathedrals before the Conquest, and a corona, or hoop, of hammered iron enriched with flowers and other ornaments is mentioned in a 13th-century inventory of St Paul's Cathedral. Prickets or spikes for candles, or cups for oil, were set at intervals on the hoop of such hanging lights, which sometimes attained enormous size.

In royal palaces and households of nobles 'coronas luminum' were occasionally made of gold and silver. Specimens are mentioned in an inventory of effects found in a room under the chapel in the Tower in 1325, and in the romance of

1. *Candlebeam, with eight candlesticks, from 15th-century French MS. in British Museum, showing Masque at Court of Charles VI of France. (B.M. Royal 18. E.11, F206.)*

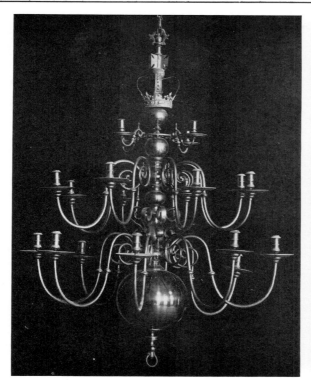

2. (*Left*) *Brass Chandelier, with globular stem and base; headed by crown. c. 1690. (Hampton Court Palace. By gracious permission of Her Majesty the Queen.)*

3. (*Right*) *Brass Chandelier, baluster stem with gadroon ornament headed by eagle; grease pans decorated with acanthus. Dated 1768. (Formerly at Hamilton Palace, Lanarks.)*

Guigamar a chamber is lit by two chandeliers of pure gold. The 'candel-beam' of the later Middle Ages was generally constructed of cross-pieces of wood, with candles affixed to spikes or cups of latten on the arms. In 1493 a widow of Bury left 'my candylbeme that hangyeth in my hall with VI bellys of laton standyng thereon'—a description which indicates that it was of unusual size and had six cups for candles on the arms. At this date the term 'belle canstyke' was sometimes applied to hanging lights, the portable variety being described as 'lesser' candlesticks.

In the medieval hall these hanging lights were frequently supplemented by tapers and torches, the holders being fixed to the walls (*see* SCONCES AND WALL LIGHTS). Even the chambers of princes seldom contained more than a single 'candelbeam'. A candlebeam with four lights is figured in a miniature from a MS. in the British Museum (Fig. 1), representing the tragical masque at the Court of Charles VI in 1393, when several courtiers were burned to death; in this instance each candlestick on the beam holds two candles, corresponding with the 'double-candlestick' mentioned in 15th-century inventories. At this time hanging lights appear to have been regarded as luxuries, for in the *Memoires* of Olivier de La Marche candlebeams painted blue and white are specially noticed in the great reception hall constructed for the marriage of Charles the Bold and Margaret of York in 1468. Brilliant illumination must have been exceptional extravagance, and even a generation later the Somerset Herald who accompanied Princess Margaret, daughter of Henry VII, on her journey into Scotland to marry King James, regarded the hall at Holyrood Palace as splendidly lit by 'six grett syerges of wax'. These were 'haunged in the same Halle for to lyght at Even,' there apparently being no other illumination.

Brass and latten chandeliers with branches do not appear to have been introduced into halls and chambers of private houses until towards the close of the Middle Ages, and the form

suggests that they 'were evolved from a common type of candlebeam which incorporated the principle of the radiating branches'. That brass chandeliers were made in England in the 15th century may be safely assumed, since Acts of Henry IV and Richard III forbid the importation of 'hanging candlesticks'. No contemporary English specimen survives, but a fine chandelier of Flemish origin and of about this date was until lately in the Temple Church at Bristol, the Virgin and Child forming the top of the shaft with a figure of St George and the Dragon below. Probably also of foreign manufacture was 'a braunche of Latten with nyne candlestickes in it, havinge an antique Woman holdinge in the one hand a scutchon', which is mentioned in an inventory of Henry VIII's possessions taken shortly after his death.

In the Tudor period candlebeams and wooden and iron coronas were still in use in the majority of houses, but metal chandeliers of an elaborate character are also found mentioned, the Guildhall at Boston in 1534 containing five, described as 'hyngynge wt lily pottes whereof the hiest of them hath V braunches and eche of the other has III braunches'. When the Duke of Wurtemberg visited Queen Elizabeth, he gave her 'a chandelier facon D'Allemagne'; and as Dinant had gained a great reputation for wares of this kind, many were, no doubt, in spite of prohibitions, imported from the Low Countries.

The brass chandeliers of the 17th century were evolved from the Gothic forms, though the transitional stages are not represented by extant English examples. The fully developed late Stuart chandeliers consisted of a moulded stem into which are slotted one or more tiers of branches, with a finial or hook for hanging at the top, and a large globe with a pendant at the bottom. The stem is made up of a number of separate pieces held together by an iron rod. The tiers of branches are often divided by a row of scrolls attached to the stem, these being of sheet metal, while the remainder is cast. Such chandeliers were made in considerable numbers in England from about the

4. Brass Chandelier, with globular gadrooned stem surmounted by eagle; arms bird-headed and grease pans worked with rococo ornament. Dated 1764.

5. Silver Chandelier, vase-shaped finial ornamented with terminal figures in French taste; bulb engraved with arabesque patterns. c. 1700. (Knole Park, Kent.)

middle of Charles II's reign for churches and public buildings, but they seem never to have been common in private houses. They depend for decorative effect upon their polished surfaces, the skilful graduation of the members composing the stem, and the scrolling of the S-shaped branches; the models were derived from foreign prototypes and similar chandeliers are often introduced in pictures of Dutch interiors by Terborch, Metsu and Gerard Dou. A chandelier from Hampton Court, dating from the Late Stuart period, is in three tiers headed by a crown, the globular base of bold dimensions contrasting with the slender and graceful arms (Fig. 2).

As these 'globe chandeliers' were cast, the original patterns were easily reproduced. Examples in churches, often dated, and with the donor's name engraved on the bowl, prove that the type was popular over a long period; but from c. 1740 it was gradually superseded by the 'vase-shaped' pattern, in which stem and globe are merged, while the branches are bolted to the interior of the body instead of being hooked on. Like the earlier globe variety, most of these late chandeliers were made for ecclesiastical use (London and the West Country, notably Bridport and Bristol, appear to have been the chief centres of production); though some of them have subsequently been transferred from churches and chapels to houses. A chandelier of exceptional elaboration and height, formerly at Hamilton Palace (Fig. 3), is inscribed 'The Gift of Jacob Rider 1768', indicating that it came out of a church. It has forty lights arranged in three tiers. The stem is gadrooned, this motif and fluting being characteristic of the 'vase-shape', while the grease pans are delicately ornamented with acanthus. Brass chandeliers retained their baroque appearance until towards the end of the century when production declined, and were scarcely affected, save in details of ornament, by the rococo and neo-classic styles. In Fig. 4, dated 1764, the globe form recalls the Late Stuart type, but rococo influence can be discerned in the bird-headed arms and the decoration of the grease pans.

In the Georgian period, apart from churches and public buildings, such as the Houses of Parliament (where they are represented in several contemporary engravings), brass chandeliers supplemented the wall-lights in the royal palaces, and in a warrant to the Duke of Montagu, Master of the Great Wardrobe, in June, 1729, 'a brass branch' at Hampton Court is included among objects to be mended.

Silver chandeliers were known in England in the 16th century. Henry VIII possessed a large number, some plain and others parcel gilt; his inventory specifies ten gilt and ten plain five-light branches of silver hung by silver chains. The earliest surviving examples are those made in Charles II's time to match silver tables, mirrors and stands in extravagantly appointed houses. In William III's Presence Chamber at Hampton Court Palace there is a specimen (Fig. 6) made by Francis Gathorne at the end of the century. The crowned escutcheons bear the emblems of the British Isles and the French fleur-de-lys, while the ornament of the stem resembles the decorative motives found on contemporary silver plate; the plain reeded arms are ringed, their solidity according with the general proportions. In the single-tier chandelier from Knole (Fig. 5) the proportions are more elegant, and the inspiration unmistakably French; the inverted pineapple forming the pendant is a very usual detail from this time onwards. A list of the contents of Windsor Castle, drawn up in 1695 and now among the MSS. in the Record Office, mentions 'one large silver branch'—a common 17th-century term for a chandelier—in the Queen's Withdrawing Room, where Celia Fiennes saw it about this date. A silver chandelier, formerly at St James's, is several times mentioned in the royal accounts for George II's reign—Benjamin Goodison (*q.v.*) charging 2s. for taking it down, and fixing it up again with 'silk lines' for the funeral of Frederick, Prince of Wales, in 1751. The silver chandelier with seventeen branches from the Worshipful Company of Fishmongers (Fig. 7) is one of the very rare examples in which

6. *Silver Chandelier, crowned escutcheons bear emblems of British Isles. By Francis Gathorne. c. 1700. (Hampton Court Palace. By gracious permission of Her Majesty the Queen.)* 7. *Silver Chandelier, in rococo taste, 1752-3. (Worshipful Company of Fishmongers.)*

rococo fantasy is fully expressed, the branches being elaborately scrolled and fishes disporting themselves amid the ornament. An inscription records that it was given in memory of Sir Thomas Knesworth to his Company in 1752; while it is known from their records to have been made by William Alexander, in business at 'ye Anchor and Key' in Wood Street.

Chandeliers of rock-crystal are mentioned in French inventories of the late 16th century, notably in that of Catherine de Medici. When Evelyn was presented to Louis XIV and the Queen Regent at the Palais Cardinal in 1649, he noticed that in the presence chamber 'hung three hugh branches of Chrystal'. In an inventory of the contents of Somerset House, drawn up after Charles I's execution, 'Two crissall Branches' valued at the large sum of £80 are listed—probably foreign importations.

In England chandeliers were made of this valuable material shortly after the Restoration, and rock-crystals were imported from Germany, Bohemia and Italy. There was a crystal chandelier at Whitehall in 1667, for in that year John Casbert, one of Charles II's upholsterers, made 'a case of taffater wh ribbons' for it at a cost of 2s. The Wheldon Account Books record a payment of £27 9s. 6d. for 'a crystal chandelier and branches' for Chatsworth. Three elaborate examples of these 'branches' hung with crystal are still to be seen at Hampton Court Palace, and it is possible that one of them is the 'Chrystal Branch for candles' which Celia Fiennes found hanging in the middle of the dining-room when she visited the palace early in Queen Anne's reign. In Fig. 8, from the Queen's Bedchamber, the stem is of silver with heads of lions and unicorns at the base amid the branches. This is not a

8. *Rock-crystal Chandelier, base formed of silver lions and unicorns. By William Griffiths, 1736 (Hampton Court Palace. By gracious permission of Her Majesty the Queen.)*

9. (*Left*) *Chandelier, carved and gilt, showing influence of contemporary French design: coronet supported by circular member of tazza form. c. 1695. (Speke Hall, Lancs.)*

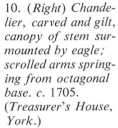

10. (*Right*) *Chandelier, carved and gilt, canopy of stem surmounted by eagle; scrolled arms springing from octagonal base. c. 1705. (Treasurer's House, York.)*

late Stuart example as the style might suggest, for when it was recently taken to pieces for cleaning, a MS. note was found within stating that:

July ye 20th 1736

This lustre and ye fellow to itt was made by William Griffiths [*q.v.*] servant to Mr. Goodison, His Majesty's cabinet maker.

The 'fellow' is perhaps one of the two other 'lustres' at the palace, of different pattern, or it has disappeared.

About the close of the 17th century chandeliers of carved and gilt wood were introduced and tended to supersede the exceedingly costly silver and rock-crystal varieties. Early specimens show unmistakable French influence, obviously inspired by the designs of Lepautre, Berain and Daniel Marot

11. *Chandelier, carved and gilt, headed by ducal coronet; wyverns' heads on lower tier of arms. c. 1720. (Chapel, Kirkleatham Hospital, Yorks.)*

12. *Chandelier, carved and gilt, one of pair; lambrequin ornament below finial; cylindrical arms spring from female masks. c. 1725. (Beningborough, Yorks.)*

13. *Chandelier, carved and gilt; bulbous stem with Indian masks and acanthus; arms intersected by knobs. c. 1730. (Treasurer's House, York.)*

14. *Chandelier, carved and gilt; corbelled base of shaft supports amorini holding festoons of flowers. c. 1740. (Houghton Hall, Norfolk.)*

15. *Chandelier, gilt and carved with foliated and floral ornament; stem surmounted by eagle displayed. c. 1740. (St Giles's House, Dorset.)*

16. *Glass Chandelier, globular stem ornamented with diamond cutting. c. 1755. (Formerly at Thornham Hall, Suffolk.)*

(Fig. 9). The two-tiered chandelier surmounted by a ducal coronet from the chapel at Kirkleatham Hospital (Fig. 11) illustrates the elaboration which such furniture sometimes attained. The base is carved in the style of contemporary silver plate, and the sweep of the broken scrolled branches is exceptionally fine, the lower tier finishing in fantastic wyverns' heads. In Fig. 12 the enriched cylindrical arms spring from finely modelled female masks.

In the succeeding decade this elegance of line gave place to the massive characteristics of furniture produced under the influence of William Kent and other contemporary architects. A chandelier designed for George II by Kent is given in John Vardy's selection from his works (pub. 1744). It shows the prevalent taste in an exaggerated form, and without considerable modification could scarcely have been executed. On the globular stem of Fig. 13 may be seen the Indian masks frequently found in chairs and tables at this time. The gilt chandelier (Fig. 15) is in the florid baroque taste of 1740, the stem being surmounted by a vigorously carved eagle displayed. In Fig. 14 on wide corbels supported by large acanthus scrolls sit amorini holding festoons of flowers; the base ends in a pineapple. This chandelier hangs in the Stone Hall at Houghton, where it has replaced Sir Robert Walpole's celebrated lantern—the subject of contemporary pasquinades. In comparison with their size, these chandeliers carried few candles; and as there was seldom more than one in each room, they must have

afforded a very indifferent light, even when supplemented by wall sconces. Extravagance in lighting was always a subject for comment, because of the comparative obscurity in which most people lived. Mrs Pendarves records that at the coronation banquet of George II, Westminster Hall was illuminated by 1,800 candles, 'besides what were on the table'. The branches holding them were gilt in the form of pyramids, and by an invention of Mr Heidegger, 'which succeeded to the admiration of all spectators', all the candles were lighted in less than three minutes.

Such extravagances were in no way representative of contemporary domestic lighting arrangements. Isaac Ware (*Complete Body of Architecture*, pub. 1746) writes that a room 'which if wainscoted will take six candles to light it, will in stucco require eight or if hung ten', and this allowance appears to him adequate, though he was concerned with the lighting of large houses. Later the consumption of candles greatly increased, and under George III saloons and ballrooms were often a blaze of light. Hanging lights were generally known as 'branches', but in 1729 a Treasury warrant refers to 'putting up chandeliers in the ball-room' at St James's, 'and sconces in the Privy Chamber'; thus differentiating between wall lights and the hanging variety. Seven years earlier Stukeley writes that the word chandelier was 'now modishly employed'.

Chippendale (*Director*, 3rd ed., 1762) states that chandeliers were then generally made of glass, but that brass was some-

17. *Glass Chandelier, with vase-shaped stem, upper arms decorated with spires. c. 1785. (Frank Partridge & Sons.)*

18. *Glass Chandelier festooned with chains and pear-shaped drops. c. 1790. (Hagley Park, Worcs.)*

times used, adding the observation, dictated by his business instincts, that 'if neatly done in wood and gilt in burnished gold [they] would look better and come much cheaper'. He favoured an entirely open construction, stating that he thought it preferable to 'solid sides'. The scarcity of wooden chandeliers dating from the second half of the century suggests that the type recommended by Chippendale did not become fashionable. In the Ball Room at Bedford House, refurnished for the fourth Duke of Bedford in 1759, were 'three large and carved gilt chandeliers with twelve branch lights each, hung with green silk lines and balance tassels'. The desire for brilliant effects led to the use of other materials. Bishop Pococke, writing (Aug., 1754) of the Duke of Cumberland's triangular tower near Sunninghill, states that in the centre of the hexagon room, decorated with festoons of fruit and flowers painted in their natural colours, was 'a branch adorned with Chelsea china, and a group of small statues in the middle of the same ware'. Ladies experimented in the construction of novel chandeliers. In 1745 'Mrs Delaney is very busy in making a shell chandelier or branch', and in 1755 she describes one made by herself and the Duchess of Portland 'as beautiful and elegant as amber, ivory, jet and mother o' pearl could make it'.

An inventory of the contents of Cannons drawn up for the first Duke of Chandos in 1725 mentions 'four glass chandeliers with ballances' in the library; in 1728 the *Daily Post* advertises 'a great quantity of Chrystal Cut Lustres,' and in 1739 Jerom Johnson, one of the most prominent glass-sellers of the period, offers for sale 'cheap, the most magnificent lustre that was ever made in England'—a claim which suggests that glass chandeliers were no longer a novelty. 'Brilliant lustres' and 'branches' were among the varieties of glassware obtainable at his shop in the Strand in 1751; while 'diamond cut and scalloped lustres' were advertised by Johnson in 1752; the one implying incised decoration in shallow star patterns, the other cutting by the hollow wheel.

In the earliest English glass chandeliers (now very rare) the curved arms are plain, and a heavy ball, ornamented with diamond-cutting hollow or in relief, forms the principal member of the shaft. Flat angular drops or pendants were added c. 1750, and the stem, built up on a silvered rod, was surmounted by a scalloped canopy, of which the introduction has been credited to Johnson. Specimens of this phase are rare, because glass chandeliers were sometimes remodelled, others regarded as unfashionable being discarded. That the production, at this time, was on a relatively small scale is suggested by a notice in the *Daily Advertiser* (Jan. 8, 1761), in which Johnson announces that he deals in crystal lustres only, and 'has made upwards of twenty'.

About 1770, under neo-classic influence, an urn motive was adopted for the shaft, which in later examples is considerably elongated in proportion to the diameter (Fig. 19). Pear-shaped drops hung in festoons from the notched or facet-cut branches, and spires of glass sometimes took the place of candles on the upper tiers (Fig. 17). Nine large chandeliers in the New Assembly Rooms, Bath, date from the time they were opened to the public in 1771, and one of those in the Tea Room is cut with the inscription 'Parker, Fleet Street, London'; all these 'lustres' were made by William Parker, who is known to have been established as a glass cutter at 69, Fleet Street c. 1760 and specialised in lighting fittings of all sorts.

19. *Glass Chandelier; shaft with multiple vase-shaped members; scrolled branches notched and festooned with drops. c. 1795.*

In chandeliers c. 1775-1800, beads and 'icicle' drops were used in great profusion, sometimes almost enveloping the shaft, which no longer figures prominently in the design (Fig. 18). The beautiful dark tone of the glass was not peculiar to any particular factory. There is no evidence that glass chandeliers were ever made in considerable numbers in Ireland, and nearly all those in English country houses and assembly rooms dating from this period, though popularly associated with Waterford, are certainly of native production. The Excise Act of 1745 prohibited the export of glass from Ireland, and the Waterford factory was not opened until 1783.

At the end of the century, long cascades of drops were substituted for short pendants, and the shaft was constructed of multiple members among which a 'Grecian' urn was often introduced. The evolution of English 'lustres' from c. 1790 to 1820 is represented in a remarkable collection of contemporary drawings until lately in the possession of Messrs Perry, whose predecessors united with Parker's firm. The purchasers' names, with the prices paid, are entered on the drawings in almost every case, and that English chandeliers had acquired a great reputation abroad is proved by the number exported. In Sept., 1791, a '20 light Lustre Richly cut with Gilt Furniture, paste arms, scroles, prisms and Tabled Drops' was shipped to William Beckford of Fonthill, then in Lisbon, another of similar pattern being made for the King of Spain. The shafts

20. *Chandelier, carved and gilt, based on a design by Thomas Hope. c. 1807. (Formerly Messrs Pratt & Sons.)*

21. *Glass Chandelier, from Wroxton Abbey, Oxon.; drops and nozzles mounted on ormolu framework. c. 1815. Ht. 6 ft., W. 4 ft. (V. & A. Mus.)*

were sometimes chased and enamelled, as in some chandeliers supplied to Lord Grenville in 1790 'on acct of the Government'. Metal bands, described in the accounts as 'silvered or Gilt Furniture', masked the joints of the stems and branches, the cutting becoming much deeper and more elaborate. At Arbury Hall, Nuneaton, there is a letter from Messrs Perry in 1804 in reply to one from Sir Robert Newdegate enquiring the price of a chandelier similar to two eight-light lustres he had bought in 1788. The firm state that they possess sketches of these lustres, but suggest that the branches require modification as 'plain arms have succeeded those cut with hollows, and are generally approved'.

Parker and Perry supplied a large number of magnificent 'lustres' to Carlton House, one made in 1808 at a cost of 1,000 guineas for the centre of the Great Drawing Room being described as 'designed to represent a fountain falling into a large reservoir'. A similar effect is achieved in the fine chandelier from Wroxton Abbey (Fig. 21). This spherical form built up on concentric metal hoops was extremely popular in the early 19th century. The arms and framework were generally of gilt metal, and the closely festooned drops were of diamond shape. J. B. Papworth, the architect, designed a number of such chandeliers about the date of Waterloo. His biographer records that specimens may yet be seen in a few houses 'possessing a beauty of colour and form and a perfectness of manufacture

still unrivalled'. Papworth suggested to the maker, John Blades of Ludgate Hill, long oblong drops full of prismatic colour which 'were so appreciated by the public that the fashion for the small and long oval or diamond-shaped drop was discarded'. For the dining and banqueting rooms at the Pavilion, Brighton, a number of chandeliers and hanging lamps were made by Parker and Perry towards the end of George III's reign, in the most extravagant Chinese taste of the time. Dragons, serpents and mandarins support lotus blooms of coloured glass holding lamps or candles, while drops of green, yellow and blue enhance the garish effect.

For great houses examples in wood or bronze continued to be made, and are illustrated by early 19th-century designers. George Smith (*Household Furniture*, 1808) writes that they are 'to be manufactured for the chief part in wood'. In Fig. 20, which bears a very close resemblance to a design (Pl. XXX) in Thomas Hope's *Household Furniture* (1807), the structure is of carved and gilded wood, the motives including the honeysuckle, gryphons and rosettes. The whole is 'ornamented with a crown of stars over a wreath of nightshade'. Smith adds that they will admit of 24 lights, if required, but the dimensions must be regulated by the size of the room, the base being at least seven feet from the ground. The craving for novelty characteristic of the last phase of Regency furniture was gratified by grotesque animal motives or concentric circles suspended from chains; but drawings in the Perry collection of c. 1820 prove that even at this late date dignified chandeliers were occasionally produced. (*See also English Glass*, W. A. Thorp, 1935. *English Brass Chandeliers*, C. C. Oman, repub. *Arch. Journal*, Vol. XCIII, 1937.)

CHANGEABLE. Textile fabric, shot or woven, with warp and weft threads of different colours, so that material changes colour under different aspects. In Robert Dudley, Earl of Leicester's bedchamber at Leicester House, 1588: 'a fielde bedsteade of Wallnutre the tester and curtains of chaungeable silke.'

CHANNEL MOULDING. Lengthened groove or fluting often found on stiles and muntins of oak furniture; in 17th century such mouldings are flat and 'stopped' at intervals on the framework (*see* CUPBOARDS, HALL, Fig. 9).

CHECKER or **CHEQUER.** Pattern of squares like those of a chess board; favourite motive, laid down in dark and light woods alternately, in 16th- and 17th-century inlay (*see* CUPBOARDS, HALL, Fig. 3).

CHEKKERS. Medieval keyboard instrument, strings plucked by metal points (*see* MUSICAL INSTRUMENTS).

CHERRY WOOD. Two indigenous varieties, *Prunus cerasus* and *Prunus avium*; wood, of close, firm texture and reddish colour, used as inlay in 17th century and for small articles of furniture. Evelyn (*Sylva*, 1664) writes that black cherry tree 'grows sometimes to that bulke, as is fit to make stooles with, Cabinets, Tables'. Stained with lime, oiled and varnished, cherry closely resembles mahogany.

CHESS, BACKGAMMON (TRIC-TRAC) AND DRAUGHTS. *See* BACKGAMMON AND CHESS BOARDS and TABLES, CARD AND GAMING.

CHESTNUT WOOD. Two indigenous varieties, horse chestnut (*Aesculus hippocastanum*) and Spanish or sweet chestnut (*Castanea vesca*). Wood of latter almost white, very like sessile fruited oak and often confused with it. Evelyn (*Sylva*, 1664) writes: 'This Timber also does well for . . . Tables, Chests, Chairs, Stools and Bedsteads.' Certain cuts of both varieties have grain similar to satinwood and were used as substitute for it, 1750-1800, in solid and as veneer. Horse chestnut yellowish in colour.

CHESTS, COFFERS, STANDARDS AND TRUNKS. The chest is the most ancient form of furniture, and from it, with the progress of civilisation, a variety of dissimilar objects has been evolved, including the settle, cabinet and chest of drawers. The nomenclature requires some explanation. Medieval literature, wills and inventories contain innumerable references to receptacles designated both 'chests' and 'coffers', the context showing in many instances where 'coffers' are mentioned that they were chests of small size, like a 'lityle grene coffre for kerchys' bequeathed by John Baset of Bury in 1463. Although it has been suggested that there was a structural difference between chests and coffers— in the one the front being housed and, sometimes, tenoned into the uprights, while the other was constructed of planks pegged or nailed together—the evidence indicates that the terms were regarded as practically interchangeable. Travelling

1. *Oak Chest, formed of a log hollowed out and banded with iron. Medieval. (Milton Bryant Church, Beds.)*

trunks of the later medieval period, covered with leather and studded with nails, were known as 'trussing coffers' or 'standards' (*q.v.*) and were made by leather-workers (*see* COFFER-MAKERS); those of a far more elaborate variety, covered with velvet or other rich materials, supplied to the Crown in the 16th and early 17th centuries, are invariably termed 'coffers' in their makers' accounts. But in general the nature of the material did not determine the use of the name. There is abundant evidence for this conclusion in medieval and Tudor times, but some entries in the inventory (1556) of Sir John Gage of West Firle, Sussex, Constable of the Tower under Henry VIII, may suffice. Among the many articles specified are: 'Item, two trussing cofers, to **carry** upon horse, covered with blacke lether of Flaunders making, bounde with iron. Item, IIII greate cofers of waynescot to laye lynyn in. Item, one great cofer of old making with high feete (obviously not a travelling trunk) to laye lynyn in. Item, II old cofers of Inglishe bourde.' Several 'chests covered in leather' figure in the inventory (1583) of Robert Dudley, Earl of Leicester's furniture at Kenilworth, Warwickshire. In the 17th century also the word 'coffer' frequently occurs in a context showing it to be applied to a wooden chest.

2. *Oak Chest, with canted lid revolving on horizontal pivot. Thirteenth-century type, but probably 15th. Ht. 1 ft. 5 in., L. 2 ft. 7 in., Depth 1 ft. 2½ in. (The late Mr W. Simpson.)*

Randle Holme (*Academy of Armoury*, MS. dated 1649) makes the distinction depend on the shape of the lid, writing that a coffer 'if it haue a streight, and flat cover, is called a chest, which in all other things represents the coffer save the want of a circular lid or cover'. The evidence reveals such a confusion in the terminology that a clear distinction is not to be obtained. Here receptacles of wood, the work of carpenters or joiners, are called 'chests'; while the term 'coffer' is reserved for travelling chests (also commonly known as 'trunks' from towards the end of the 16th century) and for receptacles with a coved or canted lid, as in Holme's definition.

The Anglo-Saxons called the chest a *loc*, assigning control of it to the lady of the household, and the Normans are said to have had examples carved and inlaid with metal and enamel. In the sparsely furnished rooms of early times chests served many purposes: as chairs, beds and practically the only receptacles for valuables. Papal Bulls and Episcopal Injunctions inform us of the religious purposes to which they were devoted before the date of any inventory; they guarded the precious relics of saints, and in them were placed jewels, vestments and church archives.

From a very early date chests were also used as collecting boxes. Jocelin of Brakelond, a monk of St Edmundsbury, records in his *Chronicle* (written 1173-1202) that two of his brethren made a hollow trunk with a hole in the lid and fastened it with an iron lock. This they caused to be set up 'near the door without the choir in the way of the people so that therein persons might put their contributions for the building of the tower'.

It was in chests that money was collected for the Crusades. In 1166 Henry II commanded a coffer to be placed in every church that his subjects might contribute to the relief of the Holy Land, directing as a precaution against theft that the three keys should be separately warded. In 1206, with the same object, Innocent III issued a general mandate exhorting the faithful to put their alms in a 'hollow trunk'. The keys were to be kept by the parish priest and a layman, and from such ordinances originated the three locks which have become associated with ecclesiastical chests. After the Crusades, a slot for money in the lid was forbidden by episcopal injunctions, on the ground that it diverted offerings that should have gone to the priest, and it was not again countenanced by the Church authorities until after the Dissolution, when the vicar and churchwardens were entrusted with the keys. Those of the type described by Jocelin were probably in use centuries before he wrote his *Chronicle*, and they continued to be made on the same lines throughout the Middle Ages. In this primitive form of construction, termed a 'dug out', a trunk split transversely is hollowed out and banded with iron, the section first removed serving as a lid (Fig. 1).

The Synod of Exeter (1287) ordered a chest to be provided in every church for the safe custody of books and vestments, and in this connection they are constantly mentioned in medieval times. Early statutes of Oxford and Cambridge prove that books belonging to the colleges were kept in chests secured by three locks, poor scholars being permitted to borrow volumes of the civil and canon law. In great religious houses, also, the chest was the primitive form of bookcase. (*See* BOOKCASES.) At Durham in the 14th century novices studied in the cloister, and their books were contained in chests, the expenses for repairing them being given in the monastery accounts. MSS. buried in chests in a muniment room were liable to decay; and early in the 16th century Bishop Sherburn of Chichester enjoins upon his Chapter that after the annual compotus 'the boxes be immediately opened and the contents turned with careful examination lest anything should perish by the boxes becoming old, or by the eating of worms, or in any other way'. As late as 1648 William Fiske of Pakenham, a substantial and cultured squire, bequeathed to his son John 'a great chest of elming borde standing in the lower gallerie for to putt therein the bookes': thus plainly indicating that there was no bookcase in the house.

The earliest framed chests now extant date from the 13th century. The front is framed in wide uprights or 'standards', the ends being sometimes tenoned into the uprights at an oblique angle and reinforced with cross-bars of wood (Fig. 2). In this specimen the canted lid is without hinges, revolving on a horizontal pivot, or 'pin hinge', a device seldom found after the 13th century. The flanges open with the lid working in a slot in the back stiles, an arrangement designed for greater security, while in some examples an iron plate of pear or kite shape prevents the pivot from being withdrawn. The feet of the Stoke D'Abernon, Surrey, chest seen in Fig. 3 are worked into small shafts on the inner side, and the front is decorated with chip-carved roundels. There is a slot for money in the lid and below it a till or tray with a false bottom concealing a well. These tills continued to be used for the collection of alms in defiance of episcopal injunctions, being occasionally so contrived that on the withdrawal of a pin they tilt up; the lock-plates in this instance are of much later date. At Chichester Cathedral there is another fine example of this type, the roundels being spaced as on the Stoke D'Abernon chest and retaining traces of the original red ochre decoration.

A large number of 13th-century chests are preserved in churches and museums. Repeated ecclesiastical enactments partly account for their existence, but the lawlessness of the age caused many domestic chests to be entrusted to churches. While they remained in private houses they were a permanent temptation to thieves; the loss from them of fur-lined gowns and other valuables at the hands of insurgents is several times deplored in the *Paston Letters*. Medieval testators sometimes directed that their plate, jewels and muniments should be deposited in 'some sure abbaye' to await the owner's coming-of-age; thereafter the contents were removed, but the chest was left behind as a thank-offering. At Oxford the common chest of the university, from which any master of arts might borrow three pounds on depositing security, remained in St Frideswide's down to the Dissolution. Such provisions for the relief of poverty were not confined to the universities and other corporate bodies. In 1371 a Lord Mayor of London gave a chest with three locks and 1,000 marks therein to be lent to young men, the recital of a *de profundis* or *pater noster* being all that was required before they received assistance. Chests, indeed, are inseparably associated with the promiscuous charity of those times.

From the close of the 13th century strap hinges were generally employed in place of pivots, the fronts and sides being often banded with foliated iron scrollwork of beautiful design, plated and applied over velvet or cloth. The construc-

3. *Oak Chest with pivoted lid; front and wide stiles carved with roundels. c. 1300. Ht. 2 ft. 1½ in., L. 3 ft. 11 in., Depth. 1 ft. 6½ in. (Stoke D'Abernon Church, Surrey.)*

4. *Oak Chest formed of planks nailed together and iron-banded; lid decorated in tempera with armorial shields and fabulous monsters; the lock missing. c. 1340. Ht. 2 ft. 1 in., L. 6 ft. 4 in., Depth 1 ft. 4 in. (Sir William Burrell Coll., Glasgow.)*

5. *Oak Chest; the front decorated with carved and painted tracery in two arcades. Late 14th century. Ht. 3 ft., L. 5 ft. 3 in., Depth 2 ft. 4 in. (Faversham Church, Kent.)*

6. *Oak Chest, front carved with the emblems of the four Evangelists and stiles with Gothic tracery. Late 14th century. Ht. 2 ft. 5¼ in., L. 5 ft. 7½ in., Depth 2 ft. 5½ in. (Dersingham Church, Norfolk.)*

7. *Oak Chest front, carved in high relief with a representation of the Nativity, with the Annunciation and Coronation of the Virgin. c. 1430. Ht. 2 ft. 5 in., L. 4 ft. 2 in. (V. & A. Mus.)*

8. *Oak Chest, front carved with two knights tilting; stiles with figures under architectural canopies. Early 15th century. Ht. 2 ft. 5 in., L. 4 ft. ½ in., Depth 2 ft. 2 in. (Harty Church, Isle of Sheppey.)*

9. *Chest, carved with the owner's name, 'N. Fares', framed in a vine pattern; front decorated with volutes terminating in roses; base arcaded; hinges later. Possibly used as a counter. Late 15th century. Ht. 1 ft. 5½ in., L. 3 ft. 6½ in., Depth 1 ft. 6 in. (V. & A. Mus.)*

10. *Standard covered with leather and banded with iron. Early 16th century. Ht. 2 ft. 3 in., L. 4 ft. 4 in.; Depth 2 ft. 2 in. (Woodbridge Church, Suffolk.)*

tion remained unchanged, but the fronts were now sometimes carved with an arcade of Gothic tracery, the outer stiles being ornamented with fabulous monsters in horizontal panels. The Faversham chest of Fig. 5 is constructed of massive boards without stiles, and the front is decorated with two rows of tracery divided by applied buttresses and resting on a diapered base. A coffer of exactly similar design is at Rainham church in the same county, and both these fine examples retain considerable traces of the original tempera decoration.

In a splendid chest at Dersingham, Norfolk, church (Fig. 6) the front is divided into panels carved with the symbols of the four evangelists. The outer uprights of this masterpiece are enriched with delicate Pointed tracery on a diapered ground, the whole being enclosed within borders carved with birds and flowers. The original lid, part of which is missing, was formerly surrounded by the inscription *Iesus Nazarenus Crucifixsus Rex Iudeorum*. Again on this example remains of polychrome decoration may be seen.

From the 14th century onwards the front was occasionally treated in a realistic manner, jousts and deeds of arms being portrayed on the panel. The chest (Fig. 8) is a specimen of these so-called 'tilting chests', the front being spiritedly carved with two knights in armour tilting, with their squires in the background; while on the stiles are figures under battlemented canopies in civil costume of c. 1400. The encounter of St George with the Dragon was another popular subject at this period on chests of Low Country origin, though no indubitable English specimen appears to have survived. On the celebrated York chest the story is represented in a series of episodes. Among the steep-pitched roofs in the background may be noticed a crow-stepped gable, a familiar Flemish detail, which, with the general character of the carving, indicates a foreign origin. In the Low Countries comparable examples exist.

The execution of such elaborate chests demanded a skill far in excess of that of the carpenter, and with the development of their art the makers formed a guild of their own. In 1328 the lesser craft of cofferers is mentioned in a list of mysteries authorised to elect their own officers, and by 1422 they had, apparently, attained to major rank.

The medieval passion for colour and gilding found an outlet in the embellishment of woodwork. The *Polychronicon* of Ranulph Higden (translated into English by John of Trevisa, 1357) relates that Fair Rosamond, the mistress of Henry II, had a coffer on which were represented, no doubt in colour, 'various figures moving like life, as giants, beasts and birds flying to and fro'; and the celebrated chest in Newport church, Essex, dating from c. 1300, is painted inside the lid in oils with the Crucifixion and figures of the Virgin Mary, St John, St Peter and St Paul. The armorial bearings which decorated a row of shields on the front of this chest have disappeared, and a sunken band of foliated leadwork below has been renewed.

The remarkable chest (Fig. 4), formerly in the office of the Chancery Court, Durham, was originally decorated throughout in tempera, and inside the lid, on a green diapered ground, are painted four shields, a centaur running a tilt against a dragon, and at either end the rampant figures of a lion and griffin. The shields are blazoned as follows: 1. *Gules: a cinquefoil ermine, within a bordure sable charged with bezants;* 2. *Gules: a cross argent between four cinquefoils ermine;* 3. *England quartering France Ancient;* 4. *Gules: a saltire argent.*

The arms on the first shield are those of Dangervile, of county Leicester, of which family Richard de Bury, Bishop of

Durham 1335-45, was a member. Although the second cannot be definitely identified, probably the cross argent represents an augmentation granted to the bishop. The third shield, England and France quarterly, is the form used prior to 1340, indicating that the coffer was made before that date. The fourth coat is that of Nevill of Raby, created Earl of Westmorland in 1397.

The blazoning of these shields shows that the chest was made for the celebrated Bishop of Durham, Chancellor of England and High Treasurer under Edward III. Traces of the same decoration can be seen on the till fitted in the interior. Here the structure is formed of single slabs of oak pegged and nailed together without stiles, and reinforced by plain bands of iron; at the ends are twisted rings of that metal. The handles found on this and many other medieval examples were provided to facilitate transport; ropes were passed through them, and the chest, slung on poles, was borne on men's shoulders to the waggon or cart which was to carry it.

Scriptural subjects sometimes took the place of mythological, as in the chest front (Fig. 7), the treatment in this instance being distinctly English. The different scenes and the detail of costume are rendered with remarkable spirit and realism.

Towards the end of the 15th century new principles of construction were introduced from abroad, and chests begin to lose their archaic character. Framed-up panelling appears, the joints being connected with mortise and tenon; the width of the stiles was much reduced, and tracery was sometimes applied instead of being carved out of the solid. Chests on the earlier plan continued, however, to be made until after the close of the Middle Ages, and in Fig. 9 late Gothic detail is found combined with horizontal panels pegged into the stiles. The front is carved with two graceful volutes ending in large roses, and the back bears in Lombardic capitals the owner's name and a device resembling the cup of an acorn. This elaborate decoration of the back proves that the chest was intended to stand out in a room: possibly it was used as a counter (see COUNTERS). The cusped arcade is a decorative motive of foreign origin borrowed from the 'Flaunders chests' so often mentioned in contemporary inventories. These chests, often described as of 'overseas work', were of the wainscoted type, and formed the model for English craftsmen. They were decorated with biblical and mythological subjects; or with the familiar linen-fold pattern, elaborated at a later date with bunches of grapes, tassels and fringes.

Massive 'boarded chests' of archaic construction continued to be made in remote parts of the country after the introduction of panel framing, and this primitive principle of construction, though with a much less prodigal use of material, was to survive until a far later date.

In such quantities was Flemish furniture brought into England in the second half of the century that the Guild of Cofferers, 'like to be undone by the said wares', petitioned Richard III in 1483 and obtained a statute prohibiting the trade under pain of forfeiture. This enactment soon became a dead letter; the work of foreign craftsmen continued to be imported 'ready wrought', and in the second half of the 16th century the productions of English cofferers were largely supplemented by 'Dantzic chests'. This seems to have been only another name for the 'spruce coffers' of earlier times that by now had become particularly associated with the port whence they were shipped (see DANSK and SPRUCE). John Baset of Bury, in his will of 1463, expressed a wish that his 'prews coffre' should 'alwey remayne' in his house, and with it three of the 'fotyd stolys thereto'—a provision suggesting that the stools were stowed away in the coffer when not in use. By the 16th century the use of Baltic fir for chests had become so familiar that testators held a bequest of 'my spruce' a sufficient explanation.

Chests were often given or bequeathed to chantry chapels, and detailed descriptions of their contents occur in contemporary wills. In 1507 Richard Brereley, Rector of Kirk Smeaton, Yorkshire, left 'to the chaumtre at Branburgh' his 'long iron bonden kyrst for to keep ye chales ye vestments, and ye evydence belongyng to ye said chauntre', with instructions that it was to be divided into two and 'oon parte to have II lokes for ye evidence, ye keyes to be in kepyng as ye composicion shewes'.

When great nobles changed houses, their plate, linen and valuables were packed in large chests known as 'standards'. These figure constantly in the inventories of Reginald de la Pole, Duke of Suffolk, relating to his journeys between Wingfield Manor and Ewelme; they are described as 'bowden

11. *Oak Chest, the stiles frame panels carved with linen-fold. Early 16th century. Ht. 1 ft. 11¾ in., L. 3 ft. 4½ in., Depth 1 ft. 5¾ in. (V. & A. Mus.)* 12. *Oak Chest, the top rail has an incised inscription; front carved with foliated ornament and profile portraits in Renaissance taste. c. 1535. Ht. 2 ft. 1 in., L. 4 ft. 1 in., Depth 1 ft. 7 in. (V. & A. Mus.)*

13. *Oak Chest, front represents an architectural elevation; panels inlaid with arms of Hugh Offley, Lord Mayor of London, and floral arabesques; three drawers in the lower portion; arcaded stand not original. Probably made by immigrant German craftsmen. c. 1590. Ht. 3 ft. 3 in., L. 6 ft. 6 in., Depth 2 ft. 4 in. (Southwark Cathedral.)*

with yrene', painted or covered with leather, and fitted with two locks, the keys of the more important being 'in my ladies keping'. Their size is suggested by the list of the contents of a single specimen: the altar hangings, tapestry, vestments, cushions, etc., are all enumerated. John de Vere, thirteenth Earl of Oxford, directed in his will (April 10, 1509) that after his death his executors 'in as good haste as they reasonably may shall convey or cause to be conveyed such of his jewels, plate stuff and goods movable as shall be thought most convenient' in chests of this description from Castle Heding-ham to the Abbey of Bury. In an inventory of his goods there are long lists of plate and jewels 'in great standards or strong coofers' all of iron (*i.e.* banded with it), 'some with as many as VI lokkes upon the same'. When Henry VIII moved from Hampton Court to Whitehall, carts were hired to bring 'the great standards with the rich coates of the garde', and on their arrival in London a special house was set apart to contain them. Standards were not, however, invariably of vast bulk, and of five belonging to Katherine of Aragon 'covered with lether and peyntid red', none measured more than a 'yard and a quarter yard'. The term continued to be used in the traditional sense well into Georgian times: in 1713 William Johnson, coffer-maker to Queen Anne, supplied the Royal laundress with 'One large Strong Standard Trunk'.

The smaller travelling chests of the 15th and 16th centuries were known as 'trussing coffers', and for these *cuir bouilli* was a favourite covering. The leather, first prepared in oils and spirits, was sometimes incised with a pattern and painted or gilded. They were made without feet and fitted with handles to be carried in waggons or hung in pairs across the backs of sumpter horses.

Some of the coffers supplied to the Crown and members of the Royal household in the reign of Henry VIII and Elizabeth I were the elaborate and costly productions of a specialised trade. Katherine of Aragon possessed one 'covered with crymson velvett garnyshed with gilte nayles, havinge four

tilles therein, the forefront of every of them gilte', and others elaborately lined and trimmed are described in the royal coffermakers' bills of the period (*see* 'The Chest and the Coffer' and 'The Craft of the Coffermaker', R. W. Symonds, *Connoisseur*, Vol. CVII, pp. 15 and 100).

Circa 1500-25 Gothic forms were gradually invaded by Renaissance detail. Although arcaded chests were still occasionally made, the traceried front was generally discarded in favour of profile heads enclosed in medallions, the panels being sometimes elaborated with dolphins and foliated ornament. Early specimens exhibit an interesting mixture of styles, and even a century later Gothic tradition lingered on in remote parts of the country.

In Fig. 12 Gothic and Renaissance mouldings are found combined, but the conventional profile heads are entirely Renaissance in character. Until the end of the century movable chairs were so scarce that, in the majority of houses, chests and stools remained the ordinary seats and were produced in enormous quantities. The Nettlecombe inventory (1526) mentions fourteen chests of various sorts and sizes in the 'Master's Chamber' alone; and even in France, where a far higher standard of domestic comfort prevailed, writes Viollet-le-Duc, '*Du temps de Brantome encore, à la cour, chez les riches seigneurs, on s'asseyait sur des coffres ou bahuts pendant les nombreuses réunions*'.

When colour was desired, inlay was substituted for painting and gilding, and early in Elizabeth I's reign architectural features were again introduced on chests of decorative character. The celebrated example in Southwark Cathedral (Fig. 13) was given to the church by Hugh Offley, who was Sheriff of London, and an Alderman in 1588. The front is composed of arches, architraves, pilasters and pedimented windows supporting an entablature in the classical style, and the panels are inlaid in a variety of coloured wood with the arms of the Lord Mayor and his wife's family, his merchant's mark and floral arabesques. The architectural design of the front and the

14. *Oak Chest; front arcaded and inlaid with floral scrolls; rails and stiles elaborately carved. c.* 1600. (*Messrs Stair and Andrew.*)

15. *Oak Chest, stiles carved with terminal figures and front arcaded. c.* 1590. *Ht.* 2 *ft.* 4½ *in., L.* 4 *ft.* 10½ *in., Depth* 2 *ft.* 1½ *in.* (*The late Mr Ralph Philipson.*)

floral decorations are reminiscent of contemporary West German chests, but, though Offley's elder brother was prominently associated with the Baltic trade, the chest may well have been made by members of the colony of immigrant German craftsmen settled in Southwark at this date. The three drawers in the lower portion represent an innovation and the first stage in the evolution of chests of drawers.

Fantastic buildings, grotesques and animal motives were sometimes represented by inlay towards the end of the 16th century: so-called 'Nonsuch Chests' are a distinct variety of this style of decoration. The fronts are divided into panels coarsely inlaid in holly, bog oak and various coloured woods with a conventional representation of a domed and turreted building flanked by lantern-topped towers framed in intricate chequer patterns and borders of bead-and-reel. Above them is often a frieze of dormer windows, and in some examples the central panels are enclosed within projecting pedimented arches. The design bears some resemblance to a drawing of Henry VIII's celebrated palace of Nonsuch, near Cheam, Surrey, made by Jooris Hoefnagle in 1568, and to an engraving of it published in Braun's *Cities* of 1582; hence the name applied in modern times to these chests.

Very similar architectural designs—domed buildings with towers or turrets—can be found on other contemporary varieties of furniture of indubitable English origin (cf. The Great Bed of Ware, BEDS; Fig. 8), but the tinned metal hinges with engraved foliate ornament, a common feature of the type, are distinctly Teutonic in character, and chests decorated in a comparable style were made in Germany at this period. If some 'Nonsuch Chests' were produced in England by members of the German colony, the type is certainly of foreign origin.

In medieval documents there are frequent references to the injury caused by moth to linen and clothes in chests. In the early 16th century chests of cypress were introduced to counteract this danger, the wood being esteemed on account of the belief that it was a preservative against moth; the decoration was generally incised or carved in very low relief, the front and sides being dovetailed into the stiles with wide V-shaped intersections. Walnut chests are mentioned in Tudor inventories. Some of these were Italian *cassones* imported into England, like the 'fower faier flatt Venetian chests of walnutree carved and gilte with locks and keys' enumerated among the goods of Robert Dudley, Earl of Leicester, in 1588; but

English examples do not appear to have survived. Wainscot chests were still commonly used to accommodate the owner's wardrobe, and below the lid a small hanging box, or till, was often fitted to contain trinkets, ribbons and other toilet accessories. In north country inventories of this period 'Danske chystes' are entered in large numbers. Robert Barker, an alderman of Newcastle, in 1588 possessed 'one lardge Danske Chest' with 'insett worke'—*i.e.* an inlaid chest from the Baltic, possibly resembling the 'Nonsuch' type.

Instead of pilasters, the arcading of late 16th-century chests is sometimes divided by terminal figures of men and women, as in Fig. 15 where the dragons on the frieze probably indicate a Welsh origin. Signs of decadence are generally perceptible by about 1600 in both carving and decoration, a coarse floral inlay being the principal motive in the panels of arcaded chests. Even in Fig. 14—an exceptionally fine specimen—the rails and stiles are redundant in ornament; the mouldings are thin, and the construction has become much less massive. Fig. 16 is a rough household coffer formed of planks pegged together. The treatment of the panels flanking the arms and date proves that the maker possessed a decorative sense, though the quality of the carving is indifferent. An attempt at architectural design is observable in Fig. 17, where the arches are of irregular size, the centre one being nail-headed, while those on either

side are supported by small balustered columns. These arches are divided by plain stiles, the corbels intersecting the frieze being incised with vertical lines. The lid is panelled, a common feature from this time forward. The spandrels of the two small arches are incised 'E.B.' with the date 1662.

Coffers covered with velvet, 'fustian of Naples', silk and other rich fabrics, trimmed with fringes and studded with brass-headed nails figure frequently in royal inventories under the Tudors, and also in those of great nobles. The type continued in use in the first half of the 17th century, and such receptacles are found described among the contents of Charles I's palaces. At Somerset House in 1649 there was, for instance, 'a small coffer of greene vellet studded with silver gilt and foure lions and new covered with new velvett', which was sold for the large sum of £50.

Linen and clothes were still often laid down, in spite of the great increase in the number of cupboards (*q.v.*), and the chests used for this purpose, carved with the bride's name and the year of her marriage, commonly formed part of her dowry. At Ingatestone, in 1600, a 'litell room' was set apart to contain the 'lynnen' which was stored in 'a long plaine chest with two partitions having a lydd with a spring locke and key'. When Charles I's furniture was sold by the Council of State after his execution, there were immense quantities of linen and

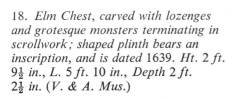

16. Oak 'borded Chest', front, carved with a foliated design, bears the Noel arms and date 1620. Ht. 2 ft. 1 in., L. 3 ft. 8 in., Depth 1 ft. 5 in. (From Mr C. G. Stirling.)

17. Oak Chest, front carved with an arcade and foliated strapwork; initials E.B. and date 1662 incised. (The late Sir Edward Barry.)

18. Elm Chest, carved with lozenges and grotesque monsters terminating in scrollwork; shaped plinth bears an inscription, and is dated 1639. Ht. 2 ft. 9½ in., L. 5 ft. 10 in., Depth 2 ft. 2½ in. (V. & A. Mus.)

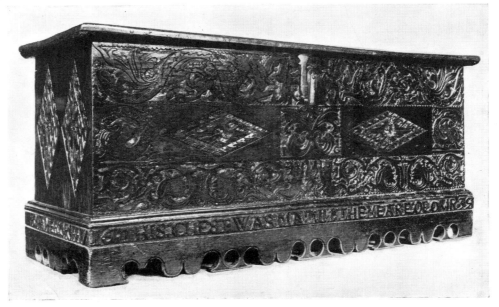

19. *Oak Chest with two drawers at base; front and stiles carved with scrolls and foliated ornament. Mid-17th century. Ht. 2 ft. 10 in., L. 4 ft. 10½ in., Depth 2 ft. (The late Mr Harold Peto.)*

20. *Oak Chest, painted with tulips and carnations in vases; stiles channel moulded. Mid-17th century. Ht. 2 ft. 2 in., L. 4 ft. 10 in., Depth 1 ft. 10 in. (V. & A. Mus.)*

21. *Oak Chest inlaid with bone; pilasters decorated with split balusters; drawers at base of walnut inlaid with lines of box. c. 1655. (From Col N. R. Colville.)*

wearing apparel belonging to Henrietta Maria in cypress chests at Somerset House, and until late in the century many householders kept their wardrobe and library in chests. In his will (1661), Captain Adam Eyre left his wife all his goods and movables 'save my apparel and bookes with the chest wherein the same are kept'.

The variety described in Stuart inventories as a 'borded' chest is represented by Fig. 18. The uprights are omitted, and planks pegged together form the front and sides. Something of traditional style is preserved in the shallow ornament of grotesque monsters terminating in scrollwork, and the deeply moulded plinth is skilfully shaped. This specimen is of elm, the carved inscription relating that it was made 'In the Yeare of Our Lord God Anno Do. 1639 by James Griffin'; the elaborate lock-plate is of a type often fitted to Stuart leather-covered trunks. The shallow ornament and addorsed S-scrolls afford an approximate guide to the date of the chest in Fig. 19, which has two drawers below the front.

In the Griffin chest (Fig. 18) traces of colour below the lock-plate show that painting was still used in the traditional manner as an accessory to carving; but, with the decline of the chest-maker's craft, it sometimes constituted the only decoration. In the example shown in Fig. 20, well within the capacities of a village carpenter, the tulips and carnations in vases were originally painted in vivid reds and greens. The applied balusters and faceted ornament of Fig. 22 are favourite motives of about the middle of the century.

A number of chests geometrically panelled and inlaid with bone were produced about the date of Charles II's restoration, and, like contemporary chests of drawers, always exhibit the same characteristics: the main structure is of oak, the polygonal panels are elaborately mitred, and the centres boldly projected. The frieze in Fig. 21 is vigorously carved, the drawers are of walnut inlaid with lines of box and the pilasters are decorated with split balusters.

Travelling trunks of the 17th century were covered with ox-hide or Russia-leather and closely studded with intricate designs in brass nails. The lids are curved and closed by means of a flanged joint to keep out the rain. Fig. 23 shows a travelling trunk once owned by Charles I and given by Henrietta Maria, with other furniture, to Henry Jermyn, Earl of St Albans. The lid bears the Royal monogram below a crown, and the front is covered with a graceful design of birds and foliated arabesques, the bottom letting down as a flap. This specimen was formerly at Rushbrooke Hall, Bury St Edmunds, and contained an embroidered shirt and other relics of Charles I.

The 'lynnen in Mrs Tomazin's charge' at Gilling Castle in 1594 was kept in a trunk, and as the inventory was drawn up to enable Sir William Fairfax to gain an accurate idea of the value of his possessions, the contents are set down with scrupulous precision, the presence of 'oon odd sheet of fine holland' being explained by a note that 'my lady', his wife, was 'wound' in its fellow. The Countess of Leicester used trunks to contain her jewellery and plate in 1634, while her linen was stored in the 'Bed Wardroppe' in the 'great blacke trunke at the bed feete' and in two others bound with iron. Sir Simon D'Ewes, writing to his brother four years later, says 'when the things in your trunk are aired (which upon your direction I shall remember to have done), I will carefullie

22. *Oak Chest, decorated with applied balusters and faceted ornament. c. 1660. (From Mr E. Lawrence.)*

23. *Travelling Trunk, covered with leather and studded with brass nails; lid bears crowned monogram of Charles I. c. 1640. (Rushbrooke Hall, Suffolk.)*

24. *Travelling Trunk, covered with leather and studded with nails; drawers in base; top bears crowned monogram of William and Mary. c. 1690. Ht. 2 ft. 3 in., L. 3 ft. 2 in., Depth 1 ft. 10 in. (V. & A. Mus.)*

25. *Walnut Chest, decorated with marquetry of birds and flowers in various coloured woods on an ebony ground; drawer in base; feet are restorations. c. 1675. Ht. 3 ft., L. 4 ft. 1 in., Depth 2 ft. ¾ in. (C. D. Rotch Collection.)*

26. *Chest, japanned in gold on a black ground; stand S-scrolled, and mounts in style of contemporary cabinets. c. 1697. (Chatsworth, Derbys.)*

27. *Chest, constructed of Chinese lacquer panels in polychrome. c. 1700. (Formerly at Holme Lacy, Herefords.)*

open and shutt the same and nothing shall be stured but your cloathes. . . .' John Aubrey kept his books in his trunk in the latter part of his life when evading his creditors, and in 1673 he wrote to Anthony Wood that they 'would be like butterflies and fly about all the country', if he were to trust the key to his brother.

Richard Pigge, coffer-maker to Charles II, supplied a large number of trunks covered with 'Russia-leather' to various members of the Court between 1667 and 1671. He made them of two kinds, with and without drawers, the handles and locks being generally described as 'of ye best'. In December, 1667, he supplied Madame Chiffinch with one 'lyned with sarcenett and quilted' for £3, charging £1 more 'for a paire of simple trunks to putt the Duke of Saxonie's Roabes in'; these were covered with 'seile skynn' and provided with girdles of ox-leather. Until late in the 18th century a coffer-maker is found among the officers of the royal household, and the Lord Chamberlain's accounts show that from 1750 to 1760, Edward Smith, who then held that office, supplied George II and various members of the Court with a large number of trunks covered with Russia-leather. The crown and monogram, so often found on these trunks, do not necessarily imply royal ownership: furniture and other accessories used in the palaces or Government service were often so stamped.

Though at the Restoration walnut became the fashionable wood it was seldom employed for chests, which continued to be made of the traditional oak. Marquetry examples are rare, the majority being of Dutch origin, but the polychromatic inlay of Charles II's time was occasionally applied to chests by English craftsmen. In Fig. 25 the front is divided by wide strappings into a centre and four spandrels, and decorated with coloured birds and flowers on an ebony ground. The normal sequence of marquetry is not to be found on chests, for the seaweed and arabesque varieties were obviously unsuited to furniture of this type. Even plain walnut chests are rare, but examples are occasionally found with a herring-bone banding and drawers at the base.

Receptacles fitted with drawers had now become common, but chests to contain linen and clothes were also made to

28. *Coffer decorated in polychrome in 'Bantam Work' on cabriole-legged stand. Coffer probably late 17th century. Stand made for it c. 1710. Mr C. R. T. Edwards.)*

29. *Chest, decorated in black and gold japan; stand supported on carved and gilt wyverns and S-scrolled legs. c. 1740. (Formerly at Kimbolton Castle, Hunts.)*

30. *Chest on stand, gilt gesso carved with arabesques and foliage on a trellis ground. c. 1720. Attributed to James Moore. (Boughton House, Northants.)*

31. *Chest of sarcophagus form on lion-paw feet; decorated in carved and gilt gesso. c. 1725. Ht. 2 ft. 7 in., L. 4 ft. 9 in., Depth 2 ft. 2½ in. (V. & A. Mus.)*

32. *Chest, gilt and elaborately carved with rococo ornament on a matted ground; the top japanned. c. 1755-60. Attributed to William Vile. (Longford Castle, Wilts.)*

33. *Elm Chest on cabriole legs; fielded panels and two drawers; shaped under-framing. c. 1720. Ht. 1 ft. 9 in., L. 2 ft., Depth 1 ft. (Mr Aubrey Jenkins.)*

34. *Mahogany Chest with drawer at base; decorated with lattice-work. c. 1760. Ht. 3 ft. 2½ in., L. 4 ft. 1½ in., Depth 2 ft. 3½ in. (Lulworth Castle, Dorset.)*

accord with contemporary japanned furniture and were sometimes mounted on elaborate stands. Like the cabinets of that time, they were either imported from the East or made in England, and decorated in imitation of oriental lacquer. When Pepys visited the Duke of York in 1661, among the furniture that attracted his attention were 'two very fine chests covered with gold and India varnish given him by the East India Company of Holland'; while lacquer trunks formed part of the cargoes of three ships sold at the East India House in 1700. Large blanket chests with domed lids were another fashionable form of bedroom furniture. The account book of the first Duke of Devonshire (September, 1697) records the arrival of japanned chests at Chatsworth, a payment being made to Henry Lobb the Joyner for '2 bills for cases of ye Japan chests'. That seen in Fig. 26 is probably one of these, the S-scrolled stand according with the date of the entry; the black and gold decoration is English with oriental motives in high relief.

A fine example (Fig. 27) is constructed of incised Chinese lacquer panels in polychrome, while a chest on a cabriole-legged stand (Fig. 28) is decorated with 'Bantam work', the rare English imitation of this Oriental variety (see JAPANNING AND LACQUER), in this instance of exceptional quality. The landscape and buildings in Fig. 29 are on the small scale of Georgian japanning, but the chest is here entirely subordinate to the very ornate stand, formed of wyverns, with a shell in the centre of the frieze and S-scrolled legs at the back.

The gilt gesso decoration fashionable on furniture in the early 18th century seems to have been rarely applied to chests. A remarkable example (Fig. 30), which may be attributed to the royal cabinet-maker, James Moore (q.v.), is mounted on its original stand, the front being divided into panels by strap-work and delicately carved with ribbons and acanthus sprays on a trellised ground. The sarcophagus type was occasionally designed by William Kent and a fine chest of this kind from Shobden, Herefordshire (Fig. 31), bears the cypher without a coronet, as the central ornament of the top, of William Bateman, created viscount in 1725; thus proving that the chest (reminiscent in shape of Italian *cassoni* of the Renaissance) was made before he was raised to the peerage. It rests on lion-paw feet and the whole surface, except the back (intended to stand against a wall), is richly decorated in gesso-work, the motives including six spiritedly carved Indian masks on the pilasters and a large scrolled shell at the base.

The lavishly enriched gilt example (Fig. 32) is of a hybrid type, for though the upper part consists of a chest, below the lifting japanned top the front opens with doors, revealing a series of mahogany drawers. Probably this remarkable piece was supplied to the first Viscount Folkestone by Vile and Cobb c. 1760. The finely carved pendants of fruit and flowers hanging from satyrs' masks on the pilasters and the aureoles forming the centre of the panels bear a strong resemblance to the carved mahogany bookcase supplied by the firm to Queen Charlotte in 1762 (see Frontispiece).

Oak chests continued to be made until well into the 18th century. In most carved examples the decoration is decadent, and sometimes merely incised, but in Fig. 33 (which resembles the oak type but is of elm) the panels are fielded, and the stand

is mounted on short cabriole legs. To this type, with drawers fitted in the stand, the term 'mule chest' is generally applied.

The old demand for a receptacle in which the bedroom hangings, linen and blankets of a large house could be conveniently stored was met by walnut and mahogany chests fitted with one or more drawers at the base. Brass handles were usually provided to lift such chests off the stands. Fig. 34 dates from c. 1760; the lattice-work decoration is very unusual, the panels of lighter mahogany on the sides being bordered by a small bead-and-reed moulding.

From 1750 to 1800 chests were in great measure superseded by other varieties of bedroom furniture. Many of the 'clothes presses' in the trade catalogues of Chippendale and his contemporaries keep the chest form, but the front is generally enclosed by doors. Chippendale (*Director*, 1754) gives several designs for furniture of this type, describing those with drawers at the bottom as 'a press and chest combined in one piece'. The inconvenience of storing clothes in a chest without partitions was obviated by fitting the interior with sliding shelves, resembling those in wardrobes of this period (see CUPBOARDS, PRESSES AND WARDROBES). Chippendale recommends that shelves of such presses be covered with baize. Two designs for 'Cloathes Chests' are given in Ince and Mayhew's *Household Furniture* (1759-63), but such furniture does not figure in later books of design, being finally superseded by chests of drawers and commodes.

CHESTS, LOBBY. 'A kind of half chest of drawers adapted for the use of a small study, lobby or lodging room. They usually consist of four drawers in height, rising to three feet in height. The top drawer is usually divided into two and sometimes there is a writing slider which draws out under the top' (Sheraton, *Cabinet Dictionary*, 1803).

CHESTS OF DRAWERS. As the name implies, chest-like constructions with the interior occupied by drawers. From c. 1550 cabinets and travelling coffers fitted with small drawers generally described as 'tilles' or 'drawer boxes', are mentioned in inventories and accounts (see CHESTS, COFFERS and CABINETS). In joined chests, a drawer at the base marks the starting-point of this development, an innovation which originated on the Continent. Hugh Offley's chest in Southwark Cathedral (probably made in 1588 by immigrant craftsmen in Southwark) has three drawers in the lower part (see CHESTS, Fig. 13); while there are two in a chest of similar character made for Gilbert Talbot, probably in 1568, at Hardwick Hall, Derbyshire. Early references suggest a kind of furniture for which a generally accepted name had not yet been found. Minsheu, for instance, in his Spanish-English Dictionary of 1599, renders the word *Caxcon* as 'a great chest or standerd with drawing chests or boxes in it'.

Early 17th-century inventories list nothing suggesting a chest of drawers, and at that time even in great establishments linen and clothes were still generally laid down in chests. Though such a method of storage was obviously inconvenient, the next stage in the evolution was delayed until c. 1650, when a hybrid form, half cabinet and half chest of drawers came into use among the prosperous classes. At first a connection with

1. *Chest of Drawers of architectural design; oak inlaid with floral designs in ivory and mother-of-pearl; pilasters and panels faced with ebony. c. 1650. (Mme Jacques Balsan.)*

architectural treatment of the front; on the doors scrolled broken pediments surmount an architrave enclosing arches in perspective. Fig. 2 is in a similar style, but with the central panels boldly projected in faceted mouldings and a free use of split baluster ornament. This style obtained for about a decade and proves that, in spite of the prevailing austerity, decorative furniture was occasionally made during the Protectorate. A structural advance is represented by Fig. 3, the doors now being discarded; a single deep receptacle is retained in the upper stage.

After the Restoration chests of drawers came into general use among the wealthier classes in place of the time-honoured chests and coffers. The love of dress spread rapidly, a natural revulsion from the deadening effects of Puritan rule, and more convenient receptacles were required for clothing, now often made of thinner materials, which would have suffered severely by compression in a chest. The lifting top with a well below, an arrangement characteristic of travelling coffers of an earlier date, is still retained in Fig. 6. This well and the drawers are lined with paper printed from wooden blocks, the ovals on the underside of the lid containing a shield of the Royal Arms as borne by Charles II. The lid is of elm, and the chest of walnut with oak drawer-linings, the front being carved with handle plates in the form of a ring with tulip-shaped devices on either side. Fig. 19 shows a remarkable instance of the strong atavistic tendency that prevailed in areas far removed from metropolitan influences. This chest of drawers, from a country house in Glamorgan, would on the evidence of style be assigned to c. 1670, but is dated 1717.

the chest is apparent in the construction: the framework is massive, and sometimes the lifting top is retained. A deep drawer in the upper or lower stage is combined with others of lesser depth enclosed by doors; or one drawer superimposed on another occupy the entire area. Bearers were fixed to the carcase, the sides of the drawers being grooved to receive them, a practice continued until after the Restoration (*see* CONSTRUCTION).

In this early type the fronts are decorated with elaborate, mitred geometrical mouldings often centring on boldly projected panels of hexagonal or octagonal form—a treatment borrowed from Flemish and German woodwork of an earlier date. The bevelled panels of some of these transitional examples are inlaid in bone or ivory and mother-of-pearl, shields with floral and animal motives figuring among the engraved ornament. For this style of ornament no close continental analogy exists, but bone and ivory had been largely employed in continental inlay since the 15th century, notably in certosina decoration; and in character the scrolls and arabesques are reminiscent of the inlay on Italian and Spanish coffers of the Renaissance (*cf. Historia Del Meuble,* L. M. Feduchi, Fig. 333). Thus, the source of inspiration for this short-lived style of decoration (a number of extant examples are dated between 1650 and 1655) is probably to be traced through Venice from the Levant.

In Fig. 1 bone and mother-of-pearl are combined with an

2. *Chest of Drawers; oak inlaid with bone and mother-of-pearl, dated 1662; Ht. 4 ft. ¾ in., L. 3 ft. 10 in., Depth 1 ft. 11¼ in. (Stourhead, Wilts.)*

3. *Chest of Drawers; oak inlaid with ivory and mother-of-pearl; two end panels of deep drawer in upper portion simulate cupboard doors. c. 1665.*

4. *Oak Chest of Drawers, geometrically panelled, and decorated with bosses, fret-cut ornaments and applied pendants. c. 1660. (The late Mr A. de Navarro.)*

By the end of Charles II's reign, these traditional forms of construction had become obsolete (save in remote parts of the country) and the last suggestions of an evolution from the chest disappear. When bone and mother-of-pearl inlay had been abandoned, geometrical mouldings and applied balusters were generally the only decoration on oak chests of drawers. Fig. 9 is exceptional because it is of yew on a foundation of oak. By this date, the gain from the practical standpoint of elevating the lower drawers some distance from the ground had been recognised, and stands were sometimes provided with baluster or spiral-turned legs like those of contemporary cabinets. The total height rarely exceeds 5 ft., thus rendering the top drawers readily accessible—an advantage lost in many of the tallboys later introduced.

For luxuriously appointed bedrooms, chests of drawers were made veneered with walnut, the tops inlaid in the fashion of contemporary tables, and the drawer fronts decorated with oval-shaped panels in a similar taste. They illustrate a familiar evolution of English marquetry (*see* INLAY AND MARQUETRY). Fig. 12 shows the normal arrangement of c. 1680, the top being divided by bands of walnut into an oval and four triangular corners. The ground between the shaped floral panels is of plain walnut, while in more elaborate specimens it is formed of oyster-pieces cut from the boughs. The original stands of such chests of drawers are sometimes fitted with a single long drawer (Fig. 11), but in most cases the supports have been renewed. Fig. 13 shows a representative specimen of arabesque marquetry. The top is decorated with oval and trefoil-headed designs, dark on a light ground, and the

5. *Combined Cupboard and Chest of Drawers of oak. c. 1660. Ht. 4 ft., L. 3 ft. 1 in., Depth 1 ft. 7 in. (J. Thursby Pelham Coll.)*

6. Chest of Drawers; walnut with elm lid and oak linings; box top and drawers lined with papers printed from wooden blocks. c. 1670. Ht. 2 ft. 9 in., L. 2 ft. 8 in., Depth 1 ft. 7 in. (V. & A. Mus.)

7. Oak Chest of Drawers on stand; drawers geometrically panelled, the divisions decorated with knobbed turning; outer framework carved. c. 1685. (Ickworth Abbey, Suffolk.)

8. Oak Chest of Drawers veneered with partridge wood and oyster-pieces of walnut; sides sycamore, stand oak. c. 1690. Ht. 3 ft. 2 in., L. 3 ft., Depth 1 ft. 10 in. (Macquoid Coll.)

9. Chest of Drawers of yew on a foundation of oak; the spiral twist between the drawers an unusual feature; handles and lock-plates not original. c. 1685. (The late Mrs H. Cordes.)

10. *Chest of Drawers veneered with walnut, on stand with spiral-turned supports. c. 1680. Ht. 4 ft. 11 in., L. 3 ft. 2½ in., Depth 1 ft. 9 in. (G. L. Riley Coll.)*

11. *Chest of Drawers, walnut with marquetry of various woods on stand with turned supports. c. 1680. Ht. 4 ft. 2½ in., L. 3 ft. 5 in., Depth 1 ft. 11½ in. (V. & A. Mus.)*

12. *Walnut Chest of Drawers decorated with floral marquetry, light on a dark ground. c. 1680. Ht. 3 ft. 1 in., L. 3 ft. 2½ in., Depth 1 ft. 11¾ in. (The late Rev. Wilfred Brocklebank.)*

13. *Chest of Drawers, walnut inlaid with seaweed marquetry. c. 1700. (The late Cora, Countess of Strafford.)*

14. (*Left*) *Chest of Drawers, veneered with oyster-pieces of walnut, on stand with turned supports; top inlaid with geometrical lines, and sides decorated with lozenges in sycamore. c. 1685. (Bourne Park, Kent.)*

15. (*Right*) *Chest of Drawers, veneered with figured burr walnut on a stand with turned supports. c. 1690. Ht. 4 ft., L. 2 ft. 6 in., Depth 1 ft. 3 in. (J. Thursby Pelham Coll.)*

drawers with the same delicate marquetry; on the sides a feathered border encloses the panels, and the stand also is enriched.

When japanning became a fashionable craze, chests of

16. *Chest of Drawers veneered with burr walnut, inlaid with sycamore; stand with double-twist turned supports. c. 1690. (J. Thursby Pelham Coll.)*

drawers were often decorated by amateurs, cabinets and other ornamental pieces of furniture being generally reserved for more practised hands. These japanned specimens are rarely found before 1690, when a knowledge of the process had been widely disseminated through the *Treatise* published by Stalker and Parker (*q.v.*). In an inventory of the contents of Kensington Palace, drawn up in 1696 after the death of Queen Mary, 'one india Jappan chest of drawers' is entered, together with other furniture similarly decorated, in the Queen's New Bedchamber. Sometimes in bedrooms plain chests of drawers of oak or deal were japanned to match the rest of the furniture. They were often mounted on arcaded stands with drawers in the frieze and turned baluster supports united by curved stretchers. Fig. 17 shows a rare and interesting specimen, the stand in this instance being deliberately Oriental in character, while the distribution of ornament is exceptionally skilful. The double chest of drawers (Fig. 18) has a hooded cresting reminiscent of the cornices on state beds of the age. These arched mouldings with intervening finials are decorated in gessowork.

Plain veneered chests of drawers, contemporary with marquetry and japanned specimens, are often remarkable for the variety of veneers, tulip, rosewood and other exotic woods being ingeniously combined with native walnut. In Fig. 8 the internal structure, framings and mouldings are of oak, but the bevels are of partridge wood, the panels of walnut oyster-pieces, and the sides of sycamore. Although it dates from c.1690, the construction is still somewhat archaic; the boldly projected panels revert to an earlier manner and the top drawer is also unusually deep.

A favourite method of enhancing the carefully chosen figured walnut veneers employed on much furniture of this class was to inlay the surface with lines of holly or boxwood in geometric patterns. Figs. 14 and 16 show this treatment.

Chests of drawers mounted on stands with spiral, twisted, or turned baluster supports were also made in walnut during the last years of the 17th century. Of these Fig. 15 is an exceptional specimen, for the proportions are elegant, the wide oversail of the cornice unusual and the delicate peg-headed legs of the stand original; whereas in most instances they have been renewed. Here material and execution are of the highest quality, and handles and lock-plates are of charming design.

References to chests of drawers in inventories and correspondence of the period are comparatively rare. Pepys records that on July 1, 1661, he bought in the City 'a fair chest of drawers' for his own chamber. Several are mentioned, though not described, in an inventory of the contents of Castle Ashby, Northamptonshire, drawn up in 1681; Richard Legh of Lyme had two in a bedroom in 1697, and four years later the Earl of Bristol paid £1 7s. 6d. for a chest of drawers at Stow-Green fair. In the lists of furniture in the Royal palaces drawn up in William III's reign, this type figures only at Kensington, where 'one wallnotree chest with drawers in it' is mentioned in the wardrobe. An inventory (1710) at Dyrham Park records only two chests of drawers in the house. It is certain, however, that many were made in the early 18th century; and at moderate prices. In his *Diary* for 1717 Mr John Tomlinson complains

18. *Double Chest of Drawers, japanned in black and gold; curved pediment decorated with brackets and finials in gesso-work gilt. c. 1700. (Alfred Morrison Collection.)*

17. *Chest of Drawers, japanned in black and gold; stand designed in the Chinese taste; handles and lock-plates original. c. 1700. (The late Lady Henry Grosvenor.)*

that at the sale of some family furniture an old-fashioned chest of drawers was valued at 18s., and notes 'one may buy a new and fashionable pair for a guinea or a little more'.

Early in the century, chests of drawers were generally simple in design, veneered with walnut, often of beautiful figure, on a foundation of pine, the drawers being of oak dovetailed in the finer manner that had become general. In the earliest specimens (c. 1710-15) they are divided by single half-round mouldings (Fig. 21), then by two such mouldings of smaller size set side by side (Fig. 20); from c. 1725 a cock-bead is often found worked in the edges of the drawers. The surface was sometimes decorated in parquetry with symmetrically arranged oyster-shells of walnut or laburnum, a treatment of which the top of the chest of drawers (Fig. 21) is an elaborate example, though not visible in the illustration. Contrasts of tone were contrived in the walnut veneers, which, as in this case, were often cross-banded with a lighter wood, and the drawers were sometimes bow-fronted with fluted pilasters at the corners. Small specimens were also made, sometimes in pairs, at this time with a folding

19. *Oak Chest of Drawers; geometrical panels and split baluster ornament. Dated* 1717. (*Pwllywrach, Glam.*)

top for writing supported on runners (Fig. 20). In one of these so-called 'bachelor chests' the frame pulls forward to support the top when open, and brackets for candles are attached to the sides (Fig. 26).

About 1700, tallboys, or double chests of drawers, were introduced, drawers replacing turned supports in the lower portion. They were surmounted either by a straight, hollow cornice, or by a curved and broken pediment; the canted corners were decorated with flutings and a slide for brushing clothes was often fitted above the top drawer of the lower portion. Fig. 23 is notable for the selection and matching of the burr walnut veneer to produce a symmetrical effect. Wide mouldings divide the two stages, and the bottom drawer centres on a semicircle starred in box and holly, a detail borrowed from Holland and often found on walnut tallboys and contemporary bureaux. Such pieces remained popular until mid-Georgian designers introduced other varieties of bedroom furniture, a combined form also being made in walnut, and later in mahogany, with the top drawer of the lower stage fitted for writing (*see* BUREAUX, Figs. 23 and 25).

The chest of drawers on stand continued to be produced in the early years of the 18th century but, instead of the twisted or peg-top headed supports of the Late Stuart type, the legs are of cabriole form and stretchers disappear. In Fig. 22 the usual canted corners are replaced by fluted columns with Corinthian capitals, the cornice being corbelled out to meet them; the stand is also exceptional, for the corners project, forming plinths to the columns, and are enriched with acanthus carving. The ivory claws of the webbed feet are a rare detail, and a mark of high quality. The tops of these tallboys, being above eye level, were seldom veneered.

Defoe (*Complete Tradesman*, 1726) states that the manufacture of chests of drawers was centralised in London; but oak specimens were also made by country joiners, and among these some interesting archaic examples are found. A pinewood chest of drawers from South Wales (Fig. 25) has a lifting top and a deep receptacle below, recalling the early phase of the evolution. It is inlaid, like many other pieces of contemporary Welsh furniture, with conventional foliated sprays in sycamore, a traditional form of decoration, while the turning of the stand is of Late Stuart character.

20. *Walnut Chest of Drawers with folding top for writing; one of a set of four. c.* 1710. *Ht.* 2 *ft.* 10¼ *in., L.* 2 *ft.* 6¼ *in., Depth* 1 *ft.* 2¼ *in.* (*Stourhead, Wilts.*)

21. *Chest of Drawers veneered with walnut parquetry and banded with sycamore. c.* 1715. *Ht.* 2 *ft.* 8½ *in., L.* 3 *ft.* 1¾ *in., Depth* 1 *ft.* 11 *in.* (*From Mr Ralph Edwards.*)

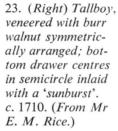

22. (*Left*) *Walnut Chest of Drawers on stand; acanthus carved corners and cabriole legs terminating in webbed feet with ivory claws; fluted columns headed by Corinthian capitals. c. 1715. Ht. 5 ft. 9 in., L. 3 ft. 5 in., Depth 1 ft. 11 in. (V. & A. Mus.)*

23. (*Right*) *Tallboy, veneered with burr walnut symmetrically arranged; bottom drawer centres in semicircle inlaid with a 'sunburst'. c. 1710. (From Mr E. M. Rice.)*

In trade catalogues of the second half of the century, chests of drawers are entirely subordinated to commodes, a term applied to most decorative pieces of furniture fitted with drawers (*see* COMMODES). On the title page of the *Director* the term chest of drawers is omitted from the list of contents in all three editions, the craze for French fashions no doubt explaining Chippendale's choice of the name. He does, indeed, in the first edition (1754) give three designs for this kind of furniture and applies the name to another in which the two stages of the front are enclosed by doors, this being the only plate described as a 'chest of drawers' in the third edition (1762). Examples in which French models are unmistakably followed are included under the heading COMMODES, but there is no clear line of demarcation between the native form and many of the pieces produced during the ascendancy of foreign taste. This fact was apparently recognised by the

24. (*Left*) *Chest of Drawers veneered with figured walnut; folding top. c. 1720–25. Ht. 2 ft. 7 in., L. 2 ft. 2 in., Depth 1 ft. 1 in. (The late Mrs Mosenthal.)*

25. (*Right*) *Chest, with drawers below, on stand with turned legs and shaped stretchers; pine with traditional inlay in sycamore. Dated 1734. Ht. 3 ft. 7 in., L. 3 ft. 2 in., Depth 1 ft. 5 in. (Nat. Mus. of Wales.)*

designers and makers, Ince and Mayhew, for instance, calling the only specimen illustrated in their *Universal System* (1759-63) 'a commode chest of drawers'. In 1758 Benjamin Goodison charged £16 16s. for 'a mahogany commode chest of drawers ornamented with carving and wrought brass handles to do, and lifting handles' for St James's Palace.

Until c. 1750 walnut was chiefly used for this type of furniture, but after that date the output of mahogany chests of drawers largely increased, French detail being often introduced even when the structural lines remained English. In Fig. 27 the central portion is in projection, each of the four long drawers being made to simulate three, a feature much adopted on American 18th-century furniture of this period.

Ordinary bedroom chests of drawers at this time were without carving, supported on plain bracket feet, and with a cock-beading round the drawers. Small chests of drawers on cabriole-legged stands survive from the period, although they are not illustrated in contemporary trade catalogues. Fig. 28 shows an excellent specimen with an enriched cornice, the handles and lock-plates being unusually good for English metal-work.

26. *Walnut Chest of Drawers; fluted pilasters pull out with the top drawer to support folding top; candle brackets hinged at corners. c. 1730-40.*

27. *Mahogany Chest of Drawers; central portion in projection; corners finishing in fluted pilasters with Corinthian capitals; base deeply moulded. c. 1750. Ht. 4 ft. 2 in.; L. 3 ft. 1½ in., Depth 1 ft. 10½ in. (Mrs Inman.)*

28. *Mahogany Chest of Drawers on cabriole legs carved with acanthus; handles in French taste. c. 1755. (Percival Griffiths Coll.)*

Fig. 29 illustrates the difficulty of classification, the serpentine curves of the front being well adapted to the elaborate handles and lock-plates in French taste; and a finely carved vine pattern in low relief decorates the consoles at the angles. The top drawer is fitted with trays, boxes and small compartments, an arrangement affording greater facilities for a Georgian beauty's toilet than the small dressing-tables of the time (*see* TABLES, DRESSING). In his bills Chippendale describes this variety as 'a commode chest-of-drawers', and in October, 1767, he supplied one to Sir Edward Knatchbull of Mersham Hatch, Kent, 'of fine wood with a dressing drawer complete' at a cost of £14 8s. An example from Badminton (Fig. 31) may be assigned to Chippendale, and here, though the chest is finely figured and the handles represent the best contemporary English metal-work, the effect depends on the carved and gilt stand (a highly exceptional feature) which is based on a design for a 'commode chest' (Plate C1) in the *Director* (1st ed.).

29. *Commode Chest of Drawers; serpentine front veneered with fiddle-back mahogany; corners carved with a vine pattern; handles and lock-plates in French taste. c. 1755. Ht. 2 ft. 8½ in., L. 4 ft. 5 in., Depth 2 ft. (J. Thursby Pelham Coll.)*

30. *(Below) Commode Chest of Drawers, veneered with Cuban mahogany; corners fluted, and bracket feet united by a carved apron; a slide below cornice. c. 1760. Ht. 2 ft. 10 in., L. 3 ft. 6 in., Depth 2 ft. (V. & A. Mus.)*

31. *(Above) Mahogany Chest of Drawers on carved gilt stand, following a design in the* Director *(1st ed. 1754). Attributed to Thomas Chippendale. (Badminton House, Gloucs.)*

32. *Mahogany Chest of Drawers on stand; taper legs headed by carved brackets. c. 1765.*

207

33. *Mahogany Chest of Drawers; serpentine break-front decorated with lattice-work; two writing slides below the cornice. c. 1760. Ht. 2 ft. 6½ in., L. 4 ft. 7 in., Depth 1 ft. 5¾ in. (Bayfordbury, Herts.)*

34. *Mahogany Chest of Drawers with serpentine front; bracket feet carved with C scrolls and foliage. c. 1760. Ht. 2 ft. 11 in., L. 3 ft. 10 in., Depth 2 ft. (Erthig, Denbighs.)*

35. *Mahogany Chest of Drawers with folding top supported on brackets in the Gothic taste. c. 1765. Ht. 2 ft. 6½ in., L. (of top), 2 ft. 7 in., Depth 2 ft. 6½ in. (F. H. Reed Coll.)*

Three other specimens which depart from the familiar type are seen in Figs. 32, 33 and 35. Runners at the front and Gothic brackets attached to the sides support the folding top in Fig. 35, and the 'block front' of the chest of drawers seen in Fig. 33 is a feature rare in England, though favoured in contemporary American furniture.

The royal accounts contain entries for payments made for a large number of chests of drawers supplied to the palaces between 1750 and 1770. Henry Williams, a joiner, charged £28 for 'eight wainscot chests of drawers with good locks and brass work' delivered at Newmarket in 1752, and one was purchased from Benjamin Goodison in 1767 'for the use of Mrs Muttlebury wet nurse to the Princess Royal'. It contained four deep drawers lined with blue paper, and was fitted with brass locks, handles, etc., the dimensions

being given as 3 ft. 9 ins. high, 3 ft. 7 ins. wide, and 1 ft. 9 ins. deep.

In spite of a large increase in clothes presses and wardrobes, tallboys continued to be made in considerable numbers during the second half of the century, and occasional allusions to them are found. Mary Kenyon, the wife of the judge, describing her new house in Lincoln's Inn Fields in 1775, says that in her bedroom is 'a large chest upon chest (so high that I must have a step-ladder to look into the five top drawers)'; while in another corner of the room was 'a small chest of dressing drawers'. In Fig. 36 the frieze and canted corners are decorated with Chinese lattice-work, the handles and lock-plates carrying out the oriental motive.

The fine tallboy shown in Fig. 37 is part of a set of bedroom furniture, which also includes two dressing tables. The serpentine front is veneered with brightly figured or 'flashed' mahogany, and the finely carved detail is in the full rococo manner; the original handles are of graceful design, merging into foliated back plates.

Later tallboys are sometimes surmounted by a swan-necked inlaid pediment; as in the case of contemporary clothes presses, the design gradually became more and more severe (Fig. 38). The word 'tallboy' appears in Gillows's cost books in 1784, used, curiously enough, as an alternative term—'A small mahogany Lobby chest or tall-boy'. This piece is shown as having five long and two small drawers, and the carcase is in one piece. In his *Household Furniture* (1808) George Smith observes that the double chest of drawers is 'an article of such general use that it does not stand in need of description'.

Late in the 18th century chests of drawers were generally of plain mahogany on a foundation of pine, oak being used for the drawer linings. Occasionally, they were carved or painted in classical taste (Figs. 39 and 41), or veneered and decorated with marquetry. Of this last treatment a fine example is seen in Fig. 40. Although there is no proof that it was produced by Chippendale's firm, it probably dates from a few years before his death in 1779, and rivals the furniture supplied by him to Harewood House.

The 'Dressing Drawers' illustrated by Hepplewhite in the *Guide* (1788) are severely simple, but those with a top drawer containing 'the necessary dressing equipage' are more decorative. He gives one with a serpentine front 'elegantly ornamented with inlaid and painted work which is applied with great beauty and elegance to this piece of furniture'. Of chests of drawers he writes, 'this article admits of little variation or ornament'. He fixes the dimensions at 3½ ft. long by 20 ins.

36. (*Above*) Mahogany Tallboy, cornice and frieze decorated with Chinese lattice-work; ogee-bracket feet boldly carved. c. 1760. (*Percival Griffiths Coll.*)

37. (*Left*) Mahogany Tallboy, serpentine front and canted corners carved with pendants of fruit and flowers, bracket feet with rococo ornament. c. 1760. Ht. 6 ft. 3 in., L. 3 ft. 10 in., Depth 2 ft. (*Cecil Higgins Museum, Bedford.*)

38. (*Right*) Mahogany Tallboy, surmounted by a dentil cornice and swan-neck inlaid pediment; fluted columns with Corinthian capitals at corners of upper stage. c. 1780. Ht. 6 ft. 10 in., L. 3 ft. 9½ in., Depth 2 ft. (*Crichel, Dorset.*)

39. *Mahogany Chest of Drawers; frieze carved with paterae and swags of husks; corners finish in taper pilasters above spirally turned feet. c. 1775 (Burley-on-the-Hill, Rutland.)*

40. *Inlaid Chest of Drawers, mounted on taper legs and veneered with harewood and satinwood; mouldings gilt. c. 1775. Ht. 2 ft. 9¾ in., L. 4 ft., Depth 1 ft. 11 in. (Syon House, Middx.)*

deep, allowing the same depth for his double chests of drawers, which are to be 5½ ft. high. These measurements, and the general characteristics, became more or less standardised.

Chests of drawers were occasionally inlaid in the late 18th century with festoons and paterae, this treatment being generally reserved for composite specimens with cupboards in the sides. Sheraton claims a top drawer fitted for the toilet as his own invention, though it was a familiar arrangement in Chippendale's time (*see* Fig. 29). He gives two designs for 'Dressing Chests', and writes that they are 'on a new plan, particularly as the common slider generally used for merely writing on is turned into a shallow drawer which contains a

41. *Chest of Drawers with cupboards in sides; banded with mahogany and painted in neo-classic taste. c. 1785. Ht. 2 ft. 8¾ in. L. 5 ft. 1 in., Depth 2 ft. ½ in. (Formerly at Woodhall Park, Herts.)*

little writing flap, which rises behind by a horse, and places for ink, sand and pens, and also dressing boxes'. The top drawer was also often fitted as a secretaire only, the front letting down by means of metal quadrants.

Chests of drawers made for bedrooms c. 1800 are generally bow-fronted, with feet turning outwards (Fig. 42), while sometimes the corners were projected in columns spirally turned (Fig. 43), or headed by foliated capitals. In a few late examples the handles are bronzed, lion masks forming the back plates. Rosewood was occasionally used instead of

42. *Mahogany Chest of Drawers; cornice and drawers cross-banded and bordered with stringing lines. c. 1795. Ht. 4 ft. 1 in., L. 3 ft. 5 in., Depth 1 ft. 10 in. (Dunn Gardner Coll.)* 43. *Mahogany Chest of Drawers; bow-fronted, with spiral-twisted columns and turned feet; brass lion-mask handles. c. 1810. Ht. 3 ft. 6 in., L. 3 ft. 8 in., Depth 1 ft. 10 in. (Dunn Gardner Coll.)*

1. *Satinwood Cheveret, with superstructure of drawers; bandings of kingwood. c. 1790. Ht. 4 ft. 8 in., L. 1 ft. 8 in., Depth 1 ft. 4 in. (Stephen Winkworth Coll.) 1. Chiffonier, one of a pair; rosewood banded with ebony, gilt mouldings and ormolu mounts. Probably designed by Henry Holland. c. 1800. Ht. (with bookcase) 4 ft. 10½ in., L. 5 ft. 7¾ in., Depth 1 ft. 1½ in. (Southill, Beds.)*

mahogany, the shapes becoming increasingly cumbrous. The double chest or tallboy, though no longer popular, was also made at this period, and George Smith (*Household Furniture*, 1808) describes one in which the height has been reduced to 'avoid the disagreeable alternative of getting on to chairs to place anything in the upper drawers'.

CHEVAL GLASS. *See* MIRRORS, TOILET.

CHEVERET. Variety of small table with drawer in frieze, tapered supports and shelf below, the top supporting movable book stand fitted with curved handle and drawers. Common in late 18th century, generally of satinwood; termed 'cheveret' in Gillows's cost books.

CHIFFONIER (also CHEFFONIER). From French *chiffonier*, defined by Littré as 'a piece of furniture with drawers in which women put away their needlework'. Chiffonier in France was a tall chest of drawers made in large numbers from c. 1750 onwards. An entirely distinct piece, termed *chiffonière*, was a small case of drawers on legs (Jauneau, *Les Meubles*, vol. 2, p. 20) sometimes with writing slide.

The earliest reference in England occurs in Chippendale's accounts for furniture supplied to Mersham Hatch: 'a neat shiffener writing table japanned green and gold, with a drawer and cut bottles'. This appears to be an English version of the *chiffonière*.

When an inventory was taken of the contents of Bedford House in 1771, 'Her Grace's Dressing Room' contained 'a small chiffonier table with drawers and brass rim' (*The Russells in Bloomsbury*, G. Scott Thomson, p. 342).

Chiffoniers figure in English trade catalogues of the early 19th century. Those illustrated in George Smith's *Household Furniture* (1808) are low shelved cupboards, described in the text as 'useful chiefly for such books as are in constant use, and not of sufficient consequence for the library'. There and in Peter Nicholson's *Practical Cabinet-maker* (1826-7) there is no distinction between the commodes and chiffoniers illustrated. In some cases the chiffonier is surmounted by a shelf with brass supports. An example from Southill represents the English type. M. J.

CHIMNEY FURNITURE comprises containers and receptacles for fuel burnt on the hearth (grate), the supports for wood fuel (andirons), and the various implements for feeding and regulating the fire (poker, tongs, shovel, fire-fork and bellows), with accessories to protect the room from ash and falling fuel (fender, hearth-rod), and the plate or slab which protects the back of the fireplace opening (fireback). The scuttle, or container of coal to make up the fire, and the chimneyboard, with which the chimney aperture was screened during the summer months, may also be included.

These implements, containers and accessories varied with the fuel burnt. In the age of wood fuel fireback and andirons were essentials; in the coal age, the grate. Mineral coal was still unpopular for household use as late as 1554, when the Venetian envoy Soranzo wrote of 'a certain sort of earth, almost mineral', found in the north, 'which burns like charcoal and is extensively used by blacksmiths, and but for a bad odour which it has would be yet more employed as it gives great heat and costs little'. That coal was used in Shakespeare's time is evident from Dame Quickly's speech to Falstaff in *King Henry IV*, reminding him of his oath when 'sitting in my Dolphin Chamber, by a sea cole fire'.

In the early 17th century coal became an important monopoly which the Long Parliament ended; and Evelyn, writing upon the nuisance of London smoke, 'the clouds of smoke and sulphur, so full of stink and darkness', attributes this largely to the growing use of coal instead of wood. In the inventory of Hampton Court (1659), however, all the important rooms are furnished with andirons, fire-shovel, tongs and bellows, and no grate is listed. Even in the early 18th century wood was still burnt in certain rooms at Dyrham, while in others are 'stove grates for burning coal' (MS. inventory, 1710). The making of a coal fire is described as a novelty by Misson: the grates are 'Iron Stoves about half a foot high', and the method of lighting the fire is 'with a Bit of linnen or paper'. None but people of the first quality, he adds, burn wood in London (*Mémoires*, 1698; trans. Oxley, 1719).

In the case of kitchens, chimney furniture includes the special form of andirons (cobirons) on which the spits rested, and the contrivances for suspending vessels over the fire (pot-bracket, pot-crane, pot-hanger).

ANDIRONS (FIRE DOG, BRAND DOG) consist of a vertical standard, a horizontal billet bar riveted to this, by means of which logs were raised above hearth level, and spreading feet or base. Frequently illustrated in illuminated manuscripts, they are generally represented with tops bent forward into a crozier form, or finishing in a cup. At Penshurst the andirons in place on the central hearth in the great hall bear the pheon badge of the Sidneys, to whom Penshurst was granted by Edward IV, and are therefore later in date than the hall. This pair of andirons is coupled by a billet bar supported in the centre, and against this bar the logs are stacked. The inventory of Cardinal Wolsey (1523-5) indicates their very varied treatment, some displaying 'my Lordes armes and Cardinall hattes on the toppes'. In the inventory taken after Henry VIII's death (1547) there are noted in the Privy Chamber at Hampton Court 'andyrons of yron, eche of them with a roose'.

In a pair of early Tudor andirons at Knole, Kent (Fig. 2), the standards terminate in bronze discs encircled by a cabled iron twist, and surmounted by a royal crown; on one disc are the arms of Henry VIII and the letters H.R., and on the other is a falcon crowned, the badge of Anne Boleyn, which limits this pair to the dates 1533-36. On each standard is a human figure; beneath is a drop handle filled with pierced arabesque tracery.

 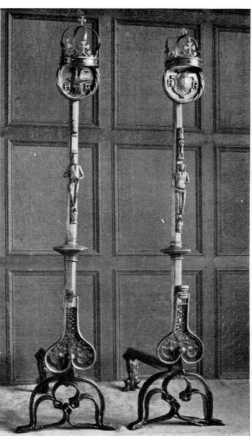 

1. *Andiron bearing the Pelham buckle on the standard. Late 15th century. Ht. 1 ft. 8½ in. (Lewes Castle Museum.)* 2. *Wrought Andirons, decorated with bronze discs; arms of Henry VIII and falcon badge of Anne Boleyn. c. 1533. Ht. 4 ft. (Knole Park, Kent.)* 3. *Cast-iron Fire Dogs, decorated with applied bronze ornament and initials E.R. Late 16th century. (Burley-on-the-Hill, Rutland.)*

  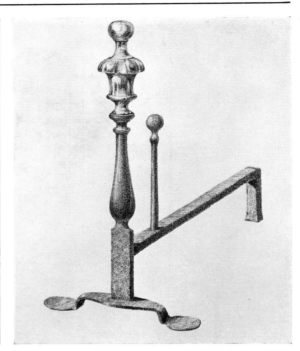

4. *Andiron, with shields of arms applied to head and to junction of billet bar. Dated 1583. (The late Sir Edward Barry.)* 5. *Drawing of an Andiron from Leeds Castle, Kent. Late 16th century. By William Twopenny.* 6. *Wrought-iron Andiron, with brass finial. First half of 18th century.*

Plain wrought-iron and latten andirons with knop finials are often mentioned in inventories from the early 17th century to c. 1750. In the Garden Chamber at Ingatestone in 1600 was 'a paire of lowe latten andirons with round heads and large knoppes on the top'.

In the early 16th century cast-iron andirons were made in the foundries of the Sussex Weald, and a considerable number have survived. They were sturdier in outline than those of wrought metal; and the standard was often formed as a short pilaster, column, or grotesque human figure. The junction of the standard and base was sometimes marked by a shield bearing arms (Fig. 4), initials, badges, or the sacred monogram 'IHS'. The base is arched, scroll-formed, or more rarely angular-stepped (Fig. 5), this type persisting until late in the century.

In a pair from Burley-on-the-Hill, Rutland, which bears the letters 'E.R.' and, on the base, the royal arms of Queen Elizabeth I supported by angels, the masks and other enrichments are of hammered bronze, applied to the iron standards (Fig. 3).

From c. 1650 there is evidence of preference for andirons with cast-iron or gilt brass enrichments, and an inventory (1641) of the Countess of Arundel's household stuff and goods at Tart Hall mentions 'a payre of great iron Andirons the upper partes thereof of cast brass, pt. guilt'.

Richer and more elaborate andirons were, in the late 17th century, ornamented with cast and pierced bass discs (Fig. 8). In enamel examples the shallow depressions which form the major part of the cast-brass fronts are filled up with opaque vitreous paste in various colours. In Fig. 7 the royal arms of the Stuarts, which form the upper portion, are supported by Atlantes, divided by a vase, while beneath their feet are convex discs of floral ornament.

Brass, latten and silver are also met with in inventories of the early Renaissance. In the inventory of the royal palaces (1649) 'a paire of andirons garnished with silver' is entered; and after the Restoration silver-enriched andirons became the fashion. The *Expense Book* of John Hervey, Earl of Bristol, records the purchase in 1690 of 'a pair of silver andirons for my dear wife her room for £13 5s.'. At Knole there is a remarkable pair of beaten silver andirons with applied cast detail. The base, of scroll-shaped profile, is faced at the sides with a finely modelled terminal satyr, while the panels are embossed with acanthus scrolls and demi-figures issuing from these scrolls, and holding up a framed female bust in high relief. This base is surmounted by a vase, and on a mound of fruit and foliage stand statuettes of boys, one holding a pair of bellows, the other a fire shovel (Fig. 9). Fig. 10 shows similar treatment of the base in brass.

With the adoption of coal as fuel these elaborate andirons lost their function, but for the smaller country house, the farmer and yeoman, wrought-iron andirons continued to be made, unadorned except for a boss as finial to the standard. Cast-iron andirons in the classic taste are met with bearing the Carron stamp.

BELLOWS. An 'instrument invented to make wind and . . . used to blow up fires for their more speedy kindling' (*Academy of Armory*, 1688) from very early times. They are listed in early inventories without particulars as to their material and ornament (*e.g.* in 1502 'a payre of belowes' is bought for Elizabeth of York for 'ijd', and in 1556 Sir John Gage of West Firle owned 'iij paier of bellowes with noses of iron'). Hand bellows consist of two boards (one of which is pierced with a venthole), a windpipe of metal and extending leather sides; serviceable bellows were of plain wood, but some surviving ones are richly decorated. Fig. 11 shows a pair of fruitwood bellows with

7. *Andiron,* **on***e of a pair in cast brass; decorated with blue, green, white and red enamel, and bearing the royal arms of the Stuarts. c. 1670. (Mulliner Coll.)* 8. *Wrought-iron Andiron, faced with cast and pierced brass ornament. c. 1670. (Lyme Park, Staffs.)* 9. *Andiron of beaten silver with applied cast ornament, surmounted by statuettes. c. 1670. (Knole Park, Kent.)* 10. *Brass Andiron, one of a pair; female head and bust applied to a scroll base. c. 1710. (Knole Park, Kent.)*

11. *Fruitwood Bellows, incised and partly painted in red. The royal arms as borne by James I. c. 1620. L. 1 ft. 11 in., W. 11 in. (V. & A. Mus.)* 12. *Bellows, decorated in marquetry with the royal crown and cypher of Charles II; handles overlaid with sheet silver. (Windsor Castle. By gracious permission of H.M. the Queen.)* 13. *Bellows, face overlaid with purl and silk needlework (front). Dated 1673. (Percival Griffiths (Coll.)*

14. *Bellows and Hearth Brush; faces of bellows and back of brush overlaid with embossed and chased silver. c. 1675. (Ham House, Surrey.)* 15. *Wrought-iron Cup Standard or Cobiron with adjustable loops for spits. (Hastings Museum).*

decoration incised and partly painted in red. On the front hood below the initials 'J.R.' is a version of the royal arms as borne by James I within the Garter motto, supported by the lion and the unicorn. On the inside of the front hood 'with the Kinges Armes on him' is among the lines of partly indecipherable verse inscription. Another pair (Fig. 13), presumably

merely decorative, has the back and front overlaid with needlework. At Windsor Castle is a pair stated to have been given by Charles II to Nell Gwynn, marquetried with coloured woods in a floriated scroll design, the royal crown and interlaced C's (Fig. 12). Another pair of bellows of identical design is in the Ashmolean Museum. A pair at Ham House, Surrey, has the back and front entirely overlaid with *repoussé* and chased sheet silver, while in the centre is engraved the cipher of the Duchess of Lauderdale (E.D.L.) with plumed mantling (Fig. 14).

During the fashion for japanning in the 18th century bellows were often decorated by that process; and in the hard winter of 1715 Lady Grisell Baillie brought on the frozen Thames 'a red Japan Bellis and brush' for 6s. The standing bellows from Knole represent an ingenious device for obtaining a stronger draught (Fig. 16).

CHIMNEY-BOARD (FIRE-BOARD). A decorated board which blocked the fireplace opening during the summer months, being painted, covered or papered. An example in the Victoria and Albert Museum dates from the early 18th century and is painted with a vase of flowers. In the Tapestry Room at Osterley, Middlesex, is a fire-board covered with a tapestry panel with a design of a basket of flowers to match the Neilson-Boucher hangings; and in the Etruscan Room was a fire-board painted in the same style, for which Robert Adam's design is preserved in the Soane Museum, London.

COAL-BOX, HOD OR SCUTTLE. A receptacle, usually of metal, for holding a supply of coal by the fireside. No example dating before the 19th century seems to have survived. In 1715 Lady Grisell Baillie spent three guineas on 'ane yron coll basket & £1 1s. 6d. upon a coper scutel'; and in 1729 Swift included coal-boxes among the 'unsightly things' that he recommended to be left about by the housemaid.

COBIRONS. Term applied to andirons for the kitchen, having hooks on the standard to support the spits (Fig. 15). In the household goods of Sir John Gage of West Firle, Sussex, 'iiij great cobirons for spittes, all good', are listed (1556).

16. *Oak Standing-Bellows, the handle and horizontal baluster attached to lever of mahogany. c. 1700. (Knole Park, Kent.)*
17. *Brass Curfew repoussé with gadrooning and a lion and acanthus. Late 17th century. (Brighton Museum.)*

CREEPERS. Small andirons standing between the tall and-irons. Holland (*Manufactures*, 1833) speaks of 'andirons proper' and also 'what were denominated creepers, a smaller sort with short necks or none at all'.

CURFEW. Term applied since the late 18th century to a hood-like metal cover 'in shape exactly like a Dutch oven'. There are good examples in the Victoria and Albert Museum, of which the earliest, dating from the first half of the 17th century, is of brass, chased with two groups of St George and the Dragon, and bordered with a *repoussé* band. Another curfew (Fig. 17) dates from later in the century.

FENDERS. The essential appliances of the hearth in the late 17th century—*e.g.* fire-irons, tongs and shovel—were hung on hooks on the jambs of the fireplace, and the wide stone or marble hearths preserved the woodwork of the house from danger from falling logs or sparks. The early hearth-rod, such as the silver example in the Duke of Lauderdale's room at Ham House, Surrey, crossed the hearthstone, and did not serve (as is the modern custom) to mask the junction of the hearth and the wood flooring. In the Miniature Room fire-place at Ham the raised hearth is protected by a wide fender

18. *Silver Firepan and Fender. c. 1675. (Ham House, Surrey.)*

19. *Steel three-piece folding Fender, pierced and engraved. Dated 1705. (The Carron Company.)*

20. *Steel Fender, pierced, engraved and studded. c. 1780.*

(Fig. 18), formed of pierced acanthus centring on a cartouche similar in style to the scroll decoration of the chimneypiece. Fenders are sometimes mentioned in domestic accounts of the early 18th century, and in 1715 Lady Grisell Baillie (*Household Book*) pays 15s. for a brass one. A decade earlier is the steel three-piece folding fender (Fig. 19), which served to contain the ashes of wood fires. The lower portion is engraved with a shield of arms and supporters. Eighteenth-century fenders are usually straight or slightly shaped strips of steel repeating the design of the fretted apron of the grate, and having no bottom plate. About 1750 there was a preference for fine pierced scroll designs occasionally ending in dragon forms; later, Robert Adam uses, in his delicate designs for the pierced portions of grates and fenders, repeated classical details, such as the anthemium (Fig. 20). A number of his grates and their accompanying fenders are still preserved in the houses that he built or completed, the elaborate examples being hand-engraved and mounted with polished studs, like the accompanying grates. Brass fenders of the late 18th and early 19th centuries are more solidly constructed, having bottom plates,

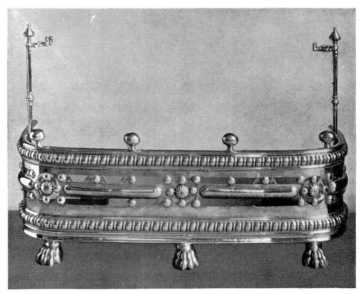

21. *Brass Fender, with cast brass feet and applied rosettes. c. 1810. (Macquoid Coll.)*

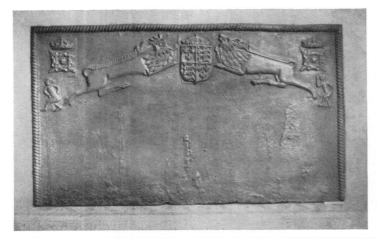

22. *Oblong Fireback edged with cable-twist; decorated with the royal arms, badges and supporters, and with two small figures. Early 16th century. (Hastings Museum.)*

23. *Fireback, decorated with border of cable-twist and with repeated shields of arms (Ayloffe). Sixteenth century. (V. & A. Mus.)*

24. *Shaped Fireback, decorated with the interlaced initials E.R., and dated 1565. (Ockwells Manor, Berks.)*

cast-brass feet and large half-round and other mouldings to strengthen the thin sheet brass, which is perforated in one or more horizontal bands (Fig. 21). The manufacture of cast-iron fenders began in Birmingham, c. 1825, and ousted from favour the more expensive fenders of steel, rolled brass and pierced steelware.

FIREBACKS (FIRE-PLATE, REREDOS). Cast-iron slabs for the protection of the brick or stone back of the fireplace opening. They were moulded by boards pressed into a bed of sand, and into this shallow cavity the molten iron was poured. Most English backs were cast in the ironworks of the Sussex Weald; though a certain number can be traced to the Forest of Dean and to centres in Yorkshire and Derbyshire, when the Sussex iron trade was decaying owing to the destruction of timber by ironmasters.

The backs can be divided into types in which the ornament is formed from movable stamps pressed into the bed of sand, and those cast from a single-piece mould, consisting of armorial bearings, or of figure and allegorical subjects. The stock ornaments or stamps include the fleur-de-lys, rosette, pieces of cable-twist, and initials. A characteristic feature of these

early plates is the bordering, cast from a cable ornament (Fig. 22).

In the armorial plates cast from a single mould the design is larger and bolder, the shield of arms occupying the centre and the remaining space being taken by supporters, or mantling, and crest (Fig. 27). Rarer than armorial bearings are designs of a topical and biblical character, such as the plate on which is represented the burning of Richard Woodman, a Sussex ironmaster, who, with his wife, was burnt at the stake in 1557. A fireback on which Richard Lennard, of Brede, Sussex, figures himself, his furnace and utensils is dated 1636, and inscribed along the top, 'Richard Lennard Founder at Bred Fournis'. Another fireback from Brede furnace is shown in Fig. 26.

During the Early Stuart period the heads of a number of backs are stepped and shaped, the subjects being of minor interest. The Sussex ironmasters borrowed new moulds and models of taller oblong shape from Holland, in which an allegorical or classical subject was framed by a rich floral border. These subjects continued in favour until the advent of the basket-grate. Of English design, however, is the back

25. *Fireback, decorated with the royal arms. Dated 1604. (The Carron Company.)*

26. *Fireback from Brede furnace. Dated 1652. (Hastings Mus.)*

27. *Fireback with shaped head; decorated with the arms of the Dacres of Hurstmonceaux with crest and mantling. Mid-17th century. Ht. 2 ft. 2½ in., W. 3 ft. 2 in. (V. & A. Mus.)*

28. *Fireback, decorated with the royal oak and the initials C.R. c. 1600. Ht. 1 ft. 11¼ in., W. 2 ft. 6 in. (V. & A. Mus.)*

29. *Fireback with figure subject on the field, and scrolled head. c. 1710. (Hastings Mus.)*

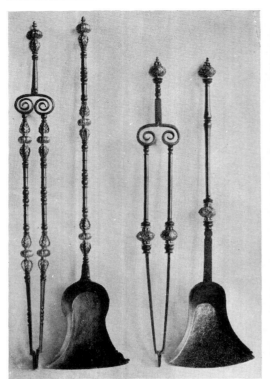

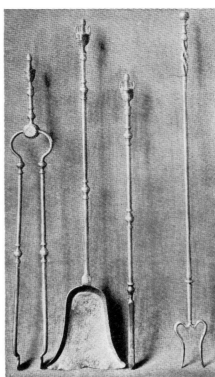

30. (Left) Iron Shovels and Tongs enriched with applied silver ornament. c. 1675. (Ham House, Surrey.)

31. (Right) Steel Fire-irons (poker, tongs and shovel) with copper urn finials. c. 1790. Right; steel Fire-fork. Early 18th century. (Macquoid Coll.)

32. (Below) Iron Fire-pan overlaid with silver. c. 1675. (Ham House, Surrey.)

known as the Royal Oak, commemorating the hiding-place of Charles II at Boscobel (Fig. 28) after the Battle of Worcester, 1651. The oak tree bears three royal crowns on its branches, and on a ribbon the legend 'the Royal Oak', and the initials 'C.R.'. In the firebacks designed under Dutch influence or cast from moulds imported from Holland the plate is thinner, sometimes measuring about $\frac{3}{4}$ in., as in the example of the early 18th century in Fig. 29, and in later firebacks, which are mechanical in design.

FIRE-IRONS. They consist, in the case of wood fuel, of tongs, fire-fork and sometimes a brush; in the case of coal, of poker, tongs and shovel. A fire-fork, to stir the logs on the hearth, appears in the inventory of the goods of Edward Ferrers, of Wood Bevington, Warwickshire (1578): '1 paier of Andirons, A fier forke, 1 fier shovell'. Tongs are of greater elaboration, consisting of two limbs connected by a hinge, pivot or spring which bring the lower ends together to take up fuel. The shovel was mainly used for coal fuel; in the inventory of the goods of Sir Thomas Kytson (1603) are entered 'one fier sholve made like a grate to seft the seacole with, and an other fier sholve'.

The design of fire-irons has not changed materially since Ham House was furnished for the Duke and Duchess of Lauderdale (1673-5). The iron stems of two pairs of shovels and tongs are enriched and tipped with silver, for, as Evelyn who) visited Ham in 1678) writes in *Mundis Muliebris*:

> The chimney furniture's of plate
> for Iron's now quite out of date.

These implements are in the Queen's Bedchamber and the North Drawing-room. The stems of one are enriched with knobs and acanthus leaves of silver (Fig. 30), while those of the other are intersected by chased knobs. The prices and materials of chimney furniture are given in Lady Grisell Baillie's *Household Books* for 1715, and include 'a pair brass tongs and shovel—14s.'. In the late 18th and early 19th

centuries excellent steel fire-irons were made, of which the stems are enriched with mouldings or enlargements, and the knobs are often formed as classical urns (Fig. 31).

FIRE-PAN. A flat pan or tray for holding burning charcoal. In Sir George Conyers's inventory (1567) is entered 'a fier pann and a pair of tonngs xxd'. At Ham House an iron fire-pan overlaid with sheet silver still exists, resting on couchant lions of silver. The *repoussé* scrollwork of the front centres on the cipher of the Duchess of Lauderdale (Fig. 32). This, no doubt, is one of two 'fire pans' mentioned in the Ham inventory of 1679.

GRATE. When sea-coal came into use, a receptacle for holding the lumps of fuel together and raised above the hearth became necessary; in the Hardwick Hall inventory (1601) 'an iron grate for sea cole' appears in the hall.

In a pamphlet *Artificiall Fire* (1644) the author writes that London ladies used to condemn the use of coal for cooking, but that it was then indispensable; and an illustration is given of a basket-grate with scroll-shaped finials to the standards of the basket, and vertical and diagonal bars in front. These

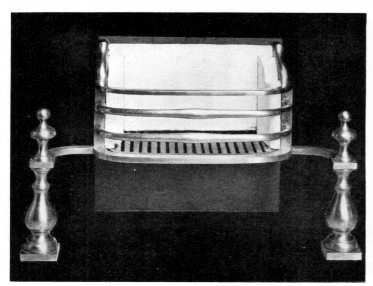

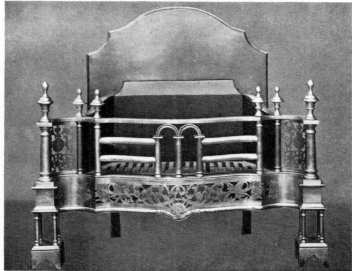

33. *Iron Basket-Grate, with baluster standards. c.* 1720. (*The Carron Company.*) 34. *Steel Basket-Grate, with apron and wings of pierced and engraved steel. c.* 1730. *Ht.* 2 *ft.* 8½ *in., W.* 3 *ft., Depth* 1 *ft.* 2½ *in.* (*Messrs Feetham.*)

standards followed the design of andirons. The front with horizontal bars or ribs was introduced before 1661, when Lamont of Newton's *Diary* recorded that 'the lady caused make a new chimney for the hall and landing of the newest fashion with long bars of iron before, with a high back all of iron behind'. Original iron grates dating from the restoration and refurnishing of the palace in 1671 may still be seen at Holyrood.

For kitchens and modest rooms a simple wrought-iron grid with unenclosed sides served to contain the fire. In their original condition these had standards and one or two bars at the bottom.

Basket grates indubitably of the early 18th century are rare. The early grate, a wrought-iron basket to hold coal together at some little distance above the hearth, was set, but not fixed, in the recess of the chimney-piece. The grate in the Stone Hall at Houghton, Norfolk, is probably original, and has side columns somewhat awkwardly attached to a fire basket with horizontal bars. The same awkward juxtaposition of columns and basket is to be seen in the grate in the dining-room at Wilton, Wiltshire. The usual material was wrought-iron, sometimes polished and finished with brass aprons, finials and other enrichments. Grates of paktong were also made (Bonnin, *Tutenag and Paktong*, p. 33). 'A steel stove grate complete' is listed among the household goods of the Countess of Warwick in 1731. A steel grate (Fig. 34) has turned pillars and pierced and engraved steel wings in which appear a coat with the royal arms and supporters.

35. *Iron Basket-Grate, with lattice front in Chinese style. c.* 1755. *Ht.* 2 *ft.* 4½ *in., W.* 2 *ft.* 4½ *in., Depth* 1 *ft.* 2½ *in.* (*Messrs Feetham.*)
36. *Steel Basket-Grate, pierced and decorated with faceted steel studs. c.* 1785. (*Lyme Park, Ches.*)

37. *Cast-iron Hob-Grate, with wrought-iron bars. c. 1770.*

38. (*Below*) *Iron Grate, with lion standards. c. 1820.* (*Lewes Castle Museum.*)

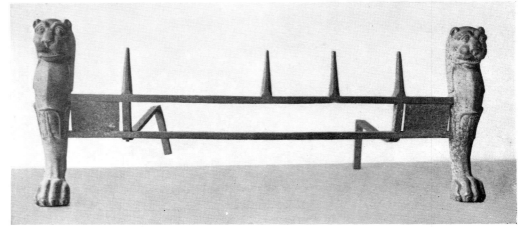

39. (*Below*) *Chimney Crane of wrought-iron. Eighteenth century. Ht.* (*including socket*) *3 ft., W. 3 ft. 2 in., L.* (*of arm*) *3 ft. 1½ in.* (*V. & A. Mus.*)

In surviving grates of the rococo period (which are rare), and in the designs in Chippendale's *Director* (1754), the bars, back-plate and standard are curved, the latter being frequently set angle-wise to the basket; and a straight line as a relief to the incessant curves is rarely found. Designs for the freestanding basket-grate, together with 'Venetian' or Philadelphia stoves 'very useful in preventing Smoak', in which the opening is narrowed by a border richly ornamen-

ted, are illustrated in Ince and Mayhew's *Household Furniture* (1759-63).

The designs of Robert Adam for grates date from 1764, for he illustrates (*Works in Architecture*, Vol. I, Pl. VII) a stove erected in brass and steel for the library of Luton Hoo, Bedfordshire, in that year. He also observes of another model designed for Luton Hoo in 1768 that, as it was the first decorated in this manner, it 'seems to have given the idea for those in this form, which now prevail so much in public and private buildings'. In Adam's designs for basket grates the ornament is treated with novel delicacy. The receptacle for coal is not large, but an appearance of stability and dignity is obtained by the prolongation on either side of the wings, which are supported by standards. The basket is often, as in the grate in the drawing-room from Lyme Park, Cheshire (Fig. 36), of semicircular shape, and the bars follow its graceful curve. The tapering standards, set wide apart, are connected by a deep perforated apron, and the spandrels immediately beneath the basket and the wings are also filled with open scrollwork, richly beaded and studded. The urn finials and the solid portions of the grate are enriched with flutings, studs and paterae. The cast-iron fireback is treated with simple cast ornament in low relief. Such an elaborate grate, with each faceted stud and button separately riveted, must have been exceedingly costly; and Mrs Lybbe Powys draws attention to a 'sweet steel grate', which cost £95, at Heythrop, Oxfordshire,

  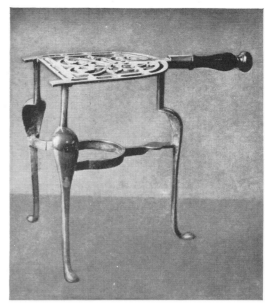

40. *Steel Footman. c.* 1770. (*V. & A. Mus.*) 41. *Iron standing Trivet; pierced and engraved brass top. Dated* 1668. (*V. & A. Mus.*)
42. *Brass standing Trivet; cabriole legs. Mid-18th century.* (*Macquoid Coll.*)

in 1778. In the Soane Museum are a number of Adam's designs for grates, sometimes showing, as in a sketch for the Earl of Coventry (dated 1765), the accompanying fender. A grate for Robert Child (1773) is exceptionally rich in treatment, with its elaborate standards of winged gryphons. The head of the back plate has a classical subject in bas-relief. In the last years of the 18th century a sarcophagus-shaped grate was introduced having a wide basket and massive standards which were occasionally enriched with applied brass ornaments, such as the anthemium. At this time the opening in enclosed grates became narrower, and this was more noticeable in the 19th century, when wide steel plates bordered by brass enrichments surrounded the basket.

Certain hob-grates, in which the fireplace opening is reduced, figure among Adam's drawings and in Glossop's *Stove-Makers' Assistant* (1771), and a great number of these were made at the Carron foundry, Stirlingshire, and at the Coalbrookdale Ironworks, Shropshire. In 1784 a visitor at the Carron works saw 'grates of all kinds, and in the best taste for coal fires, and bas-reliefs after excellent models for the back of fireplaces'.

The ornaments of cast-iron hob-grates were delightfully designed and perfectly spaced. The space on either side of the receptacle for coals is enclosed by panels or cheeks of varied shape which fill the whole width of the recess and end in hobs. A favourite pattern has a semicircular receptacle above a round arch, and the cheeks sometimes have an ogee-shaped curve (Fig. 37). The hob-grate continued in use in the early years of the 19th century; but later both the steel basket and iron hob-grate were largely superseded by more economical and labour-saving contrivances.

HEARTH BRUSH OR BROOM. For sweeping the ashes from the hearth. The example (Fig. 14) now in the Queen's Bedchamber at Ham House, is of wood overlaid with sheet silver; the handle is cylindrical and banded with twisted silver wire, which also forms the ring for suspension.

POT CRANE (CHIMNEY CRANE). A wrought-iron framework with a device for raising and lowering an arm, used for hanging pots over a fire. The usual device is a studded quadrant, which serves as a catch at different levels to the handle of the adjustable arm, which is pivoted on the bracket (Fig. 39).

TRIVET. A metal stand for a pot, kettle or other vessel placed near the fire. It stands on three legs, reaching to about the level of the top bar of the grate, and usually has a handle of turned wood. In an example dated 1668 the legs are of wrought-iron, the top of brass pierced and engraved with a baluster-shaped device, flanked by scrolls and terminating with the figure of Atlas upholding the globe (Fig. 41). A metal stand for the hearth, resting on four legs and having an oblong table-like top, in which a lifting-hole is pierced, is termed a 'footman'. In some examples the front and top are pierced in an open design (Fig. 40). Small hanging trivets were also made to be attached to the top bar of the grate. M. J.

CHIMNEY GLASS. *See* MIRRORS.

CHINESE TASTE. The taste or vogue that led to the importation of Chinese works of art and subsequently to their imitation in England. Porcelain, embroidery and small curiosities were brought back by ships trading with the East from the late 16th century onwards. In 1588 Packe published *The Historie of the Great and Mightie Kingdome of China* from the Spanish original, and three treatises on China and Japan were included by Richard Hakluyt in *The Second Voyage of the Principal Navigations, Voyages, etc.* The East India Company was founded in 1600, and early in the reign of James I specimens of oriental lacquer were being imported in sufficient quantities to give the waning taste for painted woodwork inherited from the Middle Ages a novel source of inspiration. A considerable amount of information concerning the early trade in Eastern wares is contained in the accounts of travellers' voyages and in the *Court Minutes* of the East India Company.

The minutes record (1614) that the Company had hired a 'shoppe' called 'Britain's Bourse' from 'My Lord Treasurer Salisbury . . . in his Newe Exchange, to be furnisht by them with East India Commodities'. This emporium, on the south side of the Strand, was opened in 1609 and pulled down in 1737. In 1614 also there is an entry in the minutes that 'Mr. Governor acquainted this Courte that the Skrenes which are sent unto his Majestie [James I] from Japan (being halfe a score in number) are not so good as some of those which the Company have, and did therefore wishe that nott above 2 or 3 should be presented to his Majestie and exchange some of the best of the Companies for them. . . .' At the end of the same year a sale was held in London which included 'a small truncke or chest . . . of Japan stuff guilded and sett with mother of pearle' and 'a faire contore [a Portuguese term] or cabanet guilded and inlaid with mother of pearle . . . havinge sundrie drawers and boxes' (*Court Minutes*, vol. iii, p. 327). In the minutes screens are also referred to, one being described as 'guilded and paynted with some resemblances of warfare', while two others were 'portrayde with fowles'.

Probably the earliest documentary evidence of this eastern influence on the decoration of domestic furniture is afforded by the inventory (1614) of the 'goodes and household stuffe' of Henry Howard, Earl of Northampton, then at Northampton House, near Charing Cross. Among the items enumerated were:

> A large square *China Worke* table and frame of black varnishe and golde.
> One small table of *China Worke* in golde colours with flies and wormes upon a pillar suteable.

A pair of upholstered chairs and a field bedstead were also decorated in this taste.

These objects, decorated in an exotic style, are clearly differentiated by the descriptions from an abundance of furniture painted in polychrome. In 1615 Thomas Howard, Earl of Arundel, wrote to the Countess at Arundel House asking her to buy a blue quilt which 'will serve ye bedde of Jappan exceedinge well, and fitte it for the Coller'—an early instance of the term 'Jappan'.

That the imitation of oriental lacquer had begun is proved by another letter addressed by William Smith (1616) to Arundel requesting employment. Writing from Rome he mentions among his qualifications that he has 'bene emploied by the Cardinalles and other Princes of thos parts in *workes after the Chinese fashion* which is much affected here'. There is evidence that at this period 'China worke' was differentiated from true oriental objects, often termed 'Indian'; of which the inventory of the Countess of Arundel's goods at Tart Hall (1644) affords several examples.

This early China Worke, or *chinoiserie*, is now represented by a small group of objects, of which the ballot-box in the possession of the Saddlers' Company (bearing the arms of James I and dated 1619) and two cabinets at the Victoria and Albert Museum are the most important. (*See* CABINETS, Fig. 1 and JAPANNING AND LACQUER.)

By 1670 the taste for *chinoiserie* was strongly developed in France, and a few years later *le style Bérain*, largely inspired by oriental art, afforded the basis of design for wall-paintings and tapestries. In England the fashion was less consistently

carried out, but notices of choice collections of oriental (often termed 'Indian') curiosities began to appear towards the end of Charles II's reign. Catherine of Braganza, when she came to marry the king, brought with her 'the first Oriental cabinets which had ever been seen in England'. In 1689 Evelyn describes the house of his neighbour, Mr Bohun, as 'a cabinet of elegancies, especially Indian; in the hall are contrivances of japan screens, instead of wainscot . . . the landscape of the screens represent the manner of living and country of the Chinese'. When an inventory of the contents of Kensington Palace was drawn up in 1697, after the death of Queen Mary, nearly all the furniture in the Queen's New Bedchamber was decorated in 'india Jappan'. Advertisements announcing the arrival from the East of large quantities of lacquer panels, 'screens set in frames, escretors', porcelain, etc., prove the enormous extent of the trade at the end of the century. The Kensington Palace inventory (1697) lists a large collection of Queen Mary's 'fine china', mostly oriental, arranged in shelves above doors and chimney-pieces. Porcelain displayed in this manner is seen in one of the designs by Daniel Marot, architect to William III, the room being decorated throughout in the Chinese taste. Lacquer imported from the East was soon imitated in England (*see* JAPANNING AND LACQUER), this kind of decoration affording an outlet for the post-Restoration delight in vivid colour. Oriental lacquer and English japanned cabinets set on carved and gilt stands are found in most houses furnished in the late 17th century, and instructions framed for the use of amateurs are given by Stalker and Parker in their *Treatise on Japanning and Varnishing* (1688). In 1683 Mary Verney's father wrote to her (she was then ten years old): 'I find you have a desire to learn to japan, as you call it, and I approve'.

During the early Georgian period the taste was less in evidence, though japanning was still practised, and many fashionable houses were plentifully supplied with oriental lacquer and western japan—still impossible to differentiate in inventory and sale catalogue descriptions; but before the middle of the century there was a widespread revival, and architects and designers once more turned for their inspiration to the Far East. This revived interest was stimulated by books of travel, the most important being J. B. du Halde's great work on China, published in Paris in 1735, and translated into English six years later. As early as 1749 Mrs Montagu speaks slightingly of the 'barbarous gaudy *gout* of the Chinese' sought by those sick of Grecian elegance and symmetry (though she soon had a room decorated in this manner); and Morris, in his *Rural Architecture* (1750), complains that 'the Chinese un-meaning taste' is regarded as a profitable study. A writer in the *World* (1753) observes that 'according to the present prevailing whim everything is Chinese or in the Chinese taste; or, as it is sometimes more modestly expressed, partly after the Chinese manner. Chairs, tables, chimney-pieces, frames for looking-glasses, and even our most vulgar utensils are all reduced to this new-fangled standard'. Dr Pococke, visiting Badminton in 1754, describes one bedroom as 'finished and furnished very elegantly in the Chinese manner', the bed it contained being now in the Victoria and Albert Museum (see BEDS; Fig. 31). J. Shebbeare (*Letters on the English Nation*, 1756) observes that 'every chair in an apartment, the frames of glasses and tables must be Chinese: the walls covered with Chinese papers fill'd with figures which resemble nothing in God's creation'.

The vogue, therefore, was firmly established before the appearance in 1757 of Sir William Chambers's *Designs of Chinese Buildings*, in which he disclaimed any desire to be numbered 'among the exaggerators of Chinese excellence'. On the authority of Horace Walpole, his friend Richard Bateman was 'the founder of this sharawadgi taste in England', but afterwards deserted it for Gothic 'so effectively that his every pagoda took the veil'. Architects and cabinet-makers attempting to conform to the prevalent fashion produced designs of grotesque absurdity, incongruous and overloaded with ornament, for objects which had no prototypes in the East (*see* CHIPPENDALE, DARLY, HALLETT and HALFPENNY). The more extravagant of these designs remained unrealised, but a medley of Chinese detail, often blended with rococo motives, was added to the decorative resources of the period, often with charming effect.

By 1765 the craze was on the wane, though its expressions were not universally ousted by the neo-classic revival, and ten years later the Duke of Argyll's mansion at Twickenham 'was highly Oriental in its furnishings'.

Towards the end of the century there was a revival which owed something to the influence of the Prince of Wales. His drawing-room at Carlton House, described and illustrated in Sheraton's *Drawing Book* (1793), affords the earliest evidence of his addiction to the taste. When alterations were made in the Brighton Pavilion in 1802, the prince was presented with 'several pieces of a very beautiful Chinese paper', and they were hung in a gallery painted and decorated in a corresponding style. In the Brighton Pavilion as reconstructed by Nash after 1815, the Chinese taste was exploited in a much more lavish and somewhat tawdry form. (See *A Cycle of Cathay*, W. W. Appleton, 1951, *Chinoiserie*, H. Honour, 1961.)

CHINTZ or **CHINT.** A cotton fabric painted or printed in colours or fast dyes. The process was of great antiquity in the East, and the art of staining cloths with various designs was practised in England during the Middle Ages. In 1579 Hakluyt instructed Morgan Hubblethorne, a dyer, to proceed to Persia and try to discover the manner of dyeing cloths which, he says, 'hath been an old trade in England, whereof some excellent cloths yet remain'. The importation of chintzes or 'painted callicoes' appears to have begun in the early 17th century, and in 1631 the East India Company was authorised to ship them into England. Pepys notes in his *Diary* (September 5, 1663) that he has been to Cornhill 'and after many trialls bought my wife a chint, that is a painted East Indian callico for to line her new study'. Sir Joshua Child, in a pamphlet (1677) mentions that calicoes were then brought over from India to be painted in this country, the design being drawn by hand in the East; and among the correspondence of the East India Company in 1683 is an order for '100 suits of painted curtains and vallances ready made up of several sorts and prices'. Defoe (*Weekly Review*, January 31, 1708) writes that the general fancy of the people runs upon East Indian goods, chintz and painted calicoes, which had 'crept into our houses; our closets and bedchambers, curtains, cushions, chairs, and at last beds themselves, were nothing but calicoes and Indian stuffs, and in short almost everything that used to be made of

wool or silk, relating rather to the dress of the women or the furniture of our house, was supplied by the Indian trade'. As a result of serious outbreaks among the weavers, an Act was passed in 1722 prohibiting the use and wear of all printed, stained or dyed calicoes. The law was modified in 1736, and in 1774, after Arkwright's water-frame had enabled all-cotton goods to be produced in England, the printing on cotton of English manufacture was freed from all restrictions. The importation of Indian chintzes was, however, prohibited until a considerably later date. In 1775 some curtains and bed hangings, sent to David Garrick's wife as a gift from Calcutta, were confiscated after they had been in her possession for four years. They were eventually released by the Customs and the hangings are now on the bedstead from Garrick's Hampton Villa in the Victoria and Albert Museum. In 1771 Mrs Lybbe Powys wrote that Lady Blount in her house near Ludlow 'has more chintz counterpanes than one house ever saw; not one bed without very fine ones'. In the *Guide* (1788) Hepplewhite recommends the use of printed cotton or linen for bed hangings.

CHIP-CARVING. Shallow faceted ornament executed with chisel and gouge; found in the form of roundels on the front and wide stiles of early medieval chests, and as occasional decorative motif on oak furniture until the second half of the 17th century. (*See* CHESTS; Fig. 3: BOXES; Fig. 8.)

CISTERN. *See* WINE CISTERNS AND COOLERS.

CLAPBOARD. Timber in board form imported mainly from Scandinavia and the Baltic area—where pine was the chief indigenous wood; generally used for panelling in the Tudor period and later. Term still used in the 18th century: 1725, Bradley, *Furniture Dictionary*, 'Oak Clapboard for Wainscot'.

CLASSICAL TASTE. The term used to describe the revival of Graeco-Roman forms of architecture and decoration, first apparent in the Italian Renaissance, which affected English furniture in various ways from the 16th to the early 19th centuries. For explanation and illustration of the many classical terms applied to sections of furniture and decorative motifs, *see* ACANTHUS, ACROTER, ANTEFIX, ARCHITRAVE, ASTRAGAL, CAPITAL, CORNICE, ENTABLATURE, ENTASIS, FLUTES, FRIEZE, GUILLOCHE, KEY PATTERN, MODILLION, OGEE, ORDERS, OVOLO, PATERA, PEDIMENT, PEDESTAL, PLINTH, VITRUVIAN SCROLL, VOLUTE.

Classical decoration, introduced by a few immigrant Italian artists, first affected English furniture in the early 16th century and, in the form of roundels and attempts at conventional Renaissance motives, was applied by English craftsmen, often incongruously, to traditional Gothic forms. After the Reformation, Italian influence was replaced by that of German and Flemish artists and craftsmen, whose debased forms and versions of classical decoration were widely imitated, largely through imported pattern-books. (*See* STRAPWORK.) It was not until the 17th century that classicism on Italian models finally triumphed, first through the Palladian architecture of Inigo Jones (*q.v.*) and later through Wren's anglicised baroque. Furniture, however, in spite of the growing use of classical decoration, was not fully affected until William Kent (*q.v.*) and other architects, in the Palladian revival of the early Georgian period, designed furniture to conform with their architectural schemes. Cabinet-makers were then encouraged to study the five Orders, and much case furniture of the time had pronounced architectural features. After the phase of rococo (*q.v.*), from c. 1760, the design and decoration of furniture were profoundly influenced by the neo-classic style of Robert Adam which is seen freely adapted in Hepplewhite's *Guide* (1788) and other pattern-books of the period. Shortly before 1800 the close adaptation of antique forms, based on Greek and Roman models, became apparent in English furniture design, at first carried out in an archaeological and scholarly manner by Henry Holland and Thomas Hope (*qq.v.*), but later with the classical elements often travestied or misinterpreted, and mixed with other styles. This development is illustrated by George Smith, Sheraton (in his later publications) and other contemporary designers. E.J.

CLOCK CASES. With the mechanism of clocks we are here only concerned in so far as at different periods it affected the character of the case. Originally the striking of a clock was the all-important consideration, and, probably, many early medieval clocks had neither dials nor hands, but told the time only by striking the hour; or even announced it by a single blow, upon which a larger and more sonorous bell would be struck by hand. A reminiscence of this last-named procedure is furnished by those jointed automata, representing men in armour, or grotesque figures, known as 'striking jacks', that beat upon a bell, of which examples survive.

Though public clocks equipped with 'jacks' for striking were not uncommon, a chamber clock so fitted is rare, but an example of exceptional interest, dating probably from the 16th century, is illustrated in Fig. 1, in which the figure surmounting the clock strikes the hours on the large bell with the hammer in his hands, and at the quarters strikes the two smaller bells by means of levers. Striking clocks of much more intricate and elaborate character were occasionally produced towards the end of the Tudor period, and Paul Hentzner, visiting Whitehall Palace in 1598, observed 'a piece of clockwork, an Aethiop riding upon a Rhinoceros, with four attendants, who all make their obeisance when it strikes the hour: these are put into motion by winding up the machine'. Such curiosities can, however, have been made only for princes or great nobles.

Early hanging clocks were weight-driven, necessitating an adequate space beneath the mechanism for the fall of the weights, and for the most part were fixed clocks of large size. The domestic clock which the well-to-do householder could afford probably made its appearance c. 1500. In that year Peter Henlein is said to have discovered a new motive power, adopting an expansive spring coiled within a drum or 'barrel' as a prime mover—a principle which was not perfected until a quarter of a century later and resulted in the production of a compact spring-driven clock.

During the second half of the 16th century small, portable, spring-driven table clocks were produced in large numbers in Germany, particularly in Augsburg, and on a lesser scale in France and the Low Countries. They were equipped with metal cases, usually gilt brass or copper, but sometimes silver. The dial was set horizontally on top of the movement, which was enclosed in a cylindrical, square or hexagonal case. Some of these clocks must have been imported into England during the 16th century, but their price would have confined their use to the wealthy. Towards the close of that period these low-built horizontal models were mostly superseded in Germany by higher standing clocks in which the dial was placed vertically; the movement being accommodated on the same lines as in a contemporary weight-driven clock.

It was in France that the English clock-makers of the late 16th century found their models. Very few signed English clocks of that period exist, but there are a number of unsigned examples which may well be of English manufacture. The first English spring clocks show definite traces of French influence, in both construction and ornament. Like the French maker, the English clock-maker of the early 17th century produced both types of table clock, *i.e.* with face set vertically and horizontally. He followed the French fashion of a plain rectangular case surmounted by finials at the corners and a pierced domical top containing the alarm. The classic example of this type of clock is in the British Museum. It is signed by Bartholomew Newsam, who in 1572 was granted the reversion of the office of clock-maker to Queen Elizabeth I. Newsam died in 1595; the clock, of about that date in a case of gilt engraved brass, is only about 6½ ins. high.

The finest known English clock of this period is of horizontal construction. The movement is signed by David Ramsay, clock-maker to James I. Ramsay learnt his craft in France, and when he came to England he probably brought French workmen with him. The case of the Ramsay clock, which can be dated between 1603 and 1610, is certainly French work. It is of finely engraved gilt brass with medallions but, measuring 4 ins. high and 4½ ins. wide, like the Newsam clock can scarcely be classified as furniture. These small-sized, metal-cased, spring-driven clocks did not long remain in favour in England; though a few examples dating from the second half of the 17th century, probably made to special order, still exist.

From the time of Elizabeth I to the last quarter of the 17th century the bulk of the smaller English domestic clocks were enclosed in cases of metal, generally brass. They appear to have been made in considerable numbers from c. 1600, the first common form being a weight-driven, brass-cased mural clock which was hung against the wall or set on a bracket, with the chains and weights hanging down and exposed, the pendulum superseding the balance (or 'swing wheel') sometime after 1657.

The early domestic time-keepers, known as 'lantern' or 'bird-cage' clocks (Fig. 2), were constructed entirely of metal, the case being rectangular and of brass, with a framing composed of four turned corner pillars, usually in the form of columns of the Doric order, connecting top and bottom plates, and ending below in ball feet and above in vase-shaped finials. The spaces between the pillars were occupied by fixed back and front plates and hinged side doors, while front and sides were headed with fretted crestings, and the whole was surmounted by a hemispherical bell. To the front or dial-plate a circular band, or horary circle, was attached, graduated into twelve hours, distinguished by Roman numerals, or 'chapters', the quarter-hours being marked by minor subdivisions around the inner edge of the band. With few exceptions, the time was

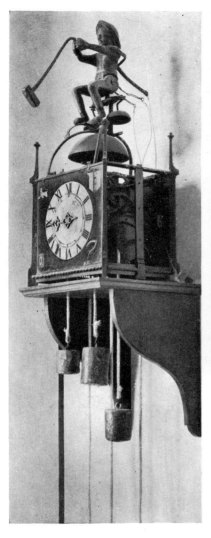

1. (*Left*) *Hanging Clock, with automaton for striking; in iron case with painted dial; the movement subsequently converted to the pendulum control. Sixteenth century. Ht. 26 in., W. 11¾ in., Depth 9 in.* (*Sir William Burrell Coll.*)

2. (*Above, left*) *Brass-cased Lantern Clock by 'Davis Mell in Crutched Fryers Londini'. c. 1665-70. Ht. 12¼ in., W. 5 in., Depth 6 in.* (*J. Drummond Robertson Coll.*)

3. (*Above, right*) *Hanging Clock with wooden hood and bracket. By Thomas Tompion, London. c. 1670. Ht. 16½ in., W. 10⅜ in., Depth 6½ in.* (*Mr Brian E. A. Vigers.*)

indicated on early 'lantern' clocks by means of a single pointer, or hand, the hours being struck on the bell. Such clocks were wound by pulling down the lengths of chain or cord opposite to those from which the weights were suspended, the descent of the weights being generally accomplished in approximately thirty hours. They were attached to the wall by means of a hook and staple. Except in size and matter of detail, these 17th-century brass-cased clocks of the 'lantern' variety differ little from each other; and indeed it is possible that all the components had a common origin.

In an early treatise on the construction of clock movements a chapter is devoted to an explanation of the method to be adopted in 'converting a twelve-hour balance-clock into a Pendulum', *i.e.* the short or 'bob' pendulum. The clock illustrated in Fig. 1 provides an instance of such later conversion—a comparatively simple matter. In England, though the minute-hand appeared occasionally, it was not in common use upon clocks before 1670, and was often omitted by provincial makers quite late in the 18th century. Early specimens of the lantern clock were small in size, the hour-circle being narrow and contained within the width of the framework. Towards the end of the 17th century the diameter of the hour-circle was increased until it projected in front of, and appreciably beyond, the corner pillars of the frame, the band itself being widened and the numerals increased in height. The open

frets, which form so characteristic a feature around the base of the bell, were often adorned with an engraved armorial shield and supporters, with a central vase and conventional floral scrolls, with scrolls alone, or with crossed dolphins; and they often bore the name and locality of the clock-maker. Lantern clocks were not originally fixed into wooden cases, but, with improvements in horological science and increasing regard for time-keeping qualities, a wooden outer case or 'hood' embodying a backboard and supporting brackets made its appearance some time before 1670. An example of a thirty-hour wall clock, constructed in the manner of a lantern clock with turned brass corner pillars, but with the innovation of a square dial and enclosed in a wooden 'hood' case, is illustrated in Fig. 3.

The great event in the history of horology was the introduction of the pendulum as a regulator. No practical application of the discovery seems to have been made until the time of Vincenzio Galilei, son of Galileo, the famous astronomer, who is stated to have first set up a pendulum clock in Venice in 1649. The invention was never brought into prominence until it came into the hands of the Dutch mathematician and physicist Christian Huygens van Zulichem (1629-95)—the 'Mr Zulichem' of Evelyn's *Memoirs*—who produced a clock controlled by a pendulum in 1657, and whose friend and countryman, Ahasuerus Fromanteel, appears in the following year to have

  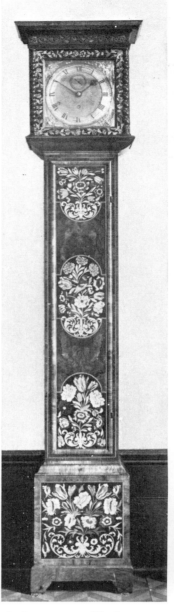 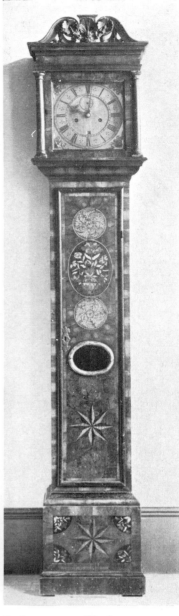

4. *Long-case Clock; case panelled and veneered with ebony. Movement by Johannes Fromanteel. c. 1675. Ht. 6 ft. 7 in. (Dunn Gardner Coll.)*

5. *Long-case Clock; case veneered with 'mazer-wood' and decorated with parquetry. Movement by Thomas Wheeler. c. 1680. Ht. 6 ft. 5½ in. (Drummond Robertson Coll.)*

6. *Long-case Clock; case veneered with walnut and decorated with marquetry in panels. Movement by Johannes Fromanteel. c. 1680-85. Ht. 6 ft. 9½ in. (F. Garrett. Coll.)*

7. *Long-case Clock; case veneered with walnut oyster-pieces decorated with insertions of parquetry and marquetry; carved cresting. Anonymous. c. 1685. Ht. 6 ft. 9 in. (The late Mr Ingleson C. Goodison.)*

been the first clock-maker to introduce pendulum clocks into this country.

An advertisement in the *Commonwealth Mercury* of November 25, 1658, refers to the manufacture and sale of pendulum clocks in England by Fromanteel:

> There is lately a way found for making clocks that go exact and keep equaller time than any now made without this regulator ... and are not subject to alter by change of weather, as others are, and may be made to go a week, or a month or a year, with one winding up, as well as those which are wound up every day, and it is very excellent for all house clocks that go either with springs or weights; and also steeple clocks, that are most subject to differ by change of weather. Made by Ahasuerus Fromanteel, who

made the first that were in England. You may have them at his house, on the Bankside, in Moses Alley, Southwark, and at the sign of the 'Mermaid' in Lothbury, near Bartholomew Lane end, London.

On the introduction of the pendulum, clocks assumed a different character. Catgut lines were substituted for the chains or cords, and barrels were introduced, round which the line was wound, and, a greater length of line being employed, clocks were made to go for eight days or more instead of thirty hours; while a chime of bells often supplemented the striking of the hour and its quarter-divisions.

Domestic clocks of this period may be divided into two

classes—those driven by falling weights and those of which the motive force is a coiled spring. Spring-driven table clocks enclosed in decorative wooden cases enriched with mounts of gilded metal were made early in the second half of the 17th century. These were evidently designed to be seen from all sides, a glazed door being provided in the back of the case through which the swinging of the short 'bob' pendulum, the fine workmanship of the pierced cock and engraving of the metal backplate of the movement would be visible. The narrow, long case, extending to the floor, and protecting the weights, also made its appearance at this period.

Although the short pendulums of Huygens and Fromanteel quickly superseded the balance as a controller of household clocks shortly after 1657, thereby improving their time-keeping qualities, it remained for Dr Hooke to discover that the real merits of the pendulum had been obscured by making it short, light and swinging in a very large arc. He exhibited a clock before the Royal Society in 1666 provided with a long and heavy pendulum having relatively a very small swing.

Writing in 1675, 'J. S. (John Smith) of London, Clock-Maker', the author of *Horological Dialogues*, alludes to the relative merits of the balance, short pendulum and long pendulum thus:

As to their regularity, I shall say only this much, that those clocks, who have their motion regulated by a pendulum are more excellent than those who are regulated by a Balance, and those that are regulated by a long pendulum are far more excellent than those that are regulated by a fhort one.

He thus affords an indication that clocks fitted with the long pendulum were at that time apparently also in general use.

The most important supplementary invention of this period was the 'anchor' escapement, the invention of Dr Hooke, or possibly of William Clement, a London clock-maker. With

8. *Table or Bracket Night Clock in case veneered with ebony. Movement by Edward East. c. 1680. Ht. 17 in. (Dunn Gardner Coll.)*

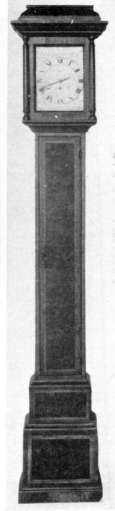

9. *Miniature Long-case Clock by 'Eduardus East, Londini'. Ht. 4 ft. 8 in.*

10. *Spring Clock; case veneered with olive wood and ebony; turned columns, brass capitals. Movement signed 'Thomas Tompion Londini Fecit.' c. 1675. (Mr Percy G. Dawson.)*

11. *Table or Bracket Clock; case veneered with kingwood; domical top of pierced and chased brass. Movement by Johannes Fromanteel. c. 1685-90. Ht. 1 ft. 2¾ in., W. 9⅜ in., (V. & A. Mus.)*

12. *Table or Bracket Clock; case decorated with marquetry of walnut and various woods. Movement by John Martin, London. c. 1700-5. Ht. 1 ft. 3¾ in., W. 10¼ in., (V. & A. Mus.)*

13. Table or Bracket Clock; case of ebonised pearwood decorated with chased brass mounts. Movement by Christopher Gould, London. c. 1690. (G. W. Wells Coll.) 14. Table or Bracket Timepiece; case of ebonised pearwood; 'basket-top' of chased brass and mounts of similar character. Movement by Thomas Cattell, London. c. 1690. (G. W. Wells Coll.) 15. Table or Bracket Clock; case overlaid with red tortoiseshell; double-tiered 'basket-top' of pierced, chased and gilded brass. Movement by George Murgatroyd, London. c. 1695. (Messrs M. Harris and Sons.)

the advent of the long pendulum and anchor escapement, the clock case obtained prominence as an important and decorative article of furniture. The productions of this period are notable as much for the decorative qualities of their cases as for the excellence of their time-keeping.

The earliest wooden clock cases were of oak veneered with ebony, kingwood, olive wood, laburnum or walnut. They were low in stature, and narrow in the trunk or 'waist', the hood enclosing the movement being flanked by twist-turned or cylindrical angle-pillars supporting an entablature, which was occasionally surmounted by an angular pediment of low pitch, or a carved and pierced cresting.

An interesting insight into the woods used in clock case-making as early as 1675 is afforded by the account book of Sir Richard Legh, of Lyme Park, Cheshire:

> I went to the famous Pendulum maker Knibb, and have agreed for one, he having none ready but one dull stager which was at 19 *l*; for 5 *l*. more, I have agreed for one finer than my Father's, and it is to be better finish'd with carved capitalls gold, and gold pedestalls with figures of boys and cherubimes all brass gilt. I wold have had itt Olive Wood, (the Case I mean), but gold does not agree with that colour, soe took their advice to have it Black Ebony which suits your Cabinett better than Walnutt tree wood, of which they are mostly made. Lett me have thy advice herein by the next.

In answer to her husband, Lady Legh assures him:

> My dearest Soule: as for the Pandelome Case I think Blacke suits anything.

16. Table Clock; case veneered with ebony and mounted with silver. The clock, spring-driven, strikes hours and quarters; to be wound once a year. Made for King William III (whose arms it bears) by Thomas Tompion, London. c. 1700. Ht. 2 ft. 4 in. (Mostyn Hall, Flint.)

17. *Long-case Clock; case veneered with finely figured walnut and decorated with ornaments of ormolu, including Royal monogram of King William III; made by Thomas Tompion, London. c. 1695-1700. (J. S. Sykes Coll.)* 18. *Long-case Clock; the case veneered with walnut; sub-plinth of chased and gilded brass; above hood a finely modelled female figure flanked by four amorini. The twelve-month timepiece movement by Daniel Quare. c. 1705. (Hampton Court Palace. By gracious permission of H.M. the Queen.)* 19. *Long-case Clock; case veneered with walnut and decorated with floral marquetry. Movement by Christopher Gould. c. 1695. Ht. 7 ft. 2 in. (Lady Capel Cure Coll.)* 20. *Long-case Clock; case veneered with walnut and decorated with arabesque marquetry. Movement by Jacob Massy. c. 1715. (Sir Leicester Harmsworth Coll.)*

In specimens of these early long cases, particularly those of ebony, the front and sides of the case are embellished with a series of finely moulded panels having raised centres. In Fig. 4 there are an angular pediment to the hood, 'scratch' mouldings and twist-turned angle pillars with carved and gilded capitals.

In addition to the use of rare, choice and beautifully figured woods for veneering, the clock case-maker of the period exploited the decorative resources of parquetry (Fig. 5) and marquetry (Fig. 6), either alone or in combination (Fig. 7). In early examples such ornament, instead of covering the entire surface, was often restricted to reserved panels of geometrical outline, the intermediate spaces being filled with 'oyster-shell' veneer. Whenever figured woods were used, the mouldings were either stained black, or were of black ebony, or were worked in facings of cross-cut wood, to exhibit the natural grain to advantage.

Carving was restricted in early long cases to such features as crestings, finials and capitals, and, more rarely, to the moulded framing round the 'bull's-eyes', or glazed apertures in the trunk-door; such carving being in soft wood and, with the exception of the cresting, usually gilded.

231

21. *Long-case Clock; case veneered with walnut. Month-going movement by Thomas Tompion. c. 1705. Ht. 8 ft. 6 in. (J. Drummond Robertson Coll.)* 22. *Long-case Clock; case veneered with walnut and embellished with ormolu and applied carving. Movement by Langley Bradley. c. 1715-25. Ht. 9 ft. 0¾ in. (The Admiralty, Whitehall.)*

Among allusions to clocks in Pepys's *Diary* is a reference to one for exhibiting the time by night:

1664 June 24—After dinner to White Hall, and there met Mr Pierce, and he showed me the Queen's bed-chamber, with her clock by her bedside, wherein a lamp burns that tells her the time of the night at any time.

English clocks of this description were made principally, if not exclusively, by Edward East, appointed to the office of 'Chief Clockmaker and Keeper of the Privy Clocks' in 1662, two examples of whose productions are given in Figs. 8 and 9. The first shows a table day-and-night clock in a case veneered with ebony, the upper portion of which can be lifted

off to permit the insertion of a light, a series of pierced numerals appearing through the curved aperture in the upper part of the dial, which is elaborately engraved and furnished with a supplementary hour-circle and pair of hands for indicating the time of day. Fig. 9 illustrates a rare miniature long-case clock with an elaborately engraved oblong dial, inscribed 'Eduardus East, Londini'. The case is veneered with walnut and inlaid with 'herring-bone' lines bordered with cross-banding. There are a slight superstructure to the hood and a double base to afford additional stability.

After the introduction of the short pendulum by Fromanteel in 1658 attention was paid to the production of so-called 'bracket' or table clocks, spring-driven and wood-encased. Surviving specimens of the earliest types by Ahasuerus Fromanteel, Edward East, Edward Staunton and others indicate a fashion for cases of pronounced architectural character, in which ebony was the favourite wood. These pedimented cases were succeeded by the square-fronted 'squat' cases, with domed tops in either wood or metal, and furnished with a top handle (Figs. 11, 12, 13). The materials used for case-making were generally ebony, ebonised pearwood, walnut and, more rarely, kingwood and wood stained or painted and overlaid with tortoise-shell, elaborate mountings of gilded brass, and even of silver, being freely employed. Marquetry cases (Fig. 12) are relatively uncommon.

Fig. 10 shows the only known clock by Thomas Tompion in a case of architectural type, and is of the pre-numbered period (c. 1675). The dial is of early character.

The dials and hands illustrated in Figs. 11, 12 and 13 show succeeding tendencies in design—hour-circles being widened and the numerals increasing in height and diminishing in thickness. Figs. 11 and 12 illustrate the numbering of the five-minute divisions within the minute-circle: in Figs. 12 and 13 these divisions are extended and the numbers engraved on a further band at the periphery.

A very decorative feature of these table clocks is the elaborate engravings on the large brass backplate to the movement, which is visible through a glazed door at the back of the case.

A development of the 'squat' case is illustrated by Figs. 14 and 15, wherein the low domical top of chased and pierced metal is elaborated into a 'basket top'. These were popular in the last quarter of the 17th century; pierced domical and basket tops serving to emit the sound of the bell or bells.

Owing largely to the encouragement of the Royal Society, the productions of British clock-makers in the last quarter of the 17th century surpassed those of all other countries. Among the most famous of the many distinguished makers of this early period were Edward East, Joseph Knibb, Henry Jones, Thomas Wheeler, Thomas Tompion, Samuel Watson and Daniel Quare. Of these, Thomas Tompion (1638-1713), clock-maker to Charles II, and maker of many fine clocks for William III, was of outstanding ability. To him several important inventions are due, and his 'advent marks a distinct epoch in the history of horological art. Throughout his career he was closely associated with some of the leading mathematicians and philosophers of his time. The theories of Dr Hooke and the Revd Edward Barlow would probably have remained in abeyance but for Tompion's skilful materialization of them.' An important example of Tompion's work is

23. *Long-case Clock; case veneered with walnut. Movement by Joseph Windmills. Dated 1710. Ht. 9 ft. 8½ in. (Paymaster-General's Office, Whitehall.)*

24. *Long-case Clock; case veneered with walnut. Movement by Richard Street, London. c. 1715. Ht. 8 ft. 9 in. (Min. of Works. Whitehall.)*

25. *Long-case Clock; case decorated with blue japan. The movement by Claudius Du Chesne. c. 1725. Ht. 8 ft. 6 in. (J. Drummond Robertson Coll.)*

illustrated in Fig. 17 in the form of a long-case clock made, apparently, to the order of William III, whose cipher it bears. It goes for three months without rewinding, is fitted with a perpetual calendar, and is enclosed in a finely proportioned tall-case, veneered with richly figured walnut wood. The mounts are pierced and chased ormolu with a figure of Minerva on the top, the gilded metalwork forming an effective contrast to the colour of the woodwork.

There is a close correspondence between the case-work of this handsome clock and the remarkable 'wheel' barometer, also made by Tompion for William III (*see* BAROMETER CASES AND FRAMES; Fig. 6). Both bear the Royal cipher, within crossed palm-branches, and both are enriched with scrolled and voluted trusses, and have moulded rectangular

bezels framing the dials, and similar applied, pierced and chased spandrel ornaments of a pattern peculiar to Tompion and his assistants.

A long-case timepiece by the celebrated maker Daniel Quare (1648-1724) is illustrated in Fig. 18. It is a one-year timepiece enclosed in a tall-case of walnut, the veneer with which it is overlaid having acquired a pale yellowish-golden hue. Like the Tompion clock (Fig. 17), it stands on a sub-plinth with chased and gilded brasswork, and is surmounted by a spiritedly carved female figure, flanked by four amorini. Along the bottom of the dial-plate are three subsidiary dials relating to the rising and setting of the sun, the latitude and equation-of-time mechanism.

As early as 1675 the author of *Horological Dialogues*,

26. Long-case Clock in narrow case with wing pieces for a short light bob pendulum; case decorated with scarlet japan. Thirty-hour movement by Markwick Markham. c. 1730. Ht. 5 ft. 6 in.; W. of 'waist', 4⅛ in. (Cold Ashton Manor, Gloucs.)
27. Long-case Clock; case decorated with red japan. c. 1730-35. Ht. 8 ft. 4 in. (V. & A. Mus.)

indicating various denominations of clocks current at that time, classifies certain of them 'from the time they continue in motion at once winding up', and mentions

> some going 16 hours, some 30 hours, some 8 days, some 5 weeks, some 3 months, some 6 months, and some a year.

An advertisement in the *London Gazette* (April 15-19, 1697) refers to several varieties made by Joseph Knibb:

> At the Clock Dyal, in Suffolk Street near Charing Cross, on Fryday, the 23rd inst; will begin the ſale of a great Parcel of very good Pendulum Clocks; ſome do go a year, ſome a quarter of a year, ſome a month, ſome a week, and ſome 30 hours; ſome are Table Clocks, ſome repeat themselves, and ſome by pulling (a string), repeat the hours and quarters: made and sold by Joseph Knibb, at his Houſe, at the Dyal, in Suffolk Street, aforementioned.

All the principal makers seem to have made such clocks.

One of the most remarkable clocks, from a horological point of view, in a case of ebony mounted with silver and surmounted by a figure of Britannia, is illustrated in Fig. 16. This is a spring-driven twelve-month table clock, which strikes the hours and quarters, and was made by Tompion for William III. The movement is attached to a base-plate supported on scrolled silver feet, the case being made in one piece to slide over the mechanism, and having a glazed aperture in the lower portion to show the swinging pendulum.

Two long-case clocks (Figs. 19 and 20) are representative types of clock cases popular c. 1695-1715, in which marquetry is the chief decorative feature. In both cases the groundwork is of walnut or sycamore veneer, the pattern being no longer restricted to reserved panels, but extending all over the front surfaces (excluding the mouldings, which are worked in finely figured cross-cut wood). Fig. 19 has a flat-topped hood and is decorated with floral marquetry in various light-toned woods on a darker ground.

Fig. 20 is an important and finely proportioned specimen of a late marquetry clock case. Below the hood is a concave moulding which early in the 18th century was preferred to the convex or ovolo moulding hitherto in vogue. The dial is arched and the hood surmounted by a domical superstructure, with finials of carved and gilded wood. The trusses below are similarly decorated. A moulded architrave follows the lines of the dial. Every appropriate surface is decorated with fine arabesque marquetry, which is continued also over the concave moulding below the hood, the cylindric pillars and curved dome.

Thanks to legislation in 1698, when clock-makers were compelled to put their names on all clocks and watches from their workshops, it has been possible to accumulate an immense amount of accurate and detailed information relating to the principal British horologists, particularly those of the capital, and to assign an approximate date to their productions. References to case-makers in the registers of members of the Clockmakers' Company are, however, rare and of the most meagre description.

In a list of members of the Clockmakers' Company from its inception in 1631 to the year 1732, contributed to the *Architectural Journal*, 1883 (vol. xl, p. 193), appears the name of Richard Blundell, 'Case-maker', in 1682, having previously been warned for practising the art without being admitted. Samuel Bennett, whose name appears in the register in 1716, is possibly the cabinet-maker (*see* BENNETT, SAMUEL).

Many names of 'Frenchmen' appear, so designated, in the lists of clock-makers working in England after 1685, the date of the Revocation of the Edict of Nantes—and probably much of the fine clock-making and case-making of the late 17th and early 18th centuries was the work of immigrants.

Early in the 18th century a fashion arose for long cases of plainer character; these were generally executed in finely figured walnut veneer with, occasionally, a little inlay in the form of simple rectilinear cross-cut or 'herring-bone' bandings and lines. A plain walnut long-case clock of high quality, with the movement by Tompion, is given in Fig. 21. Such cases rely for their effect on fine proportion, elegance of form and line, choice material and excellent workmanship. The clock-case illustrated in Fig. 22 shows, however, that special situa-

28. *Table Clock in case decorated with red japan. Movement by George Graham. c. 1735. Ht. 2 ft. 8 in., W. 1 ft. 4 in. (Edward Hudson Coll.)*

29. *Table Clock in case overlaid with tortoise-shell and mounted with ormolu. Movement by George Graham. c. 1735-40. Ht. 1 ft. 10 in. (Mr F. H. Green.)*

30. *Cartel Timepiece in carved and gilded wood case. Movement by James Scholefield, London. c. 1750-55. (E. L. Rice Coll.)*

tions evoked the utmost resources of the case-maker. In this example, to give prominence to the arms of the Board of Admiralty, for whom the clock was made, the brass dial is enlarged into an oblong, the upper part being shaped into a serpentine curve. Above that is an arched cornice and domical superstructure with turned, carved and gilded vase-shaped finials, and carved and gilded wood festoons of flowers; while the canted corners of hood and trunk are adorned with 'drops' in ormolu. Instead of the customary panel, forming the trunk door, a panel of bevelled mirror-glass is inserted. Langley Bradley, maker of the timepiece movement in this fine case, was an eminent horologist, and Master of the Clockmakers' Company in 1726. In 1698 Bradley's shop was at the sign of the 'Minute Dyall in Fanchurch St.', in which year the well-known marquetry-case clock, assigned to this maker, in the Dean's Vestry, St Paul's Cathedral, was purchased, as appears by the following extract from the Cathedral accounts:

ffor a pendulum Clock for the South East Vestrey that goes eight dayes in a Wallnut Tree inlade Case £14.00.00.

During the early years of the 18th century the height of clock-cases increased as rooms at this period tended to become more lofty. Clock-dials were augmented in height by the addition of serpentine, segmental and semi-circular or 'arched' tops. In an example (Fig. 23) made for one of the public offices by Joseph Windmills in Anne's reign, and dated 1710, the space provided by the arched top to the dial is devoted to an applied achievement of the royal arms, supporters, and monogram 'A.R.'.

Calendar-circles, tide-tables, moon-phases, strike-silent

levers, automata and many other auxiliary attachments were exhibited in the arched spaces thus provided; or a convex tablet with the maker's name and locality, flanked by applied ornaments of pierced and chased brass.

Fig. 24 illustrates one of the tall long cases of Anne's reign. This example, which is of oak veneered with finely figured walnut, has a dome-topped hood; unusual features are the arch-topped recess in the base and the carved and gilded scroll feet. Carving was rarely employed on these early 18th-century cases save for accessories—finials, trusses, etc.—and was executed usually in softwood stained a deep brown, or finished with gilding, either mat or burnished.

From c. 1710 to 1750-60 there was a vogue for clock cases decorated with japan (*see* JAPANNING AND LACQUER), the favourite ground colours being red, green, blue, black and, more rarely, yellow; or mottled and variegated in imitation of tortoise-shell or aventurine. The applied ornamentation was in gold or polychrome. Late 17th-century japan clock cases are very rare, and most English examples date from about the end of Anne's reign to c. 1750.

Figs. 25, 26, 27 and 28 show examples of japan decoration applied to long cases and a table clock. In the example in Fig. 25 the ground colour of the case is blue; red, of a vivid scarlet hue, is employed in Figs. 26 and 27. Fig. 26 shows an uncommon example of a thirty-hour short-pendulum movement in a narrow miniature long case fitted with wing pieces necessitated by the wide oscillation of the pendulum, the 'bob' of which can be seen, when in motion, through the circular glazed apertures in the wings. Markwick Markham, of the Royal Exchange, whose name is inscribed on a tablet

31. Hanging Clock in a trunk case of figured mahogany decorated with gilded wood carving. c. 1760. Ht. 5 ft. 10 in., W. 2 ft. 5 in. (V. & A. Mus.) 32. Musical Table Clock in case of carved mahogany; based on a design in Chippendale's Director, *3rd ed. Movement by Alexander Cumming. c. 1765. (Messrs Stoner and Evans.) 33. Hanging Clock in case of mahogany, with sliding hood and bracket. Movement by John Ellicott, London. c. 1765. (Hall of the Mercers' Company.)*

in the arched portion of the dial, was a well-known maker who conducted an evidently extensive business with the Turkish market.

Fig. 29 illustrates a bracket clock of somewhat unusual form, material and ornamentation, enclosing a fine movement by George Graham dating from c. 1735-40. The case is of wood overlaid with tortoise-shell or turtle-shell and mounted with ormolu. Graham (1673-1751) was assistant and successor to Tompion and one of the foremost British horologists.

Charles Clay (d. 1740) specialised in the making of the most elaborate, intricate and ingenious musical clocks. By 1723 he had become clock-maker to the Board of Works, and in 1736 he 'had the honour of exhibiting to his Majesty at Kensington his surprising musical clock, which gave uncommon satisfaction to all the Royal Family present, at which time her Majesty, to encourage so great an artist, was pleased to order fifty guineas to be expended for numbers in the intended raffle'. This clock has been identified, but 'the most curious and remarkable' of all Clay's achievements, the 'Musical Machine, Call'd the Temple of the Four Grand Monarchies of the World', which cost upwards of £4,500, now exists only in a mutilated state in the Cupola Room at Kensington Palace. It was once in the possession of Princess Augusta, wife of Frederick, Prince of Wales. Other specimens of this talented craftsman's work still survive.

An instance of the attempt made in America to follow prevailing fashions in English furniture is found in a letter (December 20, 1738) from Thomas Hancock, a wealthy merchant of Boston, to his agent in England, Francis Wilks:

I Desire the favour of you to procure for me and Send with my Spring Goods a Handsome Chiming Clock of the newest fashion —the work neat & good, with a Good Walnutt Tree Case Veneer'd work, with Dark lively branches,—on the Top instead of Balls, let there be three handsome Carv'd figures, Gilt with burnished Gold. I'd have the Case without the figures to be 10 ft. long, the price not to Exceed 20 Guineas . . . .

From c. 1725 mahogany supplanted walnut for clock cases and remained the favourite material. With the rise of the rococo style a highly decorative type of mural clock case known as the 'cartel' came into vogue. The cases, boldly carved in softwood and gilded, often with burnished gold, were popular during the vogue for asymmetric rococo forms and ornamentation inspired by continental influence. In Fig. 30 a circular silvered dial, with a moulded bezel of gilded brass, is framed in rococo scrollwork with floral ornament and surmounted by an eagle, with outstretched wings, carrying in its beak a tasselled cord. From 1740-60 the hanging clock and the table or bracket clock eclipsed the long-case clock in popular favour.

Two further examples of the hanging or mural clock case are illustrated in Figs. 31 and 33. The first is an unusually ornate example of a hanging clock, having a bold dial, which at a later period, and in simpler form, had a considerable vogue under the name of 'Act of Parliament clock', being exhibited in public situations after the tax on clocks and other time-keepers imposed by Pitt in 1797.

34. Bracket Clock in pagoda-topped case of mahogany carved and decorated with fret-cutting.¾Movement by Thos. Wynn, London. c. 1765-70. 35. Balloon Bracket Clock in case of ebonised pearwood. Movement by Julian Leroux, Charing Cross. (G. W. Wells Coll.) 36. Musical Table or Bracket Clock in case of ebonised pearwood decorated with gilt brasswork. Movement by Stephen Rimbault. c. 1760. (G. W. Wells Coll.)

At the premises of the Royal Society of Arts in the Adelphi, London, is another of these bold mural time-keepers, in a baluster-shaped trunk case of finely figured mahogany, mounted with ormolu. This, as an inscription records, was made and presented by Thomas Grignion to the Society (of which he was one of the first members) in 1759. Fig. 33 illustrates a form of combined clock and clock-bracket—a type made in limited numbers—embodying the hood and large dial characteristic of the long case, with the short pendulum and console of the bracket clock.

Towards the middle of the 18th century there were considerable modifications in the designs of clock cases which were sometimes elaborately carved. Chippendale published a number of designs, few of which, owing, no doubt, to the innate conservatism of clock-makers, appear to have been executed. Fig. 32 shows a case for a table-clock closely resembling one of Chippendale's designs (*Director*, 3rd ed., 1762, Pl. CLXV). Alexander Cumming (c. 1732-1814), the maker of the movement, was a noted horologist and the author of a valuable treatise, *The Elements of Clock and Watch-work* (1766). There is a remarkable barometric clock, made by him to the order of George III, at Buckingham Palace; and mural clocks of the types shown in Figs. 31 and 33 are found bearing his

37. Musical Table or Bracket Clock in case of figured mahogany elaborately decorated with mounts of ormolu. Movement by Higgs and Evans, Royal Exchange. c. 1775. Ht. 2 ft. 8 in. (Edward Hudson Coll.)

38. *Long-case Clock in case of carved mahogany. Columns pierced and fretted. c. 1775. Ht. 8 ft. 4½ in. (Henry Hirsch Coll.)* 39. *Long-case Clock in case of mahogany, inlaid. Movement by John Myers, Southwark. c. 1780-85. Ht. 7 ft. 4½ in. (V. & A. Mus.)* 40. *Long-case Clock; case veneered with figured mahogany and inlaid. Movement by Edwd. Shepley, Manchester. c. 1790. Ht. 7 ft. 7 in. (V. & A. Mus.)*

name, one of which, though of plainer design, is at Somerset House.

Clock cases of pronounced rococo character were occasionally incorporated into the designs of those overmantel mirror frames of carved and gilded wood which were so prominent a feature in the decorative schemes of the mid-Georgian era.

A pagoda-topped mahogany bracket clock case (Fig. 34) illustrates the application of fretted lattice and other Chinese motives popularised by Chippendale's *Director* and other trade publications. Fig. 36 shows a musical bracket clock by Stephen Rimbault of St Giles's. This maker excelled in the production of clocks of complicated mechanism operating groups of mechanical figures—working, playing or dancing. In the

example (Fig. 36) the case is bell-topped and mounted with ormolu, the dial being of brass with a silvered hour-circle, mock pendulum and brass frets. Two small auxiliary dials are provided respectively for the 'strike-silent' lever and for setting the musical selection, which is apparently performed by a party of musicians in the upper part of the dial. In Fig. 37 is seen a musical clock in a finely proportioned case of figured mahogany enriched with mountings of ormolu. The clock plays a variety of airs, and also chimes the hours and quarters, when the dancing figures in the upper portion of the dial are set in motion. The makers, Higgs and Evans, of the Royal Exchange, enjoyed practically a monopoly of the Spanish market towards the end of the 18th century, when clocks of English manufacture were highly esteemed abroad.

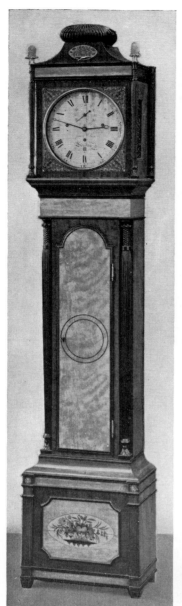  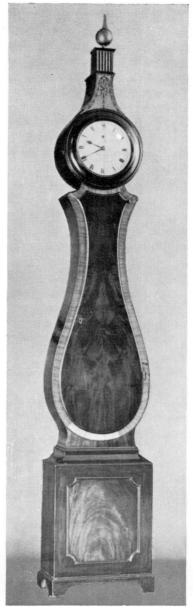 

41. Long-case Clock in case veneered with mahogany and inlaid satinwood. Chiming movement by James Wilson, London. c. 1795. (Francis Mallet Coll.) 42. Balloon Long-case Clock in case veneered with satinwood, inlaid and painted in grisaille. Movement by Benjamin Vulliamy. c. 1795. (Bank of England.) 43. Long-case Clock in baluster-shaped case veneered with mahogany and inlaid. Movement by Cragg, Southampton. c. 1785. (Lamport Hall, Northants.) 44. Regulator Timepiece in lancet-topped case veneered with mahogany and inlaid with brass and ebony. Dial inscribed 'Widdowson & Veale, London'. c. 1810. (Country Life Ltd.)

From the late 17th century down to the present there was a very large export trade in clocks to Portugal. The Marquis de Pombal, when virtual dictator, is said to have ordered 200 clocks for public offices from England. Many still retain them, and other clocks by well-known English makers are found in Portuguese country houses and in sacristies, some with English movements in cases of native origin.

A type of clock case favoured by certain makers in the latter part of the 18th century is that known as the balloon (Fig. 35); it has a circular dial, either flat or convex, silvered or enamelled, and a 'waist' contracted in graceful curves. Balloon bracket clock cases were usually executed either in ebonised pearwood mounted with ormolu or in finely figured mahogany inlaid with cross-cut bandings of kingwood, tulip-

wood or rosewood, and enriched with such motives as sand-shaded shells, rosettes or panels of stained marquetry.

The long-case clock, eclipsed for a time in popularity by the table or bracket clock, was again in favour from c. 1755 to 1760, being made in large numbers all over England, and varying greatly in proportion and design. The earlier examples were executed usually in dark, close-grained mahogany and adorned with carving and fretwork; from c. 1770 cases were often made of finely figured wood, the effect being enhanced by inlay and painting. At first the dials were of brass, and arched, with a matted centre, silvered hour-circle, and applied spandrels or corner-pieces, the moulded hood entablature following the segmental or semicircular curve of the dial-top, a feature generally repeated in the arched heading of the trunk door.

45. Mantel Timepiece in case veneered with satinwood, inlaid with rosewood; ormolu mounts. Movement by Vulliamy. c. 1795. Ht. 1 ft. 5 in. (Bank of England.)

46. Bracket Clock in lancet-topped case of mahogany inlaid with Egyptian motives. Movement by Brockbank and Atkins. c. 1795-1800. (Bank of England.)

47. Bracket Clock in chamfered-top case veneered with mahogany; mouldings of brass. Movement by R. Rolfe, Clerkenwell. c. 1820.

Fig. 38 is an example of fine quality, with a scrolled broken pediment, fretted tympanum and pilasters, the door of the trunk being flanked by engaged columns of the Ionic order with hollow fretted shafts, while the angles of the base are relieved with chamfered quoin-blocks. The phases of the moon are exhibited in the arched portion of the dial which, in other contemporary examples, formed a field for equation-tables, tide-tables, calendar-work, and the popular devices of rolling ships and moving figures attached to an arbour and oscillating with the pendulum. Miniature long-case clocks were made in limited numbers at this period, corresponding in proportion and design with the tall cases.

A good example of the restrained and effective use of inlay in a clock case of excellent proportions is illustrated in Fig. 39. The general lines of this case are characteristic of a type which attained considerable popularity among London makers in the last quarter of the 18th century. The whole field of the arched dial is silvered, with applied silvered hour-circle and 'strike-silent' circle; the chased pierced spandrel ornaments are also applied and of gilded brass.

Fig. 40 illustrates a late 18th-century case with a scrolled ogee pediment or 'horn-top'. It is a Lancashire example of characteristic wide girth, with high base and stunted trunk-door. It has a square, painted dial without seconds-dial or other auxiliary indications.

This period, notable for the rise of the provincial clock-maker, is marked by the employment for casework of choice curl-figured mahogany, sometimes inlaid. The dial-plates were often of iron japanned cream-white and gaily painted with pastoral subjects, or sprigs and bouquets of flowers. In those of brass the dial-plates were burnished or silvered, the central compartment enclosed by the hour-circle being enriched with engraving—fine cursive lettering within cartouches, or labels of scrollwork or floral festoons; the spandrel ornaments were usually of pronounced rococo character. Plainer cases

were of oak banded with mahogany and inlaid with stock motives such as sand-shaded fans, shells or paterae.

Three cases of somewhat unusual form are illustrated in Figs. 41, 42 and 43. The third has an elegant baluster-shaped case of inlaid mahogany, with a circular white dial framed in a deep moulded bezel. A less elaborate example of the baluster-shaped case, enclosing a timepiece movement by the celebrated maker George Graham, dated 1741, is among the small collection of the Clockmakers' Company in the Guildhall. The clock case (Fig. 41) corresponds very closely to one of the designs published by Sheraton in the *Drawing Book* (Pl. 29, dated 1793). At the angles of hood and trunk are reeded and carved balusters, the corners of the base being reinforced with fluted pilasters.

Figs. 42 and 45 illustrate two of the more remarkable clocks now in the Bank of England and doubtless made for it. The first is apparently a balloon-case bracket clock on a term-shaped pedestal, but actually clock and pedestal are integral, affording accommodation for the movement, long pendulum and weights of the familiar 'grandfather' clock. The case is veneered with satinwood of rich colour and fine figure, inlaid with cross-cut rosewood, and painted in grisaille. The moulded bezel of the convex dial is enriched with lines of pearling and is finely chased.

Several very elegant variations of this pedestal-shaped body were devised during the last quarter of the 18th century, when the designs of clock cases and other articles of furniture were closely allied to the decoration of apartments for which they were intended. Some of these cases are distinguished by unusual excellence of material and workmanship, inlay, carving and ormolu being associated. Wedgwood's letters to Bentley contain references to the productions of Matthew Boulton at Soho, where ormolu of high quality, even rivalling that of France, was being produced:

I had no conception of the quantity of D'Or Moulu they have

sold chiefly abroad. You remember a poor Venus weeping over the Tomb of Adonis—a Timepiece. How many do you imagine they have sold of this Group? 200 at 20 guineas each. . . .

Again, on November 21, 1768, he writes:

Mr. Boulton proposes an alliance betwixt the Pottery and Metal branches. . . . We can make things for mounting with great facility and dispatch . . . These things will do for the East India Co. & they give any price for fine things 20 or £30,000 a piece for Clocks I am told is a common price with them to give. One of this sort we have seen to-day though I believe not of that price.

A London clock-maker, James Cox, of Shoe Lane, Holborn, one of whose ormolu-cased clocks, bearing the Royal arms, was in the Donaldson collection, made a number of elaborate and costly musical clocks and automata, enclosing them in cases of the richest materials, prior to 1773, when there was a prospect of the interior of India being opened to British enterprise.

The little vase-shaped timepiece illustrated in Fig. 45 is of satinwood, inlaid and painted in grisaille, and embellished with highly finished mountings of ormolu. The maker of this and of the clock illustrated in Fig. 42, Benjamin Vulliamy, of Pall Mall, was one of a notable family of makers of Swiss origin who settled in London early in the 18th century, successive members holding the office of clock-maker to the reigning sovereign. Benjamin made numerous clocks and time-pieces to the order of George III, many of which were enclosed in cases of uncommon form and excellent workmanship. A writer of *A Description of Blenheim* (1814) thus refers to an example by this maker in the Blue Drawing-room:

A beautiful and curious clock on a new construction by *Vulliamy*, stands on the chimney-piece. A Serpent bending down its head from the top of a small urn, round which the hours are arranged, points out the time with its sting: and on the same urn an elegant figure of Contemplation leaning, gives the whole a singular and rather monumental air.

A clock case in the Chinese style, with a movement by Vulliamy, and a barometer case *en suite*, made to the order of George IV for Brighton Pavilion, are now at Windsor Castle. Notable examples by Vulliamy, with fine metalwork and carved marble figures, mounted on inlaid and painted pedestals, are at Syon House, Middlesex, and Buckingham Palace.

In Lady Mary Coke's *Journal* is a reference to a clock for the king (George III) made by Pinchbeck, the case of which was designed by Sir William Chambers; among Robert Adam's original drawings (Soane Museum) are some inscribed 'Front, and Profile, of a Bracket for a Clock for His Majesty'.

The bracket clock case in Fig. 46 represents a type current at the end of the 18th and beginning of the 19th centuries; the movement is from the workshops of one firm, Brockbank and its successors, but the design of the case was, apparently, the common property of many contemporary makers. Although not shown in the illustration, there are with this and other examples clock-brackets *en suite* with the case for attachment to the wall—a feature from which clocks of this type derive their popular name of bracket clocks.

By c. 1800 the type of long-case timekeeper known as a 'regulator' was made extensively, the term denoting a precision timepiece with a long 'seconds' pendulum, dead-beat escapement and movement of the highest class, designed solely for the accurate measurement of time, and without any additions, such as striking mechanism, or calendar-work. Regulator

1. *Close-Stool, made to simulate a travelling trunk, and covered with red velvet panelled with silver galon; interior lined with padded silk. Mid-17th century. Ht. 2 ft., L. 1 ft. 7½ in., Depth 1 ft. 5½in. (Hampton Court Palace. By gracious permission of H.M. the Queen.)*

clocks are found usually in cases of excellent material and fine workmanship, in the design of which, however, ornament was subordinated to use. Their dials were generally silvered all over, or white-enamelled, with two subsidiary dials indicating hours and seconds respectively (Fig. 44).

From about 1800 bracket clock cases, like other contemporary furniture, exhibit characteristics in design and ornament of the Regency style. Mahogany, ebony, satinwood and rosewood were the chief materials; the use of brass inlay, and inlay of ebony in lighter woods, either alone or with brass, was very general. The eight-day striking bracket clock (Fig. 47) is a typical example. I. C. G. (Revised).

CLOSE-STOOLS. From the end of the 15th century movable close-stools were used in palaces and great houses, superseding the garde-robes, or structural privies, which were the only conveniences afforded by the primitive hygiene of medieval times. Close-stools were among the varieties of furniture provided at this time by coffer-makers to the Crown. They were probably of box form, and the Royal Wardrobe accounts of the period show that they were covered with velvet or 'fustian of Naples', studded with gilt nails and elaborately trimmed. One of four such richly upholstered close-stools in an inventory of the contents of Somerset House in 1547, the first year of Edward VI (Harleian M.S., 1419), is described as 'covered with grene vellat fringed with Venice gold and grene silke and embraudered with the Kinges armes and badges'. At Ingatestone, Essex, in 1600 there was 'a high close stoole with a loose cover all covred over with black vellett'.

A close-stool at Hampton Court (Fig. 1) is of the box or trunk type, covered with red velvet bordered with silver galon

2. *Close-Stool, veneered with burr walnut; top inlaid with the coronet and cipher of second Earl of Warrington. c. 1710. Ht. 1 ft. 9½ in., L. 1 ft. 7½ in., Depth 1 ft. 2½ in. (Dunham Massey Hall, Cheshire.)*

and lined with padded silk—probably of later date. The lock-plate and lifting-handles are of patterns used in the mid-17th century, and a date about the time of the Restoration may be assigned to it. In the Kings' Gallery at Kensington Palace, in 1697 was a 'crimson velvett close stoole gold fringe and lace round it with a velvett seat'. At Knole there is one which corresponds with this description and is probably among the furniture removed as perquisites by the 6th Earl of Dorset. For such close-stools pewter pans were commonly provided. When an inventory of the contents of Ham House, Surrey, was drawn up in 1679, there were two 'cedar close stoole boxes' in dressing-rooms; another decorated with black and gold japan 'in Ye Wardrobe' is still in the house. The box type remained in use, though no longer covered with fabric, into the early years of the 18th century, and a close-

stool from Dunham Massey, Cheshire (Fig. 2), dating c. 1710, is veneered with figured burr walnut, cross-banded and bordered with ebony. In the first half of the 18th century pot-cupboards or night tables (*see* TABLES, NIGHT) were introduced, together with 'close-stool chaires'. In a Warrant (1730) two such chairs of walnut are ordered to be provided 'for their Majesties'. (*Lord Chamberlain's Warrant Book I*, p. 333.)

CLOTH OF ESTATE. Ornamented cloth spread over throne or chair reserved for persons of exalted rank; often took the form in the Middle Ages of a canopy suspended above a chair, and made of richest materials—velvets, silks, satins and even cloth-of-gold. Hangings in an inventory of Duke of Richmond (1526) include 'oone Clothe of Astate, of cloth of golde of Damask making, frenged with golde and red silke'.

CLOTHES PRESS. *See* CUPBOARDS, PRESSES AND WARDROBES.

CLOTHS OF GOLD, SILVER AND TISSUE. In the 13th century these rich stuffs were introduced into England from Spain and Italy. A web of silk was commonly used, but more costly varieties were composed almost entirely of gold or silver. Silk predominated in cloth of tissue, which was often of various colours, crimson and purple being often mentioned.

In early inventories occasionally there are descriptions of bed-hangings worked with cloth-of-gold, and at Knole, Kent, the curtains, valances and tester of a bed of Charles II's reign are all of this material. (*See* BEDS; Fig. 15.) At Glemham Hall, Suffolk, there was formerly a suite of walnut furniture, c. 1685, covered with cloth-of-silver with a salmon-coloured pattern woven into it.

CLUB FOOT. Resembling the head of a club, and often ending with a circular extension of about half an inch; appeared as terminal in England c. 1705, and used with cabriole or straight leg until the late 18th century. (*See* CHAIRS; Fig. 60.)

COAL BOX, HOD or **SCUTTLE.** *See* CHIMNEY FURNITURE.

COASTERS (or **SLIDERS**) **AND BEER WAGGONS.** Devices of various forms for circulating food and bottles on a dining-table. Mme du Bocage, when in London in 1750, wrote: 'After the desert . . . the cloth is taken away and the women retire. The table is of fine Indian wood, and very smooth, little round vessels called sliders which are of the

1. *Coaster, papier mâché, japanned black, and decorated in gold. c. 1800. Ht. 1¼ in., diameter 5 in. (Macquoid Coll.)*

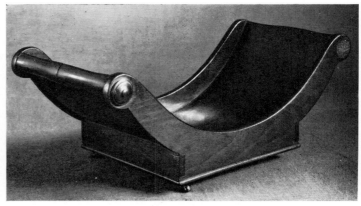

2. *Mahogany Cheese Coaster. c. 1790. Ht. 6 in., L. 1 ft. 5¼ in., W. 7¾ in. (The late Stanley May.)*

same wood, serve to hold the bottles, and the guests can put them round as they think proper.' Describing his tour in England towards the end of George IV's reign, Prince Pückler-Muskau writes: 'Three decanters are usually placed before the master of the house, generally containing claret, port, and sherry or madeira. The host pushes these on stands, or in little silver waggons on wheels, to his neighbour on the left . . . and so the circuit is made.'

A rimmed tray to hold one decanter or several bottles was generally employed. Some examples are fitted with small wheels, but usually the bottoms were of highly polished wood covered with baize, to slide conveniently along the table. In addition to mahogany referred to by Mme du Bocage, coasters. towards the end of the 18th and in the early 19th centuries. made of papier-mâché, japanned wood, silver or Sheffield plate were fashionable, but are not furniture in the ordinary connotation of the term.

A different type of coaster on wheels was also made for the convenient circulation of beer. In some examples the stand is waisted or shaped to take a jug or leather black-jack at one end and the drinking-cups at the other. A number of coasters, or waggons for beer, have also survived from the second half of the 18th and early years of the 19th centuries, in the form of trolleys to be wheeled along the floor, with a barrel, sometimes brass-bound, above. At Stratfield Saye, Hants., a barrel on a stand with a projecting platform is painted with the names of Wellington's victories arranged in circles between the metal hoops, and centres on 'Waterloo' above a ducal coronet.

Another variety of coaster was used for the circulation of cheese. Sophie V. la Roche, while staying at Normans, the English hostel at Helvoetsluys, Holland, before setting out for England in 1786, recorded that at lunch she partook of 'cheese, served in a beautiful carved mahogany cart and rolled on four

4. *Beer Coaster, painted red and bearing inscription 'Waste Not; Want Not'. A leather black-jack and five horn drinking vessels. Late 18th century. L. 1 ft. 7 in., W. 10½ in. (The late Mr H. H. Edmondson.)*

brass castors from one guest to another'. An example from about this time is given in Fig. 2.

COB-IRON. *See* CHIMNEY FURNITURE

COCK BEAD or **COCKED BEAD.** Small projecting moulding applied round edges of drawer fronts on mahogany and walnut furniture; introduced c. 1730 and continued in use throughout the 18th century. Sheraton (*Cabinet Dictionary*, 1803) states that strips of brass were sometimes used for this purpose.

COCK-HEAD HINGE. *See* METAL MOUNTS, METAL-WORK AND ORMOLU.

COFFER. *See* CHESTS.

COFFER-MAKERS. Company mentioned for the first time in 1328 in a list of 'divers misteries of London'. In 1373 the Coffer-makers petitioned to be allowed two Wardens and Surveyors with control of apprentices, powers of search, etc. In 1483 the guild, 'like to be undone' by the importation of Flemish furniture, petitioned Richard III and obtained a statute prohibiting the trade under pain of forfeiture. This petition affords proof that the Coffer-makers produced wooden chests which then and until a much later date were termed 'coffers' in wills and inventories. (*See* CHESTS.) But the Cofferers also produced trussing coffers and standards covered with leather and banded with iron to contain the owner's clothes and other portable goods during travelling. In 1517 the Company of Leathersellers (which had absorbed the Coffer-makers) obtained powers to search and oversee standards

3. *Mahogany brass-bound Beer Coaster, supported on turned balusters and on a stand with wheels. Late 18th century. (Tabley Hall, Ches.)*

1. *Mahogany Commode on lion-paw feet; front and sides of bombé shape; corners carved with acanthus; handles and lock-plates original. c. 1740. Ht. 2 ft. 11 in., L. 4 ft., Depth 2 ft. 5 in. (C. D. Rotch Coll.)*

'covered and made of leather and trussing coffers together with other leather commodities'.

In the 16th century Coffer-makers employed by the Crown supplied large quantities of coffers, chairs, desks, close-stools and stools covered with velvet, cloth-of-gold and other rich materials, which were secured by brass nails and trimmed with silver or gold lace. This was a highly specialised trade, but the 'coffers' of wood entered in large numbers in Tudor and Stuart inventories of domestic furniture were made by carpenters and joiners. (*See also* 'The Craft of the Coffer-Maker', R. W. Symonds, *Connoisseur*, March, 1941, pp. 100-5 and 133, and *History and Antiquities of the Company of Leathersellers*, W. H. Black.)

COFFERED PANEL. Deeply sunk panel, the reverse of fielded. (*See* FIELDED PANEL.)

COIN. Term for a corner cupboard (French *encoignure*) occasionally used in the 18th century. Ince and Mayhew (*Universal System*, 1759-63) give two designs for 'Ecoineurs' and the *Description* of Horace Walpole's villa at Strawberry Hill, Middlesex (1782), mentions 'A Coin of old Japan' in the gallery.

COLUMNS. *See* ORDERS.

COMMODES. The term borrowed from France, where it was apparently first applied to a low *armoire* with drawers, doubtless in allusion to its superiority to a plain chest in the matter of convenience. The *Dictionnaire de Trévoux* gives 'commode' as a new word in 1708, in which year the Duc d'Antin reported to Louis XIV that he had inspected two commodes commissioned by the King from Guillemar of Paris and found them complete except for the drawers. A decade later the commode was still regarded as a novelty. The Duchesse de Berry presented one to the daughter of the Duchesse d'Orléans, who in March, 1718, explained to a correspondent that 'a commode is a large table with deep drawers'; while, also in 1718, Sobry (in his *Architecture*) writes 'coffers or arks are commonly called commodes. Some have a lid, others have

drawers.' Boule's ponderous specimens were known as *commodes en tombeau* because of their resemblance in form to the sarcophagi placed on tombs at that period. Many such pieces, ornamented with brass and tortoise-shell, were among the furniture destroyed when his *atelier* was burnt in August, 1720.

By the time of the accession of Louis XV in 1715 the commode was no longer tomb-like, but in its subtle curves and exuberant ornament faithfully expressed the rococo spirit. The great French *ébénistes* inlaid their commodes with flowers, birds, trophies and musical instruments, Cressent, the Caffieris, Gouthière and many other masters lavishing their skill on the metal mounts.

With the setting in of gallican fashions under George II the shape was copied in England for the drawing-rooms and saloons of great Palladian houses; but it was long before anything comparable to the elegance of French specimens was achieved. These early commodes are entirely of mahogany, inlay not being attempted until about 1760; handles and escutcheons are generally the only metal enrichments. Such pieces have the heavy characteristics of the 'lion period'.

The 'French commode' is a prominent item in 18th-century trade catalogues, and, as no fashionable drawing-room was complete without one, great attention was bestowed on them by leading makers. Chippendale calls them 'commode tables', and illustrates a variety of forms in the *Director*. He contemplated their use in bedrooms, fitted with sliding shelves for clothes. He also designed 'commode-clothes-presses', explaining that they are presses with a commode pedestal part. (*See* CUPBOARDS, PRESSES AND WARDROBES.) Ince and Mayhew (*Universal System*, 1759-63) state that a commode (from their design) in the French taste published by the Society of Upholsterers and Cabinet-Makers 'has been executed from a plate and much admired'. References in contemporary bills

2. *Mahogany Commode ('a French set of Drawers') made for Sir Hugh Smithson; lion-headed consoles at angles. 1739. (Alnwick Castle, Northum.)*

3. *Mahogany Commode, one of a pair; child-headed consoles; panels carved with ovals clasped by acanthus. c. 1750. (Goodwood, Sussex.)*

4. *Mahogany Commode; front and sides shaped and divided by flat pilasters; corners and aprons carved in rococo taste. Attributed to Thomas Chippendale. c. 1755. Ht. 2 ft. 8 in., L. 4 ft. 8 in. (Mulliner Coll.)*

are rare, but in the accounts (1756-61) of Benjamin Goodison there is an entry of a 'mahogany commode chest of drawers ornamented with carving and wrought brass handles to do', which he supplied to the Duke of York.

In view of the wide application given to the term it is difficult to draw a clear distinction between the native form of chest of drawers (*see* CHESTS OF DRAWERS) and commodes divided in a similar manner, but in this section are included specimens in which the French shape is unmistakably followed or the purpose is primarily decorative; such pieces being made for saloon or drawing-room.

For convenience of reference, the commodes illustrated are arranged in four groups: mahogany, japanned, marquetry and

painted. Fig. 1 is made throughout of dark Cuban mahogany the colour of bronze, in the ponderous style of c. 1740. The plain handles and lock-plates are admirably in accord with the dignified proportions, while the form approximates to sarcophagus shape.

Two remarkable commodes (Figs. 2 and 3) are in a style associated with William Vile (q.v.); though ovals and circles clasped by acanthus are motives used by other makers, and the first considerably ante-dates his earliest documented work. The commode in Fig. 2 was made in 1739 for Sir Hugh Smithson, later Duke of Northumberland, and formed part of the furnishing of his family seat, Stanwick, Yorkshire. In that year it is mentioned in a letter from his wife to the Countess of

5. *Mahogany Commode. After a design dated* 1753 *in the* Director (1st ed.). *Attributed to Thomas Chippendale.* (*From Basset Down, Wilts.*)

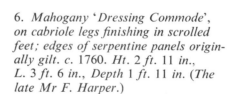

6. *Mahogany 'Dressing Commode', on cabriole legs finishing in scrolled feet; edges of serpentine panels originally gilt. c.* 1760. *Ht.* 2 *ft.* 11 *in., L.* 3 *ft.* 6 *in., Depth* 1 *ft.* 11 *in.* (*The late Mr F. Harper.*)

Hertford. She writes that in Sir Hugh's dressing-room 'between the windows stands, covered with marble, a French set of Drawers much ornamented with Brass gilt'. This small commode is carved in the most ornate style of the period. The lion-headed consoles with paw feet are vigorously modelled, while the florid mounts enhance the decorative effect. The escutcheon of the middle drawer is set in a circle clasped by acanthus. A pair at Goodwood, Sussex (Fig. 3), are among the masterpieces of English baroque furniture. Here ovals, headed and based with acanthus, decorate the front and sides, a motif employed both by Vile and Benjamin Goodison (q.v.). These splendid pieces are of serpentine form with lifting tops and false drawers. Front and sides are faced with child-headed consoles masterly in modelling; the ornament is

carved with extraordinary vigour, while the finely designed brass lock-plates and handles are delicately finished.

The example from Raynham Hall, Norfolk (Fig. 4), though technically admirable, is open to criticism in both proportion and design. It bears a strong resemblance to Plate XLIV in the *Director* (1754), and no example affords more convincing proof that the gaiety and lively fancy of contemporary *rocaille* designs could not survive the process of translation. The carving is of very high quality but excessively elaborate; the failure to capture the true French spirit is even more conspicuous in the scrolled legs. This piece is entered as a 'Sideboard' in a list of the contents of Capt. Townshend's room at Raynham (1757), and a label on the back bears the same description.

In marked contrast to the previous example, the proportions

are masterly in Fig. 5, which rivals the elegance of Parisian models, though without their exuberant decoration. This fine commode is based on Plate XLIII in the *Director* (1754). The long sweeping lines of the cabriole corners are foiled by the scrolled base and by the delicate interlaced pattern between the drawers. The carving in a light flashed mahogany is notable for its vigour and certainty.

Studied simplicity is again the characteristic of Fig. 6, a type termed by Chippendale a 'dressing commode'. The ornament is confined to serpentine panels in projection, carved with a small leaf moulding originally gilt. The legs, wide at the shoulder, are decorated with cabochon and acanthus, ending in scrolled feet. Such pieces served for the toilet of fashionable ladies before the general introduction of small dressing-tables elaborately fitted and enclosed by flaps. (*See* TABLES, DRESSING.) Fig. 7 is French in inspiration, but a few years later and on simpler lines, the corners taking the form of cabriole legs headed by female busts in

ormolu. The influence of the classical revival is discernible here and in Fig. 8, the front is slightly serpentined; the doors and sides are carved with large fluted circles, the spandrels being filled with foliated ornament, and the bottom rail is decorated with paterae and swags.

Japanned commodes were produced contemporaneously with the mahogany specimens, and oriental panels were sometimes framed up in the structure. They were in demand for bedrooms decorated in the Chinese taste, as at Badminton, Gloucestershire, and Nostell, Yorkshire. The contents of the Badminton room have been dispersed, but at Nostell the furniture designed by Robert Adam, and japanned in green and silver, remains. Fig. 9 shows a transitional example coinciding with the inception of the neo-classic style. The black-and-gold japanning is flat, and the disconnected design, in which heads and bodies of figures are mutilated, shows that imported Chinese panels have been cut up to form the front of a commode. In Fig. 10 the drawers are enclosed by doors, an arrangement more normal in England than in France. Here the panels and borders are of oriental incised lacquer, or 'Bantam work', but the keel-shaped corners and the apron are ordinary English japan of c. 1765. The decoration is in polychrome on a black ground, and the top is surrounded by a gadrooned metal border. All the curved surfaces in such pieces must have been made in that form before they were lacquered, panels of suitable shape being imported from China.

In a fine convex-fronted commode probably designed by Adam for Osterley (Fig. 11), rich pictorial japan decoration is set off by pilasters and bandings of chased ormolu. The tapered, reeded feet are of a type favoured some years later by leading French *ébénistes*. The commode seen in Fig. 12 was made in 1771 for Nostell, with other japanned furniture, by Chippendale's firm. Here the contrast of the silver-and-gold ornament and the pea-green ground is most effective, while the drawing of the detail is highly accomplished.

7. *Mahogany Commode with cabriole-shaped corners; base scrolled, and ormolu mounts in French taste. c. 1765. Ht. 2 ft. 5 in., L. 4 ft. 1 in. (H. Percy Dean Coll.)*

8. *Oak Commode, gilt, with red Brescia marble top; carved in neo-classic style; corners of slight cabriole form. c. 1765. Ht. 3 ft., L. 4 ft. 7½ in., Depth 2 ft. 3½ in (Lady Lever Art Gallery, Port Sunlight.)*

9. *Commode; the serpentine drawer fronts decorated with a continuous design in black and gold Chinese lacquer. c. 1765. (St Giles' House, Dorset.)*

10. *Commode with panels of Oriental incised lacquer in polychrome, and framings in English taste; corners and feet mounted in ormolu. c. 1765. (Ragley Hall.)*

With the introduction of mahogany, marquetry had been abandoned, but early in George III's reign this form of decoration was revived. By Chippendale's firm and other fashionable makers it was carried out in a variety of exotic woods on a satinwood ground, much of the ornament being stained and shaded. French inlay was at first imitated, with the admirable result seen in Fig. 13. The ornaments and flowers assimilate more nearly in tone with the background than in later Stuart marquetry, and a greater variety of delicate colours is employed. In the commode chest of drawers in Fig. 14 the sides and front are inlaid with scattered bouquets of flowers. The angles are mounted with ormolu headed by terminal figures. We know that Chippendale sold commodes in the style of Fig. 13 as

late as 1770, for at Nostell there is one of similar workmanship, described in his bill (December 22, 1770) as 'a large antique commode curiously inlaid with various fine woods. . . .' Another very similar piece at Hatfield House has the brass mounts from the same castings as those on the Nostell specimen.

Fig. 15 shows a serpentine-fronted commode of the highest quality, the inlay representing vases of flowers on a satinwood ground, noticeably rich and subdued in colour. These are based with acanthus and festooned with husks, the whole being enclosed within a wide honeysuckle border. The top is inlaid with fruit and foliage, the effect of modelling being skilfully obtained; the drawers in the interior are veneered with hare-

11. *Commode, decorated with black and gold Oriental lacquer and mounted with ormolu. Probably designed by Robert Adam. c. 1770. Ht. 3 ft., L. 5 ft. (Osterley Park, Middx.)*

12. *Commode, japanned green, gold and silver. Made by Thomas Chippendale in 1771. Ht. 3 ft., L. 4 ft. 8 in. (Nostell Priory, Yorks.)*

13. *Commode in French taste, with serpentine front and sides; veneered and marquetried with bouquets of flowers in vases. c. 1765. (Donaldson Coll.)*

Adam's characteristic rendering of neo-classic detail was intended to be painted rather than inlaid. But for expensive commodes in the neo-classic style marquetry decoration was freely employed: it was introduced also on the curvilinear type and those made in pairs to occupy corners at the end of a room.

Shortly after Louis XVI's accession (1774) a revival of French influence appreciably modified the severity of the neo-classic style, and in Fig. 16 its characteristic motives are seen combined with metal mounts and form of a contemporary French commode. The bull with ivory hoofs and horns inlaid in an ebony oval recalls the decoration of satinwood furniture

wood cross-banded with mahogany, and the handles are of ivory. This commode may be attributed to John Cobb, who supplied another very similar in style to Paul Methuen of Corsham, Wiltshire, in 1772. A commode in the possession of the Earl of Ilchester also closely resembles the Corsham example, and the anthemium ornament, inverted on the top border, occurs in all three pieces.

In Fig. 17 classical influence is very apparent. The frieze exactly corresponds to that of a library table at Harewood executed by Chippendale, and in both pieces the taper pilasters with metal rams' heads below the capitals are almost identical. Adam's designs for commodes at the Soane Museum represent them as straight-fronted or elliptical, the front or ends being enclosed by doors, and the drawings suggest that

14. *Commode in the French style; decorated with marquetry. c. 1780. Ht. 3 ft., L. 4 ft.*

249

15. (*Above, left*) *Satinwood serpentine-fronted Commode; top inlaid with fruit and foliage in an oval; doors decorated in a similar manner and festooned with husks set within a honeysuckle border; ormolu mounts. By John Cobb. c. 1770. Ht. 2 ft. 11 in., L. 3 ft. 3 in., Depth 2 ft. ½ in. (V. & A Mus.)*

16. (*Above, right*) *Commode in French style, veneered with satinwood; front inlaid with a bull on an ebony oval, and sides with classical amphorae. c. 1770. Ht. 2 ft. 9 in., L. 4 ft. 8 in. (Lady Lever Art Gallery.)*

17. (*Above*) *Satinwood Commode, banded with mahogany and tulipwood and decorated with marquetry in neo-classic taste; pilasters mounted in ormolu with ram-headed capitals. c. 1770. Ht. 3 ft., L. 4 ft. 10 in., Depth 2 ft. 1 in. (Lady Lever Art Gallery, Port Sunlight.)*

18. *Commode, veneered with harewood; side panels diapered in coloured woods; projecting centre inlaid with classical figure in metal framing, the other mounts corresponding in style. c. 1770. (The late Mr F. Harper.)*

19. *Satinwood Commode inlaid with various woods and mounted with ormolu. Attributed to Thomas Chippendale. c. 1770. (Renishaw Hall, Derbys.)*

20. *Commode, one of a pair, veneered with harewood and inlaid with figure subjects; tablet in centre of frieze, mouldings and pilasters mounted in ormolu. From designs by Robert Adam. c. 1773. H. 3 ft., L. 5 ft., Depth 2 ft. (Osterley Park, Middx.)*

21. *Commode, veneered with satinwood and inlaid in neo-classic taste with various coloured woods, ivory and ebony; pilasters and feet mounted in ormolu. By Thomas Chippendale c. 1773. Ht. 3 ft. 2 in., L. 7 ft. 7 in., Depth 2 ft. 3 in. (Harewood House, Yorks.)*

22. *Satinwood Commode with marquetry decoration and painted ovals; applied metal-work frieze. c. 1780. Ht. 2 ft. 10 in., L. 4 ft. 10½ in. (Lady Lever Art Gallery, Port Sunlight.)*

23. *Satinwood Commode inlaid with various coloured woods. Made by William Gates for George, Prince of Wales, in 1781. (Buckingham Palace. By gracious permission of H.M. the Queen.)*

at Harewood, Yorkshire. This imitation of the French is carried further in Fig. 18, obviously the work of one who had studied the Parisian masters. The central figure, inlaid on a ground of harewood, is surrounded by festoons and sprays of metal laurelling, repeated on drawer fronts, corners and legs. The panels on either side, inlaid with a diaper of coloured woods, let down and push under a series of drawers; the construction, the drawing of the figure and the character of the metal-work establish the English origin. In the Lady Lever Art Gallery, Port Sunlight, Cheshire, there is another example, very similar in design and decoration, the central panel being inlaid with a figure of Diana in a wooded landscape.

At this period commodes were often placed below tall pier glasses, occupying a position between the windows in important rooms, an arrangement adopted in both the drawing-room and state bedchamber at Osterley. The pair of ormolu-mounted commodes in the drawing-room (Fig. 20) are among the finest furniture designed by Adam for that house, but the maker has not been identified. They are inlaid in the centre of each panel with figure medallions in light woods on a dark ground (Venus and Cupid in one instance, Diana with her hounds in the other) flanked by slender candelabra and festoons. In the centre of the satinwood frieze is a panel of ormolu with griffins flanking a profile female head; while the mouldings are of the same material, which, treated *à jour*, is also used to decorate the sunk pilasters dividing the semi-circular front. This series of commodes in the neo-classic style culminates in the examples in Figs. 19 and 21, which are among the outstanding productions of Chippendale's final phase. The Harewood commode is veneered with the finest West Indian satinwood and inlaid throughout in classical taste. The doors are decorated with figures of Minerva and Diana in coloured woods and ivory on an ebony ground. The concave lunette forming the knee-hole is most skilfully made of narrow satinwood staves, and the pilasters are headed with metal leaves, repeated on the round taper feet. This commode

was supplied by Chippendale and Haig to Edwin Lascelles in 1773 and is described in their account as follows:

A very large rich commode with exceeding fine antique Ornaments curiously inlaid with various fine woods, drawers at each end and enclosed with folding doors, with Diana and Minerva and their emblems curiously inlaid and engraved, a cupboard in the middle part with a cove door, a dressing drawer in the top part, the whole elegantly executed and varnished with many wrought brass antique Ornaments finely finished .. £86 0. 0.

The commode at Renishaw, Derbyshire (Fig. 19), can be confidently assigned to Chippendale. A comparison with the Harewood commode leaves no doubt of their common origin; though differing in detail the style of the inlay is unmistakable. The lobed pendants at the base of the ormolu-mounted pilasters figure in the same position on the inlaid library table

24. *Commode, one of a pair; concave tambour front; doors and pilasters inlaid with classical ornament on a rosewood ground. c. 1785. Ht. 2 ft. 11¼ in., L. 4 ft. 2¾ in., Depth 1 ft. 10 in. (Henry Hirsch Coll.)*

25. *Semi circular Commode, veneered with harewood and satinwood; roses inlaid on a satinwood oval are naturalistic; remaining decoration in neo-classic taste. c. 1785. Ht. 2 ft. 11 in., L. 4 ft. 3½ in., Depth 1 ft. 9 in.*

at Harewood, while the design of both commodes is strikingly similar. The unusual and very effective decoration on the concave ends has a parallel on a pair of cabinets formerly at Panshanger, Hertfordshire. (*See* CABINETS; Fig. 4.) So excellent are the inlay, veneer and craftsmanship of these marquetry commodes made in the decade 1765-75 that the best specimens rival the works of the great French *ébénistes*. The ornament was sometimes adapted from classical friezes and Roman mosaics, while shading and modelling were cleverly produced by burning the surface of a light wood with hot sand.

References in the Walpole and Selwyn letters prove that commodes continued to be imported from France in spite of the excellence of English productions. When George Selwyn was in Paris (November, 1766), the Earl of March wrote asking him to supervise the carrying out of such an order: 'Pray don't let the commode be too much ornamented. J'aime le grand simple comme le Prince: but as it will be a principal piece at the end of the room, between the windows, it must be handsome so as to be an object.' Earlier in 1766 Horace Walpole had obtained designs for commodes for Anne Pitt from Poirier, the *marchand-mercier* (at the *Couronne d'Or*).

By 1780 the form of commodes had again undergone modification; the semicircular shape was now in fashion, the front often opening as a single large door. In the inlaid commodes of this time the decoration, though graceful in line, is frequently ill-adapted to the general design, the sense of spacing and proportion being curiously fallible. Paterae, husks, medallions and large classical vases figure prominently in the repertory of ornament. Hepplewhite (*Guide*, 1788) writes of commodes: 'This piece of furniture is adapted for a drawing-room; within are shelves which answer to a closet or cupboard —may have one principal door in the front or one at each end; are made of various shapes, and, being used in principal rooms, require considerable elegance. The panels may be of

satinwood, plain or inlaid; the top also and border round the front should be inlaid.' Sheraton observes of commodes: 'these pieces . . . are never intended for use but for ornament'. The inlay of his school is graceful, but small in style; nor is it so brilliant in colour as earlier marquetry. The art was now in its decline, and after 1775 was gradually superseded by painted decoration.

26. *Painted Commode; top of buff-coloured marble; ground of panels pea-green; ovals with figure subjects after Angelica Kauffmann. c. 1790. Ht. 3 ft. 6½ in., L. 3 ft. 8 in. (Lady Lever Art Gallery, Port Sunlight.)*

27. *Satinwood Commode;
frieze inlaid with a honeysuckle
design in coloured woods; sides
with classical amphorae; circle
in centre painted with a figure
subject; edges surrounded with
a reed-and-ribbon moulding in
brass. c. 1785.*

Fig. 23 shows one of a pair made by William Gates in 1781 for the Prince of Wales's apartments at Buckingham Palace, where they still form part of the furnishings. They cost £80 and are described in the bill as '2 very fine sattin wood inlaid Commode Tables to stand under piers with Cime Circular fronts . . . the doors, drawers and tops neatly engraved with urns, vases, flowers, and other ornaments in woods of different colours'. The same maker was probably responsible for another fine pair (Fig. 24), reputed to have come from Brighton Pavilion. They have concave tambour fronts, the two convex ends serving as a field for the decoration, which consists of buff-and-green vases and laurelling on a rosewood ground. The mahogany top is inlaid with a large double band of rushes in their natural colours tied with ribbons.

In the commode seen in Fig. 25 the quiet tones of the harewood veneer and the delicate ornament show the elegance of the final phase of inlay. The urns on the sides, supported on tripods, are neo-classic, but the small scale of the decoration and the naturalistic treatment of the roses inlaid in an oval on the cupboard door are characteristic of the marquetry in vogue c. 1790-1800.

Marquetry was supplanted in the closing years of the century by painted decoration. As early as 1778 Adam designed a white-painted commode with gilt mouldings and coloured urns and wreaths for Sir John Griffin; while in 1783 George Brookshaw supplied the Prince of Wales with 'an elegant commode highly finished with a basket of flowers painted on the front . . . and sprigs of jessamine all over the top and also on the fronts'. Hepplewhite (*Guide*, 1788) observes that 'the panels of commodes may be of satinwood, painted or inlaid'. At first these forms were generally combined. In the fine

example (Fig. 22) painted figure subjects set in circular gilt mouldings are associated with marquetry in the classical taste, while the frieze is enriched with ormolu on a ground of boxwood stained green.

Towards the end of the century these painted commodes began to deteriorate, but fine specimens were still occasionally produced. Fig. 26 is an attractive example of c. 1790. The colour of the buff marble top is repeated in the borders of the panels, on which the familiar festoons, pendants and paterae are rendered on the diminutive scale then in vogue. The medallions are after Angelica Kauffmann, the largest being a copy of her *Cupid Asleep*. These ovals are the work of a highly competent copyist, drawing and colour being alike excellent.

The example (Frontispiece) is of concave and convex form and admirable proportions. The ground is a deep ivory-white, diapered with a delicate green network, knotted with rose; the reeded colonnettes and bandings are gilt, the water leaf capitals and pineapple feet indicating the approach of Regency style. The frieze is painted with a graceful scrolling of poppies, centring on a rayed head surrounded by Cupids; the top is edged with a broad border of garlanded flowers. The painting retains its original brilliancy, and represents the highest expression of this phase of decoration.

In the Regency period the serpentine and semicircular plans are discarded in favour of a rectangular form, and the commode is sometimes flanked by tapering fluted columns resting on peg-top feet and surmounted by a marble slab. Models of this kind derive from France, and Weisweiller's influence is particularly apparent. Sheraton (*Cabinet Dictionary*, 1803) shows one 'adapted to stand under a large glass, either in a pier or at the end of a room'. The frieze is to be inlaid with brass on a dark ground, and the doors are to be filled with brass trellis-work backed by silk curtains. He also alludes to commodes 'used by ladies to dress at, in which there is a drawer fitted up with suitable conveniences'. In spite of the obvious incongruity, commodes were sometimes designed in a bastard classical style, and several examples, 'intended for those Drawing Rooms used also as living rooms', are given in George Smith's *Household Furniture* (1808). They were to be 'made of satinwood, rosewood or in gold on a white ground, or japanned in imitation of finer woods; the tops either of real marble or japanned in imitation'. Later in the Regency there was a revival of the ponderous form of the commode with metal inlay in the style of Boulle and ormolu mounts of Louis Quatorze character (Fig. 28). The rare examples were produced by specialists in this style of decoration. (*See* BULLOCK, J., and GAIGNEUR, LOUIS LE.)

COMPOSITION or **'COMPO'.** A mixture of whiting, resin and size, heated and amalgamated; pressed into moulds while still plastic, then, when set, fixed by glue or panel pins to the surface to be ornamented; much used by Adam and by furniture-makers in late 18th century.

CONCERTINA MOVEMENT. Folding frame of card-tables, much used as alternative to gate-leg in the 18th century, especially before 1750. Back half of frame hinged to fold in upon itself. (*See* CONSTRUCTION; Fig. 8.)

CONSOLE. Architectural term (from the French) applied to variety of bracket, usually scroll-shaped in profile. In 18th-century classical style furniture brackets of this form sometimes support the frieze. (*See* BOOKCASES; Fig. 18.) Tables fixed to a wall and supported only at the front by legs, an eagle, etc., are also called consoles, this particular variety being introduced from France. (*See* TABLES, SIDE.) Bailey's *Dictionarum Britannicum* (1730): 'a sort of bracket or shouldering piece, having a projecture and serving to support a cornice and bear up figures, etc.'

CONSTRUCTION. In English furniture, construction may be said to have begun when the woodman or carpenter ceased to make his chest from the trunk of a tree—the inside rudely chopped and chiselled out, with a lid of one thick plank. These hewn chests are the earliest examples of movable furniture still in existence, and the earliest may perhaps date from soon after the Conquest, though they continued to be made until towards the end of the 15th century. The smith banded them with wrought-iron straps and hinged the lids.

With the introduction of constructed furniture, the basic principles of furniture design began to evolve. These included a knowledge of the growth of trees suitable for the purpose, and the proper times and methods of felling and seasoning to secure sound workable timber; also the production and skilful use of tools used in conversion and in fashioning the actual pieces.

The earliest method of construction applied to articles of box form, *e.g.* chests and standing cupboards, dates from the 12th or 13th century. It consisted in using stout planks, either split or sawn from the log, crudely put together with oak pins or wrought-iron nails at the angles. The planks were reduced in thickness as the pit saw came into general use, and this simple method remained common in country districts for making

28. *Commode, one of a pair, rosewood inlaid and mounted with brass. c.* 1820. *Ht.* 3 *ft.* 1 *in.,* L. 3 *ft.* 10 *in., Depth* 1 *ft.* 8 *in.* (*V. & A. Mus.*)

small chests and boxes down to the early 18th century. (*See* CHESTS; Fig. 16.)

An early chest of riven planks is shown in Fig. 1a. The construction is typical of the period, and the majority of its members retain the tapering section, which is the result of riving the planks from the trunk. The angle posts have long slots or mortises in which the horizontal planks are housed, and oak pins are driven through to secure them. The side planks incline inwards from the bottom, a usual feature which allows the cross-tie at each end to occupy a very strong position; the two rear posts are again slotted at the top to take the ends of the lid, a stout oak pin being passed through to form a 'pin hinge'. Fig. 1b shows a chest with panelled front, but with sides and back of plain boards, indicating the transition from one method to another. Later, in the 16th century and in the 17th, larger and better-quality chests were panelled on all four sides, and often the lid also, but throughout this period the sides of small examples of country make were of thin sawn boards, the structure being secured at the angles by oak pins or iron nails.

The most important event in the construction of English furniture was the introduction, in the second half of the 15th century, of rectangular framing filled in with thin panels, though it can hardly be said to have become general until a hundred years later. This ensured that the object would be economical of material, light enough to be portable, and so put together that the natural tendencies of warping, twisting, splitting and shrinkage could be adequately counteracted. Panelled framing was the method adopted and it was introduced from the Continent. This was joinery in the true sense of the word, and at first the mouldings were worked on the solid (as on door and window frames of timber houses) and had mason's mitres at the angles—*i.e.* mitres were also worked on the solid. This necessitated 'masoning' or chiselling the mouldings (Fig. 12)—

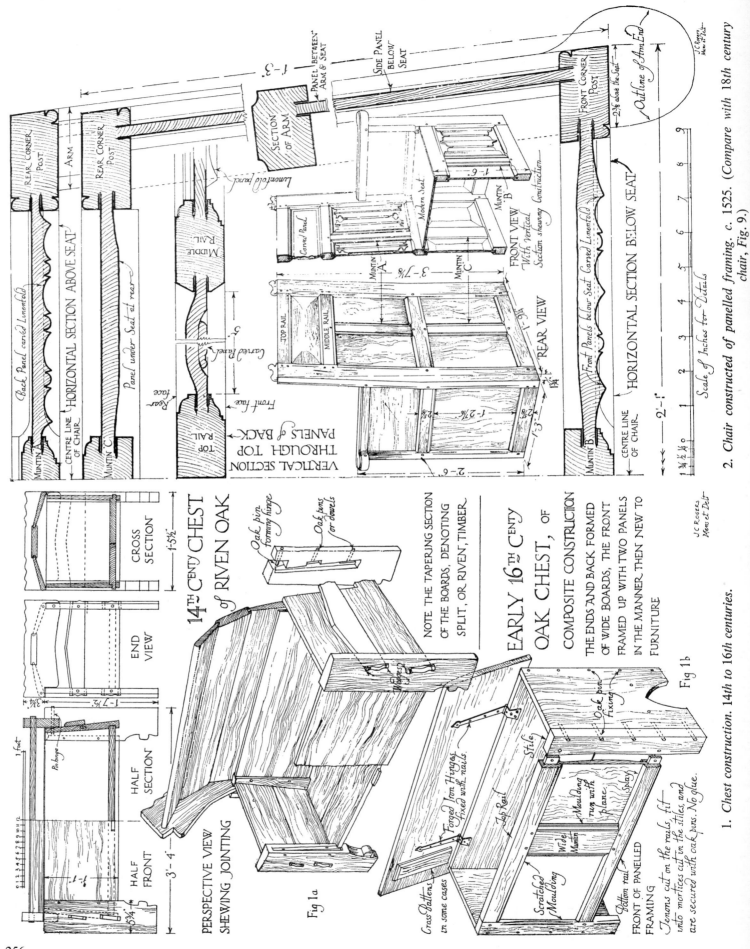

CROSS SECTION

END VIEW

HALF SECTION

HALF FRONT

PERSPECTIVE VIEW SHEWING JOINTING

14TH CENTY CHEST of RIVEN OAK

Fig 1a

Oak pin forming hinge

Oak pins or dowels

NOTE THE TAPERING SECTION OF THE BOARDS, DENOTING SPLIT, OR RIVEN, TIMBER.

EARLY 16TH CENTY OAK CHEST, OF COMPOSITE CONSTRUCTION

THE ENDS AND BACK FORMED OF WIDE BOARDS, THE FRONT FRAMED UP WITH TWO PANELS IN THE MANNER THEN NEW TO FURNITURE

Fig 1b

Oak pin Fixing

Forged Iron Hinges Fixed with nails

Stile

Top Rail

Moulding run with Plane

Splay

Wide Muntin

Cross Battens in some cases

Scratched Moulding

Bottom rail

FRONT OF PANELLED FRAMING

Tenons cut on the rails fit into mortices cut in the stiles, and are secured with oak pins. No glue.

REAR CORNER POST

REAR CORNER POST

ARM

Back Panel carved Linenfold

CENTRE LINE OF CHAIR

HORIZONTAL SECTION ABOVE SEAT

Panel under Seat at rear

MIDDLE RAIL

Linenfold panel

SECTION OF ARM

PANEL BETWEEN ARM & SEAT

SIDE PANEL BELOW SEAT

Carved panel

Rear face

Front face

Carved panel

VERTICAL SECTION THROUGH TOP PANELS of BACK

TOP RAIL

FRONT VIEW With Vertical Section shewing Construction

Carved Panel

Modern Seat

MUNTIN A

MUNTIN C

MUNTN B

TOP RAIL

MIDDLE RAIL

REAR VIEW

FRONT CORNER POST

Outline of Arm End

HORIZONTAL SECTION BELOW SEAT

Front Panels below Seat Carved Linenfold

CENTRE LINE OF CHAIR

MUNTIN B

Scale of Inches for Details

1. Chest construction. 14th to 16th centuries.

2. Chair constructed of panelled framing. c. 1525. (Compare with 18th century chair, Fig. 9.)

J C ROGERS Mens et Delt

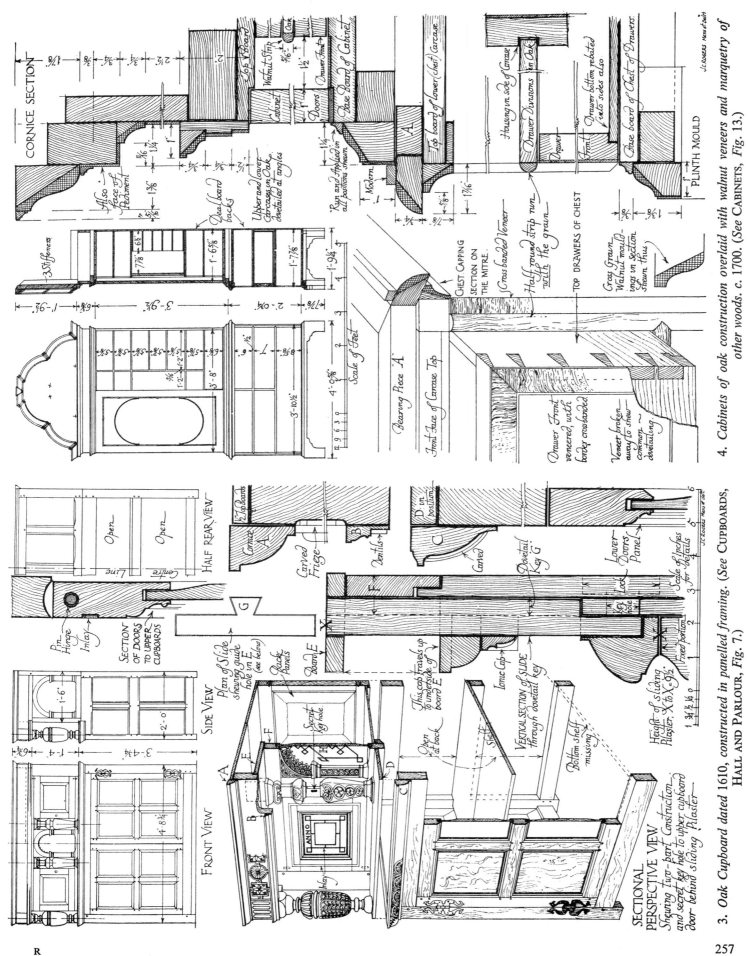

4. Cabinets of oak construction overlaid with walnut veneers and marquetry of other woods. c. 1700. (See CABINETS, *Fig. 13.*)

3. Oak Cupboard dated 1610, constructed in panelled framing. (See CUPBOARDS, HALL AND PARLOUR, *Fig. 7.*)

a laborious process, discontinued in the 16th century in favour of the joiner's mitre, the actual joint on the line of intersection of the mouldings (Fig. 13). Panelled framing achieved the essentials of strength and durability combined with lightness; the rails and stiles average between $2\frac{1}{2}$ ins. to 3 ins. wide by 1 in. to $1\frac{1}{2}$ ins. thick, and the panels vary between $\frac{3}{8}$ in. and $\frac{3}{4}$ in. thick in the middle (the backs being roughly adzed), tapering to a $\frac{3}{16}$ in. tongue to fit tightly in the groove formed in the framing.

In pre-Restoration work the width of each panel was kept small enough to be within the compass of a quarter-cut board; consequently panels are out of one piece almost invariably.

A panelled front in Tudor and Jacobean work is bounded by the two side posts or stiles, which continue to the floor, and the top and bottom rails; the latter are continuous from stile to stile, and have tenons cut on their ends which slide into mortise holes cut in the corresponding positions in the stiles. The number of intermediate stiles varied according to the size and type of work. The panels, having been cut to requisite sizes and taper-trimmed at the back on all sides to tongue in the grooves, were inserted while the framework was being assembled. The joints were lightly tapped together, and left in this state in the workshop for several weeks—or, perhaps, months—to become properly set; then, glue being dispensed with, the joints were driven up tight with a mallet. Holes were bored in the framing—one or two, to pass through each tenon—roughly squared and tapered oak pins being driven through until tightly wedged in the holes, and then trimmed off flush. Setting joints in glue was seldom done, owing to the difficulty of obtaining and keeping the glue fresh: moreover, its use was hardly necessary with pinned tenons, though, doubtless, an added source of strength to open frames of tables and chairs. In 1632 a Committee of the Court of Aldermen decided that the joiners were entitled to make: 'all tables of wainscote, walnutt or other stuffe, glued with frames, mortesses, and tennants'.

The fact that pins are often found standing a little in front of the framing is due to the shrinkage of the wood, in which the pins, being of end grain, have not participated. Mouldings, either 'scratched' or run with the plane, decorated the edges of the framing around the panels, and deep, narrow grooves were cut on the side faces of the stiles and rails where panels were required to be housed (Figs. 1b, 2 and 3). In the first half of the 17th century it became customary to decorate furniture with applied mouldings glued and bradded in position, and this method (in addition to mouldings on the solid) has been continued until modern times.

The cross-grain mouldings on walnut furniture constituted a distinct variation in treatment, thin strips of walnut being glued to the carcase, with grain running across the direction or width, and moulded in position to the required profile (Fig. 4). Bold cornices were successfully constructed by forming the largest and widest member either as a cavetto or a swell frieze, shaped on the carcase wood and faced with vertical grain veneer. Mortise and tenon joinery applied to panel framing suffered a sharp decline c. 1660, with the introduction of veneering; but for open framing, e.g. tables, chairs, stools, it maintained an unchallenged position.

Towards the end of the 17th century, when in walnut chairs there was a marked emphasis on height and vertical lines,

sound construction by means of mortise and tenon was often sacrificed to the dowel-and-socket method of fixing the top, or cresting rails, and seats; and for attaching the legs of tables and stands to their upper framework.

To secure broad, flat surfaces for walnut and mahogany veneers, carcases were built up of oak or deal boards, about 1 in. thick, glued side by side; these were trimmed to shape and secured along the abutting edges of sides, top and bottom with rows of dovetails set in glue (Fig. 5b). Panelled framing was reserved for parts unsecured at the edges, such as cabinet and cupboard doors.

This system of obtaining broad, flat surfaces was defective, for it afforded little or no provision against expansion and contraction. Consequently, cracked tops and sides are common. The earliest drawers were nailed together, and dovetailing first appeared in English furniture at the drawer sides of Elizabethan court cupboards, presses, etc., in conjunction with the groove running on a bearer fixed to the side of the carcase (Fig. 5a). This method ceased after 1660 (except in pieces of country origin), when, in the case of chests of drawers, the carcases had horizontal divisions between drawers, on which the drawer sides rested and slid (Fig. 5b). Accompanying this improvement, the dovetails became smaller, and, therefore, increased in number, being still more closely spaced and finely cut in 18th-century work.

The comparative diagrams of chests of drawers (Figs. 5a and 5b) illustrate the marked change in construction from the traditional frame and panel joinery retained in 17th-century specimens and the new type with broad, flat surfaces, housed and dovetailed together, that became predominant when walnut was adopted, and lasted, with only minor alterations, throughout the 18th century. In drawer fronts of later oak chests of drawers there is generally a very deep drawer immediately below a shallow top drawer, and below are two more of medium depth. In walnut and mahogany examples the drawers are equal in depth, or gradually increase towards the base. The fronts of drawers in veneered walnut have the joints and the grain of the veneer vertical and arranged so that the grain balances; there are also borders of veneer, usually cross-banded, and very often an intermediate 'feather' or herring-bone strip. In later specimens faced with mahogany veneer the grain runs horizontally, and there are no joints. Late in the 17th century the cross-banded border was backed on to a walnut strip, which projected beyond the drawer on all sides and formed a moulding, half-round in section. This is to be found also in early mahogany drawers worked on the solid. A few years later two conjoined half-round mouldings were employed, concurrently with and followed by a small projecting cock bead; in this case it formed a projecting rim in front of the drawer face, as Fig. 5b shows. It is found on some walnut-faced drawers, and was very popular throughout the mahogany period.

Carcases intended to be overlaid with veneers were commonly of fine-quality deal and pine throughout the walnut and mahogany periods. Oak was similarly used, particularly in walnut and the more expensive early mahogany furniture. In the second half of the 18th century Honduras mahogany was often used as a ground for veneers, and, occasionally, on very fine work, the ground is of Cuban wood, though usually this was reserved for veneers.

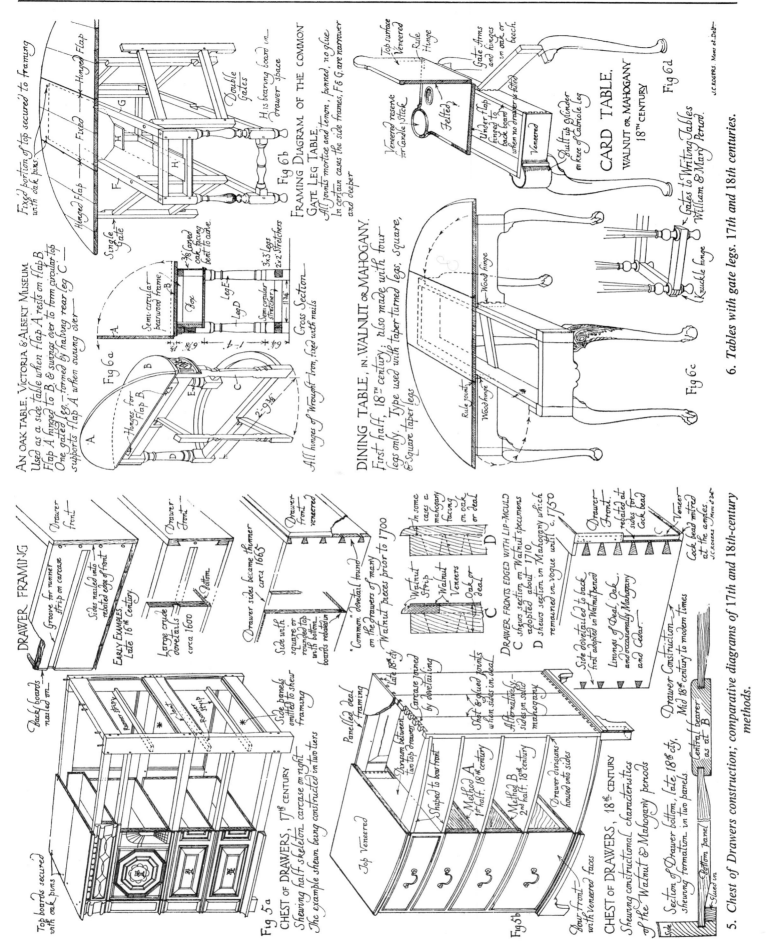

Fixed portion of top secured to framing with oak pins

Hinged Flap — Fixed — Hinged Flap

Double Gates

His bearing board in drawer space

F — G — H

Single Gate

Fig 6b

FRAMING DIAGRAM OF THE COMMON GATE LEG TABLE.
All joints mortice and tenon, pinned, no glue
In certain cases the side frames, F & G, are narrower and deeper

AN OAK TABLE. VICTORIA & ALBERT MUSEUM
Used as a side table when flap A rests on flap B
Flap A hinged to B, & swings over to form circular top
One gated leg — formed by hinging rear leg C —
supports flap A when swung over

Fig 6a

Semi-circular bearwood frame

Box

Leg D

Leg E

⅜" Cored oak facing bent to curve

3×3 Legs

2×2 Stretchers

Semi-circular stretcher

Cross Section

All hinges of wrought iron, fixed with nails

Hinges for Flap B

A

B

C

D

E

2'-9¾"

Top surface Veneered

Rule Hinge

Gate Arms and hinges in oak or beech

Veneered reserve for candle stick

Felted

Under flap hinged to back board when no drawer is fitted

Veneered

Built up cylinder on knee of cabriole leg

CARD TABLE.
WALNUT or MAHOGANY
18TH CENTURY

Fig 6d

Gates to Writing Tables
William & Mary Period

Knuckle Hinge

Wood hinge

Rule joint

Wood hinge

DINING TABLE, IN WALNUT or MAHOGANY.
First half, 18TH century; also made with four legs only. Type used with taper turned legs, square, & square taper legs.

Fig 6c

6. *Tables with gate legs. 17th and 18th centuries.*

DRAWER FRAMING

Drawer front

Groove for runner strip on carcase

Sides nailed into rebated edge of front

EARLY EXAMPLES
Late 16TH Century

Drawer Front

Bottom

Large crude dovetails
circa 1600

Drawer sides became thinner
circa 1665

Drawer Front veneered

Side with square or rounded top with bottom boards rebated

"Common" dovetail found on the drawers of many walnut pieces prior to 1700

Walnut Strip

Walnut Veneers

Oak or deal

In some cases a mahogany facing on oak or deal

C

D

DRAWER FRONTS EDGED WITH LIP-MOULD
C shews section on walnut specimens adopted about 1710
D shews section on mahogany which remained in vogue until c. 1750

Drawer Front, rebated at sides for Cock bead

Veneer

Cock bead mitred at the angles

Side dovetailed to back first adopted on walnut period

Linings of deal, oak, and occasionally mahogany and cedar.

Drawer Construction
Mid 18TH century to modern times

Top boards secured with oak pins

Back board nailed on

Runner strip

Side panels omitted to shew framing

CHEST of DRAWERS, 17TH CENTURY
Shewing half-skeleton carcase on right
The example shewn being constructed in two tiers

Fig 5a

Panelled deal framing

Division between two top drawers

Carcase joined by dovetailing

Shaped to bow front

Slat & glued joints when sides in deal

Alternatively sides in solid mahogany

Drawer divisions housed into sides

Late 18TH cy

Top Veneered

Bow Front with Veneered faces

CHEST of DRAWERS, 18TH CENTURY
Shewing constructional characteristics of the Walnut & Mahogany periods

Fig 5b

Section of Drawer bottom, late 18TH cy, shewing formation in two panels

Side

Central bearer as at B

Bottom panel

Glued in

Drawer Construction

5. *Chest of Drawers construction; comparative diagrams of 17th and 18th-century methods.*

J.C.ROGERS Mens et Delt.

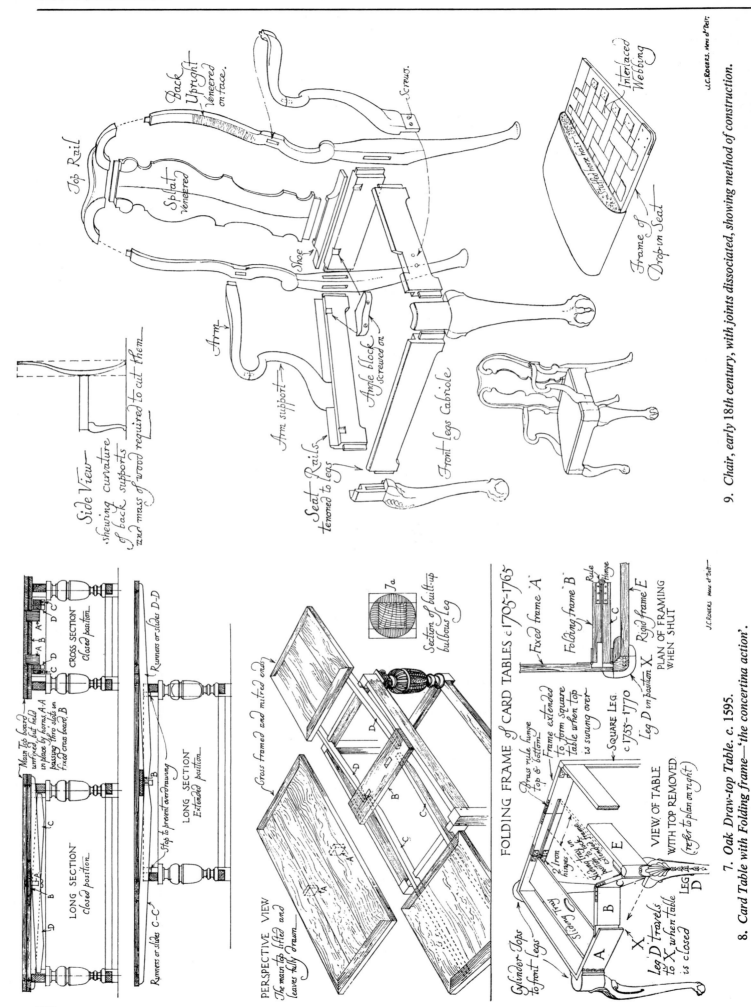

J.C.ROGERS. Mens et Delt.

Top Rail

Back Upright veneered on face.

Screws.

Splat veneered

Side View
shewing curvature
of back supports
and mass of wood required to cut them.

Arm

Arm support

Shoe

Angle block screwed on

Seat Rails
tenoned to legs

Front legs Cabriole

Frame of
Drop-in Seat

Interlaced
Webbing

Stuffed horse hair when...

9. Chair, early 18th century, with joints dissociated, showing method of construction.

Main Top board
unfixed, but held
in place by horns A-A
passing thro slots in
fixed cross board B

LONG SECTION
closed position

Stop to prevent overdrawing

LONG SECTION
Extended position.

CROSS SECTION
Closed position

CROSS SECTION
D-D

Runners or slides C-C

Cross framed and mitred ends

PERSPECTIVE VIEW
The main top lifted and
leaves fully drawn.

7a

Section of built-up
bulbous Leg

FOLDING FRAME of CARD TABLES c 1705–1765

Fixed frame 'A'

Folding frame 'B'

Rigid frame E

Leg D on position X

PLAN OF FRAMING
WHEN SHUT

Press rule hinge
top & bottom

Frame extended
to form square
table when top
is swung over.

SQUARE LEG.
c 1755–1770

Rule

Hinge

VIEW OF TABLE
WITH TOP REMOVED
(refer to plan on right)

2 from
hinges

Sliding blockframe...

A B E

Cylinder Tops
to front legs

X
Leg D travels
to X when table
is closed

LEG
D

J.C.ROGERS. Mens et Delt.

7. Oak Draw-top Table. c. 1595.

8. Card Table with Folding frame—'the concertina action'.

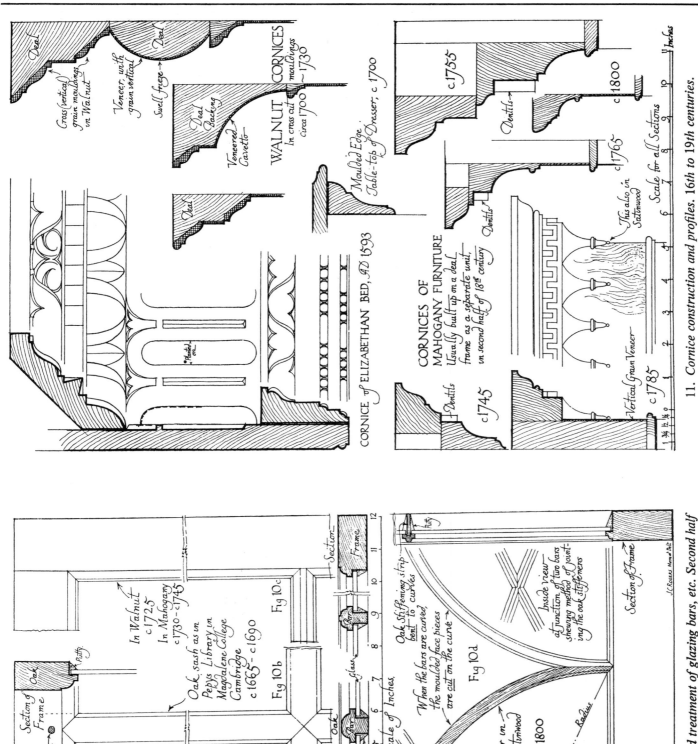

11. Cornice construction and profiles. 16th to 19th centuries.

WALNUT CORNICES

- Cross (vertical) grain mouldings in Walnut
- Veneer, with grain vertical
- Swell frieze
- Deal
- In cross cut mouldings circa 1700
- ~1730
- Deal
- Deal Backing
- Veneered Cavetto
- Deal

CORNICE of ELIZABETHAN BED, A.D. 1593

Moulded Edge. Table-top of Dresser, c. 1700

CORNICES OF MAHOGANY FURNITURE
Usually built up on a deal frame as a separate unit, in second half of 18th century

- c. 1755
- c. 1800
- Dentils
- c. 1765
- This also in Satinwood
- Dentils
- c. 1745
- Dentils
- Vertical Grain Veneer
- c. 1785

Scale for all Sections

10. Cabinet Doors; construction and treatment of glazing bars, etc. Second half of 17th and 18th centuries.

- Section of Frame
- oak pins
- Putty
- Section of Oak
- Glass pane
- Half round Cross grain moulding in Walnut glued to oak c. 1675 – c. 1705 Fig 10a
- In Walnut c. 1725 In Mahogany c. 1730 – c. 1745
- Oak sash as in Pepys Library in Magdalene College Cambridge c. 1665 – c. 1690 Fig 10b
- Fig 10c
- Section Frame
- Cross Grain Walnut Veneer
- Oak Frame
- Walnut
- Oak
- Putty
- Section
- Oak
- Putty
- Glass
- Oak
- Bars
- Bars
- Bars
- Scale of Inches
- Frame

- Oak Stiffening strip bent to curves
- When the bars are curved, the moulded face pieces are cut on the curve
- Fig 10d
- Inside view at junction of two bars shewing method of jointing the oak stiffeners
- 36 Astragal Bar in Mahogany or Satinwood c. 1750 – c. 1800
- Glass pane
- Joints
- Radius
- Frame mortised & tenoned.
- Section of Frame.

J. C. Rogers Menst. Delt.

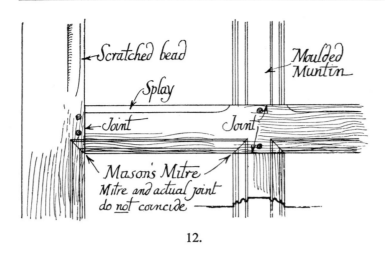

12.

Until the introduction of metal screws, late in the 17th century (and for many years after that in country districts), the fixed tops of tables, dressers, etc., were secured by oak pins driven from the top down into the under frame. After c. 1700 the manufacture of screws slowly improved, and they soon became the sole means of securing table tops. (*See* SCREWS.)

Several devices were employed for parts of furniture-framing capable of adjustment, the earliest of any importance being the sliding mechanism of tables with draw-leaves. The diagram of this type of table (Fig. 7) shows it to have an unfixed top in three portions. The uppermost board is of normal length and is registered in position by two horns, which project from its under-surface and pass through slots in a central fixed cross-board; the top can thus rise and fall, but cannot move laterally. Abutting on each side of the fixed cross-board are two sliding leaves fitted with two raking arms or runners on their undersides. When these are withdrawn at each end, they rise (causing the top to rise also) until they are just free of the main top, when the latter immediately becomes free to drop back on its central seating and is then flush with the drawn leaves. The majority of these tables have heavy bulbous legs, which, in some cases, were built up (Fig. 7a).

No less ingenious than the draw-top tables are those of smaller size, arranged with gate legs and hinged flaps to fold into a very small compass. The constructional characteristics of several types are shown in Figs. 6a, b, c and d. An interesting specimen is (Fig. 6a) a side-table with a semicircular top—a precursor of the card-table of like form. The double top is hinged at the joint, the upper leaf swinging over to provide a circular top. The underleaf can then be raised as the lid of a box contrived in the framing. The left-hand leg is sawn in halves vertically, and is framed to a stretcher and frame arm also of half thickness; these are hinged with iron butterfly hinges, so forming a swinging gate to support the upper top flap when open. A curious feature is the carved frieze of the under-frame—only $\frac{3}{8}$ in. thick—bent to semicircular form and nailed in position. The common type of gate-leg table is given in Fig. 6b, the left side having one gate, while, on the right, double gates are shown; the gates swing on oak pin pivots driven through the framing.

Eighteenth-century types in which stretchers are omitted are given in Figs. 6c and d. The dining-table shows the new method of hinging the gates: a true hinge accurately formed in wood, generally of oak or beech, with a stout wire core. The

central, fixed portion of the top was no longer held down by oak pins, but by metal screws passing obliquely through the under-frame and so into the under-surface of the top.

An earlier type of card-table had a folding frame instead of the hinged gate (Fig. 8). The drawing shows the folding action, all joints being dependent on metal hinges of rule or butt form screwed in place. The sliding tray, which often held a box of cards, served to keep the framing rigid when opened out.

Measured drawings of an early box chair and a dated cupboard are given in Figs. 2 and 3. (*See* CHAIRS, Fig. 3, and CUPBOARDS, HALL AND PARLOUR, Fig. 7.) The chair is of panelled framing throughout, with a box seat constructed of quarter-sawn oak. The cupboard (Fig. 3) is of panelled box formation with good mitred mouldings and enrichments, both carved and inlaid woods. It is constructed in two parts, the lower member having an open back. The two small doors of the top cupboards have oak pin hinges and can be locked, yet both lock and keyhole are at first invisible. The carved pilasters placed on either side of the central arched panel are in two parts, the uppermost of each being a disguised slide which travels upwards in a dovetail slot and discloses the keyhole—not on the door, as usual, but on the main framing: the lock is therefore fixed to the framing, and the bolt is shot into the door stile.

A walnut chair, with all joints dissociated, is shown in Fig. 9. A notable feature is the curvature of the back legs and supports, which necessitated a large piece of wood and much waste, unless several were cut together. The structural characteristics are typical also of mahogany chairs. The shaping of the cabriole leg demanded considerable skill. First a piece of wood of the requisite size, close in grain and free from knots and shakes, would be selected. The outline curves were then marked on it with a template, and, at the knee, mortises were cut to house the tenons of the seat rail. The craftsman next clamped one end on the bench and cut the profiles marked on the wood with a bow saw. A curved leg of rectangular section would thus be obtained, and if not left square, as in some examples, the leg was placed in a lathe to turn the pad foot (unless it was to be carved in *pied de biche* form), and the arrises were reduced on the bench with spokeshave and rasp, leaving the knee rough if carved ornament were intended. There was now a vertical face on either side of the knee which is retained in some examples, while others are rounded off with an applied

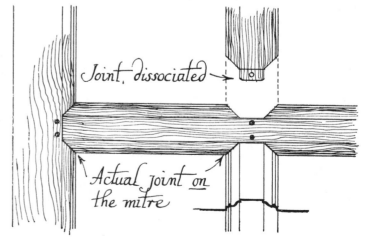

13.

knob; though generally in later cabriole chairs a shoulder-piece is dowelled or glued on at each side, thus continuing the curve of the leg.

Fig. 10 shows the development in the glazing of cabinet doors from the reign of Charles II to that of George III. The earliest form has a stout, half-round, walnut-faced bar standing above the surface of the veneered frame (Fig. 10a); alternatively, the oak was not veneered, and the bar—a large astragal—was sunk to the depth of a fillet (Fig. 10b). (See BOOKCASES; Fig. 1.) The early 18th-century type with stout ovolo bar is given in Fig. 10c, the panel being still rectangular. This was followed by thin bar-work, in which many curved forms were possible (Fig. 10d). The glazing of cabinet doors was effected by rebating the frame and the bars to receive the panes of glass, and holding them in position with putty applied from the back or inside.

Until c. 1750 rectangular panes were employed in conjunction with stout bars, as in Figs. 10a, b and c. In the period 1750-1800 the narrow mahogany astragal became general, with much curved work after the manner of tracery; this necessitated a variety of shapes for panes, and in some cases carving was glued to the glass. The glass used in the second half of the 17th century and for several decades in the 18th was, owing to methods of manufacture, of unequal thickness, never truly flat and often curved. These characteristics gave a pleasing play of light on the panes.

Cornice profiles are detailed in sectional form in Fig. 11. Walnut cornices are of the cross-cut type backed on to pine or oak with broad profiles in veneer (Fig. 4). The mahogany cornices were, with a few early exceptions, run with the grain, on the bench, before cutting to length and fixing in position, the flat friezes being usually in vertical grain veneer, often relieved with banding.

COQUILLAGE. From the French *coquille*, shell-fish, applied in furniture to carved rococo motive of shell form. surrounding a cabochon (q.v.). Much used in mid 18th century as the central ornament on chair rails, frames of side-tables, etc. (*See* CHAIRS; Fig. 112.)

CORBEL. Architectural term for bracket supporting super-incumbent weight; friezes of Tudor bedsteads and early 17th-century chests and chests of drawers sometimes intersected by such brackets. (*See* CHESTS OF DRAWERS; Fig. 2.) There is similar treatment on much 18th-century furniture.

CORINTHIAN ORDER. *See* ORDERS.

CORNICE, CORNISH. Architectural term for the horizontal moulded projection forming the top member of an entablature; used also in the 17th and 18th centuries for wooden boxes or holders from which valances and curtains were festooned. In royal accounts for William and Mary's reign 'cornishes' of this type are often mentioned and, designed in various styles, are illustrated in several 18th-century trade catalogues. In Hepplewhite's *Guide* (1788) they are scalloped, decorated with paterae and festoons, and surmounted by ostrich feathers and vases. The description states they 'may be executed in wood painted and japanned or in gold. A mixture of these two manners produces an elegant and grand effect.' Sheraton (*Cabinet Dictionary*, 1803) writes 'Cornices are

now made much lighter than formerly'. He adds that windows were often 'crowned with gold and richly painted cornices'.

COROMANDEL WOOD (*Diospyros melanoxylon*) or Bombay ebony from the Coromandel coast. Sheraton (*Cabinet Dictionary*) writes that it is 'lately introduced into England (from India) and much used by cabinet-makers for banding. Resembles black rosewood, but is intermingled with light stripes'.

CORONA. Circular hanging light, usually made of one or more metal hoops. (*See* CHANDELIERS.)

COSTERS (COSTRINGS). From old French *costier*, hanging for walls of room, etc. In 1463 John Baret, of Bury, bequeathed to his niece the 'costerys old grene wonostede' in his parlour, and to another beneficiary 'a tester with II costers smale palyd of buckram blew . . .' *i.e.* the canopy with curtains of a bed. The schedule of household goods attached to the will of Sir William Compton, of Compton, Warwickshire, who was Chancellor of Ireland under Henry VII and died in 1528, specifies a number of such hangings in different chambers—*e.g.* 'In the Parlour—Item a Costrings of Tappistrye Imagery lined wt Canvas conteynyng oon hundred and fourty sticks square at xxd. xi. li. xiis, ivd.'

COUCHES AND DAY-BEDS. The line of demarcation between couch, day-bed, sofa and settee is difficult to draw, for one is generally defined in terms of another (the *New English Dictionary* gives 'day-bed' as 'a sofa, couch, or lounge'). In this section are included pieces of furniture primarily intended for reclining.

Throughout the Middle Ages beds were often placed in the principal living-rooms, and served for purposes of repose in the daytime; but they were sometimes supplemented in great establishments by long benches on which cushions were arranged. Among the furniture of the bedroom prepared by Edward IV at Windsor Castle for the Lord of Grouthuse, Governor of Holland, there was 'a couch with feather beds, hanged about like a tent, knit like a net'; this was certainly for use in the daytime, the bed itself being fully described. These early couches are occasionally figured in illuminated manuscripts (*see* BEDS; Fig. 1), and allusions to them occur in metrical romances.

The day-bed, as a distinct variety of furniture, was probably introduced from the Continent by the foreign artists and craftsmen employed by Henry VIII in the equipment of his new palaces. By the end of the 16th century the term had become familiar. In Shakespeare's *Richard III* (1594) Buckingham observes that the Duke of Gloucester 'is not lolling on a lewd day-bed'. Another reference occurs in *Twelfth Night* (1600): Malvolio speaks of coming 'from a day-bed where I have left Olivia sleeping'. In the 'character' of Queen Elizabeth I in Nichols's *Progresses* (1788-1805), it is related that the queen 'after a light meal would rest awhile upon an Indian couch curiously and richly carved'.

Even in great establishments couches were probably still rare; they do not figure in the Lumley inventory (1591), although the house contained a large number of padded stools and other contemporary novelties; nor in the enormous aggregation of costly furniture belonging to Robert Dudley,

1. *Oak Day-Bed; ends painted with floral arabesques and arms of Shrewsbury and Talbot; cushion covered with the original rose damask; valances of later date. c. 1600. Ht. 3 ft., L. 7 ft., W. 3 ft. 1½ in. (Hardwick Hall, Derbys.)*

2. *Day-Bed covered with crimson velvet, fastened to beech framework by gilt nails and trimmed with crimson fringe; ends let down on iron ratchets. c. 1610-20. Ht. 3 ft. 5 in., L. 5 ft. 8 in., W. 1 ft. 10 in. (Knole Park, Kent.)*

Earl of Leicester, at Kenilworth and Leicester House, listed in the inventories of 1583 and 1588. A bench, made more comfortable with loose cushions, served the need of those unacquainted with the luxury of courts. Shakespeare refers to the practice of 'sleeping upon benches after noon', and in Overbury's *Characters* (1613) the Ordinary Fencer uses a bench 'in the vacation of the afternoons' as his day-bed.

The early form, developed from the bench by the addition of panelled ends, was made of oak, the lower portion being hung with valances, and the cushions often being covered with rich material. A rare specimen in the Long Gallery at Hardwick Hall, Derbyshire (Fig. 1), is painted throughout a deep chocolate red and decorated in colour with the arms of Shrewsbury and Talbot surrounded by floral arabesques. The long cushion is covered with the original rose damask, and the valances have been renewed at a later date. That such day-beds were now becoming abundant in large houses may be gathered from the following dialogue in Fletcher's *Rule a Wife and have a Wife* (1624):

> Margarita: Is the great couch up, the Duke of Medina sent?
> Altea: 'Tis up and ready.
> Margarita: And the day-beds in all chambers?
> Altea: In all, lady!

In early 17th-century inventories and correspondence references to couches sometimes occur. A list of 'Householde-stuffe' belonging to Henry Howard, Earl of Northampton (1614), mentions, among the contents of the Long Wardrobe at Northampton House, near Charing Cross, 'a cowche of crimson leather printed border wise with silver and golde, one long and two short cushions suteable to the same, lined with bayse coulored velvete and laced about with gold lace'.

Early in the 17th century, a new form of day-bed had been introduced to match the contemporary upholstered chairs and stools. Such couches resembled a settle in construction, but

3. *Oak Couch; knobbed legs, spirally turned stretchers; part of the leather covering renewed. c. 1660. (The late Mrs F. H. Leggett.)*

4. *Day-Bed of walnut, caned; back adjustable by means of a cord. c. 1665. Ht. 2 ft. 9 in., L. 5 ft. 8 in., W. 1 ft. 10 in. (Morris and Co.)*

5. *Walnut Day-Bed, elaborately carved; back divided into two caned panels, legs scroll-shaped. c. 1680. (Lady Assheton-Smith Coll.)*

6. *Oak Day-Bed; legs and uprights baluster turned, central stretcher knobbed, seat sunk for a squab. Late 17th century. Ht. 2 ft. 9½ in., L. 5 ft. 3½ in., W. 2 ft. (Rev. Meyrick Jones Coll.)*

7. *Walnut Day-Bed, upholstered in blue damask; ends finish in volutes, seat rail gadrooned. c. 1685. (Belton House, Lincs.)*

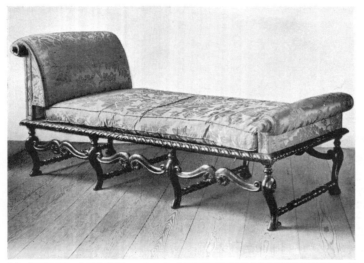

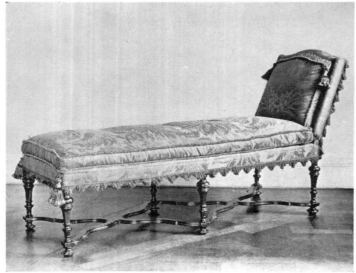

8. *Walnut Day-Bed upholstered in crimson silk; taper baluster legs united by serpentine stretchers. c. 1695. L. 5 ft. 8 in., W. 2 ft. (Lockleys, Herts.)*

were now padded and covered throughout, the ends letting down on a toothed steel ratchet to enable the occupant to repose. They were generally destroyed when the coverings had worn out, the woodwork being of little value, but a specimen at Knole Park, Kent, retains the original upholstery (Fig. 2). Similar couches were plentiful in France under Louis XIII, and they may be seen in Abraham Bosse's engravings of domestic interiors, but they were rare in this country except at Court and in the houses of great nobles. Lord Herbert of Cherbury had two of these luxuries at his Westminster house in 1641. A black velvet couch in the billiards-room was embroidered with silk and silver, and had a cushion to match 'trimmed with silver lace spangled'; while in the withdrawing-room was another described as 'long', the green velvet upholstery being 'wrought with green silke and hanged with green fringe'. When the contents of the Royal palaces were dispersed after Charles I's execution, a number of couches covered with velvet and trimmed with gold lace were included in the sale. One of the earliest mentions of day-beds at the French Court is in connection with Henrietta Maria's life in exile. Mlle de Montpensier wrote that in 1656, at the Château de Chilly, '*la reine d'Angleterre s'assit sur un lit de repos, et son cercle fut plus grand qu'il n'avoit jamais été, tout ce qu'ily avoit de princesses et duchesses à Paris y étant*'.

Cromwellian couches reflect the spirit of a time when indulgence in luxury was discouraged. They were made in oak, with seats and backs covered in cowhide to match the angular and uncomfortable chairs of that time, and in some instances served a dual purpose, being used as both a couch and a settee (Fig. 3). The ends rake outwards or let down on a ratchet to support the occupant's head, an arrangement borrowed from the earlier and more luxurious type. There is little padding, the leather, sometimes lightly incised, being stretched over the framework and secured by rows of brass-headed nails. In the lower portion, the box-like structure of early Stuart day-beds is replaced by plain columnar supports united by square stretchers, knobbed turning in conjunction with a spiral twist being also sometimes employed. A revived interest in colour

9. *Gilt Walnut Day-Bed, upholstered in rose damask, embroidered with strap-work of coloured silks; framework carved with a floral pattern, and scrolled legs united by serpentine stretchers. c. 1690. Ht. (of seat) 2 ft., L. 5 ft. (Penshurst Place, Kent.)*

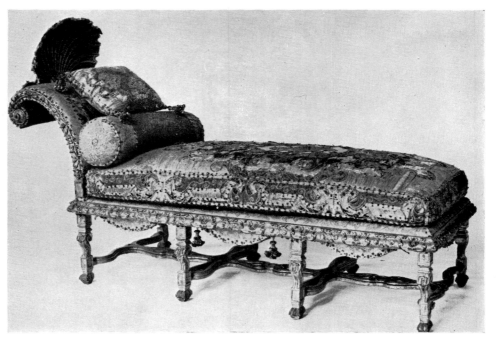

10. *Gilt Day-Bed, upholstered in flowered Genoa velvet, trimmed with tasselled fringe; cresting bears the coronet and cipher of the first Duke of Leeds. c. 1695. L. 5 ft. 2 in., W. 2 ft. 6 in. Formerly at Hornby Castle, Yorks. (Mrs David Gubbay.)*

11. *Walnut upholstered Day-Bed; cabriole legs, headed by escallop shells hipped above seat rail; turned baluster stretchers. The covering modern. c. 1715. L. 6 ft. 8 in., W. 3 ft. 4 in. (Houghton Hall, Norfolk.)*

12. *Day-Bed, japanned in gold and silver on a scarlet ground. By Giles Grendey. c. 1730. Ht. 3 ft. 3 in., L. 6 ft. 4 in. (V. & A. Mus.)*

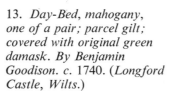

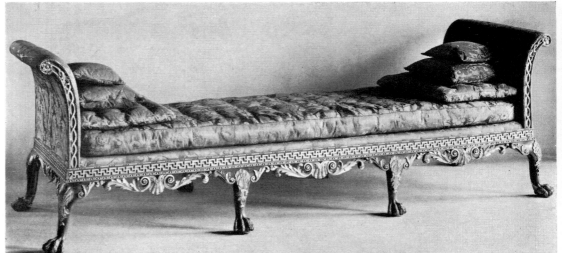

13. *Day-Bed, mahogany, one of a pair; parcel gilt; covered with original green damask. By Benjamin Goodison. c. 1740. (Longford Castle, Wilts.)*

may be detected in some of the later specimens, stamped and lacquered leather being imported from the Continent as a covering.

With the Restoration a new type was introduced from France, where *lits de repos* had become plentiful under Louis XIV. These day-beds are of true couch form, sometimes with a hinged and adjustable back-rest at one end. They were made in walnut and caned, following the evolution of contemporary chairs; the cushions, now generally missing, were covered with velvet, damask or needlework. In Fig. 4, an early specimen, the back is adjustable by means of a cord, and, like the seat, is filled with a panel of canework. Fig. 5 has the scrolled form of leg first introduced c. 1675, and shows the delight in lavish enrichment characteristic of Restoration taste. The broad stretchers, centring on amorini supporting a vase of flowers, repeat the motive of the cresting, and even the seat rail is carved. About 1680, decorated scrolls in juxtaposition sometimes replaced carved stretchers, and they are repeated in the back, where the uprights are of baluster form. These simplified versions of the fashionable type sometimes have a stretcher on one side only, showing that they were intended to stand against a wall. Day-beds with an adjustable back were also occasionally made in oak, but these followed an independent evolution, turned balusters forming legs and uprights (Fig. 6).

At the end of Charles II's reign upholstered day-beds were introduced, covered, like settees and winged armchairs of the period, with damask or figured Genoa velvet. In this new type the back is a fixture, and there are generally eight legs. The ends in Fig. 7 roll over and finish in volutes, also found on settees of this time; the seat rail is gadrooned, and the cross-stretchers are formed of bead-and-reel turning. An inventory (1688) drawn up for Sir John Brownlow, who had recently refurnished Belton House, Lincolnshire, mentions 'a couch chaire with a cushion' in 'My Lady's Chamber', a description probably referring to this specimen. The legs and stretchers on the day-bed seen in Fig. 8 are in the style of the closing years of the century, but the Carolean type persisted into William III's reign. In 1690 a charge from Thomas Roberts is entered in the royal accounts 'for a couch carved both sides very rich with figures, scroles, flowers and leaves in the Railes [*i.e.* stretchers] and Cherubims heads on the feet, and a small head board carved rich with scroles and leaves and cypher and two angells holding up the Crowne, the angells, crowne and cypher gilt with gold and all the lower part of the couch japand black'.

The walnut and gilt day-bed in Fig. 9 is one of a celebrated set (*see* CHAIRS; Fig. 52) in which the legs have square cappings and inward scrolls in conjunction with serpentine

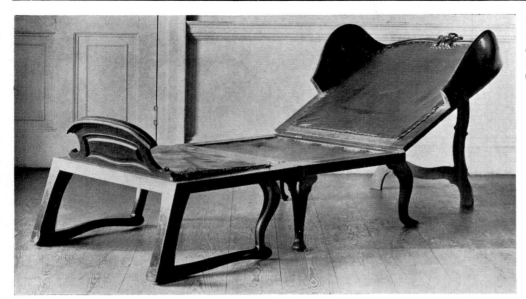

14. *Mahogany folding Couch; the winged back adjustable by a hinged support. c. 1730. Ht. 4 ft. 4 in., W. 2 ft. 7 in., L. (extended) 7 ft. 5 in. (Padworth House, Berks.)*

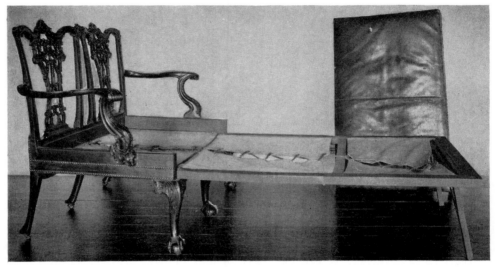

15. *Mahogany Couch Settee; back of double chair form, with serpentine cresting and ribbon-pattern splats. When in use as a settee, the leather-covered seat is closed with a double fold. c. 1755. Ht. 3 ft. 3 in., W. 4 ft. (Nostell Priory, Yorks.)*

stretchers. This example is probably the work of Thomas Roberts. The scrolled back is surmounted by a large carved escallop covered with rose damask and black velvet, and between the legs are lunette-shaped valances of damask on wood, with tassels. The cover matches the great panels of embroidered *appliqué* work that hang on the walls of a state room at Penshurst, and the set was, no doubt, acquired by Philip, third Earl of Leicester.

A day-bed from Hornby Castle, Yorks. (Fig. 10), is one of the most important surviving specimens of late Stuart furniture on account of both design and upholstery. It is in the form of a contemporary *chaise longue*, the woodwork of beech, painted black and gilt, being carved throughout with a small nulling. The scrollwork of the cresting centres on an escutcheon bearing the cipher and coronet of Thomas Osborne, created Duke of Leeds in 1694. The snail-headed arms finish on vase-shaped supports, and the taper legs, a pattern recently introduced from France, are connected by oval stretchers tenoned into oblongs. The flowered velvet of the upholstery is on a deep cream satin ground, the edges being trimmed with the tasselled fringe.

Genoa velvets, with silks imported from France and Italy, were the favourite upholstery for day-beds under William III; but other materials were also used. In the 'Large Old Eating

Roome' at Hampton Court in 1695 was 'a couch two squabbs and two boulsters covered with yellow white and crimson brocatella'. In an 'estimate of the charges . . . for his Maties Service at Hampton Court' at the end of the century there is an entry of £15 10s. 'for one long couch frame richly carved round the back and seat finely gilt'.

By this time the habit of reclining had become general even in remote country houses; and at Dyrham Park, Gloucestershire, in 1710, there were five couches in different rooms, each provided with two or three cushions and covered with 'strip'd plush' or gilded leather. Congreve (*The Way of the World*, 1700) makes Lady Wishfort decide to receive her lover in her little dressing-room: 'There's a couch—yes, yes. I'll give the first impression on a couch. I won't lie, neither, but loll and lean upon an elbow, with one foot a little dangling off jogging in a thoughtful way.'

Day-beds of the early 18th century have cabriole legs in conjunction with plainly turned stretchers. An example from Houghton, Norfolk (Fig. 11), was no doubt transferred by Sir Robert Walpole from the older house. Here the upholstery is modern; but on another specimen at Houghton, of later date, the squab and three cushions are covered with the original green damask embroidered with needlework in silver thread.

269

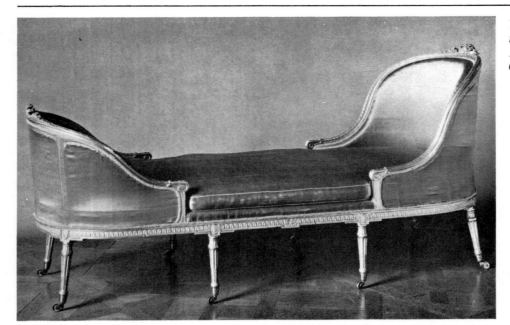

16. *Carved and gilt Couch of 'Duchesse' type with tub-shaped ends. c. 1780. Ht. 3 ft. 4½ in., L. 7 ft. 3 in., W. 2 ft. 6 in. (Chatsworth, Derbys.)*

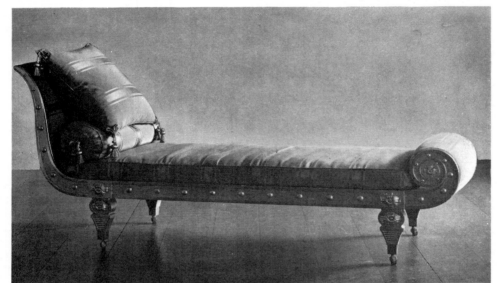

17. *Gilt Couch, one of a pair. c. 1800. Ht. 2 ft. 11 in., L. 7 ft. (Southill Park, Beds.)*

18. *Couch, japanned black and gold, one of a pair. c. 1800. (Mr Ronald Tree.)*

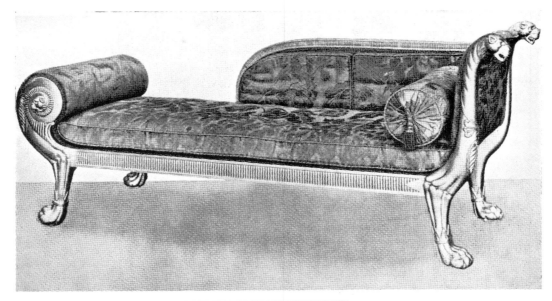

19. *Couch of carved and gilt wood Part of a set made by the firm of Gillow in 1805. Ht. 2 ft. 8½ in., L. 6 ft. 8 in. (V. & A. Mus.)*

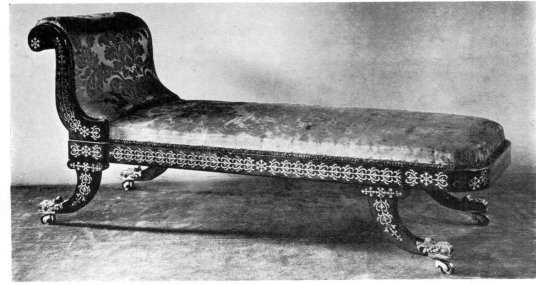

20. *Rosewood Couch, inlaid with foliated ornament in brass. c. 1810. (From Messrs Lenygon and Morant.)*

Another type with a cane or upholstered seat and an open back, of which the design was derived from contemporary chairs, was also occasionally made at this period. The majority of examples dating from the first half of the 18th century are of walnut or mahogany, but Fig. 12 shows a fine japanned day-bed by Giles Grendey, forming part of a set.

Two magnificent day-beds with scrolled double ends (Fig. 13) were supplied by Benjamin Goodison (*q.v.*) for the Picture Gallery at Longford Castle, Wiltshire, in 1740. They are of mahogany, richly carved and parcel-gilt, with scallops on the knees, lion's-paw feet and pierced aprons below the gilt key pattern on the seat rail. The fretwork is *appliqué* over the original green damask upholstery, which matches the hangings on the walls. At each end is a graduated set of cushions recalling an earlier fashion.

Some of the couches made at this time were convertible, and in a curious specimen of this dual-purpose furniture (Fig. 14) the back is adjustable by means of a hinged support, and like the seat, is made to fold up.

In Fig. 15, one of a set of ribbon-back furniture at Nostell Priory, Yorks., the treatment of splat and cresting exactly corresponds with that of a chair already illustrated (*see*

CHAIRS; Fig. 106). Here the functions of a settee and couch are ingeniously combined; the leather seat is removable, and the frame, supported by trestle legs, folds under it.

A variety of designs for convertible upholstered couches is given in the *Director* and other trade catalogues of the period; but many are of such fantastic character that they were probably never executed. Chippendale shows two with padded backs which, he says, are what the French call *Péché Mortel* (*q.v.*). He explains that they are 'sometimes made to take asunder in the middle; one part makes a large easy-chair, and the other a stool, and the feet join in the middle'. As he considered this junction unsightly, he recommended 'a pretty thick mattress' to conceal it, and gave the dimensions as 6 ft. long and 2 ft. 6 ins. to 3 ft. broad. Couches for alcoves, with elaborately carved and draped canopies, were also among the novelties offered to the public, and of these Chippendale gives an extravagant design. Ince and Mayhew (*Universal System*, 1759-63) show a similar arrangement, but in this case the tester is made to take off, and is concealed in a recess under the seat. These designers appropriate the term *birjair* to a half-couch with a seat about 3 ft. long and a back 'made to fall down at pleasure'. They also illustrate the *chaise longue* or 'single headed couch', which continued to be made on similar lines until the end of the century.

By 1788, when Hepplewhite's *Guide* was published, new forms had been introduced, and couches were often made in satinwood, tapestry or striped silk being the usual coverings. A couch with tub-shaped ends he calls a 'Duchesse': it is allotted to large and spacious ante-rooms, being formed of 'two barjier chairs of proper construction with a stool in the middle'. On each part either there was a loose squab, or the cushions were stuffed over the frame and covered with cotton or silk. The type was already in use; John Russell (q.v.) in 1781 had supplied the Prince of Wales's apartment at the Queen's House in St James's Park (Buckingham Palace) at the cost of £11 10s. with 'a mahogany Duchesse frame . . . in three parts, to stuff and cover over, the ends made as two Bergier chairs, with carved moulding tops, the elbows neatly carved and fluted, the front feet termed, turned and fluted, the middle part as a square stool'. Sheraton (*Drawing Book*, 1791-4) gives a design for a 'Duchesse' of large size which can be converted into a bed. The ends, when detached from the middle stool, are to serve as small sofas. He also experimented with the *chaise longue*, which, he states, is intended for repose after dinner, it being so contrived that the extension could be packed away in the sides of the chair. Fig. 16 shows a couch of the 'Duchesse' type, but here the ends are irremovable.

During the Regency the classic forms of couch were introduced from France. They were made in mahogany, satinwood, rosewood, or a soft wood painted and gilt. In the fully developed type the ends scroll over; there is often an arm-rest on one side occupying half the length, and the legs curve outwards and finish in scrolled brass ornament or with brass paw feet having castors attached. The gilt couch (Fig. 17) is an early specimen of the classic type, while Fig. 19, carved with lion terminals in the Egyptian style, formed part of a large set of furniture made by the firm of Gillow for Kinmel Park, Denbighshire, in 1805. The framework of rosewood couches is generally inlaid with stringing lines, more elaborate specimens (Fig. 20) being enriched with metal *appliqués*, gilt or bronze carvings. At Crawley House, Bedfordshire, there is a pair described in the accounts of Colliss, an upholsterer, for 1806, as 'two handsome Grecian couches with squabbs and feather bolsters'; like the chairs supplied by the same maker, they are painted to imitate coromandel wood inlaid with lines of brass (*see* Introduction; Fig. 19). Hope (*Household Furniture*, 1807) gives a number of designs for couches in Egyptian taste; while George Smith (1808) writes that they are 'an article admissible in every room'.

COUNTERPANE (COUNTERPOINT).

Term for a bed-covering, a fabric sewn on both sides. In John Russell's *Boke of Curtasye* (c. 1440) the groom of the chamber lays 'the counturpyn . . . on beddys fete'. The inventory of Katherine of Aragon's goods (1533) mentions a 'counterpoynte of skarlette and in length IIII yards—sore perisshid withe mowthis'. John Baker, upholsterer to James I, was paid 'for two counterpoynts of plush both sides alike, sewed with silk'. From this time onwards they were often made to match the hangings of important beds (*see* BEDS; Fig. 15). Towards the end of the 17th century the term 'counterpane' appears.

272

COUNTERS AND COUNTERBOARDS.

Tables or chests with the tops marked out into spaces with distinguishing symbols for calculating and counting money. Until the 16th century all the everyday calculations now done on paper were worked out with the aid of one of these objects. From the Middle Ages until the 17th century records of counters in various forms are abundant. In a will (1493) of William Honyboorn, a dyer of Bury, 'the counter standying in my plour' is bequeathed to his wife on condition that 'she bye another for my daughter Anneys to the value of VIII's'. Another Bury testator in 1505 bequeaths 'a tabyll callyd a counter' and contemporary wills contain allusions to counters with 'trestylles' or a 'paire of trestylles', which were obviously of table form.

The counter was often fitted with a closed receptacle and had locks and keys. In 1507 Richard Brerely, Rector of Kirk Smeaton, left to the parish church the 'countyr' in his chamber 'for to kepe ye evydence thereto belongying and other ornaments'.

The forms of counter in use at this period are shown in Figs. 1 and 2. The first is reproduced in Shaw's *Specimens of Ancient Furniture* (1832, Plate XIX) and was then at Hill Hall, Essex. In Shaw's drawing the panel at the back, which, though also carved in Early Renaissance taste, differs appreciably, has been substituted for that at the front. The horizontally divided folding top is, however, shown as in Fig. 1, and this example (which has been considerably restored) retains the 'board', or ground shelf, below. In Fig. 2 the top slides on bearers attached to the sides, and this convenient arrangement, which facilitates access to the interior without disturbing the counters, is found in a small group of such chests.

Counters were sometimes covered with cloths or carpets like contemporary cupboards. In 1557 Jane Lawson, the last Prioress of the Convent of Nerham, had in the hall 'II Flanders counters wth ther carpetts' valued at 20s. This type of table

1. *Oak Counter with hinged top and cupboard below, carved with Renaissance ornament; hinged top renewed. c. 1530. Ht. 2 ft. 8 in., L. 3 ft. ½ in., Depth (open) 2 ft. 10½ in. (Penshurst Place, Kent.)*

2. *Oak Chest on stand, probably a Counter; front panels carved with parchemin ornament and sides with linen-fold; sliding top and the back foot-rail renewed; c. 1550. Ht. 2 ft. 9 in., W. 4 ft., Depth 2 ft. 2 in. (S. W. Wolsey Ltd.)*

fitted with a cupboard was also in use on the Continent. In a late 15th-century French tapestry, 'Arithmatic', in the Cluny Museum, a lady is shown seated at a 'counter' of this kind, the top being covered with a carpet which would certainly have been marked out for calculating, for there is evidence that marked cloths were often used for this purpose. In a picture by Jan Steen at Belvoir Castle, Leicestershire, painted c. 1670 and showing a family at dinner in a farmhouse, the girl at one end of the table is seated at what is clearly a counter used as a stool, in style dating from c. 1500. The back is panelled with linen-fold, and there are buttressed ends, the top extending (as in Fig. 1) considerably beyond them on either side.

Another variety was not of table form, but consisted of several counting-boards fitting one within another. In an inventory of the goods of the Guild of the Blessed Virgin Mary of Boston (1534) 'a Counter the biggest of the neist' (*i.e.* nest) is entered in the 'Parlor in the Chauntree'. The inventory (1556) of Sir John Gage's goods lists a 'counter board having two leaves'.

CRADLES. 'A little bed or cot properly mounted on rockers, but often extended to a swing-cot or a simple cot or basket bed neither rocked nor swung' (*New Eng. Dict.*). The earliest form found in pre-Conquest illuminated manuscripts was constructed on the same primitive principle as contemporary chests, a log split transversely being hollowed out, thus rendering the provision of rockers unnecessary. Sometimes cradles were merely baskets of osiers, in which the child was placed swathed in swaddling bands. A miniature in the *Speculum Historiae* of Vincent de Beauvais, translated into French by Jean de Vigny c. 1450, shows St Ambrose sleeping in a cradle which is provided with rockers and has turned uprights surmounted by finials. The type suspended on posts appears to have been introduced into England at about this date, though it is found somewhat earlier in French inventories.

Princely cradles reproduced in miniature the magnificence of state beds; they were often elaborately painted, and in inventories of the French Crown these *berceaux de parement*, or ornamental cradles, often occur. Among the jewels and furniture reclaimed from England as having belonged to Isabel of France before her marriage to Edward II were a cradle of gold and another described as of silver, 'bel et gracieux'. The coverings were often exceedingly costly, and are occasionally mentioned in medieval inventories and domestic accounts. Margaret of Flanders, aunt of Edward IV, bought a cradle for her children, of which the making and decoration were entrusted to different artists. It was painted, inlaid and furnished by Jehan de Néauville, draper, of Paris, who supplied a coral-coloured counterpoint, a furrier adding to its adornment 1,200 ermine skins.

The children of princes and great nobles were often provided with two cradles, one 'a cradell of estate', the other for ordinary use. A manuscript in Leland's *Collectanea* (1552), but probably of 15th-century date, contains a detailed description of both varieties. It opens with an account of 'Things that must be had for the Princes Boddy',—'Pillowes', 'Pane' or ermine-trimmed coverlet of velvet, and cloth-of-gold. The 'litell Cradell of Tre' is to be mounted 'on a Forme', the woodwork being 'imbroderyd and paynted with fyne Goulde, and devised'. It is to measure 1¼ yds. in length, and, in breadth, 12 ins., with 'IIII Pomelles of Silver and gylte, II like Pomelles for the same Frame; V Bokelles of silver on eyther side the cradle without Tonges, for the swadle Bands'. The 'cradell of Estate' is to be larger: 5 ft. in length and 2½ ft. wide, 'coveryd with crymson cloath of Goulde'. It is to have pomells, or finials,

1. *Oak Cradle, traditionally that of Henry V as a child; box formed of moulded boards, pegged together, and buttressed uprights surmounted by long-tailed birds. Late 15th century. Ht. 2 ft. 10 in., L. 3 ft. 2 in., Depth 1 ft. 8 in. (By gracious permission of H.M. the Queen.)*

2. *Carved oak Cradle, said to have been used for James I; turned rocking-posts; the sides inlaid with a chequer pattern in holly and box. c. 1580. (From the Earl of Mar and Kellie.)*

3. *Hooded Cradle, covered with crimson velvet, fringed and panelled with galon studded with gilt nails. First quarter of the 17th century. (Badminton, Gloucs.)*

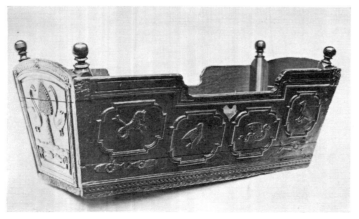

4. *Oak Cradle, carved with birds and fabulous monsters enclosed in shaped panels. c. 1605. (The late Mrs H. Cordes.)*

like its fellow, the coverings being almost identical; but here the pomells are to be 'gylte with the King and Queenes Armes'. Cradles were put within the curtains of the bed at night, which at that period frequently stood in an alcove. In *Piers Plowman* (earliest text 1362), Langland writes of the mother 'wakynge a nyghtes . . . to rocke the cradel', and a miniature in the 14th-century *Romance of Alexander* shows a cradle standing beside a bed within easy reach of the mother's hand.

The cradle seen in Fig. 1 is probably the only Gothic specimen in existence. It came originally from Courtfield, Monmouthshire, and as Henry V was born in Monmouth in 1388 and sent to Courtfield to be nursed, tradition has associated it with the infancy of that king; the cradle, however, is of late 15th-century date. The box, formed of moulded boards pegged together, is attached to the uprights by rings and iron staples. These posts are surmounted by long-tailed birds, the feathering being faithfully rendered, and the buttresses are carved with trefoil decoration in Gothic style. Probably a strap was laced through the large holes below the top to secure the child. This cradle was several times engraved in the 18th century, when a fabulous antiquity was ascribed to it. Horace Walpole (August 15, 1774) writes that near Gloucester he 'found in a wretched cottage, a child in an ancient oaken cradle, exactly in the form of that lately published from the cradle of Edward II'. He bought it for 5s., but doubted whether he would 'have fortitude enough to transfer it to Strawberry Hill'. In the *View of the Wardrobe Stuff of Katherine of Arragon* there are two entries relating to a cradle which must have held Queen Mary when a baby, thus dating from the first quarter of the 16th century, for she was born in 1516. The magnificence of the hangings shows that 'cradells of Estate' continued to be made for Royal children as in earlier times:

> Item, a ceelour, testour, and counterpoynte for a cradille paned of yalowe clothe of golde, and crymsene velvette lyned with grene bokerhame, havinge single valaunce fringid withe blewe and red silke myxid withe Venysse golde, withe IIII curteynes paned of red and blewe sarcenette, everye of them cont' in depthe one yarde III quarters, and in bredithe one yard quarter.

The second entry is concerned with mattresses, which were covered with holland cloth and 'filled with wulle'.

Cradles of the Elizabethan age show no important change in construction, for turned rocking-posts and even hoods are found represented in medieval manuscripts. The fine specimen shown in Fig. 2 is said to have been used by James I, though its style indicates a rather later date than the infancy of the King, who was placed in the care of Annabella Murray, Countess of Mar and wife of the Regent, in 1566. It has a turned rocking-post at each corner, and the back is headed by a carved lunette; the sides are inlaid with a chequer pattern in holly and box, the base is carved with bold gadroons, and the rockers are shaped. The turned knobs on which the bedding was usually hung are, in this instance, replaced by iron staples. An oak cradle at Hatfield House, Hertfordshire, bears the initials 'A.R.', and these initials probably stand for Anne of Denmark, wife of James I. Fig. 4 was also probably made in the early years of that king's reign and is exceptional in both form and decoration. The rockers are missing, but rocking-posts are set within the framework. On both sides

5. *Hooded oak Cradle; top rail carved with grotesque dolphins, geometrically moulded sides centring in a mask. c. 1640. (J. Thursby Pelham Coll.)*

6. *Hooded oak Cradle, decorated with shallow carving, bosses and applied pendants. Back bears date 1663 and the sacred monogram. Ht. 2 ft. 9 in., L. 3 ft. 4 in., Depth 1 ft. 7 in. (Lygon Arms, Broadway.)*

birds and fabulous monsters decorate the shaped panels, and at the head two swans are carved on either side of a cone-shaped tree and there are fishes in the water below. Many cradles were also made of wicker, but, owing to their perishable nature, have long since disappeared. They are often represented in pictures by Nicholas Maes and other Dutch artists, while Evelyn records that in England rural householders used plaited lime twigs in the manufacture of cradles.

In Elizabethan inventories rooms specially set apart for children's use are occasionally mentioned. There was a 'nurserye' in Sir William Ingilby's house at Padsidehead in 1583, and another at Ingatestone, Essex, a few years later. The Shuttleworths of Gawthorpe bought 12 yards of frieze 'for cradle blankets' in January, 1613, and early in Charles I's reign the steward at Naworth paid 28s. 7d. for a red flannel cradle cloth with gold lace 'for Mr Thos. Howarde's child'. Like their elders, children were half buried under a mountainous pile of bedclothes, for a high temperature in the nursery and an absence of ventilation were considered indispensable to health. Evelyn (*Diary*, January 27, 1658) writes that his 'deare son', aged five, died on that day, in his opinion, 'suffocated by ye women and maids that tended him, and cover'd him too hot with blankets as he lay in a cradle near an excessive hot fire in a close room'.

Fig. 3 shows a hooded cradle of traditional form, but in this apparently unique example the entire surface is covered with crimson velvet fringed and panelled with galon studded with gilt nails. Turned wood rocking-posts are here replaced by 'pomelles' covered with velvet. A cradle belonging to Charles I, and sold after his death, probably resembled this specimen. It is described in the inventory drawn up by order of the Council of State as 'covered with carnation vellvet', and it realised £3 10s. Fig. 5, with gabled hood, geometrical mouldings, and top rail covered with grotesque dolphins, is a fine specimen of this time. It was a much plainer cradle of

which Mary Verney contemplated the purchase in 1647, when her son Ralph had just been sent home to Claydon from abroad. Writing to Roades, the steward, from London, she tells him to 'speak to Mrs Allcock to lett the nurse have a cradle; one of the worst will sarve her turne and a hard pillow'.

In Fig. 6 the back bears the date 1663, with the sacred monogram headed by a cross, a very unusual ornament on a 17th-century cradle and one that suggests that its original owners were Roman Catholics. In September, 1666, just after the Great Fire, Sir Ralph Verney, asked to find a cradle for a relative who was expecting an addition to his family, could hardly discover one, 'such things being very deare now, as all

7. *Hooded oak Cradle with fielded panels. Early 18th century. (Brede Church, Sussex.)*

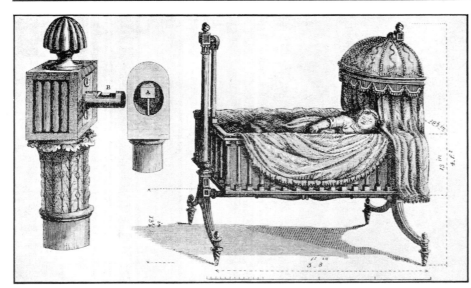

8. *Design for 'a Swinging Crib Bed', from Sheraton's* Cabinet Dictionary, 1803.

1. *Oak Cupboard of 'Credence' type; originally fitted with a canopy and projecting base; panels carved with bunches of grapes and vine leaves. c.* 1540. (*From Mr Murray Adams-Acton.*)

their stores are burnt'. In Fig. 7 the panels are fielded in the early 18th-century manner, the shape of the hood being also characteristic of that time. A passage in *Lady's Delight* (1715) shows that cradles supported on posts in the medieval fashion were in use at the end of Anne's reign. Children 'when they cry or feel Pain, or will not sleep are to be pacified . . . or singing or by rocking in cradles or hanging beds'.

In the middle of the century there was a noticeable change in the design of such furniture. Few counterparts of the solid oak cradle appear to have been made in mahogany; and wicker, which we know to have been used for this purpose under the Tudors, was then generally employed in the manufacture even of royal cradles. This change was probably due to hygienic causes, as the destruction after illness of this lighter variety did not entail serious sacrifice. The royal accounts contain several entries for cradles, supplied by Catherine Naish for the numerous children of George III. In 1766 she charged £13 2s. 'ffor a superfine split wicker cradle very large, a Pair of neat mahogany Rockers to do with carved Roses'; the next year she supplied another at the same cost. At the end of the century the majority of important cradles were of the swing-cot type, often surmounted by a hood, and with the sides formed of turned columns and panels of canework. In his *Cabinet Dictionary* (1803) Sheraton illustrates 'a Swinging Crib Bed' (Fig. 8). The name has been 'given to the swinging beds lately contrived to lull infants to sleep with'. He observes that a plainer variety is made by Mr Holinshade, of King Street, Drury Lane, who, instead of a dome, uses a waggon top. The diagram is intended to explain the mechanism, the cradle being swung by means of a clock spring (A), which hooks on to B, 'an iron center screwed to the standard'. This device was apparently borrowed by Sheraton from Holinshade, also of King Street, Drury Lane,

who informed him that in a little time he would have so improved it that the cradle would swing by itself for an hour and a half. An example which swings for twenty minutes is in the Victoria and Albert Museum. George Smith's *Household Furniture* (1808) shows a crib in Gothic taste 'suitable to many mansions in this country and should be of mahogany or oak, the enrichments carved either plain or gilt; the furniture cotton or silk'.

CREDENCE (Italian *credenza*). Side-table on which vessels were placed before being served at table; use in 1565 (cited in *New Eng. Dict.*): 'when the Pope is sitting at the table, the noblest man within the court . . . shall be brought to the Pope's credence to give him water' (Jewel, *Defence of the Apology*, 1611, p. 377). Not apparently used in any English domestic records, and now obsolete (except for the table by an altar for the elements before consecration). Cupboard on legs or uprights made in the Middle Ages and in early Renaissance times in France, but a type of great rarity in England. In 'credence' of English origin (Fig. 1) the panels are carved with grapes, vine leaves and Tudor roses.

CRESTING. Carved decoration above the top rail of a chair, settee or day-bed; also the ornamental detail surmounting cabinets, mirrors, picture-frames, etc. The cresting on Stuart walnut chairs was often very elaborately carved (*see* CHAIRS; Fig. 33); it was omitted in plain walnut and mahogany chairs and settees, but was an important central decoration on the top rail of more elaborate seat furniture of the rococo period (*see* CHAIRS; Fig. 106). From the reign of Charles II onwards there was a great variety of ornamental crestings on mirrors.

CREWEL-WORK. Embroidery of fine worsted with which bed-hangings and ornamental cloths were often worked in the

16th and 17th centuries. 'A carpet cloth of crewells, which is of divers colours, and in the middest and eyther end wrought over with goulde' (will of Lady Elizabeth Askwith, 1608). In the Victoria and Albert Museum there is a set of crewell-embroidered bed-hangings dating from c. 1650.

CROCKET or **CROCHET.** Ornament from Gothic architecture, often found in medieval woodwork (*see* top centre panel, CUPBOARDS, FOOD; Fig. 2). Of various forms, sometimes enriched with carving, but generally ending in a curve or roll. Crockets formed of two short scrolls in juxtaposition were often introduced on the curved front legs of 17th-century X-shaped chairs.

CROFT. Small writing cabinet. The example in Fig. 1, made by the firm of Seddon, bears the explanation on the maker's label that the cabinet was 'called a croft from a gentleman who first directed them to be made' (Rev. Sir Herbert Croft, Bt., 1757-1816). The label also enumerates the various advantages claimed for these pieces, among them that of 'communicating an early turn for something like order and regularity'; they may at any time 'be moved up stairs or down, without disturbing any of the papers they contain: they may easily be moved on a porter's head. . . .' The use of eight or ten crofts is contemplated in large libraries.

CROSS-CUT BANDING or **CROSS-BANDING.** Border of veneer in which grain runs across band; treatment adopted on drawer fronts of Charles II walnut furniture and continued throughout the 18th century in a variety of woods. (*See* CONSTRUCTION.)

CUIR BOUILLI. *See* LEATHER.

CUPBOARD CLOTHS. From the Middle Ages until the Late Stuart period tables and various forms of cupboards were generally covered with ornamental cloths. In 15th-century illuminated manuscripts silver vessels are sometimes shown arranged on the top of a dresser or aumbry spread with a cloth of white diaper or damask, the ends of which fall down on either side. John Russell (*Boke of Nurture*, c. 1440) recommends the butler to 'cover thy cuppeborde . . . with the towelle of diapery'. A variety of rich materials was used for this purpose in the Tudor period. Katherine of Aragon's inventory (c. 1533) mentions a large number of table carpets and cupboard cloths, the following being among the less elaborate:

> A cupboarde clothe of velvette of sundrye colours, wroughte carpettwise, cont' in lengthe II yardis quarter and in bredithe one yarde di.

Others more magnificent are fully described in the inventories of Henry VIII. In the 17th century, Turkey work, arras, worsted and embroidery appear to have been the favourite materials.

CUPBOARDS, PRESSES AND WARDROBES. In this section are included receptacles enclosed by doors, and those with a cupboard above and drawers in the lower portion. The modern term 'cupboard' has gradually acquired such a comprehensive significance that, to enable their respective evolutions to be followed conveniently, the principal varieties are treated under separate headings. (*See* CUPBOARDS—CORNER, COURT, FOOD, HALL AND PARLOUR, LIVERY and STANDING.) Receptacles enclosed with doors were generally

1. *Mahogany Croft or filing cabinet. c. 1790.*

known as aumbries in the Middle Ages, the cupboard being an open structure of shelves or 'bordes' on which to set cups. Many passages in medieval literature prove that it was primarily intended for display. In John Russell's *Boke of Curtasye* (c. 1450) there are directions for arraying the cupboard with plate; and in an account of the ceremonies used on the 'taking of her chamber' by Elizabeth of York, wife of Henry VII, we are told that the room contained a 'riche cupborde well and richly garnyshed', *i.e.* with flagons and spice plate set out on the shelves.

In the second half of the 15th century 'cupboards with aumbries' begin to appear in inventories, the description implying that part of the open shelves was enclosed by doors; and early in Henry VIII's reign, the term 'cupboard' was sometimes applied to what had hitherto been known as an aumbry. In the inventory (1527) of Cardinal Wolsey's possessions, no fewer than 21 'cupboards of Waynescote' are listed, 'whereof V be close cupboards', *i.e.* enclosed. But the old meaning of the word did not become obsolete until the 16th century was well advanced. In Elizabethan inventories aumbries, cupboards and presses are sometimes found used as apparently interchangeable terms.

By the end of James I's reign 'close' or 'joyned' cupboards with solid doors had become plentiful in large houses, and a number are listed in the inventory taken at Walton for Sir Thomas Fairfax (1624). Such cupboards, when fitted either with shelves for linen or pegs to hang clothes, were known as 'presses' or 'pressours', a term of considerable antiquity applied in the Middle Ages to a variety of aumbry, Chaucer's Miller having 'his presse covered with faldyng reed'. In 16th-century literature presses are generally mentioned in connection with the owner's wardrobe; towards the end of that century they figure constantly in inventories, and it is noticeable that, unlike cupboards intended for display, they are seldom or never stated to have been made of walnut. Among the linen and

1. *Interior of a physician's house showing two 'Joyned Cupboardes,' or aumbries; from a translation of the* Liber de Proprietatibus *written at Bruges for Edward IV. c.* 1480. (*Brit. Mus. Royal* 15E II, f. 165.)

goods that the owner of a well furnished house at Cockenden 'fownde' after the death of his wife in 1610 was 'a fayere wainscott presse to hang thereon clothes, with the lock and key'. At Ingatestone, Essex, in 1600, Sir William Petre had cupboards of this kind in almost every room, 'the great ioyned presse to sett in plate' having shelves and four doors in the lower portion fitted with locks. Presses sometimes formed part of the panelling, as at Ingatestone; where, however, these fixtures were greatly outnumbered by the movable variety.

The manuscript illustration in Fig. 1 is from a translation of *Liber de Proprietatibus*, written in Bruges by Jean du Ries for Edward IV. Two 'joyned cupboardes' are shown in the house of a physician, the one on the right having its lower stage filled with linen-fold and corresponding to the 'cupborde Wth an Aumbry'.

On the Continent, hanging cupboards or *armoires* are found, panelled with linen-fold or carved in Renaissance manner, with profile heads, dolphins and foliated arabesque; but examples of indubitable English origin do not appear to have survived. One of the 'great ioyned presses' of the 16th century, obviously intended for linen or clothes, may be seen in Fig 2. Filleted stiles intersect the panel mouldings, the proportions of the latter being still almost Gothic; the wide rail dividing the piece into stages affords additional evidence that the press was not made long after 1550. Presses fitted with drawers were already known in Henry VIII's reign, and one owned by the King was 'made with drawing tilles full of evidences' relating to the estates of Sir Nicholas Carew, and 'other mens landes'. The exact cost (£3 0s. 8½d.) of making a large oak cupboard with the interior entirely occupied by rough boxes is given in *The Chamberlains' Accounts of Stratford-on-Avon* in 1594. This 'cubborde of boxes', made, no doubt, for the muniments

of the Corporation, is now in Shakespeare's birthplace. An inventory (1601) at Chatsworth, Derbyshire, mentions 'a cubberd with tilles' in the 'high gatehouse chamber', which was probably of similar construction. At this date, 'cupboard' and 'presse' were often used as interchangeable terms, and it is not possible from inventories to determine the character of the receptacle described.

The next group shows a variety of oak 'wainescott cuboardes'. Fig. 3, one of the 'great pressours' of this age, is of unusual interest, because it is made of pearwood and carved with remarkable finish. It is enclosed by two doors divided into four tiers of panels. The frieze, carved with vases containing conventional flowers, has in the centre of the left-hand panel the head and bust of a man wearing a ruff and pointed beard. This is balanced on the right by an oval boss carved with the arms of Dormer impaling Clifford. The delicate enrichment of the arches and spandrels in the arcade is contrasted with bolder strapwork below.

In another press of c. 1650 (Fig. 4) the upper portion forms a hanging cupboard which extends behind the lower range of panels, an arrangement intended to exclude dust. The frieze bears the names of Henry Croxton and Isabel Croxton, and on the panels strapwork ornament is ingeniously varied; the drawers in the lower portion were originally fitted with yew knobs, corresponding to long pegs of the same wood generally found in the interiors of such pieces. Fig. 5 structurally resembles earlier presses, having drawers and a lower range of panels, decorated with shallow carving. By country craftsmen

2. *Oak Press; panelled doors with filleted stiles; cornice not contemporary. Second half of* 16th century. (*Ockwells Manor, Berks.*)

3. *Press of pearwood; doors divided into four tiers; in the frieze a male bust and a boss with arms of Dormer impaling Clifford. c. 1625. (Messrs Acton Surgey.)*

4. *Oak Press, for clothes, with two drawers at base; frieze bears the names of owners; panels carved with strapwork. c. 1650. (Ockwells Manor, Berks.)*

cupboards and presses of this character were made until much later and were by no means invariably of oak. Fig. 12 is an example in applewood, probably dating from c. 1750; the ventilation in the upper doors indicates that this portion was used to contain food. A combined settle and bacon cupboard was one of several hybrid forms of furniture that attained a certain popularity in cottages and farmhouses about this time. In such pieces there are cupboard doors with fielded panels in both back and front, two deep drawers being fitted below the seat.

The decoration of 17th-century presses was generally confined to carving, but examples are sometimes found in the west of England with friezes picked out in colour, a survival of the medieval practice of painting woodwork. Among Charles I's possessions sold by order of the Commonwealth was a press covered with leather embossed. Walnut cupboards decorated with marquetry are extremely rare, but Fig. 6 shows an example which at one time formed part of the furniture in the Admiralty, Whitehall. The pediment centres on a royal crown, swords of office and an anchor, this insignia probably marking the restoration of the Duke of York (later James II) to his office of Lord High Admiral in 1684, which he had been forced to resign on the passing of the Test Act in 1673. The cupboard is elaborately inlaid with large sprays of acanthus, flowers and amorini in varied shades of brown and yellow. The pilasters cleverly represent the applied twists often found on furniture at this time, a treatment repeated on the inside of the doors. The lines of the piece are clumsy and the cutting of

5. *Oak Press with cupboard doors and drawers; foliated scrolls and conventional ornament. c. 1670. Ht. 5 ft. 11 in., L. 5ft., Depth 1 ft. 8 in. (Fred Skull Coll.)*

6. *Walnut Wardrobe on arcaded stand with drawers; inlaid throughout with holly and brown woods on an ebony ground; doors similarly decorated on inner sides. Made for James II when Duke of York (probably by Dutch immigrant craftsmen), and formerly in the Admiralty, Whitehall. c. 1685. Ht. 8 ft., L. 6 ft. 3 in., Depth 1 ft. 10 in.*

7. *Wardrobe veneered with walnut on a foundation of oak; double-hooded cornice. c. 1710. (Col N. R. Colville.)*

8. *Mahogany Cupboard; broken pediment supported on carved corbels; pilasters faced with pendants finishing in tasselled drapery. c. 1735. (Mereworth Castle, Kent.)*

9. *Mahogany Cupboard with fielded door panels; cornice centres in a lion's mask and paws; gadrooned stand with paw feet. c. 1745. (Percival Griffiths Coll.)*

10. *Mahogany Cupboard, composed of a centre and two wings, containing eight doors; the cornice and pediment deeply moulded c. 1750.* 11. *Oak Wardrobe with two doors in upper portion and drawers below; frieze carved with key pattern; fielded panels flanked by angle columns. c. 1740. Ht. 6 ft. 10 in., L. 5 ft. 6 in., Depth 1 ft. 8½ in. (Hardwick Hall, Derbys.)* 12. *Cupboard of applewood; shaped cornice, octagonal door panels; upper portion ventilated for food. Mid-18th century. (Messrs Morris and Co.)*

the marquetry somewhat coarse, and while the insignia must be regarded as strong evidence of native origin, Dutch influence is strongly marked.

In the first half of the 18th century cupboards often formed part of the painted deal panelling of rooms in large houses, this arrangement tending to supersede the heavy oak presses hitherto employed. Very few walnut presses appear to have been made, but Fig. 7 with a double-hooded cornice is veneered with that wood on oak. Mahogany cupboards of this time are almost as rare. Fig. 8 was probably bought by John Fane for Mereworth Castle, Kent, c. 1736, when he succeeded his brother as seventh Earl of Westmorland. The pronounced architectural style accords with the character of the house, designed by Colin Campbell. In Fig. 9, of a decade or so later, architectural feeling is less pronounced. The fielded panels of the upper doors repeat the lines of the cornice, which centres on a lion's head and paws, while a boldly gadrooned stand carries out the animal motive; like contemporary bureaux, the piece is made in two divisions for convenience in transit, and brass handles are fixed to the sides. Oak presses and wardrobes were still occasionally made in the first half of the century, even for large houses, and Fig. 11 is an exceptionally distinguished example.

A large number of designs for clothes-presses are given in their pattern-books by Chippendale and his contemporaries, the type with doors in the upper portion, enclosing sliding shelves or trays, and drawers below, being more favoured than hanging wardrobes, which were usually simple. Fig. 15 is what Chippendale calls a 'commode clothes-press', *i.e.* a press 'with a commode pedestal part', an almost identical design (Fig. 14), dated 1754, being illustrated in the first

13. *Mahogany Clothes-Press probably by Giles Grendey; doors with serpentine fielded panels; stand richly carved with rococo ornament. c. 1750. Ht. 5 ft. 7 in., L. 4 ft. 1½ in. (V. & A. Mus.)*

14. (*Left*) *A 'Commode Clothes-Press', from a design by Thomas Chippendale. (Director, 1st ed., 1754, Pl. CII.)*

15. (*Right*) *Mahogany 'Commode Clothes-Press'; lower portion of* bombé *form; corners and feet elaborately carved in rococo taste. c. 1755. Ht. 6 ft. (Mr. John Newbould.)*

edition of the *Director*. The *bombé* form of the lower stage imposed an exacting task on the maker. A serpentine example (Fig. 16) also has its prototype in the *Director* (1st ed., Pl. CIII), the canted corners being decorated with lattice-work. In his notes Chippendale refers to this design as 'a Cloathes-Press in the shape of a Commode', a description no doubt based on the serpentine curves.

A clothes-press (Fig. 13), which may be attributed to Giles Grendey (*q.v.*), shows an attempt to exploit the decorative possibilities of this type of furniture. The cornice is enriched with a guilloche pattern, while the long sweeping lines of the raised serpentine panels are broken at the centres. This press is mounted on a stand with a scrolled convex apron, richly decorated with rococo motives on an incised diaper ground, a treatment characteristic of this maker. The interior is lined with cedar, the adjustable shelves and drawers below being also of that wood.

An example (Fig. 18), purely decorative in character, may

16. (*Left*) *Mahogany Clothes-Press; serpentine front, canted corners decorated with lattice-work, and wide bracket feet in Chinese taste. Based on a design in the Director, 1754. c. 1755. Ht. 6 ft., L. 4 ft. 2 in., Depth 2 ft. (Percival Griffiths Coll.)*

17. (*Right*) *Mahogany Clothes-Press; the panels mottled and framings decorated with paterae. c. 1765. Ht. 7 ft. 10 in., L. 3 ft. 6 in., (The Duke of Buccleuch.)*

18. *Mahogany Cupboard on lion-paw feet; frieze carved with swags of fruits and flowers; doors panelled with false drawers. Attributed to William Vile. c. 1760. Ht. 4 ft. 9 in., L. 4 ft. 7 in., Depth 2 ft. 3½ in. (Howard Reed Coll.) 19. Wardrobe, japanned in gold and silver on a green ground. By Thomas Chippendale. 1771. Ht. 5 ft., L. 4 ft. (Nostell Priory, Yorks.)*

be attributed to William Vile (*q.v.*). In design and character it resembles a set of cupboards in the private apartments at Buckingham Palace made by Vile for Kensington Palace. The swags of fruit and flowers on the frieze are most vigorously carved, and recall those on the bookcase made by Vile and Cobb for Queen Charlotte in 1762. (*See* BOOKCASES, Fig. 14).

When classical taste was fully established, paterae, husks, and honeysuckle ornament formed part of the decoration on elaborate hanging cupboards, while on presses an inlaid frieze was often surmounted by a swan-necked pediment. In Fig. 17 the construction suggests a hanging wardrobe, but the interior is fitted with shelves above four long drawers, the normal arrangement in such 'cloathes-presses'. Here the panels are formed of mottled Spanish mahogany and framed in delicate mouldings headed by spear-shaped points; in the paterae enrichments classical influence is already discernible, but the cornice and the wide bracket feet are still in the rococo style.

Few examples of japanned wardrobes survive, but there is one in the Chinese bedroom at Nostell Priory, Yorks., which Chippendale supplied for the room with other japanned furniture in 1771 (Fig. 19). The japanning is very accomplished, while classical detail (the fluted frieze and pendants of husks on the canted corners) is combined with chinoiserie decoration. The wardrobe (Fig. 21) is one of the pieces of japanned furniture made for Garrick's villa at Hampton-on-Thames, probably by Chippendale's firm. 'Japan'd' wardrobes are entered in the bills (1771-2) for furnishing the actor's house in the Adelphi. The treatment is purely classical, and there is a bookcase of very similar design among Adam's drawings in the Soane Museum. The fine cupboard in Fig. 24, one of a pair, is

again in the classical taste. Among the Adam drawings at the Soane is a 'Cloathes Press for the Earl of Coventry' dated 1764, of which the central portion is almost identical with these outstanding examples.

Chippendale's accounts show that he supplied many wardrobes and cupboards for bedrooms, and formerly at Mersham Hatch, Kent, there were inexpensive cupboards which were obtained from the firm in 1767. An example (Fig. 20) may be identified with one supplied by Chippendale for £10 10s., and described as 'a large Mahogany cloths press with folding doors and sliding shelves cover'd with Marble paper and Bays Aprons and drawers in the underpart'. The marble papers may still be seen in the interior. The firms of Gillow, Seddon and Shearer also probably made many such pieces.

In an inlaid clothes-press (Fig. 22) the figure of the mahogany is remarkable; the swan-neck pediment is perforated in Gothic tracery, the cornice is arcaded and the drawers are banded with satinwood. The presses shown in Hepplewhite's *Guide* (1788) have straight cornices and are of severe design. The author writes that they are 'of very considerable consequence, as the convenience experienced in their use make them a necessary piece of furniture; they are usually plain, but of the best mahogany'. This wood was not, however, invariably used, and as early as 1769 Chippendale and Haig supplied Sir Edward Knatchbull of Mersham Hatch, Kent, with 'a large commode clothes-press made of Black Rosewood', at a cost of £14 14s. It had folding doors, with drawers below, and the shelves were covered with marble paper. The presses made by this firm were sometimes very elaborately constructed, fine veneers and inlay being occasionally combined with japanned

20. (*Left*) Mahogany Clothes-Press with sliding shelves enclosed by doors; drawers below. Supplied by Chippendale and Haig to Sir Edward Knatchbull in 1767. (*Mersham Hatch, Kent.*)

21. (*Right*) Wardrobe of painted pine, made for David Garrick; the doors, enclosing hanging cupboards, are glazed. c. 1770. Ht. 8 ft. 3½ in., L. 5 ft. 5 in., Depth 2 ft. 3¼ in. (*V. & A. Mus.*)

ornament. In 1772 Garrick paid Chippendale and Haig for:

A very large Inlaid Press of Fustick and black Rosewood with sundry other ornaments. Curiously Inlaid with various fine woods, the middle part to hold a BED, the Ends for Shelves, Cloakpins, Night Tables, etc., enclosed with Doors, very neat Shap'd Doors with Carv'd ornaments, hung with pin hinges on Sliding parts Glaz'd with Looking Glass and Back'd with Mahogany, very neat carv'd Cornice. Japan'd to match the Fustick Wood, etc. £65 10.

Garrick's inlaid press cost nearly twice the sum charged by Chippendale for another 'very large mahogany cloathes press

of Exceeding fine wood in a commode-shape', which he supplied to Nostell in 1767.

The large wardrobes of this period consist of a clothes-press flanked by slightly recessed hanging cupboards. Sheraton (*Drawing Book*, 1791-4) describes the interior arrangements of these pieces thus: 'The upper middle part contains six or seven clothes press shelves, generally made about six or seven inches and a half deep, with green baize backed to the inside of the front to cover the doors with. The wings have each of them arms to hang clothes on made of beech with a swivel in their

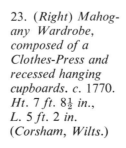

22. (*Left*) Mahogany Clothes-Press, inlaid with satinwood; Gothic tracery in pediment, cornice arcaded. c. 1770. (*Percival Griffiths Coll.*)

23. (*Right*) Mahogany Wardrobe, composed of a Clothes-Press and recessed hanging cupboards. c. 1770. Ht. 7 ft. 8½ in., L. 5 ft. 2 in. (*Corsham, Wilts.*)

24. (Left) Mahogany Cupboard on plinth, one of a pair; carved in neo-classic taste; based on a design by Robert Adam, 1764. (Formerly Combe Abbey, Warwicks.)

25. (Right) Mahogany Cupboard of elliptical form banded with satinwood; upper stage fitted with shelves and enclosed by tambour shutters. c. 1790. (Messrs Hotspur.)

centre which slips on to an iron rod fixed by plates screwed on to each side of the wings.' The cornice of Fig. 23 is surmounted by a lattice-work swan-necked pediment decorated with slender mahogany urns, and the drawers in the lower stage are serpentine. This example is of exceptional interest, for originally it formed one of the 'press bedsteads' advertised in 18th-century trade catalogues, the doors letting down to support the bedding (see BEDS, PRESS). The large wardrobe (Fig. 27) was supplied by the younger Thomas Chippendale in 1796 and is described in his bill. Here all the detail—the 'goloss in the

frieze and carved mouldings'—are atavistic in character, fully consonant with an earlier phase of the neo-classic style. The middle part is 'fitted up as a cloathes Press, the shelves lined, the Baize aprons and the front edges made of cedar . . . with Bramah's patent lock to the whole'. A cupboard (Fig. 25) is exceptional, for all the surfaces are curved, which demanded a high degree of skill in construction. The upper stage, fitted with shelves, is enclosed by tambour shutters of unusually large dimensions.

The taste for painted decoration affected presses and ward-

26. (Left) Satinwood Clothes-Press; lunette-shaped pediment and painted decoration. c. 1785. (Messrs M. Harris and Sons.)

27. (Right) Mahogany Clothes-Press; made by the younger Thomas Chippendale in 1796. (Harewood House, Yorks.)

28. *Mahogany Cupboard; fluted pilasters and arched centre; flanked by false drawers. c. 1755. Ht. 2 ft. 7 in., L. 4 ft., Depth 2 ft. 4½ in. (Ickworth Park, Suffolk.)*

robes, in common with other varieties of furniture, towards the end of the 18th century. Deal was generally used in their construction, the shallow pediments and ovals on the doors being picked out with arabesques and garlands of flowers in polychrome. Because it is of satinwood Fig. 26 is unusual. The examples illustrated in pattern books of the early 19th century

are designed in the Regency style. They were made in rosewood and mahogany inlaid with brass lines and ornamented with honeysuckle paterae of the same metal

The evolution of the clothes-press and wardrobe is largely explained by a change in the character of the garments they were made to contain. In Tudor and early Stuart times the padded trunk hose, doublets and farthingales of fashionable society were suspended in presses such as Figs. 2 and 4, ruffs, hats and hose being kept in chests. When the costume, both of men and women, was made of thinner materials, which could be folded and laid away, drawers and sliders figured prominently in their construction, serving also to accommodate minor accessories such as shoes, ruffles and fichus. In the 18th century women's dresses could also be conveniently folded, for the hoop in which they were distended during the greater part of that period was removable, and however many the dresses, a single hoop would serve for all. At this period cupboards were also introduced into other pieces of furniture of table form for libraries and reception rooms. In one of these composite pieces (Fig. 28) the form is that of a library table with the front framed in fluted pilasters and the central cupboard flanked by false drawers. The spandrels of the central arch are carved with an interlaced acanthus, and the metalwork is unusually fine.

CUPBOARDS, CORNER. Cupboards made for the corners of a room and fitted with solid doors; those with the upper portion glazed for the purpose of displaying china are classified as cabinets (*see* CABINETS). That corner cupboards were known in the first half of the 17th century is

1. *Hanging Corner Cupboard; japanned black and gold on a red ground; curved cornice supported on columns; vase-shaped finials and cresting carved with fruit and flowers. c. 1700.*

2. *Hanging Corner Cupboard, veneered with burr walnut; curved moulded cornice, fluted pilasters. c. 1715. Ht. 3 ft. 11 in., L. 2 ft. 7½ in. (The late Mr. Martin Buckmaster.)*

3. *Hanging Corner Cupboard of pine painted and grained to resemble mahogany; gilt enrichments and floral pendants in polychrome. c. 1750. (Fred Skull Coll.)*

4. *Corner Cupboard in two stages; veneered and cross-banded with walnut. c. 1710. (Robert Frank Coll.)*

5. *Japanned Corner Cupboard on stand with cabriole legs, one of a set of four. c. 1715. (Messrs Phillips, Hitchin.)*

6. *Oak Corner Cupboard on stand with turned supports; fielded door panels. c. 1720. (Mrs Inman.)*

proved by a reference in Charles I's inventory to 'one little three cornered cupboard'; but they do not appear to have become general until the reign of William and Mary. At that time they were introduced as receptacles for china, particularly the novel and highly-prized tea services. Decorative Oriental porcelain and Dutch delft ware were displayed upon the tops of cabinets, scrutoires, chimney-pieces and shelves (*see* SHELVES), china in daily use being kept in small corner cupboards, to be under the supervision of the mistress.

The earliest examples are of the hanging variety and generally apanned. In 1699 Gerreit Jensen (*q.v.*) charged for 'polishing a corner cupboard in the late Queen's apartments at Kensington'; and in an inventory of the contents of that palace drawn up in the same year, 'two india Jappan corner cubborts with blacke carved feet' are entered as in the Queen's New Bedchamber. In the *Postman* (March 8-10, 1711), Isaac van den Helm, a Dutch cabinet-maker resident in London, offers corner cupboards for sale; but by then this variety was fully naturalised in England. Fig. 1 shows a fine example made about the time of Anne's accession. The doors, framed in pilasters, are decorated by an accomplished hand; the hooded cornice and vase-shaped finials recall the design of contemporary scrutoires, while the cresting is vigorously carved. In the early 18th century many of these japanned cupboards were surmounted by a tier of shaped shelves for china, while

those in the interior were of serpentine outline. Japanned corner cupboards were also made in two stages, and Fig. 5 shows one of a set of four made for the angles of a room and mounted on stands, a very exceptional feature. Here there is a pedimented upper section enclosed by a door faced with a mirror plate above a double tier of drawers. The decoration is in gold relieved by touches of brown and black on a green ground. Lady Grisell Baillie in 1715 purchased a 'Japan corner cupboard', probably of this type, for it is stated to have had 'a table fixt to it'; while contemporary walnut examples (Fig. 4) were sometimes designed with convex fronts, straight cornice or broken pediment. In Fig. 2, of the hanging variety, the figure of the burr walnut veneer is remarkable, the hooded top being supported on fluted pilasters and the curves repeated on the fielded door panel.

In the early 18th century, corner and alcove cupboards often formed part of the deal panelling of rooms. 'Every corner', wrote Celia Fiennes, 'is improved for cupboards and necessaries, and the doors to them made suitable to the wainscot.' These alcoves provided an effective setting for china, and in wainscot rooms rendered movable corner cupboards superfluous. By c. 1750 glazed china cabinets were also becoming plentiful, and, consequently, corner cupboards, with the exception of one particular type, ceased to be fashionable. This type, derived from France and termed a 'coin', from the

7. *Mahogany Corner Cupboard in two stages; lattice-work pediment; canted corners fluted and headed by capitals. c. 1765. (A. H. Hannay Coll.)*

8. *Mahogany Hanging Corner Cupboard; fluted pilasters and inlaid frieze of satinwood; fillets of fielded panels also of satinwood. c. 1785. Ht. 4 ft. 5 in., L. 3 ft. 4 in., Depth 2 ft. 10 in. (A. Dunn Gardner Coll.)*

French *encoignure*, was a corner cupboard on legs, with a superstructure of graduated shelves. Ince and Mayhew (*Universal System*, 1759-63) illustrate two designs for 'Encoineurs', which are convex below and with an upper stage consisting of four diminishing shelves. In the gallery at Strawberry Hill, Horace Walpole had two 'coins of old Japan', and early in George III's reign Lady Mary Coke wrote to a correspondent expressing regret that the 'coins' she ordered before going to Vienna do not resemble the commode chest of drawers and must be sent back.

By country carpenters corner cupboards were made throughout this period on traditional lines, with doors hung on 'H' hinges and shelves shaped in the early manner. For the construction oak, pine and a variety of other woods were used, the interiors being almost invariably painted dull red or pale green. A chest of drawers sometimes forms the lower portion of those in two stages, while in another type of standing cupboard the front opens as two long doors, and the back is curved to fit a recess. Such examples generally present a medley of styles and are difficult to date. Corner cupboards do not figure in 18th-century trade catalogues, but they were occasionally made in the prevailing taste. Fig. 3 has a broken pediment centring on a vase with perforated ornament below of rococo character; the heading of the central panel is serpentined, and the stiles are decorated with pendants of fruit and flowers painted in their original natural colours. An unusually fine example in two stages (Fig. 7) has a swan-neck pediment filled with a Gothic fret, wide canted corners fluted and headed by composite capitals and paterae ornament.

In the second half of the century this variety of furniture was mainly confined to cottages and farmhouses, thus remaining almost unaffected by the development of successive fashions. The influence of contemporary taste is, however, perceptible in the shells and paterae with which late specimens are often decorated. In Fig. 8 not only are the frieze and fluted pilasters of satinwood, but the traditional fielded panels are relieved by satinwood fillets. A shell inlaid on the centre of the door and small chequer borders are typical at this time of country-made pieces, in which friezes and bandings of mahogany often decorate an oak structure. Like their predecessors, Regency designers do not illustrate corner cupboards, and in the early years of the 19th century production was confined to the provinces, where examples, coarsely carved and inlaid, continued to be made by country craftsmen.

CUPBOARDS, COURT. The term until lately has been erroneously applied to the cupboard in two stages with an overhanging canopy supported on columns (*see* CUPBOARDS, HALL AND PARLOUR; Figs. 5 and 7); but the evidence from inventories is conclusive that the type of sideboard in three tiers was known to its original owners as a court cupboard.

In the medieval and early Renaissance periods the cupboard was an open framework, a 'borde' upon which to set cups (*see* INTRODUCTION and CUPBOARDS, PRESSES AND WARDROBES), and though in the second quarter of the 16th century the word began to acquire its modern significance, it was still often applied to a structure formed of superimposed shelves.

The term 'court cupboard', which begins to appear in inventories towards the end of Elizabeth I's reign, seems to have been derived from the French *court* and the epithet 'short'

1. *Walnut Court Cupboard carved and inlaid; the friezes open as drawers. c. 1590. Ht. 3 ft. 11 in., L. 4 ft. 2 in., Depth 1 ft. 6 in. (V. & A. Mus.)*

2. *Oak Court Cupboard, shelves supported on square columns; carved lion masks and inlaid geometrical patterns. c. 1600. Ht. 3 ft. 10½ in., L. 4 ft., Depth 1 ft. 4 in. (Mr G. L. Riley Coll.)*

is obviously applicable to sideboards of the type here illustrated. They are rarely above about 4 ft. high, and lower than the presses in two stages that have been confounded with them in modern nomenclature. (*See* CUPBOARDS, HALL AND PARLOUR.) Such cupboards are mentioned generally in a connection which shows they were used for the display of plate; while references to a 'myddle bottom' or a 'lowe bottom' imply the middle or lowest shelf of the open structure with three tiers. It is probably to this variety, rather than to the enclosed press, that William Harrison alluded when in 1587 he wrote that silver and pewter vessels for drink 'are seldom set out on the table, but each one, as necessity urgeth, calleth for a cup of such drink as him listeth to have, so that when he hath tasted of it, he delivereth the cup again to some one of the standers by, who . . . restores it to the cupboard from which he fetched the same'. In *Romeo and Juliet*, when the hall is cleared for revels, the servants are told to remove 'the court cupboard' and 'looke to the plate'; and in Chapman's *Monsieur d'Olive* (1606) there is a less familiar allusion to 'my court cupboard with its furniture of plate'. As early as 1575 two 'court cubbordes' in the Great Chamber at Lambeth Palace are described in an inventory of Archbishop Parker's goods as already 'olde'. In the Turret Chamber at Hardwick Hall, Derbyshire, in 1601 there was an inlaid court cupboard and 'a carpet for it of cloth of tyssue and black wrought velvet with red and white silk fringe', which would have been spread on the upper shelf; while 'a fayer court cubbered coloured redd and varnished with a drawer and cubberd cloth of Indyan stuff' was among the contents of a large house at Cockesden (1610). When the inventory of the possessions of the Earl of Northampton, the Lord Privy Seal, was drawn up (1614), 'A court cupboard of walnut-tree inlaid' in the Lower Library was valued at 15s.

In 1643 Cranborne Manor, Dorset, was plundered by the troops of Lord Hertford and Prince Maurice, and, among many valuables, six court cupboards were carried away. At Whitehall, during the Protectorate, there were 'two old courte cupboards in the late King's withdrawing room', these being reclaimed by Cromwell's family after his death. Such furniture was not confined to the wealthy classes. In a selection of the inventories of husbandmen, yeomen and artisans in a single county covering the first twenty years of the 17th century more than a score of court cupboards are listed (*Bedfordshire Records Society*, Publications XX, 1938).

The earliest examples of the sideboard type date from the last years of the 16th century. 'A courte cupboarde of wainscott wth a mydell bottom' in the Cellar Chamber at Ingatestone, Essex, in 1600 and two others in the Dyninge Parlor 'wth lowe bottoms' (or shelves nailed on the rails of the bottom stage) were clearly of this kind. In the inventory of Sir Francis Carew of Beddington, Surrey (1596), 'a court cubberd wth two drawers and lockes to them' is listed. These drawers were probably intended for knives and spoons, forks in the first half of the 17th century being still rarely used.

In Fig. 1, an example made of walnut, both friezes open as drawers which run in grooves (*see* CONSTRUCTION). Here the cornice is boldly carved with egg-and-tongue, the upper frieze being decorated with chequer pattern, and the bulbous supports are finely modelled. The top and middle shelf of such a court cupboard would have been carpeted, thus setting off the 'vessels of silver' which, Harrison writes, were to be found even in the houses of yeomen and farmers. In Fig. 4 the frieze centres on the pansy badge of the Fittons, who intermarried with the Newdigates of Arbury, and the supports are headed with fleurs-de-lys and a shield with the initials of the owner and the date 1607. In design and ornament Fig. 2

3. *Walnut Court Cupboard, sideboard type; the upper frieze supported on lions, the lower on winged gryphons. Dated 1606. (Ashmolean Museum, Oxford.)*

4. *Oak Court Cupboard; supports of upper stage headed by a fleur-de-lys and a shield bearing initials J. N. with date 1607; pendant below frieze bears the pansy badge of the Fittons. (Arbury Hall, Warwicks.)*

5. *Oak Court Cupboard; upper frieze inlaid with scroll patterns and supported on gryphons. c. 1610. (Christ Church, Oxford.)*

6. Oak Court Cupboard; cornice arched; traditional leaf ornament. c. 1640. Ht. 4 ft. 2 in., L. 3 ft. 11½ in., Depth 1 ft. 6½ in. (J. Thursby Pelham Coll.)

is an interesting departure, for the shelves rest on square columns with moulded bases and capitals, instead of on the usual vase-shaped supports. This example is of oak and fruitwood profusely inlaid with geometrical patterns. The lions' masks on the lower frieze are pierced laterally through their mouths, the centre mask serving as a clutch to open the drawer.

In a few examples grotesque animals or birds take the place of corbels and bulbous supports. The lavishly carved court cupboard of Fig. 3 has the upper stage supported on lions, each holding a scrolled shield. On one shield is the English rose, on the other the Scotch thistle, these emblems proving a date after James I's accession in 1603. The lower frieze, ornamented with lions' masks and elaborately carved with strapwork, rests upon winged gryphons, while the upper frieze and both shelves are inlaid. This remarkable cupboard is of walnut, oak being used for the internal structure.

In Fig. 5 the top shelf rests on lion-headed gryphons, while the middle platform is supported on the more usual cup-and-cover bulbs. The supports in Fig. 6, dating from towards the middle of the century, have become attenuated and are without decoration. The upper shelf is supported on depressed arches. In later specimens supports have dwindled to turned and ringed balusters, while in the carving there is a repetition of stereotyped patterns applied to the structure without regard to symmetry. Court cupboards of this character continued to be made into the early 18th century for yeomen and farmers, but among the prosperous classes they were superseded by side tables and alcove cupboards, or buffets, which served as repositories for plate, glass and china. (*See* BUFFET and TABLES, SIDE.)

CUPBOARDS, FOOD. A type ventilated in various ways for food. Illuminations in late medieval manuscripts, representing scenes in halls and chambers, show cupboards enclosed by doors pierced with tracery, the tops being draped with 'cupboard clothes' on which silver vessels are set out. Such cupboards are described in contemporary inventories as fitted with 'presses' or 'ambries'; for until after 1500 the term 'cupboard' retained its traditional meaning of a board on which to set cups (*see* CUPBOARDS, PRESSES, etc.). That the piercing of the panels was not merely decorative but intended for ventilation may be safely inferred.

The earliest surviving food cupboards date from the end of the 15th century and were, no doubt, used in the great hall or in the solar, the withdrawing-room of the heads of the household. Fig. 1 shows an example of eastern counties' provenance, a region in which continental influence was particularly strong. Here the front is divided into two tiers of panels by drawers or 'tilles' which slide in and out without runners. Three of the panels open as doors, those in the upper tier and in the roundel below being pierced, while all the panels are carved with tracery of remarkable delicacy, strongly reminiscent of the French flamboyant style. But the strap hinges and the two lock-plates, which have a pierced cresting, are of English workmanship. A celebrated standing cupboard for food, was found at a farmhouse at Burwarton in Shropshire (Fig. 2). The panels at the front, two of which form doors, are perforated in Perpendicular window tracery and devices of disputed significance. It has been suggested that the cupboard belonged to Arthur, Prince of Wales, because the devices on either side of the lower door resemble feathers, while the crocketed gable above perhaps represents the letter 'A'. The prince lived for a time at Tickenhall Manor, Worcestershire, not far from Burwarton, and also at Ludlow

1. Oak Food Cupboard; the panels carved with Gothic tracery; original iron mounts. Late 15th century. (Burrell Coll.)

2. (*Left*) *Oak Standing Cupboard for food; panels pierced and carved with tracery, a crocketed gable and devices resembling feathers. c.* 1500. *Ht. 5 ft. 4½ in., L. 4 ft. 1½ in., Depth 2 ft. (V. & A. Mus.)*

3. (*Above*) *Oak Standing Cupboard for food; panels and doors pierced and carved with foliated patterns, tracery and linenfold; carved underframing centres in a pendant. c.* 1530. *Ht. 4 ft. 2 in., L. 4 ft. 6 in., Depth 1 ft. 8 in. (Col. N. R. Colville.)*

4. (*Left*) *Oak Food Cupboard; door and flanking panels pierced in late Gothic tracery, and framed in channel mouldings; two shelves in interior. Early* 16th *century. Ht. 2 ft. 1 in., L. 3 ft. 2 in., Depth 1 ft. 6 in. (V. & A. Mus.)*

5. (*Below*) *Oak Splay-fronted Food Cupboard, carved and inlaid with chequer pattern; deep frieze supported on bulbous columns c.* 1610. (*Frank Partridge and Sons.*)

Castle, from the time of his marriage to Katherine of Aragon in November 1501 to his death in 1502—facts which give plausibility to the theory. Traces of vermilion colour are still discernible. Another food cupboard (Fig. 3) represents the same school of carving and was also found in a West-Country farmhouse. Still essentially Gothic in character, it dates from a time when Renaissance ornament had been already introduced. Three of the openwork panels in the upper stage are roughly carved with grapes and vine leaves; the doors are pierced with geometrical wheels, and the linen-fold is of a late variety. The spandrels of the underframing are filled with Gothic leafage. Both these cupboards have a moulded framework, but the food cupboard of Fig. 4 is formed of planks pegged together and finished near the edges by a rude channel moulding. In the side panels the two tiers

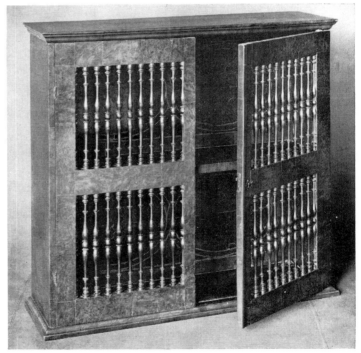

6. *Oak Food Cupboard; frieze supported on columns; panels of lower stage carved with cartouches. c. 1640. (Mallett and Sons.)*

7. *Oak Food Cupboard; cornice corbelled out; front and sides perforated, centre panel opening as a door. c. 1650. Ht. 2 ft. 10 in., L. 3 ft. 2½ in., Depth 1 ft. (Fred Skull Coll.)*

8. *Food Cupboard, veneered on oak with walnut; doors filled with finely turned balusters. Late 17th century. Ht. 3 ft. 1 in., L. 3 ft. 2½ in., Depth 11½ in. (A. Dunn Gardner Coll.)*

of late Gothic tracery are divided by a carved diaper of trefoil ornament.

Towards the end of the 16th century these food cupboards with openwork panels in the Gothic style were superseded by another variety made to hang against a wall, with turned spindles in the doors and framework carved and often inlaid in the Elizabethan manner. In Fig. 5 the front is splayed, both sides and rails being coarsely inlaid and the frieze out of scale with the remainder of the structure. About the mid-17th century another variety was made with a canopied super-structure for earthenware. In Fig. 6, a fine example of the more familiar type, the columns and vigorously carved strap-work cartouches are rare features, while the food cupboard in Fig. 7 is also exceptional. Later examples are generally of rough construction, but Fig. 8 is the work of a skilful joiner. It is veneered throughout with walnut, an extremely rare feature, the elegant turned balusters being also of that wood; on its inner surface the back is inlaid with boxwood ovals. Food cupboards of this kind are also found in churches, where they were used to contain bread distributed to the poor in accordance with the wills of charitable persons. At St

Albans Abbey there are two good examples, dating from Charles I's reign and still devoted to their original purpose.

In the 18th century this type was rarely made, being replaced by a larger variety, with the top portion ventilated for food, and by the combined settle and bacon cupboard, sometimes found in farmhouses.

CUPBOARDS, HALL AND PARLOUR. To desig-nate the varieties included in this section, the terms 'buffet' and 'court cupboard' have been used in recent times, but they are now proved to be misnomers (*see* CUPBOARDS, COURT). The evidence of inventories points to the conclusion that the varieties here grouped together were known to their

1. *Cupboard with a low superstructure for the display of plate.*
c. 1470. (From a French Manuscript in the British Museum.
Royal 15 E. II., f. 165.)

original owners as 'cupboards' or 'presses'. Though all those illustrated were obviously intended for use in living-rooms, halls and parlours, rather than bedrooms, the characteristic features, notably the bulbous cup-and-cover supports (which they share with the court cupboard), are not described in inventories, and it is, therefore, impossible to identify them in lists of household goods. For instance: 'Two fyne marketrie cupboards' entered in the inventory (1590) of Lumley Castle, Durham, were probably used in living-rooms, but whether they were open or enclosed by doors the description does not determine. These cupboards are divided into two groups: (1) those with doors and panels in the upper stage, and (2) those in which both stages are enclosed. The first type may be sub-divided into the straight- and splay-fronted varieties and is structurally closely related to contemporary court cupboards (*see* CUPBOARDS, COURT). It also suggests an evolution from the medieval cupboards on stands used for the display of plate (Fig. 1). Cupboards of this kind, fitted with an 'ambry' or 'presse', draped and with the plate set out on top, are often figured in late medieval manuscripts. The first example (Fig. 2) dates from about the end of Henry VIII's reign, and, unlike the majority of these polygonal 'cupboards wth aumbries', is probably of native origin, the character of the linen-fold panelling at the sides and the coarsely executed Renaissance ornament on the panels and doors supporting that inference. This cupboard represents the type to which the term 'credence' is now popularly applied without any contemporary authority (*see* CREDENCE). Fig. 3, of about the date of the Lumley inventory, corresponds with the many articles in that vast aggregation of furniture set down as being of 'walnutree and marquetree'. The frieze is inlaid with the favourite chequer pattern in ebony, holly and cedar; the doors and central panel, deeply recessed and set in the wide mouldings of the time, are decorated with simple geometrical designs in the

same woods and framed in corbelled-out stiles carved with acanthus. The stand has massive bulbous supports, the top rail being carved with a flat guilloche pattern. Oak is employed in the internal structure of this piece, as in the majority of walnut specimens. The upper portion of a cupboard which descended from the original owner, Sir Anthony Drury of Beesthorpe, Yaxham, Norfolk, to the late owner, Mr Robert Woodhouse, so closely corresponds in detail that it may be assigned to the same maker, and it affords a remarkable instance of a pattern duplicated by an Elizabethan craftsman (*see* 2nd ed. *D.E.F.*, Vol. II, 1954, p. 191, Fig. 4). For so late a date the straight-fronted cupboard of Fig. 4 is an unusually attractive example, with elegantly turned balusters and vigorously carved gadrooning on the lower frieze.

In splay-fronted cupboards the upper and lower friezes often open as drawers, an arrangement also found in court cupboards. Grotesque lions' heads form corbels to the upper frieze in Fig. 5, carving and inlay combining to produce a rich effect: the bold, vigorous handling of the Elizabethan age survives, but the conventional floral inlay (which has close parallels on chairs) indicates a date after 1600. The design of the lower stage is exceptional, cupboards flanked by pilasters providing additional space on either side of the deeply re-cessed central panel. The filling in of the space in that stage is alone requiredfor this example to correspond with the presses of the succeeding group—a difference in design which no contemporary inventory description could suggest. In Fig. 6, a late splay-fronted cupboard, the faceted ornament on the

2. *Oak Cupboard of polygonal form, carved with linen-fold and Renaissance ornament. c. 1540. Ht. 4 ft. 6 in., L. 4 ft. 1 in., Depth 2 ft. (Mr Murray Adams-Acton.)*

3. (*Above, left*) *Walnut straight-fronted Cupboard, inlaid with various woods. c. 1590. Ht. 3 ft. 10 in., L. 4 ft. 4 in., Depth 1 ft. 3½ in. (Macquoid Coll.)*

4. (*Above*) *Oak Cupboard with panels flanking a cupboard door; turned baluster supports, applied pendants; drawers gadrooned. c. 1630. (Quenby Hall, Leics.)*

5. *Oak splay-fronted Cupboard; cupboards flanked by pilasters in lower stage; inlaid with floreated scrolls and chequer pattern; drawer in frieze, grotesque lions' heads forming corbels. c. 1610.*

6. *Oak splay-fronted Cupboard; turned supports and faceted ornament; stretchers restored. Late 17th century. Ht. 3 ft. 9 in., L. 4 ft. 1 in., Depth 1 ft. 5 in. (Lygon Arms, Broadway.)*

friezes and panels, though carved in the solid, is reminiscent of the applied decoration so often found on furniture at this time.

The second, or entirely enclosed type, was certainly used in halls and living-rooms; and, since these presses or cupboards afford ample storage space and are fitted with shelves, in them

were doubtless kept cups, flagons and other silver vessels, which were taken out for display during meals. The canopied upper stage suggests an evolution from the more elaborate medieval dresser or plate cupboard (*see* DRESSERS), to which they are clearly related in proportion and general design. In early examples (as in the partly enclosed contemporary type)

7. (Left) Oak Hall Cupboard, dated 1610; panels in upper portion inlaid with geometrical designs; pilasters contrived as secret receptacles; cornice moulding not original. Ht. 5 ft. 4 in., L. 4 ft. 11 in., Depth 2 ft. 1½ in. (V. & A. Mus.)

8. (Right) Oak Hall Cupboard, carved and inlaid with various patterns; centre door flanked by grotesque caryatides. c. 1620. Ht. 5 ft. 5 in., L. 5 ft., Depth 2 ft. (W. Simpson Coll.)

the upper stage rests on bulbous supports and the carving is in the style of the later English Renaissance, inlaid decorative patterns being employed on the flat surface of the finer specimens.

In Fig. 7 the pilasters are contrived as secret receptacles, the capitals lifting up and the arcaded motif being repeated on the sides. A shelf is fitted midway in the interior of the lower stage, but the cupboard is open at the base, no boards having ever been fastened to the framework to form a bottom. The next example (Fig. 8) is some years later in date and much

more ornate, geometrical and chequered patterns figuring prominently in the inlaid decoration. The crudely rendered foliage on the frieze contrasts with the sharply cut and admirably disposed ornament on this member in Fig. 7. On the outer stiles flutes are combined with split balusters, an early instance of the use of such ornament. In Fig. 9 the upper stage centres on two arches flanked by plain panels in the doors. Here the supports are of yew, vigorously carved, their ruddy colour contrasting effectively with the darker oak. In the carving of Fig. 11, an unusually ornate specimen of

9. (Left) Oak Hall Cupboard, carved with various patterns; supports of yew; cornice moulding not original. c. 1625. (Ockwells Manor, Berks.)

10. (Right) Oak Hall Cupboard, dated 1658; turned pendants at corners of frieze; upper stage carved with conventional patterns. (Ockwells Manor, Berks.)

11. (*Left*) *Oak Hall Cupboard, richly carved with foliated scroll patterns; decoration of columnar supports an unnsual feature; cornice and plinth modern. Mid-17th century.* (*Late Mr W. J. Fieldhouse.*)

12. (*Right*) *Oak Hall Cupboard; frieze supported on tnrned balusters, and panels of upper portion conventionally carved; framework notched. c. 1675.* (*Late Mr Oliver Baker.*)

about the same date, foliated chain patterns the ingeniously varied. The decorated columnar supports are an exceptional feature, the introduction of a thistle on the upper doors suggesting a Scottish origin. Conventional carved ornament is confined to the upper stage in the Cromwellian court cupboard dated 1658 (Fig. 10) and the panelled lower portion has a door in the centre, thus departing from the normal arrangement. About this time turned pendants often take the place of the traditional supports, though a more slender type of baluster was also employed. In some Late Stuart examples the length

is greater than the height, decorative character being now sacrificed to the provision of storage space. Such cupboards were no longer fashionable, and among the wealthy classes after the Restoration they were largely replaced by walnut and japanned cabinets as ornamental furniture for halls and living-rooms. The division of the cupboard doors into one horizontal and two vertical panels is characteristic of this period, and may be also observed in Figs. 12 and 14.

This type continued to be produced by country craftsmen on traditional lines until a much later date, the conventional

13. (*Left*) *Oak Hall Cupboard of* 'tri-darn' *type, dated 1696; cornice moulded; middle shelf carved with a leaf pattern; upper doors fielded.* (*Late Mr Oliver Baker.*)

14. (*Right*) *Oak Cupboard of* 'tri-darn' *type, dated 1702.* (*Late Mr A. de Navarro.*)

15. *Oak Hall Cupboard* (Cwpwrdd Deuddarn); *the cornice with turned pendants. Cardiganshire. Mid-18th century. Ht. 6 ft., L. 4 ft. 6½ in. (Nat. Mus. of Wales.)*

An account of such a distribution is found in the *Liber Niger* (1483), where we are told that every retainer received 'for his Livery at night, half a chet loaf, one quart of wine, one gallon of ale; and for winter livery from All-Hallowtide till Easter, one percher wax, one candle wax'. A generation later Cavendish described the dispensing of liveries in his account of the splendid reception given by Wolsey to the Grand Master and Maréchal of France, who, with a retinue of 100 gentlemen-in-waiting, visited the cardinal at Hampton Court in October, 1527. While Wolsey talked to his guests after supper 'all their liveries were served to their chambers', and throughout the house every room was furnished with a lavish supply of silver vessels, together with a torch, a loaf of bread and a roll of the finest flour. Such provisions would have required a cupboard of considerable size. The ordinary livery consisted of bread, beer and candles; and Edmund Spenser, in his *View of the State of Ireland* (1596), uses the word in a still narrower sense, writing that in great Irish houses 'the liverye is sayd to be served up for all night, that is theyr nyghtes allowance of drinke'.

The liveries were kept in cupboards in the bedrooms that they might be available in the night, and from the early 16th century there are many references to 'livery cupboards', though no adequately informative descriptions. The building contract for Hengrave, Suffolk, in 1516 specifies that the hall is to be fitted with cupboards made without doors in 'ye facyon of livery'; but at that time livery cupboards were sometimes enclosed, *e.g.* 'a lyvery cupberd with II almeris' at The Vyne, Hampshire, in 1541; and others are sometimes stated to be fitted with locks and keys. At Ingatestone, Essex, in 1600 there were a number of these cupboards in the bedrooms, the tops covered with 'cloth of Turkey work' or some other material; one was of 'walnutree carved', while another, in 'Mr Petre's lodgings', had 'a bottom and two close cup-

ornament growing more decadent in execution. In the 18th century it was confined to simple incised patterns, while sometimes decoration was entirely dispensed with, the panels being fielded within a moulded framework (Fig. 15). In Wales the cupboard in two stages was known as a *cwpwrdd deuddarn* (two-piece cupboard), the later variety with a canopy supported on balusters and an extra shelf for the display of pewter and earthenware being termed a *cwpwrdd tridarn*—in three stages. They were produced in large numbers for all classes in a rural community and, save in details of ornament, varied little throughout the course of the century. It was customary to provide such cupboards as marriage gifts, or they were commissioned by the newly married couple. Many examples thus bear not only the initials of the owners but also the date of construction. The Welsh and border counties type is illustrated in Figs. 13 and 14. From early in the 18th century in England such pieces were gradually superseded by the familiar farmhouse dresser.

CUPBOARDS, LIVERY. Cupboards of this kind are often mentioned in inventories of the 16th and 17th centuries, but the descriptions do not afford sufficient evidence to determine their character. The term was derived from the allowance of food and drink—beer, bread, spiced wine and other commodities—which in great establishments were *livré*, or delivered out to members of the family, guests and retainers.

1. *Cupboard with canopy; the lower stage supported on turned balusters. Possibly a livery cupboard. c.* 1600. (*S. W. Wolsey Ltd.*)

boards' with locks and keys. A third was provided with a 'myddl pticon' (partition), and no fewer than six of these cupboards are stated to have had a 'bottom' or lower shelf. The aumbries and cupboards dating from the late medieval period to the second half of the 17th century and pierced with tracery or with turned balusters in the doors for the ventilation of the contents (*see* CUPBOARDS, FOOD) lack the bottom board and so do not accord with these descriptions. Probably one of the varieties so designated is represented in Fig. 1; but the evidence is not conclusive, and apparently more than one variety was so called. The sides of this cupboard are pierced with holes for ventilation. The turning indicates an early 17th-century date, though in the mouldings and door hinges with trefoil heads the Gothic tradition still lingers.

In the inventories of yeomen, husbandmen and artisans down to the Restoration, livery cupboards are often listed. A widow of Bury in 1649 bequeathed to her daughter 'a posted settwork bedstead and livery cupboard to it', the association of the two pieces of furniture implying that the cupboard contained food for consumption at night.

CUPBOARDS, STANDING. References to 'standinge cubbordes' are sometimes found in early inventories. Two examples to which the term is now popularly applied are illustrated under CUPBOARDS, FOOD (Figs. 2 and 3). An inventory of the contents of Howard House (1558) mentions 'a standinge cubbord havinge a curious carved frame of antiques with divers inlaid workes'.

CUPS (CUPPES). Stands to support plumes at the four corners of the tester of state beds introduced in the 16th century, and in beds of the late Stuart period generally of vase-shaped form (*see* BEDS; Figs. 15 and 18).

CURFEW. *See* CHIMNEY FURNITURE.

CURRICLE or **CURUL CHAIR.** Term used by Sheraton (*Cabinet Dictionary*, 1803) for a chair of classical pattern with semicircular back and elongated seat; *sella curulis* of the Roman senator no doubt suggested the original pattern.

CURTAIN CORNICES. *See* CORNICES, CORNISH.

CURTAINS. *See* HANGINGS.

CUSHIONS. Cases of woven stuff, leather or needlework stuffed with some material, such as hair, down or feathers. Round and square cushions, with tasselled corners gathered in at the sides, are often in early illuminated manuscripts shown arranged on benches and settles, the coverings generally matching the bed-hangings, and are found entered in medieval inventories and wills. In the hall of the Priory at Durham in 1446 were 'VI Quishons cum leonibus coronatis . . . scriptura de le Roi'. At Kenilworth Castle in 1583, apart from those on chairs and stools, 19 cushions are separately listed among the goods of the Earl of Leicester. Many were embroidered, as, for example, 'a large cushion of needlework, the grounde crimson silke wroughte with flowers, of gold, silver and greene silke, fringed with golde and silke, lyned with crimson satten, withe IIII buttons and tasselles at the corners'. It measured 1 yd. by 1 ft. 6 ins.

In great houses, in the 16th and 17th centuries, cushions were used for chairs and window seats and also on the floor. The inventories of Katherine of Aragon and Henry Fitzroy, Duke of Richmond (d. 1527) mention several sets of rich cushions, *e.g.*

> Item, foure square cusshyns, the outsides of everye of theme clothe of tissue, and the backsides pleyne clothe of golde, everye of theme cont' III quarters of a yarde square and upon theme alle VII knoppis withe tasselis of red silke and Venysse golde.

A large 16th-century example, in a fine state of preservation, is embroidered in relief on a satin ground with figures, animals, flowers and other motives (Fig. 1).

Damask and velvet were also favourite materials, while at Leicester House, in 1588, among many others, four square cushions are inventoried 'all of blacke and purple figured

1. *Cushion cover embroidered in coloured silks and silver-thread on a white satin ground. Late 16th century. L. 3 ft. 5 in., W. 1 ft. 10 in. (V. & A. Mus.)*

satin, and made of an old gowne of my Lady's'. The Hardwick Hall inventory (1601) shows that house to have been plentifully supplied with cushions for the chairs and window seats. They were of silk or velvet with fringes, tassels and buttons, the embroidery being very fully described. A number of these cushions still survive with the embroidery—figures, animals, birds, etc.—reapplied on later material.

Graduated sets of cushions, three or four in number, were often made for use on day-beds. Examples dating from c. 1600 can be seen at Hardwick, and a set embroidered in Queen Anne's reign was formerly at Quenby, Leicestershire. With the development of upholstered furniture in James I's reign, loose cushions diminished in number; those described in later inventories are comparatively plain. From the end of the 17th century they were covered with velvet, damask, needlework, tapestry and various other materials, striped silk being often used in the late Georgian period. They contributed greatly to the comfort of the luxurious sofas which became fashionable in the 18th century. Chippendale in the *Director* reminds the reader that they must not be omitted even when not shown in the design. For large sophas a bolster and a pillow at each end and also cushions at the back were provided.

CUSP (Lat. *cuspis*). Point or pointed end, term first applied by Sir J. Hall (*Gothic Architecture*, 1813) to 'small pointed ornament very common in Gothic windows'. Various forms of cusps in medieval architecture were reproduced on contemporary woodwork and furniture. Cusps as carved ornament revived c. 1750 during the ascendancy of the Gothic style; introduced by Chippendale and contemporaries into chair splats, crestings of cabinets and lattice-work of panels, etc. (*see* CABINETS; Figs. 43 and 48).

CYPRESS (*Cupressus sempervirens*). A native of Persia and the Levant, hard, very durable, reddish wood, close-grained and compact. In 1397 John of Gaunt bequeathed a 'little box of cypress wood' in his will, and in 1504 a widow of Bury left 'my coffyr of syprys'. Evelyn in *Sylva* mentions its use for chests: 'resisting the worm and moth and all putrefaction to eternity'. According to him (writing in 1664) cypress until lately was 'to be found only among the curious, whereas we see it now in every garden rising to as goodly a bulk and stature as most which you shall ever find in Italy'.

DAMASK. Silk figured fabric, largely used for hangings and upholstery; name derived from Damascus, which, in the 12th century, achieved world-wide reputation for the weaving of splendid patterned stuffs. Italy, Venice and Genoa were the chief European sources of supply until the late 17th century. This material was introduced into England in the early Middle Ages. By the sumptuary laws of Edward IV the wearing of it was prohibited to anybody below the degree of a knight, except the officers of the King's household.

Damask was sometimes used for the hangings of contemporary state beds. It is said to have been first manufactured in England c. 1570, when a number of Dutch and Flemish weavers settled here as a result of the Duke of Alva's ravages in the Low Countries. It appears that throughout the Tudor period damasks of various colours cost about 8s. a yard; while, in 1613, Sir Richard Boyle noted in his *Diary* that he had paid an upholsterer £3 for covering chairs, stools and 'a

window cusshen' with 5 yards of damask. The term by then was also applied to linen with a woven pattern in imitation of the silk (*Northumberland Household Books*).

Blue and red damasks were constantly used for the extravagantly upholstered beds of the late 17th century (*see* BEDS; Figs. 19, 21 and 22), such hangings being often imported, but also being woven at Spitalfields, Norwich and other places. By Charles II's time, English silk-weaving had become a flourishing industry. A proclamation for its encouragement was issued as early as 1638, damask being mentioned among the fabrics that were to be bought at home. After the Revocation of the Edict of Nantes (1685) letters of naturalisation were granted to a large number of Huguenot refugee silk weavers, who much improved the design of silk fabrics. References to damask hangings and upholstery constantly occur in contemporary literature, *e.g.* Celia Fiennes records that at Windsor (c. 1702) there were 'Damaske chaires and window curtaines' in the large dining-room; a half-tester bedstead in the King's bedchamber being hung with 'Crimson and Green damaske, inside and outside the same hangings'. Despite the excellence of Spitalfields silks, French and Italian damasks were still considered preferable by those who could afford them, as by the Duchess of Marlborough, who obtained patterns of yellow and green damask and ordered sufficient to make chair covers and window and door curtains all *en suite* in the Italian manner. She writes (1707): 'My Lord Rivers has two pieces making of yellow damask. He sent the pattern from England drawn upon paper. The only difference is that when it is a new pattern they must be paid for setting the loom.' As a result of the fashion for foreign materials, the bulk of the silk produced at home was sold as 'French make', whether this was actually the case or not.

Damask, imported or of native manufacture, remained in demand throughout the 18th century. Chippendale's bills contain numerous entries of damask covers and hangings supplied by him, or made up from material in his clients' possession. He charges Sir Edward Knatchbull of Mersham Hatch, Kent (October, 1772), £52 10s. for '150 yds of fine Blue Mix'd Damask at 7s.' For state beds this material was a favourite hanging. Ince and Mayhew (*Universal System*, 1759-63) write that a dome bed which 'may be esteemed among the best in England' was hung with blue damask and richly fringed. Figured mixed materials of silk and wool, or silk and cotton, and fabrics of figured worsted and cotton were also known as 'damask'.

DANSK (DANSKE, etc.). Danish, or, more frequently in a commercial context, from the city of Danzig and adjacent area. The term is often found in inventories, bills of lading, etc., of the 16th century and is also used in a generic sense for commodities of various kinds imported by the Eastland Merchants from Prussia and the shores of the Baltic, gradually replacing the earlier term of 'spruce' (*q.v.*). Allusions to Danske furniture, particularly chests and utensils, were abundant c. 1585-1625. In the will (1592) of a merchant of Newcastle-upon-Tyne, no fewer than eight 'Dannske Chiste(s)' are listed (*Surtees Society*, XXXVIII, pp. 215-17).

DARNIX, DORNECK, DORNIX. This coarse variety of woven fabric, made at Tournay in Flanders (of which the Flemish name was 'Dorneck'), was introduced into England in the 15th century and apparently used mainly for hangings. By an Act of 1552 Norwich obtained a monopoly of the manufacture of the material, which had been produced earlier at Pulham in Norfolk. Charles I's Book of Rates gives the duties paid on the various imported varieties, and also on those made in England—'Darnix . . . called coverlets'.

DAVENPORT. A small writing table with a sloping-top desk above a case of drawers. In the late 18th-century records of the firm of Gillow the entry 'Captain Davenport, a desk' occurs; presumably this was the origin of the term. One of the few extant early examples of that time is illustrated.

DAY-BEDS. *See* COUCHES AND DAY-BEDS.

DEAL. A sawn board, usually more than 9 ins. wide and not more than 3 ins. thick. The term was introduced from Low German, with the importation of such boards from Frisia and the Baltic, and, as timber grown there was usually pine or fir, the word is associated with these woods. It is occasionally mentioned as used for furniture, *e.g.* in a Howard House inventory (1588): 'a table of fine deale' in the great dining-chamber. From the early Georgian period, when panelling was painted, deal replaced oak. There are two general varieties of the Scots pine (*Pinus sylvestris*), yellow and red deal. The former appears to have been used almost exclusively in carcase work (when oak was not so used) for veneered furniture c. 1660-1750; but after 1750 much of the deal used was the red variety. Sheraton's *Cabinet Dictionary* (1803): 'from Deel, Dutch for a part, quantity or degree of. Hence fir or pine timber being cut into thin portions they are called deals.'

DECANTER STANDS. *See* COASTERS and BEER WAGGONS.

DENTELS, DENTILS. A series of small rectangular blocks with spaces between, generally placed in a cornice moulding and, more rarely, within the break of a pediment. Dentilled cornices are often found on mahogany bookcases and cupboards (*see* those Sections).

DERBYSHIRE SPAR, 'BLUE-JOHN' (*Radix Amethysti*). Coloured crystalline stone which has been found only in caverns of Tray Cliff, Castleton, Derbyshire. The varieties shade from blue, green and yellow to the rich amethyst purple, which is the most familiar. The first-recorded use of blue-john in Britain dates from 1743; and c. 1760 Robert Hall, of Castleton, started manufacture on a considerable scale. Large quantities were exported to France where the spar was known as *bleu-jaune* (hence 'blue-john'). Between 1762 and 1775 vases, candelabra and cassolettes, made of the spar and mounted in ormolu, were produced by Matthew Boulton at his Soho Works near Birmingham. (*See* BOULTON, M., and PERFUME BURNERS.)

DESKS, READING, WRITING AND MUSIC. A piece of furniture on which to read or write, the distinctive feature being a sloping front to support a book or writing material. Under this heading many dissimilar objects are included. The desk principle, embodied in a sloping front, is closely connected with the evolution of bookcases and enters into the structure of bureaux, the latter representing a more

1. *Davenport veneered with rosewood; a brass gallery above the desk, a drawer and writing slide at side. c. 1800. Ht. 3 ft., W. 1 ft. 6 in., Depth 1 ft. 6 in. (Mr Reginald Leon.)*

modern development, in which desk and chest of drawers are generally combined. The fittings of medieval collegiate and monastic libraries differed appreciably from those designed for private use. When permanent libraries were established by colleges in the 15th century, the fittings were adapted from the desk or lectern used in the services of the Church. These massive oak desks, designed to accommodate several readers, were ranged down the sides of a large room occupying spaces between the windows; the volumes were secured by chains to a bar fixed above or below the sloping front. The library at Oxford, furnished by Duke Humphrey c. 1450, was provided with books in twelve 'deskes' like 'half a strete' (metrical translation of Palladius' *De Re Rustica*). This arrangement was also adopted by individual colleges and by the great monastic foundations. Three desks of this time with Gothic finials and tracery are preserved in the cathedral library at Lincoln; they formed part of the fittings of an earlier building, and are probably the only English medieval examples now in existence. These and later examples of collegiate library fittings cannot, however, be classified as domestic furniture.

Medieval craftsmen displayed great ingenuity in the construction of desks for private scholars, so contriving them that they often combined the functions of a book-rest, writing-board and locker in one piece. A favourite form had a shelf enclosed by doors in the lower portion. Sometimes they revolved on a spiral column, or were made in several stages.

1. (*Left*) *Revolving Desk, on a bracket and a panelled base; from an MS. of* Le Miroir Historial. *c. 1485.* (*Brit. Mus., Royal 14. E. I. f. 3.*)

2. (*Right*) *Oak Desk with hinged lid and well for books; back and sides arcaded with late Gothic tracery. c. 1500. Ht. 3 ft. 2 in., L. 2 ft. 9 in., Depth 1 ft. 9 in.* (*V. & A. Mus.*)

Fig. 1 is from a Flemish manuscript of the time of Henry VII. It represents a Carmelite monk writing in his cell, the book being kept open by two chains with weights attached. The desk, on a bracket, is supported on a linen-fold panelled base; access to additional writing material is obtained by a circular hole at one end, a device obviating the necessity of opening the lid when the writer was at work. In another composite variety one or more circular tables are surmounted by a book-rest,

the height being adjustable by means of a central screw fitted into a columnar stand. Yet another type is seen in Fig. 2, the lid being hinged and the interior serving as a well for books.

In addition to the varieties already discussed, many small portable desks were in use throughout the Middle Ages; they were often extremely elaborate, and in French royal inventories specimens made of ebony or ivory are listed. After the invention of printing, books diminished notably in size, and as they no longer required a massive lectern to support them, portable desks gradually superseded the cumbrous structures of earlier days. Throughout the 16th century, with the exception of a few cabinets, they were the only form of furnitures designed specially for writing, a sufficient number being in existence to prove that they were fairly abundant at that time. English references to them are rare even in lists of the royal possessions; but 'a desk covered with black velvette and garnysshed withe gilt nayles' is included in the list of Katherine of Aragon's wardrobe stuff, and, as the word was not strictly used, it is possible that some of her many 'boxes' would now be termed desks. In Henry VIII's inventory (1547) a considerable number are fully described. The king seems to have had a special fancy for desks containing a variety of small implements. In the closet next to his privy chamber there were two desks 'havinge a paiere of scyssores a payer of compas and a penne knyfe cased in metal'. A desk, evidently made for Henry VIII, though not identifiable in this inventory, is seen in Fig. 3, the interior being decorated with painted and gilt leather. The outside is covered with shagreen, and this, with the metal mounts, dates from towards the end of the 17th century. The lids of the small drawers in the interior (to which access is gained by means of the fall-down front) are painted with a head of Christ in a roundel, with St George, the patron saint of England, and with the profile heads of 'Paris de Troy' and 'Helen de Greci' on a ground of arabesques. Below the lid, decorated inside with a circular strapwork enclosing the

3. *Desk fitted with drawers and tills, decorated throughout in colour; the underside of a tray below the lid bears the royal arms of Henry VIII. c. 1525. Ht. (open) 1 ft. 8½ in., L. 1 ft. 4½ in., Depth 11½ in.* (*V. & A. Mus.*)

4. *Oak Desk; front and sides carved with a floral guilloche pattern; hinges and lock-plate later. c. 1590. Ht. 1 ft. 1 in., L. 2 ft., Depth 1 ft. 5 in. (The late Mr Oliver Baker.)*

5. *Oak Desk, inlaid with floral arabesques in various coloured woods within a bead-and-reel border. c. 1590. Ht. 9½ in., L. 2 ft. 1 in., Depth 1 ft. 4½ in. (Col. N. R. Colville.)*

6. *(Right) Oak Desk, carved with a traditional vine pattern, lozenges and roses; consoles at corners. c. 1605. Ht. 1 ft. 2 in., L. 2 ft. 1 in., Depth 1 ft. 6 in. (V. & A. Mus.)*

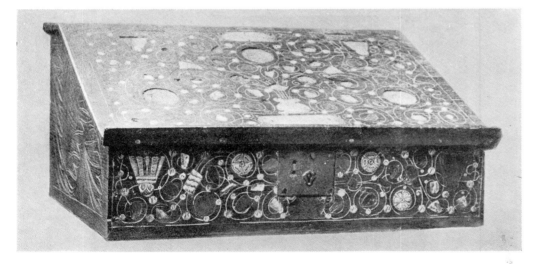

7. *Oak Desk, inlaid with arabesque patterns in bone and mother-of-pearl; sides incised, 'John Wells' and date 1651 engraved on lid; the ledge modern.*

badges of Henry and Katherine of Aragon, is a tray, which, when lifted, forms a double lid. On the inner surface this tray bears the royal arms with children blowing trumpets as supporters, and on either side are figures of Mars and Venus under Renaissance canopies from woodcuts by the celebrated German engraver Hans Burkmayer. On the rim of the tray is a restored inscription on vellum, which reads 'Henrico Octavo Regi Angliae de . . . Religiones Christianae Maxime Protector Tribuo Servo'. The painted decoration is probably the work of a foreign craftsman domiciled in England, and this remarkable desk must date before 1527 when Henry's divorce from Katherine was first publicly discussed. Much early Renaissance furniture was painted, but few English specimens have survived. References to desks are rare in early inventories of domestic furniture, but in 1556 Sir William More, of Loseley, Surrey, owned 'a deske of chestnut tree' and 'a little other deske to wryte on'.

Fig. 4 is what Cooper called (*Bibliotheca Eliotae*, 1584) 'a littell holowe desk lyke a coffer, whereupon men do write'; a desk of about the same date (Fig. 5) is inlaid with box, holly

8. *Oak Desk; front carved with heraldic lions, flanked by borders decorated with a floral guilloche. Initials and date 1679. (The late Col. Claude Lowther.)*

9. *(Right) Walnut Desk, inlaid with lines of holly, on a stand with plain cabriole legs. c. 1715. (Bourne Park, Kent.)*

10. *(Left) Desk, japanned with birds and floral patterns in reds and greens on a buff ground; interior fitted with drawers and pigeon-holes; lower portion of* bombé *form. c. 1720. Ht. 9 in., L. 1 ft. 4½ in., Depth 11 in. (V. & A. Mus.)*

11. *(Below) Desk, veneered with satinwood inlaid with classical motives, banded with mahogany and edged with ebony and ivory; interior re-fitted. c. 1785. Ht. 1 ft. 2½ in., L. 1 ft. 9¼ in., Depth 11½ in. (A. Dunn Gardner Coll.)*

and sycamore stained in various shades of greens and browns. This arabesque inlay was derived from cabinets imported from Italy under Henry VIII, but Fig. 6 is entirely English in character, and an exceptionally fine example. The interior is provided with rough drawers and a tray, suggesting that the fittings of bureaux at a later date were based on precedents afforded by these portable desks. In these early specimens the slope of the lid is less acute than it subsequently became.

In the first half of the 17th century desks were still the only form of furniture specially designed for writing. In the inventory of Henry Howard, Earl of Northampton (1614), 'A Desque with a Cabinett therein of crimson velvett laced' is entered, the description implying that the exterior was covered with fabric, like travelling coffers and close-stools of the period. Among Charles I's possessions dispersed after his execution was 'a faire Desk richly embroydered with silver and silk wherein is a silver inke pott and sand box'. Fig. 7 shows a

rare example of an oak desk decorated with bone and mother-of-pearl, in the manner of contemporary chests of drawers (*q.v.*). In Fig. 8 the lid is only slightly inclined, and retains the thumb-moulded edge that served as a finish in earlier desks (*cf.* Fig. 4). The front was obviously carved by a village craftsman imbued with the traditions of an earlier style.

With the general introduction of bureaux towards the end of the 17th century, these small desks were not discarded, but continued to be made with drawers and pigeon-holes in the interior, reproducing the arrangement adopted in the larger pieces (*see* BUREAUX). They were veneered with walnut and other woods or decorated with the fashionable japanning (Fig. 10). In 1683 the Duke of Lauderdale had at his rooms in Whitehall 'a little writing desk of plum-tree wood'; and in 1690 Gerreit Jensen (*q.v.*) supplied for Kensington Palace 'a writing desk pinewood with a table to draw out'. If walnut desks inlaid with floral or seaweed marquetry were occasionally made, examples do not appear to survive. The more highly finished specimens, veneered with walnut, were sometimes mounted on a cabriole leg stand (Fig. 9) and used by ladies as miniature bureaux.

Portable desks retained a measure of popularity throughout the 18th century; but, with the large increase in writing accommodation of all kinds, they gradually lost their decorative character, the majority being made of plain mahogany. Cowper received (December, 1785) as a present from Lady Hesketh 'the most elegant, the compactest, the most commodious desk in the world'. It was portable, for 'a certain fly-table . . . affords a convenient stand', and the slope (like some contemporary specimens) was apparently lined with baize: 'How pleasant it is to write upon such a green bank!'

In the Royal Accounts of this period the purchase of a number of mahogany desks is recorded. John Bradburn (*q.v.*) made one with '3 bottles to turn out at the ends with a Lock to suit the Hings, Key and 2 Brass Stops to stop it from sliding

12. *Conversation picture by Philip Mercier showing Frederick, Prince of Wales and his sisters in the gardens of Kew Palace; the music-desk in the foreground has a revolving top, and on the harpsichord is a desk supported by a ratchet, 1733. (Nat. Portrait Gall.)*

on the table'. *The Book of Prices*, 1788, gives four designs for desks elaborately fitted with boxes, trays and other small receptacles. Satinwood was now generally used in place of mahogany, but so great was the variety of bureaux and escritoires at this time that few ordinary desks seem to have been made. Fig. 11 shows a fine decorative example of inlaid satinwood. It represents the last phase of this particular

  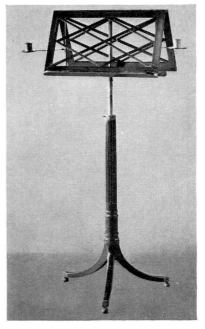

13. *Mahogany Reading-Desk on tripod stand; the vase-shaped stem finely carved. c. 1755. (Percival Griffiths Coll.)*
14. *Mahogany triangular Music-Desk or stand, with three music rests. c. 1770.*
15. *Mahogany Music-Desk; an adjustable lattice-work top on a fluted tripod stem. c. 1800.*

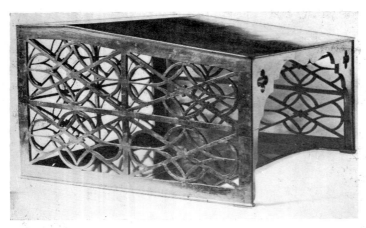

16. *Mahogany portable Reading-Desk, the sides filled with lattice-work quatrefoils. c. 1760. Ht. 1 ft. 3 in., L. 2 ft. ½ in. (Worshipful Company of Carpenters.)*

evolution that calls for notice; rosewood desks of the Regency period are occasionally found, but possess little decorative interest.

DESKS—MUSIC AND READING. A number of desks or stands were made in the second half of the 18th century to support books or music. In trade catalogues and bills of the period they are described as 'desks', and here the contemporary term is adopted. Benjamin Goodison (*q.v.*) supplied several mahogany desks of this character to the royal palaces between 1750 and 1765, one having 'a Pillar and Claw to raise up and fix at different Heights'. John Bradburn (*q.v.*), a few years later, altered a large desk of this kind at George III's command, and charged £7 5s. for 'making it lower and making the Candlesticks slide in order to give room for the books'. For the library at St James's he made one with a drawer containing a cut-glass ink and sand bottle, 'the whole mounted on a Pillar and Claw on strong casters'. Music-desks were also fitted to harpsichords and other musical instruments. In 1752 Goodison made a desk 'with Brass stays and Catches and Candlesticks with deep Rims, etc.' at a cost of £3, which he carried from London to the Pavilion at Hampton Court and fitted to a harpsichord. Both varieties can be seen in the conversation picture in Fig. 12. The stand of the music-desk, seen in the foreground, is apparently not adjustable, but the top revolves; on the harpsichord is another desk, supported by a ratchet, a usual arrangement at this time.

Chippendale does not illustrate tripod desks in the *Director* (1754), but Fig. 13 is about the date of its publication. These desks with carved stands resembling those in use for small tables and fire screens are illustrated in several trade catalogues of the time. Ince and Mayhew (*Universal System*, 1759-63) effected an improvement by attaching candlebranches to the sides of the desks, and Hepplewhite made them more readily adjustable by substituting 'a staff which slides in the stem' for the ratchet hitherto used for adjusting the top. Sheraton illustrates two of very similar design.

In Fig. 15, dating from c. 1800, may be seen the 'sliding staff' described by Hepplewhite, supported on a spider-legged base. The top, constructed for two performers, has the usual candle-branches on either side. This type was often made in rosewood, with a brass rest, in the period 1800-25.

A portable variety, made specially for reading, is seen in the decorative Master's desk of the Worshipful Company of Carpenters (Fig. 16). This was intended to be placed on the table when the Master addressed the members, and it is still used on such occasions.

DIMITY. A fine durable cotton cloth, originally woven in two threads. The manufacture appears to have been at first confined to Italy, and Guiccardini (*Description of the Low Countries*, 1560) states that Antwerp imported from Venice 'Dimities of many fine sorts'. Dimity was manufactured in England early in the 17th century, and is mentioned as an article of home production by Lewis Roberts in 1641. At that time, however, it was a woollen material. For Lord Mansfield's 'field bedstead' at Kenwood, Hampstead, William France in 1768 made the hangings out of the Chief Justice's own 'Dimotty'. Twenty years later Hepplewhite wrote (*Guide*) that, for beds, white dimity 'gives an effect of elegance and neatness truly agreeable'.

DOGWOOD (*Cornus Sanguinea L.*). A small tree, native of Great Britain; sap wood light yellow, heart brilliant yellowish red. It appears to have been used in inlay in the 16th and 17th centuries. Evelyn (*Sylva*, 1664) includes it among the hardest woods 'which are best to receive politure, and for this purpose linseed or the sweetest nut oyl does the effect best'. J.C.R.

DOLE CUPBOARDS. *See* CUPBOARDS, FOOD.

DORIC ORDER. *See* ORDERS.

DORNIX. *See* DARNIX, DORNECK, DORNIX.

DOSSER. A term applied in the Middle Ages to hangings round the walls of a hall behind the seats, and also to the ornamental covering at the back of a chair. They were made of arras, silks, velvets and other costly materials, richly embroidered. The *Boke of Curtasy* (1430-40) refers to 'the dossers cortines to hang in halle'. Alienor, Viscomtesse de Furnes, lady-in-waiting to Isabella, wife of Philip the Good, Duke of Burgundy, in her treatise on court etiquette (c. 1450), explains the term and describes the kind of dosser then in use in France and England: 'It should be as wide as three widths of cloth of gold, and made just like the canopy of a bed.' The term appears to have been seldom used after the 15th century.

DOVETAILING. *See* CONSTRUCTION.

DRAW, DRAWING or DRAW-OUT TABLES. *See* TABLES, DINING and CONSTRUCTION.

DRAW LEAF. *See* CONSTRUCTION; Fig. 7.

DRAW RUNNER or DRAW SLIP. Narrow strips of oak fitted into the carcases of bureaux with slant flaps. Small brass pull on face of runners enables them to be pulled forward to support opened flap. In use throughout the 18th century. The term 'loper' is applied to this type of runner. J.C.R.

DRAWER RUNNER. *See* CONSTRUCTION; Fig. 5a.

DRAWERS, NEST OF. Number of small drawers framed together in the form of a box or fitted into another piece of furniture.

1. (*Left*) *Oak Dresser, panelled with linen-fold; coved canopy within two bands of pierced ornament; top moulding missing, the handles modern, and structure repaired. c. 1500. (Badminton, Gloucs.)*

2. (*Above*) *Oak Dresser; moulded panels, drawer fronts carved with a scroll pattern; stiles and rails channelled. c. 1635. Ht. 2 ft. 10 in., L. 7 ft., Depth 2 ft. 1 in. (The late Mr Martin Buckmaster.)*

DRESSERS. In the medieval hall the dresser occupied a position of pre-eminence, and on it were placed the flagons, cups and spice plate, arranged in order, 'the largest firste, the richest in the myddis, the lightest before'. An open framework of shelves, it was a cupboard in the medieval sense—a 'borde' upon which to set cups, with a receptacle sometimes fitted between the shelves. The court cupboard of the late Tudor and Stuart periods was evolved from it, and Cotgrave (*Dictionary*, 1611) renders the term dressoir as 'a cupboard, a court cupboard (without box or drawer) only to set plate upon'. On the Continent dressers were built up of many stages (their number indicating the degree of the owner). The woodwork was often painted in colour and gilt, a magnificent setting being afforded for the plate by hangings of cloth of gold, velvet or damask. In 1396, at the marriage of Isabella of France with Richard II of England, the dresser in the hall, where a splendid entertainment was given, is described as '*couvert des noble vaisselles et de grande richesse*'. In 1503 the herald who accompanied Princess Margaret, daughter of Henry VII, on her journey into Scotland to marry King James IV, noted in the chamber at Holyrood Palace, where the banquet was served after the wedding, 'a riche Dresser after the Guyse of the countre', from which 'the Lord Grays the Father served the King with water for to wash, and the Erle of Hunteley berred the Towaylle'. The instructions given in a late 15th-century manuscript, *Ffor to serve a Lord*, prove that such structures were occasionally taken down and removed from the hall after the feasting.

Towards the end of the medieval period the hangings became less ornamental, a cloth of white diaper or damask being the usual covering; the ground shelf was often carpeted in the 16th century with knotted coloured wools known as 'Turkey work' (*q.v.*). In the halls of princes and great nobles this elaborate erection was also used as a sideboard on which dishes were placed:

'. . . and if it be a day of estate II squyres for the body schal go to the Dresser and bere II of the fyrst dysshes both at the fyrst course and the seconde'

are the instructions given in *Certeyn Artycles for the Regulatyng of the Householde of Henry VIII.* Lockers, or aumbries, were occasionally fitted between the shelves at this time, but the building contract for Hengrave (1516) provided that the dressers on the dais are to be without doors in 'ye facyon of livery'.

From Leigh's *Armorie* (1562) we learn that a drum was sounded in great establishments to warn gentlemen of the household to repair to the dresser, whence, observing a strict ceremonial, they carried the dishes to their lord. Cavendish records that when Wolsey entertained the French ambassadors after the ratification of the Treaty of Hampton Court there was a dresser 'made for the time in length of the breadth of the nether end' of the Presence Chamber. It was six desks high, 'full of gilt plate, very sumptuous and of the newest fashion; and upon the nethermost desk garnished all with plate of clean gold. . . . This cupboard was barred in round about that no man might come nigh it; for there was none of the same plate occupied or stirred during the feast for there was sufficient besides.' The entirely open structure with a canopy of rich material was not the only English 15th-century type.

In England the line of demarcation between cupboard and dresser was never clearly drawn, and to such an example as Fig. 1, where the lower portion is enclosed by doors, the term 'cupboard' would probably have been applied. In spite of considerable repair, it preserves its original form, and has always been in the possession of the Somersets, first at Troy House, Monmouth, and more recently at Badminton, Gloucestershire. The canopy resembles in style those of contemporary chantries and tombs. Such canopies were a

307

3. *Oak Dresser; corbelled-out cornice, geometrically panelled drawers, and two cupboards in the lower stage. c. 1600. Ht. 2 ft. 10½ in., L. 7 ft. 1 in., Depth 1 ft. 11½ in. (J. Thursby Pelham Coll.)*

4. *Oak Dresser; ogee-moulded cornice, geometrically panelled drawers, and vase-shaped balusters headed by brackets; stretchers not original. c. 1665. Ht. 2 ft. 9 in., L. 6 ft., Depth 1 ft. 9 in. (Lygon Arms, Broadway.)*

5. *Yew Dresser; geometrically moulded drawer fronts and five turned baluster supports. c. 1670. Ht. 2 ft. 9 in., L. 7 ft. 10 in., Depth 1 ft. 9½ in. (Messrs Stair and Andrew.)*

6. *Oak Dresser; front supports shaped. c. 1670. Handles later. (Mr Stuart Allcroft.)*

7. *Oak Dresser; front supports spirally turned. c. 1675. (Frank Partridge and Sons.)*

8. *Oak Dresser, composed of drawers and a central cupboard; door panels fielded, and inlaid with stars. c. 1710. (Marple Hall, Cheshire.)*

9. *Oak Dresser, with superstructure of shelves; frieze cusped and foliated, door panels fielded and shaped; the back-boards original. c. 1730. Ht. 6 ft. 10 in., L. 5 ft. 2 in., Depth 1 ft. 9 in. (Geffrye Museum, London.)*

common feature of the more elaborate late medieval dressers, or plate cupboards, and appear to have been termed 'hances', from the French *hance*, a raised part ('Evolution of the Cupboard', by R. W. Symonds, *Connoisseur*, November, 1943, pp. 91-3). The coved ceiling, with foliated bosses at the intersection of the ribs, is contained within two bands of perforated ornament and supported by spandrels filled with Gothic quatrefoils. The back is panelled with the same large linenfold that fills the front and sides. A very similar dresser may be seen in Holbein's famous drawing of Sir Thomas More and his family; as in the Badminton example, the lower portion is enclosed by cupboard doors. This form of dresser developed into the cupboard, or press, with an overhanging canopy resting on bulbous supports. References in wills and domestic accounts of the Elizabethan period to this type of furniture are comparatively rare. The inventory (1592) of Robert Mitforde, a Newcastle merchant, mentions 'a wainscotte dresser' in the hall; but such terse entries do not determine the character of these dressers. Early in the 17th century dressers are generally mentioned in connection with servants' quarters, and even the shelves in the scullery are so described.

About 1650 dressers reappeared in hall and parlour, but shorn of their medieval splendour. Stuart examples are almost invariably found without a superstructure, but the top sometimes shows that uprights were fastened to it, the shelves being secured by staples to the wall. In Fig. 2 the drawer fronts are lightly carved with a running scroll pattern and the whole of the

lower portion is occupied by cupboards. Fig. 3 is a specimen dating from c. 1650 with a corbelled-out cornice and the elaborately mitred mouldings characteristic of this time; in the lower portion are plain panelled doors, and the carved knob handles are original. Fig. 4 shows another example panelled in a similar taste, but here vase-shaped balusters headed by cut brackets and united by stretchers form a stand. The use of yew for large pieces of furniture was very exceptional at this date, but Fig. 5 shows a dresser made of that wood throughout; at the front are five balusters, of a later type than the last example, thus obviating the need for stretchers. In Fig. 6 the mouldings are Carolean, and the supports resemble in design those often found on small contemporary gate-leg tables. As exceptional as the yew dresser is the example in Fig. 7 supported on legs with a spiral twist. The back legs of all these dressers are merely flat posts, and they never exceed two in number.

Dressers continued to be made in oak on traditional lines for farmers and yeomen long after they had been supplanted by walnut and mahogany side-tables in fashionable houses. In a type dating from the early 18th century there is a central cupboard, and the doors are sometimes fielded, inlaid (Fig. 8), cock-beaded and banded with walnut. At about this time a superstructure of shelves reappears, recalling the medieval fashion. Similar dressers were common throughout the 17th century in Holland, and examples closely resembling the English type may be seen in domestic interiors of Dutch *genre* painters of that age. An early Georgian dresser (Fig. 9) has an unusual cusped frieze with the fielded, ogee-headed

10. *Oak Dresser, banded with mahogany, on cabriole legs; cupboards surmounted by swan-neck pediments with metal paterae, inlaid with figures of Britannia. c. 1780. Ht. 6 ft. 10 in., L. 7 ft., Depth 1 ft. 8 in. (Mr Aubrey Jenkins.)*

door panels characteristic of the time. In the majority of cases the backs of these dressers are additions, but here the boards are original.

Country craftsmen, having once adopted the cabriole leg, continued its use after it had ceased to be fashionable in London, and belatedly adopted motives drawn from contemporary fashionable furniture. From c. 1750 they made dressers with dentelled cornices and side cupboards in the upper portion, and the frieze was elaborately fretted. Fig. 10 shows a fine specimen of this last phase. The lines of the frieze are repeated on the apron, and the escalloped shelf-fronts are an exceptional feature. Dressers were now made for homely use, and in great houses they had long been relegated to the kitchen. There were no later developments of the type.

DRESSING GLASSES. *See* MIRRORS, TOILET.

DUCHESSE. *See* BEDS and COUCHES.

DUMB-WAITERS. Defined by Sheraton (*Cabinet Dictionary*, 1803) as 'a useful piece of furniture, to serve in some respects the place of a waiter, whence it is so named'. In the *Avant Courier* (February 25, 1771) they are described as an English invention consisting of tiers or trays affixed to a central stem, and the writer states that at about this time their use had spread to France and Germany. They were first made in England at a considerably earlier date, and, although not represented in the trade catalogues of Chippendale and his contemporaries, are sometimes mentioned in bills and inventories. The first Lord Bristol bought one in 1727 from Robert

Leigh, a cabinet-maker, and 'Dumb-waiters on casters' appear in a list of the stock of James Faucon in an advertisement in the *Daily Post* (February 16, 1731). In 1750 Benjamin Goodison charged £4 4s. for 'two mahogany Dumb-Waiters on Castors' supplied by him to Kensington Palace. At this period 'two board' waiters are sometimes mentioned in accounts, one of this kind 'with the edges of each board neatly carved' being supplied by William Vile in 1762 to the Queen's House in St James's Park.

These pieces of furniture were generally placed diagonally at the corner of a dining-table for the diners to help themselves when the servants had withdrawn, and held additional plates, knives and forks, and dessert and cheese. In her *Diary* (1784) Miss Mary Hamilton notes that at a dinner 'we had dumb-waiters so our conversation was not under any restraint by ye Servants being in ye room'.

For after-dinner drinking, bottles and glasses were placed on the tiers of revolving trays. In his *Memoirs* (1755) Captain P. Drake states that as 'soon as supper was over' a bottle of burgundy, with a flask of champagne, and the necessary glasses, was laid on the table, 'with a supply of those wines on a Dumb-waiter'. J. T. Smith (*Nollekens and his Times*, 1828) writes that in the sculptor's dining-room towards the end of the 18th century 'close to Mrs Nollekens' left elbow, stood a dumb-waiter with cheese, a slice of butter, a few water-cresses, and a change of plate, of knives and forks'.

Dumb-waiters generally consist of three circular trays increasing in size from top to bottom, and revolving on a standard with tripod feet. In Fig. 1 the vase-shaped stem is

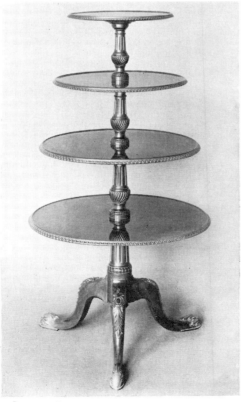

1. *Mahogany Dumb-Waiter; stem of triple vase-shape form, carved with acanthus; tripod stand realistically carved as eagles' legs. c. 1740. (Percival Griffiths Coll.)* 2. *Mahogany Dumb-Waiter; supports fluted and gadrooned, trays edged with leaf moulding. c. 1760. Ht. 4 ft. 2 in., extreme W. 2 ft. 3½ in. (A. Dunn Gardner Coll.)* 3. *Mahogany Dumb-Waiter, the trays shaped and bordered with fretwork. c. 1765. (Duchess of Roxburghe Coll.)*

4. *Mahogany Dumb-Waiter, the lower tray divided into compartments. c. 1795. Ht. 4 ft. 11 in., extreme W. 2 ft. 4½ in. (Clandon Park, Surrey.)* 5. *Rosewood Dumb-Waiter, inlaid with ebony; hinged trays and swing supports for bottles or candles; base flanked by lyres. c. 1810. Ht. 4 ft. 4½ in., extreme W. 2 ft. 1 in. (Edward Knoblock Coll.)* 6. *Mahogany Dumb-Waiter; trays with perforated brass galleries on a fluted column; a zinc-lined octagonal receptacle, lion-paw feet of brass. c. 1800. Ht. 4 ft. 9 in., extreme W. 2 ft. 2½ in. (F. Behrens Coll.)*

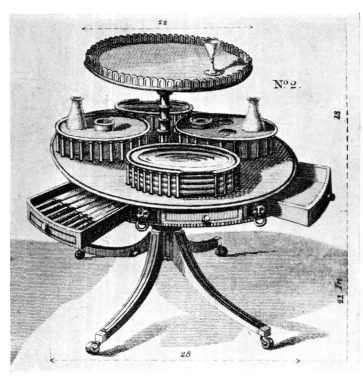

7. *Design for a Dumb-Waiter with drawers on a spider-legged stand. From Sheraton's* Cabinet Dictionary, *1803.*

finely decorated with acanthus, and the tripod takes the form of eagles' legs and claws, the carving of feathering and scaling being notably vigorous. The trays are so shallow that, to avoid warping, wood of the highest quality must have been selected. In Fig. 2 the base resembles those of tripod tables in the *Director* style; the four trays are edged with a small leaf moulding, the graduated supports being fluted and gadrooned. Enrichment was generally confined to the shaft, but in another mid-century example (Fig. 3) instead of the usual shallow rims there are trays shaped with re-entrant curves and bordered with a light 'Gothic' fretwork.

Towards the end of the 18th century new varieties were introduced. Sheraton writes that they were all made of mahogany and intended for the dining-parlour, plates and wine-glasses being placed on them. He gives two designs in his *Cabinet Dictionary.* The first, a shaped table with four reeded legs and two curved shelves, is 'partly from the French taste', and on the top is a slab of thin marble, 'which not only keeps cleaner and looks neater than mahogany, but also tends to keep the wine cool when a bottle for present use is placed upon it'. The shelves are for plates and a knife tray, the holes for the decanters having tin cases, japanned white, fitted into them. The second dumb-waiter (Fig. 7) has four spider legs and is elaborately equipped, while the knife drawer has a 'tin case to fit loose in'.

An instance of the archaeological Spirit of Regency

design is seen in Fig. 5, a rosewood dumb-waiter with the lower section of the shaft designed in the form of a double classical lyre. Here the oblong trays are hinged at the sides and fitted with drawers, candle stands being provided below the bottom tier. Fig. 6 is a rather earlier example, the zinc-lined receptacle being probably intended to hold dirty cutlery and plates. The use of dumb-waiters at this time is further shown in another of Sheraton's designs, where he illustrates one placed within the arc of a 'Grecian' or crescent-shaped table, at which the diners recline on settees. The upper tray at this time was often supported on slender brass columns resting on the tray below, the reeded tripod stand finishing in brass feet.

DUMMY-BOARD FIGURES.

Dummy-board figures, fashionable in this country in the 17th and 18th centuries, consist of flat boards, painted in oils with human and other figures, and shaped to the contours of the subjects represented. The outline of these dummies was first drawn on wood, which was cut out and bevelled from the back and then painted.

That they were not intended as fire-screens is shown, among other evidence, by the fact that they were, in many cases, originally destined to stand attached directly to, or at a very short distance from, the wall and fixed to it by staples and hooks, the staple being driven into a cross-piece of wood running from shoulder to shoulder behind the figure. In the castle of Schaumberg near Nassau, a number of such figures were formerly to be seen standing round the dining-room, within a few inches of the wall, to which they were partly attached by rings and staples. There also existed in the grand apartments of the monastery of St Florian, near Ling, on the Danube, a series of figures of soldiers standing near the doors

of the different rooms. Most of the dummies existing in England at the present day are fixed on blocks with a strut at the back, to stand independently. It is evident, therefore, that these dummies were ornamental and not intended to serve any practical purpose. Of animate objects, cats, dogs, pigs and macaws may be mentioned, but they were normally represented on a very small scale. Among human beings, children were popular, while maid-servants and soldiers were also favoured for representation. Many modern copies have been produced.

Dummy-board pictures had their origin in the Low Countries, and, in the case of some of the earlier examples, it is often difficult to determine whether they are Dutch or English. Most of the later figures, notably the military ones, with British uniforms, were undoubtedly made in England. The first dummy figures, which form a distinct group, are those representing maid-servants. The earliest are dressed in the costume of c. 1630. An example (Fig. 1) of this date in the Victoria and Albert Museum wields a broom, and wears a green gown with epaulets, and open sleeves showing white underneath: another forming the pair holds a mirror. These figures came originally from East Sutton Park, Kent. There was an identical figure of a sweeping housemaid at Lulling-stone Castle, Kent, and one of the same date is at Stoneleigh Abbey, Warwickshire. The fashion for the lady housemaid appears to have lasted well into the 18th century; and a figure in a similar pose, but wearing a dress of c. 1720, is at Castle Howard, Yorkshire. In Fig. 2 a maid-servant is represented, and there is another very similar one at Dyrham Park, Gloucestershire, described in the inventory of 1710 as 'a woman payring of an apple'.

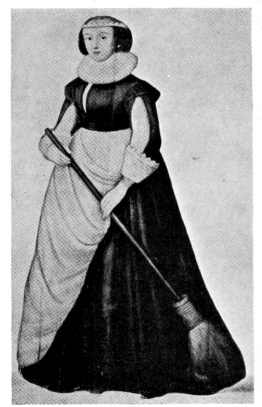  

1. *A Lady Housemaid. c. 1630. Ht. 5 ft. (V. & A. Mus.)* 2. *A Maid-Servant peeling an apple. c. 1710. Ht. 3 ft. 9 in. (Knole, Kent.)*
3. *Gentleman in costume of c. 1745. Ht. 5 ft. 5½ in. (V. & A. Mus.)*

4. *Gentleman in full-bottom wig. c. 1690. Ht. 6 ft. 2 in. (V. & A. Mus.)* 5. *Boy in frogged coat holding three-cornered hat. c. 1715. (The late Mr Ralph Philipson.)* 6. *Girl in costume of c. 1705. Ht. 3 ft. 6½ in. (Mr Ralph Edwards.)*

Another class of dummy-board is represented in Fig. 4. This imposing figure wears a full-bottom wig, lace cravat over a red tie, or bow, and a green coat with gold embroidery on the sleeves, front and buttons. In his left hand he holds his gloves. Of slightly later date is a pair of figures of a lady and gentleman at Knole, Kent. Male costume of the time of George II is well represented in Fig. 3.

Children are found of all dates, from c. 1600 to 1800. A figure of a child, about 4 feet high, dressed in a costume of c. 1630, is at Sudeley Castle, Gloucestershire. Good examples of the time of Queen Anne are shown in Figs. 5 and 6.

Another interesting group is formed by figures of soldiers. Several examples of these are illustrated by J. S. Ferguson in Vols. XLVII and LII of the *Architectural Journal*, among them being figures of grenadiers, identified as belonging to the 2nd or Queen's Regiment (later the Royal West Surrey Regiment), and dating between 1714 and 1727. Another soldier of about the same date, and supposed to represent a grenadier of the 3rd Regiment of Foot Guards, was at Canons Ashby, Northamptonshire (Fig. 7). Fig. 8 shows a late example of a dummy-board, dating from c. 1820 and representing a Jewish pedlar displaying his wares.

EASELS. A wooden frame designed to support a picture and to enable an artist to place it at a convenient height when painting. They are sometimes shown in medieval pictures and illuminations, St Luke, as the patron saint of artists, being commonly represented working at an easel. In this early form, holes for pegs to permit the picture to be raised at will are pierced in the uprights at desired heights (Fig. 1). Four uprights appear to have been more usual than a single support.

7. *Grenadier, of Third Regiment of Foot Guards (?). c. 1725. Ht. 7 ft. (Canons Ashby, Northants.)* 8. *Jewish Pedlar. c. 1820. Ht. 4 ft. 4½ in. (V. & A. Mus.)*

1. *Easel, with a single support at back; from an illuminated manuscript of the* Romant de la Rose. (*British Mus., Harley* 4425.)

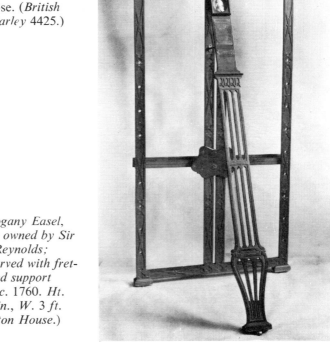

2. *Mahogany Easel, formerly owned by Sir Joshua Reynolds; frame carved with fretwork, and support pierced. c. 1760. Ht. 6 ft. 2½ in., W. 3 ft. (Burlington House.)*

Stands of this type remained in use until they were superseded in the 18th century, when a rectangular framework was substituted for the traditional form, and the shelf supporting the picture was often elevated by means of a ratchet. Sir Joshua Reynolds' mahogany easel (Fig. 2) shows that they were sometimes treated as decorative pieces of furniture. In addition to those intended for work in a studio, small easels were also made to stand on a table and support a book or picture. Of this type examples were made of turned rosewood in the early years of the 19th century.

EBONY. Black wood of great hardness, weight and closeness of texture, which comes chiefly from species of *Diospyros*. True ebonies belong to the family *ebonaceae*, but the timbers of all this family are not necessarily black. Also there are a number of black woods that belong to other families. The freedom of ebony from shrinkage and warping, its resistance to decay and the smoothness of its surface caused it to be esteemed during certain periods, especially for veneering cabinets and mirror-frames in the Low Countries in the 17th century. In England ebony and ebonised wood were in fashion for the cases of clocks during the late 17th century and were occasionally used for other furniture (*see* STANDS, CANDLE). When an inventory was drawn up (March, 1696-7) of the contents of Kensington Palace, there were in the Old Bedchamber 'One Ebbine Cabbonete plated with silver and Looking Glass . . . and stands of ebbone plated with silver and Looking Glass'; which are entered among the objects that 'the Queen bespoke of Mr Johnson [*see* JENSEN, GERREIT] and came in after her death'.

EBONY, GREEN. Name formerly given to a rare growth of the ash. Evelyn writes (*Sylva*, 1664):

Some ash is curiously camleted and veined, I say, so differently from other timber, that our skilful cabinet makers prize it equal with Ebony, and give it the name of Green Ebony.

ECHINUS *See* EGG-AND-TONGUE.

EGG-AND-TONGUE. Enrichment often carved on ovolo moulding in classical architecture, and used in a similar manner in furniture and wood-work, from the late 16th century onwards. Egg-shaped, alternating with a dart-like ornament, and from its fancied resemblance to a sea-urchin also known by the Latin term *echinus*. Often carved on 18th-century mahogany furniture designed in classical taste (*see* BOOKCASES; Fig. 7).

EGYPTIAN TASTE. The term given to a short-lived attempt to naturalise Egyptian forms and symbols in furniture, dating from the end of the 18th and beginning of the 19th centuries. Egyptian influence can be discerned in ancient Greek and Roman art, in ornaments like the palmette and anthemion, and above all in the sphinx; which, in its Greek form, became a favourite motive at the time of the Renaissance and was often used by classicising designers like Kent and Adam. With the deeper study of classical architecture in the 18th century a certain interest was aroused in Egyptian remains, a number of which were discovered in Europe, mainly at Rome, where they had been brought in imperial times. Among them were the fallen obelisks which, since the Renaissance, had been re-erected one by one by the Popes and excited widespread curiosity on account of their hieroglyphic inscriptions. In 1748 a gallery of Egyptian relics was opened in the Capitoline museum; others were to be found in private collections like that of Sir Hans Sloane, acquired by the English government in 1754, and that of the Comte de Caylus,

315

who in 1752 began to publish his *Recueil d'Antiquités Egyptiennes, Grecques, Etrusques et Romaines*.

Piranesi was probably the first artist to exploit for decorative purposes the ancient style thus gradually being brought to light, and in his designs for chimney-pieces (*Diverse Maniere di Adornare i Cammini*, 1769) he made free use of mummies, fanciful hieroglyphs, sphinxes, figures painted in profile after the Egyptian manner, etc. That the style had reached France by the 1780s is proved by an inventory of 1782 which shows that the Duc d'Aumont had obtained from Gouthière 'deux tables de jaspe vert, à gaines de style égyptien'. But the vogue did not become widespread until Napoleon's expedition to Egypt in 1798 invested everything Egyptian with a strong topical interest in France and England alike. The artist Denon accompanied the armies and his profusely illustrated *Voyage dans la Haute and dans la Basse Egypte* (1802) was soon translated into English and furnished English designers with a rich repertory of Egyptian ornament. In France, Denon himself led the fashion by commissioning Jacob to make him a set of bedroom furniture in the Egyptian style from his own designs.

In England Thomas Chippendale, the younger, was among the first to adapt the style to furniture, notably in the two tables made for Stourhead, Wiltshire, in 1804 and 1805, both decorated with 'carved Egyptian heads'. (*See* TABLES, LIBRARY; Figs. 32 and 34.) In his *Encyclopaedia* of this date Sheraton provided a few fantastic pseudo-Egyptian designs. Thomas Hope, the chief English exponent of the Egyptian manner, designed and furnished a special room at his town house in Duchess Street, to contain his collection of Egyptian antiquities, which is illustrated and described in his *Household Furniture* (1807). The armchairs are even more eclectic than the decoration, 'the crouching priests supporting the elbows being copies from an Egyptian idol in the Vatican, the winged Isis in the rail from a mummy-case from the Institute at Bologna, the canopuses from the one in the Capitol, and various other ornaments at Thebes, Tentyris, etc.'

Hope warned young artists against the indiscriminate use of the style, on the grounds that the hieroglyphics were unintelligible and that the impressive scale of the original could not be reproduced. Modern imitation in flimsy materials had nothing 'to compensate for their want of elegance and grace, and can only excite ridicule and contempt'. The warning proved ineffectual and for a brief time Egyptian detail became the vogue. In Ackerman's *Repository* (1809) it is stated to have been superseded, but as late as 1826 P. and M. A. Nicholson in their *Practical Cabinet-Maker, Upholsterer and Complete Decorator* mention the Egyptian style with the Greek and Roman as one of the three styles on which contemporary furniture might be based. P.W.J. (*See* also *Regency Furniture*, Clifford Musgrave, 1961.)

ELM (*Ulmus procera*). The ordinary English variety; the wood is of brown tone, fibrous, hard and flexible, but liable to warp; tough and difficult in working and very subject to worm. It is rare to find specimens dating before the early 17th century; but many survive from the Georgian period—such as chairs of country origin. Wych elm (*Ulmus glabra*), often termed Scotch elm, being indigenous to Scotland, is harder than *procera*, straighter and finer in grain and is also very

suitable for bending. It is preferred for furniture-making on account of its figure and for taking a good polish. In the Middle Ages it was greatly prized for making long-bows. Evelyn (*Sylva*, 1664) records that elm was used for the tops of shovel-board tables of great length. It was commonly used in the 18th century for the seats of Windsor chairs.

Owing either to lopping or accidental causes, the trunk of the elm is often marked by protruding masses of gnarled or burr wood; these portions were valued for veneers and employed on cabinet-work of the early 18th century, and again towards its close, more particularly on boxes, etc. There appears to have been an attempt in the second half of the century to treat elm with acids and stains to simulate mahogany; reference to this practice—or experiment—is to be found in the *Annual Register*, 1764. J.C.R.

EMBROIDERY. *See* NEEDLEWORK.

ENAMELLING. During the second half of the 17th century enamel was used as an ornament on several varieties of furniture. Vitreous paste was used to decorate brass castings, filling the shallow cells which form much of the surface. This opaque paste is left in the rough, with the original fire-glaze on it, not polished down to an even surface, as in the case of champlevé enamels. In some cases brass ridges form narrow borders in the enamelled surface; in others the metal forms the design, the enamel being applied only to the ground, as in the framing of an octagonal mirror (*see* MIRRORS; Fig. 3). The colours in late Stuart enamel are light turquoise, white, green, black, purple and red, all specimens dating c. 1660-85. Nothing is known of the origin of this type of enamel. The enamels produced at Battersea and in South Staffordshire in the second half of the 18th century (of which a large number of candlesticks were made) were an entirely distinct variety (*see* ANDIRONS, in CHIMNEY FURNITURE, SCONCES). (M. J.)

ENTABLATURE. Horizontal structure in classical architecture, *i.e.* architrave, frieze and cornice. Each order has a distinctive entablature (*see* ORDERS). Adapted to furniture and wood-work from the 16th century, free rendering of an entablature being found on many bookcases and cabinets (*see* BOOKCASES; Fig. 1).

ENTASIS. Swelling in the middle of a shaft or column, originally introduced by the Greeks into the Doric Order; found in columns supporting the frieze in Georgian furniture designed under architectural influence; and more pronounced in ribs filling the shield-shaped backs of some late 18th-century chairs (*see* CHAIRS; Fig. 148).

ESCRITOIRE. *See* BUREAUX, etc.

ESCUTCHEON. Armorial term applied to the shield-shaped surface on which a coat-of-arms, monogram or other device is depicted (*see* MIRRORS; Fig. 38). Keyhole plate also termed escutcheon.

ESSENCE VASES. *See* PERFUME BURNERS and ESSENCE-POTS or VASES.

ETRUSCAN STYLE. A form of decoration in the 18th century supposed to be derived from ancient Etruscan ornament. The Adam brothers (*Works in Architecture*, Vol. II, 1779) claim to have introduced this style 'which differs from anything hitherto practised in Europe'. They derived inspiration from vases and urns then regarded as of Etruscan origin, though many of these objects are now known to have been brought from Greece or Greek colonies. Similar motives were introduced in French furniture and decoration, but the Adams' claim to priority appears to be established.

Rooms in the Earl of Derby's house in Grosvenor Square, London, and the Countess of Home's, 20 Portman Square, were the chief examples of the new style. In the 'Etruscan rooms' by James Wyatt and Biagio Rebecca at Heveningham, Suffolk, and by Thomas Leverton at Woodhall, Hertfordshire, the motives are derived from Pompeian and Raphaelesque decorations and not directly from 'Etruscan' vases.

The peculiarity of the colouring, with figures, vases and other classic ornament in terra-cottas and browns relieved against delicate backgrounds of blue and biscuit colour, was a distinctive feature. The Etruscan Room at Osterley, Middlesex, the only example by Adam that survives, still retains most of its original furniture; the design for one of the armchairs (no longer in the room) is dated 1764 (*see* SCREENS; Fig. 17).

A measure of influence in spreading the taste must be assigned to *Antiquités Etrusques, Grecques et Romaines*, the plates of Sir William Hamilton's Collection published in Naples, 1766. Wedgwood drew upon this source for his new wares, and gave the name Etruria to the works he opened in 1769. The Hamilton Collection was brought to England in 1772 and purchased for the British Museum. M.J.

FEATHER BANDING or HERRING-BONE IN-LAY. Banding of veneer of two strips placed together, with the grain of each running diagonally, thus producing feather or herring-bone effect; often found on drawer fronts of late 17th- and early 18th-century walnut furniture.

FENDERS. *See* CHIMNEY FURNITURE.

FIELDED PANEL. A panel in which the edges are bevelled, having a flat field in the centre (*see* CUPBOARDS, PRESSES AND WARDROBES; Fig. 8). 'You may (if you will) bevel away the outer edges of the Pannels, and have a Table in the middle of the Pannel' (J. Moxon, *Mechanick Exercises*, 1694).

FILIGREE PAPER DECORATION. The first forms were derived from solid gold and silver filigree. When the use of precious metals was found too costly, they were imitated in materials of less value. At first, the rinds of papyrus and the barks of various trees were used, and later parchment and paper painted in colours, with the edges gilt, enriched with metal threads and beads, and made into elaborate and intricate patterns. In the 15th and 16th centuries this kind of decoration was used in England for figures of saints, relics, etc.; it died out shortly after the Reformation and few early examples survive.

Filigree, rolled paper or mosaic-work was revived in this country c. 1650. It then consisted of narrow strips of crimped and plain paper, coloured and gilt, stiffened, rolled and twisted. These paper rolls, sometimes elaborated with small shells, seeds and metal threads, were joined together and worked up into a pictorial decoration to ornament, *inter alia*, boxes and mirror frames. In an early example (Fig. 1) the rolled paper is contemporary with the stump-work medallions, the figures wearing the costume of c. 1650.

1. *Mirror Frame, decorated with rolled paper and stump-work medallions. c. 1650. Ht. 2 ft. 4 in., W. 2 ft. 6 in. (The late Viscount Leverhulme.)*

2. *Oval panel for pole-screen, decorated with filigree-work; medallion painted with figure subjects. c. 1785. Ht. 1 ft. 3 in., W. 1 ft.*

3. *Cabinet on stand; decorated with filigree-work; coloured engravings, suspended from festoons of imitation pearls. Ht. (on stand) 4 ft. 10 in., W. 2 ft., Depth 1 ft. 5½ in. (Lady Lever Art Gallery, Port Sunlight.)*

4. *Patterns for filigree-work from* The New Ladies' Magazine *for 1786.*

Filigree decoration was a favourite recreation for ladies in the 18th century. Princess Elizabeth, daughter of George III, was provided by one of the Royal tradesmen with a 'box made for filigree work with ebony mouldings, lock and key, and also a tea caddy to correspond': to these were added a supply of filigree paper. The cabinet (Fig. 3) represents the apogee of this craft. It is covered with tight little rolls of brilliantly coloured paper, arranged in patterns to simulate mosaic. The medallions, coloured engravings, are suspended from and surrounded by imitation pearls, and the doors are lined with painted satin bordered with glass jewels. A contributor to *The New Ladies' Magazine*, 1786, gives an account of the origin and progress of paper filigree-work, and supplies 'A Profusion of neat elegant patterns and models of ingenuity and delicacy suitable for tea-caddies, toilets, chimney-pieces, screens, cabinets, frames, picture ornaments, etc.' The writer adds, 'The Art affords an amusement to the female mind capable of the most pleasing and extensive variety; it may be readily acquired and pursued at a very trifling expense'. A correspondent in the magazine states that fine filigree may be seen 'at the first shop in Mount Street by Berkeley Square'. In the Victoria and Albert Museum are a number of caddies (*see* TEA-CADDIES) and an elaborate royal arms of Queen Anne's reign decorated in this manner.

FILLET. An architectural term for a small band or fascia used to separate mouldings from the Middle Ages onwards; often found worked on larger mouldings of furniture.

FINIAL. An architectural term for a decorative terminal; a great variety of finials were used from the 15th century onwards, often surmounting the uprights of chairs, four corners of bed testers, cornices of cabinets, etc. (*see* BEDS; Fig. 18; and CABINETS; Fig. 49).

FIR. *See* DEAL.

FIREBACK, FIRE-PLATE or REREDOS; FIRE-DOGS or ANDIRONS; FIRE-IRONS; FIRE-PAN. *See* CHIMNEY FURNITURE.

FLOWER-BOXES. Ornamental boxes or stands for growing bulbs in the house were introduced in Charles II's reign, when the craze for this form of floral culture had spread from Holland to England. A Ham House, Surrey, inventory (1679) mentions 'seaven boxes carv'd and guilt for Tuby Roses', among the contents of the Long Gallery; and that number of boxes, of painted wood decorated with gilt swags, are still in the house. In the 18th century they were generally of semicircular form, fitted with glasses for the bulbs or lined with zinc. Early examples are sometimes painted or japanned in Chinese taste (Fig. 1); later they are found inlaid and painted in neo-classic style (Fig. 2 and *see* STANDS, CHINA AND FLOWER).

FLUTES or FLUTINGS. Architectural term for hollows or channels cut perpendicularly in columns of classical orders and separated by a sharp edge or fillet. In furniture, flutes are a favourite ornament, being found on columns, pilasters, friezes, etc., from the 16th century onwards (*see* CHESTS OF DRAWERS; Fig. 27).

FOOD or DOLE CUPBOARDS. *See* CUPBOARDS—FOOD *and* LIVERY.

FOOTMAN. *See* CHIMNEY FURNITURE.

FOOTSTOOLS. *See* STOOLS.

FORCER, FORCET, FOSSELET. A common diminutive for chest in the Middle Ages. Among the goods of William Honeyboorne, of Bury 'a litell spruce forcer' is entered in 1493. The term is rendered by Palgrave (1530) as equivalent to casket. In the first half of the 17th century forcers are mentioned among the effects of husbandmen and small farmers (*Bedfordshire Records Society* Publications, XX). In 1610, when an inventory was taken at a house in Cockenden after the death of the owner's wife, there was 'In the Garret over my Wive's Chamber a very good wainscott forser, with a strong lock and key, and which Frances hath wont to put cloathes in'.

FORMS. *See* BENCHES AND FORMS, SETTLES.

FRAMES. *See* MIRRORS *and* PICTURE FRAMES.

FRETWORK, CUTWORK AND LATTICE-WORK. In furniture these are practically interchangeable terms for wood cut into patterns more or less intricate, and used either as perforated ornament or 'blind', *i.e.* on a solid ground. During the ascendancy of Chinese and Gothic tastes, fretwork in both these styles figured prominently in the structure and ornament of a great variety of objects, blind and pierced frets being often associated on the same piece (*see* CABINETS; Fig. 25). Pierced galleries on small tables were generally constructed of three thicknesses of mahogany veneer glued together. By the mid-18th century latticework intended for garden ornaments was commonly called 'Chinese Railings', the term being now used with a wider significance.

FRIEZE. In classical architecture, the middle division of an entablature between architrave and cornice; it is applied in a similar sense to furniture. Generally flat, but in walnut cabinets between 1675 and 1705 often of convex or barrel form; carved, inlaid or painted, conforming to decoration of successive styles.

FRINGES. *See* UPHOLSTERY.

FUSTIAN. Coarse twilled cotton cloth, often used for bed-hangings in early times. The term is probably derived from the Spanish *fuste, i.e.* substance. From the 10th century until the expulsion of the Moors, Spain was famous for cotton fabrics, fustian, woven in the same manner as velvet, being among the most important. Said to have been introduced into England by the Flemings under Edward III, but home-made fustian appears to have been a woollen fabric. From the 14th to the 16th centuries Norwich was the chief centre of manufacture. There are frequent references to a 'fustian' spread over the sheets and blankets of a bed, *e.g.* a counterpane of this material. John Russell (*Boke of Nurture*, c. 1440) instructs the 'Chamberlayne' to see that the 'fustian and shetis be clene'. *Household Ordinances* of Henry VII shows that the king had a fustian and sheet under his feather bed, over the bed a sheet, then 'the over fustian above'. By the sumptuary laws of the 15th century those with yearly possessions worth less than

1. *Pair of flower-boxes, decorated in black and gold japan; fitted with glasses and rods to support the flowers. Early 18th century. (Normanton Park, Rutland.)*

2. *Flower-Box, veneered with harewood and inlaid with a lozenge pattern; central panel decorated in colour with a group of dancing figures; glasses not original. c. 1790. Ht. 5 in., L. 1 ft. 2 in., Depth 5 in. (Mr Harold Davis.)*

40s. were forbidden to wear 'any fustian of Naples', a rich material used for covering coffers and close-stools by upholsterers to the Crown under Henry VIII and Elizabeth I. Between 1612 and 1640 several entries of sums spent on the purchase of fustian appear in the *Northumberland Household Books*. In the 18th century an attempt was made to exclude foreign fustian, apparently by then out of use for upholstery.

FUSTIC (*Chlorophora tinctoria*). Wood imported in the 17th and 18th centuries from tropical America; used by inlayers (Evelyn's *Sylva*, 1664) for its yellow colour. It also produced yellow dye. Chippendale's firm used it as a veneer, and in 1772 made 'a very large Inlaid Case of Fustick and Black Rosewood' for David Garrick's house in the Adelphi (*see* CUPBOARDS). Sheraton writes (1803) that it 'was used in cabinet work about twenty years since, but as it was found to turn by air and the heat of the sun to a dead brownish hue, it was laid aside as unfit for such purposes'. J.C.R.

GADROONING, KNURLING AND NULLING. Terms for a run of ornament, convex in form, carved on edges of furniture; first found on 16th-century oak, particularly on bulbous supports. For the two favourite forms, straight and curved, see middle shelf and capitals of Fig. 5 under CUPBOARDS, COURT. Mouldings carved with gadroons were freely used on furniture, notably side-tables, of the early Georgian and rococo periods; a gadrooned metal border sometimes surrounds the tops of commodes. A Treasury Warrant of 1704 refers to sconces with nozzles 'each *knurled* round with silver'.

GALON. *See* UPHOLSTERY.

GAMES-TABLE. *See* TABLES, CARD AND GAMING.

GESSO. A preparation of finely ground chalk worked up into a paste with parchment size. In medieval times it was used as the foundation for the painted and gilded decoration on wood-work. A very similar preparation was used on gilt gesso furniture, which first became fashionable under Charles II (*see* GILDING).

GILDING. The origin of the art of gilding is lost in antiquity; but that this process was applied to furniture at a very early date is proved by examples found in tombs of the Pharaohs. As early as 1700 B.C. the discovery had been made that the extreme malleability of gold allowed it to be beaten into a skin so thin that it would adhere to a preparation of plaster. On Egyptian mummy-cases some of the thin leaf-gilding resembles that obtained by the modern process.

In Europe since the Middle Ages two distinct methods of overlaying wood with gold leaf have been used, oil-gilding and water-gilding. Oil-gilding, the simpler and cheaper of the two, is also more durable and less vulnerable to damp; on the other hand, as it cannot be burnished, it never has the lustre of good water-gilding.

An early account of the two processes is given in the chapters on gilding in Cennino Cennini's *Il Libro dell' Arte* (written 1437). A comparison of the methods there described with those propounded by Stalker and Parker (*Treatise of Japanning and Varnishing*, 1688, published at the time when English gilding was being perfected) shows that the basic principles of the art had changed little in two and a half centuries; indeed, despite technical innovations, the same general rules are still observed by modern gilders.

Whichever process is used, the first concern of the gilder must be to provide a suitable ground for the gold, since a plain wooden surface is neither hard nor smooth enough. In Cennini's time the ground was made of gesso, a paste composed of chalk, gypsum, plaster or some such substance ground in water, with the addition of glue or gelatine as a binding medium. It was laid on in several thin coats, each coat being allowed to harden before the next was applied. The final surface was scraped and rubbed until it was almost as smooth and as hard as ivory. Gesso is still the normal ground for water-gilding, and is often used for oil-gilding too; but one of the advantages of oil-gilding is that it can be done on a ground less laborious to prepare. Stalker and Parker, for example, claim that the best ground for oil-gilding is composed of paint-pot scrapings, still used by some craftsmen. Alternatively, they say that the ground may be made of white lead or red ochre, ground in oil. But for water-gilding, they, like Cennini, recommend a gesso ground.

When the ground is ready, the next step is to apply a mordant, *i.e.* a substance which 'bites' on to the gold leaf and makes it adhere. At this point the oil and water processes diverge completely, the mordants used for oil-gilding being naturally sticky, whereas those used in water-gilding need to be wetted before the gold will adhere. For oil-gilding the mordants recommended by Cennini, by Stalker and Parker and by modern English handbooks are basically the same; the chief ingredient in each case is linseed oil cooked for several months in the sun until it solidifies and becomes what is known as 'fat oil'. This is mixed with white lead and verdigris, according to Cennini's prescription, or, according to Stalker and Parker and more modern authorities, with yellow ochre or raw sienna ground in linseed oil. This mordant is now usually known as 'oil gold size'. When ready the mordant is thinly applied with a brush and left for at least a day to dry; as soon as the surface is sufficiently firm, but still tacky, the leaf is laid on and the creases or loose fragments are carefully dusted off. The gold is finally polished with cotton-wool or shammy-leather, but unlike water-gilding, it cannot be burnished.

Water-gilding is always applied on a gesso ground. In Cennini's time the mordant used to make the gold adhere was composed of a substance called 'Armenian bole' (now usually known as gilders' red clay) ground with a tempera of 'glair' (water and white of egg beaten together). Variations of this formula are still commonly used, but parchment size is now generally substituted for glair. Stalker and Parker prescribe Armenian bole ground with water, to which they add a little candle grease and some size. This kind of mordant is now called 'Burnish size'. The exact composition of the mordant depended to some extent on the colour on which the gilder preferred to work. Blue was often used in the 18th century; red and yellow are also common and have the advantage of concealing any slight gaps and defects in the gilding.

The mordant is applied in several coats and allowed to harden. It is then ready for gilding; but before it can grip the leaf the surface must be made 'flowing wet' with cold water; owing to its absorbent nature it dries quickly, so that only a small patch can be treated at a time and even then considerable promptness and dexterity are required. To attain the finest effect a second coating of gold is applied; this is called 'double gilding', a process which cannot be used in oil-gilding. The final surface is gently polished with a pad, which produces a dull effect known as 'matt gilding'; if a burnish is desired, the gold is rubbed with a tool known as a burnisher. This was originally a dog's tooth set in a convenient handle, an instrument still used by some gilders. Various precious stones were also used for the purpose, and modern burnishers are usually made from highly polished agate stones.

In gesso-gilding, which originated in Italy in the Middle Ages and probably came to England from France, the same gilding process was used as that described above, but the method of handling the gesso was slightly different. The process is fully explained in a description of trades published in 1745 thus: 'The figures are first roughly cut in the wood, then the whole is covered with two or three coats of whiting to the thickness of a quarter of an inch; when this is dry, the carver wets the whiting with a brush, then finishes his figures by making such flourishes in his whiting as is agreeable to his pattern. When he has done his part to it, he sends it to the gilder'—an indication that the trades of the carver and gilder were by that time in some instances distinct.

The leaf used was obtained by beating sheets of gold between layers of vellum; in the final stages of the process the vellum was replaced by an exceptionally thin animal membrane known as 'gold beater's skin', which is still used for the purpose. The average leaf today measures about $3\frac{1}{4}$ ins. square. The colour of the leaf depends on the quality of the gold used. The purest and most brilliant is 24-carat, but it is difficult to blow out. For fine gilding, 22-carat was generally used, being far more easily applied; while for ordinary objects 15-carat was favoured. Gold of lesser quality was liable to be quickly affected by damp and had to be protected by varnish.

The gilding processes described by Cennini were doubtless also practised in England in the Middle Ages, and from early in the reign of Henry VIII there are occasional references in inventories to beds and other pieces of furniture wholly or partly gilded. But it was not until the 17th century that these processes were commonly applied to the interior decoration of houses and to furniture. Lavish use was made of oil-gilding in the redecoration of Ham House, Surrey (1638-9), by the new owner, William Murray, first Earl of Dysart. The sum of £320 was paid to Mathew Goodriche for painting and gilding. In most of the principal rooms the frieze and cornice, as well as the door and window frames, were 'gilt with fine gold in Oyll'. Water-gilding was apparently not used at all on this occasion.

Gilding (mostly by the oil process) became more common after the Restoration and was applied to furniture, notably to stands for cabinets, mirrors and picture-frames and chairs, as well as to architectural features; a set of gilt chairs, carved with dolphins, at Ham House provides a striking early example, dating from c. 1670. But the finest English gilding coincides with the building of the great Palladian houses between 1700 and 1750, the ornate and massive furniture appropriate to this architecture being eminently suitable for gesso-gilding. The art reached its apogee c. 1730, almost rivalling the excellence of the French. It continued to be practised throughout the 18th century, though after 1750 it declined somewhat from favour. Chippendale, though he often used gold to pick out salient features, and even extolled the appearance of entirely gilt furniture, relied mainly on the effects that can be obtained from bare wood. The fashion revived towards the end of the century, but the later gilding is seldom of the same high quality as the earlier, and water-gilding was neglected in favour of oil. Sheraton (*Cabinet Dictionary*, 1803) says of oil-gilding that it is the process 'chiefly used in this country, being in all cases the most durable', and of water-gilding that 'it is only proper for internal works and even in that situation requires much care to keep it from injury'. Both processes were sometimes used, for the sake of variety and contrast, on the same object, the flat surfaces being gilt in oil, while prominent mouldings and other ornaments were covered with water-gilding and burnished. A granulated effect could be created by sprinkling the surface with sand before gilding; in much English gesso-gilt furniture the ground is tooled and punched with a circular stamp.

From the Restoration onwards furniture was occasionally silvered. The processes used were similar to those employed in gilding and are described by Dossie (*Handmaid to the Arts*,

1758). Silvering was naturally cheaper than gilding, but the inferior metal tarnishes and discolours easily, a tendency which the 18th-century craftsman tried to check by applying a strong varnish over the surface.

For gilding metals a process known as fire gilding has been used from the Middle Ages, and has not been surpassed even since the invention of electro-gilding. The process is based on the fact that mercury will combine with gold to form an amalgam, which is applied to the objects to be gilded; it is then heated, whereupon the mercury evaporates, leaving the gold adhering to the metal. This method, dangerous to health, is now forbidden in England.

Glass-gilding, as used in the 18th century to ornament mirrors and picture glass, is similar in principle to the method of water-gilding on wood, the mordant used being composed of isinglass.

Only a small quantity of the decorated gilt leather used for wall-hangings, covers to furniture and screens was of English manufacture. From Elizabethan times it was mostly imported from Spain and Flanders, but later a certain amount was produced in this country (*see* LEATHER and SCREENS). This gilding was a direct copy of the French and Spanish processes. Silver leaf was invariably used, laid on the dressed leather with a preparation of size; the leaf was then lacquered with deep-coloured gold lacquer varnish. Decorations were painted in oil when the gilding was completed. P. W. J.

GIRTHES (GYRTHES). Bands of webbing used to support mattress, cushions, etc. 'A trussing bed with gyrthes' is mentioned in the will of Ralph Blakeston, 1548 (*Surtees Society*, Part I, p. 131).

GLAZING. *See* CONSTRUCTION.

GLOBE-STANDS. A globe is defined by Robert Hues (*Tractatus de Globis*, trans. Chilmead, 1639) as 'an Analogicall representation either of the Heavens or the Earth'. It is thus called, not only because it expresses 'the Sphaericall figure as well of the Heavens, as also of the Terrestiall Globe . . ., but rather because that it represents unto us in a just proportion and distance each particular constellation in the Heavens, and every severall region and tract of ground in the Earth'. In this section the scientific aspect of globes is not discussed, as only the stands can be regarded as furniture.

In England celestial globes were known in the time of the Venerable Bede (c. 673-735), and formed part of the educational apparatus in monastic schools. In the Middle Ages princes and eminent philosophers in western Europe caused globes to be constructed for the advancement of their studies. By the trans-oceanic discoveries of Columbus and his contemporaries a great impetus was given to the production of globes. Hitherto, maps had been engraved on metal or drawn by hand and pasted on a wooden ball; but in the 16th century they were often printed on paper gores, fashioned mathematically to fit a prepared surface. Thomas Blundeville, a Norfolk country gentleman devoted to scientific pursuits, states, in his *Exercises*, that Mercator's globes were in common use in England until 1592. In that year the first English terrestrial and celestial globes were published by Emery Molyneux, and a celebrated pair, bearing the royal arms and a dedication to Queen Elizabeth I, are preserved in the Middle Temple

1. *Celestial Globe, one of a pair, by Emery Molyneux; turned ebonised uprights of stand and horizon circle contemporary; the table of early 19th century date. c. 1592. Ht. 4 ft. 6 in. (The Middle Temple.)* 2. *Celestial Globe, one of a pair, on mahogany stand; plinth decorated with applied fretwork. 1757. Extreme Ht. 4 ft. 7 in. (Oriel College, Oxford.)* 3. *Celestial Globe, one of a pair, by George Adams, on mahogany tripod stand. c. 1770. Ht. 2 ft. 9 in. (Christ Church, Oxford.)*

library. They were repaired by J. and W. Newton in 1818, when the stands were renovated, but the columnar ebonised supports and broad wooden horizon circle forming the upper portion are probably original (Fig. 1). Hakluyt (*Principal Navigations*, 1589) mentions the approaching publication of these globes by 'M. Emmerie Mollineux of Lambeth'. A considerable number were manufactured and sold, some being made on a smaller scale for a cheaper edition. A Latin manual, giving directions for their use, was published by Robert Hues in 1594 and translated by Chilmead in 1639. In this treatise, widely used by 17th-century sailors, the author writes: 'The Fabrick of the frame is thus: First of all there is a base, or foot to rest upon, on which there is raised perpendicularly six Columnes or Pillars of equall length and distance, upon the top of which there is fastened to a levell and parallel to the Base, a round plate or circle of wood, of a sufficient breadth and thicknesse, which they call the Horizon. . . .' Molyneux appears to have been the only English maker of repute before the second half of the 17th century.

At this period 'the use of globes' was considered a part of a polite education. Sherbourne, in his appendix to Henry Peacham's *The Compleat Gentleman*, first published in 1622, says that 'Mr Wright being chosen Tutor in mathematics to Prince Henry, caused a large sphere to be made for his Highness by help of some German workmen; which sphere by means of Spring work' represented the motion of the heavenly bodies. Milton held it 'seasonable to learn the use of the globes' for those engaged in the study of fortifications, and Lord Herbert of Cherbury commended celestial globes for 'particular predictions'. Joseph Moxon, who published *A Tutor to Astronomy and Geography* (1659), was the most

celebrated English globe-maker of the time, making his mathematical instruments at 'The Sign of the Atlas' in Russell Street. In 1661 Wren's globe of the moon, the first of its kind, was presented to Charles II at Whitehall, fixed on a stand of lignum vitae curiously turned and bearing an inscription to the king. It was placed among the curiosities in the royal cabinet, but no longer survives. Most of these English globes appear to have been set on comparatively plain stands; but contemporary foreign examples were sometimes very elaborately mounted. They enable the various forms of baluster supports to be exactly dated, and are often remarkable in both detail and design.

There were many English globe-makers in the 18th century, and their productions are found in various foreign libraries, often on the original stands. These prove that highly skilled craftsmen were called in to mount the globes, and show, moreover, that when thus mounted and transformed into decorative pieces of furniture they were widely exported. It is noticeable that the stands do not invariably conform to the prevailing taste, such details as the lion-paw foot being found long after it had gone out of fashion: a form of stand well calculated to support the weight, when once adopted, was not readily abandoned. Foremost among the list of early 18th-century cartographers was John Senex (d. 1749), his globes being sold later by the Adams and other makers. Senex was a Fellow of the Royal Society, and, among several other scientific works, published (1718) at the Globe in Salisbury Court *A Treatise of the Description and Use of Both Globes*. Two of his globes, now in the Bibliothèque Nationale, are dedicated in a Latin inscription with 'befitting humility' to Sir Isaac Newton and the members of the Royal Society. A

4. Armillary sphere; stand carved mahogany, with celestial sphere of brass. c. 1750. Ht. 3 ft. 2⅛ in. (V. & A. Mus.)   5. Orrery, by Benjamin Cole, in glazed case; cabriole legs of mahogany stand carved with rococo ornament. c. 1763. (Queen's College, Oxford.) 6. Terrestrial Globe, one of a pair, on mahogany stand with reeded legs; horizon circle inlaid with a small chequer. c. 1800. Ht. (of stand) 1 ft. 6 in. (V. & A. Mus.)

celestial sphere from Oriel College, one of a pair 'adjusted to the year 1740 by John Senex, F.R.S.', and made with 'Several New improvements' by Benjamin Martin in 1757, is given in Fig. 2; stands and plinths are of the latter date. They are of mahogany—the horizon circle carved with a bold egg-and-tongue moulding, the six cabriole legs ending in lion-paw feet. James Ferguson (d. 1776), a Scotch physicist and mathematician of repute, gave special attention to the construction of orreries. These instruments, invented by George Graham c. 1700 for Charles Boyle, Earl of Orrery, represented the motions of the planets about the sun by means of wheel-work. A collection of scientific instruments usually formed part of the furniture in a well-equipped country house library. At Dunham Massey, Cheshire, in 1752 the library of George, second Earl of Warrington, contained:

> Celestial Globe with a Leather cover
> Terrestrial globe with a Leather cover
> Sphere cover'd with wood and glass
> Orrery cover'd with glass.

An orrery made by Thomas Wright, of Fleet Street, 'Instrument maker to His Majesty', who published *The Description and Use of the Globes and the Orrery* in 1731, is in a glazed case and mounted on a duodecagon stand with plain baluster supports of oak. It is probably of about that date. The contemporary stand suggests that stability, not fashion, was the primary consideration. The orrery in Fig. 5 was made c. 1763 by Benjamin Cole, and given to Queen's College, Oxford, in 1763. The case is fixed on a base with rococo chased-metal mounts, bearing the names of the twelve signs of the Zodiac. The curves of the stand are skilfully calculated

7. Globe on mahogany stand designed in classical taste; supports of horizon circle boldly carved with acanthus, and modelled as lion terminals. c. 1810. (Trinity House, London.)

323

to follow the shape of the case, the cabriole legs being finely carved. Benjamin Martin, who 'improved' the Oriel globes, and published in 1760 a work on this subject, in which a section is devoted to orreries, deplores that a machine 'most useful' in providing 'Part of the Education which our English youth should have' was not so common as it should be on account of the high price. The well-known picture *The Orrery*, exhibited by Wright, of Derby, in 1766 (Derby Gallery) charmingly illustrates the part played by these instruments in the education of children. The armillary sphere (Fig. 4) was made as a decorative piece of furniture for a library, the engraved brass circles being of no practical service for scientific purposes.

In the second half of the century George Adams achieved a world-wide reputation as a maker of globes. In 1766 he published, from his shop, the sign of Tycho Brahe's Head, Fleet Street, a *Treatise* on the use of the globes he had recently put on the market. He was mathematical instrument-maker to George III, and a pair of his globes in Christ Church Library, Oxford, are dedicated to that king. They bear no date, but were probably made c. 1770, the tripod stands closely resembling those shown in their author's book (Fig. 3). After this time there are no new developments of importance in the construction of globe-stands. The late examples are generally of plain tripod form, but occasionally they are designed in the style of contemporary furniture (Fig. 6). In the vigorously carved stand of the globe from Trinity House (Fig. 7) is shown the influence of the Regency classical revival.

GOTHIC TASTE. The term used in the 18th century by inventors and admirers of mock medieval forms then introduced into architecture, decoration and furniture. Interest in Gothic art, long ignored save by a few antiquaries and by Daniel Defoe in his *Tour through the Whole Island of Great Britain*, 1724-7, which reveals a lively appreciation, revived in England early in this century. Among leading contemporary architects, Vanbrugh, Hawksmoor and Kent all practised in the style. Batty Langley published *Gothic Architecture Restored and Improved* (1742)—an audacious adaptation and travesty of medieval forms. By 1750, satire had already been directed against Gothicism in the *Scribleriad* (1751) and in early numbers of the *World*. W. Whitehead wrote in 1753 in that journal 'A few years ago everything was Gothic; our houses, our beds, our books, our couches. . . .' In the 1750s the leading exponents of the style were Sanderson Miller, a Warwickshire squire, Horace Walpole, John Chute, of The Vyne, and Richard Bentley. The decorations of Strawberry Hill, Middlesex, and also much of the furniture were in this taste 'in its most intense degree', and were termed by its votaries 'true Gothic'. This was exceptional. The leading cabinet-designers and makers (*e.g.* Chippendale) seldom did more than introduce details of what they considered Gothic into pieces of furniture, of which the leading lines were still of classic origin. Thus in the *Director* Chippendale illustrates 'A Gothic Sideboard' (Plate LX, 3rd ed., 1762) of which the legs are enriched with cusped arches and the rail has rococo ornaments flanked with Chinese frets. A 'Clothes Chest' (Plate CXXVIII) is on a frame with the same mixed motives. A 'Bason Stand' (Plate LV) has base and top composed of baroque scrolls, but 'in the Middle hath four Gothic Pillars and an Arch'. Several bookcases are similarly treated, but there is one (Plate C)

324

which, as an exception, does come near to the 'pure Gothic' of those designed by Bentley for the Strawberry Hill library, which have their counterpart at Arbury, Warwickshire. Of the chamber organs, although one is 'according to the modern Architecture'—*i.e.* of classic design—another has cusped arcading and flamboyant finials much like the bookcase; while Plate CVI is described as 'an Organ in the Gothic taste', and the comment is made that 'as most of the Cathedral Churches are of Gothic Architecture it is Pity that the Organs are not better adapted'.

Gothic ornament also figures prominently in the pattern-books of other contemporary cabinet- and chair-makers, the vogue lasting until some years after the inception of the neo-classic style. Manwaring, for instance, was advertising the 'Most Approved Patterns' for Gothic chairs in 1766, and Edward Edwards made a cabinet in this taste for Horace Walpole as late as 1783 (*see* CABINETS; Fig. 48). But the style as Chippendale and his school interpreted it was virtually independent of its origins in the past and represented a new fashion in ornament. This decorative convention was peculiar to England, and there is no evidence on the Continent of a parallel cult. An attempt was made to revive this taste during the Regency, and in *Household Furniture* (1808) George Smith published some elaborate designs in the style, notably a state bed loaded with tracery and cusping (Plate XXVIII).

GRAINING. A process of painting furniture and woodwork, by which the colour and figure of a more costly wood was counterfeited in one of a cheaper kind; first adopted in England towards the end of the 16th century for the imitation of oak and walnut, being subsequently extended to other woods. Graining continued to be practised in Georgian times. (*See Art of Painting in Oyles*, J. Smith, 1676).

GRATES. *See* CHIMNEY FURNITURE.

GRENOBLE WOOD. The term often used in inventories of the late 17th century for the French variety of common walnut (*Juglans regia*). (*See* WALNUT.)

GRISAILLE. Style of painting in various grey tints to represent solid bodies in relief; often found in friezes and medallions on satinwood and painted furniture. (*See* BUREAUX; Fig. 42.)

GROTESQUE (*Grottescu* J. Florio, *A World of Words* 1598, corruption of the Italian). Term for carved, painted or inlaid ornament of extravagant and fanciful characters, representing figures, animals, etc., having no counterpart in nature. Also called in 16th and 17th centuries 'anticke worke'. (*See* MIRRORS; Fig. 54.)

GUERIDON. *See* STANDS, CANDLE.

GUILLOCHE. Ornament derived from classical architecture and formed of two or more bands twisted over each other making a continuous pattern; interspaces are, at times, filled with conventional roses. Used on furniture from c. 1550 to c. 1800, carved, painted and inlaid (*see* CUPBOARDS, HALL; Fig. 3).

HAKE. *See* POTHANGER, under CHIMNEY FURNITURE.

HAREWOOD. Greenish-grey wood, sycamore or maple stained with oxide of iron. A modern term, probably a rendering of 'airs-wood' and 'airewood', both of which appear to derive from German *ehren-holz*—for maple, which closely resembles sycamore and is of the same genus. Evelyn (*Sylva*, 1664) states that airewood was used by instrument-makers. The *Evening Post* (May 30, 1723) advertises that Wm. Tabel: 'the famous Harpsichordmaker . . . has also some fine Airs-wood for finishing the insides, to dispose of'. The term generally used for dyed sycamore and maple in the late 18th century was 'silverwood' (*q.v.*). 'Harewood' also now applied to West Indian (San Domingo) satinwood.

HARPSICHORD (HARPSICAL, HARPSICON). *See* MUSICAL INSTRUMENTS.

HARRATINE. Linen fabric used for drapery of beds in the 18th century. The Duke of Newcastle, writing to the Duke of Montagu (September, 1711) refers to 'six field Bedsteads with crimson harateen furnitures'. In 1752 William Reason, upholsterer to George II, charges £2 1s. 11d. 'for 15½ yds. of Harateen to new cover a 4 leaved screen' in one of the royal palaces.

HEARTH-BRUSH. *See* CHIMNEY FURNITURE.

HEARTH-ROD. *See* CHIMNEY FURNITURE.

HERCULANEUM. The name given by Sheraton (*Cabinet Dictionary*, 1803) to upholstered chairs in pronounced classical taste, which are 'so named on account of their antique style of composition'.

HERRING-BONE BANDING. *See* FEATHER BANDING.

HINGE. *See* METAL MOUNTS.

HOLLY (*Ilex aquifolium*). Hard, white wood with slightly flecked grain; used by joiners for inlay work in solid on oak and walnut furniture of the Tudor period, and by marquetry cutters in the late 17th and in the 18th centuries; sometimes stained when foliage, etc., was represented in semi-natural tints. Evelyn (*Sylva*, 1664): 'It is the whitest of all hard woods, and therefore used by the Inlayer.' J. C. R.

HOOF-FOOT. A motif, in a variety of forms, used as a terminal to legs of furniture from remote antiquity, especially by Egyptians. Introduced into England from the Continent at the end of the 17th century. Goat's hoof found on early cabriole chairs (*see* CABRIOLE and CHAIRS; Fig. 57).

HOOP-BACK. A form of chair-back in which the curves of uprights and top rail merge into each other. (*See* CHAIRS.)

HORSEBONE. A term used in the late Stuart period for inward scroll in the structure of seat furniture. A pair of stools at Hampton Court Palace made by Thomas Roberts 1700-1 are described in his bill as having 'the foreparts carved horse-bone'.

HORSEHAIR. A form of covering for furniture woven from the manes and tail-hairs of horses, with linen or cotton warp. It first became popular c. 1775, being chiefly used on chairs the upholstery of which was exposed to hard usage. Hepplewhite (*Guide*, 1788): 'Mahogany chairs should have

1. *'Sudbury's Hutch', in St James's Church, Louth; doors carved with portraits of Henry VII and Elizabeth of York, the central panel bearing the combined badges of York and Lancaster below a crown; the structure, of oak, has been restored. c. 1495. Ht. 3 ft. ½ in., L. 5 ft. 3 in., Depth 2 ft. 2½ in.*
2. *Silver Testoon of Henry VII; the portrait of the King resembles that on 'Sudbury's Hutch.'*

seats of horsehair, plain, striped, chequered, etc., at pleasure . . .' Mixed with wool or hair of other animals, it was used as stuffing for the seats and backs from the early 17th century onwards (*see* UPHOLSTERY).

HUTCH. Term derived from the French *huche*. In the will of Alicia Langham, of Snaylwell '1 spruce hutche' is entered in 1448; and other contemporary references show that for making hutches this wood, spruce or fir from the shores of the Baltic, was often used, while some hutches were probably imported from that area. The term appears to have been applied both to chests of rough construction and to more

3. *Oak Hutch or Bread Cupboard; panels perforated in diaper patterns. c. 1620. Ht. 2 ft. 9 in., L. 3 ft., Depth 1 ft. 8 in. (V. & A. Mus.)*

ornamental receptacles on legs with one or more doors in front. A well-known example of the latter type (Fig. 1) was given to Louth parish church, Lincolnshire, by a vicar named Sudbury, incumbent 1461-1504. In the church accounts, where notices of its repair at various dates occur, it is always spoken of as 'Sudbury's Hutch'. The doors are carved with profile portraits of Henry VII and his consort, Elizabeth of York, framed in Renaissance arches, but with traditional Gothic trefoils in the spandrels. These portraits are of exceptional interest, the king's head closely resembling that on the silver testoons, or shillings, of the reign. Although the queen wears her hair down, as at her coronation in 1487, the hutch probably dates from c. 1495, for Henry's crown and that surmounting the badges of Lancaster and York on the central panel are of the arched or 'imperial' type adopted on his later coinage. On the silver shilling Henry substituted a realistic portrait of himself in profile for the conventional full-face hitherto used. It is reasonable to suppose that the carver of this hutch copied a testoon (Fig. 2) as the most readily available portrait of the king.

In domestic hutches clothes were commonly stored, and under Elizabeth, Tusser writes (*Husbandry*) of the hutch as a food cupboard, the special care of provident householders.

> The eye of the master enricheth the hutch
> The eye of the mistress availeth as much.

Cotgrave (*Dictionary*, 1611) identifies the term with a 'Binne' or 'kneading Trough'. In the 17th century hutches often figure in the inventories of yeomen and farmers in the eastern counties, enumerated among the contents of halls, parlours and bedrooms. The term appears to have been used with latitude, and there are entries in inventories which seem to indicate hutches of cupboard form fitted with doors. In 1681 Mary Wilks, of Writtle, possessed 'one great hutch with a set of striped linsey woolsey curtaines, three payre of course sheetes, some pewter and other thing in it'. Fig. 3 shows a type, apparently of eastern county origin; the panels are perforated in diaper patterns, which suggests that such examples were used for bread.

'INDIAN' GOODS. From c. 1600 to 1750 a comprehensive term for any Oriental object imported into Europe. (*See* JAPANNING AND LACQUER.)

INK-STAND. *See* STANDISH.

INLAY AND MARQUETRY. Methods of decorating the surface of furniture with geometrical, floral and arabesque patterns, classical motives and other devices. Inlay was employed on oak and walnut furniture in the 16th and 17th centuries (*see* CHESTS; Fig. 13). It consisted of marking the outlines of the pattern on the actual surfaces to be decorated, sinking the surfaces about $\frac{1}{8}$ in. within these lines, and fitting therein an assortment of small pieces of light- and dark-coloured woods. The woods used in this 'cut-in' inlay were ash, beech, bog oak, ebony, fruit woods, holly, poplar, sycamore, yew, etc.; bone, ivory, tortoise-shell and mother-of-pearl were also used.

In inventories of this period the term 'markatree' was often applied to this form of decoration, and in some extant examples the process (in the modern sense of that term) is foreshadowed,

the oak ground being covered with a 'skin' of various woods about $\frac{1}{8}$ in. thick. Marquetry was introduced in conjunction with veneered walnut furniture after the Restoration, the chief varieties being floral and 'seaweed' or arabesque (*cf.* CHESTS, Fig. 25; CABINETS, Figs. 9 and 10).

The methods of cutting the patterns in the veneers varied in detail according to whether it was a floral design (needing numerous woods) or a seaweed or arabesque pattern (for either of which only one wood was used to contrast with the ground). They may be described thus:

(1) *The General Process.* The design for a panel was drawn on paper, the lines being pricked through to underlying sheets to make the necessary copies; or the pricked sheet was dusted over with a coloured powder which, passing through the perforations, marked the design faintly on the paper underneath. The layers of veneer to be used for the pattern and for the ground were secured with panel pins or were glued together with a sheet of paper interposed between them, to enable easy separation; the paper bearing the design was then pasted on top, and the set gripped in the 'chops' of the 'donkey', the terms for the marquetry-cutter's vice and bench. The craftsman then cut along the lines of the design with a fine frame saw. Normally the set of veneers was covered on both sides with a sheet of common wood, owing to the saw making a ragged cut on the exposed faces. The veneers were then separated by splitting the interleaved papers or withdrawing the pins. The pattern design would now have been cut through the whole depth of the assembled veneers. As only one layer would be required for each compartment of the design or pattern, it follows that there would have been a rejected surplus—*e.g.* if four veneers had been cut, then three would be rejected for each compartment, though not the same three in each case because of the different colours demanded by the design. It was usual to retain the light woods for the pattern and dark ones for the 'ground'.

The next operation was to fit the selected pieces of light wood to one another, and into the spaces cut in the 'ground' layer; after this, to hold the assembled panel, a sheet of paper was glued over the whole and allowed to dry in a press. The carcase's surface was planed, scraped and roughened with the toothing plane, and given a thin coat of good glue, which was allowed to dry. The marquetry panel was then laid in position, held with veneer pins, and glued down by means of a hot 'caul'—a fairly stout piece of wood, slightly convex on the underside and a little larger than the panel. It was first made very hot and then quickly cramped down over the marquetry with hand-screws: the convex surface ensured that pressure began at the centre and continued to the edges. The heat from the caul passed through the veneers and liquefied the glue previously applied; as it became cold the glue set again and after about thirty-six hours the caul could be safely removed. A further period of about a week was allowed for the glue under the marquetry to harden before the scraping of the paper from the surface and the smoothing off preparatory to polishing.

(2) *Floral Marquetry.* This was the vogue c. 1660-90 (until c. 1715 on clock-cases), in which several woods were employed, many being stained to obtain the desired colours. Evelyn (*Sylva*, 1664) mentions some of the coloured woods used: '. . . such as are naturally so: Berbery for yellow, Holly for white. Our

Inlayers use Fustic, Locust or Acacia, Brazile, Prince and Rose wood for yellow and reds, with severall others brought from both Indies.' To which may be added: box, holly, sycamore, and, for the ground, plain straight-cut walnut, figured walnut and burr walnut, also lignum vitae, and coromandel, kingwood and laburnum.

It was generally found impossible to treat the whole panel in one operation; thus the design was cut into convenient sections, the necessary veneers were chosen for the correct colours, and, after they had been glued together as before described, the portion of the design which they were to represent was pasted on them and, when they were dry, the cutting proceeded. Each section was prepared in this way, the superfluous layer of veneer being removed, and kept together in separate trays until the whole design had been cut. Great care and skill were necessary in fitting the portions to one another and into the background.

Engraving the surfaces of the marquetry does not seem to have been employed until the second half of the 18th century. Portions of the design (e.g. leaves) were shaded by being dipped into hot sand; of this Evelyn (*Sylva*) writes: 'When they would imitate the naturall turning of leaves in their curious compartments and bordures of flower works, they effect it by dipping the pieces so far into hot sand as they would have the shadow'.

(3) *Seaweed or Arabesque Marquetry*. Fashionable c. 1690, marking the culmination of the marquetry-cutter's skill. The method was more straightforward, inasmuch as only two woods were used—box or holly for the pattern, and walnut for the ground, sometimes in association with parquetry. The operation proceeded as described in (1); the fineness of the scrolling patterns demanded extreme care and a very fine saw, kept exactly on the lines of the pattern and held at a slight angle, which overcame the trouble of a wide joint caused by the saw gate.

Marquetry was revived c. 1765, and for important examples by Chippendale and other contemporary cabinet-makers, *see* CABINETS and COMMODES. The decoration was of light-coloured woods, *e.g.* box and holly in a ground of mahogany, satinwood or harewood veneers; in the more elaborate pieces a variety of other stained and exotic woods was also used. The designs were at first naturalistic and inspired by contemporary French marquetry, but later they were in neo-classical taste, being usually arranged in panels and in the frieze of the entablature.

From c. 1790 to 1800 marquetry was, to a considerable extent, superseded by painting. The laying of veneers with scrolls and foliated ornament in brass and various patterns in ebonised wood came into favour in the Regency period, couches and sideboards providing prominent instances of this treatment (*see* COUCHES AND DAY-BEDS; Fig. 20; PARQUETRY AND VENEER.) J. C. R.

IONIC ORDER. *See* ORDERS.

IRISH CHIPPENDALE. Popular term applied to mahogany furniture of Irish origin with flat and disconnected carving made c. 1740-65. In Irish side-tables of c. 1740 there is a distinctive convention in the rendering of lion masks and paw feet; aprons are often of exaggerated depth, while foliated

scrolls and other motives are relieved against incised diaper patterns on punched ground. Furniture imported from England supplied models for native craftsmen.

JAPANNING AND LACQUER. These terms, as generally applied, are very comprehensive. The sap of the *Rhus vernicifera*, 'lac-tree' (grown in China, Japan and Malaya), applied in successive coats on wood or some other substance, is the basis of the art of lacquering, as practised from remote antiquity in the East. This sap was not available in Europe, where imitation was arrived at by a method essentially different and more appropriately termed japan than lacquer. In *The Handmaid to the Arts* (1758) Robert Dossie writes that 'by japanning is to be understood the art of covering bodies by grounds of opake colours in varnish; which may be either afterwards decorated by painting or gilding, or left in a plain state'. The wood, treated with a mixture of whitening and size, was then coated with two or more applications of varnish composed of gum-lac, seed-lac or shellac, which are different preparations of the resin broken off the twigs of the trees on which it is deposited by an insect, the *Coccus lacca*, and dissolved in spirits of wine, other gums and substances being also employed. 'Bantam work', an imitation of incised lac, *papier-mâché*, and japanning on metal are variations of the ordinary process.

The word 'Indian' appears to have been applied from the end of Elizabeth I's reign promiscuously to any oriental object imported into Europe; this was due to the prevailing ignorance of Far Eastern geography. The distinction is, however, clearly drawn by Van Linschoten in an account of

1. *Design for Japan Decoration, from Stalker and Parker's* Treatise, 1688.

2. *From Edwards and Darly's* New Book of Chinese Designs, 1754.

his voyage to the East Indies (English translation, 1598). He writes that, while in India lacquer-work of all kinds is much used for furniture, 'the fayrest workmanshippe thereof cometh from China'. He mentions in support of this statement imported tables, cupboards, boxes 'and a thousand such like things that are all covered and wrought with Lac of all colours and fashions'. At this time the English and Portuguese were already trading with Japan and China, and, no doubt, some of these lacquer objects had found their way into this country. Within a few years furniture decorated in oriental taste, of native production, is mentioned in inventories, notably that (in 1614) of the contents of the Earl of Northampton's London house (*see* CHINESE TASTE for other early examples). In 1615 Thomas Howard, Earl of Arundel, writes to the Countess at Arundel House, asking her to buy a blue quilt which 'will serve ye bedde of Jappan exceedinge well. . . .'

Extant examples of English furniture decorated with 'China worke' are a ballot box in the possession of the Saddlers' Company, and a set of a dozen roundels and two cabinets, in the Victoria and Albert Museum. Foliated scrollwork in gold and silver figures prominently in the decoration of the cabinets (closely resembling that on the ballot box) with figures in pseudo-oriental costume and palm tree foliage (*see* CABINETS; Fig. 1). The decoration on all these objects, painted black on a prepared ground and thinly varnished, may be assigned to the same hand.

This taste did not become widespread until Charles II's reign, when oriental curiosities were largely imported by the East India Company (founded 1599), among them Chinese and Japanese lacquer panels which were inserted or wholly made up into pieces of furniture. These oriental panels appear to have been offered for sale in London shops, for in the first Earl of Bristol's *Expense Book* (1689) there is an entry for payment for twelve leaves of 'cutt Jappan Skreens', and in 1701 there is another entry: 'Paid Medina for a pair of Indian Cutt Jappan skreens.' About 1700, notices appear in the *London Gazette* advertising for sale 'Jappan Cabinets', both Indian and English; and the term 'japan' was then used without any definite geographical implication. The fashion for this decoration received a powerful stimulus from the

close relations between the courts of Charles II and Louis XIV, who collected oriental works of art on a vast scale through the Compagnie des Indes; in France in the 1680s large quantities of furniture *façon de Chine* were also made. Workshops for the imitation of oriental lacquer, called *laquage*, were installed at the Gobelins factory, though very few of its productions survive. Later, Mme de Pompadour possessed suites of lacquered furniture of the highest quality.

The Dutch, who after 1602 obtained a monopoly of the trade with Japan, professed to supply the West, and undertook to have furniture sent to China to be decorated. This must have been an expensive procedure, and Captain William Dampier (*Collection of Voyages*, 1688) complains that the joiners in Tonkin were greatly inferior to European craftsmen, and 'in laying the lac upon good or fine joyned work they frequently spoil the joints, edges or corners of drawers or cabinets'. He records that for this reason a certain captain, on his second voyage to Tonkin, took out with him an 'ingenious joyner' with a supply of deal boards 'to make fashionable Commodities to be lackered here'. Of the wares produced there Dampier observes that they are 'not inferior to any but that of Japan only, which is esteemed the best in the world'; though he adds 'there seems not any considerable difference in the Paint or Varnish'.

Some Dutch japanning of this period is remarkable for both quality of surface and excellence of design. It has been suggested that to instruct native craftsmen, lacquer workers were imported from China and Japan. In the Notarial Archives of Amsterdam of the 17th and 18th centuries, there are many references to 'lack-werkers' (or 'Japanish Verlakkers'). In an interesting contract (1704) one of them, Johannes Konnigh, engages himself for the next three years to make and deliver tea-tables, door panels for cabinets, etc., in his finest manner and paint them in gold or colour to the satisfaction of his employer.

In 1692 in England Edward Hurd and James Narcock petition the Crown, setting forth that by great study and expense they have brought the art of lacquering after the manner of Japan to 'such a degree of curiosity and durableness as to equal any brought from India', and pray for letters patent for the sole use and benefit of the invention for fourteen years. In 1697 the 'Patentees for Lacquering after the manner of Japan' offer 'cabinets, secretaires, tables, stands, looking-glasses and tea-tables'. In Scotland, even as late as 1705, a petition was presented to Parliament by Sarah Dalrymple for permission to carry on a japanning manufactory. It is not always possible to determine from the wording of these petitions whether japanning on wood or metal was in question; moreover, contemporary allusions often leave a doubt as to the nationality of the furniture and decoration. By far the greater part of English japanning is anonymous, but in the 18th century furniture and decoration of this kind were supplied by Chippendale (*e.g.* COMMODES; Fig. 12) and other leading firms. Early in George III's reign, when Sir William Chambers was carrying out alterations to the Queen's House (now Buckingham Palace) a japanned room was repaired at the great cost of £572 12s. by the cabinet-maker W. Vile (*q.v.*), who charged for 'new drawing and securing' the old japan and 'making a quantity of New Japan to make out the old to fit different walls'. In 1767, shortly after these alterations,

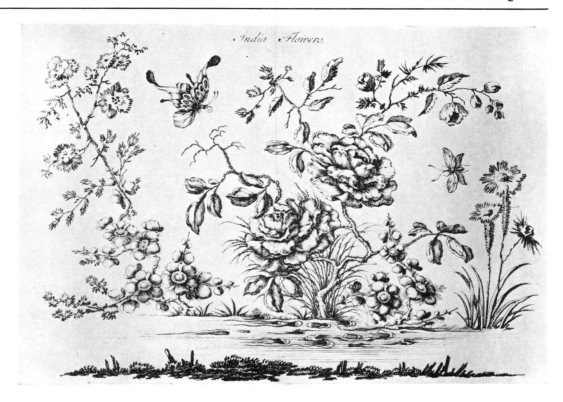

3. *Design for japanned ornament from* The Ladies Amusement. *c.* 1760.

Mrs Lybbe Powis describes this room as 'panelled in the finest Japan'.

John Stalker and George Parker probably gleaned most of the technical information for their *Treatise of Japanning and Varnishing* (1688) from Dutch craftsmen. Their crude designs, called 'Patterns for Japan-work in imitation of the Indians for Tables, Stands, Frames, Cabinets, etc.', have a strong imprint of Dutch influence, particularly in the costumes worn by some of the figures (Fig. 1). It is claimed that the patterns are exact imitations of the oriental; but the authors add that 'the artist has endeavoured to help these designs a little where they were lame and defective'. They refer to the process always as 'Japan' or 'Indian work'.

Despite the florid style the technical information is readily comprehensible, while late Stuart English japan-work is found to embody the directions given. Subsequent writers plagiarised freely from the *Treatise of Japanning*, among them Salmon, in the eighth edition of his *Polygraphice* (1701), and the 'Great Mr Boyle' (*i.e.* Hon. Robert Boyle, F.R.S., 1627-91), who professed to teach how to make 'black or gilt Japan Ware as light as any brought from the East Indies with proper directions for making the hardest and most transparent Varnishes'. An article on japanning in the *Dictionarium Polygraphicum* (1735), while heavily indebted to the *Treatise*, gives some interesting directions for 'taking off Japan Patterns' from a 'draught' or design.

Stalker and Parker, after discussing the various varnishes and gums used, explain how to overlay the object made of wood, such as deal, oak, pear-tree or olive, with a preparation of 'whiting and parchment size in as many layers as deemed necessary, permitting it to drie between every wash'. It must then be polished and varnished, following the detailed directions till the surface 'glissen and reflects your face like a mirror'. Precise descriptions are given of the instruments required for the many processes, such as varnishing pencils, Dutch rushes,

goose, duck and swallow quills. The colours advocated for the groundwork are: 'Black Japan, Red Japan, Chestnut Color, Blew Japan, Olive Color, Yellow, Green, Counterfeit Tortoiseshell'.

The directions for 'Blew Japan' are very complicated, many applications and washings with ground white lead, smalt and the clearest isinglass-size being indispensable if the finest results are to be obtained. Several shades of red japan were employed, the most important being common red, the deep dark and the light pale red. This brilliant decoration was too obtrusive to be used save in a very sparing manner, while blue japan was apparently rarely attempted, as genuine specimens are extremely scarce.

Stalker and Parker give the following as the most useful metal dusts: 'Brass Dust, Silver Dust, Green Gold, Dirty Gold, Powder Tin, Natural Copper, Artificial Copper, Adulterate Copper', noting that the first 'cannot be made in England fit for use', the best coming from Germany, and that the second is 'not good in England'. These are to be applied with either gold-size or gum water. The metal dust so often used in the decoration of red japanned cabinets is not tarnished silver, but powdered tin.

After the black or coloured ground was sufficiently polished, the picture or design was drawn on in gold-size or vermilion mixed with gum water, the parts to be raised, such as rocks, houses, figures, animals, being put in with a paste of gum arabic water and whiting, sometimes further thickened with fine sawdust, and dropped on with a rush pencil-stick. Raised portions were subsequently polished and gilt with the various metal powders. These decorations included human figures, fauna, flora and buildings with landscape background, all of a pseudo-oriental character. In amateur japanning, motives borrowed from various sources were often assembled incongruously in a single design. Decoration in high relief gradually gave way in England to a flatter style more suited

329

to the delineation of the conventional flowers and foliage that became popular in Georgian times.

According to Stalker and Parker, there were two kinds of so-called 'Bantam-work', flat and incised; but beyond saying that the former 'was done in colors mix't with a gum water', they give no account of the process. The incised variety was done on a foundation of deal or some other coarse, soft wood, a whiting and size preparation being applied in successive thin layers till at times it reached a depth of ¼ in. This, when dry, was blackened or covered with some uniform tint, varnished, and polished 'with a gentle and easie hand'. The design was then drawn, the parts carved out with a graver to the depth of the composition, tinted with colours mixed with gums, and occasionally slightly gilt; the whole design was often surrounded by a conventional border, also cut out and coloured. This particular variety was called 'Bantam-work', probably because the Dutch settlement on the western coast of Java was at first the principal market for oriental incised lacquer. Stalker and Parker refer to 'Bantam-work' in 1688 as 'almost obsolete and out of fashion', and add: 'I think no person is fond of it or gives it house-room except some who have made new cabinets out of old skreens and from that large old piece by the help of a Joyner made little ones, such as stands or Tables, but never consider the situation of their figures . . . so torn and hacked . . . you may observe the finest hodgpodg and medley' (see MIRRORS; Fig. 14). They were mistaken; Coromandel screens and cabinets were imported in the 18th century, and English imitations, later than 1688, survive (see CHESTS; Fig. 27).

It is comparatively easy to distinguish between 17th- and 18th-century oriental work intended for the European market and English japan, apart from the quality of the ground, perhaps the decisive indication. In oriental examples, the drawing of figures and animals is notably superior; faces and costumes are unmistakably Eastern. In some exceptional examples, however, particularly those of Dutch origin, ground and ornament are of such high quality that an Eastern origin is likely to be attributed to them. The lack of vitality generally noticeable in the design, compared with true lacquer, is largely explained by the decoration being often traced from imported panels or designs in pattern books. Very little of the abundant Parisian and Venetian japanning of the late 17th and early 18th centuries seems to have been imported into England.

The taste for japanned furniture was still strong in the mid-18th century; Chippendale states (*Director*) that some of his designs are suitable for this style of decoration. Ince and Mayhew also supplied japanned goods, while Edwards and Darly (*New Book of Chinese Designs*, 1754) provide a number of suitable designs (Fig. 2). Though the rage for chinoiseries was still widely prevalent, Robert Dossie (*Handmaid to the Arts*, 1758) states that japanning is 'not at present practiced so frequently'. Dossie observes that 'one principal variation in the manner of japanning is the using or omitting any priming or undercoat on the work to be japanned. In the older practice such priming was always used'. He states that another variation from the earlier method is the laying on of colours with gum water instead of varnish, but adds that for cabinets and other such pieces water-colours on an undercoat tempered with isinglass and honey 'will not be much inferior in appear-

ance to that done by the other method; and will last as long as the old japan'. Examples of fine japan decoration are found as late as 1770 on furniture designed by Robert Adam for Osterley, Middlesex, and Nostell, Yorkshire (see COMMODES; Fig. 11: CUPBOARDS, PRESSES AND WARDROBES; Fig. 19). On a suite for Garrick's bedroom in his Hampton villa the surface is merely paint and varnish, which c. 1775-1800 replaced the true japanning process. The japan-work alluded to in Hepplewhite's *Guide* (1788) as a fashion 'which has arisen within these few years' was a degenerate survival of the old form of decoration carried out on a black unprimed ground with the numerous coats of varnish formerly applied now reduced to a minimum, bronze powder being often substituted for gold leaf in the designs. In the Regency period exceptions to the degenerate practice are found; sometimes grounds of red and yellow were employed, sprinkled with metal dust imitative of gold and silver to produce a glittering effect.

The quantity of indifferent japanning that has survived is accounted for by the vast amount produced by amateurs, and the value they set on their work. Sir Ralph Verney, in a letter (1689), agrees to pay 'A Guiney entrance and 40/- more to buy materials' for his daughter Molly to be taught the art at school. Stalker and Parker write severely of the 'impotent fellows who pretend to teach young ladies an art in which they themselves have need to be instructed'. There is an entry (1694) in Lady Grisell Baillie's *Household Book*: 'To materialls to japan £3. . . .'. That these amateur efforts were prized is proved by the will of Elizabeth (second wife of the first Earl of Bristol), who died in 1741 and left her eldest son, Lord Hervey, 'My cabinet, chest, large skreen and small skreen being white japan of my own work in confidence that he will preserve them for my sake'. Amateur japanning was a veritable rage in early Georgian times. Mrs Pendarves, writing to her sister in 1729, says: 'Everybody is mad about Japan work, I hope to be a dab at it by the time I see you. I will perfect myself in the art and bring materials with me.' A work professing to teach a new and curious method of japanning, and to make black and gilt 'Japan-Ware as Beautiful and Light as any brought from the East Indies', dedicated in 1732 to Sir Robert Walpole's first wife, was intended for the benefit of such enthusiasts. *The Ladies Amusement or Whole Art of Japanning Made Easy* was published c. 1760 and illustrated with several hundred designs by Pillement and other artists (Fig. 3). Though worthless as a practical guide to the process, it contains some amusing advice on the pitfalls to be avoided when designing either in the European or the Chinese taste. Horace Walpole, son of Sir Robert, evidently did not regard these amateur attempts with favour, as he alludes to 'two vile china jars that look like the modern japanning by ladies'; yet the *Description* of his villa at Strawberry Hill (1782) mentions a cabinet japanned by his mother, Lady Walpole.

Japanning on metal is a variation of the process practised in England from the beginning of the 18th century. Thomas Allgood (*q.v.*) at Pontypool, South Wales, discovered c. 1660 a substance capable of application under heat to the surface of metal. The manufacture was carried on and developed by his son, Edward Allgood (b. 1681), who is credited with the invention of 'Pontypool Japan'. From this centre japanning on metal soon spread to Birmingham and London. In 1729, the firm of Gumley and Turing, cabinet-makers to the king, included among their accounts 'japanning four fine large tin receivers in Red with neat drawings in silver and fixing them up with silver chains to the large double-branched plates sconces'; and on March 15, 1742, William Heath, near Charing Cross, advertised (*Daily Advertiser*) 'a parcel of curious copper brown Tea-kettles and lamps, the colour of China, burnt in after the Indian manner, which for curious work and colour exceed any that come from Holland or any other place'. The japan was applied on a variety of metals, and among the objects manufactured were trays and caddies, the ground being often decorated with painted ornament in gold and colours. The Birmingham speciality was decoration in colour, for, according to Dr Richard Pococke, who visited Pontypool in 1756, the ware produced there was adorned with Chinese landscapes and figures in gold only, and not with colour as at Birmingham. That city was for a long time the greatest centre for elaborately decorated japanned tea-trays, and John Baskerville (*q.v.*), the celebrated printer, is said to have made a fortune there as a japanner before 1750.

JOINERS. Artisans who fit together or join wood to construct a piece of furniture. The Brotherhood of the Guild of St. James's Garlickhythe (est. 1375) was the ancient livery of the Joiners' Company. In 1440 the 'Mystery of the Joyners of the City of London' was allowed to elect two Wardens with power of search. The joiners were also organised in provincial centres, notably York and Chester. At York the Memorandum Book records their ordinances, which antedate those of the Carpenters and were passed in 1413. In 1530 the two guilds in that city amalgamated, and in 1563 other 'wrights', *e.g.* carvers and sawyers, were admitted to the combined guild. In one of the ordinances, rules are laid down for the precise amount of wood to be used for cupboards, tables, chairs and stools.

In the mid-15th century references appeared in inventories to furniture made by joiners: *e.g.* in 1448 Canon Norton of York had '1 *cathedra lignea* (wooden chair) de junyour worke XIId'. The charter of the London Company was granted in 1570, and in 1575 an order was promulgated that 'foreigners' 'using the art of Joinery' must submit themselves 'to the reasonable orders of the Joiners'. In 1613 power of search over makers of cupboards, trunks and boxes was confined to the joiners by the Lord Mayor, and in 1632, the joiners having become involved in a dispute with the Carpenters (*q.v.*), the Court of Aldermen, to end it, decreed that joiners were entitled to the exclusive manufacture of the following articles:

All sorts of Bedsteads whatsoever (onlie except Boarded Bedsteads and nayled together).
All sorts of Chayres and stooles which are made with mortesses or tennants.
All tables of wainscotte wallnutt or other stuffe glewed with fframes mortesses or tennants.
All sorts of formes framed made of boards with the sides pinned or glewed.
All sorts of chests being framed duftalled pynned or glued.
All sorts of Cabinets or Boxes duftalled pynned or glued.

The Joiners were also involved in a dispute with the Turners, and in the following year the Court of Aldermen dealt with the division of labour between the two companies, recognising that 'the arts of turning and joining are two several and distinct trades', and awarding a number of articles—bedposts, joined stools, etc.—to the Turners. References to furniture made by

joiners are occasionally found in domestic accounts of this period. In 1604-5 the steward of the Shuttleworths, of Gawthorpe, Lancashire, entered a payment of 11s. 1d. to 'a joyner, V days at the table in the inner rome'.

It appears that towards the end of the 17th century there were various specialised industries within a single guild. In 1699 the cane-chair-makers enrolled in the Company appealed to it for support against the Basket-Makers, and in a petition to Parliament about the same date protesting against the 'quantities of cabinet wares, manufactured after the English fashion' lately imported from the East Indies, the Joiners referred to the 'great numbers of Artificers, members of the said Company . . . bred up in the said art or mystery of making Cabinets, Scrutores, Tables, Chests and all other sorts of cabinet-work in England. . . .'

Batty Langley (Introduction to the *City and Country Builder's and Workman's Treasury of Designs*, 1740) writes depreciatingly of cabinet-makers as despising architecture, and observes that it is 'a very great difficulty' to find one cabinet-maker in fifty 'that can make a Book Case, etc., indispensably Fine, after any one of the Five Orders, without being obliged to a Joiner for to set out the Work'. By this time the importance of the Joiners' Company had greatly declined, and although an act of Common Council laid down in 1724 that all joiners in London should take up their freedom in the Company under a certain penalty, they were no longer able to enforce the ordinances. At York an attempt to do so was made as late as 1788. (*See* J. B. Jupp, *An Historical Account of the Worshipful Company of Joiners*, 1848, 2nd ed. 1887, and *Woodwork in York*, J. B. Morrell, 1950).

KETTLE-STANDS. *See* STANDS, KETTLE.

KEY PATTERN or **GREEK FRET.** Enrichment widely used among ancient Greeks, and produced in many varieties by interlacing lines at right angles. Sometimes the pattern is interrupted by paterae set in squares, but a 'perfect fret' forms a continuous meander. Key pattern was often carved, inlaid or painted on furniture from c. 1720 to 1820 (*see* CHAIRS; Fig. 134).

KINGWOOD (species of *Dalbergia*, allied to rosewood). First imported from Brazil and described in 17th-century inventories as 'prince's wood' (*q.v.*), being used as a veneer or for parquetry decoration (*see* BUREAUX; Fig. 1); revived c. 1770, and from then on employed as cross-banding in borders, etc. Liable to be confused with some cuts of rosewood (also species of *Dalbergia*), but generally lighter in tone; name apparently dates from c. 1850.

KNIFE-CASES. Knife-cases stood on the buffet or side-table in 18th-century dining-rooms. Early examples were made of walnut, usually in pairs. In the MS. version (from 1649) of Randle Holme's *Academy of Armory* (1688), an open knife-case is illustrated, one of the drawings showing knives and forks in position. In 1727 Lord Bristol bought for himself at the Duke of Shrewsbury's sale 'ye case of 12 gilt knifes, 12 spoons and 12 forks'; but the material of which it was made is not stated. From this time onwards, cases in wood or shagreen are mentioned. In 1738 Peter Faneuil, when ordering

1. (*Left*) *Drawing of Knife-Case, from the manuscript (dated* 1649) *of Randle Holme's* Academy of Armory.

2. (*Above*) *Knife-Case, one of a pair; veneered with mahogany, the silver mounts by John Carter, London. Hall-marked* 1770. (*Mr L. G. G. Ramsey.*)   3. *Mahogany Knife-Case, inlaid with herringbone stringing. c.* 1770. *Ht.* 1 *ft.* 2 *in., W.* 9 *in., Depth* 7 *in.* (*Edward Hudson Coll.*)   4. *Mahogany Knife-Case, inlaid and banded with satinwood.* 1785. *Ht.* 1 *ft.* 2½ *in., W.* 9 *in., Depth* 11 *in.* (*Edward Hudson Coll.*)

5. (*Below*) *Vase Knife-Case; mahogany inlaid with stringing, flutes and paterae. c.* 1780. *Ht.* 1 *ft.* 7 *in.* (*A. Hannay Coll.*)   6. *Vase Knife-Case, veneered with chestnut and sycamore, and inlaid. c.* 1780. *Ht.* (*closed*) 1 *ft.* 7 *in.* (*V. & A. Mus.*)   7. *Vase Knife-Case of satinwood, painted. c.* 1780. *Ht.* 2 *ft.* 5½ *in.* (*V. & A. Mus.*)

from London furniture and silver for his house in Boston, begged a friend to procure for him 'a shagreen case' to be fitted with silver-handled forks and knives and silver spoons, the case to 'be the same with that Mr Baker sent me lined with a red velvet'. The interiors of knife-cases are divided into many small rectangular partitions, the knives and forks being inserted handles upwards; the spoons were inserted bowls upwards, thus displaying the objects in tiers on the slope. The mountings of these cases are, in certain cases, of silver, pierced (Fig. 2), and sometimes engraved with the owner's name.

Wooden box knife-cases of the later 18th century are generally made in mahogany and sometimes inlaid (Figs. 3 and 4), the fronts of the finer specimens being of curved or serpentine form. Their manufacture appears to have been localised, for Sheraton states (*Drawing Book*, 1791) that they are not 'made in regular cabinet shops'. They may be 'executed in the best taste by one who made it his main business, *i.e.* John Lane, No. 44 St. Martin's Le Grand, London'. The lid is often inlaid with a boxwood and ebony star, and the partitions cut for the knives and spoons are edged with a narrow chequer inlay. Among trade-cards of the cutlery trade, knife-boxes are sometimes illustrated. Thomas Squire, cutler, who appears in the London Directory (1784), used a knife-box as his sign; and knife-boxes are advertised on the trade-cards of Joseph Gibbs, cutler, New Bond Street, and John Folgham, shagreen case-maker, Wood Street, London, who announced that he 'makes and sells all sorts of shagreen Fish skin and mahogany cases'.

A pair of English knife-boxes decorated in enamel on a white ground, with knives and forks with handles of the same enamel, formerly in the Mulliner Collection are dated c. 1770 and are apparently unique. In the late 18th century, a new form, the vase case, was introduced, which was 'usually made of satin or other light woods', and stood at each end of the sideboard or on a pedestal (Hepplewhite's *Guide*, 1788). The partitions for knives are here arranged concentrically about the central tube or stem, to which the lid was secured, being kept up by a spring when required. The body is sometimes divided by vertical lines of stringing, while a vase knife-case (Fig. 7) is painted with medallions and festoons. A second example (Fig. 6) is elaborately inlaid. The vase case continued

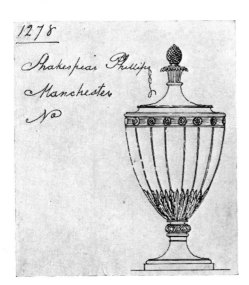

8. *Sketch of Vase Knife-Case. From Gillow's Cost Books*, 1796.

to be designed on graceful lines until the last years of the 18th century. In Gillow's cost books (1796) a design is shown for a 'vause knife-case' divided into facets by stringing, the base of the vase being carved with water leaf. Examples of high quality with decorative motifs, distinctive of the Regency period, are rare. From the early 19th century, knife-cases are found affixed to pedestal sideboards, and the foot is elongated while the body becomes heavy and angular in form. M. J.

LABURNUM (*Laburnum vulgare*). Hard, durable wood of yellowish tint, marked with varied brown streaks; first used in furniture in parquetry veneer popular after the Restoration. *See* OYSTER-PIECES and PARQUETRY.

LACQUER. *See* JAPANNING and LACQUER.

LAMBREQUIN. Ornament derived from drapery with escalloped or tasselled edge; of French origin, it figures in the designs of Jean Berain, Daniel Marot and other French decorative artists; occasionally found on English furniture in the late 17th and early 18th centuries (*see* BRACKETS; Fig. 1).

LAMPS. The meaning of this term has undergone a change with the development of lighting arrangements. Thus, the French writer Savary defines a lamp early in the 18th century as 'a vessel to contain oil or other substance, which by means of a cotton wick serves to give light during the night'. Here a lamp is taken to imply a vessel, irrespective of the shape, in which oil is burnt with a wick.

From the age of the Roman occupation many terra-cotta and a small number of bronze hand-lamps survive. Similar types were used by the Anglo-Saxons, and until the end of the 17th century a wick laid in an open vessel continued to be used, a primitive form which still survives in the Scottish 'cruzie'. During the Middle Ages lamps of this kind were sometimes placed in the chambers of the upper classes, in preference to candles. Lamps of precious metals enriched with jewels are often entered in French royal inventories, but no examples of comparable magnificence are found in English medieval records. Wicks were generally of hemp, pith or vegetable fibre, cotton being extremely dear.

Chandeliers, candle-beams and lanterns were the ordinary means of lighting in the 16th century, and, even at its close, the Hardwick and Chatsworth inventories, drawn up for the luxury-loving Countess of Shrewsbury, contain no references to lamps. Fumes and the constant need for cutting the wick and refilling with oil were disadvantages inseparable from their use. Nevertheless, the inventory of the fashionable and cultured Lord Herbert of Cherbury mentions a lamp and no other form of illumination in the bedroom of his Westminster house in 1641. The character of such lamps is uncertain, but in France considerable progress had been made in the principles of their construction. A self-feeding lamp is said to have been devised by Jérôme Cardan (d. 1576), and this type was still used in the mid-18th century. Most improvements appear to have been effected on the Continent, Lesparre's thirty-hours variety (advertised in a Paris newspaper in 1749) being among the most notable. There is no proof that these contrivances were adopted in England, but lamps continued to be used in bedrooms, as in the previous century. The *Gentleman's Magazine* (June, 1731) records that a lady of quality was burnt in her chamber 'as it is judged from a lighted Lamp which stood in the midst of the Room, and surprized her in a Fit'. This means of lighting is not represented in the trade catalogues of Chippendale and his contemporaries, but their bills show that it was occasionally adopted in preference to wax candles. In 1768 Chippendale charged £6 to Sir Edward Knatchbull, of Mersham Hatch, for '4 Glass lamps very neatly mounted with Chased Brass Ornaments and Black pedestals and Glass lamps for Oil in the inside'.

Hanging oil-lamps for various situations were designed by Robert Adam for his clients, and designs for them are shown in the *Works in Architecture* (1775). The notes state that they are intended for staircases, halls, lobbies, passages, and between columns from the centres of arches, etc. An example by Adam is seen in Fig. 1. The hanging lamps given in Hepplewhite's *Guide* (1788) are very similar; he writes that they are 'necessary to complete a suit of furniture', and the ornaments should be of brass-work. This is the traditional type, unaffected by recent French improvements.

The first important innovation to be generally adopted in England was the 'Argand lamp' perfected in 1780-3, and called after its Swiss inventor. The burner consisted of two concentric tubes with the wick between them; an arrangement which allowed a double current of air. When a little later the flame had been protected by a glass funnel, its brilliance was greatly increased. Sophie V. La Roche, a German novelist who visited England in 1786, records (September 15, 1786) 'we finished the evening at tea investigating Argand lamps of all

descriptions'. She describes the invention, and admires a shop in Bedford Street where lamps by Argand and others were displayed 'forming a really dazzling spectacle; every variety . . . crystal, lacquer and metal ones, silver and brass in every possible shade'. James Watt, then in partnership with Matthew Boulton (*q.v.*), interested himself in the subject of lighting, and a large number of Argand lamps were produced in the famous Soho Works, Birmingham. A circular of 1797 from the firm gives 'directions for using Argand and Co.'s patent lamps, made and sold by Matthew Boulton of Soho'. An example, now adapted for electric light, is seen in Fig. 5, the fluted urn being originally filled with colza, a heavy oil which descended to the burner by gravitation. An alternative method was to force the oil upwards by a mechanised device from a container below the level of the wick. Lamps on a similar principle are found in the Althorp accounts for 1790, D. Smith supplying to Earl Spencer 'by Order of Mr Holland', at a total cost of £11 1s.:

> 3 Japand Fountain Lamps with Large Round Glass Reflectors
> 3 Sprouted Fountain Lamps each with three multiplying Glass Reflectors.

Wedgwood also concerned himself with the production of lamps, and numbers were made at his Etruria Works of jasper and polished basalt in the classical style. He advertised (1787) 'lamps of two colours, adapted to Argand's patent lamp, the brilliant light of which being thrown on the bas-reliefs, has a singular and beautiful effect'.

Towards the end of the 18th century metal standard and

1. *Brass-mounted Hanging Lamp on the staircase at Osterley, designed by Adam. c. 1775.*
2. *Design for Hanging Lamp for oil by Robert Adam, from* Works in Architecture, *1775.*
3. *Bronze Hanging Lamp, decorated in classical taste. c. 1800. Ht. 4 ft. 7 in., W. 2 ft. 2½ in.* (*Corsham Court, Wilts.*)
4. *Bronze Hanging Lamp with gilt enrichments. By James Delville. Dated 1817. (Southill Park, Beds.*)

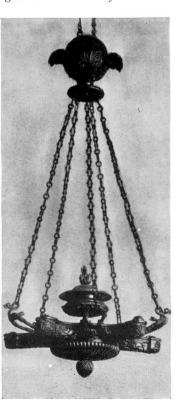

5. *Sheffield-plated Lamp on pedestal; of the Argand type. c. 1790. Ht. 1 ft. 1½in. (Hitchin Park, Herts.)*
6. *Bronze Standing Lamp. c. 1800. (Stratfield Saye, Hants.)*

7. *Gilt brass Standard Lamp with lions at base. c. 1800. Extreme Ht. 8 ft. 10 in. (Syon House, Middx.)*

hanging lamps were designed in classical and Egyptian taste. In 1773 Adam made a drawing for some lamp standards for Apsley House, five feet being the suggested height; a later example of this type is seen in Fig. 7. It is one of a set, mounted on contemporary mahogany and gilt pedestals, in the Hall at Syon, Middlesex, the four burners being fed from the centre vase.

Ancient Roman lamps of bronze or terra-cotta afforded models to designers of the Regency period. A bronze hanging lamp at Corsham Court, Wiltshire (c. 1800), is decorated with masks and 'Grecian' ornament, while another example (Fig. 4) is engraved with the maker's name.

The account books of Messrs Perry show that between 1812 and 1820 they supplied a large number of Grecian lamps with lotus burners, entries for 'Gothic borders' in connection with them suggesting a curious mixture of styles. Most of the burners and chains are stated to be French. Standing lamps at this time were similar in design and often placed on a tall pedestal or stand, following Roman precedent (Fig. 6). Such lamps were ranged along the walls of a saloon or gallery.

LANTERNS. Receptacles for a light, enclosed by some substance which protects it from draught and permits of reflection. There are many variations in the spelling of the word; 'lanthorn' perhaps is the commonest, because early lanterns were generally of horn. Lanterns were familiar in classical antiquity and were commonly employed throughout the Middle Ages. Towards the end of the 15th century domestic lanterns of *verre crystallin*, or glass made to simulate crystal,

begin to appear in French Crown inventories, but the filling was usually of horn until a much later date.

Carved wooden lanterns were often decorated in colour, and the Hengrave inventory (1503) mentions 'one great lanterne with glasse sett in joyner's work paynted', at the Great Chamber door. In Henry VIII's inventory (1547) are listed 'one Lanterne of white marble wth a curteyne of yellowe and white sarcenette paned togither', and another of 'white tynne plate to hang upon a wall'. Latten (*q.v.*) was also a favourite 16th-century material. At Leicester House (1590) there was 'upon the stayres a lanthorne of white lattyn', and in the wardrobe there were twelve others of this metal. The Hardwick Hall inventory (1601) lists 'a great glass Lanthorn in the half pace at the stair head', in which position it still hangs (Fig. 1). That horn remained the usual filling is proved by many allusions in Elizabethan literature, Dekker's *Seven Deadly Sinnes* (1605): 'candle light's coach is made all of Horne'. At this period lanterns were found most serviceable in passages, staircases and halls, where draughts were inevitable.

The 17th century saw no new development of importance in the form of lanterns. They do not figure in Stuart royal inventories, where chandeliers and sconces are often mentioned. The parts of an ordinary domestic lantern are enumerated by Randle Holme in his *Academy of Armory* (1688). The filling is of horn, and though the annexed engraving shows the lantern to have been of rude form, the type was obviously intended for use in a house, the remaining objects on the plate being all domestic furniture and applicances.

In the early 18th century glass lanterns were made with frames of copper, brass or walnut, wood being generally used

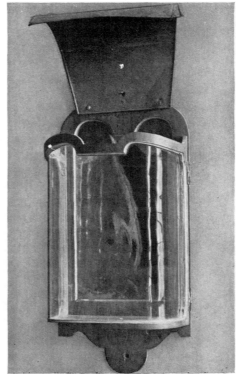

1. *Octagonal leaded Lantern of green bottle-glass. c. 1600. (Hardwick Hall, Derbys.)* 2. *Walnut Wall Lantern, with gilt mouldings. c. 1720. Extreme Ht. 2 ft. 10 in., W. 1 ft., Depth 8½ in. (Hampton Court Palace. By gracious permission of H.M. the Queen.)* 3. *Brass octagonal Lantern, headed by a royal crown; base decorated with terminal figures. Supplied by Benjamin Goodison to Hampton Court Palace. 1729-33. (By gracious permission of H.M. the Queen.)*

for the wall variety. They now begin to appear frequently in inventories and domestic accounts. In 1720 Gumley and Moore made for Kensington Palace '2 Glass Lanterns in brass fframes with Ballance Balls for the new staircase . . . 171s'; while Sir J. Hall of Dunglass, East Lothian, paid £1 3s. in 1721 'for a Wallnuttree Lanthorn with Glass and Glass Nossell and Sockett'. A few years later a large number were supplied under the Lord Chamberlain's Warrant for the various royal palaces. For the Prince of Wales's and the Princess Royal's apartments at Windsor a dozen 'side lanterns in walnut tree frames' were delivered, each holding a single candle.

For the Stone Hall at Houghton, Norfolk, Sir Robert Walpole obtained a copper gilt lantern, which held eighteen candles. As an instance of his extravagance, a Tory 'squib' relates how a visitor to Houghton, on entering, was taken into a glass room which he thought was the porter's lodge, but proved to be the lantern. In 1750, Horace Walpole, five years after the death of his father, Sir Robert, wrote to Mann:

> My Lord Chesterfield has brought the Houghton lantern the famous lantern that produced so much patriotic wit. My brother has bought a much handsomer at Lord Cholmondelley's sale, for with all the immensity of the celebrated one, it was ugly and too little for the hall.

On the Queen's Great Staircase at Hampton Court Palace hangs an octagonal lantern supplied by Benjamin Goodison (*q.v.*) between 1729 and 1733 at a cost of £138, and described in his accounts as 'a large glass Lanthorn with a wrought brass frame and a gold Crown to the top' (Fig. 3). The fine mahogany lantern (Fig. 4) is one of a set of eight made by

William Vile in 1763 for the hall of Buckingham Palace at a cost of £26 5s. each, and now at Kensington Palace. In Pyne's engraving of 1819 glass lanterns are shown on the newels of the staircase of Kensington Palace, but they have since disappeared. They are described in the accounts (1729) as '6 lanthorns, 12 inches square and 17 high, with a shade over each, and two flat sockets for candles'. Besides the wooden variety of 'side lantern', a simple form in which the candle is protected by a glass shade, globular, bell-shaped, cylindrical or square, was largely used in the 18th century. 'Globular and Bell-fashioned lanterns' are offered in the *Daily Advertiser* of May 16, 1744. Among the designs of the Society of Upholders and Cabinet Makers (1760) are several lanterns in Gothic, Chinese and rococo taste. Chippendale (3rd ed. *Director*, 1762) gives designs of various shapes for halls, passages or staircases—one 'in the form of an egg', another 'very large' and exuberantly decorated. The notes state that they 'are generally made of brass cast from wooden moulds', but Fig. 7, which closely corresponds with a design in the *Director* (3rd ed. Plate CLIII), is of carved and gilt wood. Ince and Mayhew (*Universal System*, 1759-63) illustrate similar types, also some staircase lights of lantern form 'mostly designed to fix on the handrail'. They write that they have executed several in wood 'at a much less expense than brass'. That the former kind was sometimes comparatively expensive is proved by a note of the price on a drawing for one by Matthias Lock, in the Victoria and Albert Museum; it was to cost £25 5s., and of this £22 is allowed for the carving. Figs. 2 and 5 show two wall lanterns, one of the early, the other of the mid-18th century in rococo taste. A small portable lantern (Fig. 6) is

4. *Mahogany hexagonal Lantern, headed by a royal crown; framework finely carved; base of brass. By William Vile, 1763. (Kensington Palace.)* 5. *Mahogany Wall Lantern; scrolled framework and base carved with acanthus. c. 1755. (Percival Griffiths Coll.)* 6. *Mahogany Portable Lantern in Chinese taste. c. 1755. Ht. 1 ft. 7 in., W. 10 in., Depth 7 in. (Percival Griffiths Coll.)*

7. *Lantern carved and gilt in rococo taste. Based on Plate CLIII of the* Director, *3rd edn. 1762.* 8. *Octagonal Lantern of gilded ironwork in neo-classic taste; uprights formed as female-headed consoles. Designed by Robert Adam for Sir Lawrence Dundas. c. 1770.* 9. *Brass hexagonal Lantern; cornice surmounted by honeysuckle ornament; ram-headed uprights with hoof feet. c. 1775. (P. Meyer Coll.)*

an example of chinoiserie, while the *Description* of Horace Walpole's villa at Strawberry Hill, Middlesex (1782), mentions that 'in the well of the staircase, by a cord of black and yellow hangs a Gothic lantern of tin japanned designed by Mr Bentley and filled with painted glass'. By details of ornament, such as columns and cusping, an attempt was made to reproduce medieval forms.

A number of lanterns, generally made of brass or copper, were designed for large houses in the classical style by Robert Adam and other architects. Honeysuckle ornament, festoons of husks, rams' heads and terminal figures are familiar decorative details; while the traditional scrolled framework of the top generally supports a crown or vase-shaped finial (Fig. 9). A splendid example in gilded ironwork was designed by Adam for 19, Arlington Street, c. 1770 (Fig. 8).

Lanterns of a similar character were introduced by Henry Holland at Carlton House, where there were 'six superb lanterns of lacquered brass' in the Great Hall. 'Athenian' Stuart designed a finely chased hexagonal brass lantern for Spencer House, and among the goods which D. Smith, a cabinet-maker, supplied in 1700 to Lord Spencer at Althorp by Holland's order were:

> 2 Long Square Handsome Taper Copper Lanthorns with neate Pearsed and Cheased taper Frett Borders. (£26 5s)

In the same year Beckwith and Co. supplied, for £9 12s., to the Queen's Lower Lodge at Windsor '8 square mahogany side Lanthorns with silvered backs'. During the Regency period lanterns were largely superseded by lamps of classic design for halls.

LARCH (*Larix decidua*). Deciduous conifer widely distributed in northern Europe; straight grain, fairly free from knots. It warps badly. In the late 18th century larch was sometimes used for carcase work. On good soil produces yellowish-white timber like yellow deal; on poor soil timber is reddish-brown.

LATTEN. *See* CHANDELIERS.

LEATHER. Skins or hides of various animals boiled in a special preparation to secure flexibility (*cuir bouilli*), stamped, gilt and painted, used on travelling chests or standards in medieval England (*see* CHESTS). Tanned and decorated leather was used for covering small articles of furniture and cushions in the 16th century, also for backs and seats of X-shaped chairs. It is often mentioned in the inventories of Katherine of Aragon and Henry VIII, and probably the queen introduced the fashion from her own country. Among Katherine's household stuff (1534) were many chairs and stools with cushions of 'lether lyned withe yalowe Cotton to the same'.

Ox- or cow-hides, sometimes lightly tooled, were favourite coverings for chairs c. 1650-60, and on travelling trunks of the 17th century, secured and ornamented with brass-headed nails. Gilt and coloured leather was occasionally used. In 1658 the Rector of Claydon, Buckinghamshire, wrote to Sir Ralph Verney that he 'should like very well the painted leather for a suit of chairs and stools'; and in the early 18th century a correspondent in the *Spectator* states that she prefers 'the fashionable gilt leather for furniture to the work of the needle'.

'Russia leather' also figures often as covering for chairs in the later Stuart period in royal accounts. Red morocco is mentioned c. 1750 in cabinet-makers' accounts as a covering for chairs, and Chippendale stated it 'will have a fine effect'. Later in the century leather was often used for chairs exposed to hard usage, and even for backs and seats of some 'more elegant kind of chairs'. Hepplewhite (*Guide*, 1788) recommends 'red or blue morocco leather'.

In the Middle Ages leather, chiefly from Spain, was widely used for hanging, but apparently seldom in England before the end of the 17th century, although there are a few references of an earlier date. In a chamber at Hardwick Hall there were in 1601 'six pieces of guilt lether hanginges twelve foote deep'. In the second half of the 17th century Spain was no longer the main source of supply; the industry was also carried on in the Low Countries, France, Italy and, to a minor extent, England. Among *Domestic Papers* of Charles II's reign is a petition (1660) from Hugh Robinson, who had learnt in Amsterdam 'how to make leather more bright than gold', and is ready to impart this information. At Ham House, Surrey, the 'marble dining room' is hung with gilt leather hangings mentioned in a 1679 inventory; and 'fine gilt leather to hang a room' for Hampton Court was quoted at 5s. per skin in 1699.

LIBRARY STEPS. 'Placed in a library for the use of raising a person so as to reach any book'—Sheraton (*Cabinet Dictionary*, 1803). Library steps do not appear to have come into general use until c. 1750. In private houses in the previous century books were often locked away in chests, while the few bookcases of that period in existence are comparatively small, and the volumes on the upper shelves could be easily reached by standing on a stool or chair. Before Pepys obtained his first book-press from 'Simpson the joiner' (1666) his books are stated (*Diary*) to have been 'lying one upon another on my chairs'. But at Ham House, Surrey, the library, dating from the time of the Duke and Duchess of Lauderdale, is fitted with shelves, and the inventory of 1679 mentions among the contents 'one foulding ladder of cedar'. The room still contains oak library steps of pulpit form with desk and seat, probably made c. 1700. In an inventory (1725) of the first Duke of Chandos's furniture at Cannons, Middlesex, 'a walnutt tree steps' is entered in the library. Steps of this time are extremely rare, but a dual-purpose example (Fig. 1) is in the form of a type of early Georgian writing-chair, in padouk (*q.v.*). Here the seat is hinged at the front and, when a catch is released, swings over with the back, a flight of four steps being thus provided. Though the mechanism is simple, it is identical with that found on examples dating from the Regency period, and for this specialised form of furniture an obsolete chair model was probably employed.

Library steps are rarely represented in trade catalogues, but Ince and Mayhew give two designs (*Universal System*, 1759-63), the first in the Chinese taste, 'intended for a large room', while the other is of smaller size and made to fold up. Fig. 4 is an example of about this date, the framework being filled with 'Chinese railing'. Such pieces of furniture were often ingeniously contrived to serve a dual purpose, and in Fig. 3 shaped treads are fitted between twelve reeded legs, the large stool when turned on end affording a somewhat precarious means of ascent to the upper shelves of a bookcase. A more practical

1. *Library Steps and Armchair combined; made of padouk. Style of c. 1730, but probably dates from later in the century. (V. & A. Mus.)*
2. *Same Armchair converted into Library Steps; back and seat hinged at the front. Ht. (open) 2 ft. 5 in., L. 3 ft. 7½ in.*
3. *Mahogany stool and Library Steps. c. 1760. Ht. 1 ft. 8½ in., L. 3 ft. 9 in., Depth 1 ft. 8 in. (Bayfordbury, Herts.)*
4. *Mahogany Library Steps, framework filled with Chinese railing; a book-rest supported on a strut. c. 1765. (Dyrham Park, Gloucs.)*

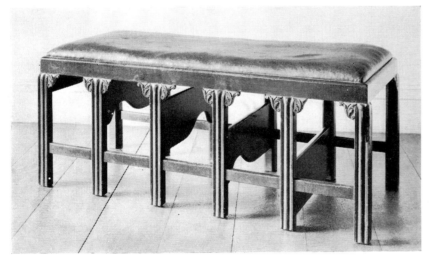

combination of a stool and steps is at Harewood House, the case being decorated in marquetry of various coloured woods on a mahogany ground (Fig. 5). This example is not included in Chippendale's accounts for the furnishing of Harewood, but in style closely resembles the inlaid commodes supplied by him to Edwin Lascelles.

These steps generally formed part of the furniture in well-appointed libraries of the late 18th century, elegance and utility being skilfully combined. Fig. 8 shows an example from Syon House, Middlesex, the gilt stool being designed in neo-classic taste. The design is often more satisfactory when no combination is attempted and the steps are confined to their original purpose. An example (Fig. 7) at Althorp, Northamptonshire, was supplied by John King, cabinet-maker, to Earl Spencer in 1790. It cost £45, and is thus described in his bills:

For a large Mahogany Circular Library Steps 9 ft high with Mahogany Hand Rails up Do. and brass wires and green silk curtains in Mahogany frames instead of bannisters with Mahogany Bookshelf and Seat the steps all carpeted with Wilton Carpet on large brass castors compleat.

5. *Mahogany Library Steps; the case, in the form of a stool, inlaid with various woods. Attributed to Thomas Chippendale. c. 1770-5. (Harewood House, Yorks.)* 6. *Mahogany Library Steps; turned balusters and painted neo-classic ornament. c. 1775. (Formerly at Blenheim Palace.)* 7. *Mahogany Library Steps, with seat and book-rest; brass wire-work originally backed with green silk curtains; on the steps Wilton carpet. Supplied to Earl Spencer in 1790 by John King. Ht. 9 ft. (Althorp, Northants.)*

8. *Gilt Stool and Library Steps combined; frieze fluted and the taper legs headed by leaf capitals. c. 1780. Ht. (open) 3 ft. 1 in., L. 3 ft. 4 in., Depth 1 ft. 6½ in. (Syon House, Middx.)* 9. *Design from Sheraton's* Drawing Book, 1791-4, *for Library Steps folding into a Pembroke table.*

10. *Mahogany Library Chair and Steps combined. By Morgan and Saunders. c. 1811. (Trinity College, Oxford.)*

11. *Same chair folded to form steps.*

At this date steps were often enclosed in a library or Pembroke table, and Sheraton (Appendix, *Drawing Book*, 1791-4) illustrates two specimens of this kind. He explains that the more elaborate design (Fig. 9) 'was taken from steps that have been made by Mr Campbell, Upholsterer to the Prince of Wales. They were first made for the King, and highly approved of by him, as every way answering the intended purpose'. Sheraton had seen other varieties made by different persons but, in his opinion these 'must have the decided preference both as to simplicity and firmness when they are set up'; an operation which could be done in half a minute. The top step was then 5 ft. 5 ins. from the ground, and on the hand-rail a small flap was provided 'so that a gentleman, when he is looking at any book in his library, may note down a passage from it without the trouble of going down again'. The second design, 'though not so generally useful will come vastly cheaper', the steps folding up and sliding into a drawer enclosed by a flap. These steps can be had 'from Mr Robert Campbell and Son, Mary-le-Bone Street, London'. An example of the less expensive variety described by Sheraton is at Heveningham Hall, Suffolk. A set, exactly similar in design, at the Victoria and Albert Museum bears the inscribed label of Francis Hervé (*q.v.*).

Similar combinations continued to exercise the ingenuity of cabinet-makers in the early 19th century. *Ackermann's Repository* (July, 1811) published an illustration of a 'Library Chair' supplied by Morgan and Saunders, of Catherine Street, Strand. The notes explain that it is 'considered the best and handsomest article ever yet invented, where two complete pieces of furniture are combined in one—an elegant and truly comfortable armchair and a set of library steps' A mahogany armchair is hinged at the seat rail, the back turning over to form a set of four library steps (Fig. 10). These types finally solved the problem of combining library steps with another piece of furniture.

LIBRARY TABLES. *See* TABLES, LIBRARY.

LIGNUM VITAE (*Guaiacum officinale*). A native wood of the West Indies, imported in the 17th and 18th centuries; dark brown, strongly veined and streaked with black; extremely hard when seasoned. It was used as oyster-shell parquetry in the late Stuart period, and occasionally in small veneered pieces in the 18th century. J. C. R.

LIMA WOOD. *See* BRAZIL WOOD.

LIME (*Tilia vulgaris*). Close-grained, soft and smooth wood; pale yellow or white in colour. It cuts equally well with or across the grain and was thus greatly favoured by carvers. It came into use in Charles II's reign; much used by Grinling Gibbons and his school for decorative carving of picture and mirror frames. Employed occasionally by turners. J. C. R.

LINEN-FOLD PATTERN. Carved ornament largely used for decoration of panels in wood-work and furniture. The name derives from the resemblance to linen arranged in narrow upright folds. This pattern was probably introduced here by Flemish craftsmen. In furniture of English origin the treatment is generally simple, folds being ogee-shaped at top and bottom (*see* CHAIRS; Fig. 3: CHESTS; Fig. 11).

LINEN-PRESS. A contrivance for pressing linen when damp. It is placed between two boards, pressure being regu-

1. *Linen-press of oak and walnut; upper board raised by a spiral screw. c. 1650. Ht. 1 ft. 10 in., W. 1 ft. 4 in. (V. & A. Mus.)*

lated by a spiral screw. Linen-presses of the 17th century on stands of table height are of Dutch origin. A small English movable example is illustrated.

LINEN, PRINTED. *See* CHINTZ OR CHINT.

LOOKING-GLASSES. *See* MIRRORS.

LOPER. *See* DRAW RUNNER or DRAW SLIP.

LUNETTE. As applied to furniture, a design of half-moon shape, generally filled with carving, inlay or painting. It is found on oak furniture and is a favourite motif in the decoration of 18th-century satinwood commodes (*see* COMMODES; Fig. 21).

LUSTRE. Term applied in the first half of the 18th century to cut-glass pendant drops for chandeliers, and also to a chandelier itself (*see* CHANDELIERS).

LUSTRING or **LUTESTRING.** Glossy silk fabric with a ribbed pattern, used for furniture upholstery in the 17th and 18th centuries. Towards the end of Charles II's reign its manufacturers were incorporated as the Royal Lustring Company, and an advertisement (*London Gazette*, 1697) states 'their warehouse shall be opened every day to sell Allamodes, Renforces and Lustrings'. In the 18th century large quantities of this material were also imported from France and Italy.

MAHOGANY. Genus *Swietenia*; indigenous to Central America, Northern South America and the West Indies. The sources of supply during the 18th and early 19th centuries were the West Indian islands of Jamaica, San Domingo, Puerto Rico and Cuba and Honduras on the mainland. In origin the name belongs to the timber of *Swietenia*, but as the demand grew the species of many other genera producing a comparable timber were employed and described as mahogany.

Mahogany was known in England as early as 1671, when it was listed in John Ogilby's *America* among the rich varieties of timber grown in Jamaica and often exported. It is mentioned in advertisements, accounts and bills of lading from c. 1720; and its first appearance in the accounts of royal tradesmen dates from 1724, when Gumley and Moore (*q.v.*) supplied a 'mahogany supping table and two mahogany desart tables'. It was occasionally used for the panelling of rooms, *e.g.* by Sir Robert Walpole at Houghton, Norfolk.

About 1730 large quantities began to arrive in England, Jamaica being a main source of supply. Catesby (*Natural History*, 1743) writes of the mahogany tree: 'The excellence of this wood for all domestick uses is now sufficiently known in England.' In San Domingo, the Spanish settlement, trees growing within easy access of a seaport were cleared first, but the formidable country inland and the absence of communications precluded removal of wood of considerable weight. The island produced mahogany of hard texture, straight grain and dark colour, with little figure. For satisfactory working when the wood was seasoned, highly tempered steel tools were required, and carving in this material by accomplished craftsmen in its vigour, crispness and finish is often suggestive of chased bronze.

Towards 1750 the Cuban variety came into general use, being less laborious in conversion and easier to work. Certain growths and cuts were found to possess a fine figure, *e.g.*

'fiddle-back', 'roe' (with 'dark flakes' giving the effect of light and shade) and 'curl'—'the confused filling in of the space between forks or the springing of branches' (Royle, *Descriptive Catalogue of Woods*). Cuban mahogany is also dark and rich in colour, the finest specimens being reserved for veneers (generally on a basis of red pine); large pieces were cut for two doors of wardrobes, etc. The San Domingo variety was stated (Sheraton's *Cabinet Dictionary*, 1803) to be 'not much in use', no doubt owing to preference for mahogany showing figure.

Honduras mahogany (from forests near the coast in that part of Central America), lighter in weight and with more open grain, was largely imported in the second half of the 18th century, and was (Sheraton, *Cabinet Dictionary*, 1803) 'the principal kind of mahogany in use among cabinet-makers'. It is sometimes known as baywood (after the bay of Honduras); colour lighter than in other varieties, figure not conspicuous.

Mahogany did not appreciably affect the design of furniture until towards the middle of the century. Great widths of mahogany board made this wood ideal for large areas such as leaves of table tops, which were made in one piece instead of in separate sections as when walnut was used; its strength allowed the construction of furniture in which portions were built up of open frets (*see* BUREAUX; Fig. 35: TABLES, VARIOUS; Fig. 22), and the making of slender constructional elements, as in the splatwork of chairs of the rococo phase, 1745-65. Mahogany remained in use for library and dining-room furniture throughout the late 18th and early 19th centuries, but it was replaced for 'dressed apartments' c. 1770 by satinwood and other lightly-coloured woods, and in the Regency period to a considerable extent by rosewood. M. J.

MAPLE. The name given in England to the tree *Acer campestris*, which should more accurately be called sycamore (*q.v.*); wood is white and more or less veined, and it polishes well. Used in marquetry, often stained, in the 17th and 18th centuries, and occasionally as veneer (*see* BAROMETER CASES AND FRAMES; Fig. 6). The Lord Chamberlain in 1730 ordered the repair of '12 maple wood chairs with matted seats' at St James's Palace. Bird's-eye maple (American sugar maple) was often used as veneer in the Regency period.

MARBLE SLABS FOR TABLE-TOPS. The use of marble for table-tops, following Italian precedent, was not usual in England until the 18th century, but many of the tables in an inventory drawn up (1590) by the steward of Lord Lumley have marble slabs, and a contemporary table with a top of variegated marbles (*see* TABLES, VARIOUS; Fig. 3) is now at Aston Hall, Birmingham.

Celia Fiennes notes c. 1700 'a white marble table behind the doore as a sideboard' at Hampton Court, but not until c. 1720 did marble-topped tables begin to be an important feature in furnishing. At this time it was customary to stain common white marble in imitatation of more costly varieties. Marble slabs were usually imported in the 18th century, but that valuable quarries were worked in England and Ireland is proved by contemporary references.

The quality of marble table-tops was a subject which greatly interested *virtuosi* in the early Georgian period, and no trouble or expense was too great to get rare specimens from Italian palaces. In 1764, the younger Matthew Brettingham,

Lord Leicester's agent in Italy, despatched in one ship alone seven cases of marble tables (MS. account book at Holkham, Norfolk). At Badminton, Gloucestershire (1754), Dr Pococke noticed several beautiful tables in the rooms, 'some of Alabastra fioreto, one or two of porphery'. Towards 1800, as tables became lighter in construction, the marble slab was not so thick, and rare varieties were less in demand (*see* SCAGLIOLA). M. J.

MARBLING. Painting of wood to produce the effect of marble; practised occasionally on wood-work and furniture early in the 17th century. It was used in imitation of figured wood on panelling and columns from that time until the Regency period. The chief varieties of furniture treated in this manner were tables and commodes.

MARQUETRY. *See* INLAY AND MARQUETRY.

MEDALLION. A circular, oval or square device. Carved profile heads on 16th-century oak chairs, chests and boxes were sometimes set in medallions, and a painted or inlaid ornament similarly enclosed was often used on 18th-century furniture (*see* CHAIRS; Fig. 4: COMMODES; Fig. 21).

METAL MOUNTS, METAL-WORK AND OR-MOLU. There are three reasons for metal mounts on furniture: for opening and shutting lids and doors, *i.e.* hinges, locks and handles; as a protection against damage and wear and tear; as a direct means of construction. It is often found, especially with iron mounts, that one particular mount may serve a dual or even triple rôle.

English smiths were highly skilled in the art of forging iron when furniture was in its most primitive state; thus metal mounts occurred on the earliest type, *i.e.* the dug-out chest or coffer, an example of which, showing a hasp and staple-plate, occurs in CHESTS; Fig. 1. If the internal space in dug-out chests was of any size, the wood had to be bound together with iron straps, or cramps, as, being cut from a single trunk, it might otherwise, in time, split and become useless. This reinforcement is also shown in the example cited.

Aumbries, another early type of furniture, also provided scope for the metal worker. A fine example of the late 13th century in Chester Cathedral has for its most prominent feature a mass of protective scrollwork distributed evenly over the surface of its four doors. The ends of the scrolls are fashioned into decorative forms, obtained by hammering the metal with dies while it was in a state of white heat. This method, an important part of early English smithcraft, went out of use in the 14th century. The hinges are of the square butterfly type, quite independent of the scrollwork.

End handles and rings were not common on early chests, as, except in the case of travelling coffers, it was often desirable to make them as immovable as possible. Fig. 2 shows an end handle which, although of the late 16th century, is of a type used two centuries earlier.

Chests of the 14th century were generally fitted with one or more locks, the common type being that on a chest at the Victoria and Albert Museum (Fig. 1). The movement was sunk into the wood-work, the face-plate flush, and the hinged hasp was accommodated between two upright prongs joined at the bottom and attached to the face of the lock. This prevents an instrument from being forced between hasp and plate, and is a distinctive feature of locks of chests and caskets of the 14th and 15th centuries. Chests of box formation were usually made with external straps of iron to strengthen the construction, some having the whole outside surface covered with straps and scrollwork.

Although wood pin-hinges were common in 12th- and 13th-century chests, metal hinges were also in general use, especially for dug-out or heavily strapped chests, in which case some straps on the lid were finished off to form part of the hinges.

Butterfly-hinges (Fig. 5) were almost the only type used on cupboard doors until the 15th century, when the door half of the hinge became elongated in the form of a strap, and was later elaborated on Flemish lines (Fig. 7A).

A hasp lock of distinctive type dating from the 15th century (Fig. 4) is of rectangular form, with cable-twist edges, and, on the face, three square bars bearing a chamfered ornament, the two outer bars fixed, the centre one swinging sideways to expose the keyhole. Locks on this principle, but without Gothic character, continued to be used until late in the Stuart period.

During the 15th century cabinet locks and hinges became more decorative. The sides of the locks remained rectangular, but with the corners extended in the form of a fleur-de-lys or other leaf-like motif: they were fitted with ring handles (*see* Figs. 7B and 7C; AUMBRY; Fig. 1).

The cupboards made for hall and parlour in the 16th and early 17th centuries, though richly carved, gave little scope to the metal-worker. The doors were fitted, as a rule, with a concealed lock, the keyhole being protected by a shaped vertical escutcheon, at the bottom of which, either attached or on a separate plate, was an iron handle in the form of an inverted heart. This handle was a much favoured pattern, persisting in similar form until the 18th century on oak dressers and table drawers of rural manufacture.

French and Flemish types of strap-hinges were used in the 16th century to some extent; most common, however, was the butt type, with only the barrel showing.

A surface hinge of the 16th century (Fig. 3) is of particular interest, as it illustrates the development of the butterfly-hinge into the prototype of the 17th-century cock's-head.

A favourite form of cabinet fastening on the Continent, also sometimes used here in the 16th century, had the fixing bolt sliding on the outside, instead of inside, as before. Fig. 6 shows a double bolt, fixed to the middle stile of a cabinet, the bolts sliding right and left and engaging in ornamental sockets attached to either door. Another form on the same lines, but with only one bolt, and made to fix on the door, had an internal movement for locking the bolt. Two operations were necessary, first to shoot the bolt, and then to turn the key, locking it.

In the second half of the century Renaissance forms were replacing Gothic. A Gothic plate with rope-twist edges and pierced top fret is found on a few boxes with Renaissance carving, while c. 1570-80 this type gave place to an iron hasp-plate with a distinct Renaissance outline (Fig. 8).

It appears that until about 1600 cabinet mounts were the work of the ordinary blacksmith—plain forgings with the occasional use of punch, chisel and file—but after that date locksmithing, which includes other forms of cabinet mounts, became more of a separate industry. The 17th century saw a

2. *Wrought-iron End Handle from oak chest. Late 16th century. L. 9¾ in.*

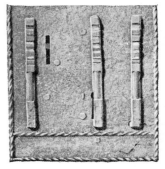

1. *Wrought-iron Hasp Lock from oak chest. 14th century. W. 7¾ in.*

3. *Wrought-iron Cabinet Hinge from Suffolk. 16th century. W. 2⅞ in.*

4. *Wrought-iron Chest Lock. 14th-15th century type.*

5. *Wrought-iron Buttery-hinge, from oak food cupboard. Mid-17th century. W. 3⅞ in*

6. *Wrought-iron Double Cupboard Bolt from Suffolk. 16th century. W. 3¼ in.*

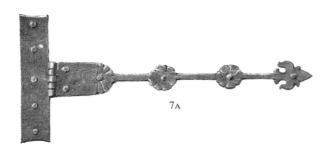

7A

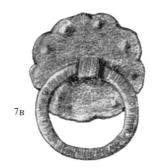

7B

7C

7. *Wrought-iron Strap-hinge (A), Ring Handle (B) and Lock (C). 15th century. (See AUMBRY; Fig. 1.)*

vast increase in the demand for furniture, and mounts increased accordingly, a number of new forms being introduced.

Much greater attention had been paid c. 1575-1600 to the value of chamfering the edges of mounts, and this method of finishing was to develop in the next hundred years into the most conspicuous feature.

Chest hasp-locks, other than the plain rectangular type, which was a stock-in-trade article, so common on many chests and boxes of all periods, became elaborate in outline, taking a semi-armorial form (*e.g.* Fig. 10). Much effect is gained by chamfering and stop-chamfering, the latter being a method which, by means of irregular cutting, makes the face of the plate take a more decorative outline than the back. This is well illustrated in Fig. 9, an early 17th-century double strap-hinge from a writing-box in the Victoria and Albert Museum.

A notable feature of the period was the surface hinge, generally known as the 'cocks-head' owing to its form of outline. It was used, in a great variety of size and design, on corner cupboards and similar pieces. Stop-chamfering is characteristic of almost all these hinges (Fig. 11). Another variety made on the same principle was the 'H' hinge which, instead of curved plates working on a central barrel, had two vertical plates, with the outline of each treated symmetrically. This long-persisting variety is shown in Figs. 13, 14, and 15. With the cocks-head hinge the metal varies in thickness, being drawn towards the extremities and the greater thickness being against the hinge. This treatment is found in many early examples, and enhances their charm.

A type of metal mount which appears suddenly in England was that used on japanned cabinets copied from Chinese examples in the second half of the 17th century. These mounts consist of double lock-plates, corner and angle plates. Although the general characteristics are Chinese, compared with the originals, detail and engraving are generally coarse.

Another class of brass mount, similar in treatment, though different in design, is the harpsichord hinge, that illustrated in Fig. 12 being on an instrument in the Victoria and Albert Museum.

These early brass mounts, including those on skin-covered travelling trunks, mark the beginning of a brass monopoly in cabinet mounting. This metal soon became popular because it was a good colour and easy and soft to work, and, by casting, a pattern could be reproduced quickly and accurately. This change produced an entirely different kind of craftsmanship, for iron mounts could be made by the smith from bar or plate to the finished article, but with brass various stages were necessary, and with each stage a man skilled in a particular process was needed. Firstly, the designer or carver of the model; then the moulder, who made the mould and ran the casting; and thirdly, the chaser or finisher, who cut away the faults in the casting and filed up the chamfered edges and surfaces. Polishing and gilding or lacquering, which prevented the metal from tarnishing, were the final stages.

8. *Wrought-iron Hasp Lock, from an oak box. 16th century. (See BOXES, Fig. 2.)*

9. *Wrought-iron Double Strap-hinge from a writing-box. 17th century. L. 6¾ in. (V. & A. Mus.)*

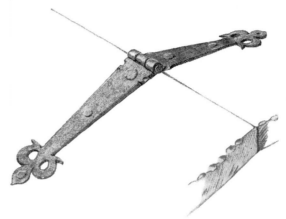

Brass mounts were introduced to harmonise with the lighter forms of furniture made in increasing numbers from the end of the 17th century. The earliest examples were generally rather heavy, as may be seen from the handle of Fig. 18 with a bulbous drop suspended by a square-shaped eye, which is attached through the back-plate to the drawer by a split-metal tang. Similar handles, but of more florid design, were made in silver for Charles II chests of drawers and cabinets.

Handles on this principle, but less decorative, were used on late 17th- and early 18th-century cabinets, the usual form being that shown in Fig. 16A.

A yet simpler type is the tear-drop or acorn, fitted with a small circular plate (Figs. 16B and 16C). It was at this period

10. *Wrought-iron Hasp Lock from a carved elm chest. Of semi-armorial form. First half 17th century. W. 6¼ in.* 11. *Wrought-iron 'Cocks-head' Hinge. 17th century. W. 3¾ in. From Suffolk.* 12. *Brass Hinge from a Harpsichord. Second half 17th century. W. 3¾ in.* 13. *Wrought-iron 'H' Hinge. 16th century. L. 5 in. From Suffolk. (All from the V. & A. Mus.)*

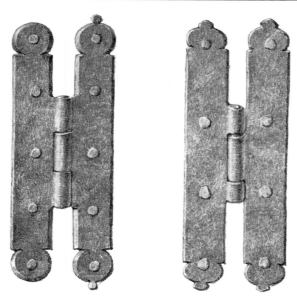

14. Wrought-iron 'H' Hinge. 17th century. 15. Wrought-iron 'H' Hinge. 18th century. L. 7 in. (Both from the V. & A. Mus.)

that Birmingham, long engaged in the iron industry, first took an active part in making brass castings. This trade steadily developed, and contemporary pattern books prove that furniture mounts formed a large part of the output.

The escutcheon or keyhole-plate was an important detail in the 18th century. The example in Fig. 17c relies on outline and punch marks for its effect, but the more common variety was in the form of a cartouche with modelled ornament covering the surface (Figs. 17a and b).

After the Stuart period an entirely new form of cabinet mount, the loop handle, with flat-shaped plate and chamfered edges (Fig. 23), was to become, with certain modifications, the chief type throughout the first half of the 18th century. The only connecting link with its predecessor, the small drop, was the manner of fixing the handle to the plate by an iron or brass double tang. This method, however, soon gave way to the cast knob, into which the ends of the loop handle engaged. These knobs formed the face of the pins which secured the back-plate to the drawer by means of a nut threaded to the inner end; the surface of the plate was sometimes ornamented by engraved lines and punch marks (Fig. 20). This type was elaborated between 1710 and 1730 by cutting out the centre of the plate to form scrollwork (Figs. 19 and 21). Escutcheons were made *en suite* with such handles, but c. 1750 a small flush key plate of brass often took its place and it is found in conjunction with ornate handles.

A new variety was introduced c. 1750. With this the loop handle was retained, but, in place of the one-piece cast plate, two small circular plates, or 'roses', were used (Fig. 22). On these lines handles to suit many different styles were made. All these 18th-century types continued to be the stock-in-trade of Birmingham manufacturers until a much later date, and are illustrated in the trade lists in the Department of Engravings at the Victoria and Albert Museum.

The loop handles also show a distinct, though not so noticeable, change in the first half of the 18th century. With the earliest form the handle was thin, the ends curving inwards and ending in a knob, which enabled them to be held in position by the metal tang. With the passing of the tang fixing, the loop was hung from the inner sides of the knobs and ornamented by a baluster-like detail in the centre, also a

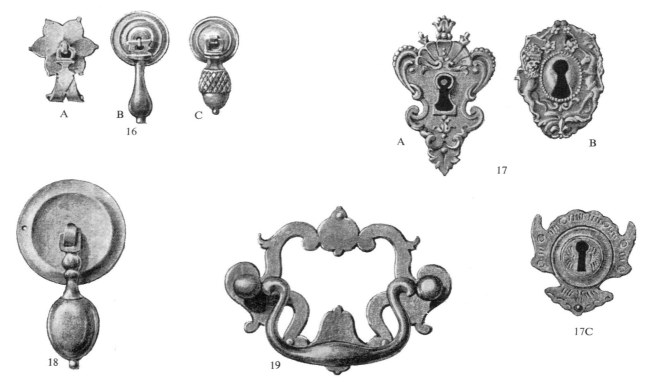

16. Cast-brass Drop Handles. (A) Late 17th- and early 18th-century type. (B, C) Early 18th-century types. 17. Cast-brass Escutcheons, early 18th-century types. (A, B) Cast and chased ornaments. (C) Ornamented with punch marks. 18. Cast-brass Drop Handle, late 17th and early 18th-century type. L. 7¼ in. 19. Loop Handle of cast brass, first half 18th-century.

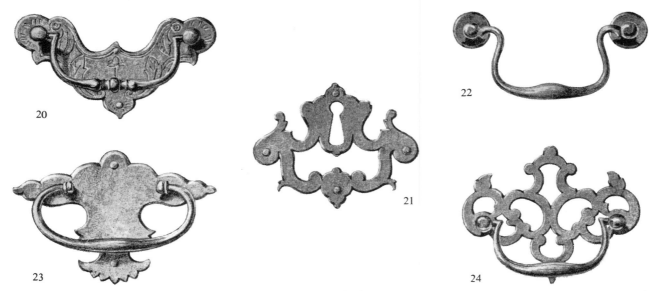

20. *Loop Handle of cast and engraved brass, early* 18th *century.*   21. *Escutcheon, first half* 18th *century.*   22. *Loop Handle of cast brass, late* 18th *century.*   23. *Loop Handle of cast brass, early* 18th *century.*   24. *Loop Handle of cast brass, second half* 18th *century.*

prominent feature in the buckle handles used on cabinets and, more especially, on doors of the 18th century. Later, the baluster was discarded for a plain heavy swelling, the ends of the handles curving inwards.

French influence in English furniture mounts began to be apparent c. 1750, and they were mostly rococo in design until the classical revival. French-style mounts were seldom lavishly used on English furniture, although on a few 18th-century cabinets and commodes metal-work is sometimes used solely as decoration in the form of friezes and crestings. Later in the Regency style, motifs and beadings were applied, and on rosewood brass inlay was often introduced.

The chasing is usually of indifferent quality, and betrays

ignorance. Chasing (*i.e.* carving in metal) must have been introduced with comparative suddenness, and many craftsmen who undertook this work could not have mastered the French styles sufficiently to do justice to the designs. Faults in the casting are often not chased up to the intended form, but blinded over, giving a blurred and unintelligible effect.

Some of the flamboyant mounts used by Chippendale and other leading cabinet-makers for decorating commodes in the French taste were probably made here by French craftsmen, or supplied direct from France to specific instructions from the cabinet-maker (Fig. 25); though soon after the establishment of Matthew Boulton's manufactory at Soho near Birmingham in 1762 (*see* BOULTON, MATTHEW) English mounts of com-

25. *Designs from Chippendale's* Director, *third edition* (1762), *for cast and chased Cabinet Handles and Escutcheons.*

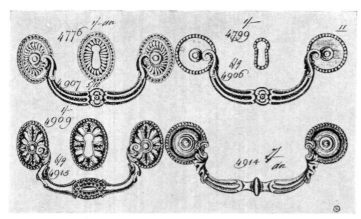

26. *Designs for stamped Back-Plates, from a trade list. c.* 1790
1810. (*Print Room, V. & A. Mus.*)

parable quality were made. For commodes, cabinets, side-boards, pedestals and other furniture in the neo-classic taste, brass mounts in the form of ram's heads, festoons of husks and other classical ornaments were used, and some of these may be by Boulton. Such mounts, and many other types, were gilded. This was not done solely to give an added beauty, but also to protect the metal from tarnishing. Work thus treated is referred to in England as 'ormolu', and the process of gilding was briefly as follows: First, some mercury was heated in a crucible and, at the required temperature, pure gold was added. This, on forming an amalgam, was allowed to cool. The paste thus produced was laid out on a flat surface and applied to the brass-work with a wire brush, the article thereupon appearing to be painted a bright silver. It was then washed and subjected to a burning temperature, when the mercury dissipated in fumes, leaving the gold fast, and ready to be polished or burnished.

The continuous back-plate was reintroduced between 1775 and 1800, but in a different form. It was of sheet brass, ornamented by stamping, a method developed and improved by two Birmingham brass-founders, John Marston and Edward Bellamy, whose patent is dated August, 1779. They described their method as 'stamping upon plated metal, gilt, and other metals . . . all sorts of figures, decorations, ornaments and other devices for cabinet furniture and lock furniture'. The plates of metal were pressed into dies and the hollow at the back was filled in with a composition. Escutcheons and door furniture were also made on similar lines. The collection of pattern books in the Victoria and Albert Museum includes many designs for handles, such as the Prince of Wales's feathers, the Irish harp, Scottish thistle, a cock, rose and 'sun in splendour'. Others showed cast loop handles on stamped roses (Fig. 26). From c. 1800 small brass knobs, ornamented or plain, tended to supersede the loop handles on tables and chests of drawers, and a 'knob' cast with a lion's mask with a ring in the mouth was also often used for drawer furniture; applied mounts, consisting of paterae, water-leaf, entwined rods and other classical motifs are sometimes found on cabinets, bookcases and tables in the Regency style. The finest of them, as on pieces at Southill, Bedfordshire, and formerly at Deepdene, Surrey, were probably carried out by a French 'bronzist'. J. S. L.

MIRRORS (LOOKING-GLASSES). In the Middle Ages mirrors were generally of metal, for, though glass was known, and the method of backing it with a metallic substance understood, it was too full of impurities for a satisfactory reflection to be obtained. Hanging mirrors were not introduced until late in the Middle Ages. Steel and crystal were the usual materials, but in 1507 two inhabitants of Murano, near Venice (where glass factories existed from early in the Middle Ages), claimed to have perfected the manufacture of glass mirrors and secured a monopoly for twenty years. Experiments had certainly been made before that date, and in French inventories mirrors of *verre crystallin*, or glass simulating crystal, occur towards the end of the 15th century. They are sometimes represented in contemporary Flemish pictures. In Van Eyck's portrait of Jan Arnolfini and his wife (1434) a mirror of convex form hanging on the wall clearly reflects the contents of the room, and a similar mirror on the counter of the goldsmith's shop in the so-called *Legend of S. Eloy and S. Godeberta*, a picture by Petrus Christus, is apparently of crystal, for it is splintered at the edge. In a miniature from a Flemish MS. of the *Romant de la Rose* (Fig. 1) a lady is seen contemplating herself in another mirror of this kind; the size is deliberately exaggerated to allow of the reflection. More than a century later, mirrors of glass were so rare and costly that one of small size, presented by the Venetian Republic to Marie de' Medici on the birth of her eldest son (1601), was accounted a worthy offering. A small Italian mirror frame of ebony inlaid with ivory, at the Victoria and Albert Museum (7,354-61), is of about this date and retains its original opaque glass. Other Italian Renaissance examples in the Museum with finely carved walnut frames all enclose plates of burnished steel.

Under the early Tudors mirrors forming part of domestic furniture were of steel, enclosed by shutters or curtains to prevent oxidisation. An inventory of the contents of Hornby, Yorkshire (1523), mentions several of these 'glasses to look in', and Henry VIII's inventory (1547) shows that he possessed a number, also described as 'glasses', although stated to have been of steel. The king's mirrors were set in frames of wood, painted or covered with various coloured velvets and richly embroidered with pearls, knots of silk, gold and jewels. Among those at Westminster was a 'rounde lookinge glass in a wooden frame painted under glass wth the armes of England, Spayne and Castile'. This was, no doubt, of Italian origin, a specimen of the art now known as *verre eglomisé* (*q.v.*). Like his predecessors, Henry appears to have depended on foreign craftsmen for his mirrors; the Privy Purse Expenses (1532) record a payment 'to a Frenchman for certayne looking-glasses'. There is no proof that the king's mirrors hung on walls; they may have been placed on tables and chests, and they were certainly sometimes supported on stands, like 'a standing glass with imagery made of bone'.

The inventory of the splendid furniture at Leicester House (1588) records 'three great glasses, one standing in a verie faire frame, with beares and ragged staves on the top, with a steele glass in it, the other II of cristall'. Mirrors are seldom mentioned in Elizabethan inventories, but contemporary literature supplies many references. Shakespeare in 1597 must have been familiar with crystal or glass specimens, as in *Richard II* the mirror that the king dashed to the ground was 'crack'd in a hundred shivers'. Paul Hentzner, visiting Hampton Court Palace (1598), observed among the furnishings of the hall 'a very clear looking-glass, ornamented with columns and little images of alabaster'. For her toilet, Elizabeth I used metal and crystal; but her palaces probably contained mirrors of Venetian glass. Products of a like nature could now be obtained from France, Henry II having granted letters patent to an Italian gentleman (1552) for the manufacture of looking-glasses '*à la façon de Venise*'. Mirrors forming part of the furniture of a room were still rare even in great houses, and no English specimen of the 16th century is known to survive.

Although glass was made at Chiddingfold, Surrey, from the 14th century onwards, and early in Elizabeth's reign a number of foreigners obtained patents for the manufacture of drinking vessels and panes for glazing, mirrors of glass do not appear to have been produced in this country until early in the 17th century. The first manufacturer on a large scale was Sir Robert Mansell (b. 1573), who started business in 1615 before he retired from the Navy 'with the help of many expert strangers from foreign parts. . . '.

At about the same time the importation of glass had been entirely forbidden, and in March, 1620, the Venetian ambassador wrote to the Doge and Senate that 'by this order they also mean to prohibit looking glasses, of which they make a quantity here'. A few months later he reported that Mansell 'had some business at Venice and has had relations for many years with the Muranese, especially some who made good mirrors'. Mansell had secured the services of several Venetians

2. *Mirror in moulded and reeded octagonal frame veneered with tortoise-shell. c.* 1650. (*The late Sir Edward Barry.*)

banished from their own country, and when in 1623 he obtained a renewal of an existing patent he was able to show that he had procured employment for 500 persons in the 'making, grinding, and foyling of looking-glasses', that branch of his business being established in Lambeth. Examples of the factory's output do not appear to have survived. The order prohibiting the importation of Venetian glass was revoked in 1624, but Mansell succeeded in organising the glass industry on a national scale and 'started or absorbed glasshouses' in a number of towns in England, Scotland and Wales.

In 1615 the use of wood during the manufacture of glass was forbidden, as the forests were becoming seriously depleted, and sea coal was substituted. As a consequence, mirror plates were often disfigured by spots owing 'to the action of the coal fire on the lead flux contained in the mixture'. How difficult it was to get a clear reflection is suggested by a letter (1639) from Lady Brilliana Harley to her son Edward at Magdalen Hall, Oxford. 'Dear Ned', she writes, 'if theare be any good looking-glasses in Oxford, chuse me one aboute the biggnes of that I use to dress in, if you remember it. I put it to your choys, because I think you will chuse one, that will make a true ansure to onse face.'

At this time hanging mirrors began to play a part in decorative schemes, and were even found in remote country houses. An inventory (1633) of the contents of Chastleton House, Gloucestershire, mentions 'one faire looking-glass with a canopy', no doubt an ornamental hood or cresting. At Tart Hall in the Strand (1641), the Countess of Arundel had two large looking-glasses in ebony frames hanging on the walls.

1. *Miniature from a Flemish manuscript of the* Romant de la Rose, *a convex mirror in a moulded frame. c.* 1480. (*Brit. Mus. Royal* 4425.)

3. (*Above left*) *Mirror of octagonal form, decorated in blue and white enamel with fruit, flowers and amorini in high relief. c. 1670. (Col N. R. Colville.)*

4. (*Above*) *Mirror in frame; gilt, carved with putti, flowers and acanthus; on cresting an Earl's coronet. c. 1680. Ht. 4ft. 10½in., W. 3ft. 2½in. (Burghley House, Lincs.)*

5. (*Left*) *Mirror frame carved in soft wood. School of Grinling Gibbons. c. 1680. (Sudbury Hall, Derbys.)*

Until late in the 18th century the plates were made from blown cylinders of glass, slit open, flattened on a stone and polished, the backs being silvered by mercury floated over tinfoil. In 1648 Lady Verney wrote from Claydon, Buckinghamshire, to her husband, Sir Ralph, that she had had the quicksilver renewed in the large mirror, and the frame re-gilt. A few months earlier she had written, 'Here is a great looking glass . . . your sisters have threatened if they (the steward and "Mr Francis") would not lett them have itt to bring a troupe of horse to breake down the walls where t'was'—an indication of the value set on looking-glasses at that time.

In the inventory of Charles I's possessions sold after his execution, many mirrors framed in ebony inlaid with mother-of-pearl and yellow amber are enumerated, as well as others of needlework. One of the latter variety is described as 'a Large looking-glass sett in a frame of needlework embroydered with 3 faculties and the 7 Liberall sciences'. The difficulty of producing a plate of any considerable size thick enough to

6. *Mirror in carved and gilt frame; a stork, hen and chickens at sides, with billing doves at base above clasped hands. School of Grinling Gibbons. c. 1685. (Bramshill, Hants.)*

bear grinding had not yet been overcome, and a large mirror with leaves belonging to the king contained no fewer than 41 glass plates. Metal mirrors continued in use after the Restoration. In Charles I's *Book of Rates* (1642), small mirrors of steel pay 13s. 4d. the dozen, and a larger variety £1 6s. 8d. They are found again in the lists of merchandise imported and paying excise in 1657 and 1660. Several metal mirrors inherited by Charles I were disposed of when the contents of his palaces were dispersed, including a 'large looking-glass of steel' with 'Cardinals arms on ye topp', and another having silver plates, both probably dating from the 16th century.

After the Restoration George Villiers, second Duke of Buckingham, obtained the sole right to produce mirror plates, and was, in July, 1663, granted a patent for 14 years. Ignoring Mansell's enterprise, Buckingham claimed that the manufacture of mirror glass 'was not known or heretofore used in England'. Probably with the aid of Italian immigrant workmen Buckingham's glass-house was established at Vauxhall, where it was managed by an Englishman, John Bellingham,

7. *Mirror decorated with stump-work; figures representing Charles II and Catherine of Braganza; mouldings of tortoiseshell and panels bordered with silver galon. c. 1680. Ht. 3 ft., W. 2 ft. 4 in. (Percival Griffiths Coll.)*

8. *Mirror in convex moulded frame veneered with walnut; on cresting kneeling amorini support a crown. c. 1685. (Ixworth Abbey, Suffolk.)*

9. *Mirror in frame decorated with floral marquetry; on cresting a profile head below a Duke's coronet. c. 1675. Ht. 5 ft. 2 in., W. 3 ft. 5¾ in. (Ham House, Surrey.)*

behold'. The plates let into the wainscot, in such cases, were, no doubt, comparatively small, for though, in 1677, Evelyn pronounced Vauxhall glasses to be 'far larger and better than any that come from Venice', they seldom exceeded three feet in length. About the same time George Hudson, a glass-maker, supplied Charles II with two mirrors described as 'large', though only 25 ins. long, and Anthony Wood records that when Lady Clayton, wife of the Warden of Merton, bought 'a very large looking-glass' in 1674 at a cost of £10, it did not permit her to see her whole person, but only 'her ugly face and body to the middle'. Pepys alludes (*Diary*) to the purchase of a mirror on December 16th, 1664 'which cost me £5.5 and 6s. for the hooks'. This he considered 'a very fair glasse'. In the *Present State of England* (1683) the claim is made that 'England now excels all the world in every branch of this beautiful manufacture'.

From towards the end of Charles II's reign mirrors occupied a conspicuous position in luxuriously appointed rooms. They were commonly placed between windows, with a table and pair of stands or *guéridons* below them (*see* TABLES and STANDS). The plates, with a flat bevelled edge, when they have survived, are often dim and pitted with rust. To give the glass the property of reflection an amalgam of tin and

10. *Mirror in frame veneered with walnut, and decorated with floral marquetry; semicircular cresting within fret-cut border. c. 1685. Ht. 4 ft. 3 in., W. 2 ft. 6½ in. (Percival Griffiths Coll.)*

from 1671 to 1674. Although the pre-eminence of Vauxhall plates was generally recognised, the Duke did not retain a monopoly: others were granted patents about the same time. There is evidence that many of the plates used for looking-glasses were imported. The letters of John Greene, glass-seller of the Poultry, to Alessio Morelli, a well-known Venice glass-maker, between 1667 and 1672 afford particulars and sketches of large orders for mirror-plates, some of which are to be diamond cut (*Journal of the Society of Arts*, December 4, 1925).

The importation of mirrors was forbidden by Proclamation in 1664, and in the same year the London Glass-sellers were incorporated, their jurisdiction being confined to the City and seven miles round. In 1675 among the 85 members of the company there were 'no less than twenty grinders of mirror plates' (*English Glass*, W. A. Thorpe, 1935). There is a special reservation in the Glass-sellers' Charter of the rights of one Thomas Tilson, merchant, for the sole making of glass for mirrors. The decorative possibilities of glass were quickly realised by those rich enough to exploit them, and the walls of rooms were sometimes entirely lined with mirror plates. In 1667 Sir Samuel Morland built a fine room at Vauxhall 'the inside all of looking-glass and fountains very pleasant to mercury was applied to the back until early Victorian times, when the 'silvering' process with a coating of pure silver was substituted.

In the late Stuart period the materials used for the frames ranged from veneers of walnut, olive and laburnum to silver, chased and embossed; marquetry, japan, beads and needle-work were common, and tortoise-shell and ebony are also found.

The first group, ebony and tortoise-shell, represents an alien taste dating back to Charles I's reign (*see supra*). The pattern originated in Italy, but, by the Restoration, it was widely distributed in France, Holland and England; the manufacture presented little difficulty, and there is no reason to suppose that all examples found in this country were imported. Square, or more rarely, octagonal in shape, two distinct types of these mirrors can be recognised. In the one (Fig. 2) tortoise-shell pressed on moulded wood forms the complete frame; in the other, plain surfaces of the shell are contained within rippled ebony borders, resembling those found in oak on Stuart chests of drawers. One of the latter type, from which the tortoise-shell veneer is missing, enclosing a steel plate, is at Cotehele House, Cornwall. By a backing of paint the colour of the shell was varied at will, gilding being employed to produce a golden effect. In 1679 the Duchess of Lauderdale had two large mirrors framed in tortoise-shell in her bedroom at Ham House, Surrey. Mirror frames of identical

12. *Mirror in frame veneered with walnut, inlaid with acanthus scrolls and ciphers of the first Duke of Leeds. c. 1690. (Col N. R. Colville.)*

shape were veneered with ebony, or wood stained to resemble it, and sometimes incised with floral patterns. Fig. 3 is more representative of Carolean taste. The design of fruit, flowers and winged amorini is in high relief, the ground being filled with blue and white enamel. (For other examples of late Stuart enamel, *see* CHIMNEY FURNITURE and SCONCES.)

A less costly method of producing a gay and decorative effect is represented by frames decorated with stump-work or beads. The shapes are sometimes polygonal and the mouldings almost invariably of tortoise-shell, the panels being bordered by silver galon, as in Fig. 7, where the usual figures of Charles II and Catherine of Braganza are introduced (*see* MIRRORS, TOILET).

While stands for cabinets, carved in deal or lime and silvered or gilded, became plentiful soon after the Restoration, con-temporary mirrors similarly treated are rare. A few early examples are overlaid with burnished silver leaf, skilfully composed and coarsely carved in the style of the Grinling Gibbons school. A fine frame (Fig. 4), gilded and carved, with an inner ovolo moulding, japanned, is at Burghley House,

Many frames were carved by Gibbons and his followers in pear and lime woods to contain pictures or mirrors, the sur-vival of the original plate being the only conclusive evidence that a particular specimen was intended for a glass. In Fig. 5 this is the case, and Gibbons was employed in the decoration

11. *Mirror in frame veneered with walnut, inlaid with foliated arabesques and eagles in buff and brown; escalloped cresting. c. 1688. Ht. 1 ft. 11¾ in., W. 1 ft. 4½ in. (Macquoid Coll.)*

of Sudbury Hall, Derbyshire. The carving is on a large scale, but lacking in the delicacy associated with the master. In Fig. 6, though the glass is modern, the scale of the carving would have overwhelmed any small picture. The frame was probably carved to commemorate a wedding, for at the sides are a stork and a hen with chickens, emblematical of love and plenty, clasped hands below two billing doves forming the base. These frames formed an integral part of the decorative scheme on panels enriched with festoons and garlands of flowers.

Veneered and japanned mirrors of c. 1685 often had their plates framed in wide convex mouldings, generally surmounted by a large perforated cresting. For plainer specimens straight-cut walnut veneer was used, or a symmetrical arrangement of oyster-pieces, the effect being enhanced by lighter coloured rings formed of the sappy portions of the wood. Some walnut frames have a cresting carved with amorini supporting a crown (Fig. 8).

In inventories of this time mirror frames of olive, 'prince's wood', laburnum and grenoble wood (see WALNUT) are also mentioned. William Farnborough, cabinet-maker, supplied Charles II with several such mirrors, one of 'grenoble' costing as much as £50 in 1677. Many frames of this time were decorated with marquetry—the floral variety (Fig. 10), large-scale foliated arabesques (Fig. 11) and, towards the end of the century, 'seaweed' or endive patterns (Fig. 12). At Ham House a mirror has the convex frame inlaid with scrollwork and jasmine flowers of ivory relieved against an ebony ground (Fig. 9). In the centre of the cresting is a profile bust within a wreath, resembling that on a mirror in the Royal Collection at Windsor. (The coronet above dates this fine specimen after the creation of the Lauderdale dukedom in 1672.) The Ham inventory (1679) lists 'one table, stands and looking glass frame of ebony flowered'. A table consonant in style still stands below the mirror, but the stands have disappeared.

In the final phase of intricate arabesques, the marquetry is again often 'reserved' in panels and, though the continuous treatment was by no means rare, inlay on this small scale covering the whole frame produces an over-elaborate effect. These mirrors were made to match the marquetry tables and

13. *Mirror in convex moulded frame, decorated in black and gold japan; semi-circular cresting with fret-cut border. c. 1685. (Hampton Court. Leominster.)*

14. *Mirror in frame, decorated with Chinese incised lacquer; in centre of cresting, coronet and cipher of Ralph, first Duke of Montagu. c. 1685. (Boughton House, Northants.)*

chests of drawers over which they hung. They were sometimes suspended by brightly coloured strings or ribbons. Lord Hatton, brother of the Duke of Lauderdale, had a walnut mirror with blue strings and tassels in his chamber at Ham House in 1679.

Evelyn (*Mundus Muliebris*, 1690) mentions a 'Large looking-glass richly Japan'd' among the contents of a fashionable lady's dressing-room. In addition to the ordinary black and gold variety, red, blue and green are found. At this time the imitation of tortoise-shell was in request and Stalker and Parker wrote (1688) that ' 'tis still in vogue and favouring by many for glass frames'. The incised form of japanning, or 'Bantam work' (*see* JAPANNING AND LACQUER), was never extensively practised in England, and is very rare on mirror frames. It is stated by Stalker and Parker to have been out of fashion when their *Treatise* was published, but panels imported

15. *Mirror with table of ebony decorated with plaquettes of silver; the mirror bears the hall-mark of 1680. A pair of stands completes the set. (Knole Park, Kent.)*

16. *Mirror in frame embossed in silver with amorini and swags of fruit; pediment bears the cipher of Charles II, probably once surmounted by a crown. c. 1670. Ht. 6 ft. 11 in., W. 4 ft. 2 in. (Windsor Castle. By gracious permission of H.M. the Queen.)*

from the East were often cut up to form cabinets, tables, and mirror frames. In Fig. 14 the panels from an imported screen have been cut without regard to the pattern. At Ham House there is a mirror with Chinese incised lacquer frame of similar form with accompanying 'Bantam work' table, though not the flanking stands which were generally provided. Account books and inventories of the period have many references to the purchase of such sets. The Earl of Bristol (1696) obtained from Gerreit Jensen (*q.v.*) a black japanned mirror with table and stands, and in the same year Jensen supplied an 'India Japan looking-glass' for Queen Mary's new bedchamber at Windsor.

Contemporary, and similar in general outline, were the mirrors decorated with plaquettes, or entirely covered with silver embossed and chased. The fashion is generally held to have originated at the Court of Louis XIV, where large sums were certainly lavished on such luxuries; but so early as 1640

17. *Mirror in frame decorated with embossed silver; the pediment bears the royal arms and supporters with a cartouche engraved with the cipher of William III. c. 1697. Ht. 7 ft. 6 in., W. 3 ft. 11½ in. (Windsor Castle. By gracious permission of H.M. the Queen.)*

Evelyn noticed tables of 'massy silver' in a palace at Genoa, a date which suggests that Italy has a prior claim to the introduction of the vogue. It spread to England soon after the Restoration—indeed silver-mounted mirrors and tables are among the earliest examples that can be dated in the post-Restoration baroque style. The most important survivals are now in the Royal Collection at Windsor, though the 'great looking glass of beaten massive gold' given by the Queen Mother which Evelyn saw at Hampton Court in June 1662 has long disappeared.

A table overlaid with embossed silver was given to Charles II by the City of London in 1670 (*see* TABLES, VARIOUS; Fig. 9), and a mirror without a cresting decorated with foliated scrolls and masks closely resembles it in style. A very large mirror (Fig. 16) bearing the cipher of Charles II differs from the table in design. The pediment has lost some portions of the cresting,

probably a royal crown, above the escutcheon. The frame is embossed with swags of fruit, linked by ribbon bands on the sides, with lively amorini sporting amid the leaves. A table, largely of solid silver, by Andrew Moore of Bridewell (*see* TABLES, VARIOUS; Fig. 10) with a mirror to match (Fig. 17) was given also by the Corporation of London to William III. The frame of the mirror repeats the string of fruit and flowers that is contained in the cavetto frieze of the table. The crown above the cartouche on the pediment is a modern replacement. Celia Fiennes, visiting Windsor Castle just after the accession of Queen Anne, observed in the drawing-room 'glass frames' of silver with other pieces of furniture of the same kind. The fashion persisted into the early years of the 18th century. Fig. 15, from Knole, Kent, is shown with the table to match; the mirror bears the hall-mark of 1680-1 and the combined initials of the fifth Earl of Dorset's widow and her second husband Henry Powle, Master of the Rolls. The cipher is surmounted by a countess's coronet, and the silver plaquettes, in this instance, are applied on an ebony frame. At Knole there is a set of greater magnificence. There was a mirror frame of ebony and silver in the Yellow Satin Room at Ham House in 1679.

In the last years of the century the taste for gilt wall mirrors became more pronounced, and the character of the design was largely transformed. The square shape went out of fashion, the height was notably increased, and the space within the arched heading was commonly filled with mirror glass instead of with a panel veneered and inlaid. On the cresting, decorated with finials and carved with foliated scrolls, the owner's crest, cipher or coronet was often introduced. The main area, owing to increasing height, was formed of two or more plates; the borders were also of glass, bevelled and framed in gilt mouldings, or ornamented with sapphire-blue bandings and rosettes (Figs. 19, 21, 22, 25). This bevelling, with the cutting of the borders, was generally done by hand, though in the *London Gazette* (1698) there is an advertisement announcing a patent by which borders can be 'cut most curiously hollow and with a better lustre than any heretofore done'.

At this time borders were also decorated in *verre eglomisé* (*q.v.*) on a red, green or black ground, the gold arabesque designs being at times exceedingly intricate and beautiful. Although this art was derived from France, it was now practised by English craftsmen. The *London Gazette* (May, 1691) has an advertisement to the effect that the art of painting on glass 'is continued at Mr Winches a Glass-Painter in Bread Street near Cheapside, where any gentleman may be accommodated in any anneal'd Draughts of Effigies whatever'. From such artists, no doubt, the makers of mirror frames obtained their painted glass borders.

In Fig. 18 the cresting is elaborately carved and centres on a pheon, the crest of the Sydneys, surmounted by an earl's coronet, the mirror having been made for Philip, fifth Earl of Leicester. The ground of the borders is a transparent red, covered with foliated arabesques, birds and Berainesque dancing figures. Probably much of this kind of decoration was carried out by Huguenot refugees for insertion in English frames.

In the next examples the borders are of looking-glass, plain or cornered with an open-carved strapwork inspired by contemporary French taste. Fig. 19 shows carved strapwork

18. *Mirror with borders decorated in red and gold* verre eglomisé; *the cresting, of carved wood gilt, centres in a pheon. c. 1695. Ht. 9 ft. 6 in. (Penshurst Place, Kent.)* 19. *Mirror in carved gilt frame; cresting surmounted by coronet of first Lord Coningsby. c. 1700. (Hampton Court, Leominster.)* 20. *Mirror in carved gilt frame; cresting surmounted by a plumed female mask. c. 1715. Ht. 11 ft. 6 in. (Hampton Court Palace. By gracious permission of H.M. the Queen.)*

applied over glass borders, surmounted by the coronet of Lord Coningsby, created an Irish baron in 1692. Here the curves are elaborate and of great elegance. In Fig. 20, one of a pair in the Public Dining-room, Hampton Court Palace, the joints of the bevelled borders are covered by slips of moulded wood, on one of which the word 'Gumley' is carved in slight relief. A pair of mirrors, also by this maker, are in the State Bedroom at Chatsworth, Derbyshire, and on the glass frame of one of them his name is scratched (*see* GUMLEY, J.). In a petition presented to Parliament concerning a glass-house set up by him at Lambeth in 1705, it is stated that the trade in looking-glass plates had so improved 'that they serve not only for Furniture and Ornament in Her Majesty's Dominions at Home, but are likewise in great esteem in foreign parts; the Venetians themselves buying of these Plates, and preferring them to their own'. Gumley claimed to have improved the size and quality, and reduced the price by 20 per cent. In 1714 he furnished the upper part of the New Exchange in the Strand 'with the largest and finest Looking-glasses in Frames and out of Frames, according to the newest fashions, to the surprize of all Foreigners and others for their largeness and excelling all other Nations for goodness and cheapness'. The same year

Richard Steele (the *Lover*) described Gumley's gallery, observing: 'It is a modest computation that England gains £50,000 a year by exporting this commodity, for the service of foreign nations.' That large mirrors were comparatively cheap in the early 18th century may be gathered from Defoe's *Complete Tradesman* in which, writing of the fittings of a tradesman's premises in 1710, he commends that there should be 'one very large pier glass seven foot high in the Backshop'.

The royal accounts for 1695 show that the rooms at Windsor contained a number of mirrors with glass borders. In Queen Mary's New Bedchamber there was 'A Lookinge Glass the frame all covered with looking glass', and her dressing-room contained another of similar character. An unusually elaborate example of this type, delicately engraved and with sapphire-blue bandings decorated with rosettes, is seen in Fig. 21 from King William's bedroom at Hampton Court Palace, where it is framed in oak mouldings between the windows.

Fig. 22 shows one of several mirrors despatched and put together at Burley-on-the-Hill, Rutland, in 1711, the date being given by correspondence between the Earl of Nottingham and the makers, Richard Robinson and Thomas Howcraft.

357

21. *Mirror with glass borders, sapphire-blue bandings, and fragmentary crown and cipher of William III. c. 1700. (Hampton Court Palace.)* 22. *Mirror with cut-glass borders in walnut frame; Earl of Nottingham's coronet and crest. 1711. (Burley-on-the-Hill, Rutland.)* 23. *Mirror in carved and gilt frame; cresting carved with scrolls and eagles' heads. c. 1715. (Castle Howard, Yorks.)*

The earl points out that the frames need careful attention, it being necessary, by reason of the slips of glass, to instruct the joiners very exactly. Howcraft proposes to send down his mirror in sections, packed in a wooden box, and to mount it on the spot; he had 'bin with ye Waginer and he says that in case the wagin should overturn or any other casolity should happen he wont be responsible'. One of these mirrors cost £82 1s. 6d., the bill including such items as 'sholoping ye end glasses and cutting ye scroops—£3; a coat of arms (at the top) £6. 10. 0; 23 ft. of glass borders 6 in. wide £9.4.0.; ten gilt Roasors (Roses) £2.10.0.' The 6-in. borders and the crest at the top may be seen in this example.

Concurrently with these glass bevelled mirrors another variety was produced under Anne and George I, the frames being of carved wood, gilt or decorated with patterns in low relief (Figs. 23 and 24). Occasionally, silvered gesso decoration was employed, while for less important houses a plain walnut variety was produced on similar lines. Japanned mirrors, contemporary with the above, followed the same general design (Fig. 26). In the *London Gazette* (1703), the loss of five mirrors 'in Japan'd Frames with cross bars, all damaged by water' is advertised. The upper plate of these tall and narrow

frames is often ornamented with a pattern in so-called 'brilliant cutting', which leads the eye up to the cresting.

By 1695 English glass had greatly improved in quality, and in that year an excise of 20 per cent. was imposed on mirror plates; but after protests from the makers, who claimed they had brought the art 'to such perfection as to out-do the world', this tax was reduced and it was abolished in 1699. Vauxhall no longer enjoyed a virtual monopoly, and in the early 18th century was eclipsed by the Bear Garden Glass House, Bank Side, Southwark. In the *Postman* (1700) Vauxhall offers for sale 'Large Looking-glass Plates, the like never made in England before'. These were 'six foot in length and proportionable breadth'; but, two years later, the Bear Garden proprietors advertised plates of 90 ins., 'of lively colour, free from Bladders, Veins and Foulness incident to the large plates hitherto sold'. About this date Gerreit Jensen supplied mirrors of similar height (some with 'border of rought glass round about them') to the royal palaces; one for St James's measured 'about 81 inches by 45 inches'. This glass with its table and stands cost £215.

After 1720 Vauxhall again recovered its pre-eminence, and under the management of Dawson, Bowles and Co. 'was

24. *Mirror in carved and gilt frame; cresting surmounted by eagle. Attributed to John Gumley. c. 1715. (Hampton Court Palace.)*
25. *Mirror in frame with glass borders; cresting and mouldings of carved and gilt wood. c. 1715. (Chevening, Kent.)* 26. *Mirror in frame japanned scarlet with chinoiserie detail; cresting carved and gilt. c. 1715. (From Mrs David Gubbay.)*

carried on with amazing success' for another sixty years. The processes of blowing, grinding, polishing and silvering practised at this time are explained in the *Dictionarium Polygraphicum* (1735).

Between c. 1690 and 1700 mirrors designed in relation to the panelling over mantelpieces were introduced, the frames being of walnut, of glass, decorated with japan, or of carved wood gilt. In 1697 Celia Fiennes, after visiting Lord Orford's house, Chippenham Park, near Newmarket, observed that in the best drawing-room 'there was no looking-glass but on ye chimney piece and just opposite in ye place a Looking-glass used to be was 4 pannells of glass in length and 3 in breadth set together in ye wanscoate'.

Several of the rooms at Hampton Court Palace contain overmantels with glass borders so arranged that they afford a vista through the rooms. In the mirror in William III's bedroom, the semicircular heading is contained within carved oak mouldings, having sapphire blue glass borders studded with rosettes of white glass. In Fig. 28 the walnut framing of the mirror is skilfully adapted to the oak mouldings above. Engraving and *verre eglomisé* decoration are found combined in Fig. 27, the glass arches being contained within a carved gilt frame. The tympana are decorated in gold and black, with delicate arabesques, and in the spandrels above are graven knots of flowers. On the centre panel are the arms of Dashwood with their crest, a gryphon's head ermine erased; also introduced on the pilasters, the mirror probably commemorated the marriage of Richard, younger brother of the first baronet of Northbrook, with Mary Jarret, of London, in 1697. Overmantel mirrors were sometimes very large, occupying the whole area between chimneypiece and cornice.

The design of overmantel mirrors of the early 18th century, with elaborately shaped crestings decorated in gilt gesso, resembles that of contemporary pier glasses. A fine example (Fig. 29) has the arms of Richard Lockwood (b. 1672) in the centre of the deep cresting, which is carved with acanthus and eagles' heads. This overmantel mirror is part of a set, two upright glasses of similar design being provided with it to hang between windows. In Fig. 30, obtained by Robert Ashhurst for the new house at Hedingham Castle, Essex, c. 1725, a carved frame is combined with glass pilasters; at the corners are satyr masks, a motif freely introduced on all kinds of gilt furniture in the early Georgian period. The overmantel mirrors in this gilt gesso group are all composed of three or

359

27. *Overmantel Mirror in a carved gilt frame; tympana decorated in gold and black* verre eglomisé; *centre compartment bears Dashwood arms and crest, those on either side cipher M.J.D. c.* 1700. (*Heydon Hall, Norfolk.*)

28. *Overmantel Mirror in walnut moulded frame with serpentine heading, designed in relation to the oak panelling of the room. c.* 1710. (*Canons Ashby, Northants.*)

29. *Mirror in frame carved and decorated with gilt gesso; on shield in pediment arms of Lockwood impaling Cutts. c.* 1715. *Ht. 3 ft. 4 in., W. 5 ft. 4 in.*

30. *Mirror in carved and gilt frame with glass pilasters; serpentine heading centres in the Ashhurst crest, and their arms are emblazoned in the dexter cartouche; at corners satyr masks. c. 1725. (Hedingham Castle, Essex.)*

31. *Overmantel Mirror in walnut frame parcel gilt with serpentine mouldings; upper portion encloses a wooded landscape in oils. c. 1745. Ht. 5 ft. W. 4 ft. 8 in. (Formerly at the Star and Garter Hotel, Kew Bridge.)*

32. *Mirror in carved and gilt frame; scrolled cresting centres in an escallop shell; on the shaped base candle branches. c. 1715. (Seaton Delaval, Northumb.)* 33. *Mirror in carved and gilt frame; corners of cresting finish in eagle heads; candle branches renewed. c. 1715. Ht. 4 ft. 2 in., W. 2 ft. 5½ in. (Mr Ralph Edwards.)* 34. *Mirror in carved and gilt frame; borders of painted glass with figures in late Stuart costume. c. 1715-20. (Doddington Hall, Lincs.)*

more plates, but this was not invariably the case, and in 1715 Lady Grisell Baillie paid £14 for a chimney glass 'in one piece, 54½×22½'.

A simpler type was introduced c. 1720 to stand on a mantel-shelf. The height was reduced, the curved heading omitted, and the mirror became rectangular, the severity of its outline being broken by mitred corners or projecting scroll-pieces at the sides, on which candle-branches were sometimes fixed. Carved mouldings divide the horizontal plate from those on either side in some examples, while in others the overlapping of the bevels keeps the plates in position. Above the glass pictures were often framed; birds, fruit and seascapes being favourite subjects. In Fig. 31 the gilt serpentine mould-ing and delicate pendants of fruit and flowers already betray rococo influence. This mirror was formerly in the coffee-room of the Star and Garter Hotel, Kew Bridge, and was no doubt made for the position it occupied over the fireplace. In Sir William Stanhope's sale at his Albemarle Street house (1733) 'a chimney glass of 3 large Plates 51 ins. by 3 ins. in a fine carv'd and gilt Frame and a Top for a Picture' was included. Ince and Mayhew (*Universal System*, 1759-63) illustrate 'Four Designs of Chimney Glasses and Pictures over them'.

In the reigns of Anne and George I the frames of the large pier glasses that occupied the space between windows were generally of carved wood gilt, but sometimes the borders were still of glass set within mouldings. They occur in Fig. 35, one of a pair from Erthig, Denbighshire, where James Moore (*q.v.*) supplied a number of mirrors and pier glasses between 1720 and

1726. Here the candle-branches, usual at this date, are also of glass, and the mirrors may be identified with 'a pair of large Looking glass Sconces in carved and gold frames with double glass branches' for which Moore charged £12 10s. in 1720. Silvering was occasionally substituted for gilding, and another large mirror in the saloon is probably the 'fine large Sconce, silver-framed', for which John Meller, the owner of Erthig, paid £21 in 1723. In an inventory (1725) of Cannons, Middle-sex, for the first Duke of Chandos 'a piere glass in a silver'd frame, £50' is entered. Another exceptional treatment is seen in Fig. 26, where the frame is japanned, and on a brilliant scarlet ground, floral sprays and other Chinese details are painted, with diapered reserves.

In addition to these long pier glasses a smaller type of hanging mirror was produced. The plates were approximately square, with a shaped cresting and base, the mouldings and flat surfaces being decorated with fine gesso ornament. The carved decoration of the cresting resembled that of con-temporary pier glasses; at the base candle-branches were generally fixed to a small shaped plate (Figs. 32 and 33). The first examples are marked by mastery of line and delicacy of ornament, combined with a treatment distinctly English. Though such mirrors tended to standardisation, some depart appreciably from the norm. In Fig. 34 the frame has an unusual feature in the broad border of painted glass, while Fig. 37 is one of 'three glass sconces in carved and gilt frames with two wrot arms each' made for Frederick, Prince of Wales, by Benjamin Goodison in 1732-3. The cresting centres on the

(5. *One of a 'pair of Large looking-glass Sconces in carved and gold frames with double glass branches'. By James Moore, 1720. Erthig, Denbigh.)* 36. *Mirror in walnut frame with shaped fret-cut cresting and base. c. 1720. Ht. 4 ft. 6 in., W. 2 ft. 2 in. (G. L. Riley Coll.)* 37. *Mirror, carved and gilt, one of three made for Frederick, Prince of Wales, 1723-33. By Benjamin Goodison. (Hampton Court Palace. By gracious permission of H.M. the Queen.)*

38. *Mirror in carved and gilt frame; cartouche within pediment bears the Bowes crest. c. 1735. Ht. 5 ft. 10 in., W. 3 ft. 3 in. (Streatlam Castle, Northumb.)* 39. *Mirror frame and console table of carved wood, originally gilt, later painted white; pediment of mirror centres in a feathered female mask; caryatides at sides. c. 1735. (Wentworth Woodhouse, Yorks.)* 40. *Mirror in carved gilt frame; a shell within pediment; the frieze centres in a sun-rayed female mask. c. 1735. (Ragley Hall, Warwicks.)*

41. *Mirror in carved and gilt oval frame, probably designed by William Kent; the cresting centres in the coronet of the Prince of Wales. Attributed to Benjamin Goodison. c. 1735. Ht. 5 ft. 10½ in. (V. & A. Mus.)* 42. *Mirror in walnut frame parcel gilt; pediment frames a cartouche. c. 1740. Ht. 4 ft. 11 in., W. 2 ft. 9 in. (C. D. Rotch Coll.)* 43. *Mirror in carved and gilt frame probably designed by William Kent; the acanthus cresting centres in a female mask. c. 1735. (Ditchley, Oxon.)*

three feathers, and the mirrors are still in the Prince's Drawing-room at Hampton Court Palace. Inexpensive mirrors veneered with cross-grained walnut were also made with shaped crestings and bases, the moulded edges and central ornament of the cresting being generally gilt.

From c. 1725 the design of pier glasses was directly inspired by their architectural setting. A broad moulded architrave was surmounted by a classical entablature, the frieze often centred on a mask, and the broken pediment framed an armorial cartouche, shell, or feathered female head; the architrave ended in base scrolls, and the sides were generally edged with floral pendants, drapery and husks. This architectural treatment, consonant with the character of Palladian houses, appears in a fully developed form in Figs. 38, 39, 40, 42. What could be made of these classical motives by a skilful designer can be seen in the first example, a mirror added to the contents of Streatlam Castle, Durham, during the ownership of Sir George Bowes, who held the estates from 1721 to 1760. In Fig. 44 the effect of the fine design and carving is marred by the loss of the escutcheon, but the disposition of drapery is admirable, and in the double break of the head, there is already a touch of rococo. The mouldings on such mirrors were often made to correspond with those on cornices, doors and window architraves, and in Fig. 40 the shell-and-dart on the cornice of the room is repeated on the frame of the mirror,

the double shell being somewhat fortuitously related to the depressed pediment.

Such leading architects as Gibbs, William Kent and John Vardy designed mirrors of this kind for their clients. A console table corresponding in style was often placed beneath these pier glasses, as in Fig. 39, where both pieces have been painted white to match the later panelling of the room. In this architectural type the gilding was sometimes confined to the mouldings and salient ornament, the frame being veneered with mahogany or walnut. Such mirrors, with the console or 'slab' tables to match them, were regarded as an important part of interior decoration. In William Jones's *Gentlemens or Builders Companion* (1739) they are the only furniture illustrated, the rest of the book being devoted to architectural detail. Mirrors were among the most expensive varieties of furniture—mainly on account of the heavy cost of the glass—and entries in the royal accounts prove that when the frames became dilapidated they were often repaired and the gilding was renewed. Regilding was often done by the oil process (*see* GILDING), but other frames were painted over in Victorian times to match the decoration of the room.

Oval mirrors were also much in demand at the time. With the examples (Figs. 41, 43) carved in baroque taste Kent's name may be associated. The first was probably designed by him for Frederick, Prince of Wales, and made by Benjamin

44. *Mirror in carved and gilt frame; escutcheon missing from centre of pediment; sides edged with drapery. c. 1745. (Pepys Cockerell Coll.)* 45. *Mirror in carved and gilt frame; cipher and coronet of the first Duke of Richmond engraved on the upper plate; on cresting a plumed female head. c. 1740. (Goodwood, Sussex.)* 46. *Mirror in gilt frame carved in rococo taste. c. 1755. (Tyttenhanger, Herts.)*

Goodison; the second is from Ditchley; he is known to have co-operated there with James Gibbs, the builder of the house.

In the early 'forties mirror frames began to be affected by rococo influence in both design and decoration, and the architectural type was soon superseded. Such frames were particularly subject to this influence, presenting a favourable field for the expression of the style 'in its most advanced degree'. The process was gradual and there are transitional examples. In Fig. 45, one of a set of three mirrors at Goodwood, made for the first Duke of Richmond, rococo scrolls are mixed with acanthus foliage and bunches of rushes which are still baroque in character. In excellence of modelling the plumed female head and the mask are strongly reminiscent of the work of Benjamin Goodison (*q.v.*). Fig. 47 is characteristic of the early phase of the style. The frame is still comparatively solid, but C-scrolls figure more prominently and the shell on base and cresting has become a version of the French *coquillage*. The charming proportions and detail of this example show how soon the new style was successfully assimilated. In Fig. 46 the framework is formed of large contrasted C-scrolls and the floral pendants are delicately carved. A set of four mirrors now at Windsor Castle was originally in Kensington Palace, being later moved to the 'Queen's House in St James's Park' (Buckingham Palace). As George III abandoned Kensington on his accession, the mirrors may

be dated before 1760. The framework is carved with great virtuosity in the full rococo taste, agitated storks being perched on the lateral scrolls (Fig. 49).

Amid the amazing variety of these mirrors it is seldom possible to recognise the work of individuals, but Chippendale's *Director* (1st ed., 1754) and other contemporary pattern books show whence the craftsmen derived their ideas. In these publications the rococo is not the only style. The Gothic of Horace Walpole and his friends—pointed arches, tracery and cusping—is shown applied to mirrors; while no other variety of furniture presented such an opportunity for exploiting the fantastic versions of Chinese ornament popularised by the books of Halfpenny and Edwards and Darly. Extravagant conceits, impossible in mahogany, could be carried out on a pinewood frame, even if some remained 'unrealised aspirations'.

Lock and Johnson (*q.v.*) were prolific designers of this class of furniture; both were also carvers with assistants in their employ. Lock's designs are less extravagant than those of Johnson, who had a marked partiality for human and animal motifs. Linnell never published his numerous drawings (*see* LINNELL, JOHN). The openwork basket with drooping flowers and the small floral pendants detached from the frame of Fig. 48 occur with such trifling modifications in Linnell's designs that this mirror may reasonably be assigned to him.

365

In Fig. 50 the ornament is of fragile delicacy, and the effect of elegance is enhanced by the narrow gilt mouldings that divide the glass. Fig. 51 is in Chinese taste and corresponds with Plate CXLIII in the *Director* (1st ed.), the only appreciable difference being that here a Negro replaces a mandarin under the pagoda canopy. Other mirrors in the same house, on the evidence of their correspondence with designs, may confidently be assigned to Chippendale. The japanned and gilt mirror (Fig. 54) is another example of chinoiserie. The columns, broken by polygonal intersections, end in pointed finials surrounded by foliage, while under the pagoda an emaciated monkey is seated. The rush motive figures prominently in Fig. 52, long rhythmical curves and festoons of husks below the cresting foreshadowing the classical revival. As an earlier period, console tables carved in the same style were often placed below these tall pier glasses (Fig. 61).

47. *Mirror in gilt frame carved with C-scrolls and ancathus; floral pendants at sides; serpentine brass candle branches attached to base. c. 1750. (The Vyne, Hants.)*

48. *Mirror in gilt frame carved in rococo taste; glass borders and candle branches at base. One of a pair from Bramshill, attributed to John Linnell. c. 1755.*

49. *Carved and gilt mirror, one of a set of four; foliated scrollwork, floral pendants and storks figure among the decorative motives. c. 1755. Ht. 5 ft. 5 in., W. 3 ft. 11 in. (Windsor Castle. By gracious permission of H.M. the Queen.)*

50. *Mirror in carved gilt frame; a pineapple forms the cresting; glass divided by gilt mouldings. c. 1755. (Castle Howard, Yorks.)*
51. *Mirror in carved gilt frame, one of a pair; based on a design in first edition of Chippendale's* Director, *1754. Ht. 8 ft. 8½ in., W. 4 ft. 10 in. (Crichel, Dorset.)* 52. *Mirror with glass borders; gilt frame carved with rush fronds. c. 1765. (Dingley Hall, Northants.)*

At this time Anglo-Chinese taste was very consistently carried out; the walls were hung with imported hand-painted paper, and the window curtains were of Chinese embroideries or brightly coloured chintz. In such interiors the glass of mirrors was sometimes painted at the back with birds, figures and landscapes to carry out the Oriental illusion. The subjects were either executed in the East on glass sent out for the purpose, or painted by European artists in imitation of the Chinese. Fig. 55 shows a fine example, the drawing of birds and foliage proving the glass to have been painted in China.

Circles and ovals in a variety of styles are shown in contemporary pattern books. Fig. 53, described in The Vyne (Hampshire) inventory (1754) as a 'round Looking Glass in a gilt frame', has the head of Apollo in the centre, with sun-rays masking the junction of four separate plates. Here oak leaves, spiritedly carved, form the circle, the candle-branches repeating the motif. A pair of oval mirrors (Fig. 56) can be assigned to Thomas Johnson, carver and designer (*q.v.*) and are based on Plate 55 in his *One Hundred and Fifty New Designs* (1758). Fig. 57 again suggests his responsibility. Below the vase finial a figure of Diana holding a hunting horn sits on a quiver of arrows, while in the centre of the pendant is a group of dead game, a pointer and fowling piece.

53. *Circular Mirror in a frame of carved oak leaves; head of Apollo in centre. c. 1750. (The Vyne, Hants.)*

54. (*Left*) *Mirror in Chinese taste; carved frame japanned and gilt; on cresting a grotesque monkey. c. 1760. (Wentworth Woodhouse. Yorks.)*

55. (*Right*) *Mirror painted behind the glass by a Chinese artist; gilt frame carved in rococo taste; candle branches at sides. c. 1760. (Lennoxlove, Haddington.)*

56. (*Left*) *Mirror in carved and gilt frame, one of a pair. Attributed to Thomas Johnson, c. 1760. Corsham Court, Wilts.)*

57. (*Right*) *Mirror in carved and gilt frame; figure of Diana below finial; dead game and a pointer at base. c. 1760. Ht. 8 ft. 8 in., W. 4 ft. 1 in. (Cobham Hall, Kent.)*

58. *Mirror in carved gilt frame with glass borders. Probably by Thomas Chippendale. c. 1765. Ht. 7 ft., W. 4 ft. 6 in. (V. & A. Mus.)*

59. *Overmantel Mirror in gilt frame, carved with long-tailed birds and rococo ornament. c. 1755. (Dingley Hall, Northants.)*

60. *(Below) Overmantel Mirror in carved and gilt frame. c. 1750. Ht. 2 ft. 4 in., W. 3 ft. 10 in. (Macquoid Coll.)*

61. *(Right) Pier Glass, one of a pair, gilt and carved with rococo ornament; console table in same style. c. 1755. (Hagley Park, Worcs.)*

62. *Overmantel Mirror in gilt frame, carved with rococo ornament; English Chinoiserie paintings on glass. c. 1755. (Bramshill, Hants.)*

63. *Overmantel Mirror of pine, originally painted; the carved ornament is carried down the marble fireplace below. c. 1755. Ht. 10 ft. 6¾ in., W. 6 ft. 5 in. (V. & A. Mus.)*

64. *Overmantel Mirror in carved and gilded frame; Ganymede and the eagle form the cresting. Based on Plate XXXVI in Thomas Johnson's* One Hundred and Fifty New Designs, 1758. *Ht. 4 ft. 2 in., W. 4 ft. 4 in. (V. & A. Mus.)*

65. Overmantel Mirror in gilt frame, carved with rushes and C-scrolls; in upper portion is picture of the Grand Canal, Venice. c. 1760. Ht. 3 ft. 6 in., extreme W. 4 ft.

66. Overmantel Mirror in carved gilt frame; rococo C-scrolls combined with classical ornament. c. 1765. (Ramsbury Manor, Wilts.)

In Chippendale's 'Designs for Glass Frames' in the *Director*, long-beaked birds, rush fronds and floral sprays figure prominently, and Fig. 58, one of a pair, where the carving is most lively and vigorous, is strongly reminiscent of these designs and is probably from his workshop. Entries in the royal accounts and existing examples prove that mirror frames, when they became badly worn, were regilded. Water gilding with the salient ornament burnished is commonly found on fine frames, but the oil process was also freely employed.

Overmantel mirrors were made in a variety of shapes and sizes by Chippendale and his contemporaries. The smaller specimens were still divided into three compartments (Fig. 60). The carving is more delicate in Fig. 59, the scrolls, acanthus and branches with oak leaves being skilfully combined. The openwork basket of flowers and a strong similarity in the treatment of C-scrolls suggest that the maker of Fig. 48, probably John Linnell, was also responsible for the large overmantel in Fig. 62. In the carved wood-work of the frame there is a suggestion of Oriental taste, the inset paintings on glass being copies of Chinese figure subjects by a Western hand. The figure of Ganymede with the eagle on the summit of Fig. 64 and other details of the ornament are derived from Plate XXXVI in Johnson's *One Hundred and Fifty New Designs* and warrant an attribution to that carver.

Overmantel mirrors were sometimes provided with brackets contrived amid the scrollwork for the display of china. There was formerly an elaborate example in the celebrated Chinese Room at Badminton, Gloucestershire; while the royal accounts for 1766 record the purchase of a 'chimney glass' for the Queen's Closet at St James's from John Bradburn (*q.v.*). The carved frame is described as 'gilt in burnish'd gold with 46 Brackets for China with rich festoons of flowers, a

67. Mirror in carved gilt frame; one of a pair carved in neo-classic taste by John Linnell. c. 1770. (Formerly at Shardeloes, Bucks.)

68. Mirror in carved gilt frame; the acanthus scrolls of the cresting support two female figures and frame an oval of looking-glass. Designed by Robert Adam. 1772. Ht. 6 ft. 6 in. (Corsham Court, Wilts.)

69. Mirror in carved gilt frame, one of a pair; at the sides are terminal female figures. Designed by Robert Adam. 1765. (Syon House, Middx.)

70. Overmantel Mirror in carved gilt frame; caryatides, holding festoons of husks, form pilasters. Designed by Robert Adam. c. 1775. (20, St James's Square.)

crown on the top': there were 21 plates of looking-glass. The scale of such mirrors enabled designers to indulge their more extravagant fancies, frames being carved with scenes from *Aesop's Fables* or Chinese life, temples, bridges or trophies. The carved ornament was sometimes carried down the fire-place below and applied over the marble (Fig. 63): of this treatment there are many examples in contemporary pattern books, the whole elaborate structure being known as a 'chimneypiece'. Chippendale (*Director*) observes that a skilful carver may 'give full scope to his capacity in the execution of these designs', and states of a chimneypiece in which archi-tecture and ruins are introduced that it would not be amiss if the whole were modelled before it began to be executed. In such cases the carver designed the carved and gilt or painted overlay of the marble fireplace to accord with his overmantel.

Overmantel mirrors of this time, containing the original picture, are rare, but one may be seen in Fig. 65, where the size of the canvas causes the frame to appear somewhat out of scale with the lower stage. The painting is by one of Canaletto's followers, the rush motif being again introduced (cf. Fig. 64). In Fig. 66 classical ornament, congruous with the chimney-piece below, is skilfully combined with the graceful foliate scrolls of the framework. A fine Chinese wallpaper provides a decorative background.

In the mahogany mirrors of this time rococo influence is discernible only in the shaping of the fret-cut cresting and baseboard. The former was generally enlivened by a shell and gilt bird with extended wings in a pierced circle, and the inner mouldings of the frame were also gilt. Among the many varieties produced between 1750 and 1765 were convex and concave mirrors in rococo taste, which, according to Ince

72. *Design for Chimneypiece and Overmantel Mirror for the Earl of Derby's house, Grosvenor Square. From Robert Adam's* Works in Architecture. *The original drawing dated* 1774.

71. *Overmantel Mirror in gilt frame; the semicircular heading decorated in composition. Designed by Robert Adam. c. 1775.* (20, *Mansfield Street, London.*)

and Mayhew, had a 'very pretty effect in a well furnish'd room'. They were, no doubt, valued for the amusing distortion of reflected objects that resulted from the shape of the glass; and that they were no innovation is proved by an advertise-ment in the *London Gazette* (September 22, 1693) announcing the sale of 'concave looking-glasses' at the Archimedes and Three Golden Prospects in St Paul's Churchyard.

In 1740 the duty on glass, repealed in 1699, was re-enacted, and the mirror-makers' trade was seriously affected by the tax. Contemporary bills and accounts prove that the cost of the glass greatly exceeded that of the frame, and even royal cabinet-makers were careful to remove the plates when making new frames in contemporary taste. Benjamin Goodison made 'five new carved and painted pier glasses' for Kew in 1752 for £28 15s.—being able to supply them for so small a charge because he had taken the glass from the discarded mirrors. At this time plates were still made from blown cylinders;

but in 1773 a new process was adopted which facilitated the production of the immensely tall pier glasses that became so fashionable in the last quarter of the century. In 1702 the Bear Garden proprietors had advertised plates of 90 ins. but in the *Plate Glass Book* (1773) 5 ft. 6 ins. is the largest size offered to the public. In that year the method of casting glass was introduced from France (where, it is said, it had been invented c. 1670) and the British Cast Plate Glass-makers were incorporated by special Act of Parliament, setting up their factories at Albion Place, Southwark, and at Ravenshead, near St Helens, Lancashire. This casting had been practised in England to a limited extent at an earlier date. In 1691 Robert Hooke and Christopher Dodsworth were granted a licence 'to exercise and put in practice the new invention of casting plate glass, particularly looking glass plates', and the *Dictionarium Polygraphicum* (1735) observes that 'the method of running and casting large looking-glass plates has been considerably improv'd by our workmen in England. . . . We cast all kinds of borders, mouldings, etc.' Mr Bowles, of the Vauxhall Works, which were to be closed within ten years, stated in evidence before the committee when the Plate Glass-makers were incorporated that plates larger than any then in demand could be made by the old method; Vauxhall, he said, had formerly experimented in casting, but the apparatus had

long since been destroyed. He charged £37 10s. for a plate 60 ins. by 40 ins. in the rough. A passage in Lady Mary Coke's *Diary* for the following year proves that some time elapsed before the company was able to compete on equal terms with the French manufacture. Describing Lord Bute's house, she writes: 'Fine glasses there are only in one of the drawing-rooms; the rest are to be brought here, as soon as the new project for casting larger plates here than they do at Paris is brought to perfection.' The prices quoted by the manufacturers show that cabinet-makers must have made large profits on the glass of mirrors supplied to their clients, and even when the casting process was no longer a novelty, glass remained inordinately dear. Chippendale's firm, in a letter dated June 23, 1778, to Sir William Knatchbull, of Mersham Hatch, Kent, reported that they have 'forwarded by the Canterbury Coach two different designs of Glasses and frames'; and quoted for the plates to fill the piers £180 each, 'which size we have often sold for 200 guineas'. The frames were to cost £28 or £36, 'but either may be slighted and made for less'.

The author of the *Plate Glass Book* enlarges on 'the exceeding brittleness of the glass, as well as the many unavoidable Hazards and accidents it is always liable to'. An extravagant charge was exacted by tradesmen when mirrors were hired on

73. *Overmantel Mirror in carved gilt frame; on cresting a classical vase flanked by winged gryphons. c. 1775. Ht. 6 ft. 10 in., W. 6 ft. 5 in. (V. & A. Mus.)* 74. *Oval Mirror in carved gilt frame; surmounted by a vase and festooned with husks. c. 1775. (Heveningham Hall, Suffolk.)*

special occasions. Horace Walpole, describing a ball given by Lord Stanley in 1773, mentions that glasses for decorating the ballroom were lent by Lord March, as an upholsterer had asked £300 for the loan of some. On account of the complex curves of the frame, rococo mirrors were not bevelled, but bevels were worked on some large pier glasses until late in the century. The royal accounts between 1740 and 1770 contain many entries for the cleaning and repairing of mirrors; the glass was often resilvered and the frames were regilded. In 1789 a steam engine, described as 'a very curious piece of mechanism', was invented for grinding and polishing, which had hitherto been done by hand.

Adam revolutionised the design of pier glasses and mirrors of all kinds. The framing of large pier glasses became more rectangular, and, in spite of increasing height, plates were now rarely subdivided. Rococo forms soon after 1765 were succeeded by classical ornament—sphinxes, urns, medallions, arabesqued acanthus, husks and paterae. Such mirrors were invariably designed to match their architectural surroundings, and, with console tables below, formed an important part of decorative schemes.

There are mirror frames at Corsham Court, Wiltshire (Fig. 68), designed by Adam; sketches are in the Soane Museum and at Corsham. The earliest (1767) dated sketch is for the mirrors in the Picture Gallery, and there is a second (undated) design in which the cresting is less elaborate than that carried out. The design for the one in the Cabinet Room (Fig. 68) is dated March 6, 1772: it shows the seated figures on the cresting, but not the scrollwork framing the oval glass.

The two great mirrors between the windows in the drawing-room at Syon House (*see* INTRODUCTION; Fig. 12) are large in scale and in Adam's more developed classical manner. The acanthus scrolls of the cresting and base, ending in paterae and centring on honeysuckle ornament, are broadly handled, while the mouldings are very delicately carved. In Fig. 69, one of a pair of large pier glasses between the windows of the dining-room, classical ornament is rendered on a slightly smaller scale with equal perfection. Here the mitred corners at the top of the frame are supported by terminal figures, headed by acanthus husks and terminating in pendants of the same; the running pattern of scrolls and paterae that decorates the flat surface is repeated on a larger scale in the cresting. At Ken Wood, Hampstead, in the library there is a pair of mirrors with gryphons and infant bacchanals in the cresting illustrated in Adam's *Works in Architecture*. The bills of W. France (*q.v.*) indicate that the frames of these pier glasses, though designed by Adam, were made in France, and there is a charge (1768) for 'repairing and gilding them as they had been a good deal hurt by unpacking and by salt water'. The arched recesses on either side of the fireplace, which now contain bookshelves, were originally fitted with mirrors by Chippendale; and by an agreement (June 14, 1769) he bound himself to deliver 'French plate Glass in London silver'd and ready to put up' for the 'mirrors in recesses' to the amount of £340. This agreement shows that four years before the establishment of the British cast plate-glass manufacture, Chippendale was obtaining glass for an important commission of this kind from France.

In the State Bedchamber at Osterley, Middlesex, there is a large pier glass designed by Adam c. 1775, and Mrs Lybbe

75. *Overmantel Mirror in wood frame painted cream colour; ovals in grisaille on a black ground, and carved ornament gilt. c. 1790. (Shavington, Salop.)*

Powys, a few years later, stated that this was 'the first plate made in England'; meaning, no doubt, the first cast by the new process. The central plate is set in wide borders of glass in Fig. 67, a sense of lightness and delicacy pervading the whole design. This mirror is one of a pair based on a design by John Linnell 'for glass-frames in the drawing-room at Shardeloes for William Drake'.

Harewood House, Yorkshire, contains many mirrors in Adam's style, supplied by Chippendale and Haig between 1773 and 1775. Between the windows in the Long Gallery are four pier glasses surmounting gilt console tables with marble slabs dating from this time, which were supplied by the younger Thomas Chippendale in 1797. The oval medallions at the top of these mirrors are painted in the manner of Angelica Kauffmann and enriched with garlands of roses supported by cupids, the glass borders being subdivided by brackets for the display of china. There is a striking disproportion between the cost of the frame and the glass in the Harewood accounts, where 'a very large pier glass at £290' is entered, while Chippendale charged only £70 for 'a superb frame to do., with very large Antique ornaments exceeding richly Carved and highly finished in Burnished Gold'.

76. *Circular Convex Mirror in carved gilt frame; badge of the Merchant Taylors' Company supported by cornucopiae forms cresting. c. 1800. Ht. 7 ft. 6 in., extreme W. 6 ft. 6 in. (Merchant Taylors' Hall.)*

77. *Circular Convex Mirror in carved gilt frame. c. 1800. Ht. 8 ft. 4 in., W. 3 ft. 6 in. (V. & A. Mus.)*

78. *Overmantel Mirror in gilt frame; in frieze small convex mirrors. c. 1800.*

79. *Overmantel Mirror in carved and gilt frame; bevelled plates divided by reeded mouldings; cavetto frieze enclosing gilt balls. c. 1805. (The late Maj.-Gen. Sir Wilkinson Bird.)*

The imitation of one material by another led to a change in the character of mirrors between c. 1775 and 1800. The frames and salient ornament were of wood; but for delicate scrolling and paterae makers exploited a special composition on metal cores, while the minute husking was often of lead. By this method an effect of lightness and grace was obtained which would have been impossible in carved wood.

At this time painted decoration largely supplemented carving on mirrors, as on other varieties of furniture, the frames being picked out with floral patterns or painted to accord with the general colour scheme. Between 1767 and 1770 Chippendale and Haig were decorating the rooms at Mersham Hatch, and supplying Sir Edward Knatchbull with many mirrors—ovals, pier and chimney glasses—the frames being painted to match the wallpapers. In a bedroom hung with purple paper, a large pier glass was 'Japann'd' purple and white.

Adam's fertility of invention is strikingly illustrated by his designs for overmantel mirrors, of which there are a large number among his drawings, the more important being reproduced in his published *Works*. These 'glass frames' were carefully designed to accord with the marble chimneypieces below. Delicate ornament was generally carried out in composition to match the plasterwork decoration of the walls, and, in consequence, such mirrors are seldom in perfect condition. In Fig. 70 the caryatides support classical vases, and the side compartments are headed by reclining female figures. Fig. 71 from No. 20, Mansfield Street, almost exactly corresponds with a mirror designed by Adam to surmount a marble chimneypiece at the Earl of Derby's house in Grosvenor Square (Fig. 72). For different clients Adam occasionally repeated his designs; a plate in the *Works* shows a chimneypiece in the third drawing-room at Derby House, London, which is practically identical with a design made for Lord Mansfield at Ken Wood.

Adam's overmantel mirrors were frequently painted, and at the end of the century this decoration became more ornate. In Fig. 75 the ovals are painted in grisaille, the borders being decorated in carved wood gilt on a cream-coloured ground. These overmantel mirrors were by no means invariably rectangular, ovals, ellipses and other shapes being also employed. Of the long horizontal mirrors which were designed at this time, in addition to those of great height reaching to the cornice of the room, Fig. 73 is remarkable for the admirable modelling of the gryphons and the graceful foliated scrollwork. Descriptions of mirrors in the neo-classic style are found in contemporary accounts. In 1781 William Gates (*q.v.*) supplied one of this type to the Prince of Wales, charging £63 for 'a chimney glass in a carved frame with fine top to do., with clusters of flowers hanging in festoons from vases and other ornaments and husks down the two sides of the frame, all very richly gilt in burnished gold; a large plate in the middle and borders to do. Size of the frame, 7 ft. 7 in. wide.' Fig. 74 is a fine example of an oval mirror in neo-classic style, the rush fronds with festoons of husks caught up by rosettes achieving an extremely elegant effect.

In 1778 the proprietors of Minshall's Looking-glass Store advertised 'an elegant assortment of looking-glasses in oval and square frames', and offered to cut the plates in old-fashioned frames into ovals or any pattern desired—a reminder that the glass was still more valuable than the frame. Square pier glasses are stated in Hepplewhite's *Guide* (1788) to be more fashionable than oval ones.

Towards the end of the century the well-known Regency type of circular mirror was introduced from France, where some of circular form had been made since about the middle of the century. The cresting of such mirrors is usually surmounted by an eagle displayed on a finial of acanthus; in a deep cavetto border gilt balls are distributed, the outer mouldings are enriched with a ribboned reeding, and next to the glass is an ebonised fillet (Fig. 77). Scrolled candle-branches are generally attached to the side, sometimes hung with cut-glass drops. A more elaborate treatment is seen in Fig. 76, where, in place of an eagle heading, the badge of the Merchant Taylors' Company, a lamb backed by a 'sun in splendour', is supported by cornucopiae. Sometimes the dimensions rivalled those of the large pier glasses of earlier days (Fig. 77). These convex mirrors soon became so popular that, under the heading 'Mirrors', they are the only variety mentioned in Sheraton's *Cabinet Dictionary* (1803). He writes that because of the 'agreeable effect' they produce by reflecting

80. *Regency Overmantel Mirror in carved gilt frame; frieze painted, the glass convex. c. 1810. (M. Harris & Sons.)*

the perspective of rooms, and their convenience as light holders, they had become 'universally fashionable'.

Sheraton states that 'glasses for chimney pieces run various, according to the size of the fire-place, and the height of the wall above'. To save expense they were sometimes fitted up in three plates, the joints of the glass being covered with gilt mouldings or pilasters, as in the 18th century. He observes that 'it is not unusual to have a twisting branch of flowers or ribband round the reeds (of the pilasters) rising upwards and terminating in some sort of composite, Corinthian or Ionic capital'. Fig. 79 shows a typical Regency overmantel. In some examples there is a deeper frieze with a procession of classical figures in bas-relief (Fig. 78). In his *Dictionary* (1803) Sheraton devotes much space to 'Back Painting', *i.e.* the decoration of mirrors either by painting on the back of the glass or by 'mezzotinto black prints' transferred on to it, and coloured by hand. He observes that direct painting may be performed on glass without a print by persons skilled in drawing and painting on paper or canvas. A considerable number of examples decorated in this manner survive (Fig. 80).

Pier and chimney glasses, or overmantel mirrors, at this time were often of great size, but generally without notable decorative features. The large pier glasses at Southill, Bedfordshire, are an exception. Those in 'Mrs Whitbread's Room' and those between the windows in the library were supplied by Marsh and designed by Henry Holland (*q.v.*). A panel of classical ornament surmounts the moulded gilt frames, and in the case of the library pier glasses this panel is decorated in high relief with addorsed gryphons taken from a plate in Tatham's *Ancient Ornamental Architecture*. George Smith, a few years later (1808), recommended that pier glasses should not have 'any ornament or head pieces, but be carried quite to the cornice of the room'.

MIRRORS, TOILET. Small hand-glasses of burnished metal, glass or crystal, carried at the girdle or enclosed in cases (*coffres de toilette*), were in common use throughout the Middle Ages. In French royal inventories of that period, hand-mirrors enriched with pearls and precious stones constantly occur, but English medieval records afford few examples and little information concerning these highly prized luxuries, which cannot be classed as domestic furniture. The hanging mirrors introduced in the 15th century were, no doubt, used for the toilet, as they permitted a better view of the person, while another variety (shown in a miniature *Le Mirouer des Dames*, c. 1450, British Museum Royal MS.19,B.XVI), circular and mounted on a revolving stand which could be turned in any direction, was clearly well adapted for this purpose.

Mirrors placed on chests or tables are rarely represented in medieval pictures or illuminations, but one is seen supported on a hutch covered with linen drapery in a miniature in the *Vita Christi*, written at Ghent in 1479 (Fig. 1). In Italy metal plates enclosed in a frame and mounted on a stem finishing in a wide-spreading foot were in use from about this time.

At the Victoria and Albert Museum there is one of these 'standing-glasses' in walnut dating from c. 1500, very delicately carved with cartouches and emblems (1695-1861); and Henry VIII's inventory of 1547 mentions 'a standing-glasse with imagery made of bone', probably of similar construction. Several mirrors belonging to Henry, enclosed with shutters or curtains, were so elaborately embroidered with jewels that it is unlikely they were hung on the walls. Small hand-glasses were still, however, generally used for dressing, and appear very frequently in royal inventories: Queen Elizabeth I possessed a large number of metal or crystal. Dressing-table mirrors do not appear to have been in regular use until late in the 17th century. In 1601 Bess of Hardwick's looking-glass, in her chamber at Hardwick Hall, had 'a frame to set it on'; and

1. *Toilet Mirror on a hutch spread with linen cloth; a miniature of the Annunciation, from the* Vita Christi. 1479. (*Brit. Mus. Royal MS. 16 G iii F 186.*)

2. *Toilet Mirror in shaped frame decorated with stump-work; the strut at back and glass original; figures in costume of c. 1660. Ht. 1 ft. 8 in., W. 1 ft. 4½ in. (Percival Griffiths Coll.)*

3. *Toilet Mirror in oak travelling-case; mouldings of tortoise-shell; frame decorated with stump-work; back (from which the strut is missing) bears initials A.P. and date 1672. Ht. 2 ft. 4 in., W. 1 ft. 11 in. (Percival Griffiths Coll.)*

when Charles I's furniture was dispersed after his execution a standing-mirror 'set with silver gilt and embroidered with a woman in the foot' was sold for £21. Allusions to toilet mirrors are occasionally found in contemporary correspondence; but, as the productions of the first great English glass factory,

established in Southwark by Sir Robert Mansell in 1618, have long since disappeared, it is impossible to determine their precise character. Lady Brilliana Harley wrote to her son at Oxford in 1639, asking him to choose a mirror 'aboute the biggnes of that I use to dress in', but she does not say if it was to stand on her table.

The earliest surviving toilet mirrors date from about the time of the Restoration and are decorated with stump-work. They are supported on a hinged strut and sometimes enclosed in a case, the needlework and glass being framed in tortoise-shell or galon (Figs. 2 and 3). These adjustable toilet glasses were, no doubt, introduced from France, for they appear in early 17th-century representations of French domestic interiors, as in *La Vue*, an engraving (c. 1630) by Abraham Bosse.

A generation later such glasses, in carved or ebony frames supported on a strut, occur frequently in Dutch *genre* paintings of the second half of the century, by Gerard Dou (1613-75), Jacob Ochtervelt (c. 1635-1700?) and other artists. In May, 1645, Sir Ralph Verney wrote to Lady Sussex asking her to accept 'halfe a dozen combs and a little combe box boughte at Paris, wch is soe very a trifle that I durst not send it had I not remembered twould sute well, with your glasse trimmed with silver'. This is a very early reference to a dressing-glass thus ornamented. In the *Academie of Armorie* (1688), Randle Holme defines a toilet glass as 'a square mirror resting upon it[s] stay, hauing a ring also on the top of the glass to hang it by'; adding 'these sorts of glasses are most used by Ladys to look their faces in, and to see how to dress their heads and set their top knots on the foreheads upright'.

Even after the establishment of Buckingham's Vauxhall works in 1663, glass was still so highly prized that great care was bestowed on the preservation of such mirrors, which, as they accompanied the owner on her travels, were very liable to be broken. Fig. 3 shows one with a folding oak travelling

4. Silver Mirror Frame, engraved in the Chinese taste; cresting centres in a cartouche with initials H.F. c. 1675. From a toilet set formerly at Sizergh Castle, Westmorland.

5. Silver Mirror Frame, chased and embossed; classical medallion on cresting cast in low-relief; glass not original. From a toilet set bearing the London hallmark of 1683-4. Ht. 1 ft. 10 in., W. 1 ft. 5 in. (V. & A. Mus.)

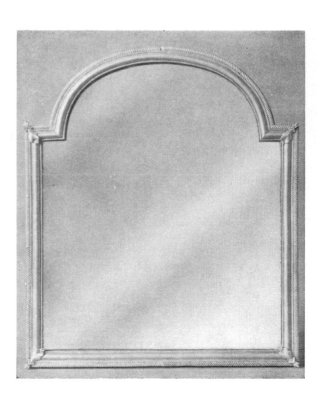

6. (Left) Engraving by one of the Bonnart brothers, representing Queen Mary, wife of William III, at her toilet; background of mirror and dressing-table draped and heavily fringed. c. 1690.

7. (Right) Silver Mirror Frame, forming part of a toilet set; the top of lunette form, and the convex mouldings bordered by a small nulling. c. 1700. Ht. 1 ft. 9 in., W. 1 ft. 5½ in. (Earl Spencer.)

8. *Toilet Mirror decorated in red and gold japan; stand fitted as a desk; drawer containing toilet requisites; glass not original. c. 1700. Ht. 3 ft. 3 in., W. 1 ft. 7¼ in., Depth 1 ft. 2⅛ in. (V. & A. Mus.)*

9. *Toilet Mirror veneered with burr walnut; pilasters pull out disclosing small receptacles. c. 1710. Ht. 3 ft. 7 in., W. 1 ft. 8 in., Depth 1 ft. 1 in. (Percival Griffiths Coll.)*

case, the back of the mirror, lined with green velvet, being dated 1672 and bearing the owner's initials 'A.P.'

The silver toilet sets introduced after the Restoration comprised a glass—supported, like the stump-work examples, by a strut—and a quantity of boxes, combs, whisks, scent-canisters and other appliances. Under Charles II the mirror belonging to such sets resembled, in design and decoration, those made in silver to hang on a wall. The frames were elaborately embossed with acanthus, amorini and sprays of flowers and foliage; the corners were masked by strappings, and the medallion on the cresting was sometimes separately cast in low relief (Fig. 5) Silver toilet glasses were also delicately chased and engraved in the Chinese taste to accord with the japanned furniture in late 17th-century bedrooms (Fig. 4). A few years later the square shape was abandoned, the solid cresting disappeared and the width of the mouldings was reduced, the curved

10. *Toilet Mirror veneered with burr walnut; serpentine drawer with cylindrical ends and shallow apron; central pigeon-hole framed in fluted pilasters. c. 1710. (G. L. Riley Coll.)*

11. *Walnut Toilet Mirror on stand with drawers; inner mouldings of glass gilt. c. 1710. Ht. 2 ft. 4 in., W. 1 ft. 4½ in., Depth 9 in. (Col N. R. Colville.)*

12. *Toilet Mirror decorated with red and gold japan. c. 1715. (Sir John Smith.)*

13. *Tortoise-shell Toilet Mirror; shaped cresting of walnut inlaid with tortoise-shell spandrels; feet and mounts of silver. c. 1720. (Knole Park, Kent.)*

heading recalling the fashion of contemporary hanging mirrors. The number of bottles, canisters and essence pots in such sets is explained by the immoderate use of cosmetics. This practice is often deplored by contemporary observers, who, far into Georgian times, denounce the excessive use of patches (worn by both sexes) and rouge.

Some of the best-known makers of silver toilet sets were Huguenot refugees; in France, so great was the consumption of silver for this purpose that Louis XIV, in 1672 and 1678,

prohibited the sale of silver mirrors under a heavy penalty. Although plate was called in by William III, elaborate silver toilet sets continued to be made. An engraving by one of the Bonnart brothers (Fig. 6) represents Mary Stuart, Queen of England, 'making up' her face before a silver toilet mirror, which has a background draped and heavily fringed to match the covering of the table, an arrangement still fashionable c. 1750. The time spent by ladies in adorning themselves was a favourite theme for satirists. Swift, in one of his longer

14. *Toilet Mirror supported on a strut; the polygonal walnut frame formed of ovolo mouldings mitred at the corners. c. 1730. (Percival Griffiths Coll.)*

15. *Toilet Mirror, veneered with walnut; shaped stretcher and bracket feet; inner mouldings of glass gilt. c. 1730.*

16. *Toilet Mirror in gilt frame carved in Chinese taste; pagoda canopy of cresting missing. c. 1755. (Tyttenhanger, Herts.)*

17. *Mahogany Toilet Mirror, bordered with a small chequer pattern in bone and ebony; the glass headed by a carved acanthus cresting. c. 1775. (Percival Griffiths Coll.)*

poems, describes Vanessa reading Montaigne at her toilet, while her maid combed her hair, and a party of glittering dames drank tea and chocolate.

After c. 1700 dressing-glasses were commonly mounted on box stands. They were japanned, or veneered with walnut, the glass being supported on finial-headed uprights by swivel screws. The stand was often a miniature version of contemporary bureaux, a long drawer, fitted with small boxes and compartments below the flap, containing toilet requisites.

This type was doubtless derived from Holland and many contemporary Dutch dressing-glasses survive. In England they were made in large quantities under Anne and George I. In 1703-4 Gerreit Jensen (*q.v.*) supplied the Queen with 'a dressing glass in a swinging frame Japan'd with an arched top'; the Dyrham Park inventory of 1710 mentions a toilet mirror in the Tapestry Bedchamber with a set of red and gold patch boxes, etc. The example in Fig. 8 is decorated in red and gold japan with crudely drawn figure subjects, landscapes and birds,

18. *Satinwood Toilet Mirror; serpentine drawers inlaid with scrolls and husks stained green. c. 1780. Ht. 2 ft. 1 in., W. 1 ft. 6 in., Depth 7¾ in. (Macquoid Coll.)*

19. *Satinwood Toilet Mirror; bow-fronted stand in two tiers banded with mahogany and inlaid. c. 1790. Ht. 2 ft. 3½ in., W. 1 ft. 6¼ in., Depth 11 in. (Col N. R. Colville.)*

the open drawer containing boxes, wisks and spools for winding silk. The shaped cresting recalls the fashion of contemporary hanging mirrors.

The walnut dressing-glasses of Anne's reign were made on similar lines; but the long drawer was often of serpentine form, and the desk portion was sometimes omitted. Most early 18th-century toilet mirrors were veneered with plain walnut on an oak foundation, the glass being sometimes framed in carved gilt mouldings (Fig. 11). Of the more costly burr walnut veneer, Fig. 10 is a notable specimen, the serpentine sweep of the interior fittings being reproduced in the drawer below the flap where the cylindrical ends terminate in pendants. The tortoise-shell dressing-glass in Fig. 13 represents the most refined Queen Anne taste. The concave centre and corners of the stand are arch-headed; the depressed bun feet, mounts and ornamented side handles are all of silver. Such toilet mirrors were placed on stands or small dressing-tables, which, as the century advanced, became more complex and were fitted with a framed glass and other toilet requisites (*see* TABLES, DRESSING).

Mirrors on box stands were not the only variety used for the toilet in the early Georgian period. The polygonal frame (Fig. 14) is supported on a strut, while in some walnut examples of c. 1740-50 the frame is rectangular without a cresting. A shaped stretcher unites bracket feet in Fig. 15, and a carved gilt moulding surrounds the glass. These small dressing-tables on trestle supports were also japanned (Fig. 12).

By c. 1750 the use of mahogany had become general in the manufacture of toilet glasses, while those designed in the Chinese taste were made of a soft wood, carved and gilt, or japanned. In the royal accounts there are many entries of the purchase of 'dressing glasses' from Benjamin Goodison and James Bradburn, the prices suggesting that the majority were severely simple. Six of these dressing-glasses, supplied by Goodison for George II's house at Newmarket in 1752, cost only about £1 each; while in 1753 Goodison repaired one 'for the king's use' and provided a travelling case for 7s. 6d. Members of the Household obtained dressing-glasses in 'plain mahogany frames and panelled back boards', generally measuring about 16 ins. by 12 ins. This type does not figure in the trade catalogues of Chippendale and his rivals, but was, no doubt, produced in large numbers by all the leading makers.

In pictures of fashionable interiors, both French and English, draped toilet mirrors are sometimes represented, and in Hogarth's *Marriage à la Mode* (1744) the mirror on the countess's dressing-table is partly hidden by heavy folds of velvet. The table was often draped and festooned with ribbons, ruchings and bows to match the mirror. A good example can be seen in the well-known picture by Zoffany, showing Queen Charlotte seated at her dressing-table in old Buckingham House, with the Princess Royal and the Prince of Wales. Ince and Mayhew (*Universal System*, 1759-63) term this arrangement a 'Lady's Toiletta', and Chippendale (3rd ed. *Director*, 1762) also illustrates these 'Draped Toylet Tables', writing of one that the glass in a carved frame is 'made to come forward with folding hinges'. Glass and table should be gilt in burnished gold, or the whole may be japanned, the hangings being of silk damask with gold fringes and tassels. These elaborate structures were intended to afford a decorative setting for Georgian beauties, who received visitors when engaged at their toilets.

Oriental embroideries or brightly coloured chintz were used for the draperies in Chinese bedrooms, the toilet mirror, designed in similar taste, helping to carry out the eastern illusion. A passage in the *Connoisseur* (April 25, 1755) describes the dressing-room of a young man of fashion as hung round with India paper adorned with little images of pagodas and Brahmins. The toilet arrangements most excited the visitor's admiration, 'a looking-glass enclosed in a whimsical frame of Chinese paling' standing on a japan table covered with the finest chintz. Few toilet mirrors of this type have survived, but Fig. 16 shows a specimen. The pagoda recesses, backed with lattice-work, are delicately carved, and in the design of the frame an imitation of oriental form is attempted.

Ordinary dressing-glasses continued to be made on traditional lines during the ascendancy of the Chinese craze, but

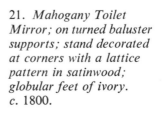

20. *Rosewood 'skeleton' Toilet Mirror, supported by struts hinged to uprights. c. 1795. Ht. 2 ft. 3 in., W. 1 ft. 8¾ in., Depth 1 ft. (Col N. R. Colville.)*

21. *Mahogany Toilet Mirror; on turned baluster supports; stand decorated at corners with a lattice pattern in satinwood; globular feet of ivory. c. 1800.*

  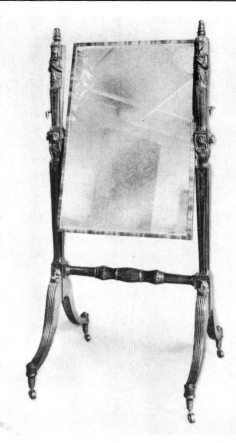

22. *Mahogany Cheval Glass with turned and ringed framework; candle branches and paw feet brass. c. 1800. (Mrs Malcolm Littlejohn.)*
23. *Satinwood Cheval Glass, inlaid and banded with zebra-wood. c. 1790. (Mrs Stileman.)* 24. *Mahogany Cheval Glass in Egyptian taste; standards headed by female terminal figures. c. 1810. Ht. 5 ft. 8½ in., W. 2 ft. 10 in.*

with the classical reaction new forms were introduced. The design was simplified: the framed mirror was often oval- or shield-shaped, and the box stand contained a single tier of drawers. Hepplewhite (*Guide*, 1788) gives 'four designs of different plans, the ornament of which may be inlaid with coloured woods or painted and varnished'.

These dressing-glasses were made in mahogany and satinwood, banded with coloured woods, or decorated with a small chequer pattern in ivory (Fig. 17). The upper surface of the stand was generally inlaid with a patera or shell, and the drawers were sometimes ornamented with sprays and swags of husks (Fig. 18). Uprights curved to accord with the shape of the glass replaced tapered standards, and as toilet requisites were now contained in the dressing-table, the stand was no longer elaborately fitted. In another late 18th-century type it was omitted, the stability of these 'skeleton glasses' being ensured by struts hinged to the uprights (Fig. 20).

These were the varieties in general use, but examples are occasionally found which show interesting departures from the prevailing fashion. The original design of Fig. 19 has, for instance, no counterpart in the pattern books of the period. As portable toilet mirrors became more simple, dressing-tables grew more complex, folding glasses being sometimes fitted in the side drawers to enable a lady to see herself at any angle. Men's dressing-tables were also so provided.

By the last quarter of the century it was possible to cast single plates of looking-glass more than 10 ft. high (*see*

MIRRORS), an improvement which led to the introduction of toilet mirrors sufficiently large to reflect the whole person (Figs. 22—24). They were known as *cheval* or 'Horse Dressing Glasses', a term derived from the four-legged frame, or horse, on which they were suspended. The glass of these standing mirrors was supported by swivel screws, or raised and lowered by leaden weights enclosed in the uprights. Sheraton elaborated this type, and in his *Drawing Book* (1791-4) shows two examples; one with toilet boxes attached to the standards which, when not in use, 'are intended to turn behind the glass', the other with a 'convenience for writing as well as for dressing which rises by a little horse'; the lower parts of the standards are lyre-shaped and, to form the strings, brass wire is let in. In his *Cabinet Dictionary* (1803) Sheraton explains that 'Horse' is used to denote 'a kind of tall dressing-glass suspended by two pillars and claws, and may, when hung by two centre screws, be turned back or forward to suit the person who dressed at them'. He adds that the glass may also be raised by means of a weight 'in the manner of a sash window'. Candle-branches were often fixed to the standards (Fig. 22). This variety remained popular with Regency designers, and George Smith (*Household Furniture*, 1808) gives some clumsy specimens in the Egyptian style. He writes that these 'Cheval Dressing Glasses' are made of mahogany, satinwood (Fig. 23) or rosewood, and 'not unfrequently executed to imitate bronzed metal', the ornaments then being gilt. They should move on castors concealed in the feet or plinths, and the inlay is to be of ebony or brass. Of the more refined Egyptian taste, Fig. 24

is a notable specimen, terminal figures in Egyptian taste forming the upper section of the standards.

At the end of the 18th century an oblong glass was substituted in the ordinary toilet mirror for the oval and shield shapes, a departure explained by the sudden change in the method of dressing ladies' hair. The towering structure of powdered curls was succeeded by a new fashion based on classical precedents, and the hair was worn flat and close to the head. The glass was supported on turned balusters or tapered uprights, and the stand was now generally square- or bow-fronted with projected corners in Regency taste. Satinwood was still occasionally used, but the majority of such mirrors were of mahogany or rosewood. Plain bandings or stringing lines replaced earlier painted or inlaid decoration, and, instead of bracket feet, the stand was often mounted on knobs of ivory or bone, handles and escutcheons corresponding in style (Fig. 21). Sheraton writes (*Dictionary*) that of this piece of furniture there are various species: 'some are fixed to a box containing three drawers about three inches deep, standing either upon small brackets or knobs for feet. The size of these dressing boxes runs from 22 to 28 inches in length and when they are serpentine they are width from 10 to 12 inches.' He states that the plates for toilet glasses of the smallest size were generally of Dutch manufacture.

Early in the 19th century fitted mirrors were occasionally produced with the toilet requisites enclosed by flaps, this type being obviously derived from contemporary washing-stands and dressing-tables constructed on a similar plan.

MODILLION. A series of projecting brackets placed below the soffit of a cornice in Corinthian, Composite and Roman Ionic orders. Rectangular blocks in the same situation in a Doric cornice are termed 'mutules'. In 18th-century furniture in an architectural manner modillions are found both below the cornice and in the pediment.

MOHAIR. A fabric occasionally used in the 17th and 18th centuries for upholstery and hangings. Originally it was a fine camlet from the hair of the Angora goat, introduced into Spain by Moors; later, the name was applied to material entirely of silk. 'Mohaire' is mentioned by Purchas early in the 17th century among 'new devised names of stuffes', and *Merchants Map of Commerce* (1638) alludes to 'mohairs of Angora', brought here by the Turkey Company. At Dyrham Park (1710) were two mohair silk beds and six mohair cushions. Chambers's *Cyclopaedia* (1741) defines it as 'a kind of stuff, ordinarily of silk, both woof and warp; having its grain wove very close'.

MONOCHORD. *See* MUSICAL INSTRUMENTS.

MOREEN (MORINE). A woollen fabric, sometimes mixed with cotton; cheap imitation of moiré (watered silk). Chippendale's bills contain items for large quantities of this material. Often used for bed-hangings in the 18th century.

MORTISE AND TENON. *See* CONSTRUCTION.

MOSAIC-WORK. *See* FILIGREE PAPER DECORATION and VERRE EGLOMISÉ.

MOTHER-OF-PEARL. A nacreous layer found on several varieties of large shells. Cut and polished, it was occasionally used in this country, in the early Stuart period, to

form delicate detail in the decoration of small objects. Figures prominently with bone and ivory in the ornament of chests of drawers and cabinets of about the time of the Restoration. In the late 18th century freely introduced on boxes and tea-caddies, which were sometimes entirely covered by highly polished shell. Mother-of-pearl sometimes found intermingled with tortoise-shell in English Buhl work.

MOULDINGS. Means by which emphasis and interest are given to parts of construction, *e.g.* cornice, frieze, plinth, edge and frames surrounding panels. Formed with moulding planes, or with scratch stocks, both having irons cut to the desired profile. Worked on solid before assembling, and also on narrow strips prepared on a bench and then applied. For description of varieties and detail diagrams *see* CONSTRUCTION. J. C. R.

MOUNTS. *See* METAL MOUNTS.

MULBERRY WOOD. The *Moraceae* family includes a great variety of important hard woods; European mulberries, *Morus nigra* and *Morus alba*, are golden brown with darker streaks, hard, heavy, tough and durable. Evelyn writes (1664) of 'the incomparable benefit of it . . . for its timber, durableness, and use for the joiner and carpenter'. He recommends that the black rather than the white variety be grown, 'which I have had sent me out of Languedoc'. This wood was used in the early 18th century to some extent as veneer for bureaux and writing cabinets.

MUNTIN. The vertical member of a framework similar to the stile, but occupying the central or intermediate position between panels. *See* CHESTS, CUPBOARDS and CONSTRUCTION.

MUSIC DESKS. *See* DESKS.

MUSICAL INSTRUMENTS. From Anglo-Saxon times a considerable variety of stringed instruments, some very richly decorated, were in use among the aristocracy and more prosperous classes, but this section is confined to those later keyboard instruments which can be classified as domestic furniture. They are not discussed in their mechanical aspects. They group themselves into two main sections: (1) keyboards in which the sounds are produced from strings, and (2) keyboards in which wind, with pipes or reeds, is employed. The first section may be subdivided into three types: (*a*) the clavichord, (*b*) the virginal, spinet and harpsichord, and (*c*) the piano. The second section will be confined to the pipe organ. The designer or decorator of keyboard instruments is limited by the requirements of the musician and the tonal value of the instrument. Until early in the 19th century many of the instruments, both English and Continental, were dated and their makers' names displayed. Sometimes, as in the case of Shudi, the celebrated harpsichord-maker of the 18th century, the master craftsman was himself a case-maker; in other cases, the musician availed himself of the skill of other artists for the various forms of decoration employed.

Section I. KEYBOARD INSTRUMENTS WITH STRINGS

(*a*) THE CLAVICHORD (CLARICORD, CLARICON). It was evolved in the 13th century from the monochord, which for ages had been used for teaching the notes of the scale required in the medieval plainsong. Early representations

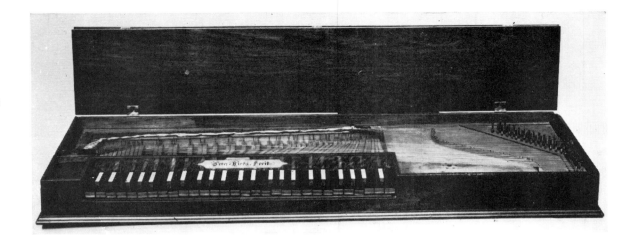

1. *Clavichord by Peter Hicks; plain mahogany case; the only old English clavichord recorded. c. 1720. Ht. 4½ in., W. 4 ft. 1 in., Depth 1 ft. 2 in. (V. & A. Mus.)*

of the clavichord are found among the 15th-century carvings on the roof of St Mary's Church, Shrewsbury, where it appears as a small, rectangular instrument with nine keys and six strings. In a Sarum breviary of the same century it appears in the like form, but with twelve keys.

In 1502 'one that sett the King's Cleyvecordes' received 13s. 4d.; and two years later Henry VII paid 10s. for 'a paire of clavycords'. The term 'pair' applied in the 16th and 17th centuries to this and other keyboard instruments and derived, probably, from the more intricate mechanism of the organ, merely implied a single and complete instrument. In the 1547 inventory of Henry VIII's possessions, mention is made of a 'paire of Claricordes' covered with gilt leather and of a similar pair covered with leather silvered. The instrument never became so popular in England as the virginal or spinet, and the only specimen of old English workmanship at present known is the small 18th-century instrument by Peter Hicks shown in Fig. 1. But in Germany, Flanders and Sweden, where the clavichord was in constant use until the beginning of the 19th century, many improvements were made about 1700, in both size and efficiency. These continental examples, decorated according to the varying styles of their periods, were occasionally brought into England.

(*b*) THE VIRGINAL, SPINET and HARPSICHORD. These are grouped together because their peculiar mechanism is identical, the strings being plucked by a quill-point (plectrum) instead of by the fingers as in the medieval psaltery from which these instruments were derived. In the 14th century mention is made by contemporary writers of an instrument with strings and keyboard, called the 'echiquier', described as of English origin. In the roll of Bishop Braybrook (1393) is the entry: 'to one playeing of the chekkers at Stepney 3/4'; and there is every reason to believe that under this name the virginal was invented in England.

The strings of the instrument were first enclosed within a rectangular case like that of the clavichord, and, owing to its popularity in convents and with ladies, it was called 'Clavicordium virginale'; hence the common English title 'virginal', which was certainly in use early in Henry VIII's reign.

During the 15th century, as seen among the carvings at Manchester Cathedral, the case also took the shape of a recumbent harp with a long straight side at right angles to the keyboard. This is the 'clavicymbal', which, under the name 'harpsichord', attained its greatest development in compara-

tively modern times. At the close of the 15th century another form—trapezoid, pentagonal or wing-shaped—was produced in Italy and called the *spinetta*, it may be because at that time 'quills' (spines) were substituted for the earlier wood, metal or leather plectra. In England, however, during the 16th and early 17th centuries at any rate, the name 'virginal' popularly covered all these forms; Henry VIII, for instance, possessed at his death thirty-five virginals of various kinds, some in cases covered with black or red leather, partly gilt, lined with black velvet, or with the lids trimmed with green Bruges satin. Two of his harpsichords are thus described:

> Twoo faire paire of newe longe virginalls made harpe-fashion of cipres with keies of ivorie havinge the Kinges armes crowned and supported by his graces beastes within a gartier guilte standinge over the saide keies, with twoo casses to them covered with blacke leather the inner partes of the liddes to the saide caeses beinge of wallnuttree with sondrie antickes of white woode wroughte in the same.

—an early example of inlaid walnut.

Fig. 2 shows 'Queen Elizabeth's virginal', which is of pentagonal form and was, like the virginals already mentioned, provided with a removable outer case. In shape, material (cypress wood) and style of decoration, it is a fine example of the Italian spinet of c. 1570; but it was possibly decorated in England. The outer case is covered with crimson Genoa velvet, and the inside lined with yellow tabby silk. At one end are emblazoned the Queen's arms, and at the other on a tree stump eradicated a falcon argent crowned and holding in its right claw a sceptre (the Boleyn badge). The painting is done on gold with carmine, lake and ultramarine.

It is about 1650 that the distinction between virginal, spinet and harpsichord becomes general: for in England the name virginal was restricted to the rectangular shape, the spinet became the title of the popular wing-shaped form, while the harpsichord, in outline like the horizontal grand piano of later days, but furnished with two keyboards, stops and other mechanical contrivances, displayed the highest standard to which this class of instrument attained.

Of the rectangular English virginal, specimens are now very rare. There are, so far as is known, only twelve examples extant, varying in date between 1641 and 1675. They are the workmanship of Gabriel Townsend, Thomas White, John Loosemore, James White, Adam Leversidge, Stephen Keene, Philip Jones, and Charles Rewallin. One of these instruments,

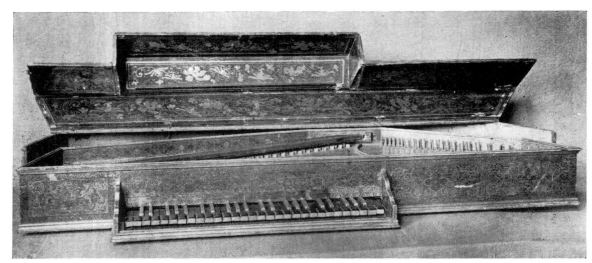

2. 'Queen Elizabeth's Virginal'; Italian instrument in case of cypress wood, possibly decorated in England; royal arms emblazoned on the left-hand panel. c. 1750. Ht. 8½ in., W. 5 ft. 5 in., Depth 1 ft. 11 in. (V. & A. Mus.)

3. *Virginal by Adam Leversidge; oak case with domed lid and embossed panels; painted under lid with figures in a landscape; original stand. 1670. (Ashmolean Museum.)*

now in the Conservatoire de Musique, Brussels, once belonged to Elizabeth Stuart, Queen of Bohemia and eldest daughter of James I. It bears the initials 'E.R.' surmounted by the royal arms of England. The case is panelled with pasteboard embossed and gilt, and the domed cover, characteristic of these instruments, has within the lid a painting of Orpheus charming the animals with his lyre. The example (1670) in Fig. 3 by Adam Leversidge is particularly fine, and resembles very closely the virginal by the same maker dated 1666, which is said to have belonged to Nell Gwynn; the painting within the domed cover represents the Mall in St James's Park, with Arlington House in the distance.

These charming works of art were destined to disappear on the introduction of the spinet—small, compact and portable. Probably the Flemish influence of the mid 17th century drew English people's attention to this particular form, which had long been used on the Continent and was known in Italy as the *spinetta traversa*. When it first appears in this country it is called, as by Pepys in 1661, 'the triangel virginall', or simply 'the triangel'. But the French fashions of the Restoration gave it a more graceful outline and its proper name 'spinette' or 'espinette'; under which latter name Pepys bought the instrument in 1668 from Charles Haward (or Hayward), the virginal-maker, for £15. Fig. 4 shows a spinet with its original stand by this celebrated maker. Some well-known craftsmen—the elder Hitchcock, Keene, Blunt, Mahoon, Slade, Harris, among them—shared in the production of this peculiarly English type, an excellent example of which is given in Fig. 5.

It is noticeable that, in both their spinets and harpsichords, the practice of the English makers was to leave the polished walnut and mahogany cases untouched, except for delicate inlay and fine strap hinges of brass; whereas the Continental mode was to overlay the wood with decorative designs in gilt or colour. But with the advent of the small rectangular piano in the second half of the 18th century the spinet, too, became obsolete, although instruments continued to be made by Culliford for the dealers Longman and Broderip until the last decade of the century.

The harpsichord (harpsicon, harpsical) differed from the simpler virginal and spinet, with their single strings and absence of means of expression, not only in its shape, as already described, but by the addition of extra strings which could be brought into use by means of stops. It is generally supposed that the instrument was indebted for an additional keyboard to Hans Ruckers, of the late 16th century, the founder of the celebrated Flemish school of harpsichord-makers bearing that name.

The earliest English harpsichord recorded is at Knole, Kent (Fig. 6). Although it has lost its lid and most of its

4. *Spinet by Charles Haward, London; walnut case with original stand of turned oak. c. 1660. (Dr W. H. Brazil.)*

5. *Spinet by Charles Brackley, London; walnut inlaid case with original turned stand. c. 1700. (Col N. R. Colville.)*

6. *Harpsichord by John Haward, London; panelled oak case with arcaded stand; spandrels carved with strapwork and fluted legs headed by split balusters. 1622. (Knole Park, Kent.)*

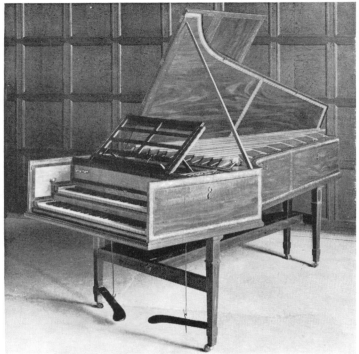

7. *Harpsichord by Jacob Kirkman, London; walnut case, interior inlaid with arabesques on ground of sycamore. 1755. (The late Mr Raymond Russell.)*
8. *Harpsichord by Shudi and Broadwood, London; mahogany, with satinwood front and bandings; original stand. 1782. (Hardwick Hall, Derbys.)*
9. *Harpsichord designed by Robert Adam for the Empress Catherine II of Russia. 1774. (From Adam's Works in Architecture.)*

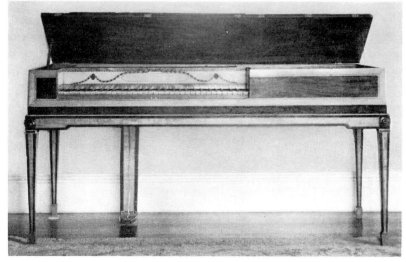

10. *Square Piano by Schrader and Hartz, London; mahogany case with stand; typical of first pianos made in England. c. 1768.*
11. *Square Piano by Christopher Ganer, London; mahogany with satinwood bandings. 1783. (From Galpin Coll.)*

12. *Square Piano by Frederick Beck, London; mahogany case veneered with satinwood and harewood, inlaid with arabesques and a medallion of Polyhymnia; beneath keyboard a music cabinet. 1777. (F. Partridge & Sons.)* 13. *Upright Square Piano by William Southwell, Dublin and London; mahogany case with satinwood and rosewood bandings; front painted with musical trophies and plaques, a later addition after Angelica Kauffmann. c. 1798. (The late Sir Walter Gilbey.)*

mechanism, it represents the skill of an English craftsman, as it bears the inscription—now indistinct—'JOHANNES [H]A[W]ARD FECIT LONDINI MDCXXII'. Thomas Mace (*Musick's Monument*, 1672) says that 'one Mr John Hayward of London' was, he had been informed, the inventor of an improved harpsichord called the 'pedall', but it is doubtful if he was this maker. Its name derived from the fact that the stops, which bring into play the three or more strings of the harpsichord, were, in this instance, moved by pedals instead of by the hand. In 1674 Charles Haward, mentioned above—and, perhaps, a relative—was employed 'for mending the harpsi-

chords and pedalls in the Great Hall in the [King's] Privy Lodgings'. The interesting instrument preserved at Knole, which is 8 ft. 4 ins. long and 2 ft. 10 ins. in greatest width, appears to have had originally one keyboard. The case and the elaborate frame or stand are of oak.

A harpsichord of the late 17th or early 18th century, by Thomas Hitchcock, is in the Victoria and Albert Museum; it has two keyboards with four stops. A fifth stop, invented c. 1700, caused one of the strings to be plucked at a different point in its length, thereby giving a more reedy tone, similar to that obtainable on the old lute. In this form the two great

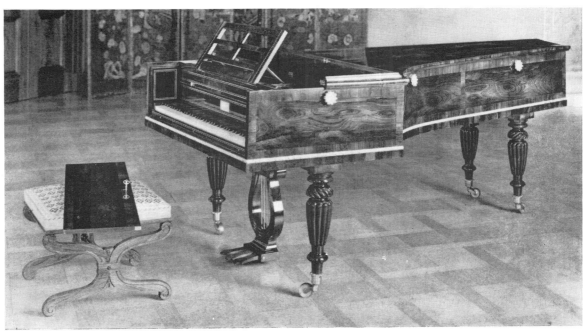

14. *Grand Piano by Clementi and Co., London; rosewood case with brass mounts and stringing lines. c. 1815. (Ickworth Park, Suffolk.)*

15. *Organ Harpsichord (Claviorganum); oak case painted with strapwork, arms and other ornaments. Inscribed 'Lodowicus Theeuwes me fesit 1579'. Harpsichord: Ht. 9 in., L. 7 ft. Organ case: Ht. 3 ft. 5 in., L. 7 ft. 7 in., W. 3 ft. 4 in. (V. & A. Mus.)*

18th-century harpsichord-makers in England—Burkat Shudi (Tschudi) and Jacob Kirkman (Kirchmann), the one Swiss and the other German—received it, both being trained in the London workshop of Hermann Tabel, a Fleming, who was, naturally, imbued with the tradition of the Ruckers. The typical harpsichord from Hardwick Hall, Derbyshire, dated 1782 (Fig. 8), is the production of Burkat Shudi (the younger) and John Broadwood, and shows the fullest development of the instrument. The 'Venetian' louvred swell, afterwards adapted to the organ, was patented by Shudi in 1769 and it is worked by a foot pedal, and another pedal. The earliest dated instrument by Shudi is of the year 1729, and a harpsichord by him, of the year 1740, with four stops and two keyboards, is now at Windsor Castle; it was formerly the property of Frederick, Prince of Wales. In 1770 Shudi took John Broadwood, his son-in-law, into partnership, and was succeeded after his death (1773) by Burkat Shudi, his son, who remained in the firm till 1782. In 1795 John Broadwood took his son, James Shudi Broadwood, into the firm; and in 1807 another son, Thomas, was added, but by this time the harpsichord had been replaced by the pianoforte. The rival harpsichord-maker, Jacob Kirkman, in 1738 married Tabel's widow, and succeeded to the goodwill of his master's business. His name is found on harpsichords and spinets until 1772; in 1773 he took his nephew, Abraham, into partnership and he is said to have died in 1778. The instruments, however, bear the joint names of Jacob and Abraham Kirkman until 1789, when Abraham took his son Joseph into partnership. In 1798 Joseph became sole proprietor. The highly decorative instrument in walnut, by Jacob Kirkman, seen in Fig. 7, is dated 1755; it is typical of the double manual English harpsi-

chord of the period. The marquetry decoration of this case is an interesting anachronism, the arabesques recalling the taste of fifty years earlier, while the long side is veneered and banded like the rest of the case (as in two or three other examples by this maker), whereas it was almost always left plain to stand against a wall. Carved cabriole legs on claw-and-ball feet are found on the stands of two other harpsichords by Kirkman, both lavishly inlaid above the keyboards with floral devices and a group of musical instruments in various coloured woods. One, at Nostell Priory, Yorkshire, is dated 1766. The other, also of 1766, is from Warley Place, Essex; it was ordered by George III for Queen Charlotte.

Robert Adam designed a harpsichord to be made for the Empress Catherine II of Russia. The general outline is reminiscent of the rectangular form found in the early 17th-century combined harpsichord and virginal. The design did not, however, commend itself to the maker, and was much altered before the work was completed.

One of the last old harpsichords made bears the name of Clementi and Co., the successors of Longman and Broderip; it is dated 1802.

(c) THE PIANOFORTE. In this final section of the stringed keyboard instruments the mechanism is entirely distinct from that of the virginal, spinet and harpsichord; and although there is a similarity in outward appearance, the strings are struck, not plucked, the principle of the falling hammer, derived from the dulcimer, having been applied to keyboard instruments by Bartolomeo Cristofori, of Florence, c. 1708. The name *piano e forte* ('soft and loud') was given to this instrument owing to its capability of expression. Cristofori, as a harpsichord-maker, adapted his invention to what is now the familiar 'grand piano' shape; but the first pianos made in England, c. 1762, by a German named Zumpe, one of Shudi's workmen, were small instruments of the rectangular virginal or clavichord shape. The specimen in Fig. 10 is typical of these early instruments, which were novelties even in 1767, when the singer Miss Brickler, at her benefit concert at Covent Garden Theatre, was accompanied by Dibdin 'on a new instrument called a Pianoforte'. Notwithstanding their plain mahogany cases and limited compass, they became exceedingly popular, and many were made by foreign workmen settled in London. John Broadwood appeared as a maker in 1773.

These small pianos from 3 ft. 6 ins. to 4 ft. 6 ins. in length were soon increased in size to over 5 ft. They were decorated in neo-classical taste, inlaid on a veneered ground, or painted with the characteristic motifs. The plain 'stand', copied from that of the spinet and harpsichord, gave way to the 'French frame', with square taper legs and brass 'furniture', or the turned legs so often shown in Sheraton's designs. Of these instruments Fig. 11 is a good example. A similar piano was made by Ganer, one of the immigrant makers called 'the Twelve Apostles', for the young Princess Amelia, daughter of George III.

An elaborately inlaid specimen by Beck (Fig. 12), with the three usual stops, in design and decoration recalls the marquetry furniture at Harewood, Yorkshire, made by Chippendale and Haig a few years earlier. The central panel is inlaid with a figure of Polyhymnia on a background of harewood with arabesques of coloured woods. A piano by Southwell (Fig. 13) depicts the earliest attempt to construct a low upright piano. The two plaques, painted after works by Angelica Kauffmann, and their surrounding fretwork are a later substitution for the original pleated silk.

The first 'grand piano' introduced into England appears to have been made by Father Wood, a monk in Rome, and to have been brought over by Samuel Crisp, of Chessington. Dr Charles Burney relates in Ree's *Cyclopaedia* (c. 1805) that 'Fulke Greville purchased this instrument of Mr Crisp for 100 guineas and it remained *unique* in this country for several years'. But nothing is known as to its actual shape, for upright as well as horizontal 'grands' had been made on the Continent before 1745. The latter variety was made in England c. 1770 by a German named Backers, though Broadwood's books do not mention this form until 1781.

One of the most highly decorated grand pianos made in the 18th century was that constructed by Broadwood in 1796 for Don Manuel de Godoy, the favourite of Queen Maria Louisa of Spain. It was designed by Sheraton (except the arrangement of the pedals) and cost 213 guineas. Its satinwood case was inlaid with Wedgwood's and Tassie's medallions, and the Prince's portrait in the oval over the keys (now missing) was painted by Alexander Taylor the miniaturist. This interesting and historical instrument was formerly the property of the first Viscount Leverhulme.

The grand piano of Fig. 14 by Clementi and Co. is in a case of finely grained rosewood, with brass stringing lines, nobs and bands; it still retains the removable front board of the harpsichord model, but the heavier carved legs and the 'lyre' attachment for the pedal mechanism, which appear only as a decorative feature in some of the 18th-century instruments, give it a much closer resemblance to the modern piano.

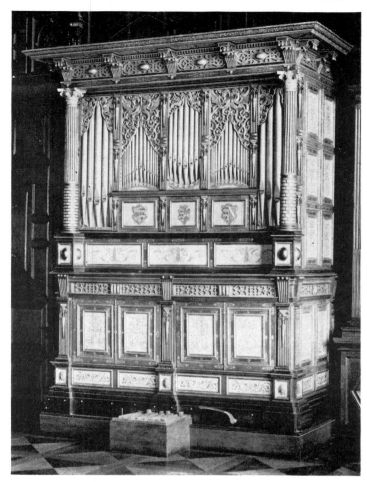

16. *Chamber Organ, probably made by a Flemish craftsman working in England, and decorated in 1611 by Roland Buckett for Robert, first Earl of Salisbury. (Hatfield House, Herts.)*

Section II. Keyboard Instruments in which Wind, with Pipes or Reeds, is employed.

With the invention of the harmonium at the beginning of the 19th century (or, rather, the adaptation of the ancient Chinese free-reed to the mechanism of the modern keyboard), the little pipe organs, which had hitherto played no unimportant part in the domestic and religious life of western Europe, disappeared. Even till the early years of the last century, they were still often to be found in many English houses. They fall into two principal groups, called respectively 'portatives' and 'positives'—to use the old terms.

(*a*) THE PORTATIVE ORGAN. This, the most portable and simple of the pipe organs, cannot be regarded as domestic furniture, and though such instruments are frequently mentioned in early inventories (*e.g.* Henry VIII's), no old English specimen is known.

(*b*) THE POSITIVE ORGAN. In medieval England this commoner and more stationary instrument was often called the 'regal' or 'a pair of regals', and although strictly this name should be reserved for an organ consisting of a reed-stop only (in which the sound is produced by the beating of a metal tongue), it was indiscriminately used for instruments possessing also 'flue' pipes of the whistle type. A positive organ of con-

siderable size is represented in a picture by Hugo Van der Goes (1476) in the royal collection.

Henry VIII, in his collection, had five small single regals, two of them being in cases of 'timbre' covered with leather, and the others in cases of 'timbre' not covered; while among the larger instruments was—

a paire of double Regalles of latten with III Stoppes of pipes couered with purple vellat embrawdered all over damaske pirles and Venice golde, and the Cover thereof the inner parte covered with crimoson vellat likewise embrawdered with damaske pirles haveing a stele Glasse in the same and the Kinges Armes and Queen Janes Armes likewise embrawdered, with a cover [to] the pipes couered with crimeson vellat likewise embrawdered, haveing a rose crowned upon the same, standing upon a foot of wainscott painted in Rabeske woorke wherein liethe the Bellowes.

17. *Large Regal, signed 'J.L.' and dated* 1650; *the walnut stand c.* 1690. (*The Duke of Atholl.*)

18. *Chamber Organ; mahogany case in Gothic style, probably constructed by Richard Bridge. c.* 1755. (*Mr J. P. Callard.*)

19. *Organ Case; mahogany carved in rococo style. From a design in Chippendale's* Director (3rd Ed. 1762). *Ht.* 11 ft. 4 in., W. 6 ft. 6 in. (*V. & A. Mus.*)

He also possessed instruments which combined the virginal with the regal or organ; this was usually termed the 'claviorganum', and a valuable example from Ightham Mote, Kent, may be seen in the Victoria and Albert Museum (Fig. 15). A harpsichord by the immigrant Flemish maker Ludovic Theeuwes, of St Martin-le-Grand is here combined with the remains of an organ contained within a 'foot' or case of wainscot, inscribed *Lodowicus Theeuwes me fesit* (sic) 1579. It is painted with strapwork and bears in medallions the arms of a branch of the Roper family partly defaced, over which later arms (now removed) had been painted. In the same museum there is also a claviorganum by Crang of London, made in 1745.

A unique oak organ case at Old Radnor, Radnorshire, carefully restored in 1872, is an example of the elaborate decoration which English artists bestowed on organs about the date of Henry VIII's accession. Late Gothic and Renaissance motifs are combined in the ornate brattishing and carved pipe-shades below, the lower panels being filled with linen-fold. Of English organs built during the 17th century, apart from large ecclesiastical organ-cases, there are three or four small specimens of great interest in existence.

The organ now in the summer drawing-room at Hatfield House, but originally in the chapel, was purchased in 1609 by Robert, first Earl of Salisbury, who built the house in

21. *House Organ by Samuel Green, London; the design probably by James Wyatt; painted in grisaille. 1790. (Heaton Park, Lancs.)*

the early years of the 17th century. It is described in the Hatfield accounts as 'a great wind instrument' which was 'bought of a Dutchman' for £1,084 6s. 8d., probably a craftsman from the Low Countries working in England. It was renovated by the famous London maker Thomas Dallam, for in 1611 he was paid 'for setting up and perfecting the greate wind instrument at Hatfield'. The case (Fig. 16) is somewhat square in outline, but the arrangement of the front flats of gilded pipes between the Corinthian pillars bearing the cornice is admirably conceived and the pipe-shades are finely carved. The instrument has been altered and enlarged. The richly decorated case is painted with delicate arabesque designs, carried out largely in gilding on a white background. The gilt pipes are partly screened by openwork wood-carvings of scrolls and gryphons. These decorations are by Roland Buckett, who painted the 'Tymber Worke of the great Stayres', the chimneypiece and some of the furniture in the King's Bedchamber and some 'pictures upon cloth for the chapel'.

Dan Bargrave's chamber organ, purchased in 1629 for £22 and now at Canterbury Cathedral, has lost nearly all its interior work; but the oak case still rests on its original stand,

20. *Chamber Organ (maker unknown); mahogany case in neo-classic style. Probably designed by Robert Adam. c. 1775. (Newby Hall, Yorks.)*

22. *Pipe and Tabor Organ by Clementi and Co., London; mahogany case inlaid with satinwood; one oval painted. c. 1800. (The late Sir Walter Gilbey.)*

and the front is closed by two folding doors bearing the shield of the Cathedral Church and the arms of the Dean. In a large English regal at Blair Castle, Perthshire (Fig. 17), the instrument, with its five divided stops, is on a walnut stand with six turned and tapered legs, and the two bellows are behind the pipes and raised alternately, as in the earlier organs. The instrument bears the initials 'I.L.', so it may be attributed to John Loosemore, the famous Exeter builder; the decorative cover over the pipes is now missing, but otherwise it is complete.

With the accession of Charles II, the English organ-builders endeavoured to repair the ravages of the Commonwealth, and the famous Bernhard Schmidt (or 'Father' Smith), from Germany, competed with Renatus Harris, an Englishman who had been living and working in France. A Treasury Warrant (December 6, 1700—*Calendar of Treasury Books*, Vol. XVI, p. 162) records a payment of £500 'to Bernard Smith, organ-maker, as royal bounty on consideration of his loss by the burning of an organ prepared by him by warrant of the late Queen [Mary of Modena] for the use of the royal chapel at Hampton Court and which by command of the late Queen

was set up in the late Popish Chapel at Whitehall pending some alterations in the said royal chapel at Hampton Court, but which was burned in the late dreadful fire in Whitehall'. Smith, who died in 1708, built many chamber organs, and some of them still exist. On the oak or mahogany cases of his and later organs famous wood-carvers and designers lavished their skill. Chippendale, in the *Director*, gives several designs for both large and small organs in the 'ordinary' or in the 'Gothic' style; a rare example of a characteristic organ-case in the latter style is shown in Fig. 18. The case of this fine instrument is decorated with delicate fretwork and applied arcading, finely carved. An organ-case in the Victoria and Albert Museum (Fig. 19) corresponds, with slight variations, to Plate CV in the *Director* (3rd ed.). The decoration throughout represents the best craftsmanship of the age. The keyboard has two manuals, with the date 1794 and the name of Lincoln, an organ-builder and harpsichord-maker who carried on business at 199 High Holborn. At that time the organ was repaired and modernised, but only the case survives.

In Newby Hall, near Ripon, Yorkshire, there is a chamber organ of which the unique and striking case was probably designed by Robert Adam (Fig. 20), though no drawing for it is known. It dates from c. 1775, when the house was being altered and redecorated by him. The instrument stands in the entrance hall, in a mahogany case with gilded pipes; a pair of short Ionic columns supporting the impost at either end. The pipe front is arranged with two flats on each side, and the central compartment is in apsidal form, the half-dome above having characteristic decoration. Above is a classic cornice, and on the lower panels are slender 'Delphic' tripods with fluted supports.

In the second half of the 18th century the popular builder was Samuel Green. He was greatly patronised by George III and, probably, the instrument for the Organ Room in the Queen's House, St James's Park, described in the Royal Accounts for 1766, was built by him in partnership with the younger Byfield. The mahogany case was supplied by John Bradburn (q.v.) and had three 'towers' in front; the stop-knobs were water-gilt; the ornaments included 'satyr-boys, musical instruments, drapery for curtains, foliage, palms, festoons of husks and other devices'. The large chamber organ with 22 stops in Heaton Park, Manchester, is Green's work (Fig. 21). The case is painted in grisaille and was probably designed by James Wyatt, the architect of the house. The medallion portrait on the front is said to represent George Frederick Handel.

A brief reference may also be made to the barrel-organs which became so popular c. 1800 and found a place in many English churches. Such automatic instruments had long been known; that ardent musician Henry VIII, for instance, had an automatic virginal, 'an instrument that goethe with a whele without playinge uppon'; and the learned Athanasius Kircher devoted the ninth book of his *Musurgia* (1650) to this special subject. In the private apartments of Buckingham Palace is the mahogany case of a large barrel-organ made for Queen Caroline c. 1735, and altered into a cabinet by William Vile (q.v.) in 1763 at a charge of £57. The front pipes have been removed and replaced by the present brass trellis-work, while below are cupboards; the decorations, consisting of 'ovals of laurels', pendants and acanthus scrolls, are fully described in Vile's bill. F. W. G. revised.

MUTULES. *See* MODILLIONS.

NEEDLEWORK. Owing to the perishable nature of textiles we can only form an idea of needlework in upholstery until the early 17th century from inventories and other records; which, however, indicate a rich variety of material and design.

In the early Tudor and Stuart periods women in large households employed their spare time in needlework and carpet-work. Outside help was sometimes sought; in the *History of Hengrave* payment for eight weeks and four days is recorded to embroiderers in 1572 at 8d. a day. In houses of the wealthy classes very rich and delicate materials, such as satin and cloth of gold, served as chair coverings, and even in luxurious establishments rich dress stuffs were not wasted, but applied to the upholstery after being worn. The Earl of Northampton's inventory of 1614 lists 'the flowers, slippes and borders of an embroidered cloke, with silver cut into pieces to embroder some furniture for the howse withall'.

In the first half of the 16th century there was an influx of French embroiderers, who were employed both in the trade and in the households of the king and nobility. Black or Spanish work in fine black silk upon linen was popular in the reigns of Henry VIII and his children, but died out after that

of James I. Two tendencies make themselves felt in the late Tudor and early Jacobean periods, one to flower ornament, the other to the use of emblems. An idea of the variety of motifes and the importance of needlework in great households may be gathered from inventories of the effects of Mary Queen of Scots (1561) and of Henry Howard, Earl of Northampton (1614), and from two MS. inventories of Elizabeth, Countess of Shrewsbury (1601). Of the latter's household stuff, 'entayled as heirlooms', there are considerable survivals at Hardwick Hall, Derbyshire. Cupboards and tables were bright with carpets and cloths, the window-sills with needlework cushions, such as the panels (Fig. 2). The vivid colouring of hangings and upholstery was reinforced by needlework and applied work. Several extant pieces bear the initials 'E.T.S.', of the Countess of Shrewsbury, and possibly she may have worked some of these herself; but that the women of her household were kept busy is clear from an entry in the Hardwick inventory of 'nyne paire of beames for embroiderers'.

In cases where the design consists (as in the 17th century) of detached floral or bird, beast and insect motives, the sources can sometimes be traced to a pattern-book, *e.g.* Richard Shorleyker's *Schole House for the Needle*. The

1. *Bedspread of velvet with Needlework medallions; worked by Mary Queen of Scots and ladies of Elizabeth, Countess of Shrewsbury. c.* 1570. (*V. & A. Mus.*)

2. *Panel of Needlework for a cushion in* petit-point: *the Sacrifice of Isaac. c.* 1590. (*Hardwick Hall, Derbys.*)

detailed illustrations in Conrad Gesner's volumes covered a large variety of birds, beasts and reptiles, while the *Theatre of Insects or Lesser Living Things* by Thomas Mouffet (English ed., 1658) accounts for the popularity of these insect motifs in the second half of the 17th century. A catalogue of plates and pictures issued by Peter Stent, in Charles II's reign, also indicates the source of embroidery designs of this period. He had for sale 'Books for Drafts of Men, Birds, Beasts, Flowers, Fruits, Flyes, Fishes'.

Of the second half of the 17th century the most frequent survivals are the boldly drawn and effective crewel embroideries on curtains and hangings, worked, as a rule, in dark blues and greens, with a small admixture of browns (Fig. 4). This type of embroidery is peculiar to England, and consists of leafy stems (generally of serpentine form) rising from a base or strip of ground varied with hillocks and sometimes diversified with small animals. In early examples, some influence can be traced to the hand-drawn and painted cloths (*palampores*) from Masulipatam (where an agency was established for the East India Company in 1611). Hangings dating from the end of the century are worked in lighter colours.

The importation of Chinese silks, embroideries and other textiles during the second half of the 17th century was followed by imitative design in the Chinese manner or 'after the Indian fashion', the majority of pieces of needlework in this taste dating c. 1690–1720. A broken and zigzag ornament and the introduction of a long-tailed, exotic bird (the Chinese phoenix) and of flowering shrubs may be noticed among these embroideries. This oriental influence disappeared as the 18th century advanced, though some isolated examples are met with. In the reign of William and Mary the fashion for needlework was stimulated by the personal taste of the Queen. Her example was followed, according to Tindal, not only by her maids of honour, but 'by all ladies of distinction throughout the kingdom'. During this reign and Anne's an additional interest is given to needlework by the presence, in fine pieces, of pictorial centres.

The pleasant colouring and individuality of the design in English needlework are its chief attractions. It differs from French embroidery in being less formal and less systematised. Sometimes the floral design is well composed, and it is probable that the needle-woman had recourse to patterns such as Robert Furber's (1734), who displays 'Four hundred curious representations of the most beautiful flowers, very useful not only for the curious in gardening, but likewise for ladies, as patterns for working and painting in water-colours'. His plates consist of well-drawn groups of flowers arranged in an ornamental vase.

An increased tendency to naturalism is noticeable in the floral designs of the mid-18th century; and a white linen quilt, dating c. 1750, is described as 'worked in flowers the size of nature, delineated with the finest coloured silks in running stitch, which is made use of in the same way as by a pen etching on paper; each flower is different, and evidently done at the moment from the original'. In this direct and patient pictorialism flowers were shaded to give the effect of relief.

Throughout the greater part of the 18th century women continued to work industriously. Embroidery played a very minor part on the covering of late 18th-century furniture, for which silk, brocade and French tapestry were fashionable. The craft of useful woolwork had declined, and ladies limited themselves to fine silk needlework on silk or satin grounds for screen panels and framed pictures, in which a popular stipple and line engraving often formed the centre. Early 19th-century needlework is of little value in design and is often executed in Berlin wools.

Needlework could be used in panels as a substitute for tapestries or woven carpets or table-cloths; it served as coverings for cushions, and also as covering (or partial covering) and enrichment of objects such as beds, caskets, chairs, stools and mirrors (*see* those sections). In the case of beds, the framework was long regarded as subordinate to the fabrics with which it was covered and apparelled.

BED-HANGINGS. As great attention was bestowed on the decoration of beds from earliest times, their hangings or apparel are often inventoried in detail. These consisted of a tester, celour, curtains and bed-coverings in the Middle Ages, the wooden framework being entirely covered by the embroidered apparel. Beds and their furniture, often embroidered with armorial devices, are found among the more important bequests in wills. In 1376 Edward, Prince of Wales, bequeaths to 'Sir Robert de Walsham our Confessor' 'a large bed of red camora, with our arms embroidered at each corner also embroidered with the arms of Hereford'; and in 1392 Richard, Earl of Arundel, leaves to his son Thomas his blue bed of silk embroidered with griffins.

When the bed, c. 1550, assumed a form consisting of a wainscot head and tester supported by two posts, the bed furniture was limited to curtains and valances. Although in the examples of Tudor beds illustrated the hangings are lacking, these were originally furnished with apparel of textiles and needlework. The 16th-century bed-hangings formerly at Oxburgh Hall, Norfolk, consist of two curtains, a valance and a large bedspread (originally a curtain). The ground of this apparel (Fig. 1) is green velvet, on which are mounted a number of embroidered medallions on canvas, some of which are initialled 'M.R.' (Maria Regina), while others bear monograms which indicate that ladies of the house of Cavendish and Talbot were also employed on them. The emblematic panels are a curious revelation of Mary Stuart's hopes and fears in 1569. The originals of many of the medallions, animals, birds and fishes, are to be found in the zoological work *Historia Animalium* by Conrad Gesner printed in Zurich, 1551-8. The large-size illustrations have been chosen, and

4. *Crewel-Work hanging, embroidered on twill ground. Late 17th century. (V. & A. Mus.)*

among them the tiger, lion, lynx, golden goose, dove and toucan. In the centre panel of the bedspread the emblematic design shows a hand grasping a sickle and pruning a vine, with the legend *Virescit Vulnere Virtus* on a scroll.

In the 17th century beds entirely covered and draped in textiles were made for the households of the rich, the most costly Carolean survival being that in the King's Room at Knole, Kent (*see* BEDS, Fig. 15). The hangings are of cloth of gold embroidered in a floral design in gold, silver and coloured silks on a ground of peach colour, now much faded; pillows and quilt are similarly embroidered.

SEAT NEEDLEWORK. In the Tudor period chairs upholstered with satin or velvet were often enriched with armorial badges and bearings in applied needlework, and in the inventory of the wardrobe of Henry VIII a crimson velvet chair is described as 'embroidered with roses and portquillaces'. In the late 16th century the framework of chairs was sometimes left in the rough and covered with richly embroidered materials, as

3. *Seat and back of armchair; frame modern. c. 1600. (Hardwick Hall, Derbys.)*

5. (*Left*) *Winged armchair, covered in Needlework; figure subjects from Ogilby's* Virgil. *c. 1720. (V. & A. Mus.)*

6. (*Above*) *Plate from Ogilby's* Virgil, *1658 (see panel of chair-back, Fig. 5).*

in those described in the inventory of Kenilworth Castle taken in 1588 (*see* CHAIRS). In a set of stools and chairs at Hardwick Hall, Derbyshire, of which the framework is modern, the seat and back are covered with embroidery on canvas in silk and gold thread, dating from c. 1610, and applied to velvet which has been renewed. The motives on the stools and single chairs are sprays, single flowers, caterpillars and butterflies powdered on the ground. In the case of two low-backed armchairs, the design is more ambitious. On the back of one a herd of deer is pursued by a pack of hounds, in allusion to the stag (both the Hardwick crest and the Cavendish supporter), while a sunburst scatters its rays over a group of fruit-bearing trees. In the second armchair (Fig. 3) the seat and sides are powdered with sprays of fruit and flowers, together with snails and newts, while in the front is the nowed snake, a Cavendish crest. On the back is seen a royal carriage, below which are formal trees and a man leading a hound and wearing the 'bombasted' breeches of James I's reign.

In the 'applied work' seat coverings of the 17th century the ornament consists of a pattern formed of stuff (or stuffs) laid on a foundation of a contrasting material. In the Spangled Bedroom at Knole, an upholstered X-framed chair is covered with red satin upon which is applied ornament in cloth of gold and silver spangles. The set of furniture to which this chair

belongs is dated c. 1610: the bed-hangings are of the same material. Dating from about 1690 is a set of gilt furniture at Penshurst Place, Kent, which is upholstered with a large-patterned rose damask, upon which is applied a design in coloured silks and black velvet edged with a narrow cord or by a tufted yellow braid. The set matches the wall-hangings in 'Queen Elizabeth's room'.

The principal and most durable material for seat covering was, however, wool needlework upon canvas. The English silk industry was undeveloped in the late 17th and 18th centuries, and the imported Italian velvets were extremely expensive and quite beyond the purse of the smaller country gentleman. In the accounts for the furnishing of Hampton Court Palace in 1699, two elbow chairs of walnut, with 'carved fore-parts and cross frames', are priced at only £2 10s., whereas their covering with 'rich Genoa velvet', and finishing with tufted and twisted silk fringe, amounted to £31 more. Many examples are in good preservation today. The covering of chairs with needlework was accounted the duty of womenfolk in country houses in the late 17th and early 18th centuries. This industry is especially characteristic of 'the age of walnut', when the stuffed-backed chairs and settees gave full scope for the worker. The needlework was fixed to the framework by close-set nails, or (in the case of chairs and settees with a movable

7. *Mahogany Settee, back and seat covered with original needlework; panels framed in floral borders. c. 1725. (Formerly at Copped Hall, Essex.)*

8. *Detail of settee, needlework of floral design enclosing landscape panel. c. 1725. (Formerly at Madingley Hall, Cambs.)*

9. *Back of chair covered in Needlework; centre panel represents Diana and attendants. c. 1730. (Dalkeith Palace, Midlothian.)*

seat) dropped into a rebate, the frame giving it the required support. Some of the finest examples date c. 1690–1715. A few have medallions in tent stitch following, on a smaller scale, the grand manner of contemporary decorative painters. For a winged armchair in the Victoria and Albert Museum c. 1720 (Fig. 5) the source of the designs is John Ogilby's *Virgil* (1658), a book rich in large plates. Following the plate facing folio 166 in this edition, Aeneas is represented on the seat holding his young son Ascanius by the hand and carrying the old Anchises (who holds in his bosom his household gods); Creusa follows, while in the distance are seen the flaming walls of Troy. Of the two subjects represented on the back, the lower (which is complete) consists of a banquet at a round table, with the chief personages, Dido and Aeneas, seated under a canopy (Fig. 6). The upper subject has been cut, but another plate in this edition gives the clue to this fragment, which represents Aeneas watching the walls of Dido's Carthage rising, while Mercury descends with a warning against dalliance. The complete subject is found on the mahogany card-table at Penshurst, of mid-18th-century date—a proof of the popularity of Ogilby's *Virgil*; and fragmentary figures, classic armour and temples appear on the inner side of the cheeks of the chair and the front face of its squab, evidence that other scenes from the great epic were attempted and ruthlessly sacrificed for upholstery purposes.

In some needlework chair coverings of finished design at Burley-on-the-Hill, Rutlandshire, the design of the double chair-back settee and the accompanying chairs—very probably the work of Lady Nottingham and her daughter—closely follow the contemporary damasks, the repeat exactly filling the chair-back (*see* SETTEES, Fig. 6).

One of the finest sets of seat coverings are those on the settee and chairs from Copped Hall, Essex, dating c. 1725 (Fig. 7). In these the centres of seat and back are occupied by figure subjects framed in a flower border. In a gilt gesso set from Madingley Hall, Cambridgeshire, consisting of two settees and chairs, the design of the centre of each settee is taken from a pair of landscapes by Jan Breughel (1568-1625).

Though under the Georges a number of chairs with stuffed backs continued to be made, there was no attempt at the ambitious figure-subjects of c. 1690–1715. Vases of flowers, pastoral scenes and subjects from Aesop's fables are met with as tent-stitch centres, and an interesting experiment in copying a textile pattern is shown in a mahogany chair in the Victoria and Albert Museum (W19—1919) of c. 1760, the back and seat of which are covered with cross-stitch needlework representing a large-patterned crimson damask. The variation in colour between the ground and pattern of the original damask is emphasised by this use of two shades of crimson.

The naturalistic tendency of the mid-18th century is observable in the coverings of the set of eight chairs, formerly at Glemham Hall, Suffolk, of which the original designs and separate studies for each flower and bird, by Lady Barbara North, daughter of the eighth Earl of Pembroke, were also at Glemham. After c. 1770 the occupation of working covers for seat furniture was superseded through the increasing use of tapestry and silk. M. J. (abbreviated).

The following terms are frequently used in needlework:

APPLIED WORK (or APPLIQUÉ). Consists in the laying of pieces of stuff upon a contrasting foundation or ground to form a pattern. The ornament is affixed to the ground and finished off round the cut edge by a cord, braid or needlework.

BARGELLO WORK (FLAME STITCH, HUNGARIAN STITCH). In this work each figure (usually a series of pointed or flame-like forms) is worked in a single colour, but in graduated shades of that colour. The work originated in Italy, where silks were used, but English work is carried out in crewels.

CHENILLE. A cord having short threads of silk or wool set at right angles to it, forming a velvety thread.

CROSS-STITCH. A stitch formed of two stitches crossing at right angles.

PATCHWORK. Consists of small pieces of various kinds of textiles, differing in colour and pattern, sewn together by the edges, generally with ornamental effect, to form an article such as a coverlet or bed-hanging.

PETIT-POINT. *See* TENT STITCH.

PURL. Fine wire closely bound with silk, which is then coiled round a fine rod and pushed off in the form of a short coiled tube. Short lengths were freely used in needlework of the late 16th and early 17th centuries.

STUMPWORK. Needlework in which the ornament (or the greater part of it) is in relief, raised by a foundation of wood or cotton-wool.

TENT STITCH. Work in which the unit is a series of parallel stitches arranged diagonally across the intersections of the threads; commonly known as *petit-point*.

NEST OF DRAWERS. A number of small drawers or tills contained in a case. Term sometimes employed in 18th century: *London Gazette* (1704) advertises 'One Nest of Drawers'.

NONSUCH. Term derived from name of palace built by Henry VIII at Cheam, Surrey, from designs of the Italian artist, Toto del Nunziata; applied to a type of inlaid decoration found on late 16th-century oak chests and occasionally on smaller objects, consisting of conventional representations of buildings. The palace was engraved by the younger Hoefnagel for Braun's *Cities* (1582), and another representation is given in Paul Hentzner's *Travels* (1598). It is shown with dormer windows, cupolas and lantern-topped towers bearing generic resemblance to the motifs on these chests, which, however, are of German origin or made by immigrant craftsmen.

NULLING. *See* GADROONING, etc.

OAK. There are more than 300 varieties of oak and the term is often inaccurately applied. The species in this country are *Quercus pedunculata* or *Q. robur*—common oak; *Q. sessiliflora*—fruited oak. European oak is of the same species as English. The wood is hard and heavy, the colour varying from white to brown, according to the soil, position in the forest, period of seasoning in water, etc. The wood of extant medieval English furniture is native oak, almost without exception, though other native woods were often used, as in later times, but, being less durable, have perished. At the close of the 17th century oak became restricted to carcase work and drawer linings in the best-quality veneered pieces. In country work it remained popular. Evelyn (*Sylva*, 1664) writes of oak:

> . . . of much esteem in former times till the finer grain'd Norway timber came amongst us which is likewise of a whiter colour. It is observed that oak will not easily glew to other wood, nor not very well to its own kind.

The extensive forests of medieval Britain were thickly stocked with oak, both the *sessiliflora* and *pedunculata* varieties. It was generally employed for furniture, and for this and other purposes was prodigally used. Mature timber was felled in great quantities; planting did not keep pace with consumption, and an Act was passed under Henry VIII enforcing the preservation of oak woods. By the middle of Elizabeth's reign the planting of oaks had become common, but these could not reach maturity for about a hundred years.

In late Tudor and Jacobean joinery a certain amount of imported oak appears to have been used. Some of this was European oak, shipped from Scandinavian and German ports under the names of clapboard and wainscot. It was softer, whiter and more easily worked than native oak.

Until the general adoption of large two-handed saws in the 16th century, the conversion of the oak trunk to scantling size had been usually accomplished by splitting the wood—riven oak. But it must have been necessary at all times to use the saw in converting trees of great age, or those in which the sap had been allowed to dry out after felling. It was discovered that oak would split fairly easily on the lines of the medullary rays, if this were done soon after felling and before the fibres had hardened. By using the beetle and wedge (or riving iron) the trunk was split into quarters; then each quarter was rent to sizes most suitable for the work required, small saws being

used for cross-cutting, and adzes and planes for dressing the surfaces. All scantlings so produced would have a wedge or taper-shaped section, which is clearly shown in Fig. 1. The broad surfaces of the boards were found to display the hard non-cellular tissue of the medullary rays—known as silver grain—which provided the surface with a fine figure, and, in the course of years, with an extremely hard crust.

The riven wood seasoned rapidly, but, even so, the boards, panels, or framing of old work have all shrunk to some extent, the hard silver grain being slightly raised above the softer wood. Riven oak possessed qualities of great hardness and durability, and very little tendency to warp. When the beetle and wedge were superseded, the timber continued to be quarter-cut, and suitable scantlings for furniture were still sawn on lines following the medullary rays.

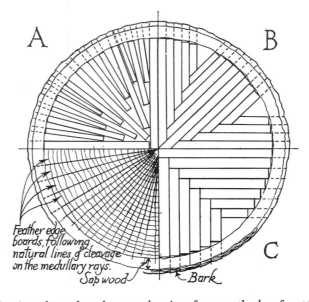

1. *Section through oak tree showing four methods of cutting.*

The diagram shows a quartered oak trunk. In quarter A are shown saw cuts following the medullary rays; in quarters B and C two other methods in which there is no waste other than that caused by the thickness of the saw. But the silver grain will be fully exposed only on those few boards which are closest to the ray lines.

In country furniture a certain amount of plain sawn oak was used in boards, such as those employed for the tops of chests and gate-leg tables, etc. To obtain this the tree was sawn up entirely on lines parallel with a diameter. With this method much wider boards were obtainable than in the case of quarter-sawn oak, but they were more liable to warp and split. Plain cut or 'mild' oak, however, had a special use when, in the second half of the 17th century, and in the 18th, furniture was decorated in japanning or veneered in walnut, and later in mahogany. Then it was found that the absence of silver grain provided a surface allowing a better equality of absorption for japan or glue, the wood being thoroughly seasoned and often cross-framed against warp.

Trees intended for conversion by saw were very generally seasoned by immersion in a river or stream, a process sometimes lasting for more than two years. The trunk, having been withdrawn from the water, lay for some weeks to dry, and, when converted, the planks, boards, billets, etc., were stacked until they became mellow and fit for joinery. In this position the oak remained probably for ten to twenty years.

The oak is always a slow-growing tree, though, in some soils and situations, the progress is slower than in others. Maturity in the best specimens is reached between 150 and 200 years. A certain amount of bog oak was used in applied and inlaid decoration in the 16th and 17th centuries; this was obtained from very ancient trees or portions of trees found submerged in peat bogs, hence the black hue.

OGEE (*Cyma reversa*). Classical moulding consisting of double curve, convex above and concave below; the reverse of *cyma recta*. Term is also applied to an arch with sides formed of two contrasted curves meeting in a point, the hollow part being uppermost. Ogee-headed glazing bars were sometimes employed in secretaires and cabinets c. 1750–1800 (*see* BOOK-CASES, Fig. 8).

OLIVE WOOD (*Olea europaea*). Southern Europe; hard close-grained wood of yellowish-green colour with dark cloudy markings. Used as veneer, generally in the form of parquetry, and for cross-grain mouldings in late Stuart period. Sir Richard Legh, of Lyme Park, Cheshire, in 1675 recorded a visit (in account book) to the 'famous Pendulum maker Knibb', and writes of a clock he proposed to buy that he 'wold have had itt of Olive Wood (the Case I mean)'. At Kensington Palace in 1696 there was 'one olive wood writing cabinet'. Continued to be used for veneers in 18th century, *e.g.* on card-tables, and occasionally in Regency period. There are also African and Indian species.

ORDERS. Columns in classic architecture, consisting of base, shaft and capital, with various subordinate members, surmounted by an entablature. Five orders usually recognised —Doric, Ionic, Corinthian, Tuscan and Composite; the last two are Roman innovations. With the object of associating the cabinet-maker's trade with architecture, plates of the five orders, with notes on their proportions and principal parts, were sometimes introduced into 18th-century trade catalogues. The first eight plates of Chippendale's *Director* (1st ed., 1754) are devoted to the Orders, and in the preface the cabinet-maker is recommended to study them as 'the very soul and basis of his Art'. Robert Manwaring (*Cabinet and Chair Makers' Real Friend and Companion*, 1765) also lays stress on the importance of the Orders, plagiarising this last sentence from the *Director*.

Columnar supports with debased versions of Ionic capitals support the tester on some Tudor bedsteads (*see* BEDS, Figs. 7 and 9), and columns and entablatures were freely introduced in 18th-century furniture designed in the classic manner: the capitals of the various Orders are sometimes accurately rendered. The Orders reappear in Sheraton's *Drawing Book* (1791–4). In his opinion 'nothing can appear more worthy of a place in a complete drawing book . . . as many cabinet-makers, and even some ingenious upholsterers, are found desirous of having a knowledge of the five orders'.

ORGAN. *See* MUSICAL INSTRUMENTS.

ORMOLU. Term *or moulu* ('ground gold') used in France from 16th century onwards to denote gold or gold leaf, ground and prepared for gilding bronze or other metals. Has since become obsolete in France, where term *bronze doré* now usually employed; but English derivative *ormolu* survives, and has been used since mid-18th century to describe objects of gilt bronze and brass, particularly when applied as mounts to furniture. The term not found in cabinet-makers' accounts of 18th century, but Matthew Boulton, chief English producer, habitually employs it. In France the casting, chasing and gilding of fine bronze ornaments for furniture was extensively carried on from the end of the 17th century. But in England the art was developed much later; until c. 1750 ornaments on furniture were usually of cast brass. Mounts of French type are occasionally found, but are mostly of foreign manufacture and inferior quality. Not until after 1760, with the advent of neo-classicism, did ormolu become really fashionable here. Some of the productions of Boulton's firm (*see* BOULTON, MATTHEW) bear comparison with those of the best French metal workers (*see also* GILDING and METAL MOUNTS). P. W.—J.

OTTOMAN (or TURKEY SOFA). Long low upholstered seat, described by Sheraton (*Drawing Book*, 1791–4) as fashionable novelty in 'imitation of Turkish mode of sitting' (*see also* SETTEES AND SOFAS).

OVOLO. Convex classical moulding of which section is usually exact quarter circle. Plain or enriched with egg-and-dart (when it is termed 'echinus') sometimes employed for cornices of furniture in 16th and 17th centuries. The japanned and marquetry frames of Charles II mirrors generally formed of ovolo mouldings (*see* MIRRORS, Figs. 9 and 13).

OYSTER-PIECES. Smaller branches of certain trees were cut transversely to produce circular or oval figures formed of annual ring markings; fitted together as parquetry (*q.v.*) and laid as veneer ground, usually associated with geometrical patterns of light-coloured woods. Oyster-pieces generally cut from walnut and laburnum saplings, but lignum vitae, king-wood, olive and some fruit woods also used (*see* CABINETS, Figs. 5 and 7). J. C. R.

PADOUK (*Pterocapus dalbergiodes*). Imported from Andaman Islands and Burma; hard and heavy, varying in colour from golden brown to deep red or crimson when first cut, red being most characteristic of Andaman variety. From c. 1720 used in solid in England for a few exceptional pieces, notably chairs. A variety of rosewood.

PAGODA MOTIVE. 'Pagoda' is corruption of Eastern name for temple or sacred tower of type common in Burma and China. In the mid-18th century publications such as Sir William Chambers's *Designs of Chinese Buildings, Furniture, etc.* (1757), popularised details of Oriental architecture, among them the characteristic roofs of spreading canopy form. These were adapted by cabinet-makers and employed to give an Eastern effect to various forms of furniture (*see* BEDS, Fig. 31, and BUREAUX, Fig. 34).

PAINTED FURNITURE. The practice of painting furniture and woodwork is of great antiquity, and was widely practised in the Middle Ages; it has persisted into modern times.

From the 12th century onwards chests and wall cupboards were frequently painted in tempera—*i.e.* opaque colours mixed with a glutinous substance (*see* CHESTS, Fig. 4). In the Tudor period colour and gilding continued to be applied to furniture. Henry VIII's possessions included a chair 'of walnuttree colour painted wth a trayle of white parcell guilte' and, among many bedsteads, one 'of wainscotte canopie facion painted redd and parcell guilte . . .' (*see also* DESKS, Fig. 3).

Early in the 17th century furniture was sometimes painted with figures and arabesque ornament in imitation of imported oriental lacquer, this taste being well represented in the Northampton inventory of 1614. Among the articles enumerated are 'a blacke field bedstead painted with flowers and powdered with gold' (*see* CHINESE TASTE).

There is ample evidence that a taste for painted furniture was widespread in the first half of the 17th century. Not only is it mentioned in the contents of palaces ('an oval table of walnuttree painted with silver and other colours', in Charles I's inventory (1649), being a typical instance), but in small households it was also plentiful. Oak and walnut bedsteads were sometimes decorated with coats-of-arms, floral sprays and other ornament in oil colours (instead of the medieval tempera), while rough country-made coffers were occasionally treated in this manner (*see* BEDS, Fig. 12, and CHESTS, Fig. 20). Under Charles II japanning with varnishes and gums to a great extent superseded painting on furniture; but the framework of walnut chairs and daybeds was sometimes picked out with coloured floral patterns. This form of decoration went out of fashion for nearly a hundred years, though cabinets and bookcases of painted pine were made in the architectural style of the early 18th century; while in much of the 'japanned furniture', supplied by Chippendale and later makers, the priming and successive coats of varnish are omitted, the colours being sometimes laid on with gum-water (Robert Dossie, *The Handmaid to the Arts*, 1758) (*see* JAPANNING). In Chippendale's bills a distinction is recognised between japanning and ordinary painting. His accounts to Sir Edward Knatchbull contain many entries for 'japanned' furniture, but in 1767 he supplied '2 Large Girandoles . . . painted Blue and White'.

The general revival of ornamental painting on furniture dates from c. 1770, but as early as 1763 a design for an organcase by Robert Adam for the Earl of Bute has a medallion with painted figures. This revival was mainly due to Adam, for furniture so treated formed an essential part of his comprehensive decorative schemes. The painting is often found on harewood and satinwood veneers in the form of borders, garlands and medallions in natural colours or *grisaille*; while, in other cases, the whole piece is painted in light colours and decorated in the same manner (*see* Frontispiece). Painted ovals and medallions were occasionally used as an adjunct to marquetry.

The usual method was to paint direct on to the primed wood, but copper panels, already decorated, were at times inserted, particularly into the fronts of commodes. The style of Angelica Kauffmann, Zucchi and other fashionable decorators undoubtedly had a far-reaching influence, and they had many imitators among the less successful artists employed by prominent cabinet-makers. Allan Cunningham (c. 1830) observed

that in the late 18th century it was the fashion for painters to be largely employed on embellishing furniture, as well as walls and ceilings. A payment to one of these minor artists for painting a table including a landscape is entered in the cost books of the Gillows firm. Most of the furniture decorated with medallions after Angelica's designs (easily accessible through engravings) date after her departure from England in 1781 (*see* BUREAUX, Fig. 41). Even an artist so well known as William Hamilton consented to decorate the medallions for a cabinet designed by Sir William Chambers and made by Seddon and Shackleton for Charles IV of Spain in 1793. By the end of the century the taste was so widespread that painting had, in great measure, superseded marquetry.

Hepplewhite (*Guide*, 1788) writes that 'the panels of commodes may be of satinwood inlaid or painted', and explains that the subjects are drawn from the 'imaginary decoration selected by Raphael, Italian engravings and also some French works'. Sheraton devotes considerable space to the subject of painted furniture. He gives (*Drawing Book*, 1791–4) 'a variety of ornaments useful for learners to copy from, but particularly adapted to the Cabinet and Chair Branches', provides detailed instructions and illustrates examples. He states (*Cabinet Dictionary*, 1803) that the general use of size and varnish colours 'constitutes this a distinct branch of painting', and deplores the low prices obtained in the country for such furniture. This would apply particularly to the beechwood chairs and settees, so popular at that time, painted with lamp black and decorated in colour or *grisaille*. By c. 1810 painting had been generally superseded by metal inlay, but in the Regency period glass panels painted in black and gold or in colours were sometimes inset in cabinets and other varieties of furniture (*see* MIRRORS, Fig. 80).

PAKTONG. Alloy of copper, nickel and zinc imported into England from China c. 1750–1800, and used in manufacture of candlesticks, grates and fenders (*see also Tutenag and Paktong*, A. Bonnin, 1924).

PANEL. Constructionally, a board held in position by a surrounding framework of rails and stiles which are grooved to receive it (*see* CONSTRUCTION). In the 16th and 17th centuries panels were carved or inlaid (*see* CHAIRS, Figs. 3 and 4, and CHESTS, Fig. 14), and, being set below the surface of the framework, are termed 'sunk'. Important variations from the rectangular panel surrounded by a moulded framework are seen in CHESTS, Figs. 13 and 15, which display architectural features in arches and pilasters. About 1650, panels were moulded on the face to represent geometrical patterns or were overlaid with false panels and stiles with broad splays or bevels and with small bolection mouldings mitred around in various patterns (*see* CHESTS, Fig. 21, and CHESTS OF DRAWERS, Figs. 2, 3, 4, 6, 8, 9). Much of this work was contemporary with furniture veneered in walnut and marquetry, and has close analogies in Holland. The influence of contemporary architectural joinery is seen in CUPBOARDS, Fig. 9. The constructional significance of the panel considerably lessened after the Restoration, when veneering necessitated broad, flush surfaces, and the word is also applied to marquetry designs arranged within a border and let into the veneer ground (*see* CHESTS OF DRAWERS, Figs. 11, 12, 13).

About 1750, panels of figured veneer, *e.g.* on a wardrobe door, were set flush with the framing and were bordered by a small bolection moulding, as seen in CUPBOARDS, *e.g.* Figs. 14, 20, 22; Fig. 24, however, illustrates true constructional panels, which were returning to fashion about 1775. Panel effects were also produced in late 18th-century painted furniture. J. C. R.

PAPIER-MACHE. A process long practised in Persia and elsewhere in the East, which came to England from France, as the name indicates. The material consisted of paper pulp made from specially prepared paper mixed with glue, chalk and sometimes fine sand. This substance, after being pressed, moulded and baked, became so hard that it could be sawn and was capable of taking a very high polish by a process resembling japanning. The use of papier-mâché was considered practicable for picture frames (*q.v.*) in England so early as 1672, though no examples of that period are known. Dossie alludes to French snuff-boxes of papier-mâché in 1758 (*Handmaid to the Arts*), and in 1763 Peter Babel, 'Designer and Modeller', Long Acre, announces himself 'One of the first improvers of Papier-Mâché Ornaments for . . . Picture-frames, etc.'; and refers to papier-mâché as 'an invention of modern date, imported by us from France and now brought to great perfection.' In 1772 Henry Clay of Birmingham (*q.v.*) patented a form of this material which he used in the construction of furniture and other objects. The *Description* of Strawberry Hill (1784) mentions a Clays-ware writing table highly varnished with blue and white ornaments in a Gothic pattern designed by the artist Paul Sandby. Edward Clarke, when on his tour in the south of England and Wales in 1791, visited Clay's manufactory. He writes 'cabinet-makers form every article as it is required, sawing it out of paper and planing it with the greatest exactness. It is then japanned and polished, and this is always done with the hand, which gives a more exquisite lustre than can be communicated by any other means'. Among the objects which attracted Clarke's notice were 'Two pier tables made for the Earl of Bristol painted with some design brought purposely from Rome'. Clay's material, known as 'paper-ware', was not papier-mâché in the strict sense of the term.

PARAGON. Woollen material, stated by worsted-weavers (1605) to be double camlet (*q.v.*). Used for hangings and upholstery in 17th and 18th centuries. In James I's reign, several entries of purchase of paragon in *Naworth Household Books*.

PARQUETRY. A mosaic of woods applied to a ground, used contemporaneously with marquetry, often in association with it. Parquetry consists in laying down thin pieces of wood of simple geometrical form carefully fitted together; employed chiefly in the early period of walnut veneered furniture. Sometimes inlaid; *e.g.* chest of drawers might have carcase and drawer fronts faced with laburnum oyster-pieces; then lines of holly or box would be let into ground in form of circles, interlacing or tangential (*see* CABINETS, Fig. 7). J. C. R.

PARTRIDGE WOOD. (*Andira inermis*). Imported from Brazil and used in small parquetry and inlay work in 17th century; close and heavy, generally of straight grain, in tones

of brown and red, the shades variously mingled and disposed in streaks resembling a bird's feather. Used sparingly as veneer in late 18th century. J. C. R.

PATERA. Architectural term for flat circular or oval ornament, favourite enrichment c. 1760–1800 on friezes, chair splats, mirror crestings, etc. (*see* CHAIRS, Fig. 160, and CHESTS OF DRAWERS, Fig. 39).

PEAR WOOD (*Pyrus communis*). Strong, heavy, and fine in grain, tinged with red, used from very early period for simple country furniture. Stained black and polished or varnished to imitate ebony, and used for applied ornament, as inlay on Elizabethan and Jacobean furniture, and for picture-frames and bracket-clocks in 17th and 18th centuries; also by carvers of Grinling Gibbons school and as veneer on some early long-case clocks and cabinets of 17th century.

PECHE-MORTEL. Term for couch borrowed from French. Horace Walpole writing to Horace Mann, Oct 3, 1743—'I could persuade myself that it is my Lord Carteret's fault that I am only sitting in a common arm chair, when I would be lolling on a *péché-mortel*'. Two couches in 3rd ed. Chippendale's *Director* (1762), Pl. XXXII, are 'what the French call *péché-mortel*'.

PEDESTAL. Sub-structure placed under columns in classical architecture, consisting of base, dado and cornice; term is applied to pieces of furniture in similar form (*see* STANDS, PEDESTAL; SIDEBOARD PEDESTALS; TABLES, LIBRARY).

PEDIMENT. In classical architecture the triangular termination over porticoes and at ends of buildings, etc.; in furniture applied to the decorative feature of similar form surmounting cornice. There is, sometimes, a triangular or scrolled pediment of low pitch above the hood in Charles II long-case clocks, but when architectural influence began to affect design of furniture in early 18th century, several varieties of this member were employed on bookcases, bureaux, cabinets, cupboards and mirrors. In the 'broken pediment' lines, either curved or straight, are stopped before reaching apex, while the 'swan-neck' form consists of opposed S curves scrolling over at the top and finishing in paterae; in both kinds the embrasure is often occupied by a vase or escutcheon. Segmental and lunette shapes were frequently adopted c. 1785–1800, and are illustrated in Sheraton's *Drawing Book* (1791–4) (*see* BOOKCASES, Fig. 19, and CUPBOARDS, Fig. 26).

PENDANT. A comprehensive term for a drop or hanging ornament, introduced on furniture in many positions (*see* MIRRORS, Figs. 46—49).

PERFUME BURNERS (also called CASSOLETS, ESSENCE VASES and ESSENCE POTS). The fashion of heating or burning substances that give out a pleasant savour has obtained widely from early times, not only as an accessory to religious ceremonial but as a domestic habit, particularly at periods and under conditions when cleanliness of home and person and ventilation of rooms were little practised. Special articles for the purpose were devised. For a Christmas performance

1. Perfume Burner, one of two having identical mounts; body of one of alabaster, other of blue-john; base rests on sphinxes; plinth with pierced and chased metal panels. By Matthew Boulton. c. 1767. Ht. 12½ in. (Mulliner Coll.)   2. Ormolu Perfume Burner on white marble plinth. c. 1770. Ht. 1 ft. 9¼ in. (V. & A. Mus.)   3. Perfume Burner, ormolu; pastille container suspended below base. By Matthew Boulton. c. 1775. (Earl of Jersey.)

in the hall at Hampton Court in 1572, together with other lighting, 'high up upon the walls there were silver sconces with candles and candlesticks with perfumes to burn at the end of the matches' (Cunningham's *Revels*, p. 63). In Evelyn's *Mundus Muliebris* (1690) cassolets are referred to among the contents of the ladies' dressing-room, and in the *Fop's Dictionary*, which serves as an appendix, the term is explained as a 'perfuming pot or censer'. In the 18th century the perfume burner was devised as an elaborate ornament for the houses of the wealthy in France, where it was called a '*Brûle parfum*'. Many French examples were imported. Perfume burners were not made at all generally in England, except by Matthew Boulton (*q.v.*), who called them sometimes cassolets, but more often essence pots or vases. A Soho inventory of 1782 lists

1 Ormolu Venus Essence Vase, white marble	15 15 0	
1 Griffin ormolu Essence Vase	7 17 6	

They generally took the form of a vase-shaped body, composed of such minerals as marble, alabaster or blue-john (*see* under DERBYSHIRE SPAR), or of Wedgwood earthenware, mounted in ormolu, which at or near the top had perforations. They were among the usual ornamental objects that Boulton supplied to royalty and wealthy subjects. Thus he wrote (in an undated letter, probably in 1767) that the king 'hath bought a pair of cassolets, a Titus, a Venus clock and some other things'.

These cassolets are probably a pair still at Windsor, of small size, but of exactly the same design as two larger examples (Fig. 1). Although identical as regards the ormolu work, the body of one is composed of blue-john, but of the other, alabaster. The workmanship of the ormolu is of high quality. The rim of the vase is deeply banded with ormolu, and has a row of open circles to let out the scented vapour. This seems to have been Boulton's favourite design, for another pair, precisely similar in size, detail and materials to those at Windsor, was formerly at Osterley Park, Middlesex, which Robert Adam was altering and redecorating for Robert Child at the time that Boulton sold the pair to George III. Though the vase shape predominated, it was not the only form employed (Fig. 2). At Osterley, a pair of carved and painted pedestals designed by Adam in 1776 (*see* STANDS, PEDESTAL AND TERM, Fig. 13) are surmounted by pastille burners of ormolu for which Boulton was probably responsible. The tapering triangular shafts are supported on sphinxes, which rest on plinths, and here the receptacle for the pastilles is of shallow dish form. In Fig. 3 the container is suspended by chains from the busts of the terms; on each face of the triangular base are classical figures in low relief.

PERNAMBUCO WOOD. *See* BRAZIL WOOD.

PIANOFORTE. *See* MUSICAL INSTRUMENTS.

PICTURE-FRAMES. There is scarcely any record of pictures in English private houses before the 15th century, and even as late as the 16th they were classed usually as chattels. Survivals from this early period are rare, being executed generally on wooden panels set in a moulded frame worked in the solid, panel and frame being in one piece. Of this character are the portraits of Richard III and Henry VII in the possession of the Society of Antiquaries, and another portrait of the latter monarch in the National Portrait Gallery (Fig. 1).

Henry VIII's inventories (1542, 1547) contain many references to pictures in the royal palaces, those painted on panels being generally designated 'tables', while paintings in tempera on canvas were habitually termed 'stained cloths', and others 'painted cloths' when oil was used as a medium.

> Itm a Table of wood wt thimage of victorye and Mars painted
> Item [a] stayned clothe wt the picture of Charles Themperor.

From these inventories occasional references to frames are to be gleaned:

> Item a Table of Salutacion of our ladye . . . the frame being of black Ibonye garnished wt silver
> Item a painted clothe wt the Tryumphe . . . sette in a frame of wood wallnuttre colloure.

The inventories also show that most of the pictures in the royal collection had curtains of sarcenet and occasionally wooden shutters.

Like practically all decorative woodwork of the Tudor period, picture-frames were embellished with painting, generally in the form of graining or marbling, and with gilding. In the National Portrait Gallery is a portrait of Henry VIII, dating from c. 1520, in a frame of wood painted and grained. The portrait of Richard Foxe, Bishop of Winchester, in Corpus Christi College, Oxford, painted about

the same time by one of the contemporaries in London of Holbein, was, until 1820, still in its original frame, which was coloured in imitation of red marble veined with green, and bore the inscription IOANNES CORVUS FLANDRUS FACIEBAT. This frame was replaced in October, 1820.

A type of frame popular for some time before and after 1600 is shown in Fig. 2, of which there are originals at Hardwick Hall, Derbyshire, and other great country houses. A very elaborate frame, lavishly embellished with carving, painting and gilding, forms the setting to Mytens's portrait of James I at Knole, Kent (Fig. 3). A manuscript in the British Museum gives the name of a frame-maker of this period—Henry Waller, 'joiner', to whom payment was made on April 20, 1613, for '6 picture frames 8 foot deep & 5 foot broad' supplied for the service of the king.

The long controversy between the Carpenters' Company and the Company of Joiners (q.v.) was settled in 1632 by an agreement containing a declaration that 'these workes next following doe properly belong to the Joyners', among those enumerated being 'Item all frames for pictures'.

Makers of picture-frames—joiners, carvers and gilders—must have been busily employed in the early part of Charles I's reign, when the king was forming his famous collection of pictures. An Issue Warrant of 1630-1 relates that 'Richard Greenbury Painter to our dearest Consort the Queen' was entitled to payment for *inter alia*:

> carving painting and guilding one great frame for the Souldier at length by Titian
> to the Carver and Joiner for mending of frames; for a straining frame for a great peece of Van Dikes.

It is not clear from the warrant whether Greenbury was the executant of the first item or merely made disbursements to others. In the accounts relating to the embellishment of (old) Somerset House, Zachary Taylor and Edward Pierce (well

1. *Early Tudor Frame and Panel in one piece. Dated 1505. Ht. 1 ft. 2½ in., W. 9⅝ in. (Nat. Portrait Gallery.)*

2. *Frame, carved, painted and parcel gilt. Probably reproducing an original of c. 1600. Ht. 3 ft. 2 in., W. 2 ft. 4½ in. (Nat. Portrait Gallery.)*

known as a decorative painter) are referred to as being engaged, in their several capacities, to carve, paint and gild the frames of pictures in the Queen's Gallery.

About this time a taste prevailed for frames, of Continental provenance, veneered with ebony or tortoise-shell and turtle-shell, either red or yellow, in combination with waved or 'rippled' mouldings of ebony or ebonised beech and other soft woods. In 1666 Pepys admired a frame of 'counterfeit tortoise-shell', which was 'most excellently done'. Tortoise-shell veneer is said to be 'still in vogue and favoured by many' for frames in Stalker and Parker's *Treatise of Japanning and Varnishing* (1688); many such frames were doubtless imported and the English origin of extant examples cannot be established. Fig. 5 shows a mid-17th century frame gilt, carved and pierced *à jour*.

The frame in Fig. 4 represents, probably, the type popular during the Commonwealth. The frames of sober black, relatively devoid of ornament, originated in patterns current in France under Henry IV, and importation again makes the nationality of existing specimens problematical.

After the Restoration (1660) picture-frames, like all other accessories of decoration and furniture, shared in the reaction in favour of greater luxury, one curious manifestation of which, the so-called *genre auriculaire*, affected frames in particular. This distinctive convention was already much employed by Continental craftsmen and is associated with Rubens's decorative *atelier*. A picture-frame composed of flattish auricular scrolls, of which many variations were popular in this country shortly after 1660, is illustrated in Fig. 6. Frames of this character are represented, in their proper environment, in paintings of interiors by Dutch and Flemish masters, their popularity in this country being, perhaps, accounted for by the fact that members of the English Court were familiar with them when in exile. At Hampton Court is a series of small-size auricular frames exhibiting interesting variations of this pattern, containing small portraits, on panel, by Theodore Roussel.

One of the most popular frames during the Restoration period consisted of a moulding with a flattish elliptical front-contour, carved with scrolls in very slight relief. A variant is carved with bay leaves, and this form is also found on frames of very narrow cross-section. At that time, also, pictures, especially portraits, were frequently enclosed within mouldings, either plain or enriched, forming elements of the then almost universally panelled wall surfaces. Fig. 7 shows a frame of an enriched bolection moulding—a type also largely used for incorporating pictures in wainscoting.

Many wood-carvers' accounts of this period relate to the fixed frames embodied in the wainscoting: in July, 1662, Henry Phillips, 'master carver to the King's Works', claims payment 'for two picture frames carved with two members . . . to stand over the windows in ye quenes bedchamber' at Whitehall Palace. References in Pepys's *Diary* relate to both categories of 'fixed' and 'portable' frames:

1666, March 17th.—To Hales's, and paid him £14 for the picture a portrait of Mrs Pepys and £1 5s. for the frame.
1669, April 30th—Thence (from 'Lilly's the varnisher') to the frame-maker one Norris, in Long Acre, who shewed me several forms of frames . . . which was pretty, in little bits of mouldings to choose from.

3. *Carved, painted and gilded Frame, decorated with scrolls, amorini and crowns. c. 1620. Ht. 7 ft. 9¾ in., W. 5 ft. 7¼ in. (Knole Park, Kent.)*

4. *Miniature Frame of ebonised softwood; 'rippled' mouldings. c. 1650. Ht. 8½ in., W. 6¼ in. (Nat. Portrait Gallery.)*

The last entry refers to Norris, 'frame-maker to the Court', whose name occurs spelt variously in many contemporary allusions. Vertue quotes a reference to him as 'Norrice', and as late as the reign of William III, 'Mr Norris' claims payment of £20 16s.:

for severall Black Ebony and paretree frames for ye Chaplains, &c., in ye yeares 1693–95, and for a Guilded frame for his Majesty's picture at Length went to Maryland 1695–6 as appears in ye bill annexed dated ye 26 Mar. 1696.

The Hon. Robert Boyle's essay *Of Man's great Ignorance of the Uses of Natural Things*, published 1672, refers to the suitability of papier-mâché for 'Frames of Pictures and Divers pieces of

5. (*Left*) *Frame of gilded limewood, moulded, carved and pierced. c. 1640. Ht. 1 ft. 8½ in., W. 1 ft. 4¼ in. (The late Mr Ingleson C. Goodison.)*

6. (*Right*) *Carved and gilt Frame. c. 1670. Ht. 2 ft. 4½ in., W. 1 ft. 11⅜ in. (Dulwich Gallery.)*

7. (*Below*) *Carved and gilt Frame with bolection moulding. c. 1675. Ht. 2 ft. 5¼ in., W. 2 ft. (Nat. Portrait Gallery.)*

8. *Carved, pierced and gilded Frame. c. 1680. Ht. 4 ft., W. 3 ft. 3¼ in. (Nat. Portrait Gallery.)*

9. (*Right*) *Frame of gilded wood; outer mouldings carved with foliage and flowers. c. 1680. Ht. 2 ft. 5 in., W. 2 ft. ½ in. (J. Pepys-Cockerell Coll.)*

10. *Frame, gilt and carved with repeating pattern of shells, scrolls and foliage. Probably by John Le Sage. c. 1685. (Lamport Hall.)*

11. *Carved and gilt Frame; arms of Elias Ashmole on cresting. Attributed to Grinling Gibbons. c. 1683. Ht. 6 ft. 2 in., W. 5 ft. 9 in. (Ashmolean Mus., Oxford.)*

12. *Frame of carved and pierced limewood c. 1685. Attributed to Grinling Gibbons. (Mr W. S. Lewis.)*

13. (*Left*) *Frame gilded and carved with scrolls and foliage; on cresting angels supporting coronet. c. 1689. (Hinchingbrooke, Hunts.)*

14. (*Above*) *Bolection-moulded Frame gilt and carved with twisted ribbon and foliage. c. 1695. Ht. 2 ft. 5 in., W. 2 ft. (Nat. Portrait Gallery.)*

15. (*Below*) *Landscape-shaped Frame of carved and gilded wood. c. 1690. Ht. 1 ft. 5½ in., W. 2 ft. ½ in. (Montague L. Meyer Coll.)*

Embossed Work and other Curious Movables'. Whether that material was used by the frame-makers of the period is uncertain, but at a later date it was extensively used for the purpose.

What type of frame was made by Norris for his royal and other patrons does not always appear, but accounts for picture-frames purchased by the Duke of Lauderdale (who had apartments at Whitehall Palace) for his wife's seat at Ham House, Surrey, c. 1675, establish that the type decorated with flattish auricular scrolls was still popular; a whole set may be seen in the long gallery at Ham House (*see* INTRODUCTION, Fig. 7).

A very ornate frame, carved, pierced and gilded, composed of acanthus scrolls and small amorini is illustrated in Fig. 8. The carved motives are common to many branches of furniture and decorative woodwork at this period. These ornate motives doubtless represent the manner of such wood-carvers as the before-mentioned Henry Phillips and his immediate successors, William Emmett and Grinling Gibbons. Emmett claimed payment of £5 in 1689 for '40 ft. of picture frame over two doors' at Whitehall Palace, and in May, 1690, he presented a bill of £8 5s. 8d. for '47 ft. 4 ins., of large Italian picture fram'd Mouldings with three Inrichments over the 2 Chimneys in the Great Roome' in the 'Thames Gallery' at Hampton Court Palace.

Another carver, John Le Sage, who was extensively em-

ployed on the woodwork of Hampton Court under Wren, made picture-frames, and even engaged in picture-dealing, at this period.

Sir Justinian Isham's account book contains the following:

1685 Aug. 13th Pd for picture frames—£10.
     Dec. 22nd. For picture frames to Le Sage—£27.
1692 Nov. 18 To Him [Le Sage] for King and Queen's picture £15.

16. *Full-length Portrait Frame gilded and carved with martial trophies.*
c. 1695. Ht. 7 ft. 1½ in., W. 5 ft. 1½ in. (Royal Hospital, Chelsea.)

17. *'Kit-Cat' Frame of carved and gilded wood. c. 1715. Ht. 3 ft., W. 2 ft.*
4 in. (Nat. Portrait Gallery.)

18. *(Right) Frame gilded and carved with gadroons and other ornament.*
c. 1730. Ht. 2 ft. 5 in., W. 2 ft. (Nat. Portrait Gallery.)

In a letter still at Lamport Hall, Northamptonshire, John Le Sage wrote from 'Flemmings Rowe neare St Martin's Lane Westminster' to Sir Justinian on September 3, 1685:

> Honoured Sir
> I have this day delivered into the Carrier at the Ram in Smithfield eight frames with the three pictures from Mr Nellers all safely packt up in fflower Boxes and the Carrier has promised to take a special care in delivering of them which I hope he will do. With my most humble service I rest
>
> Your most humble service [*sic*]
> John Le Sage

There are payments in the account book in 1685 for pictures by 'Neller' (Kneller) two being portraits of Sir Justinian and his wife. The frames are of distinctive pattern, and there are six other pictures at Lamport Hall similarly framed (Fig. 10).

Payments to this maker are also recorded in the *Diary and Expense Book* of John Hervey, first Earl of Bristol, *e.g.* in 1690

> Paid him (Le Sage) for four little pictures with carved work gilt in oil gold frames, pictures and all £11 15s.

Much of the 'gilding' executed at this period was done with silver leaf, subsequently varnished or 'lacquered' (*see* GILDING).

The frame of Fig. 15 is typical of the patterns current in the reign of William and Mary, a bolection moulding being enriched with a running pattern. This type, French in origin, was highly popular in this country, being carved and gilded, doubtless, in the first instance, by French refugee

19. *Frame, gilded and carved with sporting trophies. Attributed to Paul Petit. c. 1745. (Windsor Castle. By gracious permission of H.M. the Queen.)*

craftsmen after the Revocation of the Edict of Nantes (1685). Robert Derignee, one of these immigrants, supplied a number of frames to Kensington Palace between 1692 and 1697, described as:

> frames for pictures richly carved with flowers close and open and agreed for by our said late dear Consort the Queene and for her service at Kensington.

A frame, probably by an English carver, encloses the portrait of Elizabeth, Countess of Sandwich, painted by Kneller soon after her marriage in 1689. It is carved with scrollwork, foliage and flowers, and the cresting consists of a coronet supported by two draped angels bearing wreaths (Fig. 13). Oval and rectangular frames of this period are found in considerable numbers. The frame surrounding a full-length portrait of William III (Fig. 16) is elaborately carved with martial trophies in recognition of the king's military achievements.

Allusion has already been made to decorative carving by Grinling Gibbons and others who were frequently employed when exceptionally ornate picture frames, both fixed and portable, were required. At the Ashmolean Museum, Oxford, are three remarkable carved and gilt picture-frames—one of large size (Fig. 11) and two smaller ones of oval form—which were given by Elias Ashmole, the founder: that containing his own portrait in 1683, and the others with those of Charles II and James II in 1686–7. Ashmole's manuscript diary, in shorthand, proves that he was in communication with Gibbons, whose horoscope he cast, and there is at least a presumption

that he obtained these frames from the famous carver; though a considerable number of frames of a similar character were produced at this period, of which most must be assigned to his imitators. In the Ashmolean examples the composition is bold and effective (the distribution of the ornament is particularly skilful in the ovals), but parts of the carving are relatively coarse. The splendid frame (Fig. 12) enclosing a 'conversation' picture of Sir Robert Walpole and Catherine Shorter, his first wife, with Houghton Hall in the distance, by Eckard and Wootton, was in Horace Walpole's possession and included in the Strawberry Hill sale (1842, 22nd day, Lot 84). The frame, then painted black and gold, is described in the catalogue as by Gibbons and 'one of his finest specimens of carving . . . most beautifully designed and perfect as a work of art'. The quality of the carving and the design fully warrant the attribution, but as Gibbons died in 1721 the frame cannot have been made for the picture. It may be observed that details of ornament overlap the canvas. The pattern with variations shown in Fig. 14 was popular c. 1690–1715.

At the end of the 17th century a number of frames were commissioned for Hampton Court Palace, to which reference is made in the bills of Charles Hopson and John Le Sage (employed by the Earl of Bristol and for Lamport Hall, *see supra*). On November 5, 1700, Lord Bristol recorded in his *Diary*: 'Paid Spanger ye Dutch carver in full for picture frames . . . £37.' Pepys commissioned Sir Godfrey Kneller in 1701 to paint the portrait of Dr John Wallis, Savilian Professor of Geometry, for presentation to the University of Oxford and on July 27, 1702, Kneller wrote to Pepys:

20. *Frame of carved, pierced and gilded wood in rococo style. c. 1755. Ht. 2 ft. 11 in., W. 2 ft. 5 in. (Dulwich Gallery.)*

21. *Frame of carved and gilded wood. Probably by Thomas Chippendale. c. 1755-60.* (*Badminton House, Glos.*)

22. *Frame gilt and carved in openwork with foliate scrolls and floral motifs; plumed helmet on cresting. c. 1760.* (*Wykeham Abbey, Yorks.*)

23. *Frame with gilt and carved rococo motifs, symbols of arts and military trophies. c. 1762.* (*Doddington Hall, Lincs.*)

24. (*Left*) *Frame of carved and gilt wood; plaque on cresting with Minerva and Cupid. c. 1766. Ht. 7 ft. 10 in., W. 4 ft. 4 in. (V. & A. Mus.)*

25. (*Right*) *Circular Frame, carved and gilt; rococo ornament on cresting; mouldings reeded. c. 1765. (J. Pepys-Cockerell Coll.)*

rently, succeeded in a very lucrative business by Gerard Howard, who charged the Crown in the course of the next year upwards of £700 for 'carved gilded frames'. In 1729 he supplied two 'very rich frames' to Houghton Hall for Sir Robert Walpole. Though Howard's charges indicate that he was the principal frame-maker to the Court, he was not alone in ministering to George II's lavish demand for frames. Further accounts of Gerard Howard relate to Hampton

> I understand you have a frame making for that picture, which I desire to see put on at my house, and all packed together in a case safe. . . .

Figs. 17 and 18 illustrate patterns in vogue from the latter part of Anne's reign, and throughout George I's. The Kit-Cat portait (Fig. 17), one of the well-known series executed by Kneller for Jacob Tonson and the Kit-Cat Club (formerly at Bayfordbury, Hertfordshire, for which they were painted) gives its name to the size popular at this period and long subsequently. The earliest dated portrait was painted in 1703 and the last in 1717.

Between 1719 and 1729, large numbers of prints and miniature frames in ebonised pear wood were made by Bernard Lens, the limner, many of whose accounts for them are still preserved in the Duke of Portland's archives. In 1721 Sir Robert Walpole is indebted to John Howard in the sum of £33 'for a frame Carved and gilt with gold to Yor. Honble Picture over the Chimney'; and in 1727 the same Howard is working for the Court, and claimed 'for carved and gilded frames for His Majesty's Pictures, etc. £141. 19. 2d.' In that year he is, appa-

26. *Frame of carved and gilt wood. Probably by Thomas Chippendale. c. 1780. (Harewood House, Yorks.)*

Court, St. James's and Kensington. He charged, for example, in 1734-5

> for a very large carved and gilt fframe to a History Piece for the Great Stair Case at Hampton Court   £54. 3. 0.

Isaac Gossett (or Grossett), carver and gilder, presents an account on November 6, 1735, 'for a carved and gilt frame of her Majesty's picture at whole length'; and thirteen years later, Hogarth, writing to Gossett about the price of a frame for 'Paul before Felix', learnt that it would come to about thirty pounds if gilt, but about half as much without gilding. 'Frames' he adds, 'may be carried up to great expense'. Howard's accounts alone, during the next ten years, for picture-frames supplied to the Court, amount to nearly £1,000. In 1743–4 the cabinet-maker Benjamin Goodison (*q.v.*) supplied frames, and certain accessories, to Lady Cardigan, among them

> A picture frame Carved & Guilt in Burnish'd Gold   £1 19 0.
> a plate Glass to Do. and fixing Do.   0 8 6.

Paul Petit, the principal frame-maker to Frederick, Prince of Wales, was almost certainly responsible for the fine frame of the sporting picture of the Prince with the Dukes of Marlborough and Queensbery (Fig. 19). The canvas is dated 1742, and in 1746 Petit was paid £2 'for a Rich picture frame Carved with birds Richly ornamented neatley repair'd and Gilt in Burnished Gold to a picture of His Royal Highness painted by Mr Wootton'. The frame carved with birds and trophies shows early rococo influence, but the low cost and the reference to repairs may imply that it was made a year or two before the date of the bill.

The skilled carver, throughout the mid-Georgian period, when elaborate frames were involved, began his work after the preliminary shaping had been finished by 'joiners who make nothing but frames for looking-glasses and pictures and prepare them for the carvers' (*Description of All Trades*, 1747).

After about 1750 rococo taste increasingly influenced design and decoration of picture-frames. Fig. 20 illustrates an import-

27. *Carved and gilt Frame with gadroon ornament. c. 1758. Ht. 4 ft. 1¾ in., W. 3 ft. 3¼ in. (Nat. Gallery.)*

ant frame made about this date, elaborately carved and pierced in the prevailing style. In 1758 Thomas Johnson, carver, published *Designs for Picture Frames, Candelabra, Chimney-Pieces, etc.*, and in the 1762 ed. of the *Director* Chippendale included a number of designs for picture-frames, to which the following descriptions are annexed:

> A Frame for a Picture. The Corners are trophies of Hunting, Musick, &c. Pl. CLXXXV.

28. *'Maratti' Frame of moulded and carved wood, gilded. c. 1785-90. Ht. 2 ft. 5½ in., W. 2 ft. 1 in. (Nat. Portrait Gallery.)*

29. *'Lawrence' Frame; enrichments of composition gilded. c. 1820. Ht. 1 ft. 11 in., W. 1 ft. 7 in. (Nat. Portrait Gallery.)*

A Frame with warlike Trophies in the Corners and Middles. Pl. CLXXXVI.

A Frame for a Picture of an Engagement at Sea. Pl. CLXXXVII.

Accounts exist for picture-frames supplied by Chippendale to Nostell Priory, Yorkshire. On March 1, 1768, he charges for '41 Picture frames neatly carved in Burnish Gold of different sizes . . . £63. 10', and in the following September there is an item in his bills of £35 for 'altering picture frames adding rich carved roses and other ornaments and gilding in Burnish Gold'. Fig. 21 illustrates the close relationship between frame and picture favoured by Chippendale. Containing Reynolds's portrait of Admiral Boscawen, it has a head of Neptune on the cresting and other nautical emblems. In Fig. 22, a portrait of Viscount Downe (d. 1760) by the same artist, his military career is indicated by the plumed helmet on the cresting. In a large frame of this period (Fig. 23) symbols of the arts and military trophies are introduced among the carved enrichments. Picture-frames, highly rococo in character, designed as an integral part of the chimneypiece, figure among the original drawings of John Linnell, the portrait in one very ornate example being carefully drawn within the frame.

About 1765 the neo-classic revival begins to affect the character, and among the original drawings produced in Robert Adam's office will be found not only designs for frames, but references to the craftsmen responsible for their execution. In 1772 the name of Adair occurs in Lord Shelburne's accounts as the carver of a picture-frame carried out under Adam's direction. Two members of the Adair family, John and William, are known, John being established as a carver and gilder in Wardour Street, Soho, in 1763, while William, 'Joiner to H.M. Privy Chamber', supplied in 1773, at a charge of £67 4s., 'two rich Carved and Gilded Frames with Drive-up frame and cases for their Majesties Pictures at whole lengths'.

Fig. 24 shows an interesting example of the influence of neo-classic taste on design. The portrait, by Battoni, is dated 1766, and the frame was doubtless made on the sitter's return from Italy. Here the figure of Minerva in the cresting is not moulded but skilfully carved, like the pendants of bay leaves. The frame (Fig. 26) was probably made by Chippendale's firm for the portrait of Lady Worsley painted in 1779.

In 1763 Peter Babel, 'Designer and Modeller', Long Acre, advertised picture-frames among other productions made of papier-mâché (q.v.). In the same year Jackson, 'A Turner chiefly of Oval Picture-frames', carried on business in Tottenham Court Road. Sir Joshua Reynolds employed a frame-maker named Cribb, probably Robert Cribb, of 288 Holborn, who advertised picture-frames on his trade-card. In a letter (from Bath, April, 1762) Gainsborough, who had just painted a portrait of Richard Stevens, M.P., wrote to him: 'I have put it into the sort of frame which you was pleased to order, which comes to two guineas, the picture ten guineas, & the case seven shillings . . . and as to the frame it was done after the drawing by you sent by the best frame-maker at Bristol'. The portrait survives, with another of Stevens's sister, uniform in size, and the original frames are of comparatively simple character. Reynolds, according to James Northcote, favoured inconspicuous frames 'not above two inches deep' for his 'fancy pictures'; but those for his portraits 'were often provided by his sitters', which accounts for their more elaborate

character. Some frames have crossed palm branches forming an ellipse, a graceful form then in request.

Gainsborough's famous portrait of Mrs Siddons (Fig. 27) is contained in a contemporary frame, the principal enrichment being gadrooning. In most frames dating c. 1774-1800 the mouldings give the only indication of classical influence, and, except for husks and paterae, the decorative motives of the period are seldom employed. Leading picture-frame makers of this time were: (1) Joseph Cox, Round Court, St Martin's-le-Grand, who made and sold 'all Sorts of Carved and Gilt Frames . . . and Lacker'd & Black Frames for Paintings or Prints' for the general public; (2) Réné Stone, in 1772; (3) Isaac Gossett, later famous as a wax-modeller of portraits; (4) Adrian Maskens of Compton St., who in 1781 carved the frames for Barry's ambitious series of paintings in the lecture room of the Royal Society of Arts; (5) Kingham, of Long Acre, who made frames for the Raphael cartoons (now in the Victoria and Albert Museum) to the order of George III, at a cost of £500.

During and after the last quarter of the 18th century carved wooden frames and those of papier-mâché were largely superseded by frames with ornament of composition. The most popular pattern at the end of the 18th century and opening of the 19th, was that known as the Carlo Maratti frame (Fig. 28), the enrichments to which were made first in carved wood and later of composition. Of that material, too, are the enrichments in the typical 'Lawrence' frame (Fig. 29), of the pattern, embodying earlier motives, favoured by Sir Thomas Lawrence and current well into Queen Victoria's reign.

PIER-GLASSES. *See* MIRRORS.

PIGEON WOOD. Name now given to wood of various trees and shrubs from West Indies and South America, so called for marking or colouring. Zebra-wood (q.v.) among varieties so described. Name in inventories of late 17th to early 18th centuries, but impossible to determine sort of wood referred to. In April, 1733, at sale of Sir William Stanhope's furniture 'a pidgeon-wood corner cupboard' sold for 10s.

PILASTER. Flat pier or engaged column, slightly projecting from surface against which it is placed. Carved pilasters, with moulded bases and capitals are found on Tudor and Jacobean bedheads and chest fronts; in 18th century, fluted and with Corinthian or Composite capitals, employed to frame doors of bureaux, cabinets and cupboards. Inlaid commodes of that time often have pilasters at corner and dividing front (*see* CHESTS OF DRAWERS, Fig. 27; COMMODES Fig. 20).

PINEWOOD (*Pinus*). Genus of resin-producing trees, of natural order *Coniferae*. *Pinus sylvestris*, Scots pine, and *P. picea*, spruce fir, both native to northern parts of Great Britain in Middle Ages, and further extensively planted at end of 16th century and in James I's reign. Those species are of straight grain, rather soft and easy to work; colour white to pale yellow.

Little appears to have been used for furniture before Restoration. In 17th century large quantities of fir timber were imported; Evelyn (*Sylva*, 1664) mentioned its coming 'frome Bergen . . . Mosse (Norway) . . . long straight, clear and of a yellowish . . . colour. It is exceeding smooth to polish on, and

1. *Plateau of brass, decorated in sand-work, with oval medallions and paterae borders. Late 18th century. (Mr F. W. Phillips.)*

1. *Mahogany Plate Pail, one of pair; brass handle; sides pierced with Gothic fretwork. c. 1760. Ht. 1 ft. 1 in., W. 11½ in. (Percival Griffiths Coll.)*

therefore does well under Gilding work, and takes black equal with the Pear tree.'

The *sylvestris* wood varies in tone, pale varieties being termed yellow deal or pine, and the deeper, red deal or pine; thus some confusion has often occurred. Yellow deal largely used for carcase work in walnut-veneered furniture after Restoration, and its use continued into 18th century; towards end of that period, it seems to have been superseded by red deal. J. C. R.

PIPE-RACK. *See* RACKS AND TRAYS, PIPE.

PLANE WOOD (*Platanus acerifolia*). Maple-leaved or London plane, very white wood, close in grain, tough. Plane tree of Scotland actually *Acer pseudo-platanus*, English sycamore. Sheraton (*Cabinet Dictionary*, 1803) mentions use of plane tree: 'and in many places in the country used by Cabinet makers instead of beech for painted chairs, or the fly joint rails of card and pembroke tables'. J. C. R.

PLAQUE. Ornamental plate of metal, porcelain, etc., rectangular, round or oval in form. In late 18th century, plaques of Wedgwood were occasionally inserted into cabinets, commodes, etc. (*see* WEDGWOOD, J.), while others in bronze chased in classical taste were employed in decoration of furniture in Regency period.

PLATEAU. Ornamental stand on low plinth or feet, for centre of dining-table, constructed usually in several parts, so that it could be lengthened. Such stands, very fashionable towards end of 18th century, made of japanned wood painted with floral designs, or decorated with sand-work (Fig. 1); others were of papier-mâché with etched, gilt or coloured ornament. Later, often of looking-glass surrounded by little silver or gilt gallery, and sometimes constructed entirely of metal. Mary Frampton, 1814, describing Prince Regent's party in honour of Duke of Wellington, mentions supper-table for the Queen as 'very handsome and the plateau down the middle of the table covered with exquisite groups in silver gilt'.

PLATE PAIL. Long passages often separated kitchen and dining-room in 18th century houses and to facilitate transport of plates mahogany pails and carriers were produced, though they are not represented in trade-catalogues of the time. More elaborate specimens were polygonal, with fretwork sides and one open section to enable plates to be readily handled; in Fig. 1 tracery is in Gothic manner, but Chinese frets also employed. Such pails generally made in pairs, and, placed by fire, enabled china to be kept warm. In 1769 Chippendale's firm supplied Sir Edward Knatchbull with 'a neat mahogany plate Basket with a Brass Bow handle', probably of this type, and also with a large pail for plates bound with brass hoops.

PLATE WARMER. Although one of a pair of sideboard pedestals was usually fitted up as a plate warmer after their introduction c. 1770, a separate piece of furniture, in the form of an enclosed stand containing a receptacle for plates and heater, was occasionally made. In 1769 Chippendale's firm supplied Sir Edward Knatchbull with 'a large mahogany plate warmer lind with tin with iron box and heater and a folding top, £5 10s.'.

PLINTH. Architectural term used in furniture in distinct senses, being applied to low stands for figures or escutcheons on pediments and to the bases, often enriched with carved mouldings, on which bookcases, etc., stand. Trunks of long-case clocks are supported on plinths.

PLUM WOOD (*Prunus domestica*). Yellowish wood with heart of deep brownish red, very like West Indian mahogany; hard and heavy. Used by country cabinet-makers, also by inlayers and turners, in 16th and 17th centuries. Evelyn (*Sylva*, 1664) writes: '... pear and plum tree give the deepest red, and approached nearest in beauty to Brazil'. In the Duke of Lauderdale's room at Whitehall, 1683, was 'a little writing-desk of plum-tree wood'.

POLISHES. Processes by which the smooth and comparatively lifeless raw surfaces of wood acquire a gloss that enhances the figure or grain and, often with the addition of stain, improves the colour.

By Evelyn and subsequent writers the terms polish and varnish are used synonymously, but though both processes impart a gloss, there is a difference between them (*see* VARNISH). The earliest known polishing appears to have been the indirect result of efforts to preserve the wood by rubbing with oil, of which three kinds were used, viz., nut, poppy and linseed oil. This treatment did not become general until the medieval practice of painting furniture declined in the 16th century, when, in addition to oil polishing, the use of beeswax and turpentine came into favour. The former, especially on oak, had the effect of darkening the wood by oxidisation; the use of wax rendered the wood a light brown or golden tone by forming a film on the surface, which did not darken except by adhesion of dust. As showing the prevalence of oil polishing Evelyn (*Sylva*, 1664) mentions the following woods: 'Ebony, Box, Larch, Lotus, Terebinth, Cornus, Eugh, etc., which are best to receive politure, and for this linseed oil or the sweetest nut oyl does the effect best'; and, referring to the practice of the joiners when preparing walnut for furniture, he wrote: 'they put the boards in an oven—or lay them in a warm stable, and when they work it, polish it over with its own oyl, very hot, which makes it look black and sleek'. Again, he refers to the use of oil in the rubbing down and final polishing of surfaces treated with the new 'Japan or China vernishes'. Of wax polishing, he writes, after describing a black stain for pear tree, etc.: 'then melt some beeswax, mixing it with your lamp black and size, and when tis cold, make it up into a ball and rub it over your former black, lastly, with a polishing brush (made of short stiff Boars bristles) labour it till the lustre be to your liking.'

The use of Tripoly powder and oil in rubbing down and final polishing after varnishing was common for walnut in the 17th century and, later, for mahogany and satinwood. This was, however, a lengthy and expensive process, suitable only for fine furniture, the less costly country-made pieces being finished with linseed oil (often dyed with alkanet root) or wax-polished.

In Sheraton's *Cabinet Dictionary* (1803) the subject of polishing is dealt with at some length, the methods described being: (*a*) unsoftened wax rubbed in the wood by means of a cork for inside work, the 'clemmings' left by the wax being cleared away by rubbing on powdered brick dust under a cloth; (*b*) soft wax—'a mixture of turps and beeswax'—to which may be added 'a little red oil to help the colour of the wood': polished off with a cloth; (*c*) 'The general mode of polishing plain cabinet work'; linseed oil (either plain or stained with alkanet) with brick dust is spread over the surface and rubbed together, which produces a polishing 'putty under the rubbing cloth', 'this kind of putty will infallibly secure a fine polish by continued rubbing'; (*d*) 'Chairs are generally polished with a hardish composition of wax rubbed upon a polishing brush with which the grain of the wood is impregnated'. The mixture is specified as wax, turps, a little copal varnish and red lead, and Oxford ochre for colour. worked into a ball.

These methods continued in use until the introduction of an entirely new practice from France c. 1820. The process—'french polishing'—consists of soaking a pad with a solution of shellac dissolved in spirit and rubbing it on the surface, several coats being applied at intervals, until a pure film of shellac covers the wood with a hard, glassy shine. Much old varnished and waxed walnut and mahogany furniture was stripped and french polished; this polish, distinctive of the natural patina, wears away with use and is quickly ruined by heat.

POLLARDED WOOD. Timber of trees subjected more or less regularly to pollarding, *i.e.* removing the crown or top branches, leaving stem intact; when it is also cut at certain height from ground, it is called 'topping'. English trees generally pollarded were oak, poplar, willow and elm, and in France, walnut. This concentrates vitality in main stem, and has marked effect on grain and figure of wood. J. C. R.

POMELLS. Finials of ovoid form surmounting uprights of upholstered armchairs with X-shaped underframings, first made for royal palaces and great houses c. 1550 (*see* CHAIRS). Such pomells are generally of gilt wood or copper, and in the early Stuart period were covered with the same velvet or damask with which the chairs were upholstered.

POPLAR (*Populus spp.*) Wood whitish yellow to grey, of a close, firm texture; liable to shrink. Used in inlay, 16th and early 17th centuries; and in late 17th century in certain marquetry patterns on chests of drawers, etc., for which it was sometimes stained. J. C. R.

PRESS. *See* BOOKCASES, CUPBOARDS AND WARDROBES, AND LINEN-PRESS.

PRICKET. Spike for candle on candlesticks and chandeliers in Middle Ages, before the introduction of nozzle; term also applied to candle itself.

PRINCE or PRINCE'S WOOD. Apparently name applied in 17th and 18th centuries to species of *Dalbergia* now known as kingwood (*q.v.*). Many allusions in royal accounts and inventories of late Stuart period to furniture of 'Prince's Wood.' At Ham House, Surrey, 1679, were table and stands, cabinet and a box made of this wood, also 'scriptore of Prince wood garnished with silver'. This scriptor is still in the house (*see* BUREAUX, Fig. 1). 'Prince's Wood' applied in 18th century to a wood exported from Jamaica. 'Spanish Elm or Prince-wood is generally esteemed of the best timber woods in the island.' (P. Browne, *Jamaica*, 1756.) A species of *Cordia* from West Indies, 'neutral or chestnut brown in colour', and not liable to be confused with kingwood, is now known by that name.

PURPLEHEART. (*Genus Peltogyne*). Native of Br. Guiana and so called from colour of wood when freshly cut; used c. 1750–1800 to some extent in line inlay and veneer banding in borders, etc., on cabinets and commodes. Liable to be confused with rosewood (*q.v.*).

QUILT. Bed covering consisting of some woven material with a lining of wool, feathers or other soft substance. In early inventories bed coverings termed 'counterpoints', but quilts begin to appear in Elizabeth I's reign. At Hardwick Hall, Derbyshire, 1601, there was one 'of yellowe india stuffe embroidered with birds and beastes and white silk frenge and tassells'. An inventory (1688) of his Majesty's goods at Whitehall mentions a number of 'quilts for couches' of crimson satin, sky colour damask, etc. Sometimes used as mattresses to lie

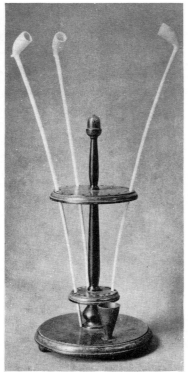

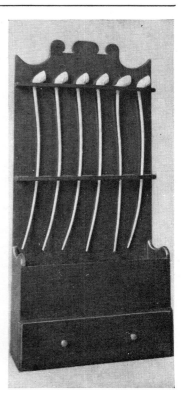

1. *Letter Rack, mahogany, carved with perforated lattice-work. c. 1755. Ht. 1 ft. 6 in., W. 2¼ in. (Percival Griffiths Coll.)* 1. *Pipe Rack; painted walnut, with turned shaft and spill holder; first half of 18th century. Ht. 1 ft. 5¼ in. (Mr Oscar Callow.)* 2. *Pipe Rack of yew; turned baluster shaft surmounted by candle nozzle; spill holders at base. Late 18th century. Ht. 1 ft. 6½ in.* 3. *Pipe Rack of pine and mahogany. Eighteenth century. Ht. 2 ft. 7 in. (Hove Mus., Sussex.)*

on. Inventory of Dyrham Park, Gloucestershire (1710) enumerates several 'under-quilts' besides 'covering' or 'upper' quilts.

RABBET or REBATE. Recess formed along edge by reducing thickness of wood; *e.g.* meeting stiles of cabinet doors often rebated together so that one could shut against the other and form dust-proof joint. Bottom edge of drawer fronts rebated to provide lodgment and fixing for bottom boards (*see* CONSTRUCTION, Figs. 4 and 5). J. C. R.

RACK, LETTER. About 1750 small mahogany hanging racks for letters or cards sometimes made in decorative form; generally vertical and divided into sections which could be pulled forward. More elaborate examples are of mahogany perforated in Chinese and Gothic lattice-work patterns

(Fig. 1). They are mentioned in contemporary bills: in 1766 Chippendale supplied '2 mahogany card racks' to Sir Rowland Winn for 10s.

RACKS and TRAYS, PIPE. In the 18th century wooden racks or stands for pipes were made in various woods and of different forms. In one type the stand supports the long churchwardens vertically round a central standard, the pipe stems passing through a perforated disc or discs; attached to the circular base are spill holders (Figs. 1 and 2). Contemporary, but on a different principle, is the example in Fig. 4. This rack is constructed to hold eleven pipes in a horizontal position one above the other, in the same way as spits and guns were accommodated above kitchen mantelpieces.

A third type (Fig. 3) is in the form of a wall fixture; it

4. *Pipe Rack of mahogany; spill holders on shaped base. Late 18th century.*

5. *Pipe Tray of mahogany; inlay of sycamore. Late Georgian type. L. 2 ft. 2½ in. (Denston Hall, Suffolk.)*

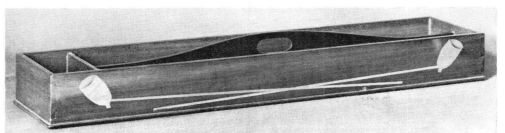

1. *Spoon Rack of oak; mid-17th century type. (Martin Buckmaster Coll.)*

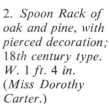

2. *Spoon Rack of oak and pine, with pierced decoration; 18th century type. W. 1 ft. 4 in. (Miss Dorothy Carter.)*

has an open receptacle for tinder box and spills and a drawer for tobacco. Such racks provided greater protection to the long, delicate stems than the earlier standing rack.

Another type was common in Georgian times—a narrow wooden tray, usually of mahogany, though sometimes of oak, divided into two partitions, like a knife box, and provided with a small receptacle at one end for tinder. These were suitable for long churchwardens (Fig. 5).

RACKS, SPOON. It is safe to assume that spoon racks for holding metal spoons were introduced in the Elizabethan period, as during this time spoons of pewter, base-metal and tinned iron were becoming common. In form these metal spoons were similar to those of silver and gold which had for centuries formed an important part of the plate chests of medieval England.

Pewter and base-metal spoons, owing to the softness of the metal, would soon have lost their form and become twisted and dented had they been kept loose in a drawer or box; so, to protect them, spoon racks came into use. The common form had a double rack for spoons, and a box, with or without a lid, at the bottom for knives and forks. Fig. 1 shows an example in oak, with a carved box with lid, the slots in the cross-bars being just large enough to permit the knob or ornamental end of the spoon handle to pass through.

Another type (Fig. 2) has four cross-bars for spoons, arranged in steps—the two upper bars for eight spoons and the two lower for seven spoons each. The top and bottom face-boards are ornamented with diaper perforations. J. S. L.

RAIL. Term for constructional members occupying horizontal position, *e.g.* seat rails of chair; top, bottom and lock rails of panelled door. Ends of rails formed as tenons to slide into mortices cut in vertical members (*see* CONSTRUCTION). J.C.R.

RAILING, CHINESE. *See* FRETWORK.

RATCHET ADJUSTMENT. Curved metal bar with series of saw-like teeth into which cog engages; ends of couches and backs of 'sleeping chairs' sometimes adjusted by this method in 17th century (*see* COUCHES, Fig. 2, and CHAIRS, Fig. 44).

RAYNES, CLOTH OF. Linen of fine quality, often used for sheets in medieval and Tudor periods; name from Rennes, where originally made.

REEDINGS or REEDS. Term for grouping of two or more beads set closely in parallel lines, either raised above or flush with a general surface, effect being reverse of fluting (*q.v.*). For an early use of reeding *see* CHESTS OF DRAWERS, Fig. 15, dating from c. 1690. At end of 18th century reeding became favourite moulding, supplanting flute in bedposts, chair legs, pilasters, etc. J. C. R.

REGAL. *See* MUSICAL INSTRUMENTS.

REGENCY TASTE. The more intensive classical revival which set in during the last years of the 18th century in England and on the Continent; *le style Etrusque* of the later part of Louis XVI's reign exercised a considerable influence on the English development. Among Englishmen, Henry Holland, Sir John Soane and Thomas Hope, a friend of the architect Percier, gave an expression to domestic decoration which is distinct from the French Empire style, and is termed the Regency; though its dates do not fully coincide with the period during which George, Prince of Wales acted as Regent (1811-20). The style originated from a closer study of Roman interior decoration and remains (notably the discoveries at Herculaneum and Pompeii), and its exponents believed that they had captured not only 'the beautiful spirit of antiquity' (as Robert Adam had claimed) but the letter. It was an archaeological revival, not an adaptation. Holland was supplied with drawings of classical antiquity and ornamental detail by his pupil C. H. Tatham (*q.v.*) from Rome. The furniture made under his supervision or from his designs for Carlton House (1793 onwards) and Southill Park, Bedfordshire (1796–1806), is an original blend of Louis XVI and Graeco-Roman elements. The singularity of the movement under Hope's influence lay in the reproduction of classical types of furniture and the adaptation of Greek and Roman motives; and, preoccupied with this idea, Hope aimed at making objects of modern use—a fire-screen, bookcase and sideboard—congruous with the classical tradition. From the early years of the 19th century not only were the forms of furniture changed but a new ideal 'Grecian severity' was the aim of cabinet-makers. Following the evidence of reliefs, vase-paintings and bronzes, the school designed sofas after Roman beds, and candlestands after Greek or Roman tripods. For furniture for which there was no classical precedent, *e.g.* bookcases and sideboards, classic originals were adapted; dwarf bookcases were designed in sympathy with the taste for furniture *d'appui*; larger bookcases were designed like a temple façade. Archaic lion masks, the swan, the hocked animal leg as a support, the 'lion monopodium' characterised the new designs. A contemporary critic (*Edinburgh Review*, July, 1807) questioned the propriety of Hope's design for a fire-screen 'in the form of a Roman shield, adorned with the fulmen of Jupiter'; and a bronze tripod is illustrated by Hope with hinges and slides 'made to take to pieces and fold up after the manner of ancient tripods'.

Cabinet-makers discarded decoration with composition ornament and painting as less durable and less in accord with classical precedent than applications and inlays of metal. Carving was sparingly employed at this period and was usually restricted to classic ornament, often bronzed or gilt, a sign of the dominance of metal technique. An element evident in Sheraton's *Encyclopaedia* (1804–6) and in Hope's *Household Furniture* (1807) is that of Egypt, a reflection of the result of Bonaparte's expedition to Syria and Egypt, 1798–1801 (*see* EGYPTIAN TASTE). The Regency period included elements which could not be combined with the archaeological version of classical art.

The 'Gothic' style (which had been revived c. 1750) was again studied. Adumbrations of this style can be found in Sheraton's *Drawing Book* (1791–4) and more pronouncedly in the *Cabinet Dictionary* (1803). Gothic ornament is illustrated in a few plates of Sheraton's *Encyclopaedia* (1804), and in George Smith's *Household Furniture* (1808). The revived Gothic (which had its adherents as a 'national style') was encouraged by the considerable amount of building in the 'Gothic' and 'Castle' styles c. 1800–25. Among the earliest Regency work which can be definitely dated is some furniture made for Stourhead, Wiltshire, by the younger Thomas Chippendale, much of which can be identified by his bills (*see* CHAIRS, Figs. 191 and 193, and SIDEBOARDS, Fig. 17). The phases of Regency style may be studied in Sheraton's *Cabinet Dictionary* (1803), the incomplete *Cabinet-makers, Upholsterers and General Artists Encyclopaedia* (1804), Hope's *Household Furniture and Decoration* (1807), George Smith's *Collection of Designs for Household Furniture and Interior Decoration in the Most Improved and Elegant Taste* (1808), *see also* issues of Ackermann's *Repository* (from 1809); Clifford Musgrave *Regency Furniture* (1961); CHIPPENDALE, JUNIOR; HOLLAND; HOPE; SHERATON). M. J. (revised).

REREDOS. *See* CHIMNEY FURNITURE—FIREBACKS.

ROCOCO TASTE. Rococo is a word that first appeared in England c. 1830, as a vernacular term borrowed from France; it is now used as the equivalent of the French *rocaille*. The latter is the name given to the distinctive form of asymmetrical ornament evolved from the baroque (*q.v.*) during the regency after the death in 1715 of Louis XIV, and extensively used by the makers of furniture between 1720 and 1755.

It is a form interposed between the heavy, pseudo-classic, the *Romain en Perruque*, of Louis XIV, and the style *à la Grecque*, which succeeded it in the later years of Louis XV. Nicholas Pineau (1684–1754) and Claude Audran (1658–1734) may be counted among the chief pioneers. Later, in the designs of Juste-Aurèle Meissonnier (1696–1750) it was developed by the exploitation of violent asymmetry and contortion. The *rocaille* has been described as a return to nature, but it was really of the utmost sophistication, and in its logical disorder and subtle lawlessness owes nothing to nature beyond the circumstance that certain natural forms were pressed into its service as a foundation on which the new conventions were based. Rocks and shells dominate the style, and the name is held to derive from the elaborate grottos with which Catherine de' Medici adorned the Garden of the Tuileries, the makers of which were termed *rocailleurs*.

In the hands of the great French *ébénistes* many of the decorative accessories of furnishing assumed new and surprising shapes, in which the dominant lines were suggested through the agency of associated curves. By such means consoles, chandeliers, mirror frames, clock-cases and guéridons achieved a sense of movement without restlessness, of asymmetry with no loss of balance. In other pieces, *e.g.* chests, chairs and tables, the new style was fettered by the traditional demand for a rectangular basis, and could only express itself by elaboration of surface ornament. Mounts of gilt bronze, cast and chased, were important accessories of the *rocaille*. After the deaths of Meissonnier (1750) and Caffieri (1755), the style quickly degenerated and fell into disfavour.

It was a style which, in its more fanciful forms, was unsuited to the sober tastes of English patrons or the capacity of English craftsmen, who mostly lacked the requisite imagination and audacity necessary for its development, though they possessed the technical skill. In England ormolu mounts were sparingly used and were relatively simple save on the finest pieces.

The English derivation of *rocaille*, in spite of the difference in spirit and temper, may be said to have dominated furniture and decoration for nearly two decades. Matthias Lock (*q.v.*), carver and gilder, and his collaborator H. Copland (*q.v.*), the chief English pioneers in this field, were producing designs (ornaments, sconces, tables, etc.) as early as the mid-forties. In Chippendale's *Director* (1st ed., 1754) the rococo is dominant, and combined with excursions into the Gothic and Chinese tastes—the former variant having no parallel in the parent *rocaille*. A similar mixture of rococo and its offshoots is found in Ince and Mayhew's *Universal System* (1759–63) and other contemporary pattern-books.

In case-furniture—tables, commodes, bureaux—experiments in the rococo were mostly tentative and unsuccessful, failing conspicuously in rhythm of line. But in mirror frames, stands, sconces and girandoles, pieces in the production of

1. Design for rustic chair from Manwaring's Cabinet and Chair Makers' Real Friend and Companion, *1765.*

which carver and gilder combined, much of the spirit and *élan* of the original was captured. For mirrors more especially the whole characteristic repertory was drawn on—naturalistic ornament, animal motives, *coquillage*, 'cartouches, pierced and tattered', C scrolls and tortuous curves in an endless variety of combinations.

The style is still dominant in the third edition of the *Director* (1762), but the classical reaction had already set in (for rococo examples *see* MIRRORS, Fig. 46; STANDS, CANDLE, Fig. 15, and Fiske Kimball, *The Creation of the Rococo*, 1943).

ROSEWOOD. Various species of genus *Dalbergia*, to which kingwood (*q.v.*) belongs, are widely distributed. *Dalbergia nigra* and *D. latifolia* (from Brazil and East Indies respectively) appear to have been chiefly used in English furniture. Dark purplish brown with variegated figure; heavy, dense and durable. Referred to by Evelyn (*Sylva*, 1664) for inlaying, and used more often in Georgian times as veneer in bandings and small panels. In 1766 Chippendale supplied Sir Roland Winn at Nostell Priory, Yorkshire, with 'A Lady's commode writing table made of tulip and rosewood . . .'. A trade name, applied to a large number of genera and species.

RUNNER. Member of rectangular section sliding in groove or slot. Term often applied to narrow strips added along bottom edge of drawer sides in 18th century to give good running surface on framing. Flaps of bureaux and secretaires, when open, supported on runners termed by cabinet-makers 'lopers' (*see* CONSTRUCTION).

RUSHES. Stalks of common rush (*juncus*) used in medieval and Tudor times as covering on stone floors in great halls and private apartments of houses. 'Mattes of flagges', or plaited rushes, often used as mattresses for beds in Tudor period. Seats of chairs and stools sometimes covered with rushes in 18th century. In 1766 Chippendale supplied Sir Rowland Winn with '12 Rush bottom chairs'.

RUSH-LIGHT HOLDER. *See* CHANDELIERS.

RUSTIC FURNITURE. In the 18th century, furniture was specially designed in the 'rustic taste' for garden buildings. Summer-houses and temples, in which people supped or dined out of doors, were often elaborate and solidly built structures, and some of the objects intended for this purpose were also suitable for ordinary domestic use, *e.g.* Windsor chairs (*see* CHAIRS, WINDSOR.) Designs for such furniture are given by W. Halfpenny, Chippendale and Manwaring. In the *Director* (3rd ed., 1762) a seat and two chairs are illustrated, Chippendale recommending the latter for arbours, summer-houses and grottos. The materials is not specified, but 'the backs may be cut out of the Solid Board'. In the *Cabinet and Chair Makers' Real Friend and Companion* (1765) Manwaring shows a number of rustic seats, which he claims are 'the only ones of the kind that ever were published'. They are to be made 'with the limbs of Yew and Apple trees, as Nature produces them', but dry and well seasoned, the bark being peeled off and pieces of appropriate shape being selected (Fig. 1). Some are carved in extravagant style, while others are painted with landscapes and various pastoral conceits. For garden temples in the Gothic and Chinese tastes these 'rude branches and limbs of trees' were replaced by furniture more in accord with the character of the building.

RUSTICATION. Architectural treatment derived from masonry in which joints are worked with grooves or channels to make them conspicuous. Chamfered coin blocks, occasionally used at corners of 18th-century tallboys, produce similar effect.

SABICU, SACQUEBU (*Lysiloma sabicu*). Grown chiefly in Central America, similar in appearance to some growths of mahogany and rosewood; hard and heavy, chestnut-brown with darker stripes. Used very sparingly from c. 1750, chiefly as veneer in bandings, but in rare instances in solid construction, or pieces were entirely veneered with the wood (e.g. Library Table, V. & A. Mus., W. 28–1938).

SANDBURNING. *See* INLAY AND MARQUETRY.

SARCENET. Silken fabric, name said to derive from its first being made by Saracens. Introduced into England as early as 13th century, but not extensively used until much later. Common material for luxurious hangings and coverings in 17th century. Hardwick Hall, Derbyshire, inventory (1601) enumerates many quilts of sarcenet, and 'a tester for a field bed of crimson taffetie sarcenet with red silk frenge and foure curtins of crimson taffetie sarcenet to yt'. Many sarcenet covers and hangings at Ham House, Surrey, 1679.

SATIN. Silken fabric with glossy surface, produced by special manner of weaving. So much of the woof is brought uppermost that it gives a more lustrous and unbroken surface to the cloth than is obtained when the warp and woof cross each other more often. Satins were first imported from China into Europe, and appear to have been known in England as early as the 13th century. They did not become common until late in the Middle Ages, the *Wardrobe Account* of Edward IV showing that the prices of different coloured satins varied considerably, black satin costing 2s. a yard, and green as much as 8s. When made with the warp and woof of pure silk, it was used only for the most luxurious furniture; but a cheaper variety, with the woof of thread, termed 'satin of Bruges', is often mentioned in inventories, the name of the town being, generally, corrupted into 'Bridges'. At Howard House in 1588 there was 'one ould chaire of yelowe satten of bridges'.

Pure satin hangings appear to have been sometimes used for beds at this time. Robert Dudley, Earl of Leicester, ordered large quantities of various colours from the Low Countries (1579) and at Kenilworth Castle had a walnut bed with 'the ceelor, tester and single Vallaunce of crymson satten paned'. In 1672 'a white satin embroidered bed' was entered in the inventory of Cobham Hall, Kent. The production of satin in England was greatly stimulated by the advent of Huguenot immigrants (c. 1685). They probably introduced the practice of painting satin, and soon afterward the material thus treated is mentioned in inventories. In 1788 Hepplewhite writes in the *Guide* that in State rooms 'where a high degree of elegance and grandeur are wanted' bed-hangings are often made of satin, figured or plain. Sheraton recommends French printed satin for the 'figures in the tablets above the front rails' of his drawing-room chairs, and George Smith (*Household Furniture*, 1808) includes painted satin among the materials suitable for expensively furnished rooms.

SATINWOOD. A great variety of woods, very widely distributed, go by this name. *Chloroxylon swietenia* (East Indian satinwood) and *Xanthoxylun flavium* (West Indian satinwood) were species used in 18th century. Both of yellow tone and vary from plain grain to rich figure, latter having clearer, more transparent grain under polish or varnish. West Indian variety imported from Guiana some years before East Indian kind, and found as veneer in much fine furniture from 1765. Used very sparingly in solid, and not extensively for chairs until c. 1800. East Indian satinwood (from Ceylon) of pale yellow introduced late in 18th century, and used until largely supplanted by rosewood after 1800. For cabinet-makers preference given to western variety by Sheraton (*Cabinet Dictionary*, 1803) 'because of its breadth and general utility'. The other sort 'runs narrow and is used only for cross-bandings'.

SAY. Thin silk fabric, also woollen material similar to bayes (*q.v.*). Figures in both senses in 17th-century inventories, context generally suggesting character. Thus, at Hardwick Hall, Derbyshire 1601—bed with sarcenet hangings with 'a canapie of yellowe saye, stayned with birdes and antikes'; obviously silk.

SCAGLIOLA. Composition in imitation of marble and other ornamental stones, consisting of finely ground plaster of Paris mixed with solution of glue, and coloured to imitate particular variety, pieces of fibrous gypsum, marble, alabaster, porphyry, etc., being worked into substance; name 'derived from number of small pieces of marble (*scaglia*) employed. Capable of taking a very high polish, and, made into slabs, it was extensively used in 18th century, among other purposes, for furniture, particularly table tops. Traces of scagliola have been discovered in early Roman decoration, but the art was revived and brought to perfection by a celebrated Italian master mason, Guido del Conte (1584–1649), a native of Lombardy. Evelyn, when travelling in Italy in 1664, admired the floors he saw there of this compound, and wrote in his *Diary:* 'I have frequently wondered that we never practised

this in England for cabinets.' Probably the earliest extant examples of scagliola in England are the panels surrounding the fireplace in the Queen's Closet, Ham House, Surrey, dating between 1673 and 1675, and assumed to have been imported from Florence. At Wilton House, Wilts., there is a carved gilt side-table with scagliola top inlaid with playing cards and an envelope bearing the name of the Venetian painter Sebastiano Ricci, who came to London c. 1709.

In the 18th century there are many records of tables and commode tops of scagliola being purchased in Italy. A top of scagliola on a side-table formerly at Ditchley, Oxfordshire (*see* TABLES, SIDE, Fig. 29), was obtained for Lord Litchfield by his brother, Admiral Fitzroy Lee, at Leghorn in 1726. Horace Walpole states that scagliola 'is a composition which was made only at Florence by Father Hugford, an Irish Friar'; and writing to Sir Horace Mann in 1747 about a commission for tables he said: 'If the original friar can make them, I shall be glad; if not, I fancy the person would not care to wait so long as you mention for what would be far less handsome than mine.' Some years later this composition was available in England, the firm of Richter and Bartoli in Newport Street being, according to Sir William Chambers, 'the best makers of Scagliola'. A bill of the firm is extant for 'two statuary tables, inlaid scagliola according to Messrs Adam's disaing at 77 guineas each' (*see* M. Brockwell, *The Nostell Collection*, 1915).

The process of making these table tops and architectural features (columns, chimneypieces, etc.) was identical. In a letter, January 1769, from Sir William Chambers to Mr W. Hall, of Whitehall in Scotland, he gives a recipe for Venetian scagliola and adds: 'If it can be of use it will give me much pleasure.' The following is an extract:

> The composition for the foundation is Bitts of Tile or well baked brick and Bitts of Marble mixed with Lime of River flints —a Sufficient quantity to bring the whole to the Consistance of a paste. Then a finer paste of the same composition but with less of marble is laid on about one and a half inches thick and after having beat it for some time then strew in bits of Marble of different kinds and beat them into the paste, then when dry put on a paste composed of Powder of tiles, lime and soap-water for otherwise it never takes a polish, this lay on the thickness of a sheet of paper and smooth and polish it with a clear polished trowel before it drys, then rub it with Linseed oyl and a woollen cloth. N.B. The Italians give what colour they please by mixing with the paste, Brown, Red, Vermilion, Yellow Occar or any other colours that agrees with Lime.

A manufactory was started by an Englishman, Vincent Bellman, in London in 1790, and this scagliola was soon in much request for slabs, short columns and pedestals to hold busts, as most rare marbles could be counterfeited at comparatively small cost. Robert Adam employed scagliola often for decoration and furniture. George Smith (*Household Furniture*, 1808) recommends it for the tops of some of his small tables.

SCALING. Imbricated surface ornament resembling scales of fish; used in early 18th century on chairs, settees and console tables (*see* TABLES, SIDE, Fig. 25).

SCONCES and WALL-LIGHTS. A variety of lighting arrangements are included under this heading. Movable lanterns, candlesticks with screens, and fixed light-holders attached to walls have all, at different times, been designated 'sconces'. Johnson's *Dictionary* (1755) defines this word as

1. Sconce of glazed yellow earthenware, with two candle sockets; moulded in relief with royal arms and crowned Tudor rose between initials 'E.R.' c. 1600. (Brit. Mus.) 2. Silver Sconce; back-plate embossed with flowers and engraved in Chinese style; tray with contemporary coat of arms. By Will Gamble, London, 1665. Ht. 1 ft. ½ in., W. 5 in. (Col N. R. Colville.) 3. Brass Sconce: on central cartouche royal crown and cipher of Charles II. c. 1680. (Windsor Castle. By gracious permission of H.M. the Queen.)

'a pensile candlestick, generally with a looking glass to reflect the light'. The term 'girandole', derived from the Italian, appears in the late 17th century, and is comprehensive, embracing both branched candlesticks and fixed brackets bearing lights.

Medieval halls were lit by candlebeams and coronas, supplemented by torches, sometimes placed in iron frames against the walls; in illuminated MSS. a single candle is often shown set on an iron pricket above the fireplace (*see* CHANDELIERS, Fig. 1). By 1470 a form of sconce with branches was already known in France, and King René of Anjou possessed twelve made of latten, some with three nozzles, others with two. When the term is found in English at this period, it generally implies a portable candlestick, as in the *Book of St Albans* (1486): 'Clymbe to her with a sconce or a lanterne that hath bot oon light.' That sconces with backplates were already known on the Continent in the early 16th century is proved by a jewelled example once belonging to Catherine de' Medici, and now in the Louvre. Cavendish's description of those owned by Wolsey suggests a similar type: 'The plates that hung on the walls to give light in the chamber were of silver and gilt, with lights burning in them.' Contemporary English specimens do not survive, but a comparison of various entries relating to lighting arrangements in a single list of household goods sometimes enables the sconce type to be recognised. Thus, John Rede, Keeper of the Royal Wardrobe, 1577, owned several 'candilsticke plates of latten', in addition to ordinary candlesticks in his rooms. In the Hardwick Hall, Derbyshire, inventory (1601) their purpose is stated: there were 'fyftene plate candlestickes of copper to hang on the walls' in the wardrobe

alone, while there were others of brass in the hall. A few earthenware sconces survive from this period, although those made in more durable materials have perished. Fig. 1 (in the British Museum) is of glazed yellow ware, moulded with the royal arms and a crowned Tudor rose between the initials 'E.R.'

Wall-lights appear to have been generally of metal until the late 17th century, a backplate with a plain flat or convex centre surrounded by embossed ornament serving as a reflector. Early in 1662 Pepys records (*Diary*) that he spent most of the morning 'hanging up pictures, and seeing how my pewter sconces that I have bought will become my stayres and entry'. The diversity of pattern at this period is indicated by Randle Holme in his fanciful treatise on blazons (*The Academy of Armory*, pub. 1688), derived from familiar objects; he writes of some 'with Faces, others with Birds, Beasts, Fish, Trees amd Flowers, some with round or oval embossed works'. Silver wall-lights became fashionable after the Restoration. They were not an absolute innovation, for there were silver sconces on the walls at Hampton Court in 1572 (Cuningham's *Revels*), and among Charles I's plate in the Tower of London were 'four large hanging wall candlesticks', afterwards sold for £121 6s. 8d.

These late Stuart wall-lights may be divided into two main types—a shaped and embossed back, generally of oval form (Figs. 4 and 5), and an enriched truss or console from which the candle-branch springs (Fig. 9). Another variety, rarely made in silver, had a flat backplate and a projecting tray in which the candle-holder was set. A sconce of this kind, dated by the hall-mark 1665 (Fig. 2), is a very early example of chinoiserie,

4. *Silver Sconce; scrolled cartouche, with applied monogram, 'A.G.', between amorini, surmounted by earl's coronet; stand modern. c. 1695. (Messrs Crichton.)* 5. *Silver Sconce, one of set of eight with shield-shaped backplates; borders, pierced, chased and embossed with fruit and foliage, are surmounted by amorini; crowned cipher of William III on cresting. c. 1690. Ht. 1 ft. 6 in., W. 1 ft. (Keele Hall, Staffs.)* 6. *Carved and gilt Wall-Light, one of pair; cartouche headed by coronet bears crest of Earls of Radnor. c. 1690. (Bramshill, Hants.)*

oriental figures being combined with embossed floral ornament. This practical form, at a later period, is often found in base metals. When made for the Crown, silver was often unmarked, and in such cases the chronology of wall-lights is obscure, as earlier models were sometimes used. Thus, the amorini and pierced acanthus foliage in Fig. 5, one of a set formerly at Keele Hall, Staffordshire, are strongly reminiscent of Restoration plate, but on the cresting is the crowned cipher of William III. Several payments are recorded in the accounts of the first Lord Bristol for sets of silver sconces at this time. In 1699 he purchased from David Willaume eight such sconces for £175. In the state apartments at Windsor Castle there are a number of brass sconces, made for Charles II, that surpass most silver examples in elaboration of design (Fig. 3).

Occasionally the branch takes the form of an arm, the hand grasping the scroll from which the candle socket springs; or a hand alone is set back on the plate, as in Fig. 7. Among Daniel Marot's drawings are sconces intended to receive backplates of looking-glass or burnished metal, and resembling the silver type then fashionable in England; while several varieties of branched wall candlesticks for execution in either wood or metal are given in the designs of André Charles Boulle. They are termed 'girandoles', a word that appears in French royal inventories c. 1660 and was used in a comprehensive sense. Although the French name was not adopted until later, English examples resembling the designs of Bérain and his contemporaries are found in both wood and metal.

In a pair of gilt wall-lights (Fig. 6) this Continental influence is apparent. They are of baluster shape headed by a coronet, and a cartouche with the crest of Robartes, Earls of Radnor.

By this time sconces with backplates or reflectors of looking-glass had already become fashionable, and five of a large size in the Council Chamber at Kensington Palace are stated to have been 'old' when the inventory was drawn up in 1697.

7. *Sconce, decorated in blue and white enamel; scroll-shaped candle branch springs from clenched hand. c. 1665. Ht. 6½ in., W. 4½ in. (Col N. R. Colville.)*

8. *Glass Sconce in metal frame, one of pair; top decorated with star. c. 1700. (Percival Griffiths Coll.)*

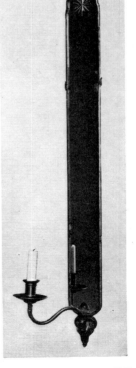

9. *Silver Wall-Light in form of truss, enriched with acanthus husks, and pendants of oak leaves and acorns. By Philip Rolless c. 1700. (Earl of Ilchester.)* 10. *Walnut Sconce framing panel of tent-stitch needlework, one of pair; brass candle branch terminate-in snake's head. c. 1700. Ht. 1 ft. 10 in., W. 1 ft. 2 in. (Percival Griffiths Coll.)* 11. *Silver Sconce, one of set of six; centre of back. plate embossed and chased with story of Actaeon; on cresting amorini support coronet of second Earl of Warrington. By Peter Archambo, London, 1730.*

The royal tradesmen supplied specimens decorated in the taste of contemporary mirrors, Gerreit Jensen charging £4 15s. for a pair of chimney sconces of wrought blue glass with double gilded branches for Lord Albemarle's lodgings in the same palace. The painting behind the glass known as *verre eglomisé* (*q.v.*) is clearly implied in the description of two large sconces 'scoloped, dimond cutt and engraved embollished with crimson and gold Mosaic work with flowers on the bodys of the Glasses', made by Philip Arbuthnot in 1703, as a gift from the Crown to the Emperor of Morocco. Such glass wall-lights were generally contained within metal borders. About this date Lord Bristol made a payment to the silversmith, David Willaume, 'for ye silver borders of eight sconces, for ye drawing-room'. A favourite early 18th-century type had a narrow back-plate of bevelled glass, straight or escalloped and ornamented with a diamond-cut pattern (Fig. 8.) Another variety, with the plate set in wood, was also in favour, and is mentioned in the Royal Accounts. In an inventory (1700) of the furniture of Henry Tomson of the Inner Temple 'a large sconce in a walnut-tree and gold frame' (*i.e.* parcel gilded) is entered among the dining-room furniture. Gumley and Moore provided for St James's Palace in 1722 'a paire of glass sconces with gilt frames and carved topps, with double brass arms'; while a few years later Benjamin Goodison supplied four large wall-lights of the same kind for the Princess Royal's use, 'hanging them up with a silk Line'.

Embossed and chased silver wall-lights continued to be made even at this period in a manner reminiscent of Restoration taste. Their diverse character is suggested by a list of plate at Kensington Palace in 1724, including:

Four pairs of Picture sconces
One pair of large Round Chimney sconces
One pair of chimney-sconces with crowns
Six small heart sconces
One pair of Sun sconces

The picture sconces mentioned perhaps represented a classical subject, like Fig. 11. The Lord Chamberlain's Warrant Book (p. 312) for December, 1729, contains an order for '6 Christial receivers for the Queen's silver sconces'. Simplified versions of these elaborate wall-lights were made in base metals generally with a plain convex-shaped plate set in a scrolled border.

Among varieties mentioned in early 18th-century inventories are 'Japan sconces', of which there were two at Dyrham Park, Gloucestershire, in 1710. A tent-stitch panel was occasionally framed for the backplate (Fig. 10), but the proximity of the candle explains the rarity of these needlework examples. In the carved and gilt gesso sconce (Fig. 12) the delicate embroidery on satin is protected by an original bevelled plate, the scrolled cresting having three ostrich feathers in the centre. These wall-lights were made c. 1729, when George II's son, Frederick, was created Prince of Wales. For his funeral in 1751 Goodison supplied a large number of black sconces, hiring them out at 3s. 9d. each.

During the early Georgian period many wall-lights were of carved and gilt wood, without a reflector, escalloped shells, masks and large acanthus scrolls generally forming part of the ornament. In a set of four gilt sconces at Knole, Kent (Fig. 14), of exceptional size, the massive scale and medley of ornament suggest William Kent's responsibility. The four candle-branches are quite inconspicuous in these grandiose and finely modelled examples. Candle-brackets surmounted by globes of glass were often fixed on the newels of 18th-century staircases and supplemented by wall-lights of similar character. In a pair of painted wood the scrolled branch, round which a serpent is twisted, springs from a bearded mask (Fig. 13).

About 1750 French taste dominated the design of wall-lights, the term 'girandole', generally adopted in trade catalogues, indicating the source of their inspiration. In them the prevailing ideal of asymmetry was fully realised, for their purpose permitted innumerable variations of form. A shaped looking-glass framed in columns and scrollwork sometimes served as a reflector, but often the branches were attached to an open-work background of carved and gilt wood, architectural detail and figure subjects being fantastically blended with rococo ornament. Among the designs of Lock and Copland are many wall-lights of this kind (Fig. 23). Both types are shown in the *Director*, a fine pair (Fig. 16) closely following a design (Pl. CLXXVIII in the 3rd edition 1762); and in Edwards and Darly's *Chinese Designs* (1754) pagodas, bells and mandarins are employed to give an oriental effect. In France chased bronze was a favourite material and, as ormolu had not attained to great excellence in this country before M. Boulton opened his works at Soho (1762), models of a French character were sometimes made in wood. The example in Fig. 17, formerly at Hagley Hall, Worcestershire, was probably carved by Thomas Johnson, and is distinctly English in design. It is based on Pl. 10 of Johnson's *One Hundred and Fifty New Designs* (1758).

Wall-lights are among the most expensive items in Chippendale's bills to Sir Edward Knatchbull, of Mersham Hatch, Kent, who, in 1767, paid £26 'for 2 large Gerandoles very richly carv'd and painted Blue and White with large Looking

14. *Gilt Wall-Light, one of set of four; carved with lion and female masks with feathered head-dresses, swags of drapery and bay leaves; four candle branches formed as serpents. c. 1730. Ht. 5 ft. 2 in., W. 2 ft. 2 in. (Knole Park, Kent.)*

12. *Gilt gesso Sconce, one of pair. c. 1730. (Mulliner Coll.)*
13. *Candle-Bracket of soft wood painted, surmounted by original glass globe. c. 1727. (Formerly at Belhus, Essex.)*

Glasses in the Backs, 2 Branches to each and Wrought Nozzles'. Several others were supplied at smaller prices, and when sending Sir Edward drawings for pier-glasses the firm wrote: 'Along with them you have a sketch of a very handsome Gerandole with Glass in the Back for your choice.' Occasionally a more ambitious treatment took the place of the favourite architectural detail, and in Ince and Mayhew's *Universal System* (1759–63) a girandole carved with the story of Phaeton is illustrated, the backplate being cut 'so that the several Rays will reflect the candle in so many different colours as to render it very beautiful'. One of a very large pair of sconces at Temple Newsam, Yorkshire, represents the rococo apotheosis of furniture of this kind (Fig. 18). The introduction of hound and stag suggests the responsibility of Lock or Johnson, whose partiality for animal motifs is evident in their designs.

The accumulation of different varieties, as the result of changing fashions, is noticeable in inventories of this period.

15. *Girandole, gilt and carved in rococo style.*
c. 1755. (Hartlebury Castle, Worcs.)

16. *Girandole, gilt and carved in rococo style.*
Closely follows plate CLXXVIII (centre)
in Chippendale's Director *(3rd ed.) 1762.*
Ht. 4 ft. ½ in. (The Marquess of Anglesey.)

17. *Girandole of pine, partly stained dark*
mahogany colour, in form of windmill
supported on rusticated arch; one of pair.
Based on design by Thomas Johnson. c. 1760.
Ht. 3 ft. 5 in., W. 2 ft. 2 in. (Formerly at
Hagley Hall, Worcs.)

18. *Girandole, one of pair; gilt and carved*
in rococo style. A stag and hound amid the
ornament. c. 1760. Ht. 6 ft. 10 in. W. 5 ft.
(Temple Newsam, Yorks.)

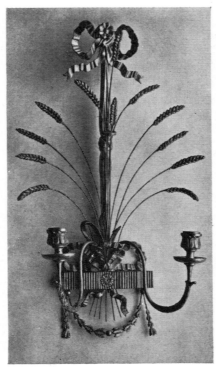

19. *Gilt Girandole with glass reflector, one of set of six; terminal female figures support swags of husks. Probably by John Linnell. c. 1775. (Osterley Park, Middx.)*

20. *Girandole of carved wood, composition and wire. c. 1790. Ht. 2 ft. 1½ in. (V. & A. Mus.)*

21. *Gilt Girandole in Regency style; part of the ornament in composition. c. 1800. Ht. 2 ft. 7½ in.*

22. (*Below*) *Glass Wall-Light with faceted branches and festoons of drops. c. 1800. (Mrs Wilfred Harris.)*

23. (*Right*) *Design for Girandole, from Lock and Copland's* New Book of Ornaments, *1768.*

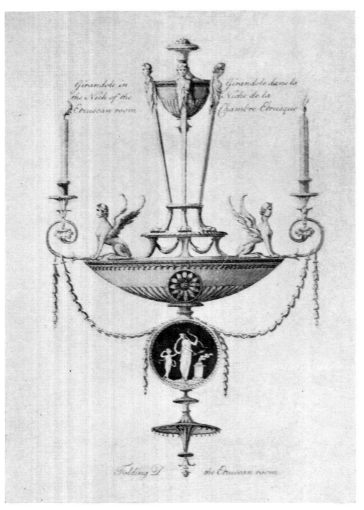

24. *Design for Girandole in Earl of Derby's house in Grosvenor Square 1773-4, from the Adam brothers'* Works in Architecture.

At the end of George II's reign Easton Maudit, Northampton-shire, contained 'glass sconces in gilt frames', others of glass only, and, in the drawing-room, a pair of gilt wood. Arthur Young, visiting Burghley House in 1768, noticed that one of the large rooms was hung with silver sconces. Among the original drawings of John Linnell (q.v.) a large number of sconces and wall-lights are included, ranging from fantastic versions of the rococo to more or less stereotyped patterns in the neo-classic style. Porcelain sconces were common in France at this period, and a few were made in English factories.

The fantastic wall-lights of the rococo period are in striking contrast to those produced in the subsequent classical phase. They were designed by Robert Adam to accord with his mirrors, and often formed part of the plaster wall decoration. In the saloon at Kedleston Hall, Derbyshire, there are examples of this type, candle-branches surmounting an oblong panel of infants framed in swags of husks. Several girandoles from the Earl of Derby's house in Grosvenor Square are illustrated in the *Works in Architecture*: the design in Fig. 24 shows one for the Etruscan Room 'elegantly carved and gilt; with the paintings by Mr Zucchi'. A set of six large carved and gilt girandoles in the Long Gallery at Osterley Park, Middlesex (Fig. 19), was probably designed and carried out by John Linnell, as he was responsible for other furniture in the house,

and the crossed swags of husks on the backplate is a motive which occurs in some of his designs. The wall-lights in Hepple-white's *Guide* (1788) are in a vernacular version of the classical taste. He writes that girandoles 'are usually executed of the best carverwork, gilt and burnished in parts. They may be carved and coloured suitable to the room.' They were often suspended from the wall by a carved ribbon, and by means of wire and composition ornament attained a remarkable degree of lightness and grace (Fig. 20). The words 'sconce' and 'giran-dole' do not appear in Sheraton's *Dictionary* (1803), but two are illustrated in the Accompaniment to the *Drawing Book* (1791–4), of such fragile character that they would be imprac-ticable in wood. At this time the more delicate ornament was modelled in composition on a wire core.

During the Regency carved and gilt girandoles were some-times surmounted by a large eagle with outspread wings, like contemporary convex mirrors (Fig. 21). In his *Household Furniture* (1808) George Smith shows wall-lights designed in this taste, one with an owl mask and birds' heads, another in an Adamitic style. He recommends that they should be finished in bronze and gold or wholly gilt, writing that 'in rooms of considerable length, where a single chandelier would not afford sufficient light, girandoles are fixed at the extremities of apartments in panels against the wall; they are equally service-able in apartments where chandeliers are not used'. Wall-lights of cut glass with S-shaped candle-branches became fashionable towards the end of the 18th century (Fig. 22).

SCREENS. The term screen has a comprehensive significance, embracing pieces of furniture of dissimilar form. Used to ward off draughts or the heat of a fire, they have been made of upright boards or a frame containing almost any material suitable for these purposes. In the Middle Ages they were usually fixtures, and the Exchequer Accounts contain entries for setting them up in the royal palaces. They were, however, sometimes movable, though it is seldom possible to deter-mine of what they were made. In the *Boke of Curtasye* (c. 1440) the Groom of the Chamber is charged to provide fuel for the chimney, and screens to protect his lord from the heat when seated at table. By Tudor times costly materials were already employed, and Henry VIII's inventory (1547) mentions 'four skrynes of purple Taphata, frynged with purple silke, standinge uppon feete of tymbr guilte silvered and painted'. Wicker was used for screens as well as chairs (Fig. 1) and at Hampton Court Palace in the Withdrawing Chamber there was 'a wycker skrine' among the King's furniture. Such screens must have remained in fashion, for fifty years later there were many in the chambers at Hardwick Hall, Derby-shire, and even Charles I's inventories enumerate a number. In the Wardrobe at Leicester House (1588) there was 'a skreen cloth of greene velvete, laid on with a little parchement lace of gould'; another was of 'painted Buckrame', also trimmed or 'laid aboute' with gold lace.

The variety of materials of which screens were made c. 1600 is suggested by the list of those at Hardwick Hall (1601). Some were elaborate, one in the best bedchamber having 'a cover for it of carnation velvet embroidered with golde and a golde fringe'. In less important rooms screens of buckram of coloured cloth and of wood were enumerated. The folding or hinged variety was already is use, and in the Hengrave

Hall (Suffolk) inventory of 1605 'one great foulding skrene of seaven foulds' is entered.

A number of elaborate pieces of needlework intended for screens were among Charles I's possessions dispersed after his execution, one embroidered all over with 'gold and silver with the Colours of England and Scotland joyned together' being sold for £7 5s. By this date the import of furniture from the East had already begun, and the King had 'two china skreens, gilt, one being broken'; while pieces of embroidery for others were of silk, or gold and silver 'china worke'. The oriental lacquer screens brought into England in Charles II's reign were often large, with as many as twelve folds, but separate panels were also imported. In 1689 the Earl of Bristol bought twelve leaves of 'cutt Jappan skreens'; buying a complete pair of screens, also of incised lacquer, a few years later. Advertisements of sales in the London press show that 'Lacquer'd boards for screens' and 'Screens set in Frames' formed part of the cargoes of East India merchantmen. When an inventory was drawn up in 1697 of the contents of Queen Mary's Lodgings at Kensington Palace, there were several 'India Chimney screens' in the late Queen's bedroom. These oriental screens soon became plentiful, even in country houses. They do not seem to have been often imitated in England, either in incised or raised lacquer, but a fine six-fold screen (decorated on both sides) is given in Fig. 2 and shows rare excellence of drawing and composition. The folding type was not always decorated with japan, various materials being used to form the panels. In 1671 John Casbert, a cabinet-maker to the Crown, charges £1 10s. 'for making a skreen with 6 leaves lined with canvas on both sides and joined with gold galloon and gilt nails'.

A very early instance of the tripod form is shown in Fig. 12, forming part of a set of chimney furniture in the Queen's Bedchamber at Ham House, Surrey, and described in the 1679 inventory as 'garnished with silver'. Though surviving specimens are scarce before the end of the century, screens of many kinds were made after the Restoration. Early in William and Mary's reign the accounts of the first Lord Bristol contain entries of 'a glass skreen for my niece Elwes', while among the furniture at St James's Palace was 'I sweet-wood wyar screene to put about a bed'.

At this date fire-screens with the uprights enclosing a sliding panel (later known as a 'horse' or 'cheval' screen) became fashionable; and two fine gilt examples (Figs. 3 and 4) are strongly imbued with French influence. In the screen from Hampton Court, which can be attributed to John Pelletier (q.v.), the carved strapwork is notably delicate, the balusters, supported on scrolled bases, recalling the decoration of contemporary silver plate. There is a sliding panel in Fig. 3 divided by a carved upright. In the King's Library at Kensington in 1697 there was a 'slidinge fire skreen, one side embroidered with silke', no doubt constructed on this principle, and there were others in different rooms, some having fringes of silver or gold. The royal accounts contain many entries of sums expended on fire-screens. When Kensington Palace was furnished for the occupation of William and Mary, Thomas Roberts (q.v.) supplied one of princewood (kingwood) 'wrought smooth and handsome'; while in 1713 he charged £2 5s. 'for a ffire screen made of the best Wallnuttree and polished' for Queen Anne's dressing-room at Hampton Court. This, probably, resembled a plain walnut example from Canons

1. *Virgin and Child by Robert Campin, showing circular Screen of wicker behind Virgin's head. Flemish. Before 1430. (Nat. Gallery.)*

Ashby, Northamptonshire (Fig. 5). Most of the elaborately carved fire-screens of this period are so French in character and design that their origin is open to doubt.

Fire-screens to match the other gilt furniture in Palladian houses of the early Georgian period are now very rare, but Fig. 6, like a side-table also formerly at Stowe, bears the crest and baron's coronet of Richard Temple, created Lord Cobham in 1714, and a Viscount in 1718. It can thus be dated within five years, and assigned with the table to James Moore (q.v.) on the evidence of style.

In a fine walnut cheval screen (Fig. 7) rococo influence is already perceptible. Most of these screens contained panels of needlework or tapestry, but other materials were also used. Thus, in 1732, Benjamin Goodison supplied the Princess Royal at St James's with 'two walnuttree fire screens with sliding frames covered with Indian paper on both sides'. At Chequers, Buckinghamshire, is a two-fold mahogany fire-screen containing four paintings signed 'F. Russell fecit, 1744,' three representing landscapes with ruins and figures, the fourth a view from St James's Palace. They were painted by a lady-in-waiting to Princess Amelia, one of George II's daughters.

Besides oriental screens, which are mentioned in almost every inventory of a great house c. 1700–50, many other varieties of folding screen were in use. Leather, painted in oils with birds and flowers in natural colours on a rayed or diapered gilt ground, was often used, and, although much of this material was imported from Spain or Flanders, a certain

amount was of English manufacture (*see* LEATHER), and the names of English makers have been found on some examples (Fig. 8). Sometimes the gilding was omitted and the leather entirely covered by figure subjects and landscapes in oils (Fig. 9). The remarkable six-leaved screen of Fig. 11 was painted in oils by a minor sporting artist, for John Knox, of Castle Rea, Sligo, in 1759. Knox is represented in several of the panels, which are in part derived from the series of large hunting scenes by Wootton in the hall at Longleat, Wiltshire. On the reverse are eighteen oil-sketches of race-horses, uniform in size, the framings, more elaborate than those in front, being in red and gold. In another fine folding screen (Fig. 10)

3. *Gilt Fire-Screen, supported on scrolled feet, with ornately carved cresting and stretcher; sliding panel of modern damask. c. 1690. (Knole Park, Kent.)* 4. *Gilt Fire-Screen; panel of red velvet with wide silver galon original. Attributed to John Pelletier. c. 1700. (Hampton Court Palace. By gracious permission of H.M. the Queen.)* 5. *Walnut Fire-Screen with sliding panel; needlework original. c. 1710. (Formerly at Canons Ashby, Northants.)*

6. *Fire-Screen, carved and gilt; cresting centres in crest and baron's coronet of Richard Temple, Lord Cobham. Attributed to James Moore. c. 1715. Ht. 4 ft. 9 in., W. 2 ft. 10 in. Formerly at Stowe. (V. & A. Mus.)*

7. *Mahogany Fire-Screen, needlework panel original. c. 1750. (Ditchley, Oxon.)*

8. *Leather six-fold Screen; decorated in gold and polychrome. Inscribed 'Holford, maker, at the Golden Lyon and Bull, St Paul's Churchyard.' Mid-18th century.*

9. *Leather six-fold Screen; decorated in oils with pastoral designs and subjects copied from pictures by Lancret and other French artists. Mid-18th century. Ht. 6 ft., W. 10 ft. 9 in. (V. & A. Mus.)*

10. *Four-fold Screen; upper panels worked with floral subjects in cross-stitch, borders simulating frames; fretted arabesques and acanthus below laid on ground of plain red fabric. c. 1750. Ht. 8 ft. 6 in., W. 9 ft. 4 in.*

11. *Six-fold Screen; hunting scenes painted by Richard Roper, signed and dated 1759; framework carved with rococo ornament and coloured olive green parcel gilt. Ht. 7 ft. 6 in. (Mrs Jersey de Knoop.)*

12. *Iron 'Screen-Stick' of tripod form, with silver finials, described in inventory of 1679; tapestry panel of later date. c. 1675. (Ham House, Surrey.)* 13. *Mahogany tripod Pole-Screen; panel of tent-stitch needlework framed in ribbon and rosette mouldings; legs carved with floral pendants and dolphin heads. c. 1750. Ht. 5 ft. 3 in., W. 2 ft. 2 in. (Percival Griffiths Coll.)* 14. *Mahogany tripod Pole-Screen, with panel of tent-stitch needlework in frame with pagoda cresting. c. 1760. Ht. 5 ft. 9½ in., W. 2 ft. 3½ in. (Holyrood Palace, Midlothian.)* 15. *Mahogany tripod Pole-Screen with panel of tent-stitch needlework; shaft and base pierced in Gothic taste. c. 1760. (Fred Skull Coll.)*

16. *Mahogany tripod Pole-Screen with panel of tent-stitch needlework; shaft formed of engaged columns. c. 1765. (Padworth House, Berks.)* 17. *Painted tripod Pole-Screen with panel of silk embroidery; designed by Robert Adam, 1777. (Osterley Park, Middx.)*

of date c. 1750 the upper panels, with their elaborate borders, are finely worked in cross-stitch on a rich red ground, while those below are framed in carved mahogany arabesques and acanthus. Paper printed with landscapes and figures in oriental taste was among the materials used for this type. As early as 1700 the Blew Paper Warehouse in Aldermanbury, London, advertised a 'great variety of Skreens' in their handbills, among 'other things of Curious figures and Colours'. In 1750 Benjamin Goodison made a 'six leaf Indian Picture Screen' for Kensington Palace, and about the same time Edward Griffiths supplied the fourth Earl of Cardigan with another containing the same number of folds 'on a mahogany frame to mount 18 Pictures'. The royal accounts contain many entries of expenses for repairing folding screens.

Tripod fire-screens with a panel adjustable by a knob on the pole became common in the first half of the 18th century. They resembled small contemporary tables constructed on the same principle, the shaft being generally vase-shaped at the base and the tripod cabriole finishing in claw feet or, more rarely, in paws. As late as 1748 Edward Griffiths supplied 'Wallnuttree pillers and claws' to the Earl of Cardigan, who was then furnishing Deene Park, Northamptonshire, and his town house. Fig. 13 shows an exceptionally fine and ornate specimen. The large basket-grates then in common use gave out such intense heat that some form of protection was needed,

and Samuel Johnson wrote at the end of George II's reign, 'we have twice as many fire-screens as chimney's'.

The 'horse' folding and tripod types are all illustrated by Chippendale. He explains that those standing on four feet are commonly called 'Horse-Fire-Screens' and the woodwork 'should be gilt in burnished gold'. Fig. 19 shows a fine mahogany example, apparently based on a plate in the *Director* (1st ed., 1754), the frame (from which later gilding has been removed) being carved in florid rococo taste. Sometimes the panel was 'intended to slide up, out of the pillars that are in each side', but here the contemporary needlework is a fixture.

Smaller folding screens, with two leaves only, were now becoming fashionable, and are illustrated in the *Director* (Fig. 28). They are mounted on slender legs connected by a stretcher, and where the frame is of lattice-work, it is to be 'cut through' to take the paper. Some years later one of these screens was supplied by Benjamin Parran (*q.v.*) for St James's Palace, and he states that for the double panels in each leaf he 'used four mandarin India pictures, 4 India flower potts, with borderings to each'. Few of this fragile type have survived.

Chippendale claims that his tripod screens, termed by him 'pillars and claws', are 'among the best of the sort'. Two fine examples of the decade 1750–60 are represented in Figs. 14 and 15. The screen at Holyrood has scroll feet headed by pierced brackets. The pole of such ornate stands generally terminates in a finial—a pineapple or an ivory urn. From c. 1760 the standard was sometimes formed of engaged columns (Fig. 16), or was flanked at the base by cusping, the legs being often of the scrolled form, which, at this time, usually replaced the cabriole.

18. *Mahogany Folding Screen, cresting carved with scrolls and acanthus; repeated below tapestry panels. c. 1765. Ht. 4 ft. 3 in., W. 4 ft. 2½ in. (Frank Partridge & Sons.)*

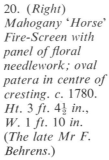

19. (*Left*) *Mahogany Cheval Fire-Screen carved with rococo ornament containing panel of tent-stitch needlework. Based on plate CXXVII in* Director (*1st ed. 1754*). *c. 1755. Ht. 3 ft. 2 in., W. 2 ft.* (*V. & A. Mus.*)

20. (*Right*) *Mahogany 'Horse' Fire-Screen with panel of floral needlework; oval patera in centre of cresting. c. 1780. Ht. 3 ft. 4½ in., W. 1 ft. 10 in.* (*The late Mr F. Behrens.*)

21. (*Left*) *Mahogany 'Horse' Fire-Screen with sliding panel of wool-work. c. 1790. Ht. 3 ft. 4½ in.* (*Edward Hudson Coll.*)

22. (*Right*) *'Horse' Fire-Screen, carved and gilt. Probably designed by Henry Holland. 1795.* (*Southill, Beds.*)

Screens characteristic of the neo-classic style are to be found in great houses designed by Adam. At Osterley Park, Middlesex, in the Tapestry Room, is a two-leaved screen framing tapestry similar to the Gobelins hangings on the walls; while in the Etruscan Room is one of tripod form (Fig. 17) matching the general scheme of decoration, and based on an Adam design in the Soane Museum entitled 'Fire screen for Mrs Child'. Screens formed a convenient means of displaying prints, water-colour drawings and paintings on silk. Even fragments of earlier tapestry were sometimes used; and in Horace Walpole's *Description of Strawberry Hill* (1784) among the screens mentioned is one with two leaves containing part of a map of Surrey and Middlesex, which, 'is a piece of the first tapestry woven in England, and came from Weston in Warwick, the seat of the Sheldons'.

By the date of Hepplewhite's *Guide* (1788), the classical reaction had greatly modified the design of pole and cheval firescreens. There was a tendency to greater lightness of construction in both varieties. The curved legs or solid base of the pole type were now generally weighted to ensure stability, the small oval or shield-shaped panels being adjusted by means of a ring and screw or a pulley. Hepplewhite observed that these screens 'may be ornamented variously with maps, Chinese figures, needlework, etc.,' and are made of mahogany or japanned wood. Gathered silk was among the favourite materials for the panels, *e.g.* Fig. 24, the standard, of pillar form, resting on an inlaid circular base, as in two designs shown in the *Guide*. The 'horse-screens' illustrated by Hepplewhite are of a severe character and work on a similar principle, sliding in grooves in the inner side of the uprights. An example based on a Hepplewhite design is seen in Fig. 21; another, a few years earlier, has a fixed panel and a cresting with an oval patera in the centre (Fig. 20).

Gilt fire-screens are exceptional at this date, but Fig. 22 shows one at Southill Park, Bedfordshire, probably designed by Henry Holland (*q.v.*). In the carved ornament—notably the water-leaf motif in which the stretcher centres—the influence of the *Directoire* style is already apparent.

23. *Tripod Pole-Screen of painted satinwood; shield-shaped panel of painted silk. c. 1785.* 24. *Pole-Screen veneered with harewood and satinwood; oval panel filled with gathered silk. c. 1790. Ht. 4 ft. 9 in. (F. Behrens Coll.)* 25. *Mahogany tripod Pole-Screen, shield-shaped panel of silk embroidery; shaft supported on columns and reeded lion-paw legs. c. 1795. (J. Thursby Pelham Coll.)* 26. *Rosewood Pole-Screen, carved and gilt; panel painted with arabesques in water-colours; probably designed by Henry Holland. c. 1805. (Southill, Beds.)*

Sheraton in the *Drawing Book*, 1791–4, enters fully into the mechanism by which his screens can be raised and lowered, producing designs readily distinguishable from those of his predecessors (Figs. 29 and 30). He writes that in the pole type a pulley is let into the hollow rods 'and a weight being enclosed in the tassel, the screen is balanced to any height'. Those framing fine prints or worked satin should be provided with a glass. Sheraton claims that a 'lyre screen' revolving on a swivel so that it can be turned to any position without moving the stand 'is constructed upon an entire new plan'. The lyre ornament is to be carved in bas-relief or burnished, 'which when planted on to a blue silk or satin ground cannot fail to produce a fine effect'. The sizes recommended for this type are

29 and 30. Two designs for Pole-Screens, from Sheraton's Drawing Book, *1791-4. 31. Design for Pole-Screen in Egyptian taste, from George Smith's* Household Furniture, *1808.*

from a carved cross-bar on the pole: rosewood was the favourite wood for this type. Cheval screens were decorated in a similar manner, and are said by Smith to be appropriate for drawing-rooms if executed wholly in carved work or gilt and varied with bronzed ornaments on a gold ground. Those made of mahogany may be inlaid with ivory. A similar type, with 'frames to slide out on the sides' and with the panels of plain coloured stuff, 'answers extremely well for Dining Rooms'.

27 and 28. Designs for Pole- and Folding-Screens, from Chippendale's Director, 1754.

about 3 ft. 6 ins. high and about 1 ft. 6 ins. wide. The designs in George Smith's *Household Furniture* (1808) are essays in the anglican version of the Empire style, and attempt to give a classical impress to this form of furniture (Fig. 31). Pole-screens, being 'articles of general use', are said to admit of every species of decoration, and may be made entirely gilt, of bronze and gold, japanned, or of mahogany, rosewood or satinwood, according to the character of a room. If expense is no object, the panels may be carved in solid wood ornamented with painted decoration; or, where the stands are of mahogany without gilding, lutestring flutes, with tassels to match, are recommended.

A distinctive feature of screens in the Regency style is the solid base or block on which the pole rests—often triangular in plan. The pole-screen (Fig. 26) was probably among the furniture designed by Henry Holland for Southill at the end of his career.

About this time the banner type became fashionable, a piece of damask or velvet hung with tassels being suspended

SCREENS, CANDLE. Candlesticks with glass shades were already in use c. 1750, but, in preference to this arrange-

1. Mahogany Candle Screen, panel notched at edges; turned shaft on tripod with paw feet. c. 1750. Ht. 1 ft. 3 in. (Percival Griffiths Coll.)

ment, small screens were occasionally made to protect the candle from draught; they were sometimes made on the principle of a pole-screen (Fig. 1, p. 441), while others were of the 'horse' type, with a solid panel sliding up and down between the uprights.

SCREWS, METAL. The use in furniture of tapering metal screws with slotted heads dates from late 17th century, early examples being small brass screws with hand-filed irregular thread (horizontal in profile), used in addition to brass pins to secure hinges. From c. 1760 lathe-made screws were made and were used for fixing hinges of gate-leg and other folding tables, and for securing fixed tops of tables; the spiral diminishing towards the point becomes more noticeable. Machine-made screws with gimlet-pointed heads came into general use c. 1850 (*see* CONSTRUCTION). Brass screws were used for visible hinges, though still in conjunction with brass pins, as on the H-type of hinge on cupboard doors.

SCRIPTOR, SCRUTOIR. Anglicised forms of escritoire —writing cabinet. In 1679 inventory, two cabinets of this kind at Ham House, Surrey, with falling fronts and mounted on stands are described as 'scriptors'. In inventory of contents of Canons, Middlesex (1725), for first Duke of Chandos, walnut 'scriptors' are entered as being in several rooms. John Radcliffe (1650–1714), the celebrated physician, in a postscript to his will (Oct. 22, 1714) refers to 'my great Scrutore' (*see* BUREAUX).

SCUTTLE. *See* CHIMNEY FURNITURE—COAL BOX.

SEATS. *See* BENCHES AND FORMS, CHAIRS, SETTEES, STOOLS.

SECRETAIRE, SECRETARY. *See* BUREAUX.

SERGE. Woollen twilled stuff manufactured on loom, often used for covers of furniture in late 17th and 18th centuries. Curtains sometimes made throughout of this material. In a room at Dyrham Park, Gloucestershire (1710), elbow chairs had 'red serge covers'. Chippendale's bills to Sir Edward Knatchbull contain several entries of 'Fine Buff Serge Cases' for stools and chairs.

SERPENTINE FRONT. Undulating curved surface, centre generally convex, ends concave. Serpentine curves, demanding great skill in construction and laying of veneers, adopted c. 1750 in place of previous rectangular forms, to secure greater elegance of outline. Seat-rails of chairs and friezes of side-tables sometimes made in this form; commodes, clothes presses and chests of drawers of that period often found with serpentine fronts. In chintz bedroom at Castle Ashby, Northants., in 1774, 'a mahogany serpentine chest of drawers'. Considerable variety found in arrangement of curves. Serpentine front largely superseded by square or semicircular forms at end of 18th century (*see* COMMODES, Figs. 15 and 27).

SETTEES AND SOFAS. The seats included under this heading are closely related. As the words are now understood, a settee implies a seat with a back and arms to hold two or more persons; while a sofa, though often of similar construc-

tion, is of large size and made to allow reclining. (For the first phase of the evolution, *see* SETTLES.)

'Sopha' is of Eastern origin; applied to a movable seat, it first appears in French literature and inventories c. 1690, but not in English until a few years later. In the East it was merely the dais or platform on which the Grand Vizier sat cross-legged in his audience hall, the person he was receiving occupying a cushion before him on the floor. As early as 1625 Purchas (*Pilgrimes*) alluded to 'a sofa spread with very sumptuous carpets of Gold . . . upon which the Grand Vizier sitteth'. The term settee, also, does not seem to have been used before the early years of the 18th century, when it is found in advertisements (*e.g. London Gazette*, No. 5494/4, 1716). Couches and day-beds are, however, described in contemporary inventories, and, probably, the compilers did not differentiate between them and large upholstered seats with a back and arms. The Dyrham Park, Gloucestershire, inventory of 1710 mentions five couches in different rooms, and it is unlikely that they were all of day-bed form.

Towards the end of the 16th century padded seats were evolved from the settle, this improvement coinciding with the introduction of upholstered furniture into luxuriously appointed houses. The earliest surviving seats of this type are at Knole, Kent, and a well-known example, which combines the dual functions of settee and couch, the end letting down on ratchets, is illustrated under COUCHES AND DAY-BEDS (Fig. 2). In Fig. 1 the wings are immovable, the legs and stretchers resembling those of contemporary farthingale chairs, and the upholstery corresponding with that of the Knole day-bed. Among the furniture of this period at Knole there is also another small settee or double chair, the forerunner of a type which later became very popular. The terms 'love seat' and 'courting chair', now applied to seats of this form, have no contemporary authority.

In their structural lines the severe rectangular seats, covered with leather or turkeywork and made to match oak Cromwellian chairs, resemble settles, but the backs and seats are not solid, the upholstery being stretched and nailed over coarse canvas. They may, thus, be classified either as settles or settees (*see* under SETTLES, Fig. 5). Occasionally they were made in walnut, and in Fig. 2 legs and uprights are formed of bobbin turning, the original leather covering being replaced by modern velvet.

With the return of Charles II (1660) the demand for luxurious furniture based on continental types led to a rapid and continuous development in this form of seat. The first variety was formed by combining two or three chair-backs, the arms being placed at either end of the seat. Genuine specimens are rare, but one from Bramshill Park, Hampshire (Fig. 4), matches a set of high-backed chairs, the backs being filled with split balusters. Made of beech or walnut and structurally weak, no doubt many similar specimens have perished. At Holyrood Palace there is a contemporary oak settee (Fig. 3). Here a third arm divides the backs, the middle upright being made thicker than those at either end to receive it.

Towards the end of the reign another variety, luxuriously padded and covered in silks and velvets, *en suite* with chairs and stools, was introduced. The backs rose well above the occupants and effectively set off gay costumes, tall head-dresses and periwigs, their height being reduced when tie-wigs and powder became the vogue. From this time onward the evolution of the woodwork corresponds closely with that of chairs.

In the fully developed Stuart settee there are often wide wings at the corners of the back, large comfortable padded rolls replace the wooden arms hitherto employed and the seats are filled with squab cushions. An example from Holyrood Palace, entirely regilt (Fig. 5), slightly precedes this development. The gold embroidery, in which are introduced two ducal coronets, with the cipher C.H., has been re-applied with modern fringe on new material. The cipher also appears on the ornate cresting and front stretchers, enclosed within the Garter; needlework and carving no doubt commemorating the Duke of Hamilton and Chatelherault, 'Keeper of the Palace of Holyrood', a hereditary office his descendants still retain. Definitely French in character, the treatment, like that of much furniture in Scotland, suggests an immigrant craftsman.

The next important innovation was the division of the back into chair shapes, which, though general at the end of Charles II's reign, was not universal. In Fig. 6 the *gros-point* covers are original, and were worked, according to tradition, by the wife and daughters of the Earl of Nottingham, the wings and outward curving arms being often adopted on both settees and armchairs at the end of the century.

When needlework was not used as a covering, velvet or damask was often adorned with elaborate fringes. Many yards of this costly trimming, composed of innumerable small tassels, edged the backs and seats of late Stuart settees; while, in some instances, fringed valances or 'bases' conceal the seat-rail. In a small settee (Fig. 7) the back is not divided into chair form, the cross-stitch covers being also elaborately fringed. The magnificent example formerly at Hornby Castle, Yorkshire (Fig. 10), in design and upholstery matches a day-

1. *Settee covered with crimson velvet fastened to beech framework by gilt nails and trimmed with crimson fringe; wings at sides. c. 1610-20. Ht. 3 ft. 5 in., L. 3 ft. 8 in. (Knole Park, Kent.)*

bed already described and illustrated (*see* COUCHES). Inspired by French taste, the straight back is headed by three scrolled escutcheons bearing the cipher and coronet of the first Duke of Leeds, and carved arms, ending in volutes, surmount solid upholstered sides. The wedge-shaped bolsters and cushions, of which originally there were five, prove it

2. *Walnut Settee; stretchers and uprights of knobbed turning; upholstery modern. c. 1660. (Francis Mallett.)*

3. *Oak Settee of double-chair form, with spiral turning and royal crowns flanked by scrolls. c.* 1680. (*Holyrood Palace, Midlothian.*)
4. *Walnut Settee of double-chair form; splats filled with split balusters; woodwork painted black picked out with floral patterns. c.* 1685. *Ht. 4 ft. 6 in., L. 4 ft. 4 in.* (*Formerly at Bramshill Park, Hants.*)

was intended to be used either as a seat or for repose at full length.

At the end of the century several varieties of back were in fashion: the division into chair form was, perhaps, the most common, but backs were also straight and, more rarely, elaborately shaped, with the chair motive omitted. In Fig. 9, formerly at Wrest Park, Bedfordshire, the high projecting wings recall an earlier fashion. This late Stuart group concludes with one from Lyme Park (Fig. 8). The back rolls over and has a deep semi-circular dip in the centre, its height providing an excellent field for the needlework representing flowers issuing from fantastic vases. These early upholstered settees with their multiple curves show remarkable fertility of invention in design. Some specimens are long enough to permit

5. *Settee of gilded wood; cipher and Garter of Duke of Hamilton and Chatelherault on elaborately carved stretchers and cresting; coronet and monogram re-applied and gilding modern. c.* 1680. (*Holyrood Palace, Midlothian.*) 6. *Walnut Settee, covered in contemporary cross-stitch needlework; elaborately scrolled front stretchers, fluted pillar legs on scroll feet. c.* 1690. (*Burley-on-the-Hill, Rutland.*)

7. *Walnut Settee, covered in cross-stitch needlework trimmed with galon and fringed; fluted pillar legs united by looped stretchers. c. 1690. Formerly at Hampton Court, Leominster. Ht. 4 ft. 6½ in., L. 5 ft. 2 in., Depth 3 ft. (V. & A. Mus.)*

8. *(Above right) Walnut Settee, with shaped and divided back and scrolled arms; woodwork and original embroidery show French influence. c. 1695. (Lyme Park, Ches.)*

9. *Walnut Settee, or sofa, covered in original needlework; pillar legs and serpentine stretchers. c. 1690. (The late Lt-Col L. C. D. Jenner.)*

10. *Gilt Sofa, covered in flowered Genoa velvet, trimmed with tasselled fringe; scrolled escutcheons bear cipher and coronet of Thomas Osborne, first Duke of Leeds; taper legs united by oval stretchers. c. 1695. Ht. 3 ft. 7½ in., Depth 2 ft. 11 in. (Formerly at Hornby Castle, Yorks.)*

445

11. *Settee with straight back covered in original needlework; plain cabriole legs and turned stretchers. c. 1710. (Formerly at Bramshill Park, Hants.)*

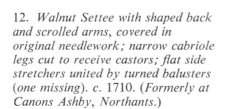

12. *Walnut Settee with shaped back and scrolled arms, covered in original needlework; narrow cabriole legs cut to receive castors; flat side stretchers united by turned balusters (one missing). c. 1710. (Formerly at Canons Ashby, Northants.)*

reclining, and would now be termed sofas; but one of the earliest English references to a piece of movable furniture called by this name occurs in the royal accounts for 1700, when Thomas Roberts (*q.v.*) made '4 large Sophas' for Hampton Court, and charged £3 for mending 'guilte Chaires and sophas in the long Gallery'. In 1702 this joiner supplied 'two large saffaws carved' to Chatsworth, Derbyshire.

Shortly after Queen Anne's accession cabriole legs supplanted the varieties hitherto fashionable, and the design of upholstered settees and sofas underwent considerable modification, the backs gradually becoming low and straight in contrast with the curves of the woodwork. The narrow legs, plain, or carved on the knees with the escallop shell, were at first united by simply turned stretchers, but towards the end of the reign

they were generally discarded. In Fig. 12 a country origin perhaps accounts for the shape of the back, and the woodwork matches that of a set of chairs (*see* CHAIRS, Fig. 67). The feet have been cut to receive castors. The woodwork is the only guide to the chronological arrangement of late Stuart settees or sofas, for often the shape was, apparently, governed by the fancy of makers and their patrons.

Towards the end of Anne's reign the design becomes more restrained, and the low back, newly introduced, is seen in Fig. 11; the woodwork is severely simple. A popular 18th-century type, now commonly termed 'love seat', is shown in Fig. 13, the legs being without stretchers and delicately inlaid. One of a pair of this kind (Fig. 14) forms part of a set of gilt walnut furniture. It is exceptional in both design and up-

13. *Walnut 'Love Seat' covered in contemporary needlework; cabriole legs delicately inlaid. c. 1715. (Frank Green Coll.)* 14. *Gilt 'Love Seat', one of pair; original coverings of cloth of gold and silver threaded with coral silk lines; cabriole legs carved on knees with cabochon and trefoil ornament. c. 1720. (Formerly at Glemham Hall, Suffolk.)*

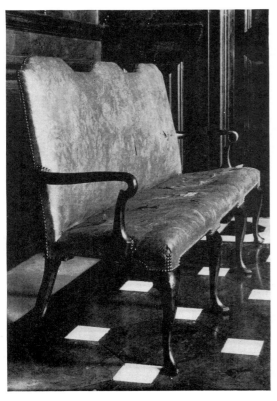

15. *Walnut Settee with shaped back, covered with stamped leather, silver on light green ground; scrolled wooden arms and plain cabriole legs. c. 1715. (Formerly at Stoke Edith, Herefords.)* 16. *Walnut Settee covered with Soho tapestry; probably by Joshua Morris. c. 1725.*

17. *Walnut Settee, parcel gilt, part of set; covered in green velvet; cabriole legs with hoof feet; pendants below seat rail broken. c. 1715. (Houghton Hall, Norfolk.)*

18. *Settee of double-chair form, veneered with figured burr walnut; splats shaped and headed by carved crestings; arms finish in eagles' heads. c. 1720. (Percival Griffiths Coll.)*

holstery, the woodwork being influenced by *Régence* taste. The covering is a woven fabric of gold and silver threads with coral silk arabesques, while the slender cabriole legs, carved on the knees with cabochon and trefoil ornament, end in decorated volutes.

Plain wooden arms had been out of fashion since Charles II's reign, but they were reintroduced early in the 18th century and from then on were often adopted for upholstered seats (Fig. 15).

In large houses sets of chairs and stools were generally supplemented by a pair of settees. About 1720 Lady Coventry, shortly after the death of her husband, offered for sale to Peter Legh, of Lyme, a set of eight walnut chairs and a settee. She wrote that the settee cost more than eight pounds without the damask, double the price of the chairs. One of a pair (Fig. 16) is covered with brilliant polychromatic tapestry, of Soho manufacture, probably by Joshua Morris and remarkable for the high quality of the design and draughtsmanship. A specimen from Houghton Hall, Norfolk (Fig. 17), forms part of a set (*see* CHAIRS, Fig. 72). Until c. 1725, when upholstered

settees were mentioned in inventories, the woodwork is generally stated to have been of walnut. In 1731 the drawing-room of the Burlington Street house of the Countess of Warwick contained a 'Walnuttree settee', part of a set, the whole 'covered with yellow damask, and serge false cases'.

Shortly before this time chair-back settees, of which the appearance under Charles II has already been noted, were reintroduced, and for the rest of the century rivalled the upholstered variety in popularity. Early specimens were of double chair-back form and made in walnut, a wood generally abandoned for mahogany c. 1735. These new and fashionable seats closely follow the evolution of contemporary chairs: in some cases the pattern exactly corresponds with that of chairs. At first the vase-shaped splats were plain and generally veneered with finely figured burr walnut; but later they developed acanthus scrolls on either side, and were occasionally united to the curved uprights by a horizontal extension (Fig. 20). At the junction of the hooped backs a shell was sometimes introduced, repeating the ornament on crestings and seat-rail (Fig. 20). It is unlikely that many of these walnut settees

19. *Walnut Settee of double-chair form; vase-shaped splats divided by single upright; seat-rail carved with satyr masks; cabriole legs with hoof feet. c. 1730. (Percival Griffiths Coll.)*

with eagle-headed arms or masks on the seat-rail (Fig. 19) were made before 1720.

A decade or so later triple chair-backs were occasionally made both in walnut and mahogany, the greater strength and resilience of the latter wood being well adapted for seats of this size. A period of about fifteen years, nearly equal to the duration of the fashion for lion-mask furniture, separates Fig. 21 from the smaller example in Fig. 22. In one the splats are still of simple vase shape, but in the other they are opened out into four uprights, a treatment which began c. 1740 and led to the subsequent openwork developments. The pronounced curves of the early hoops merged into each other with charming effect, but when square forms were generally adopted a satisfactory fusion became more difficult. At this stage of the evolution the chair-back motif is generally preserved complete; each upright being carried down separately to the seat, and the top rail forming the only connecting link. When a single upright divided the splats, owing to the width of the back,

20. *Mahogany Settee; splats connected with uprights and carved with foliated whorls; scallop shell motif predominates in decoration. c. 1720. (E. Mallett Coll.)*

21. *Settee of triple-chair form, veneered with burr walnut; arm-supports scroll outwards; cabriole legs carved with lions' masks and paw feet. c. 1730. (Percival Griffiths Coll.)*

22. *Mahogany Settee, of double-chair form; top rail finishes in whorls; splats pierced; below seat-rail acanthus-carved aprons; lion motifs and rococo ornament. c. 1745. Ht. 3 ft. 1½ in., L. 4 ft. 8 in., Depth 2 ft. 1 in. (S. B. Joel Coll.)   23. Mahogany Settee of double-chair form; openwork splats divided by single upright and top rails ending in volutes; cabriole legs and foliated ornament. c. 1750. (Percival Griffiths Coll.)*

24. *Mahogany Settee; backs and arms carved with lattice-work in Chinese style; legs and stretchers imitating bamboo. c. 1760. Ht. 3 ft. 2½ in., L. 5 ft. 4½ in. (V. & A. Mus.)*

25. *Mahogany Settee, of double-chair form; backs carved with ribbon-pattern and the cabriole legs with rococo ornament; covered in contemporary needlework. c. 1755. Ht. 3 ft. 3½ in., L. 4 ft. 2 in., Depth 2 ft. (V. & A. Mus.)*

an impression of emptiness is liable to result (Fig. 23).

Examples in the Chinese taste, c. 1750–65, embody motifs similar to those of chairs in that vogue. In a remarkable combination of strength and delicacy (Fig. 24) the curved uprights of the central chair-back at the apex cross those flanking them, while the stretchers and legs are turned to imitate bamboo. What 18th-century designers called 'the true Gothic' is seen in Fig. 26; the legs are of pillar form and the stretchers scrolled. Made to match a set of ribbon-back chairs, a finely carved example (Fig. 25) is apparently based on Pl. XVI in the *Director* (1st ed., 1754).

A fusion of styles was often attempted in such seats, straight legs carved with fretwork in low relief and perforated Chinoiserie stretchers being found in conjunction with splats which show no trace of oriental influence (Fig. 27). No doubt because they followed the patterns of chairs so closely, settees with openwork wooden backs are not illustrated by Chippendale or Ince and Mayhew, but Manwaring (*Cabinet and Chair Makers'*

26. *Mahogany Settee, of triple-chair form in the Gothic taste; taper legs connected by scroll-shaped stretchers; seat covered with contemporary needlework. c. 1760. Ht. 3 ft. 4 in., L. 6 ft. 3 in., Depth 2 ft. 1 in. (Mulliner Coll.)*

27. *Mahogany Settee of triple-chair form; splats in rococo taste, arms eagle-headed; straight legs carved with fretwork in low relief; stretchers pierced. c. 1760. (Formerly at Bramshill Park, Hants.)*

28. (*Below*) *Settee carved and gilded, covered in needlework with Chinoiserie motives; arms eagle-headed; cabriole legs carved with feathered female masks. c. 1720. Ht. 3 ft. 6 in., L. 4 ft. 7 in. (Lady Lever Art Gallery, Port Sunlight.)*

29. *Settee, carved and gilt, covered in Italian cut velvet; legs scrolled and headed by female masks; large double shell pendant; cresting carved with acanthus on imbricated ground; part of set. Ht. 4 ft. 1 in., L. 4 ft. c. 1730. (Houghton Hall, Norfolk.)*

30. *Settee, carved and gilt on a granulated ground, covered in original sea-green damask; en suite with a set of chairs with eagle-headed arms. c. 1725. Ht. 3 ft. 5 in., L. 4 ft. 6 in. (Houghton Hall.)*

451

31. *Settee, carved and gilt;
upholstered in velvet; design
attributed to William Kent. c. 1730.
Ht. to top of mask, 3 ft. 6¾ in.,
L. 5 ft. 1 in. (Wilton House, Wilts.)*

32. *(Above right) Mahogany Settee,
parcel gilt, part of set; cresting
centres in shell; cabriole legs,
decorated with 'money moulding',
are connected by large acanthus
sprays. c. 1735 (Stourhead, Wilts.)*

33. *Mahogany Settee, one
of pair; coronet of eighth
Earl of Moray in centre of
cresting; arm-supports
scrolled and headed by lion
masks, motive repeated on
cabriole legs connected by
carved aprons. c. 1740.
(Formerly at Kinfauns
Castle, Perth.)*

34. *Mahogany Settee,
parcel gilt, part of large set;
cabriole legs united to seat-
rail by wide acanthus
brackets. c. 1740-50
(Chatsworth, Derbys.)*

35. *Mahogany Settee with scrolled arm-supports set back on seat-rail; cabriole legs with claw-and-ball feet connected by carved aprons. c. 1750. Ht. 3 ft., L. 6 ft, (Percival Griffiths Coll.)*

36. *(Below) Mahogany Settee, of double-chair form upholstered in leather; seat-rail carved with ribbons and rosettes; legs of scrolled X form. c. 1750. Ht. 3 ft. 2 in., L. 4 ft. 11 in., Depth 2 ft. 4 in. (Langley Park, Norfolk.)*

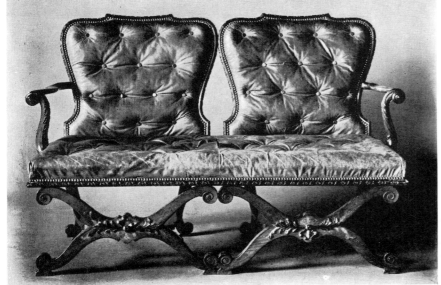

37. *(Below, left) Mahogany 'Love Seat' covered in original needlework; upholstered arms finish in lions' heads; cabriole legs carved on knees with female classical masks. c. 1730. (Duke of Buccleuch.)*

38. *(Below) Mahogany 'Love Seat'; hooped uprights and wide pierced splat; cabriole legs, hipped on to seat-rail, end in volutes. c. 1755. (Apsley House, Beds.)*

39. *Sofa with shaped back and high scrolled arms; cabriole legs of mahogany gilt carved with eagle heads, shells and acanthus. c. 1745. Ht. 3 ft. 9½ in., L. 8 ft. 4½ in., Depth 3 ft. 4 in. (Crichel, Dorset.)*

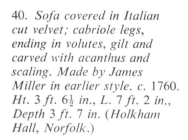

40. *Sofa covered in Italian cut velvet; cabriole legs, ending in volutes, gilt and carved with acanthus and scaling. Made by James Miller in earlier style. c. 1760. Ht. 3 ft. 6½ in., L. 7 ft. 2 in., Depth 3 ft. 7 in. (Holkham Hall, Norfolk.)*

Real Friend and Companion, 1765) gives two designs for what he calls 'Grand French Settee Chairs', *i.e.* settees with open-work backs formed of large carved acanthus scrolls, recommending that they should be made either in lime or yellow deal. In bills and inventories of the period chair-back settees can seldom be identified, but 'a settee of two seats', mentioned in a list of the drawing-room furniture at Shirburn Castle, Oxfordshire (1734), was probably of this type. Occasionally they served a dual purpose, combining the function of settee and couch (*see* COUCHES, Fig. 15).

A pair or more of upholstered settees were generally made to match large sets of walnut and mahogany chairs and stools. The carved ornament is similar to that found on the foregoing group, with such modifications as seats of this size required. Arms were either of wood or padded, and backs gradually became more uniform in height. Squab cushions were no longer fashionable, and the seats were either removable, dropping into the framework with a rebate, or, more generally, the upholstery was fastened to the seat-rail, and secured by

rows of brass-headed nails. Damask, silks, velvet, harrateen and mohair were usual coverings, while needlework or tapestry of French or Soho and Fulham manufacture was also employed. The female masks with feathered head-dresses (Fig. 28) accord admirably with the fantastic design of the gaily coloured needlework, an interesting specimen of pseudo-oriental taste reminiscent of the wall hangings in *le style Bérain*. On the magnificent mahogany settee from Copped Hall, Essex (*see* NEEDLEWORK, Fig. 7), eagle-headed arms in conjunction with the lion motif are rendered with remarkable force and realism. The outward curves of the low, padded back correspond with those of the chairs from the same set, and the wide-spreading brackets effectively break the line of the seat-rail. A similar treatment of the brackets can be seen on the Chatsworth example (Fig. 34), one of a set of six, where the S-scrolled arm supports are covered with velvet and nailed, the original system of upholstery being retained. The settee (Fig. 33) is a fine example of the same phase of decoration. It is closely similar in design and carving to a

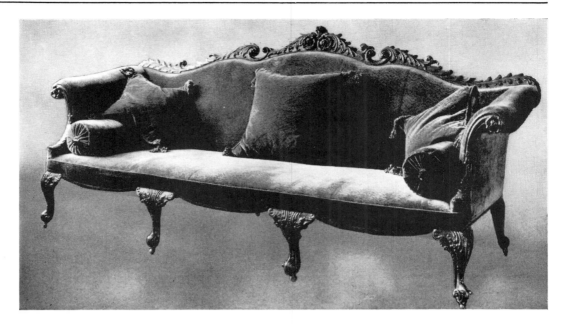

41. *Mahogany Settee with shaped back and carved cresting. c. 1760. Ht. 3 ft., L. 8 ft. 5 in. (Percival Griffiths Coll.)*

leather-covered set at Ragley Hall, Warwickshire, bearing the coronet of the second Lord Conway on the crestings. Clearly the same craftsman was responsible.

That there was considerable diversity in the treatment of the back and arms between 1725 and 1750 is shown by the examples illustrated in Figs. 28–34. The C-scroll finish of the arms was still retained at this period on upholstered settees, while a carved framing of the back was again brought into favour by Kent and his followers. This architect's designs for settees and sofas are marked by strong individuality. The baroque classicism, of which, at the time, he was the most prominent exponent, is noticeable in the gilt seat furniture he designed, his cumbrous ornament being less obtrusive on large seats. His eclectic tendency is conspicuous in the somewhat incongruous motives he attempted to combine in the settee at Houghton (Fig. 29). Large acanthus scrolls or swags of fruit with a deep pendant in the centre were his favourite devices for filling the space below the seat-rail, the large scale of the carving being well suited to the great saloons of Palladian houses. There is a settee at Holkham, typical of Kent's treatment, but, though the example in Fig. 40 is contemporary in style, the accounts afford evidence that it was

made by James Miller in 1760, when the State rooms were finished after Lord Leicester's death. The settee (Fig. 31) of eccentric proportions and with incongruous motives can be attributed to Kent.

Until c. 1750 the backs of 'love seats' were generally padded (Fig. 37), though occasionally the splats were pierced. It is probably to this variety that the Hon. Mrs Osborn refers

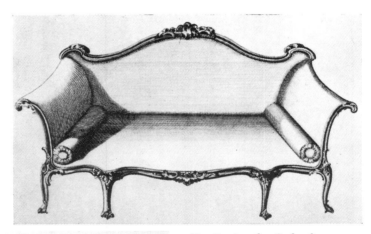

42. *Design for Sofa, from 3rd ed. of the* Director, *1762 (Pl. XXIX).*

43. *Mahogany Sofa, with shaped back and scrolled arms, probably by Chippendale's firm; decoration in rococo style; upholstery modern. c. 1760. (St Giles's House, Dorset.)*

Chippendale's indebtedness to France is apparent in the 3rd ed. of the *Director* (1762), where he gives several plates of sofas not included in the first. One—'for a grand Apartment'—is a more extravagant version of a design by Meissonier, and in a high degree fantastic. Gilding is frequently recommended by Chippendale. Both straight and cabriole legs are illustrated, while the dimensions given are from 6 to 10 ft long, and the scrolls forming the sides 18 or 19 ins high. He notes that 'when made large, they have a Bolster or Pillow at each End, and Cushions at the Back, which may be laid down occasionally and form a Mattrass'. He also shows 'a Chinese Sopha' surmounted by a pagoda canopy, and convertible into a bed. An exceptional specimen, probably from his workshop (Fig. 36), matches a set of chairs, and the X-shaped underframing represents a revival of this traditional form. The designs in the *Director* were closely followed by

44. *Mahogany Settee of curvilinear form; framework carved with gadrooning; slender cabriole legs end in volutes. c. 1760. Ht. 3 ft. 2½ in., L. 4 ft. 10½ in., Depth 2 ft. 1 in. (Henry Hirsch Coll.)*

45. *Carved and gilt Sofa; ends formed as classical female terminals. From anonymous design probably adapted by Robert Adam. c. 1762. (Philadelphia Mus. of Art.)*

46. *Carved and gilt mahogany Sofa; part of set designed by Robert Adam in 1764. Probably by Samuel Norman. (Formerly at No. 19, Arlington Street, London.)*

when she wrote (1740) about the furnishing of her house: 'I wish you would look at any of the auctions or places, they sell at in Jermyn Street, and find two old half settees, for a trifle to cover with the red damask to match the six chairs.'

From c. 1740 the influence of French taste becomes increasingly apparent in the design of upholstered settees and sofas, and rococo motives gradually supplant baroque decoration. The arms are higher, and now form a continuation of the undulating back, a fashion based on Louis XV *canapés*.

Ince and Mayhew in their *Universal System* (1759–63), but, by way of novelty, they show a 'Turkish Soffa' complete with cushions and raised on a platform of two steps. Wooden scrolls facing the padded arms and a carved cresting emphasising the subtle curves of the back are the most noticeable innovations. In Fig. 44 the curves are carefully co-ordinated almost suggesting actual movement.

Adam freely adapted the prevailing models in his designs for sofas and settees. He passed through an experimental

47. *Carved and gilt Settee, part of set covered with Gobelins tapestry woven by Jacques Neilson (1765-9). Probably by Samuel Norman. Formerly at No. 19, Arlington Street. c. 1770. Ht. 2 ft. 4¾ in., L. 4 ft. 10 in. (Philadelphia Mus. of Art.)*

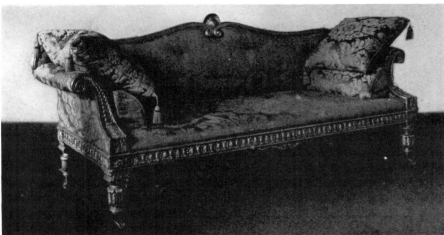

48. *Carved and gilt Sofa, one of pair; designed by Robert Adam and made by William France in 1768. (Kenwood, Middx.)*

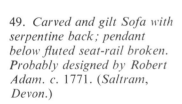

49. *Carved and gilt Sofa with serpentine back; pendant below fluted seat-rail broken. Probably designed by Robert Adam. c. 1771. (Saltram, Devon.)*

phase before the full development of his neo-classic style. Among the Adam drawings in the Soane Museum there is a design (1762) for a sofa for 'Lord Scarsdale and also executed for Mrs Montagu in Hill Street'. Fig. 45 is close to that design, the earlier motif of lion-paw feet being retained with female classical figures and masks. This example is probably by John Linnell (q.v.), to whom may also be assigned a set of four ponderous gilt settees at Kedleston, embodying mermaids and dolphins and based on drawings by him in the Victoria and Albert Museum lettered 'Lord Scarsdale's

sofa at Kedleston in Derbyshire'. In the gilt sofa (Fig. 46) the old curvilinear form is retained though the carved ornament is of classic character, the drawing in the Soane Museum being dated 1764.

The carved and gilt settee (Fig. 47), forms part of a set made for the Tapestry Room at Moor Park, and covered to match the walls with the Gobelins tapestry woven by Jacques Neilson in Paris. This set was made to receive the tapestry and is probably the work of Samuel Norman (q.v.). The seat anticipates later developments and resembles a type fashion-

50. *Mahogany Settee, covered with original buttoned leather; legs and arm-supports reeded. c.* 1785. (*Hatfield House, Herts.*)

51. *Design for 'Confidante' from Hepplewhite's* Guide, 1788.

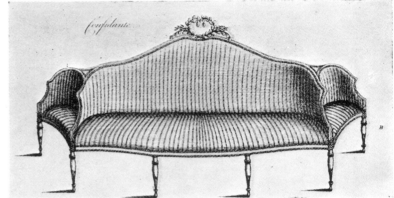

52. *Carved and gilt 'Confidante', upholstery in velvet. c.* 1785. *Ht. 3 ft. 3½ in., L. 10 ft. 10 in., Depth 2 ft. 6 in.* (*Chatsworth, Derbys.*)

53. *Painted Settee, back carved with drapery and ostrich feathers. c.* 1780. *Ht. 3 ft. 4½ in., L. 5 ft. 6 in., Depth 2 ft. 1½ in.* (*Formerly at Woodhall Park, Herts.*)

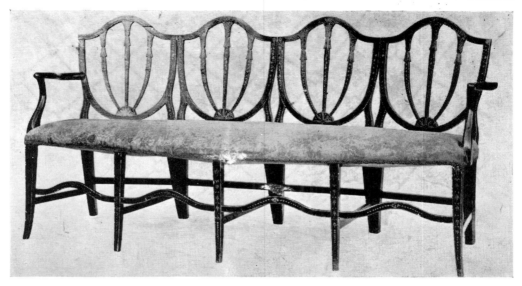

54. *Japanned Settee with four connected chair backs and taper legs united by waved stretchers. c.* 1785. (*Badminton, Glos.*)

55. (*Left*) *Mahogany Settee; triple back enclosing pierced splats in neo-classic taste. c.* 1785.

56. (*Right*) *Painted Settee, part of set, with three connected chair backs; inner ovals painted with figure subjects on original silk; seat upholstery modern. c.* 1785. (*Kyre Park, Worcs.*)

able in France under Louis XVI, but though it represents the early neo-classic phase (the 'money moulding' is a traditional motif—see Fig. 32) there is no proof that Adam was responsible for the design. One of a pair of far more solid construction (Fig. 48) was made by William France (*q.v.*) in 1768 for the library at Kenwood. He charged £50 14s. for them, and in his bills they are described as '2 sophas made to Mr Adams Design carv'd and gilt in burnish'd Gold the carving all finished in a very Elaborate manner'; the original coverings of 'crimson India silk damask' have been renewed. In Fig. 49, the back still preserves the early serpentine curves, but the delicate mouldings and fluted cylindrical legs are characteristic of Adam's later style.

The royal accounts prove that some years after George III's accession mahogany furniture, apparently unaffected by Adam's influence, was still being obtained for the King and his family. In 1767, when the classic style was already in the ascendant, Catherine Naish, joiner (*q.v.*), supplied 'for their Majesty's late bedchamber in the House in St James's Park'

(now Buckingham Palace) a large mahogany sofa on castors, of which the description suggests that it resembled earlier models. It was 'carved with a leaf on the knee and scrole bracketts, the scroles made very large and carved with a large leaf and scrole at the top to match the feet'.

Between 1772 and 1775 japanned sofas fitted with feather cushions and bolsters figured in Chippendale's bills. New varieties now appeared. A sofa at Harewood, Yorkshire, conforming to Adam's style, recalls the shape of contemporary French ottomans, defined by Bimont (1770) as 'the same thing as the sofa, save that it has no end pieces; but in default of these, the two ends of the back curve round, forming a semi-circle'. The 'confidante' was a composite piece of furniture also derived from France; it was a sofa with removable ends, which, according to Hepplewhite, take away 'and may be used as Barjier chairs'. He observed that 'an elegant drawing-room, with modern furniture is scarce complete without a confidante', and recommended that it should be made about 9 ft long. In 1779 Adam designed one of these seats for Sir Abraham

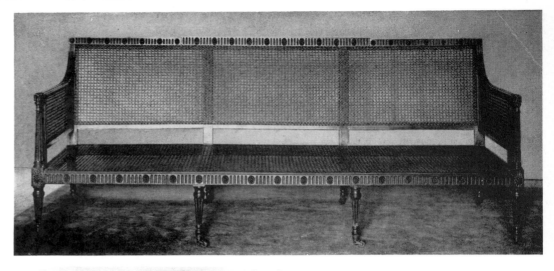

57. *Satinwood caned Settee; framework carved with paterae and flutings; legs and arm-supports tapered. c. 1785. Ht. 3 ft., L. 7 ft., Depth 2 ft. 2 in. (The late Mr Edward Dent.)*

58. *Settee, japanned wood with polychrome decoration; back and seat caned. c. 1790. Ht. 3 ft. 1 in., L. 5 ft., Depth 2 ft. 6 in. (V. & A. Mus.)*

59. *Mahogany Settee upholstered in leather; back in three divisions with framework and scrolled arms reeded; legs curve outwards. c. 1810. Ht. 3 ft. 1 in., L. 7 ft. 6 in., Depth 2 ft. 1½ in. (Burlington House, London.)*

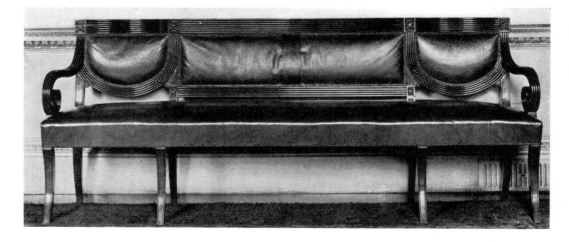

Hume; and a gilt example of the same kind is given in Fig. 52. The 'duchesse' was another ingenious combination, which Sheraton (*Drawing Book*, 1791–4) states could be taken apart to form two small sofas (*see* COUCHES).

The memoirs, correspondence and general literature of this luxurious age naturally contain occasional references to the comfortable seats on which fashionable people idled hours away. Lady Louisa Stuart, writing in 1783, reported that, when

a lady of her acquaintance visited the Duchess of Argyll, she found her 'lolling in her usual nonchalant manner upon a settee and beating the devil's tattoo with one leg over the other'. Such seats were not confined to ladies' boudoirs, but, as they generally formed part of a large set, had their place also in state and reception rooms. Seats so suggestive of careless ease were sometimes not considered sufficiently formal, and a few years earlier Mrs Delaney observed that on a visit

60. *Painted Sofa with scrolled ends; outward-curving legs finishing in brass paw feet. c. 1810. Ht. 2 ft. 10 in., L. 7 ft., Depth 2 ft. 4 in. (The late Mr Henry Hudson.)*

61. *Settee, carved and gilt, part of set; presented to Greenwich Hospital in memory of Lord Nelson, and now at the Admiralty. c. 1813. Ht. 4 ft. 9 in., L. 7 ft. 3 in., Depth 2 ft. 4½ in. Covered in green and silver tabouret.*

painted or gilt (Fig. 54), the backs of mahogany examples being generally straight and the legs of taper form. Expensive seats of this kind were often covered in tapestry of French origin or woven on English looms. Figured silks and satins were also favourite materials, while horsehair, plain, striped or chequered, was in great demand towards the end of the century. For upholstered sofas Hepplewhite (*Guide*, 1788) gives four designs, and writes that the woodwork 'should be either mahogany or japanned in accordance with the chairs; the coverings also must be the same', the dimensions varying according to the size of the room and the pleasure of the purchaser. One of these designs still retains traces of rococo influence, the back, arms and seat-rail forming a series of continuous curves, and the delicate cabriole legs ending in scroll feet. This is intended to be gilt and japanned 'of a bright colour'. Hepplewhite illustrates what he terms 'a bar-back

62. *Sofa carved with lion terminals, bronzed and gilt. By Thomas Oxenham & Sons, 1807. (Renishaw Hall, Derbys.)*

from the Princess Amelia 'all the comfortable sofas and great chairs . . . were banished for the day, and the blew damask chairs set in prim form round the room'. In *The Task* (1784) Cowper introduced the soft settee, devised by 'ingenious fancy', into the rooms of the middle class.

In the later phase of classic taste, upholstered sofas and settees became gradually more severe in design. Serpentine curves were practically confined to those made in soft wood

sofa', formed of four connected shield-shaped chair-backs, and states that 'this kind of sofa is of modern invention', though this type had long been popular. Fig. 56 shows an exceptionally fine example of this date, of triple chair-back form. Such seats were now made in mahogany, satinwood, or a soft wood japanned. To vary the repetition of shield and heart shapes, openwork carving was sometimes substituted (Fig. 53); or a large oval was introduced between the chair-backs, decorated in colour, or filled with a radiating design. The settee in Fig. 56 is of unusual interest, for, although the covering of the seat has been renewed, the ovals are filled with the original silk painted with figure subjects after Angelica Kauffmann, a decorative treatment of which few specimens survive. At this time the backs and seats of ordinary settees were often caned (Figs. 57 and 58).

Sheraton was content, in his earlier designs, with slight variations of the Louis XVI type of upholstered sofa. In the *Drawing Book* (1791–4) he shows sofas with fluted cylindrical legs and turned baluster arm supports, the arms being filled in with upholstery and provided with the familiar *manchette* or padded elbow rest. A carved cresting was sometimes retained on japanned seats, and now often centred in an oblong plaque; but when mahogany or satinwood was used there was little attempt at ornament. Sheraton recommended two sofas in a drawing-room. They are to be covered with figured silk or satin, and may have 'cushions to fill their backs, together with bolsters at each end'.

From c. 1800, by means of outward-curving, or 'sabre', legs, scrolled arms and details of ornament, upholstered settees and sofas were made to accord with other furniture designed in the Regency style (Figs. 59 and 60). In their books, George Smith and Thomas Hope favoured a far more thorough exploitation of archaeological motives, holding 'antique heads of Helmeted warriors and winged figures emblematical of freedom' as suitable for these seats as for chairs. Among Smith's designs are sofas with Egyptian ornament, even the upholstery being in that manner. He stated that ottomans should be of mahogany, with ornaments bronzed or carved in the wood, and 'are particularly useful in Picture Galleries'. A few years later a form of circular ottoman was introduced, the persons occupying it sitting back to back. Of the drawing-room at his house in Duchess Street, Hope wrote 'a low sofa, after the Eastern fashion, fills the corners of this room'; and he also provided a design for a settee of which the frieze 'contains in small the figures of the twelve great gods of the Greeks and Romans'. More representative of the qualified classicism that commended itself to most householders is the 'Grecian sofa' given by Sheraton (*Cabinet Dictionary*, 1803), which has stumpy legs headed by Ionic volutes.

A sofa at Renishaw Hall, Derbyshire (Fig. 62), was obtained by Sir Sitwell Sitwell, c. 1800. This example is one of the 'two superb sofas' supplied by Thomas Oxenham and Sons, Oxford Street, in 1807, at a cost of £120 12s. 8d.: the companion piece is no longer at Renishaw.

Even the most advanced exponents of this archaeological taste offered nothing more grotesque to the public in their books than the gilt sofa forming part of a set given in 1813 for the house of the Governor of Greenwich Hospital by the widow of John Fish, of Kempton Park, in memory of Lord Nelson (Fig. 61).

SETTEES, HALL. Seats generally without padding and upholstery, supplemented by chairs of similar character, were specially designed for halls and galleries throughout the 18th century. In an early example (Fig. 1) the panels are 'fielded' and inlaid with arabesque designs, dark on a light ground and light on dark. The back is surmounted by a moulded cornice and to the outer stiles scrolled brackets are attached. Houses such as Holkham Hall, Norfolk, contain settees congruous with the Palladian style of the architecture, and one of this type is illustrated in Vardy's selections from the designs of William Kent (1744). It resembles the hall settee (Fig. 2), in which the panelled back and characteristic mouldings of the time are incongruously combined with baluster legs. Large scrolls perforated in the Gothic taste fill the back and arms in Fig. 3, the centre panel being painted with the coronet and arms, enclosed with the Garter, of Francis Seymour, created Earl of Hertford in 1750.

Designs for similar seats for gardens and summer-houses are given in the *Director* and other trade catalogues, Manwaring recommending that they should be made of 'the limbs of Yew or Apple trees'. For the most part, these hall seats, or settees, followed the prevailing patterns of chairs, but occasionally a distinctive treatment was adopted to harmonise with their special surroundings, as in Fig. 4, designed to accord with a hall decorated in the neo-classic style. One of a set of four, carved and parcel gilt (Fig. 5), now at Buckingham Palace, was made with eight chairs to match, from designs by Henry Holland for Carlton House. Hall settees were particularly in request for board-rooms and places of assembly;

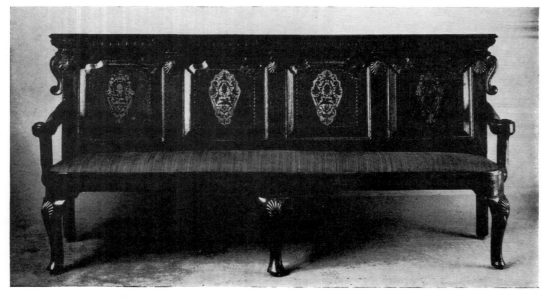

1. *Oak Hall Settee, carved with escallop shells and inlaid with arabesques in shaped panels. c. 1720. (Frank Partridge & Sons.)*

2. *Mahogany Hall Settee with panelled back, probably designed by William Kent. c. 1735. (Formerly at Devonshire House, London.)*

3. *(Above, right) Oak Hall Settee stained mahogany colour; back filled with pierced scroll work; arms and coronet of first Earl of Hertford. c. 1760. Ht. 4 ft., L. 8 ft. 5 in., Depth 1 ft. 11 in. (Ragley Hall, Warwicks.)*

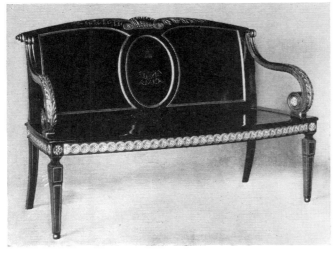

4. *Mahogany Hall Settee, with shaped back and carved cylindrical ends; decoration in classic taste. c. 1775. Ht. 3 ft., L. 6 ft., Depth 1 ft. 7 in. (A. Dunn Gardner Coll.)*

5. *(Left) Mahogany Settee, parcel gilt, one of set of four designed by Henry Holland for Carlton House. c. 1790. Cypher of Queen Victoria added. Ht. 3 ft. 2½ in., L. 4 ft. 7½ in., Depth 2 ft. 1½ in. (Buckingham Palace, by gracious permission of H.M. the Queen.)*

6. *Mahogany Hall Settee; centre oval filled with radiating design and flanked by chair backs on either side bearing crescent-shaped shields on pierced splats; seat lifts up. c. 1800. Ht. 3 ft. 3 in., L. 6 ft. 4 in., Depth 2 ft. ½ in. (Bedford Hotel, Brighton.)*

the type in use at the end of the century being well represented in Fig. 6. About this time there was a short-lived revival of the Gothic taste, and George Smith (*Household Furniture*, 1808) shows a seat in that style without cushions or upholstery, which he terms a 'hall sofa'. The distinction between hall settees and settles is in some instances indefinable (*see infra*).

SETTLES. In early inventories the terms 'settle' and 'bench' are interchangeable, but the distinctive character of the settle is the presence of arms. The name is of Anglo-Saxon origin, and as in early examples of the movable settle there was generally a locker beneath the seat, it may be taken to have originated in the chest.

Readily adaptable to a variety of purposes, like the chest, the settle was constantly used as a bed, and from the 17th century many hybrid specimens survive. Most combine the dual functions of seat and table, but in the inventory of Tart Hall (1641), a London house of the Countess of Arundel, a settle of more than ordinary complexity is mentioned: 'a great settle bedstead in fashion of a fourme'. A settle of about this date with the upper section of the back swinging over on pivots to form a table is shown in Fig. 4, while in another of these table-settles a panel from the centre of the back lets down, being supported on a shaped and pierced strut (Fig. 8). Until late in the 16th century a settle was the nearest approach to a comfortable seat in most houses, for chairs were accounted luxuries and emblems of rank.

In an inventory of goods in the possession of Henry Field, a tanner, in 1592, 'A wainscote bench' is entered with the tables and joint stools in the hall of his house; and in Shakespeare's *Henry IV* (1596) there is an allusion to 'sleeping upon benches after noon', a settle being no doubt referred to in both instances.

The earliest example that may be included in this class is a massive structure formed of hewn planks, preserved in Winchester Cathedral. It was probably made in the late Middle Ages, but cannot be dated with accuracy.

At Muchelney Abbey, Somerset, there is a fine settle (Fig. 2) dating from the first years of the 16th century. It runs across the whole south end of the Abbot's parlour, and has a return at each end, single-seated next the fireplace, but double at the opposite end. The back is kept low where the windows occur, rising to tall panels between them. The front panels of the chest beneath the seat are of simple linen-fold, while those in the back, rather more elaborate, have a frieze of pierced scroll work crisply carved.

It was a settle of this type, no doubt, which was left to his son in 1444 by John Brompton, a merchant of Beverley, Yorkshire, for the inventory of his goods mentions 'I kerven longe satill' among the furniture in his great hall. Settles 'thrown', or 'thrawne'—*i.e.* constructed of turned wood—like another included in Brompton's will, no longer exist. Movable examples are usually represented in illuminations as placed either before a fire or with their backs to a wall, in the latter position generally under a canopy of some rich material. When thus placed a settle formed a seat of honour in the householder's private apartment. A trestle table was placed in front for meals, which, after serving its purpose, was dismantled, and in winter the seat was moved back to its original position before the fire. Fig. 1 shows one long enough to accommodate the company gathered about a chessboard, before which a lady sits on a smaller bench. The settle has the usual chest beneath the lid, and here a foot-rail is provided. In another late medieval type the panelled back and sides are omitted, their place being taken by plain uprights and horizontal bars. Sometimes the back-rail was made to swing over on a pivot bar; a fine Netherlandish

1. Settle with linen-fold panels and foot-rail, from illuminated MS. of Les Trésors des Histoires *in the British Mus. (Cotton Augustus V, f. 334b.). c. 1470. 2. Oak Settle with lockers beneath seat, perforated cresting, and panels of linen-fold. c. 1500. (The Abbot's Parlour, Muchelney Abbey, Som.)*

3. *Oak Settle; back divided into two rows of panels carved with lozenges and conventional ornament; arms shaped; seat renewed. Dated 1635. Ht. 3 ft. 7 in., L. 5 ft. 2 in., Depth 1 ft. 4 in. (Mrs Ralph Edwards.)*

4. *Combined Settle-Table of oak, carved with conventional patterns; seat opens to form locker. Mid-17th century. Ht. 2 ft. 9½ in., L. 5 ft. 11 in., Depth 2 ft. 3 in. (V. & A. Mus.)*

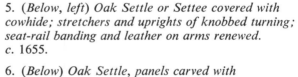
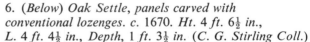

5. *(Below, left) Oak Settle or Settee covered with cowhide; stretchers and uprights of knobbed turning; seat-rail banding and leather on arms renewed. c. 1655.*

6. *(Below) Oak Settle, panels carved with conventional lozenges. c. 1670. Ht. 4 ft. 6½ in., L. 4 ft. 4½ in., Depth, 1 ft. 3½ in. (C. G. Stirling Coll.)*

7. *Settle of chestnut wood, in two stages, with applied ornament and curved back. End of 17th or early 18th century. (The late Mrs Graham Rees-Mogg.)*

8. *Oak Settee-Table; central panel of back lets down and is supported by strut. Late 17th century. (The late Mrs Graham Rees-Mogg.)*

9. *Oak Settle, dated 1681. J. Thursby Pelham Coll.)*

10. *Settle; top rail and front stretchers carved with foliage. Dated 1715. (Trinity Coll., Oxford.)*

11. Oak Settle with fielded panels; back bears initials and date 1717. (Lygon Arms, Broadway, Worcs.)

example of c. 1500 with this arrangement is in the Rijksmuseum, Amsterdam.

In view of the settle's popularity and solidity of construction, it is curious that movable specimens of Elizabethan date do not appear to have survived, while those fixed to the wall are extremely rare. The more important settles of the time were formed of a chest, with a panelled back on the medieval pattern, and were placed facing the fire in winter and with their backs to it in summer. In his dedication of *Have with you to Saffron Walden* (1596) Nash alludes to the heterogeneous collection of odds and ends kept in his 'by settle', the manuscript of his book having lain idle 'almost this two yere among old shoes and boots'. At Ingatestone Hall, Essex, in 1600 'the little rowme within Mr Kebles chamber' contained 'a bench settell with two chests and two lydds, having two locks and two keyes'. Loose cushions supplied the only approach to comfort, as settles were not upholstered like contemporary couches. After the beginning of the 17th century they were less used by the wealthier classes owing to the increase in the number of chairs, and few settles of that period survive. A specimen from Yorkshire (Fig. 3) has the wide framework and solid, shaped arms of contemporary chairs, with an irregular spacing of the panels.

The discomfort of the severe and angular type of settle produced under the Protectorate was to some extent mitigated by leather upholstery fastened to the woodwork by rows of brass nails. In Fig. 5 the back is without padding. Although this example has a close affinity to the settee (*q.v.*), in its structural lines it resembles a settle.

Oak settles of c. 1650 no longer retain the massive character-

istics of earlier times; the arms are open, but the back remains high. They are sometimes supported on turned legs united by a foot-rail, but more often the seat opens as the lid of a chest, which is occasionally divided into compartments. In the settle (Fig. 7) the back is of exceptional height and the whole structure of curved form. Above the three tiers of panels is a moulded cornice with simple applied ornament. Such furniture was strongly atavistic in character, and the thin mouldings suggest the possibility of a date early in the 18th century. Fig. 9 is a representative specimen of the late Stuart type. The turning of the legs and arm supports is bold, in marked contrast to the scratch mouldings and shallow carving of the back. Oak seats of settle form were occasionally made at this period for use in the open air. At Ham House, Surrey, there is a pair in perfect preservation with high panelled backs and arms boldly carved in the Caroline baroque style—entered in the 1679 inventory as 'Two carv'd Wainiscot benches'. They were then in 'The Cloisters' (*i.e.* the colonnade before the main entrance), and are still in the same position. Many settles made for inns and farmhouses are in existence with the decadent ornament and moulded stiles or plain bolection panels of the early 18th century. But in this type of furniture traditional influence was strong, and Fig. 10, despite the date, has the top rails and front stretchers carved with foliage in a manner reminiscent of Charles II's reign. Most later examples are severely utilitarian in character (*see also* SETTEES, HALL).

SHAG. Variety of cloth with long, coarse nap, occasionally used for hangings and upholstery in 18th century. At Dyrham Park, Gloucestershire, in 1710 were '2 Dutch Chairs with Shagg Cushions'.

SHAGREEN. Species of untanned leather obtained, originally, in Persia and Turkey, from hide of horse or wild ass. Artificial granular surface on early 17th century shagreen obtained by pressing small seeds into skins when soft and flexible; afterwards skins were shaved down, soaked in water and dyed, black and green being favourite colours. Following long drying process they became hard and rigid. This leather much used in Jacobean times for covering small desks, boxes and outer cases for valuable objects; and in 18th century it was fashionable for sideboard knife-cases, tea-caddies, boxes, etc. Shagreen later made from highly polished skins of sharks and other fish. Name 'shagreen' adopted in England from French *chagrin*, because of rasping nature of the leather. It was also name of 18th-century material apparently chiefly used as lining.

SHELL-WORK. A few boxes and caskets of the late Stuart period which are decorated with designs in coloured shells supplemented by rolled paper (*see* BOXES, Fig. 15) appear to represent the earliest English attempts in shell-work. In the 18th century it became a popular pursuit for amateurs, stands, lustres, mirror-frames and cabinets being covered with designs in minute shells; these were stuck on, occasionally coloured, and at times mingled with paper filigree ornament and painted seeds. A London gentlewoman advertised (*Edinburgh Gazette*, December, 1703) that, among other accomplishments, she will teach 'Shell-work in sconces, rocks or flowers'.

1. *Vase and flowers of shell-work. Late 18th century. Ht. of glass shade 2 ft. 2 in., diameter 10½ in. (V. & A. Mus.)*

Mrs Delaney advised that in making a lustre the shells should be left in their natural colours to imitate enamel. An entry in Boswell's *Journal of a Tour to the Hebrides* (1773) shows that by then the art had reached Scotland, and was highly esteemed; as, when in the Island of Mull, he records that Dr Johnson said of Miss McLean: 'She knows French, musick and drawing, sews neatly, makes shell-work and can milk cows, in short she can do everything'. One of a pair of vases protected by glass shades (Fig. 1) is typical of a number made in the last years of the 18th century.

SHELVES. Pieces of furniture formed of boards fixed in a frame not enclosed by doors. In the Middle Ages it was a common practice to arrange finely bound volumes on fixed shelves. Chaucer (*Miller's Tale* c. 1380) speaks of 'shelves couched at his beddes head'; and if these resembled the kind shown in contemporary illustrations, they were merely rough boards bracketed out on the wall. Shelves for books are sometimes described in early inventories as 'desks', and in 1547, in 'The hyghest Library', at Hampton Court, Henry VIII had a number covered with velvet and leather. Among the furniture bought for Lord Essex's chamber, when he went up to Trinity College, Cambridge (1577), was 'a great desks of shelves for bokes in the studye'. Wall furniture of this sort must have been customary in such rooms, for fifty years later John Earle wrote (*Cosmographie*) of a young gentleman at the University: 'his study has commonly handsome shelves'. For ordinary domestic use oak shelves, made on the lines of ventilated food cupboards, but not so deep, were commonly

used to hold plate or pewter. Early examples are generally of square form, coarsely inlaid with chequer or bead-and-reel patterns; while, in a type made during the first half of the 17th century, the top is arcaded and the frame boldly carved (Fig. 1). An example of exceptional size and elaboration, with the arcades supported on coupled columns, is given in Fig. 2, the foliated scrolls on the middle shelf and vigorously carved *amorini* below suggesting a date soon after the Restoration. These shelves were sometimes made of soft wood gilt, matching other elaborate furniture, and an inventory of Charles's possessions mentions, at Hampton Court, 'nine wooden hanging shelves gilt' valued at £9.

Of what wood shelves were made after the Restoration is not indicated in contemporary inventories. They were, probably, of walnut, and being of small decorative value liable to destruction. At his rooms in Whitehall in 1683, the Duke of Lauderdale had hanging book shelves, and, a few years later, according to Evelyn's *Mundus Muliebris* (1690), they were among the ordinary contents of a lady's dressing-room, where they supported 'romances, plays, and amorous songs'. Hanging shelves and brackets were also used to display the oriental porcelain and Delft ware enthusiastically collected at this period. Defoe writes that the passion was indulged in even to the extent of 'setting up shelves for their China-ware, when they wanted such Places, till it became a grievance in the Expense of it'. An inventory (1697) of Kensington Palace affords a detailed list of Queen Mary's china arranged on shelves over the doors, a note stating that in the 'Garden Room' alone there were '143 pieces of fine china'. How such porcelain was displayed is indicated in a design by Daniel Marot, where it is shown on fixed shelves and brackets in a room decorated in the Chinese taste. These complete wall schemes, if ever carried out, no longer survive, but movable corner shelves were also used, and four are entered in the

1. *Oak Shelves; arcaded top and corbelled cornice; framework carved and middle shelf incised and shaped. c. 1630. Ht. 2 ft. 1 in., L. 2 ft. ½ in., Depth 7 in. (J. Thursby Pelham Coll.)*

2. *Oak Shelves elaborately carved; two arcades supported on coupled columns. c. 1660. Ht. 4 ft. 4½ in., L. 3 ft. 9½ in. At St Fagan's Castle, Glam. (Welsh Folk Mus.)*

3. *Japanned Standing Shelves in Chinese taste, surmounted by pagoda canopies. c. 1755. (Kedleston Hall, Derbys.)*

4. *Mahogany Hanging Shelves with pagoda top and perforated gallery; fretwork ends canted and returned. c. 1760. Ht. 3 ft. 8 in., L. 2 ft. 10 in., Depth 9 in. (Robert Frank Coll.)*

5. *Standing Shelves japanned black and gold; pagoda roof supported on twisted columns; lower compartment of sides open lattice-work. c. 1760. Ht. 4 ft. 2 in., L. 1 ft. 8 in., Depth, 10 in. (Badminton, Glos.)*

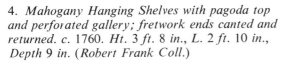

ante-chamber in the Dyrham Park, Gloucestershire, inventory (1710). In the Duchess Anne's closet at Dalkeith Palace, Midlothian, there is a set of this number for china, designed to fit into the angles of the room, and gilt and grained to resemble oak.

In the period 1700–50 china was generally kept in cabinets and in the alcoves or wall cupboards with tiers of shaped shelves supported on brackets, which were termed 'buffets'

by early Georgian designers. Movable shelves do not appear to have been much used at this time, but Bishop Pococke, when visiting (1754) the Duke of Cumberland's triangular tower near Sunninghill, noticed 'little shelves hung up' for the duke's use, one for books, the other for china. In the same year Chippendale illustrated no fewer than eleven in the *Director*, four being designs for china shelves mounted on legs. They are all in Chinese taste, except one described as

6. *Mahogany Shelves with brackets for china; carved in Chinese taste. c. 1755. Ht. 4 ft., 7 in., W. 2 ft. 10 in. (Spink & Son Ltd.)*

7. *Mahogany Hanging Shelves; pagoda top, and sides filled with lattice-work. Probably by Thomas Chippendale. c. 1760. (Nostell Priory, Yorks.)*

8. *Mahogany Hanging Shelves with seven compartments and drawers at base: veneered and inlaid in satinwood. c. 1780. Ht. 2 ft. 3½ in., L. 3 ft. 5¾ in., Depth 5¾ in. (Edward Hudson Coll.)*

9. *Mahogany Hanging Shelves, decorated with satinwood and green inlay; canted sides, cupboards and drawers. c. 1785. Ht. 4 ft., L. 4 ft. 9 in., Depth 11 in. (Sir John Ramsden Coll.)*

10. *Designs for Hanging Shelves, from Chippendale's* Director, 1754.

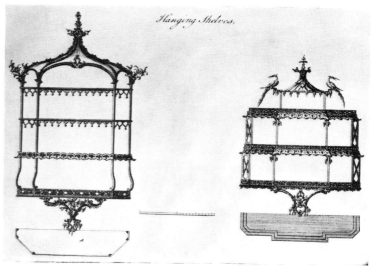

'Gothic'. He hopes that a standing shelf 'will afford some satisfaction to the beholders', claiming that it is very light, but strong; another is to be japanned, and has fretwork doors at the ends. This type is represented by the fine example from Kedleston Hall, Derbyshire, in the Chinese taste, the pagoda canopies in their fanciful elaboration approximating to some of the more extravagant *Director* designs (Fig. 3).

The space devoted to shelves was reduced in the third edition, where, however, 'shelfs for Books, etc.' were added. For two of these, in mahogany, Sir Edward Knatchbull paid £5 5s. to Chippendale's firm in 1768. Mahogany and japanned examples show how well the pagoda construction lent itself to furniture of this type, and how many were the ingenious variations (Figs. 3, 4, 5, 7). At this time shelves figure prominently in the structure of many domestic objects. Ince and Mayhew (*Universal System*, 1759–63) illustrate what they term a 'China Table and Shelf', a kind of chiffonier surmounted by pagoda-headed shelves, and their corner cupboards or *encoignures* also have a series of graduated shelves on top.

In common with more important pieces of furniture, the design of shelves was modified by the neo-classical taste, and those illustrated in the *Guide* (1788) are severely simple, alternative patterns for fretwork or solid ends being given. Hepplewhite states that they should be of mahogany, and are 'often wanted as Book-shelves in closets of Ladies' rooms; They are also used to place China on'. A late survival of the fretwork treatment is seen in Fig. 8. More typical of the hanging shelves produced in the late 18th century is Fig. 9, the canted ends being a rare feature, and the marquetry decoration recalling that of contemporary commodes. Sheraton does not illustrate shelves in the *Drawing Book*, but in his *Dictionary* (1803) writes that small open shelves are intended 'for books under present reading, and which a lady can move to any sitting-room'. He states that the usual measurements are 2 ft to 27 ins in length, mahogany or satinwood being employed 'banded on the edges of the shelves, which are seldom more than two in number, exclusive of the top and bottom'. He also mentions hanging shelves as appropriate to the tea room and breakfast room. This type of furniture did not lend itself readily to the exploitation of archaeological motifs, and few examples are extant which can be regarded as in any way characteristic of Regency design.

SHEVERET. Type of small writing table dating from c. 1790; so described in Gillow's cost books, with superstructure of drawers, fitted with handle for lifting.

SHOE-PIECE. Shaped projection on back rail of chair to receive base of splat which, before 1700, was not connected to the seat. This member, made in separate piece, continued to be used until c. 1775, when the introduction of shield and heart shapes and horizontal bars raised some inches above seat caused it to be discarded (*see* CHAIRS, Fig. 57; CONSTRUCTION, Fig. 9).

SHOVEL BOARD. *See* TABLES, CARD AND GAMING.

SHOW CASES. Pieces of furniture for the display of curios and valuables, the shape and size determined by their contents. The term 'show case' is not used in inventories or accounts. In the late Stuart period both the front and sides of cabinets

1. *Walnut Show Case with glazed doors and sides; on stand with legs of spiral turning and flat shaped stretchers. c. 1685. (Cuckfield Park, Sussex.)*

2. *Glazed Show Case, frame and stand japanned dark green and gold. c. 1755. Total Ht. 3 ft. 3 in., L. 2 ft., Depth 1 ft. ½ in.*

were sometimes glazed when to display the contents was particularly desirable. In a large walnut case mounted on a stand with turned legs (Fig. 1) may be seen a model of a two-decker ship made for Charles Sergison, commissioner of the Royal Navy under William III. By the mid-Georgian period china cabinets with glazed doors and sides were plentiful; but, so that porcelain, model ships and other objects could be viewed from all sides, show cases of table form, with movable glass tops, were sometimes made. They are not illustrated in contemporary trade catalogues, but a japanned example of c. 1755 is given in Fig. 2. Satinwood and mahogany show cases with hinged tops, to contain curios, were not made until the late Victorian period.

SIDEBOARDS AND SIDEBOARD TABLES. The term 'sideboard' was used in the 18th and 19th centuries for a piece of furniture holding plate, wine or accessories for the dining-room. It was first employed, however, in the sense of a side-table for meals (*e.g.* 'longe sytte bordes' are recorded in an inventory of 1553).

In the Middle Ages the dresser served to display the owner's plate; while cupboards of the late 16th and first half of the 17th centuries (*see* CUPBOARDS, COURT and CUPBOARDS, HALL AND PARLOUR) were repositories for vessels, glasses and dishes used during meals. In court cupboards of those periods there is ample space for display of plate on the shelves; in the enclosed variety there is also considerable storage room for the 'cups and glasses to drink in, spoons, sugar box, viall and cruces for vinegar, oyle, and mustard pot', which are mentioned in the *Academy of Armory* (1688) as the contents of such cupboards. These receptacles went out of favour among the wealthy in the period c. 1675–1700.

Soon after Anne's accession in 1702 a 'white marble table' is noted in the travel diary of Celia Fiennes as serving as a sideboard at Windsor Castle; and shortly after 1731 the Marble Parlour at Houghton Hall, Norfolk, of which one flank was lined with marble, had a marble sideboard of table form A dining-room of the reigns of Anne and the first two Georges was almost entirely devoid of cupboard or drawer furniture. Plates and dishes were set on the side-tables with a top of either wood or marble, but such tables contained nothing, and all napery must have been brought in, though cutlery was ranged in the knife boxes (*see* KNIFE CASES).

The side-table or tables for the dining-room were similar in design to the tables placed beneath the mirrors in reception rooms or in the hall. Almost invariably they had a marble or scagliola top in great houses, separately noted in inventories of this date: 'One marble table with a black frame' is listed in the great dining-room at Easton Maudit, Northamptonshire, in 1759. The walnut side table (Fig. 1) from Canons Ashby, Northamptonshire, which may be for use in either the hall or dining-room, dates from the early 18th-century decoration of the house. Under the influence of Palladian architects, the slab was sometimes supported by coupled consoles, and a carved pendant or apron was a characteristic treatment, as in the side table at Ditchley, Oxfordshire (Fig. 3), which corresponds to a design in the album of Matthias Lock's drawings at the Victoria and Albert Museum.

It was after 1750 that the dining-room received a fuller and specialised equipment, perhaps because of the taste of the English, who were (as Robert Adam notes) 'accustomed by habit, or induced by the nature of our climate', to indulge more largely in the enjoyment of the bottle than the French. Hence the finish and occasional splendour of the appointments of the dining-room, among which the sideboard and side-tables figured prominently. In the *Director* (1754) the sideboard tables which are figured, with or without marble tops, possess no drawers or enclosures, and the notes accompanying the plates are concerned only with the appearance of these simple structures. In one design the feet and rails are fretted to give it 'an aery look', as Chippendale terms it: hence no marble slab is used, as this would overweight the slight underframing. The supports in Fig. 8 correspond with one of the

1. *Walnut Sideboard Table with marble top; early cabriole legs finishing in volutes and serpentine stretchers. c. 1710. (Canons Ashby, Northants.)*

2. *Gilt Sideboard Table with marble top; legs realistically carved with tufts of hair; apron formed of acanthus scrolls with lion mask in centre. c. 1730. (Grimsthorpe Castle, Lincs.)*

3. *Painted and Gilt Sideboard Table; apron carved with mask of Hercules and lion trophies. Attributed to Matthias Lock. c. 1735. (Ditchley, Oxon.)*

4. *Gilt Sideboard Table, legs, carved with scaling, finish in scroll feet; apron has double shell in centre. c. 1735. Formerly at Devonshire House, London. (Chatsworth Estates Co.)*

5. *Mahogany Sideboard Table with marble top; legs carved with eagles' heads and acanthus; apron centring in double shell. c. 1735. (The late Hon. A. Holland Hibbert.)*

6. *Mahogany Sideboard Table; pierced and scrolled apron. Probably by Giles Grendey. c. 1760. (Ragley Hall, Warwicks.)*

7. *Mahogany Sideboard Table, one of pair; frieze carved with fretwork; shaped convex apron. c. 1760. (Hagley Hall, Worcs.)*
8. *Mahogany Sideboard Table in Gothic style; based on Pl. XXXIX in* Director, *1754. c. 1755. Ht. 2 ft. 10½ in., L. 4 ft. 10 in. Depth 2 ft. 4 in. (V. & A. Mus.)*

9. *Mahogany Sideboard Table; console supports carved with acanthus and frieze with rococo ornament. c. 1760. Ht. 3 ft., L. 7 ft. 3 in., Depth 3 ft. 4 in. (Ragley Hall, Warwicks.)*

10. *Carved and painted Sideboard Table with mahogany top and brass gallery, designed by Robert Adam (see Fig. 11). Probably by William France. c. 1770. (Formerly at Kenwood, Middx.)*

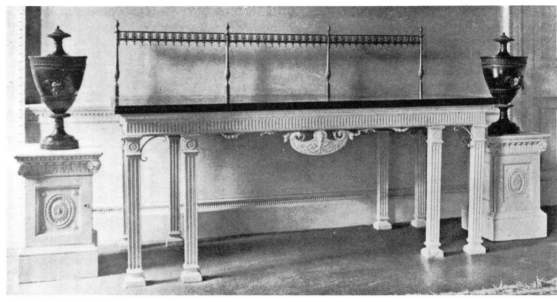

11. *Design for a Sideboard Table and pedestals for Kenwood. From Robert and James Adam's* Works in Architecture, *1773.*

alternative versions in Plate XXXIX, dated 1754 in the *Director*, for a 'Gothic Sideboard Table' with supports 'cut thro'. In most illustrations the fretted detail, however, is applied to solid rectangular legs and the frieze; no pedestals or urns accompany these tables. Fig. 7 shows a characteristic example of this period, admirable in line and delicately carved.

The grouping of sideboard and urn-surmounted pedestal is almost certainly due to Robert Adam. His dining-room furniture was varied in every case to suit the room in which it was to be placed, *e.g.* the presence of a recess at one end of the room called for a group of a sideboard, or sideboards, and pedestals in that space. In the dining-room at Kedleston Hall, Derbyshire, three marble-topped tables (which are curved in plan to fit into a recess) are painted white with gilt enrichments. Between the centre and side-tables are set pedestals surmounted by metal urns mounted with gilt brass. A sideboard table originally at Kenwood is flanked by mahogany urns on white-painted pedestals; the frame of the table is painted white and surmounted by a mahogany top mounted with a brass gallery (Fig. 10 and *cf.* Fig. 11).

A sideboard made by Chippendale in the full Adamitic style for Harewood House, Yorkshire, soon after 1770 (Fig. 12), is of rosewood mounted with a brass guilloche moulding and inlaid with a broad banding of tulipwood framing an oval; the legs are headed with drops and festoons of husks linked to a patera of chased and gilt brass. To the frieze is applied a repeating scroll and anthemion design of chased and gilt brass of high quality, as in the case of the accompanying pedestals and wine-cooler. A remarkable sideboard table

12. *Sideboard Table and pedestals; rosewood, inlaid and mounted with ormolu. By Thomas Chippendale c. 1770. Ht. of sideboard 2 ft. 9 in., L. 6 ft. 6 in. (Harewood House, Yorks.)*

13. *Mahogany Sideboard Table with marble top; frieze elaborately carved with classic ornament and vine trails; legs of baluster form. c. 1770. (Formerly at No. 20, St James's Square, London.)*

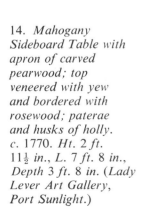

(Fig. 14) closely resembles in the character of the inlay and metalwork the Harewood sideboard (for the pedestals *see* SIDEBOARD-PEDESTALS AND URNS, Fig. 1).

At Saltram, Devonshire, where the sideboard furniture was designed by Adam in 1780, sideboard tables and pedestals (fitted into a recess) are painted green with buff enrichments to accord with the walls (*see* INTRODUCTION, Fig. 14). A side-table and pedestals designed by Adam for 20 St James's Square (now in the National Museum of Wales) are of wood painted a delicate shade of eggshell blue with the salient ornament ivory white. The frame of the table, surmounted by a slab of mahogany, rests on four fluted and tapered legs; the fluted frieze is broken by paterae and tablets. Another example from

14. *Mahogany Sideboard Table with apron of carved pearwood; top veneered with yew and bordered with rosewood; paterae and husks of holly. c. 1770. Ht. 2 ft. 11½ in., L. 7 ft. 8 in., Depth 3 ft. 8 in. (Lady Lever Art Gallery, Port Sunlight.)*

15. *Mahogany serpentine-fronted Sideboard Table with convex centre. c. 1780. (Ramsbury Manor, Wilts.)*

16. *Mahogany Sideboard Table carved with classical ornament. c. 1780. (Formerly at Woodhall Park, Herts.)*

17. *Mahogany Sideboard Table with leopard-headed fluted legs, made by the younger Thomas Chippendale in 1802. (Stourhead, Wilts.)*

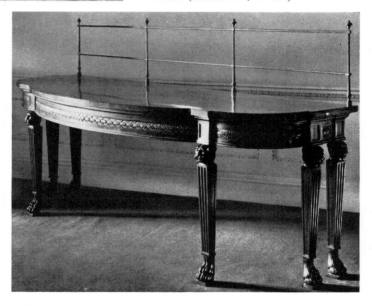

the same house (Fig. 13) has a marble top and frieze delicately carved with classic detail and vine trails.

Sideboard tables without drawers of any sort, having simply a rail 'a little ornamented' and pedestals with vases at each end, were, according to Sheraton, 'much used in spacious dining-rooms' during the last decade of the 18th century.

A reversion to the first type is the sideboard table illustrated by Sheraton, who writes that 'the most fashionable sideboards at present are those without cellarets, or any kind of drawer, having massy ornamented legs and moulded frames'. The sideboard of Fig. 17, made by the younger Chippendale in 1802, is an example. It is described in his bill as 'a large mahogany sideboard with sweep front of fine wood, carved laurel leaves on frieze, thermed feet with leopards' head and lion foot, the top inlaid with ebony'. The top of Fig. 18 is supported on vigorously carved chimaeras and the rail, with its Greek detail, is bronzed, the lyres being of wood, whereas in most instances where the motif, which was revived at this period, is introduced the strings are of metal. In George Smith's *Household Furniture* (1808) three designs of sideboards are given in which the centre table is flanked by pedestals. In a fourth design, without pedestals, a wine-cooler is added.

A useful development by the cabinet-makers of the last quarter of the 18th century is the sideboard with lateral wine drawers and cupboards. In July, 1779, the firm of Gillow (*q.v.*)

inform a client that 'We make a new sort of sideboard table now with drawers etc in a genteel style to hold bottles'; and the first mention in the royal accounts of a sideboard of this type occurs in 1782, when William Gates (*q.v.*) supplied the Prince of Wales at Windsor Castle with 'a very large mahogany sideboard table, made to fit a recess, with a shaped front, 2

18. *Mahogany Sideboard supported on carved chimaeras; rail bronzed; lyres of wood. c. 1815. (Bretton Park, Yorks.)*

19. *Mahogany and satinwood inlaid Pedestal Sideboard. (cf. Fig. 28.) c. 1785. (The late Mr S. Letts.)*

20. *Mahogany Sideboard inlaid with satinwood; tambour shutter below drawer. c. 1780. (B. Copinger Prichard Coll.)*

21. *Mahogany Sideboard, stiles carved with husks. c. 1785. (Mr F. Behrens Coll.)*

22. Mahogany Sideboard; front with convex and concave curves; banded tulipwood. c. 1785. (T. Seed Coll.)   23. Mahogany serpentine-fronted Sideboard, inlaid with holly stringing. c. 1790. Ht. 3 ft. 1½ in., L. 6 ft. 6 in., Depth 2 ft. 8 in. (A. Dunn Gardner Coll.)

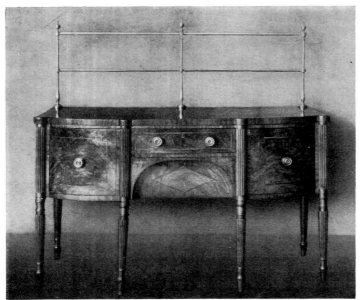

drawers made to the shape of the front, 2 do. very deep, with six divisions in each drawer lined with lead to hold wine bottles, 6 turned legs'. In the *Guide* (1788) two designs are given of sideboards with drawers; and in one 'the internal construction and convenience of the drawers' is shown. In some examples, to ensure a symmetrical exterior, the outside of one deep lateral drawer is panelled to represent two, and serves as a cellaret, while two drawers balance this on the other side. Two sideboards with cellaret drawers are illustrated in the *Cabinet Makers' London Book of Prices* (1788). In a third design by Shearer the sideboard with cellaret drawers coalesced with the flanking pedestals, forming a piece of considerable capacity, as in Fig. 19, in which the pedestals are surmounted by a tambour top and urn fixed to the receding plinth.

In form Sheraton's sideboards resemble the designs of Shearer and Hepplewhite, but they are distinguished by the use of a brass gallery at the back strengthened by a vertical

24. Mahogany Sideboard; framing of drawers and front legs reeded. c. 1795. Ht. 4 ft. 10 in., L. 5 ft. ½ in. (A. Dunn Gardner Coll.)

25. Mahogany serpentine-fronted Sideboard, inlaid with holly stringing. c. 1790. Ht. 2 ft. 8 in., L. 9 ft. 6 in., extreme Depth 4 ft. 8 in. (Edward Hudson Coll.)

26. *Mahogany Sideboard; frieze decorated with carved lion masks; fluted taper legs end in paw feet. c. 1800. Ht. 3 ft. 1 in., L. 7 ft., Depth 2 ft. 4½ in. (V. & A. Mus.)*

27. *Rosewood Sideboard inlaid with brass; tapering pedestal cupboards supporting knife-boxes. c. 1820. Ht. of back, 4 ft. 6½ in., L. 6 ft. 2 in., Depth 2 ft. 6 in. (V. & A. Mus.)*

Beside, if the sideboard be near the diningroom, the hollow front will sometimes secure the butler from the jostles of the other servants' (*Cabinet-Makers' and Upholsterers' Encyclopaedia*, 1805).

A fine example of a serpentine-fronted sideboard table with convex centre (Fig. 15) was designed to fit its position in the flank of the dining-room before the two recesses. In the small sideboard (Fig. 24) the reeded tapering legs are continued upwards in the form of engaged colonnettes, a detail characteristic of the last decade of the century.

In the early 19th century an attempt was made to design sideboards on classical lines. The cellaret drawers are sometimes extended downwards almost to the floor, the structure becomes still more massive, and the centre section often projects. Some of these Regency sideboards were of rosewood with metal inlay and stringing lines of brass. Fig. 27 shows a representative example of this period; the projecting centre is flanked by tapering pedestals, supporting knife boxes of

support serving as a candelabrum for two or more lights, which 'give a very brilliant effect to the silver ware'.

The plan of the sideboard at this time is considerably varied in existing examples, the front being straight, bow-fronted, serpentine or hollow-fronted.

At Althorp, Northamptonshire, is a set of sideboards dating from 1790, consisting of a large piece 'made to fitt in a Recess', and a pair designed for corners. In these the front is incurved, and the tapering fluted legs are carved with leaves just below the necking. In the bills of John King for 1790 £17 is charged for the large sideboard, while those for the angles cost £36, one being fitted 'with a Plate Warmer, Lined with Copper & Iron Rack Stand & Heater'. A hollow-fronted sideboard for Sir Robert Peel, of Drayton Manor, Staffordshire, appears in the Gillow cost books in 1797, and this plan, described by Sheraton as 'not usual', had certain advantages. 'If', he writes, 'a sideboard be required nine or ten feet long, as in some noblemen's houses, and if the breadth of it be in proportion to the length, it will not be easy for a butler to reach across it. . . .

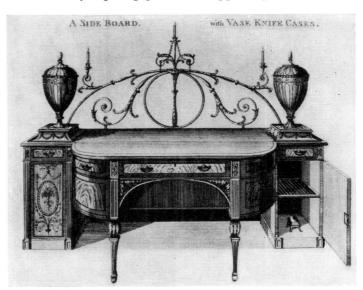

28. *Design for Pedestal Sideboard from Sheraton's* Drawing Book, 1791–4.

1. *Sideboard Pedestal and Urn, one of pair; veneered and inlaid with satinwood, rosewood, acacia and other woods, mounted with ormolu. c. 1770. Ht. of urn, 2 ft. 4¾ in., Ht. of pedestal, 3 ft. 4¾ in. (Lady Lever Art Gallery, Port Sunlight.)* 2. *Sideboard Pedestal and Urn veneered with rosewood and inlaid with satinwood; mounted with ormolu. By Thomas Chippendale. c. 1770. Ht. 6 ft., W. 1 ft. 6 in. (Harewood House, Yorks.)* 3. *Painted Sideboard Pedestal and Urn designed by Robert Adam, and made by John Linnell. c. 1770. Ht. 5 ft. (Osterley Park, Middx.)* 4. *Painted Sideboard Pedestal and Urn designed by Robert Adam, 1780. Ht. 5 in. 3½ in., W. 1 ft. 7 in. (Saltram, Devon.)*

similar form. The high, shaped back-piece is a characteristic feature. The variety on legs continued to be made, and of this kind George Smith writes (*Household Furniture*, 1808): 'these articles of so general use can scarcely be made of any other wood than mahogany, in which case the ornaments in bronze will have a good effect: sideboards may each contain three drawers, for holding naperies etc.' For the drawers brass lion-mask handles were often employed.

SIDEBOARD PEDESTALS AND URNS. Sideboard pedestals surmounted by vases or urns (introduced c. 1760) afforded an opportunity for accomplished classic design. The pedestals supplied some storage room as cellarets or plate-warmers; while the urns or vases usually served to hold iced water or water for washing the silver spoons and forks in the dining-room. In the accounts of Chippendale, Haig and Co., for the furnishing of David Garrick's house in the Adelphi (1772) one of the mahogany pedestals is described as fitted up for a plate-warmer, the other for water.

A detailed inventory in the royal tradesmen's accounts (1780) gives a contemporary description of a pair of the fine pedestals supplied to George, Prince of Wales, by William Gates for his apartment in the Queen's House in St James's Park (Buckingham Palace). These 'very fine mahogany urns on square pedestals' had 'the insides lined with lead to hold

water, the tops carved and gilt, and rich masked handles to do., gilt in water gold. The rims round the urns fluted and carved, the doors of the pedestal fronts carved: the inside of one tinned all round and Racks to hold plates, a large heater in an iron frame fixed to the bottom to warm the plates, the other with a cistern for water lined with lead.' For these Gates charged £32 10s. Sheraton (*Encyclopaedia*, 1805) explains that of the 'pedestals with vases at each end of the sideboard, one was used as a plate-warmer, while the other sometimes contained a cellaret for wine'. The vases 'are used for water for the use of the butler, and sometimes as knife cases. They are sometimes made of copper japanned, but generally of mahogany'. The practice of washing cutlery during dinner still persisted in 1808, when it is mentioned in Smith's *Household Furniture*.

The pedestals and the urns surmounting them were usually of the same material, and corresponding in style to the sideboard table, whether of mahogany (Fig. 6), satinwood (Fig. 5), rosewood (Fig. 2), or painted wood (Figs. 3 and 4). The pair of pedestals and vases flanking the dining-room sideboard at Harewood House (*see* SIDEBOARDS, Fig. 12), are veneered with rosewood inlaid with various woods, including satinwood and amboyna, and mounted with finely chased gilt brass like the sideboard.

The pedestals in Fig. 1, which rest on a rosewood base,

are chamfered at the angles; the ground of the frieze and chamfers is of rosewood inlaid with acacia, while the panels are finely inlaid in the neo-classic style. As in the case of the Harewood pedestals, the front panel opens by a spring, disclosing a cupboard and deep drawer. The vase-shaped urns are veneered with fruit-wood inlaid with bleached walnut and mounted with bands, festoons and goat-head handles of gilt brass. One of the urns is lined with lead, and has a spout, to let out the water, fixed in the plinth; the other is fitted as a knife case. The pedestals at Saltram, Devonshire (Fig. 4), designed by Adam in 1780, are painted green with buff enrichments, and in addition to these urns there is a second ornamental pair set in niches in the dining-room and painted in the style of red-figure Greek vases. At Osterley Park, Middlesex, the cylindrical pedestals, which are painted, are surmounted by two-handled urns spirally fluted (Fig. 3). This design appears in Adam's *Works in Architecture* (Vol. III, Pl. VIII) in a plate of the furniture for Syon House, Middlesex, in which two designs are given for pedestals, the Osterley pedestals and urns corresponding to the right-hand design. There is evidence that they were made by John Linnell (*q.v.*). The examples in Fig. 5 are unusual in being decorated with painting on satinwood panels bordered by harewood, a treatment somewhat unsuitable for dining-room furniture.

In the early 19th century mahogany was generally employed for pedestals as for sideboards of the table variety with which they were made *en suite* (Fig. 6). The pedestals in Smith's *Household Furniture* (1808) are without urns, but are surmounted by 'figures holding lights, of plaster bronzed'. Of the uses of these pedestals he writes that one serves as a plate-warmer, while the other 'should have a tray capable of holding six or eight bottles, which turns on a centre, also a drawer under, containing water to wash glasses during dinner'. M. J.

SILK. Textile, woven from cocoon produced by mulberry silk moth (*Bombyx mori*) and a few closely allied moths; imported into Europe in Middle Ages as article of luxury. Cultivation of silkworms and manufacture of silk introduced from China to Constantinople, probably as early as the 6th century, and thence spread to cities of northern Italy (Florence, Milan, Genoa and Venice) and France.

In England first important impulse to silk manufacture due to influx of Flemish weavers in 1585. A further influx, from France, occurred 1685 (Revocation of Edict of Nantes). A few years later Sir Josiah Child speaks of 40,000 families living by silk (*A New Discourse of Trade*). Chief centres where both silk and velvet were made were Canterbury and Spitalfields; at latter, industry flourished for more than a century, until introduction of power loom. Comparing Spitalfields brocades with Italian, it will be noticed that patterns of former are generally simpler, and floral motives more scattered, but sometimes the approximation is close. As silk thread was almost entirely imported, English manufacturers specialised in fabrics of mixed silk and wool (*see also* BROCADE, DAMASK, SARCENET, SATIN, SAY AND TAFFETY OR TAFFETA).

SILK, PAINTED. Silk on which ornament was painted used for upholstery in France in late 18th century. Painted silks also made in England, and Sheraton (*Drawing Book*, 1791–4) writes of printed and painted silks 'executed of late by Mr

5. *Sideboard Pedestal and Urn veneered with satinwood and harewood, and decorated with painting. c. 1785. (Arundel Castle, Sussex.)* 6. *Mahogany Sideboard Pedestal and Urn. c. 1815. Ht. 5 ft. 7 in., W. 1 ft. 6 in. (Syon House, Middx.)*

Eckhardt, in manufactory at Chelsea' (*see* SETTEES AND SOFAS, Fig. 56).

SILVERING. See GILDING.

SILVERWOOD. Name which in 18th century appears to have been applied to stained sycamore, also called harewood (*q.v.*). In 1772 Chippendale and Haig supplied David Garrick with 'a very large . . . commode of Silverwood with folding doors' and two Pembroke tables similarly veneered.

SLAB FRAMES. See TABLES, SIDE.

SLAT. Term for thin, narrow piece of wood, *e.g.* horizontal bars in ladder-back chairs (*see* CHAIRS, Fig. 37).

SLIDE or SLIDER. Terms applied to sliding panels, *e.g.* flush-framed tray or slider often fitted to chests of drawers between uppermost drawer and top in 18th century.

SNAKEWOOD. (*Colubrina species*, Central America; *Piratinera guinanensis*, British Guiana.) Heart produced deep, bright red wood irregularly marked with dark rings and spots; hard and very heavy. Used sparingly as inlay on 17th-century furniture, and as veneer in late 18th-century and Regency cabinet work.

SOFAS. See SETTEES AND SOFAS.

SOFFIT. Architectural term for underside of arch, cornice, lintel, etc.

1. *Woman spinning, from* Decretals *of Gregory IX, illuminated in England. Early* 14*th century.* (*B.M.* 10 *E. IV.*)

SPANDREL. Irregular triangular space between curve of arch and rectangle enclosing it; or between two arches. Found on panels of arcaded chests and in many other varieties of furniture in which arch motif is introduced (*see* CHESTS, Figs. 14 and 15).

SPARVER (SPERVER). Bed curtain—Fr. *Espervier*; It. *Sparviere*: used in England at least as early as 15th century. Original purpose is apparently given by Horman, *Vulg.* (1519), 167h: 'Some haue curteynes; some sparuers aboute the bedde to kepe away gnatties.' Later it developed into an ornate hanging or canopy to suspend over the bed. Sparvers were made of tapering strips of silk, velvet, linen, etc., more or less on the lines of a bell tent, and hung from the ceiling on a round wooden disc, usually painted or gilt. In English inventories of 16th and 17th centuries, beds with sparvers are as a rule differentiated from beds with testers, celors, etc. Henry VIII's inventory mentions 'oone sparver of red turque silke striped lined wth buckeram'. There are two entries of sparvers in the list of Katherine of Aragon's wardrobe stuff, one being 'lyned with blewe bokerhame'. In an inventory of 1606 there is mention of a 'sparver of wainscot' which may be taken to imply a screen (*see* BEDS, SPARVER).

SPINDLE—SPLIT SPINDLE. Member turned in lathe, the mouldings more or less balancing above and below centre, and usually of slender proportions; practically interchangeable term for baluster (*q.v.*). When sawn longitudinally and applied to flat faces of framing of chests, etc., known as 'split spindles'.

SPINET. *See* MUSICAL INSTRUMENTS.

SPINNING-WHEELS. Apparatus, usually of wood, with revolving wheel for converting wool, cotton or flax into threads, the process that prepared those materials for weaving. The earliest method of spinning was by distaff and spindle only; but a form of mechanism with a wheel must have existed by c. 1300, as an illuminated manuscript of that period gives a representation of a woman standing at a spinning-wheel, which she is turning with her right hand, working the threads with her left (Fig. 1). The *Dictionnaire des Origines*

states that in 1553 a citizen of Brunswick was the first inventor of a wheel with an attached treadle, which enabled the spinner to rotate the spindle with one foot, leaving both hands free to manipulate the threads. Continual improvements were added to this so-called 'Saxon wheel', a form of machine which soon superseded the slower process by distaff and spindle, and spinning quickly became a popular occupation for women of every class. In the middle of the 16th century Sir William Cecil presented his daughter Ann with a spinning-wheel as a New Year's gift, accompanied by a poem of his own composition in which the following occur:

> Yet for your yeres, a new yeres gift
> This huswife's toy is now my shifte,
> To set you on worke some thrifte to feele
> I send you now a spinning wheele.

About 1615 Sir Thomas Overbury of his character of the Fair and Happy Milkmaid writes: 'She makes her hand hard with labour and her heart soft with pity, and when winter evenings fall early, sitting at her merry wheel, she sings defiance to the giddy wheel of fortune.' John Aubrey (*Natural History of Wiltshire*, before 1697) observed that 'The art of Spinning is so much improved within the last forty years that one pound of wool makes twice as much cloath as it did before the Civill Warres'.

Hand spinning continued as an industry throughout the 18th century, and a spinning-wheel formed part of the furniture of almost every English farmhouse and cottage. It was also a fashionable pursuit for ladies, for whom the wheels embellished with inlay and small ivory finials were made. Mrs Delaney, when a girl, was a celebrated spinner, and Romney represented Lady Hamilton so engaged in one of his most celebrated portraits. The *Book of Trades* (1806) states that

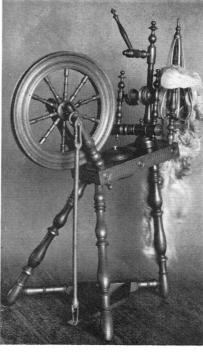

2. *Spinning-Wheel of beech, with oak supports. Late* 17*th century.* (*The late Sir Edward Barry.*) 3. *Oak Spinning-Wheel; sides of stand decorated with paterae and flutings. Second half of* 18*th century.* (*Knole Park, Kent.*)

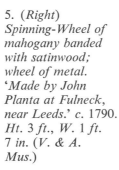

4. (*Left*) *Mahogany Spinning-Wheel with spindle gallery and drawer below. c. 1780. (J. Thursby Pelham Coll.)*

5. (*Right*) *Spinning-Wheel of mahogany banded with satinwood; wheel of metal. 'Made by John Planta at Fulneck, near Leeds.' c. 1790. Ht. 3 ft., W. 1 ft. 7 in. (V. & A. Mus.)*

many attempts have been made to render spinning machines more expeditious by means of complicated machinery: 'but the spinning-mill has not as yet been able to afford worsted yarn so cheap as that which is spun by hand'.

Spinning-wheels were generally made of several woods—yew, box, oak and beech being employed to form the various parts; while the more highly finished examples of the late 18th century were of mahogany, sometimes inlaid with shells and a chequer border. The types of baluster turning used for the supports and spindles do not afford a reliable chronological guide, as traditional patterns were maintained. Thus, in Fig. 3 the turning is of Caroline character, while the decoration proves the date to be towards the end of the following century. Late examples, however, are sometimes made in the fashion of contemporary stands, with taper legs and satinwood and sycamore bandings (Fig. 5). An engraving dated 1804 and entitled *Spinner* (from the *Book of Trades*), if compared with the manuscript illustration (Fig. 1), shows that, for cottages, the medieval type was retained with little modification.

SPIRIT-CASES. Boxes, generally of oblong form, made of mahogany and mounted in silver, fitted with bottles for spirits and placed on sideboard or side-table in dining-rooms, supplementing a cellaret (*q.v.*). Examples are rare; one, dating c. 1750, contains a dozen bottles of green glass with gilt decoration, the silver mounts, added later, being engraved with names of contents.

SPLAT or SPLAD. Vertical piece of wood, generally of shaped outline, occupying centre of chair-back. Splat shapes and designs found in great variety from c. 1700 onwards (*see* CHAIRS).

SPOON-RACK. See RACK, SPOON.

SPRUCE (SPRUS, SPREWSE). Various forms of this word used as equivalent for Pruce, Prussia, are found in wills from early in the 15th century, implying both the material and country of origin. In the latter connection it appears to have been applied in a general sense to objects shipped from ports on the shores of the Baltic. Thus, *I cistam vocatam sprusse coffre* mentioned in one of the York wills of 1445 (Surtees II,

1. *Mahogany Spirit-case, silver mounted; case c. 1760; bottles earlier, with silver mounts of c. 1800. Ht. 1 ft. 1½ in.; W. 1 ft. 9 in. (A. Dunn Gardner Coll.)*

195) was probably of fir, like much furniture imported from that area. A bequest of the owner's 'spruce' without further description is sometimes found in wills of this period.

SQUAB. Common term for removable stuffed cushion in 17th and 18th centuries. Dyrham Park, Gloucestershire, inventory (1710) mentions 'a canopy Bed and Squab with clouded silk'; while Chippendale supplied 'A fine thick hair squab' for a couch to Edwin Lascelles, Harewood House, Yorkshire, in 1773. Term also seems to have been applied to a large padded seat. In the Japan Closet at Dyrham there were 'a Squab and 2 large Cushions', probably a couch.

STAINING. The use of vegetable colouring matter dissolved in oil appears to be the earliest form of stain applied to furniture, *e.g.* alkanet root, which makes the oil red. But at least as early as the second half of the 17th century other stains were in use, as shown by Evelyn's description (*Sylva*, 1664) of beech furniture 'which to counterfeit and deceive the unwary, they wash over with a decoction made of the green husks of walnuts, etc.'. Again, 'There is a Black which joyners use to tinge their Pear tree with, and make it resemble Ebony, and likewise Fir and other woods for Cabinets, Picture Frames etc. which is this—Take logwood, boyle it in ordinary oyle, and with this paint them over, when tis dry work it over a second time with lamp black and strong size. That also dry, rub off the dusty sootiness adhering to it with a softbrush or cloth.' (For the final finishing with wax, etc., *see* POLISHES.)

In the 18th century the colour of fashionable mahogany was produced on common native woods, as walnut colour had been imparted to beech furniture a century earlier. A pair of candlestands (*see* STANDS, CANDLE, Fig. 15) and other pieces formerly in the saloon at Hagley Hall, Worcestershire, dating c. 1760, have parts of the work stained a mahogany colour, others being left in the natural wood. Sheraton observes (*Dictionary*, 1803): 'The art of staining wood was more in use at the time when inlaying was in fashion which required most of the primitive colours; at present, red and black stains are those in general use.' He gives several receipts for these stains, and one 'in repairing old furniture, to bring the new to the colour of the old mahogany'.

The earlier marquetry work on walnut required the use of stain in representing the sprays of flowers and foliage, green being obtained from verdigris in vinegar, and yellow from a tincture of turmeric. These stains were again used in marquetry panels of cabinets, etc., in the second half of the 18th century, as was also a solution of oxide of iron, generally on sycamore veneer, to which it gave a greenish-grey tone known as harewood (*q.v.*).

STANDARD. *See* CHESTS.

STANDISH. A stand to contain ink, pens and other writing materials and accessories. Term found in common use from 15th century onwards, but the form and material of contemporary standishes not known. Made of silver from the late 17th century for wealthy householders, and in base metals, pewter and lead, for poorer classes. Term still current up to date of Great Exhibition (1851) but 'inkstands' referred to in a letter of Matthew Boulton as early as 1773, and designs for them given in Vol. I of his Pattern Books. Sheraton (*Cabinet Dictionary*, 1803) writes 'Black tambour ink-stands are often

1. *Inkstand, or Standish, veneered with amboyna; mouldings rosewood, handle and lids brass. Early 19th century. Ht. (with bottles)* 8½ *in., W.* 1 *ft.* 4½ *in., Depth* 1 *ft.* ½ *in.* (*V. & A. Mus.*)

used. In these stands there is a drawer for paper, and the tambour incloses a place for ink and sand, which appear when the tambour is pushed back. These stands are about 1 foot in length and 9 inches wide.' Examples of this kind with a roll top are sometimes found in mahogany or satinwood. In the early 19th century inkstands veneered with amboyna or rosewood were fitted with ormolu handles and feet. In earlier standishes (*e.g.* those designed by Boulton) one of the glass pots was intended to hold the 'sand' or pounce for drying the paper.

STANDS. 'Stand', used in a very comprehensive sense, implies almost any kind of support, either forming a distinct object, as a candlestand, or used in connection with another piece of furniture, as a stand for a cabinet. Sheraton (*Dictionary*, 1803) recognises the wider connotation: 'it is applied to different small pieces of furniture'; a large number of varieties being enumerated. The more important kinds are here discussed alphabetically, under separate headings. The many purposes to which they could be applied preclude an exhaustive classification, *e.g.* in 1762, William Vile supplied one of the royal palaces with 'two mahogany stands, part carved and gilt, to set large glass basons of gold fish on top'.

STANDS, CABINET, CHEST AND CHEST OF DRAWERS. Elaborately carved and gilt stands, designed to afford an appropriate setting for lacquered and japanned cabinets, were first introduced in Charles II's reign. In inventories of that period they are generally mentioned together with the cabinet and described as 'frames', like 'one Indian Cabinet wth a guilt Frame carved' at Ham House, Surrey, in 1679. As they were intended to stand against a wall, the decoration was concentrated on the front and sides (*see* CABINETS, Figs. 15 and 16). The profusion of baroque ornament and bold undercutting was rendered possible by the soft woods employed—lime, fir and pear. This type was a transient fashion, soon replaced by stands less floridly carved: taper pillar legs with undulating stretchers were succeeded by the cabriole form, while the decoration was in gesso or 'japan'.

The stands for late 17th-century walnut cabinets followed a distinct evolution, the legs, sometimes of yew or chestnut woods, calculated to bear a heavy weight, being at first spirally turned and later S-scrolled (*see* CABINETS, Figs. 3, 4, 5, 7, 9, 10). Similar, but rather lower, supports were used for chests of drawers. Japanned blanket chests were also mounted on stands of ornate character, sometimes supported by grotesque monsters (*see* CHESTS, Fig. 29). During the ascendancy of the Chinese and Gothic tastes, stands were specially designed in relation to cabinets, *e.g.* one formerly in Horace Walpole's possession (*see* CABINETS, Fig. 48). This unity of treatment is also noticeable in inlaid and painted furniture. When stands are separately mentioned in 18th-century bills and inventories the term 'frame' is still employed; in 1767 Chippendale's firm made 'a very neat new frame' for an inlaid cabinet belonging to Sir Edward Knatchbull of Mersham Hatch, Kent.

STANDS, CANDLE- AND LAMP-, GUERIDON AND TORCHERE.

Movable stands to support a candle-stick or lamp were intended to supplement the fixed lighting arrangements of rooms. Inventories prove that they did not become general in France until c. 1650; while, a few years later, Pierre Richelet writes that, in his time, they accompanied fine tables and cabinets. Such stands, being sometimes made in the form of a negro holding up a circular tray, ebonised and with painted and gilt decoration, were called *guéridons*, a term applied to young Moors brought over from Africa as pages. These *guéridons* were imported into England from Italy, France and Holland. The taste for figures of this kind is indicated as early as 1638 by an entry in the *Diary* of Sir Henry Slingsby, who had 'a blackamore cast in led holding in either hand a candlestick to set a candle to give light to ye staircase'; and painted and gilt ornamental stands, in the form of negroes, are at Knole, Kent, and other great houses; a pair at Ham House, Surrey, of Italian origin is described in the 1679 inventory as 'Two Blackamore stands'. Examples of less fanciful character were already in use in the first half of the century. Charles I's inventory (1649) records 'two wooden painted frames to sett candlesticks upon' at Somerset House.

The taste for decorative candle-stands spread rapidly after the Restoration, when they were often made *en suite* to flank a side-table with mirror above. Such sets are mentioned in lists of household goods and by contemporary writers. In 1664, for example, Mary Verney was anxious to obtain 'a table and stands of the same coler'. The *Academy of Armory* (MS. dated 1649) defines a candle-stand as 'a little round table, set upon one pillar or poste, which in the foote branches itselfe out into three or four feete or toes . . . for its fast and steddy standing'. The ordinary form under Charles II was a plain or spiral baluster, circular or octagonal top, and tripod base (Figs. 1 and 2). Walnut and elm were commonly employed, but 'prince's wood' (*see* PRINCE OR PRINCE'S WOOD) and olive are also specified. The most extravagant type was entirely covered with silver, like those mentioned (in conjunction with her tables) in Evelyn's account of the Duchess of Portsmouth's apartments. Among the silver furniture at Windsor Castle is a pair of these stands bearing the cypher of Charles II (Fig. 3). The shafts are clothed with acanthus and intersected by a bulbous member with embossed floral festoons, while massive scrolls form the tripod support. There is a similar pair forming part of a set at Knole, bearing the hall-mark

1. (*Left*) *Walnut Candle-Stand; octagonal tray top, turned baluster shaft and scrolled feet. c. 1670. (Col N. R. Colville.)*

2. *Walnut Candle-Stand; polygonal inlaid top and spiral-turned shaft. c. 1680. Ht. 3 ft. 4 in. (Hardwick Hall, Derbys.)*

for 1676. Another set there is of ebony with silver mounts.

A bedroom at Boughton, Northamptonshire, in 1718 contained 'one large glass table and stands inlaid with cyphers and slates and other work on them of silver', probably obtained by Ralph, Duke of Montagu, in Charles II's time. In one of a pair (Fig. 9) made c. 1715 to accompany a mirror and table decorated with plaques and floral motives in silvered metal on a walnut ground, the metalwork is applied only to the top; the standard, of graceful baluster form, is carved with long acanthus leaves relieved against a diaper pattern and with pendants of graduated husks. Such examples did not serve for candles alone, perfume jars of oriental porcelain or silver being also placed on them.

Towards 1700, a greater variety of patterns was introduced, and ornamental stands of carved and gilt wood inspired by French design became fashionable. The tops were generally vase-shaped, and the tapered standards were enriched with gadrooning and husks, the elaborate scrolling of the feet being a noticeable feature. There are several fine examples of this new fashion at Hampton Court. A pair (Fig. 8) can be assigned to John Pelletier (*q.v.*); they were provided for 'the new gallery' (Queen's Gallery) at Hampton Court in accordance with a warrant of October 25, 1701.

In another remarkable pair from Tyttenhanger, Hertfordshire (Fig. 4), foreign influence is again apparent, and the tops are enriched with *lambrequin* ornament. The boldly carved decoration of these stands contrasts with the delicate gesso enrichment in Fig. 6, where the design on the tray top is obviously of eastern inspiration, and the feet revert to a Caroline form.

3. *Silver Candle-Stand, bearing cypher of Charles II, c. 1680. (Windsor Castle. By gracious permission of H.M. the Queen.)* 4. *Candle-Stand, carved and gilt, one of pair; design and carving show French influence. c. 1690. Ht. 5 ft. 6 in. (Tyttenhanger, Herts.)* 5. *Walnut Candle-Stand inlaid with arabesque marquetry, one of pair. c. 1690. Ht. 3 ft. 7 in. (Levens Hall, Westmorland.)* 6. *Walnut Candle-Stand decorated in gilt gesso; polygonal tray top, baluster shaft and scrolled tripod. c. 1690. Ht. 4 ft. 1 in. (J. Thursby Pelham Coll.)*

   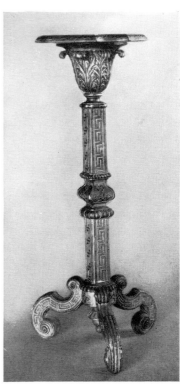

7. *Walnut Candle-Stand, baluster shaft and scrolled tripod finely carved with husks and acanthus. c. 1695. Ht. 3 ft. 2 in. (J. Thursby Pelham Coll.)* 8. *Gilt Candle-Stand, one of pair; top supported on eagles' heads; shaft tapered and base elaborately scrolled. By John Pelletier. 1701. (Hampton Court Palace. By gracious permission of H.M. the Queen.)* 9. *Walnut Candle-Stand, one of pair top mounted with silvered metal, shaft carved with acanthus and trellis work, c. 1715. (Formerly at Penn House, Amersham, Bucks.)* 10. *Gilt Candle-Stand, one of pair; vase-shaped top member carved with acanthus, shaft and tripod with key pattern. By James Moore. c. 1720. Ht. 4 ft. (Hampton Court Palace. By gracious permission of H.M. the Queen.)*

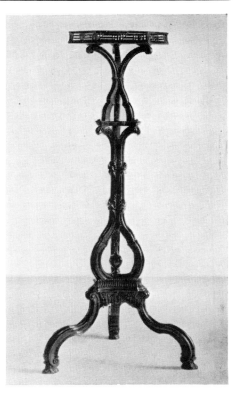

11. *Mahogany Candle-Stand; lattice-work gallery, scrolled supports and rococo ornament. c. 1755. (Messrs Hotspur Ltd.)*
12. *Gilt Candle-Stand (?) carved with interlaced branches, a bird and rococo ornament. c. 1755. Ht. 1 ft. 11 in. (Norman Adams Ltd.)*
13. *Mahogany Candle-Stand, scrolled shaft and tripod; based on design in* Director, *1762 (3rd ed., Pl. CXLIV). Ht. 4 ft. 2 in. (Percival Griffiths Coll.)*

14. *Mahogany Candle-Stand, one of pair; pierced tray top, scrolled shaft filled with lattice-work. c. 1760. Ht. 3 ft. 7 in. (Ickworth Park, Suffolk.)* 15. *Candle-Stand with metal candle branches, one of set; pinewood partly stained and carved in rococo taste. From design by Thomas Johnson. c. 1760. Ht. 5 ft. 2 in. (V. & A. Mus.)* 16. *Japanned tripod Candle-Stand, one of pair; scrolled shaft and octagonal top. c. 1760. (Bramshill Park, Hants.)*

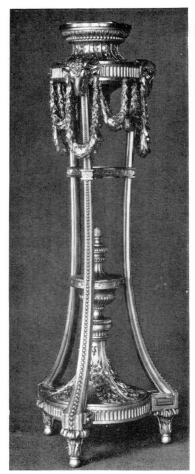  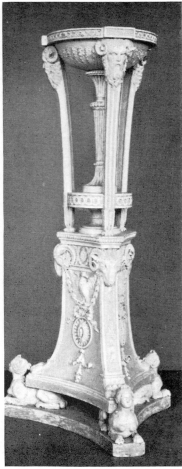 

17. *Gilt tripod Candle-Stand; top carved with rams' heads supporting swags of leaves. c. 1770. Ht. 4 ft. 10 in. (Osterley Park, Middx.)*
18. *Gilt Candle-Stand on plinth; ram-headed terminals support vase-shaped top. c. 1775. Ht. 4 ft. (Saltram, Devon.)* 19. *Pine and mahogany Candle-Stand painted egg-shell blue and ivory white; tripod carved below top with horned male masks; ram-headed plinth on sphinxes. Designed by Robert Adam. c. 1777. Ht. 4 ft. Formerly at 20, St James's Square. (V. & A. Mus.)* 20. *Mahogany Candle-Stand, shaft and circular plinth carved in classic taste. c. 1775. Ht. 4 ft. (Saltram, Devon.)*

Many stands, with tables and mirrors to match, are entered in the royal inventories under William and Mary; several were of walnut and olive wood inlaid, others being more vaguely described as 'marble coloured', or 'of some sort of fine woods'. In the Queen's New Bedchamber at Kensington in 1697 were stands 'all inlade with mettle' supplied by Gerreit Jensen (*q.v.*), who, a year before, had been paid by Lord Bristol for a pair japanned black, forming part of a set. Their fragile character explains the disappearance of such specimens, while those of inlaid walnut are extremely rare. In Fig. 5 is shown one of a pair from Levens Hall, Westmorland, the faceted tapered standard, a favourite form of support in furniture of this period, being intersected by a ringed ball of plain walnut, and inlaid, like top and base, with arabesque marquetry. The feet here are of an early pattern, but in the fine walnut stand (Fig. 7), the more fanciful double-scroll form is adopted.

Gilt candle-stands remained fashionable in the early Georgian period for large reception-rooms, the design showing the architectural influence then prevalent in furniture. The vase-shaped top member becomes larger, and is often decorated with acanthus; the shafts are of solid baluster form or, occasionally, square-sided. Though the double-scroll was at first

retained, later the base is of tripod form. This particular type is represented at Hampton Court, Penshurst Place, Kent, and Blenheim, Oxfordshire. At Hampton Court are two different pairs bearing on the tops the royal crown and cypher of George I, and the name of the cabinet-maker, James Moore (*q.v.*). One of these stands is given in Fig. 10.

A great variety of candle-stands are figured in mid 18th-century design books; Chippendale in the *Director* (3rd ed., 1762) illustrates no fewer than 17, recommending between 3 ft. 6 ins. and 4 ft. 6 ins. as convenient heights. The stand in Fig. 13 is based on a design dated 1760, and here Gothic influence is perceptible. Others show a remarkable diversity of rococo forms, and many are supplied with branching metal arms. One is surmounted by a glass globe with a candle socket, worked by a pulley, and this stand may be converted into a term for a bust. Four candle-stands from Hagley Park, Worcestershire, resemble an engraving dated 1760 (in the 3rd ed.) and, even more closely, one published by Johnson in 1758, on Pl. 13 in a volume (without title) of his designs (*see* JOHNSON, THOMAS). They are of pinewood partly stained to resemble mahogany and fitted with metal candle-branches, the top and high scrolled tripod being carved with familiar rococo motives and the standard with dolphins (Fig. 15).

21. *Satinwood inlaid Lamp-Stand, one of pair; top lined with metal. c. 1785. (Woodhall Park, Herts.)*

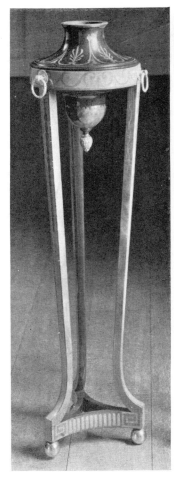

22. *Painted Stand; tripod, carved with female terminals, supports metal candle branches; column with twisted serpents springs from bowl. c. 1795. (Heveningham Hall, Suffolk.)*

23. *Gilt Candle-Stand, one of set of four; shaft and three cranes on pedestal support top. (Buckingham Palace. By gracious permission of H.M. the Queen.)*

In contrast to some of the designs shown by Edwards and Darly, or Ince and Mayhew, these fanciful examples are comparatively sober. Of an orchard scene, with an animated group collecting fruit, Ince and Mayhew assert that it 'has gained great applause in the execution'. Matthias Lock's drawings afford more convincing proof of what was actually attempted, for on one of them the costs are entered (Fig. 24). Candle-stands of a practical character were, however, designed by Chippendale and his contemporaries. In addition to those of carved mahogany, gilded, painted and japanned stands of soft wood (Fig. 16) were made at this time.

A group representing the period 1755–70 (Figs. 11, 13, 14, 15, 16) illustrates fertility of invention in the treatment of the standard. Such furniture is rarely mentioned in bills and inventories, but the royal accounts afford a few descriptions. Shortly after George III's accession, John Bradburn (*q.v.*) supplied to the Queen's House in St James's Park (Buckingham Palace) 'a neat mahogany candle-stand made to rise, neatly fluted and carved, the candlestick part made to turn out with 4 Joints on each side with double Joints and the candle stick made to take out and screw fast occassionally [*sic*]'.

The tripod base rendered candle- and lamp-stands particularly suitable for classic treatment, and the whole design was speedily transformed by Robert Adam and his followers. Specimens are given in the *Works in Architecture* which could be made either in wood or bronze, among them a 'tripod designed for the Earl of Coventry; with a vase and branches for three candles, executed in ormolu' (Fig. 25).

A type popularised by Adam consisted of three long ram-headed uprights, supporting the top and enclosing a vase or column (Figs. 17 and 18). This structure was sometimes mounted on a plinth, a snake twisted round the tripod recalling the ornament of classic originals. Among the departures from the prevailing type is an example at Saltram, Devon (Fig. 20), a vase-shaped fluted shaft being set on a decorated circular plinth. Most of these stands supported candelabra; but they were also used for perfume burners and china, while some were intended for lamps. Mahogany, gilded, painted or japanned wood remained fashionable materials, while inlaid satinwood was occasionally used (Fig. 21). A pair of candle-stands, or torchères (Fig. 19), formerly at 20 St James's Square (built by Adam for Sir Watkin Williams-Wynn, between 1771–4) formed part of the furnishings of the eating-room and are obviously related to two ink and wash sketches among the Adam drawings in the Soane Museum, inscribed 'a stand for candles for Sir W. W. Wynne [*sic*] Bart., Adelphi, 26 April, 1777'. The upper stage and all the carved ornament, of which the execution is remarkably sensitive and delicate, are of pine-wood, but Honduras mahogany has been used for the plinths and swags.

In 1781 William Gates (*q.v.*) supplied the Prince of Wales's apartments at the Queen's House (Buckingham Palace) with 'four exceeding superb tripods or stands each in a triangular form and carved with women's heads at each corner supporting a large vase to receive, a glass Lustre for Candles, a satyr's foot at bottom with rich swags in groups of flowers dropping from the women's breasts, a sun on each side in the middle with feathers and various ornament; made to a drawing chosen

489

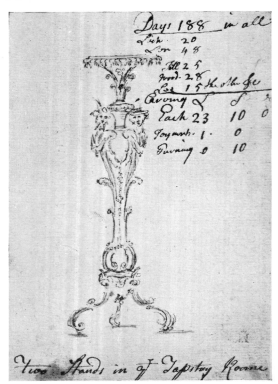

24. *Design for Candle-Stand, from album of drawings by Matthias Lock. c. 1760. (V. & A. Mus.)*

25. *Design for Candle-Stand with candelabrum, from Robert Adam's* Works in Architecture, 1773.

26. *Design for Candle-Stand from Sheraton's* Drawing Book, 1791–4.

by the Prince . . . all richly gilt with burnished gold'. For these remarkable stands the large sum of £234 was paid by the Crown.

Sheraton observes that candle-stands afford 'additional light to such parts of the room where it would neither be ornamental nor easy to introduce any other kind'. His designs appear dangerously fragile, but 'the scrolls are made of strong wire, and the ornaments cemented to them' (Fig. 26). Stands bearing candelabra, or with metal candle-branches attached, were often placed in alcoves and wall recesses in the late 18th century. At Heveningham Hall, Suffolk, are several, presumably designed by James Wyatt, who completed the house and its interior decoration c. 1790. A curious variation of the classic type is seen in Fig. 22, based on a sketch by Wyatt.

Ordinary mahogany examples of the late 18th century were of simple design with turned shafts and galleried tops; but in the Regency period gilt stands were still in demand for large houses, and Sheraton's statement that 'the style of finishing these . . . is exceedingly rich' remained true. Among the items in the younger Chippendale's bills for Sir Richard Colt Hoare, of Stourhead, Wiltshire, is a charge for £37 10s. in 1802 for 'a rich candelabrum for four lights to match your own with a variety of carved ornamental work with Goats' Heads and Lions' feet, the pillars reeded and highly finished in Burnished Gold.' More than a century later 'blackamore stands' were again revived, and many examples are extant of these figures with ebonised bodies painted on a gilt ground with brilliant floral designs.

Few elaborate stands of this time survive, but Fig. 23 shows one of a set of four 'very elegant candelabras . . . superbly carved and gilt', made by Tatham, Bailey and Saunders for the saloon at Carlton House, in 1811, at a total cost of £680. The bronze figure supporting the cornucopia of the ormolu candelabra is from a model by Etienne Falconet.

1. *Mahogany Candle-Stand with adjustable moulded top to fit base of candlestick. c. 1750. Full Ht., when top is raised, 1 ft. 2 in. (Percival Griffiths Coll.)*

STANDS, CANDLE- (PORTABLE). From c. 1750, portable variety of candle-stand was made, mouldings of top exactly fitting base of candlestick (Fig. 1). In some examples, top is adjustable by means of rod secured by a wooden screw. In early 19th century, examples with turned shafts and circular moulded bases, sometimes of rosewood.

STANDS, CHINA AND FLOWER. At the end of the 17th century when the 'custom or humour' of collecting oriental porcelain and Delft ware had become general, stands were introduced for pieces too large to be conveniently placed on other furniture. At Hampton Court Palace there are a

1. *Walnut Stand; base scrolled and carved; one of set for Delft flower holders. c. 1690. Ht. 2 ft. (Hampton Court Palace. By gracious permission of H.M. the Queen.)*

2. *Walnut Stand of vase shape, scaled and gadrooned; one of set for porcelain jars; octagonal plinth of later date. c. 1700. (Petworth, Sussex.)*

3. *Carved and gilt Stand; satyr masks at corners. Probably by William Vile. c. 1755. (The Vyne, Hants.)*

4. *Stand for porcelain flower-pots, painted in classic taste. c. 1770. Ht. 2 ft. 6½ in., L. 3 ft. 6 in., Depth 1 ft. 5 in. (Osterley Park, Middx.)*

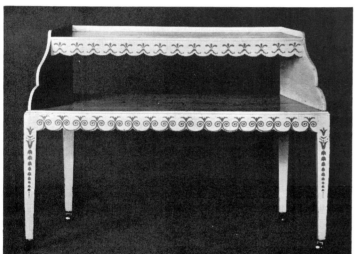

5. *(Left) Satinwood inlaid tripod Flower Stand with dished top; rams' heads and feet of ivory. c. 1775. Ht. 4 ft. (Courtauld Institute, 20, Portman Square, London.)*
6. *(Above) Designs for China Stands, from 3rd ed. of Chippendale's* Director, *1762.*

1. *Mahogany Urn Stand carved with frets; slide below pierced gallery. c. 1755. Ht. 2 ft. (Ickworth Park, Suffolk.)* 2. *Mahogany Tea-Kettle Stand; top with pierced lattice gallery. c. 1750. Ht. 1 ft. 11 in., W. 11½ in. (V. &A. Mus.)* 3. *Mahogany Tea-Kettle Stand with carved rococo decoration. c. 1755. Ht. 1 ft. 9 in., Diameter of top, 1 ft. (V. & A. Mus.)*

number of Delft flower-holders on carved walnut stands with scrolled supports (Fig. 1), and china bowls are mentioned in the Dyrham Park, Glos., inventory (1710), standing 'in ye chimney' of the principal rooms. These stands were also of vase shape, like a set at Petworth, Sussex, made for mandarin jars (Fig. 2), the octagonal plinths being added when classic busts replaced the porcelain at a later date.

With the rise of rococo taste, c. 1750, a more fanciful variety was produced. In books of designs of that time elaborately scrolled stands for china jars and figures are illustrated. Chippendale shows three of this type (Fig. 6) in the *Director* (3rd ed., 1762) which, he writes, 'may be either gilt

or japanned', while Ince and Mayhew (*Universal System*, 1759–63) give a wider selection, among them low cabriole tripods with galleried tops. A gilt stand carved in full rococo taste (Fig. 3) is likely to have been intended for china. With the classical reaction, stands for china resembled in design the tripods for candelabra, the tops being dished to hold a bowl for flowers; they were gilt, painted or inlaid (Fig. 5). Low decorated plinths were also made to support Oriental porcelain cisterns, which remained favourite ornaments in corridors and reception rooms; while painted stands with shelves mounted on legs (Fig. 4) provided much greater space than the tripod variety.

Sphinxes, lions and other Egyptian motives show the influence of the archaeological revival in examples dating from the early 19th century.

STANDS, KETTLE, URN AND TEAPOT. With the advent of specialised tea-tables in the late 17th century stands for the silver kettle and its heater were introduced. 'A small japan tea stand' is entered in an inventory of 'the King's Ma. Wardrobe Stuffe' at Windsor, in 1688, and in 1703 Gerreit Jensen (*q.v.*) supplies Queen Anne with 'a Walnutree stand for a tea pot'. As represented in early Georgian portrait groups, such stands are in the form of small tripods with round tops.

Stands of tripod form were still in use early in George III's reign and are illustrated among their designs for 'Teakettle Stands' by Chippendale and Ince and Mayhew: the example (Fig .2) resembles a design (Pl. IV) in the *Director* (3rd ed., 1762). Another variety, like a box without a lid mounted on cabriole legs, is illustrated by both firms (Fig. 8). Such stands effectively protected the flame from the draught, and were usually lined with metal. Some have a curved opening to take the spout of the kettle, and a slide below for the teapot. They do not appear

4. *Mahogany Urn Stand; serpentine top with raised edge and slide below. c. 1760. Ht. 1 ft. 10 in., W. 11 in. (Percival Griffiths Coll.)*

5. *Mahogany Stand, probably for urn, spindle gallery; scrolled supports, pierced stretcher with finial. c. 1765. Ht. 2 ft. ½ in., W. 1 ft. 1½ in. (Fred Skull Coll.)*

6. *Satinwood inlaid Urn Stand; drawer below top lined with metal and fitted with perforated draining plate; tea-caddy contemporary. c. 1785. Ht. 2 ft. 6 in., W. 1 ft. (Donaldson Coll.)*

7. *Mahogany Urn Stand with slide, fluted frieze and legs. 1785. Ht. 2 ft. 4 in., W. 1 ft. 6½ in. (Osterley Park, Middx.)*

8. *Design for 'Teakettle Stand' on four legs, from Ince and Mayhew's* Universal System, *1759–63.*

to have been an innovation, for Chippendale writes that they 'are so easy to understand that they want no explanation'. The slide for a teapot is also found below the tray top in contemporary stands of table form (Figs. 1 and 4), but there are others without a slide probably intended to hold a kettle or urn (Fig. 5). The slide was a usual feature in the late 18th-century type, and is shown by Hepplewhite in all six designs in the *Guide* (1788). The legs splay outwards, and Hepplewhite observes these stands 'may be inlaid of various coloured woods or painted or varnished', recommending a height of about 26 ins. In Fig. 6, an inlaid satinwood example, instead of the familiar raised edge or gallery, the top is enclosed on three sides, and below is a drawer lined with metal and fitted with a perforated silver plate to catch the drip. These specially designed stands appear to have gone out of fashion by c. 1800, their place being taken by small occasional tables.

STANDS, MIRROR. Among late 18th-century pieces were small framed mirrors on a shaft set on a tripod base. The glass was adjustable and could be turned in any direction. Examples are found resembling contemporary pole screens (*e.g.* at Boughton House, Northamptonshire).

STANDS, MUSIC. In the early 19th century stands were made to hold bound volumes of music, and Sheraton explains (*Cabinet Dictionary*, 1803) that the term 'Canterbury' was applied to 'a small music stand, with two or three hollow topped partitions, formed in light slips of mahogany, about

1. *Mahogany 'Canterbury'. Music Stand of type described in Sheraton's* Cabinet Dictionary, *1803. Ht. 1 ft. 11 in., L. 1 ft. 7½ in., Depth 1 ft. 3 in. (Mr Ralph Edwards.)*

1. *Gilt Term, one of set; headed by female bust bearing Ionic capital. By Benjamin Goodison, 1732–3. Ht. 4 ft. 8 in. (Hampton Court Palace. By gracious permission of H.M. the Queen.) 2. Mahogany Term, parcel gilt, one of pair. Attributed to Benjamin Goodison. c. 1740. (Longford Castle, Wilts.) 3. Mahogany Pedestal, carved and parcel gilt. Designed by William Kent. c. 1740. (Rousham, Oxon.) 4. Pedestal, painted and gilt. Designed by Robert Adam. 1765. (Formerly at No. 10, Arlington Street, London.)*

three inches apart from each other, and about 8 inches deep, for holding music books. Thes have sometimes a small drawer, 3 inches deep, and the whole length of it which is 18 inches; its width 12 inches, and the whole height 20 inches.' The legs are 'turned or plain tapered with castors, and are adapted to run under a pianoforte' (Fig. 1).

Two music stands are illustrated in G. Smith's *Household Furniture* (1808). He writes that 'they are intended for holding such music-books as are in constant use', and may be made in mahogany, rosewood, or bronzed and gilt.

Towards the middle of the 18th century portable stands on turned shafts with a circular base and a revolving adjustable desk of wood or metal were introduced to hold music scores. No examples of that period appear to survive, but *see* Philip Mercier's 'Music Party' (Nat. Portrait Gal. 1556), c. 1733.

STANDS, PEDESTAL AND TERM. These forms of stands are developments or adaptations, respectively, of the substructure placed under columns in classic architecture, and of the stones used in antiquity to mark boundaries, which

were often in the form of a human bust without arms surmounting an inverted obelisk. In the Stuart period the busts collected by the Earl of Arundel and other virtuosos were displayed on pedestals. A payment is recorded in 1639–40 'To Zachary Taylor, for Carving Tenn Pedestals of timber for marble statues to stand on with Bull's heads, festoons, fruites, leaves and flowers'. These were set up in the Great Room at the Queen's House, Greenwich.

Gilt stands both of term and pedestal form were introduced by early 18th-century architects into great Palladian houses. Their solid proportions fitted them to support heavy objects and, in addition to candelabra, they were used for vases, perfume jars, lamps and busts. When terminal figures were made for this purpose, they were headed by the bust of a child or woman bearing the capital of one of the classic orders, the tapered lower portion ending in scrolled feet or a square plinth. At Hampton Court is a set of gilt female terminals supplied by Benjamin Goodison in 1732–3 and described in his account as 'carved term-fashion' (Fig. 1). Examples designed by William Kent are at Houghton Hall, Norfolk, and others were formerly at Devonshire House. A pair at Longford Castle, Wiltshire, are of mahogany with gilt enrichments, the tapered shaft, which rests on a square plinth, being headed by a finely modelled bust of Hercules (Fig. 2). They were probably supplied by Goodison to the first Lord Folkestone for the gallery (finished 1739–40).

Other pedestals made at this time were also of tapered form, surmounted by an entablature. They supported busts, bronzes or classical vases. 'One marble bust upon a pedestal wood' occurs in a list of the household goods of Sir Robert Sutton, 1732. In the inventory (1742) of the contents of Rousham, Oxfordshire, enlarged and decorated by Kent for General James Dormer between 1738 and 1740, 22 bronze figures and 20 busts are entered, some of which were supported on pedestals (Fig. 3).

Pedestals and terms are represented in the pattern books of the mid 18th century. Chippendale (*Director*, 3rd ed., 1762) illustrates four 'terms for bustos' [*sic*], one with ornament in neo-classic taste. A few years later John Bradburn (*q.v.*) supplied the King's apartments at St James's with two stands of which the description recalls this design, for they are entered as 'two very rich antique termes for candles, ornamented with goats heads and festoons of husks on each side with rich mouldings carved and gilt with Burnished gold and statuary marble tops'. Chippendale also shows pedestals ornamented with 'emblems of war, music and poetry' similar in form to Fig. 5, a fine example of neo-classic ornament. These low stands

5. *Mahogany Pedestal with marble top; on front panel a festooned ram's head. c. 1765. (Donaldson Coll.)*

were well adapted to support large busts or even full-length statues. The long tapered variety was much used for lights. Ince and Mayhew (*Universal System*, 1759–63) show four terms suitable for either busts or lamps. In the hall of the Queen's House (Buckingham Palace) in 1763 were 'eight hexagon lanterns on Terms or carved columns . . .' and in

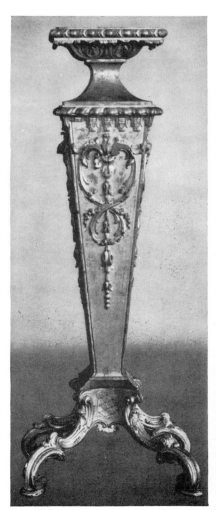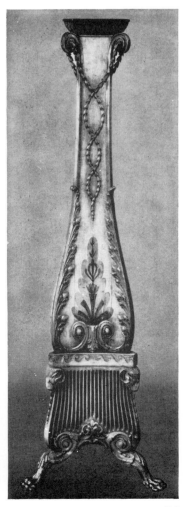

6. *Pedestal, one of pair; carved and gilt in rococo style, c. 1760. Ht. 4 ft. 7 in., W. 1 ft. 1 in. (V. & A. Mus.)*

7. *Vase Stand, one of pair; satinwood inlaid with various woods. By John Cobb, 1772. Ht. 4 ft. 4 in. (Corsham Court, Wilts.)*

8. *Stand, one of pair; carved, veneered with boxwood and inlaid. c. 1775. Ht. 4 ft. 3 in. (The late Mr. F. Behrens.)*

9. *Candelabra Stand carved and gilt; triangular pedestal painted with winged figures of Victory. Designed by James Stuart; ormolu candelabra by Matthew Boulton. Formerly at Spencer House, London. (Earl Spencer.)*

10. *Mahogany Pedestal carved with paterae and festoons of husks. c. 1775. (Padworth House, Berks.)*

11. *Painted Pedestal with original candle-holder; carved ornament in classic taste. c. 1775. (Woodhall Park, Herts.)*

12. *Pedestal, one of pair; gilt carved and painted in classic style. c. 1776. Ht. 5 ft. 9½ in. (Osterley Park, Middx.)*

13. *Design for Pedestals at Osterley Park by Robert Adam, dated 1776. (Soane Mus., London.)*

1768 Chippendale's firm supplied Sir Edward Knatchbull with 'Black pedestals and Glass Lamps for Oil'. Inlaid decoration was occasionally used at this date, and in such examples there is often a departure from the orthodox shape. In a pair of satinwood stands at Corsham, Wiltshire, made by John Cobb in 1772 (Fig. 7), the swelling curves accord with the serpentine commode they were designed to accompany, while Fig. 8 shows an obelisk form with classic enrichments carved in boxwood. One of a pair of candelabra (Fig. 9), designed by James ('Athenian') Stuart (*q.v.*) for Spencer House, affords a rare instance of painted decoration on this form of furniture. Here the pedestal is triangular in plan, each face being painted with a winged victory holding a wreath, relieved against a maroon ground.

In the late 18th century pedestals were extensively used, particularly in houses by Robert Adam and his school. Designs for pedestals, called 'terms for candles', made by Adam for Sir John Griffiths and Sir W. Williams-Wynn, are among his drawings in the Soane Museum, while in the *Works in Architecture* (2nd Vol., 1779) large vases are shown set on pedestals of gilt wood in the third drawing-room of the Earl of Derby's house in Grosvenor Square. For the collection of antique statues and busts at Newby Hall, Yorkshire, Adam designed a number of pedestals adapted to the shapes and sizes of each particular piece. The classical pedestal form admitted of little variation, but in the finely conceived pair of pedestals from the Tapestry Room at Osterley Park, Middlesex (Fig. 12), Adam departed from the established type. They are of gilt wood decorated with deli-

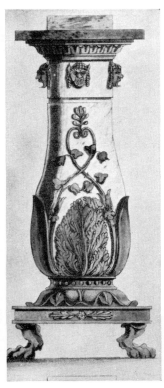

14. *Pedestal and Vase, one of pair painted in Etruscan taste; metal candle branches spring from rams' heads at corners of frieze. c. 1795. (Heveningham Hall, Suffolk.)* 15. *Design for carved and painted Pedestal, from George Smith's Household Furniture, 1808.*

cately painted medallions, the openwork carving in the lower portion being more skilfully placed than in the original design dated 1776 (Fig. 13).

Stands of this kind, according to Hepplewhite's *Guide* (1788), were 'generally made of mahogany with the ornaments carved', but examples of inlaid satinwood, or soft wood painted and gilt, are also found. When designed for busts and vases,

pedestals were painted to represent marble or match the colour of the walls. The latter treatment is well represented by a pair designed by Wyatt for the niches in the Etruscan room at Heveningham Hall, Suffolk: they are surmounted by vases (Fig. 14). Several stands of this kind were supplied by the younger Chippendale for Stourhead, Wiltshire, c. 1800, among them '2 antique pedestals to support Figures with carved goats' heads'. Falling within the province of the architect, they are not figured in the later trade catalogues, with the exception of Smith's *Household Furniture* (1808), published during the Regency phase of design. He recommends them for a number of purposes—candelabra, transparent alabaster or glass vases, busts and statues. They are to be placed in picture galleries, in halls, or on staircases, 'and need not be rejected in drawing-room, if executed in wood carved and gilt, in which case they answer conveniently to support vases or flowers or figures carrying branches of lights'. The designs illustrated are to be manufactured in wood, painted to imitate antique marble (Fig. 15). At this time there is a closer approximation to Roman originals. Pedestals were also greatly in request for lights, and Creevy, writing of a dinner party at Knowsley Hall, Lancashire, in the early 19th century, says the room was partly illuminated 'by ten great lamps on pedestals'.

STANDS, PLATE AND CUTLERY. Among the accessories introduced for the service of the dining-table in the period 1750–1800 were stands designed to hold plates, while others had the tops fitted with cross-divisions to provide space for knives, forks and spoons (Figs. 1 and 2). These stands, like dumb-waiters, were used when service in the dining-room was dispensed with, and particularly at informal supper parties. Sheraton (*Dictionary*, 1803) states they are among pieces termed 'Canterbury', being 'made to stand by a table at supper, with a circular end, and three partitions cross-wise, to hold knives, forks and plates, at that end, which is made circular on purpose'. In Fig. 1, made for plates only, the gallery is formed of turned spindles, as in one of Sheraton's designs. The Canterbury type is seen in Fig. 2.

STANDS, SALVER AND TRAY. Besides the many kinds of small table used for china in the 18th century, a

1. *Mahogany Plate Stand; one of pair formerly at Ken Wood; spindle gallery top, shelf below. c. 1790. Ht. 2 ft. 3 in.* 2. *Mahogany Plate and Cutlery Stand of 'Canterbury' type; supported on tripod with turned shaft. c. 1795. Ht. 2 ft. 3 in., L. 1 ft. 11 in., Depth 1 ft. 1 in. (A. Dunn Gardner Coll.)*

1. *Mahogany Tripod Stand, tilt-up top notched for feet of original silver tray. c. 1740. Ht. 2 ft. 2 in., Diameter 1 ft. 8 in. (Dunham Massey, Ches.)*

2. *Mahogany Salver and Plate Stand, portable type. c.* 1760. *Ht. 1 ft. 4½ in., W. 1 ft., Depth 6 in. (The late Mr F. Behrens.)*

number of stands were made to support trays on which tea or coffee services were set. At Dunham Massey, Cheshire, there are two tripods of this type (Fig. 1) with tilt-up tops notched to receive the feet of the silver trays which belong to them. An inventory of the Tea Room Gallery mentions: '2 Mahogany stands to set the silver Tea and Coffee Tables on'; while in a list of the second Earl of Warrington's possessions, drawn up in his own hand (1752), the diameter and weight of each tray or 'table' is given, both bearing the hall-mark of 1741. The small portable stand on Fig. 2 is of a type usually made to support salvers or plates, which by means of the spiral twists could be placed at various inclinations (*see* TRAYS, STANDING).

1. *Mahogany Stand, carved with swags and pendants of fruits and flowers; panels filled with strapwork. Attributed to William Vile. c.* 1760. *(Longford Castle, Wilts.)*

STANDS, VARIOUS. In the mid 18th century elaborate open-work constructions, sometimes mounted on legs and fitted with shelves, were made for the display of china, and are illustrated in Chippendale's *Director* (1754) and other contemporary trade journals (*see* SHELVES). These standing shelves afford no storage space, but there are other contemporary pieces of furniture in which shelves are combined with drawers to form a stand. Fig. 1 shows a finely carved example which can be assigned to William Vile (*q.v.*). Another exceptional stand is remarkable for high quality and admirable proportions (Fig. 2).

2. *Mahogany Stand in four stages. Back and sides with 'Chinese railing'. Upper stage, a cupboard with pierced fretwork door. c.* 1760. *Ht. 6 ft. (Messrs Hotspur Ltd.)*

STANDS, WIG. Short turned wooden standards, usually on circular bases, and finishing in bulbous knobs, or mushroom-shaped tops. The custom of wearing wigs did not become usual for ladies in England till the 16th century; Charles II introduced the fashion for men at the Restoration. Shakespeare mentions the wearing of wigs by women ('I'll get me such a colour'd periwig', *Two Gentlemen of Verona*, iv, 4, 198), and Queen Elizabeth had a large number at the time of her death. Louis XIII, prematurely bald, started the fashion for men in France. During Louis XIV's reign the wig-makers of Paris were famous throughout Europe, and at one time 1,200 were stated to have belonged to their guild, employing over 6,000 assistants. Accounts and bills show that many of the wigs worn in this country came from France. Pepys records the day in 1664 when the Duke of York first wore a periwig (*i.e.* peruke), adding that he himself 'had some thoughts but no great desire or resolution to wear a periwig yet'.

1. *Leather-covered Peruke Block on oak stand. First half of 18th century. Ht. 1 ft. 1 in. (London Mus.)* 2. *Barber's plate of Lambeth ware, showing representation of Wig-Stand. c. 1700. Diameter 9¾ in. (Brighton Mus.)* 3. *Double Wig Stand of yew. Second half of 18th century. Ht. 1 ft. 8½ in. (Mr Arthur Edwards.)*

The prices of wigs varied greatly; Lady Grisell Baillie, in 1690, pays £28 'For a long wige'; Lord Bristol, in 1698, £12 for a long periwig and £2 3s. for his son's, the boy being then under twelve. Pepys appears to have given about £3 for some of his perukes, while Mr Thomas Turner, a retired grocer living in a small way in Sussex, mentioned in his diary in 1746 that he paid '£1 15s. for a new wigg'.

During Queen Anne's reign perukes attained their fullest development in both length and width. The changes in hairdressing for both sexes were rapid, and many forms of perukes and wigs followed one another, but the fashion gradually died out for private persons in George III's reign, though it lingered on for doctors, clergymen and soldiers.

Wig stands are occasionally mentioned in inventories. Among the furniture in the New Gallery at Dyrham Park, Gloucestershire, in 1710 was a 'Peruke Block', while in the Gallery at Canons, Middlesex, 'A Powdering Trough' and 'two wigg blocks' are listed in the inventory (1725) of the first Duke of Chandos. There was another of these 'troughs' and a block in the Powdering Room. The shape and length of the stand must have been considerably affected by the prevailing fashion, a large peruke requiring far more solid support than the later tie-wig. A barber's plate of Lambeth ware (Fig. 2, in the Brighton Museum) of c. 1700 shows a representation of a wig stand that can be raised or lowered. Most surviving specimens are of late 18th-century date, but the turning of the shafts affords little guide to the chronology, traditional forms being used. In Fig. 1 the stand is of oak and the vizor-shaped block, covered in leather, is hollow, to contain small hairdressing requisites.

STATE. Chair of state or canopy over throne or state chair; thus often abbreviated from 15th century onwards. Shakespeare, *Henry IV* (1596), ii, 4, 416: 'This chayre shall bee my State.' Bacon, *New Atlantis* (1626), 19, 'Over the chair is a State made round or oval'. In royal palaces and great houses the chair, stool and canopy together sometimes formed the 'State'. An inventory of Kensington Palace (1697) lists in the Presence 'One crimson velvett State, silke fringe and His Majesty's Armes Embroydered thereon with gold and silver', including a chair of state, one foot stool and two 'high stooles', with cushions. There are contemporary canopies or 'States' at Hampton Court and Hardwick Hall, Derbyshire.

STEPS. *See* LIBRARY STEPS.

STILE. *See* CONSTRUCTION.

STOOLS. The term 'stool' had a double significance in the Middle Ages, being applied to any kind of seat for one person, and, more especially, to a seat without arms or back; it is now used in the latter sense. Chests and stools were the ordinary seats in medieval living-rooms, a chair, regarded as a symbol of authority, being reserved for the master of the household and distinguished strangers. The 'fald-stools' illustrated in the 'Eadwine' psalter (c. 1150), and later described in the *Chanson de Roland* and other metrical romances, also partook of this ceremonial character. Draped with rich material, they were the seats of princes and great nobles, and seem to have been really X-shaped chairs; though folding stools used in church services were also called by this name. In halls and parlours stools were the only readily portable seats. The hall of Finchale Priory in 1397 contained three stools, besides benches, and a number are enumerated in a list of Henry VI's furniture, with the damask and silk coverings used to drape them. John Baset, of Bury, a contemporary merchant, kept his 'three fotyd stolys' (or tripod stools) in a spruce coffer; when his will was made in 1463, he directed that the coffer, with its contents, should always remain in his house.

1. *Oak Stool of trestle form; underframe pierced; splayed and moulded uprights. Early 16th century. Ht. 1 ft. 9½ in., L. 1 ft. 10 in., Depth 11 in. (V. & A. Mus.)* 2. *Oak Stool of trestle form with carved underframe. Early 16th century.* 3. *Stool of birchwood painted, covered with velvet and fringed. c. 1610-20. (Knole Park, Kent.)*

In royal palaces rules, which later developed into strict etiquette, governed the allotment of seats on ceremonial occasions, a chair being reserved for the sovereign alone, while the members of the court occupied stools. A departure from this practice was considered worthy of notice by the herald who accompanied Princess Margaret, Henry VII's daughter, to Scotland to marry King James IV. Even after the wedding, when a banquet was held, a stool was placed for the Queen, but because it was 'not for hyr Ease' her husband ordered it to be taken away and a chair substituted.

From this period a few oak joined stools survive similar in design to late Gothic benches, splayed and moulded uprights being connected by a deep shaped underframing. Seats of this kind are represented in contemporary illuminations. Occasionally, the underframing was carved with a vine pattern and cusping (Fig. 2), or with profile heads in medallions, a favourite Renaissance ornament. The foreign craftsmen em-

ployed by the King no doubt made many of the elaborate stools described in Henry VIII's inventories (1547), introducing more luxurious seats from the continent. All the royal palaces contained large numbers covered with velvet, silk, or cloth of gold, embroidered with the king's arms and richly fringed. A list is given of 'Stools in their Cases'. Foot-stools, generally made in pairs and sometimes of walnut, were plentiful, replacing the cushions and foot carpets used for this purpose in the Middle Ages; and in the 'Guarderobe' at Nonsuch, Surrey, were a pair, 'ye fete painted and gilte couvered with nedelwoorke grene red and white in knotted wise, frynged in redd silke and gould'. There were also several 'folding stooles', covered in the same manner, and, no doubt, of the X-pattern also adopted for contemporary chairs. Although joined stools with plain wooden tops continued in common use until the late 17th century, loose cushions mitigated their discomfort. In 1556 the six stools in Sir William More's parlour at Loseley

4. *Oak Joint Stool; legs of fluted baluster form. c. 1600. Ht. 1 ft. 10 in., L. 1 ft. 6 in. (Lady Assheton-Smith Coll.)* 5. *Folding Stool of X-shape; frame of birch covered with velvet, trimmed with fringed galon. c. 1610. Ht. 1 ft. 7½ in., L. 2 ft., Depth 1 ft. 7 in. (Knole Park, Kent.)* 6. *Oak Joint Stool; carved frieze, shaped underframe, fluted baluster legs. c. 1625. (The late Mr W. Simpson.)*

7. *Oak Joint Stool; baluster-shaped chamfered legs. c. 1625. (The late Sir Edward Barry.)* 8. *Oak Joint Stool: shaped under-frame and knobbed and ringed legs. Mid-17th century. Ht. 1 ft. 9½ in., L. 1 ft. 5 in., Depth 10 in. (V. & A. Mus.)* 9. *Pearwood Joint Stool; turned baluster legs. Mid-17th century. Ht. 1 ft. 8½ in., L. 1 ft. 5¾ in., Depth 10¾ in. (V. & A. Mus.)*

10. *Oak Joint Foot-Stool. Mid-17th century. Ht. 11½ in., L. 1 ft. 4 in. (H. Clifford Smith Coll.).* 11. *Oak Stool, framework of bobbin turning. c. 1660. Ht. 1 ft. 6½ in., L. 1 ft. 8 in. c. 1660. (Mr Reginald Leon.)* 12. *Oak Stool with turned legs and stretchers; seat sunk for squab cushion. c. 1670. (The late Mr Harold Peto.)*

13. *Oak three-legged Joint Stool. Second half of 17th century. (Fred Skull Coll.)* 14. *Oak Joint Stool; spiral turning above vase-shaped members c. 1670. (Mr. H. W. Keil.)* 15. *Oak Joint Stool, drawer original, handle later. Late 17th century. Ht. 2 ft. 1½ in., L. of top 1 ft. 4 in. (Mr Golding Barrett.)*

16. *Oak Joint Stool, with top pierced for lifting; columnar legs finish in moulded feet. Late 17th century. Ht. 1 ft. 6½ in., L. 1 ft. 7½ in. (H. Clifford Smith Coll.)*
17. *Walnut caned Foot-Stool with scrolled legs and turned side stretchers. c. 1680. Ht. 7 in., L. 2 ft. 2 in., Depth 1 ft. 6 in. (Knole Park, Kent.)*

Park, Surrey, were each provided with an embroidered cushion.

Towards the end of Elizabeth's reign seats were often padded and upholstered. Sir John Harrington, writing c. 1596, says that in every merchant's hall stood 'easy quilted and lined forms and stools'; but complains that in the Queen's presence-chamber the stools were so hard that 'since great breeches were laid aside, men can scant endure to sit on them'. The inventories of Lord Lumley's various houses (1590) corroborate Harrington's statement that upholstered stools were abundant. He had an enormous number of stools, 57 of inlaid walnut and 118 of wainscot; many were cushioned, each chair, covered with silk, velvet or cloth of gold, having its accompanying stool. In 1603 the Great Chamber of Hengrave Hall, Suffolk, contained 24 stools, not counting foot-stools. Like contemporary chairs, they were sometimes made in sets at this time and upholstered to match. The Earl of Northampton's inventory (1614) lists in the Winter Dining Chamber at Northampton House 'eight highe stooles of tawney velvet with cases', and there is a similar set in another room. When stuffed and covered such seats are sometimes found described as 'buffet stools'. William Dalton, a Durham merchant, had three of this kind in his house as early as 1556.

The upholstered type, of which specimens survive at Knole, Kent, dating from c. 1610–20, corresponds with contemporary farthingale chairs, the woodwork being originally painted and gilt or covered with brocade or velvet and the padded seats trimmed with a straight silk fringe. Two 'lowe stooles' belonging to the Earl of Northampton (1614) were covered with 'striped clothe of silver frindged with yelowe and silver frindge'. The traditional X-shaped pattern, with the frame entirely covered in velvet and galon, is seen in Fig. 5.

Ordinary joint stools of this date resembled small tables of the period in design, the columnar legs being generally splayed for greater stability. In Fig. 4 they are of fluted form, and the underframing is arcaded. The subsequent evolution shows a great variety of treatment, carved and fluted legs gradually giving place to turning (Figs. 8 to 16). These oak joined stools were often made in sets to fit under a dining-table (*see* TABLES, DINING, Fig. 15); others were of such considerable length that the term 'bench' is equally applicable. The three-legged stool of medieval times continued to be made, and Shakespeare alludes to it in *Cymbeline* and other plays. This type is illustrated in Randle Holme's *The Academy of Armory* (MS. dated 1649), the author explaining that 'joynt stooles' were 'so called because all made and finished by the

18. *Walnut Stool upholstered in velvet of later date; stretchers with crown supported by amorini. By Thomas Roberts, 1689. Ht. 1 ft. 4 in., L. 1 ft. 7 in. (Hampton Court Palace. By gracious permission of H.M. the Queen.)* 19. *Circular walnut Stool, one of set of three; upholstered in Genoa velvet with tasselled fringe; scrolled stretchers centre in coronet of first Earl of Nottingham. c. 1685. (Burley-on-the-Hill, Rutland.)* 20. *Walnut upholstered Stool; pierced and carved with scrollwork; one scrolled stretcher broken. c. 1690. (Drayton House, Northants.)*

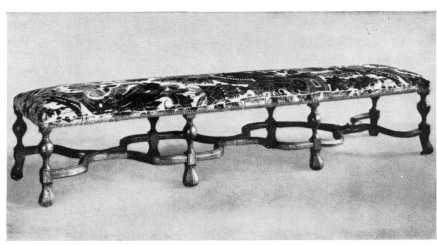

21. *Walnut Double Stool; pear-shaped legs and flat serpentine stretchers, upholstered in Spitalfields velvet. c. 1700. (Hampton Court Palace. By gracious permission of H.M. the Queen.)* 22. *Walnut Stool; faceted pear-shaped legs and scrolled feet; upholstered in Spitalfields velvet. c. 1695. Ht. 1 ft. 6 in., L. 2 ft. 2 in., Depth 1 ft. 8 in. (Hampton Court Palace. By gracious of H.M. the Queen.)*

23. *Gilt Stool; inward-curving legs united by serpentine stretchers; upholstered in grey moiré. Attributed to Thomas Roberts. c. 1700. Ht. 1 ft. 6 in., L. 2 ft., Depth 1 ft. 7½ in. (Hampton Court Palace.)* 24. *Walnut upholstered Stool, legs with faceted 'mushroom' cappings; scrolled stretchers elaborately carved. c. 1690. (Lady Assheton-Smith Coll.)* 25. *Beechwood upholstered Stool; pillar legs ending in volutes; high scrolled stretchers. c. 1690. (J. Thursby Pelham Coll.)*

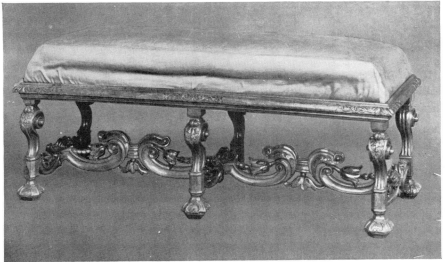

26. *Circular Stool, carved and gilt; original brocade embroidered in silk and silver thread. c. 1690. (Boughton House, Northants.)* 27. *Walnut Double Stool with mouldings 'carved round the seat'; outer covering (since removed) conceals double squab covered in figured crimson velvet. By Thomas Roberts, 1702. Ht. 1 ft. 10½ in., L. 4 ft. 3 in., Depth 1 ft. 9 in. (Hardwick Hall, Derbys.)*

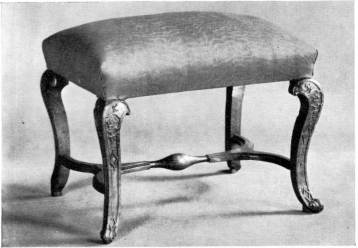

28. *Walnut Stool; fluted pillar legs with carved cappings; scrolled stretchers with central finial; original yellow silk upholstery. c. 1695. (J. Thursby Pelham Coll.)* 29. *Walnut upholstered Stool; cabriole legs carved in relief and ending in volutes. c. 1700. Ht. 1 ft. 7 in., L. 1 ft. 11½ in., Depth 1 ft. 6 in. (Hampton Court Palace. By gracious permission of H.M. the Queen.)*

joyner', distinguishing them from turned stools 'made by the turner or wheelwright ... wrought with knops and rings'. Oak joined stools continued to be used in the 18th century, and the servants' hall at Dyrham Park, Gloucestershire, in 1710 contained '18 Joint stools'. Tripod examples are given in Figs. 13 and 43.

Chairs were becoming more plentiful in Elizabethan times, but still retained their ceremonial significance. To offer one to a guest was a mark of respect, and in *Arden of Feversham* (1592) Will Shakebag tells Arden's wife to 'place Mosbie, being a stranger, in a chair, and let your husband sit upon a stool'. The rules governing the allotment of seats at Court were based on Continental precedent. In France the sovereign occupied a chair, and the right to sit on a stool or *tabouret* in his presence was reserved for the wives of princes, dukes and some of the high Court dignitaries. The etymology implies a round stool, and from their introduction tabourets appear invariably to have been upholstered. As a similar etiquette obtained in England, this name for a stool became naturalised. In 1604 'tabourets of brocade with a high cushion' were provided for the Constable of Castile when James I entertained

him at Whitehall; while 'their Majesties sat at the head of the table on chairs . . .'. The word afterwards acquired a less restricted meaning, and Blount (*Glossographia*, 1656) defines 'tabouret' as 'a little low stool for a childe to sit on'.

With the exception of those at Knole, very few upholstered stools of the first half of the 17th century survive. Constructed like contemporary chairs of a soft wood, they were probably destroyed when the upholstery had worn out. In large houses stools were generally upholstered with rich materials *en suite* with the chairs. A list of royal furniture dispersed after Charles I's execution in 1649 contains a large number of stools and foot-stools, covered, in almost every case, to match the chairs, and sold together with them, like 'two High Chaires eight high stools and 2 foot-stools of Stript Stuffe in Colours the ground Tynncell and three Cushans' (£6 10s.). Twelve 'foulding stools' at Oatelands, Surrey, upholstered with green velvet, probably resembled the Knole specimen (Fig. 5). The name was often applied, as in the Middle Ages, to what would now be termed a chair. Among Charles I's furniture at Somerset House in 1649 were 'twenty four wooden stools with Backs painted and gilt'. When an inven-

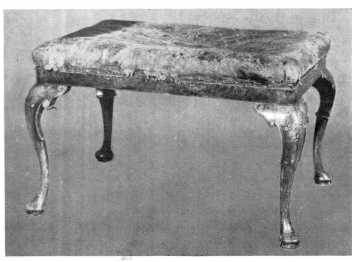

30. (*Left*) *Walnut Stool; moulded cabriole legs; leather covering original. c. 1710. (Formerly at Cold Overton Hall, Leics.)*

31. (*Right*) *Walnut circular Stool; sunk seat covered with rushes; scrolled supports. c. 1710. (Formerly at Canons Ashby.)*

32. (*Left*) *Walnut circular Stool; moulded cabriole legs, drop-in seat. c. 1710. Ht. 1 ft. 5 in. (Hardwick Hall, Derbys.)*

33. (*Right*) *Walnut Stool, cabriole legs carved with shells, claw-and-ball feet; needlework original. c. 1720. Ht. 1 ft. 2 in., L. 1 ft. 7 in. (Holyrood Palace, Midlothian.)*

tory of the contents of Kimbolton Castle, Huntingdonshire, was drawn up about this time, the stools considerably outnumbered the chairs; and this was true of most houses.

At the Restoration walnut and painted beech became the fashionable woods, and stools were made to match the new types of chair that were introduced from the Low Countries. The evolution in both varieties of furniture is practically identical, but, on stools, the florid carved stretchers of the time are usually found at back and front: thus they might be placed in any position in a room, and produced a very ornate effect (Fig. 20). Four scrolled stretchers centring on the coronet of the first Earl of Nottingham may be seen in the round stool (Fig. 19) elaborately covered in parti-coloured velvet with tassel fringe. The example in Fig. 18 was made in 1689 by Thomas Roberts (*q.v.*), a joiner who supplied a large quantity of furniture to the royal palaces during the reigns of the later Stuarts. In his bills of that year, he described two square walnut stools, matching chairs of state and carved 'with leaves and figures holding up the Crowne in the fore Raill'. Some of the plainer specimens are described in the royal joiners' accounts as 'cutt with scrowles all over'. The chairs and stools in the Venetian Ambassador's Room at Knole (Introduction, Fig. 8) may be assigned to Roberts; as also may the long stool, Fig. 27. In 1702 he supplied the

first Duke of Devonshire with 'six bankettes' (besides other seat furniture) 'all carved, with mouldings carved round the seats'.

Although most of the stools in the palaces had been dispersed like other furniture at the end of the Civil War, the loss was soon made good under Charles II, and vast quantities are again enumerated in the royal inventories of the time. A list of 'His Majesty's goods in the standing wardrobe at Whitehall' in 1688 shows the variety and elaborate character

34. *Walnut oval Stool; cabriole legs carved with escallop shells and husks; drop-in seat, claw-and-ball feet. c. 1720. (Percival Griffiths Coll.)*

35. *Walnut Stool; seat-rail centres in satyr mask; cabriole legs furred at back; paw feet. c. 1725. Ht. 1 ft. 6 in., L. 2 ft. 2 in. (Donaldson Coll.)*   36. *Mahogany upholstered Stool; lion masks and paw feet. c. 1730. (Shottisbrooke Park, Berks.)*

37. *Gilt upholstered Stool, seat-rail carved with wave pattern; pendant and 'broken' cabriole legs scaled. By Henry Williams, 1737, (Hampton Court Palace. By gracious permission of H.M. the Queen.)* 38. *Gilt upholstered X-Stool, one of large set; frame carved with acanthus and scaling. By Henry Williams, 1737. (Hampton Court Palace. By gracious permission of H.M. the Queen.)*

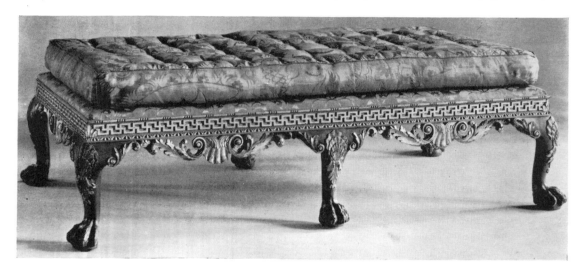

39. *Double Stool, part of set; mahogany carved and parcel gilt; squab and seat covered in original green damask. By Benjamin Goodison, 1740. L. 5 ft. 4 in. (Longford Castle, Wilts.)*

40. *Double Stool, mahogany; pendants below seat-rail and cabriole legs carved with acanthus; drop-in seat with earlier needlework reapplied. c. 1745. Ht. 1 ft. 8½ in., L. 4 ft. 4½ in., Depth 1 ft. 11 in. (Hardwick Hall, Derbys.)*

of these seats. 'Four old stooles of purple, cherry colour and gold coloured figured velvet with mixt fringe', and twelve covered with 'Turkey worke', probably dated from before the Rebellion; whereas six to match a crimson velvet bed and embroidered with gold and silver are specified as new. Foot-stools 'suiteable' to chairs of state occur in large numbers; among the entries are 'three dozen of Leather folding stooles'

and 'one dozen of cane stooles'. Contemporary specimens showing a different treatment of legs and stretchers, are given in Figs. 24, 25, 26, the tapered pillar leg, gadrooned, fluted and moulded, being particularly characteristic of this phase of design.

By Charles II's reign the *tabouret* etiquette had become extremely strict, being observed both in private houses and at

41. *Mahogany tripod Stool of kidney shape, drop-in seat; cabriole legs carved with ribbed acanthus. c. 1740. Ht. 1 ft. 1½ in., W. 9 in. (Percival Griffiths Coll.)*

42. *Mahogany Stool; shaped seat-rail carved with coquillage and foliage; legs end in dolphins' heads. c. 1755. Ht. 1 ft. 6½ in., L. 2 ft. 1½ in. (V. & A. Mus.)*

43. *Elm tripod Stool, one of pair; saddle-shaped seat, turned legs and stretchers. First half of 18th century. (Red Lion, Colchester.)*

44. *Mahogany Stool covered with earlier needlework. Based on design by Ince and Mayhew. c. 1760. Ht. 1 ft. 6½ in., L. 1 ft. 9 in., Depth 1 ft. 4 in. (Stephen Winkworth Coll.)*

45. *Mahogany Stool in Gothic taste, covered in tent stitch needlework; seat-rail arcaded; perforated legs finish in scrolled acanthus-carved feet. c. 1760. Ht. 1 ft. 4½ in., L. 2 ft. ½ in. (Percival Griffiths Coll.)*

46. *Mahogany upholstered Stool, part of set in Chinese taste. c. 1760. (Padworth House, Berks.)*

47. *Mahogany Stool, one of set of four; taper legs carved with paterae and husks. Supplied by Chippendale and Haig to Sir Edward Knatchbull in 1767. (Mersham Hatch, Kent.)*   48. *Mahogany Double Stool in Gothic taste. Made by Vile and Cobb, 1753. (The Vyne, Hants.)*

49. *Gilt Window Stool, one of pair, covered with Gobelins tapestry. Probably by Samuel Norman. c. 1770. L. 3 ft. 6 in. Formerly at Moor Park, Herts. (Philadelphia Museum of Art.)*

Court. When in England in 1669, Cosimo III, Duke of Tuscany, made gracious concessions in this matter to his hosts and hostesses at Wilton House, Wiltshire, and Althorp, Northamptonshire, causing chairs to be provided for them similar to his own, while the rest of the company sat on stools. The etiquette had lost none of its strictness at the Court of George II, by the time of Frederick, Prince of Wales's marriage. At the dinner before the wedding the royal princesses refused to appear until Frederick abandoned his demand that his bride should sit on a chair, objecting that she was not yet actually Princess of Wales.

In the first half of the 18th century, the legs, in form and decoration, follow the same evolution as in chairs, but occasionally a pattern is found particularly suited to a seat of this

50. *Mahogany Stool; shaped apron, legs end in volutes. Signed 'Strickland, Sept. 1st, 1763'. (H. W. Keil Ltd.)*

51. *Window Stool, framework carved with beading; scrolled ends finish in paterae; covered in leather. c. 1760. Ht. 2 ft. 5 in., L. 4 ft. 9½ in., Depth 1 ft. 4½ in. (Corsham Court, Wilts.)*

52. *Gilt Window Stool, with seat and scrolled ends caned. c. 1785. Ht. 2 ft., L. 5 ft. 1 in., Depth 1 ft. 3 in. (Chatsworth, Derbys.)*

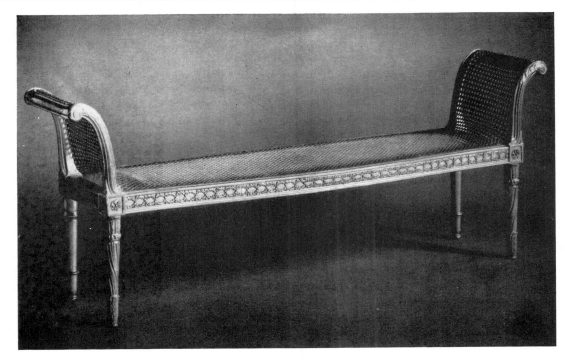

53. *Mahogany Window Stool carved in classical taste; scrolled ends; pendants below seat-rail. (Ickworth Park, Suffolk.)*

size. The round walnut stool from Canons Ashby, Northamptonshire (Fig. 31), has woodwork of unusual design, and a sunk seat covered with rushes. One of a very large gilt set from Hampton Court (Fig. 38) was made by Henry Williams (*q.v.*) in 1737, the traditional X-pattern being cleverly adapted. The large shells and scaling are characteristic of Kent, who probably supplied the design. In Fig. 37, also by this maker, the legs are of the broken cabriole form Kent sometimes employed. Lion and satyr masks were also carved on stools (Figs. 35 and 36), and at Houghton Hall, Norfolk, there is a gilt set thus decorated, matching chairs designed by Kent. At Longford Castle, Wiltshire, there is a pair of double stools (Fig. 39), part of a magnificent set of furniture made by Benjamin Goodison in 1740 (*cf.* COUCHES, Fig. 13).

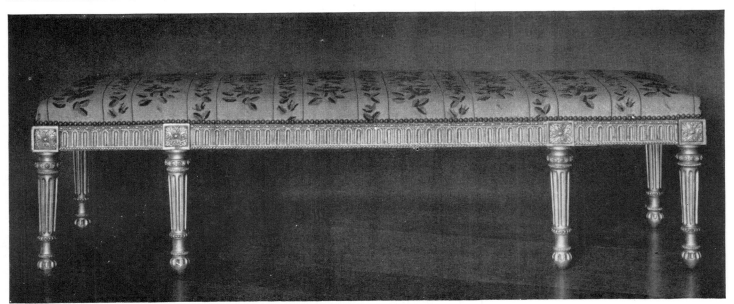

54. *Double Stool, one of three, carved and gilt. c. 1770. (Needlework later.) Ht. 1 ft. 6 in., L. 5 ft. 6 in., Depth 1 ft. 10 in. (Syon House, Middx.)*

55. *Mahogany Hall Stool, dipped seat painted with coronet and coat-of-arms. c. 1760. (Coleshill, Berks.)*

56. *Painted X-frame Stool, gilt enrichments in Egyptian taste; cushion and tassels not original. c. 1800.*

Chippendale does not illustrate this kind of seat in the *Director*, but Ince and Mayhew show designs for 'Lady's Dressing Stools' (Fig. 59) with elaborately carved and scrolled legs, one of those reproduced closely resembling a mahogany specimen (Fig. 44). Types fashionable between 1725 and 1760 may be seen in Figs. 35 to 46. The three-legged specimen (Fig. 41) is of kidney shape; while in Fig. 45 there is Gothic cusping on the seat and perforated legs, which end in a form of scrolled foot illustrated in some of the *Director* plates. The fine example in Fig. 42 has dolphin-headed feet, a terminal illustrated by Chippendale for a 'French chair' (*Director*, 3rd ed., Pl. XXI). The frets of the double stool

(Fig. 48), one of a pair included in a bill of William Vile's for Anthony Chute of The Vyne in 1753, are in Gothic taste; the guttae feet, however, are of an oriental type more often adopted in the Chinese style, of which Fig. 46 is a characteristic example. Ince and Mayhew also show what they term French stools 'for recesses of windows', much in demand for large Georgian houses. Chippendale sold a number of such seats to Sir Edward Knatchbull, of Mersham Hatch, Kent, charging £22 in 1767 for '4 long stools for the windows with scroll heads stuff'd and cover'd to match the chairs'. The covers in several instances were of leather 'brass nail'd,' and, though most were of mahogany, '3 scroll headed stools, Japand

57. *Carved and gilt Stool with X-frame in 'Grecian' taste. c. 1810. (Syon House, Middx.)*

58. *Foot-Stool; legs carved as animal terminals and painted green. c. 1810. Ht. 10 in., L. 1 ft. 5 in., Depth 1 ft. 1 in. (Chatsworth, Derbys.)*

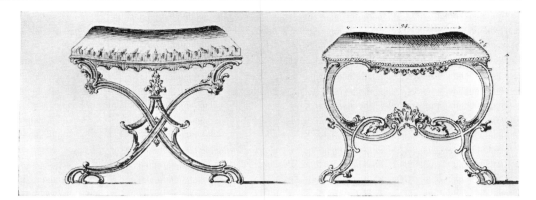

59. *Designs for 'Lady's Dressing Stools,' from Ince and Mayhew's* Universal System, 1759–63.

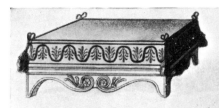

60. *Designs for Foot-Stools from George Smith's* Household Furniture, 1808.

61. *Design for a Window Stool from Hepplewhite's* Guide, 1788.

Green and white', were bought by Sir Edward in 1773. For the hall at The Hatch, Chippendale supplied two large mahogany stools and four smaller, 'without heads and made to match'. The latter cost £8 8s. and one in neo-classical style is shown in Fig. 47.

In trade catalogues of the period, single chairs are found described as 'back-stools' (*q.v.*), a term recalling the distant age when a seat with a back was comparatively rare. After 1750 stools do not seem to have been made in such numbers, but inventories prove they were plentiful in large houses, many, of course being of a considerably earlier date. At Easton Maudit, Northamptonshire, the Earl of Sussex's house, and at Chatsworth, Derbyshire, early in George III's reign, they are entered in almost every room. A 'double stool' covered with chintz in the earl's bedroom was probably four or five feet long, like Fig. 40; seats of this size in rather earlier inventories were described as 'banketts'. Mahogany stools seem to have been little used by the middle classes and were rarely made to accompany chairs in the rococo style, though at the beginning of the century both kinds of seat were commonly made in walnut to form a set.

In the great saloons and drawing-rooms of houses built and furnished by Robert Adam a formal and stately effect was obtained by long stools ranged against the walls, while in the deep window recesses others, with curved ends, were often placed. They were gilt or japanned, the legs being cylindrical and tapered, or with a slight cabriole, in the early days of the style. The ends were boldly scrolled and the decoration corresponded with that on chairs. The window stool (Fig. 51) is of the same type as one designed by Adam for Sir Lawrence Dundas, of Moor Park, c. 1764, and forms part of a set covered with Gobelins tapestry woven by Jacques Neilson. In the Corsham example (Fig. 49) the influence of the new classical taste is already apparent in the paterae enrichments and comparative severity of line. Caning was often used for this type.

Hepplewhite illustrates several stools in the *Guide* (1788), with both taper and cabriole legs, one being round and described as 'proper for a dressing stool'. The note states that the framework 'may be of mahogany or japanned, or to match the

suit of chairs, and of consequence should have the same sort of covering'. Two of the 'window stools' (Fig. 61) are stated to be 'peculiarly adapted for an elegant drawing-room of japanned furniture'. The ends are scrolled, and may be either stuffed or openwork. The example in Fig. 53 has the carved pendants below the seat-rail shown in one of Hepplewhite's designs. A double stool from Syon House, Middlesex (Fig. 54), shows the type of seat commonly used in great reception rooms, together with others of smaller size. Their formal arrangement is suggested by a passage in *The Description of Strawberry Hill* (1782), Horace Walpole writing that 'all along the wall are high stools of crimson Norwich damask, mounted on black and gold frames'.

There was no notable change in the design of stools until furniture began to be affected by the anglicised version of the Empire style. Sheraton does not illustrate them in his *Drawing Book* (1791–4), and in the *Dictionary* (1803) omits the heading 'stool'. He does, however, in the later work, note that foot-stools are 'generally stuffed with hair and covered with some kind of needlework', and shows what he calls a 'corridor stool', a long seat on dolphin legs, with scrolled wooden ends but no back. Stools in pronounced Egyptian taste are illustrated in considerable variety in *Ackermann's Repository*, Smith's

Household Furniture (1808), and other contemporary books. They were of mahogany or soft wood gilt or bronzed, and, as on chairs, the feet and hoofs of animals were generally used as terminals. An X-pattern was at this time often adopted in an attempt to reproduce the form of classical antiquity. The type in Fig. 56 is said by Smith to be 'intended as ornamental and extra seats in elegant Drawing Rooms', and for saloons and drawing-rooms stools of this kind were sometimes gilt (Fig. 57). The earlier variety with a curved seat continued in favour for halls and lobbies. The stool shown in Fig. 55 corresponds in design with a large set supplied for the library at Christ Church, Oxford, for £38 15s. by Chippendale in 1764. One of a pair from Chatsworth (Fig. 58) closely resembles a design by Smith dated 1803 (*Household Furniture*, Pl. 55).

STOOLS, BACK. *See* BACK-STOOLS.

STOOLS, GOUT. Prevalence of gout in the Georgian period, induced by hard drinking, led to production of stools specially designed to alleviate that complaint. Hepplewhite (*Guide*, 1788) illustrates a stool of this kind with top adjustable by a ratchet, writing that 'being so easily raised or lowered at either end, it is particularly useful to the afflicted'. Miniature versions of the X-stool, comfortably padded, were also produced for this purpose. The younger Chippendale's bills for furniture for Sir Richard Colt Hoare of Stourhead, Wiltshire (1804), include '2 Satin Wood Gout Stools with Scroll Elbows stuffed and covered with red Morocco leather and brass Mouldings £5 16s. 0d.'

STRAP-WORK. Interlaced and arabesque ornament of architectural origin, carved in low relief and generally in repeated patterns. This form of decoration, introduced c. 1550 largely through Flemish and German pattern books, often used in Tudor and Jacobean times on friezes and panels of oak furniture. Term also applied to interlaced and perforated scrolls which, c. 1735, replaced solid splats in chairs (*see* CHAIRS, Fig. 100, and CHESTS, Fig. 17).

STRAW-WORK. The process of embellishing cabinets, table-tops, desks, boxes, etc., by straws, which, split into required widths, bleached and dyed, were, with aid of adhesive, laid down on the object in imitation of landscapes, buildings, figures, and animals, or marquetry. This form of decoration was brought to perfection in the 17th century in Italy, Spain and France. Evelyn writes (1646) of 'curious straw worke among the nuns (of Milan) even to admiration'. An early English example of the craft is the toilet mirror (Fig. 1), the straws in various shades of brown being laid down on a silk ground. A gentlewoman advertises in the *Edinburgh Gazette* (1703) that she teaches 'Straw-Work of any sort as houses birds and beasts'.

From c. 1700 Dunstable appears to have been the chief source of production. The craft received a considerable stimulus in the Napoleonic wars, as French and Dutch prisoners were allowed to practise it as a trade, and the excellent quality of their straw-work began to compete seriously with the indigenous industry. A variety of objects—panels, work-boxes, cabinets, desks and tea-caddies—were produced by these

1. *Mirror in frame decorated with Straw-work. c. 1670. Ht. 1 ft. 10 in., W. 1 ft. 6½ in. (V. & A. Mus.)*

2. *Miniature Bureau decorated with Straw-work and stained to represent marquetry. c. 1800. (Mrs Abell.)*

prisoners 1793–1815; the prison camp or depot, Norman Cross, near Winchester, being one of the chief centres of manufacture. Several examples by Jean de la Porte, a prisoner there in 1810, are known, and a panel in the Victoria and Albert Museum (595—1906) is inscribed:

> Monsieur De leporte [Sic]
> Prisonnier de Guerre
> NORMAN CROSS
> Le Quatorzième d'Aout Mille huit cent dix.

A number of other prisoners' names are recorded. The technical accomplishment displayed in some of the pieces is remarkable, but it is not possible to distinguish between unsigned French examples and native productions. The miniature bureau on stand in Fig. 2 is an important example of straw-work; here a considerable variety of well-preserved dyes may be seen. (*See also* T. W. Bagshawe, 'Straw Marquetry', *Apollo*, Vol. XXII, pp. 283-6, and Vol. XXIII, pp. 332-5.)

STRETCHERS. Rails or bars of various kinds used to unite legs of chairs, tables, stools, etc., and to afford additional strength; plain or sometimes highly ornate, carved and moulded, following in design the sequence of styles (*see* CHAIRS, STOOLS, TABLES).

STRINGING. Narrow band or line of wood or other substance used as inlay to contrast with surrounding veneer. Light-coloured woods, *e.g.* sycamore and box, used commonly for this purpose from c. 1550 onwards: in Regency style stringing lines frequently of brass.

STUMP-WORK. *See* NEEDLEWORK.

SWAN-NECK PEDIMENT. *See* PEDIMENT.

SWEETWOOD (*Nectandra exaltata*). Lauraceous timber from West Indies, brownish in colour, tinged with green, and of hard, fine grain. Its use recorded in 16th century, *e.g.* 'a sweetwood table standing upon four bears' (the Warwick badge) at Leicester House, 1588.

SYCAMORE. Term sycamore applied in England to wood of *Acer pseudo-platanus*, more accurately described as maple, or false plane; in Scotland same wood termed plane tree. White, becoming yellow with age; fine, compact grain, and takes excellent polish. Some of this wood found with fine rippled surface similar to satinwood. Sycamore one of woods used in cutting floral marquetry on walnut furniture: and both as veneer and in solid when satinwood fashionable for fine furniture, *i.e.* c. 1765–90. At that period also dyed with a solution of oxide of iron in water. Sycamore, when polished, assumed a grey colour tinged with green, and was known as 'harewood'. J. C. R.

TABBY (also TABBINET). Kind of silk taffety with shot or variegated surface.

> Those counter-chaged Tabbies in the air
> The sun once set, all of one colour are.
>
> (Herrick: *Life is the Bodys Light*.)

Manufacture introduced here by Huguenot refugees in Charles II's reign, but 'Tabby Grogram' and others of silk shown as imports in first half 17th century. 'Queen's Bed-Chamber: curtains and valances are of a rich green corded tabby'

(Windsor Castle), (*Les Délices des Châteaux Royaux, or a Pocket Companion to the Royal Palaces of Windsor, Kensington, Kew, Hampton Court*, 1785).

TABLE COVERS. *See* CUSHIONS; TAPESTRY; TURKEY WORK.

TABLES, ARTISTS' AND READING. Early in the 18th century the needs of draughtsmen, architects and amateur artists led to the introduction of specialised tables suitable for drawing, reading and writing. In a type long popular the area of the top is increased by a pull-out front supported on the front sections of two legs. In an early example (Fig. 1) the drawer is supported by the two outer pilasters, and in the centre of the extending top is a slope adjustable by a strut; a drawer swings out from the side for drawing materials.

Some of these tables had rising tops so that the artist could sit or stand; others were mounted on a pillar with tripod feet. In 1758 Benjamin Goodison supplied George II with a mahogany writing and reading table 'with racks and stays to fix the top at different heights'. In some reading tables the 'double rising top', seen in Fig. 4, can be raised to a considerable height 'so healthy for those who stand to write, read or draw'. The top is devised on this principle in Fig. 2, an unusually elegant specimen contemporary with Fig. 4. An artist's table with 'upward and inward rising desks' is said by J. T. Smith (*Nollekins and his Times*) to have been brought into fashion by John Cobb (*q.v.*), and the painter Nathaniel Dance considered the tables so useful that he 'easily persuaded Cobb to allow him to paint his portrait in exchange for one'.

In 1767 Chippendale provided 'a very neat mahogany drawing table of very fine wood, the top made to rise' at a cost of £8 8s. for the library at Nostell Priory, Yorkshire; where that example, designed in the neo-classic style, still remains.

1. *Artist's Table, veneered with walnut; arcaded front supported on pilasters. c. 1725. (Exhibited in the Art Institute of Chicago.)*

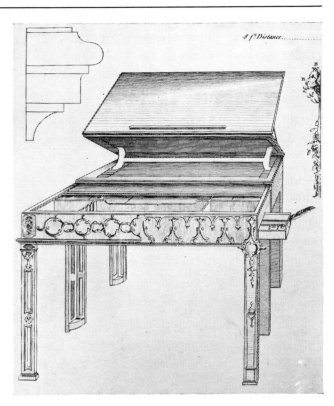

2. (*Left*) *Mahogany Artist's Table; top rises on ratchet; pierced lattice-work frieze, cluster column supports.* c. 1755. (*The late Sir Sydney Greville.*)

3. (*Right*) *Design for 'Writing and Reading Table' from Ince and Mayhew's* Universal System, 1759–63.

William France in 1770 supplied one of the tripod variety to Lord Mansfield at Ken Wood (Fig. 5), charging £6 14s. 'for a large Mahogany Reading Stand on a Stout Pillar and Claw, with a screw nutt, work'd very true, capable of screwing to rise 10 ins if required, the whole of very good Mahogany and pillar and Claw richly Carv'd'. Sheraton (appendix, *Drawing Book*, 1791–4) illustrates what he regards as an improvement on the earlier type, writing: 'This table will be found highly useful to such as draw, it being designed from my own experience of what is necessary for those who practise this art.

The top of the table is made to rise by a double horse, that the designer may stand if he please, or he may sit, to have the top raised in any direction.'

TABLES, BILLIARD. Cloth-covered tables with raised, padded sides for a game of skill, of which the origin is uncertain. It is supposed to have been first played in the open air on a piece of smooth turf, sunk and measured out, the balls being struck with long mallets or cues; when the game was adapted to indoor use, billiard tables were covered with green cloth,

4. (*Left*) *Detail of portrait* (*Rev. Edward Foyle*) *by Arthur Devis, showing table with double rising top.* c. 1760.

5. (*Right*) *Mahogany Reading Table made by William France in* 1770; *pierced brackets; tripod stand carved in rococo taste.* Ht. 2 ft. 6 in., L. 2 ft. 2 in., Depth 2 ft. 1¾ in. (*V. & A. Mus.*)

perhaps in representation of grass. Billiards is mentioned as an indoor recreation in conjunction with cards as early as 1429 in France, and at the beginning of the 16th century tables for the game, covered with a green cloth, and ivory cues, are entered in French inventories. At Howard House, 1588, the Duke of Norfolk had 'a billyard bord covered wth a greene cloth wth a frame of beache wth fower turned postes'. The inventory also mentions 'three billyard stickes and 11 balles of yvery'.

Spenser (*Mother Hubbard's Tale*, 1591, a satire on Court vices and follies) writes of 'balliards', together with dice and cards, as among the 'thriftless games'; and Shakespeare, early in James I's reign, also refers to it, making Cleopatra say to Charmian, 'Let's to billiards'. Florio, about the same date, defined the game as 'a kinde of play with balles upon a table . . .'; while Cotgrave's *Dictionary* (1611) proves that the cue was sometimes known as a billiard, explaining the word as 'The sticke where-with we touch the ball at billyards'.

Robert Burton in *The Anatomy of Melancholy* (1622) gives a list of winter amusements, including shuttle-cock, shovel-board and 'balliards'; and tables for the last-named must have been plentiful by the second half of the 17th cen-

tury, for as early as 1653 there is one described as old and 'spoyled' at Birsay House in the Orkneys. They begin to appear fairly often among the contents of great houses about this time; *e.g.* Charles I had 'a Billiard Board covered in green cloth' at Hampton Court; and though the Protector was averse to frivolous pursuits, his inventory mentions another, described as 'small'. Cotton (*Complete Gamester*, 1674) writes of billiards as 'a most gentile, cleanly and ingenious game', and continues that 'it is much approved of and played by most nations of Europe, especially in England, there being few towns of note therein which hath not a public billiard table, neither are they wanting in many noble and private families in the country'. He deals at length with the construction. A table should be somewhat greater in length than width and railed round; 'the rail or ledge ought to be a little swel'd or stuft with fine flox or cotton'. The cloth is to be green and free from knots, while 'the board must be level'd as exactly as may be, so that a Ball may run true upon any part of the Table without leaning to any side thereof'. What with ill-seasoned boards and the unevenness of floors, however, the author complains that very few tables are found true, and therefore the rare exceptions are the more esteemed. He states that, instead of pockets with nets placed at the four corners

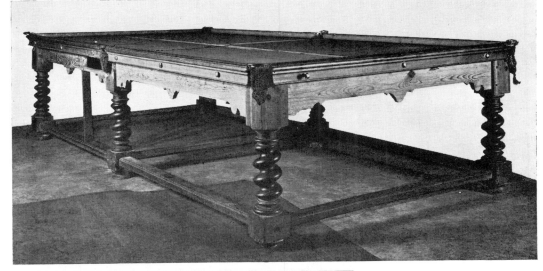

1. *Billiard Table of oak and pine with spiral-turned supports; mahogany top of later date. c. 1660. Ht. 3 ft., L. 12 ft. 2 in., W. 6 ft. 2 in. (V. & A. Mus.)*

2. *Oak Billiard Table (restored); twelve supports of baluster form. c. 1700. Ht. 3 ft. 2½ in., L. 13 ft. 6 in., W. 6 ft. 8 in. (Knole Park, Kent.)*

3. *Mahogany Billiard Table, frieze inlaid with honeysuckle in satinwood; gilt brass mounts. c. 1780. Ht. 3 ft., L. 6 ft. 1 in., W. 3 ft. 1 in. (Alnwick Castle, Northumberland.)*

and exactly in the middle of the sides, wooden boxes were sometimes used, though they were undesirable because 'a Ball struck hard is apt to fly out of them'.

Very few early billiard tables survive, no doubt because they were destroyed when superseded by improved methods of construction, but at Knole Park, Kent, there is an oak example of late 17th-century date, still preserving its original form, despite some restoration (Fig. 2). The curved mahogany cues are tipped with ivory. Another table (Fig. 1), dating some years earlier, was formerly at Rushbrooke Hall, Suffolk.

There are many allusions to the game at this period. Pepys (*Diary*) records July 17, 1665, 'Up all of us and to billiards', and, a little later, notes that he beat Captain Cocke, winning about 8s. from him and another player. In 1679 the Great Hall at Ham House, Surrey, contained 'one billiard table covered with green cloathe and a leather case to it'.

Celia Fiennes, on her travels in 1697, noted 'a Billyard Room' above the hall in the Earl of Hereford's house at Ipswich; while at Euston Hall, Suffolk, she observed in the Long Gallery 'a square in ye middle where stands a billiard table'.

Billiard tables are not represented in 18th-century trade catalogues, and seldom appear to have been designed as decorative pieces of furniture; they are absent, moreover, from the bills of Chippendale and other famous makers. Sheraton is the only celebrated designer who mentions them, writing (*Cabinet Dictionary*, 1803): 'These tables are made very large when they are full-sized ones. Their shape is an oblong about 12 ft. in length and 6 ft. in width. Billiard-table making is generally a branch of itself; though sometimes they are made in regular cabinet shops; when they are, they require the best of workmen to execute them.' Fig. 3 shows a table of this period, 6 ft. in length, with the frieze inlaid with honeysuckle and swags of ormolu capping the legs.

TABLES, BREAKFAST.

Specialised forms of table for breakfast seem to have been in use from an early date. Tudor inventories suggest that such tables were already regarded as a distinct variety. The *Privy Purse Expenses* of the Princess Mary contain an entry of 1544 'For mending the Brekefaste

borde'; about the same date there was 'a brekefaste table of walnuttree' in Henry VIII's Privy Chamber.

During the Stuart period small tables with flaps and those of gate construction, with turned legs, were doubtless used for this purpose, and are often mentioned among the contents of parlours and eating-rooms. In the 18th century the habit of rising late and breakfasting upstairs, often referred to in contemporary satires, led to the introduction of small breakfast tables, designed to match the furniture of a fashionable bedroom. Fig. 1 shows a mahogany example from Dumfries House, Ayrshire, which closely follows Pl. XXXIII in the *Director* (1st ed., 1754). Like the design, it has a shelf enclosed with fretwork, while 'the front is cut out for a recess for the knees and two folding doors to open'. The notes state that sometimes the filling is of brass wire. A fine breakfast table (Fig. 3), has one of these wirework fillings, the top being

1. *Mahogany Breakfast Table with shelf enclosed by fre two in Chinese style. Attributed to Thomas Chippendale. c. 1759. (Dumfries House, Ayrshire.)*

2. *Breakfast Table, japanned black and gold; fretwork ornament in Chinese taste. c. 1755. Ht. 2 ft. 3½ in., L. 3 ft. 3 in., Depth 2 ft. 2 in. (Hagley Hall, Worcs.)*   3. *Breakfast Table, mahogany and satinwood with floral inlay; cupboard enclosed by brass wirework. c. 1780. (Longford Castle, Wilts.)*

inlaid with a floral design, while Fig. 2 shows a japanned version of this type. Chippendale illustrates (*Director*, 3rd ed., 1762, Pl. LIII) anothe rtype resembling Fig. 4, though with stretchers, pierced in Gothic tracery.

This specialised variety appears in the royal accounts, John Bradburn in 1765 supplying the royal household with 'a good mahogany 2 Flap Breakfast Table with a Drawer on Brass Casters'. In 1766 Benjamin Goodison made another of the exceptional height of 2 ft. 9 ins., the drawer having a 'Brass Lock wrought Handle', and the castors being of leather.

George Smith's *Household Furniture* (1808) contains three designs for 'Déjuné Tables'. 'Adapted for a breakfast set of

4. *Mahogany Breakfast Table; with shaped flaps and C-scrolled stretchers. c. 1760. Ht. 2 ft. 4 in., L. 2 ft. 11 in., Depth 1 ft. 11½ in. (Macquoid Coll.)*

superb china, (they) are used in Ladies' Boudoirs or Morning Breakfast Rooms.' Two are in the Chinese taste, and the notes explain that they may be painted to match the china placed on them.

TABLES, CARD AND GAMING. (Cards, backgammon, chess and draughts). The earliest form of gaming table was, probably, a wooden board marked out with lines and placed on the floor or on a piece of furniture; as before the 15th century, when playing cards were introduced into England, the indoor games of skill and chance mentioned by contemporary writers are chess, tables (later called backgammon) and dice. Chess was well known in this country before the Conquest, and in the Middle Ages proficiency at the game was considered a polite accomplishment.

The importation of playing cards was forbidden in 1463, but in the *Paston Letters*, during Richard III's reign, 'Tabylls, schesse and cards' are referred to as the 'dysports' of the whole household, and these amusements were very popular at the Tudor Courts. Henry VIII delighted in tables, dice and shovel-board, at which games he played for high stakes (*see* BACK-GAMMON AND CHESS BOARDS).

'A paier of playeing tables', an entry often found in Tudor inventories, implies a chess or backgammon board, but the walnut table at Hardwick Hall, (Fig. 2), probably by an immigrant craftsman, was intended for games. The top, decorated with a parquetry of various woods, is inlaid with playing cards, the five of each suit at the corners, and supported on pillar legs, with T-shaped stretchers tenoned into them.

Early card games appear to have been for two or four persons. Any small table with a smooth surface would have served for dice and, when covered by a carpet or cloth, for cards. The Hardwick inventory of 1600 enumerates a number of little square and folding tables with carpets of needlework, which were probably thus used, while Sir John Harrington speaks of a 'velvet carpet' as a covering for games tables.

1. *Oil painting representing game of primero. Artist unknown. Late 16th century. Ht. 3 ft. 2½ in., W. 5 ft. 1¾ in. (Earl of Derby.)*

John Northbrooke in his *Treatise* against dicing (1579) stigmatises card playing 'as an invention of the devill'; but Queen Elizabeth I, though she played draughts and chess with Roger Ascham, was also fond of cards, and primero, introduced from Spain, was much in favour at her Court. In Fig. 1 four unidentified persons, obviously of great distinction, are playing it at a square table covered with a cloth. Shakespeare alludes to this game, making Falstaff say, 'I never prospered since I foreswore myself at Primero'.

Glecko, or gleek, was also popular, and could be played by two or three persons. Lady Anne Clifford continually mentions this amusement in her *Diary*; in 1616 there is an entry 'after supper I played Gleeko with the Steward and as I often do after dinner and supper'. E.O. tables were for a game of chance 'Euen or Odde', which was 'determined by the letters E and O being marked on that compartment of a box into which a die or ball fell'. Richard Hubolt (*Abcedarium Anglo-*

Latinum, 1552) states it to be 'a game much used now a dayes among chyldren', but later it was taken up by adults. In the Shuttleworth accounts (Gawthorpe Hall, Lancashire) there is an entry, September, 1617, 'for a little E. and O. box and sending them down 12d'. During his tour in the late 18th century, Bray, when at Althorp, Northamptonshire, noted that 'in one of the rooms is a table for play, which seems to be the original of the E.O. tables'.

In the Stuart period entries of gaming tables appear in inventories, but without such descriptions as enable their character to be recognised. In Charles I's reign the splendidly furnished rooms of the royal palaces contained a number of tables covered with velvet and other costly materials, which were, no doubt, used for cards. In addition to these are several, stated to have been for games, in the list of the royal possessions sold after the king's death. At Hampton Court was 'one table to play at Trolle Madam'.

Ombre, a three-handed game, popularised by Catherine of Braganza, but introduced before her arrival in England (as a pamphlet, *The Royal Game of Ombre*, 1660, proves), was much played at Court after the Restoration. With quadrille, a later version for four players, and picquet, it maintained its popularity into the mid-Georgian period.

Dicing was a popular diversion at Charles II's Court, and Evelyn (*Diary*, January 6, 1662) writes that according to custom 'His Majesty opened the revels of that night by throwing the dice himself in the privy-chamber, where was a table set on purpose, and lost his £100; the ladies also played very deep'. The *Compleat Gamester* (1674) states that gaming had by then 'become so much the fashion among the *beau monde* that he who in company should appear ignorant of the game in vogue would be reckoned low-bred and hardly fit for conversation'. Basset and loo were very fashionable at this date; both games could be played by a considerable number. Evelyn mentions (February, 1685, when recording the king's death) that he had the week before seen 'Twenty of the great

2. *Walnut Gaming Table, pillar supports; top inlaid with parquetry of various woods, borders with strapwork and playing cards. c. 1580. Ht. 2 ft. 10½ in., L. 3 ft. 6 in., Depth 3 ft. 5 in. (Hardwick Hall, Derbys.)* 3. *Walnut Card Table, circular folding top and three drawers in shaped frieze; supports tapered, hinged back stretchers. c. 1700. Ht. 2 ft. 6 in., L. 2 ft. 9 in., Depth 2 ft. 6 in. (V. & A. Mus.)*

4. *Walnut Card Table with folding top, inlaid with arabesque marquetry; pillar legs with Ionic capitals. c. 1690. (Mrs David Gubbay.)*
5. *Walnut Piquet Table on tripod stand, decorated with foliated scroll marquetry; flaps inlaid on underside. c. 1695. Ht. 2 ft. 4 in.
(Lady Assheton-Smith Coll.)*

courtiers and other dissolute persons at Basset round a large table'. The Countess of Sunderland, in a letter of about this time, complains that her husband plays for £5,000 a night at basset.

The earliest type of table especially designed for cards was introduced at the close of the 17th century. Such tables are veneered with walnut and usually have circular folding tops and tapered or turned legs united by shaped stretchers. Two of the back legs swing out to support the flap, and there are small drawers in the frieze (Fig. 3). The rectangular tops of another variety constructed on the same principle are occasionally covered with velvet, and were probably used both for cards and other purposes. In Fig. 4 the legs, decorated in

marquetry with leafage and arabesques, recall contemporary French designs, the capitals and ball feet being finely carved. Celia Fiennes, on her travels early in Anne's reign, mentioned that she saw at Hampton Court Palace 'a little wanscote table for tea, cards or writing'.

Picquet, a game from France played by two persons, appears to have inspired a number of particularly elegant small tables. A rare example on a tripod stand (Fig. 5) closely resembles those designed at the same period in France; it is veneered with walnut and inlaid with arabesque marquetry, instead of the brass and tortoise-shell usually employed by French craftsmen. In the 'Suping Roome' at Kensington Palace in 1697 there was a table which appears to have been of similar

6. (*Left*) *Walnut Card Table; circular folding top and cabriole legs with hoof feet. c. 1705. (J. Thursby Pelham Coll.)*

7. (*Right*) *Card Table; parquetry of contrasting veneers, cross-bandings of laburnum. c. 1715. Ht. 2 ft. 5 in., L. 2 ft. 11½ in., Depth 1 ft. 6 in. (Ickworth Park, Suffolk.)*

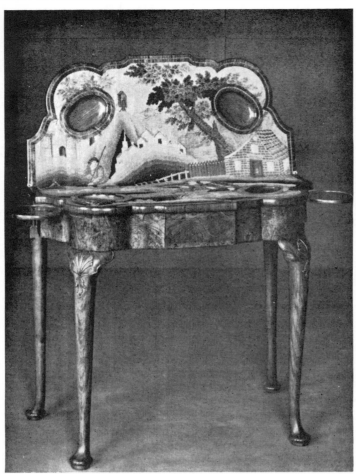

8. *Walnut Card Table; wells for counters and pull-out candle-brackets; top covered with cross-stitch needlework; borders and frieze shaped. c. 1715. Ht. 2 ft. 4 in., L. 2 ft. 8 in. (Donaldson Coll.)*

9. *Card Table with oval folding top and cabriole legs, japanned in black and gold. c. 1720. Ht. 2 ft. 5½ in., L. 3 ft. 1 in. Above: detail of top. (Cora, Countess of Strafford Coll.)*

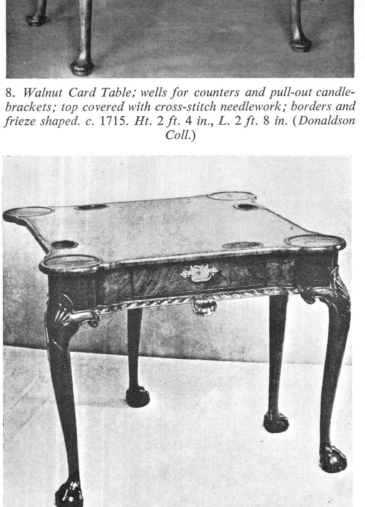

character, for it is described in the inventory as a 'small square wallnutt tree table Inlaid with white and covered with greene velvett upon a foote'.

Early in the 18th century turned and tapered supports gave way to cabriole legs, and stretchers were abolished. The folding tops were at first circular (Fig. 6), but in the next type generally square, with cylindrical corners dished to hold candlesticks (Fig. 10), wells for money or counters being also provided. The cabriole legs follow the familiar evolution and gradually become bolder, spade and club feet being succeeded by claw-and-ball and lion paw. Until c. 1715 the flap had been supported by a swing leg hinged to the back framework, so that the table, when open, looked somewhat incomplete; a folding frame with hinges was, therefore, introduced to ensure greater stability and symmetry (*see* CONSTRUCTION, Fig. 8). A square frieze is at first found below the rounded corners of the top, but later the frieze is curved to correspond with them. Before 1720 walnut was mainly employed, but other woods were also used, the table in Fig. 7, for instance, being overlaid with contrasting veneers of laburnum, set

10. *Walnut Card Table; circular corners dished for candlesticks, and wells for counters; one of the cabriole legs swings out. c. 1720. (Fred Skull Coll.)*

11. *Walnut Table with flaps for cards, chess, writing and backgammon. c. 1720. Ht. 2 ft. 5 in., L. 2 ft. 9 in., Depth (closed) 1 ft. 3 in. (Col N. R. Colville.)*

12. *(Above) Mahogany Card Table; finely carved cabriole legs, tufted and headed by lion masks; top covered with original tent-stitch needlework. c. 1730. Ht. 2 ft. 3½ in., L. 2 ft. 6 in. (Penshurst Place, Kent.)*

diagonally on the top and cross-banded. Fig. 8 shows a fine example veneered with bleached burr walnut. The needlework, representing a pastoral scene, is set in an undulating border and the frieze follows out its complex curves.

These tables were occasionally of multiple form, with extra flaps for games, writing and tea, a knuckle-joint being generally provided on the framework to keep the leaves at the required level. The example in Fig. 13 is unusual in having an additional flap for drawing and an extra leg to support both when open.

13. *Mahogany Table with two flaps, one for drawing, other for cards and backgammon; candle brackets and swing-out drawer. c. 1730. Ht. 2 ft. 4 in., L. 2 ft. 11 in., Depth 2 ft. 4 in. (A. Dunn Gardner Coll.)*

14. *Card Table veneered with burr walnut; ringed cabriole legs carved with eagle heads and acanthus. c. 1735. (Mr Andrew J. Reid.)*

15. *Tripod Card Table, japanned black and gold. Early* 18*th century. Ht. 2 ft. 3¾ in., L. 3 ft. 7½ in., Depth 3 ft. 2¼ in.* 16. *Top of same table bearing Tower Arms. (Weald Hall, Essex.)*

The table in Fig. 11 may be used for backgammon, chess, writing or cards.

Early in George I's reign, mahogany began to supersede walnut for card tables and in the decade 1725–35 lion decoration became fashionable for this type of furniture. In the fine mahogany table from Penshurst Place, Kent (Fig. 12), the realistic masks and feathering on the cabriole legs closely correspond with those on a set of contemporary chairs form-

erly at Copped Hall, Essex; the acanthus brackets start from the same six-petalled flower in both instances. The top, covered with fine *petit-point*, is dished for counters and candlesticks (*see* NEEDLEWORK, Fig. 7; CHAIRS, Fig. 78). About this time there was another variation in design, the top and frieze becoming rectangular, with the dishings for candles of similar shape. A distinct type was produced with a triangular folding top and a leg at each corner, another supporting the flap,

17. *Walnut tripod Card Table; top covered with needlework. Mid-*18*th century. Ht. 2 ft. 3¾ in., L. 3 ft., Depth 2 ft. 6¾ in. (Weald Hall, Essex.)* 18. *Walnut Card Table; serpentine frieze and cabriole legs headed by lion masks. c.* 1735. *Ht. 2 ft. 4 in., L. 3 ft. 1½ in. (Percival Griffiths Coll.)*

19. *Mahogany Card Table; folding top and frame carved with rococo ornament. c. 1760. Ht. 3 ft. 3½ in., L. 3 ft. (Henry Hirsch Coll.)*

20. *Walnut Card Table; legs carved with foliage end in volutes. c. 1760. Ht. 2 ft. 4½ in., L. 2 ft. 11½ in. (Formerly at Langley Park, Norfolk.)*

21. *Mahogany Card Table; hinged folding framework carved with Gothic fluting. c. 1760. Ht. 2 ft. 5 in., L. 3 ft. (Tyttenhanger, Herts.)*

22. *Card Table carved with rococo ornament and veneered with figured burr walnut. c. 1760. (Percival Griffiths Coll.)*

23. *Mahogany Card Table with folding top; frieze and straight legs carved wih frets. c. 1760. (Ickworth Park, Suffolk.)*

24. (*Left*) *Mahogany Card Table; corners inlaid with playing cards. c. 1760. Ht. 2 ft. 4 in., L. 2 ft. 9½ in., Depth 1 ft. 5 in.*

25. (*Right*) *Gilt Card Table; top inlaid with diaper pattern and veneered with harewood and satinwood. Attributed to Peter Langlois. c. 1770. (Syon House, Middx.)*

when open, while plain tripod tables were made, the tops being sometimes covered with needlework and the veneered borders dished for counters (Fig. 17).

Some of these early Georgian card tables were made in soft wood and japanned. A number so decorated are recorded in the inventory (1725) of the Duke of Chandos's furniture at Cannons. In His Grace's Closet there was a 'red japand Card Table with doors and drawers, the top lined wth green velvet'; there was another of these red japanned tables, now very rare, in Lord Carnarvon's bedchamber. The table with doors must have been quite exceptional in construction. Though the table in Fig. 9 is designed in the English taste of c. 1720, the decoration in black and gold japan is of unusual excellence and scarcely distinguishable from Eastern lacquer.

Card playing, stimulated by the prevailing spirit of speculation, became a positive mania during the early 18th century,

and in 1713 the *Guardian* denounced women gamesters, concluding 'There is nothing that wears out a fine face like the Vigils of the Card Table . . .'. The Revenue sought to benefit by this passion. An act of Anne's reign placed an imposition of sixpence per pack on certain cards and five shillings a pair on dice. This restriction had no effect on the upper classes, and Swift in his rhymed *Journal of a Modern Lady* represents her waiting eagerly after tea to begin play.

Pope (*Rape of the Lock*, 1712–14) describes the game of ombre played by a fashionable company 'on the velvet plain'; and in *The Basset Player*, one of the *Town Eclogues*, asks:

> But who to Bowl, or ratt'ling Dice compares
> To Basset's heav'nly Joys and pleasing Cares?

George II encouraged the rage for all forms of card playing, and headed many of the Court gambling entertainments.

26. *Mahogany Table; serpentine fluted frieze and narrow, trefoil-headed cabriole legs. c. 1780. (Culzean Castle, Ayrshire.)* 27. *Card Table of cherrywood inlaid with satinwood; folding top of mahogany. c. 1770. Ht. 2 ft. 5 in., L. 2 ft. 9 in., Depth (closed) 1 ft. 6 in. (Royal Scottish Mus., Edinburgh.)*

28. *Mahogany and satinwood inlaid Card Table. c. 1790. (Paxton House, Berwick.)* 29. *Satinwood Games Table with sliding reversible top, showing chess and backgammon boards. c. 1790. (Formerly at Hamilton Palace, Lanarks.)*

Lord Hervey writes (1733) of the high stakes prevailing at Hampton Court, and mentions that the king played at commerce and backgammon and the queen chiefly at quadrille. A little later, Benjamin Goodison (*q.v.*) supplied for His Majesty's use 'Two walnut-tree card tables covered with green velvet, one trimmed with gold lace, the other plain'; he also charged for 'new covering' several of the royal tables with velvet. An inexpensive table, made by him for one of the Court officials in 1752, is described as 'a mahogany card table with folding frame covered with green cloth'. Strict ceremonial etiquette respecting these royal amusements continued to be observed at this time. Chamberlayne (*Present State of Great Britain*, 1735) stated that, among other things, the office of groom porter is to see the king's lodgings furnished with tables, cards and dice and to decide disputes arising from cards, etc. Whist is mentioned as a game played in England in the 17th century, and Cotton wrote in 1680, 'Every child of eight hath a competent knowledge of that recreation'. Hoyle notes in 1745 that it had then become fashionable.

The card tables with square corners, introduced c. 1730, remained in favour throughout the mid-Georgian period. The edges of the folding top were generally carved with rococo mouldings, and the shaped frieze below was sometimes elaborately decorated with scrolls and foliage. The cabriole of the legs becomes more graceful, the scroll foot being a favourite termination. In the table in Fig. 21 the frieze is decorated on all four sides with flutings in Gothic taste. Finely figured walnut is used in another example of about the same date

30. *Rosewood Card Table inlaid with holly; two back legs pivot on frame. c. 1800. Ht. 2 ft. 3½ in., L. 2 ft. 11½ in., Depth 2 ft. 11 in. (Mrs Stephen Sanford.)* 31. *Card Table of calamander wood inlaid with brass and ebony; made by George Oakley in 1810. Ht. 2 ft. 4½ in., L. 3 ft., Depth 1 ft. 10 in. (Mrs Stileman.)*

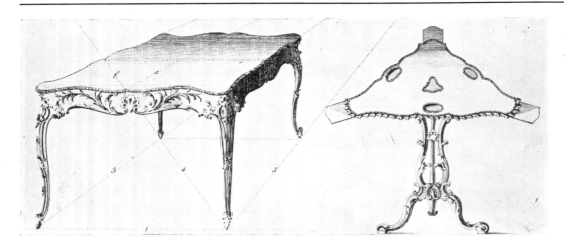

32. *Designs for Card Tables* (*that on right for 'traydrill'*) *from Ince and Mayhew's* Universal System, 1759–63.

(Fig. 22), and the curves are of exceptional elegance. The square corners characteristic of these mid-Georgian card-tables are in Fig. 24 inlaid with playing cards set diagonally, the aces of the black suits and the kings of the red. Another type has straight legs, carved, like the frieze, with lattice-work of Chinese or Gothic character (Fig. 23).

Tripod card tables with triangular tops were also made at this time, and were used for tredrille and other three-handed games. In Ince and Mayhew's *Universal System* (1759–63) a design for one of these tables is given (Fig. 32); and although japanned examples are very rare, one is illustrated in Figs. 15 and 16. Card tables are not represented in Chippendale's *Director*; nor do they figure in his surviving bills.

George III and Queen Charlotte tried to discourage gambling by forbidding it for a time in any of the royal palaces, but apparently without appreciable effect. Horace Walpole in 1770 writes of the gaming at Almacks as 'worthy of the decline of our Empire', young men losing five, ten and fifteen thousand pounds in an evening. 'Low Tables', as they were called, for small stakes, were instituted in certain houses, but did not meet with much favour. Lady Mary Coke in 1770 observed that 'Low tables at this time of the year bring out odds and ends that nobody thinks of inviting when better are to be had'. Mrs Lybbe Powys, describing a party at Fawley Court, Bucks., in 1777, wrote that there were 'two card-rooms, the drawing-room and eating-room . . . two tables at loo, one quinze, one vingt-une, many whist. At one of the former large sums pass'd and repass'd. They wanted Powys and I to play at "low loo", as they term'd it, but we rather chose to keep our features less agitated than those we saw around us.' Even in remote country villages card playing was a favourite diversion. The Rev. James Woodforde has many notes in his *Diary*, from 1767 onwards, of small sums lost and won by him when playing cribbage, loo, whist and quadrille with the squire of his parish and other friends.

In the period 1775–1800 mahogany and satinwood card-tables with tapered quadrilateral or cylindrical legs were made in a variety of shapes—broken fronted, serpentine, square, circular or oval. They were generally covered with green baize, the dishings for candles and counters being omitted, and the flaps, when open, were supported either on a single leg, on two swinging out on a central pivot, or on a hinged frame. Hepplewhite writes (*Guide*, 1788) that 'the fronts of these tables may be enriched with inlaid or painted orna-

ments; the tops also admit of great elegance in the same stiles' [*sic*]. He gives four designs 'proper for inlaid or painted tops for Card Tables'. Marquetry decoration on such furniture designed in the early neo-classic style is rare, but there is a fine pair of card tables of this character in the drawing-room at Syon House, Middlesex (Fig. 25), which may be attributed to Peter Langlois (*q.v.*). Late 18th-century types are well illustrated in Figs. 26, 27, 28. In 1781 William Gates supplied George, Prince of Wales, with two circular mahogany card tables, inlaid with different coloured woods. A detail of a small games table of this time is shown in Fig. 29; it has a sliding and reversible top.

Although gambling was freely indulged in by the Prince of Wales and his profligate associates, fewer card tables appear to have been made in the Regency period, and they receive small attention from contemporary designers, Sheraton noticing them unwillingly in his *Dictionary* (1803) with the observation that they are 'oftener used than to good purpose'. The chief London clubs at this time were notorious centres of gambling for enormous stakes. For faro, one of the games particularly favoured, a special variety of table was made, with a series of deep oval wells for counters round the edge and a recess in one side 'to enable the croupier or dealer to be nearer the play'. Inlaid tables are found in rosewood with the outward-curving feet characteristic of the time. Another type in favour is shown in Fig. 31, this particular example, formerly at Papworth Hall, Cambridgeshire, being supplied

33. *Design for inlaid Card Table from Sheraton's* Drawing Book, 1791–4.

by George Oakley (*q.v.*) in 1810 for £31 10s. It is described in his bills as 'a calamander wood circular loo table upon pedestal and claws, the top inlaid with a border of stars in brass and ebony'. While faro was fashionable in disreputable society, loo, whist and quadrille were still among the games chiefly favoured in country houses. In *Pride and Prejudice* (1813) Bingley and Jane Bennet decide that 'they both like Vingt-un better than Commerce'. When Elizabeth entered the drawing-room at Netherfield 'she found the whole party at loo'; on another evening two of the gentlemen 'were at picquet', and, at Rosings, Lady Catherine de Burgh had sent for Mr Collins 'to make up the pool of quadrille in the evening'. The combination of games and work was much in favour at this date (*see* TABLES, WORK).

TABLES, CARLTON HOUSE. *See* TABLES, LIBRARY AND WRITING.

TABLES, CHAIR. *See* CHAIR-TABLES.

TABLES, CHINA, TEA- AND SUPPER-. Tables for holding the tea and coffee equipage did not come into general use until towards the end of the 17th century. Tea had already been introduced into this country from Holland. Probably the earliest reference to it by an Englishman is in a letter from an agent of the East India Co. in Japan, 1613, asking a fellow officer in China to send him 'a pot of the best sort of chaw'. Subsequently 'three silver porringers to drink chaw in' occur in his accounts. In *Mercurius Politicus* (September 23, 1658) there is a reference to 'that excellent drink called by the Chinese *Teka*, by other nations *Tay* alias *Tea*'. At first it was chiefly regarded as medicinal, being approved of by physicians as good for various ailments and 'for clearing the sight and expelling infection'. Pepys, in 1660, alluded to the new drink, and on returning home in 1667, finds his wife 'making of tea, a drink which the Potticary tells her is good for her cold and defluxions'. Rugge's *Diurnal*

states that tea was sold in almost every street in 1659, but Thomas Garway appears to have been the first regular tea-dealer. In a broadsheet (pub. c. 1660) he states that tea 'in respect of its scarceness and dearness, it hath only been used as a regalia in high treatment and entertainments'. In spite of the high prices and heavy duty imposed, tea became much in demand and was drunk both in public places and fashionable houses. The Duchess of Lauderdale's Private Closet at Ham House, Surrey, in 1679 contained 'a Tea-Table carved and guilt', her tea being kept, together with sweetmeats, 'in a Japan box'. Roger North in his *Life* of Lord Keeper Guildford (d. 1685) observes that it was always his custom after dinner to retire with his company into a withdrawing-room 'and the tea-table followed'. Dramatists and poets railed against this new custom of evening tea-drinking, and in 1678 Henry Savill writes that some of his friends 'have fallen into the base, unworthy, Indian practice of calling for tea after dinner', in place of the pipe and bottle.

That among people of means the habit of tea-drinking had become almost universal is suggested by a petition of the Joiners' Company dating from the end of the century, against the importation of goods from the East Indies, which states *inter alia* that 6,582 tea-tables had been imported 'within these Four years'. Such tables would have been lacquered like other furniture of oriental origin, and it is surprising that no examples of this period apparently survive. Issac Van den Helm, 'Dutch Tablemaker', advertised (*The Postman*, March 5, 1711) that he 'makes and sells all sorts of fine painted Tea Tables with new fancies and that can endure boiling water'; the context showing they were japanned.

In the first Lord Bristol's *Expence Book* (1690) there is an entry: 'Paid to Medina ye Jew for a tea-table and two pairs of china cupps £10'; and a few years later as much as £2 is entered 'for half a pond of Keiser tea'. Mrs Delaney, writing in 1728, says: 'The man at the Poultry has tea of all prices, Bohea from thirteen to twenty shillings and green from twelve

1. *Walnut Tea-Table; tray top and cabriole legs. c. 1715. Ht. 2 ft. 6 in., L. 2 ft. 11 in. (A. Dunn Gardner Coll.)* 2. *Mahogany Tea- or China Table; pierced gallery and slender cabriole legs carved with acanthus; claw-and-ball feet. c. 1750. Ht. 2 ft. 4½ in., L. 2 ft. 7½ in., Depth 1 ft. 11 in. (V. & A. Mus.)*

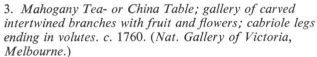
3. *Mahogany Tea- or China Table; gallery of carved intertwined branches with fruit and flowers; cabriole legs ending in volutes. c. 1760. (Nat. Gallery of Victoria, Melbourne.)*

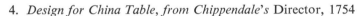
4. *Design for China Table, from Chippendale's* Director, 1754

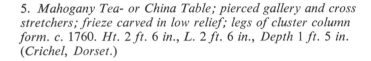
5. *Mahogany Tea- or China Table; pierced gallery and cross stretchers; frieze carved in low relief; legs of cluster column form. c. 1760. Ht. 2 ft. 6 in., L. 2 ft. 6 in., Depth 1 ft. 5 in. (Crichel, Dorset.)*

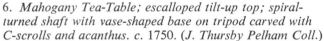
6. *Mahogany Tea-Table; escalloped tilt-up top; spiral-turned shaft with vase-shaped base on tripod carved with C-scrolls and acanthus. c. 1750. (J. Thursby Pelham Coll.)*

to thirty.' In the inventory (1725) of Cannons, drawn up for James Brydges, first Duke of Chandos, 'A large Tea Table cover'd wth silver', with a pair of stands to match, is entered as 'in His Grace's Visiting Room', the set being valued at £750. This table and its accompanying stands formed one of the sets which from Charles II's reign onwards had been made primarily for decoration, and was doubtless used by the duke for this special purpose. Tea-tables, carved and gilt, in a florid baroque taste, the tops having deep rims, are shown with the equipage in several of Hogarth's 'Conversations', e.g. *The Wanstead Assembly* (c. 1731).

About 1750 the many tea gardens in and near London, which had hitherto been popular resorts where fashionable people assembled for tea-drinking, came to be regarded as of low repute; thus it became customary for friends to drink tea in each other's homes. It was at this time that cabinet-makers turned their attention to making suitable ornamental

7. (*Left*) *Mahogany Tea-Table; spindle gallery; tripod carved with human masks and lion paws. c 1750. (Percival Griffiths Coll.)*

8. (*Right*) *Mahogany Tea-Table; serpentine top and spindle gallery; shaft spirally fluted. c. 1755. Ht. 2 ft. 6 in., Diameter 2 ft. 5½ in. (Mr Ralph Edwards.)*

tables, and a special tea-room was often constructed for this form of entertainment, sometimes decorated in the prevailing Chinese taste, and furnished with seats and tea-tables of various shapes and character, and a cupboard to hold the china. An inventory (c. 1750) of the effects at Dunham Massey Hall, Cheshire, mentions the furniture of the gallery tea-room, which includes 'Mahogany stands to set the silver Tea and coffee tables on'. In the Georgian period, the large round silver trays or salvers were often called tea- and coffee-tables. In this instance the trays bear a hall-mark of 1741. They fit on tripod mahogany stands (*see* STANDS, SALVER AND TRAY, Fig. 1).

Tea-tables of oblong shape were contemporary with the round and tray-shaped top on pillar and tripod, the tops of this latter type being often made to tilt up so that they could be placed against a wall when not in use. These tops were constructed with carved ornamental edges (Fig. 10) or lattice-work and spindle galleries (Figs. 7 and 8). In some cases there are small circular wells to hold the cups. When the furniture in Sir William Stanhope's Albemarle Street house

9. (*Left*) *Rosewood Supper-Table; octagonal centre of escalloped top and tripod inlaid with engraved brass. Probably by Abraham Roentgen, senr. c. 1740-50. (Duchess of Roxburghe Coll.)*

10. (*Right*) *Mahogany Tea-Table; edges of top carved with foliage; scrolled tripod. c. 1750. (Percival Griffiths Coll.)*

11. *Mahogany Tea-Table; top carved with* coquillage *ornament and floral sprays; tripod decorated in low relief. c. 1760. Ht. 2 ft. 4 in., Diameter 2 ft. 7 in. (V. & A. Mus.)*

12. *Mahogany Tea-Table; pierced gallery of Chinese fretwork; tripod shaft and base carved with scrolls and foliage. c. 1760. (Longford Castle, Wilts.)*

3. *Mahogany Supper-Table with circular compartments for plates; carved at junction of shaft and scrolled tripod with helmeted masks. c. 1750. Ht. 2 ft. 3½ in. (Henry Hirsch Coll.)* 14. *Mahogany Tea-Table; legs carved with rams' heads and hoofs. c. 1775-80. Ht. 2 ft. 2 in., diameter 10⅝ in. (Bassett Down, Wilts.)* 15. *Mahogany and Satinwood inlaid Tea-Table. c. 1790. Ht. 2 ft. 5 in., Diameter 2 ft. 8 in. (A. Hannay Coll.)*

was sold in 1733, the steward's hall contained among other objects 'a mahogany scollop'd Tea-table on a claw'; *i.e.* one with a shaped ornamental edge to the top and a tripod, for which 'claw' was the usual contemporary equivalent. Again, in 1759 Sir John Hall paid Young and Trotter for 'A fine Jam^a Mahogany Tea-Table with Scoloped Corners 39 × 30 on top Pillar and Claw feet with Castors £1 15.' When the tops of these tables were divided into compartments, as in Fig. 13, they served to hold the cups and saucers or the plates for supper, an informal meal often partaken of in a private chamber after returning from a play. The table in Fig. 9 is in the style of the elder Abraham Roentgen (*q.v.*), a celebrated German cabinet-maker who worked for a time in England and specialised in ivory, brass and mother-of-pearl inlay.

Chippendale shows two designs for tables (*Director*, 1754, Pl. XXXIIII), which he says are 'for holding Each a Set of China, and may be used as Tea-Tables'. Fig. 3 illustrates a remarkable contemporary example, the decoration being a *tour de force* of carving in the most ornate rococo taste. Ince and Mayhew (*Universal System*, 1759–63) illustrate the tripod type, which they call 'claw tables'. The fragile lattice-work tables, of which comparatively few genuine examples survive, were used for these purposes. They were made during the ascendancy of Chinese taste, and the legs are sometimes formed of cluster columns in imitation of bamboo (Fig. 5).

Coffee as a beverage was introduced into England c. 1650, but never obtained the same popularity as tea. Chocolate was regarded chiefly as a morning drink. The many little tables for tea and other beverages (*e.g.* Fig. 14) are accounted for by the custom in some houses of giving each guest a separate table. In the middle of the 18th century, Miss Hamilton mentions in her diary that when staying with Mrs Delaney at Bulstrode,

'it was customary to have tea at seven . . . We have each our little table'.

A variety of small portable tables 'to set about rooms' were produced in the Regency period, some of them serving among other purposes 'for the convenience of ladies drinking tea'.

TABLES, CLAP. *See* TABLES, SIDE-.

TABLES, CLAW. *See* TABLES, CHINA.

TABLES, CONSOLE. *See* TABLES, SIDE-.

TABLES, DINING- AND HALL. In this section are included the types of tables used primarily for meals, though many of them were also used for other purposes. Their use is indicated by their character and by pictorial representations, for it is not until comparatively modern times that tables stated to have been for dining are mentioned in inventories and domestic accounts. In the Middle Ages those in the master's private chamber were necessarily smaller than the dining-tables of the great hall, where it was customary for the whole household to assemble for meals. On these occasions the high table for the master and most important guests stood on the dais under a canopy, while at right angles to it down the length of the hall side-tables were placed for the rest of the company (Fig. 1). William Cely, a merchant of the Staple, who was staying with other merchants at an Englishman's house in Calais in 1483, wrote to two members of his family to inform them of a dispute between the host and the 'felly-schyppe of owre logyng'. It had been agreed that 'we schulde payne noo more for owre burdd but IIIs. IVd (Flemish) a weke at the hye tabull and IIs. VIIId. at the syde tabull'. The host wanted to raise the charge in both cases and for this

1. *Banquet, showing Dining-Table on dais, and another in body of hall. From French illuminated MS., second half of 15th century. (B.M. Facsimile. 182 Pl. 83.)*

2. *Oak Hall Table, one of pair; top supported by trestles with crocketed mouldings and cruciform feet. Late 15th century. Ht. 2 ft. 10 in., L. 27 ft. 5 in., Depth 3 ft. 1½ in. (Penshurst Place, Kent.)*

reason the Englishmen, with the exception of Cely, moved elsewhere.

In illuminated manuscripts of the 14th and 15th centuries, small tables which could be drawn up to the fire in winter are generally portrayed with shaped supports and a foot-board and are sometimes of round form; but such tables would have served for many purposes besides meals. The tables on which state banquets are taking place are also occasionally represented as round, with the guests seated on curved benches; and of these there is a large and much restored example in the castle at Winchester, which probably dates from the 15th century. The most usual type of early dining-table was of trestle construction, consisting of massive boards of oak or elm resting on a series of central supports: the tops were detachable, and the entire table was often removed after meals. Froissart, writing in 1350 of Edward III's Court, draws attention to this custom: '*Quand on eust soupe on lever les tables si demeura le dict roy en la salle.*' Chaucer, describing the Frankleyn's hospitality, alludes to:

> His table dormant in his halle alway
> Stood redy covered at the longest day.

Such tables 'wth trestelys' are often listed in 15th-century inventories. In 1444 John Brompton, a merchant of Beverley, Yorkshire, left his son '*longam tabulam pro superiore parte aulae cum tribus kerven tristes . . .*' (a long table for the upper part of the hall with three carved trestles).

Banquets from medieval times being the recognised form of hospitality and entertainment, tables of great length and solidity were required, the amount of food prepared on these occasions being stupendous. Many records of royal and private banquets are in existence, and late in the 15th century the *Bokes of Keruynge and Curtasye* set forth elaborate and detailed directions for serving meals. After grace, servants are instructed to 'lay some of the tables on the floor, and remove the trestles'.

Two massive trestle tables of the late 15th century survive at Penshurst Place, Kent (Fig. 2). Another form of trestle dining-table was also made in the early 16th century, this type having upright crocketed or curved supports at each end sawn out of very thick oak or elm planks, and united by rails and stretchers passing through the uprights and secured on the out-side with stout pegs; on these being removed the table could be taken to pieces and stacked against a wall. Tudor inventories abound in references to tables of these two types, 'a table wth trestilles' or 'a table with a payer of trestilles' recurring repeatedly in the chambers of John Rede, Keeper of the Royal Wardrobe, whose list of household goods was drawn up in 1557.

'Joyned' tables were in use in the previous century. John Brompton had in his hall (1444), besides the trestle table already alluded to, '*alia tabula vocata dormorunt*' [sic] (another table called a table dormant), *i.e.* a standing table not intended to be moved, and probably joined. Another early reference occurs in the will of John Gaywoode, a merchant prince and partner of William Canynges (1399–1474), which mentions a 'joyned' table of wainscot with four feet and 'a beast carved therein'. Such tables came into general use c. 1550, and are often noticed in the same inventories which specify the trestle variety: thus, John Rede had 'a long table upon a frame' in his 'Nether-most chamb^r'. Fig. 3 was probably made a few years before the date of his inventory and still retains traces of Gothic influence in the vase-shaped moulded supports, brackets and ogee-form underframing at the ends. These framed tables were of fixed size and too cumbersome to be moved easily; but a 'draw top' was soon introduced, a simple device (*see* CONSTRUCTION) by which the table could be extended to double its original length. In an inventory of the goods at Stationers' Hall there is an entry of 'a new joyned drawing table' in 1558, which is about the date of their introduction. The steward's accounts of the Shuttleworths, of Gawthorpe Hall, Lancashire, contain entries in 1614–15 of a payment to 'a joiner VI dayes tryeinge of tymber for the great table in the dyninge chamber'.

Figs. 5 to 15 show good examples of the fixed and extending types, ranging in date from c. 1585 to c. 1700. The bulbous or vase-shaped legs were of Flemish and German origin, introduced into England by immigrant craftsmen and through published designs such as those of Dietterlein and de Vries. In early examples the vase-shape is very pronounced, the bulbs being often carved with acanthus and gadroons, and terminating at the junction with the frame in small Ionic volutes. Fig. 5 shows the full development of those supports, and here the

3. *Oak joined Table; one of centre legs hexagonal, others of faceted vase form; ogee-shaped arch in underframing at ends. Mid-16th century. Ht. 2 ft. 11½ in., L. 11 ft. 6½ in., Depth 2 ft. 8 in. (V. & A. Mus.)*

4. *Oak Table of trestle construction, one of pair; pierced edging and supports. 1611. Ht. 2 ft. 7 in., L. 24 ft. 1 in., Depth 3 ft. 2 in. (Hatfield House, Herts.)*

5. *Oak Hall Table; inlaid frieze intersected with carved bosses; legs of bulbous form; claw feet. c. 1585. Ht. 2 ft. 11 in., L. 8 ft. 2 in., Depth 3 ft. 2 in. (Sir William Burrell Coll., Glasgow Art Gallery and Museum.)*

frieze is inlaid with architectural façades stopped at intervals by female heads projecting from ruffs; the inlay is distinctly German in inspiration, recalling that on contemporary 'Nonsuch' chests. Another exceptional example (Fig. 9) provides a remarkable contrast, for here the underframing is arcaded, and the design resembles one on Pl. M, Part 2 of de Vries's *Plusieurs Menuiseries* (pub. 1630). Fig. 8 shows a remarkable departure from the prevailing type. The richly carved frieze, intersected by grotesque masks centring on an escutcheon

with coat of arms is supported on winged monsters. This exceptional table in the character of the couchant monsters resembles a design by de Vries in his *Différents Pourtraicts de Menuiserie* (1565, Pl. 8).

During the 17th century the bulbous supports gradually changed in character, becoming less pronounced, while the legs finished top and bottom with ring mouldings (Fig. 10). The frames were carved with flutings or strapwork in low relief, or inlaid with a chequer pattern in various woods. The

6. *Oak Draw-Table; gadrooned underframing and bulbous legs headed by Ionic capitals; stretchers inlaid. c. 1600. (Col N. R. Colville.)*

7. *Oak Draw-Table; frieze inlaid with chequer patterns; legs headed by Ionic capitals; stretchers moulded. c. 1600. Ht. 2 ft. 9 in., L. 5 ft. 11 in., Depth 2 ft. 9 in. (V. & A. Mus.)*

8. *Oak Table, draw top; frieze, carved with scroll patterns and grotesque masks, centres on arms of Lambton (Yorks.). Winged monsters and lion cub corners. c. 1600. (S. W. Wolsey Ltd.)*

534

9. *Oak Draw-Table; frieze carved with gadroons, foliage and fluted bosses; columnar supports and arcaded under-framing. c. 1610. (Mr Murray Adams-Acton.)*

10. *Oak Dining-Table; frieze inlaid with chequer pattern; legs fluted. c. 1630. (Sodbury Hall, Glos.)*

11. *Oak Hall Table; fluted frieze and turned baluster legs; bears inscription and date 163–. (Mr L. J. Cadbury.)*

12. *Detail of Table illustrated in Fig. 11, showing inscription.*

13. *Oak Dining-Table with one of set of original stools; frieze and bulbous legs carved with gadroons. Dated 1686. (Treasurer's House, York.)*

14. *Oak Dining-Table; deep frieze carved with strapwork and legs vase-shaped. Dated 1697. Ht. 2 ft. 10 in., L. 12 ft. 3 in., Depth 2 ft. 10 in. (Hardwick Hall, Derbys.)*

15. *Elm Dining-Table with set of original stools; plain frieze and turned legs. Late 17th century. Ht. 2 ft. 6 in., L. 8 ft. 3 in., Depth 2 ft. 5 in. (Messrs Mallett & Son.)*

usual height of a draw-table when closed was about 2 ft 9 ins; joined stools, a foot or so lower, and benches were the normal seats at such tables. These stools were ranged under the tables when not in use, with their tops outwards, supported on the stretchers. This arrangement is shown in Fig. 15, the table and six 'jointstools' being appraised at £2 6s. in an inventory of the goods of Abram Jaggard, of Leek Wootton, Warwickshire, drawn up in 1755, probably about half a century after their manufacture.

The immovable character of these early examples caused them to descend through many generations in the same family, and Evelyn observes in a familiar passage that both in hall and parlour long tables 'were as fixed as the freehold'. In Fig. 12 is given a detail of a long table with four legs on each side, which was removed from a house in Lancashire, now divided into tenements. The inscription reads 'A Harelome To This Hous for Ever', and on the adjoining leg is the date 163–, the last figure missing.

Trestle tables continued to be used, probably because they were so readily removable when a room had to be cleared for dancing or other revels: thus, after the banquet (in *Romeo and Juliet*, written in 1597) Capulet instructs the servants to clear

16. *Walnut Gate-leg Table;*
spiral-turned supports. c. 1670.
Ht. 2 ft. 4 in., L. 5 ft. 8 in., Depth
4 ft. 10 in. (J. Thursby Pelham
Coll.)

17. *Walnut Dining-Table, made*
in two semicircular parts, attached
by iron hooks; turned taper legs.
Late 17th century. (The late Capt.
E. G. Spencer Churchill.)

and basin had taken place. It was a foreign custom that continued in use till late in the 17th century. Cardinal Wolsey possessed table-linen of damask 'with flowers paned losinge-wise' and napkins of 'Dyaper damaske work with losinges and birds-eyes'. The Littlecote, Wiltshire, accounts of 1589 contain an entry of 5s. for 'two long table-cloths'. In spite of the industry of English spinners, much of the finest linen was imported from abroad. Moryson (*Itinerary*, 1663) notes that, when at Haarlem, he saw a damask table-cloth being woven 'with the English arms and many curious figures'. At Ham House, there is a large white damask table-cloth bearing the arms of the Duke of Lauderdale and dating from c. 1675–80. This may perhaps have been imported from Holland, but by Anne's reign table-linen of English origin was universal in every household.

Pewter and wooden trenchers were used in Elizabethan times, bread having been earlier employed for the purpose.

the hall and 'turn the tables up' for dancing. Even as late as 1649 there was 'a long Table standing upon antique tressells' among Charles I's furniture at Greenwich. An early 17th-century example in which this form of construction is adhered to is seen in Fig. 4. The main trestles are pierced with arches, and the top, which is probably of later date, has a perforated strapwork edging. In 1611 William Woode, a carpenter employed at Hatfield House, Hertfordshire, charged £10 for 'settinge up of the Tables, Stooles and formes in the Hall'.

Napery was in use from an early period. The *Modus Cenandi* states that after the dining-table is set up 'a white cloth should be placed upon it'. John Russell's *Boke of Nurture* (c. 1460) gives directions that all table-linen shall be sweet and clean and 'bordclothe, towelle and napkyns foldyn alle bydene'. In the articles ordained by Henry VII for the regulation of his household, full instructions are set out for laying the dining-table with a narrow cloth of Reynes, and also with a surnape. The surnape consisted of fine extra cloths one over another, laid before those of high degree, and lifted up towards the end of a meal, and when the customary ablution with ewer

18. *Mahogany Dining-Table; shaped underframing; scrolled cabriole legs with hoof feet. c. 1720. (Bourne Park, Kent.)*

537

19. *Mahogany Dining-Table with semicircular leaves; cabriole legs carved with lion masks and acanthus; paw feet. c. 1730. Ht. 2 ft. 4 in., diameter 4 ft. 10 in. (Percival Griffiths Coll.)* 20. *Mahogany Dining-Table with two leaves; cabriole legs carved with scrolls and foliage; claw-and-ball feet. c. 1750. Ht. 2 ft. 6 in., L. 4 ft. 8¾ in., Depth 3 ft. 11½ in. (Mr Ralph Edwards.)*

21. *Mahogany Dining-Table, made in four sections. c. 1730. L. 16 ft. 2 in. (Houghton Hall, Norfolk.)*

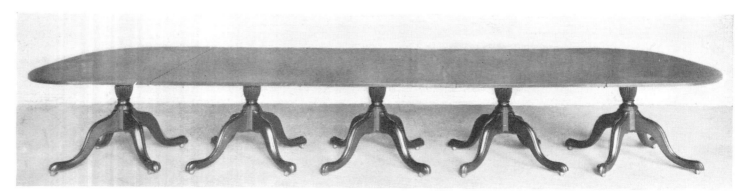

22. *Mahogany Dining-Table made in sections; on turned and reeded columns with curved legs. c. 1795. Ht. 2 ft. 6½ in., L. 15 ft. 8 in., Depth 5 ft. 10 in. (Hardwick Hall, Derbys.)*

23. *Mahogany Dining-Table; turned supports and reeded legs. c. 1795. Ht. 2 ft. 3½ in., L. 9 ft. 8 in., Depth 4 ft. 11 in. (Mrs F. H. Hamilton.)*

24. *Mahogany Dining-Table; folding leaf for extension; underframing carved with paterae and husks. c. 1775. (Basil Oxenden Coll.)*

According to the Littlecote accounts, Darrell, in 1589, paid 15d. for three dozen wooden trenchers, and 5s. for a dozen pewter trencher-plates. In the Shuttleworth accounts (Gawthorpe Hall, Lancashire) of 1612 there is an entry for two dozen plane tree trenchers, 2s. 4d. Flat wood roundels painted with figures and mottoes were used for the dry comfits and fruits that usually ended a feast; and of these there are two sets dating from James I's reign in the Victoria and Albert Museum, one being an early example of chinoiserie ornament (*see* CHINESE TASTE).

China dishes and plates, even by the 17th century, were regarded as novel and a luxury. In 1609, when King James and the Prince of Wales were invited to a banquet of great magnificence on the occasion of the launching of ships at Deptford, it was specially noted that the whole entertainment was served on long tables and in china dishes, which the guests were permitted to take away with them.

French writers of the 17th century make many comments on English manners and customs at table. Sorbière, after his journey to England in 1664, denounced the badness of English cooking even for 'the greatest Lords' Tables,' and adds 'they scarce ever make use of forks or ewers, for they wash their Hands by dipping them into a Bason of water'.

Oak joined tables continued to be used until the practice of dining in hall was discontinued, and specimens with straight legs are found dated in the carving as late as 1720. After the

Restoration rooms set apart for dining came into general use among the upper classes and the draw-top variety was superseded by oval or round tables, generally of the gate-leg type with two flaps, and made of oak, walnut, or, more rarely, yew (*see* TABLES, GATE-LEG). They were sometimes of very large size with double gates to support the heavy ends.

Shortly after the Restoration Pepys recorded the purchase of a dining-table in Wood Street for 50s., adding in a subsequent entry, 'I find my new table very proper, and will hold nine or ten people very well, but eight with great room'. On May 28, 1665, he dined with Sir Philip Warwick, and,

25. *Mahogany Dining-Table on curved supports; top banded with ebonised veneer. c. 1795. L. 7 ft., Depth 5 ft. (Ragley Hall, Warwicks.)*

26. Mahogany extending Dining-Table; detachable leaves supported on lozenge-shaped underframing and turned legs. c. 1810. L. 11 ft., Depth 4 ft. 3 in. (Mr Stanley May.)

visitors arriving unexpectedly, 'I saw one pretty piece of household stuff, as the company increaseth, to put a larger leaf upon an ovall table'. The supper given in London in 1669 by Cosimo, Duke of Tuscany, to Charles II 'was set out in the middle of the saloon on a table of oval figure convenient both for seeing and conversing . . . other guests to the number of 17 were accommodated round the table on stools'. This was probably a large gate-leg table, but in great houses the fashion was now spreading of dining at a number of small tables: there were eight cedar tables in the 'Great Dining Room' at Ham House when an inventory was taken in 1679. In 1680 Roger North noticed that the Duke of Beaufort at Badminton,

27. Design for Dining-Table from George Smith's Household Furniture, *1808.*

Gloucestershire, had 'nine original tables covered every day', and notes as peculiar that the Duke's own table is 'an oblong not an oval'. Fig. 17 shows a rare contemporary table made in two parts with turned legs and stretchers.

The gate-leg type was still popular in the early 18th century; but, with the introduction of mahogany, dining-tables were generally made with oval or circular tops and cabriole legs, one swinging out on either side to support the flaps. After 1725 the cabriole is found decorated with acanthus or lion masks (Fig. 19), but elaborate carving was rarely attempted. Some of these tables could be extended by an extra leaf, and had as many as eight legs, though in most large specimens there are six. They were also made in pairs with square flaps, so that they could be placed together when required. The mahogany dining-table at Houghton Hall, Norfolk (Fig. 21), is made in four sections on the gate principle, and supported on thirty-two baluster legs. Another, and less clumsy, method of extension, which came into use c. 1750 consisted of a centre with rectangular flaps and two semicircular ends, which when detached could be used as pier tables.

Dining-tables are not illustrated by Chippendale and his contemporaries in their trade catalogues, but in a bill to Sir Edward Knatchbull (1769) Chippendale charges for '2 Mahogany round ends to Join his Dining Tables, with 2 pair of strap Hinges, Hooks and Eyes, etc. £5'; and in 1771 David Garrick

28. Mahogany Dining-Table; on turned columns with reeded legs and paw feet. c. 1800. (F. D. Lycett Green Coll.)

29. *Mahogany Dining-Table supported on four short columns; bases elaborately carved with acanthus on lion paw feet. 1820. Ht. 2 ft 5 in., L. 19 ft. 5 in., Depth 6 ft. 4 in. (Town Hall, Liverpool.)*

paid the firm £10 10s. for 'a set of Mahogany Dining Tables with Circular Ends to Joyn together complete'. Fig. 24 represents a dining-table of about this time, with a semicircular detachable end, the flap for extending it being shown folded down in the illustration. This type is sometimes described in the bills of the period, and the royal accounts contain an entry of £24 paid in 1791 to Beckwith and France for 'a set of Mahogany dining Tables, consisting of one square frame with 2 flaps and 2 round ends with a flap to each all made to take off with strap hinges, bolt and fork fastenings, the whole or any part to Join together at pleasure, good Jamaica wood'.

There was no notable advance in the methods of enlargement until 1800, when Richard Gillow obtained a patent for an improvement in the construction of dining-tables 'calculated to reduce the number of legs, pillar and claws and to facilitate their enlargement and reduction'. In 1805 Richard Brown patented a device by which 'the two ends of the table frame are connected by pieces of wood, so joined together as to form what are commonly called lazy tongs' (Fig. 26). They did not entirely supersede the earlier methods of enlargement.

The dining-tables of the Regency period were generally made in sections which could be bolted together, each section being supported on a turned column with four curved legs (Figs. 22 and 28). Sheraton (*Cabinet Dictionary*, 1803) describes this type: '. . . there are various sorts now in use, and some under the protection of his Majesty's patent. The common useful dining-tables are upon pillar and claws, generally four claws to each pillar, with brass castors. A dining-table of this kind may be made to any size, by having a sufficient quantity of pillars and claw parts, for between each of them is a loose flap, fixed by means of iron straps and buttons so that they are easily taken off and put aside.' He adds that the size may be readily calculated by allowing 2 ft to each person. George Smith (*Household Furniture*, 1808) shows a heavy monopodium dining-table, and writes: 'This design is intended to do away with the necessity of claw feet, and will answer as well for setts of Dining as for Single Tables.'

TABLES, DRESSING-. Evidence is lacking as to what kind of table was used in the Tudor and early Stuart periods for brushes and combs and for receptacles to hold the many cosmetics, paints and salves that had been constantly used by men as well as women since the 14th century. Philip Stubbs (*Anatomie of Abuses*, 1583) complains that Englishwomen were not content with their faces but must 'adulterate the Lord's workmanship with unguents and cosmetics'. The so-called 'Secrets' of Don Alexis of Piemont, first rendered into English in Elizabeth I's reign, are replete with recipes for hair dyes, paints, powders and scarlet cloths to make the face fair; odoriferous oils to eradicate wrinkles; 'sweet suet to keepe the lips and hands from Chinks and chaps, White Italian pommades fine and sweet, suitable for great Lords etc'.

These toilet requisites were probably arranged on wainscot tables covered with a carpet or cloth, which are often entered in contemporary inventories among the contents of bedrooms. The dramatic pastoral, *Rhodon and Iris*, first played in 1631, alludes to a lady who 'daubed herself with civet, musk and amber', and enumerates some of the articles she has on her dressing-table—lip salves, confections, ointments, etc. The custom of patching for fashionable men was usual at the Courts of Elizabeth and James I. The taste could not have been common for women till later in the century, as Bulwer (*Artificial Changeling*, 1653) notes that 'Our ladies have lately entertained a vain custom of spotting their faces'. No woman of any repute ventured to paint or patch during the Commonwealth, but Pepys refers often to the excesses of the custom. At this time dressing-tables as a distinct variety of furniture are occasionally mentioned in inventories. In the *Household Expenses* of Sir Edward Dering a payment of 10s. is entered for 'two dressing-tables with drawers' in 1652, and twenty years later the Duchess's Chamber at Cobham Hall, Kent contained 'one dressing table and stand'.

After the Restoration, elaborate sets of dressing plate became fashionable for the wealthy. These generally comprised a mirror supported on a strut, salvers, porringers for possets, candlesticks, powder-boxes, caskets, brushes and combs; and needed a substantial table for their display. For those

1. *Walnut Table; chamfered tapered legs united by curved stretchers; fitted with three drawers. c. 1690. (Col N. R. Col-ville.)*

2. *Walnut Table; cabriole legs; shaped underframing, fitted with three drawers. c. 1715. Ht. 2 ft. 8½ in., L. 2 ft. 6 in., Depth 1 ft. 8 in. (Macquoid Coll.)*

unable to afford silver plate, Stalker and Parker, in their *Treatise* (1688), give various suggestions and designs for dressing-table accessories of 'Japan work', such as 'Combe boxes, halfe round frames for looking-glasses, a pincushion trunk for jewells, brushes, powder and patchboxes'; and these would be set out on a japanned table. They were spread on a table-cloth—often of rich materials—termed a 'toilet', the word

being also used for the accessories themselves when thus displayed (*see* TOILET).

Towards the end of the 17th century, painting and rougeing the face and the use of paints and powders with deleterious ingredients such as white lead, were indulged in to an inordinate extent. At this period it became the custom for ladies of fashion to receive their intimate friends of both

3. *Oak Table on cabriole legs of eccentric form. c. 1715. Ht. 2 ft. 4½ in., L. 2 ft. 8½ in., Depth 1 ft. 10 in. (A. Dunn Gardner Coll.*
4. *Table decorated with gilt gesso ornament and black and gold japan. c. 1725. (Longford Castle, Wilts.)*

5. *Walnut Table; shaped underframing and cabriole legs carved with acanthus. c. 1730. (Percival Griffiths Coll.)*

6. *Knee-hole Dressing-Table veneered with burr walnut; pilasters fluted and carved; top fitted with compartments and toilet glass. c. 1725. (Percival Griffiths Coll.)*

sexes while seated at a dressing-table. Pictures and engravings of the time show that many such tables were completely enveloped in fringed draperies (*see* MIRRORS, TOILET, Fig. 6) and had elaborately worked covers. In the first Earl of Bristol's *Diary* (1696) there is an entry 'Paid a work woman for finishing ye crimson and yellow quilt for a toilette cloath which my dear Isabella began, £5 10.' The walnut and japanned swing toilet glasses on box stands that came into fashion c. 1700 were placed on small tables veneered or japanned to match and having pillar or cabriole legs and usually two or three deep drawers to hold brushes, combs, etc. (Figs. 1 and 2). This type and the familiar small knee-hole table with drawers at the sides, which were also used for writing, remained popular throughout the first half of the 18th century, even after dressing-tables with complex fittings had become fashionable. At Dyrham Park, Gloucestershire, in 1710 there were japan tables and stands in many of the bedrooms, and the absence of any other tables shows that these must have been used for dressing. In an inventory (1718) of the Duke of Montague's furniture at Boughton, Northamptonshire, 'A Wainscott dressing table' is listed 'in the Room against Mr Cecill's Room'.

In inventories, bills and advertisements of about this time stands are often mentioned in conjunction with a table and mirror, these objects together forming a set. Probably most of such sets were used for dressing, candlesticks being placed on the stands which stood on either side of the table. Gay (*The Fan*, 1713) alludes to a dressing-table:

> There stands the Toilette, nursery of charms
> Completely furnished with bright beauty's arms
> The patch, the powder-box, pulville, perfumes
> Pins, paint, a flatt'ring glass and black lead combs.

In 1730 Benjamin Goodison (*q.v.*) supplied 'three Walnuttree dressing tables with large drawer to the Bottoms and a sliding table to each of them' for St James's Palace.

Changes of style in ladies' hairdressing rapidly succeeded one another in the 18th century, and by 1776 the mode of wearing the hair had become most extravagant in height and

7. *Knee-hole mahogany Dressing-Table; serpentine front, chamfered corners decorated with frets and wide bracket feet. Top drawer fitted with writing-board, looking-glass and toilet boxes. c. 1755. Ht. 2 ft. 8½ in., L. 3 ft. 2½ in. (Percival Griffiths Coll.)*

8. *Knee-hole Dressing-Table, japanned black and gold. Mid-18th century. (Badminton, Glos.)*

9. *Dressing-Table; figured mahogany with scrolled brass handles and escutcheons; one of pair with toilet mirrors to match. c. 1760. (Cecil Higgins Mus., Bedford.)*

10. *Mahogany Dressing-Table with folding lid; lower portion in Chinese taste. c. 1755. (Messrs Mallett & Son.)*

11. *Mahogany Dressing-Table; hinged mirror set between hexagonal cupboards. Probably by Thomas Chippendale. c. 1760. W. 3 ft. 10 in. (Formerly at Kimbolton, Hunts.)*

12. *Design for 'a Lady's Dressing Table,' from Chippendale's* Director (3rd ed.), 1762.

13. *Dressing-Table, veneered and marquetried with laburnum, satinwood and various woods. c. 1780. Ht. 2 ft. 4 in., L. 2 ft. 6 in. (V. & A. Mus.)*

14. *Satinwood Dressing-Table in Chinese taste, decorated with marquetry; hinged mirror and flanking supports headed by pagodas. c. 1770. (Private Coll., U.S.A.)*

15. *Satinwood Dressing-Table banded with mahogany; serpentine front; end drawers swing out and are fitted with looking-glasses c. 1790. Ht. 3 ft. 9½ in., L. 5 ft. 1 in., Depth 3 ft. 4 in.* 16. *Mahogany serpentine-fronted Dressing-Table, mounted on taper legs. c. 1790. (Mrs Baldwyn-Childe.)*

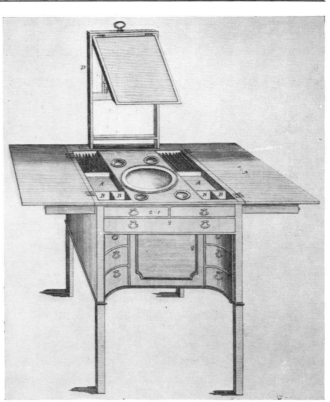

17. *Mahogany Shaving-Table; box lid encloses pull-up mirror and toilet requisites. c.* 1765. (*Mannington Hall, Norfolk.*)
18. *Design for Shaving-Table, from Chippendale's* Director (3rd ed.), 1762.

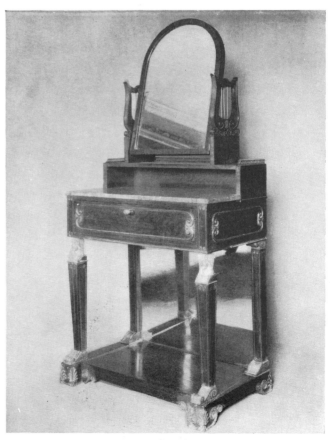

19. *Satinwood Dressing-Table banded with rosewood; made by George Oakley for Papworth Hall in 1810. Ht. (with mirror) 5 ft., L. 4 ft. 6 in., Depth 1 ft. 10½ in. (Mrs Stileman.)*   20. *Rosewood Dressing-Table; applied brass mouldings on frieze; ormolu classical heads probably of French origin. Ht. 5 ft. 6½ in., L. 2 ft. 7 in., Depth 1 ft. 7 in. (Duke of Wellington.)*

elaboration, requiring the services of a professional hairdresser to build up the edifice. The fashion was freely satirised in the *London Magazine* of 1777 and the *New Bath Guide*, while a correspondent in the *New Lady's Magazine* (1786) complained of the 'Impropriety which is making great strides of Ladies now having frisseurs for hours together straddling over them at their dressing tables'.

Tables with fittings designed for dressing begin to appear in inventories and accounts before 1750; in 1745 William Hallett (*q.v.*) supplied the fourth Earl of Cardigan with 'a mahogany Dressing Table on casters the top to lift up with a Glass and boxes, a shelf underneath with the sides and back cutt open'. At first they were generally of knee-hole pedestal form, with the top drawer divided into compartments and a small hinged glass in the centre. An early example of

21. *Mahogany Dressing-Table inlaid with ebony stars and stringing lines. c. 1810. Ht. 2 ft. 4 in., L. 3 ft. 10 in., Depth 2 ft. (V. & A. Mus.)*

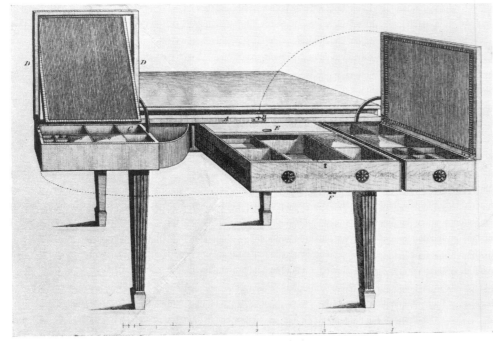

22. *Design for 'Rudd's Dressing Table,' from Hepplewhite's* Guide, *1788 (Pl. 79).*

this type, veneered with finely figured walnut, is shown in Fig. 6. The fluted pilasters are headed by trusses and the base is corbelled out: here the top lifts up, an alternative arrangement often adopted. Chippendale styles this variety 'a buroe dressing-table', observing that 'the recess should be of circular form as it looks more handsome'. The type illustrated in the *Director* is represented in Fig. 7. It has a baize-covered slide for writing, and this, when pushed back, discloses an array of compartments and toilet boxes; the hinged looking-glass can be reversed and raised again as a book-rest. Though most of these pedestal dressing-tables were of walnut or mahogany, japanned decoration was sometimes adopted, as in Fig. 8.

Dressing-tables with hinged mirrors on the top set between cupboards were also made at this time. The example formerly at Kimbolton Castle, Huntingdonshire (Fig. 11), is obviously based on Pl. LII in the third edition of the *Director* (Fig. 12) and described as 'a Design of a Dressing Table for a Lady'; the notes state that two have been made in rosewood from this design, and that 'all the ornaments are gilt'. A second

dressing-table, in this case of rosewood, with gilt enrichments, and corresponding more closely with the *Director* plate, is in the Lady Lever Gallery, Port Sunlight. It differs in many details from the Kimbolton example. Such tables were often draped, and for this purpose Chippendale recommends silk damask with gold fringe and tassels. These rich hangings are represented in contemporary pictures, and in *Marriage à la Mode* (1745) Hogarth shows a draped toilet-table in the countess's dressing-room. The unspecialised form fitted with one or more drawers employed in the Stuart period still remained popular. A pair of dressing-tables with their accompanying mirrors on box stands are designed *en suite* with an ornately carved tallboy (Fig. 9, and see CHESTS OF DRAWERS, Fig. 37), forming a bedroom set; a surprising rarity in English furniture.

The 'Chinese' taste was at this time freely exploited for bedroom furniture, but dressing-tables designed in that style are rare. The elaborate pierced lattice-work of the panels and gallery in Fig. 10 compares with the simplicity of the top enclosed in a folding lid and fitted with compartments for the

23. *Design for lady's Cabinet Dressing-Table, from Sheraton's* Drawing Book, 1791-4.

toilet. In Fig. 14 the upper structure with a mirror is flanked by three-storeyed pagoda-like supports, the cupboards being decorated with Chinese figures on tessellated floors. Below the hinged mirror is a small tambour. The table portion is fitted with a writing slide and a drawer with a ratcheted mirror and subdivisions for toilet requisites. The draw front is marquetried with urns and trophies, the handles and tapered legs indicating a date after the inception of the classical revival.

Dressing-tables with a hinged box-lid—which, when thrown open, exposes a framed mirror and what Ince and Mayhew term 'the full aparatus'—remained popular throughout the period 1750-1800. The smaller and more compact specimens fitted with drawers are called 'Shaving Tables' in catalogues of the period, the glass rising at the back, and compartments being provided for soap, bottles and razor.

Another distinct type is the 'commode dressing-table' a chest of drawers made more or less on French lines, with the top drawer containing 'the necessary dressing equipage' (*see* CHESTS OF DRAWERS, Figs. 29 and 30). Chippendale supplied several to Sir Edward Knatchbull, of Mersham Hatch Kent, between 1767 and 1770 among them one which is described in his bills as 'a commode dressing Table of Black rosewood . . . with a dressing drawer and slider covered with Green Cloth—complete £9 10s.' Hepplewhite (*Guide*, 1788) shows them with serpentine fronts, and recommends that the drawers should be ornamented with inlaid or painted work, 'which is applied with great beauty and elegance to this piece of furniture'. These ornamental tables were intended to afford a decorative setting for Georgian beauties, who received the fashionable world at their toilets. The small fitted dressing-

table has by this time attained a remarkable degree of elegance, and some examples are based on Louis XVI models. The dressing-table (Fig. 13), is elaborately marquetried. A drawer pulls out and the top can be pushed back, disclosing a mirror on a ratchet, flanked by two compartments, the lids being inlaid with male and female busts in Oriental head-dress on a brilliant green ground.

A person named Rudd, described by Hepplewhite as 'a once popular character', is said to have invented a dressing-table with two drawers in the sides to swing out and provided with mirrors on a quadrant, so that a lady could see herself at any angle (Fig. 22). Hepplewhite, when offering these tables to the public, makes a handsome acknowledgment to the original inventor: 'Rudd's Table or Reflecting Dressing Table possesses every convenience which can be wanted or mechanism or ingenuity supply'. Sheraton, on the other hand, writes disparagingly of this variety, and claims the folding side glasses as 'an addition of my own'. Judging by Shearer's designs in the *Book of Prices* (1788) he specialised in this class of furniture. He improved on Rudd's idea by fitting the front with small drawers and contriving a washing-stand between them; and even the tambour cupboard which, in one of Sheraton's designs, is to 'take a lady's hat as they wear them now', was apparently borrowed from Shearer. The principle of 'Rudd's table' as developed by Shearer is seen in Fig. 15. A book-rest rises on a ratchet in the centre, the side drawers are curved at the ends, and to close the dressing-table these sides are turned in and the glasses folded down.

Sheraton illustrated a considerable number of dressing-tables, and offered the public such complex and elaborate examples as the one shown in the design, Fig. 23. He writes that it contains every requisite for a lady to dress at, and is to be finished in a style 'neat and somewhat elegant'. The drapery behind the glass may be either real to match that below or painted in imitation of it. The right-hand drawer under this glass contains ink and sand, while 'the drawers in the cabinet part are intended to hold all the ornaments of dress, as rings, drops, etc.'. Knee-hole tables with cupboards in the centre were still occasionally made, but the type on legs with a hinged box lid or a lifting top enclosing the toilet fittings enjoyed the greatest popularity (Fig. 16). In 1791 Beckwith and France supplied one of this kind for the Princess Elizabeth, described as 'a neat mahogany dressing Table, with folding top a glass to rise, a Cupboard and drawer under, a Bason & glass soap cups'. In the early 19th century this variety gradually went out of use, and larger dressing-tables fitted with drawers were made; indeed Sheraton (*Dictionary*, 1803) defines a dressing-table as 'a small case of drawers . . . the uppermost of which is divided into conveniences for dressing'. Although a fixed swinging glass still remained popular, on many of these tables a movable toilet mirror was placed on the flat top. In Fig. 19 is seen an example made by George Oakley for Papworth Hall, Cambridgeshire, in 1810, and described in his bills.

Fig. 21 closely resembles Pl. 72 in Smith's *Household Furniture* (1808). He writes that it contains five drawers without any dressing apparatus, and the ornaments are to be formed by an inlay of ebony or carved in the mahogany. The drawers, made without handles, are to be locked by spring catches and released by springs behind. The maker has carefully followed these directions. Rosewood was sometimes used at this time with brass stringing lines or applied mouldings, and Fig. 20 shows an example designed in the 'Grecian Style'. Richard Brown (*Rudiments of Drawing Cabinet and Upholstery Furniture*, 1820) propounded the idea of making the decoration of dressing-tables symbolical. He writes that 'the Embellishments appropriate are foliage and flowers producing perfumes—and running fig-leaves to denote the dress of our first parents'.

TABLES, GATE-LEG. In this classification, based on a special method of construction, the distinctive feature is a top with flaps supported on pivoted legs, each pair being united at top and bottom by stretchers and forming a 'gate'.

Oak tables with folding tops were familiar in the early Tudor period. In 1502 John Coote of Bury St Edmunds bequeathed 'the best faldyn table' in his hall. Early in Elizabeth's reign, Archbishop Parker had one of this kind fitted with a cupboard; at Howard House in 1598 there was 'a large foulded table of walnut-tree upon a frame'. This type is entered in almost every Stuart inventory of a large house, *e.g.* 'an ovall Table of wanscote with falling sides' at Tart Hall, London, in 1641.

The evolution of turning may be studied in these tables; only approximate dates can be assigned, for the simpler forms of turning long remained popular among country craftsmen.

An early stage in the evolution is represented by a semicircular example with a folding top (Fig. 1), the right-hand back leg being halved vertically and framed to stretchers, also of half thickness, to form a gate. When the table is open the lower leaf can be raised as the lid of a box (*see* CONSTRUCTION, Fig. 6A). There is a complete gate in Fig. 2, the top being still in two sections with wrought-iron hinges secured by

1. *Oak Gate-leg Table; semicircular folding top; frieze carved with strapwork. c. 1620. Ht. 2 ft. 6½ in., Diameter 3 ft. 8 in. (V. & A. Mus.)*

nails. In Fig. 3 the solid columnar supports suggest that this table was made in James I's reign and here, in place of a pivot, the gate is secured at top and bottom by wooden hinges, a feature of early specimens.

The familiar type with a gate on either side had been evolved by about this time, the top consisting of a fixed centre section

2. *Oak Gate-leg Table; carved and arcaded underframing; legs decorated with split bosses; gate supported on ground-shelf. c. 1620-30. Ht. 2 ft. 7½ in., L. 3 ft. 1½ in., Depth 2 ft. 10 in. (Col N. R. Colville.)*   3. *Oak Table; folding top and gate attached by wooden hinges. c. 1620. (The late Mr A. de Navarro.)*

4. *Oak Table; moulded polygonal frieze and turned baluster supports; gate supported on ground shelf. c. 1650. Ht. 2 ft. 8 in., Diameter 3 ft. (Col N. R. Colville.)*

5. *Oak Gate-leg Table; supports of knob turning; drawer below top. c. 1650. Ht. 2 ft. 4 in., L. 2 ft. 11 in., Depth 2 ft. 6½ in. (Col N. R. Colville.)*

6. *Oak Table; gates with shaped supports; turned balusters on shaped base-board. c. 1660.*

7. *Oak Table; gates with shaped uprights and stretchers; ends and base-board pierced. c. 1660. Ht. 2 ft. 4 in., L. 3 ft. 9 in., Depth 3 ft. (Mr Ernest Lawrence.)*

8. *Oak Table with two gates; shaped base-board with moulded feet. Late 17th century. Ht. 2 ft. 2 in., L. 2 ft. 3½ in., Depth 2 ft. 2 in. (Col N. R. Colville.)*

9. *Walnut Table; double gates, legs of ball-and-reel turning. c. 1660. Ht. 2 ft. 5½ in., L. 5 ft. 8 in., Depth 4 ft. 5 in. (Col N. R. Colville.)*

10. *Oak Table; double gates; ringed baluster legs and stretchers. c. 1670. L. 7 ft. 8½ in., Depth 6 ft. 11 in. (Queen's College, Cambridge.)*

11. *Gate-leg Table of applewood; cupboard door enclosing two drawers. Late 17th century. Ht. 2 ft. 3 in., L. 4 ft. 1½ in., Depth 3 ft. (Col N. R. Colville.)*

12. *Oak Table; frieze carved with scroll pattern; on each gate horizontal turned rails enclosing vertical spindles. c. 1670. Ht. 2 ft. 6 in., L. 4 ft. 10 in., Depth 4 ft. 2 in. (V. & A. Mus.)*

13. *Oak Table; double gates with supports and stretchers of spiral turning. c. 1665. Ht. 2 ft. 6 in., L. 7 ft. 7½ in., Depth 6 ft. 1½ in. (Chetham's Hospital, Manchester.)*

14. *Oak Gate-leg Table; oval folding top of burr walnut. c. 1670-80. Ht. 1 ft. 11½ in., L. 1 ft. 11 in., Depth 1 ft. 5½ in. (Col N. R. Colville.)*

with hinged flaps on either side. Some examples of the first half of the century show a development from the trestle form, flat moulded uprights being pegged into a base-board with shaped feet. Later, the uprights are found simulating the profile of spiral turning (Fig. 7): vase-shaped balusters are occasionally combined with supports of this character. The joints between the hinged flaps and the fixed section of the top are square, bead and groove, or rule and joint. Although rectangular or turned stretchers usually joined both the main frame and the gates, a base-board raised on feet in the early

manner distinguishes one variety, and is found in conjunction with balusters implying by their character a date after the Restoration.

At this time large tables with two gates on each side were used for dining, and in Figs. 10 and 13 are shown two examples of exceptional size with finely turned balusters and stretchers. There are references to tables of this kind in contemporary bills and inventories, *e.g.* an entry (Windsor Castle accounts, 1686-88) of an 'Ovall Wanscott Table 6 ft 6 ins long and 4 ft 6 ins broad, with a Turned Frame (the Table made to fould).'

15. *Oak Gate-leg Table; tapered baluster supports. c. 1690. Ht. 2 ft. 2 in., L. 2 ft. 5½ in., Depth 2 ft. ½ in. (Gordon Woodhouse Coll.)*
16. *Oak Table, gates support top made to fall vertically. Late 17th century. Ht. 2 ft. 4 in., L. 2 ft. 3½ in., Depth 1 ft. 10½ in. (Gordon Woodhouse Coll.) 17. Oak Gate-leg Table; tapered baluster supports, curved front stretchers, and feet carved and shaped; receptacle below folding top. c. 1690. Ht. 2 ft. 4 in., Diameter 2 ft. 4 in. (The Misses Leeson.)*

18. (*Left*) *Satinwood Gate-leg Table; slender turned legs and stretchers. c.* 1765. *Ht.* 2 *ft.* 4½ *in., L.* 3 *ft., Depth* 2 *ft.* 7½ *in.* (*Stephen Winkworth Coll.*)

19. (*Right*) *Mahogany Gate-leg Table; slender turned legs, curved back stretchers. c.* 1765. (*The Vyne, Hants.*)

This was supplied by a joiner, William Cleere. Gate-leg tables dating from the time of the Restoration onwards were sometimes made of walnut, and more rarely of yew. But oak was chiefly used, fruitwoods—apple, pear or cherry—supplementing it in country districts.

The tops of these tables with two or more gates were made in three sections, the iron hinges being fitted on the underside, while sometimes the gates are attached to the frame by wooden staples secured by pegs. There were certain departures from the prevailing type. In some cases, instead of separate gates on either side, a single gate, pivoted on the central stretcher, served to support both flaps. A small example of this arrangement with oval top made to tilt up is given in Fig. 14. A drawer was often fitted into the main framing, while Fig. 11 recalls the table with a cupboard (*see supra*) which Archbishop Parker possessed at an earlier date.

A moulded polygonal frieze sometimes replaces the ordinary frame-work on mid 17th-century examples with a single gate, solid turned baluster uprights pegged into a ground shelf giving a massive character to such tables (Fig. 4); while the turned baluster rails and spindles tenoned midway into the gates in Fig. 12 are very exceptional. In addition to these varieties, another form, made about this time, demands notice, a folding top being supported on two gates which swing out and fit into the frame when shut. These were used for cards and writing (*see* TABLES, CARD and TABLES, LIBRARY).

Gate-leg tables were made in the first half of the 18th century, the centre section of the top being secured with screws instead of dowels, but in the early Georgian period such furniture was no longer fashionable. About 1760 there was a revival of this model in a much lighter form. The example in Fig. 19, one of three at The Vyne, Hampshire, is described in the 1776 inventory as a 'spider leg' table. The inward-curving stretchers at the back are an improvement on the original model, and designed to accommodate the sitter's legs; but Fig. 18 shows an example with two flaps and gates arranged in the traditional manner. These represent the last form of gate-leg table, which had now been adapted for drawing-room use.

TABLES, HALL. *See* TABLES, DINING-.

TABLES, HARLEQUIN. *See* TABLES, PEMBROKE.

TABLES, LIBRARY AND WRITING-. Tables specially designed for writing were not made in England until towards the end of the 17th century. In medieval illuminated manuscripts scholarly saints are represented writing at desks, which are sometimes composite pieces of furniture, a sloping writing board being mounted on a chest or table. Cabinets enclosed by flaps and small portable desks were generally used for correspondence in the Tudor and early Stuart periods, though a rude form of writing-table is suggested by a few entries in inventories. Thus, Henry VIII, who had many elaborate desks, had also 'a joyned bourde to write uppon', which was provided with another board under it. Small joined tables were probably used from this time onwards, but even Charles I's inventory does not record a specialised table for writing.

After the Restoration, bureaux and writing-tables were among the new types introduced from France. The terms are often used in an interchangeable sense; but examples fitted with a superstructure of small drawers and pigeon-holes enclosed by a sloping or fall-down front are, in accordance with current nomenclature, included under BUREAUX.

Late Stuart writing-tables were made in oak, walnut, 'prince's wood', etc., and had rectangular folding tops, two of the legs swinging out to support the flap. This type of table was also used for cards and other purposes, the legs being of baluster or tapered pillar form. Others had drawers below the top and were mounted on stands with turned supports. Such tables were often decorated with marquetry, and are mentioned in the royal accounts under William and Mary. Early in their reign (1690) Kensington Palace was supplied by Gerreit Jensen (*q.v.*) with 'a ffolding writing Table fine markatre with a Crowne & cypher', at a cost of £22 10s. (Fig. 6), 'for her Ma^{ts} service'. Decorated throughout with arabesques, dark on a light ground, it has a folding top, which in the centre bears the royal crown and cypher; the writing box is a very exceptional feature. In 1697 the Queen's apartments in the same palace contained two others of a similar kind 'inlaid with white and covered with greene velvete'. The compiler of this inventory adds: 'These the Queen bespoke of Mr Johnson & they came in after her death.' The most expensive writing-

1. *Writing-Table veneered with burr walnut; superstructure divided into compartments; scrolled legs and feet carved with acanthus. c. 1685. (Kensington Palace, London.)*

table, however, supplied by Gerreit Jensen, was ordered by the Queen in 1694 for her closet at Whitehall and cost £200. It is described as having 'a cabinet to set over it . . . with Doors finely Inleyd with Mettel'. At Windsor Castle there is another example of *marqueterie d'étain* in the manner of Boulle, of which Jensen was the only contemporary English exponent. This table, enriched with marquetry of engraved brass and pewter and bearing an ebony plaque inlaid with the cypher W.M., can be identified with the 'fine writing-desk table inlaid with metall' provided by Jensen in 1695. A closely similar table at Boughton, Northamptonshire (Fig. 5), made for the first Duke of Montague (1638–1709) is also to be

2. *Walnut Writing-Table, decorated with seaweed marquetry; legs swing out to support flap. c. 1695. Ht. 3 ft., L. 2 ft. 10 in., Depth 1 ft. 2 in. (Lady Assheton-Smith Coll.)*

assigned to Jensen, the 'desk' being mounted on taper pillar legs with gilt Ionic capitals. There is another with Ionic capitals, and as fine, at Wilton House, Wiltshire.

In Fig. 4 is seen an interesting specimen of the type used for both cards and writing. The top, surrounded by a wide crossbanding and inlaid with eight-pointed stars, has in the centre the Bowes crest, *a sheaf of arrows or, feathered and headed argent banded azure*. This table was probably made for Sir William Bowes, of Streatlam Castle, Durham, c. 1700: the marquetry decoration, which is apparently by the craftsman responsible for the cabinet from Streatlam (*see* CABINETS, Fig. 13), is therefore almost contemporary with the more familiar seaweed pattern of Fig. 3, which is, however, exceptional because veneered with kingwood. Tables of this kind afford little accommodation for writing material, but Fig. 2

3. *Walnut Writing-Table inlaid with seaweed marquetry on kingwood veneer; centre legs swing out. c. 1695.*

shows a specimen fitted with fifteen drawers, the centre legs swinging out to receive the top. Writing-tables of larger size had also been introduced by this time (Fig. 1).

Large library tables of pedestal form with drawers and cupboards did not come into general use until c. 1725, but the oak example in the Bibliotheca Pepysiana at Magdalene College, Cambridge (Fig. 7), proves that the type was already known towards the end of the 17th century. The carved mouldings resemble those of the bookcases made for Pepys by 'Simpson the joiner', and this table may also be ascribed to him. It has false drawers in the ends and glazed cupboards.

In the early 18th century small tables with three drawers in the frieze appear to have been used by ladies for correspondence and dressing (*see* TABLES, DRESSING). When mentioned in inventories, it is seldom possible to determine their

4. *Walnut Writing- or Card Table; two centre legs swing out to support top, inlaid with Bowes crest. c. 1695. Ht. 2 ft. 7 in., L. 2 ft. 9 in., Depth 2 ft. 2 in. (Col N. R. Colville.)*

5. *Writing-desk Table decorated with metal marquetry. Attributed to Gerreit Jensen. c. 1690. (Boughton House, Northants.)*

6. *Writing-Table, with movable case of drawers; walnut decorated with 'fine markatre'. Made by Gerreit Jensen for Kensington Palace, 1690. Turned supports replacements. (Windsor Castle. By gracious permission of H.M. the Queen.)*

7. *Oak Library Writing-Table, made for Samuel Pepys, probably by 'Simpson, the joiner'. c. 1670. Ht. 2 ft. 4½ in., L. 5 ft. 5 in., Depth 3 ft. 8 in. (Pepys Library, Magdalene College, Cambridge.)*

8. *Writing-Table, 'knee-hole' type; boxwood stringing lines; cupboard door inlaid as arch; angles chamfered and reeded. c. 1720. (G. L. Riley Coll.)*

character. Thus, in 1711 the family parlour at Dyrham Park, Gloucestershire, contained 'a Walnut Tree writeing Table', and 'A large Walnut-tree library Table cover'd with green Cloth' was included in the sale of the contents of Sir William Stanhope's house in Arlington Street, in April, 1733. Another variety much in use at this period was the small table with a recessed centre, or 'knee-hole', and drawers on either side (Fig. 8).

For the great libraries, so characteristic of Palladian houses, mahogany tables of dignified proportions and massive construction were designed. They were English versions, freely adapted, of the type already established in France towards the end of the previous century. For the English type lion-headed terminals, floral pendants and elaborate mouldings were carved in solid mahogany and sometimes gilded. This modification of a foreign form is well illustrated by the library table at Houghton Hall, Norfolk (Fig. 9), used by Sir Robert Walpole, the legs and stretchers being distinctly French in inspiration and somewhat atavistic in design. Most early Georgian examples were of open pedestal form, but

9. *Mahogany Library Writing-Table; pillar legs, carved in low relief and united by flat, shaped stretchers, are in earlier style. c. 1720. Ht. 2 ft. 7 in., L. 6 ft. 4 in., Depth 3 ft. 2 in. (Houghton Hall, Norfolk.)*

10. *Mahogany Library Writing-Table with carved and gilt enrichments; panels divided by lion-headed terminals. c. 1730. (Rokeby Park, Yorks.)*

11. *Mahogany Library Writing-Table with carved and gilt enrichments; designed (to stand against wall) by William Kent for the Earl of Burlington. c. 1735. (Chatsworth, Derbys.)*

occasionally a cupboard was fitted in the centre. These tables were well suited to architectural treatment, and afforded a good opportunity for the lavish enrichment favoured by Kent and his contemporaries. They occupied a position in the middle of the room, and their ornament was carefully calculated to accord with the plaster decoration; they were designed as an integral part of a general decorative scheme.

Lion terminals give a monumental effect to the great polygonal library table from Rokeby, Yorkshire, the gilt ornament throughout being large in scale (Fig. 10); while the decoration is more restrained in the example formerly at Devonshire House (Fig. 12). In Fig. 11 is a table designed by Kent for Lord Burlington's villa at Chiswick. Owl-headed terminals

with claw feet are introduced as appropriate to a library, the owl being the emblem of Athena, Goddess of Learning. After c. 1740 massive terminals are rarely introduced and mouldings become noticeably more delicate; from this time onwards elaborate handles are employed. The table, Fig. 14, made for the first Lord Leicester, is of a less cumbrous type; is mounted on sturdy cabriole legs finishing in vigorously modelled paw feet, the outer pair of legs pulling out to support the top drawers which form a desk.

Chippendale's *Director* and Ince and Mayhew's *Universal System* (1759–63) prove what close attention was bestowed on library and writing-tables by the mid-century. In the first edition of Chippendale's book (1754) six of the former are illustrated,

12. *Mahogany Library Writing-Table with carved and gilt enrichments; decoration same on both sides. Designed by William Kent for the Earl of Burlington. c. 1735. Formerly at Devonshire House. (Chatsworth, Derbys.)*

13. *Mahogany 'Gothic Writing-Table' resembling design (Pl. LII) in 1st ed. of Chippendale's Director. c. 1755. Ht. 2 ft. 5½ in., L. 3 ft. 9 in., Depth 2 ft. 3 in. (Hon. Mrs R. Fellowes Coll.)*

14. *Mahogany Library Table, carved and parcel gilt; cabriole legs with lion-paw feet. c. 1740. (Handles c. 1770.) Ht. 2 ft. 4½ in., L. 3 ft. 9 in., Depth 2 ft. 6 in. (Holkham Hall, Norfolk.)*

15. *Mahogany Library Table; trusses flanking doors, oval foliated wreaths; mounts later. The design follows Pl. LXXXIII in Chippendale's Director 1st ed. c. 1755. Ht. 2 ft. 8 ins., L. 8 ft., Depth 4 ft. (Formerly at Combe Abbey, Warwicks.)*

16. *Mahogany Library Table with sliding top and adjustable desk; front (which pulls out) and sides divided by lion-headed terminals. Attributed to William Vile, c. 1750. Formerly at Ashburnham Place, Sussex. (V. & A. Mus.)*

17. *Mahogany Library Table; back and front fitted with open compartments flanked by lion-headed terminals with brass rings. Attributed to Thomas Chippendale. c. 1760. Ht. 2 ft. 8¼ in., L. 6 ft. 5 in., Depth 4 ft. 4 in. (Badminton, Glos.)*

18. *Mahogany Library Table; lion-headed terminals with paw feet; pendants and swags of husks in neo-classic style. Supplied by Thomas Chippendale in 1767. Ht. 2 ft. 8 in., L. 6 ft. 6 in., Depth 4 ft. (Nostell Priory, Yorks.)*

19. *Mahogany 'Commode-Buroe-Table'; made in two parts, and of serpentine form. c. 1765. (Althorp, Northants.)*

20. *Library Writing-Table; veneered with rosewood and inlaid with various coloured woods in neo-classic taste; ormolu mounts finely chased. Attributed to Thomas Chippendale. c. 1770. Ht. 2 ft. 9 in., L. 6 ft. 10 in., Depth 4 ft. (Harewood House, Yorks.)*

21. *Library Writing-Table inlaid in classical taste; metal mounts, pilasters of rosewood and panels veneered with harewood. Probably by John Linnell. c. 1775. Ht. 2 ft. 6 in., L. 6 ft., Depth 3 ft. 2 in. (Osterley Park, Middx.)*

22. *Mahogany Writing-Table;
curved cupboards in knee-hole recesses; ovals veneered with darker
mahogany; stringing lines of satinwood. c. 1785. Ht. 2 ft. 8½ in., L.
5 ft. 9½ in., Depth 3 ft. 10½ in.
(Horse Guards, Whitehall.)*

23. *Mahogany Writing-Table; lion-
headed terminals at corners pull
out, and hinged brackets support
folding top. c. 1740. (Percival
Griffiths Coll.)*

were substituted for the original mounts in the Regency period.
A similar variety, fitted with a cupboard in the centre, forming
a knee-hole, is termed by Chippendale a 'Commode-Buroe-
Table' in the third edition of the *Director* (1762): the notes
state that if the recess for the knees is of circular form it
will look 'more handsome'. In an example of this type from
Althorp, Northamptonshire, the central cupboard is straight
and those on either side are concave (Fig. 19). Cluster columns
were sometimes placed at the angles, consoles with floral
pendants being an alternative treatment.

and eleven in the third edition. They are all of the open pedestal
type, and, besides a remarkable variety of ornament, show a
careful regard for convenience. In one, the middle drawer
'goes from Front to Front, for holding Maps, Prints, etc';
another, with convex ends, has a 'Top, which rises with a
double Horse' to form a desk. They were sometimes made
with drawers on one side and doors on the other, containing
upright partitions for folio volumes. The table in Fig. 13
closely resembles a design (Pl. LII) for 'a Gothic Writing-
table' in the *Director* (1st ed.). Chippendale observes that
'This table has been made more than once from this design,
and with a better appearance when executed than in the drawing'. The outstandingly fine library pedestal table (Fig. 15)
closely follows a design (Pl. LXXXIII) in the *Director* (1st ed.),
the alternative right-hand pedestal having been adopted.
This and other pieces of fine mid-18th-century furniture were
probably made for William, fifth Baron Craven (1705–69),
for Combe Abbey by Chippendale's firm. The character of
the bronze neo-classic masks and handles suggests that they

24. *Mahogany Library Writing-Table; three drawers; gadroon
moulding and acanthus-carved cabriole legs with paw-and-ball
feet. c. 1750. (Mr Anthony de Rothschild.)*

25. *Mahogany 'Rent-Table'; polygonal satinwood centre in top; drawers inscribed with days of week. c. 1770. Ht. 2 ft. 4½ in., Diameter of top, 4 ft. 5 in. (Crichel, Dorset.)*

26. *Mahogany Writing-Table; top enclosed by flaps; rising compartment in back fitted with drawers and pigeon-holes; concave tambour cupboard. c. 1770. (Mr J. B. Taylor.)* 27. *Writing-Table of satinwood banded with kingwood; upper drawer divided into compartments with sliding lids. c. 1790. Ht. 2 ft. 9 in., L. 2 ft., Depth 1 ft. 7½ in. (V. & A. Mus.)*

Fig. 16 shows a fine example which may be attributed to William Vile, the lion terminals and oval wreaths clasped with acanthus having close parallels on this maker's authenticated furniture. The front pulls forward and the well, covered by a sliding panel, is fitted with compartments, while the top is hinged to form a rising desk supported on a ratchet. A large brass escutcheon and mounts, apparently not original, and notably out of scale, have been lately removed.

The celebrated library table at Nostell Priory, Yorkshire (Fig. 18), was supplied by Chippendale's firm to Sir Rowland Winn in 1767, and is thus described in the bills:

To a large mahogany library table of very fine wood with doors

on each side of the bottom part and drawers within on one side and partitions on the other, with terms to ditto carved and ornamented with lions' heads and paws with carved ovals in the pannels of the doors and the top covered with black leather, and the whole compleately finished in the most elegant taste   £72 10 0.

Neo-classic influence is discernible only in the paterae, swags and pendants of husks, though some of the furniture at Nostell Priory was made to Adam's designs. The decoration is the same on both sides, the carving throughout is of superlative quality and the traditional lion terminals are employed. Terminals of this kind, but without the paw feet, may also be seen in the table at Badminton, Gloucestershire (Fig. 17), which can be attributed to Chippendale's firm (the fourth Duke of Beaufort subscribed to the *Director*). Of these tables Chippendale observes that 'they frequently stand in the middle of a room, which requires both sides to be made useful'. The royal accounts contain some interesting entries of this type of furniture. In 1766 John Bradburn supplied the Queen with 'an extraordinary neat mahogany round Library Table' which cost £6 more than the Nostell Priory specimen. It had twelve drawers, four cupboards and four rising desks for reading and writing, with invisible spring locks in the top, the ordinary locks being made 'to suit the Queen's Key'.

Lighter forms of writing-table are also well represented in contemporary trade catalogues, and are notable for the in-genuity displayed. Of these, perhaps the most highly specialised were the 'Reading and Writing Tables' made for the use of draughtsmen (*see* TABLES, ARTISTS' AND READING); but even those for ordinary use were often very elaborate. Evidence of the care bestowed on the writer's convenience is afforded by the notes on the writing-tables illustrated in the *Director* (3rd ed., 1762): however ornamental the design, practical needs are kept well in view. In one variety a compartment fitted with drawers and pigeon-holes draws up at the back and is level with the top when the flaps on either side are turned in to close the table (Fig. 26). This compact and service-able form recalls the somewhat later designs of Shearer, who excelled at providing the maximum of convenience in a small space.

28. (*Left*) *Design for a 'Lady's Writing Table,' from Sheraton's* Drawing Book, 1791–4.

29. *Writing-Table; mahogany, veneered and decorated with marquetry of various woods: desk enclosed by sliding cylindrical top. c. 1785. Ht. 3 ft. 1½ in., L. 2 ft. 8½ in., Depth 2 ft. 1 in. (Syon House, Middx.)*

30. *Mahogany 'Carlton House' Table; satinwood stringing lines, tapered legs with reeded cappings. c. 1795. Total Ht. 3 ft. 3 in., L. 5 ft. 8 in. (Reuben Sassoon Coll.)*

Mahogany writing-tables without a superstructure were also made. An early specimen with a folding top supported on brackets which draw out with the lion terminals is given in Fig. 23. A familiar type, popularly known as a rent-table, was introduced early in George III's reign, and continued to be made into the 19th century. The tops are circular or of polygonal form and the drawers, bearing labels, served to keep the documents relating to the various properties on an estate, among other purposes. Of this type Fig. 25 is an early and exceptionally fine example.

In bills of the period 'writing table' often occurs. John Bradburn charged £10 5s. in 1765 for supplying the Queen's Presence Chamber at St James's with 'a Good Mahogany Writing Table the ffront to Draw forward with a Sliding Board lined with cloth and Drawers and partitions for papers etc.'. The legs pulling out with the top drawer was a favourite arrangement, but sometimes the maker's fondness for com-

31. *Rosewood Writing-Table; scrolled acanthus-carved supports headed by lion masks and ending in paws. c. 1810. Ht. 2 ft. 5 in., L. 5 ft., Depth 2 ft. 6 in. (Heveningham Hall, Suffolk.)*

32. *Mahogany Writing-Table made by the younger Thomas Chippendale for Stourhead, Wilts., in 1804. Ht. 2 ft. 5 in., L. 4 ft. 11½ in., Depth 3 ft. 6½ in.*

33. *Mahogany pedestal Library Table; applied bronze ornaments and frieze inlaid with key pattern in brass on ebony ground; cupboard doors mounted with owl emblem of Goddess Athena within bay wreaths. c. 1805. L. 7 ft. (Capt. J. Musker.)*

34. *Mahogany Library Writing-Table made by the younger Thomas Chippendale for Stourhead in 1805. Ht. 2 ft. 6½ in., L. 8 ft. 3 in., Depth 3 ft. 11 in.*

posite terms renders a particular variety hard to identify. Thus, Chippendale and Haig supplied Sir Edward Knatchbull with 'a neat Commode Shiffeneer Writing-Table Japand Green and Gold wᵗ a drawer and cut bottles', probably of commode form with a superstructure of cupboards or drawers (*see* CHIFFONIER).

Adam's influence did little to change the form of library tables, but the decoration was transformed by the neo-classic style. Rosewood and satinwood now supplemented mahogany, and inlay of classical character, stained and shaded, superseded elaborate carved ornaments. Chippendale's firm provided an unrivalled specimen of the new style (Fig. 20) for Harewood House, Yorkshire, which had lately been completely redecorated by Adam and the design, if not by the architect, is very clearly under his influence. This table, made c. 1775, is 'comparable in technical brilliance with the finest achievements of the French cabinet-makers of the 18th century', and shows to what degree of perfection the revived art of marquetry had been brought by that date. The

table from Osterley Park (Fig. 21) is a simpler specimen of neo-classic design, probably by John Linnell (q.v.).

These elaborately inlaid tables are confined to a few great houses; but many tables of this type were produced, without carved enrichments, and depending mainly on carefully contrasted veneers. The classical style affected library tables by imposing a greater severity of line, and in the designs given by such makers as Hepplewhite and Shearer ornament is subordinate to use. At this period one pedestal was often fitted with drawers while the other contained cupboards. There was a large variety of shape, and serpentine sides calculated to display the quality of the veneers were favoured: curved cupboards as in Fig. 22, required most careful workmanship. Sheraton, offering the public a design for an oval library table with rising desks fitted in the end drawers (Fig. 42) explains that it is 'intended for a gentleman to write on, or to stand or sit to read at'; and adds that it has been already executed for the Duke of Kent, with the exception of the desk drawers, which are suggested as an improve-

35. *Mahogany Library Writing-Table on turned column with reeded legs; hinged sloping sections fitted with partitions above drawers; in top, inkpots. c. 1800. Ht. 2 ft., L. 4 ft. 7 in., Depth 4 ft. 7 in. (Castle Ashby, Northants.)* 36. *Rosewood Library Table; brass mounts and winged paw feet gilt; polygonal top fitted for books. c. 1820. (Normanton Park.)*

565

37. *Rosewood Library Table; bronzed and gilt leopard monopodia. c. 1810. L. 5 ft. 6 in., W. 3 ft. 6 in. (Ayer & Co. Ltd.)*

38. *Rosewood Writing-Table with lion-headed X-supports; top bordered with gallery, and drawers with beading of brass. c. 1805. (Southill, Beds.)*

ment. He writes that the style of finishing 'ought to be in the medium of that which may be termed plain or grand, as neither suits their situation. Mahogany is the most suitable wood, and the ornaments should be carved or inlaid, what little there is'; adding that, where expense is no object, the strength, solidity and effect of brass mouldings make them very desirable. The top is to be lined with leather or green cloth, and the piece is moved on castors hidden in the plinth.

Several new forms of writing-table had been evolved, among the best known being the 'Carlton House' type (Fig. 30) called after the house assigned to the Prince of Wales on his coming of age in 1783. This form of table is illustrated in the 2nd edition of *The Cabinet Maker's Book of Prices*, 1792, Pl. 21, inscribed 'Hepplewhite', and in the Appendix to Sheraton's *Drawing Book* (Fig. 41, the design dated 1793), but the name is first found in Gillow's Cost Books (1796) applied to a design which was executed for the Earl of Derby two years later. Sheraton describes the plate as a 'Lady's Drawing & Writing Table'. The notes state that it is to be made either in mahogany or satinwood with a brass rim round the top part. The rising desk in the middle is to slide forward, and will 'then serve to draw upon'. The tiers of drawers at each end in Fig. 30 are shown in the *Book of Prices* version of the design. In the centre of the writing space a board rises on a rack, a common feature in this eminently practical type. A rosewood table of this kind with similar legs is at Buckingham Palace, and is stated to have been originally in the Prince Regent's bedroom at Carlton House. Plain writing-tables with two drawers in the frieze were also much used for correspondence and official business. John Russell and Benjamin Parran supplied one some years earlier to the Council Office, Whitehall; the top was 'covered with green cloth and banded round'.

Smaller and more elegant models were produced in large numbers at this period: the tops are often enclosed by flaps (Fig. 27), while in some specimens a writing board supported

39. *Rosewood Writing-Table with scrolled supports. c. 1805. Ht. 2 ft. 4½ in., L. 5 ft. ½ in., Depth 2 ft. 3½ in. (Earl of Sandwich.)*

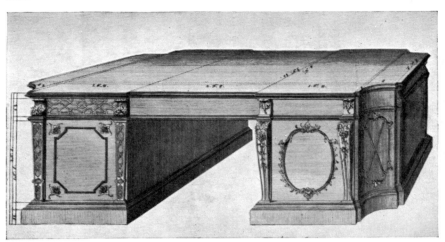
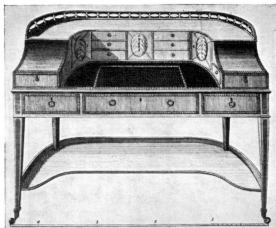

40. *Design for Library Writing-Table, from 1st ed. Chippendale's* Director, 1754.
41. *'A Lady's Drawing and Writing-Table,' from Sheraton's* Drawing Book (*Appendix*), 1793.

42. *Design for Library Table, from Sheraton's* Drawing Book, 1791–4.
43. *Design for Writing-Table, from George Smith's* Household Furniture, 1808.

on a ratchet is fitted in the centre, and a screen rises up at the back. Of the design in Fig. 28 Sheraton writes: 'The convenience of this table is that a lady, when writing at it, may both receive the benefit of the fire, and have her face screened from the scorching heat.' It is to be 'made of satinwood, cross-banded, japanned, and the top lined with green leather'; to raise the screen, the patera in the centre of the back is pressed, thereby releasing a spring. Examples based on this design are extant. Small tables with a superstructure of drawers, made separately and provided with a handle, were also made for writing, Sheraton explaining that they are convenient for moving from one room to another. The drawer below the top was divided for ink, sand and pens: in Gillow's Cost Books this model is termed a 'Sheveret'. Among the ingenious varieties made in the late 18th century was what is termed in the *Cabinet Maker's Book of Prices* 'A Lady or Gentleman's Screen Writing Table'. In construction it resembled a tall cheval screen, the upper part fitted with drawers and pigeon-holes, a board letting down on a quadrant with shallow cupboards below.

Tambour and cylinder writing tables were also in favour. An example at Syon House, veneered with harewood and a variety of coloured exotic woods (Fig. 29), is of superlative quality. The cupboard door in the centre of the interior is decorated with a full-length female figure in oriental costume.

Early in the 19th century pedestal library tables and those of other kinds for writing began to be affected by the archaeological revival of the Regency style. Egyptian terminals, heavy scrolled legs with lion-paw feet and reeded columns headed by water-leaf now became fashionable, brass bandings and ebonised inlay being freely employed. Two examples from Stourhead, Wiltshire (Figs. 32, 34), made by the younger Chippendale in 1804–5, are very characteristic of this new manner, the second one (1805) being thus described:

A large mahogany Library table with pedestals and drawers inside pedestals, mahogany pannelld doors, thermed legs with Philosopher's heads carved on Do. 4 end therms with Egyptian heads, the top part fitted up with drawers of fine wood, the whole made to take to pieces, and strong iron castors £115.

In another Regency example of the pedestal type (Fig. 33) the frieze is inlaid with a Greek key pattern in brass on an ebony ground. The cupboard doors are both enriched with bronze owls, the emblem of Athena, and the Greek characters *alpha* and *theta*, the first two letters of her name, within a bay wreath, while the flanking pilasters have bronze capitals and paw feet, the sides being also mounted with bronze ornaments and lion-mask lifting handles. A library table (Fig. 37) is supported on monopodia resembling those shown in the designs for such a table in George Smith's *Household Furniture* (1808), though it lacks the shaped ground-shelf of this example. The frieze of another table of this kind illustrated by Smith 'is intended as an inlay of ebony' and 'the chimeras may be carved in wood or bronzed' (Fig. 43).

Dating from this time are many library tables on a turned column with curved legs or a solid base resting on animal feet, partitions for books being often fitted below the top (Fig. 36). The variety with a revolving circular top, described as 'a round mahogany library table' appears in Gillow's Cost Books in 1798. In a specimen (Fig. 35) the top is hexagonal. Each sloping section is hinged, and when opened reveals partitions: there are six inkpots, and three bone labels on which initials are inscribed. In addition to these familiar types, special varieties of a curious character were produced. A design in *Ackermann's Repository* (1810) for 'Pitt's cabinet writing table' 'forms externally a handsome globe', and becomes a flat-topped table when two quarters are let down. This is described as 'a humble tribute of respect to a late illustrious statesman'.

Another type of writing-table, at this time generally made of rosewood, had drawers in the frieze and curved or yoke-shaped supports at either end, the top being sometimes enclosed on three sides by a brass gallery (Fig. 38).

TABLES, NIGHT. Towards 1750 the close-stools (*q.v.*) of box form covered with fabric, veneered with walnut or sometimes japanned, were superseded by another variety consisting of a cupboard mounted on legs or a stand. Fig. 2 shows an early example designed to fit into a corner, its pagoda moulding and pierced brackets being in the Chinese taste.

Chippendale does not illustrate this type of furniture in the *Director*, but 'night tables' are represented in later trade catalogues. The example (Fig. 1) resembles a design given by Ince and Mayhew in the *Universal System* (1759–63), the front being 'lined with silk to show the fret', as they recommend, while the panels at the sides are solid. In the second half of the century these night tables were generally designed on similar lines to the small enclosed washing stands of the period, with which indeed they were often combined. A favourite form which long remained popular is seen in Fig. 3, an example supplied by Chippendale and Haig to Sir Edward Knatchbull, of Mersham Hatch, in 1769. Sheraton (*Drawing Book*, 1791–4) writes that night tables or 'pot cupboards' intended for 'genteel bedrooms are sometimes finished in satinwood and in a style a little elevated above their use'. Of this more decorative treatment Fig. 4 shows an excellent specimen. A tambour shutter, a common feature in this kind of furniture, encloses the cupboard, and there are scrolled lifting handles at the sides. The corner variety is also illustrated in the *Drawing Book* (Pl. XXIII) and is 'to answer the purpose of a wash-hand stand occasionally'. In the *Cabinet Dictionary* (1803) Sheraton observes that 'common night tables have a tray top, with holes on each side to lift them up; the doors of the cupboard part are sometimes reeded (Fig. 5) and at other times fold . . .'. The usual sizes are given as 22 ins across, and from back to front 18 ins to $20\frac{1}{2}$ ins, the height 32 ins. He refers to two other types: 'balance night tables have the appearance of a small commode standing upon legs', and those made 'to imitate the appearance of a small lobby chest of drawers, having the top hinged behind so that it may lift up to a perpendicular position'. Fig. 7 shows the chest of drawers form to which Sheraton refers. There was no notable change in design

1. *Mahogany Night Table; fretwork gallery; side panels solid and door lined with silk behind openwork design. c.* 1760. (*Percival Griffiths Coll.*)   2. *Mahogany Night Table of pentagonal form, top pagoda-moulded; legs arcaded with Chinese fret. c.* 1755. *Ht.* 2 *ft.* $3\frac{1}{4}$ *in., W.* 1 *ft.* 4 *in., Depth* $11\frac{3}{4}$ *in.* (*Percival Griffiths Coll.*)   3. *Mahogany Night Table with tray top. Supplied by Chippendale and Haig in* 1769. (*Mersham Hatch, Kent.*)

4. (*Left*) *Satin-wood Night Table, banded with rose-wood and inlaid; corners keel-edged; cupboard enclosed within tambour shutter. c. 1780. Ht. 2 ft. 6¼ in., W. 1 ft. 9¼ in., Depth 1 ft. 6¼ in. (Formerly at Wood-hall Park, Herts.)*

5. (*Right*) *Mahogany Night Table; tray top; reeded doors; projecting corners and legs turned. c. 1790. Ht. 3 ft. 1½ in., W. 1 ft. 11 in., Depth 1 ft. 4½ in. (Petworth, Sussex)*

during the Regency period, but after that time tables of this kind became more and more ponderous and ungainly, like other pieces of bedroom furniture.

TABLES, OCCASIONAL (or to serve a variety of purposes). *See* TABLES, VARIOUS.

TABLES, OYSTER. Variety used for consumption of oysters in 17th and 18th centuries—probably boards mounted

on trestles. The first Earl of Shaftesbury in his account of Henry Hastings (1551–1650) states that he had an oyster table in his parlour 'which was in constant use twice a day all the year round'. When the contents of Sir William Stanhope's house in Arlington St were sold in 1733 there was 'a neat red Wood Oyster Table' in the fore parlour.

TABLE, PATENT. *See* TABLES, DINING-, and TABLES, VARIOUS.

6. *Mahogany Night Table, inlaid with stringing lines in darker wood, projecting corners and turned supports. c. 1800. Ht. 2 ft. 5 in., W. 1 ft. 3¾ in., Depth 1 ft. 2½ in. (Edward Hudson Coll.)*

7. *Satinwood Night Table, inlaid with mahogany stringing lines; recessed balusters in corners; concave drawers with lion-mask handles. c. 1800. Ht. 3 ft. 1½ in., W. 2 ft. 3½ in., Depth 1 ft. 11½ in. (Petworth, Sussex.)*

TABLES, PEMBROKE AND SOFA. Pembroke tables have extending tops, the flaps on either side being supported on hinged wooden brackets; they were generally made with four tapering legs, while for the later 'sofa' variety various forms of support were employed. According to Sheraton, they derive their name from that 'of the lady who first gave orders for one of them, and who probably gave the first idea of such a table to the workmen...', possibly the Countess of Pembroke (1737–1831). They begin to figure in accounts c. 1750. In 1766 Chippendale supplied one of mahogany with a writing drawer to Nostell Priory, Yorkshire. The example in Fig. 1 is contemporary with the publication of the *Director* (1754) and the stretcher corresponds with that in one of Chippendale's designs for 'breakfast tables', which were often of the Pembroke type. The Chinese taste applied to this particular variety is seen in Fig. 2.

From c. 1770 Pembroke tables were often made of inlaid satinwood, while painting was also employed for their embellishment, as in Fig. 3, which shows one from the Etruscan Dressing Room at Osterley Park. Hepplewhite (*Guide*, 1788) writes that they may be of various shapes, square and oval being the most fashionable. He pronounces them to be the most useful tables of their class, admitting 'of considerable Elegance in the workmanship and ornaments'; and to show what may be attempted in inlaid and painted decoration he gives two designs for the tops. Fig. 4 represents a specimen of this elaborate inlay, the ormolu mounts on the feet being an unusual feature. A year earlier Beckwith and France made for the royal household 'a neat satinwood Pembroke Table, a bordered pannel inlaid in centre, a drawer, good brass lock and key, 2 wrought wreath rings, and on brass socket castors, the whole highly varnish'd and polish'd'. About this time Mrs Papendick records, in an account of her drawing-room, that the furniture had been removed from the Princess Royal's apartments and includes two card tables 'and a Pembroke table made to match'.

These tables served for meals, and, according to Sheraton, were suitable 'for a gentleman or lady to breakfast on'. The description in the *Drawing Book* states that the style of finishing them sometimes borders on elegance, satinwood being used 'with richly japanned borders round their tops', and ornamented drawer fronts. In Jane Austen's *Emma* (1816) the heroine introduced a dining-table 'which none but Emma could have had power to place there, and persuade her father to use, instead of the small-size Pembroke, on which two of his daily meals had for forty years been crowded'. In 1800 Jane Austen wrote to her sister about the arrival at Steventon of some new furniture:—'The Pembroke has got its destination by the sideboard and my mother has great delight in keeping her money and papers locked up.'

An ingenious variety, a 'Harlequin' Pembroke, was introduced towards the end of the century, the distinctive feature being a box-like structure, fitted with drawers or small receptacles, which was concealed in the body of the table and made to rise by means of weights. Sheraton claims that such pieces will serve not only for breakfast, but also for writing and are very suitable for a lady. He explains that the name is given 'for no other reason but because in exhibitions of that sort, there is generally a great deal of machinery introduced in the scenery'. He claims that they are offered to the public on an improved plan, a friend having supplied him with the idea. In the descriptive notes he explains that the nest of drawers or till 'can be raised to any height, gradually, until at length the whole is out'; and, when let down until it is level with the rest of the top, can be secured 'so that if the whole table were turned upside down the till would still keep its place'. A contemporary example (Fig. 5) has two rising tills. One contains two drawers, the uppermost being divided for pencils and colours, while the other receptacle, a fixture, is intended for work, and has a wool-winder inside. George Smith terms the version of this type shown in his *Household Furniture* (1808) 'an appendage to the Ladies' Boudoir', and states that it is so

1. *Mahogany Table of Pembroke type; based on Pl. LIII (rt.), Director, 3rd ed., 1762. (Mr Ralph Edwards.)* 2. *Mahogany Table of Pembroke type, designed in Chinese taste. c. 1760. Ht. 2 ft. 4 in., L. (extended) 3 ft. 7 in., Depth 2 ft. 1 in. (Frank Partridge & Sons.)*

3. *Pembroke Table painted in Etruscan taste; probably designed by Robert Adam. c. 1770. (Osterley Park, Middx.)*

4. *Pembroke Table, mahogany and satinwood inlaid; ends convex, taper legs with ormolu mounts. c. 1785. (James Ivory Coll.)*

5. *'Harlequin' Pembroke Table, veneered with harewood and inlaid with various woods; ovals of burr walnut. c. 1790. Ht. 2 ft. 4 in., L. 2 ft. 2 in., Depth 1 ft. 6 in. (V. & A. Mus.)*

6. *Pembroke Table; veneered rosewood, banded satinwood; top and tray below inlaid with circles of mulberry wood. c. 1790. Ht. 2 ft. 5½ in., L. (extended) 3 ft. 6 in., Depth 2 ft. (Hardwick Hall, Derbys.)*

7. *Pembroke Table, veneered with satinwood; painted decoration. c. 1790. (Frank Partridge & Sons.)*

8. *Mahogany Pembroke Writing-Table with sliding top; the bandings of kingwood. c. 1790. Ht. 2 ft. 4 in., L. (extended) 3 ft. 3 in., Depth 2 ft. 4 in. (Bayfordbury, Herts.)*

9. *Pembroke Table, veneered satinwood inlaid with ebony. c. 1800. Ht. 2 ft. 4½ in., L. 2 ft. 6 in., Depth 2 ft. 10 in. (V. & A. Mus.)*

10. *Sofa Table, gilt and painted; top enclosed with flaps. c. 1800. Ht. 2 ft. 2 in., L. 2 ft. 11 in., Depth 1 ft. 8½ in. (Mr R. P. Fane.)*

11. *Sofa Table of zebra wood; turned supports. Made by George Oakley in 1810. Ht. 2 ft. 3½ in., L. (extended) 5 ft., Depth 2 ft. 2½ in. (Mrs Stileman.)*

12. *Sofa Table; veneered rosewood with satinwood bandings. Made by the younger Thomas Chippendale in 1802. Ht. 2 ft. 5 in., L. (extended) 5 ft. 6 in., Depth 3 ft. 1 in. (Stourhead, Wilts.)*

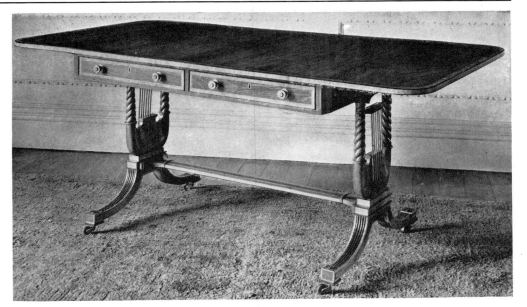

13. *Sofa Table of calamander wood; curved supports and brass mounts. c. 1810. (Lady Victoria Sackville Coll.)*

14. *Sofa Table; lyre-shaped supports; classical ornament, ivory colour 'stopped out' on black ground. (Mr A. Wyndham Green.)*

contrived as to form a writing, work, drawing and breakfast table as occasion may require. A small escritoire rises by springs, and one of the drawers is fitted 'with the necessary apparatus to the work table'. Great numbers of small tables with brackets on the Pembroke principle were made in the last decade of the 18th century.

Many of the sofa tables which became popular about this time were also fitted with fly brackets. 'They are', writes Sheraton, 'those used before a sofa, and are generally made between 5 and 6 ft long and from 22 ins to 2 ft broad'. The more serviceable kind had two drawers, and a plate in the *Drawing Book* shows an example with a sofa 'that a stranger may more clearly see the use of such tables'. Ladies, it is added, chiefly occupy them to draw, write or read upon. A variety of patterns were employed, the legs being sometimes of curved or X form (Fig. 10). Turned columns in conjunction with inward curved legs and brass lion-paw feet, or lyre-shaped supports, are also found, as in two early 19th-century examples (Figs. 11, 12) supplied by George Oakley and the younger Thomas Chippendale respectively. The brass inlay favoured at this time in preference to painted or marquetry

15. *Sofa Table; calamander wood with brass inlay and ormolu mounts; ends draw out below top. c.* 1815. *Ht. 2 ft. 5 in., L. 3 ft. 3 in., Depth 2 ft. 1 in. (Collection of Her late Majesty Queen Mary.)*

16. *Sofa Table; amboyna inlaid with brass; one of three made in* 1816 *for Princess Charlotte. Ht. 2 ft. 4¼ in., L. (extended) 4 ft. 9½ in., Depth 2 ft. 2 in. (Buckingham Palace. By gracious permission of H.M. the Queen.)*

17. *Design for Pembroke Table from Hepplewhite's* Guide, 1788.

18. *Design for 'Harlequin' Pembroke Table from Sheraton's* Drawing Book, 1791–4.

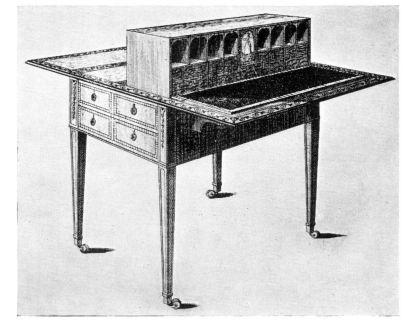

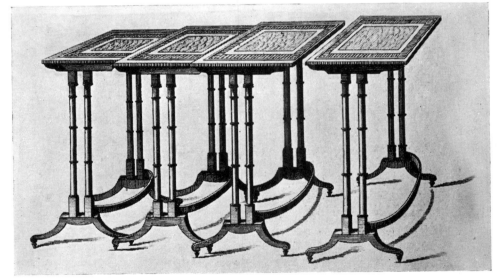

1. *Set of 'Quartetto' Tables; mahogany, tops inlaid with metal stars. By George Oakley, 1810. Ht. (enclosed)* **2** *ft. 5 in., L. 1 ft. 6 in., Depth 1 ft.* (*Mrs Stileman.*)

2. *Set of 'Quartetto' Tables; turned mahogany. c. 1810.* (*Leighton Hall, Lancs.*)

3. *Design for set of 'Quartetto' Tables, from Sheraton's* Cabinet Dictionary, 1803.

decoration in coloured woods is seen in a fine amboyna table (Fig. 16), one of three in the Royal Collection made for Princess Charlotte in 1816. Another of these tables, of cala-mander wood with brass inlay, is not only of remarkable quality but also exceptional because, instead of the normal folding flaps, the ends draw out beneath the top, which falls into position between them (Fig. 15). The sofa tables illustrated by George Smith are designed in the 'Grecian' style and are to be manufactured in mahogany, rose- or satinwood, the en-richments being carved and bronzed or gilt. They are recom-mended as furniture for a drawing-room, breakfast parlour or library, and can be fitted with a chess-board, concealed by a sliding panel in the top.

TABLES, PIER-. See TABLES, SIDE-, CONSOLE-, AND PIER-.

TABLES, QUARTETTO. Small tables made in gradua-ted sizes to fit one below another in sets of four, hence the name. Sheraton (*Cabinet Dictionary*, 1803) contemplates their use for needlework, writing that they are 'made to draw out of each other, and may be used separately'; while George Smith (*Household Furniture*, 1808) assigns them to drawing-rooms, where they 'prevent the company rising from their seats, when taking refreshments'. A set made by George Oakley for Papworth Hall, Cambridgeshire, in 1810 is seen in Fig. 1: and another, of unusual design with three tiers of stretchers uniting the legs (Fig. 2), is from Leighton Hall, Lancashire, a house owned by Richard Gillow and containing several pieces of furniture which can be assigned to his firm.

TABLES, RENT. See TABLES, LIBRARY AND WRITING-.

1. *Oak Shovel-board Table on turned bulbous supports; drawer at one end to receive coins or metal discs. (Repaired.) c. 1620. Ht. 3 ft., L. 30 ft. 2 in., Depth 3 ft. (Littlecote, Wilts.)*

TABLES, SHOVEL- OR SHUFFLE-BOARD. Long narrow tables, sometimes with shallow dishes or nets at the ends, for a game invented in the 15th century. Coins or flat discs were driven from the edge of the table by a blow with the palm of the hand, the objectives being compartments marked out with transverse lines on the smooth polished top. Shovel-board was popular in England in the Tudor period and, according to Nicolas, was a favourite pastime of Henry VIII. In the Privy Purse expenses for 1523, there is an entry of £IX, 'paied to my lord Wylliam for that he wanne of the kinges grace at shovillaborde'. In 1542 the game was prohibited by law, but the enactments soon proved ineffective.

In the early Jacobean ballad, *The Old Courtier of the Queen*. there is a reference to a 'Shovel-a-board Table whereon meat

2. *Oak Shovel-board Table; frieze of pierced carving; twenty turned baluster supports. c. 1665. L. 23 ft. 6 in. (Astley Hall, Lancs.)*

never stood'. The game was much played during the 17th century, and in the *Anatomy of Melancholy* (1st ed., 1621) Burton recommends it as a winter amusement. The inventory (1641) of the possessions of the Countess of Arundel at Tart Hall, near St James's Park, mentions in the Greate Roome 'a long shovel Board Table with a cou^r of old yellow Buckram'; while at Ludlow Castle, one of the royal palaces, there was a 'Shovell Board Room', the long table it contained for playing the game being sold after Charles I's execution. Like other diversions, it was frowned on during the Protectorate, and in 1656 one of the Verney family remonstrated with a correspondent for playing it 'on Sondaies contrary to order'.

Pepys soon after the Restoration mentions that he found Sir William Batten's clerks playing shuffle-board at the 'White Hart,' Woolwich, in their master's absence. Towards the close of the century it seems to have been condemned by the authorities, together with other gambling games, as in 1692 N. Luttrell records that the Justices of the Peace of Middlesex had lately made an order prohibiting certain unlawful games, including cards, dice and 'shovellboard', in all public places.

These tables were often put together in the halls or taverns where they were intended to remain. Evelyn, writing of his father's time, alludes to the shuffle-board being 'as fixed as the freehold'; while Plot (*Natural History of Staffordshire*, 1686) mentions one measuring over ten yards in length, which was built up of 260 pieces, and 'so accurately joined and glew'd together that no shuffleboard whatever is freer from Rubbs and Castings'.

As the game was much favoured in country houses, tables of various lengths and of fine execution were made. A notable example at Astley Hall, Lancashire (Fig. 2), was undoubtedly made for the gallery, which was added to the house in 1665–6. It is supported on twenty ringed baluster legs, resting on cross-stretchers, and has a frieze of pierced carving; each section being different and separated from the one next to it by a carved panel. At the end the frieze is solid, and ornamented with a double vine trail, of which a single trail is continued throughout the length of the back. On one of the sections the royal crown, supported by thistles, figures prominently. To ensure a smooth surface, a parquet made up of pieces of thin boarding, forming a herringbone pattern is laid over the oak boards. A 'swallowing dish', as it is termed in a poem of the period, is seen fixed to the end of the table in Fig. 2, and some of the metal discs, about $1\frac{1}{2}$ in. in diameter, are preserved in the gallery. A plain table at Littlecote, Wiltshire (Fig. 1), represents the ordinary large type, but small shuffle-boards were also made, the divisions incised on the top alone indicating their purpose. These tables were generally made entirely of oak, but the tops were occasionally of yew, or other woods capable of taking the high polish necessary for the game. In the 18th century shuffle-board appears to have lost the popularity it had long enjoyed as a fashionable amusement, but when the inventory of Cannons, Middlesex, was drawn up (1725) for the first Duke of Chandos, the Stone Gallery contained 'A Shuffle board table 33 foot Long', valued at £8.

TABLES, SIDE-, CONSOLE- AND PIER-.
Tables intended to stand against the walls of a room and ornamented with a view to their situation. Console-tables are so called because they are of bracket construction and fixed against a

1. *Oak Side-Table; spandrels of front carved with foliage; top renewed. c. 1525. (Formerly at Canons Ashby, Northants.)*

wall, without legs at the back. Pier-tables derive their name from the architectural term for that part of a wall which is between the windows of a room, the tables being designed to stand in that position. Neither variety was introduced until furniture in important rooms was treated as part of the general scheme of decoration and somewhat formally distributed.

The side-tables used in 15th-century halls mark the starting-point of this development from chests, which were often used as tables in the earlier Middle Ages. Large examples resemble a low armoire in construction, the panels being carved with linen-fold or tracery; in some cases they are fitted with drawer tops, though these have probably been substituted at a later date. Such pieces could be used as serving tables, while they also afforded convenient room for storage, one or more of the panels in the front usually opening as a cupboard door. In Fig. 2 the doors retain their original lock-plates and are boldly carved with late Gothic tracery.

Probably such pieces of furniture were confined to large establishments where the head of the house was waited on by retainers. In the directions *For to serve a Lord*, written about the end of the 15th century, it is explained that after the high table has been provided for, 'thenne salte selers shall be sette upon the syde-tablys'. Contemporary illuminations show standing-salts and other silver vessels thus arranged on the tables, which are often draped. It is seldom possible to identify them in inventories of the period, the furniture in a room generally being briefly entered without any mention of its position. These cupboard-like structures were not the only variety in use c. 1500, and Fig. 1 shows an example obviously designed as a serving-table. The top and shelf below are comparatively modern, but the depressed arches with leaf carving in the spandrels of the upper stage and the scratch mouldings are of late Gothic character. What proportion of the 'tables on frames' in 16th-century inventories were designed to stand against a wall cannot be determined, but most surviving specimens of this type are carved or inlaid on all four sides, and, therefore, clearly intended for a central position. By the middle of the Stuart period tables of similar design to those used for dining were sometimes used as sideboards for serving meals. They are found with a straight frieze carved in low relief on one side only (Fig. 3), or the underframing is arcaded and centres on a pendant. Lord Herbert of Cherbury had 'a side table' in the dining-room of his Westminster House when a list of his goods was drawn up in 1641.

After the Restoration many small walnut tables with twisted or baluster legs united by shaped stretchers were made. In some of these there is a drawer in the frieze, and the back stretcher is straight, clearly indicating that they were not intended to stand out in a room (Fig. 10). They are found plain or decorated on three sides only with marquetry, 'a little table with a drawer' being a fairly common entry in inventories of the time. Pepys records that on September 13, 1665, when visiting Sir W. Hickes's house in Essex, the wind, blowing

into the dining-room through an unlatched door, 'flung down a great bowpot ("bough-pot" for boughs or cut flowers) that stood upon the side-table'.

About 1680 S-scrolled legs and spherical feet were adopted for the more important side-tables (Fig. 4). The majority are of walnut, plain or decorated with floral marquetry (Fig. 6); but they were also japanned (Fig. 5), and gilt examples are found dating from the reign of William and Mary, the tops being ornamented with delicate patterns in carved gesso. A side-table (Fig. 7) represents the arabesque phase of marquetry. Many of these tables formed part of a set (now seldom found complete) and stood below a pier glass, being flanked by guéridons, or stands.

Tables overlaid with silver, embossed and chased, were sometimes made in this extravagant age to stand against a wall accompanied, like the walnut examples, by mirror and stands, also of silver. At Knole there is a remarkable side-table of this character bearing the hall-mark of 1680 (Fig. 8).

2. *Oak Side-Table; centre and door panels carved with late Gothic tracery; lock-plates original. c. 1485. Ht. 2 ft. 5 in., L. 5 ft. 6 in., Depth 2 ft. (Lord Rochdale Coll.)*

3. *Oak Side-Table; frieze carved in low relief, turned supports. c. 1650. L. 10 ft., Depth 2 ft. 9 in. (Lady Henry Grosvenor Coll.)*

4. *Walnut Side-Table with marble top; S-scrolled legs ending in volutes and bun feet. c. 1680. Ht. 2 ft. 7 in., L. 4 ft. 6 in., Depth 2 ft. 3 in. (Lt-Col L. C. D. Jenner Coll.)* 5. *Side-Table, japanned black and gold; drawer in frieze and scrolled legs. c. 1685. Ht. 2 ft. 4½ in., L. 3 ft. 1½ in., Depth 2 ft. 2½ in. (Castle Ashby, Northants.)*

6. *Walnut Side-Table decorated with floral marquetry; top bears initial 'M' for Ralph Montagu; legs scrolled and stretchers curved. c. 1685. (Boughton, Northants.)* 7. *Side-Table decorated with arabesque marquetry; single long drawer; bandings of tulip wood c. 1690. L. 3 ft. 2 in., Depth 2 ft. 2 in. (Mulliner Coll.)*

The top represents the musical contest between Marsyas and Apollo, and is set in richly embossed borders, while at the corners are a coronet and the combined initials of the fifth Earl of Dorset's widow and her second husband, Henry Powle. The coronet supported by amorini appears in relief in the centre of the deep apron, and the legs are of S-scrolled pattern. Silver tables were not always made *en suite* with mirrors and stands, and are sometimes decorated on all four sides, no apron being introduced. In such cases they are suitable for a central position in a room (*see* TABLES, VARIOUS). Complete sets with side-tables intended for wall decoration are often entered in the royal accounts under Charles II and William III. In the Windsor Wardrobe, 1695, among other furniture, are mentioned:

A Table carved and gilded, a large glass and two Stands suitable. In the Large Old Eating Roome, an olive wood Table, glass, & stands, inlaid and imbossed with brass.

The second set was doubtless the work of Gerreit Jensen (*q.v.*).

A few side-tables carved in the style of Grinling Gibbons were made in this period. They stand somewhat apart from the main evolution, and are sculpturesque in character with the structure subordinated to the ornament. In Fig. 9 the disposition of the carved ornament is masterly, the cherubs' heads beneath long pinions being most skilfully combined with wreaths of fruit and flowers. The gilt cherub terminals in a remarkable side-table (Fig. 13) decorated in polychrome incised lacquer also represent the Gibbons school of carving. Upon the top is a design of a Chinese building in a rocky landscape, edged by an incised scroll border. This table dates from c. 1688, the year in which Stalker and Parker in their *Treatise* on japanning state that incised lacquer or 'Bantam Work' was 'almost obsolete and out of fashion'.

In gilt side-tables produced under William III French influence is clearly apparent, the tapered legs with gadrooned capitals, foliated strapwork pendants and elaborately scrolled stretchers having their counterparts in the designs

8. *Set of silver-mounted furniture; Side-Table, Mirror and Stands, in the King's Bedchamber at Knole, Kent. The Side-Table overlaid with sheet silver bearing London hallmark of 1680. The apron centres in the cypher surmounted by an earl's coronet flanked by winged amorini.* 9. *Side-Table of limewood gilt, carved with cherubs' heads and swags of fruit. Style of Grinling Gibbons. c. 1680. (Formerly at St Donats's Castle, Glam.)*

of Bérain and Daniel Marot. Many skilled French craftsmen were then domiciled in England. A fine specimen of this ornate taste may be seen in the small side-table (Fig. 12). An example at Chatsworth (Fig. 14) is probably from the hand of one of the French immigrants known to have been employed there. It is of the highest quality and original in design, the legs, headed by tasselled *lambrequin* ornament,

already suggesting the cabriole form. The scagliola top of the gilt side-table (Fig. 15) bears the cypher of Queen Anne below a royal crown, the Queen having presented it to Lord Trevor of Bromham, President of the Council and Lord Privy Seal.

Console or 'clap' tables of bracket construction appear to have been introduced early in the 18th century, French inventories suggesting that the fashion became prevalent at the

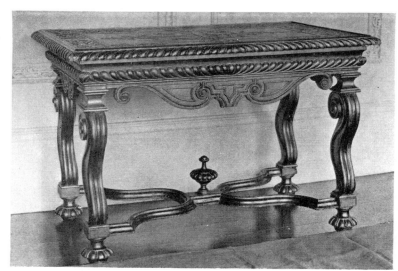

10. *Walnut Side-Table decorated with foliated scroll marquetry; spiral supports, front and side stretchers shaped. c. 1690. (Col N. R. Colville.)* 11. *Side-Table of carved and gilt wood; gesso pattern on top; gadrooned carving, scrolled legs and looped stretchers. c. 1695. (Formerly at Hampton Court, Herefords.)*

12. *Side-Table of carved and gilt wood, top decorated in gesso; pendants, pillar supports and scrolled stretchers elaborately carved. c. 1700. Ht. 2 ft. 7 in., L. 3 ft. 2 in. (Formerly at Hampton Court, Herefords.)*

13. (*Above*) *Gilt Side-Table with polychrome incised 'Bantam work'; legs carved as cherub terminals, united by serpentine cross-stretchers. c. 1685. Ht. 2 ft. 7½ in., L. 3 ft. 11 in., Depth 2 ft. 2 in. (Col N. R. Colville.)*

14. *Side-Table, carved and gilt wood, with marble top; foliated pendants, lambrequin ornament heading curved supports. c. 1700. (Chatsworth, Derbys.)*

15. *Side-Table, carved and gilt; top inlaid with crown and cypher of Queen Anne; pillar supports and scrolled diagonal stretchers centring in urn. c. 1710. (Windsor Castle. By gracious permission of H.M. the Queen.)*

16. *Side-Table with marble top, gilt and decorated with carved gesso; mask in centre of frieze; cabriole legs prolonged in scrolls below frame. c. 1710. (Col N. R. Colville.)*

17. *Walnut Side-Table with marble top; convex underframing with shell pendant; cabriole legs carved with shells and husk pendants. c. 1710. Ht. 2 ft. 11½ in., L. 4 ft. 11½ in., Depth 2 ft. 6 in. (Col N. R. Colville.)*

18. *Side-Table, gilt gesso; crowned cypher of George I on top and apron. Incised 'Moore'. c. 1715. (Buckingham Palace. By gracious permission of H.M. the Queen.)*

19. *Side-Table, gilt and decorated with carved gesso; monogram in centre of top. c. 1710. Ht. 2 ft. 6 in., L. 3 ft. 2 in., Depth 1 ft. 10½ in. (Lord Plender Coll.)* 20. *Gilt Side-Table with marble top; apron, carved with swags of oak leaves, centres in escutcheon bearing Preston arms. c. 1715.*

21. *Mahogany Side-Table; frieze carved with wave pattern, and cabriole legs with acanthus ornament; marble top. c. 1725. (Hardwick Hall, Salop.)* 22. *Side-Table; walnut top; scrolled legs of chestnut carved with acanthus and 'money moulding'; shaped blocks support scrolls. 1732–3. Ht. 2 ft. 9 in., L. 3 ft. 3 in., Depth 2 ft. (Hampton Court Palace. By gracious permission of H.M. the Queen.)*

court of Louis XIV. They were generally placed below pier glasses and early in Anne's reign Celia Fiennes mentions 'a clap table under ye large looking glass between ye windows' at Hampton Court Palace. In the principal rooms of large houses a side-table with a pair of stands and a mirror to complete the group remained popular. At Dyrham Park, Gloucestershire, in 1710 there were no fewer than eighteen of such sets. Some of the tables enumerated were of walnut or 'prince's wood' inlaid, while others were japanned and had leather covers, no doubt to protect them from rough usage. In two instances the table is stated to have been of white marble, a reference to the top.

Marble table tops were much in demand at this period, and were often imported from Italy at great expense. They are found on plain walnut examples (Fig. 17) and also on the elaborate carved and gilt side-tables which played such an important part in the decoration of early Georgian rooms. Scagliola or mosaic were occasionally substituted for marble, while gesso tops were also employed (Fig. 19). Many tables with marble slabs were used as sideboards in dining-rooms throughout the first half of the 18th century, and corresponded in design with the tables placed below mirrors in halls and reception rooms (*see* SIDEBOARDS).

There is a great diversity of treatment in side-tables of the first half of the century. Conventional animals and birds were introduced as supports, while sphinxes, female terminals and figures of *putti* are used in conjunction with boldly scrolled supports. Such examples represent the monumental side-tables of Venetian palaces adapted by architects to English use. Furniture of this character afforded an admirable opportunity for William Kent, whose Italian travels had enabled him to study it in the country of its origin. The carving is extremely accomplished in some of the side-tables designed by him, and the sculpturesque quality of the figures is especially noticeable in celebrated examples from Houghton Hall (Figs. 24 and 25), where they are introduced together with large acanthus ornament, swags and scaled supports. It seems likely, however, that these figures were modelled, if

23. *Side-Table carved in low relief and silvered; glass top bears Meller arms. By James Moore, 1726. (Erthig, Denbigs.)*

24. *Side-Table, carved and gilt; on pendant Sir Robert Walpole's crest within Garter flanked by female sphinxes on scrolls; marble top. Designed by William Kent. c. 1730. Ht. 3 ft. 6 in., L. 7 ft. 5 in., Depth 3 ft. 4 in. (Houghton Hall, Norfolk.)*

25. *Side-Table, carved and gilt; scrolled legs and stretchers decorated with scale pattern; swags of oak leaves; child seated on shell in centre; marble top. Designed by William Kent. c. 1730. Ht. 2 ft. 10 in., L. 8 ft., Depth 2 ft. 8 in. (Houghton Hall, Norfolk.)*

26. *Side-Table of mahogany with gilt enrichments; top with brass lattice banding supported by six female-headed scrolled terminals on plinth. c. 1730. Ht. 2 ft. 9 in., L. 3 ft. 8 in., Depth 2 ft. 1 in. (Fitzwilliam Mus., Cambridge.)*

27. *Gilt Side-Table with marble top; design probably by Henry Flitcroft. c. 1736. (Formerly at Ditchley, Oxon.)*

28. *Side-Table, carved and painted; shaped to curve of room; at front, wolves support frieze and flank composition of foliated scrolls and swags of oak leaves centring in female mask; marble top. c. 1735. (Longford Castle, Wilts.)*

29. *Side-Table, carved and gilt; eagle terminals and swags of fruit centring in shell pendant; scagliola top inlaid with arms of Earl of Litchfield impaling those of his wife, Frances Hales. c. 1726. Ht. 2 ft. 9 in., L. 4 ft. 9 in. Formerly at Ditchley, Oxon. (V. & A. Mus.)*

30. *Side-Table, carved and gilt; the top inlaid with various stones on a black marble ground; eagle terminals, and the apron formed of swags of fruit with a pendant in centre. c. 1730. (Formerly at Devonshire House.)*

31. *Side-Table, carved and gilt; fluted frieze, acanthus ornament and female mask in centre of apron; marble top. c. 1730. (Formerly at Hornby Castle, Yorks.)*

32. *Side-Table, carved and gilt; below frieze floral swags and acanthus foliage centring in lion's mask; marble top. c. 1730. L. 4 ft. 7 in. Formerly at Wentworth Woodhouse, Yorks. (No. 10, Downing Street.)*

33. *Side-Table, carved and gilt; eagle displayed, festoons of flowers and scrolled legs headed by satyr masks; marble top. c. 1730. (St Giles's House, Dorset.)*

34. *Side-Table, carved and gilt; scrolled supports scaled; below frieze acanthus foliage and floral swags centring in pendant; marble top. c. 1730. Ht. 2 ft. 10½ in., L. 4 ft. 6 in., Depth 3 ft. 1 in. (Temple Newsam, Yorks.)* 35. *Console-Table, carved and gilt; supported at front by interlaced dolphins; marble top. c. 1730. Ht. 2 ft. 10 in., L. 3 ft. 1½ in., Depth 1 ft. 8 in. (Ramsden Coll.)*

36. *Console-Table, carved and gilt; plinth supports eagle displayed, standing on rock; marble top. c. 1730. (Lady Capel Cure Coll.)*

37. *Mahogany Side-Table; cabriole legs, carved with floral pendants, end in paw-and-ball feet; marble top. c. 1745. Ht. 2 ft. 11 in., L. 4 ft. 11½ in., Depth 2 ft. 6 in. (Formerly at Langley Park, Norfolk.)*

38. *Mahogany Side-Table, frieze centres in mask amid pierced coquillage; scrolled terminal supports with female heads; marble top. Based on plates in B. and T. Langley's* Treasury of Designs *(1740). c. 1745. Ht. 2 ft. 9¾ in., L. 5 ft. 3½ in., Depth 2 ft. 6 in. (V. & A. Mus.)*

39. *Side-Table; scrolled legs headed by satyr masks; carved and gilt decoration in rococo style; marble top. c. 1745–50. Ht. 3 ft. 2½ in., L. 5 ft. 7 in., Depth 2 ft. 10 in. (Temple Newsam, Yorks.)*

40. *Limewood Side-Table; frieze centres in plumed mask; motif repeated on feet of cabriole legs, carved with scrolls and foliage. c. 1740. (Duchess of Roxburghe Coll.)*

41. *Mahogany Side-Table, legs; carved with acanthus and scrolls, end in paw feet; marble top. c. 1750. (Percival Griffiths Coll.)*

42. *Mahogany Side-Table; pierced lattice-work frieze with pendant of scrolls and husks in centre; marble top. c. 1760. Ht. 3 ft. ½ in., L. 5 ft. 6½ in., Depth 2 ft. 9½ in. (Crichel, Dorset.)*

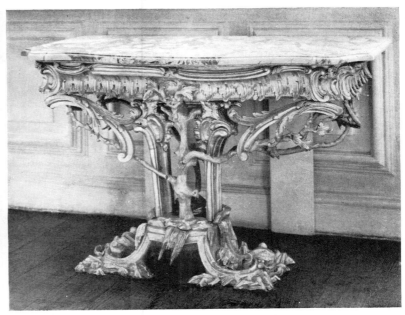

43. Console-Table, carved and gilt, one of pair; ornament shows rococo influence; top carved in low relief. c. 1750. (Temple Newsam, Yorks.)   44. Console-Table, carved and gilt; rococo decoration with oak branches introduced; marble top. Probably by Thomas Johnson. c. 1755. Ht. 2 ft. 6½ in., L. 4 ft. 3 in., Depth 2 ft. 3 in. (Corsham Court, Wilts.)

not carved, by an Italian sculptor (G. B. Guelfi), who is known to have accompanied Lord Burlington on his return in 1715 to England. In Fig. 24 the pendant bears Sir Robert Walpole's crest encircled by the Garter conferred on the Prime Minister in 1726. Sphinxes, more coarsely rendered, occur on an example at Badminton, Gloucestershire, and also on another formerly at Ditchley (Fig. 27), where they are addorsed on either side of an ornamental urn.

The monumental and richly carved side-table (Fig. 28) was supplied to the first Viscount Folkestone at Longford Castle, and specially made to fit the circular end of the dining-room. An almost identical example (now in the Victoria and Albert Museum) was formerly at Coleshill, Derbyshire (which came to the first Earl of Radnor through his marriage with the Pleydell heiress); though the detail is less finely executed.

The terminal treatment is seen to great advantage in a mahogany table partly gilt (Fig. 26). The facile execution and academic rendering of the faces suggest the work of a foreign craftsman, but the design has nothing of Italian exuberance and the mouldings are characteristically English. A table from Ditchley (Fig. 29) in design closely resembles one probably designed by Kent for Devonshire House. The slab was made for the second Lord Litchfield in Florence, the centre of marble inlaying and scagliola manufacture, in 1726. It is inlaid within an oval medallion with the arms of the second Earl of Litchfield (1689–1743) impaling those of his wife, Frances Hales, surrounded by foliated scroll-work, fruit and flowers. Two oval vignettes flank the arms, one a view of Roman ruins, the other a harbour scene in which is represented the ship of Admiral Fitzroy Lee. He writes (July 26, 1726) to his brother, Lord Litchfield: 'I have seen this morning your table (*i.e.* the slab) which is entirely finish't only the armes and supporters which I writ to you of ten months ago, and you have not sent them yet which is a great pity, for I am sure it will be the finest of the sort in Europe.'

Other side-tables of the early 18th century, which are less

baroque in character, also show an interesting variety of design. The same details of ornament—bold acanthus, 'money mouldings', wave and key patterns—are found on them as on the more extravagant type. In place of heavily carved aprons, there is sometimes an arrangement of scrolls below the frame (Fig. 16). On a side-table incised 'Moore' (*see* MOORE, J.), at Buckingham Palace, the crowned cypher of George I appears in the centre of the apron (Fig. 18). The taper legs and yoke-shaped stretchers recall the style in vogue under William III. Moore was also responsible for the

45. Mahogany Side-Table, carved with fret and diaper patterns; shelf pulls out below top. c. 1765. (Longford Castle, Wilts.)

589

46. *Side-Table, carved and gilt, one of pair; top of Italian verd-antique marble. Probably designed by 'Athenian' Stuart. c. 1765. Ht. 3 ft. 1¼ in., L. 6 ft. 3 in., Depth 2 ft. 4½ in. (Formerly at Spencer House, London.)*

47. *Side-Table, carved and gilt; top of agate inlaid; it corresponds with design by Robert Adam dated 1765. Probably by Samuel Norman. (Formerly at 19 Arlington Street, London.)*

admirably designed 'silver table with a glass top and coat of arms cut in it' from Erthig Park, Denbighshire (Fig. 23), which figures in his accounts for furniture supplied to the house in 1726. Gilding was generally favoured in state apartments, but a very large number of mahogany side-tables were produced in this period for use in lesser rooms and to serve as sideboards.

Console-tables constitute a separate group, and, after c. 1725, afford a continuous evolution. An eagle with wings displayed standing on a rock (Fig. 36) grasping a tortoise with one claw, was at first the favourite form of support. The carving of these birds is remarkable in the finer specimens, their feathers

and the nervous grip of their claws being rendered with striking realism. Such tables were generally made in pairs, but few now remain in the positions for which they were designed and matching examples are rarely found. Comparatively few eagle consoles now retain the carved apron pieces at the sides which served to conceal the unsightly metal or wooden struts employed to secure the table to the wall. In the fine side-table in Fig. 33 an eagle bracket is combined with scrolled legs headed by satyr masks. A pair of dolphins supporting the top on their interlaced tails was another treatment sometimes adopted (Fig. 35).

In works published by the architectural designers of this

48. *Side Table, carved and gilt, one of a pair; classic decoration and ram-headed supports; swags between pairs of rams' heads missing. From a design by Robert Adam dated 1773. (Formerly at 20 St James's Square, London.)*

49. *Side-Table, carved and gilt, one of pair; top inlaid with various coloured woods on rosewood ground. Attributed to Thomas Chippendale. c. 1775. Ht. 2 ft. 10 in., L. 5 ft. 9 in. (Harewood House, Yorks.)*

50. *Side-Table; top overlaid with battern of specimen marbles; frieze and paluster legs fluted and carved in classic taste. Probably designed by Thomas Leverton. c. 1775. Formerly at Woodhall Park, Herts. (Buckingham Palace. By gracious permission of H.M. the Queen.)*

51. *Mahogany Side-Table, decoration in classic taste; sphinxes flanking urn in centre of frieze; marble top. c. 1770. (Christ Church, Oxford.)*

52. *Console-Table, carved and gilt; top of satinwood inlaid with various woods. Attributed to Thomas Chippendale. c. 1775. (Harewood House, Yorks.)*

53. *Mahogany Pier-Table carved in classic taste. c. 1775. (Formerly at Woodhall Park, Herts.)*

54. *Mahogany Pier-Table carved in classic taste. c. 1780. (Formerly at Hampton Court, Herefords.)*

55, 56. *Gilt Side-Table, top of marble inlaid with coloured composition; frieze decorated with painted ovals. Designed by Robert Adam in 1775. Ht. 2 ft. 11 in., L. 5 ft. 6 in., Depth 2 ft. 4 in. (Tapestry Room, Osterley Park, Middx.)*

57. *Pier-Table of mahogany inlaid with various woods; top decorated with musical instruments and arabesques. c. 1780. Ht. 2 ft. 11 in., L. 4 ft. 8 in. (Donaldson Coll.)*

58. *Mahogany Console-Table, top quartered and inlaid with oval of amboyna. c. 1780. Ht. 2 ft. 11½ in., L. 3 ft., Depth 1 ft. 5½ in. (F. Behrens Coll.)*

59. *Mahogany Pier-Table; top banded with satinwood; frieze decorated with arcade and paterae in boxwood. c. 1780. Ht. 2 ft. 10 in., L. 4 ft. 8 in., Depth 1 ft. 9½ in. (Stephen Winkworth Coll.)*

60. *Side-Table, satinwood and rosewood; top and frieze inlaid with floral sprays; metal bandings and ormolu mounts. c. 1785. Ht. 3 ft. 1 in., L. 5 ft., Depth 2 ft. 5½ in. (The late Mr Anthony White.)*

period, console- and side-tables figure prominently. They are illustrated with the large pier glasses they were made to accompany by William Jones in his *Gentlemens or Builders Companion* (1739), a work in which no other furniture is represented. In the selection from William Kent's designs published by Vardy in 1744, plates of side-tables for Sir Robert Walpole and others compare unfavourably with those actually executed. There is in the Victoria and Albert Museum a drawing for a table for Houghton Hall, dated 1731, by Kent with cornucopias supporting a satyr mask below the frieze, and another, almost identical in design, is now at Marlborough House. Six of the consoles and side-tables 'for Rooms of State' shown by Thomas and Batty Langley in their *Trea-*

sury of Designs (1740) were pilfered from Nicholas Pineau's *Nouveaux Desseins de Pieds de Tables*.

After 1740 these ponderous baroque models declined in favour, though gilt side-tables of massive construction are also found dating from the rococo phase (Fig. 39). The 'Sideboard tables' shown in Chippendale's *Director* (1754) are to be made of mahogany, these models being equally suitable for saloon or dining-room. Fig. 37 shows a fine representative example.

The ornamental English side-tables designed in the Gothic and Chinese styles between 1750 and 1760 had straight legs (Fig. 42); but for those in rococo taste the cabriole was retained (Fig. 39). It is found as late as 1788 in Hepplewhite's

61. *Pair of Pier-Tables; mahogany and satinwood inlaid. c. 1785. Ht. 2 ft. 10 in., L. 2 ft. 6 in., Depth (joined) 2 ft. 4 in. (Stourhead, Wilts.)* 62. *Pier-Table, carved and gilt; painted panel in centre of frieze; floral festoons of composition on metal cores. c. 1790. Ht. 2 ft. 11 in., L. 4 ft. 11 in., Depth 2 ft. 1½ in. (Audley End, Essex.)*

designs, and is characteristic of side-tables based on contemporary French models. Chippendale's designs include a far more florid console variety, intended for gilding and described as 'Frames for marble slabs'; while Ince and Mayhew, illustrating the same type, direct that they are to be 'in Piers under glasses'. In the ornament of such side-tables designers permitted their fancies to run riot, but it was impossible to carry out the more extravagant. Of Fig. 68 Chippendale wrote that it 'is supported by two piping Fauns, leaning against two Vines, intermixed with Foliage, etc.', and it will have a grand appearance 'if executed with judgement'. Tables to stand below mirrors were supplied by Chippendale and Haig to their clients. In 1768 Sir Edward Knatchbull, of Mersham Hatch, Kent, obtained one with an oval top 'very neatly inlaid'; while Edwin Lascelles of Harewood House, Yorkshire, in 1775 spent £60 on a large pier-table of fine yellow satinwood with antique ornaments and 'Emblematic Heads of Ivory', the frame being finished in burnished silver.

Many contemporary accounts contain large items for marble slabs. In 1764, Lord Leicester's agent in Italy despatched '9 marble tables', or slabs, to Holkham, Norfolk. The tops for a pair of tables from Spencer House (Fig. 46), were ordered by Lady Spencer two years later. On June 26, 1766, Gavin Hamilton writes to her from Rome: 'The marble slabs of *verd antique* veined of the dimensions mentioned will come to fifty five crowns a piece according to the calculations of Seg^n Domenico de Angiolis in the Piazza di Spagna, who I am told has the greatest choise of all sorts of antique marble, for this price he offers the finest sort of *verd antique*.' On April 2, 1767, Hamilton reports that the slabs were on their way to England. There is reason to suppose that the frames to receive them were designed by 'Athenian' Stuart.

The prevailing fondness for asymmetrical and tortuous forms is shown in the console-tables of the mid 18th century. In the example from Corsham Court, Wiltshire (Fig. 44), the awkward blend of scrolled supports with oak branches and foliage has parallels in the designs of Thomas Johnson. In a

fine pair at Temple Newsam, Yorkshire (Fig. 43), rococo influence is clearly perceptible; the motives are co-ordinated and the ornament carved with great spirit and verve. Fashionable models were translated into vernacular terms, while at this time also a considerable variety of small mahogany side-tables carved in the prevailing taste were produced for minor reception rooms.

This variety of furniture was particularly susceptible to neo-classic influence, for mirrors and pier-tables, forming an important part of mural decoration, could not be left to the caprice of a cabinet-maker in houses for which Adam, and other prominent contemporary architects, were responsible. In the collection of Adam's designs at the Soane Museum his activities in the designing of such furniture are impressively shown. The example from 19 Arlington Street (Fig. 47) accords with a design dated 1765, and was probably among the furniture supplied to the house by Samuel Norman (*q.v.*).

63. *Side-Table, one of pair; gilt with painted decoration. Made for the Prince of Wales (afterwards George IV). c. 1795. Ht. 2 ft. 8 in., L. 3 ft. 10 in., Depth 1 ft. 9 in. (V. & A. Mus.)*

64. *Mahogany Side-Table, one of pair; lion monopodia; frieze inlaid with ebonised scrolls. c. 1810. (Goodwood House, Sussex.)*

65. *Mahogany Console-Table supported by gilt lion monopodia; plate glass behind rear supports. One of pair. c. 1810. (Mr Ralph Dutton.)*

66. *Slab of scagliola forming top of Fig. 65.*

carved with honeysuckle, the traditional satyr mask is retained, but the swags of husks springing from acanthus on metal cores contrast with the massive aprons of the earlier phase.

Though most neo-classic side-tables were gilt, they were also executed in mahogany. An interesting example from the Senior Common Room, Christ Church, Oxford, is finely carved with heterogeneous classical motives (Fig. 51).

Pier-tables for drawing-rooms in the late 18th century were usually of satinwood inlaid or painted, but sometimes of soft wood japanned, with the edges and carved portions gilded, the painted decoration being reserved for the top. Most were semicircular, and made in pairs so that they formed a round table when joined together. Hepplewhite wrote in 1788 that pier-tables 'are become an article of much fashion: and, not being applied to such general use as other tables, admit, with great propriety, of much elegance and ornament'. He gives details of inlaid tops, and in his 'Plan of a Room', showing the proper distribution of the furniture, three pier-tables are illustrated under glasses between the windows.

The enrichment is purely classical, though the third edition of the *Director*, in which rococo predominates, had been published only three years before. Fig. 48 shows a side-table designed by Adam for 20 St James's Square, and is characteristic of his fully developed manner. This new fashion, in which ram- and female-headed terminals are combined with swags and classical detail, was soon adopted by the leading makers. Among Adam's drawings are to be found plans and elevations for side-tables at Nostell Priory, Yorkshire (dated 1775), of which the identity of the maker is unknown. The tops of those for the hall are to be 'statuary slabs', but scagliola (*q.v.*), a material now becoming popular, replaces it in the saloon. For the design of the pair of side-tables (Fig. 49) in the Music Room at Harewood, Yorkshire, among the masterpieces of English furniture, Adam is not known to have been responsible, but though not included in his extant bills, an attribution to Chippendale is fully justifiable. Here the tops are inlaid on a rosewood ground in a variety of coloured woods with a design of foliated sprays centring on a classical oval, a broad band of tulip wood forming the borders. In the centre of the frieze,

Instead of marquetry, the tops of some of these pier-tables were of marble inlaid with coloured composition, a variety of scagliola. This method was exploited by Adam, and is seen to advantage on the top of the Osterley pier-table (Figs. 55, 56), where the frieze is decorated with painted oval medallions. The design is dated 1775 (*see* ADAM, ROBERT, Fig. 1). The imitation of one material by another was much favoured at this time, and delicacy of effect was obtained by mounting swags of composition flowers on wire cores (Fig. 62). Console-tables came under the influence of classical design, and the example seen in Fig. 52 from Harewood is an admirable solution of the difficulties presented by the cabriole form.

Sheraton writes of pier-tables in his *Drawing Book* (1791-4) that, as they are 'merely for ornament under a glass, they are generally made very light'. The tops, he observes, are sometimes solid marble, but more often of satinwood 'with a cross-band beyond it'. The frames are to be gilded, or painted white with gilt enrichments. Sheraton comments on one important innovation: 'Stretcher rails have of late been introduced to these tables, and it must be owned that it is with good effect,

596

67. *Design for Console-Table from Ince and Mayhew's* Universal System, *1759-63.*
68. *Design for Side-Table from 3rd ed. of Chippendale's* Director, *1762.*

as they take off the long appearance of the legs, and make the under part appear more furnished; besides they afford an opportunity of fixing a vase or basket of flowers, which, with their reflection when there is a glass behind, produces a brilliant appearance.' The stretchers and central vase appear in a design in the *Drawing Book* (Fig. 70). In 1791 Beckwith and France supplied one of the royal palaces with 'a neat demi elliptical pier table top, exceeding fine satinwood highly japan'd in colours and varnished on a carv'd frame, gilt in best burnished gold, & a bordered Damask leather cover, lind green Baize and bound gilt leather, for the top'.

Sheraton illustrates the Prince of Wales's Chinese drawing-room at Carlton House, with one of the pair of remarkable tables in the revived Chinese taste, veneered with ebony and lavishly mounted with ormolu, which were probably obtained for the Prince from the celebrated *ébéniste* Adam Weisweiler. Sheraton also illustrates the sides and ends of a drawing-room which he states to be based on hints derived from those of the Prince of Wales and Duke of York. On one side three pier glasses are shown with console-tables below, and Sheraton

writes: 'The pier tables have marble tops and gold frames, or white and gold. The glasses are often made to appear to come down to the stretcher of the table; that is a piece of glass is fixed behind the pier table, separate from the upper glass, which then appears to be in continuation of the same glass, and, by reflection, makes the table appear double.' Another side-table, one of a pair, with gilt and painted decoration, (Fig. 63), was made for Carlton House and is stamped G. IV. R. at the back. The semi-elliptical top is painted primrose yellow and decorated with medallions in grisaille on a chocolate ground. That in the centre, of oblong shape, represents a chariot with figures and is adapted from a picture by Guido Reni (1575–1642) representing Aurora scattering flowers before the chariot of the sun. The frieze is carved with a design of linked paterae; the two convex sides are in the form of false drawers enriched with crossed laurel sprays. The form and decoration are exceptional and possibly this fine pair of side-tables was designed by Henry Holland.

In the archaeological revival, based on the Directoire and Empire style, which began in the closing years of the century,

69. *Design for Pier-Table from Hepplewhite's* Guide, *1788.*
70. *Design for Pier-Table from Appendix to Sheraton's* Drawing Book, *1791-4.*

Egyptian terminal figures and animal-headed supports were incorporated into the design of pier-tables. An attempt was made by George Smith and Sheraton in his later works to impart 'Grecian severity' or a recognisable Egyptian form even to this variety of furniture; but Thomas Hope's devotion to classical precedent would not allow of mirrors with pier-tables below them. In the view of the room which contained his Egyptian Collections (*Household Furniture*, 1807, Pl. 8) he does, however, show pier-tables set against two of the walls, which, unlike the rest of the furniture, have no distinctive Egyptian character.

George Smith writes that such tables are the decoration of apartments of consequence, 'their beauty consisting greatly in the execution and proper conception of the parts ornamented with chimeras'. They are to be made in rosewood or in imitation of marble, the gilding in matt gold being calculated to produce 'a solid and metal-like appearance' (*Designs for Household Furniture*, 1808). He allows, however, mahogany in rooms which contain it, and examples in that wood are often found with lion monopodia designed on the lines of contemporary sideboards; which indeed many of them were intended to supplement. Bronzed metal is recommended for the decorative parts: a silvered plate of looking-glass may be placed at the back for the sake of reflection (Fig. 65). Marble and scagliola slabs were in fashion for such tables, and here the detail of the classic vases is carefully rendered. George Smith shows console-tables with a terminal figure of bizarre design supporting the marble slab, a backboard extending from the dado above the slab and being provided with a projecting shelf (*Household Furniture*, 1808, Pl. 121). This innovation does not appear to have met with favour.

TABLES, SOFA. *See* TABLES, PEMBROKE AND SOFA.

TABLES, SPIDER. Form of gate-leg table with slender turned legs and stretchers introduced c. 1750 and thus named in contemporary bills (*see* TABLES, GATE-LEG, Figs. 18, 19).

TABLES, SUPPER-; TABLES, TEA-; TABLES, TRIPOD. *See* TABLES, CHINA.

TABLES, VARIOUS. Tables have developed from a few simple types, used as occasion arose for different purposes; hence the term 'occasional table', now commonly employed. In the course of time more and more new varieties were introduced, and their history is one of increasing specialisation. Thus, towards the end of the 17th century, side-tables began to be made in increasing numbers; while tables for cards and games, dressing, writing, needlework and other employments were gradually evolved. Throughout the evolution, however, vast numbers of tables intended for general purposes have been produced. Representative specimens of successive periods are given in this section, supplemented by some unusual forms not readily classified.

During the Middle Ages most tables were movable, narrow boards of great weight being laid on trestles. But this was not always so; the table 'dormant' had its tops secured to the supports, and remained fixed in its place. In the first half of the 16th century, tables with frames constructed by the joiner came into use; it was long, however, before they superseded the trestle form, and the two varieties constantly recur in the same inventory. John Rede, Keeper of Mary Tudor's wardrobe, at his death in 1557 had tables with one or more 'payer of trestilles' in most of the bedrooms in his large house; but he had others also, stated to have been 'uppon a frame'. Nearly a hundred years later there was 'a Long Table standing upon Antique tressells', when the inventory of Charles I's possessions at Greenwich was taken.

Tables with folding tops were known in the 15th century, and among the goods of 'My Maister in his Chambre' the compiler of the inventory of Sir John Fastolfe (d. 1459) enters one of this kind. These early tables, large or small, were by no means invariably of oak, 'spruys' or fir from the Baltic being often specified (*see* SPRUCE).

By the end of the Tudor period the number of small tables, suitable for many purposes, had largely increased. They figure in all the principal bedrooms of great houses, and are generally stated to be covered with a carpet of needlework or tapestry. At this time walnut, either of native growth or imported, was freely used, and the decorative aspect of tables was fully con-

1. *Walnut Centre Table, inlaid with various woods; top decorated with coats of arms, musical instruments and other devices; inner surfaces of stretchers painted. c. 1570. Ht. 2 ft. 11½ in., L. 9 ft. 11 in., Depth 4 ft. 2½ in. (Hardwick Hall, Derbys.)*

sidered when they were destined for a place in important rooms. The table in Fig. 1 is probably the most elaborate example of Tudor inlay on this kind of furniture. The walnut top is decorated, in three horizontal divisions, with musical instruments, coats-of-arms, playing boards, cards, a music book and other devices. The arms are Talbot impaling Hardwick, Cavendish (with crescent for Henry Cavendish) impaling Talbot, the crests of the families with their mottoes being also represented amid intricate strapwork. In the centre of the top is a cartouche with the legend:

> The Redolent smel
> of aeglentyne [sweetbriar]
> We stagges exavet [exalt]
> To the deveyne.

This table was probably made for Elizabeth (Bess) of Hardwick at the time of her marriage to her fourth husband, the Earl of Shrewsbury, in 1568, and the arms represented commemorate also the marriage of her son, Henry Cavendish, and her daughter, Mary, with a daughter and son of Lord Shrewsbury. The tapered pillar legs with depressed capitals are inlaid with festoons of flowers; the deep stretchers are also inlaid, the inner surfaces being painted with a strapwork pattern. The top is formed of a thick veneer of walnut on a core of deal.

In the small oak tables of the 16th and early 17th centuries arcaded friezes and fluted or gadrooned columnar legs witness to the influence of Renaissance taste. A fine example belonging to the Armourers' and Braziers' Company bears the date 1606 carved in the spandrels of the arcade, and closely resembles another table in the possession of the Carpenters'

2. *Drawings of Tables in inventory of John, Lord Lumley, 1590.*

3. *Table, oak, with top of inlaid marble; frieze and baluster legs carved with strapwork. c. 1595. Ht. 2 ft. 11¼ in., L. 4 ft., Depth 4 ft. (Aston Hall, Birmingham.)*

4. *Oak octagonal Table; frieze intersected by fluted corbels; vase-shaped legs gadrooned; folding top. c. 1600. (Ashmolean Mus., Oxford.)*

5. *Oak Table; fluted columnar legs; leaves of oval top supported on brackets with pivoted uprights. c. 1610. (Col N. R. Colville.)*

Company. Another fine table, also octagonal, has a folding top, supported by the centre leg, which pulls out from the back frame (Fig. 4); this table was given by Elias Ashmole to the University of Oxford in 1679. Fig. 5 shows an interesting precursor of the gate-leg type, the folding top being supported on brackets with pivoted uprights.

From early Tudor times there appears to have been a demand for tables of a composite character. Of these, Henry VIII's inventory (1547) specifies a number. In the King's Library at Windsor was 'a table in the myddes of the house with a cupboard in yt'; while 'among the stuffe deliuered to

the Lady Elizabeth' by the King, her father, were 'a table of waynscotte having iii leaves w a frame underneath ye same like onto a presse', and 'a table with tilles in it standing upon iv carved pillors, ye same table being couered with green cloth and fringed with greene silke fringe'. The list in which these two examples occur is headed 'Tables of sondrie sortes standing in sondrye places'. The variety termed 'lyverey', which were probably fitted with a cupboard to contain the allowances of food made to members of the household, are expressly stated to have been the 'work of carpentars'.

As early as 1590 some of Lord Lumley's 25 tables 'of walnut-

6. *Oak Table carved with flutes; bulbs at base of columnar legs. c. 1610. Ht. 2 ft. 3½ in., L. 3 ft., Depth 1 ft. 11 in. (The late Mr Walter Simpson.)* 7. *Oak Table with stretchers and uprights of spiral turning. c. 1670. (A. de Navarro Coll.)*

8. *Centre Table decorated on core of oak with plates of silver elaborately embossed and chased; given to Charles II by citizens of London. c. 1670. Ht. 2 ft. 10 in., L. 3 ft. 5½ in., Depth, 2 ft. 3½ in. (Windsor Castle. By gracious permission of H.M. the Queen.)*

9. *Centre Table veneered with burr maple; top, inlaid with silver lines, supported on scrolls terminating in female heads and tasselled cushions. c. 1685. Ht. 2 ft. 7½ in., L. 3 ft. 9 in., Depth 2 ft. 4½ in. (Chatsworth, Derbys.)*

tree and Markatre' had tops inlaid with marble in the Italian manner. Some of the tables shown in the original drawings (Fig. 2) are distinctly Italianate, but in a rare example of about this date (Fig. 3) the frame with its columnar supports is unmistakably English, while the top is of polychrome *pietre dure* inlaid with a perspective design of Italian inspiration.

Painted furniture appears in the Northampton inventory of 1614, 'a large square China worke table and frame of blacke varnish and golde' being no doubt decorated in Oriental taste like contemporary cabinets, of which a few specimens survive (*see* CABINETS, Fig. 1). When an inventory (1641) of the contents of Tart Hall, London, was drawn up for the Countess of Arundel, the drawing-room contained 'A little Ebony Square

Table inlayde with Torteaux shels', which was probably obtained from Holland.

The royal palaces after Charles I's execution in 1649 contained many tables of unusual character. At Hampton Court was 'one faire Table of Walnutt Tree garnished with mother of pearle gilt'; while the contents of Somerset House included a 'marble Table inlayed upon a gilt frame square given to the Queen by Lady Banings'.

With the Restoration in 1660 the age of specialised tables begins, and distinct varieties suitable to the requirements of a luxurious and pleasure-loving society were produced. From this period a large number of examples survive, which do not appear to have been intended for any one specific purpose, the 'little joyned table' of early Stuart inventories being now often made with legs and stretchers of spiral turning (Fig. 7); many small gate-leg examples were for general use (*see* TABLES, GATE-LEG). Decorative tables designed to stand in the middle of a room closely resemble those of the side and console varieties, except that the ornament is on all four sides. Veneers of walnut, olive, maple, kingwood (prince's wood) and laburnum took the place of the traditional solid oak, and marquetry decoration was freely employed. The table in Fig. 9, dating from the time of the first Duke of Devonshire, is veneered with maple-wood; broken scrolls with female heads support small tasselled cushions, and the top is inlaid with lines of silver. Terminal figures were occasionally introduced as supports, a fashion which lasted into the 18th century and was of Italian origin.

Tables of 'massy silver' were noticed by Evelyn in a Genoese palace in 1644; and Louis XIV expended vast sums on furniture of this kind for Versailles. The fashion was introduced into England before the outbreak of the Civil War, for 'a silver Table and Frame all layed over with silver' was among Charles I's possessions, and when sold by the Council of State

11. Centre Table; top walnut, frame of limewood; carved by Grinling Gibbons and given by him to John Evelyn. c. 1680-5? (Evelyn Coll., at Christ Church, Oxford.)

in 1650 realised £120. Existing examples of this extravagant manner of furnishing date from after the Restoration, when sets comprising a table, stands and mirror were sometimes made. The table presented to Charles II by some citizens of London c. 1670 has a core of oak covered with thin sheets of silver embossed and chased (Fig. 8). This example was intended for a central position, for the frieze is enriched on all four sides. The other table from Windsor Castle (Fig. 9), supported on caryatides of solid silver, was presented to William III, also by some citizens of London. It was made by Andrew Moore of Bridewell, whose monogram it bears; the engraving,

by another hand, is signed 'R.H.Scap'. In the centre of the top are the royal arms of England, trophies and banners, each bearing the monogram 'W.R.'; at the four corners are crowned shields engraved with the emblems of the British Isles, which also appear within escutcheons on the frieze embossed with fruit and flowers. Among the decorative motives on the top is the crowned reversed cypher 'W.M.R.' and the motto 'Je Main Tien Dray' inscribed on a fold of drapery.

Silver enrichments applied on a frame of ebony were also in favour, this less extravagant fashion being borrowed from

12. *Centre Table, carved and decorated with gilt gesso. Probably by James Moore. c. 1700. (Boughton House, Northants.)*

13. *Centre Table; top of Oriental lacquer; frame decorated with English japan. c. 1690. (Boughton House, Northants.)*

14. *Table of yew wood; octagonal form with folding top. c. 1715. Ht. 2 ft. 6 in., L. 2 ft. 6 in., Depth 2 ft. 4 in. (Fred Skull Coll.)*
15, 16. *Centre Table decorated with carved gesso; in centre of top, marquess's coronet surrounded by strapwork; legs headed by plumed Indian masks. c. 1725. Ht. 2 ft. 6 in., L. 2 ft. 10 in., Depth 1 ft. 10 in. (Chatsworth, Derbys.)*

17. *Mahogany Table, one of three made for East India House. c. 1735. Ht. 2 ft. 8 in., L. 8 ft. 5½ in., Depth 3 ft. 6 in. (Commonwealth Relations Office.)*

18. *Centre Table of gilt wood; top inlaid with various marbles; legs, headed by lion masks, united by swags of drapery centring in shell. c. 1725. (Penshurst Place, Kent.)*

19, 20. *Table decorated with black and gold japan; in centre of top, Tower arms impaling Cambe. Mid-18th century. Ht. 2 ft. 3½ in., L. 2 ft. 5 in., Depth 1 ft. 8 in. (Weald Hall, Essex.)*

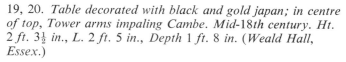

21. *Mahogany Table; top shaped and frieze carved with frets; cabriole moulded legs end in volutes. c. 1760. Ht. 2 ft. 2½ in., L. 3 ft. 1½ in., Depth 2 ft. (Audley End, Essex.)*

22. *Mahogany extending Table; legs pierced to match fretwork gallery; top divided into two compartments. c. 1765. (Longford Castle, Wilts.)*

23. *Mahogany Table, satinwood inlay; revolving top made to fold in sections. c. 1785. Ht. 2 ft. 5 in., L. 1 ft. 6 in., Depth 1 ft. 6 in. (Stephen Winkworth Coll.)*

24. *Mahogany Table with triangular folding flap; baluster fluted legs carved with gadroons, flutings and water leaf. c. 1780. (F. Behrens Coll.)*

25. *Table veneered with tulipwood, walnut and sycamore; decorated with marquetry and mounted with ormolu. c. 1785. Ht. 2 ft. 4 in., L. 2 ft. 6 in., Depth 1 ft. 7 in. (Leopold Hirsch Coll.)*

26. Satinwood Table, with superstructure of shelves and cupboards; marquetry decoration and kingwood bandings. c. 1785. Ht. 4 ft. 5 in., L. 4 ft. 5½ in., Depth 1 ft. 9 in. (Hatfield House, Herts.)

Holland. A restored example at Ham House, Surrey, with female terminal figures bears the monogram and coronet of Elizabeth, Countess of Dysart, on a silver plaque in the centre of the top and on the cornerpieces, proving that it was made before she became Duchess of Lauderdale in 1672. It is entered in the inventory of 1679 as an 'ebony table garnished with silver'. Another ebony table with silver mounts, at Knole, Kent, has a mirror and stands to match.

Centre tables in the late 17th century were similar to those intended to stand against a wall. A highly exceptional example, Fig. 11, is authenticated by a description in John Evelyn's *Inventory of Wotton House* as having been given to him by Grinling Gibbons in gratitude for his introduction of the artist to Charles II. The top is of walnut and the frame of lime 'incomparably carved with 4 Angels, flowers and frutages'. Scagliola was occasionally used for the tops at the end of the century, and an example formerly at Drayton, Northamptonshire, bears the arms of the second Earl of Peterborough with acanthus and floral ornament, all inlaid in that substance. A centre table with gilt gesso decoration at Boughton, Northamptonshire (Fig. 12), is of remarkably rich design and is probably by James Moore, to whom other furniture at Boughton can be assigned (*see* CHESTS, Fig. 30); the stretchers are of the type used by him and the legs are headed by the small Ionic capitals found on several of his tables—in this instance ornamented with swags of husks. In the centre of the top is the cypher of Ralph Montagu as Earl; this dates the piece between 1689 and 1705. The earliest reference in accounts to Moore occurs in the Duke of Montagu's domestic expenses for 1708, and this table antedates any other piece that can be assigned to him (*see* MOORE, JAMES).

Tables decorated with panels of oriental lacquer, cut up for the purpose, or with English japan, when made for the centre of a room, were decorated on all four sides. In Stalker and Parker's *Treatise* on japanning (1688) the method of making 'little (pieces) such as stands or Tables' out of old screens is referred to, and a centre table (Fig. 13) provides an instance of this practice. The top is made up of Chinese scenes in polychrome cut lacquer on a dark ground. The rest of the surface is japanned with flower-sprays and foliage flatly painted in pseudo-oriental taste.

Tables of an unfamiliar character are occasionally entered in the royal accounts at this period. Gerreit Jensen, in 1689, supplied the Crown with 'a wallnuttree Dophin Table' at a cost of £3; but its character is uncertain, for dolphins do not appear to have been introduced as supports until c. 1725. At

27, 28. Occasional Table; top of maple wood bound with brass containing pietre dure *panel; legs with ormolu enrichments. c. 1800. Ht. 2 ft. 3½ in., L. 2 ft. 8½ in., Depth 1 ft. 10 in. (Southill, Beds.)*

29. *Occasional Table; top, with brass gallery, of kingwood; support gilt and carved in Egyptian taste. c. 1805. Ht. 2 ft. 5½ in., L. and Depth 1 ft. 8 in. (Southill, Beds.)* 30. *Circular Table veneered with zebra wood; fillets on scrolled legs and paw feet gilt. c. 1810. (Mr Ralph Dutton.)*

Dyrham Park, Gloucestershire, in 1710, japan as a decoration is well represented on tables which are not assigned to any distinct purpose. One of this class, but of a later date, is seen in Figs. 19 and 20, the finely decorated top contrasting with the simple character of the frame. The occasional tables of Queen Anne's reign rely on the judicious use of veneers, mostly of walnut, and represent a reaction from the marquetry enrich-

ments of the previous generation. In the small folding example seen in Fig. 14 one leg swings out to support the top, which with the frame is inlaid with boxwood stringing lines.

Sober dignity and mastery of line (more apparent in the specialised varieties) were succeeded by florid enrichment and a revived use of gilding. Such forms of support as caryatides, sphinxes and eagles were reserved for the monumental

31. *Circular Table, mahogany inlaid with ebony and silver. From a design (Pl. XXXIX) in Thomas Hope's* Household Furniture, *1807. Ht. 2 ft. 5 in., Diameter 3 ft. 6 in. (V. & A. Mus.)* 32. *Centre Table of maple wood; brackets and lyre-shaped supports carved and gilt. c. 1810. (Mr Ralph Dutton.)*

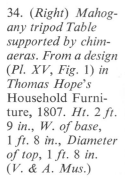

33. (Left) Rosewood Table with inlaid marble top and metal mounts. c. 1810. Ht. 2 ft. 7 in. (Castle Ashby, Northants.)

34. (Right) Mahogany tripod Table supported by chimaeras. From a design (Pl. XV, Fig. 1) in Thomas Hope's Household Furniture, 1807. Ht. 2 ft. 9 in., W. of base, 1 ft. 8 in., Diameter of top, 1 ft. 8 in. (V. & A. Mus.)

side-tables of this period, those intended for a central position having legs decorated with lion or human masks, the friezes and aprons being elaborately carved on all four sides. In a table of this class (Fig. 18) the sculpturesque treatment of the lion masks and shaggy manes is particularly noticeable; the imported slab is inlaid with various marbles in a geometric pattern. Gesso decoration is represented in Figs. 15 and 16. This delicate enrichment was possible only in carved gesso, and in contemporary mahogany examples similar motives are more broadly handled. Three massive mahogany tables, made for the East India Office in Leadenhall Street (completed in 1729) and removed after its demolition in 1861 to the Council Room of the India Office, are carved on the legs with a male mask finishing above in acanthus leaves hipped on to the frieze (Fig. 17). There is a central pendant composed of a finely modelled female mask set within a shell and flanked by acanthus, but the decoration on all four legs indicates that these magnificent examples were intended to stand one at the end of the room and the others with chairs set behind them on either side. Although mahogany and walnut were the fashionable woods, in country districts oak and many other indigenous varieties were freely used.

When trade catalogues were first published, the age of specialisation was far advanced, and the tables shown by Chippendale, Ince and Mayhew, Hepplewhite and Sheraton are all assigned to some specific purpose. Centre tables suitable for general use, though not illustrated separately by the makers, were produced in large numbers, and in style closely resembled the specialised varieties. An example (Fig. 21) with serpentine fret-carved frieze and elegant cabriole legs ending in volutes is representative of centre tables about 1760, a pierced gallery being alone required to complete the resemblance to what Chippendale terms a 'tea or china table'. Fig. 22 shows a curious extending table; the legs are pierced to match the fretwork gallery, and the top is divided into two compart-

ments which fold upon each other when the table is closed. Classical taste is apparent in the carved enrichments of the example in Fig. 24 with a triangular folding top.

In the second half of the 18th century patents were taken out by several craftsmen for ingenious varieties of tables, collapsible or extending devices being the usual principles in these inventions. A typical instance is afforded by A. G. Eckhardt's 'Portable Table', for which the patent was obtained in 1771. In the specification the maker states that 'he had by long study and pains found out and invented a new Portable Table with Double or Single Folding Flaps and folding Feet . . . so contrived as to answer all the Purposes of the Common Table, and at the same time to lay in the compass of a small Box'. Among the advantages claimed, in addition to the small space occupied, is 'the facility of changing the sides of the flaps at pleasure, the one of which being of any beautiful wood, and the other covered with green cloth, it will then occasionally serve either as a tea table or as a card or writing table'. At the Victoria and Albert Museum there is a plain mahogany example corresponding in every detail with Eckhardt's patent. A similar desire for economy of space prompted the making of small tables in graduated sizes to fit one below another (see TABLES, QUARTETTO). At this period there were many methods of enlargement, and one of the most satisfactory is shown in Fig. 23, the top revolving on a pivot and being made in folding sections. The delicate floral marquetry of the late 18th century was well adapted to the enrichment of small drawing-room tables, and is sometimes found in conjunction with ormolu mounts, the designs being based on contemporary French models (Fig. 25). A curious composite form with inlaid decoration was apparently designed for a deep alcove at Hatfield House, Hertfordshire (Fig. 26).

In the Regency period, mahogany, rosewood or zebra wood was usually employed; the enrichments were bronzed or gilt, and applied metal ornament was freely used. The animal

1. *Mahogany Wine-Table of horseshoe shape; brass rail, two japanned metal coasters sliding in well. c. 1810. Ht. 2 ft. 4½ in., L. 7 ft. 9 in., Depth 5 ft. 11 in. (Trinity Hall, Cambridge.)*

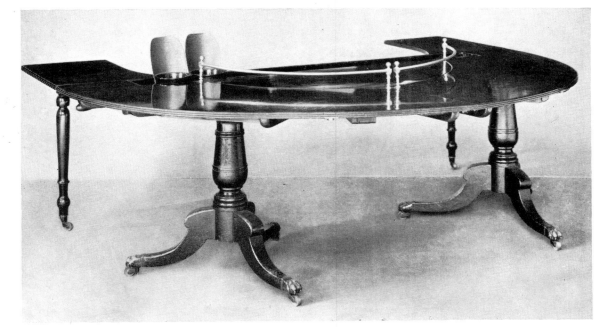

2. *Design for 'A Gentleman's Social Table,' from* The Cabinet-Maker's Book of Prices, 1793.

centre for biscuits; while coasters attached to a metal rod, or sliding in a well (Fig. 1), were provided to hold the bottles. Unless they were secured by such means the narrow surface of the horseshoe top increased the risk of accidents. This shape was not universal, several varieties of wine-table being made. In the *Cabinet-Maker's Book of Prices* (1793), a design by Hepplewhite is given for 'A Gentleman's Social Table' (Fig. 2). It is to be 4 ft long, with 'a pillar and claw in the hollow part, the top of ditto turn'd to receive the bottom of a tin or copper cylinder, two feet over and made to turn round, a mahogany top fitted into the cylinder, and cut to receive five tin 'bottles'. The table (Fig. 3) is unusual and complicated.

supports advocated by Hope with classical and Egyptian motives were favoured for centre tables as for side-tables in the early 19th century, while lyre-shaped supports are also found (Fig. 32), the absence of hinged flaps alone differentiating such tables from the sofa variety. Small occasional tables from Southill (Figs. 27-29) were probably designed by Henry Holland and in elegance of form are exceptional at this period. In Figs. 27 and 28 the legs are decorated with applied ormolu, and in the centre of the mahogany top is a fine *pietre dure* panel of Florentine origin and earlier date. The circular table (monopodium) of high quality (Fig. 31) was designed by Thomas Hope for his house in Duchess Street, London. So great is the variety of tables made for general use that the evolution can be only imperfectly represented.

TABLES, WINE-. Among specialised varieties produced towards the end of the 18th century were tables intended for after-dinner drinking. The large consumption of liquor, characteristic of the period, was usually indulged in when the meal was over, and for these potations fireside tables of horseshoe form were specially suitable. Some had folding screens as a protection against the heat, and a network bag in the

3. *Mahogany Wine-Table; drum, consisting of two concentric circles opened from below, contains japanned metal coasters and small receptacles of Wedgwood ware. c. 1800. Ht. 2 ft. 5 in., Diameter 3 ft. 6 in. (Hatfield House, Herts.)*

4. *Mahogany Wine-Table; tilt-up top with spaces for decanters and goblets; border for suspending glasses. Late 18th century. Ht. 2 ft. 8 in., Diameter 2 ft. 3 in. (A. Dunn Gardner Coll.)*

In the centre of the top is a drum consisting of two **concentric** circles which are pushed up from below. The inner circle is removed first and discloses a mahogany slab fitted with three japanned metal coasters. In partitions at the bottom of the drum are three crescent-shaped receptacles of buff-coloured ware, stamped 'Wedgwood', for light refreshments.

Another type of wine-table allows for the entertainment of a large party, and was probably intended to help servants in handing round wine during dinner (Fig. 4). The top tilts up and has a platform with spaces for decanters and goblets, while the wine glasses hang by the feet in notches contrived in the edge. The care bestowed on the design of these tables serves to recall the habits of an age when 'intoxication was expected, as a matter of course, to conclude the evening's entertainment'.

TABLES, WORK-. The variety known as a 'work-table' with small drawers or lifting top disclosing a well and fitted with receptacle for reels, shuttles and bobbins, etc., was not introduced before the second half of the 18th century, and is one of the many specialised forms characteristic of that age.

In Tudor and Stuart times the wools, silks and implements for embroidery were doubtless kept in small chests, wooden stools with lifting tops, and boxes. The accessories for needlework in the 16th century were highly treasured, beads, spangles, metal threads and coloured silks being imported from Italy and Holland. No regular manufacture of needles in England appears to have been started till after 1650, a charter of incorporation in 1656 for a Needle Makers' Company being the first record of the kind. No specialised examples of this period survive, but small oak or walnut tables with raised edges round the top (Fig. 1) were made in the late 17th century.

1. *Table of painted wood with tray top, probably for needlework or tea; scrolled legs. c. 1690. Ht. 2 ft. 1½ in., L. 1 ft. 9½ in. (Formerly at Bramshill, Hants.)* 2. *Mahogany Work-Table; shaped frieze decorated with fretwork. Made by William Vile for Queen Charlotte in 1763. (Buckingham Palace. By gracious permission of H.M. the Queen.)*

610

3. Work-Table, painted grey with gilt enrichments; top decorated with representation of firmament; green silk bag original. c. 1770. Ht. 2 ft. 6 in., L. 1 ft. 6 in., Depth 1 ft. 1 in. (Osterley Park, Middx.) 4. Mahogany Work-Table with two tiers of serpentine inlaid drawers, bow handle and bag; handles of ivory. c. 1785. (James Ivory Coll.) 5. Walnut Work-Table on slender cabriole legs; screen pulls up; frame decorated with floral marquetry. c. 1770. (Donaldson Coll.)

These 'bead tables', though equally convenient for other purposes such as tea, may have been used for coloured bead work which became a popular pursuit after the Restoration.

The work done by ladies in the 18th century was most varied, ranging from coarse worsted-work hangings and carpets to all manner of fine embroidery in silks, wool, feathers, beads and even hair (*see* NEEDLEWORK). Fitted work-tables of this period were not suitable for embroidery on a large scale, for they are generally of slight construction, and designed with regard more to elegance than utility, being only intended for delicate forms of fancy work. An exception is the table which William Vile supplied to Queen Charlotte in 1763, (Fig. 2). It is among the outstanding masterpieces of contemporary craftsmanship, and obviously designed for practical use. No work-table is illustrated in Chippendale's *Director*, but Sheraton expended much ingenuity on his designs, among them being 'Tambour Tables' used by ladies on a pillar and claw (or tripod base) with a frame for needlework so contrived that the 'work may be turned to any position'.

An open table with a falling ledge and a shelf below he calls in the *Drawing Book* (1791–4) 'A French Work Table', adding 'the style of finishing them is neat, being commonly made of satinwood with a brass moulding round the edge of the rim'. The example in Fig. 9 is obviously based on Sheraton's design. The pouch variety he writes of as 'a table with a bag used by the ladies to work at, in which bag they deposit their fancy needlework. Of such tables there are two designs . . . where observe the work bags of both tables are suspended to a frame which draws forward in which frame is a lock which

shoots its bolt up into the under edge of the rail of the top.' Sheraton adds that one of his designs was taken from a table executed by Mr M'Lean (*see* MCLEAN, JOHN) in Mary-le-Bone Street, 'who finishes these small articles in the neatest manner . . . The edges should be of brass and the ground of black rosewood when they are required to be elegant otherwise they may be made of mahogany.' An elaborately fitted pouch table decorated with Tunbridge ware is illustrated under that heading.

The suspended pouch was also adopted by other designers and makers, and attached to small satinwood Pembroke tables with painted tops (Fig. 7) and to portable tables with curved wood handles and a superstructure of small drawers (Fig. 4). In Fig. 3 there is a hinged lifting top, and this example has a delicate raised ornament carved and gilt in neo-classic taste. In Gillow's cost books (1795 and 1798) a tripod pillar work-table with two extending leaves and one with a circular top, 'an imitation of marble, finely japan'd', are illustrated.

In the early 19th century lyre-shaped supports were in fashion, and some attempt was made to design work-tables on classical lines. Tub and globe shapes were also favoured, the top of the latter variety being made to revolve behind the lower portion: an example in the royal collection at Buckingham Palace, inlaid with the signs of the Zodiac, is mounted on a tripod carved with draped satyrs' masks and parcel gilt. Many small screen-tables were made (Figs. 5 and 8). Sheraton explains that they are intended for a lady to write or work at near the fire, the screen part behind protecting the face. In the late Georgian period work-tables were sometimes con-

6, 7. (*Left*) *Satinwood painted Work-Table with flaps supported on brackets; pleated silk bag; top painted with figure subject in French taste. c. 1785. Ht. 2 ft. 6 in., L. (open) 2 ft. 5 in., Depth, 1 ft. 6 in. (Walter Raphael Coll.)*

8. (*Above*) *Satinwood Work-Table with screen; turned taper legs and stringing lines of ebonised wood. Made by George Oakley, 1810. Ht. 2 ft. 6 in., L. 1 ft. 7½ in. (Mrs Stileman.)*

9. *Satinwood Work-Table with three trays and shaped supports; based on design by Sheraton. c. 1790. (Pepys-Cockerell Coll.)*

10. *Work-Table of calamander wood; adjustable writing board, brass gallery and slide inlaid with chess-board. 1800. Ht. (closed) 2 ft. 5½ in., L. 2 ft. 6 in., Depth 1 ft. 4½ in. (Mrs Stileman.)*

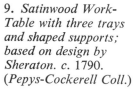

structed with folding flaps, which when turned back disclosed a chess-board; others had a rising desk covered in leather and a chess- or backgammon-board to draw out. George Smith (*Household Furniture*, 1808) gives five designs for work-tables (Pls. 76–78), one fitted with a backgammon-board and 'concealed drawers'. A circular table with four goat legs intended 'to afford convenience for writing by having part of the top hinged in front to rise up. This rising top when it is let down locks into the frame and secures the bag where the work is.' The work-bag is to be of lute-string or satin, and 'these articles of furniture may be made to imitate bronze and gold with

11. *Mahogany Work-Table of tub shape; two lower sections supported on brass rods. c. 1810. (Donaldson Coll.)*

12. *Work-Table, japanned red and decorated in Chinese taste; tray top. c. 1815. (Mrs David Gubbay.)*

13. *Design for lady's Work-Table from Sheraton's* Drawing Book, 1791-4.

parts of antique marble, or executed in scagliola, the edges secured by an ormolu rim'.

TABLES, WRITING-. *See* TABLES, LIBRARY.

TABOURET. Low seat or stool. 'A little stool for a child to sit on . . . in France the priviledge of the Tabouret is of a stool for some particular Ladies to sit in the Queen's presence' (Blount, *Glossary*, 1661). At that time and considerably later strict etiquette governed use of the tabouret in France, and regulations connected with it were also adopted at the English Court. (*See* STOOLS).

TAFFETY or TAFFETA. Name applied in early times to plain woven silks, and more recently to fine smooth silken stuff with lustre or gloss. In 16th century 'Spanish taffetye' is mentioned at 6s. a yard, and also 'linnen taffetye', a cheaper imitation in linen. Employed for cushions and hangings; Hardwick, Derbyshire, inventory 1601, recording 'a long quition of cloth of golde and black stript tuffaffetie', and also a bed with 'fyve curtins of carnation taffety'. In Lord William Howard's *Household Books* (early 17th century) 'an ell of green taffety' costs as much as 16s. It continued to be used fairly extensively for hangings, and in 1710 'a scarlet Taffeta Silk Bed' was in one of the rooms at Dyrham Park, Gloucestershire. Chambers's *Cyclopaedia* (1714) states that there are taffeties of all colours—'some plain, others striped with gold, silver, silver silk, etc., others chequered, others

613

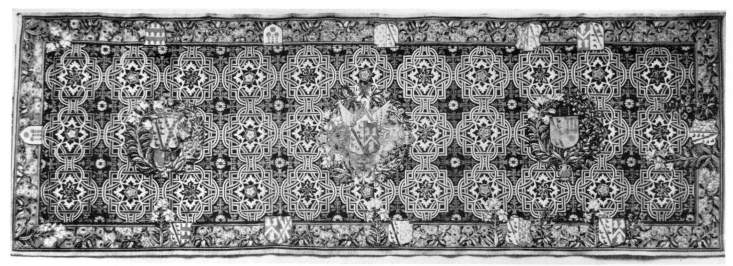

1. *The Luttrell Armorial Table-Cover, c. 1520. Ht. 6 ft. 7 in., W. 18 ft. 3 in. Formerly at Cotehele House, Cornwall. (Sir William Burrell Collection, Glasgow.)*

2. *Long Cushion-Cover with arms of Walker Jones and his wife (who acquired Chastleton House in 1602). (Lt.-Col Henry Howard.)*

flowered'. It adds that the silk must be of the finest kind. Sheraton's account of taffety in his *Cabinet Dictionary* (1803) is taken from Chambers's *Cyclopaedia*.

TALL-BOY. *See* CHESTS OF DRAWERS.

TAMBOUR. Series of narrow mouldings or reeds of wood glued transversely or vertically side by side to stout canvas backing, to form sliding doors to sideboards, cabinets, etc., also as rolltop covers to writing-tables. Ends of tambour fit into grooves provided on inner sides of a writing-table or other object, thus guiding top in direction required. Tambour covers fashionable in France c. 1750 and extensively used in England towards end of century. William Gates (*q.v.*), royal cabinet-maker, supplied to crown in 1780 'an exceedingly fine satinwood writing-table with a Tambour Top

neatly inlaid . . .'. In Hepplewhite's *Guide* (1788) tambour writing-tables described as 'very convenient pieces of furniture'; but Sheraton (*Cabinet Dictionary*, 1803) represents them as 'almost out of use being both insecure and liable to injury'; adding, however, that tambour doors often introduced in small pieces when no great strength or security required, *e.g.* 'pillar and claw', night tables and pot cupboards (*see* TABLES, NIGHT, Fig. 4).

TAPESTRY. Here confined to table- and cushion-covers and omitting wall-hangings. A table-cover (Fig. 1) of c. 1520 is probably (but not certainly) of early English weaving, commemorating the marriage of Sir Andrew Luttrell, of Dunster and Quantoxhead, and Margaret, daughter of Sir Thomas Wyndham, of Felbrigg, Norfolk, with other family alliances, on a black field almost covered by geometrical patterns in yellow, brown and green, with roses, various flowers and blue foliage, suggestive of earlier stained glass windows. The floral border shows the arms of Luttrell impaling Beaumont, Scrope quartered with Tibetot, Audley, Hill and Courtenay of Powderham respectively. The tapestry formerly hung in Cotehele House, Cornwall.

In the mid-16th century there was an immigration of foreign weavers for various causes. Some settled at Sandwich in 1561, and their first work, six cushions, was presented to Secretary Cecil. The mid-century also witnessed the founding by William Sheldon of an important manufactory in Warwickshire which wove hangings, cushion-covers and other furnishings for country-house use. At Chastleton House, Oxfordshire, were formerly three small finely woven Sheldon pieces for cushion-covers, one with the subject of Plenty; the others were heraldic and connected with the Jones family of Chastleton. Of the three cushion-covers, one is in the Barber Institute, Birmingham, and another is shown in Fig. 2. A fairly large number of cushion-covers, usually woven in sets, can with reasonable certainty be ascribed to Sheldon's looms; there are examples in the Victoria and Albert Museum, the Royal Scottish Museum, the Lady Lever Art Gallery, the Burrell Collection, Glasgow, and a number of private collections. A table-cover and cushion to match with rich floral decoration, at Sudeley Castle, Gloucestershire, are perhaps the nearest link in style with the four large and imposing tapestries of the Seasons, dated 1611, at Hatfield House, Hertfordshire, which were woven after the designs of Martin de Vos, and are generally ascribed to the Sheldon looms.

In 1674 Ralph Montagu purchased the celebrated Mortlake tapestry works, founded by James I; and, as he had already bought the Mastership of the Great Wardrobe from the Earl of Sandwich, he controlled a number of tapestry weavers who worked there under Francis Poyntz, bringing them into connection with Mortlake. The magnificent Mortlake and Soho hangings at Boughton, Northamptonshire, include a set of four table-covers with Montagu's armorial bearings as earl, which indicates a date between 1688 and 1710. George Smith Bradshaw of Soho, c. 1720, wove six covers for chairs and one for a settee (formerly at Belton House, Lincolnshire), the settee bearing his name and that of Stranyer, a minor Dutch painter, who doubtless supplied the design. Other covers of high quality were produced at Soho under George I by John Vanderbank, a weaver of Flemish origin, and probably also by Joshua Morris (see SETTEES Fig. 16); later (1750–5) at Fulham. Thereafter there was little demand for English tapestry covers, needlework and other materials replacing them.

TEA-CADDIES AND CHESTS. Small boxes or cases for holding tea, an expensive commodity in the late 17th and early 18th centuries. In 1665 Thomas Garway advertised that he had tea for sale from 16s. to 50s. a pound, and in 1728 a London tea merchant had 'tea of all prices, Bohea from thirteen shillings to twenty shillings, and green from twelve to thirty shillings'.

The word caddy is a corruption of *catty* (*Kāti*), a weight used in the Eastern Archipelago and China, equal to a little more than a pound avoirdupois, and in the *Madras Courier*

of 1792 'tea in quarter chests and caddies' is advertised. The early term for caddies (in use until the late 18th century) was 'tea-chests'. Dean Swift (*Directions to Servants*, 1729) writes of 'small chests and trunks, with lock and key, wherein they keep the tea and sugar'. The term caddy must have come into use between 1762, when in *The Director* (3rd ed.) Chippendale illustrated 6 'tea chests', and 1788, when Hepplewhite's *Guide* illustrated both tea-caddies and tea-chests. Sheraton observes (*Cabinet Dictionary*, 1803) that the word caddy is *now* applied to various kinds of tea-chests of square, octagonal and circular shapes.

In most cases, tea-chests, defined in 1775 as 'a small kind of cabinet in which tea is brought to table', were either partitioned for black and green tea or fitted with canisters (often loosely called caddies) for the two varieties, which were blended to suit the taste of the consumer. Tea-caddies were in most cases small and portable objects, but a mahogany case for tea (Fig. 1) is, with its stand, of some considerable size. This case, with a receding moulded top, has its chamfered angles decorated with a simple Chinese fret. The top lifts off, and

1. *Mahogany Tea-Chest containing four metal canisters. c. 1755. (Percival Griffiths Coll.)*

2. *Mahogany Tea-Caddy, with carved scroll corners; gilt brass mounts in rococo taste. c. 1750. L. 11 in. (Fred Skull Coll.)*

3. *Mahogany Tea-Caddy; silver mounts bear maker's mark, 'I.W.'. 1765. (Mr L. Hugh Smith.)*

4. *Shagreen Tea-Caddy, mounted; cut glass canisters, silver mounts and lids. Dated 1768. (Royal Academy, Ht. 6 in., Burlington House, Piccadilly.)*

5. *Tea-Caddy, veneered with satinwood and inlaid in classical taste. c. 1770. (Pepys-Cockerell Coll.)*

6. *Tea-Caddy, veneered with green tortoise-shell. c. 1790. Ht. 4½ in., L. 7½ in., Depth 3⅞ in. (Macquoid Coll.)*

7. *Tea-Caddy, veneered with mahogany and rosewood; decorated with floral marquetry. Silver mounts c. 1790. Ht. 6 in., Diameter 4⅞ in. (Mr Ralph Edwards.)*

8. *Tea-Caddy, overlaid with filigree and powdered pearl-shell. c. 1790. Ht. 5 in., L. 5½ in., Depth 4¼ in.*

discloses four metal canisters of which two have hinged lids, while a third has a small cap.

The tea-chests figured in the *Director* are miniature bombé or shaped chests, resting on scroll feet and mounted with brass or silver handles and lock-plates. The enrichments are either carved, as in the mahogany caddy of Fig. 2, or of applied metal. Another example (Fig. 3) is notable for the effective use of silver mounts, marked 'I.W.', the initials of an unrecorded silversmith: a similar case bears the same initials and the date 1765. A few years later is the caddy of Fig. 5; veneered with satinwood and other woods in neo-classical taste.

During the 18th century caddies were made of a large variety of materials. They were of solid or veneered wood, inlaid or painted. The wooden cases were overlaid with ivory, filigree, tortoise-shell, or straw-work (the latter material (*q.v.*) a speciality of French prisoners-of-war). A metal caddy might be of silver or copper, japanned or enamelled; and there was also a considerable production of 'Clay's Ware' or papier-mâché caddies during the second half of the century.

In wooden caddies the plan varied from square to oblong, hexagonal and octagonal; during the late 18th century oval,

11. *Tea-Caddy of ivory and ebony; set with composition medallions by James Tassie of King George III, Queen Charlotte, and their children.* 1818. (*Coll. of Her late Majesty Queen Mary.*)

9. *Ivory Tea-Caddy inlaid with ebony lines. c. 1800. Ht. 5¼ in., L. 4 in. (V. & A. Mus.)*

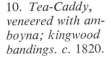

10. *Tea-Caddy, veneered with amboyna; kingwood bandings. c. 1820.*

pear and urn shapes were in vogue, resembling in miniature contemporary knife-cases. The carcase, in most caddies veneered with wood, dating from the second half of the 18th century, is of mahogany. The interior is lined with lead foil. Occasionally a caddy of fanciful form was made, such as the miniature model of Carlton House, made by William Potter, of Cornhill, in 1786, and valued by him at 100 guineas. It was subsequently raffled, subscriptions for tickets amounting to 880 guineas. The maker gained the prize, and this caddy is now in the London Museum.

Tunbridge Wells was for a long period a centre for inlaid caddies and other small articles (*see* TUNBRIDGE WARE), and in 1762 Samuel Derrick, sending from the town as presents some of its curious toys, included 'the prettiest tea chest he could lay his hands upon'. A small oval inlaid maplewood example in the Victoria and Albert Museum is signed Gillows, Lancaster; and in the cost books of that firm, prices and drawings of simple veneered caddies are given. Caddies were also decorated by engraving on the surface of the wood, in which the incisions are filled up with colour, and by applied engravings or prints.

While the inlaid caddies were the work of cabinet-makers or trained craftsmen, the decoration by straw-work and filigree was undertaken by amateurs in the second half of the 18th and early 19th centuries. One of the royal tradesmen, Charles Elliott, in 1791 supplied Princess Elizabeth, the third daughter of George III, who dabbled in painting and domestic crafts, with fifteen ounces of different filigree paper, one ounce of gold paper, and a box made for filigree work with ebony mouldings, lock and key, lined inside and out, and also 'a tea caddé to correspond with the box'. The panels of such caddies were filled in by amateurs, for whom designs were published in 1786 in the *New Ladies' Magazine* (*see* FILIGREE). Caddies of the last years of the 18th century were, like larger objects, often painted. An oval example is coloured a dull black, and painted on either side with a grisaille medallion and grouped flowers; the handle is silver. To the early years of the 19th century belong specimens overlaid with engraved mother-of-pearl or with ivory, divided by metal, tortoise-shell or ebony mouldings, and wooden caddies veneered with rosewood, maple, or amboyna of sarcophagus shape (Fig. 10). A remarkable example (Fig. 11) is decorated inside and out with ebony and ivory, and set with medallion portraits of George III and Queen Charlotte, George, Prince of Wales, and Frederick, Duke of York, executed in white enamel composition by James Tassie, the well-known Scottish modeller. It was made in 1818 to the order of the Corporation of Bath for presentation to Queen Charlotte, who died, however, in the autumn of that year, before the caddy could be given to her.

In the period 1780–1800 metal caddies were also made of silver or Sheffield plate. M.J.

TEA CANISTERS. *See* TEA-CADDIES.

TEA POY. (Spanish *apoyo*, prop or stay.) Defined as . . . 'a small three-legged table or stand, or any tripod'; and 'a table with a receptacle for tea or a tea caddy' (*New English Dictionary*). In George Smith's *Household Furniture* (1808) two tea poys are figured as small stands with tray top and central shaft, 'used in drawing-rooms to prevent the company rising from their seats when taking refreshments'. A rosewood specimen (Fig. 1) is decorated with parquetry of various woods arranged in geometrical patterns (Tunbridge Ware,

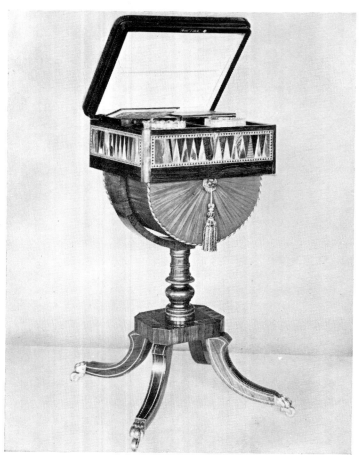

1. *Rosewood Tea Poy with parquetry of various woods (Tunbridge Ware). c. 1820. Ht. 2 ft. 7 in., W. 1 ft. 5½ in., Depth 1 ft. 5½ in. (V. & A. Mus.)*

q.v.). The receptacle is fitted with two lidded compartments and two others containing circular cut-glass bowls. Below is a drawer of semicircular form covered with pleated silk, which fits within a curved bar secured to the turned shaft.

TENON AND MORTISE. *See* CONSTRUCTION, Fig. 1.

TERM or THERM. *See* STANDS, PEDESTAL.

TESTER. *See* CELURE.

THROWN. *See* CHAIRS AND TURNING.

THUYA. *Tetraclinis articulata.* Imported into this country in 18th century from North Africa; warm brown in colour, richly marked with wavy lines interspersed between masses of small 'birds' eyes' resembling those in amboyna. Appears to have given trouble in many instances owing to partial disintegration when laying veneer. Used with walnut and mahogany veneers; highly decorative burr wood. J.C.R.

TILL. Box or drawer fitted in larger piece of furniture, *e.g.* at one end of medieval chests and in Tudor and Stuart oak presses and cupboards. Press in Henry VIII's possession was 'made wth drawing tilles full of evidences'.

TOILET (TOILETTE, TWILET, etc.). Term originally used for cloth or cover for dressing-table, on which were spread accessories of toilet. Phillips (*New World of English Words*, 1696) defines toilet as 'kind of table cloth or carpet of silk, sattins, velvet or tissue spread upon a table in a Bed-chamber'. Term, however, also used for accessories spread on this cloth or cover (in 1662 John Evelyn described at Whitehall 'the great looking-glasse and toilet of beaten and massive gold . . . given by the Queen Mother'); and also for a box containing these accessories (Chambers's *Cyclopaedia*, 1727–41—'toilet, the dressing box wherein are kept the paints, pomatum, essences, patches, etc.; the pincushions, powder-box, brushes, etc. which are esteemed parts of a lady's toilet)'. In the stage directions of *Man of Mode*, by George Etherege (1676), one scene opens in 'A dressing room with a table covered with a Toilet'.

In the late 17th and early 18th centuries the word in the odd form of 'twilet' or 'twilight' occurs in inventories and accounts:—William Farnborough (1689) supplied 'Two cedar tables for ye Twilight' for Kensington Palace. The inventory (1725) of the contents of Cannons record that a closet contained 'A mahogany Twylet Chest' valued by the compiler at £3. Princess Augusta, second daughter of George III, writing of a visit paid by the King and royal family to Lord Harcourt at Nuneham, Oxfordshire, in August, 1785, stated that her brother, Prince Ernest (later Duke of Cumberland), in his bedroom had 'got a toilette, too, with fine japan boxes on it.' (*The Daughters of George III*, D. M. Stuart, 1939.)

TOILET MIRRORS. *See* MIRRORS, TOILET.

TORCHERES. *See* STANDS-, CANDLE, and STANDS, PEDESTAL.

TORTOISE-SHELL. Term for shell or scales of tortoise and other allied chelonians, particularly *Caretta imbricata*, shell of which is very brilliant, finely marked and semi-transparent. Tortoise-shell becomes plastic after being heated, retaining when cold any form to which it may have been moulded. The shell was widely used in Italy and the Low

1. *Mahogany Towel-horse with turned top rail. c. 1790. Ht. 4 ft., L. 3 ft. (Hardwick Hall, Derbys.)*

2. *Mahogany Towel-horse with folding leaves mounted on curved feet. c. 1790. Ht. 4 ft., L. 2 ft. 4 in. (G. B. Croft Lyons Coll.)*

Countries in the 17th century to decorate cabinets and tables, and as a veneer in combination with ebony mouldings for mirror and picture-frames. Such furniture was also fashionable in England (*see* MIRRORS and PICTURE-FRAMES), but the bulk of it was of foreign origin. Sir Ralph Verney in 1650, when in Italy, contemplated buying a cabinet for a friend in England 'of Tortus Shell garnished out with very thin silver guilt or Brasse'. In 1679 there were two large mirrors framed in tortoise-shell in the Duchess of Lauderdale's bedroom at Ham House, Surrey. Dampier (*Voyages*, 1703) wrote that 'The Hawksbill-Turtle of Brazil is most sought after . . . for its shell, which . . . is the clearest and best-clouded Tortoise-Shell in the World'. Its popular use in England as decorative inlay on furniture was borrowed from A. C. Boulle, the celebrated *ébéniste*, who employed coloured shells in conjunction with brass inlay for table-tops, cabinets, etc. Very thin sheets of tortoise-shell were tinted at the back, green or deep yellow being favourite colours; and these were much used as veneer in the 18th century on boxes, mirror frames, tea-caddies, brackets and clocks. In the Lady Lever Art Gallery, Port Sunlight, there is a pair of English side-tables of c. 1780, 3 ft 3 ins long, veneered with clear tortoise-shell on a coloured mottled ground of red, green and yellow. (*See also* LANGLOIS, PETER.)

TOWEL-HORSES. Wooden frames mounted on feet, with two or more cross-bars, either in one piece or made to fold. Probably they began to be generally used for hanging towels after introduction of specially designed washing-stands, c. 1750; but frames, no doubt of similar construction, appear in inventories much earlier. At Dyrham Park, Gloucestershire (1710), were two horses 'for drying of cloaths'. In royal accounts they are rather more fully described. Thus, in 1750, Henry Williams charged £1 12s. 'for a Folding Drying Horse,

with Two Leaves'; while early in George III's reign Catherine Naish (*q.v.*) provided 'a neat Mahogany Airing Horse with Claw Feet' for Prince Edward's nursery in Kew Palace. In the *Cabinet Maker's Book of Prices* (1793) details of the cost of 'Chamber Clothes Horses' are given: one of 3 ft square is to have three rails and be mounted 'on common ogee feet'; another of the same height, having two leaves, is 4 ft wide when open. Surviving examples are generally of about this date, and were no doubt used for both airing clothes and hanging towels. The folding type is often found mounted on shaped brackets, which may correspond with the 'common ogees' referred to in the *Book of Prices*, depressed cabriole legs finishing in pointed club toes being also well adapted to ensure stability (Fig. 2). Early in the 19th century towel-horses became heavier in construction, with turned rails and uprights.

TRACERY. Architectural term for ornamental stonework in Gothic windows, and applied on tombs, screens, etc.; also for similar decoration on furniture (for medieval examples *see* CHESTS, Fig. 5, and CUPBOARDS, FOOD, Figs. 2 and 3). Debased varieties of medieval tracery were introduced in the decoration of furniture designed in the Gothic taste (*q.v.*), c. 1750. They were freely used as carved enrichments, while they also figure prominently in the splats of chairs and as astragals in the glazing of cabinets, etc. Tracery of this kind also used by George Smith and other Regency designers for furniture in Gothic or 'Old English' style (*see* CHAIRS, Fig. 189; CABINETS, Fig. 48).

TRAVERSE. Curtain or screen placed or drawn across a room; also a partition of wood; screen. Occurs often in royal wills and inventories of 16th century. Henry VIII possessed large number of traverses, including one 'of redde and yellowe satten lyned wth buckram being foure yeards square verey worne and stayned'.

TRAYS AND VOYDERS. Trays are defined by Shera-ton (*Cabinet Dictionary*, 1803) as 'boards with rims round them, on which to place glasses, plates, and a tea equipage'; he enumerates several other purposes for which they served. They have been made in many shapes and sizes and of a variety of materials, but in this section those of silver are not represented, as they form part of domestic plate and are not among the permanent furniture of rooms.

Trays used in the Middle Ages to remove dirty plates and broken food from the table were known as 'voyders', and this term is found in comparatively modern inventories. In the directions 'For to serve a Lord' in the *Babees Book* (written c. 1475) we are told that 'the kerver muste . . . have a voyder to geder in all the broke brede, trenchours, cromys lying upon the tabill'. Clearing away dishes and food was not the only purpose for which trays were used: when Edward VI was presented with sweetmeats and confections after his coronation banquet, they were brought to him in 'a goodly voyde'.

The material used for these early trays is not specified, but in 16th-century inventories, pewter voyders are occasionally entered. Thomas Heywood (*A Woman Killed with Kindness*, 1607) introduces a serving-man 'with a voyder and a woodden knife to take away all', probably intending knife and tray to be both of wood. After the Restoration, trays of fanciful decorative character were made of beads threaded on wire (Fig.1).

Few trays survive dating before c. 1750, but from then a considerable variety are found designed in successive styles, for the service of the dinner-table and for the tea equipage. They were introduced for the latter purpose shortly after tea came into general favour. Among the japan ware in the Dyrham Park, Gloucestershire, inventory of 1710 were '2 hand Tea Tables', a common term for trays at that time. Japanned wood seems to have been the favourite material, walnut

being rarely, if ever, mentioned. Lady Grisell Baillie paid 5s. in 1715 'for a japan Lief to hand about Tee'; while early in George I's reign 'Four India tea boards' occur in the inventory of the Duke of Montagu's furniture at Boughton, Northamptonshire. An oak tray from a Sussex cottage (Fig. 2), with perforated ornament, the date and owner's initials, shows this variety of furniture was not confined to large houses.

Ornamental mahogany trays appear to have been seldom made before 1750. In the *Director* (1st ed., 1754) Chippendale illustrates 'Four plans or designs for Tea-Trays or Voiders', with a separate detail of the fret pattern appropriate to each. Ince and Mayhew (*Universal System*, 1759–63) show trays of similar character (Fig. 11), and also describe them as 'voiders', the traditional term. A tray with pierced edges (Fig. 4) recalls these designs. In 1762 William Vile (*q.v.*) supplied '2 Neat Mahogany Tea Boards with rims all Round for the Queen's House in the Park at St James', and, about the same time, an octagon tray 'with a cuttwork rim'.

Although the trays shown in mid-18th-century trade catalogues were intended to be made of mahogany, japanned woods still remained popular. In 1764 the drawing-room at Chatsworth, Derbyshire, contained an 'old Tea table on it two Indian Waiters', a teapot hooped with silver, cups and saucers. A fine example of about this time, decorated with the arms of Tower of Weald Hall and landscapes in black and gold japan, is given in Fig. 3.

Lattice-work and scrolled handles had hitherto formed the favourite ornament of trays; but with the re-introduction of marquetry they became more decorative in character. Hepplewhite (*Guide*, 1788) writes: 'For Tea trays a very great variety of patterns may be invented; almost any kind of ornament may be introduced'. He points out that suitable and proper designs may be chosen from the various kinds of inlaid table-tops. They are to be inlaid with various coloured woods (Figs. 5 and 6), or painted and varnished, and afford an

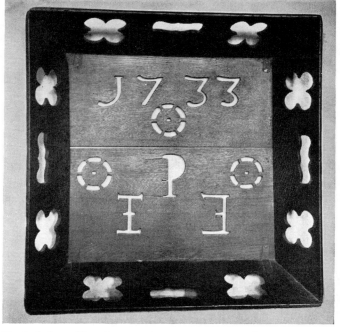

1. *Tray; coloured beads threaded on wire. c. 1680. Ht. 4½ in., L. 2 ft., W. 1 ft. 9 in. (London Mus.)*   2. *Oak Tray of country origin, with pierced ornament; owner's initials and date 1733. L. 1 ft. 7 in., W. 1 ft. 6 in. (Mr Nathaniel Lloyd.)*

3. *Tray decorated in black and gold japan; in centre, arms and crest of Tower of Weald Hall. Mid-18th century. L. 1 ft. 3 in., W. 9 in. (Weald Hall, Essex.)*

4. *Mahogany Tray; pierced and shaped edges; handles scrolled. c. 1760. Ht. 3 in., L. 1 ft. 10 in., W. 1 ft. 5 in. (B. Copinger Prichard Coll.)*

5. *Tea-Tray; fan-shaped centre of sand-burnt holly; wide border of inlaid rosewood and inner of willow stained green; brass handles. c. 1780. (Mulliner Coll.)*

6. *Tea-Tray; central oval of mahogany within inlaid borders; outer broad band of satinwood inlaid with holly stained green. c. 1780. (Mulliner Coll.)*

7. *Mahogany Tea-Tray inlaid with satinwood; handles gadrooned. c. 1785. L. 2 ft. 9½ in., W. 1 ft. 8½ in. (James Ivory Coll.)* 8. *Circular Tea-Tray inlaid with satinwood paterae; ground of burr walnut, bandings mahogany. c. 1785. Diameter 1 ft. 7 in. (Martin Buckmaster Coll.)*

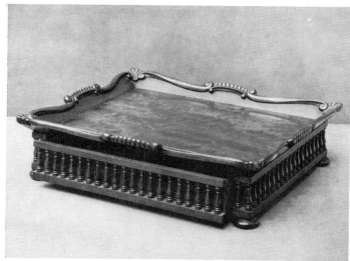

9. *Tea-Tray of japanned metal; decorated with sheep-shearing scene. c. 1820. L. 2 ft. 5½ in. (Edward Hudson Coll.)*

10. *Mahogany Tray with drawer. Early 19th century. Ht. 3¾ in., L. 1 ft. 2 in. (Brighton Mus.)*

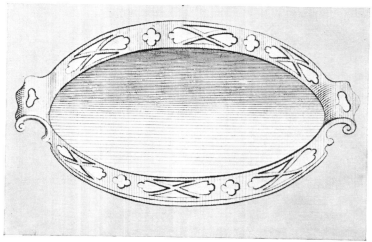

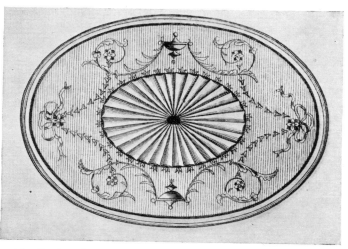

11. *Design for Tray or 'Voyder' from Ince and Mayhew's* Universal System, *1759-63.*

12. *Design for Tea-Tray from Hepplewhite's* Guide, *1788.*

opportunity for 'much taste and fancy'. The gadrooned mahogany handles in Fig. 7 are unusual, a plain brass grip being generally fitted to this type. The round tray of Fig. 8 is an exceptional specimen.

Sheraton makes no reference to trays in his *Drawing Book* (1791–4), but devotes considerable space to them in his *Cabinet Dictionary* (1803), explaining that mahogany dinner-trays are for taking up dishes and plates to the dining-table. The sides are to be 3½ ins deep all round, with handle holes in each, the maximum length being 32 ins and width 2 ft. Full-sized tea-trays are stated to be of nearly the same measurements, but nothing is said of their decoration. Among the other types alluded to is one to hold knives, made with two partitions and brass handles. These were in use considerably earlier, and Sheraton directs the maker to notice that the sides 'are square up, not sloped as formerly'. Small mahogany trays with a raised edge and a drawer were also made to hold beads at this period (Fig. 10). At the end of the century elaborate marquetry was superseded by plainer decoration. In 1797 the trade card of Charles Pryer, cabinet-maker of 472, Strand, announces that, among other articles, he sells oval trays wholesale and retail, and illustrates an example inlaid with an oval shell.

Rosewood was occasionally employed in the Regency period, but by then woods were to a large extent replaced by other materials. Tea-trays of japanned metal decorated with floral subjects, groups of figures and landscapes (Fig. 9) were much in demand; many were made of papier-mâché by Henry Clay.

TRAYS, STANDING. In the 18th century trays were often mounted on legs or folding stands and used, in Sheraton's words, 'as a sideboard for the butler, who has the care of the liquor at a gentleman's table'; while others served as dumb waiters and for tea. This composite form of furniture first

2. *Japanned papier-mâché Tray; oval decorated with waterfowl on black ground; top of gilt stand rabbeted for tray. Late 18th century. Ht. 2 ft. 4 in., L. 2 ft. 7 in., W. 2 ft. ½ in. (Syon House, Middx.)*

appears early in the Georgian period. The example in Fig. 1 was probably brought into the dining-room laden with bottles of wine and glasses, and placed by the host, the inner curve being intended to facilitate transport.

Shortly after 1750 mahogany trays were made for butlers' use, set on the familiar X-shaped folding stand. The sides of the trays were sometimes pierced (Fig. 4) and carved with lattice-work. Sheraton (*Cabinet Dictionary*, 1803) writes: 'These trays are made of mahogany, half inch Honduras will do for the sides, but the bottoms ought always to be made of Spanish, or other hard wood, otherwise the glasses and slop will leave such a print, on soft wood, as cannot be easily erased.' He gives the measurements as from 27 ins to 30 ins long and 20 ins to 22 ins wide, and says that one end should be made nearly open 'for the convenience of having easy access to the glasses'. The type of tray shown in Fig. 5 accords with Sheraton's description and long remained popular. In the Regency period the folding stands were generally turned and ringed, later becoming rectangular in section. Another variety of butler's tray was hinged in the centre to fold up with the legs.

Late in the 18th century oval trays were occasionally made, fitting into stands with tops of corresponding shape. At Syon House, Middlesex, there is a pair of japanned papier-mâché examples, the ovals decorated with landscapes and birds and the edges with a leaf pattern (Fig. 2). On one, the

1. *Mahogany semicircular Butler's Tray on stand; shaped under-framing and cabriole legs. c. 1720. (The late Lady Henry Grosvenor.)*

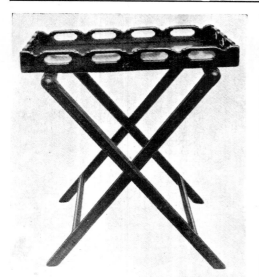
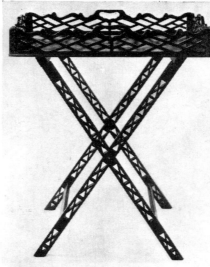

3. Mahogany Butler's Tray with folding stand. c. 1765. Ht. 2 ft. 2 in., L. 1 ft. 11 in., W. 1 ft. 4 in. (James Ivory Coll.) 4. Mahogany Butler's Tray and stand with pierced lattice-work decoration. c. 1760. 5. Mahogany Butler's Tray with brass-bound corners; folding stand turned and ringed. c. 1800. Ht. 2 ft. 9 in., L. 2 ft. 7 in., W. 2 ft. (The late Mr Anthony White.)

signature 'Clay, London' appears, and they were no doubt obtained from one of the shops which Clay had established in London for the sale of his work (*see* CLAY, H.).

TRESTLE. *See* TABLES-, DINING-; and TABLES, VARIOUS.

TRIDARN. A Welsh term for a cupboard or press in three stages (*see* CUPBOARDS).

TRIVET. *See* CHIMNEY FURNITURE.

TRUCKLE or TRUNDLE BED. *See* BEDS, TRUCKLE, TRUNDLE or WHEILBED.

TRUNK. *See* CHESTS, etc.

TRUSS. Architectural term for bracket or corbel (*q.v.*); applied to furniture in same sense.

TRUSSING BED. *See* BEDS, TRUSSING.

TULIP-WOOD. Species of *Dalbergia*; hard and heavy; yellowish, shading to red with variegated stripes. Imported from Brazil in second half of 18th century and employed as veneer in cross-banded borders. Sideboard at Harewood House, Yorkshire, made by Chippendale's firm c. 1770, has wide banding of tulip-wood surrounding top (*see* SIDEBOARDS, Fig. 12).

TUNBRIDGE WARE. An industry started in the mid-17th century, taking its name from the town in which it originated. Of the first phase no specimen appears to survive. Early in the following century the ware took the form of simple coarse inlay in different coloured woods.

Tunbridge Wells gradually became a fashionable resort after the discovery of its medicinal springs by Lord North in 1616, and the industry was much patronised by visitors. About 1697 Celia Fiennes wrote in her *Journeys* that she found 'the shopps in Tunbridge filled with all sorts of Curious wooden Ware which this place is noted for (the delicate neate and

1. Tunbridge Ware; Mahogany pouch Work-Table with rising desk, veneered with various woods; embroidery implements in drawer. c. 1800. Ht. 2 ft. 6 in., L. 1 ft. 10 in., Depth 1 ft. 6 in. (Miss Theresa Dent.)

2. Top of same Table (Fig. 1).

thin ware of wood both white and Lignum-vitae wood)';
and Mrs Pendarves in 1727 mentioned that she was sending
her sister '2 Tunbridge Voiders' (trays). The inlay was at first
of geometrical character, but later developed into representations of landscapes, dwellings and animals, surrounded by
running floral borders. These were built up from minute
chequers, made from strips of different woods, which after
being slit to the required sizes were glued together in a set
mosaic-like pattern, then cut out with a fret-saw, applied as thin
veneer, and afterwards rubbed down and highly polished;
one design could therefore be repeated many times. This
kind of decoration lent itself chiefly to the embellishment of
small table-tops, trays, desks, boxes and tea-caddies, the
larger pieces of furniture being usually ornamented with
veneers of inlay such as on the work-table with a rising desk
for writing (Fig. 1). It is entirely covered with veneers in
various woods, the reels, bobbins and other working implements being each made from a foreign wood. The centre
portion of the top (Fig. 2) shows the favourite arrangement of
cubes, each visible side being inlaid with a different wood, a
contemporary key to these having been preserved with the
table.

A characteristic of the craft is that only woods in their
natural colours were used, and much ingenuity was expended
in procuring the variety of tints required from different
shrubs and trees. Specimens of the principal woods used
in the construction of Tunbridge ware may be seen in the
museum at Kew; these include, besides native products,
purplewood, partridge, tulip, zebra and ebony woods.

TURKEY WORK. Also known as set-work in the 17th
century. An imitation of carpets woven with knotted pile in
Asia Minor, Persia and elsewhere in the Middle East, known
as Turkey carpets. There are two methods of production:—
(1) that in which weaving follows techniques of Turkey carpets, having knotted woollen pile; (2) that in which wool is
drawn through canvas ground and knotted to form pile.
Turkey work was made from early 16th century to mid-18th

century, but in references in accounts and inventories, 'work
of Turkey making' may refer to either English Turkey work or
oriental carpets. In some instances, however, English origin
is specified, *e.g.* inventory (1614) of Earl of Northampton's
Household Stuff, where a 'Turkie carpett of Englishe worke'
has 'the Earl of Northampton, his arms'.

Turkey work was used for covering seats and backs of
chairs, for cushions and also (more rarely) for rugs and carpets. It continued to be used as late as George II's reign for
chair-coverings, and a Treasury warrant to the Master of the
Great Wardrobe (September, 1729) specifies 'four dozen of
Turkey worked chairs' for House of Commons, and in October
a large number ordered for 'the House of Peers' (*see*
CHAIRS, Fig. 78).

TURNERS AND TURNING. 'Turning' comprises the
whole art of shaping wood, metal, ivory or other hard substances into forms having a curved shape, and of engraving or
incising figures or curved lines on a smooth surface, by cutting
into the substance with chisels and gouges while the member
is revolving in a lathe.

A familiar process to the Romans, doubtless they employed
it during their occupation of Britain. Among the City of
London records of the various medieval trade or craft guilds
mention is occasionally made of turners—*e.g.* in 1310 six
turners appeared before the Mayor and Aldermen and entered
into undertakings regarding vessels used as measures.

An important list of ordinances for the better working of the
guild and conduct of members was approved by the Court of
Aldermen in 1478; but it was not until after 1604 that a charter
of incorporation as a City Company was obtained.

Prior to that event the Company has no records, having lost
nearly all of them in the great fire of 1666. There is evidence,
however, that the Company sought to ensure that all freemen
admitted were competent workmen and that they vigorously
exercised their right of search to see that turnery ware offered
for sale was properly made. Chairs made by strangers and
foreigners about the City were ordered to be brought to
Turners Hall to be searched, and would then be bought at
prices fixed by the Masters and Wardens; which were 6s. per
dozen for plain matted chairs, and 7s. per dozen for turned
matted chairs. Chairs and stools were often chosen as test or
proof pieces, which had to be approved before a turner could
set up as a master workman. Thus in 1609 Richard Freeman
was ordered to make a high chair for a child, and Ambrose
Busher a small stool for a woman. From these records it is
clear that at the dates mentioned, and no doubt before those
years, turners were concerned not alone with the actual
turning of members or parts of furniture, but were responsible
for its complete construction, at least in the case of chairs.

In 1633 the Court of Aldermen, in response to a complaint
by the turners that the joiners 'assume unto themselves the
art of turning', laid down that 'turning and joyning are two
several and distinct trades and we conceive it very inconvenient that either of these trades should encroach upon the
other, and we find that the Turners have constantly for the
most part turned bedposts and the feet of joyned stools for
the Joyners and of late some Joyners who never used to turn
their own bedposts and stool feet have set on work in their
own houses some poor decayed Turners, and of them have

learned the feate and art of turning which they could not do before. And it appeareth unto us by custom that the turning of Bedposts, Feet of tables, Joyned stools do properly belong to the trade of a Turner and not to the art of a Joyner and whatsoever is done with the foot as have treddle or wheel for turning of any wood we are of opinion and do find that it properly belongs to the Turners.'

The crude wooden type of dead centre lathe was known from very early times, but few of its pre-16th-century products survive. Simple spindle shapes constitute most early patterns, in which there is little more than ringing by small V cuts and shallow hollows formed with the gouge. Chairs constructed entirely of turned members, and known as 'thrown' chairs, were made in the Middle Ages and down to Charles II's reign (see CHAIRS, Fig. 9).

Bulbous supports became popular towards the end of the 16th century, many being of considerable diameter and in some instances built up (see CONSTRUCTION, Fig. 7A). At this period, also, the classic column with plain shaft was used for tables and stands, such features coinciding with the rapid spread of the Renaissance style (see GLOBE-STANDS, Fig. 1, and TABLES). In oak furniture of the Stuart period there was a gradual reduction in the diameter and in the quality and extent of carved enrichment (see CUPBOARDS, COURT, Fig. 6). The spindle and baluster profile were produced in great variety, though still clumsy in proportion. During the second quarter of the 17th century, monotonous repeats of the knob and ball and reel were popular (see CHAIRS, Fig. 21), and the twist or spiral cut made its appearance c. 1650, early attempts being probably hand-cut rather than lathe-turned, though even when a lathe was used the spiral was largely finished by rasping.

After the Restoration, on walnut furniture baluster and spindle forms were almost entirely supplanted for a few years by the twist, of which many types were produced between 1660 and 1700 (see CHAIRS, Fig. 30). In James Moxon's *Mechanick Exercises* (pub. in monthly parts 1677–83) there is a section on turning which illustrates a contrivance for imparting a twist or spiral: in describing it Moxon says: 'you set it to that slope you intend the swash on your work shall have' (aswash=aslant). By this means the spiral could roughly be shaped and then finished off with rasps, whereas the ordinary lathe only allowed of cuts at right angles to the axis.

Plot (*Staffordshire*, 1686) writes: 'As for Turner's work, I have seen nothing equal to that of the same person (John Ensor, of Tamworth), who hath contrived an engine to turn wreath work . . . being able to make not only two but 3 or 4 twists, or more if he pleaseth, and that in so little time that he can turn 20 of these, whilst one is cut or raspt, the only ways they could make such a work at London and Oxford, that I could ever hear of.'

Baluster turning had revived in the last quarter of the 17th century, but the styles of the 18th century in walnut and mahogany afforded little scope to the turner prior to c. 1760, his work being restricted to such pieces as tripod tables with central pillar, which were baluster or column turned, often with spiral grooving or fluting. The classical revival brought turning into favour for legs of tables, chairs, bedposts, etc. At this time turning was enriched by carving in relief and by fluting, reeding, etc., as on bedposts (see BEDS, Fig. 37).

These characteristics were also to be seen at the end of the century, and little change is noticeable until c. 1805. During the Regency period the twist was revived, a new variety taking the form of a stout rope with bold rounded strands (see CHESTS OF DRAWERS, Fig. 43).

TUTENAG. *See* PAKTONG.

UPHOLDER. 'Upholster'; later 'upholsterer': artisan who made or finished articles of furniture in which textiles and materials used for stuffing them were employed. Connotation of the term has varied greatly in different periods.

An early reference occurs in the *Calendar of Close Rolls*, 18, Henry VI, under the date July 8, 1440, to William Kent, citizen and 'upholder' of London. The Upholders' Guild was already in existence by 1459, for in that year there is an entry in the account books of the Carpenters' Company 'Resseivd of the Bredered of the Upholders for the Hall (*i.e.* for hiring it) 3s. 3d.'. In 1465 the Upholders obtained a grant of arms from Edward IV. In 1489 they entered into an association or partnership with the Skinners, though still maintaining their corporate existence. Writing of Birchin Lane in Cornhill Ward, Stow observed that 'this lane, and the high streete neare adioyning . . . in the raigne of Henry the sixt, had yee for the most part dwelling Fripperers or Upholders that solde olde apparell and householde stuffe' (*Survey*, 1598); but the Upholders' status improved gradually, and probably from the end of the 16th century most of their activities were concerned with furniture.

Sir Richard Boyle's diary (1613) records payment to 'the uphoulster for sylck ffringe and making up the chaires and stools and window cusshen of damask'; and in 1628 Lord Cork paid 'Mr Angell my upholster' for hangings, bedding and cushions. Charles I granted the Guild a Charter in 1626 by which they were empowered to supervise all work executed by the craft, but the regulations are not recorded.

Upholsterers first figure prominently in the royal tradesmen's accounts of the Lord Chamberlain and Master of the Great Wardrobe after the Restoration, in connection with the new and luxurious types of furniture which were introduced in Charles II's reign. At the Restoration Robert Morris was appointed to the office of King's Upholsterer, and within twenty-one months the indebtedness of the crown to this tradesman for carpets, chairs, couches and bedsteads amounted to the enormous sum of £10,000. At this time the accounts afford considerable evidence of a differentiation of function between the craftsmen employed in the production of upholstered furniture, joiners being mainly responsible for making the frames of chairs and stools, etc., while uphosterers (*e.g.* John Casbert, *q.v.*) supplied the stuffing and covered them, also providing the hangings of beds. This differentiation is illustrated in estimates for furniture, upholstery, etc., of various apartments at Hampton Court Palace, dated 1699, and signed by the Earl of Montagu, Master of the Great Wardrobe (Victoria and Albert Museum MSS., R.G. V. 6). In these estimates the cost of the frames and that of the upholstery of seat furniture, beds, etc., are entered separately—*e.g.*

For the frames of one Elbow Chair two back chairs and a fire screen carved and Jappand black £5 18.

1. *Detail of armchair; upholstered with appliqué embroidery on damask ground and trimmed with silk fringe. Early 17th century. (Knole Park, Kent.)*

For mouldings to putt round the hangings and two Cornices over the window Curtains, carved £4.

For the Upholsters' Worke in makeing the Hangings and Window Curtains covering the Chaires and fire screene and finding all materialls as feathers, nailes, Tacks, dyed Lynnen, Silk Thread, Gerth Webb (*e.g.* canvas webbing to support the seats) etc., £13 16.

For the charges of the Upholsters men to goe to Hampton Court to put up the said furniture £1 10.

For the charges of the Joyners men on the said account £1.

R. Campbell, the author of the *London Tradesman*, 1747, writes of the upholder that he 'was originally a species of Taylor, but by degrees has crept over his Head, and set up as a Connoisseur in every article that belongs to a House. He employed journeymen in his own proper calling, cabinet-makers, glass-grinders, looking-glass framers, carvers for chairs, Testers and Posts for Beds, the Woolen Draper, the mercer, the Linen Draper and several species of smiths and a vast army of tradesmen and other mechanic branches.' The extant bills of Chippendale's firm prove that upholstery formed an important part of its business (*see* UPHOLSTERY), and other prominent tradesmen such as the partners William Ince and John Mayhew, George Smith Bradshaw and William France (*q.v.*) styled themselves 'Upholsterers and Cabinet-Makers', a separate department for upholstery being maintained by such firms. In the second half of the century the Society of Upholsterers and Cabinet-Makers published trade catalogues at intervals (the first, *Household Furniture in Genteel Taste*, 1760) and had premises of their own in Aldgate.

UPHOLSTERY. The earliest forms of upholstery in England were connected with state canopies and beds, the MS. illustrations of medieval times showing elaborately draped beds, while the wooden seats and chairs have merely a loose squab and a few small cushions. Many references to upholstered beds are found in early inventories and wills, one bequeathed by Joane, Lady Bergavenny in 1437, having six mattresses, six pillows, cushions, blankets and sheets, in addition to rich velvet hangings. Sir John Fastolf's inventory (c. 1460) mentions 'pillows of downe and lavendre', 'Pillowes of Grene silk,' others of 'Rede Felwet', 'A cover of grene silke to a bedde lyned with blue silk', and a 'Cover for a bedde of new arras'.

Bedding for the wealthy in the late 15th and early 16th centuries was composed of feathers, wool, down and 'bastard down', the last a vegetable substance. Animal hair was also used and precautions were taken by the Upholsterers' Guild (founded before 1460) to ensure that this was sanitary and that no corrupt bedding was sold in fairs or markets.

Lists of royal household goods of the Tudor period, such as Henry Duke of Richmond's inventory (1535), Katherine of Aragon's taken after the divorce, and the immense list of Henry VIII's possessions (1547) enumerate many velvet embroidered beds, and prove that both chairs and stools were elaborately upholstered with rich materials with fringes of silk and gold thread. Rich costume fabrics were sometimes used for this purpose. Among the 'stuff as is in the removing Guardrobe of Bedds' of Queen Elizabeth I (1559) was 'blak vellat enbranderid very richely with borders of damaske and venice golde being part of a gowne of our late Brother's of famous memorye Kinge Edward the VIth and frengid with golde and silke garnished wth reben and gilt nayles', which was used to cover a chair and two stools. Under Elizabeth I upholstered furniture must have been fairly general, as Sir John Harrington, towards the end of the century, writes, 'The fashion of cushioned chayres is taken up in every merchant's house'. About this time the upholstery of beds became more and more elaborate (*see* BEDS). Some of the more luxurious furniture of the early 17th century relied for effect on rich upholstery.

After the Restoration a new type of bed became popular,

2. *Detail showing cornice of state bed with plumes and tasselled fringes (see Beds, Fig. 26). Late 17th century. (Knole Park, Kent.)*

3. *Portion of tissue curtains with tasselled fringe on the Knole bed.*

4. Canopy of late 18th-century bed; festooned valance of painted wood. (Chatsworth, Derbys.)

the carved woodwork of back and tester was entirely covered with silk or velvet glued on. When draped, fringed and plumed, these were triumphs of the upholsterer's skill (*see* BEDS, Figs. 15, 16 and 18). The feathers in the cups at the corners of the testers (which had been in use since Elizabethan times) were expensive items, and the accounts of Robert Crofts, feather dresser to Charles II, show how frequently they required renewing and repairing. Richard Bealing, in 1690, supplied King William III with a set of plumes with fine sprigs costing £50. Less costly beds were hung with woollen materials, such as serge, mohair or cloth.

A vast expenditure in upholstery occurred in the 17th and 18th centuries after the death of an important person, the house being hung with black and the widow receiving condolences reclining in a black-draped bed. When Sir Ralph Verney died in 1696, his son John directs that, besides the provision of a mourning bed, much of the house should be hung with 'black baize', and 'a dozen chairs and three great tables' covered with it. Instances are recorded of upholders hiring out the black cloth and baize hangings.

A diversity of materials was employed for early upholstery. In Tudor times cow-hide, ornamental leather, plain and embroidered velvet, satin, cloth, tapestry and needlework were used; later the variety appears almost endless. In 1715 Lady Grisell Baillie pays £5 for 'A Yellow Callamanca easie chair'; and cloth, brokadel, harretine, velvets, mohair, silks, damasks, embroidery, tapestry, horsehair-cloth, leather, painted satins, lutestring and taffetas are all enumerated as coverings during the century. Oriental chintzes for bed hangings, curtains and chair-covers were in use from towards the end of Charles II's reign.

Few examples of early upholstery exist, but the day-bed (COUCHES Fig. 2) and chair (Fig. 22) at Knole, are good specimens of the type entirely covered with material. Walnut cane-seated day-beds and chairs were made comfortable by thin squabs and cushions, and, when more luxurious chairs were required, they were padded with hair or wool, covered with velvet and fringed. Sometimes these chairs were covered with a plain fabric with a removable ornamental case. This method is seen in a chair of c. 1690 (Fig. 53), which is padded in wool, tightly upholstered in white taffeta, the loose outer case of velvet being secured to nails by eyelet holes.

The upholsterer's trade must have reached its zenith during the 18th century, judging by the large number of rooms then hung in damasks and cut velvets, with curtains and furniture to match. Fashions in dress influenced the manner of uphol-

5. Fringes of 17th and 18th centuries. (V. & A. Mus.)

stering chairs, particularly c. 1720, when the maximum space was required for the voluminous skirts, and hard bolsters became popular on couches, with flat cushions fastened to the back. Allusions to upholstery were numerous in the 18th century. Mrs Lybbe Powys, in 1757, writes of having seen a chamber at Chatsworth, Derbyshire, in quiet taste with 'a most elegant bed and furniture of fine print set upon nankeen'. She describes the best drawing-room at Eastbury, Dorset (Bubb Doddington's house), in 1760 as 'Hung and furnished with cut velvet, the state bed-chamber hung with crimson velvet, furniture the same, the bed with gold and lined with a painted Indian satin'. In 1767 Lady Mary Coke mentions a new room at Lady Holdernesse's with 'Hangings, chairs and window curtains of three coloured damask'. At this time the upholstery of chairs was more closely studied in relation to the human form, and comfort was obtained from elaborate padding with horse-hair, waste silk and wool. The buttoned, or *capitonné*, style of upholstery, used on walls and furniture, was known here by 1788, when Mary Frampton mentions it as a novelty in Mrs Fitzherbert's new house in Pall Mall, Adam also gives it as a proposed covering for a chair design.

It is obvious that when tightly strained coverings on chairs became the fashion, the material would quickly rub and perish. This necessitated frequent renovation; new damask, needlework and even old dresses were used. The deep chair-rail rebated to take an upholstered seat was introduced from Holland in William and Mary's reign. This type of seat was convenient because it could be easily renovated, and continued in use throughout the greater part of the 18th century.

Chippendale (*Director*, 1754) gives some recommendations concerning upholstery. When writing of beds he is content with such vague directions accompanying a design as 'The drapery may be silk damask with gold fringes and Tassels'. But about other furniture he is more explicit: of some chairs he writes: 'These seats look best when stuffed over the Rails, but are most commonly done with brass Nails in one or two Rows and sometimes the nails are done to imitate fret-work. They are usually covered with the same stuff as the window curtains.' For 'French' chairs 'Both the backs and seats must be covered with Tapestry or other sort of needlework'. Chairs after the Chinese manner 'Have commonly Cane Bottoms with loose Cushions, but if required may have stuffed Seats and Brass Nails'. Of sofas he explains, 'When made large they have a bolster and pillow at each end and cushions at the back'. The firm's accounts prove that their upholstery charges formed large and costly items. In 1769 Chippendale charged Sir Edward Knatchbull of Mersham Hatch, Kent, £14 for a four-post bed, and for its upholstery £30 13s. 5d. One of the firm's letters shows how Chippendale and Haig endeavoured to fall in with their clients' tastes, and that they proposed to submit patterns to Lady Knatchbull that she might cover '2 large Barjairs' (large armchairs) with needlework. Both Chippendale in this letter and William France in his accounts for Kenwood also refer to serge as suitable for outer cases; and in 1768 France charged Lord Manfield for three scroll-headed sofa frames for the windows, covered in damask and 'For 3 serge cases to do. of crimson serge with silk strings, £2 8s.'. He alludes in his bills to the making up of Lord Mansfield's materials, such as 'India silk damask of your own for chair covers'.

Hepplewhite (*Guide*, 1788) observed that 'a high degree of Elegance' may be shown in bed draperies, and that they 'may be executed of almost every stuff which the loom produces'. In particular he recommends white dimity, plain or corded, which, with a fringe with a gymp head, 'produces an effect of elegance and neatness truly agreeable'. He adds that the 'Manchester stuffs have been wrought into Bed-furniture with good success', and also considers printed cottons and linens 'very suitable'. For hangings of a dark pattern a green silk linen will have a good effect. Sheraton's designs (*Drawing Book*, 1791–4) for bed draperies are based on contemporary French fashions. The hangings illustrated are very voluminous, entailing the use of a large quantity of material, fringe, galon and tassels. For the hangings of a 'Sofa Bed' he contemplated the use of 'rich silk' in conjunction with a frame painted white and gold. The upholstery shown in the designs of Thomas Hope and George Smith were intended to recommend it to a classical taste; a noticeable feature are the stuffed projecting backs, which were often covered in delicate materials, such as painted satin or taffeta.

FRINGES. Of the effect of completion of a richly upholstered bed in the second half of the 17th century with embroideries, fringes, cords, tassels and plumes we can form some idea by the few surviving examples; and in this elaboration the fringe of silk and gold thread played a considerable part.

When furniture, such as beds and seat furniture, began to be covered, a braid or fringe served a purpose in masking the bare joins and seams where the material was tacked down to the wooden framework. But fringes were also used for decoration, for the cushions which were found in profusion in wealthy houses from Elizabeth's time onwards were also usually fringed.

The early fringes that have survived, such as that trimming a chair of X form at Knole, dating from James I's reign, hang straight from a netted heading of silk, and with the straight silk strands metal threads are combined. These rich fringes were probably bought from upholsterers or London merchants, and are usually entered in accounts as a separate purchase; *e.g.* in the accounts of the Elizabethan estate of Grafton Manor there is entered payment to Edward Lyttleton 'for a ffrynge of blew silk & gold for stoles & a copbord cloth bought by him at London'. In the X-framed chair (Fig. 1), which is covered with an appliqué of cloth of gold on a ground of red satin, the deep fringe of red silk is carried round the lower edge of the seat, of the arms and of the stretchers, while the back is divided into two panels by a fringe. In addition to this hanging fringe, a narrow fringe—termed *molet* in French—serves to edge the cushion.

In the tasselled or tufted fringes in which the ball or tassel is made of floss silk—popular after the Restoration—the fringe was first woven, and the tufts and tassels were afterwards attached. By the time the *Academy of Armory* was written (MS. version 1649), Randle Holme was able to enumerate several varieties for fringing a bed, such as 'Inch fringe, caul fringe, tufted fringe, snailing fringe, gimpe fringe with tufts & Buttons, & Vellum fringe'. In bills silk fringes are described as 'tufted, twisted & Faggoted'. This elaboration of trimming was a speciality of refugee upholsterers whose names appear in the accounts for furnishing the royal palaces and great houses. In the details from the state bed at Knole (Figs. 2 and 3), dating from the reign of Charles II, the varied fringes, both close and hanging, can be seen, edging the cornice and head board and valances. The cost of such richly furnished beds must have been enormous: in 1693 when Queen Mary gave some velvet stuffs to Canterbury Cathedral, the tufted fringe of silver and purple cost her £500. Another bed of which the velvet furniture is richly fringed is that made for Sir Dudley North, which was formerly at Glemham Hall, Suffolk (*see* BEDS, Fig. 16). Here the broad bands of applied ornament on the cornices and valances are edged with ball fringe, and the head board and curtains are bordered with fringes of close-set balls.

Under William III the fashionable elaboration in beds was wood imitative of drapery or architectural motives pasted with damask or velvet. Fringes were, therefore, used to edge these ornaments (*see* BEDS, Fig. 19). On the state bed formerly at Dyrham Park, Gloucestershire, a narrow ball fringe edges the cornice of red velvet, while the deep shaped and gallooned valance is bordered with a ball fringe of red and faded olive green, which matches the two colours of velvet employed (*see* BEDS, Fig. 23). The broad flat galon finishing

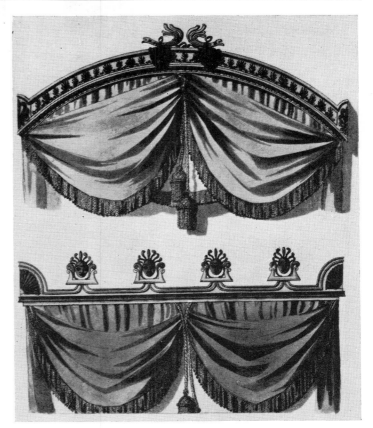

6. *Two designs for bed cornices with festooned drapery from George Smith's* Household Furniture, *1808.*

at the corners in a volute is also found decorating the edges of some contemporary seat furniture.

The making of fringes has been described as the 'ordinary pastime' of ladies at this period. The first Duchess of Beaufort employed at Badminton, 'diverse gentlewomen at work upon embroidery and fringe-making, for all the beds of State were made in the house'; Lettice Legh, of Lyme Hall, writes to Frances Legh in 1690 for knotted fringe, with directions for its making as well as for 'any other worke that may be done by candlelight with ease to the eyes'—a matter of moment with the slender lighting equipment of the day. In the same year Gerreit Jensen (*q.v.*) supplied Queen Mary with '2 engines to make fringe'. When the fringes were not made by the ladies of the house, the details of their make and style were closely scrutinised. Sarah, Duchess of Marlborough, in 1708 was proposing in the interests of economy to import from Italy a quantity of damasks, velvets and fringes for trimmings. It was at this period, when beds attained an immense height in keeping with that of rooms, that their upholstery and fringing were carried to extreme limits.

Fringes were comparatively little used after c. 1720, but were revived during the invasion of French fashions during the last years of the 18th century.

URNS. *See* KNIFE-CASES and SIDEBOARD PEDESTALS.

VALANCES. *See* BEDS and UPHOLSTERY.

VARNISH. Two kinds of varnish appear to have been generally used on English furniture: first, oil, and later, spirit. The body of these varnishes was composed of (*a*) the base or solvent, either a drying oil or a volatile spirit, and (*b*) resinous substances, such as the copals, lac, etc.

Oil varnish seems to have been the first used in this country, but whether there was more than one kind, and the nature of its composition, is not positively known. It is reasonable to suppose, however, that a resin such as copal was dissolved in linseed, poppy or walnut oil. These oils, when applied in thin coats without any resinous addition, form a thin glossy film by oxidisation, but the process is very slow unless the oil has been previously boiled, or a drier added; the latter aid was probably familiar in the 16th century. References to painted and varnished beds occur at this period. In the Grafton and Shuttleworth accounts (*see* BEDS) a joiner is paid for varnishing beds 'with walnottree collers', while a Kenilworth inventory (1588) describes a walnut bedstead with 'Pillars redd and varnished'. At Gawthorp the cost of the preparation at 1s. 6d. a pound is recorded.

After the Restoration, oil varnish was still widely used. Evelyn (*Sylva*, 1664) refers to it as 'Joyners Vernish' at 6d. per pound; he writes also: 'of the extracted oyle (of Juniper) with that of nuts, is made an excellent good vernish for pictures, for woodwork, and to preserve polished iron from rust'. At this period spirit varnish was introduced into England and began to some extent to supersede the traditional methods. Evelyn refers to it as 'that incomparable secret of the Japan and China vernishes which has hitherto been reserved so choicely among the virtuosi' (the ingredients being spirits of wine and gum lac); 'they varnish their work with china varnish, which infinitely excels linseed oil'. Stalker and Parker (*Treatise of Japanning*, 1688) state that both seed-lac and shell-lac were used on late 17th-century furniture, to be polished with the aid of tripoli, etc. They give a decided preference to the former variety, writing of the 'Shell-Lac-varnish' that 'though it may be polished, and look well for the present, yet like a handsome Ladies beautiful face, it has no security against the injuries of time . . .'.

The several coats of lac varnish were applied at short intervals and when hard the surface was rubbed down with 'dutch reeds'. More coats of varnish were applied and the surface again cut down with tripoli powder and olive oil or water; lastly one or two coats of varnish were given, and finally the surface was polished by friction, as described under POLISHES.

The composition of furniture varnish was much improved in the 18th century, greater tenacity and elasticity being obtained. In 1759 the Society for the Encouragement of Art, etc., offered a reward of £20 for 'making one quart at least of the best, most transparent and colorless varnish equal in all respects to Martin's at Paris'.

In some of Chippendale's bills pieces of furniture are described as varnished. About 1820 the introduction of French polish superseded varnishing. J.C.R. (*see also* JAPANNING AND LACQUER).

VELVET. Silk textile fabric having short, dense, piled surface, looped or cut. Besides plain velvet, in which the whole surface is covered with an even pile, velvets were treated by producing piles of different lengths (pile upon pile, or double pile), by brocading with silk, or with a ground of gold tissue.

The earliest centres of velvet-making in Europe, dating from the 13th century, were the cities of Lucca, Genoa and Florence; later the craft was taken up in the Low Countries, and in the 16th century 'velvet of Bruges' attained some reputation.

In England, though there was little production of velvet until the immigration of French silk weavers after the Revocation of the Edict of Nantes (1685), there are records of isolated attempts at velvet-making, as, for instance, that of George Damice, an Italian weaver, who practised his trade under Edward IV's protection, weaving velvets among other rich fabrics by the King's high command in a house assigned to him at Westminster, and instructing others in the same mystery (Proceedings in Chancery in the Reign of Edward IV, 1461). In 1587 it is stated that 'wrought velvets, branched satins and other curious silk stuffs' had been 'altogether brought out of France and other parts beyond the seas', and that the art of weaving these cloths 'was never known or used in England until about this year (1587) when perfect art was attained thereto.'

After the Revocation of the Edict of Nantes the English silk industry, centred in Spitalfields, became a flourishing trade; and in a petition presented by the Weavers' Company in 1713 to Parliament the silk trade of London was stated to be twenty times greater than it was in 1664. Both plain and figured velvets were made at Spitalfields. A specimen of velvet-weaving exists in the state bed at Hampton Court (formerly at Windsor Castle) which is stated to be 'of rich flower'd velvet made in Spitalfields by order of Queen Anne' (*The English Connoisseur*, vol. II, pl. 199) (*see* BEDS, Fig. 20). The chair and stools in the room are also covered with the same crimson, gold and white figured velvet that was supplied by John Johnson and Co., Mercers, the total amount being 321 yards of velvet at 1s. 8d. a yard. The importation of Italian velvets was still desired by the owners of great houses, such as Kimbolton Castle, Huntingdonshire; Knole, Kent; Houghton Hall, Norfolk (*see* BEDS, Fig. 26; CHAIRS, Figs. 46, 47 and 54; also UPHOLSTERY). The Duchess of Marlborough, writing in 1708 to the Earl of Manchester at Venice, when ordering a vast quantity of damasks and velvets, tells him that she prefers plain velvets, though 'figured velvets of general colours are in fashion'; but she would 'mightily like to see a pattern of figured velvet without any mixture of colours'. Others, however, preferred the bright and florid designs characteristic of late 17th-century Venice; and Celia Fiennes, in her travels through England, noted at Burghley, Northamptonshire, two velvet beds, 'figured crimson, green, severall coullours in one'. A state bed and a pair of armchairs *en suite* answering to that description are still in the house. There was little further development in design, the same patterns and colourings being repeated until the mid 18th-century. After that time velvet declined in favour and was replaced by lighter fabrics for both wall and seat coverings.

Utrecht velvet, made of worsted, mohair, or mohair and cotton, was also used for hangings and upholstery.

Plush is a textile fabric with a pile or nap longer than that of velvet. In the *Drapers' Dictionary* it is described as a long-napped velvet, and it is stated that cotton, silk, wool or any kind of hair may be used in its manufacture. In the Gilded Room at Dyrham Park, Gloucestershire, were, in 1710, 'chairs of Striped plush'. M.I.

VENEER. Veneering consists of laying down sheets or pieces of veneer-cut wood on solid structural members by means of glue; it was practised to only a very limited extent before the Restoration. Evelyn (*Sylva*, 1664), urging a greater use of cedar, says: 'It might be done with moderate expense, especially in some small proportions and in Faneering as they term it.' The term in its modern form (*i.e.* veneer) did not come into use until a much later date, but when an inventory of the contents of Cannons was drawn up for the first Duke of Chandos in 1725, His Grace's cabinet contained 'A Large Wallnutt wood Veneir Bueroe'. Before the introduction of machinery, all veneers were cut with a hand-saw, it being possible to obtain six or eight from an inch of wood. The method of laying down a sheet of veneer was generally similar to that employed with a panel of marquetry work (*see* INLAY AND MARQUETRY); but for small areas, such as borders, the splays of fielded panels, curved work, etc., a 'veneering hammer' was used. This tool was like a toothed scraper, the handle being at right angles to the blade, and was pushed forward to squeeze out the hot glue from under the veneer, which, to make it more pliable, had been soaked in heated size before laying.

In costly work veneers displaying the greatest variety and richness of figure were chosen, and to obtain this, cuts were made at various angles, and irregular growths, such as burrs and the boles and root-wood of ancient trees, were reserved for the veneer cutter.

The curved fronts of some chests of drawers and commodes were veneered by the continental method of laying sandbags over the undulating surfaces until the glue was set. J.C.R.

VERRE EGLOMISE. Process of decorating glass by drawing and painting on the underside and backing the decoration with metal foil, generally gold or silver leaf. The name is derived from that of a Jean-Baptiste Glomy (d. 1786), a designer, framer and collector of works of art, who lived at the junction of the Rues de Bourbon and Saint-Claude, Paris, and is credited with inventing a method of framing prints with black and gold fillets painted from behind the glass. But there appears to be no reason to suppose that Glomy used a backing of metal foil. Thus, Glomy's name has become arbitrarily attached to a process of great antiquity which was practised in the Near East (*i.e.* Damascus) at a very early date, and widely in Italy, to decorate goldsmiths' work in the period of the High Renaissance: many examples are extant. Verre églomisé panels with a backing of metal foil are incorporated in the well-known Vyvyan Salt at the Victoria and Albert Museum, the motives of flowers and fruit being derived from Geoffrey Whitney's *Choice of Emblems* (pub. 1586).

Mirrors with glass borders which became fashionable at the end of the 17th century were sometimes decorated with verre églomisé in gold and silver foil relieved against a ground of black, red, or more rarely green: this style of decoration was introduced from France, and surviving specimens show strong French influence, notably that of Jean Berain's designs. The process consisted of applying 'some fine impress cut in paper' to the glass to be decorated, which had been previously varnished; when the varnish was dry the paper was moistened on the blank side and drawn off, leaving the 'lines of the picture perfect and distinct on the varnish side of the glass . . .' (*Dictionarium Polygraphicum*, 1735, Vol. I, p. 114). After filling in with colour, an 'additional and improving beauty' was given by overlaying all colours except the ground with leaf silver (*see* MIRRORS, Fig. 18).

VIRGINAL. *See* MUSICAL INSTRUMENTS.

VITRUVIAN SCROLL. Enrichment called after Vitruvius, celebrated Roman architect; though of earlier origin. It consists of a series of scrolls connected with one another and forming a continuous pattern, resembling waves; freely used on furniture by architectural designers of early 18th century, mainly for decoration of friezes (*see* TABLES, SIDE-, Fig. 21).

VOLUTE. Architectural term for spiral scroll forming chief feature of Ionic capital, also spiral conformation (*see* ORDERS).

VOYDER. *See* TRAYS AND VOYDERS.

WAINSCOT (WAGENSHOT, etc.). 'A shipper's label or consignment word for "parcels" of wagon wood for wagon (wain) construction; and, of course, suitable for many other uses of builders or carpenters.' The term was used on the Baltic wharves, whence large quantities of timber from the Middle Ages onwards were shipped to England and other European countries. The word in its English form came to be applied in the 17th century to timber used for furniture and also for panelling—'tables of wainscote, walnut or other stuffe' (E. B. Jupp, *Historical Account of the Worshipful Company of Carpenters*). Large quantities of planks were at this period imported from the coasts of the Baltic and the Low Countries at Lynn and other East Coast ports. In an agreement (dated October, 1611) for the making of desks, seats and writing tables for the Chapter library at Hereford and the Bodleian, Oxford, it is specified that 'Richard Rogers of the citie of Hereford, carpenter . . . shall waynescot . . . the sayd libraries'. The smaller sizes of split oak imported were known as 'clapboard' (*q.v.*), which was in demand for panelling. Evelyn (*Sylva*, 1664) mentions 'Clapboard for wainscot'.

WALL-LIGHTS. *See* SCONCES.

WALNUT. There are two varieties of walnut, *Juglans regia* and *Juglans nigra*, both used in England. Some walnut was used during the early Renaissance, and it is evident from inventories of great houses in the Elizabethan period, such as that of Lord Lumley (1590), that the best pieces of furniture were made of this timber; Bacon mentions walnut as best for tables, cupboards and desks (*Naturall Historie*, 1616), and, though some of the supplies were probably imported, the existence of walnut furniture in midland districts and in comparatively small country houses (proved by contemporary inventories) suggests that much of the wood was of native origin.

From the Restoration to the close of George II's reign both varieties of walnut were in use for veneer and in construction, matching and contrasting veneers being much in demand for case and seat furniture in the first quarter of the 18th century. A decided figure is usually found only in the stump at a point where the roots begin to spread from the base, and near the crotches. A small proportion of trees produced a valuable veneer from burrs.

Walnut timber was imported to supplement the wood from plantations in the southern counties. Several notable plantations are recorded dating from the middle years of the 17th century. Sir Francis Slydolf, of Mickleham, Surrey, at his death in 1656, had made a considerable revenue from the 'inumerable' walnut trees he had planted years before; and in 1683 Sir Josiah Child's 'prodigious cost in planting' whole square miles of walnut trees at Wanstead, Essex, was noted by Evelyn.

Evidence of imports from France in the early 17th century is to be found in the diary of the Earl of Cork (May, 1613, *Lismore Papers*, Vol. I, p. 23) when 'planks of walnuttree' were 'received out of France'. The importation was on a much larger scale after the Restoration, though Evelyn (*Sylva*, 1664) dwells on its comparative scarcity: 'were the timber in greater plenty amongst us we should have far better utensils of all sorts for our Houses, as chairs, stools, Bedsteads, Tables, Wainscot, Cabinets, etc., instead of the more vulgar beech'.

From this time to c. 1750 the demand for European walnut was constant. In the royal tradesmen's accounts the wood used is often stated to be 'Grenoble wood' or 'French walnut-tree'; and, according to Evelyn, Grenoble walnut was 'much prised by cabinet makers'; also 'that which we have from Boulogne, very black in colour, and so admirably streaked, as to represent natural flowers, landskips and other fancys'. The severe winter of 1709 destroyed most of the walnut trees in central Europe, and the timber became so scarce in France that its export was prohibited in 1720. But, at least in England, the cessation of continental supplies was counterbalanced by regular importation of the larger, sounder black walnut from Virginia, which caused a falling off in the planting of native walnut. Dr Hunter's 1776 edition of Evelyn's *Sylva* states: 'Formerly the walnut tree was much propagated for its wood, but since the importation of mahogany and the Virginia walnut it has considerably decreased in reputation'; while *Chambers's Encyclopaedia* (1786) states that the timber had almost gone out of use.

Juglans regia is widely distributed in many parts of Europe, Turkey, Persia, Northern India and China. It provides a timber fine and uniform in texture, which takes a smooth finish, and is an excellent carving wood. Density and colour vary according to the sort and situation, but in general the wood is a pale brown with brown and black veinings. Sheraton (*Cabinet Dictionary*, 1803) states that the timber of the *Juglans regia* is much paler than the Virginia and 'cannot be used but for the most common purposes'.

Juglans nigra (black walnut) is similar to *Juglans regia* in both weight and texture, but the timber is of a uniform deep brown colour with considerable markings and veinings. It grows in large quantities in the eastern states of the United States. Its quality as a cabinet wood was realised early in the 17th century, and it was considered 'of precious use for tables, cabinets and the like' in 1632. 'Black Walnut' was recommended by Evelyn, who suggested planting the trees in England, 'if we were careful to procure them out of Virginia where they abound'. 'Virginia walnut' was stated in 1731 to have been shipped from Virginia and Maryland to the value of £15,000 annually. The timber has only a small amount of sapwood, and shows a mottled or waved figure at the root and crotches. Sheraton (*Cabinet Dictionary*, 1803) writes that 'the black virginia (walnut) was much in use for cabinet work about forty or fifty years since, but is now quite laid aside'. Some furniture

made of the timber of this tree in England closely resembles in colour faded mahogany. M.J.

WARDROBES. *See* CUPBOARDS.

WASHING-STANDS. In the medieval and Tudor periods the flat-bottomed metal basins and ewers used in bed-chambers for washing purposes were placed on any convenient chest or table. One of the directions in 'How to order your Mayster's Chamber at night to bedwarde' from Rhodes's *Boke of Nurture* (1530) is 'Array your Cupboord with a Cupboorde Cloth, wyth your Basyn, Ewer, Candle light and Towell'. Many elaborate instructions were given in early times for the taking of baths, but lesser ablutions are less often noticed. Andrew Boorde, early in Elizabeth I's reign, recommended a person on rising to 'Wasshe your handes & wrestes, your faces & eyes and your teeth with fountain water'; and in the *Dyet for the Healthfull Man*, by Sir John Harrington (1524), 'dentrifices and clensers of teeth' are advocated, and advice given on getting up to 'Wash all the instruments of the sences with cold water'.

These instructions suggest that there were the necessary facilities to carry them out in bed-chambers. From the second half of the 16th century onwards small tables with a single drawer doubtless served as wash-stands and for the washing requisites. Toothbrushes seem to have been unknown in this country until c. 1650, and in 1694 an English friend wrote to Sir Ralph Verney in Paris asking him to enquire 'for the new little brushes for making cleane of the teeth'.

There was a manufacture of soap in England in the 14th century, and in the Elizabethan age sweet-scented soap and 'odiferous white sopes' are mentioned. The numerous recipes for making 'Sweet soape balls' that appear in the *Lady's Delight*, written in the latter part of the 17th century, indicate that much was made in the houses. There is an entry in Lady Grisell Baillie's accounts for 1716: '4 Wash balls 1/s.'

In the Tudor period ewers and basins were of brass, pewter or silver in the houses of the wealthy. Cardinal Wolsey owned many washing-sets of solid silver. In the household books of Lord North (1576) there is an entry: 'For the use of the Quene, a rownd bason and ewer, with a pot of silver weighing 57 oz.' In an inventory of Cromwell's goods many pewter basins are entered; and at the end of the 17th century, ewers and basins of delft ware were imported in large quantities. In Sir John Hall's accounts for 1720 there are several payments for 'Dutch basins for bed-rooms'. Silver was also used in Georgian times. In the inventory of George, Earl of Warrington, written by himself (1752), there is an entry of silver washing-plate which bears a hall-mark of ten years earlier:

> A Bason to wash my mouth
> A Hand Bason
> Wash-ball box.

A piece of furniture specially designed as a washing-stand does not appear until towards the middle of the 18th century. An early example resting on four cabriole legs carved with shells is given in Fig. 1. The top opens and is sunk in the centre to support a basin: below is a drawer for toilet requisites and at either side are slides for candles. Chippendale (*Director*, 3rd ed., 1762) gives three designs for 'Bason Stands' (Fig. 7). Such furniture was supplied by his firm to Sir Edward Knatchbull for Mersham Hatch, Kent, and among

1. *Mahogany Washing-Stand on carved cabriole legs; lifting top, interior fitted for basin; drawer below, at each end a candle slide. c. 1740.*

2. *Mahogany Washing-Stand; frieze carved with fretwork; flaps to enclose top missing. c. 1760. Ht. 2 ft. 10 in., L. 1 ft. 9 in., Depth 1 ft. 4 in. (Corsham Court, Wilts.)*

many mentioned in the bills for 1768–9 are 'a very neat Commode Bason stand of black rosewood, £3. 3.,' 'a neat Bason stand Japan'd Green and gold £2. 10'; and, in 1773, 'A Wash hand stand for front Bed Chamber'. Later designers provided washing-stands ingeniously constructed to disguise their real purpose; when closed they looked like a small table, a miniature chest of drawers or a cabinet, and were for bedrooms used also as sitting-rooms. Sheraton (*Cabinet Dictionary*, 1803) writes of a basin-stand as 'a piece of furniture much in use and as generally known'. He gives their size and variety, the common square basin-stand being generally made of Honduras wood and measuring from 13 ins to 15 ins square and 34 ins high. The stretcher should not be less than 13 ins from the underside of the drawer 'to allow

3. *Mahogany Washing-Stand; top enclosed by flaps supported on brackets. c. 1770. Ht. 2 ft. 8½ in., L. (open), 3 ft. 2 in., Depth 1 ft. 6 in. (Hardwick Hall, Derbys.)*

4. *Mahogany Washing-Stand with shaving-glass; banded with satinwood. c. 1790. Ht. 4 ft. 1½ in., L. 3 ft. 5½ in., Depth 1 ft. 7 in. (A. Dunn Gardner Coll.)*

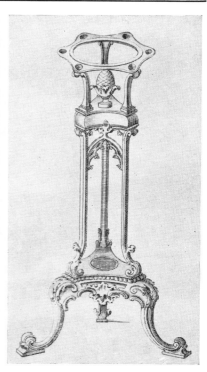

5. *Mahogany Washing-Stand with lifting top; shaving-glass and candle slides, c. 1790. Ht. 4 ft. 7 in., L. 1 ft. 10 in., Depth 1 ft. 10 in. (Hardwick Hall, Derbys.)*

6. *Mahogany tripod Basin-Stand; scrolled supports and cabriole legs finely carved with volutes and foliage. c. 1755-60. Ht. 2 ft. 7 in., Diameter of top, 1 ft. 9 in. (Exeter College, Oxford.)*

7. *Design for a 'bason stand,' from Chippendale's* Director *(3rd ed., 1762.)*

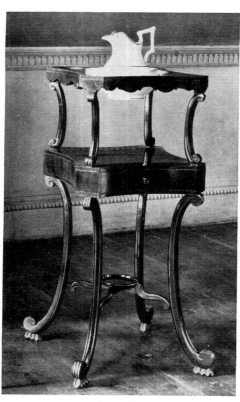

8. *Mahogany Basin-Stand with scroll supports; shaped edge to top; one drawer. c. 1760. (Kyre Park, Worcs.)* 9. *Mahogany tripod Basin-Stand. c. 1770. Ht. 2 ft. 5½ in. (Edward Hudson Coll.)* 10. *Mahogany Basin-Stand; slender cabriole legs, satinwood inlay and stringing lines. c. 1785. Ht. 2 ft. 6 in. (Messrs. Mallett and Son.)*

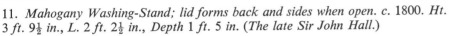

11. *Mahogany Washing-Stand; lid forms back and sides when open. c. 1800. Ht. 3 ft. 9½ in., L. 2 ft. 2½ in., Depth 1 ft. 5 in. (The late Sir John Hall.)*

12. *Corner Washing-Stand japanned in colours; lifting top. c. 1790. Ht. 2 ft. 7½ in., L. 2 ft., Depth 1 ft. 5 in. (V. & A. Mus.)*

13. *Design for a 'Corner Basin-Stand,' from Sheraton's Drawing Book, 1791-4.*

sufficient height for the bottle'. He explains that sometimes they may be enclosed by doors and so form a cupboard. Of a design for a corner wash-stand (Fig. 13), he writes:

'This basin-stand has a rim round the top, and a tambour door to enclose the whole of the upper part in which is a small cistern. The lower part has a shelf in the middle on which stands a vessel to receive the dirty water conveyed by a pipe from the basin. These sort are made large, and the basin being brought close to the front gives plenty of room. The advantage of this kind of basin-stand is that they may stand in a genteel room without giving offence to the eye—their appearance being somewhat like a cabinet.'

Early examples of the tripod type were sometimes elaborately carved with rococo ornament (Fig. 6), while others were made with four legs and a shelf midway to hold the receptacle for soap. In 1784 John Russell and Benjamin Parran supplied for his Majesty's house at Newmarket 'A Wainscote Bason stand with a Dressing glass to slide up and down in a frame with racks and a spring fastening, a white stone Bason, 2 Glasses for soap and a Drawer in front with a brass pendant ring, a bottom shelf cut out with a turned ring for a bottle'. The size, 14 ins by 14 ins by 2 ft 8½ ins high, indicates how small these articles of furniture were, even when intended for royal palaces. Shearer (*Cabinet-Makers' Book of Prices*, 1788) gives drawings for both corner and combination wash-stands, some of which he suggests could be placed in a recess and have a curtain to draw in front of them. Another favourite pattern at the end of the century was one that closed down

(Fig. 11), the lid when raised serving as a protection to the wall. Wash-stands were also designed in the Regency style. George Smith (*Household Furniture*, 1808) gives three designs (one in the Egyptian taste with chimera feet), and observes that they admit of some variety in woods for their manufacture, such as mahogany, satinwood or rosewood, with bronzed metal embellishments.

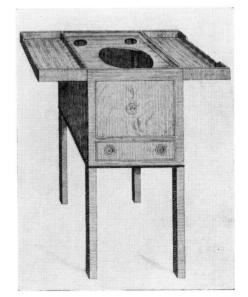

14. *Design for a 'Bason Stand,' from Hepplewhite's Guide, 1788.*

1. *Rosewood What-not mounted with ormolu; one of pair. c.* 1800. (*Southill Park, Beds.*)

2. *What-not; wood painted black with white stringing lines, one of pair; rings of columns gilt, marble top. c.* 1800. (*St Giles's House, Dorset.*)

WHAT-NOTS. Portable stands intended to carry or display a variety of objects; usually rectangular in plan with shelves arranged in tiers supported by turned columns at the angles. The first published reference to a what-not occurs in 1808 in the *Correspondence* of Sarah, Lady Lyttleton, but one of the type now so described is figured eight years earlier in Gillow's Cost Books. The term does not occur in Sheraton's *Cabinet Dictionary* (1803). Sometimes they were fitted with a drawer or drawers, as in Fig. 2. Mahogany was also used for their construction and the supports of late examples are often spirally twisted. The type is particularly associated with the Victorian period.

WILLOW (*Salix*). Very numerous species; soft though tough wood, pale brown with numerous flecks when seasoned. Light, resilient, flexible, it will take good polish, and in 17th and 18th centuries was dyed black to simulate ebony for both inlay and applied ornament. Oziers, saplings of *Salix aquatica*, mentioned by Evelyn (*Sylva*, 1664) as used for chairs. References to 'twiggen' or 'wicker', *i.e.* of willow, occur in 16th- and 17th-century inventories (*see* CHAIRS). J.C.R.

WINE CISTERNS AND COOLERS. In considering the form of the various articles used as receptacles for wine in bottles it is often difficult to make a clear distinction between the different types; the 'fountain' or cistern for bottles, which was known as 'wine cooler', might, when provided with a cover, serve equally as a case for bottles, *i.e.* a cellaret (*see* CELLARETS). Portable vessels in which wine bottles were set during meals appear to have been used from early times, and the reference in the will of Sir John Fastolfe to a 'fountayne of latynne (latten) to set in pottys of wine' shows that they were already in use in the 15th century.

Many representations of bowl-shaped cisterns filled with wine bottles occur in 16th- and 17th-century tapestries and pictures of banquets; while in the picture attributed to Van Bassen at Hampton Court (dated 1637) of Charles I and his Queen dining in public (probably at Theobalds), a cistern of this kind is clearly shown containing short-necked flasks.

Cisterns of various materials, either of marble or stone, of silver, pewter, bronze or copper, or else of wood, are often mentioned in late 17th- and early 18th-century inventories. There is little doubt that most were for cooling wine in ice, and household accounts of the time contain many references to charges for cartage and labour for filling ice houses. They seem occasionally to have served the double purpose of washing plates, cutlery and glasses during the meal.

In a French conversation manual of 1605 (*The French Garden*) the lady of the house draws a distinction between two types of cisterns, ordering her butler to 'put cleane and fresh water in the tubbes, that of copper, the other of wood, the one to keep the drink fresh, and the other to refresh the glasses and cuppes, to the end that we may drink fresh, for it is very hot'.

1. *Wine Cistern or Cooler of copper, japanned and decorated with chinoiserie motives. Made in* 1699. *Ht.* 1 *ft.* 7 *in., L.* 3 *ft.* 9 *in., W.* 1 *ft.* 5 *in.* (*Chatsworth, Derbys.*)

2. *Wine Cistern or Cooler of silver. Dated 1720. Ht. 1 ft. 9 in., L. 3 ft. 4 in. (Worshipful Company of Grocers.)*

3. *Mahogany Wine Cooler, carved with gadroons and satyr masks; mounts of gilt metal. c. 1730. (Althorp, Northants.)*

4. *(Right) Mahogany Wine Cooler with gilt metal mounts; it resembles a design in Chippendale's* Director, *1st ed. (Pl. CLI, Fig. 1). c. 1755. (Formerly at The Fort, Bristol.)*

5. *Wine Cooler; mahogany inlaid with satin and other woods. c. 1775. Ht. 1 ft. 8½ in., L. 2 ft. 9½ in. (Stourhead, Wilts.)*

6. *Wine Cooler; mahogany, brass hoops and tap. c. 1800. (Pepys-Cockerell Coll.)*

7. Conversation picture by Zoffany, the 'Ferguson Group,' painted in 1781; *Wine Cooler in foreground.* (*Viscount Novar.*) 8. *Painted Wine Cooler; sarcophagus-shaped body carved with flutes; stand with lion terminals. c.* 1810 (*Stourhead, Wilts.*)

The silver cisterns for bottled wine were very elaborate. In Defoe's novel *Roxana*, the heroine speaks of her 'great cistern for bottles which cost a hundred and twenty pounds'; and several huge silver cisterns are in existence, dating from 1681 into George I's reign; *e.g.* one (dated 1701), which was made for the first Duke of Marlborough, belongs to Earl Spencer; another (dated 1720) is the property of the Worshipful Company of Grocers (Fig. 2). Among the plate at Cannons when an inventory was drawn up for the first Duke of Chandos in 1725 were two cisterns, the 'large cistern' comparable in size to some extant examples weighing 2,158 oz. and valued at £1,025 5s. 9d., an enormous sum in early Georgian currency. An interesting specimen of a copper cistern japanned and decorated with Chinese figures was purchased for the Cavendish family in 1699 (Fig. 1). James Gibbs's *Book of Architecture* (1739) contains designs for marble 'cisterns for Buffets'; and cisterns of the kind in marble and stone are often met with, sometimes as fixtures in the dining-room.

Wooden cisterns or wine coolers lined with lead appear to have come first into use c. 1730, and Fig. 3 shows a fine example. It is carved on the sides with gadroons and rests on cabriole legs decorated with satyr masks and paw feet. Chippendale (*Director*, 1754) advises that one of the four designs he gives be 'made of wood or Marble and cut out of the solid; the others may be made in parts, and joined with Brasswork'. A wine cooler of c. 1755 which may be compared with one of his design is shown in Fig. 4. The finest wooden wine cooler in neo-classic taste is that at Harewood House, Yorkshire, which was made by Chippendale's firm. It is of rosewood richly mounted in ormolu with bandings, festoons and satyr masks (*see* SIDEBOARDS, Fig. 12). The inlaid example shown in Fig. 5 is of about the same date.

In later Georgian times the wine cooler was generally a plain mahogany tub hooped with brass and standing on four legs. Mary Kenyon in a letter to her mother (October 30, 1775) wrote that among the furniture in the parlour of her new house in Lincoln's Inn Fields was 'a handsome cistern of mahogany with brass hoops etc. under the sideboard'. A typical example of a brass-bound wine cooler filled with bottles and glasses is shown in a picture by Zoffany, representing William Ferguson commemorating with his friends his succession to the estate of Raith in 1781 (Fig. 7). The wine cooler itself is still preserved at Raith, where the picture was painted. A later variety of this type, of c. 1800, is fitted with a brass tap and rests on a 'pillar and claws' pedestal (Fig. 6).

The taste for wine led to great extravagance. Dr Shaw (*The Juice of the Grape: or, Wine Preferable to Water*, 1724) refers to the frequent use of champagne; and in 1789 it is recorded that 'Port and Champagne are exceedingly dear on account of the duties: notwithstanding this the consumption of these wines is very great in London'. In Ireland the habit of drinking appears to have been even more pronounced than in England. The Irish, according to Mrs Delaney, were very extravagant, and people with not more than a thousand a year dispensed burgundy and champagne, the most expensive wines.

Sheraton does not distinguish in his *Cabinet Dictionary* (1803) between the cellaret and the wine cistern and cooler, and in his *Encyclopaedia* (1805) writes that cellarets 'are not so generally used as they were, and amongst the higher classes are wholly laid aside', their place being taken by the sarcophagus form 'in the figure of ancient stone coffins'. A wine cooler (Fig. 8) is characteristic of the Regency archaeological phase of design. It is one of those described in the accounts of the younger Thomas Chippendale as '3 Sarcophagus's carved and painted white and part bronze; a Medusa's head in the centre'. H.C.S.

WINE KEEPER. *See* CELLARETS.

WINE WAITER. Open wagon or case on legs to contain bottles of wine or spirits in a dining-room; fitted with castors to allow contents to be circulated. This type of Georgian furniture, possibly of Irish origin, is now rare. The wine waiter (Fig. 1) is formed like an oblong stool with fixed tray partitioned for bottles or decanters and hand grip in centre.

1. *Mahogany Wine Waiter with partitions for bottles; stand carved with foliage in low relief. Irish. c. 1750. (Mulliner Coll.)*

WOOD-WORM or WOOD-BEETLE. Wood-worm is the term commonly applied to the species of grub or larva which germinates in wood, devours it and turns it to powder; the beetle being the same insect when fully developed. There are two principal wood-boring insects which are generally

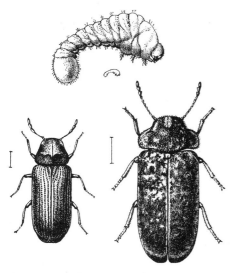

1. (*Top*) *Larva of furniture beetle.* (*Left*) *The furniture beetle.* (*Right*) *The 'death-watch' beetle.* (*Magnified six times.*)

2. *Exit holes* ('*worm holes*') *of the furniture beetle, natural size.*

3. *Section through the same piece of wood.*

included under the title of wood-worm. One, the *Xestobium tessallatum*, is known as the 'death-watch' beetle; the other, the *Anobium domesticum* or *punctatum*, as the furniture beetle. The former, the larger insect, confines its attention mainly to timberwork, and seldom attacks ordinary movable furniture. The life histories of both these insects are very much the same, each having four distinct stages during its development. The beetle lays its eggs, from which the grubs or larvae are hatched; these, when fully grown, change into the pupae or chrysalides, and these in turn merge into the winged beetle.

The so-called furniture worm, the grub of the beetle, is the insect which more commonly attacks furniture, panelling and small wooden articles; walnut, ash, beech, elm and soft woods, and also the sap wood of oak, being particularly vulnerable. The eggs are laid by the beetle usually in June, in cracks or crevices in the wood, and the larva or grub emerges in about three weeks. It tunnels inwards, and when full size alters its course in the wood and comes near to the surface. Here it passes from the larval to the pupal stage, and after an interval the beetle emerges from the chrysalis and bores its way through the thin wall of wood. The holes made by the beetle are commonly known as 'worm holes'. The indication that the grub is active in the wood is the appearance of the yellow powder, composed of rejected fragments of the wood and of the excrement of the larvae, which can be found emerging from the worm holes. The time occupied to complete the whole development of the insect from the egg to the beetle is uncertain, but it is calculated to last about two years.

Numerous methods for the treatment of wood infected by the wood-worm are recommended and are discussed in detail in a pamphlet (*Furniture Beetles*, Economic Series No. II) published by the British Museum (Natural History). The use of warm parchment size is also of value for hardening up the worm-eaten wood.

WORK-BOX. See Boxes.

WORK-TABLES. See Tables, Work-.

YEW (*Taxus*). A wood of very ancient use in England; hard, elastic and of reddish brown tone. In 17th and 18th centuries used in veneer work, and from 16th century in constructional framings of country-made pieces. A few pieces, *e.g.* gate-leg tables, are made throughout of the wood. Also found used in backs of some Windsor chairs of 18th century. Yew burrs similar to amboyna. Wood long used for drawer knobs, pegs, etc., and in 17th century for parquetry.

ZEBRA-WOOD. (*Pithecolobium racemiflorum*, South America.) Light brown in colour, very strongly marked with wide bands of deep brown, generally in severe contrast. Hard, heavy, durable; used as veneer in late 18th-century work, generally in cross-banded borders. Occasionally the entire surfaces were veneered with zebra-wood (*see* Bureaux, Fig. 53). By 1820 there was 'no more to be had for love or money' (*see* Bullock, John).

DESIGNERS, CABINET-MAKERS, ETC.

ADAIR, JOHN AND WILLIAM (fl. c. 1763 and 1773–99). John Adair, established as carver and gilder in Wardour Street, Soho, c. 1763; and William Adair, joiner to H.M. Privy Chamber, in 1773 supplied 'two rich carved and gilded frames for their Majesty's Pictures in whole Length'. Carving and gilding of mirrors and tables was done by 'Adair Carver' in 1766 and 1778 for Sir William Lee at Hartwell House, Aylesbury; John Adair supplied Lord Anson with frames and carved capitals for Shugborough Hall, Staffs., between 1763–9. William Adair worked for the crown between 1799 and 1805, and in the former year supplied three small sofas for the Queen's House (Buckingham Palace). The address of 'Adair carver and gilder' is given in a directory (1799) as 55, King Street, Golden Square.

ADAM, ROBERT (1728–92). Architect and designer of decorations and furniture: the second son of William Adam, who had a large architectural practice in Scotland. At first trained under his father, Robert went to Italy in 1754, and, returning to England in 1758, began practising in London. He believed that the subjects of decoration and furnishing were

1, 2. A Side Table and top for Osterley Park, 1775.

within the province of the architect, and that only thus could a complete and consistent result be obtained. In a lecture delivered in 1812, Sir John Soane witnessed to the far-reaching change which he brought about in the whole domain of domestic equipment:

> The light and elegant ornaments, the varied compartments in the ceilings of Mr Adam, imitated from Ancient Works in the Baths and Villas of the Romans, were soon applied in designs for chairs, tables, carpets and in every other species of furniture. To Mr Adam's taste in the ornament of his buildings and furniture we stand indebted, inasmuch as manufacturers of every kind felt, as it were, the electric power of this revolution in art.

Cabinet-makers abandoned the rococo, Chinese and Gothic styles, which still hold the field in the third (1762) edition of Chippendale's *Director*, and produced furniture founded in large measure on the pieces for which Adam had himself made careful and exact drawings and which he had seen set in their destined positions.

At the date of Chippendale's third edition Robert Adam was already architect of Croome Court, Worcs., for Lord Coventry, of Bowood, Wilts., for Lord Shelbourne, of Kedleston, Derby., for Sir Nathaniel Curzon, of Osterley, for Robert Child, the banker, and of Syon, for the Duke of Northumberland. His plan for carrying out Northumberland's wish for a suite of rooms at Syon 'entirely in the antique style' is dated 1761. His designs for wealthy clients are set forth in *Works in Architecture*, which he and his brother James began publishing in parts in 1773. Syon occupies more than one part, and there are several plates of its furniture (1765), as also of pieces for Lords Derby, Coventry and Mansfield, for the Duke of Bolton and for Sir Laurence Dundas. Nowhere did he design more richly than at Osterley, where Horace Walpole considered hall, library and eating-room '*chefs-d'oeuvre* of Adam' and a drawing-room 'worthy of Eve before the Fall'. He doubtless refers to the room hung with Boucher-Nielson tapestries, and for which Adam designed, among other furniture, a gilt-framed, marble-topped semi-circular table, the drawings for which are reproduced, Figs. 1 and 2.

Though *le goût grec* was already widespread in Paris by the late 1750s, and the neo-classic style is at least adumbrated in a few extant pieces of furniture produced for a small Parisian circle, Adam paid only one brief visit to Paris late in 1754 and appears to have arrived at his style in furniture designing independently of French inspiration. The rococo curves and exuberances of the Louis XV period are what Chippendale still called 'French' in 1762, and it was fully a decade after that date that in France itself they were ousted by the straight lines and restrained details of the first phase of the Louis XVI style. Adam may be regarded as the protagonist of the classical revival in England and revolutionised the character of the applied arts.

In the design of metalwork and furniture he was an innovator evolving new forms and adapting familiar elements from his wide and eclectic repertory. His furniture was specially designed for each client, and there are few duplicates among his sketches in the Soane Museum. Among his chief innovations may be noted the group of sideboard, table, pedestals and urns (*q.v.*), stands for lights of classical form and door furniture. In his designs for Northumberland House (1770–4) he shows a novel decorative use of mirrors. Between 1758 and his death in 1792, his style underwent considerable modifications. An example of his first manner is the set of seat furniture from 19, Arlington Street, a house altered by the architect for Sir Abraham Hume, of Moor Park, Herts., which is solidly constructed and severely classical in decoration (*see* CHAIRS, Fig. 138). The settee and chairs closely correspond with a design dated 1764 in the Soane Museum.

In the furniture at Harewood House, Yorks. (c. 1770–5) the influence of Adam's style is clearly perceptible, most conspicuously in the designs of mirrors, a picture frame and a console-table (*see* PICTURE FRAMES, Fig. 26 and TABLES,

4. *A Chimney Glass for* 20 *Portman Square*, 1775.

SIDE-, Fig. 49), forming an integral part of the mural decoration for which he was responsible. There marquetry on a ground of veneer is employed for a number of pieces by Chippendale in a masterly manner, but no designs for furniture at Harewood are known to survive. So far as can be judged from coloured drawings without descriptive notes, most of Adam's furniture was apparently intended to be painted and gilded, but a pair of marquetry commodes at Osterley (*see* COMMODES, Fig. 20) are from his designs. About 1778–80 the accent is on colour and an elegance of form 'spidery in its delicate fineness'. In 1778 Horace Walpole sounded a note of disapproval when referring to the small scale of the ornament of some of the furniture at Osterley (*Letters*, July 16, 1778). He pronounced the state bed to be 'too theatrical and too like a modern head-dress' (Fig. 3 and BEDS, Fig. 35), and regretted that 'from Kent's mahogany we are dwindled to Adam's filagree; grandeur and simplicity are not in the fashion'. During this last period, Adam made much use of painted decoration, in the form of both panels and medallions (sometimes painted on copper and applied) and decorative detail painted directly upon the wood (*see* KAUFFMANN, PERGOLESI and ZUCCHI), thus bringing furniture into still closer relation with interior decoration.

The cabinet-makers Samuel Norman, William France and Thomas Chippendale (*qq.v.*) are among those known to have been associated with Adam in some of his undertakings. He covered the whole ground of household equipment. Among the vast collection of his drawings now preserved in the Soane Museum, there are designs not only for furniture but also for carpets and curtain cornices, lanthorns and lamps, wall lights and firegrates, clocks and inkstands. There are also examples of

3. *A Bed for Osterley Park*, 1776.

silversmith's work. Adam had great fertility of invention; he was an able draughtsman, ceaselessly active and with a comprehensive grasp of his profession in all its branches. (See *The Architecture of Robert and James Adam*, Arthur Bolton, 1922, *The Age of Adam*, James Lees-Milne, 1948, and *The Furniture of Robert Adam*, Eileen Harris, 1963.)

ARBUTHNOT, PHILIP. The accounts of the Lord Chamberlain's Department for the year 1703–4 contain the entry:

> Philip Arbutnot (*sic*) Cabinet-Maker. For a present from Her Matie to the Emperor of Morocco. For Two large Sconces with double Branches, finely gilded, being three foot deep scoloped, dimond cutt and engraved embollished with crimson and gold Mosaic work with flowers on the bodys of the Glasses.

In the *Daily Courant*, Jan. 14, 1716, he announced that he was 'designing to leave off his trade', and advertised a large assortment of furniture, including 'Cabinets both English and Japan'.

BAILEY AND SAUNDERS. Cabinet-makers, No. 13, Mount St. This firm (formerly Tatham and Bailey) was employed by George, Prince of Wales, in connection with the furnishing of Brighton Pavilion. In 1817 they made 'four large chairs' superbly carved and gilded for the music room, and two side-tables of rosewood and satinwood supported by Chinese dragons for the banqueting room; these tables cost £430 each. They also supplied a set of 36 japanned chairs, which furniture is still in the Royal Collection (*see* TATHAM, THOMAS).

BEALING, RICHARD. An upholsterer, whose name appears in the royal tradesmen's accounts during the reigns of William III and Anne. He charged, Dec., 1692, for 'a fine carved couche frame, with rounde ends of walnuttree, fully carved', for stuffing it, and 'for making of the couch and covering the same with velvett'; and in 1698 for 'making ye scarlet and white damask bed, very fine, and covering all ye carving of ye Tester, head board and cornices and base mouldings' for Kensington Palace. In 1711 described as 'her Majesty's upholsterer' (*Calendar of Treasury Papers* 1708–11).

BECKWITH, SAMUEL. In partnership with William France (*q.v.*); among royal cabinet-makers 1784 to 1810, when he supplied furniture for the Queen's House in St James's Park (Buckingham Palace). In 1795 he supplied a 'neat mahogany worktable' to the Earl of Verulam at Gorhambury, Herts., his address being given as 101, Great St Martin's Lane. After William France's death Beckwith was in partnership with another member of France's family, Edward, described as an 'upholder' in contemporary directories.

BELCHIER, JOHN. Cabinet-maker 'at the Sun in St Paul's Churchyard'. Supplied furniture to Mr Purefoy of Shalstone Manor, Bucks., 1735–49. Billhead announces: 'All sorts of cabbinet work, chairs, glasses and coach glasses made and sold'. A walnut bureau-cabinet with panel of mirror glass (at offices of Triangle Valve Co., 315, Regent St.) bears his label. Died 1753—'a very eminent cabinet-maker, aged near 70 years'.

BELL, DANIEL. Cabinet-maker whose premises near St Martin's Lane were destroyed by fire in Oct., 1728, with the loss of 'valuable Foreign wood', and damage 'in Walnut-tree Plank only' at an estimated £500 (*British Gazette* and *Daily Journal*). He announced (*Daily Journal*, Oct. 17) that he had

taken new premises 'opposite to my late Dwelling House'. In partnership with Thomas Moore 1734; a set of 10 walnut chairs with other furniture was supplied to the 'Hon. Counsellor Rider' by this firm for Sandon Hall, Staffs.

BELL, HENRY AND **PHILIP.** Cabinet-makers 'at the White Swan against the South Gate in St Paul's Churchyard'. A walnut bureau c. 1745 bears Henry Bell's trade label with this address and states that he 'makes and sells all sorts of the finest Cabinet Goods—Looking Glasses, Coach Glasses and Chairs'. Died 1740 succeeded by Elizabeth Bell and later by Philip Bell, probably his son; latter's name occurs in London directories 1767–74 and on his label, found on several pieces of furniture. Firm of G. and J. Coxed and T. Woster (*q.v.*) occupied same premises earlier in the century.

BENNETT, SAMUEL. London cabinet-maker of early 18th century. No details of his life are known, but two fine bureau-

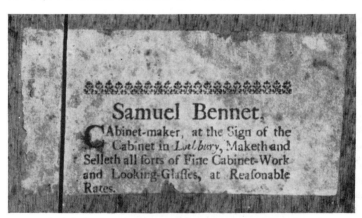

1. *Trade-label of Samuel Bennet, in drawer of a walnut bureau.*

bookcases are inlaid with his name and 'London fecit' (*see* BUREAUX, Fig. 19). Label in a cabinet drawer of a third bureau-bookcase gives his address 'at the Sign of the Cabinet in Lothbury', where he was working in 1723. Died 1741.

BENTHAM, SIR SAMUEL (1757–1831). Naval architect, engineer and inventor; invented and patented almost every known variety of woodworking machine at close of 18th century. Soon after 1779 he invented the first planing machine.

BLADWELL, JOHN (1725–68). Chair-maker, Bow Street, Covent Garden. Goods supplied to the Duke of Bedford at Woburn in 1732 included 'five neat mahogany chairs carved after Lady Holderness's pattern with elbows'; and in 1752 'six neat Chinese chairs and six neat strong Pembrook chairs'.

BLAND, CHARLES. Cabinet-maker to Charles II. In 1672 supplied to the king 'a bed of needlework richly wrought with silver trimmed with silver and gold fringes, with all other necessaryes thereunto belonging bought by his Majesty's especiall command for her Grace the Duchess of Monmouth'; also 'two large elbow-chaires of needleworke richly wrought of blew and gold, the other of silver and pincke'. (Great Wardrobe Accounts, Record Office.)

BOLTE, ADRIAN. Cabinet-maker to Charles I; his petition for readmission to that post under Charles II is among the State Papers, Domestic, June, 1660, and his name occurs in the Great Wardrobe Accounts early in Charles II's reign.

BOROUGH (OR **BURROUGH**), **JOHN,** AND **FARN-BROUGH, WILLIAM.** Cabinet-makers to Charles II, figuring in the Lord Chamberlain's Household Accounts; Farnbrough much more frequently than his partner, who is not mentioned until 1677, when they both supplied two large glass table and stands for Windsor at £50 each. Farnbrough was employed by the King in 1672, chiefly making dressing-tables and stands of exotic woods and walnut. He continued to supply the court under William and Mary with large quantities of furniture of a similar character. The Heal collection of trade cards has a bill in the name of 'John Burrough at ye Looking-Glass Cornhill' (June 17, 1662) which includes 'a large Cabenett £55'.

BOSIN (OR **BOSON**), **JOHN** (fl. c. 1738–43). A carver whose work for Richard Hoare (Hoare Bills, Victoria and Albert Museum) included 'several ornaments, as foliage festoons, etc., to a headboard, footboard and sides of a bedstead, done in mahogany'. George Vertue described him as 'a man of great ingenuity who undertook great works in his way for the prime people of quality and made his fortune very well in the world'; adding that he died in 1743. (Vertue's *Notebooks, Walpole Society*, Vol. XXII, p. 116.)

BOULTON, MATTHEW (1728–1802). English developer and leading producer of fine wares in ormolu; extended his father's Birmingham toy maker's business by founding new works at Soho and starting there in 1762, in partnership with John Fothergill, a manufactory of ormolu, Sheffield and silver plate, clocks, etc. His ormolu was soon competing with and largely ousting French objects both here and on the Continent and even found a ready market in France. He sought to make goods of first-rate quality but cheap and in large quantities. In 1770 James Adam suggested to him the manufacture of ormolu 'in an elegant and superior style', and his reply shows that he contemplated some kind of arrangement with the Adam brothers. Robert Adam supplied him with sketches for some of his cassolets or perfume burners (*q.v.*). Three years before this, however, a magnificent pair of blue-john candelabra had been ordered from Boulton for Queen Charlotte by George III. He also supplied a pair of cassolets and a square-cased bracket clock of this same material, richly mounted in ormolu; all of these are still in the Royal Collection. Similar articles became usual in wealthy houses, for which he had special sales of his goods at Christie's auction rooms. In 1775 he entered into partnership with James Watt and brought him to Soho to perfect his steam-engine; and 'soon after my connection with Mr B. he declined the ormolu business'. His friend, James Keir, in an obituary notice, observed that 'the ormolu vases and ornaments were found too expensive for general demand'. Boulton is said at one time to have had 35 chasers tooling his castings, and to have employed 700 workmen in 1791. (*Torrington Diaries*, Vol. 1, p. 49, 1934.)

A series of large volumes with hundreds of designs (including many original drawings) for plate and objects in stone and ormolu, sold with the effects of the Boulton and Watt factory in 1850, are now at the City of Birmingham Central Library. The designs in the first pattern-book give a wealth of information concerning Boulton's early productions of silver, Sheffield plate and ormolu-mounted wares; among the drawings is one of Queen Charlotte's candelabra. The catalogues of the sales at Christie's (Apr., 1771, and May, 1778) also throw a flood of light on his activities. In the earlier sale the wares sold were mainly of blue-john and ormolu—vases and urns, essence pots, clocks, etc. (See *Matthew Boulton*, H. W. Dickinson, 1937, and *The M. Boulton Pattern Books*, W. A. Sealby and R. J. Hetherington, *Apollo*, Feb. and Mar., 1950.)

BRADBURN, JOHN. Cabinet-maker who supplied large quantity of furniture to the royal household 1773–6. Employed by Vile and Cobb (*q.v.*), and became cabinet-maker to the crown in partnership with William France (*q.v.*) after the retirement of Vile in 1763. Apparently carving was his speciality and is fully detailed in his bills. His first premises were in Hemmings Row, off St Martin's Lane (1758); in 1767 he moved to 8, Long Acre. Resigned as royal cabinet-maker July, 1777, and died 1781. In his will (Aug., 1780) described as of 'the parish of Wandsworth . . . gentleman'. A secretaire-cabinet at Buckingham Palace was made by Bradburn for the Princess Royal in 1774, and a 'mahogany pillar and claw table neatly carved', covered with 'needlework in being' at Kew Palace is included in his bills (1767). He charges also for a 'Crown' for two 'very rich tabernacle frames' on portraits by F. Cotes and N. Dance in the Royal Collection. He supplied a large quantity of furniture hangings, etc., to John Chute of The Vyne, Hants., to a total of £1,052 in 1765–7. Some of the items can still be identified, notably two large mahogany 'sophas' and chairs forming a set. The bills are headed 'To John Bradburn and the Executors of the late M^r W^m. France'; the last payment recorded (£400) was in 1776 after the death of France.

BRADSHAW, GEORGE SMITH. Cabinet-maker, for a time in partnership with Paul Saunders in Soho; the Holkham, Norfolk, accounts for the panels of Saunders' Pilgrimages to Mecca (dated 1756–8) show that the partnership existed in 1756. It was dissolved Oct., 1758 (*London Gazette*), Bradshaw continuing in Greek Street and Saunders in Soho Square; those with claims on the partnership were 'to bring their Accounts of Mr Mayhew (*see* INCE, W.) at Mr Bradshaw's'. Bradshaw was employed by the Admiralty 1764–74 providing furniture for the First Lord's house.

BRADSHAW, WILLIAM. Prominent furniture-maker of mid-Georgian period. His name is in the accounts of the second Earl Stanhope at Chevening, Kent, 1736, when he was paid £1,200; probably a gilt set of chairs and love seats there was supplied by him. Entries for small payments to Bradshaw (1738–9) are in the expense book of first Earl of Bristol. He was also employed by the first Earl of Leicester at Holkham, Norfolk, and among the household accounts for 1740 is: 'To Mr Bradshaw for mending tables, cabinet work and furnishing Mr Coke's apartment in the London House £85'. He supplied the fourth Earl of Cardigan and his wife at Deene Park, Northants., and Dover House, Dover Street. His name occurs in the accounts for furnishing Longford Castle, Wilts. (Lord Folkestone), 1737–50. He supplied a carpet and hung tapestry. He was probably 'William Bradshaw Esq.', who subscribed to Chippendale's *Director* (1754).

BRODSTOCK, WILLIAM. Upholsterer and cabinet-maker to Charles II, first appears in royal accounts Feb., 1667; bills mainly for small amounts.

BROOKSHAW, GEORGE. Employed at Carlton House 1783–6; supplied Prince of Wales in 1783 with an 'elegant commode highly finished with a basket of flowers painted in the front and sprays of jasmine all over the top, and ditto on the front, the body with carved and gilt mouldings and legs'. His account (in Royal Archives, Windsor Castle) gives address 48, Great Marlborough St.

BROWN, JOHN. Cabinet-maker and upholsterer at 'The Three Cover'd Chairs and Walnut Tree, the East Side of St Paul's Church Yard, near the School'; where his business was 1728–44. His card advertises chairs, all sorts of cabinet-work, sconces, pier and chimney-glasses, mahogany and other tables and window blinds 'best painted of any in London'.

BULLOCK, GEORGE. (d. before 1820). Furniture-maker whose work is described by R. Brown (*Rudiments of Drawing Cabinet and Upholstery Furniture*, 1820) as sometimes too 'massy and ponderous... considerably overcharged with buhl', but with 'great novelty without absurdity, as well as happy relief in his ornaments'. Maria Edgworth mentions at Aske Hall, Yorks., 1820, 'fine tables of Bullock's making, one of wood from Brazil, Zebrawood and no more to be had for love or money'. (*Life and Letters*, Vol. I, pp. 275–6.) Made pair of cupboards inlaid with brass and mounted with ormolu for Blair Castle, Perth., 1817. M. J.

CAMPBELL, ROBERT. Cabinet-maker of Little Marylebone Street, Golden Square, largely employed in furnishing of Carlton House for the Prince of Wales. His 'Estimate of Works' at the Prince's instructions totalled £10,500 in 1789, and some fine examples of late 18th-century furniture in the Royal Collection have been attributed to him (see *Buckingham Palace*, H. Clifford Smith, 1931). Campbell and Sons were among subscribers to the *Drawing Book* (1791–4), and Sheraton writes 'two designs for library steps were taken from steps made by Mr Campbell, upholsterer to the Prince of Wales, and first made for the King'. Campbell's patent for library steps was taken out in 1774.

CARTER, JOHN. Architect and antiquarian draughtsman. Among the many architectural drawings which he published in *The Builder's Magazine* between 1774 and 1778 are a few designs in a personal neo-classic style (see *English Furniture Designs*, P. Ward-Jackson, 1958). A drawing attributed to Carter (not noted above) is in the Dep. of Engravings, V. and A. Mus., for a mirror for the Earl of Derby.

CASBERT, JOHN. Upholsterer to Charles II, constantly in Lord Chamberlain's accounts 1667–73 for curtains, canopies of state, hangings, Turkey carpets, etc., and also for furniture (beds, chairs, stools and screens). He appears to have been entrusted with decoration of royal yachts *Monmouth*, *Cleveland* and *Henrietta*.

CASEMENT, WILLIAM. Designer and probably maker of furniture; responsible for two plates in *The Cabinet Maker's Book of Prices*, c. 1760. A. W. Casement, perhaps son or grandson of above, was among subscribers to first ed. of Sheraton's *Drawing Book* (1791–4).

CATIGNOU, JAMES. Cabinet-maker who supplied a quantity of furniture for the royal palaces under William III

(1692–3), *e.g.* for Hampton Court '12 round stooles carved handsome'.

CAUTY, WILLIAM. Cabinet-maker whose trade-card with a bill on the back, dated 1757, gives address 'at ye sign of the Chair and Curtains, the West End of Somerset House in the Strand'. In 1770 in King's St., St James's (Westminster Poll Book), where he advertised on a trade-label found in a chest of drawers that his beds, sofas and chairs are 'finished so as no Vermin of any Denomination can ever possibly exist in either (Warranted Gratis) by a new and infallible method . . . done nowhere else but at the above shop'. Westminster City Rate Book records c. 1780 he had not paid rates; marginal note 'poor, Give him time'.

CHAMBERS, SIR WILLIAM (1726–96). Celebrated architect who designed furniture for some of his buildings. Of old Scottish family trading as merchants at Gothenburg, Sweden, he went, aged 16, on Swedish East India Co.'s ship to China; hence his *Designs of Chinese Buildings and Furniture* (1757), *Dissertation on Oriental Gardening* (1772) and Chinese pagoda at Kew. He made it clear, however, that he did not seek 'to promote a taste so much inferior to the antique and so very unfit for our climate'. He turned to architecture at the age of 18 and studied for many years in Italy. Soon after his return to England in 1755 he was appointed (probably by the influence of Lord Bute) to teach architecture to the Prince of Wales

1. *Sir William Chambers: design for an overmantel mirror frame.* (*Soane Mus.*)

(later George III), and embellish Kew Gardens for the Princess Dowager of Wales; he became Surveyor-General and Comptroller of the Works (1782). George III allowed him to use the title of Knight of the Polar Star granted by the King of Sweden in 1772, and he was known as Sir William. He had a good private practice as architect, chiefly among the King's friends. He published his *Treatise on Civil Architecture* (1759; 3rd ed., with additional plates, 1791). His designs include a vase, candle-socket on a sphinx, and pedestal in the form of a term; the latter and its fellow with female head (original drawings for both in the Soane Mus.) appear to have been made for the Duke of Marlborough at Blenheim. But Chambers was responsible for more important furniture still at Blenheim—a state bed with domed top and military trophies on the cornice, and mirrors and console table in the cabinet room (see *Furniture at Blenheim*, D. Green and M. Jourdain, *Country Life*, Apr. 20, 1951). A letter from M. Boulton to Thomas Wright, clock-maker, 1771, reveals that 'Mr Chambers' designed a clock-case for the king, which Boulton carried out in ormolu at his Soho works. Next to Somerset House, Chambers's best London building was Carrington House, Whitehall (demolished), and among his remaining drawings are designs for furniture there, including a side-table. In 1773 he designed for Charles IV of Spain an organ combined with bureau and jewel cabinet, William Hamilton, R.A., being responsible for the very ornate painted decoration. (This piece of furniture no longer exists.) His favourite craftsmen were Benoni Thacker, cabinet-maker, and Samuel Alken, wood-carver. The considerable collection of his designs (Soane and V. and A. Museums) include decorative schemes and other pieces of furniture, one of them a wall-mirror frame 'for my own house'. An inscription on a small satinwood table records that it was commissioned and designed by Chambers and executed by George Haupt, the famous Swedish cabinet-maker, in London, Feb., 1769. (*Burlington Magazine Monographs*, 1929.)

CHANNON, J. Cabinet-maker, west side of St Martin's Lane. 'J. Channon fecit' appears on plate on one of pair of fine rosewood bookcases inlaid with brass, 1740, at Powderham Castle, near Exeter (*see* BOOKCASES, Fig. 6). 'Channon Senior' and 'Channon Junior' were among subscribers to Chippendale's *Director* (1754).

CHILLINGWORTH AND **BURNETT, THOS.** Upholders and Appraisers, King's Arms, Harp Alley, Fleet Ditch, 1724, and King's Arms by St Mary-le-Strand, c. 1740. Succeeded by Thomas and Gilbert Burnett, cabinet-makers and upholsterers, at latter address. Thomas Burnett supplied furniture to Lord Leigh of Stoneleigh Abbey, Warwick., to a total of £3,000–£4,000, 1764–5. A pair of mahogany commodes with curved keel-shaped corners, c. 1765, and another of similar design were probably supplied by Burnett (Christie's, May 6, 1962, Lots 53 and 54).

CHIPPENDALE, THOMAS (1718–79). Born 1718 at Otley, Yorks., son of village carpenter; probably sent to London by local patron and apprenticed to cabinet-maker there; married Catherine Redshaw 1748. Thereafter Poor Rate books of St Martin-in-the-Fields show he lived at Conduit Court and Spur Alley Ward, and at Somerset Court (later Northumberland Court, Strand) before moving in 1754 to 60 and 61,

1. *Thomas Chippendale: design for French Chair. Dated* 1753. (*Director, 1st ed.*)

St Martin's Lane; where he rented two houses and remained until he died. Partners were James Rannie (*q.v.*) and, later, Thomas Haig; the firm's premises were extensive and included shop, timber-yard and workshops.

His great reputation is due to *The Gentleman and Cabinet-Maker's Director*, first published 1754, with second edition (virtually a reprint) 1755, and third enlarged edition 1762 (in weekly parts 1759–62); the first two editions have 160 engraved plates, and the third 200, illustrating almost every type of mid-century domestic furniture. The plates bear Chippendale's signature, 'T. Chippendale del.' and usually the engravers' names; Darly and Muller being employed in all three editions, while others were used only for the third. The high-flown preface was probably drafted by a literary hack though signed by Chippendale. List of subscribers, including prominent peers together with cabinet-makers and members of associated trades, was printed in the first edition only.

Though Chippendale signed the *Director* plates, and wrote in the preface 'I frankly confess that, in executing many of the drawings, my pencil has but faintly copied out those images that my fancy suggested'; thus claiming the designs as his own. It has been contended that many of the engraved plates were inventions of other furniture designers, particularly Lock and Copland (*q.v.*), who have been described as 'Chippendale's ghosts'. (*The Creators of the Chippendale Style*, F. Kimball and E. Donnell, *Metropolitan Museum Studies*, Vol. I, Part II,

2. *Design for Gothic Chair. Dated* 1754. (Director, 1*st ed.*)

May and Nov., 1929.) Further examination of the evidence, particularly that of the original drawings signed by Chippendale, has restored to him the credit for at least a considerable number of the designs; and probably for all of those for case furniture. (New Edition Chippendale's *Director*: Intro. by Ralph Edwards, 1957; *English Furniture Designs of the 18th Century*, P. Ward Jackson, 1958.)

Although furniture designs had been published in Europe 200 years earlier, nothing on the *Director* scale had been attempted. Architectural treatises sometimes included a few designs for movables; Chippendale's book was not only confined to furniture but illustrated almost every type in use. Most of the designs were in the rococo, Gothic or Chinese fashions. Some of the 'carver's pieces' were impractical, and many of the designs were intended to be executed, not in mahogany, but in soft wood and japanned or gilded. Chippendale's accounts and correspondence prove that for most of his career he was not a working cabinet-maker, but the organiser of a highly successful firm which furnished and decorated important houses.

The *Director* plates show mainly an anglicised version of the French *rocaille*, but during his latter years Chippendale produced, under Robert Adam's influence, furniture very different in character from that commonly associated with his name.

The third edition of the *Director* (1762) remains thoroughly rococo in conception, though many of the earlier plates were replaced by new designs for furniture and interior decoration. But by this date the neo-classic style was already in the ascen-

dant, and most of our evidence about Chippendale's firm and its productions comes from the accounts he rendered to Adam's clients. He usually supplied mahogany furniture for hall and dining-room, gilt and inlaid pieces for the saloon and japanned furniture for bedrooms.

The most valuable surviving accounts are those for Nostell Priory (1766–70) and Harewood House, Yorks. (1772 onwards), which provide full descriptions of furniture still in its original position. The Harewood bills, dated from 1772, illustrate the final, most accomplished phase of Chippendale's work, when marquetry decoration in the neo-classic style predominated. At Nostell Priory (where there are examples of his successive styles) is the magnificent mahogany library table, perhaps the finest of its type in existence (*see* TABLES, LIBRARY, Fig. 18); while an inlaid commode with metal mounts, an adaptation of the Louis XV style, shows the brilliant technique eminently characteristic of his finished work. The magnificent furniture at Harewood includes the famous Diana and Minerva commode, inlaid with various woods and ivory, which is a masterpiece of craftsmanship (*see* COMMODES, Fig. 21). There are also detailed accounts for Mersham le Hatch, Kent (1767), where much of the furniture has been identified (including simple bedroom pieces), and for David Garrick's house in Adelphi Terrace (1771–2), the contents of which have not survived. The MS. accounts in the Victoria and Albert Museum describe minutely the furniture supplied to Garrick's town house, and the Museum possesses the japanned bedroom furniture from his villa at Hampton, which was probably by Chippendale's firm (*see* CUPBOARDS, Fig. 21).

Other records of Chippendale's activities have enlarged the

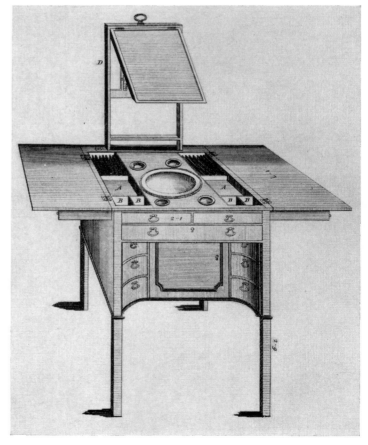

3. *Design for a Shaving Table. Dated* 1761. (Director, 3*rd ed.*)

4. (*Left*) *Design for Commode Table. Dated* 1760. (*Director, 3rd ed.*)

5. (*Right*) *Design for Candelabrum.* (*Director, 3rd ed.*)

canon of his work. The *Director* states that a bedstead was made for the Earl of Pembroke's house in Whitehall, and at Wilton a large bookcase of remarkable quality and two smaller bookcases can be attributed to Chippendale (*see* BOOKCASES, Fig. 15). The Pembroke papers included a receipt (June 21, 1770) for £460 5s. 'for the four Bonds now delivered up with interest' by his Lordship to Chippendale and Rannie (*q.v.*), and the Earl paid £243 in May, 1773, in full settlement of 'all demands'.

Chippendale also had business relations with Lord Mansfield (Kenwood for 'French Plate Glass'), Lord Shelbourne (Lansdowne House), the Earl of Dumfries (Dumfries House, Ayrshire), the Duke of Atholl (Blair Castle, Perthshire)—furniture at Blair can still be identified from entries in the accounts, notably a rosewood bookcase and a state bed (*Director*, 3rd ed., 1762) supplied in 1759—and the Duke of Portland, to whom he supplied two gilt mirrors in the *Director* style in 1766, and C. W. Bamfylde (Hestercombe, Somerset).

Apart from furniture authenticated by bills, there is a much larger group more or less corresponding to *Director* designs. Though such resemblances cannot afford conclusive proof, there is a strong case for attribution where the furniture is obviously by a master craftsman and in a house whose owner subscribed to the *Director*—conditions fulfilled at Arundel, Alnwick, St Giles's House, and Badminton. Attribution to Chippendale is also justified, on the evidence of high quality and correspondence of design, or close stylistic resemblance to authenticated pieces, in instances such as mirrors at Crichel, a library table formerly at Coombe Abbey, an inlaid commode at Renishaw, and a pair of cabinets formerly at Panshanger *see* MIRRORS, Fig. 51, TABLES, LIBRARY, Fig. 15, COMMODES, Fig. 19, and CABINETS, Fig. 41). These lists might be considerably extended.

In the Court of Bankruptcy proceedings in 1773 concerning the notorious Teresa Cornelys of Carlisle House, Soho Square,

Chippendale was one of the principal creditors and an assignee of her estate. It is most probable that he had been employed on the furnishings of Carlisle House.

Chippendale was not the only begetter of the English rococo style in England, and his work in that manner on the whole is not superior to the authenticated productions of William Vile (*q.v.*). But in his last phase (1770–9), under Adam's influence, he produced marquetry furniture (much of it mounted with finely chased ormolu) which rivals the achievements of the great French *ébénistes*. He was certainly supreme among English cabinet-makers as an exponent of the neo-classic style

6. *Design for Hall Lantern. Dated* 1761. *See Lanterns, Fig.* 9. (*Director, 3rd ed.*)

1. *Giovanni Baptista Cipriani: design for a painted pedestal. c. 1780.*

in cabinet-making. (See also *Georgian Cabinet-Makers*, R. Edwards and M. Jourdain, 3rd ed., revd., 1955.)

It is widely believed in Portugal that Chippendale visited that country after the publication of the *Director*, which afforded patterns for many native cabinet-makers. Unpublished and at present inaccessible documents at Braga are said to supply the evidence (information from the Duke of Palmella). Chippendale is also known to have imported French furniture; and in 1769 he was fined by the Customs for under-valuing 'five Dozen of Chairs, unfinished' which he had imported from France.

CHIPPENDALE, THOMAS, JUN. (1749–1822). Cabinet-maker and artist, eldest son of T. Chippendale's 11 children; presumably trained in the St Martin's Lane workshop, where he carried on his father's business after 1779, trading as Haig and Chippendale; member of Society of Arts, exhibited five pictures at Royal Academy 1784–1801. He opened another shop at 57, Haymarket (1814) and removed thence to 42, Jermyn St. (1821). Haig retired in 1796; Chippendale went

bankrupt 1804, when a large quantity of 'beautiful cabinet work of the first class' was sold, but was soon in full practice again. His firm enjoyed a considerable reputation; he was paid £170 by the Earl of Pembroke (1790), £1,424 by Charles Hoare, of Luscombe, Devon (1796–1808), and several thousand pounds by Sir Richard Colt Hoare of Stourhead, Wilts. (1795–1820). Library tables, chairs (*see* CHAIRS, Fig. 191) and other furniture in this house can be identified by the bills, which include charges for paper-hanging, curtains and upholstery. Some of the satinwood and mahogany furniture at Luscombe closely resembles examples at Stourhead. Accounts dated 1796–7 show that he was employed by Lord Harewood; he supplied four carved and gilt side-tables in the Gallery at Harewood which mark the transition between the earlier classical manner and the Regency style; among the largest items is £124 10s. for a mahogany table—more than for a very elaborate one supplied to Stourhead in 1805. In 1819 he spent some months at Raynham Hall, Norfolk, where he was paid £1,200 by Lord Townshend.

Chippendale's furniture, of a high level of craftsmanship, includes excellent specimens of the less extravagant Regency taste. He visited Paris towards the end of his life and brought back a sketch book illustrating Empire furniture. He published in 1779 *Sketches for Ornament*, a small quarto with four plates. (See also *Georgian Cabinet-Makers*, R. Edwards and M. Jourdain, 3rd ed., revd., 1955.)

CIPRIANI, GIOVANNI BAPTISTA (1727–85). Florentine artist who came to England 1755 and soon made a reputation for painted decoration in public buildings and houses. His classical and allegorical figure subjects probably inspired much of the painted ornament on late 18th-century furniture, though there are no existing examples known to be by his hand; in one instance at any rate a commode (for Mrs Montagu) was painted by him 'with four muses in his very best manner'. A design for a painted pedestal, from a water-colour by Cipriani, is seen in the accompanying illustration. On the foundation of the Royal Academy in 1768 he was elected a member.

CLAY, HENRY. Japanner and inventor of the ware named after him. In youth he was apprenticed to John Baskerville, who from 1740–9, before he became a printer, manufactured japanned goods at Birmingham. Clay patented his invention, a kind of *papier-mâché*, in 1772. The patent specifies that among other purposes it was intended for making highly varnished panels for cabinets, bookcases, screens, tables, trays, etc. For the decoration of caddies, dressing-cases and other small objects he employed cameos of Wedgwood's ware. In 1778 Horace Walpole paid Clay £14 5s. 6d. for two waiters, a card-rack, 'tea cade', and a table. G. C. Lichtenberg, the Hanoverian scholar and scientist, while staying in England, visited Clay's factory at Birmingham in Oct., 1775, 'where the excellent japanned ware, which is also copied in Brunswick, is manufactured, besides paper boxes, tea-caddies and panels for coaches. . . . They make there coffee-trays of paper and all kinds of other vessels, black with orange figures in the style of Etruscan vases which are indescribably handsome. A tea-caddy costs three guineas.'

Clay is said to have left Birmingham in 1802 and opened a shop for the sale of his tea-trays in Bedford St., Strand, subsequently removing to 17–18, King St., Covent Garden, where he sold various kinds of furniture made by his process. In the Osterley accounts there is an entry (1804) for four guineas to 'Henry Clay, Japanner in Ordinary to His Majesty', his premises then being in King St. His process is described in E. D. Clarke's *Tour through the South of England, Wales and the Borders of Scotland* (1791). (See also *English Papier Mâché*, G. Dickinson, 1925.)

CLEYN, FRANCIS (1582–1658). German artist and designer, b. at Rostock; court painter to Christian IV of Denmark; appointed in 1624 designer to Mortlake tapestry works, a position he held until his death. Responsible for mural decoration at Ham House, Surrey, and for the 'Gilt Room' at Holland House (destroyed), where 'chairs, carved and gilt, with large shells for backs . . . were undoubtedly from his designs, and are evidences of his taste'. (Horace Walpole, *Anecdotes of Painting*, 1762–71. *See also* CHAIRS, Fig. 12.)

COBB, JOHN (d. 1778). Cabinet-maker and upholsterer at 72, St Martin's Lane, partner of William Vile (*q.v.*) 1750–65; then alone until his death. Described by J. T. Smith (*Nollekens and his Times*, 1828) as a 'singularly haughty character'; frequently employed by George III for cabinet-work 'of the most elaborate and expensive sort'. He left property and £20,000 'to support ye name of Cobb as a private gentleman'. The firm supplied furniture to The Vyne, Hants. (1752–3), Came House, Dorset (1756–62), Edgcote, Northants. (1758), Sir Charles Hanbury-Williams for his town house in Upper Brook St. (1758), Strawberry Hill (1770), and Corsham, Wilts. (1772), where an 'extra neat' inlaid commode closely resembles one from Holland House and a smaller one in the V. and A. Mus. (*see* COMMODES, Fig. 15). The bill to Sir Charles (£437 19s. 6d.) is headed 'Messrs Cobb and Vile,' receipted by Cobb (the order of the names is reversed in earlier and later bills) and includes items for upholstery and papering rooms. It shows that the firm supplied not only costly furniture but also simple, inexpensive pieces which, if they survive, cannot be identified. After Cobb's death the business was continued by one Jenkins, his foreman, and W. Strickland (*q.v.*), Vile's nephew. (See also *Georgian Cabinet-Makers*, R. Edwards and M. Jourdain, 3rd ed., revd., 1955.)

COLE, GEORGE. Prominent 'Upholder' of Golden Square, 1747–74. He supplied the Duke of Atholl with three finely carved mahogany console tables and '3 very nice carved and gilt glass frames' for Blair Castle in February, 1763 (another of the set was ordered for Dunkeld House and is probably by Thomas Johnson). At Corsham Court there are bills for 'Mr Cole the Upholsterer' for a total of £234 between 10 March 1761 and 25 November 1763; these probably include mirrors by Johnson. (See 'Some Cabinet-Makers at Blair Castle' A. Coleridge, *Connoisseur*, Vol. CXLVI, No. 590, pp. 25–45.)

COLLINS, WILLIAM. Presumably the maker of the set of 'Fish Furniture' at the Admiralty, given to Greenwich Hospital in 1813, as a torchère in the set bears his name. A pair of candelabra at the Bowes Museum also inscribed. Not to be confused with William Collins, of Tothill St., who died in 1793.

COPLAND, H. A designer who published *A New Book of Ornaments*, 1746, with cartouches which are among the earliest examples of English rococo. He published another book under the same title in collaboration with M. Lock (*q.v.*) in 1752

1. *H. Copland: design for an escutcheon from* New Book of Ornaments. *Dated* 1746.

containing sconces, tables, stands, etc., 2nd ed. 1768. Six plates in R. Manwaring's (*q.v.*) *Chairmakers' Guide* (1766) may be assigned to Copland. These chairs, having wide interlaced scrolls in the back as a characteristic feature, are quite different in style from the plates in Chippendale's *Director*, most of which have been attributed on inadequate evidence to Copland (see *Met. Mus. Studies*, Vol. I, Part II, 1929, F. Kimball and E. Donnell). These are the only furniture designs attributable to Copland, since it is impossible to distinguish between his and Lock's designs in their joint publications. (See *English Furniture Designs of the 18th Century*, P. Ward-Jackson, 1958.)

COXED, G. AND **J.,** AND **WOSTER, T.** Cabinet-makers working c. 1690–1736. Labels bearing the names of these three makers have been found on several pieces of furniture, including two bureau-cabinets c. 1700 and 1720 respectively. These and other pieces which may be assigned to Coxed and Woster are very distinctive in being veneered with burr elm, crossbanded with kingwood and inlaid with stringing lines of pewter; the use of metal inlay having been introduced into England by Gerreit Jensen (*q.v.*). The firm's most complete advertisement reads: 'At the White Swan, against the south gate in St Paul's Churchyard, London, makes and sells Cabinets, Scrutores, Desks and Bookcases, Buro's, Chests of Drawers, Whisk, Ombre Dutch and India Tea-Tables; all sorts of Looking-

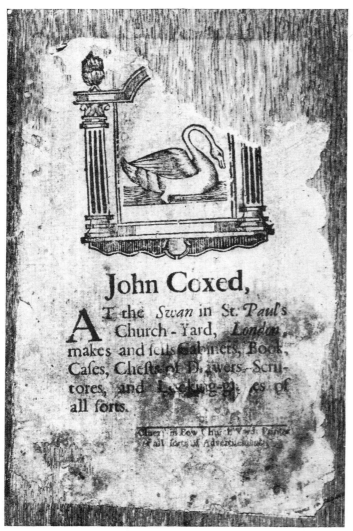

1. Trade-label used by the firm of Coxed and Woster.

Glasses, Large Sconces, Dressing Sets and Wainscot-Work of all sorts at Reasonable Rates. Old Glasses New Polished and Made Up Fashionable.' Another engraved label (Fig. 1) of rather earlier date bears the name of J. Coxed only. In Apr., 1735, Thomas Woster rendered a bill to Richard Hoare, of Barn Elms, for a 'strong wainscot table' and a 'large wainscot press', at a total cost of £9 12s. 6d.

The occupants of the White Swan have been traced from the end of Elizabeth I's reign, and in the 18th century Henry Bell and Philip Bell, 'cabinet-maker and upholder' (*q.v.*) issued advertisements from the same address. Woster's death is recorded in the *Daily Post*, Dec. 14, 1736.

CROFTS, ROBERT. Feather dresser to Charles II; his bills in the royal accounts show that feather plumes on the testers of state beds were frequently renewed or repaired.

CROOK, BENJAMIN. Cabinet-maker at the George and White Lion, St Paul's Churchyard c. 1730–48. Trade-label in walnut card-table of c. 1730 and on other pieces.

CROXFORD, FRANCIS. Chair- and cabinet-maker (address unknown), advertisement in the *Daily Post* (July 12, 1733) of the sale of his stock in trade indicates that he was not only a maker on a considerable scale but also 'eminent in his profession for his many and beautiful designs'.

CRUNDEN, JOHN. Architect and designer, author of *The Joyner and Cabinet-maker's Darling* (1765), containing Chinese and ornamental frets probably used for furniture in the Chinese taste, and other works of similar character.

DAGUERRE, DOMINIQUE. Refugee French dealer; specialist with his partner, M. E. Lignereux, in furniture inlaid with Sèvres porcelain plaques; fled to London 1793. Styled *Marchand privilégé de la Cour*. Supplied furniture to Louis XVI from his shop in Rue St Honoré, Paris. In 1789 sent bill to English crown for £1,659 for 'carving and gilding done by S. Nelson by order of Mr Dagare'. In London continued partnership with M. E. Lignereux in Sloane St., whence he supplied much costly furniture for Carlton House, including gilt armchairs and sofas, still in the Royal Collection, bearing his label. Claimed £15,000 in settlement of the Prince of Wales's debts. (See H. Clifford Smith, *Buckingham Palace*, pl. 169–70, and F. J. B. Watson, *Wallace Collection Catalogues, Furniture*, 1956.)

DARLY, MATHIAS. Designer, publisher, engraver and caricaturist; said to have begun work as an architect, afterwards setting up as publisher with George Edwards in the Strand, where he taught engraving, etc. Published *A New Book of Chinese, Gothic and Modern Chairs* (1750–1), with 'crude and feeble' designs (*Met. Mus. Studies*, Vol. I, Pt. 2, p. 122, 1929), and a *New Book of Chinese Designs* (1754) jointly with Edwards,

1. Mathias Darly: chimney furniture from New Book of Chinese Designs, *1754.*

'calculated to improve the present taste'. The latter contains a few plates of furniture among many designs for bridges, temples and garden houses, which, although far removed from the true spirit of oriental art, show distinct originality, the chimney furniture (Fig. 1) being doubtless for a Chinese room. In 1754 Darly engraved many of the plates for the first ed. of Chippendale's *Director*. His most important work, *The Compleat Architect* (1770), was formerly ascribed to another author of the same name. About this time, in a letter to the Liverymen of London, he styled himself 'Math. Darly Citizen and Clock maker': possibly he was admitted to the guild as a designer. His contemporary fame rested mainly on his political prints ('the famous caricature print seller'—*Nollekens and his Times*, J. T. Smith, 1828). Darley died c. 1780.

DECAIX, ALEXIS. French metal worker mentioned in Hope's *Household Furniture* (1807) as having executed 'the most complete and enriched portions' of his furniture; also in Royal Archives, Windsor Castle, as bronze and ormolu manufacturer; at 43, Old Bond St., and 15, Rupert St. (Holden's *London Directory*, 1809–11).

DELABRIERE, LOUIS A. Decorative painter employed by Henry Holland (*q.v.*) at Carlton House. Appears in Prince of Wales's Debt Book, July, 1795, when established in Tenterden St.; may perhaps be identified with Louis Alexandre Delabrière who before the Revolution was architect to the Comte d'Artois, later Charles X. Responsible for painted decoration of ceilings and overmantel in boudoir at Southill, Beds. Panels of pair of rosewood parcel gilt pole screens in that house were 'painted by Delabrière' (inventory, 1816), and decoration of chairs 'with painted Tablet backs' may be assigned to him. (*See* SCREENS, Fig. 26, and *Southill, The Furniture and Decoration*, F. G. B. Watson, 1951, p. 26.)

DE LA COUR, WILLIAM (d. 1767). Painter, stagedesigner, engraver and ornamentalist presumably of French origin, who worked in England and published eight books of *rocaille* ornament (the fifth entirely devoted to designs for furniture) between 1741 and 1747. His engravings are among the earliest examples of the rococo style printed in England. De la Cour was working in London in 1740 and in Edinburgh 1757–67, where he was Director of a School of Design. (See *English Furniture Designs*, P. Ward-Jackson, 1958.)

DERIGNEE, ROBERT. Carver who supplied carved and gilt furniture to royal palaces under William and Mary. In 1691 made, at cost of £20, for Kensington Palace 'a great wainscott frame for a glasse 10 feet long and seven feet wide . . . carved with figures and gilt gold'. Paid in 1707 for carver's work for Duke of Montague.

DOMINIQUE (DOMINIC), JEAN. Gilder and brassfounder, who executed work in ormolu for Carlton House 1783–6 (*Buckingham Palace*, H. Clifford Smith, 1931, p. 103).

EDWARDS, EDWARD (1738–1806). Son of chair-maker and carver; at age of 15 began to work with his father in shop of William Hallett (*q.v.*), where he 'drew patterns for furniture' and 'sought every opportunity of looking at works of art'. In 1760 opened evening school in Compton St., Soho, to teach drawing to 'several young men who either aimed to be artists, or to qualify themselves to be cabinet or ornamental furniture

makers'. Elected A.R.A. 1773, went to Italy to study art 1775. On his return was engaged by Horace Walpole at Strawberry Hill, where he designed a cabinet and stand in the Gothic style. (*See* CABINETS, Fig. 48.) Appointed 'Teacher' of Perspective at the Academy, 1788: and frequently exhibited there. A portfolio of his sketches of ancient furniture, etc., is in the V. and A. Mus.

ELLIOTT, CHARLES (b. 1752). Upholsterer and cabinetmaker of 97, New Bond St. Supplied furniture for the royal palaces 1783–1810, and was paid a regular salary for carrying out extensive repairs. A bill of the firm is extant at Langleys, Essex; much of the furniture, chiefly of inlaid satinwood, supplied June, 1797, to Feb., 1798, still exists. The bill is endorsed 'part of the furniture of drawing-room besides this, the stoves in both rooms, chairs and tables in the green drawingroom, window curtains and carpets in do, girandoles, bronze figures and two pier glasses'. Other items are '2 satinwood commodes neatly cross-banded', and 'a pair of oval satinwood tables on claws cross-banded and varnished'. Bedroom furniture made *en suite* for the house may also be attributed to Elliott. Nemmich writes (1807) that 'Elliott & Co. and France are the Royal upholsterers. These two firms, together with the undertakers, made arrangements for Nelson's funeral' (*Neueste Reise durch England, Schottland und Irland*). William Francis, Elliott's brother-in-law, made a partner in 1809, later took over the business at 104, New Bond St.

ENSAR, GEORGE. See TURNERS AND TURNING.

FARNBROUGH, WILLIAM. See BOROUGH, JOHN.

FENTHAM, THOMAS. 'Carver, Gilder and picture frame maker' recorded in directories 1783–96 at 'No. 52 opposite Old Round Court, Strand'. From 1802–11 at 136, Strand. His trade-label, behind a mirror in the neo-classic style at 10, Downing St., announces that he 'sells all sorts of picture, print and looking-glass frames. . . . Various sorts of dressing glasses, rich girandoles and green and blue Venetian Window blinds.' Another label (Heal Coll.) adds 'Glass Grinder' to his activities.

FERGUSON, JOHN. Shopkeeper or cabinet-maker who sent account in 1690 for 'a very large fine japan looking glass and frame, table and stands bought by her Majesty's command'. In 1686 Mary Ferguson petitioned for delivery of 'white wood boxes, Tunbridge deskes' which had been sent by her to Holland to be lacquered (*Calendar of Treasury Books*, Dec. 8, 1686).

FLAXMAN, JOHN (1755–1826). Celebrated sculptor and draughtsman. When aged about twenty joined Josiah Wedgwood and designed wax models for classical friezes and portrait medallions in Wedgwood ware. Wedgwood writes to Bentley (July, 1775), 'suppose you were to employ Mr Flaxman to model some figures. They would do for Tablets, Vases, inlaying, etc.' The suggestion was acted on, and Flaxman's first bill to Wedgwood is dated in that year. Later, Flaxman was employed on many of the more celebrated groups produced at Etruria; but designs for cameo plaques, sometimes found on late 18th-century commodes and secretaires, were generally by lesser men. (*See* WEDGWOOD, JOSIAH.)

FORT, ALEXANDER. Master joiner employed at royal palaces in William III's reign. Payment to him is entered in Kensington Palace paybook (1691) for frame for marble table and in royal tradesmen's accounts (Lord Chamberlain's Office, 1689) for 'a carved walnuttree table to set flowers on'.

FRANCE, WILLIAM (ALSO **BECKWITH AND FRANCE**) of Long Acre, Cabinet-maker. His name appears among the royal tradesmen in 1765, and he was also employed by the first Lord Mansfield at Kenwood and Bloomsbury Square, between 1768–71. He was responsible for most of the furniture at Kenwood, and, although Chippendale was paid £340 for 'French plate glass' for the 'mirrors in recesses' in the library, the frames were made by France. The glass was to be delivered within three months, and, when it was not forthcoming, a first instalment of £170 was paid by Lord Mansfield to France, who guaranteed that it should be returned if Chippendale failed to carry out his contract (*Architecture of Robert and James Adam*, A. T. Bolton, 1922). The glass was delivered within three months, when Thomas Chippendale Junior and France signed a receipt for the second instalment.

Although the contents of Kenwood have been dispersed, the pier glasses between the windows in the library are still in position and, with much of the other furniture supplied by France, can be identified in his bills, which range from '8 Cabriole Elbow chairs . . . covered with damask' and '2 very elegant screens' (still on either side of the fireplace)—clumsy versions of the rococo—to furniture in the neo-classic taste, such as two mirror frames 'all enriched with the most delicate Antique Ornaments and Arches of light ornaments'. 'A large mahogany reading stand', for which he charged in 1770, is now in the V. and A. Mus. (*see* TABLES, ARTISTS' and READING, Fig. 5).

He succeeded W. Vile (*q.v.*) as cabinet-maker to the crown in 1764 (Lord Chamberlain L.C. 5/57); was apparently in partnership with John Bradburn (*q.v.*) in 1765 and in 1774 he was referred to as 'the late William France'. The firm of France and Beckwith continued to be employed by the crown until early in the 19th century. After the death of William, Edward France, described as an upholder, was entered in contemporary directories as at 101, St Martin's Lane, and in 1787 France was in partnership with Samuel Beckwith. Among the subscribers to Sheraton's *Drawing Book* (1791) was 'France, Cabinet-Maker to his Majesty, St Martin's Lane'. In that year France and Beckwith were paid for 'a large mahogany sideboard, a pedestal at each end', and several tables, under the heading 'work done by Order of the Lord Chamberlain's Office for his Majesty's Service'. The firm supplied the Earl of Verulam with 'a neat mahogany work table' in 1795, and in 1799 'three cornices over curtains, richly carved and gilt' for the great saloon in the 'Queen's House in the Park' (Buckingham Palace).

GAIGNEUR, LOUIS LE. French cabinet-maker who opened a 'buhl factory' in 1815 at 19, Queen St., Edgware Rd, and supplied a 'buhl library table' for Carlton House in the same year at a cost of £250.

GATES, WILLIAM. Cabinet-maker who succeeded John Bradburn (*q.v.*) as tradesman to the Great Wardrobe; his warrant of appointment is dated 1777. His name is often recorded in royal accounts between 1777–83. He appears to have specialised in inlaid furniture; for examples which can be assigned to him *see* COMMODES, Figs. 23 and 24. A key which locks the pair has a bronze bow cast with the Prince of Wales's plume, crown and motto. These specimens prove that Gates was one of the most accomplished makers of marquetry furniture in neo-classic style. For first quarter of 1783 he was in partnership with Benjamin Parran (*q.v.*).

GAUBERT, GUILLAUME. Of Panton St., 'maker of ornamental furniture'. He claimed £1,133 19s. 8d. for ornaments at Carlton House in 1795. M. J.

GERN—. Cabinet-maker of Newcastle House, St John's Square, Clerkenwell. Abraham Roentgen the elder (*q.v.*) was employed by him when he came to England c. 1731, and in 1756 he sent over one of his assistants to Gern 'to perfect himself'.

GIBBONS, GRINLING (1648–1721). Carver and designer; born at Rotterdam (possibly trained there in the workshop of Artus Quellin, the sculptor) but, according to Thomas Murray (a contemporary portrait painter), 'of English parents' and 'came into England about nineteen years of age'. Nothing is known for certain of his training and early years. An entry by John Evelyn in his diary, Jan. 18, 1671, describes how he discovered the young man, in a 'solitary thatched house' near Deptford, at work on a reproduction in wood of a *Crucifixion* by Tintoretto, including a frame that he thought already showed the carver's particular bent and genius, 'there being nothing in Nature so tender and delicate as the flowers and festoons about it, and yet the worke was very strong'. This carving (which is probably identical with one in the possession of the Earl of Stamford) Evelyn endeavoured to induce the King and Queen to buy, but failed; another carving, the *Stoning of Stephen*, is now in the V. and A. Mus. It was through Lely and Evelyn that Gibbons was brought to the notice of Hugh May, the architect, who gave him his first commissions, notably the carving in the Chapel Royal, Windsor Castle (c. 1680); and Wren too soon availed himself of Gibbons' remarkable powers as a wood carver. Drops of fruit and flowers, coarsely rendered, were used in mural schemes in Holland and had been employed by Inigo Jones; while carvings in wood from the workshop of Artus Quellin in Antwerp foreshadow Gibbons in handling. He gave to the motives hitherto employed an 'airy lightness' and vastly enlarged the naturalistic repertory, drawing upon the vegetable world, the human form and wrought objects. Extraordinary dexterity of handling distinguishes his schemes of mural decoration in lime or pear wood on large-panelled and bolection-moulded wainscoting, of which the saloon at Petworth, Sussex, is the outstanding example.

The only piece of secular furniture that can be identified as by Gibbons on documentary evidence is 'a table of walnut tree curiously vein'd and vernish'd standing on a frame of lime-tree, incomparably carved with 4 Angels, flowers and frutages' (*see* TABLES, VARIOUS, Fig. 11), which Evelyn records in his MS. Inventory of Wootton House, was given him by Gibbons in acknowledgement of the service Evelyn had rendered the artist by recommending him to Charles II. There can, however, be no doubt that he carved frames such as the one containing a picture of the Walpole family formerly at Strawberry Hill (*see* PICTURE FRAMES, Fig. 12). But Gibbons was the head or most prominent member of a considerable school, and much of the output traditionally assigned to him in churches, colleges and country houses has been shown to be by other carvers, whose work in some instances suffers little by comparison with his. Portugal provides an instance of the pervasive influence of Gibbons' style. In the sanctuary at Santa Cruz in Coimbra there is a carved and gilt mirror frame of Portuguese origin which might plausibly be assigned to a gifted member of his school.

Gibbons was no mere craftsman. He was also an able designer, an excellent draughtsman and an accomplished sculptor as well. Among his drawings in the library of All Souls, Oxford, are delicate pen and ink sketches for the enrichment of chimney-pieces for the Presence Chamber and a bedchamber of a royal palace (probably Whitehall, destroyed in 1696). A few of Gibbons' letters, bills and agreements survive. They show that he had a very imperfect command of the English language. On Oct. 12, 1682, he wrote to Elias Ashmole, who appears to have obtained from him three carved picture frames now in the Ashmolean Mus. (*see* PICTURE FRAMES, Figs. 11 and 12), asking him to cast his horoscope 'as I haen onder taken a consarne of great Consequens and in order theer onto sent a fackto (factor?) last monday beiand seas I would fain knouw waser I and my partners theer in Consarnd shall haen sucksess or no . . .' (MS. Ash. 243: information supplied by Dr Kurt Josten). Shortly before his death he was described in a list of craftsmen at Blenheim as 'Carver Commissioner of ye Board of Works' and his address given as Bow St., Covent Garden. (*See also* David Green, *Grinling Gibbons*, 1964, and M. Whinney and O. Miller, *English Art*, 1625–1715.)

GIBBS, JAMES (1682–1754). One of the most successful architects of his time. Many of his drawings are preserved in the Ashmolean, Oxford, including those used in his *Book of Architecture* (1728), and also some unpublished sketches for interiors and furniture, pedestals, vases, etc. Among them are several mirrors, and a chandelier for St Martin-in-the-Fields, which he had built (1721). One of his mirrors is of octagonal form; the other designs are of architectural character. At Blenheim there are a domed state bed and two mirrors from his designs. Gibbs's few drawings for furniture are in the baroque idiom and show no strong individuality.

GILBERT, JOHN. Carver, cabinet-maker and 'Upholder to his Majesty', of Great Queen St. Supplied the Mansion House (1752) with 'eight rich carved frames with glass and branches gilt with Burnish gold for the great parlour; also six brackets richly carved for the vestibule'. Bill for carving 'by order of Messrs Adams Esq. [sic],' for Lord Shelburne, in Berkeley Square (Lansdowne House) 1767–8, totals £313 4s. 3½d.; most items are for carved decoration, but among them are a gilded mirror and two 'table frames'.

GILDING, EDMUND. Chair- and cabinet-maker, Red-cross St. Employed by Alderman Hoare 1742 and 1744, and by Sir Richard Hoare, 1754 (MS. bills of Hoare family, V. and A. Mus.). The business was carried on from 1757 by his son, Francis Gilding, whose address (1760–90) is given as 113, Aldersgate St.

GILLOW, FIRM OF. Cabinet-makers. Robert Gillow, joiner, founder of the firm, moved to Lancaster from Kirkham and was made a freeman of the borough 1727–8. Records of the firm go

1. *Grinling Gibbons: pen and ink design for enrichment of a chimney-piece. (Soane Mus., London.)*

back to 1731 and show that it was then concerned with building and surveying. In 1757 Robert's son, Richard, was taken into partnership at the age of twenty-three. Two other sons, Robert and Thomas, also entered the business. About 1760 land was leased and premises were opened at 176, Oxford St. The furniture for the London branch, which was managed by Robert Junior, was for many years made at Lancaster. Entries of goods (which were for long despatched by sea to London) appear on a small scale in the Gillow books as early as 1740, and among exports sent by Robert Gillow and other merchants to Riga are a mahogany dressing chest and a 'snap table'. The firm of Gillow also carried on a flourishing trade with the West Indies.

In 1771 Gillow and Taylor were carrying on business as upholsterers and cabinet-makers, and in 1779 the style of the firm was Gillow, Robert, Richard and Thomas. In 1790 it was Robert Gillow and Co., 'upholders', and in 1811 (on the death of Richard) G. and R. Gillow and Co., merchants and cabinet-

1. *Richard Gillow.* (1734–1811.)

makers. Some years later the Gillows ceased to be connected with the business, though it was still carried on under their name.

The firm was employed by Mrs Piozzi, soon after her marriage in 1794, to refurnish Streatham Park 'in modern style, supremely elegant', but (she adds) 'not expensive'. The bills, however, after protracted negotiations, were settled for £2,070. In the same year the second Lord Palmerston, then furnishing Broadlands, assured his wife that Gillow 'thinks he can supply any quantity I may want of the vine-leaf pattern' (*i.e.* linen). P. A. Nemmich, a German visitor to London in 1807, wrote of the firm as 'the first grade salesmen and manufacturers in London; they deal extensively in home and overseas trade and maintain employees in different parts of England; their work is good and solid, though not of the first class in inventiveness and style'. The existing examples fully justify this verdict, and the series of cost books in which rough sketches are inserted show that Gillows were distinctly conservative, producing certain models some years after they had ceased to be fashionable. The books also show that they were careful to obtain the finest materials. In 1800 Richard Gillow was granted a patent for a 'telescopic dining-table' (*see* TABLES, DINING, Fig. 26). In 1822 his third son, Richard (b. 1773), bought Leighton Hall in North Lancs., from a cousin. There are a number of pieces of furniture in the house which resemble designs in the cost books, and were doubtless supplied by the firm c. 1800–10.

From the early 'nineties the firm sometimes stamped their case furniture with the name 'Gillows' or 'Gillows, Lancaster', (there are several good satinwood examples of this date so stamped at Shugborough Hall, Staffs.), and appear to have been

the only English makers to adopt this practice before Victorian times (*see* BUREAUX, Fig. 52). After 1820 most of their productions were stamped. The Lancashire connections of the firm explain the large number of clients from the northern counties whose names are recorded in the cost books. A considerable quantity of mahogany, rosewood and parcel gilt furniture supplied by Gillows between 1803–13 is at Broughton Hall, Yorks. The family were Roman Catholics, and their business was patronised by their co-religionists. (See also *Georgian Cabinet-Makers*, R. Edwards and M. Jourdain, 3rd ed., revd., 1955.)

GOLE, CORNELIUS. Cabinet-maker employed by William III and Mary; his bills among the royal accounts show that he supplied the King and Queen with several pieces of fine furniture; among them, in 1691, a carved, inlaid and lacquered table with a pair of stands to match. These, 'for her Majesty's service at Whitehall', cost £20.

GOODISON, BENJAMIN. Cabinet-maker, at the Golden Spread Eagle, Long Acre, 1727. He supplied a large quantity of mahogany and walnut furniture to the royal palaces 1727–67.

At Hampton Court Palace several pieces can be assigned to him on the evidence of the royal accounts, notably the brass octagonal lantern headed by a royal crown on the Queen's Great Staircase, which cost £138 in 1729 (*see* LANTERNS, Fig. 3). Among the new furniture supplied by Goodison for the apartments of Frederick, Prince of Wales, in 1732–3 were 'three glass sconces in carved and gilt frames, with two wrought arms each, for the Prince of Wales'. These small mirrors, carved and gilt with the Prince's plume of feathers, hang in the Prince of Wales's drawing-room. The gilt stands 'carved term fashion' (*see* STANDS, PEDESTAL, Fig. 1), which were supplied at the same time, finish in female heads supporting Ionic capitals. Among items in his accounts for the royal family are a number of mirrors, carved and gilt tables, 'frames', 'a mahogany commode chest of drawers ornamented with carving and wrought Brass handles to Do.', 1758–9, and parcel-gilt mahogany furniture.

In his will Goodison stated that the Prince of Wales was 'indebted unto me in a considerable sum of money'. Among his other patrons the most regular were the first and second Viscounts Folkestone, who bought a large quantity of furniture from him for Longford Castle, Wilts., 1737–47. He was employed exclusively for furnishing the picture gallery 1739–40, where the magnificent pedestals (*see* STANDS, PEDESTAL, Fig. 2), gilt side-tables, day-beds and stools (all upholstered with the original green damask) can be assigned to him. The disappearance of Goodison's name from the Longford Castle accounts coincides with the advent of one 'Griffiths, Cabinet-Maker' (*q.v.*), who had been his assistant.

At Holkham Hall, Norfolk, accounts include a charge by Goodison 'for a mahogany table press carv'd and gilt . . . for ye gallery', the sides being carved with ovals clasped by acanthus, which resemble those employed by W. Vile (*q.v.*). There are carved and gilt tables in the house, which may be credited to Goodison. He was employed by the fourth Earl of Cardigan for furnishing Deene Park, Northants., and Dover House, London. The accounts (1739–45) include chiefly picture frames, small items and repairs. He also enjoyed the patronage of Sarah, Duchess of Marlborough, 'who employed him in her many houses'.

Goodison was in the front rank of contemporary makers. The furniture which can be definitely attributed to him is boldly designed with the ornament large in scale and admirably executed. A favourite motif in his repertory was long opposed acanthus scrolls centring in a shell, crown or plume of feathers. His will (dated May 29, 1765) was proved in Dec., 1767. He left about £16,000 and was succeeded by his son, the younger Benjamin Goodison, and his nephew and partner, Benjamin Parran (*q.v.*).

GORDON AND TAITT, FIRM OF. Upholsterers and cabinet-makers. William Gordon was among subscribers to the *Director* (1754), and from 1770–9 the firm (Gordon and Taitt) sent in several detailed bills for furniture and repairs to the first Earl Spencer for work at Althorp, Northants., and Wimbledon; probably this firm made some of the fine mahogany furniture at Althorp. They appear in London directories as Gordon and Taitt in King St., 1768–70, and later in Little Argyle St., Golden Square. Gordon's name disappears after 1779; John Taitt, upholsterer and cabinet-maker, is at Swallow St., Piccadilly, 1779-85, and at 254, Oxford St., 1785–99. Richard Taitt, upholsterer and joiner, of Jermyn St., worked for the royal household 1793-5, and John Taitt from 1793–6.

Georgina Lady Spencer, doing up her dower house at St Albans in 1784, constantly mentioned one of the Taitts, who probably made the cabinet given her by her friends 1783–4, and now at Althorp. Chairs, settees and candlestands all of mahogany were supplied to Blair Castle, Perth (1753–6), by either William or John Gordon of Swallow St., Argyle Buildings, from whom there is a bill at the castle dated 1748.

GRANGER, HUGH. Fl. 1692–1706 at 'the Carved Angell, in Aldermanbury'. His trade-label, found on a walnut cabinet, a walnut bureau with japanned interior and two chests of drawers, veneered with olive wood and parquetry, states that he supplied 'all sorts of Fashionable Household Goods at Reasonable Rates'. Sale of his stock advertised in *Daily Courant*, Aug. 24, 1706.

GREGSON, MATHEW (1749–1824). Born in Liverpool and for many years in business as upholsterer there. In 1817 he published *History and Antiquities of the County Palatine and Duchy of Lancaster* in three folio parts, and was elected F.S.A. Prominent in developing public institutions of Liverpool. In V. and A. Mus. a satinwood urn table with painted decoration in green and yellow (W. 45–1935) is inscribed under flap in ink 'M. Gregson, Liverpool, 1790'.

GRENDEY, GILES (1693–1780). 'In St John's Square, Clerkenwell.' Member of Joiners' Company; liveryman 1729, elected master 1766. Only known bills of this maker for furniture are three for small sums made out 1732–9 to Richard Hoare, of Barn Elms. These bills show he carried out repairs and used old glass belonging to his patron for some of the mirrors; a few simple pieces of furniture are entered. His trade-label states he 'makes and sells all sorts of cabinet goods, chairs and glasses'. In the Longford Castle accounts payment is recorded (1739) of £68 to 'Greenday, chairmaker'. His name appears ('Grindey') in the London Directory, 1753. A number of richly carved chairs and stools exist, having legs similar to an upholstered chair bearing Grendey's label, and as the design is unusual, it may be inferred that they came from his

workshop. That he exported furniture on a considerable scale is suggested by an account of a fire (Aug., 1731) in which he lost goods, 'packed for exportation next morning', worth £1,000. Among the goods he sent abroad was a set of furniture (*see* COUCHES AND DAY-BEDS, Fig. 12) decorated with japan of a brilliant sealing-wax colour, which was, until 1935, in the possession of the Duke of Infantado, at the Castle of Lazcano, Spain. This consists of a day-bed (now in the V. and A. Mus.), six armchairs and twenty single chairs. Grendey's label is affixed beneath the seat rail of one of the armchairs. These pieces are decorated with finished japanned detail in gold and silver and rest on paw feet. Several other pieces with Grendey's label are known, japanned or in mahogany, dating 1745–50. The characteristic shaping of the panels and low relief carving found on mahogany examples thus authenticated justify other attributions to this maker (*e.g.* CUPBOARDS AND WARDROBES, Fig. 13). (See also *Georgian Cabinet-Makers*, R. Edwards and M. Jourdain, 3rd ed., revd., 1955.)

GRENE OR **GREENE,** FAMILY OF. Coffer-makers to the crown from about the middle of Henry VIII's reign until early in James I's. William Grene, first holder of the office was apparently succeeded in 1553 by John, and 'from 1566 to his death in 1600 Thomas, brother of John, was Royal coffer-maker'. His son John (II), d. 1608, was the last member of the family employed by the crown. During this period a large number of chairs, travelling coffers, close stools, etc., covered with velvet, cloth-of-gold and other materials and richly trimmed, were supplied to the royal household, the total cost amounting to many thousands of pounds. William Grene and John the Elder were Wardens of the Leathersellers' Co., their connection being explained by the fact that the Company controlled the manufacture of leather-covered standards and trussing coffers, and that the Grenes practised a craft very similar in technique. (See 'The Craft of the Coffer-Maker', by R. W. Symonds, *The Connoisseur*, March, 1941, pp. 100–105.)

GRIFFITHS, EDWARD. Cabinet-maker; assistant to Benjamin Goodison (*q.v.*), 1743; later set up business on his own account. Between 1746–9 supplied the fourth Earl and Countess of Cardigan with a number of inexpensive tables, picture frames, screens and boxes, being also employed to execute repairs to their furniture at Dover House, Dover St. During these years Griffiths' name occurs in accounts for furnishing Longford Castle, Wilts., for the first Lord Folkestone; entry (1747) records that £88 15s. was paid to him 'for gilding the drawing-room'. Edward Griffiths, cabinet-maker, was subscriber to *Director* (1754).

GUIBERT, PHILIP (d. 1729). Upholsterer who supplied Windsor Castle and Kensington Palace with furniture towards the end of William III's reign. In 1697 he supplied 'a couch of carved walnutree, the headboard carved with his Ma'ties cyphers and ornaments belonging to it' for £6, and in the same year 'a fine black soffa of a new fashion, filled up with fine hair, and its cushion filled up with downe, the frieze and cheeks all molded and fringed' for £16. In 1698 P. Gibbard (*sic*) petitioned for payment of £1,695 5s. 3d. due for furnishing his Majesty's bedchamber and dining-room at Windsor and his house at Hounslow and other lodgings; £1,000 was paid 'in part of his claim'. A bill at Rousham, Oxon., shows that a craftsman named Guibert, probably a relative, worked there in 1739 under William Kent.

GUMLEY, JOHN. The earliest notice of John Gumley appears in *A Collection for the Improvement of Husbandry and Trade* (Apr. 6, 1694), where the sale is advertised of 'all sorts of cabinet work, as Japan Cabinets, Indian, and English, with Looking Glasses, Tables, Stands, Chest of Drawers, Scrutores, writing Tables and dressing suits of all sorts'. There were two Gumleys, Peter and John. From the first-named the Earl of Bristol bought £29's worth of China and Japan ware in 1693. In 1705 John set up a glass house at Lambeth. Richard Steele, writing (*Spectator*, 1712) of debt of the glass trade to the 'witty and inventive Duke of Buckingham', maintained that everyone would prefer to deal 'with my diligent Friend and Neighbour Mr Gumley, for any goods to be prepared and delivered on such a day', rather than with 'that illustrious Merchant'.

Gumley took all the upper part of the New Exchange in the Strand and furnished it as a looking-glass shop, and a notice of this venture also appears in the *Lover* (Apr. 24, 1714). In 1715 Steele (the *Lover*, May 13) described Gumley's gallery over the New Exchange as 'a place where people may go and be very well entertained, whether they have or have not a good taste . . . we have arrived at such perfection in this ware, of which I am speaking, that it is not in the power of any Potentate in Europe to have so beautiful a mirror as he may purchase here for a trifle'. Other furniture was also displayed. 'In the midst of the walk are set in order a long row of rich tables, on many of which lie cabinets, inlaid or wholly made of corals, ambers, in the like Parts.' Besides this warehouse, Gumley had a house and shop in Norfolk St.

A mirror framed in glass borders, in the public dining-room at Hampton Court, has 'Gumley' carved on the gilt slip inter-secting the glass panels of one pilaster (*see* MIRRORS, Fig. 20). Gumley was in partnership with James Moore (*q.v.*) and among bills in Lord Chamberlain's office (Aug., 1714, to Michaelmas, 1715) is an entry from Gumley and Moore's account for sup-plying 'a large glass in a glass frame and ffestoon finely done with carved and gilt work £149'. Gumley is doubtless the maker of the fine mirror in the King's writing-closet at Hampton Court. The inscription 'John Gumley, 1703' is scratched on the lower part of a mirror at Chatsworth. There are two mirrors of this date in the State bedroom, about 12 feet in height; the bevelled frames are divided into sections, the joints of which are banded by glass ornaments, some of sapphire blue glass. In the tall cresting the arms of the Duke of Devonshire are worked in shaped and engraved glass in the one mirror, and the Garter star in the other. These are the mirrors referred to in Whilden's account book: '1703. Paid Mr Gumley for

1. *Gilt slip, carved with the name 'Gumley'. From a mirror at Hampton Court Palace.*

two large Looking Glasses £200. Paid Mr Chadwick for going to Chatworth with ye glasses £16.' Payment was made to Gumley and Moore in 1720 on behalf of Lord Burlington for brackets (chandeliers) and sconces supplied to Chiswick House. Gumley was paid for looking-glasses supplied to Thomas Coke (later Earl of Leicester) at Thanet House, Great Russell St., soon after his marriage to Lady Margaret Tufton in 1718.

After Gumley's death the firm was continued by his mother. The furniture supplied in 1729 by 'Mrs Elizabeth Gumley and Co.', cabinet-makers, for St James's Palace and Kensington did not meet with approval. The *Daily Journal* (Dec. 20, 1729) reports that it had been inspected by the Comptroller of the Great Wardrobe, who found the work ill done and recom-mended that the charge, which amounted to £512 12s., should be reduced to £361 10s. 6d. Finally Mrs Gumley and her partner William Turing (*q.v.*) were dismissed 'on account of their notorious impositions'.

Gumley made a fortune from his business and owned Gum-ley House, Isleworth. His daughter married William Pulteney, Earl of Bath.

HADDOCK, ELKA. Cabinet-maker. He rendered bills with small charges to General Dormer, of Rousham, Oxon. (1737), and to Lord Pembroke at Wilton House (1742–3). In 1739 made 'Sella Curulis' for Dilettante Society.

HAIG, THOMAS. Cabinet-maker and upholsterer, who had probably acted as book-keeper to James Rannie (*q.v.*), first partner of the celebrated Thomas Chippendale. Rannie died 1766, and in that year there was a sale of Chippendale's stock at 60, St Martin's Lane. In 1771 Chippendale took Haig into partnership. In June, 1770, Haig signed a receipt for £460 paid by the Earl of Pembroke and 'due from his Lordship to ye Partnership boghte of Thomas Chippendale and the late James Rannie' (Wilton House accounts). The accounts for the furnishing of Harewood House, Yorks., and Garrick's house in the Adelphi are made out to Chippendale, Haig and Co.; and among several letters from the firm to Sir Edward Knatch-bull, of Mersham Hatch, Kent (1770–8), two were written and signed by Haig. It is probable that he attended mainly to the business side of the enterprise. After Chippendale's death (1779), his eldest son, Thomas, carried on the business in part-nership with Haig until 1796, when the latter withdrew. In the Wilton accounts (1790–1) the style of the firms is Haig and Chippendale. The dates of Haig's birth and death are unknown.

HALFPENNY, W. AND **J.** Architects and designers of furniture. W. Halfpenny's first architectural work appeared in 1725. Between 1750–2 he and his son John published in parts their *New Designs* for Chinese temples, etc., with a few designs for chairs and chimneypieces with mirrors above them. The chairs have cabriole legs and Chinese railing in the back, an incongruity not found in any later trade catalogue. *Rural Architecture in the Chinese Taste* (1751–2) was a similar ven-ture. These books (with a work by Darly, *q.v.*) are the earliest known publications of the kind, but Halfpenny states that 'the Chinese manner' had been 'already introduced here with success'. In 1752 he brought out two other architectural works —one exploiting the Gothic, the other the Chinese taste. The later instalments of *New Designs* were published with 'the assistance of my son John Halfpenny'. The plates in these

1. (*Left*) *Design for a Pier Glass, from Hepplewhite's* Guide, *1788.*

2. (*Right*) *Design for a Shield-back Chair, from the same.*

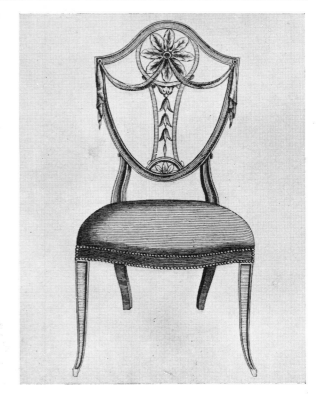

pattern-books are 'unintentionally absurd', and are castigated by contemporary satirists. In his *Ancient Masonry*, Batty Langley refers to the father as 'alias Hoare'.

HALLETT, WILLIAM (1707–81). Among the most fashionable furniture-makers of George II's reign. He was employed at Holkham, Norfolk, by Thomas Coke, first Earl of Leicester, and in the accounts for Mar., 1737, £3 5s. is shown as having been paid 'to Mr Hallett for a Pattern chair for Holkham'.

In Lord Folkestone's accounts this maker was paid considerable sums from 1737–40 and occasionally until 1767; his name also appears in accounts of the fourth Earl of Cardigan in 1745. His first address (1732–53) is Great Newport St. In 1753 he took premises in St Martin's Lane and Long Acre, next door to William Vile (*q.v.*). In 1755 Horace Walpole paid a bill to him for £73 11s. 4d., among the items being '8 black Gothic chairs'.

Edward Edwards, A.R.A. (*q.v.*), worked in his shop for three years, and while with him 'drew patterns for furniture', presumably for his master to carry out. Walpole associates Hallett's name with the Chinese taste and writes of his 'mongrel Chinese'. In an advertisement in a New York paper (1771) one of Hallett's former employees explains that he had been for eleven years his foreman.

After the sale of Cannons, the Duke of Chandos's house in Middx., in 1754, Hallett bought the site and estate and 'built himself a house on the centre vaults of the old one'. He retired in 1769. He married the daughter of James Hallett, of Dunmow, Essex, and died Dec., 1781. He is shown in a family group by Francis Hayman holding a plan of Cannons in his right hand. (See also *Georgian Cabinet-Makers*, R. Edwards and M. Jourdain, 3rd. ed., revd., 1955.)

HAUPT, GEORGE (1741–84). Celebrated Swedish cabinet-maker, partly trained in England. In petition to Swedish Guild (Feb. 10, 1770), Haupt prayed to be admitted master cabinet-maker, stating that he had been appointed court cabinet-maker in the previous July, while still a journeyman. He was in England at the time of his appointment and is known to have been employed by Sir William Chambers (*q.v.*). A small satinwood table, sold some years ago in London, was inscribed; *Cette table a été commandée et desinée par Mr Chambers Premier Architect de sa Majesté Brittanique et Exécutée par son très humble serviteur—George Haupt, Swedois London le 4 de Fevrier 1769.* This table was inlaid with festoons of laurel, with coloured marbles inset in the top. The furniture made by Haupt during his first active years in Stockholm shows traces of the influence of contemporary English style; much of it was in mahogany with or without gilt mounts. (See *George Haupt*, Böttiger, Stockholm, 1901. *Allg. Lex. Der Bil. Kstlr.*, Thieme Becker, art. *George Haupt*, G. M. Silfverstolpe, 1923. *Burl. Mag. Monograph Georgian Art*, Furniture, O. Brackett.)

HEPPLEWHITE, GEORGE (d. 1786). Cabinet-maker and designer. Apprenticed to firm of Gillow of Lancaster (*see*

3. *Design for a Sideboard, from Hepplewhite's* Guide, *1788.*

Pier Tables.

4. *Table to be placed against a wall, from Hepplewhite's* Guide.

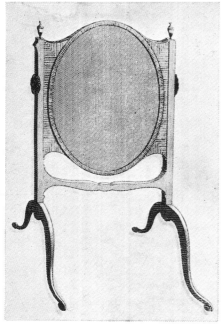

5. *Design for a Fire Screen, from the same.*

GILLOW), and subsequently came up to London, where he opened a shop in Redcross St., St Giles, Cripplegate. On his death, administration of his estate granted to his widow, Alice, who carried on the business. In 1788 appeared the *Cabinet Maker and Upholsterers' Guide*, with nearly 300 designs 'from drawings by A. Hepplewhite & Co. Cabinet-makers', a folio volume, of which new editions were published 1789 and 1794. Only considerable changes are in 3rd ed., where a section devoted to chairs has been freely revised and contains a wide selection of chairs with square backs—a form by then fashionable and also represented in Sheraton's *Drawing Book* (1791–4). Ten designs in *Cabinet-Makers' London Book of Prices* (1788) are signed 'Hepplewhite' or 'Heppelwhite'; but plates in *Guide* bear no name, and degree of Hepplewhite's personal

responsibility cannot be determined. Aim of the book is set out in the preface—'to unite elegance and utility, and blend the useful with the agreeable'. Attempt at originality is expressly disclaimed—'we designedly followed the latest or most prevailing fashion only, purposely omitting such articles, whose recommendation was mere novelty'. On the whole the designs are unimaginative, in ornament employing the familiar neo-classic repertory, and conservative, *e.g.* the cabriole leg was retained for some chairs and tables. The firm justified publication of another work on cabinet-making because 'English taste and workmanship have of late years been much sought for by surrounding nations'. Besides foreigners, the book was also intended to benefit 'our own countrymen and artisans whose distance from the metropolis makes even an imperfect knowledge of its improvement acquired with much trouble and expense'. On the designs in the *Guide* is based the popular idea of 'Hepplewhite furniture', which was not the creation of any one individual but a collective expression of prevailing taste. That Hepplewhite was no real innovator is proved by the *Cabinet-Makers' Book of Prices*, in which his designs are scarcely distinguishable from those of other contributors. The *Guide* however remains by far the best exposition of the neo-classic style rendered into vernacular form for cabinet-makers: it epitomises *fin de siècle* taste—rational, simple and, withal, extremely elegant and refined. The credit for introducing oval-, heart- and shield-shaped chair backs does not belong to Hepplewhite. He observes that one of his chairs (Pl. X in all eds. of the *Guide*) 'has been executed with good effect for the Prince of Wales' and it is possible that Hepplewhite was the first cabinet-maker to use the familiar three feathers as a decorative motive; but the name of his firm does not appear in the royal accounts. Much of the furniture based on his designs was in satinwood inlaid with various exotic or stained woods. Sheraton wrote in 1791: 'notwithstanding the late date of Hepplewhite's book, if we compare some of the designs, particularly the chairs, with the newest taste, we shall find that this work has already caught the decline, and perhaps, in a little time, will suddenly die in the disorder'; probably the alterations in the 3rd ed. are to some extent accounted for by Sheraton's strictures. It is noticeable that Hepplewhite and Co. are not among subscribers to the *Drawing Book* in which this opinion is expressed. Correspondence between existing furniture and a plate in the *Guide* is rare, though most of the designs are simple and readily reproduced. A painted armchair with three feathers in the back at Marsh Court, Hants., is virtually identical with Pl. X. How long the business was carried on is not known.

HERVE, FRANCES. Chair-maker of 32, Lower John St., Tottenham Court Rd., who worked for the Prince of Wales at Carlton House, 1783–9, and supplied upwards of £3,000 worth of furniture under the direction of Henry Holland (*q.v.*). A set of library steps bearing Hervé's label is in the V. and A. Mus. His name occurs in the Althorp accounts (1789–91) as maker of a set of furniture in *Louis Seize* style —a 'fauteuil à la Reine' and 'six cabriole back stools' (*i.e.* chairs) painted white with the carved enrichments gilt. His name appears in London directories as late as 1796.

HINTZ (OR HINTS), FREDERICK. Cabinet-maker, at the Porcupine, Newport St., probably of German origin.

Daily Post (May 22, 1738) has advertisement of 'a choice Parcel of Desks and Book-cases of mahogany, Tea-Tables, Tea chests, Tea boards, etc., all curiously made and inlaid with fine figures of Brass and Mother of Pearl', the notice concluding: 'They will be Sold at a very reasonable Rate, the Maker, Frederick Hints, Designing soon to go abroad.' This shows that Hintz practised the Boulle technique of metal inlay (*see* BRASS, INLAY OF). Labels of Frederick Hinds, Ryders Court, Leicester Fields, presumably same maker or relative, have been found on some stringed instruments dated 1740–76 (Lütgendorff, *Die Geigen-und-Lautenmacher*, 1913).

HODSON, JOHN. Upholder and cabinet-maker, Hodson's Looking Glass and Cabinet Warehouse, Frith St., Soho (1727–44). Supplied tripod table, fine carved and painted side-table, and wine-cooler for Duke of Atholl, Blair Castle, 1738, and furniture for Lord Monson, 1735 and 1741. Hodson apparently specialised in japanned and lacquered work. See 'J. Hodson and Some Cabinet-Makers at Blair Castle,' A. Coleridge, *Connoisseur*. Apr., 1963.) A bill of 1744 is receipted by P. Smagget for 'Hodson and Self'.

HODSON, ROBERT. Cabinet-maker, 'The Cabbinet in Ffrith Street, Soho'. Made for Sir Edward de Bouverie an elaborately fitted bureau of peculiar design with 'extraordinary locks . . . and plac'd it upon strong brass wheels or castors that you may more easily move it to the fire'. (Letter from Hodson to Sir Edward, Sept. 8, 1724, at Longford Castle, Wilts.)

HOLLAND, HENRY (1746–1806). Architect instrumental in introducing Graeco-Roman detail in England; enlarged Carlton House, Pall Mall, and 'improved' Woburn and Southill, Beds., and Althorp, Northants. Began work at Carlton House 1783, and held appointment of architect to the Prince of Wales. Eight carved and gilt pedestals with finely modelled terminal figures were designed by him c. 1795 for the Throne Room at Carlton House, and are now at Buckingham Palace. The Royal Collection also contains a set of mahogany and gilt settees, which are probably by Holland and are shown in a plate in Pyne's *Royal Residences* forming part of furniture of entrance hall, Carlton House.

At Southill, 1795–1800, Holland accomplished in the decoration of the interior a remarkably impressive blend of late Louis XVI and Graeco-Roman styles. Much of the furniture was supplied by Marsh and Tatham (*q.v.*) and made under Holland's supervision or from his designs, which incorporate not only classical detail from drawings made in Italy by his pupil, Tatham, but also show the influence of the French *ébéniste* Weisweiller, notably in the use of ormolu colonnettes at the corners of commodes. There are at Woburn and Althorp several pieces of furniture probably designed by him (*see also* F. B. J. Watson, *Southill: a Regency House*, 1951).

HOPE, THOMAS (1769–1831). Author and virtuoso, son of John Hope, of Amsterdam, banker and merchant; studied architecture at early age, and travelled widely, sketching architectural remains in Egypt, Sicily, Turkey, Syria and Spain. He left Holland for England at time of French occupation (1794). Here he employed his considerable fortune in collecting ancient and modern sculptures, and designing the furniture and decoration of his London house in Duchess St., Cavendish Square, and of his Surrey home, Deepdene. In his *Household Furniture and Interior Decoration* (1807) the designs carried out at Duchess St. are illustrated, and in these he shows a scholarly gift for adapting elements, Greek and Egyptian, to furniture. The novelty of the fittings and furnishings of his London house was commented on by Dance, who was of the opinion that it would 'contribute to emancipate the public taste'. *Household Furniture* was not well received by the critics, and a writer in the *Edinburgh Review* (July, 1807) condemns the articles in general as 'too bulky, massive and ponderous to be commodious for general use. . . . Let anyone look at the chairs in the Egyptian room (Plate 8) or that on Plate 22, with their enormous pediments, friezes and massive bronze ornaments and say whether

1. *Henry Holland: drawing of a stand for a Lamp. c.* 1790.

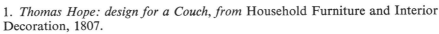

1. *Thomas Hope: design for a Couch, from* Household Furniture and Interior Decoration, 1807.

it is possible for such things to come into general use as articles of furniture till aldermen wear armour.'

Hope's designs for furniture have the interest of being 'exclusively confined in its representation to objects where effects had already been tried and had been approved of' (*Blackwood's Magazine*, Vol. X, p. 200). He found difficulty in obtaining artisans in London to carry out his designs, and after 'most laborious search' entrusted them to Decaix, a French metal-worker, and Bogaert, a wood-carver born in the Low Countries. Examples from Deepdene of furniture designed by Hope are a bookcase (*see* BOOKCASES, Fig. 28) with lion-headed supports to the upper stage and metal mounts and ornament, and tables supported on chimaeras (*see* TABLES, VARIOUS, Fig. 34). Hope was also author of the romance *Anastasius*; his furniture and collection at Deepdene remained practically undisturbed until their sale, July 18, 1917.

HUNT, PHILIP (fl. c. 1680–1730). Cabinet-maker 'at ye Looking Glas and Cabenet at East end of St Paul's Church Yard', maker (1720) of the half-tester bedstead, perhaps the finest of its kind, in the state bedroom at Erthig, Denbigh (*see* BEDS, Fig. 24). His trade-card bears the interlaced cypher of William III and Mary with royal supporters and design of a marquetry mirror and cabinet. It announces that he makes 'Cabenetts, Looking Glasses, Tables and Stands, Scretors, Chests of Drawers, and Curious inlaid Figures for any worke'.

INCE, WILLIAM, AND **MAYHEW, JOHN.** Cabinet-makers, upholsterers, partners in business. The *Public Advertiser* (Jan. 27, 1759) announced that Messrs John Mayhew, who served his time with Mr Bradshaw (*see* BRADSHAW, GEORGE SMITH) and William Ince, who served his time with the late Mr West (*see* WEST, J.), 'having taken the house of Mr Charles Smith, cabinet-maker and upholsterer, opposite Broad Street, Carnaby Market . . . begs [*sic*] leave to inform . . . [customers, etc.] . . . commands executed in the neatest taste'.

Between 1759–62 the partners brought out the *Universal System of Household Furniture*, which in its final form was a large folio, dedicated to the Duke of Marlborough, and containing about 100 plates. The name of the firm was 'Mayhew and Ince,' but the order is reversed on the title page, probably because Ince, the predominant partner, provided a large majority of the designs. The address is given as Broad Street, Golden Square, 'where every article in the several Branches treated of is executed on the most reasonable terms with the utmost neatness and punctuality'. By 1779 the partners had moved to 20 and 47, Marshall Street, Carnaby Market, and the firm is found there in directories until 1811.

The *Universal System* was, to a considerable extent, based on the *Director*, though it has far fewer designs: Ince was among the subscribers to Chippendale's work. The book was intended to appeal to a large public, and Ince and Mayhew wrote that 'In furnishing all should be with Propriety. . . . Elegance should always be joined with a peculiar neatness through the whole House, or otherwise an immense expense may be thrown away to no purpose'; their taste, however, obviously inclined to the lavish and ornate. The designs are in the rococo convention with a considerable admixture of the Gothic and Chinese. Some are obvious plagiarisms from Chippendale, especially those for chair-backs. Although the preface states that the directions for executing the various articles are given, the notes contain little explanation. Of varieties of furniture not included in the *Director*, tripod tables are the most important. There is a metal-work section at the end of the book, which includes a staircase railing, grates and brackets for lanthorns. The notes are in French and English, showing that the authors hoped to obtain foreign custom, and a trade-card of the firm announces that they have 'an assortment of French furniture consigned from Paris'. It is stated that a candlestand 'has gained great applause in execution', and a state bed (Pl. XXXII, for which the original drawing by Ince in the V. and A. Mus.

is the only one of the firm known) 'may be esteemed among the best in England'. A large canopied sofa is stated to have been made for Lady Fludyer, wife of Sir Samuel Fludyer, Lord Mayor of London, 1761. Writing at the end of the century, Sheraton pronounced the *Universal System* 'to have been a book of merit in its day, though much inferior to Chippendale's'. He referred to it as 'Ince's book'. The partners contributed some designs to *Household Furniture . . . for the Year 1760*, identifiable by comparison with plates in the *Universal System*.

In 1768 Lady Shelburne, then engaged in furnishing Shelburne (later Lansdowne) House, records a visit to 'Mayhew and Inch's [*sic*] where is some beautiful cabinet work'. She ordered 'two pretty glass cases for one of the rooms in my apartments, which, though they are only deal, and to be painted white, he charges £50 for'. In Oct., 1769, the firm supplied the Earl of Coventry with 6 fine carved and gilt 'Large Antique Elbow chairs' and a 'Large Architect Pier Frame, fluted richly carv'd . . . gilt in the very best Double Burnished Gold' for the Tapestry Room at Croome Court (now in the Metropolitan Mus.). The partners were employed by the second Viscount Palmerston for furnishing his town house in Hanover Square. He wrote to his wife that Ince had been altering the sofa in her dressing-room and that she might have 8 'new painted' chairs of his to match it for two guineas or perhaps somewhat less. In Nov., 1796, Palmerston received an additional account from Ince for £700. Before settling it he complained to Lady Palmerston, who replied that she was 'much surprised and truly sorry to hear that Ince persists in making out such a bill . . . having so long witheld the particulars of his account'.

Mrs Piozzi in a letter dated 1802 mentions that she is expec-

1. *Ince and Mayhew: design for a lady's Dressing-Table, from the* Universal System, *1759-63.*

ting 'furniture . . . from Mayhew and Ince, to decorate pretty Brynbella', her house near Flint. A mahogany china cabinet, now in the Copenhagen Mus., bears Ince and Mayhew's label, printed in French and English (*see* CABINETS, Fig. 36). For a mahogany stool of unusual form which closely follows a design in the *Universal System*, *see* STOOLS, Fig. 44.

On June 7, 1792, the Westminster Fire Office ordered 18 new chairs for the directors and one for the chairman. On June 13, 1793, they instructed the clerk to complain of the charge.

2. *Two designs for Parlour Chairs, from the* Universal System.

3. *Design for a lady's 'Toiletta,' or draped dressing-table and mirror, from the same work.*

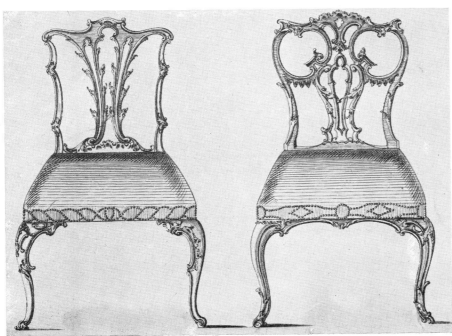

1. *Thomas Johnson: design for a Candle-stand*, 1758.

Among the bills discharged (June 20, 1793) was 'Mayhew and Ince—Chairs etc. £102 9s. –d.'. At the premises of the Fire Office, 27, King Street, Covent Garden, there are now two armchairs and 22 single chairs, of which total 18 were supplied by Ince and Mayhew in 1793, while 6 were supplied 20 years later by the same firm. The chairs are of mahogany, the backs being carved in openwork with the Prince of Wales's feathers above a portcullis, the badge of the office (founded 1717).

John Mayhew and William Ince were directors at various dates between 1761–98. Mayhew was in partnership with Samuel Norman (*q.v.*) in 1758.

JENSEN, GERREIT (GERRIT) (fl. c. 1680–1715). Cabinet-maker to the royal household, whose activities extend from the reign of Charles II to the end of Queen Anne's. Of Dutch or Flemish origin, his name is often found anglicised to Garret Johnson in contemporary records. Phillips (*Annals of the Joiners' Company*) quotes instances of 'Gerrard' or 'Garrett' Johnson being fined by this Company in the late 17th century.

Jensen's first bill in the royal household accounts is dated 1680, and gives particulars of 'a cabinet and frame table-stands and glass' sent as a gift to the Emperor of Morocco. He was one of the London craftsmen engaged for the fitting and decoration of Chatsworth, Derbys., as rebuilt by the first Duke of Devonshire, and he appears as having provided the glass for the south and east fronts between 1688–98. He was also paid in 1692 for japanning the closet. The 'Japan closet' (now called the State sitting-room) was wainscoted with 'hollow burnt Japan' (incised lacquer) intersected by mirror glass at each corner. Jensen was paid for 'framing moulding, and cutting of the Japan, and joyning it into panels'. The closet was dismantled in 1700, but the sides of two chests in the state drawing-room japanned with peacocks and other birds are probably survivors of this decoration. Jensen's name (anglicised to Johnson) appears in the *Diary* of the first Earl of Bristol; he was paid for a black set of table and stands.

From the royal household accounts and inventories it can be gathered that Jensen's furniture was decorated with marquetry or japan, and in some instances inlaid with metal; and that he supplied mirrors framed in ebony, olivewood and japan. Two pieces at Windsor Castle, of William III's reign and enriched with 'fine' or arabesque marquetry, may be attributed to Jensen, a writing-table and a cabinet with glass doors (*see* TABLES, LIBRARY AND WRITING, Fig. 6, and CABINETS, Fig. 14). The royal household accounts in William III's reign show that Jensen supplied mirrors and glass panels for Hampton Court. A mirror there can be assigned to Jensen on the evidence of his bill (1699) for 'a pannel of glass 13 feet long with a glass in it of 52 inches with a Crown and cypher in glass and other ornaments' (*see* MIRRORS, Fig. 21).

An inventory of goods at Kensington (1697) mentions tables, looking-glasses, and stands, the frames all inlaid with metal, which were 'bespoke by the Queen and came in after her death from Mr Johnson'. Other sets and a pair of folding writing-tables all of 'Wallnott tree inlaid with white' were also supplied by Jensen. A desk-table at Windsor Castle, inlaid with metal and bearing an ebony plaque inlaid with the cypher W.M., is doubtless the 'fine writing-desk table inlaid with metall'. supplied by Jensen in 1695; he seems to have been the only craftsman of the period in England employing the Boulle technique of metal inlay.

A similar table at Boughton, Northants., made for the first Duke of Montagu (1638–1709), and another at Wilton House, Wilts., with gilt Ionic capitals can also be assigned to Jensen. There is an entry in his accounts for 1699–1700 for sending a servant to 'pollish and whiten a Beuro inlaid with mettal' Several existing pieces are decorated with 'fine' or arabesque marquetry, which is very accomplished from the technical standpoint, while the design is obviously indebted to French models. Jensen was responsible for the glasses and framework of the overmantel mirrors in Queen Mary's Gallery at Kensington, Grinling Gibbons being paid for the carving.

From the building accounts of the royal palaces in the reign of William and Mary it is evident that Jensen had the monopoly of supplying fixed mirrors over the chimneypieces and in the window piers. He is referred to as 'cabinett-maker and glasse-seller' in a document reappointing him cabinet-maker to the crown. At Drayton House there are a table and pair of stands inlaid with metal in his manner, and (on the analogy of the Japan Closet at Chatsworth) he may be held responsible for a small japanned room on the ground floor. A table at Deene Park with similar inlay may also be assigned to him. Jensen also worked at Burghley House, where he was paid £8 15s. for a cabinet in 1682, and £50 in 1685. All these houses are in Northants.

In Queen Anne's reign the furniture supplied by Jensen is, for the most part, less elaborate, japanning and gilding superseding marquetry as decoration. For the Queen's drawing-room at St James's he provided gilt tables, stands and mirrors at a cost of £450. His will (Aug. 15, 1715) shows he had two houses and a warehouse in St Martin's Lane, and a notice in the *Daily Courant* earlier in that year stated that he had 'left off trade'. (See also *Georgian Cabinet-Makers*, R. Edwards and M. Jourdain, 3rd, ed., revd., 1955.)

JOHNSON, THOMAS. Carver and designer of furniture. His name, with the address Grafton St., Soho, appears in

1. *William Jones: design for a Console-Table, from the* Gentlemen's or Builders Companion, 1739.

Mortimer's *Universal Director* (1763), where he is described as 'Carver, Teacher of Drawing and Modelling and author of a book of Designs for Chimney pieces and other oranaments; and of several other pieces'. His first book of designs, *Twelve Girandoles* (1755), gives his address as Queen St., near Seven Dials. A larger work for carvers' pieces, frames, candlestands, candelabra, tables and lanterns, was issued in monthly parts 1756-8, with no title, and in a second edition as *One Hundred and Fifty New Designs* in 1761. The book is dedicated to Lord Blakeney, 'Grand President of the Antigallican Association'. Johnson, who describes himself as 'a truly antigallic spirit'. touched the climax of fantasy in his designs. He claimed that the 150 plates 'may all be performed by a master of his art', making the assertion with greater confidence as he is well satisfied that he can execute them himself. In some he shows a liking for animal motives and naturalistic treatment of foliage, as in the girandole (Pl. LV in his *New Designs*, 1761), the original of a pair of mirrors at Corsham, Wilts. He was a spirited draughtsman with a fertile imagination and considerable powers of composition in the full rococo style, but several of his designs are impracticable without modification or 'sleighting' as Chippendale terms it (e.g. Pls. 25 and 33). But he was also a craftsman, and the small quantity of carving that can be confidently assigned to him is lively and accomplished. (For further attributions and a highly eulogistic estimate of Johnson as carver and designer, see *Thomas Johnson and English Rococo*, Helena Hayward, 1964.)

JONES. 'Mr Jones, Upholsterer', supplied 1737-8 some important furniture (chairs, settees and couches) to the first Lord Leicester at Holkham, Norfolk. No other details of this maker known.

JONES, INIGO (1573–1652). This famous architect, who introduced the true principles of classic design into England (the Banqueting House, Whitehall, was completed 1622), was, according to Vertue, in his youth 'put apprentice to a joiner in Paul's Churchyard'. No designs for furniture unquestionably by him are known, but in the Palladian revival of the early 18th century elements in the architectural style of Jones and his pupil, John Webb (1611–72), were adapted for cabinets, bookcases and other furniture.

JONES, WILLIAM (d. 1757). In 1739, when living in King St., Golden Square, published the *Gentlemens or Builders Companion*, including 20 designs of side-tables (Fig. 1) and pier glasses. They are representative of furniture designed for early Georgian houses by architects, while some tables show contemporary French influence, notably that of N. Pineau. Jones's book has no text except a description of the plates.

KAUFFMANN, ANGELICA (1741–1807). Artist, born at Coire, Switzerland; showed a precocious talent for painting and travelled in various Italian cities in search of commissions, many well-known English people being among her sitters. She settled in London c. 1766, married a valet (1767), elected R.A. (1768); in 1781 she married A. Zucchi (*q.v.*), and departed with him for Italy, 1782. She was employed by the Adam brothers, and ceiling and mural decorations by her are to be found in several of their houses. Sir John Soane, in a MS. note, recorded that Robert Adam patronised Angelica Kauffmann and Zucchi on all occasions. Joseph Moser, a contemporary artist, writes that 'in the elegant manufactures of London, Birmingham, etc.' the prints from her picture of Sterne's Maria 'assumed an incalculable variety of forms and dimensions, and were transferred to numerous articles of all sorts and sizes, from a watch case to a tea-waiter'. Many of the painted medallions on contemporary furniture were undoubtedly inspired by her works, and a few of high quality may be from her hand (*see* COMMODES, Fig. 26), but there is no documentary evidence.

KENT, WILLIAM (1686–1748). Architect, painter, landscape-gardener and designer of decoration and furniture.

1. *A design for a Table, by William Kent, published by J. Vardy, 1744.*

He was sent to Italy in 1709 by a group of friends to study painting, and supported by them until his return to England in 1719. He became acquainted with many English noblemen, including Thomas Coke (afterwards Earl of Leicester) and Richard, third Earl of Burlington, 'the Apollo of the Arts', who became his constant friend and employer. It was as a decorative painter at Kensington Palace, and at Houghton and Holkham Halls, Norfolk, that he made his reputation. His decorative paintings and designs for furniture for Houghton date from c. 1726–30. In the houses in which he decorated the interiors furniture forms part of a unified scheme. His designs cover a wide range of objects, for he was 'not only consulted for furniture, glasses, tables, chairs, etc., but for plate, for a barge, for a cradle' (Horace Walpole, *Anecdotes of Painting*). Some examples of furniture designed by Kent are figured in Vardy's *Some Designs of Mr Inigo Jones and Mr Kent* (1744), and these, together with existing pieces at Houghton, Holkham, Raynham, Rousham, and Wilton show his highly individual style. In his work enrichments and carved mouldings are large in scale, and acanthus foliations, masks and demi-figures are freely used. The structure is over-weighted with ornament—often, writes Walpole, 'immeasurably ponderous' —but Kent's furniture was designed in relation to its environment and the effect of the whole is 'audacious, splendid, sumptuous and of finished technique, and as these qualities were in demand, Kent was supreme in his own generation'. (*See also* W. Kent, *Designs of Inigo Jones*, 1727; J. Vardy, *Some Designs of Mr Inigo Jones and Mr Kent*, 1744; M. Jourdain, *The Work of William Kent*, 1948.)

LANE, JOHN. Sheraton (*Drawing Book*, 1791–4) writes that knife-cases, which he illustrates, 'are not made in regular cabinet shops' but are 'executed in the best taste by one who makes it his main business, *i.e.* John Lane, No. 44 St Martin-le-Grand, London'.

LANGLEY, BATTY (1696–1751) AND **THOMAS** (b. 1702). The elder brother was architect, designer, etc., the younger mainly engraver and draughtsman. In 1740 they pub-

lished the *City and Country Builder's and Workman's Treasury of Designs*, which went through four editions, and, among its 400 plates, includes 25 designs for furniture. Described as in 'the French manner', they are obviously based on the engravings of Berain, Marot and A. C. Boule. A console-table (Fig. 1) and five others 'for Rooms of State' by Thomas are transcripts from Nicholas Pineau, while a dressing-table (in the 1750 ed.) is taken from a German designer, J. J. Shübler

2. *A design for a Chair, by William Kent, from the same source.*

1. *Console-Table, with alternative legs and stretchers, designed by Thomas Langley*, 1739.

(*Connoisseur*, Sept., 1943, p. 36), and a clock from a design by J. F. Lauch. B. Langley's *Ancient Architecture Restored* (1742), though containing no furniture designs, was the first attempt to introduce the Gothic style into ordinary domestic interiors. Horace Walpole pronounced him a 'barbarous architect'. A pair of carved and gilt side-tables at The Vyne, Hants, closely correspond with a plate in the *Treasury* (*see* J. Lees-Milne, 'John Chute at the Vyne', *Connoisseur*, June, 1960, and P. Ward-Jackson, *English Furniture Designs of the 18th Century*, 1958).

LANGLOIS, PETER (PIERRE ELOI). B. 1738 in Paris, probably of same family as French *ébénistes* 'les sieurs Langlois' mentioned in *Livre Commode* (1692) as imitating *'fort bien les meubles de la Chine'* (*Chinoiserie*, H. Honour, 1961, p. 60). He had a fashionable and distinguished clientèle. Supplied 'a large inlaid commode table' (£78) for Woburn Abbey, Beds., 1760; 'two commodes and two coins' (encognures) for Strawberry Hill, Middx., 1763, and also an inlaid writing box. Caroline, Lady Holland, proposed in same year to give her sister, Lady Louisa Connolly, 'a commode table, bureau or *coins*', because 'I hear she likes L'Angley's inlaid things . . . really they are lovely and finish a room so well' (*Correspondence of Emily, Duchess of Leinster*, ed. B. Fitzgerald, Vol. I, 1949). 'A table inlaid woods by L'anglois' bought by first Duchess of Northumberland, probably a card table with inlaid top at Syon House, Middx. George Montague (1766) thought it 'a burning shame' that Langlois had left 'three parts of the japan' entrusted to him by John Chute of The Vyne lying about in his house. Langlois supplied a marquetry commode for Earl of Coventry, Croome Court, Worcs., 1764.

LA PIERRE, FRANCIS (d. 1717). French upholsterer, Pall Mall, who supplied hangings, carpet and beds for the Great Wardrobe, 1690–6. In Sept., 1697, paid £102 (an instalment of a total of £470) for a state bed for Chatsworth, Derbys., to which he also supplied velvets and brocades. In that year he was prosecuted as an enemy alien (*Calendar of Treasury Papers*, 1697–1701/02, p. 49).

LE GAIGNEUR, L. C. *See* BUHL.

LEVERTON, THOMAS (1749–1824). Architect, born at Woodford, Essex, son of a builder. Commissions included many houses in Bedford Square, notably No. 1, and Woodhall Park, Herts., which he built for Sir Thomas Rumbold from plans drawn up in 1777. 'The slender grace of his furniture matches the lively treatment of the rooms.' Though documentary evidence is lacking, some of the furniture formerly in the house may be assigned to Leverton as designer on the evidence of style. (See *Country Life*, Apr. 26, 1930, pp. 611–13, and SIDEBOARDS, Fig. 16; STANDS, PEDESTAL, Fig. 11; and TABLES, SIDE-, Fig. 50.)

LEWGAR, JOHN. Coffer-maker to crown under James I. Supplied (1623–4) at cost of 50s. 'one large flatt coffer covered with hide leather lyned wth bayes for the carriage of his higs [Charles, Prince of Wales] silver bathine sestome' (cistern).

LIGHTOLLER, THOMAS. Architect, carver and designer; collaborated with Morris and Halfpenny (*q.v.*) in *Modern Builder's Assistant* (1742). About this date started to supervise alterations at Burton Constable, Yorks., for William Constable. Responsible for much of the decoration there, and his drawings exist for several pieces of furniture, notably two gilt side-tables with fluted legs and frieze in staircase hall; apparently designed c. 1766, they show a curious anticipation of style associated with the Regency.

LINNELL, JAMES (1760–1836). 2 Streatham St., Bloomsbury; carver, gilder, picture-frame maker and print seller, father of John, the well-known artist.

LINNELL, JOHN (d. 1796). 28, Berkeley Square; carver, cabinet-maker and designer, according to Charles Heathcote Tatham, 'in the first line of his profession', a statement borne out by surviving particulars of his clients.

The V. and A. Mus. has a large collection of Linnell's original drawings, the most important, entitled 'A miscellaneous collection of original designs made and for the most part executed during an extensive practice of many years in the first line of his profession by John Linnell, upholsterer, carver and cabinet-maker'—a selection made by Tatham and intended for publication.

Of same family as William Linnell (*q.v.*) and probably as James (*q.v.*), father of the artist, Linnell's designs include a large variety of pieces of furniture, some of which are coloured; many of a later group (1773–81), chiefly mirror frames, bear his clients' names.

In 1763 Linnell began providing furniture and upholstery for Shardeloes, Bucks., and by the end of that year the bill amounted to £1,056. Bills of the next three years suggest that he almost completely refurnished Shardeloes. A number of items have been identified, *i.e.* a pair of mirrors (*see* MIRRORS, Fig 67), a set of sofas and 'French' chairs (1768) 'gilt in parts in Burnish gold', and the dining-room sideboards and pedestals; the latter with their urns 'like Mr Child's' closely resembling those at Osterley, where Linnell was employed. A rococo marble chimneypiece and overmantel mirror for that house (now in the V. and A. Mus.) is from his design, while on the evidence of another drawing he was probably also responsible for the lyre-back satinwood chairs in the library. Accounts there show he supplied other furniture.

He was an admirable draughtsman, and his designs range in style from accomplished versions of the rococo and Chinese tastes, through a skilful blend of rococo and neo-classic detail,

 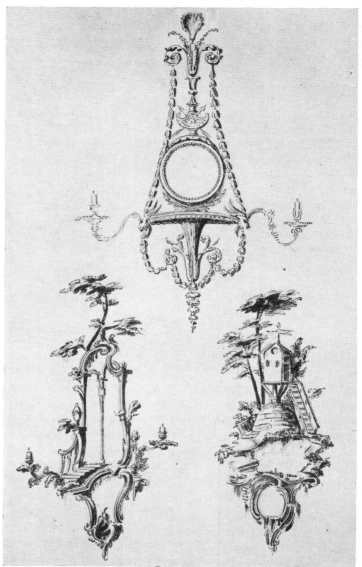

1. *Design for a Mirror, from an original drawing by John Linnell. c. 1755. (V. & A. Mus.)* 2. *Design for three Wall-lights by John Linnell; the right-hand lower drawing signed and dated 1763; the left-hand drawing is about the same date; the upper is in classical style. (V. & A. Mus.)*

to a duller interpretation of the classical revival. He had a large and fashionable clientèle, including the Duke of Cumberland, the Duchess of Ancaster, the Earl of Carlisle, Lady Salisbury, Lord Cadogan and W. Blathwayt, of Dyrham Park, Glos. Entries of payments to John Linnell occur in the accounts of Sir William Lee, of Hartwell, Bucks. His executors carried out part of the furnishing of Ammerdown, Somerset, for Samuel Joliffe in 1795. They supplied the more important furniture, including two side-tables in the dining-room, 'gilt in burnished gold in the best manner'. Though controlling a large business, Linnell produced his own designs.

LINNELL, WILLIAM (d. 1763). Carver and upholsterer. In bills rendered 1739–52 to Richard Hoare, first baronet, of Barn Elms, Surrey, which total nearly £1,100, describes himself as carver, and several of most important items are for picture and mirror frames. Besides carving he also supplied tables and chairs. One bill includes a note on 'the exact prime cost of the chairs, and what they stand me in per chair'. The

cost of each was £4 7s., excluding the coverings (apparently supplied by Hoare).

Between 1749–58 supplied a considerable quantity of furniture to William Drake, of Shardeloes, Bucks. It was probably this William Linnell who was employed by Mrs Montague, the 'Queen of the blues', in 1752. When decorating a house in Hill Street, she wrote to her cousin, Gilbert West, that 'if Mr Linnell designs to gild the bird he sent me in a drawing of, it will look like the sign of an eagle at a laceman's door. If japanned in proper colours, it will resemble a bird only in colour, for in shape it is like a horse.' A letter of Nov. 16, 1752, shows she was disturbed by the cost of Linnell's decorations, as Richard Hoare had been. Apparently the charges were for the decoration of a japanned room and its contents. Among them are said to have been a japanned cabinet and writing-table now at Came House, Dorset. (See *Chinoiserie*, Hugh Honour, 1961, p. 138.)

'William Linnell, carver', appears in the *Universal Director* (1763). After his death his 'large and genuine stock in trade at his late House and Ware rooms in Berkeley Square' was sold by auction. Among many varieties of furniture were included 'magnificent large Pier and other glasses . . . Derbyshire and Italian marble tables, mahogany chairs and settees, Dressing, Dining and card tables, commodes'. The house was No. 28, a large building in the north-east corner of the square. He was succeeded at his address by John Linnell (q.v.).

LOCK, MATTHIAS (fl. c. 1740–69). Carver and designer, of whose life no particulars known; accomplished ornamentalist and pioneer in introduction of English rococo style. Between 1740–69 published 11 books of designs, two in collaboration with H. Copland (q.v.), five being second editions. A gifted draughtsman, as an exponent of English versions of French *rocaille*, with Copland monopolised this field for a decade before publication of Chippendale's *Director*. In the V. and A. Mus. a large number of drawings by Lock c. 1740–65, for mirrors, chairs, pier-tables, girandoles, etc., some tinted. The majority not inscribed, but on seven sketches are memoranda of charges for carving (1742–4), and on some notes recording days spent by Lock and assistants. These annotated sketches allow identification of pieces of furniture supplied to second Earl Poulett, of Hinton House, Somerset, c. 1745–50, including carved and gilt mirror frame (now in V. and A. Mus.), side-table *en suite*; also pair of stands and side-table still at Hinton House. Other clients known from a diary are Lord Holderness, Mr Bradshaw—perhaps William Bradshaw (q.v.) and the Earl of Northumberland. A side-table c. 1740, in baroque style, formerly at Ditchley, Oxon., corresponds with a sketch in Lock album (see SIDEBOARDS, Fig. 3). There is a gap in Lock's publications between 1752–68. A group of Lock's drawings in the Museum Collection (bought from his grandson, 1862) are intermingled with seven original drawings for Chippendale's *Director*, and others by Chippendale or from his workshop, which suggests that during this period Lock was employed by Chippendale; but evidence not conclusive. *The New Book of Pier Frames* (1769) has first engraved designs for furniture of neo-classic revival: designs lack spontaneity and distinction of Lock's rococo drawings. In 1746 at Nottingham Court, Castle St., Long Acre; in 1752 near ye Swan, Tottenham Court Rd. (See also *Georgian Cabinet-Makers*, and *The Creators of the Chippendale Style*, Met. Mus. Studies, May, 1929; and J. F. Hayward, 'Furniture . . . by Matthias Lock for Hinton House, Som.,' *The Connoisseur*.)

McLEAN, JOHN. Cabinet-maker, Little Newport St., Leicester Square (1774), and as McLean and Son, Upper Terrace, Tottenham Court Rd., and 34, Marylebone St. (1793); also at No. 58 (1809–14). Trade card indicates that he specialised in 'elegant Parisian furniture'. For secretaire bearing his label *see* BUREAUX, Fig. 55. Entered among master cabinet-makers, Sheraton's *Cabinet Dictionary* (1803), where design for work-table said to be 'taken from one executed by Mr Mclean in Marylebone Street . . . who finishes these small articles in the neatest manner'. In 1806–7 he furnished Middleton Park, Oxon., for Earl of Jersey throughout and provided great quantity of carpets and curtains; his bill amounted to £4,793 11s. 10d. His detailed accounts are at Osterley Park. After 1814, succeeded by William McLean, probably the 'son' in the former style of the firm. Several tables and secretaires bear firm's label with 58, Marylebone St. address.

MANWARING, ROBERT. Designer, cabinet- and chair-maker, Haymarket. In 1765 published *The Cabinet and Chair-Maker's Real Friend and Companion*, containing upwards of 100 designs for chairs, stools and garden seats 'calculated for all People in different stations of life' (2nd ed., 1775). Manwaring claimed that, with few exceptions, he had either executed all the designs in his shop or seen them 'completely finished by others'; and asserted that they were 'actually originals and not

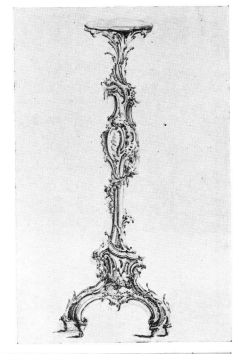

1. *Design for a Candle-stand, from* A New Book of Ornaments *by Lock and Copland*, 1768.

1. *Design for Chair, from Manwaring's* Cabinet and Chair-Maker's Real Friend and Companion, 1765; *the bracket below the seat rail is a characteristic detail.*

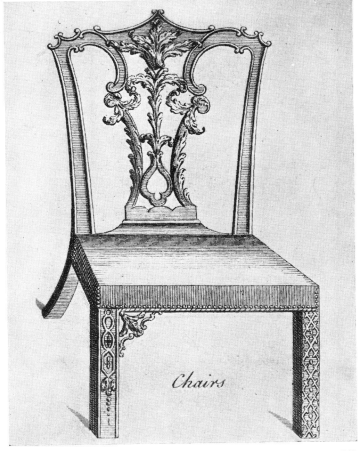

Chairs

2. *Another chair from the same book.*

pirated copies'. He praised his own work in extravagant terms, describing his Gothic and Chinese chairs as 'elegant and superb'. Some have been made in mahogany and others 'in Pear Tree for Japanning'. Some 'very beautiful designs' were intended to be executed with limbs of yew, apple or pear trees. In 1760 Manwaring had contributed upwards of 20 plates to the Society of Upholsterers' *Household Furniture in Genteel Taste*, and in 1762 appeared *The Chairmakers' Guide*, with designs 'for Gothick, Chinese, Ribbon and other chairs, couches, settees, burjairs, French, dressing and corner stools . . . by Robert Manwaring, cabinet-maker and others'. He failed to capture the rococo spirit and in his books the engravings are crude and faulty in perspective, but the best designs have a distinct individuality, and were probably much more satisfactory when executed. Massive framework, undulating uprights and an openwork bracket introduced at the junction of leg and seat rail (Fig. 1) are characteristic details in Manwaring's designs for chairs (*see* CHAIRS, Figs. 121, 123). Sheraton (preface to *Drawing Book*, 1791) pronounced that *The Chairmakers' Guide* contained only 'what a boy might be taught in 7 hours'.

MAROT, DANIEL (1663–1752). Architect, decorator and furniture designer, born Paris, son of Jean Marot, designer and engraver. When already launched on promising career, as a Protestant he sought refuge in Holland in 1684, the year before Revocation of Edict of Nantes. Entered service of William

Prince of Orange and was employed by him on important architectural works; after the Prince's accession to the English throne styled himself *Architecte de roy de la Grande Bretagne*. In many of his designs he introduced the royal arms and cypher with an inscription to the effect that the object was designed for the king. Evidence that he was in England 1694–6 and again in 1698. Married Catherine Golle of family of Pierre Golle, famous French *ébéniste*. Payments to Marot (1698) for total of 1,800 guilders during his stay in England from the King's patrimony in Holland. Documentary proof that he was employed on the gardens of Hampton Court Palace; he was probably consulted on decoration of interior, where some rooms have features strongly reminiscent of his style: a set of Delft vases in the palace are from his designs. Marot produced a great number of designs of a highly decorative baroque character, ranging from schemes for completely furnished rooms to tapestries, damasks and silver plate, among them a room decorated throughout in Chinese taste (*q.v.*). Some of these designs were derived from Berain, 'modified only in minor regards'; influence of Pierre Lepautre also apparent. He was 'creator of a national provincial variant' of Louis XIV style. Decoration for state beds in his designs fantastically elaborate (Fig. 2); several examples approximate to his style,

1. *Designs for upholstered Chairs and Stools, Bed Valances and Pelmets; from a collection of Daniel Marot's designs published early in 18th century.*

2. *Design for a State Bed, from the same source.*

notably the state bed from Melville House, Fife (*see* BEDS, Fig. 17).

Furniture supplied by Jean Pelletier (*q.v.*) and other aliens to Hampton Court, Chatsworth, Boughton, etc.—reminiscent of Marot's designs. His engraved works widely known in England and exercised powerful influence. First collected edition of designs (many previously published in parts) published at The Hague, 1702: *Œuvres du Sieur D. Marot, architecte de Guillaume III, roy de la Grande Bretagne, contenant plusieurs pensées utiles aux architectes, peintres, sculpteurs, orfèvres* . . . 2nd enlarged ed., Amsterdam, 1712. Another collection, undated, with title in Dutch and Latin, published later. A gifted and versatile baroque designer.

MARSH, WILLIAM. Cabinet-maker and upholsterer (later Edward, Marsh and Tatham, Tatham and Bailey, etc.). Marsh of Mount St., 'upholsterer and cabinet-maker', appears in London *Directory* (1778); he supplied furniture on large scale to Carlton House and Brighton Pavilion after 1795. Some fine furniture made by Marsh and partners for Carlton House still in Royal Collection. Tatham appears in Lord Chamberlain's accounts for furniture supplied to Crown in 1802 (see *Buckingham Palace*, H. Clifford Smith, 1931), and in 1806 firm rendered bill for over £6,000. It was also responsible, between 1801–13 at a cost of nearly £10,000, for some of the finest furniture at Southill, Beds. (*see* CABINETS, Fig. 56), and Rev. S. Johnes writes in 1800 of boudoir there 'Marsh's cabinets are superb, and he has made some frames for the glasses with a large bead that has a very good effect in the gilding'. Inexpensive furniture supplied to Viscount Grimstone (Gorhambury accounts, 1787–8); furniture to total of £715 to Lord Villiers (Osterley accounts, 1804). In 1807 title Tatham and Bailey; as such they were 'the Prince's chief upholsterers'. Thomas Tatham, senior partner, brother of Charles H. Tatham, the architect (*q.v.*).

MASTERS, WILLIAM. Cabinet-maker, Golden Fleece, Coventry St., Piccadilly. Only recorded productions at Blair Castle, Perthshire, to which between 1751–6 supplied furniture, including side-table, four-poster bed with Gothic shafts and set of chairs (see *Country Life*, Nov. 11 and 18, 1949).

MAYHEW, JOHN. (*See* INCE, WILLIAM.)

MILLER, JAMES. Carver, retained by Lady Leicester at Holkham, Norfolk, after death of first Lord Leicester 1760, at salary of £50 a year. Inventory of 1760 shows state rooms then unfurnished, and Miller carved frames for chairs and tables in East Drawing-room and green State bedchamber, also window cornices (*see* C. W. James, *Chief Justice Coke*, 1929, p. 280).

MOORE, JAMES (c. 1670–1726). Cabinet-maker, partner of John Gumley (*q.v.*) from 1714 until his death. Established in Dock St. (1720); also recorded as living in 'Short's Gardens, St Giles-in-ye-Fields'. Entry in Earl of Bristol's *Diary* (1710): 'To Mr. James Moore for a walnut-tree chest—£8 10s'; and Lord Bristol paid him in 1712 'in full of the bill for glass piers, scones, etc. £33 10'.

Moore adopted the practice, apparently peculiar to him, of incising his name on some pieces of his gilt gesso furniture. It is found on a set consisting of a gilt gesso table and stands of unusual design in the Queen's Audience Chamber, Hampton Court Palace (*see* STANDS, CANDLE, Fig. 10). A gilt gesso table in the Queen's bedchamber there, supported on straight legs and lion paw feet, is also the work of the partners, Moore and Gumley, between Aug., 1714, and Michaelmas, 1715. The gilt table on the Ministers' Staircase, Buckingham Palace, like that in the Audience Chamber, Hampton Court, bears the crowned cypher of George I on the apron and top (*see* TABLES, SIDE, Fig. 18). Above the crown is incised the maker's name. Two gilt tables at Windsor Castle have rectangular legs finishing in bulbous carved feet, and at Boughton, Northants., a table closely corresponds in design, indicating Moore's employment by the second Duke of Montagu (Master of the Great Wardrobe). In some account books of the Duke of Montagu's agent Moore's name occurs twice.

At Erthig, Denbighshire, there is an account of purchases by the owner, John Meller, receipted by Moore (1722–6), which include mirrors, sconces and a silver table with a glass top and coat-of-arms (*see* TABLES, SIDE, Fig. 24). A second gesso table, which is gilt, is probably by the same hand, and all the group of mirrors (*see* MIRRORS, Fig. 35) are also from the firm.

A gesso table formerly at Stowe, Bucks., and now in the V. and A. Mus. (W30–1947), can be assigned to Moore on the evidence of style. The top bears the cypher and baron's coronet of Richard Temple, Lord Cobham, and as he was created Lord Cobham in 1714 and a viscount in 1718, the table can be dated within five years. A gilt fire-screen (also in the Museum) was probably made at the same time, as the cresting bears the coronet and cypher of Cobham before he became a viscount (W40–1949).

Moore was employed by Sarah, Duchess of Marlborough, as clerk of the works at Blenheim, after the departure of Vanbrugh (1716) who refers to him contemptuously in a letter as '. . . your Glassmaker Moor'. The nature of his activities at Blenheim has not emerged. The Duchess in a letter (July 2, 1714) recommends her correspondent to consult 'my Oracle, Mr Moore, for he certainly has very good sense and I think him very honest and understanding in many Trades besides his own'. Moore gave evidence in a lawsuit brought against Henry Joynes, one of the controllers at Blenheim, by the Duchess in 1724. Joynes's assistant Jefferson affirmed that Moore and Bobart, another controller, were rogues: 'its hard to tell which is the Biggest, for Bobart has as bad a name in this country as the other has in London'. In an inventory (1740) of the Duchess 'a black Lacquered table of Mr Moore's' is mentioned. This has not been identified, but in the palace there are gilt gesso tables with marble tops with large pier glasses above them which may confidently be assigned to Moore on the evidence of style.

These and other pieces (e.g. a pair of tables with japanned tops at Plas Newydd, Anglesey) which can be attributed to Moore are all of high quality and distinguished by rich treatment of carving and gesso detail. A distinctive feature is the straight leg with a foliated and scrolled projecting member at the top (see TABLES, SIDE, Fig. 18). He was a designer of conspicuous originality. Moore's entire stock is advertised in the *Daily Post*, July 1, 1728, to be sold.

At the close of his career Moore evidently carried out William Kent's designs for furniture for the 'new apartment' designed by Kent at Kensington, for in the firm's accounts 1723–5 'four large sphinx stands for tables' and two 'fine sphinx table frames' are entered as supplied for that palace. In Pyne's illustrations of Kensington Palace a marble slab supported by couchant sphinxes is shown in the old dining-room, while there are four small tables or stands of similar design in the Cupola Room, another similar table being shown in the Queen's bedroom. Pyne attributed the design to Kent. Moore was paid for 'branches and scones' supplied to the Earl of Burlington for Chiswick House, March–April 1720 (*Earls of Creations*, James Lees-Milne, 1962, p. 149.)

James Moore, the younger, was appointed cabinet- and chair-maker to Frederick, Prince of Wales, in 1732, and died in 1734. Sharington Davenport, of Davenport House, Shropshire, enters in an account book, Feb., 1731: 'Paid Mr Moore ye Upholsterer 29. 0. 0.' (*See* David Green, *Blenheim Palace*, 1951, and R. Edwards and M. Jourdain, *Georgian Cabinet-Makers*, 3rd ed., revd., 1955.)

MOORE, THOMAS (d. 1738). Cabinet-maker in St Martin's Lane, in partnership with Daniel Bell (*q.v.*). In May and June, 1734, they supplied 'The Hon. Counsellor Rider' with furniture for which bills are receipted: 'Daniel Bell and Self, Thos. Moore'; but bills for further consignments, Oct. 31–Dec. 18, 1734, are receipted by Moore only. In

these later bills two sets of 'handsome walnut-tree chairs . . . with Lyons faces on ye knees and Lyons Paws' are recorded. Some of these chairs are still at Sandon Hall, Staffs.

MOORE, WILLIAM. Cabinet-maker, fl. 1782–1815; set up business in Dublin 1783, after having worked for considerable period with Ince and Mayhew. A commode at Welbeck Abbey, Notts., was made by Moore 1782 for third Duke of Portland (sent to Ireland as Lord-Lieutenant, Apr., 1782). In advertisement in *Dublin Evening Post* (May, 1782) Moore informed 'those who may want Inlaid work' that 'he has brought the manufacture to such perfection, to be able to sell for almost one half his original prices', and that 'as the greatest demand is for Pier-Tables, he has just finished in the newest taste a great variety of patterns, sizes and prices, from three guineas to twenty'. Moore mentions among his advantages 'long experience at Messrs Mayhew and Ince, London'. Between 1794–1815 Moore described his kind of business as 'Cabinet and Pianoforte maker'. An inlaid harewood commode in the V. and A. Mus. (W. 56–1925) has been attributed to Moore on stylistic grounds, and also a side-table, formerly at Lismore Castle, Co. Waterford.

MORANT, GEORGE (fl. 1814–37). Founder of well-known firm of decorators and cabinet-makers, 88, New Bond St. In earliest bill-heads describes himself as 'Ornamental Painter and Paper-hanging Manufacturer', but later (under William IV) as 'Carver, Gilder, Decorator and Upholsterer'. Decorated Farnborough Hall, and the Pavilion, Farnborough, 1820–2, for Mrs Luke Foreman, and it appears that he supplied much of the furniture.

MOREL (NICHOLAS) AND HUGHES. Cabinet-makers and upholsterers, 13, Great Marlborough St. Described in accounts for furnishing Carlton House as 'Upholsterers Extraordinary to His Royal Highness' (George, Prince of Wales). Firm supplied quantity of expensive furniture to the Prince, and was paid (1812) £951 12s. for 'six large elegant bergère chairs carved chimeras' (*see* CHAIRS, Fig. 200). Morel's name first occurs in 1795, and some time after 1812 he became partner in the firm of Seddon (*q.v.*).

MORGAN AND SAUNDERS (1801–17). Upholsterers and cabinet-makers, Trafalgar House, 16 and 17, Catherine St., Strand. Took out patents for various forms of mechanical furniture; 'Imperial' extending dining-tables, sofa beds, portable chairs, 'Brass Screw' bedsteads, etc., illustrated and described in firm's trade label. Their show-room illustrated in *Ackermann's Repository*, Aug., 1809, and patent library steps, July, 1811 (*see* LIBRARY STEPS, Figs. 10 and 11). They employed a large number of 'mechanics', and their premises were very extensive. Supplied Nelson's cabin furniture for the *Victory* and received a large order just before the battle of Trafalgar in 1805 for furnishing his seat at Merton, Surrey, making for it what was known as the 'Trafalgar patent sideboard'.

NAISH, CATHERINE. 'Joiner', address unknown. In the Lord Chamberlain's accounts payments to her are entered for cradles 'as usual' for George III's children, a mahogany state bedstead, the head-board 'supporting a crown', and, in 1766, a set of 12 mahogany chairs 'with hollow seats', now at Buckingham Palace.

NELSON, S. Carver, gilder and upholsterer, employed by Robert Adam at Shelburne House (1769) and Kenwood. In the collection of Adam's designs (in Soane Mus.) are a drawing of 'a term for the great staircase at Ken Wood' and a note: 'Mr Nelson to make one complete, if that is liked he is to do three more,' Also paid (1791) for carving and gilding 'in ye best Burnish Gold' the 'tops of glass frames' at Spencer House (MS. Accounts at Althorp, Northants.).

NEWMAN, EDWARD. Master of Worshipful Co. of Joiners (1749), carved 'A proper Handsome Master's chair' for the Co. 1754. It is in ornate Gothic style.

NEWTON, JAMES. Cabinet-maker and upholsterer, 63, Wardour St. In 1804 supplied Lord Villiers with furniture to total of £437 (Osterley Park accounts).

NIX, GEORGE. Cabinet-maker, King St., Covent Garden, who 'although of low origin . . . raised himself to eminence in his profession and from the honest and pleasant frankness of his conversation was admitted to the tables of the great' (*Memoirs*, Sir William Jones, 1806, Vol. I, p. 10). Supplied furniture to fourth Earl of Dysart for Ham House, Surrey, and did repairs there (1729–34). At the end of Nix's bill for £437 13s. 6d., Lord Dysart noted that £235 3s. 6d. was still outstanding 'for which he has my bond payable in three years from Nov. 29, 1734'.

NIXON, JAMES. Cabinet-maker, 123, Great Portland St., in 1817. His trade-card within a small chiffonier or cabinet on a table, decorated with boulle work, at Castle Ashby, advertises 'Louis XV furniture'.

NORMAN, SAMUEL. Cabinet-maker and carver, who with his partners, James Whittle and John Mayhew, purchased lease of 'the late Mr West's house and warehouses in King Street, Covent Garden', and advertised (*General Evening Post*, 1758) that 'they continue to carry on the Upholstery and Cabinet as well as the carving and gilding businesses, in all their branches'. In 1759 a fire entirely consumed the house in King St., and Mayhew went into partnership with Ince (*q.v.*).

Between 1754–60 Norman executed various commissions for the fourth Duke of Bedford at Woburn Abbey, including the redecoration of the picture gallery and principal drawing-room. One of the bills for this work is headed: 'To Samuel Norman, Cabinet-maker, Carver, etc. at the Royal Tapestry Manufactory, Soho Square, October 1760.' Among the furniture supplied were a 'Grand State Bed' and an elaborate mirror, described thus in the bill:

1759. For making and carving that exceeding large and grand oval frame, with eagles, a shield and rich 'Saggs', festoons of flowers twisting round 'Flora's' head, top and rich flowers curiously finished and gilt in burnished gold complete £97 10 0.
For a plate of best glass to ditto 49 by 38 complete £65 3 0.

Another bill (1760) is in the name of William Norman, but the receipt is signed by Samuel, which suggests that William was a relative and member of the firm. Norman's prices were high and the Duke had them checked by another firm. On this occasion the charges were confirmed, but a further account for £378 was reduced by £20. There are a number of fine mirrors, probably by Norman, at Woburn.

In Mortimer's *Universal Director* (1763) Norman, of Soho Square, is described as 'Sculptor and carver to their Majesties, and Surveyor of the curious Carvings in Windsor Castle'. In 1763 he is mentioned as having supplied Sir Lawrence Dundas (for whom 19, Arlington St. was altered and redecorated by Robert Adam 1763–6) with furniture 'to the amount of ten thousand' (mainly for Moor Park). The gilt set from Dundas's town house, consisting of a sofa and chairs (designed by Adam, 1764), was probably made by Norman (*see* CHAIRS, Fig. 138, and SETTEES AND SOFAS, Fig. 47). Mrs Harris wrote Aug., 1763, that she had spent the whole morning with him 'partly at Whitehall and partly at his warehouse, and had given what are, for us, I think, large orders, though not so great as those of Sir Lawrence Dundas'. For the Arlington St. furniture assigned to Norman, Adam's drawings are in existence: the craftsmanship is of good quality.

OAKLEY, GEORGE. Upholsterer and cabinet-maker, 22, St Paul's Churchyard; trade-card dated 1786. In 1796 the firm's style was Oakley and Kettle, in 1799 'George Oakley'. In 1800 the firm became Oakley, Shackleton and Evans, 8, Old Bond St., and in 1803 appeared as subscribers to Sheraton's *Dictionary*. In 1804 the London correspondent of the *Journal der Luxus und der Moden* (Weimar) wrote that 'all people with taste buy their furniture at Oakeleys, the most tasteful of the London cabinet-makers'. In 1810 Oakley supplied furniture to Papworth Hall, Cambs., including an 'elegant satinwood winged wardrobe fitted with drawers and clothes shelves and enclosed by panelled doors . . . £75', a 'mahogany winged library case in the Grecian stile, the doors fitted with brass trellis wire and quilled silk curtains with best locks and keys', and sets of 'Grecian-shaped' dining-room and hall chairs.

OKELEY, JOHN. Cabinet-maker, born at Bedford 1752, a pupil of Abraham Roentgen at Neuwied, Germany, 1766–c. 1770. Address (as subscriber to Sheraton's *Drawing Book* 1803) St Paul's Churchyard.

OLD, WILLIAM, AND **ODY, JOHN.** At the Castle, in St. Paul's Churchyard. Label in drawer of walnut writing cabinet, c. 1720, gives this address, and states that the firm 'makes and sells all sorts of cane and Dutch chairs. . . . And also all sorts of the best Looking Glass and Cabinet Work in japan, walnut tree and wainscot at reasonable rates.' Ody made liveryman of Joiners' Co., 1723. In 1738 entire stock-in-trade, 'goods in the chair and cabinet-making way, belonging to the late widow Old', were offered for sale on the premises.

PAINE, JAMES (1725–89). Architect, who according to Gwilt, divided the practice of the profession with Sir Robert Taylor 'until Robert Adam entered the list'. Among collection of Paine's drawings in V. and A. Mus. are designs for a wall-bracket surmounted by vase-shaped candelabrum, tripod candlestand and three pier-glasses. Appears to have occasionally made himself responsible for furniture forming part of the decorative scheme in houses erected by him, and at Brocket Hall, Herts., are four bookcases, painted white with gilt enrichments which may be attributed to Paine (*see* BOOKCASES, Fig. 17). President of Society of Artists, 1771.

PARDOE, JOHN. Cabinet-maker (fl. c. 1710–48), 'Cabinet and Chair, next to Temple Bar in ye Strand' (removed from

1. *Patterns for inlaid and painted ornament, from a portfolio of original drawings by Pergolesi (1772–92).*

'against St Clements Church'). Charged Richard Hoare, of Barn Elms, for 'a mahogany writing desk on a frame with special partitions and drawers' (1740). Sale of stock announced in *Daily Advertiser*, Mar. 12, 1748.

PARKER, GEORGE. *See* STALKER, J., and JAPANNING AND LACQUER.

PARKER AND PERRY. Firm of providers of cut-glass chandeliers, lustres and candelabra in last years of 18th century and in early 19th. Founded by William Parker in Fleet Street, 1756, a few years later their style became 'Parker and Perry'; changed to Perry & Co. 1817, when business moved to 78, New Bond St. Firm continued in existence until recently, and large collection of designs, accounts and notebooks formerly in its possession affords much valuable information as to the character of chandeliers and other lighting arrangements produced for many prominent patrons at home and abroad. All the fine and very expensive cut-glass 'lustres' now in the Royal Collection at Buckingham Palace were supplied by Parker and Perry to Carlton House for George, Prince of Wales, their first estimate (£1,500) for 'lustres' being given to Henry Holland (*q.v.*), 1789. (*See* CHANDELIERS, and *Buckingham Palace*, H. Clifford Smith, 1931.)

PARRAN, BENJAMIN. Cabinet-maker and upholder, the Golden Spread Eagle, in Long Acre, subscriber to Chippendale's *Director* 1754. In partnership with his uncle, Benjamin Goodison (*q.v.*), who died 1767, then with the younger Benjamin Goodison; they supplied furniture (mostly at low prices) to the crown 1767–84. For the first quarter of 1783 he was in partnership with William Gates (*q.v.*) and in following years with John Russell (*q.v.*).

PELLETIER, JEAN. Carver and gilder who supplied carved and gilt frames for tables, stands, screens and mirrors to the Crown in William III's reign. Two sets of stands at Hampton Court Palace can be assigned to him on the evidence of his accounts (*see* STANDS, CANDLE, Fig. 8):

674

For carving and guilding six pairs of large stands at £30 per pair—£180.
For carving and guilding two pairs of large stands   £70.

One of these sets was provided in accordance with a warrant dated Oct. 25, 1701, 'for the new gallery' (Queen's Gallery). A fine fire-screen at the Palace (*see* SCREENS, Fig. 4) can also be attributed to him. Pelletier was presumably of French origin, and his stands, of high quality in design and carving, closely follow contemporary Louis XIV models. In the accounts of the Dukes of Montagu the name of Thomas Pelletier, carver and gilder, appears between 1707–10 as supplying frames for Boughton, Northants.

PERGOLESI, MICHELE ANGELO (fl. c. 1760–1801). Decorative artist, engraver and designer. Of the date and place of birth nothing is known, but he appears to have come to this country from Italy before 1770 at Robert Adam's invitation, and to have co-operated with Adam in his decorative schemes. Pergolesi published *Designs for Various Ornaments* in 14 parts 1777–1801 (the first 12 dedicated to the Duke of Northumberland, d. 1786, and the 13th to his widow). The prospectus indicates that he was extensively employed as a decorative artist, and his designs, mainly for ornamental panels 'in the Etruscan and Grotesque styles', prove that some of the detail affords suitable patterns for inlaid and painted ornament (Fig. 1). Several of the oval medallions bear a striking resemblance to those on coeval painted furniture

2. *A Candelabrum from Pergolesi's* Designs for Various Ornaments, *published between* 1777 *and* 1801.

(see MIRRORS, Fig. 75). In the V. and A. Mus. there is a design for a table in classical taste, c. 1780, by Pergolesi 'for the Duke of Northumberland'. (See P. Ward Jackson, *English Furniture Designs of the 18th Century*, 1958, No. 260).

PERRY, ALEXANDER. *Daily Post*, Mar. 15, 1733, advertised 'The rich stock in Trade of Mr Alexander Perry, an eminent Cabinet-maker, at the Great White House in King Street, Bloomsbury end near Holborn ... fine walnut-tree and mahogany chairs cover'd in the newest fashion, cover'd or uncover'd with Spanish Leather, Damask or Mohair; with other Chairs, from two shillings apiece to Forty; several fine Dressing Chairs, Shaving Chairs, Close-stool Chairs and Easy Chairs'.

PETIT, PAUL. Employed chiefly as frame-maker by Frederick, Prince of Wales, and after his death in 1748, by his widow, Augusta, Dowager Princess of Wales, to 1753. He rendered bills for gilding, cleaning and making picture frames, gilding barges, etc. (£650 in 1749). He was presumably an immigrant and member of family of French *ébénistes* active from c. 1735 to the end of the century. (See Salverte, Comte F. de, *Les Ébénistes du xviiie Siècle*, 4th ed., 1953, and Millar, O., *Pictures in the Royal Collection*, 1963, Cat. No. 547.)

PHENE, SAMUEL AND NICHOLAS. 'Upholster and Sworn Appraiser of the Golden Plow, the Corner of Little Moorgate, London Wall.' Samuel's card announces that he 'Buys and sells all manner of Household Goods ... (in Mahogany Walnuttree or Wainscot) ... with all manner of Upholstery, Cabinet and Brasiery Goods new and old at very reasonable Rates'. Thomas Jones was taken into partnership c. 1760, and they are found at the Golden Plow in London directories between 1763–8 as upholders and sworn appraisers. Nicholas Phene then appeared as upholder at 17, Brokers Row, 1774–84; in 1790 the address was 80, London Wall; in 1802, 18, Little Moorgate; and in 1809, London Wall again. Under the style of Phene and Williamson the firm was still in existence early in Queen Victoria's reign.

PHILLIPS, JOHN. A small bureau-bookcase veneered with finely figured walnut dating from c. 1715 (now in America) bears this maker's label within one of the lower drawers, inscribed, without ornament, 'John Phillips at The Cabinet, St. Paul's Churchyard'. He announced (*Daily Post*, Feb. 3, 1732) that he 'is removed from St Paul's Churchyard to the Cabinet against St Peter's Church in Cornhill near the Royal Exchange'.

PISTOR, THOMAS (d. 1711). 'At the cabinet on Ludgate Hill.' *Spectator*, Mar. 21, 1711, advertises that on those premises 'still remains to be sold, at very low rates, the following goods of Mr. Pistor, lately deceased.... Three fine japan'd and walnut cabinetts, five walnut, one India scrutore ... three fine Princewood strong Boxes ... India japan'd glass table ... one japan'd chimney glass, some japan'd swing glasses.' A fall-front cabinet veneered with kingwood formerly in the Ionides Collection has inscription in interior: 'Mr Thomas Pistor, Lady's Hill, London'.

PRICE, RICHARD. St Martin's Lane; 'His Maties' Joyner to his Great Wardrobe' (admitted 1678). He provided a large quantity of furniture for royal palaces during Charles II's reign. In 1676 charged for fitting up bedstead for Windsor,

and for 'four lyons feet carved for the same bed', and in 1682 one for the King's new bedchamber at Whitehall, described as French, *i.e.* in the French taste, as was much of Price's furniture made for the crown. In the same year charged for 'two fformes of walnutwood wrought with mouldings and scrowles with great Bases on the foot and of the Dutch turne'. For the Queen at Windsor in 1681 he supplied 'a caned chair with elbows to move with Joynts and a ffootstool with Iron Workes to fold'. References to Dutch turning in his bills recognise the difference between English and foreign types of turning at this time. He died 1683, and in bills for Michaelmas, 1684, Elizabeth Price, 'relict and administrator' of Richard Price, sent in account.

PRITCHARD, WILLIAM. Cabinet-maker, Philip Lane, Aldermanbury. At Rousham, Oxon., pedestal library table of c. 1760, and glazed bureau-bookcase, probably made some years later, bear Pritchard's trade-label with above address, which has also been found on other pieces.

RANNIE, JAMES. Cabinet-maker and upholsterer; first partner of Thomas Chippendale, but date when they entered business relations, and particulars of Rannie's career are unknown. Died 1766, when *Public Advertiser* announced sale at 60, St Martin's Lane, of 'The entire genuine and valuable Stock in Trade of Mr Chippendale and his late Partner Mr Rennie, deceased, Cabinetmakers and Upholsterers'. Thomas Haig, taken into partnership some years later, is said to have been Rannie's book-keeper.

REASON, WILLIAM. Upholsterer, Long Acre, often employed in royal palaces towards end of George II's reign; for instance, in 1752–3 he re-covered a four-leaved screen with harateen, and trimmed it with silk garnished with brass nails 'for Mr Schroider, the King's Page'. 'Dismissed for cheating his majesty.'

ROBERTS, RICHARD. Chair-maker. Employed by crown c. 1714–30. On Oct. 21, 1717, received warrant to 'provide eighteen chairs with bending backs and girt web bottoms for His Majesty's dining-room', and relative account specifies 'eighteen chairs made of the best walnut-tree bended backs fully carved and polished'. This description supplemented by entry in Receipts Book: 'Received from H.M.'s great Wardrobe, eighteen walnut-tree chairs, India backs and girt web bottoms and silk upon that, for H.M.'s eating room at Hampton Court.' These chairs have been identified with the remainder of a set in Hampton Court Palace, and 'India' must relate to the pierced carving on the splat, which is of Indo-Portuguese character; 'bended' refers to the curvature of the back.

In 1727 Roberts supplied '4 new carved lyons' gilded to the base of the Coronation chair in Westminster Abbey for £7. 'Mr Roberts' described as 'chairmaker to His Majesty' in *London Journal*, Oct. 19, 1728, which reported attempt to break into his house in Air St., Piccadilly. This was Richard Roberts' house, as he was employed by the Court at that date, and it is likely that he was a son of Thomas (*see* below).

ROBERTS, THOMAS. 'Joiner.' Address unknown; supplied royal palaces with seat furniture and fire-screens c. 1685–1714. Most important single item in accounts is 'large rich fire skreene, the top piece carved both sides into leaves and cyphers, the pillows [*sic*] into festoons and flowers and two firepotts on top, the two claws into Lyons and mouldings and foldings, the bottom railes in festoons and flowers', supplied 1697 for Windsor Castle. In same year charged 'For two Pattern chairs and two stooles made to show the King'. In 1689, craved allowance of £7 10s. 'for 6 forms Irish turning and varnished'.

Roberts was also employed at Chatsworth, and paid in 1702 for 'walnut armchairs, two large saffaws and six bankettes', 'all carved, with mouldings carved round the seats'—an unusual feature (see CHAIRS, Fig. 55, and STOOLS, Fig. 27).

The gilt day-bed at Penshurst, a state bed and a set of gilt stools in the Venetian Ambassador's room at Knole, may also be assigned to Roberts on the evidence of his documented work (see COUCHES AND DAY-BEDS, Fig. 9, and INTRODUCTION, Fig. 8). As an able craftsman, he had distinctive characteristics in the treatment of ornament, notably in foliated scrolls on seat rails. The influence of contemporary French design is apparent in some of his work. After 1714 Thomas Roberts is succeeded in the royal accounts by Richard Roberts. In 1729 a craftsman named Thomas Roberts sent Sir Robert Walpole a bill for £1,420 8s. 7½d. for work done at Houghton. His connection with the firm of royal tradesmen has not been determined, but possibly the elder Roberts in the crown's service sent in this large bill after his retirement.

ROENTGEN, ABRAHAM (1711–93). German cabinet-maker, who practised marquetry and engraving on wood for some years in England, and popularised mid-Georgian style in Germany. Born at Mülheim on the Rhine, and taught cabinet-making by his father. After practising at The Hague, Rotterdam and Amsterdam, came to London c. 1731, where he was employed by cabinet-maker named Gern at Newcastle House, St John's Square, Clerkenwell. Seems to have remained in England until 1738 and specialised in 'engraving, marquetry and the mechanics of cabinet-making'; is said to have been 'employed and highly paid by the most skilful cabinet-makers'. On return home settled near Frankfurt, and in 1740 attempted to emigrate as missionary to Carolina; shipwrecked on Irish coast, and worked for short time in Galway. Returning to Germany, he settled c. 1750 at Neuwied, near Coblenz. In 1756 sent one of his assistants to former employer Gern in London to perfect him in the trade, and in 1766 Roentgen again visited England and brought back John Okeley (q.v.), who was apprenticed to him for several years and then returned home. At Neuwied Roentgen produced a quantity of fine furniture in English style of mid-18th century, and several examples in German collections are obviously based on plates in Chippendale's *Director*. Most of his furniture is made of fruit woods; for inlay he used fine brass lines with engraved ornament, ivory and mother-of-pearl (see TABLES, CHINA AND TEA, Fig. 9).

David Roentgen, Abraham's celebrated son, styled himself *Englischer Kabinettmacher*, but there is no evidence that he was ever in England. He substituted coloured woods for the type of marquetry used by his father, and his furniture was mainly intended for the French market. The elder Roentgen retired 1784. (See *Abraham und David Roentgen*, Hans Huth, Berlin, 1928; *Connoisseur*, Vol. XCII, No. 384, Aug, 1933.)

RUDD. Inventor, according to Hepplewhite's *Guide* (1788), of 'the most complete Dressing Table made', called after this

'once popular character'; stated by Sheraton (*Cabinet Dict.*, 1803) to be 'not much in present use'. (*See* TABLES, DRESSING.)

RUSSELL, JOHN. Chair-maker, upholsterer and cabinet-maker; employed by the crown 1773–1810; chair-maker to the King. Business first in New Bond St., and after 1793 at 12, Broker Row, Moorfields (Kent's *Directory* and *Universal British Directory*). In 1773 Russell supplied 'for his Majesty's House at Kew' set of carved mahogany forms, now in Royal Collection, and in 1808 provided Prince Regent with 'a double-headed couch bedstead richly carved with figures and ornaments, Egyptian heads, gilt leaves, chased honeysuckle, lyres' (£209 10s.). In 1784 Russell was in partnership with Benjamin Parran (q.v.).

SAPP, ROBERT. 'Upholsterer', who supplied quantity of furniture, window curtains, carpets, etc., to 'New Treasury', Whitehall, completed 1734–7. Sapp's bill dated June 28, 1739. Among items for 'the Honble Secretary Fox's Room etc.' (i.e. Stephen Fox, created Earl of Ilchester 1756) were 'a mahogany desk of curious wood, £5 10s.', and '6 Wallnuttree chairs with compass backs and seats and wallnuttree Elbows, the backs and seats stuffed with curled hair and covered with Spanish leather and trimmed with large brass nails guilt, £22 1s.' Early Georgian furniture at the Treasury—a set of 12 Cuban mahogany carved chairs (see CHAIRS, Fig. 82), a large library table *en suite* with the set, and a gilt throne chair have been attributed to Sapp, but on inadequate evidence. (*See* W. A. Thorpe, 'Tradition in Treasury Furniture,' *Country Life*, Vol. CIX, pp. 42–4.) No other particulars concerning him are known.

SAUNDERS, PAUL. Chief arras-maker in the office of the Great Wardrobe (c. 1758–71) and cabinet-maker. Partner of George Smith Bradshaw (q.v.) in Greek St., Soho. Partnership dissolved 1758, when Saunders carried on business in Soho Square. His Pilgrimage to Mecca tapestries at Holkham signed and dated 1756–8. Payments in 1757–9 Holkham accounts to 'Mr. Sanders' [sic] for three sets of carved and gilt mahogany chairs, and for 'ye modell of ye state bed', etc.

SEDDON, GEORGE (1727–1801). Founder of a firm of cabinet-makers which carried on a large business in the second half of the 18th and first half of the 19th centuries. The son of John Seddon, of Blakelea, Lancs., he was apprenticed to a George Clemapon, a cabinet-maker in Cripplegate (1743), and appears to have set up business at London House, Aldersgate St., c. 1750. A liveryman of the Joiners' Co. in 1737 and master in 1795. Subscribed to the 1st ed. of Chippendale's *Director* (1754). In 1768 a fire burnt down his premises, damage being computed at £20,000. He was then employing 80 cabinet-makers and the *Annual Register* refers to him as 'one of the most eminent cabinet-makers of London'. Soon started business again in new and improved premises close to the original site. From there furniture was supplied to the new Somerset House, completed in 1780, and the firm's bills extend from 1779–89. It continued to enjoy a high reputation down to c. 1850. William Hickey records in his *Memoirs* (1791) that he 'purchased a very capital billiard table, made by Seddon's, at the price of one thousand sicca rupees', i.e. £188 sterling, for his house at Calcutta.

Sophie von La Roche, a German traveller, describes in her

diary a visit she made to Seddon's in 1786. Four hundred craftsmen were employed—joiners, carvers, gilders, mirror-makers, upholsterers, workers in ormolu and locksmiths. No other cabinet-maker of the period is known to have owned business on so great a scale. In the annual stocktaking (Dec., 1789) the total valuation was £118,926, carpets alone being over £9,000. The diarist observes that Seddon 'is for ever creating new forms', implying that he was a designer as well as cabinet-maker. He died at his house in Hampstead in 1801.

Seddon's son, George, was taken into partnership in 1785, and his elder son, Thomas, in 1788. From 1793 to 1800 George Seddon's son-in-law, Thomas Shackleton, was in the partnership; the firm was then known as Seddon, Sons and Shackleton. Thomas Seddon in that year charged £11 0s. 6d. for 'a Trick-track table, etc.' supplied to Lord Ducie (Osterley Park accounts). In 1802 the style reverted to Seddon and Sons. In George IV's reign Nicholas Morel became a partner; they were among the tradesmen to whom the King became indebted for large sums.

Of Seddon's surviving output the most important are two sets of seat furniture, one of mahogany, the other of painted satinwood (see CHAIRS, Fig. 169), made for D. Tupper, of Guernsey, in 1790 (part of one with a card-table *en suite* at Woolbeding, Sussex, through descent). The bill totalled £414 11s. 6d., and the firm is described as 'cabinet-makers, upholsterers, also manufacturers of British Cast Large Plate Glass'. A similar satinwood armchair at the V. and A. Mus. (W.59–1936) may also be attributed to the Seddons. With few exceptions the identified pieces show little individuality. An important one was the very elaborate satinwood cabinet, made from Sir William Chambers's design for Charles IV of Spain, com-

1. *Portrait of George Seddon.* 1727-1801. *Painter unknown (V. & A. Mus.)*

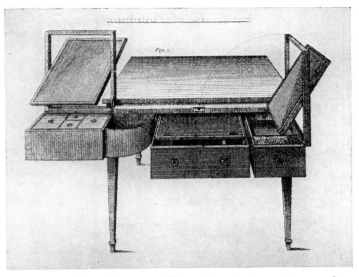

1. *Design for a dressing-table with swinging mirrors, from* Thomas Shearer's Household Furniture, 1788.

2. *Design for a Sideboard with alternative ends, from the same source.*

bining functions of bureau, jewel case, dressing-table and organ. Decorated by William Hamilton with painted oval panels of the four seasons and other emblematical subjects, it was broken up after 1908, when it was shown at the Franco-British Exhibition. A cradle made by Seddons in 1814 for Joanna Southcott's 'Prince of Peace' is now in the Peel Park Mus., Salford. The scale of the enterprise justifies the assumption that much fine furniture was produced by Seddons which can no longer be identified. (*See also* R. Edwards and M. Jourdain, *Georgian Cabinet-Makers*, 3rd ed., revd., 1955.)

SHEARER, THOMAS. Cabinet-maker and designer. He contributed 17 out of the 20 plates in the 1788 edition of the *Cabinet-Maker's London Book of Prices* (a trade catalogue giving the labour and material costs of the various articles), the remaining plates being anonymous. Shearer's designs show bureaux bookcases, sideboards, and bedroom furniture, distinctive in character and competently drawn (Figs. 1 and 2). Notable features are a sideboard with cellaret drawers united for the first time to the flanking pedestals

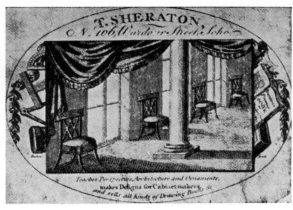

1. *Design for a library table from Sheraton's* Encyclopaedia, 1805.

2. *Thomas Sheraton's Trade Card. Early 19th century. (Mr David Citroen.)*

(*see* SIDEBOARDS) and wine tables, termed 'gentlemen's social tables'; great ingenuity is displayed in the fittings of dressing-tables and washing-stands. Sheraton compared the *Book of Prices* favourably with Hepplewhite's *Guide*: 'Whether they had the advantage of seeing Hepplewhite's book before theirs was published I know not; but it may be observed that their designs are more fashionable and useful than his in proportion to their numbers.' Sheraton's praise clearly refers to Shearer. His address is not known; nor does it appear that any bills survive.

SHERATON, THOMAS (1751–1806). Born at Stockton-on-Tees, Durham, brought up in poor circumstances, and trained as 'journeyman cabinet-maker'. He seems to have settled in London about 1790, at 41, Davies St., at 106, Wardour St. (1795) and later at 8, Broad St., Golden Square. There he devoted himself to drawing and authorship. He published 1791–4 the *Cabinet-Maker and Upholsterer's Drawing Book* in four parts (3rd ed., 1802). In 1803 he brought out the *Cabinet Dictionary* (with plates) 'containing an explanation of all the Terms used in the Cabinet, Chair and Upholstery Branches, with Directions for Varnishing, Polishing and Gilding'. The last of his schemes, entitled the *Cabinet-Maker, Upholsterer, and General Artist's Encyclopaedia*, produced but one volume, published 1805, the year before his death. It suggests that his mind was beginning to give way, and contains a number of

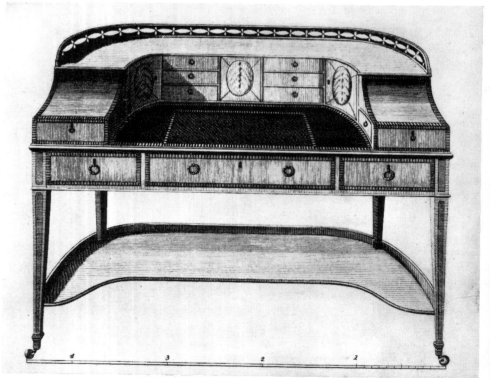

3. *Design for a secretaire, from Sheraton's* Drawing Book, 1791-4.   4. *Original drawing for a mirror, signed Thos. Sheraton. c. 1790. (V. & A. Mus.)*

5. *Design for an armchair, from Sheraton's* Drawing Book, *1791-4.*

6. *Design for a cylinder writing-table, from the* Cabinet Dictionary, *1803.*

articles which have no bearing on the title. He was also responsible at different dates for various religious and philosophical treatises. In 1800 he was called as a Baptist minister for the connection at Stockton-on-Tees.

An obituary notice in the *Gentleman's Magazine* (Nov., 1806) contains the following account: 'In Broad Street, Soho, after a few days illness of a phrenitis: aged 55, Mr Thomas Sheraton, a native of Stockton-on-Tees, and for many years a journeyman cabinet-maker, but who since the year 1793 has supported himself, a wife and two children by his exertions as an author.' Then follow references to his publications, and the notice concludes: 'He was a very honest, well-disposed man; of an acute and enterprising disposition; but like many other self-taught authors, showing the want of a regular education in his writings. He has left his family, it is feared, in distressed circumstances.' Further light is thrown on Sheraton's life and character in the *Memoirs of Adam Black*, the publisher, who came to London in the early years of the 19th century, and was employed by Sheraton for a brief time to write articles for the *Encylopaedia*. After describing Sheraton's home as 'half-shop, half-dwelling house', Black adds: 'He understands the cabinet business . . . he has been, and perhaps is, a preacher; he is a scholar, writes well, draws in my opinion masterly, is an author, bookseller, stationer, and teacher. How comes it to pass that a man of such abilities and resources is in such a state? I believe his abilities and resources are his ruin in this respect, for by attempting to do everything, he does nothing.'

Under the generic term 'Sheraton' is classified much of the furniture produced in England between c. 1790–1800, especially such as was made of satinwood, and countless examples have been unwarrantably attributed to him. But though Sheraton published illustrations of furniture in the typical manner of his period, there is no evidence that he possessed a workshop or executed the designs illustrated in his books. Nor were his designs confined to the typical satinwood furni-

ture of the end of the 18th century, for the drawings in his later publications include many extravagant examples of the Regency styles.

The *Drawing Book* is by far the most important of his works. The first half of the book is given up to elaborate and complicated dissertations on perspective geometry, architecture and drawing. But in the second half (Part III), the designs are excellent in draughtsmanship and the descriptive notes contain fuller technical information than can be found in any other book of designs. It is not clear from the text whether all the illustrations were Sheraton's own invention, or whether some of them were drawings of the finished work of other cabinet-makers. In his introduction to Part III the author writes: 'The design of this Part of the Book is intended to exhibit the present taste of furniture, and at the same time to give the workman some assistance in the manufacturing part of it.' Later he says: 'I have made it my business to apply to the best workmen in different shops, to obtain their assistance in the explanation of such pieces as they have been most acquainted with.' Of a library table, 'It has already been executed for the Duke of York, excepting the desk drawers, which are here added as an improvement'. In describing a plate on which knife-cases are illustrated he observed: 'As these cases are not made in regular cabinet shops, it may be of service to mention where they are executed in the best taste, by one who makes it his main business: *i.e.* John Lane, No. 44, St Martin's-le-Grand, London.'

The *Drawing Book* provides a valuable summary of the fashions of c. 1790–1800, and even though the degree of his responsibility for the designs must remain doubtful, Sheraton can be held largely responsible for the marked difference in the neo-classic style as represented in Hepplewhite's *Guide* (1788), and in his own publication, in which late Louis XVI influence is perceptible. That at this period Sheraton was gifted with a remarkable sense of style and with an ability to use and improve on ideas obtained from various quarters cannot be questioned.

1. *Design for a Library Chair or 'fauteuil' with pedestal and stand. From George Smith's* Household Furniture, *1808.*

Several extant pieces of furniture are virtually identical with, or closely related to, designs in the *Drawing Book*, but such correspondences do not indicate that they were made by Sheraton. Nothing is known of his activities as a maker, whereas his book had a very large circulation (about 700 cabinet-makers, joiners and upholsterers subscribed to it in all parts of England), and there can be no doubt that as a repertory of designs it was widely exploited.

SMITH, GEORGE. Cabinet-maker, upholsterer and designer, who in 1808, being then at 15, Princes St., Cavendish Square, published *A Collection of Designs for Household Furniture and Interior Decoration*, the most comprehensive work of the Regency period. On the title-page he describes himself as 'Upholder Extraordinary to His Royal Highness the Prince of Wales'; but he is not known to have supplied furniture to the Prince. The 158 plates in colour (dated 1804–7) include various designs for rooms, showing the decoration and arrangement of the furniture. Smith observes that 'the superb style in which Household Furniture . . . is now executed and the classic elegance which guides the form of cabinet-work render a publication of Designs . . . absolutely necessary'. He claims that those given by him are studied from the best antique examples of the Egyptian, Greek and Roman styles, some 'after the Gothic, or old English fashion and according to the costume of China', being added to augment their variety. In their selection the wants of 'elegant and polite life' have been considered, 'whether lived in an extensive mansion or a social villa'. They are eclectic, drawing freely on Hope, Sheraton and classical sources. He was much indebted to Denon's *Voyage dans la Basse et la Haute Egypte* (1802), for his detail.

In 1812 Smith published a *Collection of Ornamental Designs after the Manner of the Antique*, for the use of 'Every Trade dependent on the Fine Arts', in which 'the purest antique ornament is accommodated to modern embellishments'. In 1828 he produced another large volume, illustrated in colour and entitled the *Cabinet-Maker's and Upholsterer's Guide, Drawing Book, and Repository of New and Original Designs for Household Furniture*. This ambitious work opens with an 'Historical View of the Origin of the Art in this Country', from the Normans downwards. Smith observes that his own *Household Furniture* has been rendered wholly obsolete by the change of taste and rapid improvements of the previous twenty years. His new book, besides the designs, contains long treatises on geometry, perspective and ornamental drawing. He now describes himself as 'Upholsterer and Furniture Draughtsman to His Majesty, and principal of the drawing Academy, Brewer Street (41) Golden Square'.

Smith states that he had been employed 'by some of the most exalted characters in the country to manufacture many of the Designs, some of which have been considered the most difficult to be executed'. In his *Guide* he points out that he has forty years' experience in both theory and practice, has been patronised by George IV and received 'the most flattering testimonials from Mr Thomas Hope'. His *Household Furniture* standardised the Regency style and covered a very wide range. The dates of his birth and death are unknown.

STALKER, JOHN, AND PARKER, GEORGE. Authors of *Treatise of Japanning and Varnishing* (1688), a quarto volume illustrated by 'Above an Hundred distinct Patterns of Japan-Work. . . '. Besides giving recipes for imitation of Oriental lacquer and technical information on the subject (*see* JAPANNING AND LACQUER), it discusses staining of woods for marquetry, polishing, gilding, etc. Three issues appeared within a year of publication. In A the work is stated to be by John Stalker of the Golden Ball in St James's Market; in B it is by Stalker and Parker; and in C by Parker and Stalker. All three published at Oxford, and an 'Epistle to the Reader' is signed by Stalker in each, from which it may be inferred that he was primarily responsible.

STRICKLAND, WILLIAM. 'Nephew to the late Mr Vile' (*see* VILE, W.), 75, Long Acre, where he carried on business with 'Jenkins, late foreman to Mr Cobb' (*see* COBB, J.). A mahogany stool (*see* STOOLS, Fig. 50) with carved cabriole legs and scroll feet is signed below seat rail 'Strickland, September 1, 1763'. In that year Strickland signs receipts for upholstery materials delivered to the Great Wardrobe, in some instances on behalf of Vile and Cobb.

STUART, JAMES (1713–88). Well-known architect and protagonist of classical revival inaugurated at end of George II's reign. Travelled in Italy and Greece. First volume of *Antiquities of Athens* (1762), in which he collaborated with Nicholas Revett (responsible for the measured drawings), gained him name of 'Athenian' Stuart; second published by his widow in 1788, and third in 1795. This work caused the 'Grecian gusto to reign supreme'; or, as Robert Adam writes, 'Mr Stuart with his usual elegance and taste has contributed greatly towards introducing the true style of antique decoration' (*Works in Architecture*, 1st Vol., 1773). Stuart designed or remodelled several important town and country houses. Between 1760–5 carried out decoration of interior of Spencer House for first Lord Spencer, and designed suite of carved and gilt furniture for painted room, consisting of four settees and six armchairs, besides pair of pedestals for candelabra (*see* STANDS, PEDESTAL AND TERM, Fig. 9). The whole suite 'bears the impress of a man to whom furniture designing was a rare adventure'.

SYMPSON. Joiner employed by Samuel Pepys in furnishing and decoration of his house in Seething Lane, 1663–8; supplied presses for books now in Bibliotheca Pepsyiana, Magdalene College, Cambridge (*see* BOOKCASES), and also made chimney-pieces for diarist. Christian name unrecorded.

TAITT, JOHN. Upholsterer and cabinet-maker; partner of William Gordon, 1768–70, in King St., Golden Square (*see* GORDON AND TAITT). Partnership seems to have been dissolved after 1779; Taitt moved to 75, Swallow St., then to 254, Oxford St. (until 1799).

TATHAM, CHARLES HEATHCOTE (1772–1842). Architect who exercised considerable influence on furniture design in early 19th century. Son of Ralph Tatham (d. 1779); at 19 became pupil of Henry Holland (*q.v.*), who helped him to visit Italy, where he travelled extensively for about three years. In Soane Mus. there is volume of his drawings containing studies executed in various Italian cities; and when in Rome (1796) he sent Holland, then engaged on decoration and equipment of Carlton House, drawings for 'various bronzes for lights composed from the Antique. . . .' In his letters he commented on new interest in Grecian style, which he understands 'is gaining ground in England'. His drawings also include Egyptian antiquities in Rome. After his return he received number of important architectural commissions. Published 1796–9 *Etchings of Ancient Ornamental Architecture at Rome and in Italy* (several eds.). By this means he sought to reform prevailing taste, and *Dictionary of Architecture* pronounces that 'to him, perhaps more than to any other person, may be attributed the rise of the Anglo-Greek style' (under heading *Furniture*). His brother Thomas was partner in firm of Marsh and Tatham (*see* MARSH, WILLIAM, and TATHAM, THOMAS), and at Southill, Beds., where these fashionable cabinet-makers were largely employed, certain details of furniture are taken from C. H. Tatham's designs.

TATHAM, THOMAS (b. 1763). 13, Mount St., elder brother of architect C. H. Tatham. In 1802 joined firm of William Marsh, of Mount St., from 1795 principal cabinet-makers to George, Prince of Wales. Tatham became head of firm Marsh and Tatham in 1809; shortly afterwards firm's style was 'Tatham and Bailey, upholsters to His Royal Highness the Prince of Wales', of 14, Mount St. (Holden's *Directory*. 1809–11). In 1811 firm was Tatham, Bailey and Saunders; in 1817, Bailey and Saunders (H. Clifford Smith, *Buckingham Palace* 1931). Thomas Tatham died 1818 at Brighton, leaving estate of £60,000 (*Gentleman's Magazine*, Jan. 1, 1818).

THACKER, BENONI. Craftsman employed by Sir William Chambers (*q.v.*) in making furniture at Carrington House, Whitehall, and elsewhere. In Chippendale's *Director* (1st ed., 1754) he appears among list of subscribers, described as 'carpenter'.

TROTTER, JOHN. 43, Frith St., Soho, cabinet-maker and upholder; appointed upholder to George II, and termed by Lord Barrington (writing 1763) 'the honestest man in London of his profession'. Superseded by William Vile (*q.v.*).

TURING, WILLIAM (fl. 1723–30). Looking-glass maker at Eagle and Child, Bedford St., and (1723–6) 'over against the New Exchange'. After Michaelmas, 1721, Turing appeared in Great Wardrobe accounts in partnership with John Gumley, but in 1729 employment of Mrs Gumley and Turing 'as cabinet-makers for the Wardrobe' terminated (*see* GUMLEY, JOHN). His appeal (1730) for re-employment rejected (*Treasury Letter Book*, Vol. XVIII, p. 420, and *Calendar of Treasury Papers*, 1729–30).

VARDY, JOHN (d. 1765). Architect, Clerk of the Works at Whitehall and St James's (1749). Closely associated with William Kent and published *Some Designs of Mr Inigo Jones and Mr William Kent*, 1744. There are a number of designs by Vardy both at the V. and A. Mus. and at the R.I.B.A.; several are strongly reminiscent of Kent, while others show he studied the French rococo style. In the R.I.B.A. collection are drawings for a pair of carved and gilt side-tables and pier glasses, designed for the 3rd or 4th Duke of Bolton, and intended for Hackwood, Basingstoke, where they still are. He also designed other furniture for the duke (1761), probably for Grosvenor Square and for Milton Abbey, Dorset. In the Iolo Williams bequest to the British Museum (Dept. of Prints and Drawings) there are two designs by Vardy, each for a baroque console with a mirror over it. (*See* A. Coleridge, 'John Vardy and the Hackwood Suite', *The Connoisseur*, Jan., 1962.)

VILE, WILLIAM (d. 1767). Cabinet-maker and upholsterer of 72, St Martin's Lane, who with his partner John Cobb (*q.v.*) takes the leading place among furniture manufacturers employed by the crown early in George III's reign. He had worked for the Prince of Wales before his accession to the throne and for the Prince's mother, the Dowager Princess of Wales.

Vile, who died in Sept., 1767, described himself in his will (dated Aug., 1763) as 'of the parish of St Martin's in the fields, Cabinet maker and upholder', and bequeathed to his wife Sarah 'two houses now in my possession situate at Battersea Hill'. He gave legacies to relatives in Somerset. Vile states that for many years he had been and is now 'engaged with my co-partner John Cobb in very extensive branches of trade', and appoints William Hallett (*q.v.*) and Charles Smith as trustees. Vile and Cobb in 1752–3 rendered bills to Anthony Chute, of The Vyne, Hants, for upwards of £120, including a charge of £28 16s. for a set of '8 Large Mahogany Stools' part of a set still in the house (*see* STOOLS, Fig. 48). References to Vile appear in the Strawberry Hill accounts (1765) and in Lord Folkestone's accounts at Longford Castle., Wilts. He was first employed at Longford in 1760 and frequent payments to him and to his partner, Cobb, are entered up to 1767.

In some pieces which can be assigned to the firm there is a distinctive style of enrichment by carved pendants and applied wreaths clasped with acanthus and festoons of fruit and flowers; or pendants hanging from a lion's or satyr's mask (*see* CHESTS, Fig. 32). The wreath motif was also used by other makers.

The first entry referring to Vile in Lord Folkestone's accounts is a protest against his high prices, and those invoiced in the royal accounts are also high. At Came House, near Dorchester,

1. *Grand Piano of satinwood banded with mahogany; decorated with medallion of Wedgwood ware and dated* 1798. (*Alec Hodson and Benton Fletcher Coll., Hampstead.*)

an account is preserved for furniture supplied by the firm to Hon. John Damer. It dates between 1756–62 and covers both furniture and the gilding of a ceiling. A mahogany settee and chairs at Came are doubtless part of a set of '10 good mahogy Back stool chairs . . . with the sopha to match' supplied in July, 1761.

Identified pieces by Vile, dating from the early years of George III's reign, are of superlative quality and individual in design. Among the finest and most characteristic are the bureau-cabinet with a fretwork superstructure (*see* BUREAUX, Fig. 32) and 'Queen Charlotte's jewel cabinet' (*see* CABINETS, Fig. 32) made of 'many different kinds of fine wood . . . and inlaid with Ivory . . . neatly Ingraved'. The break-front bookcase of the Corinthian order (*see* BOOKCASES, Fig. 14) is an outstanding masterpiece of design and rococo carving. The wreaths on the lower stage are closely similar to the 'ovals of laurels' added by Vile to the base of an early Georgian cabinet (also at Buckingham Palace) when it was being converted from an organ case.

Vile's identified *oeuvre* has now attained considerable dimensions, and examples which may be attributed to him on stylistic grounds will be found illustrated in the relevant sections (*see* CABINETS, Fig. 33; COMMODES, Figs. 2 and 3). The commode from Alnwick, Northumb., precedes by about a decade the earliest documented works by Vile, while the Good-wood piece is among the masterpieces of English baroque furniture. In the period 1750–60 pride of place among contemporary cabinet-makers must be assigned to Vile, whose extant work is equal, if not superior, to anything known to have been produced by Chippendale while working in the rococo style. It is not possible to determine the degree of individual responsibility of Vile and his partner Cobb during the period of their

association; but Vile was the senior partner, and the furniture for which Cobb alone is known to have been responsible is in the neo-classic manner and decorated with marquetry. (*See also* R. Edwards and M. Jourdain, *Georgian Cabinet-Makers*, 3rd ed., revd., 1955.)

VULLIAMY, FIRM OF. Founded by Justin Vulliamy, partner of Benjamin Gray, who obtained the appointment of clock-maker to the Crown in 1742. In 1786 a German visitor, who paid a visit to Vulliamy's, 'witnessed works of exquisite beauty and perfection'. . . . 'It is no prejudice on my part to state that no Paris invention comes up to those which I saw here; and truly, ideas for practical use cannot be more nobly represented' (*Sophie in London*, 1788, p. 100). Benjamin Lewis Vulliamy (1780–1845), third in succession of this family, introduced several peculiarities and improvements into the clocks made by the firm. He was made free of the Clockmakers' Company in 1809, admitted to the Livery in 1810 and five times filled the office of Master. Vulliamy was employed from 1806 onwards by the Prince of Wales not only to make and repair clocks, but also to supply or mend metal work, mounts and a variety of other objects. A pair of candelabra of ormolu, marble and ebony at Harewood House, is signed 'Vulliamy, London, 1811'.

WEDGWOOD, JOSIAH (1730–95). Famous potter. Shortly after he had established his works at Etruria, between Burslem and Stoke-on-Trent, he began to produce cameo plaques of his celebrated jaspar ware for the decoration of furniture. As early as 1774 a few cabinet-makers in Birmingham and other Midland towns were said to be using cameos and encaustic paintings for this purpose. Wedgwood proposed to have drawings and catalogues made of the latter, but apparently

1. *Drawer of mahogany writing table, signed by David Wright. (V. & A. Mus.)*

the project was not realised. His London showrooms, towards the end of his career, were in Greek St., Soho, and here these plaques were on sale. Sheraton (*Drawing Book*, 1791–4) wrote of a commode: 'In the frieze part is a tablet in the centre, made of an exquisite composition in imitation of statuary marble. These are to be had of any figure, or on any subject at Mr Wedgwood's, near Soho Square. They are let into the wood and project a little forward. The commode should be painted . . .'. The piano, Fig. 1, illustrates the use of this decoration.

WHITTLE, JAMES. King's Street, Covent Garden. Carver, gilder, cabinet-maker and decorator. Supplied the Earl of Cardigan in 1742–3 with carved and gilt mirror frames and tables; among them 'two rich tables like the Duke of Montagu's with Boys heads'. In partnership with Samuel Norman (*q.v.*) and John Mayhew (*q.v.*) in 1758 (Mayhew ceased to be a partner the following year) and the firm was then styled Whittle and Norman; though when the premises in King Street were destroyed on Dec. 23, 1759, they are referred to by the *Public Advertiser* as 'Mr Norman's'. Between 1754–60 the firm was employed at Bedford House and also at Woburn, to which they supplied a large quantity of furniture, including a number of fine mirrors. 'A magnificent pier-glass' of rococo character in the Drawing-Room at Holkham is stated by the architect Matthew Brettingham (1761) to be 'by Whittle', and he appears to have been responsible for other large carved and gilt mirror frames and console-tables in the state rooms.

WILLIAMS, HENRY. London joiner, address unknown; supplied chairs and large mahogany frame for marble table to Sir Paul Methuen, 1729. Name appears among those of tradesmen employed by crown 1729. In 1737 provided two armchairs and two large sets of stools with carved and gilt frames for Hampton Court Palace, for Frederick, Prince of Wales (*see* STOOLS, Fig. 38). The two armchairs are at Windsor Castle. Supplied large quantity of inexpensive furniture to royal palaces; among items in bills are a number of wainscot chests of drawers, and a library table with drawers and knee-hole. Also repaired some royal furniture, and charged £2 14s. 'For fetching home nine Walnuttree Chairs being very much out of Repair, taking them all to pieces New Jointing them, mending Scraping and polishing Do.' His accounts continue to 1728, when Catherine Naish (*q.v.*) replaced him as joiner.

WILMOTT, THOMAS. 16, John St., Oxford St., cabinet-maker and undertaker. A set of mahogany chairs dating from early 19th century in Palace of Tullgarn, near Stockholm, all bear his trade-label. The goods he supplied are specified as 'Imperial Dining Tables, Sofas, Chair-Beds on an improved principle'. In 1802 T. Wilmot (*sic*) of this address was among subscribers to Sheraton's *Cabinet Dict.*; he was still in business there in 1824.

The term imperial dining-table was applied late in the 18th century by Gillow and Co. (*see* GILLOW, FIRM OF) to dining-tables which might be lengthened by the insertion of loose leaves. Much furniture in the style of Sheraton was exported to Scandinavia, or made by Norwegian and Swedish craftsmen in a similar style, at end of 18th and early in 19th centuries. Princess Sophia Albertina inherited Palace of Tullgarn 1803. The set of chairs with Wilmott's label are of inexpensive type made for dining-rooms.

WRIGHT, DAVID. This maker's signature inscribed on bottom of one of oak-lined drawers in mahogany knee-hole writing-table of fine quality at V. and A. Mus., 'David Wright Fecit Lancaster August 11, 1751' (Fig. 1). Possibly this craftsman, of whom no further details known, employed by Gillow of Lancaster (*see* GILLOW, FIRM OF). Thomas Pennant (*Tour in Scotland*, 1776) describes Lancaster as 'famous in having some very ingenious cabinet-makers settled there'. Such signatures extremely rare on English furniture. (*See* STRICKLAND, W.)

WRIGHT, F. AND W. Billhead describes them as 'Upholsterers and Cabinet Makers to His Majesty's Stamp Office, 410, Oxford Street, opposite Rathbone Place'. Bill to Earl of Jersey for £115 signed by W. Wright, dated Mar., 1805.

WYATT, EDWARD (fl. c. 1794–1811). Carver, 360, Oxford St. For many years repaired cabinet work, picture frames, etc., at Windsor Castle. In accounts for furnishing Carlton House, 1811, Wyatt's bill amounts to £756 for the year (H. Clifford Smith, *Buckingham Palace*, 1931). Buried in Merton Church, Surrey. Trade-card c. 1790 reproduced in *London Furniture Makers*, A. Heal, 1953.

WYATT, JAMES (c. 1800). Label 'Jas Wyatt upholsterer and cabinet-maker, No. 37, Eagle Street, Red Lion Square, Holborn' found beneath commode veneered with cedar wood and enriched with panels of rosewood inlaid with mother-of-pearl (illustrated in *Georgian Cabinet-Makers*, 2nd ed., 1946, Fig. 173). Label addressed to Hon. Richard Ryder (1766–1832), son of first Earl of Harrowby.

WYATT, JAMES (1748–1813). Celebrated architect, born in Staffs., apparently taken by Richard Bagot, a gentleman of that county, to Italy; spent 6 years there (4 in Rome). Returned to England c. 1768, elected A.R.A. 1770. His fashionable vogue dates from his selection as the architect of the Pantheon, Oxford St., opened 1772. Succeeded Sir William Chambers in 1796 as Surveyor-General to Board of Works. Among furniture designed by him were cabinets (executed by cabinet-maker named Rouch) for sets of Tassie's reproductions of gems sent to Catherine the Great of Russia. A volume of his drawings shows details of his furniture for Heveningham, Suffolk.

ZUCCHI, ANTONIO PIETRO (1726–95). Venetian artist who achieved great reputation for painted decoration. In 1754 accompanied Robert Adam on tour through Italy and Dalmatia; in 1766 came to England at Adam's invitation, being employed by him to decorate ceilings and walls in a number of houses. The carved and gilt girandoles in the first drawing-room at the Earl of Derby's house, Grosvenor Square, were decorated with classical plaques by this artist (*see* SCONCES, Fig. 24). He designed frontispiece for *Works in Architecture* (1st vol., 1773) and engraved many of the plates. Elected A.R.A. 1770, and 1781 married Angelica Kauffmann (*q.v.*). They returned to Italy 1782. Sir John Soane records that Zucchi and Angelica were employed by Adam 'on all occasions'; but while designs on several pieces of late-18th century painted furniture are copied direct from pictures by his wife, no specimen which can be traced to Zucchi is known.